D0995254

LANGENSCHEIDT'S UNIVERSAL GERMAN DICTIONARY

GERMAN-ENGLISH
ENGLISH-GERMAN

New edition

LANGENSCHEIDT

NEW YORK · BERLIN · MUNICH
VIENNA · ZURICH

Contents

Abbreviations Used in this Dictionary

Die Tilde (~, bei veränderter Schreibung des Anfangsbuchstabens ℒ) ersetzt entweder das ganze Stichwort oder den vor dem senkrechten Strich (|) stehenden Teil davon oder ein bereits mit einer Tilde gebildetes Stichwort, z. B. **birth** ... **~day** = **birthday**; **ap|prov|al** ... **~e** = **approve**; **after** ... **~noon: good ~** = **good afternoon; lord** ... **the ℒ** = **the Lord.**

The tilde (~, when the initial letter changes: ℒ) stands for the catchword at the beginning of the entry or the part of it preceding the vertical bar (|) or for a catchword already having a tilde. Examples: **birth** ... **~day** = **birthday; ap|prov|al** ... **~e** = **approve; after** ... **~noon: good ~** = **good afternoon; lord** ... **the ℒ** = **the Lord.**

---

a. auch, *also.*

abbr. abbreviation, Abkürzung.

acc accusative (case), Akkusativ.

adj adjective, Adjektiv.

adv adverb, Adverb.

aer. aeronautics, Luftfahrt.

agr. agriculture, Landwirtschaft.

Am. American English, amerikanisches Englisch.

anat. anatomy, Anatomie.

appr. approximately, etwa.

arch. architecture, Architektur.

ast. astronomy, Astronomie.

attr attributively, attributiv.

biol. biology, Biologie.

bot. botany, Botanik.

Brit. British English, britisches Englisch.

bsd. besonders, *especially.*

chem. chemistry, Chemie.

cj conjunction, Konjunktion.

colloq. colloquial, umgangssprachlich.

comp comparative, Komparativ.

cond conditional, Konditional.

contp. contemptuously, verächtlich.

dat dative (case), Dativ.

dem demonstrative, Demonstrativ...

ea. einander, *one another, each other.*

eccl. ecclesiastical, kirchlich.

econ. economics, Wirtschaft.

e-e, *e-e* eine, *a* (an).

electr. electricity, Elektrizität.

e-m, *e-m* einem, *to a* (an).

e-n, *e-n* einen, *a* (an).

e-r, *e-r* einer, *of a* (an), *to a* (an).

e-s, *e-s* eines, *of a* (an).

et., *et.* etwas, *something*.

etc. et cetera, *and so on*, und so weiter.

f feminine weiblich.

fig. figuratively, bildlich.

gen genitive (case), Genitiv.

geogr. geography, Geographie.

geol. geology, Geologie.

ger gerund, Gerundium.

gr. grammar, Grammatik.

hist. history, Geschichte.

hunt. hunting, Jagd.

ichth. ichthyology, Ichthyologie.

impers impersonal, unpersönlich.

indef indefinite, Indefinit...

inf infinitive (mood), Infinitiv.

int. interjection, Interjektion.

interr interrogative, Interrogativ...

irr irregular, unregelmäßig.

j-m, *j-m* jemandem, *to someone*.

j-n, *j-n* jemanden, *someone*.

j-s, *j-s* jemandes, *someone's*.

jur. jurisprudence, Recht.

konkr. konkret, *concretely*.

ling. linguistics, Sprachwissenschaft.

lit. literary, literarisch.

m masculine, männlich.

mar. maritime terminology, Schiffahrt.

math. mathematics, Mathematik.

m-e, *m-e* meine, *my*.

med. medicine, Medizin.

metall. metallurgy, Metallurgie.

meteor. meteorology, Meteorologie.

mil. military terminology, Militärwesen.

min. mineralogy, Mineralogie.

mot. motoring, Kraftfahrwesen.

mst meistens, *mostly*, usually.

mus. music, Musik.

n neuter, sächlich.

od. oder, *or*.

opt. optics, Optik.

orn. ornithology, Ornithologie.

o.s., *o.s.* oneself, sich.

paint. painting, Malerei.

parl. parliamentary term, parlamentarischer Ausdruck.

pass passive voice, Passiv.

ped. pedagogy, Pädagogik.

pers pron personal pronoun, Personalpronomen.

phot. photography, Fotografie.

phys. physics, Physik.

physiol. physiology, Physiologie.

pl plural, Plural.

poet. poetical, dichterisch.

pol. politics, Politik.

poss possessive, Possessiv-.

post. postal service, Postwesen.

pp past participle, Partizip Perfekt.

pred predicative, prädikativ.

pres present, Präsens.

pres p present participle, Partizip Präsens.

pret preterit(e), Präteritum.

print. printing, Buchdruck.

pron pronoun, Pronomen.

prp preposition, Präposition.

psych. psychology, Psychologie.

rail. railway, Eisenbahnwesen.

rel relative, Relativ...

rhet. rhetoric, Rhetorik.

S., S. Sache, thing.

s. siehe, see, refer to.

Scot. Scottish, schottisch.

s-e, s-e seine, his, one's.

sg singular, Singular.

sl. slang, Slang.

s-m, s-m seinem, to his, to one's.

s-n, s-n seinen, his, one's.

s.o., s.o. someone, jemand (-en).

sp. sports, Sport.

s-r, s-r seiner, of his, of one's, to his, to one's.

s-s, s-s seines, of his, of one's.

s.th., s.th. something, etwas.

sub substantive, noun, Substantiv.

subj subjunctive (mood), Konjunktiv.

sup superlative, Superlativ.

tech. technology, Technik.

tel. telegraphy, Telegrafie.

teleph. telephony, Fernsprechwesen.

thea. theatre, Theaterwesen.

u., u. und, and.

univ. university, Hochschulwesen.

v/aux auxiliary verb, Hilfsverb.

vb verb, Verb.

vet. veterinary medicine, Tiermedizin.

v/i intransitive verb, intransitives Verb.

v/refl reflexive verb, reflexives Verb.

v/t transitive verb, transitives Verb.

vulg. vulgar, vulgär.

zo. zoology, Zoologie.

Zs., zs. zusammen, together.

Zssg(n) Zusammensetzung (-en), compound word(s).

△ For all German nouns which are not compounds formed from other independent nouns, *gen sg* and *nom pl* have been indicated.

△ The irregularity of German verbs is shown by the abbreviation *irr.* The user should consult the list of irregular verbs (see pp. 646–654).

Key to German Pronunciation

The phonetic alphabet used in this dictionary is that of the International Phonetic Association (IPA).

Vowel length is indicated by [ː]. [ˑ] placed over a vowel indicates that the vowel in question is non-syllabic. Stress is shown by [ˈ]; it is placed at the onset of the stressed syllable. [-] stands for a whole phonetic syllable or a sequence of phonetic syllables, e.g. **entgegengesetzt** [-gəzɛtst] instead of [ɛntˈgeːgəngəzɛtst]. The glottal stop [ʔ] has been omitted when the first sound of an entry word is a vowel, e.g. **Abend** [ˈaːbənt] instead of [ˈʔaːbənt].

A. Vowels

Symbol	German example	Remarks
[iː]	Vieh [fiː]	as in see
[i]	Bilanz [biˈlants]	short, otherwise like [iː]
[ɪ]	mit [mɪt]	as in hit
[eː]	weh [veː]	as in day
[e]	legal [leˈgaːl]	short, otherwise like [eː]
[ɛː]	zähmen [ˈtsɛːmən]	as in bed, but opener
[ɛ]	wenn [vɛn]	short, resembles [ɛː]
[ə]	Zacke [ˈtsakə]	as in ago, but closer
[yː]	Düse [ˈdyːzə]	resembles French u in muse
[y]	Physik [fyˈziːk]	short, otherwise like [yː]
[ʏ]	Hütte [ˈhʏtə]	short, opener than [yː]
[øː]	böse [ˈbøːzə]	long, resembles French eu in feu
[ø]	möblieren [møˈbliːrən]	short, otherwise like [øː]
[œ]	Hölle [ˈhœlə]	short, opener than [øː]
[uː]	gut [guːt]	as in boot
[u]	Musik [muˈziːk]	short, otherwise like [uː]
[ʊ]	Bulle [ˈbʊlə]	as in bull
[oː]	Boot [boːt]	as in port, but closer
[o]	Modell [moˈdɛl]	short, otherwise like [oː]
[ɔ]	Gott [gɔt]	as in got, but closer

[aː]	Basis ['baːzɪs]	as in *father*
[a]	Hand [hant]	short, otherwise like in [aː]
[ɛ̃ː]	Teint [tɛ̃ː]	long, approximately the *a* in *bad*, but nasalized
[õː]	Fonds [fõː]	long nasalized [o], but opener than this
[õ]	Champignon ['ʃampɪnjõ]	short, otherwise like [õː]
[ã ː]	Ensemble [ãˈsãːbəl]	long nasalized [a]
[ã]	Pension [pãˈzi̯oːn]	short nasalized [a]
[aɪ]	Beil [baɪl]	diphthong as in *while*
[aʊ]	Haus [haʊs]	diphthong as in *house*
[ɔʏ]	heute ['hɔʏtə]	diphthong as in *boy*

B. Consonants

Symbol	German example	Remarks
[ʔ]	beeilen [bəˈʔaɪlən]	glottal stop (forced stop between one word or syllable and a following one beginning with a vowel)
[ŋ]	Ding [dɪŋ]	as in *thing*
[l]	lallen ['lalən]	as in *light*
[r]	1. rot [roːt]	rolled or flapped consonant, with the uvula or with the tip of the tongue; also uvular fricative
	2. Heer [heːr], Heers [heːrs]	mostly weak uvular fricative after long vowels in final position or before consonant
	3. Wasser ['vasər], bessern ['besərn]	very weak uvular fricative in [ər] in final position or before consonant
[v]	Welt [vɛlt]	as in *vice*
[s]	Gasse ['gasə]	as in *miss*

[z]	Faser ['fa:zər]	as in *blazer*
[ʃ]	Masche ['maʃə]	as in *cash*
[ʒ]	genieren [ʒe'ni:rən]	as in *measure*
[ç]	mich [mɪç]	voiceless palatal fricative. It can be made by unvoicing a fricative [j].
[j]	ja [ja:]	as in *yes*
[x]	Bach [bax]	similar to Scottish *ch* in *loch*

For list of suffixes normally given without phonetic transcriptions, see p. 644.

Key to English Pronunciation

The length of vowels is indicated by [:] following the vowel symbol, the stress by ['] preceding the stressed syllable.

[ɑː]	as in *father*		[uə]	as in *poor*
[ʌ]	as in *but, come*		[u]	as in *put*
[æ]	as in *man*		[r]	as in *rose*
[ɛə]	as in *bare*		[ʒ]	as in *jazz*
[ai]	as in *I, sky*		[ʃ]	as in *shake*
[au]	as in *house*		[θ]	as in *thin*
[ei]	as in *date*		[ð]	as in *father*
[e]	as in *bed*		[s]	as in *see*
[ə]	as in *ago, butter*		[z]	as in *zeal*
[iː]	as in *sea*		[ŋ]	as in *ring*
[i]	as in *big*		[w]	as in *will*
[iə]	as in *here*		[f]	as in *fast*
[əu]	as in *boat*		[v]	as in *vast*
[ɔː]	as in *door*		[j]	as in *yes*
[ɔ]	as in *god*		[ɑ̃]	as in French *blanc*
[ɔi]	as in *boy*		[ɔ̃]	as in French *bonbon*
[əː]	as in *girl*		[ɛ̃]	as in French *vin*
[uː]	as in *shoe*			

A

Aal [a:l] *m* (-[e]s/-e) eel.

Aas [a:s] *n* (-es/*no pl*) carrion, carcass.

ab [ap] *prp* from; from ... (on); from ... on(ward[s]); *adv colloq.* off; ~ **und zu** *adv* now and then; **von jetzt** ~ *adv* from now on.

abändern ['apʔɛndərn] *v/t* alter, modify.

Abart ['apʔa:rt] *f* (-/-en) variety.

Abbau ['apbau] *m* (-[e]s/ *no pl*) reduction; *Bergbau*: exploitation, working; Sen *v/t* reduce; *Maschinen etc.*: dismantle; *Bergbau*: exploit.

ab|beißen ['apbaɪsən] *v/t* (*irr*) bite off; **~bekommen** *v/t* (*irr*) get off; **s-n Teil** *od.* **et. ~bekommen** get one's share; **~berufen** *v/t* (*irr*) recall; **~bestellen** *v/t* countermand; *Zeitung etc.*: cancel one's subscription to; **~biegen** [-bi:gən] *v/i* (*irr*) turn off; **nach rechts** *od.* **links ~biegen** turn right *od.* left.

Abbildung ['apbɪlduŋ] *f* (-/-en) picture, illustration.

ab|binden ['apbɪndən] *v/t* (*irr*) untie, undo; *med.* ligature, tie off; **~blenden**

v/t Scheinwerfer: dim *od.* dip (*v/i*: the headlights); **~blendlicht** *n* dimmed headlight(s *pl*); **~brechen** *v/t*, *v/i* (*irr*) break off (*a. fig.*); *Gebäude*: demolish; *Zelt*: strike; *fig.* stop; **~bremsen** *v/t*, *v/i* slow down *od.* up, brake; **~brennen** *v/t*, *v/i* (*irr*) burn down; **~bringen** *v/t* (*irr*): **j-n von** ~ dissuade s.o. from; **~bröckeln** *v/i* crumble; **~bürsten** *v/t* brush (off).

Abc [a:be:'tse:] *n* (-/*no pl*) ABC, alphabet.

ab|danken ['apdaŋkən] *v/i* resign; *Herrscher*: abdicate; **~decken** *v/t* uncover; *Tisch*: clear; *zudecken*: cover (up, over); **~dichten** *v/t* make s.th. watertight.

Abdruck ['apdruk] *m* (-[e]s/ˆe) impression, (im)print; Sen *v/t* print; *Artikel*: publish.

abdrücken ['apdrʏkən] *v/i* fire.

Abend ['a:bənt] *m* (-s/-e) evening, night; **Guten** ~! Good evening!; **am** ~ in the evening; **heute** ~ tonight; **morgen** *od.* **gestern** S tomorrow *od.* last night; **~brot** *n* S. **Abend-**

essen [ˈɛsn] n (evening) twilight, dusk; **~essen** n evening meal; dinner; bsd. spätabends: supper; **~kleid** n evening dress od. gown; **~kurs** m evening classes pl; **~land** n (-[e]s/no pl) the Occident; **~mahl** n (-[e]s/-e) eccl. the (Holy) Communion, the Lord's Supper; **2s** adv in the evening; **~zeitung** f evening paper.

Abenteuer [ˈaːbəntɔyər] n (-s/-) adventure; **2lich** adj fig. wild, fantastic.

aber [ˈaːbər] cj but; **oder ~** cj or (else).

Aber|glaube [ˈaːbərglaubə] m (-ns/no pl) superstition; **2gläubisch** adj superstitious.

abermals [ˈaːbərmaːls] adv again, once more.

abfahr|en [ˈapfaːrən] v/i (irr) leave, start, depart; Schiff: sail; v/t carry od. cart away; **2t** f (-/-en) departure; mar. sailing; **2ts-lauf** m downhill (race).

Abfall [ˈapfal] m (-[e]s/ᵘe): oft **Abfälle** pl waste, refuse, Am. a. garbage; **~eimer** m dustbin, Am. garbage od. trash can; **2en** v/i (irr) Blätter etc.: fall (off); Gelände: slope (down).

abfällig [ˈapfɛlɪç] adj unfavo(u)rable; disparaging.

Abfallprodukt n (-[e]s/-e) by-product; waste product.

ab|fangen [ˈapfaŋən] v/t (irr) catch; Brief etc.: intercept; mot., aer. right; **~färben** v/i Farbe: run; **~fassen** v/t write, compose, pen; **~fertigen** [-fɛrtɪɡən] v/t dispatch; Zoll: clear; Kunden: serve, attend to; **~feuern** [-fɔyərn] v/t fire (off), discharge.

abfind|en [ˈapfɪndən] v/t (irr) satisfy; entschädigen: compensate; **sich ~en mit** v/refl resign o.s. to; **2ung** f (-/-en) satisfaction; compensation.

ab|fliegen [ˈapfliːɡən] v/i (irr) leave (by plane); aer. take off, start; **~fließen** v/i (irr) drain od. flow off.

Abflug [ˈapfluːk] m (-[e]s/ᵘe) take-off, start; departure.

Abfluß [ˈapflʊs] m (-sses/ᵘsse) flowing off; drain; See: outlet; **~rohr** n waste-pipe, drain-pipe.

Abfuhr [ˈapfuːr] f (-/-en) fig. rebuff.

ab|führen [ˈapfyːrən] v/t lead away; Geld: pay; **~end** adj med. laxative, purgative; **2mittel** n laxative.

abfüllen [ˈapfʏlən] v/t decant; **in Flaschen ~** bottle.

Abgabe [ˈapɡaːbə] f (-/-n) Ball: pass; econ. sale; Steuer: tax.

Abgang [ˈapɡaŋ] m (-[e]s/ᵘe) departure; thea.

exit; leaving; ~**szeugnis** n (school-)leaving certificate, Am. a. diploma.

Abgas ['apga:s] n (-es/-e) waste gas; mot. exhaust (gas).

abgearbeitet ['apgəˀarbaɪtət] adj worn-out.

abgeben ['apge:bən] v/t (irr) deliver; leave; give; Arbeit: hand in; Ball: pass; Erklärung: make; **sich ~ mit** v/refl occupy o.s. with.

abge|bildet ['apgəbɪldət] adj in the picture; ~**brannt** adj fig. colloq. hard up, sl. broke; ~**griffen** adj Buch: well-thumbed; ~**härtet** adj hardened.

abgehen ['apge:ən] v/i (irr) leave, depart, start; Brief etc.: be dispatched; Weg: branch off; Knopf etc.: come off; fig. go od. pass off.

abge|hetzt ['apgəhɛtst] adj exhausted; ~**legen** adj remote, distant; ~**macht** ~**l** it's a deal!; ~**magert** adj emaciated; ~**neigt** adj disinclined, averse; ~**nutzt** adj worn-out.

Abgeordnete ['apgəˀɔrdnətə] m, f (-n/-n) deputy, delegate; Deutschland: member of the Bundestag od. Landtag; Brit. Member of Parliament, Am. Congress|man, -woman.

abge|schlossen ['apgəʃlɔsən] adj fig. complete; ~**sehen:** ~ **von** adv apart

(Am. a. aside) from; ~**spannt** adj fig. exhausted, tired; ~**standen** adj stale, flat; ~**storben** adj numb; dead; ~**stumpft** adj fig. indifferent; ~**tragen** adj threadbare, shabby.

ab|gewöhnen ['apgəwø:nən] v/t: **j-m et.** ~ break od. cure s.o. of s.th.; **sich das Rauchen** ~ give up smoking; ~**grenzen** v/t mark off; fig. define.

Abgrund ['apgrʊnt] m (-[e]s/~e) precipice, chasm.

ab|hacken ['aphakən] v/t chop od. cut off; ~**haken** [-ha:kən] v/t Liste: tick off; ~**halten** v/t (irr) hold; **j-n von et.** ~**halten** keep s.o. from doing s.th.; ~**handen** [ap'handən] ~ **kommen** v/t (irr) get lost.

Abhandlung ['aphandlʊŋ] f (-/-en) treatise.

Abhang ['aphaŋ] m (-[e]s/~e) slope, incline.

abhängen ['aphɛŋən] v/t Bild etc.: take down; rail. uncouple; ~ **von** v/i depend (up)on.

abhängig ['aphɛŋɪç] adj: ~ **von** dependent (up)on; 2**keit** f dependence.

ab|härten ['aphɛrtən] v/t harden (**gegen** to); **sich** ~**härten** harden o.s.; ~**hauen** v/t (irr) cut od. chop off; v/i colloq. be off; ~**heben** v/t, v/i (irr) tel-

Abhilfe

eph. lift the receiver); cut (the cards); lift *od.* take off; *Geld:* (with)drw; **sich ~heben von** sand out against; **~heilen** *-v/i* heal (up); **~hetzen: sich ~** *v/refl* rush, hurry.

Abhilfe ['aphilfə] *f* (*-/no pl*) remedy.

ab|holen ['apho:lən] *v/t* fetch; call *od.* come for; **~holen lassen** *v/t* send for; **j-n von der Bahn ~holen** go to meet s.o. at the station; **~horchen** *med.* sound; **~horchen** *v/t teleph.* listen in to; intercept; **e-n Schüler ~hören** hear a pupil's lesson.

Abitur [abi'tu:r] *n* (*-s/no pl*) school-leaving examination.

ab|kaufen ['apkaufən] *v/t* buy *od.* purchase from; **~kehren** *v/t* sweep off; **sich ~kehren von** *v/refl* turn away from; **~klingen** *v/i* (*irr*) *Schmerz:* ease off; **~klopfen** *v/t Staub:* knock off; *Mantel:* dust; *med.* sound; **~knicken** *v/t, v/i* snap *od.* break off; **~kochen** *v/t* boil; *Milch:* scald.

abkommen ['apkɔmən] *v/i* (*irr*): **~ von** get off; *Thema:* digress from; **vom Wege ~** lose one's way; **2** *n* (*-s/-*) agreement.

ab|koppeln ['apkɔpəln] *v/t* uncouple; **~kratzen** *v/t* scrape off; **~kühlen** *v/t, v/i* cool; **sich ~küh-**

len *v/refl* cool; *fig.* cool down.

ab|kürzen ['apkyrtsən] *v/t* shorten; *Wort etc.:* abbreviate; **den Weg ~en** take a short cut; **2ung** *f* abbreviation; short cut.

ab|laden ['apla:dən] *v/t* (*irr*) unload; *Schutt:* dump.

Ablage ['apla:gə] *f* (*-/-n*) files *pl.*

ab|lagern ['apla:gərn]: **sich ~** *v/refl* settle; be deposited; **~lassen** *v/t* (*irr*) drain (off), run off; *Dampf:* let off.

Ablauf ['aplauf] *m* (*-[e]s/ ~e*) *Verlauf:* course; expiration, end; **nach ~ von** at the end of; **2en** *v/t* (*irr*) *Absätze:* wear down; *v/i* (*irr*) run off; drain off; *Frist, Paß:* expire; *Uhr:* run down.

Ableben ['aple:bən] *n* (*-s/ no pl*) death, *jur.* demise.

ab|lecken ['aplɛkən] *v/t* lick (off); **~legen** *v/t Kleidung:* take off; *Akten etc.:* file; *Geständnis:* make; *Eid, Prüfung:* take; *v/i Schiff:* sail; take off one's (hat and) coat.

Ableger ['aple:gər] *m* (*-s/ -*) layer, shoot.

ab|lehnen ['aple:nən] *v/t* decline, refuse; *Antrag etc.:* turn down; **~end** *adj* negative; **2ung** *f* refusal; rejection.

ab|leiten ['aplaitən] *v/t* divert; *fig.* derive.

ab|lenken ['aplɛŋkən] *v/t*

divert (**von** from); **2ung** *f* diversion; distraction.

abliefer|n ['apliːfərn] *v/t* deliver; **2ung** *f* delivery.

ablös|en ['apløːzən] *v/t* detach, remove; take off; *mil.* relieve; *Amtsvorgänger:* supersede; **sich ~en** come off (time); *Person:* alternate, take turns; **2ung** *f* relief.

abmach|en ['apmaxən] *v/t* remove, detach; *fig.* settle, arrange, agree on; **2ung** *f* arrangement, settlement, agreement.

abmagern ['apmaːgərn] *v/i* lose weight, grow lean *od.* thin.

Abmarsch ['apmarʃ] *m* (-es/*no pl*) start; *mil.* marching off.

abmelden ['apmɛldən]: **sich ~** *v/refl* give notice of one's departure.

abmes|sen ['apmɛsən] *v/t* (*irr*) measure; **2sung** *f* measurement.

ab|montieren ['apmɔn-tiːrən] *v/t* take down, dismantle; **~mühen** [-myː-ən]: **sich ~** *v/refl* drudge, toil; **~nagen** *v/t* gnaw off; *Knochen:* pick.

Abnahme ['apnaːmə] *f* (-/ *no pl*) decrease, diminution.

abnehme|n ['apneːmən] *v/i* (*irr*) *Mond:* wane; lose weight; decrease; diminish; *v/t* take off, remove; *teleph. Hörer:* lift; *med.* amputate; *econ.* buy, purchase; **j-m et. ~n** take

s.th. from s.o.; **2r** *m econ.*: buyer; customer.

Abneigung ['apnaɪɡʊŋ] *f* (-/-en) aversion, dislike.

ab|nutzen ['apnʊtsən], **~nützen** [-nʏtsən] *v/t*: (**sich**) **~** wear out.

Abonn|ement [abɔn(ə)-'mãː] *n* (-s/-s) subscription (**auf** to); **~ent** [abɔ'nɛnt] *m* (-en/-en) subscriber; **2ieren** [-'niːrən] *v/t* subscribe to, take in.

Abordnung ['apʔɔrdnʊŋ] *f* (-/-en) delegation.

ab|pfeifen ['appfaɪfən] *v/t* (*irr*): **das Spiel ~** stop the game; **~pflücken** *v/t* pick, pluck, gather; **~plagen** [-plaːɡən]: **sich ~** *v/refl* toil; **~prallen** [-praːlən] *v/i* rebound; **~putzen** *v/t* clean; wipe off; **~rasieren** *v/t* shave off; **~raten** *v/t* (*irr*): **~ von** dissuade from, advise against; **~räumen** *v/t* clear (away).

abrechn|en ['apʀɛçnən] *v/t* deduct; **mit j-m ~en** *v/i* get even with s.o.; **2ung** *f* settlement (of accounts); deduction.

abreiben ['apraɪbən] *v/t* (*irr*) rub off; *Körper:* rub down; polish.

Abreise ['apraɪzə] *f* (-/ *rare* -n) departure, start; **2n** *v/i* depart, leave, start.

abreißen ['apraɪsən] *v/t* (*irr*) tear *od.* pull off; *Gebäude:* pull down; *v/i* break off; *Knopf etc.:* come off;

2kalender *m* tear-off calendar.

ab|richten ['aprɪçtən] *v/t Tier:* train; *Pferd:* break (in); **~riegeln** s. **verriegeln.**

Abriß ['aprɪs] *m* (-sses/ -sse) outline, summary.

ab|rollen ['aprɔlən] *v/t* unroll; uncoil; unwind; **~rücken** *v/i* move away; *mil.* march off.

Abruf ['apruːf] *m:* **auf ~** on call.

abrunden ['aprʊndən] *v/t* round (off).

abrupt [ap'rʊpt] *adj* abrupt.

Abrüstung ['aprʏstʊŋ] *f* (-/-en) disarmament.

abrutschen ['aprʊtʃən] *v/i* slip off.

Absage ['apzaːgə] *f* (-/-n) cancellation; **2n** *v/t* cancel, call off.

absägen ['apzɛːgən] *v/t* saw off.

Absatz ['apzats] *m* (-es/ ⁀e) *Schuh:* heel; *Treppe:* landing; *print.* paragraph; *econ.* sale.

ab|schaffen ['apʃafən] *v/t* abolish; **~schälen** *v/t* peel (off), pare; **~schalten** *v/t* switch off, turn off *od.* disconnect; **~schätzen** *v/t* estimate, value.

Abschaum ['apʃaʊm] *m* (-[e]s/*no pl*) scum; *fig. a.* dregs *pl.*

Abscheu ['apʃɔy] *m* (-[e]s/*no pl*) horror, ab-

horrence; **2lich** *adj* abominable, horrid.

abschicken ['apʃɪkən] *v/t* send off, dispatch; post, *bsd. Am.* mail.

Abschied ['apʃiːt] *m* (-[e]s/*no pl*) parting, leave-taking; **~ nehmen** *v/i (irr)* take leave (**von** of); **~sfeier** *f* farewell party.

ab|schießen ['apʃiːsən] *v/t (irr)* shoot off; *hunt.* shoot, kill; *Waffe:* discharge; *Rakete:* launch; *aer.* shoot *od.* bring down; **~schirmen** [-ʃɪrmən] *v/t:* **~ (gegen)** shield (from); screen (from).

Abschlag ['apʃlaːk] *m* (⁀s/ ⁀e) *econ.* discount, rebate; **2en** [-ʃlaːgən] *v/t (irr)* knock *od.* beat *od.* strike off; *Kopf:* cut off; *Angriff:* beat off, repulse; *Bitte etc.:* refuse; **~(s)zahlung** *f* instal(l)ment.

abschleifen ['apʃlaɪfən] *v/t (irr)* grind off.

Abschlepp|dienst ['apʃlɛpdiːnst] *m* (-[e]s/-e) breakdown (*Am.* wrecking) service; **2en** *v/t mot.* tow; **sich 2en mit** *v/refl* trail *od.* toil along with; **~seil** *n* tow(ing)-rope; **~wagen** *m* breakdown lorry, *Am.* wrecking car.

abschließen ['apʃliːsən] *v/t (irr)* lock (up); end, finish, complete; *Versicherung:* effect; *Vertrag etc.:* conclude; **e-n Handel ~** strike a bargain; **~d** *adj* final; in conclusion.

Abschluß ['apʃlus] *m*
(-es/ᵛe) conclusion;
~**prüfung** *f* final examination, finals *pl*; ~**zeugnis** *n* leaving certificate.

ab|schmieren ['apʃmiːrən] *v/t* lubricate, grease;
~**schnallen** [-ʃnalən] *v/t* unbuckle; **Skier:** take off;
~**schneiden** *v/t* (*irr*) cut (off); slice off; **gut** *od.* **schlecht** ~**schneiden** *v/i* come off well *od.* badly.

Abschnitt ['apʃnɪt] *m*
(-[e]s/-e) *math.* segment;
print. section, paragraph;
Kontroll2: counterfoil, *Am. a.* stub; **Reise:** stage; **Entwicklung:** phase; **Zeit:** period.

ab|schöpfen ['apʃœpfən] *v/t* skim (off); ~**schrauben** [-ʃraubən] *v/t* screw off; ~**schrecken** [-ʃrekən] *v/t* deter; ~**schreiben** *v/t* (*irr*) copy; **Schule:** crib; 2**schrift** *f* copy, duplicate; ~**schürfen** [-ʃyrfən] *v/t* graze, abrade.

Abschuß ['apʃus] *m*
(-sses/ᵛsse) **Rakete:** launching; *aer.* shooting down, downing; ~**rampe** *f* launching pad *od.* platform.

ab|schüssig ['apʃysɪç] *adj* steep; ~**schütteln** *v/t* shake off; ~**schwächen** [-ʃweçən] *v/t* weaken; ~**schweifen** *v/i* digress; ~**segeln** *v/i* set sail, sail off.

absehlbar ['apzeːbaːr]

adj: **in** ~**er Zeit** in the not-too-distant future;
~**en** *v/t* (*irr*) foresee; **es abgesehen haben auf** aim at; ~**en von** refrain from; disregard.

abseits ['apzaɪts] *adv*
~ 2 *n* (-/-) *sp.* offside; ~ (*gen*) *od.* **von** *prp* off.

absende|n ['apzɛndən] *v/t* send off, dispatch; post, *Am.* mail; 2**r** *m* sender.

absetzen ['apzɛtsən] *v/t* set *od.* put down; *j-n:* remove, dismiss; **Passagier:** drop, put down; **Waren:** sell; **Theaterstück:** take off; *v/i* stop, pause.

Absicht ['apzɪçt] *f* (-/-en) intention; 2**lich** *adj* intentional; *adv* intentionally, on purpose.

absolut [apzo'luːt] *adj* absolute.

ab|sondern ['apzɔndərn] *v/t* separate; *med.* secrete; **sich** ~**sondern** seclude o.s.; ~**sorbieren** [apzɔr'biːrən] *v/t* absorb; ~**spenstig** ['apʃpɛnstɪç] ~ **machen** *v/t* entice away (*dat* from); ~**sperren** [-ʃpɛrən] *v/t* lock (up); **Wasser, Gas:** cut *od.* shut off; **Straße:** block; ~**spielen** [-ʃpiːlən] *v/t* play; **Tonband:** play back; **sich** ~**spielen** *v/refl* happen, take place.

Absprung ['apʃpruŋ] *m*
(-[e]s/ᵛe) jump.

abspülen

abspülen ['apʃpy:lən] *v/t* wash off *od.* away; *Geschirr:* wash up.

abstammen ['apʃtamən] *v/i* be descended; 2**ung** *f* descent.

Abstand ['apʃtant] *m* (-[e]s/ᴗe) distance.

abstauben ['apʃtaubən] *v/t* dust.

absteche|n ['apʃteçən] *v/i* (*irr*) contrast (**von**, **gegen** with); 2**r** *m* excursion, trip.

ab|stehen ['apʃte:ən] *v/i* (*irr*) stick out; ~**steigen** *v/i* (*irr*) descend; *Pferd:* dismount, alight; *Fahrrad:* dismount; *Hotel:* put up (**in** at); ~**stellen** *v/t* put down; *Gas etc.:* turn off; *Auto:* park; ~**stempeln** *v/t* stamp.

Abstieg ['apʃti:k] *m* (-[e]s/-e) descent; *fig.* decline.

abstimm|en ['apʃtimən] *v/i* vote (**über** on); *v/t* harmonize (**auf** with); balance; 2**ung** *f* voting; vote.

abstoßen ['apʃto:sən] *v/t* (*irr*) push off; *j-n:* repel; ~**d** [-t] *adj* repulsive.

abstreiten ['apʃtraitən] *v/t* (*irr*) deny.

Ab|sturz ['apʃturts] *m* (-es/ᴗe) fall; *aer.* crash; 2**stürzen** *v/i* fall; *aer.* crash.

absuchen ['apzu:xən] *v/t* search (**nach** for).

absurd [ap'zurt] *adj* absurd, preposterous.

Abszeß [aps'tses] *m* (-sses/-sse) abscess.

Abtei [ap'tai] *f* (-/-en) abbey.

Abteil [ap'tail, 'aptail] *n* (-s/-e) compartment; 2**en** ['aptailən] *v/t* divide; *arch.* partition off; ~**ung** [ap'tailuŋ] *f* department; *Krankenhaus:* ward; ~**ungsleiter** *m* head of a department.

abtragen ['aptra:gən] *v/t* (*irr*) *Gebäude:* pull down; *Hügel:* level; *Kleidung:* wear out.

abtreib|en ['aptraibən] *v/i* (*irr*) *med.* have an abortion; 2**ung** *f med.* abortion.

abtrennen ['aptrenən] *v/t* detach, separate; sever.

abtret|en ['aptre:tən] *v/t* (*irr*) *Gebiet:* cede; *v/i fig.* retire; 2**r** *m* doormat.

ab|trocknen ['aptrɔknən] *v/t* dry; wipe (dry); ~**tupfen** [-tupfən] *v/t* mop (up); dab; ~**wägen** [-vɛ:gən] *v/t* (*irr*) consider carefully, weigh; ~**wälzen** *v/t* shift; ~**wandeln** *v/t* vary, modify; ~**warten** *v/i* wait and see.

abwärts ['apverts] *adv* down, downward(s).

abwasch|bar ['apvaʃba:r] *adj* washable; 2**becken** *n* sink; ~**en** *v/t* (*irr*) *s.* **abspülen**.

Abwässer ['apvɛsər] *pl* sewage *sg*; *Industrie:* waste water *sg*.

abwechs|eln ['apvɛksəln] *v/i* alternate; **einander** *od.* **sich ~eln** take turns; **~elnd** *adj* alternate; **2(e)lung** *f* change; *Zerstreuung:* diversion; **zur 2(e)lung** for a change.

Abwehr ['apveːr] *f* (*-/no pl*) defen|ce, *Am.* -se; **2en** *v/t* ward off; *Angriff, Feind:* repel, repulse.

abweichen ['apvaiçən] *v/i* (*irr*) deviate.

abweisen ['apvaizən] *v/t* (*irr*) refuse, reject; rebuff; **~d** *adj* unfriendly, cool.

ab|wenden ['apvɛndən] *v/t* turn away (*a.* **sich**); *Unheil, Blick:* avert; **~werfen** *v/t* (*irr*) throw off; *Bomben:* drop; *Gewinn:* yield.

abwer|ten ['apveːrtən] *v/t* devaluate; **2tung** *f* devaluation.

abwesen|d ['apveːzənt] *adj* absent; **2heit** *f* absence.

ab|wickeln ['apvikəln] *v/t* unwind, wind off; **~wiegen** *v/t* (*irr*) weigh (out); **~wischen** *v/t* wipe (off); **~würgen** *v/t mot.* stall; **~zahlen** *v/t; ~zählen** *v/t* count; **2zahlung** *f* instal(l)ment.

Abzeichen ['aptsaiçən] *n* (*-s/-*) badge.

ab|zeichnen ['aptsaiç-nən] *v/t* copy; draw;

Schriftstück: initial; **~ziehen** *v/t* (*irr*) take off, remove; deduct; *Bett:* strip; *Schlüssel:* take out; *v/i mil.* withdraw; go away; *Rauch:* clear away.

Abzug ['aptsuːk] *m* (*-[e]s/*ᵉe) *mil.* withdrawal; *Waffe:* trigger; *math.* deduction; *phot.* print; *print.* proof.

abzüglich ['aptsyːkliç] *prp* less, minus.

abzweig|en ['aptsvaigən] *v/i* branch off; **2ung** *f* turning, bifurcation.

ach [ax] *int.* oh!, ah!; **~ so!** oh, I see!

Achse ['aksə] *f* (*-/-n*) axis (*a. pol.*); *tech.* axle(-tree).

Achsel ['aksəl] *f* (*-/-n*) shoulder; **die** *od.* **mit den ~n zucken** shrug one's shoulders; **~höhle** *f* armpit.

acht [axt] *adj* eight; **in ~ Tagen** a week today, in a week's time; **vor ~ Tagen** a week ago; **sich in 2 nehmen** be careful.

Acht *f* (*-/no pl*) attention; **außer 2 lassen** disregard; **sich in 2 nehmen** be careful.

achte ['axtə] *adj* eighth; **2l** *n* (*-s/-*) eighth (part).

achten ['axtən] *v/t* respect; **~ auf** pay attention to; **darauf ~, daß** take care (that).

achtens ['axtəns] *adv* eighth(ly).

Achter ['axtər] *m* (*-s/-*)

(figure) eight; *Rudern:* eight; **~bahn** f big dipper, *Am.* roller coaster.

acht|geben ['axtge:bən] *v/i (irr)* be careful; pay attention to; **gib acht!** look out!, watch out!; *s.* **aufpassen auf;** **~los** *adj* careless.

Achtung ['axtuŋ] f (-/no pl) attention; respect; **~!** attention!, caution!; **~, Stufe!** mind the step!

acht|zehn(te) ['axtse:n-(tə)] *adj* eighteen(th); **~zig** *adj* eighty; **~zigste** *adj* eightieth.

ächzen ['ɛçtsən] *v/i* groan, moan.

Acker ['akər] m (-s/⁻) field; **~bau** m (-[e]s/no pl) agriculture; farming.

addieren [a'di:rən] *v/t* add (up).

Adel [a:dəl] m (-s/no pl) nobility, aristocracy; **2ig** *adj* noble.

Ader ['a:dər] f (-/-n) vein; artery.

adieu [a'diø:] *int.* farewell, *colloq.* cheerio.

Adjektiv [atjekti:f] n (-s/ -e) *gr.* adjective.

Adler ['a:dlər] m (-s/-) eagle.

adlig ['a:dliç] *adj* noble; **2e** m (-n/-n) nobleman; peer.

Admiral [atmi'ra:l] m (-s/ -e) admiral.

adoptieren [adɔp'ti:rən] *v/t* adopt.

Adreßbuch [a'drɛsbu:x] n directory.

Adress|e [a'drɛsə] f (-/-n) address; **2ieren** [adrɛ'si:-rən] *v/t* address, direct.

Advent [at'vɛnt] m (-[e]s/ no pl) Advent.

Adverb [at'vɛrp] n (-s/ -ien) *gr.* adverb.

Affäre [a'fɛ:rə] f (-/-n) (love) affair; matter, business.

Affe ['afə] m (-n/-n) monkey; *Menschen2:* ape.

affektiert [afɛk'ti:rt] *adj* affected.

Afrika|ner [afri'ka:nər] m (-s/-) African; **2nisch** *adj* African.

After ['aftər] m (-s/-) anus.

Agent [a'gɛnt] m (-en/ -en) *(pol.* secret) agent; **~ur** [agɛn'tu:r] f (-/-en) agency.

Aggress|ion [agrɛ'sio:n] f (-/-en) aggression; **2iv** [agrɛ'si:f] *adj* aggressive.

Ägypt|er [ɛ'gyptər] m (-s/ -) Egyptian; **2isch** *adj* Egyptian.

ah [a:] *int.* ah!

aha [a'ha] *int.* aha!, I see!

Ahle ['a:lə] f (-/-n) *tech.* awl.

ähneln ['ɛ:nəln] *v/i* be like, resemble.

Ahnen ['a:nən] *pl* ancestors *pl,* forefathers *pl.*

ahnen *v/t* guess; suspect.

ähnlich ['ɛ:nliç] *adj* similar *(dat* to); like; **2keit** f (-/-en) likeness, resemblance, similarity.

Ahnung ['a:nuŋ] f (-/-en)

presentiment, foreboding; notion, idea; **2slos** *adj* unsuspecting.

Ahorn ['aːhɔrn] *m* **-s(-e)** maple(-tree).

Ähre ['ɛːrə] *f* **(-/-n)** *bot.* ear.

Akademie [akade'miː] *f* **(-/-n)** academy; **~ker** [aka'deːmikər] *m* **-s/-)** university graduate; **2sch** *adj* academic.

akklimatisieren [aklimatiˈziːrən]: **sich ~** *v/refl* acclimatize.

Akkord [a'kɔrt] *m* **-[e]s -e)** *mus.* chord; **im ~** *econ.* by the piece; **~arbeit** *f* piece-work; **~lohn** *m* piece-wages *pl.*

Akku ['aku] *m* **-s/-s)** *s.* **Akkumulator.**

Akkumulator [akumuˈlaːtɔr] *m* **-s/-en)** battery.

Akkusativ ['akuzatiːf] *m* **(-s/-e)** *gr.* accusative (case).

Akrobat [akroˈbaːt] *m* **(-en/-en)** acrobat.

Akt [akt] *m* **-[e]s/-e)** act(ion), deed; *thea.* act; *paint.* nude.

Akte ['aktə] *f* **(-/-n)** document; *abgelegte:* file; **~n** *pl* a. papers *pl;* **~nmappe** *f,* **~ntasche** *f* briefcase.

Aktie ['aktsiə] *f* **(-/-n)** share, *Am.* stock; **~nge-sellschaft** *f* joint-stock company, *Am.* stock corporation.

Aktion [ak'tsioːn] *f* **(-/-en)** campaign, *Handlung:* action; *mil.* operation.

aktiv [ak'tiːf] *adj* active; **2** *n* **(-s/rare -e)** *gr.* active (voice); **2ität** [aktiviˈtɛːt] *f* **(-/-en)** activity.

aktuell [aktu'ɛl] *adj* current; up-to-date.

Akusti|**k** [aˈkustik] *f* **(-/no** *pl)* acoustics *pl (Lehre: sg);* **2sch** *adj* acoustic.

akut [aˈkuːt] *adj* acute.

Akzent [ak'tsɛnt] *m* **-[e]s/-e)** accent; *Betonung: a.* stress *(a. fig.).*

akzeptieren [aktsepˈtiːrən] *v/t* accept.

Alarm [a'larm] *m* **(-[e]s -e)** alarm; **2ieren** [alarˈmiːrən] *v/t* alarm.

albern ['albərn] *adj* silly, foolish.

Album ['album] *n* **(-s/Alben)** album.

Alge ['algə] *f* **(-/-n)** alga; seaweed.

Algebra ['algebra] *f* **(-/no** *pl)* algebra.

Alibi ['aːlibi] *n* **(-s/-s)** alibi.

Alimente [aliˈmɛntə] *pl* support sg.

Alkohol ['alkohoːl] *m* **(-s/-e)** alcohol; **2frei** *adj* non-alcoholic, soft; **2isch** *adj* alcoholic.

all [al] *pron* all; *jeder:* every; **vor ~em** *adv* most of all.

All *n* **(-s/no** *pl)* the universe.

Allee [a'leː] *f* **(-/-n)** avenue.

allein [a'laɪn] *adj* alone; only; **~stehend** *adj Person:* alone in the world;

single; *Gebäude etc.*: isolated; detached.

allemal ['alə'ma:l]: **ein für** ~ adv once and for all.

aller|best ['alər'best] *adj* very best; ~**dings** adv indeed; *int.* certainly!; ~**erst** ['alər'ʔe:rst] *adj* very first; **zu** ~ **erst** adv first of all.

Allergie [aler'gi:] *f (-/-n)* allergy.

aller|hand ['alər'hant], ~**lei** *adj* all kinds od. sorts of; ~**letzt** *adj* very last; ~**meist** *adj* most; **am** ~**meisten** adv most of all; ~**nächst** *adj* very next; ~**neu(e)st** *adj* very latest; ~**wenigst**: **am** ~**en** adv least of all.

allgemein ['algə'maɪn] *adj* general; *üblich*: common; **im** ~**en** adv in general, generally; **2heit** *f* general public.

Alliierte [ali'i:rtə] *m, f (-n/-n)* ally.

all|jährlich ['al'jɛ:rlɪç] *adj, adv* annual(ly); ~**mählich** [al'mɛ:lɪç] *adj, adv* gradual(ly); **2tag** *m* everyday life, daily routine; ~**täglich** *adj, adv* daily; *fig.* common; ~**zu** adv (much) too; ~**zuviel** adv too much.

Alm [alm] *f (-/-en)* alpine pasture, alp.

Almosen ['almo:zən] *n (-s/-)* alms *pl.*

Alpen ['alpən] *pl* the Alps *pl.*

Alphabet [alfa'be:t] *n (-s/*

-e) alphabet; **2isch** *adj* alphabetical.

Alptraum ['alptraʊm] *m (-s/ᵛe)* nightmare.

als [als] *cj nach comp*: than; *ganz so wie*: as; *nach Negation*: but; *zeitlich*: when, as; ~ **ob** as if, as though.

also ['alzo] *cj* therefore.

alt [alt] *adj* old; aged; ancient; *schal*: stale; second-hand.

Altar [al'ta:r] *m (-[e]s/ᵛe)* altar.

Alte *m, f (-n/-n)* old man od. woman; **die** ~**n** *pl* the old people *pl.*

Alter ['altər] *n (-s/no pl)* age; **im** ~ **von** at the age of; **er ist in meinem** ~ he is my age.

älter ['eltər] *adj (comp of* **alt)** older; senior; **der ᵉe Bruder** the elder brother; ~**e Dame** elderly lady.

altern ['altərn] *v/i* grow old, age.

Altersheim ['altərshaɪm], **Altenheim** *n (-s/ -e)* old people's home.

Alter|tum ['altərtu:m] *n (-s/* antiquity; ~**tümer** *pl* antiquities *pl.*

ältest ['eltəst] *adj (sup of* **alt)** oldest; *Schwester etc.*: eldest.

alt|klug ['altklu:k] *adj* precocious; ~**modisch** *adj* old-fashioned; **2papier** *n* waste paper; **2stadt** *f* old (part of a) town od. city.

Aluminium [alu'mi:nĭum]

n (**-s/no pl**) aluminium; *Am.* aluminum; **~folie** *f* tin foil.

Amateur [ama'tø:r] *m* (**-s/-e**) amateur.

Amboß ['ambɔs] *m* (**-sses/-sse**) anvil.

ambulant [ambu'lant] *adj:* **~er Patient** outpatient; **2z** *f* (**-/-en**) ambulance. [ant.]

Ameise ['a:maɪzə] *f*(**-/-n**)

Amerikan|er [ameri'ka:-nər] *m* (**-s/-**) American; **2isch** *adj* American.

Amme ['amə] *f* (**-/-n**) (wet-)nurse.

Amnestie [amnɛs'ti:] *f* (**-/-n**) amnesty.

Ampel ['ampəl] *f* (**-/-n**) hanging lamp; traffic light(*s pl*).

Ampulle [am'pʊlə] *f* (**-/-n**) ampoule.

amputieren [ampu'ti:-rən] *v/t* amputate.

Amsel ['amzəl] *f* (**-/-n**) blackbird.

Amt [amt] *n* (**-[e]s/ᵘer**) office; *Aufgabe:* duty; (telephone) exchange; **2-lich** *adj* official.

Amulett [amu'lɛt] *n* (**-[e]s/-e**) amulet, charm.

amüs|ant [amy'zant] *adj* amusing, entertaining; **~ieren** *v/t* amuse; **sich ~ieren** *v/refl* enjoy o.s., have a good time.

an [an] *prp* at; upon; in; against; to; by; **am 1. März** on March 1st; **von ... ~** from ... on.

Analyse [ana'ly:zə] *f* (**-/-n**) analysis.

Ananas ['ananas] *f* (**-/-, -se**) pineapple.

Anarchie [anar'çi:] *f* (**-/-n**) anarchy.

anatomisch [ana'to:mɪʃ] *adj* anatomical.

Anbau ['anbau] *m* (**-[e]s/no pl**) *agr.* cultivation; (*pl* **-ten**) *arch.* annex(e), extension; **2en** *v/t* grow; *arch.* build.

anbehalten *v/t* keep on.

anbei [an'baɪ] *adv* enclosed.

an|beißen [an'baɪsən] *v/t* (*irr*) bite into; *v/i Fisch:* bite; **~beten** *v/t* adore, worship.

Anbetracht ['anbətraxt] *m:* **in ~** considering.

an|bieten [an'bi:tən] *v/t* (*irr*) offer; **~binden** *v/t* (*irr*) bind, tie (up).

Anblick ['anblɪk] *m* (**-[e]s/-e**) sight; spectacle; **2en** *v/t* look at; glance at.

an|brechen ['anbrɛçən] *v/t* (*irr*) *Vorräte:* break into; *Flasche:* open; *v/i* (*irr*) *Tag:* break, dawn; **~brennen** *v/i* (*irr*) burn; **~bringen** *v/t* (*irr*) bring; fix, attach; **~brüllen** *v/t* roar at.

An|dacht ['andaxt] *f* (**-/-en**) devotion; prayers *pl*; **2dächtig** [-dɛçtɪç] *adj* devout.

andauern ['andauərn] *v/i* continue, go on; **~d** *adj* continual, constant.

Andenken ['andɛŋkən] *n* (-s/*no pl*) memory, remembrance; **zum ~ an** in memory of; (-s/-) keepsake, souvenir.

ander ['andər] *adj* other; *verschieden:* different; *folgend:* next; **ein ~er** another; **nichts ~es** nothing else; **unter ~em** among other things; **~erseits** *adv* on the other hand.

ändern ['ɛndərn] *v/t, v/refl:* **(sich)** ~ alter, change.

andernfalls ['andərnfals] *adv* otherwise, (or) else.

anders ['andərs] *adv* different(ly); *andernfalls:* otherwise; **jemand ~** s.o. else; **~ werden** change; **~wo** *adv* elsewhere.

anderthalb ['andərt'halp] *adj* one and a half.

Änderung ['ɛndəruŋ] *f* (-/-en) change; alteration.

andeuten ['andɔytən] *v/t* hint; imply.

Andrang ['andraŋ] *m* (-[e]s/*no pl*) rush, run.

an|drehen ['andre:ən] *v/t Gas etc.:* turn on; *Licht: a.* switch on; **~eignen** *v/t:* **sich ~** appropriate, seize; *Kenntnisse:* acquire.

aneinander [an'ʔaɪ'nandər] *adv* together; **~geraten** *v/i* (*irr*) clash.

anekeln ['an'ʔe:kəln] *v/t* disgust, nauseate, sicken.

anerkennen ['an'ʔɛrkɛnən] *v/t* (*irr*) acknowledge, recognize; *lobend:* appreci-

ate; **~ung** *f* acknowledg(e)ment, recognition; appreciation.

anfahren ['anfa:rən] *v/i* (*irr*) start; **j-n ~** *v/t* run into s.o.; *fig.* snap at s.o.

Anfall ['anfal] *m* (-[e]s/*~e*) fit, attack; **~en** *v/t* (*irr*) attack.

anfällig ['anfɛlɪç] *adj* susceptible (**für** to).

Anfang ['anfaŋ] *m* (-s/*~e*) beginning, start; **2en** *v/i* (*irr*) begin, start.

Anfänger ['anfɛŋər] *m* (-s/-) beginner, learner.

anfangs ['anfaŋs] *adv* at the beginning.

Anfangsbuchstabe [-bu:xʃta:bə] *m* (-ns/-n) initial (letter); **großer ~** capital (letter).

an|fassen ['anfasən] *v/t packen:* seize; *berühren:* touch; **mit ~fassen** *v/i* lend a hand; **~fechten** *v/t* (*irr*) contest; dispute; **~fertigen** [-fɛrtɪgən] *v/t* make, manufacture; **~feuchten** ['anfɔyçtən] *v/t* moisten, wet; **~feuern** [-fɔyərn] *v/t sp.* cheer; **~flehen** *v/t* implore.

Anflug ['anflu:k] *m* (-s/*~e*) *aer.* approach (flight); *fig.* touch.

anforder|n ['anfordərn] *v/t* demand; request; **2ung** *f* demand; request; **2ungen** *pl* requirements *pl.*

Anfrage ['anfra:gə] *f* (-/-n) inquiry.

anǀfreunden ['anfrɔyndən]: **sich ~** *v/refl* make friends; **~fühlen: sich ~** *v/refl* feel.

anführǀen *v/t* lead; *zitieren:* quote; *täuschen:* dupe, fool; **2er** *m* (ring)leader; **2ungszeichen** [-tsaɪçən] *pl* quotation marks *pl*, inverted commas *pl.*

Angabe ['anga:bə] *f* (-/-n) declaration, statement; (*-/no pl*) *colloq.* bragging, showing off; **~n** *pl* information *sg;* directions *pl.*

angebǀen ['ange:bən] *v/t (irr)* declare, state; *einzeln:* specify; *Namen, Grund:* give; *v/i colloq.* brag, show off; **2er** *m colloq.* braggart; **~lich** *adj* supposed.

angeboren ['angəbo:rən] *adj* innate, inborn; *med.* congenital.

Angebot ['angəbo:t] *n* (-ǀe|s-e) offer; *Auktion:* bid; *econ.* supply.

angeǀbracht ['angəbraxt] *adj* appropriate, suitable; **~bunden** *adj* : **kurz ~** curt, short; **~heitert** *adj colloq.* slightly tipsy.

angehen ['ange:ən] *v/i (irr) colloq.:* go on; begin, start; *v/t* *j-n:* concern; **das geht dich nichts an** that is no business of yours.

angehörǀen ['angəhø:rən] *v/i* belong to; **2ige** *pl* relations *pl*, relatives *pl.*

Angeklagte ['angəkla:ktə] *m, f* (-n/-n) the accused, defendant.

Angel ['aŋəl] *f* (-/-n) *Tür:* hinge; fishing-rod.

Angelegenheit ['angəle:gənhaɪt] *f* (-/-en) business, concern, affair, matter.

angelehnt ['angəle:nt] *adj:* **~ sein** *Tür:* be ajar.

Angelǀgerät ['aŋəlgərɛ:t] *n* (-[e]s/-e) fishing-tackle; **~haken** *m* fishhook; **2n** *v/i, v/t* fish; **~rute** *f* fishing-rod; **~schnur** *f* fishing-line.

angeǀmessen ['angəmesən] *adj* suitable; adequate (*dat* to); **~nehm** [-ne:m] *adj* pleasant; **~regt** [-re:kt] *adj* animated, lively; **~sehen** [-ze:ən] *adj* respected.

Angesicht ['angəzɪçt] *n* (-s/-er) face, countenance; **2s** *prp* in view of.

angespannt ['angəʃpant] *adj fig.* tense.

Angestellte ['angəʃtɛltə] *m, f* (-n/-n) employee; **die ~n** *pl* the staff *sg.*

angeǀwandt ['angəvant] *adj* applied; **~wiesen** [-vi:zən] *adj:* **~ auf** dependent (up)on.

angeǀwöhnen ['angəvø:nən] *v/t:* **sich ~** get into the habit of; **2wohnheit** *f* habit.

Angina [aŋ'gi:na] *f* (-/-**Anginen**) angina, tonsillitis.

Angler ['aŋlər] *m* (-s/-) angler. **[nɪʃ]** *adj* Anglican.

anglikanisch [aŋli'ka:-

angreif|en ['angraɪfən] *v/t* (*irr*) touch; *feindlich:* attack; *Gesundheit:* affect; *chem.* corrode; **2r** *m* aggressor.

angrenzen ['angrɛntsən] *v/i* border (**an** on).

Angriff ['angrɪf] *m* (-[e]s; -e) attack, assault.

Angst [aŋst] *f* (-/-e) fear (**vor** of); **ich habe** ~ I am afraid.

ängst|igen ['ɛŋstɪgən] *v/t* frighten, alarm; **~lich** *adj* fearful, timid.

anhaben ['anha:bən] *v/t* (*irr*) have on.

anhalt|en ['anhaltən] *v/i* (*irr*) continue, last; stop; **den Atem** ~**en** *v/t* hold one's breath; **~end** *adj* continuous; **2er** *m* hitchhiker; **per 2er fahren** hitchhike; **2spunkt** *m* s.th. to go on, *Hinweis:* clue.

Anhang ['anhaŋ] *m* (-[e]s; ~e) appendix, supplement; followers *pl.*

anhäng|en ['anhɛŋən] *v/t* attach; **2er** *m* adherent, follower; *Schmuck:* pendant; *Schild:* label, tag; *Wagen:* trailer; **~lich** *adj* devoted, attached.

an|häufen ['anhɔʏfən] *v/t:* (**sich**) ~ accumulate; **~heben** *v/t* (*irr*) lift, raise.

Anhöhe ['anhø:ə] *f* (-/-n) rise, hill.

anhören ['anhø:rən] *v/t* listen to; **sich** ~ *v/refl* sound.

Ankauf ['ankaʊf] *m* (-[e]s; ~e) purchase.

Anker ['aŋkər] *m* (-s/-) anchor; **2n** *v/i, v/t* anchor.

Anklage ['ankla:gə] *f* (-/ -n) accusation, charge; **2n** *v/t* (*gen,* **wegen**) accuse (of), charge (with).

anklammern ['ankla-mərn] *v/t* clip s.th. on; **sich** ~ *v/refl* cling (**an** to).

Anklang ['anklaŋ] *m:* ~ **finden** meet with approval.

an|kleben ['ankle:bən] *v/t* stick on; *mit Leim:* glue on; *mit Kleister:* paste on; **~kleiden** [-klaɪdən] *v/t* dress (*a.* **sich**); **~klopfen** *v/i* knock (**an** at); **~knipsen** *v/t* switch on; **~kommen** *v/i* (*irr*) arrive; **~kommen auf** depend (up)on; **~kreuzen** *v/t* tick.

ankündig|en ['ankʏndɪ-gən] *v/t* announce; **2ung** *f* announcement.

Ankunft ['ankʊnft] *f* (-/no *pl*) arrival.

an|lächeln ['anlɛçəln] *v/t* smile at.

Anlage ['anla:gə] *f* (-/-n) *Bau:* construction, building; *Vorrichtung:* installation; *Werk:* plant; *Anordnung:* plan, layout; *zu e-m Schreiben:* enclosure; *econ.* investment; *Fähigkeit:* talent; **~n** *pl* grounds *pl,* park.

anlangen ['anlaŋən] *v/i* arrive (**in, an** at); *fig.* concern.

Anlaß ['anlas] m (**-sses/**
⁻sse) occasion; cause.

anlassen ['anlasən] v/t
(irr) Kleidung: leave od.
keep on; Licht etc.: leave
on; tech. start; **£r** m mot.
starter.

anläßlich ['anleslıç] prp
(gen) on the occasion of.

Anlauf ['anlauf] m (**-s/ᵘe**)
start; sp. run; **£en** v/i (irr)
start (up); run up; **Metall**:
tarnish; Spiegel etc.: cloud
over; v/t mar. call at.

anlegen ['anle:gən] v/t
put (**an** to, against); Garten: lay out; Straße: build;
Verband: apply; Vorräte:
lay in; Geld: invest; v/i mar.
land; **£stelle** f landing-
stage.

anlehnen ['anle:nən] v/t
Tür: leave od. set ajar;
(**sich**) **~ an** lean against
od. on.

anleiten ['anlaıtən] v/t instruct; **£ung** f instruction.

anliegen ['anli:gən] v/i
(irr) fit close od. tight(ly); **£**
n (**-s/-**) request.

anmachen ['anmaxən]
v/t colloq. fasten, fix; Feuer: make, light; colloq.
Licht: switch on; Salat:
dress; **~malen** v/t paint;
~maßend [-ma:sənt] adj
arrogant.

Anmeldeformular ['an-
mɛldəfɔrmula:r] n (**-s/-e**)
registration form; application form; **£egebühr** f registration fee; **£en** v/t an-

nounce; notify; **sich £en**
bei make an appointment
with; **~ung** f registration;
appointment.

anmerken ['anmɛrkən]
v/t mark; see, notice; **laß**
dir nichts ~en! don't
give yourself away; **£ung** f
note; **Fußnar**. a footnote.

Anmut ['anmu:t] f (**-/no pl**)
grace, charm; **£ig** adj
charming, graceful.

annageln v/t nail on; **~-**
nähen v/t sew on; **~nä-**
hernd ['annɛ:ərnt] adj approximate.

Annahme ['anna:mə] f (**-/**
-n) acceptance (a. fig.);
fig. assumption.

annehmbar ['anne:m-
ba:r] adj acceptable; Preis:
reasonable; **~en** [-ne:mən]
v/t (irr) accept (a. v/i); take;
fig. suppose, assume, Am.
guess; **sich ~en e-r Sache**
od. j-s: take care of s.th. od.
s.o.; **£lichkeit** f amenity.

Annonce [a'nõ:sə] f (**-/-n**)
advertisement.

anonym [ano'ny:m] adj
anonymous.

Anorak ['anorak] m (**-s/**
-s) anorak.

anordnen ['an?ordnən]
v/t arrange; order; **£ung** f
arrangement; order.

anpacken v/t seize,
grasp; **~passen** v/t adapt,
adjust; **~pflanzen** v/t
cultivate, plant; **~pro-**
bieren v/t try on; **~rech-**
nen v/t charge; credit.

Anrecht ['anrɛçt] n (**-[e]s/**

-e) right, title, claim (**auf** ~
-e) incentive.

Anrede ['anreːdə] f (-/-n)
address; 2n v/t address,
speak to.

anregen ['anreːgən] v/t
stimulate; suggest; ~**d** adj
stimulating.

Anreiz ['anraɪts] m (-es/
-e) incentive.

Anrichte ['anrɪçtə] f (-/-n)
sideboard; 2n v/t Speisen:
prepare, dress; Schaden:
cause.

Anruf ['anruːf] m (-s/-e)
call; 2en v/t (irr) call;
teleph. ring up, colloq.
phone, Am. call (up).

anrühren ['anryːrən] v/t
touch; mix.

Ansage ['anzaːgə] f (-/-n)
announcement; 2n v/t an-
nounce; ~**r(in** f) m an-
nouncer.

an|schaffen ['anʃafən] v/t
procure, get; purchase; ~-
schalten v/t switch od.
turn on.

anschauen ['anʃaʊən] v/t
look at; view; ~**lich** adj
clear, vivid, graphic.

Anschein ['anʃaɪn] m
(-[e]s/no pl) appearance;
allem ~ **nach** to all
appearances; 2end adv
apparently.

anschicken ['anʃɪkən] v/
refl: **sich** ~, **et. zu tun**
get ready to do s.th.

Anschlag ['anʃlaːk] m
(-[e]s/⁺e) touch; tech.
stop; notice; Plakat:
placard, poster, bill; (crim-

inal) attempt; ~**brett** n no-
tice-board, Am. bulletin
board; 2en v/t (irr) touch;
strike; Plakat: post od. put
up; v/i knock (**an** against).

anschließen ['anʃliːsən]
v/t (irr) connect; **sich** ~
j-m: join; ~**d** adj, adv
subsequent(ly); after-
wards.

Anschluß ['anʃlus] m
(-sses/⁺sse) connection,
a. connexion; ~ **finden**
an make friends with; ~
haben an rail., Boot:
connect with; ~**zug** m rail.
connection.

an|schmiegen ['anʃmiː-
gən] v/refl: **sich** ~ an nestle up to; ~**schmieren** v/t
(be)smear; fig. colloq.
cheat; ~**schnallen** v/t:
sich ~ fasten one's seat-
belt; ~**schnauzen** ['an-
ʃnaʊtsən] v/t colloq. snap
at; ~**schneiden** v/t (irr)
cut; Thema: broach; ~-
schrauben v/t screw on;
~**schreien** v/t (irr) shout
at.

Anschrift ['anʃrɪft] f (-/
-en) address.

an|schuldigen ['anʃʊldi-
gən] v/t accuse; ~**schwel-
len** v/i (irr) swell (a. fig.);
Fluß: rise; fig. increase; ~-
schwemmen ['-ʃvɛmən]
v/t wash ashore.

ansehen ['anzeːən] v/t
(irr) (take a) look at; see;
regard, consider; 2 n (-s/
no pl) prestige; respect.

ansehnlich ['anzeːnlɪç]

adj considerable; good-looking.

an|sengen ['anzɛŋən] *v/t* singe; **~setzen** *v/t* put (**an** to); **anstücken**: add (**an** to); *Termin*: fix, appoint.

Ansicht ['anzɪçt] *f* (*-/-en*) sight, view; *fig. s.* **Meinung**; **~karte** *f* picture postcard; **~ssache** *f* matter of opinion.

ansiedel|n ['anziːdəln] *v/t* (**sich**) ~ settle; **2lung** *f* settlement.

anspann|en ['anʃpanən] *v/t* stretch; harness (*to the carriage*); *fig.* strain; **2ung** *f fig.* strain.

anspielen ['anʃpiːlən] *v/i*: ~ **auf** allude to, hint at.

Ansporn ['anʃpɔrn] *m* (*-[e]s/no pl*) spur; **2en** *v/t* spur on.

Ansprache ['anʃpraːxə] *f* (*-/-n*) address, speech.

ansprechen ['anʃprɛçən] *v/t* (*irr*) speak to, address; **~d** *adj* appealing.

anspringen ['anʃprɪŋən] *v/t* (*irr*) leap at; *v/i Motor*: start.

Anspruch ['anʃprʊx] *m* (*-[e]s/ᵉe*) claim (**auf** *acc.*); **2slos** *adj* modest; simple; **2svoll** *adj* hard to please, fastidious.

Anstalt ['anʃtalt] *f* (*-/-en*) establishment; institution.

An|stand ['anʃtant] *m* (*-[e]s/no pl*) good manners *pl*; decency, propriety; **2-ständig** [-ʃtɛndɪç] *adj* de-

cent; respectable; *Preis*: reasonable; **2standslos** [-ʃtantsloːs] *adj* readily, without hesitation.

anstarren ['anʃtarən] *v/t* stare *od.* gaze at.

anstatt [an'ʃtat] *prp* (*gen*) instead of.

ansteck|en ['anʃtɛkən] *v/t* pin on; fasten on; *Ring*: put on; *med., fig.* infect; **~end** *adj med.* infectious (*a. fig.*), *Berührung*: contagious; **2ung** *f* catching; **2ung** *f* infection, contagion.

an|stehen ['anʃteːən] *v/i* (*irr*) queue (up), line up; **~steigen** [-ʃtaɪgən] *v/i* (*irr*) rise, ascend; *fig.* increase; **~stellen** *v/t* employ; *colloq. Tun*: do; **s. an-, einschalten**; **sich ~stellen** *v/refl* queue (up), line up.

Anstieg ['anʃtiːk] *m* (*-[e]s/-e*) ascent; rise.

an|stiften ['anʃtɪftən] *v/t* instigate; **~stimmen** *v/t* strike up.

Anstoß ['anʃtoːs] *m* (*-es/ᵉe*) *Fußball*: kickoff; *fig.* initiative; **~ erregen** give offence; ~ **nehmen** *an* take offence at; **2en** *v/t, v/i* (*irr*) push; knock; nudge; **auf j-s Gesundheit 2en** *v/i* drink (to) s.o.'s health.

anstößig ['anʃtøːsɪç] *adj* shocking.

anstrahlen ['anʃtraːlən] *v/t* illuminate; *j-n*: beam at.

anstreiche|n ['anʃtraɪçən] v/t (irr) paint; Fehler etc.: mark, underline; 2r m house-painter.

anstrengen ['anʃtrɛŋən] v/t exert; strain; (a. Augen); try; j-n: fatigue; **sich ~en** exert o.s.; **~end** adj strenuous; trying (**für** to); **2ung** f exertion, strain, effort.

Anstrich ['anʃtrɪç] m (-s/ -e) (coat of) paint.

Anteil ['antaɪl] m (-s/-e) share, portion; **~ nehmen an** take an interest in; sympathize with; **~nahme** [-naːmə] f (-/no pl) interest; sympathy.

Antenne [an'tɛnə] f (-/-n) aerial.

Antibiotikum [antibi'oː tikum] n (-s/-ka) antibiotic.

antik [an'tiːk] adj antique.

Antilope [anti'loːpə] f (- -n) antelope.

Antiquar|iat [antikva ri'aːt] n (-[e]s/-e) secondhand bookshop; **2sch** [an ti'kvaːrɪʃ] adj secondhand.

Antiquitäten [antikviˈteː tən] pl antiques pl; **~laden** m antique shop.

antiseptisch [anti'zɛptɪʃ] adj antiseptic.

Antlitz ['antlɪts] n (-es/ rare -e) face, countenance.

Antrag ['antraːk] m (- -[e]s/ʉe) offer, proposal; parl.: motion; **~steller** [-ʃtɛlər] m (-s/-) applicant.

an|treffen ['antrɛfən] v/t (irr) find; **~treiben** v/i (irr) drift ashore; v/t drive (on); **~treten** v/i (irr) line up; v/t Amt, Erbe: enter upon; Reise: set out on.

Antrieb ['antriːp] m (-s/ -e) drive, propulsion; fig. impulse.

antun ['antuːn] v/t (irr) j-m et. ~ do s.th. to s.o.; **sich et. ~** lay hands on o.s.

Antwort ['antvɔrt] f (-/ -en) answer, reply; **2en** v/i, v/t answer, reply.

an|vertrauen ['anfər trauən] v/t (en)trust; confide; **~wachsen** v/i (irr) take root; fig. increase.

Anwalt ['anvalt] m (-[e]s/ ʉe) s. Rechtsanwalt.

Anwärter ['anvɛrtər] m (-s/-) candidate, aspirant.

anweis|en ['anvaɪzən] v/t (irr) zuweisen: assign; anleiten: instruct; befehlen: direct, order; **2ung** f assignment; instruction; direction, order.

anwend|en ['anvɛndən] v/t (irr) use; apply; **2ung** f application; use.

anwesen|d ['anveːzənt] adj present; **2heit** f (-/no pl) presence.

anwidern ['anviːdərn] v/t s. anekeln.

Anzahl ['antsaːl] f (-/no pl) number, quantity.

anzahl|en ['antsaːlən] v/t pay on account; **2ung** f first instal(l)ment, deposit.

anzapfen ['antsapfən] *v/t* tap.

Anzeichen ['antsaiçən] *n* (-s/-) symptom, sign.

Anzeige ['antsaigə] *f* (-/-n) notice; *Zeitung*: advertisement; ∼n *v/t* notify; advertise; *Thermometer*: indicate; *Thermometer*: read; report *s.o.* to the police.

anziehen ['antsi:ən] *v/t* (*irr*) *Schraube*: tighten; *Kleidung*: put on; *j-n*: dress (*a.* sich); *fig.* attract; ∼d *adj* attractive.

Anzug ['antsu:k] *m* (-[e]s/ᵙe) suit.

anzüglich ['antsy:kliç] *adj* personal.

anzünden ['antsyndən] *v/t* light, kindle; *Streichholz*: strike; *Gebäude*: set on fire.

apathisch [a'pa:tiʃ] *adj* apathetic.

Apfel ['apfəl] *m* (-s/ᵙ) apple; ∼mus [-mu:s] *n* (-es/-e) apple-sauce; ∼saft *m* apple juice; ∼sine [apfəl-'zi:nə] *f* (-/-n) orange; ∼wein *m* cider.

Apostel [a'pɔstəl] *m* (-s/-) apostle.

Apostroph [apo'stro:f] *m* (-s/-e) apostrophe.

Apotheke [apo'te:kə] *f* (-/-n) chemist's shop, pharmacy, *Am.* drugstore; ∼r *m* chemist, *Am.* druggist.

Apparat [apa'ra:t] *m* (-[e]s/-e) apparatus; telephone; **am** ∼! speaking!; **am** ∼ **bleiben** hold the line.

Appartement [apart(ə)-'mã:] *n* (-s/-s) flat, *Am.* apartment.

appellieren [apɛ'li:rən] *v/i* appeal (**an** to).

Appetit [ape'ti:t] *m* (-[e]s/-e) appetite; ∼lich *adj* appetizing.

applaudieren [aplau-'di:rən] *v/i* applaud; ∼s [a'plaus] *m* (-es/*no pl*) applause.

Aprikose [apri'ko:zə] *f* (-/-n) apricot.

April [a'prɪl] *m* (-[s]/*no pl*) April.

Aquarell [akva'rɛl] *n* (-s/-e) water-colo(u)r.

Aquarium [a'kva:rĭʊm] *n* (-s/-rien) aquarium.

Äquator [ɛ'kva:tɔr] *m* (-s/*no pl*) equator.

Araber ['a(:)rabər] *m* (-s/-) Arab; **ᵃisch** [a'ra:bɪʃ] *adj* Arabian, Arab(ic).

Arbeit ['arbait] *f* (-/-en) work; labo(u)r; job; ∼en ['arbaitən] *v/i* work; labo(u)r; ∼er(in *f*) *m* worker; ∼geber [-ge:bər] *m* (-s/-) employer; ∼nehmer [-ne:mər] *m* (-s/-) employee.

Arbeits|amt ['arbaits-ʔamt] *n* (-[e]s/ᵙer) labo(u)r exchange; ∼kraft *f* worker, hand; **ᵃlos** *adj* out of work, unemployed; ∼lose [-lo:zə] *m, f* (-n/-n) unemployed person; **die** ∼**losen** *pl* the unemployed pl; ~**losengeld** n, ~**losenunterstützung** f unemployment benefit, colloq. dole; ~**losigkeit** f (-/no pl) unemployment; ~**pause** f break; ~**platz** m job; ~**tag** m workday; 2-**unfähig** adj incapable of working; ständig: disabled; ~**zeit** f working time; working hours pl; ~**zimmer** n study.

Archäologie [arçeo'lo:gə] m (-n/-n) arch(a)eologist; ~**ie** [-lo'gi:] f (-/no pl) arch(a)eology.

Architekt [arçi'tɛkt] m (-en/-en) architect; ~**ur** [-tɛk'tu:r] f (-/-en) architecture.

Archiv [ar'çi:f] n (-s/-e) archives pl; record office.

Arena [a're:na] f (-/-**Arenen**) arena; bullring.

arg [ark] adj bad.

Ärger ['ɛrgər] m (-s/no pl) Verdruß: vexation, annoyance; Zorn: anger; 2**lich** adj vexed, angry; annoying, vexatious; 2n v/t annoy, vex; **sich** 2n be angry.

Arglwohn ['arkvo:n] m (-[e]s/no pl) suspicion; 2-**wöhnisch** adj suspicious.

Arie [a:riə] f (-/-n) aria.

arm [arm] adj poor.

Arm m (-[e]s/-e) arm; Fluß: branch.

Armaturenbrett [arma'tu:rənbrɛt] n (-[e]s/-er) dashboard.

Armband ['armbant] n

(-[e]s/-**er**) bracelet; ~**uhr** f wrist watch.

Armee [ar'me:] f (-/-n [-ən]) army.

Ärmel ['ɛrməl] m (-s/-) sleeve; ~**kanal** m the (English) Channel.

ärmlich ['ɛrmlɪç] adj s. **armselig.**

armselig ['armze:lɪç] adj poor; wretched, miserable; schäbig: shabby.

Armut ['armu:t] f (-/no pl) poverty.

Aroma [a'ro:ma] n (-s/-**Aromen**) flavo(u)r.

Arrest [a'rɛst] m (-[e]s/-e) arrest; ~ **bekommen** be kept in.

arrogant [aro'gant] adj arrogant.

Art [a:rt] f (-/-en) kind, sort; bot., zo. species; Weise: manner, way.

Arterie [ar'te:riə] f (-/-n) artery.

artig ['a:rtɪç] adj good, well-behaved; civil, polite.

Artikel [ar'ti:kəl] m (-s/-) article (a. gr.); econ. a. commodity.

Artillerie [artɪlə'ri:] f (-/no pl) artillery.

Artist [ar'tɪst] m (-en/-en) performer, artiste.

Arznei [a:rts'naɪ] f (-/-en), ~**mittel** n medicine.

Arzt [a:rtst] m (-es/**e**) doctor; physician.

Ärztin ['ɛ:rtstɪn] f (-/-nen) (woman of. lady) doctor; 2**lich** adj medical.

As [as] n (-ses/-se) ace.

auf

Asche ['aʃə] f (-e/rare -n) ash(es pl); **~nbahn** f cinder-track, mot. dirt-track; **~nbecher** m ash-tray; **~rmittwoch** m Ash Wednesday.

Asiat [a'zīa:t] m (-en/-en) Asian, Asiatic; **2isch** adj Asian, Asiatic.

asozial [a(:)zotsīa:l] adj antisocial; asocial.

Asphalt [as'falt] m (-[e]s/-e) asphalt.

Assistent [asıs'tent] m (-en/-en), **~in** f assistant.

Ast [ast] m (-es/⁓e) branch, bough.

Aster ['astər] f (-/-n) aster.

Asthma ['astma] n (-s/no pl) asthma.

Astro|naut [astro'naut] m (-en/-en) astronaut; **~nomie** [-no'mi:] f (-/no pl) astronomy.

Asyl [a'zy:l] n (-s/-e) asylum.

Atelier [ate'līe:] n (-s/-s) studio.

Atem ['a:təm] m (-s/no pl) breath; **außer ~** out of breath; **~ holen** draw od. take breath; **2los** adj breathless; **~zug** m breath.

Äther ['ɛ:tər] m (-s/no pl) ether.

Athlet [at'le:t] m (-en/-en), **~in** f athlete; **2isch** adj athletic.

atlantisch [at'lantıʃ] adj Atlantic.

atmen ['a:tmən] v/i breathe.

Atmosphäre [atmo'sfɛ:-rə] f (-/-n) atmosphere.

Atmung ['a:tmuŋ] f (-/no pl) breathing.

Atom [a'to:m] n (-s/-e) atom; in Zssgn: atomic, nuclear; **2ar** [ato'ma:r] adj atomic; **~bombe** [a'to:m-] f atomic od. atom bomb, A-bomb; **~energie** f atomic od. nuclear energy; **~forschung** f atomic od. nuclear research; **~kraftwerk** n nuclear power station; **~reaktor** m s. **Reaktor**; **~waffe** f nuclear weapon.

Attent|at ['atənta:t] n (-s/-e) (attempted) assassination; **~äter** [-'tɛ:tər] m (-s/-) assassin.

Attest [a'test] n (-es/-e) certificate. [dummy.]

Attrappe [a'trapə] f (-/-n)|

Attribut [atri'bu:t] n (-[e]s/-e) attribute; gr. a. attributive.

ätzend ['ɛtsənt] adj corrosive, caustic (a. fig.); fig. biting.

au [au] int. oh!; ouch!

auch [aux] cj also, too; even; **~ nicht** neither, nor.

Audienz [au'dīents] f (-/-en) audience.

auf [auf] prp (dat) (up)on; in; at; from; to; up; **~ (... zu)** towards; **~ deutsch** adv open; **~ und ab gehen** walk up and down, walk to and fro; int.: **~!** up!

aufatmen ['aufʔa:tmən] *v/i* breathe (heave) a sigh of relief.

Aufbau ['aufbau] *m* (-[e]s/*no pl*) building; construction; **2en** *v/t* erect, build; construct.

auf|bekommen *v/t* (*irr*) *Tür:* get open; *Aufgabe:* be given; **~bewahren** *v/t* keep; preserve; **~bieten** *v/t* (*irr*) summon (up); **~binden** *v/t* (*irr*) untie; **~blasen** *v/t* (*irr*) blow up, inflate; **~bleiben** *v/i* (*irr*) sit up; *Tür* etc.: remain open; **~blenden** *v/i mot.* turn the headlights to full beam; **~blicken** *v/i* look up; **~blühen** *v/i* blossom (out); **~brausen** *v/i* fly into a passion; **~brechen** *v/t* (*irr*) break *od.* force open; *v/i* burst open; *fig.* set out; **2bruch** *m* (-[e]s/ *rare* ⁓e) departure, start; **~brühen** *v/t s.* aufgießen; **~bügeln** *v/t* press, iron; *Bettdecke:* turn down; *fig.:* expose; disclose; **~drängen** *v/t* force *od.* obtrude (up)on; **~drehen** *v/t* turn on; **~dringlich** [-drɪŋlɪç] *adj* obtrusive; **2-druck** *m* (-[e]s/-e) imprint; *Briefmarken:* surcharge.

aufeinander [aufʔaɪˈnandər] *adv* one upon the other; **~folgend** *adj* successive; consecutive; **~prallen** [-pralən] *v/i* col-

lide.

Aufenthalt ['aufenthalt] *m* (-[e]s/-e) stay; delay; **~ haben** *rail.* stop; **~sgenehmigung** *f* residence permit; **~sraum** *m* lounge.

Auferstehung ['aufʔerˌʃte:uŋ] *f* (-/*no pl*) resurrection.

auf|lessen *v/t* (*irr*) eat up; **~fahren** *v/i* (*irr*) *Person:* start up; **~fahren auf** *mot.* run into; **2fahrt** *f* drive, *Am.* driveway; **~fallen** *v/i* (*irr*) be conspicuous; **j-m ~fallen** strike s.o.; **~fallend,** **~fällig** *adj* striking; *Kleider:* flashy; **~fangen** *v/t* (*irr*) catch.

auffass|en ['auffasən] *v/t* comprehend; *deuten:* interpret; **2ung** *f* interpretation; view.

auffinden ['auffɪndən] *v/t* (*irr*) find, discover.

aufforder|n ['auffordərn] *v/t* ask; invite; request; **2ung** *f* invitation; request.

auffrischen ['auffrɪʃən] *v/t* freshen (up).

aufführ|en ['auffy:rən] *v/t thea.* (re)present, perform; *eintragen:* list, enter; **sich ~en** *v/refl* behave; **2ung** *f thea.* performance.

auffüllen ['auffʏlən] *v/t* fill up.

Aufgabe ['aufga:bə] *f* (-/ -n) task; duty; problem; homework; *Preisgabe:* abandonment; *Geschäfts*2:

giving up.

Aufgang ['aʊfgaŋ] *m* (-[e]s/ⸯe) *ast.* rising; stair-case.

auf|geben ['aʊfge:bən] *v/t* (irr) give up; abandon; *Anzeige:* insert; *Brief:* post, *Am.* mail; *Telegramm:* send; *Gepäck:* register, *Am.* check; *Hausaufgabe:* set, *Am.* assign; **~gehen** *v/i* (irr) open; *Naht:* come open; *hochgehen:* rise.

aufge|legt ['aʊfgəle:kt] *adj* disposed; in the mood; **gut** *od.* **schlecht ~legt** in a good *od.* bad mood; **~schlossen** [-ʃlɔsən] *adj fig.* open-minded; **~weckt** [-vɛkt] *adj fig.* bright.

auf|gießen ['aʊfgi:sən] *v/t* (irr) *Tee:* make, brew; **~greifen** *v/t* (irr) *fig.* take up; **~haben** *v/t* (irr) *colloq. Hut:* have on; *Aufgabe:* have to do; *v/i Geschäft:* be open; **~halten** *v/t* (irr) keep open; *anhalten:* stop, detain; *Verkehr:* hold up; **sich ~halten** *v/refl* stay.

aufhängen ['aʊfhɛŋən] *v/t* hang (up); *tech.* suspend; **⸮r** *m* tab.

auf|heben ['aʊfhe:bən] *v/t* (irr) lift (up); raise; pick up; *aufbewahren:* keep, preserve; *abschaffen:* abolish; *Versammlung:* break up; **~heitern** [-haɪtərn] *v/t* cheer up; **sich ~heitern** *v/refl* brighten (up); **~hellen** [-hɛlən] *v/t:*

(sich) ~ brighten (up); ~ **hetzen** *v/t* incite, instigate; **~holen** *v/t* make up for; *v/i* gain (**gegen** on); **~hören** *v/i* cease, stop, *Am.* quit; **~kaufen** *v/t* buy up; **~klären** *v/t* clear up (*a.* sich), enlighten (**über** *a.* sich); **~kleben** *v/t* paste up; **~knöpfen** *v/t* unbutton; **~kochen** *v/t*, *v/i* boil up; **~krempeln** [-krɛmpəln] *v/t* turn *od.* roll up; **~laden** *v/t* (irr) load; *electr.* charge.

Auflage ['aʊfla:gə] *f* (-/ -n) *Buch:* edition; *Zeitung:* circulation.

auflassen ['aʊflasən] *v/t* (irr) *colloq.:* leave open; *Hut:* keep on.

Auflauf ['aʊflaʊf] *m* (-[e]s/ⸯe) crowd; *Speise:* soufflé; baked sweet *od.* savo(u)ry pudding; **⸮en** *v/i* (irr) *Zinsen:* accrue; *Schiff:* run aground.

auf|legen ['aʊfle:gən] *v/t* apply; *Platte:* put on; *Buch:* print, publish; *teleph.* hang up (*a.* v/i); **~lehnen: sich ~** *v/refl* rebel, revolt; **~lesen** *v/t* (irr) gather, pick up; **~leuchten** *v/i* flash (up).

auflös|en ['aʊflø:zən] *v/t* undo, loosen; *Versammlung:* break up; *Ehe, Geschäft etc.:* dissolve; *Rätsel:* solve; **(sich)** **~en** *chem.* dissolve; **⸮ung** *f* (dis)solution); disintegration.

aufmachen ['aʊfmaxən]

v/t open; *Knoten:* undo; *Schirm:* put up.

aufmerksam ['aufmɛrkza:m] *adj* attentive; **j-n ~ machen auf** call s.o.'s attention to; **2keit** *f* attention.

aufmuntern ['aufmuntərn] *v/t* cheer up.

Aufnahme ['aufna:mə] *f* (-/-n) *Empfang:* reception; *Zulassung:* admission; *phot.* photograph; **e-e ~ machen** take a photograph; **~gebühr** *f* admission fee; **~prüfung** *f* entrance examination.

auf|nehmen ['aufne:mən] *v/t* (*irr*) take up; *Diktat etc.:* take down; *geistig:* take in; admit; receive; *Verhandlungen etc.:* enter into; *phot.* take; *filmen:* shoot; *mus. etc.:* record; **~passen** *v/i Schule:* be attentive; *vorsichtig sein:* look out; **~passen auf** look after; pay attention to; **~platzen** *v/i* burst open.

Aufprall ['aufpral] *m* (-s/ *no pl*) impact; **2en** *v/i:* **~ auf** crash into.

Aufpreis ['aufprais] *m* (-es/-e) extra charge.

auf|pumpen ['aufpumpən] *v/t* pump *od.* blow up; **~räumen** *v/t* clean up, tidy (*v/i:* up).

aufrecht ['aufrɛçt] *adj* upright (*a. fig.*), erect; **~erhalten** *v/t* (*irr*) maintain, uphold.

aufreg|en ['aufre:gən] *v/t*

excite; **sich ~en** get upset (**über** about); **2ung** *f* excitement.

auf|reiben ['aufraibən] *v/t* (*irr*) *Haut:* chafe; *fig.* wear out; **~reißen** *v/t* (*irr*) rip *od.* tear open; *Straße:* tear up; *Tür:* fling open; *Augen:* open wide; *v/i* split, burst; **~richten** *v/t* set up, erect; **sich ~richten** sit up; **~richtig** *adj* sincere; candid; **~rollen** *v/t* roll up; unroll; **~rücken** *v/i* move up.

Aufruf ['aufru:f] *m* (-[e]s -e) call, summons; **2en** *v/t* (*irr*) *j-n:* call s.o.'s name.

Aufruhr ['aufru:r] *m* (-[e]s/-e) uproar, tumult; riot, rebellion.

Aufrüstung ['aufrystʊŋ] *f* (-/-en) (re)armament.

aufsagen ['aufza:gən] *v/t* recite, repeat.

Aufsatz ['aufzats] *m* (-es/ ʾe) essay; *Schul2:* composition; *tech.* top.

auf|saugen ['aufzaugən] *v/t* absorb; **~schieben** *v/t* (*irr*) slide open; *fig.* put off, postpone, adjourn.

Aufschlag ['aufʃla:k] *m* (-s/ʾe) impact; extra charge; *Mantel:* lapel; *Hose:* turnup; *Ärmel:* cuff; *Tennis:* service; **2en** ['aufʃla:gən] *v/t* (*irr*) open; *Zelt:* pitch; *v/i* strike, hit; *Tennis:* serve.

auf|schließen *v/t* (*irr*) unlock, open; **~schneiden** *v/t* (*irr*) cut open; *Fleisch:*

cut up; v/i *colloq.* brag, boast.

Aufschnitt ['aʊfʃnɪt] *m* (-s/*no pl*) (slices *pl* of) cold meat, *Am.* cold cuts *pl.*

auf|schnüren ['aʊfʃny:-rən] *v/t* untie; *Schuh:* unlace; **~schrauben** *v/t* unscrew; screw (**auf** on); **~schrecken** [-ʃrɛkən] *v/t* startle; *v/i* start (up).

Aufschrei ['aʊfʃraɪ] *m* (-s/-e) shriek, scream.

aufschrei|ben ['aʊfʃraɪ-bən] *v/t* (*irr* write down; **~en** [-ʃraɪən] *v/i* (*irr*) cry out, scream.

Aufschrift ['aʊfʃrɪft] *f* (-/-en) inscription; *Brief:* address; label.

Aufschub ['aʊfʃu:p] *m* (-[e]s/ᵘe) delay.

aufschürfen ['aʊfʃʏrfən] *v/t Haut:* graze.

Aufschwung ['aʊfʃvʊŋ] *m* (-[e]s/ᵘe) *econ.* boom.

aufsehen ['aʊfze:ən] *v/i* (*irr*) look up; **2** *n* (-s/*no pl*) sensation; **2erregend** cause a sensation; **~erregend** *adj* sensational.

Aufseher ['aʊfze:ər] *m* (-s/-) overseer, supervisor.

aufsetzen ['aʊfzɛtsən] *v/t* put on; *Dokument:* draw up; **sich ~** *v/refl* sit up.

Aufsicht ['aʊfzɪçt] *f* (-/*no pl*) inspection, supervision; **~srat** *m* board of directors.

auf|spannen ['aʊfʃpa-nən] *v/t Schirm:* put up; **~**

~sparen *v/t* save; reserve; **~sperren** *v/t* unlock; **~spießen** [-ʃpi:sən] *v/t* pierce; *mit Hörnern:* gore; **~springen** *v/i* (*irr*) jump up; *Tür:* fly open; *Haut:* chap; **~stacheln** [-ʃta-xəln] *v/t* goad, incite; **~stampfen** *v/i* stamp (one's foot).

Auf|stand ['aʊfʃtant] *m* (-[e]s/ᵘe) insurrection, uprising, revolt; **~ständische** [-ʃtɛndɪʃə] *m, f* (-n/-n) rebel.

auf|stapeln ['aʊfʃta-pəln] *v/t* pile up; **~stecken** *v/t* pin up; *Haar:* put up; **~stehen** *v/i* (*irr*) stand up; rise, get up; stand open; **~steigen** *v/i* (*irr*) rise, ascend; *Reiter:* mount.

aufstell|en ['aʊfʃtɛlən] *v/t* set *od.* put up; *Kandidaten:* nominate; *Rechnung:* draw up; *Rekord:* set up, establish; **2ung** *f* nomination; list.

Aufstieg ['aʊfʃti:k] *m* (-[e]s/-e) ascent; *fig.* rise.

auf|stoßen ['aʊfʃto:sən] *v/t* push open; *v/i Essen:* repeat; *Person:* belch; **2strich** *m* spread; **~stützen:** **sich ~** *v/refl* lean (**auf** on); **~suchen** *v/t Ort:* visit; go to see; **~tanken** *v/t, v/i* fill up; (re)-fuel; **~tauchen** *v/i* emerge; *fig.* turn up; **~tauen** *v/i, v/t* thaw; **~teilen** *v/t* divide (up).

Auftrag ['auftra:k] *m* (-[e]s/^ze) commission; order (*a. econ.*), instruction; **₂en** [-tra:gən] *v/t (irr) Speisen*: serve; *Farbe*: lay on.

auf|treffen ['auftrefən] *v/i* (*irr*) strike, hit; **~trennen** *v/t* undo; **~treten** *v/i (irr)* tread; *thea. etc.*: appear; behave; *Schwierigkeiten*: arise.

Auftrieb ['auftri:p] *m* (-[e]s/-e) buoyancy; impetus, drive.

Auftritt ['auftrit] *m* (-s/-e) *thea.* scene (*a. fig.*); *Schauspieler*: appearance.

auf|wachen ['aufvaxən] *v/i* wake (up); **~wachsen** *v/i (irr)* grow up.

Aufwand ['aufvant] *m* (-[e]s/*no pl*) expense, expenditure; extravagance.

aufwärmen ['aufvermən] *v/t* warm up.

Aufwartefrau ['aufvartə-frau] *f* (-/-en) charwoman, *Am. a.* cleaning woman.

aufwärts ['aufverts] *adv* upward(s).

auf|waschen ['aufvaʃən] *v/t (irr)* wash up; **₂wasser** *n* dishwater.

auf|wecken ['aufvekən] *v/t* wake (up); **~weichen** *v/t* soak; soften; *v/i* become soft, soften; **~weisen** *v/t (irr)* show.

aufwert|en ['aufve:rtən] *v/t* revalue; **₂ung** *f* revaluation.

auf|wickeln ['aufvikəln]

v/t: (**sich**) **~** wind *od.* roll up; **~wiegeln** [-vi:gəln] *v/t* stir up, incite; **~wiegen** *v/t (irr) fig.* make up for; **~wirbeln** *v/t* whirl up; *Staub*: whirl up; **~wischen** *v/t* wipe up; **~zählen** *v/t* enumerate.

aufzeichn|en ['auftsaiç-nən] *v/t* draw; note down; record; **₂ung** *f* note; record.

aufziehen ['auftsi:ən] *v/t (irr)* draw *od.* pull up; *öffnen*: (pull) open; *Uhr etc.*: wind (up); *Kind*: bring up; **j-n ~** tease s.o.

Aufzug ['auftsu:k] *m* (-s/^ze) lift, *Am.* elevator; *thea.* act.

aufzwingen ['auftsviŋən] *v/t (irr)*: **j-m et. ~** force s.th. upon s.o.

Augapfel ['aug^ʔapfəl] *m* (-/^z) eyeball.

Auge ['augə] *n* (-s/-n) eye; *Sehkraft*: sight; *bot.* eye, bud; **im ~ behalten** keep an eye on; *fig.* bear in mind; **aus den ~n verlieren** lose sight of.

Augen|arzt *m* eye specialist; **~blick** *m* moment, instant; **₂blicklich** *adj* instantaneous; *vorübergehend*: momentary; *vorwärtig*: present; *adv* instant(aneous)ly; *at present*; **~braue** *f* eyebrow; **~licht** *n* (-[e]s/*no pl*) eyesight; **~lid** *n* eyelid; **~zeuge** *m* eye-witness.

August [au'gust] *m* (-[e]s,

         auseinandersetzen

-/no pl) August.

Auktion [aʊk'tsɪo:n] *f* (*-/ -en*) auction.

Aula ['aʊla] *f* (*-/Aulen, -s*) (assembly) hall, *Am.* auditorium.

aus [aʊs] *prp* (*dat.*) out of; from; of; for; by; in; by ~ **diesem Grunde** for this reason; *adv* out; over; *auf Geräten:* **an** - ~ **on** - **off**.

aus|arbeiten ['aʊs²arbaɪtən] *v/t* work out; *sorgsam:* elaborate; ~**atmen** *v/i*, *v/t* breathe out; ~**bauen** *v/t* extend; develop; ~**bessern** [-bɛsərn] *v/t* mend, repair.

Ausbeute ['aʊsbɔʏtə] *f* (*-/ no pl*) profit; *Ertrag:* yield; *Bergbau:* output; 2**n** *v/t* exploit (*a. fig.*).

ausbild|en ['aʊsbɪldən] *v/t* develop; train, instruct; educate; *mil.* drill; 2**ung** *f* development; training, instruction; education; *mil.* drill.

ausbleiben ['aʊsblaɪbən] *v/i* (*irr*) stay away, fail to appear.

Ausblick ['aʊsblɪk] *m* (*-[e]s/-e*) outlook, view.

aus|brechen ['aʊsbrɛçən] *v/i* (*irr*) break out; ~**breiten** [-braɪtən] *v/t* spread (out); stretch; **sich** ~ **breiten** spread.

Ausbruch ['aʊsbrʊx] *m* (*-[e]s/²e*) outbreak (*a. fig.*); *Vulkan:* eruption; *Flucht:* escape; *Gefühl:* outburst.

aus|brüten ['aʊsbry:tən] *v/t* hatch (*a. fig.*); ~**bürsten** [-byrstən] *v/t* brush.

Ausdauer ['aʊsdaʊər] *f* (*-/ no pl*) perseverance; 2**nd** *adj* persevering.

ausdehn|en ['aʊsde:nən] *v/t* (**sich** ~) extend; expand; 2**ung** *f* extension; expansion.

aus|denken ['aʊsdɛŋkən] *v/t* (*irr*) think *s.th.* out; devise, invent; *vorstellen:* imagine; ~**drehen** *v/t s.* ausschalten.

Ausdruck ['aʊsdrʊk] *m* (*-[e]s/²e*) expression.

ausdrück|en ['aʊsdry-kən] *v/t* press, squeeze (out); *Zigarette:* stub out; express; ~**lich** *adj* express.

ausdrucks|los ['aʊs-drʊkslo:s] *adj* expressionless; *leer:* blank; vacant; ~**voll** *adj* expressive; 2**weise** *f* mode of expression; style.

Ausdünstung ['aʊsdynstʊŋ] *f* (*-/-en*) odo(u)r; smell.

auseinander [aʊs²aɪ-'nandər] *adv* apart; broken up; ~**bringen** *v/t* (*irr*) separate; ~**fallen** *v/i* (*irr*) fall apart; *fig.* break up; ~**gehen** *v/i* (*irr*) *Versammlung:* break up; *Meinungen:* differ; *Freunde:* part; *Menge:* disperse; ~**nehmen** *v/t* (*irr*) take apart; *tech.* dismantle.

auseinandersetz|en *v/t:* **sich** ~ **mit** *Problem:* grapple with; *j-m:* argue

auserlesen

with; 2**ung** f discussion; argument.

auserlesen ['aus?ɛrle:-zən] adj exquisite, choice.

ausfahr|en ['ausfa:rən] v/i, v/t (irr) go od. take for a drive; Baby: take out (in the pram); 2t f departure; Ausflug: drive, ride; gateway, drive; exit, way out.

ausfall|en ['ausfalən] v/i (irr) fall out; Maschine etc.: break down; nicht stattfinden: be cancel(l)ed; Ergebnis: turn out; ~**end** adj insulting; 2**straße** f arterial road.

aus|fegen ['ausfe:gən] v/t sweep (out); ~**findig** adj: ~ **machen** find out; ~**fließen** v/i (irr) flow od. run out.

Ausflucht ['ausfluxt] f (-/ ⁅e): Ausflüchte **machen** make excuses.

Ausflug ['ausflu:k] m (-[e]s/⁅e) excursion, trip.

ausfragen ['ausfra:gən] v/t question (über about), sound (über on).

Ausfuhr ['ausfu:r] f (-/ -en) export(ation).

ausführen ['ausfy:rən] v/t execute, carry out; econ. export; j-n: take out.

Ausfuhrgenehmigung f (-/-en) export permit od. licen|ce (Am. -se).

ausführlich ['ausfy:rlıç, aus'fy:rlıç] adj detailed; umfassend: comprehensive; adv in detail, at (some) length.

Ausführung ['ausfy:ruŋ] f (-/-en) execution; workmanship; model, make.

Ausfuhr|verbot ['aus-fu:rfɛrbo:t] n (-[e]s/-e) export ban; ~**zoll** [-tsɔl] m (-[e]s/⁅e) export duty.

ausfüllen ['ausfylən] v/t fill in (bsd. Am. out).

Ausgabe ['ausga:bə] f (-/ -n) distribution; Buch: edition; Geld: expense, expenditure.

Ausgang ['ausgaŋ] m (-[e]s/⁅e) exit, way out; end; result; ~**spunkt** m starting-point.

ausgeben ['ausge:bən] v/t (irr) give out; Geld: spend; **sich ~ für** pass o.s. off for.

ausge|beult ['ausgə-bɔylt] adj baggy; ~**bucht** [-bu:xt] adj booked up; ~**dehnt** [-de:nt] adj extensive, vast.

ausgehen ['ausge:ən] v/i (irr) go out; Haare: fall out; Geld, Vorräte: run out; end.

ausge|lassen ['ausgəla-sən] adj lively, boisterous; ~**nommen** [-nɔmən] prp except; ~**rechnet** ['aus-gə'rɛçnət] adv: ~ **er** he of all people; ~ **heute** today of all days; ~**schlossen** [-ʃlɔsən] adj impossible; ~**schnitten** [-ʃnıtən] adj low-necked; ~**sucht** [-zu:xt] adj exquisite; choice; ~**zeichnet** [-tsaıçnət] adj excellent.

ausgiebig ['ausgi:biç] *adj*
abundant, plentiful; *Mahlzeit:* substantial.

aus|gießen ['ausgi:sən]
v/t (irr) pour out; **~glei-
chen** [-glaiçən] *v/t (irr)*
equalize (*a. sp.*);
compensate; **~gleiten** *v/i
(irr)* slip; **~graben** *v/t
(irr)* dig out *od.* up; excavate.

Ausguß ['ausgus] *m
(-sses/*vsse) sink.

aus|halten ['aushaltən]
v/t (irr) endure, bear,
stand; **~händigen** [-hɛn-
dɪɡən] *v/t* deliver, hand
over.

Aushang ['aushaŋ] *m
(-[e]s/*ve) notice.

aus|hängen ['aushɛŋən]
v/t hang *od.* put out; *Tür:*
unhinge; **~harren** [-ha-
rən] *v/i* hold out; **~helfen**
v/i help out; **~höhlen**
[-hø:lən] *v/t* hollow out;
~holen *v/i:* (**mit der
Hand**) **~** raise one's hand;
~horchen *v/t* sound,
pump; **~kehren** *v/t/i* sweep
(out); **~kennen** *v/refl
(irr):* **sich ~ in** (*dat*) know
a place; know all about
s.th.; **~kleiden** *v/t tech.*
line, coat; **~klopfen** *v/t*
beat (out); *Pfeife:* knock
out; **~knipsen** *v/t colloq.*
s. **ausschalten; ~kom-
men** *v/i (irr):* **~ mit** *et.:*
manage with; *j-m:* get on
with.

Auskunft ['auskunft] *f (-/*
ve) information; = **~s-**

büro *n* inquiry office, *Am.*
information desk.

aus|kuppeln ['auskup-
pəln] *v/t* declutch; **~la-
chen** *v/t* laugh at; **~la-
den** *v/t (irr)* unload.

Auslage ['ausla:gə] *f (-/
-n)* display, show; **~n** *pl*
expenses *pl.*

Ausland ['auslant] *n
(-[e]s/no pl):* **das ~** foreign countries *pl;* **ins** *od.*
im ~ abroad.

Ausländ|er ['auslɛndər]
m, **~erin** *f* foreigner;
2isch *adj* foreign.

Auslands|aufenthalt *m*
stay abroad; **~korre-
spondent** *m* foreign
correspondent; **~reise** *f*
journey abroad.

aus|lassen ['auslasən] *v/t
(irr) Fett:* render down;
Saum: let down; *Wort:*
leave out, omit; miss out;
2ungszeichen *n* apostrophe.

aus|laufen ['auslaufən]
v/i-i leak; end; *mar.* (set)
sail; **~leeren** *v/t* empty.

aus|legen ['ausle:gən] *v/t*
lay out; *Waren: a.* display;
deuten: interpret; *Geld:*
advance; **2ung** *f* interpretation.

ausleihen ['auslaiən] *v/t
(irr)* lend, *Am. a.* loan.

Auslese ['ausle:zə] *f (-/no
pl)* selection; **2n** *v/t (irr)*
pick out, select; *Buch:* finish reading.

ausliefer|n ['ausli:fərn]
v/t deliver; *Verbrecher:* ex-

tradite; **2ung** f delivery; extradition;

aus|löschen ['auslœʃən] v/t Licht: put out, switch off; Feuer etc.: extinguish (a. fig.); wipe out (a. fig.); **~losen** [-lo:zən] v/t draw lots.

auslöse|n ['auslø:zən] v/t tech. release; Gefangene: ransom; Pfand: redeem; fig. start; **2r** m release.

aus|lüften ['auslyftən] v/t air; **~machen** v/t betragen: amount to; Feuer: put out; Licht etc. s. **ausschalten**; vereinbaren: agree on, arrange; **würde es Ihnen et. ~machen zu ...?** would you mind (ger) ...?

Ausmaß ['ausma:s] n (-es/-e) extent.

ausmessen ['ausmesən] v/t (irr) measure.

Ausnahme ['ausna:mə] f (-/-n) exception; **2slos** adv, adj without exception; **2sweise** adv (just) for once.

aus|nutzen ['ausnutsən] v/t utilize; Gelegenheit: take advantage of; j-n, et.: exploit; **~packen** v/t unpack; **~pressen** v/t squeeze (out); **~probieren** v/t try, test.

Auspuff ['auspuf] m (-[e]s/-e) exhaust; **~gase** [-ga:zə] pl exhaust fumes pl; **~topf** m silencer, Am. muffler.

aus|radieren ['ausradi:-rən] v/t erase; **~rangieren** [-rãːʒiːrən] v/t discard; **~rasieren** v/t: den Nacken ~ shave the neck clean; **~rauben** v/t rob; **~räumen** v/t empty, clear out; **~rechnen** v/t calculate.

Ausrede ['ausre:də] f (-/-n) excuse; **2n** v/i finish speaking; **2n lassen** hear s.o. out.

ausreichen ['ausraiçən] v/i suffice, be enough; **~d** adj sufficient.

Ausreise ['ausraizə] f (-/-n) departure; **2n** v/i leave (a country); **~visum** [-viːzum] n (-s/-visa) exit visa.

aus|reißen ['ausraisən] v/t (irr) pull od. tear out; v/i colloq. run away; **~renken** [-reŋkən] v/t dislocate; **~richten** v/t Botschaft: give; erreichen: accomplish, achieve; **~rotten** [-rɔtən] v/t exterminate.

Ausruf ['ausru:f] m (-[e]s/-e) cry; exclamation; ling. interjection; **2en** v/t (irr) cry out, exclaim; **~ezeichen** n, **~ungszeichen** n exclamation mark (Am. a. point).

ausruhen ['ausru:ən] v/t: (sich) ~ rest.

ausrüst|en ['ausrystən] v/t fit out, equip; **2ung** f outfit; equipment.

ausrutschen ['ausrutʃən] v/i slip.

Aussage ['aʊszaːgə] f (-/ -n) statement; declaration; jur. evidence; gr. predicate; 2n v/t state, declare; v/i jur. give evidence.

aus|saugen ['aʊszaʊgən] v/t suck (out); **~schalten** v/t Licht: switch off; Gas etc.: turn off od. out; **~scheiden** v/t (irr) eliminate; med. secrete; v/i retire (**aus** from); be eliminated, aufgeben: drop out; **~scheren** [-ʃeːrən] v/i pull out; **~schimpfen** v/t scold; **~schlafen** v/i (irr) get enough sleep; sleep late.

Ausschlag ['aʊsʃlaːk] m (-[e]s/ ^{u}e) med. rash; Zeiger: deflection; 2en v/i (irr) Pferd: kick; Zeiger: deflect; v/t knock out; fig. reject; 2gebend adj decisive.

ausschließen ['aʊsʃliːsən] v/t (irr) shut od. lock out; fig.: exclude; ausstoßen: expel; **~lich** adj exclusive.

Ausschluß ['aʊsʃlʊs] m (-sses/ˇsse) exclusion; expulsion.

aus|schmücken ['aʊsˌʃmʏkən] v/t decorate; fig. embellish; **~schneiden** v/t (irr) cut out.

Ausschnitt ['aʊsʃnɪt] m (-[e]s/-e) Kleid: (low) neck; Zeitung: cutting, clipping; fig. section.

ausschreiben ['aʊsʃraɪbən] v/t (irr) write out;

Rechnung etc.: make out; Stelle: advertise.

Ausschreitung ['aʊsʃraɪtʊŋ] f (-/-en) riot.

Ausschuß ['aʊsʃʊs] m (-sses/ˇsse) Vertretung: committee; (no pl) substandard goods pl.

aus|schütteln ['aʊsʃʏtəln] v/t shake out; **~schütten** v/t pour out; spill; **~schweifend** adj dissolute.

aussehen ['aʊszeːən] v/i (irr) look; 2 n (-s/no pl) look(s pl), appearance.

aussein ['aʊszaɪn] v/i colloq.: be out; be over.

außen ['aʊsən] adv (on the) outside; **nach** ~ outward(s).

Außen|bordmotor ['aʊsənbɔrdmoːtɔr] m (-s/-en) outboard motor; **~handel** m foreign trade; **~minister** m foreign minister, Brit. Foreign Secretary, Am. Secretary of State; **~politik** f foreign policy; **~seite** f outside; **~seiter** [-zaɪtər] m (-s/-) outsider; **~welt** f outer od. outside world.

außer ['aʊsər] prp (dat) out of; except; besides; **~wenn** cj unless; **~dem** cj besides, moreover.

äußere ['ɔʏsərə] adj exterior, outer, outward; 2 n (-n/no pl) exterior, outside; outward appearance.

außer|gewöhnlich ['aʊsərgevøːnlɪç] adj excep-

tional; **~halb** [-halp] *prp*
(*gen*) outside, out of; *jenseits*: beyond.

äußerlich ['ɔʏsərlɪç] *adj*
external, outward.

äußern ['ɔʏsərn] *v/t* utter,
express.

außerordentlich ['au-
sər?ɔrdəntlɪç] *adj* extraordinary.

äußerst ['ɔʏsərst] *adj, adv*
outermost; *fig.* utmost; ex-
treme(ly).

außerstande ['ausər-
'ʃtandə] *adv* unable.

Äußerung ['ɔʏsərʊŋ] *f* (*-/
-en*) utterance, remark.

aussetzen ['auszɛtsən] *v/t*
Belohnung: offer; *et., j-n,
sich*: expose (*dat* to); **et.**
auszusetzen haben
an find fault with; *v/i* stop;
Motor: a. fail; **mit et.**
interrupt s.th.

Aussicht ['auszɪçt] *f* (*-/
-en*) view (**auf** of); *fig.*
chance; **~slos** *adj* hopeless, desperate.

aus|söhnen ['auszøːnən]:
sich ~ (mit) *v/refl* become
reconciled (with); **~sor-
tieren** [-zɔrtiːrən] *v/t* sort
out; **~spannen** *v/t fig.*
(take a) rest, relax;
~sperren *v/t* shut out;
lock out; **~spielen** *v/t*
Karte: play; *v/i* **beim Kar-
tenspielen**: lead.

Aussprache ['ausʃpraː-
xə] *f* (*-/-n*) pronunciation,
accent; talk, discussion;
2sprechen *v/t* (*irr*) pro-
nounce; express; *v/i* finish

speaking; **~spruch** *m* remark.

aus|spucken *v/t* spit out;
v/i spit; **~spülen** *v/t* rinse.

ausstatten ['ausʃtatən]
v/t furnish, supply; **2ung** *f*
equipment; furnishings *pl*;
Buch: getup.

aus|stehen ['ausʃteːən]
v/i (*irr*) *econ.* be outstanding; *v/t* endure, bear;
~steigen *v/i* (*irr*) get out
od. off, alight.

ausstell|en ['ausʃtelən]
v/t exhibit, display; *Rechnung, Scheck*: make out;
Paß: issue; **2er** *m* exhibi-
tor; **2ung** *f* exhibition,
show.

aussterben ['ausʃtɛrbən]
v/i (*irr*) die out.

Aussteuer ['ausʃtɔʏər] *f*
(*-/no pl*) trousseau.

aus|stopfen *v/t* stuff,
pad; **~stoßen** *v/t* eject;
Schrei: utter;
Seufzer: heave; *fig.* expel;
~strahlen *v/t, v/i* radiate;
~strecken *v/t* stretch
(out); **~streichen** *v/t* (*irr*)
strike out *od.* out; **~strö-
men** *v/i* stream out; *Gas,
Dampf*: escape; *Geruch*: exhale; **~suchen** *v/t* choose,
select.

Austausch ['austauʃ] *m*
(*-[e]s/no pl*) exchange;
2en *v/t* exchange.

austeilen ['austailən] *v/t*
distribute.

Auster ['austər] *f* (*-/-n*)
oyster.

austragen ['austraːgən]

v/t (*irr*) *Briefe etc.*: deliver; *Wettkampf*: hold.

Australi|er [aʊs'traːliər] *m* (-s/-) Australian; **2sch** *adj* Australian.

aus|treiben ['aʊstraɪbən] *v/t* (*irr*) drive out; *vertreiben*: *a.* expel; **~treten** *v/t* (*irr*) tread *od.* stamp out; *Stufen etc.*: wear down; **~treten aus** *v/i* leave, resign from; **~trinken** *v/t* (*irr*) drink up; finish; **~trocknen** *v/t* dry (up); *Boden, Kehle*: parch; *v/i* dry up; become dry *od.* parched; **~üben** *v/t* exercise; *Beruf*: practi|se, *Am.* -ce, follow; *Einfluß, Druck*: exert.

Ausverkauf ['aʊsfɛrkaʊf] *m* (-[e]s/ᵈe) sale; **2t** *adj* sold out; *thea. a.* full house.

Auswahl ['aʊsvaːl] *f* (-/*no pl*) choice, selection; *econ.* assortment.

auswählen ['aʊsvɛːlən] *v/t* choose, select.

Auswander|er ['aʊsvandərər] *m* (-s/-) emigrant; **2n** *v/i* emigrate; **~ung** *f* emigration.

auswärts ['aʊsvɛrts] *adv* out of town; **von ~** from another place *od.* town.

aus|waschen ['aʊsvaʃən] *v/t* (*irr*) wash out; **~wechseln** *v/t*: ~ (**gegen**) (ex)change (for), exchange.

Ausweg ['aʊsveːg] *m* (-[e]s/ᵈe) way out.

Ausweiche ['aʊsvaɪçə] *f* (-/-n) road widening, *Am.* turnout; **2n** *v/i* (*irr*) make way (*dat* for); evade, avoid (*a. fig.*); **2nd** *adj* evasive.

Ausweis ['aʊsvaɪs] *m* (-es/-e) identity card; **2en** [-vaɪzən] *v/t* expel; **sich 2en** prove one's identity; **~papiere** *pl* identification papers *pl*; **~ung** *f* expulsion.

aus|weiten ['aʊsvaɪtən] *v/t*: (**sich**) ~ widen, stretch, expand; **~wendig** [-vɛndɪç] *adv* by heart; **~werten** [-veːrtən] *v/t* evaluate; *verwerten*: exploit; **~wickeln** *v/t* unwrap; **~wirken: sich ~ auf** *v/refl* affect; **~wischen** *v/t* wipe out; **~wringen** *v/t* (*irr*) wring out; **~zahlen** *v/t* pay (out); pay *s.o.* off; **sich ~zahlen** pay; **~zählen** *v/t* count (out); **2zahlung** *f* payment.

auszeichnen ['aʊstsaɪçnən] *v/t* mark; *fig.* distinguish (**sich** o.s.); **2ung** *f* marking; *fig.* distinction, hono(u)r; *Orden*: decoration; award, prize.

ausziehen ['aʊstsiːən] *v/t* (*irr*) draw out; *Kleid*: take off; undress (*a.* **sich**); *v/i* **aus e-r Wohnung**: move (out).

Auszug ['aʊstsuːk] *m* (-es/ᵈe) departure; removal; *Buch etc.*: extract, excerpt; *Konto*: statement (of account).

Auto ['auto] *n* (-s/-s) (motor-)car; ~ **fahren** drive, slip-road; motor.

Autobahn ['autoˌbaːn] *f* (-/-en) motorway, *Am.* superhighway, freeway; ~**ausfahrt** *f* (motorway) exit, slip-road; ~**einfahrt** *f* access road, slip-road; ~**gebühr** *f* toll; ~**zubringer** [-tsuːˌbrɪŋər] *m* (-s/-) feeder road.

Autobiographie [autobiogra'fiː] *f* (-/-n) autobiography.

Autobus ['autobus] *m* (-ses/-se) (motor-)bus; (motor-)coach; ~**bahnhof** *m* bus station; ~**haltestelle** *f* bus stop.

Autofähre [autoˈfɛːrə] *f* (-/-n) car ferry; ~**fahrer** *m* motorist, driver.

Autogramm [auto'gram] *n* (-s/-e) autograph.

Autohändler ['autoˌhɛndlər] *m* (-s/-) car dealer; ~**hilfe** *f* breakdown service; ~**karte** *f* road map; ~**kino** *n* drive-in cinema.

Automat [auto'maːt] *m*

(-en/-en) slot-machine, vending-machine; ~**enrestaurant** *n* automat; ~**ion** [automaˈtsǐoːn] *f* (-/ no *pl*) automation; 2**isch** [auto'maːtɪʃ] *adj* automatic.

Automechaniker ['automeçaːnikər] *m* (-s/-) car mechanic; ~**mobil** [automoˈbiːl] *n* (-s/-e) *s.* Auto; ~**mobilklub** *m* automobile association.

Autor ['autor] *m* (-s/-en) author.

Autoreisezug *m* rail. motorail train.

Autorin [au'toːrɪn] *f* (-/-nen) author(ess).

autorisieren [autoriˈziːrən] *v/t* authorize; ~**tär** [autoriˈtɛːr] *adj* authoritarian; 2**tät** [autoriˈtɛːt] *f* (-/-en) authority.

Autostraße *f* (motor) road; ~**verkehr** *m* (motor) traffic; ~**verleih** *m* [autoferˈlai] *m* (-[e]s/-e) car hire (*Am.* car rental) service; ~**zubehör** *n* (car) accessories *pl*.

Axt [akst] *f* (-/ᵘe) ax(e).

B

Baby ['beːbi] *n* (-s/-s) baby.

Bach [bax] *m* (-[e]s/ᵘe) brook.

Backbord ['bakbort] *n* (-[e]s/-e) *mar.* port.

Backe ['bakə] *f* (-/-n) cheek.

backen ['bakən] *v/t, v/i* bake.

Backenbart *m* (side)whiskers *pl, Am.* sideburns *pl*; ~**zahn** *m* molar (tooth).

Bäcker ['bɛkər] *m* (-s/-) baker; ~**ei** [bɛkə'rai] *f* (-/

-en) baker's shop; bakery.

Back|hähnchen ['bak-hɛ:nçən] n (-s/-) fried chicken; ~obst n dried fruit; ~ofen m oven; ~stein m brick.

Bad [ba:t] n (-[e]s/ˇer) bath; s. Badeort.

Bade|anstalt ['ba:dəˀan-ʃtalt] f (-/-en) baths; ~anzug m bathing-costume, bathing-suit; ~hose f (swimming- od. bathing)trunks pl; ~kappe f bathing-cap; ~mantel m bathrobe; ~meister m bath attendant; 2n ['ba:dən] v/t bath; Augen, Wunde: bathe; v/i have od. take a bath; im Freien: bathe; 2n gehen go swimming; ~ort ['ba:dəˀɔrt] m (-[e]s/-e) spa; seaside resort; ~strand m (bathing) beach; ~tuch n bath-towel; ~wanne f bath(tub); ~zimmer n bathroom.

Bagger ['bagər] m (-s/-) excavator; 2n v/t, v/i excavate.

Bahn [ba:n] f (-/-en) course; railway, Am. railroad; mot. lane; ast. orbit; sp. track; Eis2: rink; Kegel2: alley; **mit der ~** by train; **~damm** m railway (Am. railroad) embankment; 2en ['ba:nən] v/t: **sich e-n Weg ~** force one's way; ~hof ['ba:nho:f] m (-[e]s/ˇe) (railway, Am. railroad) station; ~steig m (-[e]s/-e) platform; ~übergang m level (Am. grade) crossing.

Bahre ['ba:rə] f (-/-n) stretcher.

Bakterie [bak'te:riə] f (-/-n) bacterium, germ.

bald [balt] adv soon; fast: almost, nearly; **so ~ wie** as soon as.

Balken ['balkən] m (-s/-) beam; Dach: rafter.

Balkon [bal'kɔːn; bal'kõ:] m (-s/-s, -e) balcony.

Ball [bal] m (-[e]s/ˇe) ball; dance, ball.

ballen ['balən] v/t Faust: clench.

Ballen m (-s/-) bale; anat. ball.

Ballett [ba'lɛt] n (-[e]s/-e) ballet.

Ballon [ba'lɔːn; ba'lõ:] m (-s/-s, -e) balloon.

Ball|saal m ballroom; ~spiel n ball-game.

Bambus ['bambus] m (-, -ses/-se) bamboo.

banal [ba'na:l] adj commonplace, banal.

Banane [ba'na:nə] f (-/-n) banana.

Band¹ [bant] n (-[e]s/ˇe) volume.

Band² n (-[e]s/ˇer) band; ribbon; Meß2, Ton2, Ziel2: tape; anat. ligament; fig. (pl -e) bond, tie.

bandagieren [banda'ʒiː-rən] v/t bandage.

Bande ['bandə] f (-/-n) gang, band.

bändigen ['bɛndigən] v/t

tame; subdue (*a. fig.*); *fig.*
restrain.
Bandscheibe ['bantʃaɪ-
bə] *f* (-/-n) intervertebral
disc.
bang(e) [baŋ, 'baŋə] *adj*
anxious, uneasy; **mir ist ~**
I am afraid.
Bank¹ [baŋk] *f* (-/ᵕe)
bench; *Schul2:* desk.
Bank² *f* (-/-en) *econ.* bank;
~beamte *m* (-n/-n) bank
clerk *od.* official; **~ier**
[baŋ'kiːe:] *m* (-s/-s) bank-
er; **~konto** *n* (-s/-ten)
account; **~note** *f* (bank)-
note, *Am.* (bank) bill.
bankrott [baŋ'krɔt] *adj*
bankrupt.
Bann [ban] *m* (-[e]s/-e)
ban; *fig.* spell.
Banner ['banər] *n* (-s/-)
banner.
bar [baːr] *adj:* **(in) ~ (in)**
cash.
Bar *f* (-/-s) bar; nightclub.
Bär [bɛːr] *m* (-en/-en)
bear.
Baracke [ba'rakə] *f* (-/-n)
barrack, hut.
barfuß ['baːrfuːs] *adj*
barefoot.
Bargeld ['baːrgɛlt] *n*
(-[e]s/*no pl*) cash, ready
money.
barmherzig [barm'hɛr-
tsɪç] *adj* merciful.
Barometer [baro'meːtər]
n (-s/-) barometer.
Barren ['barən] *m* (-s/-)
metall. bar, ingot; *sp.* parallel bars *pl.*
Barriere [ba'rĭeːrə] *f* (-/

-n) barrier.
Barrikade [bari'kaːdə] *f*
(-/-n) barricade.
barsch [barʃ] *adj* rude,
gruff, rough.
Bart [baːrt] *m* (-[e]s/ᵕe)
beard; *Schlüssel:* bit.
bärtig ['bɛːrtɪç] *adj* beard-
ed.
Barzahlung ['baːrtsaː-
luŋ] *f* (-/-en) cash payment.
Basar [ba'zaːr] *m* (-s/-e)
bazaar.
Basis ['baːzɪs] *f* (-/-Basen)
base; *fig.* basis.
Baskenmütze ['baskən-
mʏtsə] *f* (-/-n) beret.
Bast [bast] *m* (-es/-e)
bast; *Geweih:* velvet.
basteln ['bastəln] *v/t*
make, build; *v/i* make
things with one's hands.
Batterie [batə'riː] *f* (-/-n)
battery.
Bau [bau] *m* (-[e]s/-ten)
building; (*pl* -e) *Tier2:*
burrow, den, *Fuchs:* earth.
Bauarbeite|n ['bauʔar-
baɪtən] *pl* construction
work; **~r** *m* construction
worker.
Bauch [baux] *m* (-[e]s/ᵕe)
abdomen, belly; *Schmer2:*
paunch; **~schmerzen** *pl,*
~weh [-veː] *n* (-s/*no pl*)
stomach-ache *sg,* belly-
ache *sg.*
bauen ['bauən] *v/t* build;
construct.
Bauer¹ ['bauər] *m* (-n, -s/
-n) farmer.
Bauer² *n, m* (-s/-) (bird-

bedauern

cage.

Bäuer|in ['bɔyərɪn] f (-/
-nen) farmer's wife;
2**lich** adj rustic.

Bauern|haus n farm-
house; 2**hof** m farm.

bau|fällig ['baufɛlɪç] adj
out of repair, dilapidated;
2**gerüst** n scaffold(ing);
2**herr** m owner; 2**holz** n
timber, Am. lumber;
2**jahr** n: ~ 1982 1982
model od. make.

Baum [baum] m (-[e]s/⸚e)
tree.

baumeln ['baumәln] v/i:
~ **mit** (dat) dangle od. swing
s.th.

Baum|stamm ['baum-
ʃtam] m (-[e]s/⸚e) (tree-)
trunk; ~**wolle** f cotton.

Bauplatz ['bauplats] m
(-es/⸚e) building plot od.
site.

Bausch [bauʃ] m (-es/⸚e)
wad, pad; 2**en** v/t: **sich** ~
bulge, swell out.

Bau|stein ['bauʃtain] m
(-[e]s/⸚e) brick; Spiel-
zeug: a. (building) block;
~**stelle** f building site;
~**unternehmer** m build-
ing contractor; ~**werk** n
building.

Bayer ['baiər] m (-n/-n)
Bavarian; 2**isch** adj Bavarian.

Bazillus [ba'tsilus] m (-/
Bazillen) bacillus, germ.

beabsichtigen [bә'?ap-
zıçtıgən] v/t intend, mean.

beacht|en [bә'?axtən] v/t
pay attention to; befolgen:

observe; ~**lich** adj considerable.

Beamt|e [bә'?amtə] m (-n/
-n), **-in** f (-/-nen) official, officer; civil servant.

beängstigend [bә'?ɛŋs-
tıgənt] adj alarming;
~**anspruchen** [-'?an-
ʃpruːxən] v/t claim, de-
mand; Zeit, Raum: take
up; tech. stress; ~**anstan-
den** v/t object to; ~**an-
tragen** v/t apply for;
~**antworten** v/t answer,
reply to; ~**arbeiten** v/t
work (on); ~**aufsichti-
gen** v/t supervise; Kind:
look after; ~**auftragen**
v/t commission; ~**bauen**
v/t build on; agr. cultivate,
till.

beben ['be:bən] v/i shake,
tremble; Erde: quake.

Becher ['bɛçər] m (-s/-)
cup.

Becken ['bɛkən] n (-s/-)
basin, Am. a. bowl; anat.
pelvis.

bedächtig [bә'dɛçtıç] adj
deliberate.

bedanken [bә'daŋkən] v/
refl: **sich bei j-m** ~ thank
s.o.

Bedarf [bә'darf] m (-[e]s/
no pl): **an** (dat) need
(of); econ. demand (for);
~**shaltestelle** f request
stop.

bedauerlich [bә'dauər-
lıç] adj deplorable.

bedauern [bә'dauərn] v/t
j-n: feel sorry for, pity; et.:
regret; 2 n (-s/no pl) re-

gret; pity; ~swert adj pitiable.

bedeck|en [bə'dɛkən] v/t cover; ~t adj Himmel: overcast.

bedenk|en [bə'dɛŋkən] v/t (irr) consider ~lich adj doubtful; dangerous

bedeuten [bə'dɔʏtən] v/t mean; ~d adj important; beträchtlich: considerable.

Bedeutung [bə'dɔʏtuŋ] f (-/-en) meaning; Wichtigkeit: importance; 2slos adj insignificant; 2svoll adj significant.

bedien|en [bə'di:nən] v/t serve; wait on; tech. operate; Telefon: answer; sich ~en help o.s.; v/i serve; bei Tisch: wait at (Am. on) table; Karten: follow suit; 2ung f (-/-en) waiter, waitress; shop assistant; (no pl) service.

Bedingung [bə'dɪŋuŋ] f (-/-en) condition; 2slos adj unconditional.

bedrängen [bə'drɛŋən] v/t press hard, beset.

bedroh|en [bə'dro:ən] v/t threaten; ~lich adj threatening.

bedrücken [bə'drʏkən] v/t depress, deject.

Bedürfnis [bə'dʏrfnɪs] n (-ses/-se) need; want; ~nisanstalt f public convenience, Am. comfort station; 2tig adj needy, poor.

beleilen [bə'ʔaɪlən]: sich ~ v/refl hasten; hurry; ~eindrucken [bə'ʔaɪn-druk̍ən] v/t impress; ~einflussen [bə'ʔaɪnflu-sən] v/t influence; ~einträchtigen [bə'ʔaɪntrɛç-tɪgən] v/t impair; injure; ~end(ig)en [bə'ʔɛn-d(ɪg)ən] v/t end; finish; ~erben v/t: j-n ~ be s.o.'s heir.

beerdig|en [bə'ʔe:rdɪ-gən] v/t bury; 2ung f funeral; 2ungsinstitut n undertakers pl.

Beere ['be:rə] f (-/-n) berry.

Beet [be:t] n (-[e]s/-e) bed.

be|fahrbar [bə'fa:rbar] adj passable, practicable; ~fangen [bə'faŋən] adj embarrassed; ~fassen: sich ~ mit v/refl engage in, occupy o.s. with; deal with.

Befehl [bə'fe:l] m (-[e]s/-e) command; order; 2en v/t (irr) command; order.

be|festigen [bə'fɛstɪgən] v/t fasten, fix, attach (an to); mil. fortify; ~feuchten v/t moisten.

befinden [bə'fɪndən]: sich ~ v/refl be; 2 n (-s/no pl) (state of) health.

befolgen [bə'fɔlgən] v/t follow; obey.

be|fördern [bə'fœrdərn] v/t convey; carry; transport, forward; promote (zum Major to) major); 2ung f fig. promotion.

be|fragen [bə'fra:gən] v/t question; interview;

~**freien** [bə'fraɪən] v/t free, rescue; ~**freundet** [bə'frɔyndət] adj: ~ **sein** be friends.

befriedi|gen [bə'fri:dɪgən] v/t satisfy; ~**gend** adj satisfactory; **2gung** f satisfaction.

befruchten [bə'frʊxtən] v/t fertilize.

befugt [bə'fu:kt] adj authorized.

Befund [bə'fʊnt] m (-[e]s/ -e) result; findings pl.

be|fürchten [bə'fʏrçtən] v/t fear; ~**fürworten** [-'fy:rvɔrtən] v/t support, advocate.

begab|t [bə'ga:pt] adj gifted, talented; **2ung** f gift, talent.

begegn|en [bə'ge:gnən] v/i: (**sich**) ~ meet; **2ung** f meeting.

be|gehen [bə'ge:ən] v/t (irr) Verbrechen: commit; Fehler: make; ~**gehren** [bə'ge:rən] v/t desire.

begeister|n [bə'gaɪstərn] v/t: **sich** ~ **für** become enthusiastic over, ~**t sein** be delighted; **2ung** f enthusiasm.

Begier|de [bə'gi:rdə] f (-/ -n) desire; **2ig** adj eager, desirous.

begießen [bə'gi:sən] v/t (irr) water; Braten: baste.

Beginn [bə'gɪn] m (-[e]s/ no pl), **2en** s. **Anfang, anfangen.**

be|glaubigen [bə'glaʊbɪgən] v/t attest, certify;

~**gleichen** v/t (irr) pay, settle.

begleit|en [bə'glaɪtən] v/t accompany; **j-n nach Hause** ~**en** see s.o. home; **2er** m companion; **2ung** f company; mus. accompaniment.

be|glückwünschen [bə-'glʏkvʏnʃən] v/t congratulate; ~**gnadigen** [-'gna:dɪgən] v/t pardon; ~**gnügen: sich** ~ **mit** v/refl be content with; ~**graben** v/t (irr) bury; **2gräbnis** [-'grɛ:pnɪs] n (-ses/-se) funeral; ~**greifen** [-'graɪfən] v/t (irr) comprehend, understand; ~**greiflich** adj: **j-m et.** ~ **machen** make s.o. understand s.th.; ~**grenzen** [-'grɛntsən] v/t bound; limit, restrict.

Begriff [bə'grɪf] m (-[e]s/ -e) idea, notion; **im** ~ **sein zu** be about to, be going to.

begründen [bə'grʏndən] v/t establish, found; give reasons for.

begrüß|en [bə'gry:sən] v/t greet, welcome; **2ung** f greeting, welcome.

be|günstigen [bə'gʏnstɪgən] v/t favo(u)r; ~**haart** [-'ha:rt] adj hairy; ~**haglich** [-'ha:klɪç] adj comfortable, cosy, snug; ~**halten** v/t (irr) retain; keep (**für sich** to o.s.); remember.

Behälter [bə'hɛltər] m (-s/

behandeln

-) container; box; *Flüssig-keit:* tank.

behandel|n [bə'handəln] *v/t* treat (*a. med.*); *Thema:* deal with; **2lung** *f* treatment.

beharren [bə'harən] *v/i* persist (**auf** in).

behaupt|en [bə'hauptən] *v/t* assert (**sich** o.s.); maintain; **2ung** *f* assertion.

be|heben [bə'he:bən] *v/t* (*irr*) remove; *Schaden:* repair; **~helfen** *v/refl:* **sich ~ mit** make shift with; **sich ~ ohne** do without; **~helfsmäßig** [bə'hɛlfsmɛ:sɪç] *adj* temporary, makeshift; **~hend(e)** [bə'hɛnd(ə)] *adj* nimble, agile.

beherrsch|en [bə'hɛrʃən] *v/t* rule (over), govern; *Lage etc.:* be in control of; *Sprache:* have command of; **sich ~en** control o.s.; **2ung** *f* (*-/no pl*) command, control.

be|hilflich [bə'hɪlflɪç] *adj:* **j-m ~ sein** help s.o. (*bei* with); **~hindern** *v/t* hinder; obstruct.

Behörde [bə'hø:rdə] *f* (*-/-n*) *mst* authorities *pl*.

behutsam [bə'hu:tza:m] *adj* cautious; gentle.

bei [baɪ] *prp* (*dat*) *räumlich:* by, near; at, with; *zeitlich:* by, in, during; on; (*present*) at; **~ Schmidt** care of (*abbr.* c/o) Schmidt; **~ j-m** at s.o.'s (house *etc.*), with s.o.; **~ Tag** by day; **~ s-r Ankunft** on his arrival; **~**

Tisch at table; **~ der Arbeit** at work; **j-n ~m Namen nennen** call s.o. by his name; **~ günstigem Wetter** weather permitting.

bei|behalten ['baɪbəhaltən] *v/t* (*irr*) keep up, retain; **~bringen** *v/t* (*irr*) *Niederlage, Wunde etc.:* inflict (*dat* on); **j-m et. ~bringen** teach s.o. s.th.

Beichte ['baɪçtə] *f* (*-/-n*) confession; **2n** *v/t* confess.

beide ['baɪdə] *pron* both; *unbetont:* two; **alle ~** both; **e-r von ~n** either of them; **nur wir ~** just the two of us.

beieinander [baɪʔaɪ'nandər] *adv* together.

Beifahrer ['baɪfa:rər] *m* (*-s/-*) (front-seat) passenger; assistant driver; *sp.* co-driver.

Beifall ['baɪfal] *m* (*-[e]s/no pl*) approval; applause.

beifügen ['baɪfy:gən] *v/t* *Brief:* enclose.

Beigeschmack *m* (*-[e]s/no pl*) slight flavo(u)r; taste.

Beihilfe ['baɪhɪlfə] *f* (*-/-n*) aid; *finanzielle:* allowance; *Stipendium:* grant.

Beil [baɪl] *n* (*-[e]s/-e*) hatchet; chopper; ax(e).

Beilage ['baɪla:gə] *f* (*-/-n*) *Zeitung:* supplement; *Speisen:* vegetables *pl*, side-dish, *colloq.* trimmings *pl*.

beiläufig ['baɪlɔyfɪç] *adj* casual.

belanglos

beilegen ['baɪleːgən] *v/t* enclose; *Streit*: settle.

Beileid ['baɪlaɪt] *n* (-[e]s/ *no pl*) condolence, sympathy.

beimessen ['baɪmesən] *v/t* (*irr*) attach (*dat* to).

Bein [baɪn] *n* (-[e]s/-e) leg.

beinah(e) ['baɪnaː(ə)] *adv* almost, nearly.

beisammen [baɪ'zamən] *adv* together.

Beisein ['baɪzaɪn] *n* (-s/*no pl*) presence.

beiseite [baɪ'zaɪtə] *adv* aside, apart.

beisetz|en ['baɪzetsən] *v/t* bury; **2ung** *f* funeral.

Beispiel ['baɪʃpiːl] *n* (-[e]s/-e) example; **zum** ~ for example; **2haft** *adj* exemplary; **2los** *adj* unexampled.

beißen ['baɪsən] *v/t, v/i* (*irr*) bite; ~**d** *adj* biting, pungent.

Bei|stand *m* (-[e]s/*no pl*) assistance; **2stehen** *v/i* (*irr*) assist, help.

Beitrag ['baɪtraːk] *m* (-[e]s/**e) contribution; share; *Mitglieds2*: subscription; *Zeitung*: article; **2en** *v/t* (*irr*) contribute.

beitreten ['baɪtreːtən] *v/i* (*irr*) join.

Beiwagen ['baɪvaːgən] *m* (-s/-) side-car.

bejahen [bə'jaːən] *v/t* answer in the affirmative; ~**d** *adj* affirmative.

bejahrt [bə'jaːrt] *adj* aged.

bekämpfen [bə'kɛmpfən] *v/t* fight (against); *fig.* oppose.

bekannt [bə'kant] *adj* known (*dat* to); **j-m mit j-m** ~ **machen** introduce s.o. to s.o.; **2e** *m, f* (-n/-n) acquaintance, *mst* friend; ~**geben** *v/t* (*irr*) announce; ~**lich** *adv* as is generally known; **2machung** [-maxuŋ] *f* (-/-en) publication; public notice; **2schaft** *f* acquaintance.

bekennen [bə'kɛnən] *v/t* (*irr*) admit; confess; **sich schuldig** ~ *jur.* plead guilty.

beklag|en [bə'klaːgən] *v/t* lament; **sich ~en** complain (**über** *of*, about); **2te** *m, f* (-n/-n) defendant, *the* accused.

bekleid|en [bə'klaɪdən] *v/t* clothe; dress; **2ung** *f* (-/*no pl*) clothing, clothes *pl.*

bekommen [bə'kɔmən] *v/t* (*irr*) get; receive; obtain; *Zug etc.*: catch; *Kind*: be going to have; *Krankheit*: get, catch; *Hunger etc.*: get; *v/i j-m*: agree with; ~**kräftigen** *v/t* confirm; ~**laden** *v/t* (*irr*) load; *fig.* burden.

Belag [bə'laːk] *m* (-[e]s/ **e) covering; coat(ing); *Zunge*: fur; *Brot*: filling, spread.

belager|n [bə'laːgərn] *v/t* besiege; **2ung** *f* siege.

belanglos [bə'laŋloːs]

adj unimportant; **~lasten** [-'lastən] *v/t* load; *Konto*: charge, debit; *jur.* incriminate; *fig.* burden; **~lästigen** [-'lɛstɪgən] *v/t* molest; trouble, bother; **2lastung** *f* load; *fig.* burden; **~laufen** *v/refl* (*irr*): **sich ~ auf** amount to; **~lebt** [-'le:pt] *adj* Straße: busy, crowded.

Beleg [bə'le:k] *m* (-[e]s/-e) document; **~schein** voucher; 2*en v/t Platz*: reserve; *beweisen*: prove; *Vorlesungen*: enrol(l) for; **ein Brötchen mit e.** 2*en* put s.th. on a roll, fill a roll with s.th.; **~schaft** *f* personnel, staff; 2*t adj* engaged, occupied; *Platz*: taken; *Hotel etc.*: full; *Stimme*: thick, husky; *Zunge*: coated, furred.

belehr|en [bə'le:rən] *v/t* teach; inform.

beleibt [bə'laɪpt] *adj* corpulent, stout.

beleidig|en [bə'laɪdɪgən] *v/t* offend, *stärker*: insult; **~end** *adj* offensive, insulting; 2*ung* *f* offen|ce *Am.* -se, insult.

beleucht|en [bə'lɔʏçtən] *v/t* light (up), illuminate; 2*ung* *f* light(ing); illumination.

Belgi|er ['bɛlgɪər] *m* (-s/-) Belgian; 2**sch** *adj* Belgian.

belicht|en [bə'lɪçtən] *v/t phot.* expose; 2*ung f phot.* exposure; 2*ungsmesser m* exposure meter;

2*ungszeit f* (time of) exposure.

belieb|ig [bə'li:bɪç] *adj* any; **jeder ~ige** anyone; **~t** *adj* popular (**bei** with); 2*theit f* popularity.

beliefern [bə'li:fərn] *v/t* supply.

bellen ['bɛlən] *v/i* bark.

belohn|en [bə'lo:nən] *v/t* reward; 2*ung f* reward.

belüg|en [bə'ly:gən] *v/t* (*irr*) **j-n ~** lie to s.o.; **~malen** *v/t* paint; **~mängeln** [-'mɛŋəln] *v/t* find fault with.

bemerk|en [bə'mɛrkən] *v/t* notice, perceive; *äußern*: remark; **~kenswert** [-'mɛrkənsve:rt] *adj* remarkable (**wegen** for); 2*kung f* remark.

bemitleiden [bə'mɪtlaɪdən] *v/t* pity; **~swert** [-sve:rt] *adj* pitiable.

bemüh|en [bə'my:ən] *v/t* trouble; **sich ~en** *v/refl* trouble (o.s.); *endeavo(u)r*; 2*ung f* trouble; endeavo(u)r, effort.

benachrichtig|en [bə'na:xrɪçtɪgən] *v/t* inform, notify; *econ.* advise; 2*ung f* information; notification; *econ.* advice.

benachteilig|en [bə'na:xtaɪlɪgən] *v/t* place *s.o.* at a disadvantage; 2*ung f* disadvantage.

benehmen [bə'ne:mən] *v/refl* (*irr*): **sich ~** behave (o.s.); 2 *n* (-s/*no pl*) behavio(u)r, conduct.

beneiden [bə'naɪdən] v/t envy (**j-n um et.** s.o. s.th.); **~swert** [-veːrt] adj enviable.

benennen [bə'nɛnən] v/t (irr) name.

Bengel ['bɛŋəl] m (-s/-) (little) rascal, urchin.

benommen [bə'nɔmən] adj stunned.

benötigen [bə'nøːtɪgən] v/t need, want, require.

benutz|en [bə'nʊtsən] v/t use, make use of; Bus etc.: take; **2er** m user; **2ung** f use.

Benzin [bɛn'tsiːn] n (-s/ -e) chem. benzine; mot. petrol, Am. gasoline, colloq. gas.

beobacht|en [bə'ʔoːbaxtən] v/t observe; genau: watch; **2er** m observer; **2ung** f observation.

bepacken [bə'pakən] v/t load.

bequem [bə'kveːm] adj convenient; easy; comfortable; Person: easygoing; faul: lazy.

berat|en [bə'raːtən] v/t, v/i (irr) j-n: advise; et.: discuss (**über et.** s.th.); **sich ~en** confer; **2er** m adviser; **2ung** f consultation, conference.

berauben [bə'raʊbən] v/t deprive (gen of).

berechn|en [bə'rɛçnən] v/t calculate; econ. charge; **~end** adj calculating; **2ung** f calculation.

berechtig|en [bə'rɛçti-

gən] v/t entitle; authorize; **~t** adj entitled; qualified; Anspruch: legitimate.

Bereich [bə'raɪç] m (-[e]s/ -e) area; reach; fig. scope, sphere; Wissenschaft etc.: field, province; **2ern** v/t enrich (**sich** o.s.).

Bereifung [bə'raɪfʊŋ] f (-/ -en) tyres pl, (Am. nur) tires pl.

bereit [bə'raɪt] adj ready; **~en** v/t prepare; Freude etc.: give; **~halten** v/t (irr) hold s.th. ready; **~s** adv already; **2schaft** f readiness; **~stellen** v/t place s.th. ready; provide; **~willig** adj ready; adv readily.

bereuen [bə'rɔʏən] v/t repent (of).

Berg [bɛrk] m (-[e]s/-e) mountain; **die Haare standen ihm zu ~e** his hair stood on end; **2ab** [-'ʔap] adv downhill (a. fig.); **2auf** [-'ʔaʊf] adv uphill (a. fig.); **~bahn** f mountain railway; **~bau** m (-[e]s/no pl) mining.

bergen ['bɛrgən] v/t (irr) recover; j-n: rescue.

berglig ['bɛrgɪç] adj mountainous; **2mann** m miner; **2rutsch** [-rʊtʃ] m (-[e]s/-e) landslide; **2steiger** ['-ʃtaɪgər] m (-s/ -) mountaineer, climber.

Bergung ['bɛrgʊŋ] f (-/ -en) recovery; Menschen: rescue.

Bergwerk ['bɛrkvɛrk] n (-[e]s/-e) mine.

Bericht [bə'rɪçt] *m* (-[e]s/
-e): ~ **(über)** report (on),
account (of); 2**en** *v/t* report; *Presse:* a. cover
(**über** et. s.th.); ~**erstatter** [-ɛr'ʃtatər] *m* (-s/
-) reporter; correspondent.

berichtigen [bə'rɪçtɪgən]
v/t correct.

bersten ['bɛrstən] *v/i* (*irr*)
burst (**vor** with).

berüchtigt [bə'rʏçtɪçt] *adj*
notorious (**wegen** for).

berücksichtigen [bə-
'rʏkzɪçtɪgən] *v/t* consider.

Beruf [bə'ru:f] *m* (-[e]s/
-e) calling; *Gewerbe:*
trade; vocation, occupation, *colloq.* job; *höherer* ~:
profession; 2**en** *v/refl* (*irr*):
sich ~ auf refer to; 2**lich**
adj professional.

Berufs|ausbildung *f* vocational *od.* professional
training; ~**beratung** *f*
vocational guidance;
~**kleidung** *f* working
clothes *pl*; ~**schule** *f* vocational school; ~**sportler**
[-ʃpɔrtlər] *m* professional;
2**tätig** [-tɛ:tɪç] *adj* working; ~**tätige** *m*, *f* (-**n**/-**n**)
employed person; **die**
~**tätigen** *pl* the working
people *pl*.

Berufung *f* (-/-en) *Ernennung:* appointment; reference (**auf** to); ~ **einlegen** *jur.* appeal.

beruhen [bə'ru:ən] *v/i*: ~
auf be based on; **et. auf**
sich ~ lassen let a matter

rest.

beruhig|en [bə'ru:ɪgən]
v/t quiet, calm; soothe;
sich ~en calm down;
2**ungsmittel** *n* sedative.

berühmt [bə'ry:mt] *adj* famous, celebrated.

berühr|en [bə'ry:rən] *v/t*
touch; 2**ung** *f* contact,
touch.

Besatzung [bə'zatsʊŋ] *f*
(-/-en) crew; *mil.* occupation troops *pl.*

beschädig|en [bə'ʃɛ:dɪ-
gən] *v/t* damage; 2**ung** *f*
damage (*gen* to).

beschaffen [bə'ʃafən] *v/t*
procure; provide; *Geld:*
raise; 2**heit** *f* state, condition.

beschäftig|en [bə'ʃɛftɪ-
gən] *v/t* employ, occupy;
keep busy; 2**ung** *f* employment; occupation.

beschämen [bə'ʃɛ:mən]
v/t make s.o. feel ashamed;
~**d** *adj* shameful; humiliating.

Bescheid [bə'ʃaɪt] *m*
(-[e]s/-e): ~ **bekommen** be informed; ~ **geben** let s.o. know; ~ **wissen** know.

bescheiden [bə'ʃaɪdən]
adj modest; 2**heit** *f* modesty.

bescheinig|en [bə'ʃaɪnɪ-
gən] *v/t* certify, attest; acknowledge; 2**ung** *f* certification; *Schein:* certificate;
Quittung: receipt; *Bestätigung:* acknowledg(e)ment.

be|scheren [bə'ʃe:rən] *v/t*

j-n ~ give s.o. presents; ~**schießen** v/t (irr) fire od. shoot at od. on; bombard; ~**schimpfen** v/t ~ abuse, insult.

Beschlag [bə'ʃlaːk] m (-[e]s/ᵛe) metal fitting(s pl); **mit** ~ **belegen** seize; monopolize; 2**en** v/t (irr) tech. fit, mount; Pferd: shoe; v/i v/refl Fenster, Wand: steam up; Spiegel: cloud over; 2**nahme** [-naːmən] v/t seize; confiscate; mil. requisition.

beschleunig|en [bə'ʃlɔynɪgən] v/t hasten, speed up; mot. accelerate; 2**ung** f acceleration.

beschl|ießen [bə'ʃliːsən] v/t (irr) end; close; sich entscheiden: resolve, decide; 2**uß** [-'ʃlus] m (-sses/ᵛsse) decision.

be|schmieren [bə'ʃmiːrən] v/t (be-)smear; ~**schmutzen** v/t soil, dirty; ~**schneiden** v/t (irr) cut, clip; Haare, Hecke etc.: trim, clip; fig. cut down, curtail; ~**schönigen** [bə'ʃøːnɪgən] v/t gloss over.

beschränk|en [bə'ʃrɛŋkən] v/t confine, limit, restrict; **sich** ~**en auf** confine o.s. to; 2**ung** f limitation, restriction.

beschreib|en [bə'ʃraɪbən] v/t (irr) Papier: write on; fig. describe; 2**ung** f description; account.

beschrift|en [bə'ʃrɪftən]

v/t inscribe; label; 2**ung** f inscription.

beschuldig|en [bə'ʃuldɪgən] v/t (gen) accuse (of [doing] s.th.), bsd. jur. charge (with); 2**te** m, f(-n/-n) the accused; 2**ung** f accusation, charge.

beschützen [bə'ʃytsən] v/t protect.

Beschwer|de [bə'ʃveːrdə] f (-/-n) complaint (a. med.); 2**en** [-'ʃveːrən] v/t burden; **sich** 2**en** v/refl complain (über about, of; bei to); 2**lich** adj tedious.

be|schwichtigen [bə-'ʃvɪçtɪgən] v/t appease, calm (down); ~**schwingt** [-'ʃvɪŋt] adj elated, elevated; ~**schwipst** adj colloq. tipsy; ~**schwören** v/t (irr) et.: take an oath on; j-n: implore, entreat; ~**seitigen** [-'zaɪtɪgən] v/t remove; do away with.

Besen ['beːzən] m (-s/-) broom.

besessen [bə'zesən] adj obsessed (von by).

besetz|en [bə'zetsən] v/t occupy (a. mil.); Stelle: fill; thea. cast; Kleid: trim; ~**t** adj engaged, occupied; Platz: taken; Bus etc.: full up; teleph. engaged, Am. busy; 2**ung** f thea. cast; mil. occupation.

besichtig|en [bə'zɪçtɪgən] v/t visit, see; inspect (a. mil.); 2**ung** f visit (gen to); inspection (a. mil.); sightseeing.

besiedeln

besied|eln [bə'ziːdəln] v/t settle; **bevölkern:** populate; **2lung** f settlement.

besiegen [bə'ziːɡən] v/t conquer; defeat, beat.

Besinnung [bə'zɪnʊŋ] f (-/ no pl) reflection; **Bewußtsein:** consciousness; **2slos** adj unconscious.

Besitz [bə'zɪts] m (-[e]s/ no pl) possession; **2en** [bə-'zɪtsən] v/i (irr) possess; **~er** m possessor, owner, proprietor.

besohlen [bə'zoːlən] v/t (re)sole.

Besoldung [bə'zɔldʊŋ] f (-/-en) pay; Beamte: salary.

besonder [bə'zɔndər] adj particular, special; **~s** adv especially; hauptsächlich: chiefly.

besonnen [bə'zɔnən] adj prudent, calm.

besorg|en [bə'zɔrɡən] v/t get, procure; do, manage; **2nis** [-'zɔrknɪs] f (-/-se) apprehension, fear, anxiety; **~niserregend** [-'ʔɛr-'reːɡənt] adj alarming; **~t** adj uneasy, worried (**um** about); **2ung** f: **~en machen** go shopping.

besprech|en [bə'ʃpreːçən] v/t (irr) discuss, talk s.th. over; Buch etc.: review; **2ung** f discussion; conference; review.

bespritzen [bə'ʃprɪtsən] v/t splash, (be)spatter.

besser ['bɛsər] adj better; superior; **um so ~** all the

better; **~n** ['bɛsərn] v/t (make) better, improve; **sich ~n** get od. become better, improve; **2ung** f improvement; **gute 2ung!** I wish you a speedy recovery!

best [bɛst] adj best; **~en Dank** thank you very much; **am ~en** adv best.

Bestand [bə'ʃtant] m (-es/⁴e) Vorrat: stock; (no pl) (continued) existence; **~ haben** last.

beständig [bə'ʃtɛndɪç] adj constant, steady; dauerhaft: lasting; Wetter: settled.

Bestandteil [bə'ʃtanttaɪl] m (-[e]s/-e) part; component; Mischung: ingredient.

bestärken [bə'ʃtɛrkən] v/t confirm, strengthen.

bestätig|en [bə'ʃtɛːtɪ-ɡən] v/t confirm, attest; Behauptung etc.: verify; Empfang: acknowledge; **sich ~en** prove (to be) true; **2ung** f confirmation; attestation; verification; acknowledg(e)ment.

Beste ['bɛstə] m, f (-n/-n) the best (one); **~** n the best (thing).

bestechen [bə'ʃtɛçən] v/t (irr) bribe.

Besteck [bə'ʃtɛk] n (-[e]s/ -e) knife, fork and spoon; cutlery.

bestehen [bə'ʃteːən] v/t (irr) Prüfung: pass; v/i exist; **~ auf** insist (up)on;

~ aus consist of.

be|stehlen [bə'ʃteːlən] v/t (irr) steal from; **~steigen** v/t (irr) Berg: climb (up); Pferd: mount; Thron: ascend.

bestell|en [bə'ʃtɛlən] v/t order; Zimmer etc.: book, bsd. Am. reserve; make an appointment with; Boden: cultivate, till; Grüße: give; **zu sich ~en** ask to come; **♀ung** f order; booking, bsd. Am. reservation.

Bestie ['bɛstiə] f (-/-n) beast; fig. a. brute.

bestimm|en [bə'ʃtimən] v/t determine, decide; Preis: fix; Termin, Ort: a. appoint; **~en für** mean for; **~t** adj determined, firm; Absicht etc.: definite; adj, adv certain(ly); **♀ungsort** [-'ʃtimuŋsʔɔrt] m destination.

bestraf|en [bə'ʃraːfən] v/t punish (**wegen, für** for); **♀ung** f punishment.

bestrahlen [bə'ʃtraːlən] v/t med. irradiate.

Bestreb|en [bə'ʃtreːbən] n (-s/no pl), **~ung** f effort.

be|streichen [bə'ʃtraɪçən] v/t (irr) spread; **~streiten** v/t (irr) deny.

bestürz|t [bə'ʃtʏrtst] adj dismayed; **♀ung** f (-/no pl) consternation, dismay.

Besuch [bə'zuːx] m (-[e]s/ -e) visit; call; Besucher: visitor(s pl); **♀en** v/t visit; call on; Schule etc.: attend; **~er** m visitor, caller;

~szeit f visiting hours pl.

be|tasten [bə'tastən] v/t touch, feel, finger; **~tätigen** [-'tɛːtɪgən] v/t tech. operate; Bremse: apply; **sich ~tätigen** v/refl work, busy o.s.

betäub|en [bə'tɔʏbən] v/t stun (a. fig.), daze; med. an(a)esthetize; **♀ung** f (-/ no pl) med.: an(a)esthetization; Zustand: an(a)esthesia; fig. stupefaction; **♀ungsmittel** n narcotic, an(a)esthetic.

Bete ['beːtə] f (-/-n): **rote ~** beetroot, red beet.

beteilig|en [bə'taɪlɪgən] v/t give a share (**an** in); **sich ~en** v/refl take part (in), participate (in); **♀te** m, f (-n/-n) person od. party concerned; **♀ung** f participation; share.

beten ['beːtən] v/i pray.

beteuern [bə'tɔʏɐn] v/t protest.

Beton [be'tõː; be'tɔːn; be-'tɔŋ] m (-s/-s) concrete.

beton|en [bə'toːnən] v/t stress; fig. a. emphasize; **♀ung** f stress; fig. emphasis.

be|trachten [bə'traxtən] v/t look at; fig. consider; **~trächtlich** [-'trɛçtlɪç] adj considerable.

Betrag [bə'traːk] m (-[e]s/ ♀e) amount, sum; **♀en** [-'traːgən] v/t amount to; **sich ♀en** v/refl behave (o.s.); **~en** n (-s/no pl) behavio(u)r, conduct.

betreffen [bə'trɛfən] v/t (irr) concern; **was ... betrifft** as for, as to; **~d** adj concerning; concerned, in question.

be|treten [bə'tre:tən] v/t (irr) step on; eintreten: enter; adj verlegen: embarrassed; **~treuen** ['trɔyən] v/t look after.

Betrieb [bə'tri:p] m (-[e]s/-e) business, firm; Fabrik: plant, works (a.) workshop; Am. a. shop; fig. bustle; **außer ~** out of order; **in ~** working.

Betriebs|ferien pl works holidays pl; **~leitung** f management; **~rat** m works council; **~unfall** m industrial accident.

be|trinken [bə'trɪŋkən] v/refl (irr): **sich ~** get drunk; **~troffen** ['-trɔfən] adj affected (**von** by).

Betrug [bə'tru:k] m (-[e]s/no pl) fraud; deceit; **2trügen** ['-try:gən] v/t (irr) deceive; cheat; **~trüger** m cheat; fraud; impostor.

betrunken [bə'trʊŋkən] adj drunken; pred drunk; **2e** m, f (-n/-n) drunk.

Bett [bɛt] n (-[e]s/-en) bed; **~bezug** m plumeau case; **~couch** f studio couch; **~decke** f blanket.

betteln ['bɛtəln] v/i beg (**um** for).

Bett|gestell ['bɛtgəʃtɛl] n (-[e]s/-e) bedstead; **2lägerig** ['-lɛːgərɪç] adj bed-

ridden, confined to bed; **~laken** n sheet.

Bettler ['bɛtlər] m (-s/-) beggar.

Bett|tuch ['bɛttuːx] n (-[e]s/-ᵘer) sheet; **~vorleger** m bedside rug; **~wäsche** f bed-linen; **~zeug** n bedding, bedclothes pl.

betupfen [bə'tʊpfən] v/t dab.

beugen ['bɔygən] v/t bend, bow (dat to).

Beule ['bɔylə] f (-/-n) bump, swelling; im Blech: dent.

be|unruhigen [bə'ᵘunruːɪgən] v/t make s.o. anxious; **sich ~unruhigen** v/refl worry; **~urlauben** ['-ᵘurlaubən] v/t give s.o. time off; vom Amt: suspend; **~urteilen** v/t judge.

Beute ['bɔytə] f (-/no pl) booty, spoil(s pl); e-s Tieres: prey (a. fig.).

Beutel ['bɔytəl] m (-s/-) bag; zo., Tabaks2: pouch.

Bevölkerung [bə'fœlkəruŋ] f (-/no pl) population.

bevollmächtig|en [bə'fɔlmɛçtɪgən] v/t authorize; **2te** m, f (-n/-n) authorized person od. agent, proxy, deputy.

bevor [bə'foːr] cj before.

bevor|stehen [bə'foːrʃteːən] v/i (irr) be approaching; be near; Gefahr: be imminent; **j-m ~stehen** await s.o.; **~zu-**

gen [-tsu:gən] *v/t* prefer.

bewach|en [bə'vaxən] *v/t* guard, watch; **2ung** *f* guard; escort.

bewaffn|en [bə'vafnən] *v/t* arm; **2ung** *f* (*-/no pl*) armament; *Waffen:* arms *pl.*

bewahren [bə'va:rən] *v/t* keep, preserve; **~ vor** save from.

bewähr|en [bə've:rən] *v/refl:* **sich ~** stand the test; **sich ~ als** prove to be; **sich nicht ~** prove a failure; **2ungsfrist** *f jur.* probation.

be|waldet [bə'valdət] *adj* wooded, woody; **~wältigen** [-'vɛltɪgən] *v/t* overcome; *master;* **~wandert** *pred adj* (well) versed.

bewässer|n [bə'vɛsərn] *v/t* water; *Land etc.:* irrigate; **2ung** *f* watering, irrigation.

beweg|en [bə've:gən] *v/t, v/refl:* (**sich**) ~ move, stir; *v/t* (*irr*): **j-n ~ zu** induce *od.* get s.o. to; **2grund** *m* motive; **~lich** *adj* movable; *Person, Geist etc.:* agile, active; **~t** *adj Meer:* rough; *Leben:* eventful; *fig.* moved, touched; **2ung** *f* movement; motion (*a. phys.*); **in 2ung setzen** set in motion; **~ungslos** *adj* motionless.

Beweis [bə'vais] *m* (*-es/-e*) proof (**für** of); **~(e** *pl*) evidence (*bsd. jur.*); **2en** *v/t* (*irr*) prove; **~material**

n evidence; **~stück** *n* (piece of) evidence; *jur.* exhibit.

bewerb|en [bə'verbən] *v/refl:* **sich ~ um** apply for; *kandidieren:* stand for, *Am.* run for; **2er** *m* applicant; **2ung** *f* application; candidature; **2ungsschreiben** [bə'verbuŋsʃraibən] *n* (*-s/-*) (letter of) application.

be|werten [bə'verten] *v/t* rate; **~willigen** [-'vɪlɪgən] *v/t* grant, allow; **~wirken** [-'vɪrkən] *v/t* cause, bring about.

bewirt|en [bə'vɪrtən] *v/t* entertain; **~schaften** [bə'vɪrtʃaftən] *v/t agr.* cultivate, farm; *Gut etc.:* manage, run; *Waren:* ration; *Devisen:* control; **2ung** *f* (*-/no pl*) entertainment.

bewohn|en [bə'vo:nən] *v/t* inhabit, live in, occupy; **2r** *m* inhabitant, occupant.

bewölk|en [bə'vœlkən] *v/refl:* **sich ~** cloud over; **~t** *adj* clouded, cloudy, overcast; **2ung** *f* clouds *pl.*

bewunder|n [bə'vundərn] *v/t* admire (**wegen** for); **2ung** *f* admiration.

bewußt [bə'vust] *adj* deliberate, intentional; **sich ~ sein** be aware of; **~los** *adj* unconscious; **2sein** *n* (*-s/no pl*) consciousness.

bezahlen [bə'tsa:lən] *v/t* pay; *Ware:* pay for; *Schuld:* pay off, settle; **2ung** *f* payment; settlement.

bezaubernd [bə'tsau-
bərnt] adj charming, en-
chanting.
bezeichnen [bə'tsaiç-
nən] v/t mark; describe;
call; **~end** adj characteristic; 2ung f name.
bezeugen [bə'tsɔygən]
v/t testify (to).
beziehen [bə'tsi:ən] v/t
(irr) cover; *Wohnung:* move
into; *Waren, Zeitung:* get;
ein Kissen ~en put a
clean case on a pillow; *das
Bett ~en* put clean sheets
on the bed; **sich ~en auf**
refer to; 2ung f relation;
in dieser ~ in this
respect; **~ungsweise** cj
respectively; or rather.
Bezirk [bə'tsɪrk] m (-[e]s/
-e) district, *Am.* a. precinct.
Bezug [bə'tsu:k] m (-[e]s/
ve) covering, case; *Kis-
sen:* a. slip; **~ nehmen
auf** refer to.
Bezüge [bə'tsy:gə] pl
earnings pl.
bezwecken [bə'tsvɛkən]
v/t aim at, intend; **~zwei-
feln** v/t doubt, question.
Bibel ['bi:bəl] f (-/-n)
Bible.
Biber ['bi:bər] m (-s/-)
beaver.
Bibliothek [biblio'te:k] f
(-/-en) library; **~ar** [-te-
'ka:r] m (-s/-e) librarian.
biblisch ['bi:blɪʃ] adj bib-
lical.
biegen ['bi:gən] v/t (irr):
(sich) ~ bend; um e-e

Ecke ~ turn (round) a
corner; **~sam** adj flexible;
2ung f bend.
Biene ['bi:nə] f (-/-n) bee;
~nkönigin f queen bee;
~nkorb m, **~nstock** m
(bee)hive.
Bier [bi:r] n (-[e]s/-e)
beer; **helles ~** pale beer,
ale; **dunkles ~** dark beer,
stout, porter; **~deckel**
[-dɛkəl] m (-s/-) beer-mat;
~krug m beer-mug.
Biest [bi:st] n (-es/-er)
beast, brute.
bieten ['bi:tən] v/t (irr) offer; *Auktion:* bid; **sich ~**
offer itself, arise.
Bilanz [bi'lants] f (-/-en)
balance; *Aufstellung:* bal-
ance-sheet.
Bild [bɪlt] n (-es/-er) picture; photograph; illustration; *Gemälde:* painting;
fig. idea.
bilden ['bɪldən] v/t: (sich)
~ form; *fig.* educate (o.s.).
Bild|erbuch ['bɪldərbu:x]
n (-[e]s/ver) picture book;
~hauer ['bɪlthauər] m
(-s/-) sculptor; 2lich adj
figurative; **~nis** n portrait;
~röhre f (television)
tube; **~schirm** m screen.
Bildung ['bɪldʊŋ] f (-/-en)
forming, formation; (*no pl*)
Aus2: education.
Billard ['bɪljart] n (-s/-e)
billiards sg.
billig ['bɪlɪç] adj cheap, in-
expensive; **~en** [-lɪgən] v/t
approve of; 2ung f (-/no
pl) approval.

Blässe

Binde ['bɪndə] f (-/-n)
band; *med.* bandage; *s.*
Damenbinde; ~**glied**
n connecting link; ~**haut** f
anat. conjunctiva; ~**haut-
entzündung** [-enttsyn-
dʊŋ] f (-/-en) conjunc-
tivitis; **2n** ['bɪndən] *v/t*
(*irr*) bind; tie; *Krawatte:*
knot; **2nd** *adj* binding; ~**r**
m (neck)tie; ~**strich** *m* hyphen.

Bindfaden ['bɪntfaːdən]
m (-s/ᵘ) string; *stärker:*
pack-thread.

Bindung ['bɪndʊŋ] f (-/
-en) binding (*a. Ski*); *fig.*
tie, link, bond.

Binnen|land ['bɪnənlant]
n (-[e]s/ᵘer) inland, interior; ~**schiffahrt** f inland navigation.

Biographie [biogra'fiː] f
(-/-n) biography.

Biologie [biolo'giː] f (-/*no
pl*) biology.

Birke ['bɪrkə] f (-/-n)
birch(-tree).

Birne ['bɪrnə] f (-/-n) pear;
electr. bulb.

bis [bɪs] *prp, adv räumlich:*
to, as far as; *zeitlich:* till,
until (*a. cj*), to, by; **zwei** ~
drei two or three; **alle** ~
auf all but, all except.

Bischof ['bɪʃɔf] *m* (-s/ᵘe)
bishop.

bisher [bɪs'heːr] *adv* until
now, so far.

Biß [bɪs] *m* (-sses/-sse)
bite.

bißchen ['bɪsçən]: **ein** ~
adj a little, a (little) bit of;

adv a little (bit).

Bissen ['bɪsən] *m* (-s/-)
bite; mouthful, morsel.

bissig ['bɪsɪç] *adj* biting (*a.
fig.*); **Achtung,** ~**er
Hund!** beware of the dog.

Bitte ['bɪtə] f (-/-n) request
(**um** for); **2n** ['bɪtən] *v/t,
v/i* (*irr*): ~ **um** ask for; **bitte** please; (**wie**) **bitte?** (I
beg your) pardon?; **bitte**
(**sehr**)! not at all, you're
welcome.

bitter ['bɪtər] *adj* bitter.

Bittschrift ['bɪtʃrɪft] f (-/
-en) petition.

blähen ['bleːən] *v/i med.*
cause flatulence; *v/t* Segel:
swell; **sich** ~**en** *v/refl Segel:* swell out; **2ungen** *pl*
flatulence, wind.

Blam|age [bla'maːʒə] f (-/
-n) disgrace, shame;
2ieren *v/t:* **sich** ~ make a
fool of o.s.

blank [blaŋk] *adj* shining,
shiny, bright.

Bläschen ['blɛːsçən] *n* (-s/
-) small blister.

Blase ['blaːzə] f (-/-n)
Luft: bubble; *Haut:* blister
(*a. tech.*); *anat.* bladder;
2n ['blaːzən] *v/t, v/i* (*irr*)
blow.

Blas|instrument ['blaːs-
ʔɪnstrumɛnt] *n* (-[e]s/-e)
wind instrument; ~**ka-
pelle** f brass band.

blaß [blas] *adj* pale (**vor**
with); ~ **werden** turn
pale.

Blässe ['blɛsə] f (-/ *no pl*)
paleness.

Blatt

62

Blatt [blat] n (-[e]s/ˇer) leaf; Papier2 etc.: sheet; Säge: blade; Karten: hand; (news)paper.

blättern ['blɛtərn] v/i: ~ in leaf through.

Blätterteig ['blɛtərtaık] m (-[e]s/-e) puff pastry.

blau [blau] adj blue; colloq. drunk, tight; **~er Fleck** bruise; **~es Auge** black eye; 2beere f bilberry.

bläulich ['blɔylıç] adj bluish.

Blausäure ['blauzɔyrə] f (-/no pl) prussic acid.

Blech [blɛç] n (-[e]s/-e) sheet metal; plate; Back2: baking-sheet; fig. colloq. rubbish; **~büchse** f, **~dose** f tin, Am. can; **~schaden** m mot. body-work damage.

Blei [blai] n (-[e]s/-e) chem. lead.

bleiben ['blaibən] v/i (irr) remain, stay; **am Apparat ~** hold the line; **~d** adj lasting; **~lassen** leave s.th. alone; stop s.th.

bleich [blaiç] adj pale (vor with); **~en** v/t bleach; blanch.

bleiern ['blaiərn] adj (of) lead, leaden (a. fig.); 2stift m (lead) pencil; 2stiftspitzer m pencil-sharpener.

Blende ['blɛndə] f (-/-n) blind; phot. diaphragm, (f-)stop; ~ **8** f-8; 2n ['blɛndən] v/t blind, dazzle.

Blick [blık] m (-[e]s/-e) look, glance; Aussicht: view; **auf den ersten ~** at first sight; 2en ['blıkən] v/i look, glance; v/t: **sich 2en lassen** show o.s.

blind [blınt] adj blind; Spiegel etc.: dull; ~ **werden** go blind; **~er Passagier** stowaway.

Blinddarm ['blın(t)darm] m (-[e]s/ˇe) (vermiform) appendix; **~entzündung** f appendicitis.

Blinde ['blındə] m, f (-n/-n) blind man od. woman.

Blinden|anstalt f institute for the blind; **~hund** m guide dog; **~schrift** f braille.

blinkeln ['blınkən] v/i shine; Sterne, Licht: twinkle; signal, flash; 2r m mot. trafficator, indicator.

blinzeln ['blıntsəln] v/i blink, wink.

Blitz [blıts] m (-es/-e) lightning; **~ableiter** [-ʔaplaitər] m (-s/-) lightning-conductor; 2en ['blıtsən] v/i flash; sparkle; **es blitzt** it is lightening; **~licht** n flashlight; **~schlag** m (stroke of) lightning; 2schnell adj with lightning speed, like lightning; **~würfel** m flash cube.

Block [blɔk] m (-[e]s/ˇe) block; Schreib2: pad; **~ade** ['ka:də] f (-/-n) blockade; **~haus** n log cabin; 2ieren [-'ki:rən] *v/t* block (up); *v/i* Räder: lock; *Bremsen:* jam; **~schrift** *f* block letters *pl.*

blöd|e(e) [blø:t, 'blø:də] *adj* imbecile; *dumm:* stupid; **2sinn** *m* rubbish, nonsense; **~sinnig** *adj* idiotic, stupid, foolish.

blöken ['blø:kən] *v/i* bleat.

blond [blɔnt] *adj* blond(e), fair(-haired).

bloß [blo:s] *adj* bare, naked; mere; *adv* only; **~legen** *v/t* lay bare, expose; **~stellen** *v/t* expose.

blühen ['bly:ən] *v/i* blossom, bloom; *fig.* flourish, thrive.

Blume ['blu:mə] *f* (-/-n) flower; *Wein:* bouquet; *Bier:* froth.

Blumen|geschäft *n* florist's (shop); **~händler** *m* florist; **~kohl** *m* cauliflower.

Bluse ['blu:zə] *f* (-/-n) blouse.

Blut [blu:t] *n* (-[e]s/*no pl*) blood; **2arm** ['-ʔarm] *adj* bloodless, *med.* an(a)emic; **~bad** *n* massacre, **~druck** *m* blood pressure.

Blüte ['bly:tə] *f* (-/-n) blossom, bloom, flower; *fig.* prime, heyday.

Blut|egel ['blu:tʔe:gəl] *m* (-s/-) leech; **2en** ['blu:tən] *v/i* bleed.

Blütenblatt ['bly:tənblat] *n* (-[e]s/*er) petal.

Bluterguß ['blu:tʔergus] *m* (-sses/*sse) effusion of

blood; **~gruppe** *f* blood group; **2ig** *adj* bloody; **~kreislauf** *m* (blood) circulation; **~probe** *f* blood test; **~spender** *m* blood donor; **2stillend** *adj* styptic, sta(u)nching; **~sverwandte** *m, f* (-n/-n) blood relation; **~transfusion** *f* blood transfusion; **~ung** *f* bleeding, h(a)emorrhage; **~vergießen** [-ferɡi:sən] *n* (-s/*no pl*) bloodshed; **~vergiftung** *f* blood-poisoning; **~verlust** *m* loss of blood; **~wurst** *f* black pudding.

Bö [bø:] *f* (-/-en) gust, squall.

Bock [bɔk] *m* (-[e]s/*e) buck; *Ziegen2:* he-goat; billygoat; *Widder:* ram; *Turngerät:* buck; *Gestell:* trestle; **2ig** *adj* stubborn, obstinate.

Boden ['bo:dən] *m* (-s/*) ground; *agr.* soil; *Gefäß, Meer:* bottom; *Fuß2:* sole; *Dach:* loft; **~kammer** *f* garret, attic; **~los** *adj* bottomless; *fig.* unbounded; **~schätze** *pl* mineral resources *pl.*

Bogen ['bo:gən] *m* (-s/-, *) curve, bend; *Geige:* bow; arch; *Waffe, Papier:* sheet; **2förmig** [-fœrmiç] *adj* arched; *arch.* arcade; **~gang** *m* arcade; **~schießen** *n* (-s/*no pl*) archery; **~schütze** [-ʃytsə] *m* (-n/-n) archer.

Bohle ['bo:lə] *f* (-/-n) thick plank, board.

Bohne

Bohne ['boːnə] f (-/-n) bean; ~nkaffee m coffee.

bohnern ['boːnərn] v/t polish, wax.

bohreln ['boːrən] v/t, v/i bore, drill; 2r m drill; _Hand2_.: gimlet.

böig ['bøːɪç] adj squally, gusty; _aer._ bumpy.

Boiler ['bɔylər] m (-s/-) boiler, heater.

Boje ['boːjə] f (-/-n) buoy.

Bolzen ['bɔltsən] m (-s/-) bolt.

bombardieren [bombar-'diːrən] v/t bomb, bombard (a. fig.).

Bombe ['bɔmbə] f (-/-n) bomb; ~nangriff m air raid; ~r m bomber.

Bonbon [bõ'bõ] m, n (-s/-s) sweet, Am. candy.

Boot [boːt] n (-[e]s/-e) boat; ~sfahrt f boat trip; ~sverleih ['-sferlaɪ] m (-[e]s/-e) boat hire.

Bord¹ [bɔrt] n (-[e]s/-e) shelf.

Bord² m (-[e]s/-e) _mar._, _aer._: **an ~** on board, aboard; **von ~ gehen** go ashore; ~stein m kerb, Am. curb.

borgen ['bɔrgən] v/t et.: borrow; _j-m et._: lend, Am. a. loan.

Borke ['bɔrkə] f (-/-n) bark.

Börse ['bœrzə] f (-/-n) stock exchange; _Geld2_: purse; ~nkurs m quotation; ~nmakler m stockbroker.

Borste ['bɔrstə] f (-/-n) bristle.

Borte ['bɔrtə] f (-/-n) border; _Besatz_: braid.

bösartig ['bøːsʔartɪç] adj malicious, vicious; _med._ malignant.

Böschung ['bœʃʊŋ] f (-/-en) slope, bank.

böse ['bøːzə] adj bad, evil, wicked; _zornig_: angry, Am. mad; 2 n (-n/no pl) evil.

boshaft ['boːshaft] adj wicked, malicious.

Botanilk [bo'taːnɪk] f (-/no pl) botany; 2sch adj botanical.

Bote ['boːtə] m (-n/-n) messenger.

Botschaft ['boːtʃaft] f (-/-en) message; _Amt_: embassy; ~er m ambassador.

Bottich ['bɔtɪç] m (-[e]s/-e) tub; tun, vat.

Bouillon [bul'jõ] f (-/-s) consommé, bouillon, broth.

boxlen ['bɔksən] v/t, v/i box; 2en n (-s/no pl) boxing; 2er m boxer; 2kampf m boxing-match, fight.

boykottieren [bɔyko'tiːrən] v/t boycott.

Branche ['brãːʃə] f (-/-n) line (of business).

Brand [brant] m (-[e]s/ᵘe) fire, conflagration; _med._ gangrene; _bot._ blight, mildew; in ~ geraten catch fire; ~blase f blister; 2en ['brandən] v/i surge, break; ~salbe f burn ointment; **~stiftung** [-ʃtɪftʊŋ] f arson; **~ung** f surf, breakers pl.

braten ['braːtən] v/t, v/i (irr) roast; Rost: grill; Pfanne: fry; Äpfel: bake; 2 m (-s/-) roast (meat); Keule: joint; 2**fett** n dripping; 2**soße** f gravy.

Brat|... ['braːt-] fried od. grilled ...; **~huhn** n roast chicken; **~kartoffeln** pl fried potatoes pl; **~pfanne** f frying-pan; **~röhre** f oven.

Brauch [braux] m (-[e]s/ᵛe) custom; 2**bar** adj useful; 2**en** ['brauxən] v/t need, want; erfordern: require; Zeit: take.

Braue ['brauə] f (-/-n) eyebrow.

brauen ['brauən] v/t brew; 2**rei** [brauə'raɪ] f (-/-en) brewery.

braun [braun] adj brown; **~ werden** ge a tan.

Bräun|e ['brɔynə] f (-/ no pl) (sun) tan; 2**en** ['brɔynən] v/t, v/i brown; Sonne: tan.

Brause ['brauzə] f (-/-n) rose; **~(bad** n) f shower (-bath); **~(limonade)** f fizzy lemonade; 2**n** ['brauzən] v/i roar; have a shower.

Braut [braut] f (-/ᵛe) fiancée; am Hochzeitstag: bride.

Bräutigam ['brɔytɪgam] m (-s/-e) fiancé; am Hochzeitstag: bridegroom.

Braut|jungfer ['brautjʊŋfər] f (-/-n) bridesmaid; **~kleid** n wedding dress; **~paar** n engaged couple; am Hochzeitstag: bride and bridegroom.

brav [braːf] adj honest; artig: good.

brechen ['brɛçən] v/t, v/i (irr) break; Strahlen etc.: refract; erbrechen: vomit.

Brei [braɪ] m (-[e]s/-e) pulp; Mus: mash; Kinder2: pap; 2**ig** adj pulpy, mushy.

breit [braɪt] adj broad, wide; 2**e** ['braɪtə] f (-/-n) breadth, width; geogr. latitude.

Brems|belag ['brɛmsbəlaːk] m (-[e]s/ᵛe) brake lining; **~e** ['brɛmzə] f (-/-n) zo. gadfly, horsefly; tech. brake; 2**en** ['brɛmzən] v/t, v/i brake; slow down od. up; **~spur** f skid marks pl; **~weg** m braking distance.

brenn|bar ['brɛnbaːr] adj combustible, inflammable; **~en** ['brɛnən] v/i (irr) burn; be on fire; Wunde, Augen: smart; Nessel: sting; **~er** m burner; 2**essel** ['-nɛsəl] f (-/-n) stinging nettle; 2**holz** n firewood; 2**material** n fuel; 2**punkt** m focus; 2**stoff** m fuel.

Brett [brɛt] n (-[e]s/-ər) board; shelf.

Brezel ['breːtsəl] f (-/-n) pretzel.

Brief [bri:f] m (-[e]s/-e)
letter; ~bogen m (sheet
of) notepaper; ~kasten m
letter-box, pillar-box, Am.
mailbox; 2lich adj, adv by
letter; ~marke f (postage)
stamp; ~papier n notepaper;
~tasche f wallet;
~träger m postman, Am.
mailman; ~umschlag m
envelope; ~wechsel m
correspondence.

Brillant [bril'jant] m (-en/
-en) brilliant, cut
diamond; 2 adj brilliant.

Brille ['brilə] f (-/-n) e
a pair of glasses pl od.
spectacles pl; Schutz2:
goggles pl.

bringen ['briŋən] v/t (irr)
bring; fort~, hin~: take; zu
Bett ~ put to bed; nach
Hause ~ see s.o. home; in
Ordnung ~ put in order;
zur Welt ~ give birth to.

Brise ['bri:zə] f (-/-n)
breeze.

Brit|e ['bri:tə, 'bri:tə] m
(-n/-n) Briton; die ~en pl
the British pl; 2isch adj
British.

bröckeln ['brœkəln] v/i
crumble.

Brocken ['brɔkən] m (-s/
-) piece; Erde, Stein: lump.

Brombeere ['brɔmbe:rə]
f (-/-n) blackberry.

Bronchitis [brɔnçi:tis] f
(-/-tiden) [-'ti:dən]) bronchitis.

Bronze ['brõ:sə] f (-/-n)
bronze.

Brosche ['brɔʃə] f (-/-n)
brooch.

Broschüre [brɔ'ʃy:rə] f (-/
-n) booklet, brochure.

Brot [bro:t] n (-[e]s/-e)
bread; Laib: loaf; belegtes ~ (open) sandwich;
~aufstrich m spread.

Brötchen ['brø:tçən] n
(-s/-) roll.

Brotrinde ['bro:trɪndə] f
(-/-n) crust.

Bruch [brux] m (-[e]s/²e)
Knochen: fracture; med.
hernia; math. fraction; Versprechen:
breach; Eid, Gesetz:
violation.

brüchig ['brʏçɪç] adj
brittle.

Bruch|landung f crash-landing;
~rechnung f
fractional arithmetic, fractions
pl; ~stück n fragment;
~teil m fraction.

Brücke ['brʏkə] f (-/-n)
bridge; Teppich: rug;
~npfeiler m pier.

Bruder ['bru:dər] m (-s/²)
brother; eccl. (lay) brother,
friar.

Brühe ['bry:ə] f (-/-n)
broth; klare: clear soup;
Suppengrundlage: stock.

brüllen ['brʏlən] v/i roar,
bellow; Rinder: low; v/t
roar.

brumm|en ['brumən] v/i,
v/t Tier: growl; Motor:
purr; fig. grumble; ~ig adj
grumbling.

brünett [bry'nɛt] adj brunette.

Brunft [brunft] f (-/²e) s.

Bügel

Brunst.

Brunnen ['brʊnən] m (-s/
-) well; *Quelle:* spring;
Spring₂: fountain.

Brunst [brʊnst] f (-/ᵕe)
männliches Tier: rut, *weibliches Tier:* heat; rutting
season.

brüsk [brysk] *adj* brusque,
abrupt; short.

Brust [brʊst] f breast;
chest, *anat.* thorax; (woman's) breast(-s *pl*); bosom;
~korb m chest, *anat.* thorax; **~schwimmen** n
breaststroke; **~warze** f
nipple.

Brut [bru:t] f (-/-en)
brood, hatch; *Fische:* fry.

brutal [bru'ta:l] *adj* brutal;
2ität [-tali'tɛːt] f (-/-en)
brutality.

brüten ['bry:tən] *v/i, v/t*
brood, sit (on eggs); **~**
über brood over.

brutto ['brʊto] *adv* gross.

Bube ['bu:bə] m (-n/-n)
Karten: knave, jack.

Buch [bu:x] n (-[e]s/ᵕer)
book; **~druckerei** f
printing office.

Buche ['bu:xə] f (-/-n)
beech(-tree).

buchen ['bu:xən] *v/t* book.

Bücher|brett [by:çər-
brɛt] n (-[e]s/-er) book-
shelf; **~ei** [by:çə'rai] f (-/
-en) library; **~schrank** m
bookcase.

Buchfink ['bu:xfɪŋk] m
(-en/-en) chaffinch; **~-
halter** m bookkeeper; **~-
haltung** f bookkeeping;

~händler m bookseller;
~handlung f bookshop,
Am. bookstore.

Büchse ['byksə] f (-/-n)
box, case; *Blech₂:* tin, *Am.*
can; *Gewehr:* rifle;
~nfleisch n tinned (*Am.*
canned) meat; **~nöffner**
[-ˀœfnər] m (-s/-) tin-
opener, *Am.* can opener.

Buchsta|be ['bu:xʃta:bə]
m (-n/-n) letter; **2bieren**
[-ʃta'bi:rən] *v/t* spell.

Bucht [bʊxt] f (-/-en) bay;
kleine: creek.

Buchung ['bu:xʊŋ] f (-/
-en) booking, reservation.

Buck|el ['bʊkəl] m (-s/-)
Höcker: hump, hunch;
humpback, hunchback;
2(e)lig *adj* humpbacked,
hunchbacked.

bücken ['bʊkən] *v/refl:*
sich ~ bend (down),
stoop.

Bückling ['bʊklɪŋ] m (-s/
-e) bloater; *fig.* bow.

Bude [bu:də] f (-/-n) stall;
colloq. den, place.

Büfett [by'fe:, by'fɛt] n
(-[e]s/-s) sideboard, buffet; *kaltes ~* buffet supper *od.* lunch.

Büffel ['byfəl] m (-s/-)
buffalo.

Bug [bu:k] m (-[e]s/*rare*
-e) *mar.* bow; *zo.* nose.

Bügel [by:gəl] m (-s/-)
Brille: bow; *Kleider:* handle; *Kleider:* coat hanger,
clothes-hanger; *Steig₂:*
stirrup; **~brett** n ironing-
board; **~eisen** n iron;

~falte f crease; 2frei adj non-iron; drip-dry; 2n ['by:gəln] v/t, v/i iron, press.

Bühne ['by:nə] f (-/-n) platform; thea. stage; ~nbild n stage design; setting, décor.

Bullauge ['bʊlʔaʊgə] n (-s/-n) porthole, bull's eye.

Bulle ['bʊlə] m (-n/-n) bull.

Bummel ['bʊməl] m (-s/-) stroll; 2n ['bʊməln] v/i stroll, saunter; trödeln: dawdle, waste time; ~zug m colloq. slow train.

Bund[1] [bʊnt] m (-[e]s/ᵘe) (waist-, neck-, wrist)band; pol. union, federation, confederacy.

Bund[2] n (-[e]s/-e) bundle; Radieschen: bunch; n, m Schlüssel: bunch.

Bündel ['byndəl] n (-s/-) bundle, bunch.

Bundes... ['bʊndəs-] in Zssgn: federal ...; ~genosse m ally; ~kanzler m Federal Chancellor; ~republik f Federal Republic; ~staat m federal state; ~wehr f (-/no pl) German Federal Armed Forces pl.

Bündnis ['byntnɪs] n (-ses/-se) alliance.

Bungalow ['bʊŋgalo] m (-s/-s) bungalow.

Bunker ['bʊŋkər] m (-s/-) air-raid shelter.

bunt [bʊnt] adj colo(u)rful;

bright, gay; 2stift m colo(u)red pencil, crayon.

Burg [bʊrk] f (-/-en) castle.

Bürge ['byrgə] m (-n/-n) jur.: guarantor; surety; für Einwanderer: sponsor; 2n v/i: ~ für vouch for; stand surety od. bail for; sponsor s.o.; guarantee s.th.

Bürger ['byrgər] m (-s/-) citizen; ~krieg m civil war; ~meister m mayor; ~steig [-staik] m (-[e]s/-e) pavement, Am. sidewalk.

Büro [by'ro:] n (-s/-s) office; ~angestellte m, f clerk; ~stunden pl office hours pl.

Bursche ['bʊrʃə] m (-n/-n) boy, lad, colloq. chap, Am. a. guy.

Bürste ['byrstə] f (-/-n) brush; 2n ['byrstən] v/t brush.

Bus [bʊs] m (-ses/-se) s. Autobus.

Busch [bʊʃ] m (-[e]s/ᵘe) bush, shrub.

Büschel ['byʃəl] n (-s/-) bunch; Haare: tuft; Stroh, Haare etc.: wisp.

buschig ['bʊʃɪç] adj bushy.

Busen ['bu:zən] m (-s/-) bosom, breast(s pl).

Bushaltestelle ['bushaltəʃtelə] f (-/-n) bus stop.

Bussard ['bʊsart] m (-[e]s/-e) buzzard.

Buße ['bu:sə] f (-/-n) Sühne: atonement, penance; = ~geld n fine.

büßen ['by:sən] v/t atone for; pay for; v/i do penance.

Büste ['bystə] f (-/-n) bust; ~nhalter m brassière, colloq. bra.

Butter ['butər] f (-/ no pl) butter; ~blume f buttercup; ~brot n (slice od. piece of) bread and butter; ~brotpapier n greaseproof paper; ~milch f buttermilk.

C

Café [ka'fe:] n (-s/-s) café, coffee-house.

Camping ['kɛmpɪŋ] n (-s/ no pl) camping; ~platz m camping-ground, camping-site.

Cello ['tʃelo] n (-s/-s, Celli) (violon)cello, 'cello.

Celsius ['tsɛlzius] n: 5 Grad ~ (abbr. 5° C) five degrees centigrade.

Champagner [ʃam'panjər] m (-s/-) champagne.

Champignon ['ʃampinjõ, -jɔŋ] m (-s/-s) champignon, (common) mushroom.

Chance ['ʃã:sə, 'ʃaŋsə] f (-/-n) chance.

Chaos ['ka:ɔs] n (-/no pl) chaos.

Charakter [ka'raktər] m (-s/-e [karak'te:rə]) character; 2isieren [-teri'zi:rən] v/t characterize; 2istisch [-'tɪstɪʃ] adj characteristic; ~zug m trait.

charmant [ʃar'mant] adj charming; 2e [ʃarm] f (-s/no pl) charm, grace.

Charterflug ['tʃartər-flu:k] m (-[e]s/⁓e) charter

flight; ~maschine f charter plane.

Chauffeur [ʃɔ'fø:r] m (-s/ -e) chauffeur, driver.

Chef [ʃef] m (-s/-s) head, chief, colloq. boss; ~arzt m head od. chief physician.

Chemie [çe'mi:] f (-/no pl) chemistry; ~kalien [-mi'ka:liən] pl chemicals pl; ~ker ['çe:mikər] m (-s/-) chemist; 2sch ['çe:mɪʃ] adj chemical.

Chiffre ['ʃifrə] f (-/-n) code, cipher; Anzeige: box number.

Chinese [çi'ne:zə] m (-n/ -n) Chinese; 2isch [çi'ne:zɪʃ] adj Chinese.

Chinin [çi'ni:n] n (-s/ no pl) quinine.

Chirurg [çi'rʊrk] m (-en/ -en) surgeon.

Chlor [klo:r] n (-s/no pl) chlorine; ~oform [kloro'fɔrm] n (-s/no pl) chloroform.

Cholera ['ko:lera] f (-/ no pl) cholera.

Chor [ko:r] m (-[e]s/⁓e) chancel, choir; Sänger: choir; Gesangsstück: chorus.

Christ [krɪst] *m* (-en/-en)
Christian; **~baum** *m*
Christmas tree; **~entum**
['krɪstəntu:m] *n* (-s/*no pl*)
Christianity; **~kind** *n*
(-[e]s/*no pl*) the infant Je-
sus; **~lich** *adj* Christian.

Chrom [kro:m] *n* (-s/*no
pl*) chromium.

chronisch ['kro:nɪʃ] *adj*
chronic.

circa ['tsɪrka] *adv* about,
approximately.

Conférencier [kõferã-
'sie:] *m* (-s/-s) compère,
Am. master of ceremonies.

Couch [kautʃ] *f* (-/-es)
couch.

Coupé [ku'pe:] *n* (-s/-s)
coupé.

Cousin [ku'zɛ̃:] *m* (-s/
-s), **~e** [ku'zi:nə] *f* (-/-n)
cousin.

Creme [kre:m] *f* (-/-s)
cream.

D

da [da:] *adv räumlich:*
there; here; *zeitlich:* then;
cj begründend: as, since, because.

dabei [da'baɪ] *adv near it
od.* them; with; *im Begriff:*
about, going (**zu** to); *außerdem:* besides; **~ bleiben** stick to one's point;
~sein *v/i* (*irr*) be present
od. there.

dableiben ['da:blaɪbən]
v/i (*irr*) stay, remain.

Dach [dax] *n* (-[e]s/**~er**)
roof; **~decker** ['-dɛkər] *m*
(-s/-) roofer; **~garten** *m*
roof garden; **~kammer** *f*
attic, garret; **~rinne** *f* gutter, eaves *pl*.

Dachs [daks] *m* (-es/-e)
badger.

Dachziegel ['daxtsi:gəl]
m (-s/-) tile.

Dackel ['dakəl] *m* (-s/-)
dachshund.

dadurch ['da:durç] *adv*
for this reason, thus; by it,

by that; *cj:* **~, daß** because.

dafür [da'fy:r] *adv* for it
od. them; instead; **~** in return, in exchange; **~** seem
be in favo(u)r of it; **er
kann nichts ~** it is not his
fault.

dagegen [da'ge:gən] *adv*
against it *od.* them; *Vergleich:* by comparison; **ich
habe nichts ~** I have no
objection (to it); *cj* however.

daheim [da'haɪm] *adv* at
home.

daher [da'he:r] *adv* from
there; therefore; *bei Verben
der Bewegung:* ... along; *cj*
therefore, that is why.

dahin [da'hɪn] *adv räumlich:* there, to that place;
bei Verben der Bewegung:
... along; **bis ~** till then.

dahinter [da'hɪntər] *adv*
behind it *od.* them;
~kommen *v/i* (*irr*) find

Darm

out about it; **~stecken** *v/i* be behind it.

damallig ['da:ma:lɪç] *adj* then, of that time; **~s** *adv* then, at that time.

Dame ['da:mə] *f* (-/-n) lady; *beim Tanz*: partner; *Karten, Schach*: queen.

Damen|binde *f* sanitary towel (*Am.* napkin); **~friseur** *m* hairdresser; **2haft** *adj* ladylike; **~toilette** *f* ladies' room, powder-room.

damit [da'mɪt; 'da:mɪt] *adv* with it *od.* them; *cj* so that; **~ nicht** in order that ... not.

Damm [dam] *m* (-[e]s/~e) *Stau2*: dam; *Deich*: dike, dyke.

dämmer|ig ['dɛmərɪç] *adj* dim; **~n** ['dɛmərn] *v/i* dawn (*a. fig. colloq.*: **j-m** on s.o.); grow dark; **2ung** *f* twilight, dusk; *morgens*: dawn.

Dampf [dampf] *m* (-[e]s/~e) steam, vapo(u)r; **2en** ['dampfən] *v/i* steam.

dämpfen ['dɛmpfən] *v/t Lärm, Stoß etc.*: deaden; *Stimme*: lower; *Licht*: soften; *s. dünsten*.

Dampfer ['dampfər] *m* (-s/-) steamer; **~maschine** *f* steam-engine.

danach [da'na:x] *adv* after it *od.* them; *später*: afterwards; *entsprechend*: accordingly; **ich fragte ihn ~** I asked him about it.

Däne ['dɛ:nə] *m* (-n/-n)

Dane.

daneben [da'ne:bən] *adv* next to it *od.* them; beside it *od.* them; *cj außerdem*: besides, moreover.

dänisch ['dɛ:nɪʃ] *adj* Danish.

Dank [daŋk] *m* (-[e]s/ *no pl*) thanks *pl*; **~barkeit**: gratitude; **Gott sei ~!** thank God!; **2 prp** (*dat*) owing *od.* thanks to; **2bar** *adj* thankful, grateful; *lohnend*: rewarding; **2en** ['daŋkən] *v/i* thank; **2e (schön)** thank you (very much); **nichts zu ~en** don't mention it.

dann [dan] *adv* then; **~ und wann** (every) now and then.

daran [da'ran] *adv* at (by, in, of, on, to) it *od.* them; **nahe ~ sein zu** be on the point of *ger.*

darauf [da'rauf] *adv räumlich*: on it *od.* them; *zeitlich*: after (that); **~hin** ['-'hɪn] *adv* after that.

daraus [da'raus] *adv* out of it *od.* them; from it *od.* them; **was ist ~ geworden?** what has become of it?

Darbietung ['da:rbi:tuŋ] *f* (-/-en) performance.

darin [da'rɪn] *adv* in it *od.* them; in there.

darlegen ['da:rle:gən] *v/t* explain.

Darleh(e)n ['da:rle:ən] *n* (-s/-) loan.

Darm [darm] *m* (-[e]s/~e)

intestine(s *pl*), bowel(s *pl*), gut(s *pl*).

darstell|en ['da:rʃtelən] *v/t* describe; show; 2**ung** *f* representation.

darüber [da:ry:bər] *adv* over it *od.* them; *quer:* across it *od.* them; *davon:* about it; ~ **hinaus** beyond it; in addition.

darum [da'rum; 'da:rum] *adv* (a)round it *od.* them; for it *od.* them; *cj* therefore.

darunter [da'runtər] *adv* under it *od.* them; beneath it *od.* them; *dazwischen:* among them; *weniger:* less; **was verstehst du ~?** what do you understand by it?

das [das] *s.* **der;** ~ **heißt** that is (to say).

dasein ['da:zaın] *v/i* (*irr*) be there *od.* present; exist; 2 *n* (*-s/ no pl*) existence, being, life.

dasjenige ['dasje:nıgə] *s.* **derjenige.**

daß [das] *conj* that.

dasselbe [das'zɛlbə] *s.* **derselbe.**

dastehen ['da:ʃte:ən] *v/i* (*irr*) stand (there).

Daten ['da:tən] *pl* data *pl* (*a. tech.*); facts *pl*; particulars *pl*; **~verarbeitung** *f* data processing.

datieren [da'ti:rən] *v/t* date.

Dativ ['da:ti:f] *m* (*-s/-e*) *gr.* dative (case).

Dattel ['datəl] *f* (*-/-n*) *bot.* date.

Datum ['da:tum] *n* (*-s/ Daten*) date.

Dauer ['dauər] *f* (*-/ no pl*) duration; *Fort2:* continuance; period; **von ~ sein** last; 2**haft** *adj* lasting; durable; 2**n** ['dauərn] *v/i* continue; last; *Zeitaufwand:* take; 2**nd** *adj* lasting; permanent; constant; **~welle** *f* permanent wave, *colloq.* perm.

Daumen ['daumən] *m* (*-s/-*) thumb.

Daunendecke ['daunəndɛkə] *f* (*-/-n*) eiderdown (quilt).

davon [da'fɔn] *adv* of it *od.* them; *fort, weg:* off, away; *darüber:* about it.

davor [da'fo:r] *adv* before it *od.* them, in front of it *od.* them; **er fürchtet sich ~** he is afraid of it.

dazu [da'tsu:] *adv* to it *od.* them; *Zweck:* for it *od.* them; about it; *überdies:* besides; **~gehören** belong to it *od.* them; **~kommen** *v/i* (*irr*) arrive; join; be added; **~tun** *v/t* (*irr*) add.

dazwischen [da'tsvıʃən] *adv* between them, (in) between; **~kommen** *v/i* (*irr*) intervene; happen.

Debatte [de'batə] *f* (*-/-n*) debate.

Deck [dɛk] *n* (*-[e]s/-s*) deck.

Decke ['dɛkə] *f* (*-/-n*) cover(ing); blanket; (travel[l]ing) rug; *Zimmer:* ceiling; **~l** ['dɛkəl] m (-s/-) lid, cover; (book) cover; **2n** ['dɛkən] v/t cover; **den Tisch 2n** lay the table.

Deckung ['dɛkuŋ] f (-/no pl) cover.

defekt [de'fɛkt] adj defective, faulty; **2** m (-[e]s/-e) defect, fault.

definieren [defi'ni:rən] v/t define; **2tion** [-fini'tsio:n] f (-/-en) definition.

Defizit [de'fi:tsit] n (-s/-e) deficit, deficiency.

Degen ['de:gən] m (-s/-) sword; *Fechten:* épée.

dehnbar [de:nba:r] adj elastic; **~en** ['de:nən] v/t extend; stretch.

Deich [daiç] m (-[e]s/-e) dike, dyke.

Deichsel ['daiksəl] f (-/-n) pole, shaft(s pl).

dein [dain] poss pron your; **der, die, das ~e** yours; **~etwegen** ['dainət've:-gən] adv for your sake; because of you.

Dekan [de'ka:n] m (-s/-e) dean.

Deklination [deklina-'tsio:n] f (-/-en) gr. declension; **2ieren** [-'ni:-rən] v/t gr. decline.

Dekorateur [dekora-'tø:r] m (-s/-e) decorator; window-dresser; **~ation** [-ra'tsio:n] f (-/-en) decoration; (window-)dressing; *thea.* scenery; **2ieren** [-'ri:rən] v/t decorate; dress.

delikat [deli'ka:t] adj köstlich: delicious; delicate; **2esse** [-ka'tɛsə] f (-/-n) delicacy; *Leckerbissen:* a. dainty; **2essengeschäft** n delicatessen.

Delphin [dɛl'fi:n] m (-s/-e) dolphin.

dementieren [demɛn'ti:-rən] v/t deny.

dementsprechend ['de:m²ɛnt'ʃprɛçənt] adv accordingly; **~nach** ['de:mna:x] adv, cj according to that; therefore; **~nächst** ['dem'nɛ:çst] adv soon, shortly.

Delle ['dɛlə] f (-/-n) colloq. dent.

Demokrat [demo'kra:t] m (-en/-en) democrat; **~ie** [-kra'ti:] f (-/-n) democracy; **2isch** [-'kra:tiʃ] adj democratic.

demolieren [demo'li:rən] v/t demolish.

Demonstration [de-mɔnstra'tsio:n] f (-/-en) demonstration; **2ieren** [-'stri:rən] v/i, v/t demonstrate.

demontieren [demɔn'ti:-rən] v/t dismantle.

Demut ['de:mu:t] f (-/no pl) humility.

demütig ['de:my:tiç] adj humble; **~en** [-tɪgən] v/t humble, humiliate.

denkbar ['dɛŋkba:r] adj conceivable, imaginable; **~en** ['dɛŋkən] v/i, v/t (irr) think; **~en an** think of; remember; **sich et. ~en**

imagine s.th.; **2mal** [-ma:l] *n* (-[e]s/-er) monument; *Ehrenmal*: memorial; **~würdig** *adj* memorable; **2zettel** *m* fig. lesson.

denn [dɛn] *cj* for, because; **es sei ~, daß** unless, except.

dennoch ['dɛnɔx] *cj* yet, still, nevertheless.

denunzieren [denun'tsi:rən] *v/t* inform against.

deponieren [depo'ni:rən] *v/t* deposit.

der [der], **die** [di], **das** [das] *definite article* the; *dem pron* that, this; he, she, it; **die** *pl* these, those, they; *rel pron* who, which, that.

derartig ['de:r'a:rtɪç] *adj* such.

derb [dɛrp] *adj* coarse, rough; *Schuhe*: stout; *Person*: sturdy; *Ausdrucksweise*: blunt.

dergleichen ['de:r'glaɪçən] *dem pron*: **nichts ~** nothing of the kind.

der-, die-, dasjenige ['-je:nɪgə] *dem pron* he, she, that; **diejenigen** *pl* those.

der-, die-, dasselbe ['-'zɛlbə] *dem pron* the same; he, she, it.

desertieren [dezɛr'ti:rən] *v/i* desert.

deshalb ['dɛs'halp] *cj, adv* therefore; **~, weil** because.

desinfizieren [dɛs?ɪnfi-'tsi:rən] *v/t* disinfect.

Dessert [dɛ'se:r] *n* (-s/-s) dessert, sweet.

destillieren [dɛstɪ'li:rən] *v/t* distil.

desto ['dɛsto] *adv* (all, so much) the; **~ besser** (all) the better; **~ mehr** (all) the more.

deswegen ['dɛs've:gən] *cj, adv* s. **deshalb.**

Detail [de'taɪ] *n* (-s/-s) detail.

Detektiv [detɛk'ti:f] *m* (-s/-e) detective.

deuten ['dɔytən] *v/t* interpret; *Sterne, Traum*: read; *v/i*: **~ auf** point at.

deutlich ['dɔytlɪç] *adj* clear, distinct.

deutsch [dɔytʃ] *adj* German; **2e** *m, f* (-n/-n) German.

Devisen [de'vi:zən] *pl* foreign exchange *sg od.* currency *sg.*

Dezember [de'tsɛmbər] *m* (-s/*no pl*) December.

dezimal [detsi'ma:l] *adj* decimal.

Dia ['di:a] *n* (-s/-s) *s.* **Diapositiv.**

Diagnose [dia'gno:zə] *f* (-/-n) diagnosis.

diagonal [diago'na:l] *adj* diagonal.

Dialekt [dia'lɛkt] *m* (-[e]s/-e) dialect.

Dialog [dia'lo:k] *m* (-[e]s/-e) dialog(ue).

Diamant [dia'mant] *m* (-en/-en) diamond.

Diapositiv [diapozi'ti:f] *m* (-s/-e) slide.

Diät [di'ɛ:t] *f* (-/-en) diet.

dich [dɪç] *pers pron* you; ~ **(selbst)** yourself.

dicht [dɪçt] *adj* thick; ~ **an** *od.* **bei** close to.

dichten ['dɪçtən] *v/i* compose *od.* write poetry, *etc.*; *v/t* compose, write; **2r m** poet; author.

Dichtung[1] ['dɪçtʊŋ] *f* (-/-en) poetry; *Prosa:* fiction; poem, poetic work.

Dichtung[2] *f tech.* gasket, seal.

dick [dɪk] *adj* thick; *Person:* fat, stout; **2icht** ['dɪkɪçt] *n* (-s/-e) thicket; **~köpfig** [-kœpfɪç] *adj* stubborn.

die [di] *s.* **der**; *Artikel: pl* the.

Dieb [di:p] *m* (-[e]s/-e) thief; **~stahl** [-ʃta:l] *m* (-[e]s/∨e) theft, *jur. mst* larceny.

diejenige ['di:je:nɪgə] *s.* **derjenige.**

Diele ['di:lə] *f* (-/-n) board, plank; *Vorraum:* hall, *Am. a.* hallway.

dien|en ['di:nən] *v/i* serve (j-m s.o.); **2er m** (man-, domestic) servant; **2erin** *f* (woman-)servant, maid; **2st m** [di:nst] *m* (-[e]s/-e) service; **im** *od.* **außer 2st** on *od.* off duty.

Dienstag ['di:nsta:k] *m* (-[e]s/-e) Tuesday.

Dienst|bote ['di:nstbo:-tə] *m* (-n/-n) (domestic) servant, domestic; **2frei**

adj off duty; **2freier Tag** day off; **~leistung** *f* service; **2lich** *adj* official; **~mädchen** *n* maid(servant), help; **~stunden** *pl* office hours *pl*; **2tuend** [-tu:ənt] *adj* on duty.

dies [di:s], **~er** ['di:zər], **~e** [-zə], **~es** [-zəs] *dem pron* this (one); he, she, it; **~e** *pl* these; they.

dieselbe [di:zɛlbə] *s.* **derselbe.**

dies|mal ['di:sma:l] *adv* this time; for (this) once; **~seits** [-zaɪts] *adv, prp* on this side (*gen* of).

Differenz [dɪfe'rɛnts] *f* (-/-en) difference.

Diktat [dɪk'ta:t] *n* (-[e]s/-e) dictation; **~or** [-'ta:-tɔr] *m* (-s/-en) dictator; **~ur** [-ta'tu:r] *f* (-/-en) dictatorship.

diktieren [dɪk'ti:rən] *v/t* dictate.

Ding [dɪŋ] *n* (-[e]s/-e) thing; **vor allen ~en** above all.

Diphtherie [dɪfte'ri:] *f* (-/-n) diphtheria.

Diplom [di'plo:m] *n* (-[e]s/-e) diploma, certificate.

Diplomat [diplo'ma:t] *m* (-en/-en) diplomat, diplomatist; **2isch** *adj* diplomatic (*a. fig.*).

dir [di:r] *pers pron* (to) you; ~ **(selbst)** yourself.

direkt [di'rɛkt] *adj, adv* direct; **2ion** [-rɛk'tsi̯o:n] *f* (-/-en)   management;

board of directors; **2or** [-'rɛktɔr] *m* (-s/-en) director, head, manager; *Schule:* headmaster, *Am.* principal; **2orin** [-rɛk'toː-rɪn] *f* (-/-nen) headmistress, *Am.* principal; **2rice** [-rɛk'triːsə] *f* (-/-n) manageress; **2übertragung** *f* live broadcast.

Dirig|ent [diri'gɛnt] *m* (-en/-en) conductor; **2ieren** [-'giːrən] *v/t* conduct.

Dirne ['dɪrnə] *f* (-/-n) prostitute.

Diskont [dɪs'kɔnt] *m* (-s/ -e) discount.

Diskothek [dɪsko'teːk] *f* (-/-en) discotheque.

diskret [dɪs'kreːt] *adj* discreet; **2ion** [-kre'tsioːn] *f* (-/no *pl*) discretion.

Diskus ['dɪskʊs] *m* (-/-se, -ken) *sp.* discus.

Disku|ssion [dɪsku'sioːn] *f* (-/-en) discussion; **2tieren** [-'tiːrən] *v/i, v/t* discuss (**über** et. s.th.).

disqualifizieren [dɪs-kvalifi'tsiːrən] *v/t* disqualify.

Distanz [dɪs'tants] *f* (-/ -en) distance (*a. fig.*); **2ieren** [-tan'tsiːrən] *v/ refl:* **sich ~ von** dissociate o.s. from.

Distel ['dɪstəl] *f* (-/-n) thistle.

Distrikt [dɪs'trɪkt] *m* (-[e]s/-e) district.

Disziplin [dɪstsi'pliːn] *f* (-/ -en) discipline.

dividieren [divi'diːrən] *v/t* divide (**durch** by).

doch [dɔx] *cj, adv* but, though; however; yet; **also ~!** I knew it!; **komm ~ herein!** do come in!; **nicht ~!** don't!; *nach negativer Frage:* **~!** yes, ...

Docht [dɔxt] *m* (-[e]s/-e) wick.

Dock [dɔk] *n* (-[e]s/-s, -e) dock.

Dogge ['dɔgə] *f* (-/-n) Great Dane.

Dohle ['doːlə] *f* (-/-n) (jack)daw.

Doktor ['dɔktɔr] *m* (-s/ -en) doctor.

Dokument [doku'mɛnt] *n* (-[e]s/-e) document; **~afilm** [-mɛn'taːrfɪlm] *m* (-[e]s/-e) documentary (film).

Dolch [dɔlç] *m* (-[e]s/-e) dagger.

Dolmetscher ['dɔlmɛt-ʃər] *m* (-s/-) interpreter.

Dom [doːm] *m* (-[e]s/-e) cathedral.

Donner ['dɔnər] *m* (-s/-) thunder; **2n** *v/i* thunder; **es donnert** it is thundering; **~stag** [-staːk] *m* (-[e]s/-e) Thursday.

Doppel ['dɔpəl] *n* (-s/-) duplicate; *Tennis:* doubles *sg, pl;* **~bett** *n* double bed; **~decker** [-dɛkər] *m* (-s/ -) double-decker; **~gänger** [-gɛŋər] *m* (-s/-) double; **~punkt** *m* colon; **~stecker** *m* two-way adapter; **2t** ['dɔpəlt] *adj* double; *adv* twice; **~zent-ner** *m* quintal, 100 kilogram(me)s *pl*; **~zimmer** *n* double room.

Dorf [dɔrf] *n* (-[e]s/ˇer) village.

Dorn [dɔrn] *m* (-[e]s/-en) thorn (*a. fig.*); (*pl* -e) *Schnalle*: tongue; *Rennschuhe*: spike; **2ig** *adj* thorny.

Dorsch [dɔrʃ] *m* (-[e]s/-e) cod(fish).

dort [dɔrt] *adv* (over) there; **~her** ['-'heːr] *adv* from there; **~hin** ['-'hɪn] *adv* there.

Dose ['doːzə] *f* (-/-n) box; *Konserven2*: tin, *Am.* can; **~nöffner** *m* ['-n'ɔefnər] *m* (-s/-) tin opener, *Am.* can opener.

Dosis ['doːzɪs] *f* (-/Dosen) dose (*a. fig.*).

Dotter ['dɔtər] *m*, *n* (-s/-) yolk.

Dozent [do'tsɛnt] *m* (-en/-en) (university) lecturer.

Drache ['draxə] *m* (-n/-n) dragon; **~n** *m* (-s/-) kite.

Draht [draːt] *m* (-[e]s/ˇe) wire; **2los** *adj* wireless; **~seilbahn** *f* s. Seilbahn.

drall [dral] *adj* plump, buxom.

Drama ['draːma] *n* (-s/-men) drama; **~tiker** [dra'maːtikər] *m* (-s/-) dramatist, playwright; **2tisch** *adj* dramatic.

dran [dran] *adv colloq.* s. **daran**; **ich bin ~** it's my turn.

Drang [draŋ] *m* (-[e]s/*rare* ˇe) pressure; *fig.* urge.

drängen ['drɛŋən] *v/i* be pressing *od.* urgent; *v/t* press (*a. fig.*), push; *fig.* urge; **sich ~** *v/refl* crowd, throng.

drauf [drauf] *adv colloq.* s. **darauf**; **~ und dran sein zu** be on the point of *ger*.

draußen ['drausən] *adv* outside; out of doors.

Dreck [drɛk] *m* (-[e]s/*no pl*) *colloq.* dirt; filth; **2ig** *adj* dirty; filthy.

dreh|bar ['dreːbaːr] *adj* revolving, rotating; **2bleistift** *m* propelling pencil; **2bühne** *f* revolving stage; **~en** ['dreːən] *v/t*, *v/i* turn; *Film*: shoot; **2stuhl** *m* swivel-chair; **2tür** *f* revolving door; **2ung** ['dreːuŋ] *f* (-/-en) turn; *um Achse*: rotation.

drei [drai] *adj* three; **2eck** ['-ʔɛk] *n* (-[e]s/-e) triangle; **~eckig** *adj* triangular; **~fach** ['-fax] *adj* threefold, treble, triple; **2rad** *n* tricycle.

dreißig ['draisɪç] *adj* thirty; **~ste** *adj* thirtieth.

dreist [draist] *adj* bold; *frech*: saucy.

dreizehn(te) ['draitseːn-(tə)] *adj* thirteen(th).

dreschen ['drɛʃən] *v/t* (*irr*) thresh; *colloq. prügeln*: thrash. (train.)

dressieren [drɛ'siːrən] *v/t*)

Drillinge ['drɪlɪŋə] *pl* triplets *pl.*

drin [drɪn] *adv colloq. s.* **darin.**

dringen ['drɪŋən] *v/i (irr):* ~ **auf** insist on; ~ **aus** *Geräusch:* come from *od.* through; ~ **durch** penetrate, pierce; ~ **in** penetrate into; **~d** *adj* urgent, pressing; *Verdacht:* strong.

drinnen ['drɪnən] *adv* inside; indoors.

dritte ['drɪtə] *adj* third; **2I** ['drɪtl] *n* (-s/-) third; **~ns** *adv* thirdly.

Drog|e ['dro:gə] *f* (-/-n) drug; **~erie** [drogə'ri:] *f* (-/-n) chemist's shop, *Am.* drugstore; **~ist** [dro'gɪst] *m* (-en/-en) chemist, *Am.* druggist.

drohen ['dro:ən] *v/i* threaten, menace.

dröhnen ['drø:nən] *v/i* roar; boom.

Drohung ['dro:uŋ] *f* (-/-en) threat, menace.

drollig ['drɔlɪç] *adj* amusing, comical.

Dromedar [drome'da:r] *n* (-s/-e) dromedary.

Droschke ['drɔʃkə] *f* (-/-n) *s.* Taxi.

Drossel ['drɔsəl] *f* (-/-n) thrush; **2n** *v/t tech.* throttle.

drüben ['dry:bən] *adv* over there, yonder.

drüber ['dry:bər] *adv colloq. s.* **darüber.**

Druck [drʊk] *m* (-[e]s/-ᵉe) pressure; *Hände2:*

squeeze; *(pl* **-e)** print. print(ing); **~buchstabe** *m* block letter; **2en** ['drʊkən] *v/t* print.

drücken ['drykən] *v/t* press, push; *Hand etc.:* squeeze; **~ vor** *colloq. Arbeit etc.:* shirk; *v/i Schuh:* pinch; **~d** *adj Wetter:* oppressive, close.

Druck|er ['drʊkər] *m* (-s/-) printer; **~erei** [-kə'raɪ] *f* (-/-en) printing office; **~knopf** *m* snap-fastener; **~sache** *f* printed matter; **~schrift** *f* block letters *pl.*

drum [drʊm] *adv colloq. s.* **darum.**

drunter ['drʊntər] *adv colloq. s.* **darunter; es geht ~ und drüber** everything is topsy-turvy.

Drüse ['dry:zə] *f* (-/-n) gland.

Dschungel ['dʒuŋəl] *m* (-s/-) jungle.

du [du:] *pers pron* you.

ducken ['dʊkən] *v/refl:* **sich ~** crouch.

Dudelsack ['du:dəlzak] *m* (-[e]s/-ᵉe) bagpipes *pl.*

Duft [dʊft] *m* (-[e]s/-ᵉe) scent, fragrance, perfume; **2en** ['dʊftən] *v/i* smell **(nach** of); **2end** *adj* sweet-smelling, fragrant.

dulden ['dʊldən] *v/t* endure; suffer; tolerate, put up with.

dumm [dʊm] *adj* stupid; **2heit** *f* stupidity; stupid *od.* foolish action; **2kopf** *m* fool.

durchgehen

dumpf [dʊmpf] *adj* musty, stuffy; *Ton, Schmerz:* dull.

Düne ['dy:nə] *f* (*-/-n*) dune, sand-hill.

Dung [dʊŋ] *m* (*-[e]s/no pl*) dung, manure.

düngel|n ['dʏŋəln] *v/t* dung, manure; *bsd. künstlich:* fertilize (*a. v/i*); **2r** *m* (*-s/-*) *s. Dung; Kunstdünger:* fertilizer.

dunkel ['dʊŋkəl] *adj* dark; *trüb:* dim; *fig.* obscure; *Vorstellung etc.:* faint, vague; **es wird ~** it is growing dark; **2** *n* (*-s/no pl*) = **2heit** *f* (*-/no pl*) dark(ness).

dünn [dʏn] *adj* thin; *Luft:* rare.

Dunst [dʊnst] *m* (*-[e]s/ᵉe*) vapo(u)r, steam; haze, mist.

dünsten ['dʏnstən] *v/t, v/i* steam; *Fleisch, Obst etc.:* stew.

dunstig ['dʊnstɪç] *adj* hazy, misty.

Dur [du:r] *n* (*-/no pl*) *mus.* major (key).

durch [dʊrç] *prp* (*acc*) through; by; **~aus** ['~aus] *adv* absolutely, quite; **~aus nicht** not at all; **~blättern** ['~blɛtərn] *v/t* leaf through.

Durchblick ['dʊrçblɪk] *m* (*-[e]s/-e*) = **~auf** view of; **2en** *v/i* look through.

durch|bohren ['dʊrçbo:rən, dʊrç'bo:rən] *v/t* pierce; bore through; **~brechen** ['~brɛçən] *v/t,*

v/i (*irr*) break through; break apart od. in two; **~brennen** *v/i* (*irr*) *Sicherung:* blow; **~dringen** ['~drɪŋən] *v/i* (*irr*) penetrate; [~'drɪŋən] *v/t* (*irr*) penetrate; pierce.

durcheinander [dʊrç?aɪ'nandər] *adv* in confusion *od.* disorder; **2** *n* (*-s/no pl*) mess, confusion; **~bringen** *v/t* (*irr*) confuse; *Begriffe:* mix up.

durchfahr|en ['dʊrçfa:rən] *v/i* (*irr*), [~'fa:rən] *v/t* (*irr*) go (*pass, drive*) through; **2t** ['dʊrçfa:rt] *f* (*-/-en*) passage (through); *Tor:* gate(way); **2t verboten!** no thoroughfare.

Durchfall ['dʊrçfal] *m* (*-[e]s/ᵉe*) diarrh(o)ea; **2en** ['~falən] *v/i* (*irr*) fall through; *Examen:* fail; *thea.* be a failure.

durchführen ['dʊrçfy:rən] *v/t* lead *od.* take through; *vollenden:* carry out *od.* through; *verwirklichen:* realize.

Durchgang ['dʊrçgaŋ] *m* (*-[e]s/ᵉe*) passage; **kein ~!** no thoroughfare; private; **~sverkehr** *m* through traffic.

durchgebraten ['dʊrçgəbra:tən] *adj* well done.

durchgehen ['dʊrçge:ən] *v/i* (*irr*) go through; *Pferd:* bolt; *v/t prüfen:* go *od.* look through; **~d** *adj* continuous; **~der Zug** through train.

durchgreifen ['dʊrçɡraɪfən] *v/i* (*irr*) *fig.* take drastic measures *od.* steps; **~d** *adj* drastic; radical.

durch|halten ['dʊrçhaltən] *v/t* (*irr*) keep up; *v/i* hold out; **~hauen** *v/t* (*irr*) chop through; *fig.* give *s.o.* a good hiding; **~kommen** *v/i* (*irr*) come *od.* pass through; *Kranker:* pull through; *Examen:* pass; **~kreuzen** [-'krɔʏtsən] *v/t Plan etc.:* cross, thwart; **~lassen** [-lasən] *v/t* (*irr*) let pass *od.* through; **~lässig** [-lɛsɪç] *adj* pervious (*to light, etc.*), permeable (*to water, etc.*); **~laufen** [-laufən] *v/i* (*irr*) run *od.* pass through; *v/t Schuhe etc.:* wear out; [-'laufən] *v/t* (*irr*) *Stufen, Abteilungen etc.:* pass through; **~lesen** ['-le:zən] *v/t* (*irr*) read through; **~leuchten** ['-lɔʏçtən] *v/i* shine through; [-'lɔʏçtən] *v/t med.* X-ray; **~löchern** [-'lœçərn] *v/t* (*irr*) perforate; **~machen** ['-maxən] *v/t* go through; **2messer** ['-mɛsər] *m* (**-s/-**) diameter; **~näßt** [-'nɛst] *adj* soaked, drenched; **~queren** [-'kve:rən] *v/t* cross, traverse.

Durchreise ['dʊrçraɪzə] *f* (**-/no pl**) journey *od.* way through; **2n** ['-raɪzən] *v/i*, [-'raɪzən] *v/t* travel *od.* pass through; **2nde** *m*, *f* (**-n/-n**) person passing

through, *Am. a.* transient.

durch|reißen ['dʊrçraɪsən] *v/t*, *v/i* (*irr*) tear (in two); **2sage** ['-za:ɡə] *f* (**-/-n**) announcement; **~schauen** ['-ʃaʊən] *v/i* see *od.* look through; [-'ʃaʊən] *v/t fig.* see through.

durchscheinen ['dʊrçʃaɪnən] *v/i* (*irr*) shine through; **~d** *adj* translucent.

Durchschlag ['dʊrçʃla:k] *m* (**-[e]s/-e**) carbon (copy); **2en** [-'ʃla:ɡən] *v/t* (*irr*) pierce; *Kugel:* penetrate; **~papier** ['dʊrç-] *n* carbon(-paper).

durchschneiden ['dʊrçʃnaɪdən] *v/t* (*irr*) cut through.

Durchschnitt ['dʊrçʃnɪt] *m* (**-[e]s/-e**) average; **im ~** on an average; **2lich** *adj* average; ordinary; *adv* on an average; normally.

durch|sehen ['dʊrçze:ən] *v/i*, *v/t* (*irr*) see *od.* look through; look *s.th.* over; go over *s.th.*; **~setzen** *v/t* put through; *mit Gewalt:* force through; **sich ~setzen** get one's way; be successful; **~sichtig** [-'zɪçtɪç] *adj* transparent; clear; **~sickern** ['-zɪkərn] *v/i* seep through; **~sieben** ['-zi:bən] *v/t* sieve, sift; **~sprechen** *v/t* (*irr*) discuss, talk over; **~stöbern** [-'ʃtø:bərn] *v/t* ransack, rummage; **~streichen** ['-ʃtraɪçən] *v/t* (*irr*) strike *od.* cross out; **~suchen** ['zu:xən] *v/t* search; **~wachsen** ['-vaksən] *v/t* streaky; **~weg** ['-vɛk] *adv* throughout, without exception; **~wühlen** ['-vy:-lən, '-vy:lən] *v/t* ransack, rummage; **2zug** *m* draught, *Am.* draft; **~zwängen** ['-tsvɛŋən] *v/t*: **sich ~** squeeze o.s. through.

dürfen ['dyrfən] *v/aux* (*irr*): **ich darf** I am allowed to; I may; **du darfst nicht** you must not.

dürftig ['dyrftiç] *adj* poor; scanty.

dürr [dyr] *adj* dry; *Boden etc.*: barren, arid; *mager*: lean, skinny; **2e** *f* (-/-n) dryness; barrenness.

Durst [durst] *m* (-es/*no pl*)

---

thirst (**nach** for); **~ ha-ben** to be thirsty; **2ig** *adj* thirsty.

Dusche ['duʃə] *f* (-/-n) shower(-bath); **2n** *v/i* have a shower(-bath).

Düse ['dy:zə] *f* (-/-n) nozzle; *aer.* jet; **~nflugzeug** *n* jet aircraft *od.* plane, *colloq.* jet; **~njäger** *m aer.* jet fighter.

düster ['dy:stər] *adj* dark, gloomy (*a. fig.*); *Licht:* dim.

Dutzend ['dutsənt] *n* (-s/-e) dozen.

dynamisch [dy'na:miʃ] *adj* dynamic(al).

Dynamit [dyna'mi:t] *n* (-s/ *no pl*) dynamite.

Dynamo [dy'na:mo] *m* (-s/-s) dynamo, generator.

D-Zug ['de:tsu:k] *m* express (train).

E

Ebbe ['ɛbə] *f* (-/-n) ebb (tide), low tide.

eben ['e:bən] *adj* even; *flach:* plain, level; *math.* plane; *adv* exactly; just.

Ebene ['e:bənə] *f* (-/-n) plain; *math.* plane; *fig.* level.

eben|falls ['e:bənfals] *adv* also, likewise; **~so** [-zo:] *adv* just as; **~soviel** *indef pron* just as much *od.* many; **~sowenig** *indef pron* just as little *od.* few.

Eber ['e:bər] *m* (-s/-) boar.

---

ebnen ['e:bnən] *v/t* level; *fig.* smooth.

Echo ['ɛço] *n* (-s/-s) echo.

echt [ɛçt] *adj* genuine; *Farbe:* fast; *Dokument:* authentic.

Eck|ball ['ɛkbal] *m* (-[e]s/ ⸚e) *sp.* corner-kick; **~e** ['ɛkə] *f* (-/-n) corner; *Kante:* edge; *s.* **Eckball;** **2ig** *adj* angular; **~platz** *m* corner-seat; **~zahn** *m* canine tooth.

edel ['e:dəl] *adj* noble; **2stein** *m* precious stone.

Efeu ['eːfɔy] m *-s/no pl* ivy.

egal [e'gaːl] *adj colloq.* s. gleich.

Egge ['egə] f (-/-n) harrow; **2n** v/t harrow.

egoistisch [ego'ɪstɪʃ] *adj* selfish.

ehe ['eːə] *cj* before.

Ehe f (-/-n) marriage; *Ehestand:* a. matrimony; **~bruch** m adultery; **~frau** f wife; **2lich** *adj* conjugal; *Kind:* legitimate.

ehemalig ['eːəmaːlɪç] *adj* former, ex-...; late.

Ehe|mann ['eːəman] m (-[e]s/*er*) husband; **~paar** n married couple.

eher ['eːər] *adv* sooner; *lieber:* rather; **je ~, desto besser** the sooner the better.

Ehe|ring m wedding ring; **~scheidung** f divorce; **~schließung** [-ʃliːsʊŋ] f (-/-en) marriage.

Ehre ['eːrə] f (-/-n) hono(u)r; **2n** v/t hono(u)r.

Ehren|bürger m honorary citizen; **~gast** m guest of hono(u)r; **~mitglied** n honorary member; **~wort** n word of hono(u)r.

ehr|erbietig ['eːrʔɛrbiːtɪç] *adj* respectful; **2furcht** f: **~ (vor)** respect (for); awe (of); **2gefühl** n sense of hono(u)r; **2geiz** m ambition; **~geizig** *adj* ambitious.

ehrlich ['eːrlɪç] *adj* honest; **2keit** f honesty.

Ehrung ['eːrʊŋ] f (-/-en) hono(u)r.

Ei [aɪ] n (-[e]s/-er) egg; *physiol.* ovum.

Eiche ['aɪçə] f (-/-n) oak (tree); **~l** f (-/-n) acorn.

Eichhörnchen ['aɪçhœrnçən] n (-s/-) squirrel.

Eid [aɪt] m (-[e]s/-e) oath.

Eidechse ['aɪdɛksə] f (-/-n) lizard.

eidesstattlich ['aɪdəsʃtatlɪç] *adj:* **~e Erklärung** statutory declaration.

Eidotter ['aɪdɔtər] m, n (egg) yolk.

Eier|becher ['aɪərbɛçər] m (-s/-) egg-cup; **~kuchen** m omelet(te), pancake; **~schale** f egg-shell.

Eifer ['aɪfər] m (-s/no pl) zeal, eagerness; **~sucht** f jealousy; **2süchtig** *adj* jealous (auf of).

eifrig ['aɪfrɪç] *adj* eager, keen.

Eigelb ['aɪgɛlp] n (-s/-e, -) (egg) yolk.

eigen ['aɪgən] *adj* own; *besonder:* particular; peculiar; **~artig** [-aːrtɪç] *adj* peculiar; **~händig** [-hɛndɪç] *adj* personal; *adv* with one's own hand(s); **~mächtig** *adj* arbitrary; without authority; **2name** m proper name; **~s** *adv* expressly; specially.

Eigenschaft ['aɪgənʃaft] f (-/-en) quality; *Sachen:* property; **in s-r ~ als** in his capacity as.

eigensinnig ['aɪgənzɪnɪç] *adj* obstinate.

eigentlich ['aɪgəntlɪç] *adj* actual; proper.

Eigen|tum ['aɪgəntuːm] *n* (-s/ver) property; **~tü-mer** *m* (-s/-) owner, proprietor.

eigenwillig ['aɪgənvɪlɪç] *adj* individual; self-willed.

eignen ['aɪgnən] *v/refl*: **sich ~ für** *od.* **zu** be suited for.

Eil|bote ['aɪlboːtə] *m* (-n/-n) express (messenger); **~brief** *m* express letter.

Eile ['aɪlə] *f* (-/no pl) haste, hurry; **2n** *v/i* hasten, hurry; *Brief, Angelegenheit:* be urgent.

eilig ['aɪlɪç] *adj* hasty, speedy; *dringend:* urgent; **es ~ haben** be in a hurry.

Eilzug ['aɪltsuːk] *m* (-[e]s/ve) fast train.

Eimer ['aɪmər] *m* (-s/-) bucket, pail.

ein [aɪn] *indef article* one; a, an; **~ander** ['anˈʔandər] *pron* one another, each other.

ein|äschern ['aɪnˈʔɛʃərn] *v/t* burn to ashes; *Leiche:* cremate; **~atmen** *v/t, v/i* breathe (in), inhale.

Ein|bahnstraße ['aɪnbaːnʃtraːsə] *f* (-/-n) one-way street; **~band** *m* binding, cover.

ein|bauen ['aɪnbauən] *v/t* build in; **~berufen** *v/t* (irr) call; *mil.* call up, *Am.* draft.

Einbettzimmer ['aɪnbet-tsɪmər] *n* (-s/-) single room.

einbiegen ['aɪnbiːgən] *v/i* (irr): **~ in** turn into; **~ nach** turn to.

einbilden ['aɪnbɪldən] *v/refl*: **sich et. ~** imagine, think, **2ung** *f* imagination; *Dünkel:* conceit.

einbreche|n ['aɪnbreçən] *v/i* (irr) break through; break in; **~n in** *Haus:* break into; **2r** *m* (-s/-) nachts: burglar; tagsüber: housebreaker.

Einbruch ['aɪnbrux] *m* (-[e]s/ve) housebreaking; burglary.

ein|bürgern ['aɪnbyr-gərn] *v/t* naturalize; **~bü-ßen** *v/t* lose; **~deutig** [-dɔytɪç] *adj* clear.

eindring|en ['aɪndrɪŋən] *v/i* (irr): **~ in** enter; penetrate (into); **~lich** *adj* urgent.

Ein|druck ['aɪndruk] *m* (-[e]s/ve) impression; **2drücken** *v/t* push in; **2drucksvoll** *adj* impressive.

ein|er, **~e**, **~(e)s** *indef pron* one.

einerlei ['aɪnərlaɪ] *adj s.* **gleich;** **2** *n* (-s/no pl) monotony, humdrum.

einerseits ['aɪnərzaɪts] *adv* on the one hand.

einfach ['aɪnfax] *adj* simple, plain; *Mahlzeit:* frugal; *Fahrkarte:* single, *Am.* one-way; **2heit** *f* (-/no pl) simplicity.

Einfahrt

Einfahrt ['aɪnfaːrt] f (-/
-en) entry; entrance; *s.*
Autobahneinfahrt.

Einfall ['aɪnfal] *m* (-[e]s/
ᵉe) *mil.* invasion; *fig.* idea,
inspiration; **2en** *v/i* (*irr*)
fall in, collapse; **2en** in
mil. invade; **j-m 2en** occur to s.o.

ein|fangen ['aɪnfaŋən] *v/t*
(*irr*) catch, capture, seize;
~farbig *adj Stoff:* selfcol-
o(u)red, plain; **~fassen**
v/t edge, border; **~fetten**
[-fɛtən] *v/t* grease.

Einfluß ['aɪnflʊs] *m*
(-sses/ᵉsse) influence;
2reich *adj* influential.

einfrieren ['aɪnfriːrən]
v/i, v/t (*irr*) freeze (in).

Einfuhr ['aɪnfuːr] f (-/
-en) import(ation); **2führ-
ren** *v/t econ.* import; introduce; *in ein Amt:* instal(l).

Eingang ['aɪŋaŋ] *m*
(-[e]s/ᵉe) entrance; *von
Waren:* arrival.

einge|bildet ['aɪŋəbɪl-
dət] *adj* imaginary; *dün-
kelhaft:* conceited; **2bo-
rene,** *m* (-n/-n) native;
~fallen *adj* sunken, hollow.

eingehen ['aɪŋeːən] *v/i*
(*irr*) come in, arrive; *bot.,
zo.* die; *Material:* shrink; **~
auf** agree to; *Einzelheiten:*
enter into.

Eingemachte ['aɪŋə-
maxtə] *n* (-n/no *pl*) pre-
served fruit; preserves *pl.*

eingeschrieben ['aɪŋə-
ʃriːbən] *adj* registered.

Eingeweide ['aɪŋəvaɪ-
də] *pl* intestines *pl*, bowels
pl; Tiere: entrails *pl.*

eingewöhnen ['aɪŋə-
vøːnən] *v/refl* ~ *sich* acclimatize, settle down.

ein|gießen ['aɪŋiːsən] *v/t*
(*irr*) pour (out); **~gießen**
in pour into; **~greifen** *v/i*
(*irr*) intervene; interfere.

Eingriff ['aɪŋrɪf] *m* (-[e]s/
-e) *med.* operation.

einhängen ['aɪnhɛŋən]
v/t, v/i Telefon: hang up.

einheimisch ['aɪnhaɪmɪʃ]
adj native; **2e** *m, f* (-n/-n)
native; resident.

Einheit ['aɪnhaɪt] f (-/-en)
unity; *phys., math., mil.*
unit; **2lich** *adj* uniform.

einholen ['aɪnhoːlən] *v/t*
catch up with; *Zeitverlust:*
make up for; *colloq.* buy.

einig ['aɪnɪç] *adj* united; ~
sein agree; **sich nicht** ~
sein differ; **~e** ['aɪnɪgə]
indef pron some, several;
~en ['aɪnɪgən] *v/t* unite;
sich ~en come to an
agreement; **~ermaßen**
[-gər'maːsən] *adv* to some
extent; somewhat; **~es** *indef pron* something; **2ung**
f unification; agreement.

einjährig ['aɪnjɛːrɪç] *adj*
one-year-old; one year's.

Einkauf ['aɪnkauf] *m*
(-[e]s/ᵉe) purchase; **2en**
v/t buy, purchase; *v/i:* **2en
gehen** go shopping;
~stasche f shopping bag;
~szentrum *n* shopping
centre (*Am.* -er).

ein|kehren ['aɪnke:rən]
v/i put up od. stop (in at);
~kleiden v/t clothe.

Einkommen ['aɪnkɔmən]
n (-s/-) income; ~steuer f
income-tax.

Einkünfte ['aɪnkʏnftə] pl
income sg.

einladen ['aɪnla:dən] v/t
(irr) load (in); invite; 2ung
f invitation.

Einlaß ['aɪnlas] m (-sses/
≈sse) admission; Zutritt:
admittance.

einlassen ['aɪnlasən] v/t
(irr) let in, admit.

Einlauf ['aɪnlauf] m (-[e]s/
≈e) med. enema; 2en v/i
(irr) Zug: pull in; Schiff:
enter the harbo(u)r; Material: shrink.

einlege|n ['aɪnle:gən] v/t
pickle; Film ~n load a
camera; 2sohle f insole,
sock.

Einleitung ['aɪnlaɪtʊŋ] f
(-/-en) introduction.

ein|liefern ['aɪnli:fərn]
v/t: in ein Kranken-
haus ~ take to hospital;
~lösen v/t Wechsel: hon-
o(u)r; Scheck: cash; ~ma-
chen v/t preserve; in Do-
sen: tin, Am. can.

einmal ['aɪnma:l] adv
once; one day; auf ~ all at
once; nicht ~ not even;
~ig adj fig. unique.

einmischen ['aɪnmɪʃən]
v/refl: sich ~ meddle, interfere.

Einmündung ['aɪnmʏn-
dʊŋ] f (-/-en) junction.

Einnahme ['aɪnna:mə] f
(-/-n) taking; ~nahmen
pl takings pl, receipts pl;
2nehmen v/t (irr) take;
Geld: earn, make, bei Ge-
schäften etc.: take; Platz:
take up, occupy.

ein|ordnen ['aɪnɔrdnən]
v/t put in its place; Briefe
etc.: file; ~packen v/t
pack (up); einwickeln: wrap
up; ~pflanzen v/t plant;
~reiben v/t (irr) rub (s.th.
in); ~reichen v/t send od.
hand in.

Einreise ['aɪnraɪzə] f (-/
-n) entry; ~genehmi-
gung f entry permit;
~visum n entrance visa.

ein|reißen ['aɪnraɪsən] v/t
(irr) tear; Haus: pull down;
~renken [-rɛŋkən] v/t
med. set; fig. put od. set
right.

einrichten ['aɪnrɪçtən] v/t
equip, fit up; Wohnung:
furnish; fig. arrange;
2ung f establishment;
equipment; furniture; in-
stitution.

eins [aɪns] adj one.

einsam ['aɪnza:m] adj
lonely, solitary; 2keit f
loneliness, solitude.

einsammeln ['aɪnzaməln]
v/t collect.

Einsatz ['aɪnzats] m (-[e]s/
≈e) inset, insertion; Spiel2:
stake.

ein|schalten ['aɪnʃaltən]
v/t switch od. turn on; sich
~schalten intervene;
~schenken v/t pour

Einschnitt

Einschnitt

(out); **~schicken** v/t send in; **~schlafen** v/i (irr) fall asleep; **~schläfern** [-ʃlɛːfərn] v/t lull to sleep; *Tier:* put to sleep; **~schlagen** v/t (irr) *Nagel:* drive in; *zerbrechen:* break, smash; *einwickeln:* wrap up; *Weg:* take; v/i *Blitz, Geschoß:* strike; **~schließen** v/t (irr) lock in od. up; *umgeben:* enclose; *mil.* surround; *fig.* include; **~schließlich** *prp* (gen), *adv* including; **~schmieren** v/t grease; **~schneiden** v/i (irr): **~ in** cut into; **~schneidend** *adj fig.* drastic.

Einschnitt ['aɪnʃnɪt] *m* (-[e]s/-e) cut; *Kerbe:* notch.

einschränken ['aɪnʃrɛŋkən] v/t restrict, confine; *Ausgaben:* reduce, cut down; **sich ~** economize.

Einschreibe|brief ['aɪnʃraɪbəbriːf] *m* (-[e]s/-e) registered letter; **2n** *v/t* (irr) enter; *Mitglied:* enrol(l); *Post:* register; **sich 2n** *v/refl* enter one's name.

ein|schreiten ['aɪnʃraɪtən] v/i (irr) intervene; **~schüchtern** [-ʃʏçtərn] v/t intimidate; **~sehen** v/t (irr) *fig.* see, understand; **~seitig** [-zaɪtɪç] *adj* one-sided; *pol.* unilateral; **~senden** v/t (irr) send in; **~setzen** v/i begin; *Kälte etc.:* set in; v/t put in, insert; *Geld:* stake; use; *Le-*

ben: risk; **sich ~setzen für** v/refl stand up for; support.

Einsicht ['aɪnzɪçt] *f* (-/-en) *fig.* insight, judiciousness; **2ig** *adj* judicious; sensible.

einsilbig ['aɪnzɪlbɪç] *adj* monosyllabic; *fig.* taciturn.

ein|sinken ['aɪnzɪŋkən] v/i (irr) sink (in); **~sparen** v/t save; **~sperren** v/t shut od. lock up; imprison.

Einspruch ['aɪnʃprʊx] *m* (-[e]s/⸚e) objection, protest; *jur.* appeal; **~ erheben (gegen)** object (to), protest (against).

einspurig ['aɪnʃpuːrɪç] *adj* single-lane.

einst [aɪnst] *adv* once.

ein|stecken ['aɪnʃtɛkən] v/t pocket (a. *fig.*); *Brief:* post, *Am.* mail; **~steigen** v/i (irr): **~ in** get into; *Bus:* get on; **alles ~!** all aboard!

einstellen ['aɪnʃtɛlən] v/t *Arbeitskräfte:* engage, employ, hire; *aufgeben:* give up; *Zahlungen etc.:* stop, cease; **~en (auf)** *Mechanismus:* adjust (to); *Radio:* tune in (to); **die Arbeit ~en** strike, *colloq.* down tools; **sich ~en** v/refl appear; **sich ~en auf** be prepared for; adapt o.s. to; **2ung** *f* engagement; *Zahlungen:* stoppage; adjustment; *innere:* attitude.

ein|stimmig ['aɪnʃtɪmɪç]

adj unanimous; ~**stöckig** [-ʃtœkɪç] *adj* one-stor|eyed, -ied.

ein|studieren ['aɪnʃtudi:-rən] *v/t* study; *a. thea.* rehearse; 2**sturz** *m* collapse; ~**stürzen** *v/i* fall in, collapse.

einstweilen ['aɪnst'vaɪ-lən] *adv* for the time being.

ein|tauchen ['aɪntauxən] *v/t, v/i:* ~ **in** dip od. plunge into; ~**tauschen** *v/t* exchange (**gegen** for).

einteil|en ['aɪntaɪlən] *v/t* divide (**in** into); classify; ~**ig** *adj* one-piece; 2**ung** *f* division; classification.

eintönig ['aɪntø:nɪç] *adj* monotonous.

Eintracht ['aɪntraxt] *f* (-/ *no pl*) harmony.

eintragen ['aɪntra:gən] *v/t* (*irr*) enter; *amtlich:* register; **sich** ~ register, *Hotel a.* check in.

einträglich ['aɪntrɛ:klɪç] *adj* profitable.

ein|treffen ['aɪntrɛfən] *v/i* (*irr*) arrive; *sich erfüllen:* come true; ~**treten** *v/i* (*irr*) enter; *fig.* happen; ~**treten** *v/i* join.

Eintritt ['aɪntrɪt] *m* (-s/*no pl*) entry, entrance; *Einlaß:* admittance; ~ **frei!** admission free; ~ **verboten!** no admittance; ~**sgeld** *n* entrance fee, admission (fee); ~**skarte** *f* admission ticket.

ein|trocknen ['aɪntrɔk-nən] *v/i* dry up; ~**ver-**

standen [-ferʃtandən] *adj:* ~ **sein** agree.

Einwand ['aɪnvant] *m* (-[e]s/¨e) objection.

Einwander|er ['aɪnvan-dərər] *m* (-s/-) immigrant; 2**n** *v/i* immigrate; ~**ung** *f* immigration.

einwandfrei ['aɪnvant-fraɪ] *adj* perfect.

ein|weichen ['aɪnvaɪçən] *v/t* soak; ~**weihen** *v/t* inaugurate; **j-n** ~**weihen** in initiate s.o. into; ~**wenden** *v/t* (*irr*) object (**gegen** to); ~**werfen** *v/t* (*irr*) throw in (*a. fig.*); *Fenster:* smash, break; *Brief:* post, *Am.* mail; *Münze:* insert.

einwickel|n ['aɪnvɪkəln] *v/t* wrap (up); 2**papier** *n* wrapping paper.

einwillig|en ['aɪnvɪlɪgən] *v/i* consent; 2**gung** *f* consent.

einwirken ['aɪnvɪrkən] *v/i:* ~ **auf** act (up)on; *beeinflussen:* influence.

Einwohner ['aɪnvo:nər] *m* (-s/-), ~**in** *f* (-/-nen) inhabitant; resident.

Einwurf ['aɪnvurf] *m* (-[e]s/¨e) *sp.* throw-in; *Briefkasten:* slit; *Automat:* slot; *Einwand:* objection.

Einzahl ['aɪntsa:l] *f* (-/*no pl*) *gr.* singular.

einzahl|en ['aɪntsa:lən] *v/t* pay in; 2**ung** *f* payment; *Bank:* deposit.

einzäunen ['aɪntsɔʏnən] *v/t* fence (in).

Einzel ['aɪntsəl] *n* (-s/-)

Tennis: singles *sg, pl;*
~**handel** *m* retail trade;
~**heiten** *pl* particulars *pl,*
details *pl;* 2**n** ['aintsəln]
adj single; *für sich allein:*
individual; *abgetrennt:*
separate; *Schuh etc.:* odd;
im 2**nen** in detail; ~**zimmer** *n* single room.

einziehen ['aintsi:ən] *v/t
(irr)* draw in; *Erkundi-
gungen:* make (**über** on,
about); *v/i Mieter:* move in;
~ **in** *Mieter:* move into.

einzig ['aintsiç] *adj* only;
single; *alleinig:* sole; ~**artig** *adj* unique.

Eis [ais] *n (-es/no pl);
Speise:* ice cream; ~**bahn**
f skating-rink; ~**bär** *m* polar bear; ~**diele** *f* ice-
cream parlo(u)r.

Eisen ['aizən] *n (-s/-)* iron.
Eisenbahn ['aizənba:n] *f
(-/-en)* railway, *Am.* railroad; ~**er** *m* railwayman.

Eisenwaren ['aizənva:-
rən] *pl* hardware *sg,* iron-
ware *sg.*

eisern ['aizərn] *adj* iron, of
iron.

eis|gekühlt ['aisgəky:lt]
adj iced; chilled; 2**hok-
key** [-hɔki] *n (-s/no pl)* ice
hockey; ~**ig** ['aiziç] *adj* icy
(*a. fig.*); ~**kalt** ['ais'kalt]
adj ice-cold, icy; 2**kunst-
lauf** *m (-[e]s/no pl)* figure
skating; 2**lauf** *m (-[e]s/no
pl)* skating; 2**läufer** *m*
skater; 2**würfel** *m* ice
cube; 2**zapfen** *m* icicle.

eitel ['aitəl] *adj* vain;

2**keit** *f* vanity.

Eiter ['aitər] *m (-s/no pl)*
matter, pus; 2(**e)rig** *adj*
purulent, festering; 2**ern**
v/i fester, suppurate.

Eiweiß ['aivais] *n (-es/rare
-e)* white of egg; *biol.,
chem.:* protein; albumen.

Ekel [e:kəl] *m (-s/no pl)*
disgust, loathing; 2**erre-
gend** [-ʔɛrrə:gənt] *adj*
nauseating, sickening;
2**haft** *adj* disgusting, repulsive; 2**n** *v/refl:* **sich ~
(vor)** be nauseated (at);
fig. be disgusted (with),
feel disgust (at).

Ekzem [ɛk'tse:m] *n (-s/-e)*
eczema.

elastisch [e'lastiʃ] *adj*
elastic.

Elch [ɛlç] *m (-[e]s/-e)* elk,
moose.

Elefant [ele'fant] *m (-en/
-en)* elephant.

elegant [ele'gant] *adj* elegant, smart.

Elektri|ker [e'lɛktrikər] *m
(-s/-)* electrician; 2**sch** *adj*
electric(al).

Elektrizität [elɛktritsi-
'tɛ:t] *f (-/no pl)* electricity;
~**swerk** *n* power-station,
power-house.

Elektro|gerät [e'lɛktro-
gərɛ:t] *n (-[e]s/-e)* electric
appliance; 2**nisch**
[elɛk'tro:niʃ] *adj* electro-
nic.

Element [ele'mɛnt] *n
(-[e]s/-e)* element.

Elend ['e:lɛnt] *n (-[e]s/no
pl)* misery; *Not: a.* need,

distress; 2 *adj* miserable, wretched; needy, distressed; **~sviertel** *n* slums *pl.*

elf [ɛlf] *adj* eleven.

Elfenbein [ɛlfənbaɪn] *n* (-[e]s/*no pl*) ivory.

elfte [ɛlftə] *adj* eleventh.

Ellbogen [ˈɛlboːgən] *m* (-s/-) elbow.

Elster [ɛlstər] *f* (-/-n) magpie.

Eltern [ɛltərn] *pl* parents *pl;* **~teil** *m* parent.

Email [eˈmaɪ(l)] *n* (-s/-s), **~le** *f* (-/-n) enamel.

Emigrant [emiˈgrant] *m* (-en/-en), **~in** *f* (-/-nen) emigrant.

Empfang [ɛmˈpfaŋ] *m* (-[e]s/ᵉe) reception (*a.* Radio); Erhalt: receipt; 2en *v/t (irr)* receive.

Empfänger [ɛmˈpfɛŋər] *m* (-s/-) receiver (*a.* Radio); Geld2: payee; Brief2: addressee.

empfänglich [ɛmˈpfɛŋlɪç] *adj* susceptible (**für** to).

Empfangs|bestätigung [ɛmˈpfaŋsbəʃtɛtɪgʊŋ] *f* (-/-en) (acknowledg[e]ment of) receipt; **~chef,** *m,* **~dame** *f* receptionist; **~schalter** *m* reception desk.

empfehl|en [ɛmˈpfeːlən] *v/t (irr)* recommend (**j-m et.** s.th. to s.o.); 2ung *f* recommendation; Gruß: compliments *pl.*

empfind|en [ɛmˈpfɪndən]

v/t (irr) feel; **~lich** *adj* sensitive (**gegen** to); Person: touchy; 2ung *f* sensation, feeling.

empor|ragen [ɛmˈpoːrraːgən] *v/i* tower, rise; **~steigen** *v/i (irr)* rise, ascend.

empör|t [ɛmˈpøːrt] *adj* indignant, shocked; 2ung *f* indignation.

emsig [ɛmzɪç] *adj* busy, industrious.

Ende [ˈɛndə] *n* (-s/-n) end; **am ~** at od. in the end; eventually; **zu ~ sein** be at an end; be over; **zu ~ gehen** end; knapp werden: run short; 2n [ɛndən] *v/i* end.

End|ergebnis [ˈɛntʔergeːpnɪs] *n* (-ses/-se) final result; 2gültig *adj* final; 2lich *adv* finally, at last; 2los *adj* endless; **~runde** *f,* **~spiel** *n sp.* final; **~station** *f* terminus, terminal; **~summe** *f* (sum) total; 2ung *f* [ɛndʊŋ] *f gr.* ending.

Energ|ie [enɛrˈgiː] *f* (-/-n) energy; 2isch [eˈnɛrgɪʃ] *adj* vigorous, energetic.

eng [ɛŋ] *adj* narrow; Kleidung: tight; dicht: close; innig: intimate.

Engel [ˈɛŋəl] *m* (-s/-) angel.

Engländer [ˈɛŋlɛndər] *m* (-s/-) Englishman; **die ~** *pl* the English *pl.*

englisch [ˈɛŋlɪʃ] *adj* English.

Engpaß

Engpaß [ˈɛŋpas] *m* (-sses/ᵛsse) defile, narrow pass; *fig.* bottle-neck.

engstirnig [ˈɛŋʃtɪrnɪç] *adj* narrow-minded.

Enkel [ˈɛŋkəl] *m* (-s/-) grandchild; grandson; ~**in** *f* (-/-nen) granddaughter.

enorm [eˈnɔrm] *adj* enormous.

Ensemble [ãˈsãːbəl] *n* (-s/-s) *mus.* ensemble; *thea.* company.

entbehr|en [ɛntˈbeːrən] *v/t* do without, spare; *vermissen*: miss; ~**lich** *adj* dispensable; *überflüssig*: superfluous; 2**ung** *f* want, privation.

Entbindung [ɛntˈbɪndʊŋ] *f* (-/-en) *med.* delivery, confinement; ~**heim** *n* maternity hospital.

entdeck|en [ɛntˈdɛkən] *v/t* discover; 2**er** *m* discoverer; 2**ung** *f* discovery.

Ente [ˈɛntə] *f* (-/-n) duck.

enteign|en [ɛntˈʔaɪɡnən] *v/t* expropriate, dispossess; ~**erben** *v/t* disinherit; ~**fallen** *v/i* (*irr*): **j-m** ~ *fig.* escape s.o.; ~**falten** *v/t* unfold (*a.* **sich**); *Fähigkeiten*: develop.

entfern|en [ɛntˈfɛrnən] *v/t* remove; **sich** ~**en** *v/refl* go away, leave; ~**t** *adj* distant, remote; 2**ung** *f* removal; distance; 2**ungsmesser** *m phot.* range-finder.

entfliehen [ɛntˈfliːən] *v/i* (*irr*) flee, escape.

entführ|en [ɛntˈfyːrən] *v/t* kidnap; *Flugzeug*: hijack; 2**er** *m* kidnap(p)er; *Flugzeug*: hijacker; 2**ung** *f* kidnap(p)ing; *Flugzeug*: hijacking.

entgegen [ɛntˈɡeːɡən] *prp* (*dat*) contrary to; against; *adv* towards; ~**gehen** *v/i* (*irr*) go to meet; ~**gesetzt** [-ɡəzɛtst] *adj* opposite; *fig.* contrary; ~**kommen** *v/i* (*irr*) come to meet; *fig.* meet s.o.'s wishes); ~**kommend** *adj* obliging; ~**nehmen** *v/t* (*irr*) accept, receive; ~**sehen** *v/i* (*irr*) look forward to; ~**strecken** *v/t* hold *od.* stretch out (*dat* to).

entgegn|en [ɛntˈɡeːɡnən] *v/t* reply; ~**gehen** *v/i* (*irr*) escape; ~**gleisen** [-ˈɡlaɪzən] *v/i* be derailed; ~**gleiten** *v/i* (*irr*): **j-m** ~ slip from s.o.'s hands.

enthalt|en [ɛntˈhaltən] *v/t* (*irr*) contain, hold; **sich** ~**en** (*gen*) abstain *od.* refrain from; ~**sam** *adj* abstinent; 2**ung** *f* abstention.

enthüllen [ɛntˈhʏlən] *v/t* uncover; *Denkmal*: unveil; *fig.* reveal, disclose.

enthusiastisch [ɛntuˈzɪastɪʃ] *adj* enthusiastic.

entkleiden [ɛntˈklaɪdən] *v/t*: (**sich**) ~ undress; ~**kommen** *v/i* (*irr*) escape; get away; ~**laden** *v/t* (*irr*) unload; (**sich**) ~**laden** discharge.

entlang [ɛntˈlaŋ] *prp, adv* along.

entlass|en [ɛntˈlasən] *v/t* (*irr*) dismiss, discharge; **2ung** *f* dismissal, discharge.

ent|lasten [ɛntˈlastən] *v/t* relieve, exonerate; **~laufen** *v/i* (*irr*) run away (*dat* from); **~legen** [-ˈleːgən] *adj* remote, distant; **~lüften** *v/t* ventilate; **~mutigen** [-ˈmuːtigən] *v/t* discourage; **~nehmen** *v/t* (*irr*) take (*dat* from); **~nehmen aus** *fig.* gather from; **~reißen** *v/t* (*irr*) snatch away (*dat* from); **~rinnen** *v/i* (*irr*) escape (*dat* from).

entrüst|en [ɛntˈrʏstən] *v/t lit.* fill with indignation; **sich ~en** be indignant (**über** *at s.th.*, with *s.o.*); **~et** *adj* indignant; **2ung** *f* indignation.

entschädig|en [ɛntˈʃɛːdigən] *v/t* compensate; **2ung** *f* compensation.

entscheid|en [ɛntˈʃaidən] *v/t u/refl:* (**sich**) decide; **~end** *adj* decisive; *kritisch:* crucial; **2ung** *f* decision.

entschließ|en [ɛntˈʃliːsən] *v/refl* (*irr*): **sich ~** decide, make up one's mind; **~schlossen** [-ˈʃlɔsən] *adj* resolute, determined; **2schluß** *m* (*-sses/-sse*) resolution, decision, determination.

entschuldig|en [ɛntˈʃʊl-

digən] *v/t* excuse; **sich ~en** apologize (**bei** to); **2ung** *f* excuse; apology; *int.* sorry!, (I beg your) pardon!

Entsetz|en [ɛntˈzɛtsən] *n* (*-s/no pl*) horror; **2lich** *adj* horrible, terrible.

entsinnen [ɛntˈzɪnən] *v/refl* (*irr*): **sich ~** remember.

entspann|en [ɛntˈʃpanən] *v/refl:* **sich ~** relax; *pol.* ease (up); **2ung** *f* relaxation; *pol.* easing.

entsprech|en [ɛntˈʃprɛ-çən] *v/i* (*irr*) (*dat*) correspond (to, with); *Beschreibung:* answer (to); *Anforderungen etc.:* meet; **~d** *adj* corresponding; *angemessen:* appropriate (*dat* to).

entspringen [ɛntˈʃprɪŋən] *v/i* (*irr*) *Fluß:* rise.

entstehen [ɛntˈʃteːən] *v/i* (*irr*) arise, originate; **2ung** *f* origin.

entstellen [ɛntˈʃtɛlən] *v/t* disfigure; *fig.* distort.

enttäusch|en [ɛntˈtɔy-ʃən] *v/t* disappoint; **2ung** *f* disappointment.

entweder [ˈɛntveːdər] *cj:* **~ ... oder** either ... or.

ent|weichen [ɛntˈvaiçən] *v/i* (*irr*) escape; **~wenden** *v/t* steal, pilfer; **~werfen** *v/t* (*irr*) *Vertrag:* draft; *Muster:* design; *flüchtig:* sketch, outline; *Garten:* plan.

entwert|en [ɛntˈveːrtən]

v/t devaluate; *Briefmarke, Fahrkarte:* cancel; **2er** *m* cancel(l)ing machine; **2ung** *f* devaluation; cancel(l)ation.

entwick|eln [ɛnt'vɪkəln] *v/t:* **(sich)** ~ develop; **2lung** *f* development.

ent|wirren [ɛnt'vɪrən] *v/t* disentangle; **~wischen** *v/i colloq.:* **j-m** ~ give s.o. the slip.

Entwurf [ɛnt'vʊrf] *m* (-[e]s/⁻e) draft; design; sketch; plan.

ent|ziehen [ɛnt'tsiːən] *v/t* (*irr*) deprive (**j-m et.** s.o. of s.th.); **~ziffern** [-'tsɪfərn] *v/t* make out.

entzück|end [ɛnt'tsʏkənt] *adj* delightful, charming; **~t** *adj* delighted.

entzünd|en [ɛnt'tsʏndən] *v/t* light, kindle; **sich ~en** *med.* become inflamed; **~et** *adj* inflamed; **2ung** *f* inflammation.

entzwei [ɛnt'tsvaɪ] *adj* in two.

Epidemie [epide'miː] *f* (-/-n) epidemic.

Epilog [epi'loːk] *m* (-[e]s/-e) epilog(ue).

Episode [epi'zoːdə] *f* (-/-n) episode.

Epoche [e'pɔxə] *f* (-/-n) epoch.

er [eːr] *pers pron* he; *Sache:* it.

Erbarmen [ɛr'barmən] *n* (-s/*no pl*) pity, mercy.

erbärmlich [ɛr'bɛrmlɪç]

adj pitiful; **elend:** miserable.

erbarmungslos [ɛr'barmʊŋsloːs] *adj* merciless, relentless.

erbauen [ɛr'baʊən] *v/t* build, construct; **2r** *m* builder, constructor.

Erbe¹ ['ɛrbə] *m* (-n/-n) heir.

Erbe² *n* (-s/*no pl*) inheritance, heritage; **2n** *v/t* inherit.

erbeuten [ɛr'bɔʏtən] *v/t* capture.

Erb|in ['ɛrbɪn] *f* (-/-nen) heiress; **2lich** *adj* hereditary.

er|blicken [ɛr'blɪkən] *v/t* see; **~blinden** [-'blɪndən] *v/i* go blind; **~brechen** *v/t, v/refl, v/i* (*irr*): **sich ~** vomit.

Erbschaft ['ɛrpʃaft] *f* (-/-en) inheritance.

Erbse ['ɛrpsə] *f* (-/-n) pea.

Erd|beben ['eːrtbeːbən] *n* (-s/-) earthquake; **~beere** *f* strawberry; **~boden** *m* earth, ground; **~e** [eːrdə] *f* (-/*no pl*) earth; *Bodenart:* ground, soil; **2en** *v/t electr.* earth; **~geschoß** ['eːrt-] *n* ground (*Am.* first) floor; **~kugel** *f* globe; **~kunde** [-kʊndə] *f* (-/*no pl*) geography; **~nuß** *f* peanut; **~öl** *n* (mineral) oil; **~reich** *n* (-[e]s/*no pl*) ground, earth.

erdrosseln [ɛr'drɔsəln] *v/t* strangle.

erdrücken [ɛr'drʏkən] *v/t*

erhellen

crush to death; **~d** adj fig. overwhelming.

Erd|rutsch [ˈɛːrtrʊtʃ] m (-[e]s/-e) landslide (a. pol.), landslip; **~teil** m continent.

er|dulden [ɛrˈdʊldən] v/t suffer, endure; **~eignen** v/refl: **sich ~** happen.

Ereignis [ɛrˈʔaɪɡnɪs] n (-ses/-se) event; **2reich** adj eventful.

erfahren [ɛrˈfaːrən] v/t (irr) learn, hear; erleben: experience; adj experienced, expert; **2ung** f experience.

erfassen [ɛrˈfasən] v/t seize, grasp.

erfinden [ɛrˈfɪndən] v/t (irr) invent; **2er** m inventor; **2ung** f invention.

Erfolg [ɛrˈfɔlk] m (-[e]s/-e) success; Ergebnis: result; **2los** adj unsuccessful; **2reich** adj successful.

erforder|lich [ɛrˈfɔrdər-lɪç] adj necessary; **~n** v/t require, demand.

Erforschung [ɛrˈfɔrʃʊŋ] f (-/no pl) exploration.

erfreu|en [ɛrˈfrɔʏən] v/t please; entzücken: delight; **~lich** adj pleasant; delightful.

erfrier|en [ɛrˈfriːrən] v/i (irr) freeze to death; **2ung** f frost-bite.

erfrischen [ɛrˈfrɪʃən] v/t refresh; **2ung** f refreshment.

er|froren [ɛrˈfroːrən] adj frost-bitten, **~füllen** v/t

fulfil(l); Pflicht: perform; Bitte: comply with; Forderungen: meet; Zweck: serve; **~gänzen** [-ˈgɛn-tsən] v/t complete; nachträglich hinzufügen: supplement; Warenlager: replenish; **~geben** v/t (irr) show, prove; yield; **sich ~geben** v/refl surrender; **sich ~geben** in resign o.s. to.

Ergebnis [ɛrˈgeːpnɪs] n (-ses/-se) result, outcome; sp. result; score; **2los** adj unsuccessful.

ergehen [ɛrˈgeːən] v/i (irr): **über sich ~ lassen** suffer; **wie ist es ihm ergangen?** how did he fare?

ergiebig [ɛrˈgiːbɪç] adj productive, rich.

ergreifen [ɛrˈgraɪfən] v/t (irr) seize, grasp; Verbrecher: capture; Gelegenheit, Maßnahme: take; Flucht: take (to); Beruf: take up; fig. move, touch; **2ung** f capture, seizure.

erhalten [ɛrˈhaltən] v/t (irr) get, obtain; Nachricht etc.: receive; bewahren: preserve, keep; unterstützen: support; **gut ~** adj in good repair od. condition.

erheben [ɛrˈheːbən] v/t (irr) raise; **sich ~en** rise; **~lich** adj considerable.

er|hellen [ɛrˈhɛlən] v/t light (up); **~hitzen** [-ˈhɪt-sən] v/t heat; **~hoffen** v/t hope for.

erhöh|en ['ɛr'hø:ən] *v/t* raise; *fig. a.* increase; **2ung** *f* elevation; *fig.* increase; *Preise, Lohn:* rise.

erhol|en [ɛr'ho:lən] *v/refl:* **sich ~** recover; (take a) rest, relax; **2ung** *f* recovery; *Entspannung:* relaxation, rest.

erinner|n [ɛr'?ɪnərn] *v/t:* **j-n ~ an** remind s.o. of; *v/refl:* **sich ~ an** remember; **2ung** *f* remembrance (**an** of), recollection, memory.

erkält|en [ɛr'kɛltən] *v/refl:* **sich (stark) ~** catch a (bad) cold; **2ung** *f* cold.

erkenn|en [ɛr'kɛnən] *v/t* (*irr*) recognize; *wahrnehmen:* perceive (*a. fig.*), see; *fig.* realize; **2tnis** *f* (*-/-se*) realization.

Erker ['ɛrkər] *m* (*-s/-*) *arch.* bay.

erklär|en [ɛr'klɛ:rən] *v/t* explain; *aussprechen:* declare, state; **2ung** *f* explanation; statement; declaration.

erkrank|en [ɛr'kraŋkən] *v/i* fall ill, be taken ill (**an** with); **2ung** *f* falling ill; illness, sickness.

erkundig|en [ɛr'kundɪgən] *v/refl:* **sich ~** make inquiries, inquire (**nach** *j-m:* after, for, *et.:* about); **2ung** *f* inquiry.

Erlaß [ɛr'las] *m* (*-sses/-sse*) decree; **2lassen** [~] *v/t* (*irr*) remit; dispense (*j-m et.* s.o. from s.th.); *Verordnung:* issue; *Gesetz:*

enact.

erlaub|en [ɛr'laubən] *v/t* allow, permit; **2nis** *f* (*-/no pl*) permission.

erläutern [ɛr'lɔytərn] *v/t* explain.

erleb|en [ɛr'le:bən] *v/t* experience, have; see; *Schlimmes:* go through; **2nis** *n* (*-ses/-se*) experience; adventure.

erledigen [ɛr'le:dɪgən] *v/t* settle; manage; finish.

erleichtern [ɛr'laɪçtərn] *v/t* ease, lighten; *fig.* make easy; *Not, Schmerz:* relieve; **2ung** *f* relief.

erleid|en [ɛr'laɪdən] *v/t* (*irr*) suffer; endure; **~lernen** *v/t* learn; **~lesen** [~'le:zən] *adj* choice; excellent.

Erlös [ɛr'lø:s] *m* (*-es/-e*) proceeds *pl.*

erloschen [ɛr'lɔʃən] *adj* extinct.

erlös|en [ɛr'lø:zən] *v/t* release, deliver (**von** from); **2ung** *f* release, deliverance; *eccl.* redemption.

ermächtigen [ɛr'mɛçtɪgən] *v/t* authorize; **~mahnen** *v/t* admonish.

ermäßig|en [ɛr'mɛ:sɪgən] *v/t* reduce; **2ung** *f* reduction.

ermessen [ɛr'mɛsən] *v/t* (*irr*) estimate; judge; **2 n** (*-s/no pl*) judg(e)ment; discretion.

ermitt|eln [ɛr'mɪtəln] *v/t* ascertain, find out; *jur.* investigate; **2lungen** *pl jur.*

investigations *pl*, inquiries *pl*.

ermöglichen [er'mø:klɪçən] *v/t* make possible.

ermord|en [er'mordən] *v/t* murder; *meuchlerisch:* assassinate; **2ung** *f* murder; assassination.

erlmüden [er'my:dən] *v/t* tire; *v/i* get tired and fatigued; **~muntern** ['~muntərn] *v/t* encourage.

ermutigen [er'mu:tɪgən] *v/t* encourage; **2gung** *f* encouragement.

ernähr|en [er'nɛ:rən] *v/t* feed; *Familie:* support; **sich ~en von** live on; **2ung** *f* (*-/no pl*) food, nourishment, nutrition.

erlnennen [er'nɛnən] *v/t* (*irr*) appoint; **2ung** *f* appointment.

erneu|ern [er'nɔyərn] *v/t* renew; **~t** *adj* renewed; *adv* once more.

ernst [ernst] *adj* serious, grave; **2 m** (*-es/no pl*) seriousness; **im 2** in earnest; **~haft, ~lich** *adj* serious.

Ernte ['erntə] *f* (*-/-n*) harvest; *Ertrag:* crop; **~dankfest** [erntə'daŋkfest] *n* harvest festival; **2n** ['erntən] *v/t* harvest, gather, reap (*a. fig.*).

erober|n [er'?o:bərn] *v/t* conquer; **2ung** *f* conquest.

eröffn|en [er'?œfnən] *v/t* open; **2ung** *f* opening.

erpress|en [er'prɛsən] *v/t* blackmail; **2er** *m* blackmailer; **2ung** *f* blackmail.

erraten [er'ra:tən] *v/t* (*irr*) guess.

erregen [er're:gən] *v/t* excite; *verursachen:* cause; **2ung** *f* excitement.

erreich|bar [er'raiçba:r] *adj* within reach; *attainable, available;* **~en** *v/t* reach; *Zug etc.:* catch; *fig.* achieve, attain.

erlrichten [er'rɪçtən] *v/t* set up, erect, raise; build, construct; **~röten** ['~rø:tən] *v/i* blush.

Ersatz [er'zats] *m* (*-es/no pl*) replacement; substitute; *Schaden2:* compensation, damages *pl*; **~teil** *n* spare (part).

erschaffen [er'ʃafən] *v/t* (*irr*) create.

erschein|en [er'ʃainən] *v/i* (*irr*) appear; **2en** *n* (*-s/no pl*) appearance; **2ung** *f* appearance; phenomenon.

erlschießen [er'ʃi:sən] *v/t* (*irr*) shoot (dead); **~schlagen** *v/t* (*irr*) kill; **~schließen** *v/t* (*irr*) *Bauland:* develop.

erschöpf|en [er'ʃœpfən] *v/t* exhaust; **2fung** *f* exhaustion.

erschrecken [er'ʃrɛkən] *v/t* frighten, scare; *v/i* (*irr*) be frightened.

erschütter|n [er'ʃytərn] *v/t* shake; **2ung** *f* shock (*a. seelisch*); *tech.* vibration.

erschweren [er'sve:rən] *v/t* make more difficult.

erschwinglich [ɛrˈʃvɪŋlɪç] *adj* reasonable.

ersetzen [ɛrˈzɛtsən] *v/t* replace; substitute; *Auslagen*: refund; *Schaden*: compensate.

erspar|en [ɛrˈʃpaːrən] *v/t* save; **j-m et.** ~**en** spare s.o. s.th.; ²**nisse** *pl* savings *pl.*

erst [eːrst] *adv* first; *nicht früher als*: not till *od.* until; *nicht mehr als*: only.

erstarr|en [ɛrˈʃtarən] *v/i* grow stiff, stiffen; ~**t** *adj* *Finger*: stiff, numb.

erstatten [ɛrˈʃtatən] *v/t* *Auslagen*: refund; **Bericht** ~ report.

Erstaufführung [ˈeːrstʔaʊffyːrʊŋ] *f* (-/-en) first night *od.* performance, première.

Erstaun|en [ɛrˈʃtaʊnən] *n* (-s/*no pl*) astonishment; ²**lich** *adj* astonishing, amazing; ²**t** *adj* astonished.

erst|e, ~**er,** ~**es** [ˈeːrstə/ɐ, -s] *adj* first; ²**e Hilfe** first aid; *s.* **Mal.**

erstechen [ɛrˈʃtɛçən] *v/t* (*irr*) stab.

erstens [ˈeːrstəns] *adv* first(ly).

ersticken [ɛrˈʃtɪkən] *v/i, v/t* suffocate, choke.

erstklassig [ˈeːrstklasɪç] *adj* first-class.

er|strecken [ɛrˈʃtrɛkən] *v/refl*: **sich** ~ extend, stretch; **sich** ~ **über** *a.* cover; ~**suchen** *v/t* re

quest; ~**teilen** *v/t* give.

Ertrag [ɛrˈtraːk] *m* (-[e]s/ᴠe) yield; *Einnahmen*: proceeds *pl*, returns *pl*; ²**en** *v/t* (*irr*) bear, endure, stand.

erträglich [ɛrˈtrɛːklɪç] *adj* tolerable.

er|tränken [ɛrˈtrɛŋkən] *v/t* drown; ~**trinken** *v/i* (*irr*) be drowned, drown; ~**wachen** *v/i* wake (up).

erwachsen [ɛrˈvaksən] *adj* grown-up, adult; ²**e** *m, f* (-n/-n) grown-up, adult.

er|wägen [ɛrˈvɛːgən] *v/t* (*irr*) consider; ~**wähnen** *v/t* mention; ~**wärmen** *v/t* warm, heat.

erwarten [ɛrˈvartən] *v/t* await, wait for; expect; ²**ung** *f* expectation.

erweisen [ɛrˈvaɪzən] *v/t* (*irr*) prove; *Achtung*: show, pay; *Dienst*: render; *Gefallen*: do; **sich** ~**weisen als** prove (to be); ~**weitern** [-ˈvaɪtərn] *v/t* (sich) ~ expand, enlarge, extend, widen.

erwerb|en [ɛrˈvɛrbən] *v/t* (*irr*) acquire; ~**slos** *adj* unemployed.

erwidern [ɛrˈviːdərn] *v/t* *Besuch etc.*: return; answer, reply.

erwünscht [ɛrˈvʏnʃt] *adj* desired; *wünschenswert*: desirable.

erwürgen [ɛrˈvʏrgən] *v/t* strangle.

Erz [eːrts, ɛrts] *n* (-es/-e) ore.

evangelisch

erzähl|en [ɛr'tsɛːlən] *v/t* tell; narrate; **2ung** *f* narration; *Literatur*: (short) story, narrative.

Erz|bischof ['ɛrtsbɪʃɔf] *m* (-s/ᵛe) archbishop; **~engel** *m* archangel.

erzeug|en [ɛr'tsɔygən] *v/t* produce; make, manufacture; **2nis** *n* (-ses/-se) product; *agr. a.* produce.

erzieh|en [ɛr'tsiːən] *v/t* (*irr*) bring up; educate; *Tier*: train; **2er** *m* (-s/-) educator; teacher; **2ung** *f* upbringing; education; *Lebensart*: breeding; **2ungs-anstalt** [-'ʔanʃtalt] *f* (-/-en) approved school, reformatory.

erzielen [ɛr'tsiːlən] *v/t* obtain; *Preis*: realize; *sp.* score; *Einigung*: reach, arrive at.

es [ɛs] *pers pron* it; he; she.

Esche ['ɛʃə] *f* (-/-n) ash (-tree).

Esel ['eːzəl] *m* (-s/-) donkey; *fig.* ass; **~sohr** *n fig.* dog-ear.

eßbar ['ɛsbaːr] *adj* eatable, edible.

Esse ['ɛsə] *f* (-/-n) chimney.

essen ['ɛsən] *v/t, v/i* (*irr*) eat; **zu Mittag ~** (have) lunch; *Hauptmahlzeit*: dine, have dinner; **zu Abend ~** dine, have dinner; *bsd. spätabends*: sup, have supper; **auswärts ~** eat *od.* dine out; **et. zu Mittag** *etc.* **~** have s.th.

for lunch, *etc.*; **2** *n* (-s/-) eating; *Kost*: food; *Mahlzeit*: meal; lunch, dinner, supper.

Essig ['ɛsɪç] *m* (-s/*rare* -e) vinegar.

Eß|löffel ['ɛslœfəl] *m* (-s/ -) soup-spoon; **~tisch** *m* dining-table; **~waren** *pl* victuals *pl*, food; **~zim-mer** *n* dining-room.

Etage [e'taːʒə] *f* (-/-n) floor, stor(e)y; **~nbett** *n* bunk bed.

Etat [e'taː] *m* (-s/-s) budget.

Etikett [eti'kɛt] *n* (-[e]s/ -e[n]) label, ticket.

etliche ['ɛtlɪçə] *indef pron* some, several.

Etui [e'tviː] *n* (-s/-s) case.

etwa ['ɛtva] *adv vielleicht*: perhaps, by any chance; *ungefähr*: about, *Am. a.* around.

etwas ['ɛtvas] *indef pron* something; *verneinend, fragend*: anything; *adj* some; *adv* a little; somewhat.

euch [ɔyç] *pers pron* you.

euer ['ɔyər] *poss pron* your; **~(e)re** *poss pron* your.

Eule ['ɔylə] *f* (-/-n) owl.

Europä|er [ɔyro'pɛːər] *m* (-s/-) European; **2isch** *adj* European.

Euter ['ɔytər] *n* (-s/-) udder.

evangeli|sch [evaŋ'geː-lɪʃ] *adj* evangelic(al); Protestant, *Deutschland: a.* Lutheran; **2um** [-'geː-lium] *n* (-s/-lien) gospel.

eventuell [evɛn'tŭɛl] *adj*
possible; *adv* possibly,
perhaps.

ewig ['e:viç] *adj* eternal;
everlasting, perpetual;
auf ~ for ever; 2**keit** *f*
eternity.

exakt [ɛ'ksakt] *adj* exact.

Examen [ɛ'ksa:mən] *n* (-s/
-) exam(ination).

Exemplar [ɛksɛm'plaːr] *n*
(-s/-e) specimen; *Buch:*
copy.

exerzieren [ɛksɛr'tsiːrən]
v/i, v/t drill.

Exil [ɛ'ksi:l] *n* (-s/-e) exile.

Existenz [ɛksɪs'tɛnts] *f* (-/
-en) existence; 2**ieren**
[-'tiːrən] *v/i* subsist.

Fabel ['faːbəl] *f* (-/-n)
fable; 2**haft** marvel(l)ous.

Fabrik [fa'briːk] *f* (-/-en)
factory, works *sg, pl;* **~at**
[-bri'kaːt] *n* (-[e]s/-e)
make; *Erzeugnis:* product.

...fach [-fax] *in Zssgn:*
...fold.

Fach [fax] *n* (-[e]s/ᵘer)
compartment, partition,
shelf; *Schub*2: drawer; *ped.*
subject; **~arbeiter** *m*
skilled worker; **~arzt** *m*
specialist (**für** in).

Fächer ['fɛçər] *m* (-s/-)
fan.

Fach|gebiet ['fax-] *n*
branch, field, province;
~kenntnisse *pl* special-
ized knowledge *sg;*
~mann *m* expert.

Expedition [ɛkspedi-
'tsĭoːn] *f* (-/-en) expedition.

Experiment [ɛksperi-
'mɛnt] *n* (-[e]s/-e) experiment; 2**ieren** [-mɛn'tiː-
rən] *v/i* experiment.

explo|dieren [ɛksplo'diː-
rən] *v/i* explode, burst;
2**sion** [-'zĭoːn] *f* (-/-en)
explosion; **~siv** [-'ziːf] *adj*
explosive.

Export [ɛks'pɔrt] *m* (-[e]s/
-e) export(ation); 2**ieren**
[-pɔr'tiːrən] *v/t* export.

extra ['ɛkstra] *adv, adj*
extra.

extrem [ɛks'treːm] *adj* extreme.

F

Fackel ['fakəl] *f* (-/-n)
torch.

fad [faːt], **fade** ['faːdə] *adj*
ohne Geschmack: insipid,
tasteless; *schal:* stale; *fig.*
dull, boring.

Faden ['faːdən] *m* (-s/ᵘ)
thread (*a. fig.*).

fähig ['fɛːɪç] *adj* capable,
able; 2**keit** *f* (cap)ability;
talent, faculty.

fahl [faːl] *adj* pale, pallid.

fahnd|en ['faːndən] *v/i:* **~
nach** search for; 2**ung** *f*
search.

Fahne ['faːnə] *f* (-/-n) flag;
banner; *mil. a.* colo(u)rs *pl.*

Fahrbahn ['faːrbaːn] *f* (-/
-en) roadway.

Fähre ['fɛːrə] *f* (-/-n)
ferry-(boat).

fahren ['faːrən] *v/i Person, Fahrzeug:* drive, go; *Radfahrer:* ride, cycle; *mar.* sail; **mit der Bahn ~** go by train; *v/t Wagen:* drive; *Fahrrad:* ride.

Fahrer ['faːrər] *m* (-s/-) driver; **~flucht** *f* (-/no *pl*) hit-and-run driving.

Fahr|gast ['faːrgast] *m* (-es/-e) passenger; *Taxi:* fare; **~geld** *n* fare; **~gestell** *n mot.* chassis; *aer. s.*

Fahrwerk; ~karte *f* ticket; **~kartenautomat** [-?aʊtomaːt] *m* (-en/-en) (automatic) ticket(-vending) machine; **~kartenschalter** [-ʃaltər] *m* booking-office, *Am.* ticket-office; **2lässig** [-lɛsɪç] *adj* careless; **~lehrer** *m* driving instructor; **~plan** *m* timetable, *Am. a.* schedule; **2planmäßig** [-mɛːsɪç] *adj* on time *od.* schedule; **~preis** *m* fare; **~rad** *n* bicycle, *colloq.* bike; **~schein** *m* ticket; **~schule** *f* driving school, school of motoring; **~stuhl** *m* lift, *Am.* elevator; **~stunde** *f* driving lesson.

Fahrt [faːrt] *f* (-/-en) ride, drive; *Reise:* journey; *Vergnügungs2:* trip.

Fährte ['feːrtə] *f* (-/-n) track (*a. fig.*).

Fahr|werk ['faːrvɛrk] *n* (-[e]s/-e) *aer.* undercarriage, landing-gear; **~zeug** *n* vehicle.

Fakultät [fakʊlˈtɛːt] *f* (-/-en) *univ.* faculty.

Falke ['falkə] *m* (-n/-n) hawk, falcon.

Fall [fal] *m* (-[e]s/ᵂe) fall; *gr., jur., med.* case; **auf alle Fälle** at all events; **auf jeden ~** in any case; **auf keinen ~** on no account.

Falle ['falə] *f* (-/-n) trap.

fallen ['falən] *v/i* (*irr*) fall, drop; *mil.* be killed; **lassen** drop.

fällen ['fɛlən] *v/t Baum:* fell, cut down; *Urteil:* pass.

fallenlassen *v/t* (*irr*) drop.

fällig ['fɛlɪç] *adj* due.

falls [fals] *cj* if, in case.

Fallschirm ['falʃɪrm] *m* (-[e]s/-e) parachute.

falsch [falʃ] *adj* false; *verkehrt:* wrong; *Geld:* counterfeit; *Person:* deceitful; **~ gehen** *Uhr:* be wrong; **~ verbunden!** [fɛrˈbʊndən] *teleph.* sorry, wrong number.

fälschen ['fɛlʃən] *v/t* forge, fake; *Geld:* counterfeit.

Falschgeld *n* counterfeit money.

Fälschung ['fɛlʃʊŋ] *f* (-/-en) forgery; counterfeit; fake.

Falt|e ['faltə] *f* (-/-n) fold; *Rock etc.:* pleat; *Hose:* crease; *Gesicht:* wrinkle; **2en** ['faltən] *v/t* fold; **die Hände 2en** clasp one's hands; **~er** *m* (-s/-)

familiär

butterfly; moth; **2ig** adj wrinkled.

familiär [fami'llɛ:r] adj familiar; informal.

Familie [fa'mi:liə] f (-/-n) family.

Familien|angehörige [-ʔangəhø:rigə] m, f (-n/-n) member of the family; **~name** m surname, family name, Am. a. last name; **~stand** m marital status.

fanatisch [fa'na:tiʃ] adj fanatic(al).

Fang [faŋ] m (-[e]s/٨e) catch; **2en** [ˈfaŋən] v/t (irr catch.

Farb|... [ˈfarp-] colo(u)r ...; **~e** [ˈfarbə] f (-/-n) colo(u)r; Malerfarbe: paint; Farbstoff: dye; Gesicht: complexion; Karten: suit; **2echt** [ˈfarpˀɛçt] adj colo(u)r-fast.

färben [ˈfɛrbən] v/t colo(u)r; Stoff, Haare etc.: dye.

farb|ig [ˈfarbɪç] adj colo(u)red; Glas: tinted, stained; fig. colo(u)rful; **~los** [ˈfarplo:s] adj colo(u)rless; **2stift** m s. Buntstift; **2ton** m shade.

Färbung [ˈfɛrbuŋ] f (-/-en) colo(u)ring; leichte Tönung: shade.

Farn [farn] m (-[e]s/-e, **~kraut** n fern.

Fasan [fa'za:n] m (-[e]s/-e[n]) pheasant.

Fasching [ˈfaʃiŋ] m (-s/-e, -s) carnival.

Fas|er [ˈfa:zər] f (-/-n)

fib|re, Am. -er; **2(e)rig** adj fibrous; **2ern** v/i fray (out).

Faß [fas] n (-sses/٨sser) cask, barrel; Bottich: tub, vat.

Fassade [fa'sa:də] f (-/-n) façade, front.

Faßbier n (-[e]s/-e) draught (Am. draft) beer.

fassen [ˈfasən] v/t seize, take hold of; catch; enthalten: hold; Schmuck: set; grasp, understand; **sich ~** compose o.s.; **sich kurz ~** be brief.

Fassung [ˈfasuŋ] f (-/-en) Edelsteine: setting; Brille: frame; electr. socket; schriftlich: draft(ing); Wortlaut: wording, version; **die ~ verlieren** lose one's self-control; **aus der ~ bringen** disconcert; **2slos** adj disconcerted.

fast [fast] adv almost, nearly.

fasten [ˈfastən] v/i fast.

Fastnacht [ˈfastnaxt] f (-/ no pl) Shrove Tuesday, Mardi Gras.

fauchen [ˈfauxən] v/i spit.

faul [faul] adj rotten; bad; Person: lazy; **~en** [ˈfaulən] v/i rot, go bad; decay.

faulenzen [ˈfaulɛntsən] v/i idle, laze, loaf; **2r** m sluggard, lazy-bones.

Faulheit f laziness.

Fäulnis [ˈfɔʏlnɪs] f (-/no pl) rottenness, decay.

Faul|pelz m s. **Faulen-zer;** ~**tier** n sloth.

Faust [faust] f (-/∼e) fist; ~**handschuh** m mitt(en); ~**schlag** m blow with the fist, punch.

Favorit [favo'ri:t] m (-en/-en) favo(u)rite.

Februar ['fe:bruar] m (-[s]/no pl) February.

fechten ['fɛçtən] v/i (irr) fence.

Feder ['fe:dər] f (-/-n) feather; Schreib2: pen; tech. spring; ~**ballspiel** n badminton; ~**bett** n eiderdown; ~**gewicht** n featherweight; ~**halter** m penholder; ❷**nd** adj springy, elastic; ~**ung** f mot. springs pl; ~**vieh** n poultry.

Fee [fe:] f (-/-n) fairy.

fegen ['fe:gən] v/t, v/i sweep.

fehlen ['fe:lən] v/i be absent; be missing; lack, be lacking; **sie fehlt uns** we miss her; **was fehlt Ihnen?** what is the matter with you?

Fehler ['fe:lər] m (-s/-) mistake, error; tech. defect, flaw; ❷**frei** adj faultless, perfect; tech. flawless; ❷**haft** adj faulty, defective; incorrect.

Fehl|geburt ['fe:lgəbu:rt] f (-/-en) miscarriage, abortion; ~**schlag** m fig. failure; ❷**schlagen** v/i (irr) fig. fail, miscarry; ~**zündung** f mot. misfire,

backfire.

Feier ['faiər] f (-/-n) ceremony; celebration; ~**abend** m: ~ **machen** finish; ❷**lich** adj solemn; ❷**n** ['faiərn] v/t, v/i celebrate; ~**tag** m holiday.

feig [faik], **feige** ['faigə] adj cowardly.

Feige ['faigə] f (-/-n) fig.

Feig|heit ['faikhait] f (-/no pl) cowardice; ~**ling** [-lɪŋ] m (-s/-e) coward.

Feile ['failə] f (-/-n) file; ❷**n** ['failən] v/t, v/i file.

feilschen ['failʃən] v/i haggle.

fein [fain] adj fine; delicate; Qualität: highgrade; choice; Unterschied: subtle.

Feind [faint] m (-[e]s/-e) enemy; ❷**lich** adj hostile; ~**schaft** f enmity, stärker: animosity; ❷**selig** adj hostile.

fein|fühlig ['fainfy:lɪç] adj sensitive; ❷**heit** f fineness; delicacy; ❷**kost** f delicatessen sg, pl; ❷**schmek-ker** [-ʃmɛkər] m (-s/-) gourmet.

Feld [fɛlt] n (-[e]s/-er) field; Schach: square; ~**flasche** f water-bottle, Am. canteen; ~**stecher** [-ʃtɛçər] m (-s/-) s. **Fern-glas;** ~**webel** [-ve:bəl] m (-s/-) sergeant; ~**weg** m (field) path.

Felge ['fɛlgə] f (-/-n) mot. rim; sp. circle.

Fell [fɛl] n (-[e]s/-e) skin,

Fels

fur; *lebender Tiere:* coat;
*Schaf*2: fleece.

Fels [fɛls] *m* (-ens/-en)
rock; **~block** *m* rock,
boulder; **~en** [ˈfɛlzən] *m*
(-s/-) rock; **2ig** *adj* rocky.

Fenster [ˈfɛnstər] *n* (-s/-)
window; **~brett** *n* win-
dow-sill; **~laden** *m* shutter; **~rahmen** *m* window-
frame; **~scheibe** *f* (win-
dow-)pane.

Ferien [ˈfeːriən] *pl* holi-
day(s *pl*), *Am.* vacation *sg*;
parl. recess; *jur.* vacation,
recess; **~dorf** *n* holiday
village; **~wohnung** *f* holiday flat.

Ferkel [ˈfɛrkəl] *n* (-s/-)
young pig; *fig.* pig.

fern [fɛrn] *adj* far, distant,
remote; **2amt** [ˈfɛrnˀamt]
n (-[e]s/**~er**) trunk (*Am.*
long-distance) exchange;
~bleiben *v/i* (*irr*) remain
od. stay away (*dat* from);
2e [ˈfɛrnə] *f* (-/-n) distance; remoteness; **~er** *adj*
further; future; *adv* in future; *cj* furthermore, *in*
ture; *cj* furthermore;
2gespräch *n* trunk (*Am.*
long-distance) call; **~ge-
steuert** [-gəˈʃtɔyərt] *adj*
Rakete: guided; *Flugzeug
etc.*: remote-controlled;
2glas *n* (**ein** a pair of)
field-glasses *pl*; binoculars
pl; **2heizung** *f* district
heating; **2licht** *n mot.* full
(headlight) beam; **2rohr** *n*
telescope; **2schreiber**
[-ʃraibər] *m* (-s/-) tele-
printer, *Am.* teletypewrit-

er; **2sehapparat** [-zeː-
ˀapaˈraːt] *m* (-[e]s/-e) *s.*
Fernseher; **2sehen**
[-zeːən] *n* (-s/*no pl*) television; **~sehen** *v/i* (*irr*)
watch television; **2seher**
m television set; **2sehzu-
schauer** [-tsuːˈʃauər] *m*
(-s/-) television viewer;
2sicht *f* view; **2sprech-
amt** [-ʃprɛçˀamt] *n*
(-[e]s/-er) telephone ex-
change, *Am. a.* central;
2sprechzelle *f* telephone box (*Am.* booth);
2verkehr *m* long-distance traffic.

Ferse [ˈfɛrzə] *f* (-/-n) heel.

fertig [ˈfɛrtɪç] *adj* ready,
finished; *Kleidung:* ready-
made; **~bringen** *v/t* (*irr*)
manage; **~machen** *v/t*
finish, complete; (**sich**)
~machen get ready;
2stellung *f* completion.

Fessel [ˈfɛsəl] *f* (-/-n)
chain, fetter; *anat.* ankle;
Pferd: pastern; *fig.* bond,
fetter, tie; **2n** *v/t* chain; *fig.*
fascinate; **2nd** *adj* fasci-
nating.

fest [fɛst] *adj* firm (*a. fig.*);
solid; *Schlaf:* sound.

Fest *n* (-[e]s/-e) celebration; *eccl.* feast.

fest|binden *v/t* (*irr*) fas-
ten, tie (**an** to); **~halten**
v/t (*irr*) hold on to; *v/i:*
~halten *an* hold on to;
v/i: **~halten** *an fig.* cling
to; **2land** *n* mainland,
continent; **~legen** *v/t:*
sich ~ auf commit o.s. to;

~lich *adj* festive; ~machen *v/t* fix, fasten; *mar.* moor (*alle*: an to); 2nahme *f* (-/-n) arrest; ~nehmen *v/t* (*irr*) arrest; ~schnallen *v/t* strap down; ~setzen *v/t* fix, set; 2spiele *pl* festival *sg*; ~stehen *v/i* (*irr*) stand firm; *fig.* be certain; ~stellen *v/t* find out; see, perceive; 2tag *m* festive day; holiday; 2ung *f* fortress; 2zug *m* procession.

fett [fɛt] *adj* fat; *Boden*: rich; 2 *n* (-[e]s/-e) fat; grease (*a. tech.*); 2fleck *m* grease-spot; ~ig *adj* fat; *Haut*: oily; *Haare, Finger*: greasy.

Fetzen ['fɛtsən] *m* (-s/-) shred; *Lumpen*: rag.

feucht [fɔʏçt] *adj* damp, moist; *Luft*: humid; 2igkeit *f* moisture; dampness; *Luft*: humidity.

Feuer ['fɔʏər] *n* (-s/-) fire; *fig.* ardo(u)r; ~alarm [-'?alarm] *m* (-[e]s/-e) fire-alarm; ~bestattung [-baʃtatʊŋ] *f* (-/-en) cremation; 2fest *adj* fire-proof, fire-resistant; 2gefährlich *adj* inflammable; ~leiter *f* fire-escape; ~löscher [-lœʃər] *m* (-s/-) fire-extinguisher; ~melder [-mɛldər] *m* (-s/-) fire-alarm; 2n ['fɔʏərn] *v/t* shoot, fire; ~wehr [-veːr] *f* (-/-en) fire-brigade, *Am. a.* fire department; *Fahrzeug*: fire-engine; ~wehrmann *m* fireman; ~werk *n* (display of) fireworks *pl*; ~zeug *n* (cigarette-)lighter.

feurig ['fɔʏrıç] *adj* fiery; *fig. a.* ardent.

Fibel ['fiːbəl] *f* (-/-n) primer.

Fichte ['fıçtə] *f* (-/-n) spruce; ~nnadel *f* spruce needle.

Fieber ['fiːbər] *n* (-s/*rare* -) temperature, fever; ~ haben *s.* fiebern; 2haft *adj* feverish; ~n ['fiːbərn] *v/i* have *od.* run a temperature; ~thermometer *n* clinical thermometer.

fiebrig ['fiːbrıç] *adj* feverish.

Figur [fi'guːr] *f* (-/-en) figure; *Schach*: chessman, piece.

Filet [fi'leː] *n* (-s/-s) fillet.

Filiale [fi'lɪaːlə] *f* (-/-n) branch.

Film [fılm] *m* (-[e]s/-e) *Überzug*: film, thin coating; *phot.* film; *Spiel2*: film, (moving) picture, *Am. a.* motion picture, *colloq.* movie; ~aufnahme *f* *Vorgang*: filming, shooting; *Einzelszene*: shot; 2en ['fılmən] *v/t* film, *v/i* film, shoot; ~kamera *f* cine-camera, film (*Am.* motion-picture *od.* movie) camera; ~schauspieler(in *f*) *m* film *od.* screen actor (*od.* actress), *Am. colloq.* movie actor (*od.* actress); ~theater *n* cinema, *Am.* motion-picture theater.

Filter ['fɪltər] *m, tech. n* (-s/-) filter; 2n *v/t* filter; ~**zigarette** *f* filtertipped cigarette.

Filz [fɪlts] *m* (-es/-e) felt.

Finale [fi'na:lə] *n* (-s/-) *sp.* final(s *pl*); *mus.; thea.* finale.

Finanz|amt [fi'nants-ʔamt] *n* (-[e]s/ʼʼer) tax *od.* revenue office; *England:* a. office of the Inspector of Taxes; ~**en** [-'nantsən] *pl*; 2**iell** [-nan-'tsi̯ɛl] *adj* financial; 2**ieren** [-'tsi:rən] *v/t* finance; ~**minister** *m* Minister of Finance, *Brit.* Chancellor of the Exchequer, *Am.* Secretary of the Treasury.

finden ['fɪndən] *v/t* (*irr*) find; discover; *der Ansicht sein:* think.

Finger ['fɪŋər] *m* (-s/-) finger; ~**abdruck** *m* fingerprint; ~**hut** *m* thimble; *bot.* foxglove.

Fink [fɪŋk] *m* (-en/-en) finch.

Finn|e ['fɪnə] *m* (-n/-n) Finn; 2**isch** *adj* Finnish.

finster ['fɪnstər] *adj* dark, gloomy; 2**nis** *f* darkness.

Firma ['fɪrma] *f* (-/Firmen) firm, business, company.

firmen ['fɪrmən] *v/t eccl.* confirm.

First [fɪrst] *m* (-[e]s/-e) *arch.* ridge.

Fisch [fɪʃ] *m* (-[e]s/-e)

fish; ~**dampfer** *m* trawler; 2**en** *v/t, v/i* fish; ~**er** *m* fisherman; ~**erdorf** *n* fishing-village; ~**fang** *m* fishing; ~**gräte** *f* fishbone; ~**händler** *m* fishmonger, *Am.* fish dealer.

fix [fɪks] *adj* quick; clever, smart.

flach [flax] *adj* flat; *seicht:* shallow.

Fläche ['flɛçə] *f* (-/-n) surface; *geom.* area; *ebene* ~ plane.

Flachland ['flaxlant] *n* (-[e]s/*no pl*) plain.

Flachs [flaks] *m* (-es/*no pl*) flax.

flackern ['flakərn] *v/i* flicker.

Flagge ['flagə] *f* (-/-n) flag.

Flamme ['flamə] *f* (-/-n) flame; *lodernde:* blaze.

Flanell [fla'nɛl] *m* (-s/-e) flannel; ~**hose** *f* flannels *pl*.

Flanke ['flaŋkə] *f* (-/-n) flank.

Flasche ['flaʃə] *f* (-/-n) bottle; *Taschen2:* flask.

Flaschen|bier *n* bottled beer; 2**öffner** [-ʔɛfnər] *m* (-s/-) bottle-opener; ~**zug** *m* pulley.

flattern ['flatərn] *v/i* flutter; *Haare etc.:* stream, fly.

flau [flau] *adj* weak, feeble, faint; *econ.* dull, slack.

Flaum [flaum] *m* (-[e]s/*no pl*) down, fluff, fuzz.

Flaute ['flautə] *f* (-/-n) dead calm; *econ.* dullness, slack period.

Flechte ['flɛçtə] f (-/-n)
Haar: braid, plait; bot.,
med. lichen; 2en ['flɛçtən]
v/t (irr) braid, plait; Korb,
Kranz: weave.

Fleck [flɛk] m (-[e]s/
-e[n]) Schmutz, zo.: mark,
spot; Öl: smear; Blut,
Wein, Kaffee: stain; Tinte:
stain, blot; Stelle, Ort:
place, spot; Flicken: patch;
fig. blemish, spot, stain;
~enwasser [-vasər] n
spot od. stain remover; 2ig
adj spotted; stained.

Fledermaus ['fle:dər-
maus] f (-/ve) bat.

Flegel ['fle:gəl] m (-s/-)
flail; Person: lout, boor.

flehen ['fle:ən] v/i: ~ um
plead for.

Fleisch [flaɪʃ] n (-es/no pl)
flesh; Schlacht2: meat;
Frucht2: pulp; ~brühe f
meat-broth od. bouillon;
klare: beef tea; ~er m butcher; ~erei
[-ə'raɪ] f (-/-en) butcher's
shop; 2ig adj fleshy; bot.
pulpy; ~konserven pl
tinned (Am. canned) meat
sg.

Fleiß [flaɪs] m (-es/no pl)
diligence, industry; 2ig
adj diligent, industrious,
hard-working.

fletschen ['flɛtʃən] v/t:
die Zähne ~ Tier: bare
its teeth.

Flick|en ['flɪkən] m (-s/-)
patch; 2en v/t patch;
Schuhe, Dach etc.: mend,
repair; ~werk n (-[e]s/

Flieder ['fli:dər] m (-s/-)
lilac.

Fliege ['fli:gə] f (-/-n) fly;
Krawatte: bowtie.

fliegen ['fli:gən] v/i, v/t
(irr) fly.

Fliegen|gewicht ['fli:-
gəngəvɪçt] n flyweight;
~pilz m bot. fly agaric.

Flieger ['fli:gər] m (-s/-)
airman, pilot.

fliehen ['fli:ən] v/i (irr)
flee, run away (**vor** from).

Fliese ['fli:zə] f (-/-n) tile.

Fließ|band ['fli:sbant] n
(-[e]s/ver) assembly line;
Förderband: conveyor-
belt; 2en ['fli:sən] v/i (irr)
flow; Leitungswasser etc.:
run; 2end adj Wasser:
running; Verkehr: moving;
Rede: fluent.

flimmern ['flɪmərn] v/i
glimmer, glitter; Film:
flicker.

flink [flɪŋk] adj quick, nimble, brisk.

Flinte ['flɪntə] f (-/-n)
shot-gun.

Flirt [flɪrt, flœrt] m (-[e]s/
-s) flirtation; 2en ['flɪr-
tən, 'flœrtən] v/i flirt.

Flitter ['flɪtər] m (-s/-)
spangles pl, sequins pl;
~wochen pl honeymoon
sg.

Flock|e ['flɔkə] f (-/-n)
flake; Wolle: flock; 2ig adj
fluffy, flaky.

Floh [flo:] m (-[e]s/ve)
flea.

Floß [flo:s] n (-es/ve) raft.

Flosse ['flɔsə] f (-/-n) fin; *Robbe:* flipper.

Flöte ['fløːtə] f (-/-n) flute.

flott [flɔt] *adj* quick, brisk, gay, lively; *Kleidung:* smart, stylish.

Flotte ['flɔtə] f (-/-n) fleet; *Kriegs2:* navy; **~nstützpunkt** m naval base.

Fluch [fluːx] m (-[e]s/⁺e) curse; *Schimpfwort:* curse, swear-word; **2en** ['fluːxən] v/i swear, curse.

Flucht [fluxt] f (-/-en) flight (**vor** from); escape (**aus** from).

flüchten ['flʏçtən] v/i flee (**nach, zu** to); run away; *Gefangener:* escape; **~ig** *adj* fugitive (a. fig.); *kurz:* fleeting; *oberflächlich:* careless, superficial; *chem.* volatile; **2ling** [-lɪŋ] m (-s/-e) fugitive; *pol.* refugee; **2lingslager** n refugee camp.

Flug [fluːk] m (-[e]s/⁺e) flight; **im ~(e)** rapidly, quickly.

Flügel ['flyːgəl] m (-s/-) wing; *Propeller etc.:* blade, vane; *mus.* grand piano.

Fluggast ['fluːkgast] m (-[e]s/⁺e) (air) passenger.

flügge ['flʏgə] *adj* fully-fledged.

Fluggesellschaft ['fluːk-] f airline (company); **~hafen** m airport; **~kapitän** m captain; **~karte** f ticket; **~linie** f airline; **~lotse** m air traffic controller; **~platz** m airfield; **~sicherung** [-zɪçəruŋ] f air traffic control; **~steig** [-ʃtaɪk] m (-[e]s/-e) gate, channel; **~verkehr** m air traffic; **~zeit** f flying time.

Flugzeug ['fluːktsɔʏk] n (-[e]s/-e) aircraft, aeroplane, *colloq.* plane, *Am. a.* airplane; **~kanzel** f cockpit; **~rumpf** m fuselage, body; **~träger** m aircraft carrier; **~unglück** n air crash *od.* disaster.

Flunder ['flundər] f (-/-n) flounder.

flunkern ['fluŋkərn] v/i fib, tell a fib.

Flur [fluːr] m (-[e]s/-e) hall.

Fluß [flus] m (-sses/⁺sse) river, stream; flow(ing); *fig.* fluency, flux; **2ab(-wärts)** [-'ʔap(vɛrts)] *adv* downstream; **2auf(-wärts)** [-'ʔauf(vɛrts)] *adv* upstream; **~bett** ['-bɛt] n river bed.

flüssig ['flʏsɪç] *adj* fluid, liquid; *Metall:* molten, melted; *Stil:* fluent; **2keit** f fluid, liquid.

flüstern ['flʏstərn] v/i whisper.

Flut [fluːt] f (-/-en) flood; high tide, (flood-)tide; *fig.* flood, torrent; **~licht** n floodlight; **~welle** f tidal wave.

Fohlen ['foːlən] n (-s/-) foal; *männliches:* colt; *weibliches:* filly.

Föhre ['føːrə] f (-/-n) pine.

fort

Folg|e ['fɔlgə] *f* (-/-n) sequence, succession; *Hörfunkserie:* instal(l)ment, part; *Reihe:* series; *Ergebnis:* consequence; result; **2en** ['fɔlgən] *v/i* follow; *als Nachfolger:* succeed (j-m s.o.; **auf** to); *sich ergeben:* follow, ensue (**aus** from); *gehorchen:* obey (j-m s.o.); **2lich** *cj* therefore; **2sam** *adj* obedient.

Folie [fo:li̯ə] *f* (-/-n) foil.

Folter ['fɔltər] *f* (-/-n) torture; **2n** ['fɔltərn] *v/t* torture.

Fön [fø:n] *m* (-[e]s/-e) *Warenzeichen:* electric hair-dryer.

Fonds [fõ:] *m* (-/-) fund(s *pl*).

Fontäne [fɔn'tɛ:nə] *f* (-/-n) fountain.

Förderband ['fœrdər-bant] *n* (-[e]s/*ver*) conveyor-belt.

fordern ['fɔrdərn] *v/t* demand; *Entschädigung:* claim; *Preis:* ask, charge.

fördern ['fœrdərn] *v/t* further, advance; *Bergbau:* haul, raise.

Forderung ['fɔrdəruŋ] *f* (-/-en) demand; *Anspruch:* claim.

Forelle [fo'rɛlə] *f* (-/-n) trout.

Form [fɔrm] *f* (-/-en) form; *Gestalt:* figure, shape; *tech.* mo(u)ld; *sp.* form, condition; **2al** [-'ma:l] *adj* formal; **~alität** [-mali'tɛ:t] *f* (-/-en) formality; **~at** [-'ma:t] *n* (-[e]s/-e) size; **~el** ['fɔrməl] *f* (-/-n) formula; **2en** ['fɔrmən] *v/t* form; *Material:* shape, fashion.

förmlich ['fœrmliç] *adj* formal.

formlos ['fɔrmlo:s] *adj* formless, shapeless; *fig.* informal.

Formular [fɔrmu'la:r] *n* (-s/-e) form, *Am. a.* blank.

formulieren [fɔrmu'li:-rən] *v/t* formulate; *Frage etc.:* word, phrase.

forsch [fɔrʃ] vigorous, energetic; *draufgängerisch:* smart, dashing.

forsch|en ['fɔrʃən] *v/i* do research (work); **~** nach search for; **2er** *m* researcher, research worker; *Entdecker:* explorer; **2ung** *f* research (work).

Forst [fɔrst] *m* (-[e]s/-e[n]) forest.

Förster ['fœrstər] *m* (-s/-) forester.

fort [fɔrt] *adv weg:* away, gone; *weiter:* on; *verloren:* gone, lost; **~bestehen** *v/i* (*irr*) continue; **~fahren** *v/i* (*irr*) depart, leave; *mit dem Auto etc.:* a. drive off; *fig.* continue, keep on; **~führen** *v/t* continue, carry on; **~gehen** *v/i* (*irr*) go (away), leave; **~geschritten** ['-gəʃrɪtən] *adj* advanced; **~laufend** ['-laufənt] *adj* consecutive, continuous; **~pflanzen**

Foto

v/refl: sich ~ propagate, reproduce; **~schaffen** *v/t* take away, remove; **~schreiten** ['-ʃraitn] *v/i* (*irr*) advance, proceed, progress; **2schritt** *m* progress; **~schrittlich** *adv* progressive; **~setzen** *v/t* continue, pursue; **2setzung** *f:* ~ folgt to be continued; **~während** ['-vɛːrənt] *adj* continuous; *adv* constantly, always.

Foto [fo:to] *n* (-s/-s) *colloq.* photo; **~apparat** ['-ʔapaːt] *m* (-[e]s-e) camera; **~graf** [-'gra:f] *m* (-en/-en) photographer; **~grafie** [-gra'fi:] *f* (-/-n) photography; photo (-graph); **2grafieren** [-gra'fi:rən] *v/t, v/i* photograph; take a photo (-graph) (of).

Fotokopie [fotoko'pi:] *f* (-/-n) photostat.

Foyer [foaˈjeː] *n* (-s/-s) *bsd. thea.* foyer.

Fracht [fraxt] *f* (-/-en) goods *pl;* freight; *mar. a.* cargo; *Gebühr:* carriage, *aer., mar., Am.* freight; **~er** [ˈfraxtər] *m* freighter.

Frack [frak] *m* (-[e]s, -s) dress coat, tailcoat.

Frage [ˈfraːgə] *f* (-/-n) question; *gr., rhet.* interrogation; *Problem:* problem, point; **~bogen** *m* questionnaire; *für Antragsteller:* form; *§n* [ˈfraːgən] *v/i* ask; *ausfragen:* question; **~zeichen** *n* question mark.

fraglich [ˈfraːklɪç] *adj* doubtful, uncertain; *betreffend:* in question.

Fragment [fraˈgment] *n* (-[e]s/-e) fragment.

fragwürdig [ˈfraːkvʏrdɪç] *adj* doubtful, dubious.

frankieren [fraŋˈkiːrən] *v/t Brief, Paket etc.:* stamp.

Franse [ˈfranzə] *f* (-/-n) fringe.

Französe [franˈtsoːzə] *m* (-n/-n) Frenchman; **die ~osen** *pl* the French *pl;* **§ösisch** [-ˈtsøːzɪʃ] *adj* French.

Frau [frau] *f* (-/-en) woman; *Dame:* lady; *Ehe§:* wife; ~ **X** Mrs X; **~enarzt** *m* gyn(a)ecologist.

Fräulein [ˈfrɔylain] *n* (-s/-) young lady; teacher; shop-assistant; waitress; ~ **X** Miss X.

frech [frɛç] *adj* impudent, *colloq.* saucy; **2heit** *f* impudence, *colloq.* sauciness.

frei [frai] *adj* free (*von* from, of); *nicht besetzt:* vacant; *Feld:* open; **~er Tag** day off.

Freibad [ˈfraibaːt] *n* (-[e]s/ˈ~er) outdoor swimming pool; **~e** [ˈfraiə] *n* (-n/*no pl*): **im ~n** in the open (air), outdoors; **ins ~** into the open (air), outdoors; **2geben** *v/t* (*irr*) release; **j-m 2geben** give s.o. time off; *Gepäck* **2geben** free luggage (allowance); **2haben** *v/i* (*irr*) have a holiday; *im Büro etc.:* have a day off; **~hafen** m free port; **~handel** m free trade; **~heit** f liberty, freedom; **~karte** f free ticket; **Ωlassen** v/t (irr) release, set free od. at liberty; **gegen Kaution Ωlassen** jur. release on bail; **~lassung** [-lasʊŋ] f (~/no pl) release; **~lauf** m freewheel.

freilich ['fraɪlɪç] adv admittedly; bejahend: certainly, of course.

Frei|lichtbühne ['fraɪlɪçtbyːnə] f (~/-n) open-air theatre (Am. -er); **~lichtkino** [-kiːno] n (-s/-s) open-air cinema, bsd. Am. outdoor od. drive-in theater; **Ωmachen** v/t Post: prepay, stamp; **~maurer** m freemason; **Ωmütig** [-myːtɪç] adj frank; **Ωsprechen** v/t (irr) acquit; **~stoß** m Fußball: free kick; **~tag** m Friday; **Ωwillig** [-vɪlɪç] adj voluntary; **~willige** [-vɪlɪgə] m (-n/-n) volunteer; **~zeit** f (~/no pl) free (spare, leisure) time.

fremd [frɛmt] adj strange; ausländisch: foreign, alien (a. fig.).

Fremde¹ ['frɛmdə] f (~/no pl) abroad; foreign parts; **in der ~** abroad.

Fremde² m, f (-n/-n) stranger; Ausländer: foreigner.

Fremden|führer ['frɛmdənfyːrər] m (-s/-) guide;

~heim n boarding house; **~verkehr** m tourism; **~verkehrsbüro** n tourist office (bureau, agency); **~zimmer** n room.

fremd|ländisch ['frɛmtlɛndɪʃ] adj foreign, exotic; **Ωsprache** f foreign language; **Ωwort** n foreign word.

Frequenz [fre'kvɛnts] f (~/-en) frequency.

fressen ['frɛsən] v/t (irr) eat; colloq. devour.

Freud|e ['frɔydə] f (~/-n) joy; Vergnügen: pleasure; **Ωestrahlend** ['-ʃtraːlənt] adj radiant with joy; **Ωig** adj joyful; happy; **Ωlos** ['frɔytloːs] adj cheerless.

freuen ['frɔyən] v/t: **es freut mich** I am glad od. pleased; **sich ~ über** v/refl be pleased about od. with, be glad about; **sich ~ auf** v/refl look forward to.

Freund [frɔynt] m (-[e]s/-e) (boy)friend; **~in** ['-dɪn] f (~/-nen) (girl)friend; **Ωlich** adj friendly, kind, nice; Zimmer: cheerful; **~schaft** f friendship.

Friede ['friːdə] m (-ns/-n), **Frieden** ['friːdən] m (-s/-) peace.

Fried|hof ['friːthoːf] m (-[e]s/¨e) cemetery; **Ωlich** adj peaceful.

frieren ['friːrən] v/i (irr) freeze; Fenster etc.: freeze over; **mich friert** I am cold, I feel cold.

frisch

frisch [frɪʃ] *adj* fresh; *Eier:* new-laid; *Wäsche:* clean; *Brot:* new; **~ gestrichen!** [gə'ʃtrɪçən] wet (*Am.* fresh) paint!

Friseu|r [fri'zøːr] *m* (-s/-e) hairdresser; *Herren:* barber; **~se** [-'zøːzə] *f* (-/-n) (woman) hairdresser.

frisier|en [fri'ziːrən] *v/t:* **j-n** ~ do *od.* dress s.o.'s hair; **sich** ~ do one's hair; **2salon** [-za'lõː] *m* (-s/-s) hairdresser's, hairdressing salon.

Frist [frɪst] *f* (-/-en) (fixed, limited) period of time; *jur.* respite.

Frisur [fri'zuːr] *f* (-/-en) hair-style, hair-do.

froh [fro:] *adj* glad; cheerful, gay.

fröhlich ['frøːlɪç] *adj* cheerful, happy.

fromm [frɔm] *adj* pious; *Gebet:* devout.

Frömmigkeit ['frœmɪçkaɪt] *f* (-/*no pl*) piety.

Front [frɔnt] *f* (-/-en) *arch.* front, façade; *mil.* front, line; **2al** [frɔn'ta:l] *adj* frontal; *Zusammenstoß:* head-on; **~antrieb** *m mot.* front-wheel drive.

Frosch [frɔʃ] *m* (-[e]s/~e) frog.

Frost [frɔst] *m* (-[e]s/~e) frost; **~beule** *f* chilblain.

frösteln ['frœstəln] *v/i* feel chilly.

frostig ['frɔstɪç] *adj* frosty; *fig.* cold.

frottier|en [frɔ'tiːrən] *v/t*

rub down; **2tuch** *n* Turkish towel.

Frucht [fruxt] *f* (-/~e) fruit; **2bar** [-'ba:r] *adj* fertile; fruitful.

früh [fry:] *adj* early; **am ~en Morgen** in the early morning; *adv:* ~ **aufstehen** rise early; **heute** ~ this morning; **2aufsteher** ['-ʔaʊfʃteːər] *m* (-s/-) early riser, *colloq.* early bird; **~er** ['fry:ər] *adj* earlier; former; *adv* formerly, in former times; **~estens** ['-əstəns] *adv* at the earliest; **2geburt** *f* premature birth; premature baby *od.* animal; **2jahr** *n*, **2ling** ['-lɪŋ] *m* (-s/-e) spring; **~morgens** ['-'mɔrgəns] *adv* early in the morning; **~reif** *adj* precocious.

Frühstück ['fry:ʃtʏk] *n* (-[e]s/-e) breakfast; **Zimmer mit** ~ bed and breakfast; **2en** *v/i* (have) breakfast.

Fuchs [fuks] *m* (-es/~e) fox; *Pferd:* sorrel.

Füchsin ['fʏksɪn] *f* (-/-nen) she-fox, vixen.

Fuge ['fu:gə] *f* (-/-n) *tech.* joint.

füg|en ['fy:gən] *v/refl:* **sich** ~ **in** submit to.

fühlbar ['fy:lba:r] *adj* fig. sensible, noticeable; **~en** ['fy:lən] *v/t* (**sich**) ~ feel; **2er** *m* feeler.

führen ['fy:rən] *v/t* lead, guide, conduct, show; *Ge-*

schäft etc.: run; *Waren*: deal in; *Leben*: lead; *Tagebuch etc.*: keep; *Krieg*: make, wage; *v/i Pfad etc.*: lead, go (**nach, zu** to); go (**nach, zu** to); (hold the) lead; **~ zu** lead to, result in; **~d** *adj* leading, prominent.

Führer ['fy:rər] *m* (-s/-) leader (*a. pol.*); *Fremden2*: guide; *Reise2*: guide (-book); **~schein** *m mot.* driving licence, *Am.* driver's licence.

Führung ['fy:rʊŋ] *f* (-/-en) leadership; management; *Besichtigung*: conducted tour; (*no pl*) *Benehmen*: conduct, behavio(u)r; *sp.* lead; **in ~ liegen** lead; **~zeugnis** *n* certificate of good conduct.

Fuhrunternehmer ['fu:rʔʊntərneːmər] *m* (-s/-) carrier.

füllen ['fylən] *v/t* fill; *Zahn*: fill; *Kissen, Geflügel etc.*: stuff.

Füllen *n* (-s/-) *s.* **Fohlen.**

Füller ['fylər] *m* (-s/-) *colloq.*, **~feder(halter** *m*) *f* fountain-pen; **~ung** *f* filling; *Zahn*: stopping, filling; *Tür*: panel.

Fundament [funda'mɛnt] *n* (-[e]s/-e) foundation; *fig.* basis.

Fund|büro ['fʊntbyroː] *n* (-s/-s) lost-property office; **~sachen** *pl* lost property *sg.*

fünf [fynf] *adj* five; **2eck**

['-ʔɛk] *n* (-[e]s/-e) pentagon; **2kampf** *m sp.* pentathlon; **2linge** *pl* quintuplets *pl*; **~te** ['-tə] *adj* fifth; **2tel** ['-təl] *n* (-s/-) fifth (part); **~tens** ['-təns] *adv* fifthly, in the fifth place; **~zehn(te)** ['-tse:n(tə)] *adj* fifteen(th); **~zig** ['-tsɪç] *adj* fifty; **~zigste** *adj* fiftieth.

Funk [fʊŋk] *m* (-s/*no pl*) radio, wireless.

Funke ['fʊŋkə] *m* (-ns/-n) spark; *fig. a.* glimmer; **2ln** ['fʊŋkəln] *v/i* sparkle, glitter; *Stern*: twinkle, sparkle; **~n** *m* (-s/-) *fig.* *s.* **Funke.**

funk|en ['fʊŋkən] *v/t, v/i* radio, transmit; **2er** *m* radio *od.* wireless operator; **2gerät** *n* radio set; **2signal** *n* radio signal; **2spruch** *m* radio *od.* wireless message; **2station** *f* radio *od.* wireless station; **2streifenwagen** ['fʊŋkʃtraifənvaːgən] *m* (-s/-) radio patrol car.

Funktion [fʊŋk'tsi̯oːn] *f* (-/-en) function; **~är** [-tsi̯o'nɛːr] *m* (-s/-e) functionary, official; **2ieren** [-'niːrən] *v/i* work; **nicht 2ieren** *a.* be out of order.

für [fy:r] *prp* (*acc*) for; in exchange for, return for; *Schritt ~ Schritt* step by step; *Tag ~ Tag* day after day.

Furche ['fʊrçə] *f* (-/-n) furrow; *Wagenspur*: rut.

Furcht [furçt] f (-/no pl)
fear, dread; **aus ~ vor** for
fear of; **2bar** adj terrible,
dreadful.

fürchten ['fyrçtən] v/t
fear, dread; **sich ~en vor**
v/refl be afraid od. scared
of; **~erlich** adj terrible.

furchtlos ['furçtlo:s] adj
fearless; **~sam** timid,
timorous.

Fürsorge ['fy:rzɔrgə] f (-/
no pl) care; **öffentliche ~**
public welfare (work);
soziale ~ social welfare
(work); **~erziehung**
['-ʔɛrtsi:uŋ] f (-/no pl)
corrective training; **~r(in**
f) m (social) welfare
worker.

Fürsprache ['fy:rʃpra:-
xə] f (-/no pl) intercession;
~sprecher m intercessor.

Fürst [fyrst] m (-en/-en)
prince; **~entum** ['-ʔən-
tu:m] n (-s/-er) principality.

Furt [furt] f (-/-en) ford.

Furunkel [fu'ruŋkəl] m, n
(-s/-) boil, furuncle.

Fuß [fu:s] m (-es/ᵛe) foot;
zu ~ on foot; **zu ~ gehen**
walk; **~abstreifer** ['-ap-
ʃtraifər] m (-s/-) door-
scraper, doormat.

Fußball ['fu:sbal] m
(-[e]s/ᵛe) football; (no pl)
(association) football, col-

loq., Am. soccer; **~platz** m
football ground; **~spiel** n
football match; **~spieler**
m football player, foot-
baller.

Fuß|boden ['fu:sbo:dən]
m (-s/ᵛ) floor(ing);
~bremse f mot. foot-
brake.

Fußgänger ['fu:sgɛŋər]
m (-s/-) pedestrian;
~übergang ['-ʔy:bər-
gaŋ] m pedestrian crossing;
~unterführung ['-ʔun-
tər-] f subway; **~zone** f
pedestrian precinct od.
zone.

Fuß|gelenk ['fu:sgəleŋk]
n (-[e]s/-e) ankle joint;
~note f footnote; **~pfad**
m footpath; **~sohle** f sole
of the foot; **~spur** f foot-
print; mehrere: track;
~tritt m kick; **~weg** m
footpath.

Futter¹ ['futər] n (-s/no pl)
food; Vieh2: feed; Trok-
ken2: fodder.

Futter² n (-s/-) lining.

Futteral [futə'ra:l] n (-s/
-e) Brille etc.: case;
Schirmhülle: cover; Messer:
sheath.

füttern ['fytərn] v/t feed;
Kleid: line; **2ung** f feed-
ing.

Futur [fu'tu:r] n (-s/-e) gr.
future (tense).

G

Gabe ['ga:bə] f (-/-n) gift,
present; Almosen: alms pl.

Gabel ['ga:bəl] f (-/-n)
fork; **2n: sich ~** v/refl

fork, bifurcate.

gackern ['gakərn] *v/i* cackle.

gaffen ['gafən] *v/i* gape; stare.

Gage ['ga:ʒə] *f (-/-n)* salary.

gähnen ['gɛ:nən] *v/i* yawn.

Galerie [galə'ri:] *f (-/-n)* gallery.

Galgen ['galgən] *m (-s/-)* gallows *sg.*

Galle ['galə] *f (-/-n)* bile; gall; ~**nstein** *m* gall-stone, bile-stone.

Gallert ['galərt] *n (-[e]s/ -e)*, ~**e** [ga'lɛrtə] *f (-/-n)* jelly.

Galopp [ga'lɔp] *m (-s/ -e, -s)* gallop; *kurzer:* canter; 2**ieren** [-lo'pi:rən] *v/i* gallop; canter.

Gang [gaŋ] *m (-[e]s/*ᵉ**e)* walk; *tech.* running, working; *Botens* 2: errand; *Verlauf, Mahlzeit:* course; *Flur:* corridor; *zwischen Sitzreihen:* gangway, *bsd.* *Am.* aisle; *mot.* gear; **erster (zweiter, dritter, höchster)** ~ low *od.* bottom (second, third, top) gear; **in** ~ **bringen** *od.* **setzen** set going *od.* in motion; ~**art** ['gaŋ'a:rt] *f (-/-en)* gait, walk; *Pferd:* pace; ~**schaltung** ['-ʃal-tuŋ] *f (-/-en)* gear-change.

Gans [gans] *f (-/*ᵉ**e)* goose.

Gänse|blümchen ['gɛn-zəbly:mçən] *n (-s/-)* daisy; ~**braten** *m* roast goose;

~**haut** *f (-/no od.)* *fig.* goose-flesh, *Am. a.* goose pimples *pl;* ~**rich** ['gɛnzə-rɪç] *m (-s/-e)* gander.

ganz [gants] *adj* all; *ungeteilt:* entire, whole; *vollständig:* complete, total, full; **den** ~**en Tag** all day (long); *adv* quite; entirely.

gänzlich ['gɛntslɪç] *adj* complete, total, entire.

Ganztagsbeschäftigung ['gantsta:ksbəʃɛftɪ-guŋ] *f (-/-en)* full-time job *od.* employment.

gar [ga:r] *adj Speisen:* done; *adv:* ~ **nicht** not at all; ~ **nichts** nothing at all.

Garage [ga'ra:ʒə] *f (-/-n)* garage.

Garantie [garan'ti:] *f (-/ -n)* guarantee, *jur.* guaranty; 2**ren** [-'ti:rən] *v/t* guarantee.

Garbe ['garbə] *f (-/-n)* sheaf. [guard.)

Garde ['gardə] *f (-/-n)∫*

Garderobe [gardə'ro:bə] *f (-/-n)* wardrobe; cloakroom, *Am.* checkroom, *thea.* dressing-room; ~**marke** *f* check.

Gardine [gar'di:nə] *f (-/ -n)* curtain.

gären ['gɛ:rən] *v/i (irr)* ferment.

Garn [garn] *n (-[e]s/-e)* yarn; thread; cotton.

Garnele [gar'ne:lə] *f (-/ -n)* shrimp, prawn.

garnieren [gar'ni:rən] *v/t* garnish.

Garnison [garni'zo:n] *f* (-/-en) garrison.

Garnitur [garni'tu:r] *f* (-/-en) set.

garstig ['garstıç] *adj* nasty.

Garten ['gartən] *m* (-s/-) garden.

Gärtner ['gεrtnər] *m* (-s/-) gardener; **~ei** [gεrtnə'rai] *f* (-/-en) market-garden; nursery.

Gas [ga:s] *n* (-es/-e) gas; **~ geben** *mot.* accelerate; **~ wegnehmen** *mot.* decelerate; **~förmig** ['-fœrmıç] *adj* gaseous; **~hahn** *m* gas tap; **~heizung** *f* gas heating; **~herd** *m* gas stove, *Am.* gas range; **~leitung** *f* gas mains *pl*; **~ofen** *m* gas oven; **~pedal** *n* accelerator (pedal), *Am.* gas pedal.

Gasse ['gasə] *f* (-/-n) lane, alley.

Gast [gast] *m* (-es/-e) guest; visitor; *Wirtshaus*: customer; **~arbeiter** *m* foreign worker.

Gästezimmer ['gεstətsɪmər] *n* (-s/-) guestroom; spare (bed)room.

gast|freundlich ['gastfrɔyntlıç] *adj* hospitable; **~freundschaft** *f* hospitality; **~geber** [-ge:bər] *m* (-s/-) host; **~geberin** *f* (-/-nen) hostess; **~haus** *n*, **~hof** *m* restaurant; inn, (small) hotel; **~lich** *adj* hospitable; **~spiel** *n* *thea.* guest performance; **~stät-te** *f*, **~stube** *f* restaurant; **~wirt** *m* innkeeper, landlord; **~wirtschaft** *f* restaurant; public house, *colloq.* pub.

Gas|werk ['ga:svεrk] *n* (-[e]s/-e) gasworks *sg*; **~zähler** *m* gas meter.

Gatte ['gatə] *m* (-n/-n) husband; **~in** ['gatın] *f* (-/-nen) wife.

Gattung ['gatuŋ] *f* (-/-en) *bot.*, *zo.* genus; *fig.* kind, sort, type.

Gaul [gaul] *m* (-[e]s/-e) (old) nag.

Gaumen ['gaumən] *m* (-s/-) *anat.* palate.

Gauner ['gaunər] *m* (-s/-) scoundrel, *sl.* crook.

Gaze ['ga:zə] *f* (-/-n) gauze.

Gazelle [ga'tsεlə] *f* (-/-n) gazelle.

Geächtete [gə'ʔεçtətə] *m*, *f* (-n/-n) outlaw.

Gebäck [gə'bεk] *n* (-[e]s/-e) *feines*: pastry, fancy cakes *pl*; *s.* **Plätzchen.**

gebären [gə'bε:rən] *v/t* (*irr*) give birth to.

Gebäude [gə'bɔydə] *n* (-[e]s/-) building, edifice.

geben ['ge:bən] *v/t* (*irr*) give; *Karten*: deal; **es gibt** there is, there are; **was gibt es?** what is the matter?; **gegeben werden** *thea.* be on.

Gebet [gə'be:t] *n* (-[e]s/-e) prayer.

Gebiet [gə'bi:t] *n* (-[e]s/-e) territory; *Bezirk*: district; *Fläche:* area; *Fach*2: field; *Wissens*2: province; *Interessen*2: sphere.

Gebilde [gə'bɪldə] *n* (-s/ -) shape; structure.

gebildet [gə'bɪldət] *adj* educated; cultured, cultivated.

Gebirg|e [gə'bɪrgə] *n* (-s/ -) mountains *pl;* 2**ig** *adj* mountainous; ~**skette** [-skɛtə] *f,* ~**szug** *m* mountain chain *od.* range.

Gebiß [gə'bɪs] *n* (-sses/ -sse) (set of) teeth; *künstliches:* (set of) artificial *od.* false teeth, denture; *Zaum:* bit.

geboren [gə'bo:rən] *adj* born; ~**er Deutscher** German by birth; ~**e Smith** née Smith.

geborgen [gə'bɔrgən] *adj* safe.

Gebot [gə'bo:t] *n* (-[e]s/ -e) order, command; **die Zehn** ~**e** *pl eccl.* the Ten Commandments *pl;* ~**sschild** *n* mandatory sign.

Gebrauch [gə'braʊx] *m* (-[e]s/ˇe) use; 2**en** *v/t* use; ~**sanweisung** [-s-ʔanvaɪzʊŋ] *f* (-/-en) directions *pl od.* instructions *pl* for use; 2**t** *adj* secondhand; ~**twagen** *m* used *od.* second-hand car.

Gebrech|en [gə'brɛçən] *n* (-s/-) defect; 2**lich** *adj* fragile; *schwach:* infirm.

Gebrüll [gə'brʏl] *n* (-[e]s/ *no pl*) roaring; *Rind:* lowing.

Gebühr [gə'by:r] *f* (-/ -en) *Kosten:* charge; *Post:* rate; *amtliche:* fee; 2**en** *v/i* be due (*dat* to); 2**enfrei** *adj* free of charge; 2**enpflichtig** [-ənpflɪçtɪç] *adj* liable to charges.

Geburt [gə'bu:rt] *f* (-/ -en) birth; ~**enkontrolle** *f* birth-control.

gebürtig [gə'bʏrtɪç] *adj:* ~ **aus** a native of.

Geburts|datum [gə-'bu:rtsda:tʊm] *n* (-s/-**daten**) date of birth; ~**jahr** *n* year of birth; ~**ort** *m* place of birth, birthplace; ~**tag** *m* birthday; ~**urkunde** *f* birth certificate.

Gebüsch [gə'bʏʃ] *n* (-[e]s/-e) bushes *pl,* undergrowth.

Gedächtnis [gə'dɛçtnɪs] *n* (-sses/-se) memory.

Gedanke [gə'daŋkə] *m* (-n/-n) thought; idea; 2**nlos** *adj* thoughtless; ~**nstrich** *m* dash; 2**nvoll** *adj* thoughtful.

Ge|därme [gə'dɛrmə] *pl* entrails *pl,* bowels *pl,* intestines *pl;* ~**deck** ['-dɛk] *n* (-[e]s/-e) cover; menu; 2**deihen** [-'daɪən] *v/i* (*irr*) thrive, prosper.

gedenk|en [gə'dɛŋkən] *v/i* (*irr*) think of; *ehrend:* commemorate; *v/t* intend; 2**tafel** *f* (commemorative) plaque.

Gedicht [gə'dɪçt] *n* (-[e]s/ -e) poem.

Gedränge [gə'drɛŋə] *n*

(-s/no pl) crowd, throng; 2t adj crowded, packed.

gedrückt [gə'drykt] adj fig. depressed.

Geduld [gə'dʊlt] f (-/no pl) patience; 2en v/refl: sich ~ have patience; 2ig adj patient.

gelehrt [gə'ʔeːrt] adj honou(r)ed; Brief: **Sehr ~ehrter Herr N.!** Dear Sir, Dear Mr N.; ~eignet ['ʔaɪɡnət] adj fit; suitable.

Gefahr [gə'faːr] f (-/-en) danger, peril; risk; **auf eigene ~** at one's own risk.

gefähr|den [gə'fɛːrdən] v/t endanger; risk; ~lich adj dangerous.

Gefährt|e [gə'fɛːrtə] m (-n/-n), ~in f (-/-nen) companion.

Gefälle [gə'fɛlə] n (-s/-) fall, descent, gradient.

Gefallen[1] [gə'falən] m (-s/-) favo(u)r.

Gefallen[2] n (-s/no pl): ~ **finden** an take (a) pleasure in, take a fancy to od. for; 2 vi (irr) please; es **gefällt mir** I like it; sich et. 2 lassen put up with s.th.

gefällig [gə'fɛlɪç] adj pleasing, agreeable; obliging; kind; 2keit f kindness, favo(u)r.

gefangen [gə'faŋən] adj captive; imprisoned; 2e m, f (-n/-n) prisoner, captive; ~nehmen v/t (irr) take prisoner; fig. captivate;

2schaft f captivity, imprisonment.

Gefängnis [gə'fɛŋnɪs] n (-ses/-se) prison, jail, gaol; ~strafe f sentence od. term of imprisonment.

Gefäß [gə'fɛːs] n (-es/-e) vessel (a. anat.).

gefaßt [gə'fast] adj composed; ~ **auf** prepared for.

Ge|fecht [gə'fɛçt] n (-[e]s/-e) mil. engagement, action; ~fieder [-'fiːdər] n (-s/-) plumage, feathers pl.

gefleckt [gə'flɛkt] adj spotted.

Geflügel [gə'flyːɡəl] n (-s/no pl) fowl, poultry.

gefräßig [gə'frɛːsɪç] adj greedy, voracious.

gefrier|en [gə'friːrən] v/i (irr) freeze; 2fach n freezing compartment; 2fleisch n frozen meat; 2punkt m freezing-point; 2truhe f deep-freeze.

gefügig [gə'fyːɡɪç] adj pliable.

Gefühl [gə'fyːl] n (-[e]s/-e) feel; Empfindung: feeling (a. fig.), sensation; Gemütsregung: emotion; 2los adj unfeeling; insensible; 2voll adj sentimental.

gegen ['ɡeːɡən] prp (acc) towards; against; jur., sp. versus; vergleichend: compared with; **Am Entgelt:** (in exchange) for; Medikament: for; adv ungefähr: about, Am. around.

Gegenangriff ['ge:gən-ʔaŋrif] m (-[e]s/-e) counterattack.

Gegend ['ge:gənt] f (-/-en) region, area.

gegeneinander [ge:gən-ʔai'nandər] adv against one another od. each other.

Gegen|gewicht ['ge:-gəngəviçt] n (-[e]s/-e) counterbalance, counterpoise; ~**gift** n antidote, antitoxin; ~**leistung** f return (service), equivalent; ~**licht** n (-[e]s/no pl): **im** ~ against the light; ~**lichtblende** f phot. lens hood; ~**maßnahme** f counter-measure; ~**mittel** n remedy, antidote; ~**satz** m contrast; opposition; **im** ~**satz zu** in contrast to od. with, in opposition to; ~**seite** f opposite side; **2seitig** ['-zaitiç] adj mutual, reciprocal; ~**spieler** m opponent, antagonist; ~**stand** m object; fig. subject, topic; ~**stück** n counterpart; ~**teil** n contrary, reverse; **im** ~**teil** on the contrary.

gegenüber [ge:gən-'y:bər] prp (dat), adv opposite; ~**stehen** v/i (irr) be faced with, face.

Gegen|wart ['ge:gən-vart] f (-/no pl) presence; jetzige Zeit: present time; gr. present (tense); ~**wärtig** [-vɛrtiç] adj present; adv at present; ~**wert** m equivalent; ~**wind** m head

wind; ~**zug** m corresponding train.

Gegner ['ge:gnər] m (-s/-) adversary, opponent.

Gehackte [gə'haktə] n (-n/no pl) minced meat.

Gehalt¹ [gə'halt] m (-[e]s/-e) content.

Gehalt² n (-[e]s/ver) salary; ~**serhöhung** [-s²ɛr-høːʊŋ] f (-/-en) rise (in salary), Am. raise.

gehässig [gə'hɛsɪç] adj malicious, spiteful.

Gehäuse [gə'hɔyzə] n (-s/-) box; case.

geheim [gə'haim] adj secret; 2**dienst** m secret service; 2**nis** n (-ses/-se) secret; mystery; ~**nisvoll** adj mysterious.

gehen ['ge:ən] v/i (irr) go; zu Fuß: walk; weg~: leave; Maschine: go, work; Uhr: go; Ware: sell; Wind: blow; **wie geht es Ihnen?** how are you?

Geheul [gə'hɔyl] n (-[e]s/no pl) howling.

Gehilfe [gə'hilfə] m (-n/-n), ~**in** f (-/-nen) assistant.

Gehirn [gə'hirn] n (-[e]s/-e) brain(s pl); ~**erschütterung** [-²ɛrʃytə-ruŋ] f (-/-en) concussion (of the brain).

Gehöft [gə'høːft] n (-[e]s/-e) farm.

Gehölz [gə'hœlts] n (-es/-e) wood, coppice.

Gehör [gə'høːr] n (-[e]s/no pl) hearing; ear.

gehorchen [gə'hɔrçən] *v/i* obey (**j-m** s.o.).

gehör|en [gə'hø:rən] *v/i* belong (*dat*, **zu** to); ~**ig** *adj* proper, right; *colloq.* good; *adv colloq.* thoroughly.

gehorsam [gə'ho:rza:m] *adj* obedient; 2 *m* (*-s/no pl*) obedience.

Geh|steig ['ge:ʃtaɪk] *m* (*-[e]s/-e*), ~**weg** *m* pavement, *Am.* sidewalk.

Geier ['gaɪər] *m* (*-s/-*) vulture.

Geige ['gaɪgə] *f* (*-/-n*) violin, *colloq.* fiddle; ~**r(in** *f*) *m* violinist.

Geisel ['gaɪzəl] *f* (*-/-n*) hostage.

Geiß [gaɪs] *f* (*-/-en*) (she-, nanny-)goat; ~**bock** *m* he-goat, billy-goat.

Geist [gaɪst] *m* (*-es/-er*) spirit; mind, intellect; wit; *Gespenst:* ghost.

geistes|abwesend ['gaɪstəs'apve:zənt] *adj* absent-minded; ~**gegenwärtig** *adj:* ~ **sein** have the presence of mind; *schlagfertig:* be quick-witted; ~**gestört** [-gəʃtø:rt] *adj* mentally disturbed; ~**krank** *adj* insane, mentally ill; 2**zustand** *m* state of mind.

geistig ['gaɪstɪç] *adj* intellectual, mental, spiritual; ~**e Getränke** *pl* spirits *pl*.

geistlich ['gaɪstlɪç] *adj* religious, spiritual; 2**e** *m*

(*-n/-n*) clergyman; minister.

geistreich ['gaɪstraɪç] *adj* witty; ingenious; spirited.

Geiz [gaɪts] *m* (*-es/no pl*) meanness; ~**hals** *m* miser; 2**ig** *adj* mean, miserly, stingy.

Ge|jammer [gə'jamər] *n* (*-s/no pl*) lamentation(s *pl*); ~**kreisch** [-'kraɪʃ] *n* (*-[e]s/no pl*) screaming, shrieking; ~**lächter** [-'lɛçtər] *n* (*-s/-*) laughter.

gelähmt [gə'lɛ:mt] *adj* paralysed, crippled.

Gelände [gə'lɛndə] *n* (*-s/-*) area; *Boden:* ground; *Landschaft:* country; mil. terrain; ~**lauf** *m* cross-country run.

Geländer [gə'lɛndər] *n* (*-s/-*) railing(s *pl*); banisters *pl*; *Balkon:* balustrade.

gelassen [gə'lasən] *adj* calm, composed.

Gelatine [ʒela'ti:nə] *f* (*-/no pl*) gelatin(e).

ge|läufig [gə'lɔyfɪç] *adj* common; familiar; ~**launt** [-'laʊnt] *adj:* **gut** *od.* **schlecht** ~ **sein** be in a good *od.* bad humo(u)r *od.* mood.

Geläute [gə'lɔytə] *n* (*-s/-*) ringing; *Kirchenglocken:* chimes *pl*.

gelb [gɛlp] *adj* yellow; 2**sucht** *f* (*-/no pl*) jaundice.

Geld [gɛlt] *n* (*-[e]s/-er*) money; ~**anlage** *f* investment; **~ausgabe** f expense; **~buße** f fine; **~schein** m banknote, *Am.* bill; **~schrank** m strongbox, safe; **~sendung** f remittance; **~strafe** f fine; **~stück** n coin; **~wechsel** m exchange of money.

Gelee [ʒe'le:] n, m (-s/-s) jelly.

gelegen [gə'le:gən] adj situated; *passend*: convenient.

Gelegenheit [gə'le:gənhaIt] f (-/-en) occasion; *günstige*: opportunity; **~skauf** m bargain.

gelegentlich [gə'le:gəntlIç] adj occasional.

gelehrig [gə'le:rIç] adj docile; **~t** adj learned; **2te** m (-n/-n) learned man, scholar.

Geleise [gə'laIzə] n (-s/-) s. **Gleis**.

Geleit [gə'laIt] n (-[e]s/ rare -e) escort; **2en** [gə'laItən] v/t accompany, conduct; *schützend*: escort; **~zug** m mar. convoy.

Gelenk [gə'leŋk] n (-[e]s/ -e) joint; **2ig** adj supple.

gelernt [gə'lernt] adj skilled, trained.

Geliebte [gə'li:ptə] m (-n/-n) lover; f (-n/-n) mistress.

gelinde [gə'lIndə] adv: ~ **gesagt** to put it mildly.

gelingen [gə'lIŋən] v/i (irr) succeed; **es gelingt mir zu** I succeed in ger.

gellend ['gelənt] adj shrill, piercing.

geloben [gə'lo:bən] v/t vow, promise.

gelten ['geltən] v/i (irr) be valid; *Geld*: be current; ~ **als** pass for; ~ **lassen** let pass; **~d** adj: ~ **machen** *Anspruch*, *Recht*: assert.

Gelübde [gə'lypdə] n (-s/-) vow.

gelungen [gə'luŋən] adj successful.

gemächlich [gə'mɛçlIç] adj leisurely, comfortable, easy.

Gemahl [gə'ma:l] m (-[e]s/rare -e) *lit.* husband; **~in** f (-/-nen) wife.

Gemälde [gə'mɛ:ldə] n (-s/-) painting, picture; **~galerie** f picture-gallery.

gemäß [gə'mɛ:s] prp (dat) according to; **~igt** [-Içt] adj moderate; temperate (a. geogr.).

gemein [gə'maIn] adj common; mean.

Gemeinde [gə'maIndə] f (-/-n) community; *eccl.* parish; *in der Kirche*: congregation; **~rat** m municipal council; *Person*: municipal council(l)or.

Gemein|heit [gə'maInhaIt] f (-/-en) meanness; mean trick; **2sam** adj common; **~schaft** f community.

gemessen [gə'mesən] adj measured; formal; grave.

Gemisch [gə'mIʃ] n

(-[e]s/-e) mixture; **~t-warenhandlung** f grocery (store).

Gemse ['gɛmzə] f (-/-s) chamois.

Gemurmel [gə'mʊrməl] n (-s/*no pl*) murmur(ing).

Gemüse [gə'my:zə] n (-s/-) vegetable(s *pl*); *grünes:* greens *pl*; **~händler** m greengrocer.

gemütlich [gə'my:tlıç] *adj* good-natured; comfortable, snug, cosy; **2keit** f snugness; cosiness.

Gemüts|bewegung [gə'my:tsbəveːgʊŋ] f (-/-en) emotion; **~ver-fassung** f, **~zustand** m state of mind.

genau [gə'naʊ] *adj* exact, accurate; precise; *adv* just; **2igkeit** f accuracy, exactness; precision.

genehmig|en [gə'ne:mı-gən] v/t approve; grant; **2ung** f grant; approval; licen|ce, *Am.* -se; permit; *Erlaubnis:* permission.

geneigt [gə'naıkt] *adj* inclined (**zu** to).

General [genə'ra:l] m (-s/-e, -e) general; **~bevoll-mächtigte** m (-n/-n) *econ.*: universal agent; general manager; **~direktor** m general manager; director; **~konsul** m consul-general; **~konsulat** n consulate-general; **~probe** f dress-rehearsal; **~streik** m general strike; **~voll-macht** f full power of attorney.

Generation [genəra-'tsɪo:n] f (-/-en) generation.

Generator [genə'ra:tɔr] m (-s/-en) generator.

genes|en [gə'ne:zən] v/i (*irr*) recover (**von** from); **2ung** f recovery.

genial [ge'nɪa:l] *adj* brilliant.

Genick [gə'nık] n (-[e]s/ -e) nape of the neck.

genieren [ʒe'niːrən] v/ *refl:* **sich ~** feel *od.* be embarrassed.

genieß|bar [gə'niːsbaːr] *adj* eatable; drinkable; **~en** [gə'niːsən] v/t (*irr*) enjoy.

Genitiv ['ge:nıti:f] m (-s/ -e) *gr.* genitive (case).

genormt [gə'nɔrmt] *adj* standardized.

Genosse [gə'nɔsə] m (-n/ -n) *pol.* comrade; **~nschaft** f association; co(-)operative (society).

genug [gə'nu:k] *adj, adv* enough, sufficient(ly).

genüg|en [gə'ny:gən] v/i be enough; **~end** *adj* sufficient; **~sam** ['ny:kza:m] *adj beim Essen:* frugal; *bescheiden:* modest.

Genugtuung [gə'nu:k-tu:ʊŋ] f (-/-en) satisfaction.

Genus ['ge:nʊs] n (-/Genera) *gr.* gender.

Genuß [gə'nʊs] m (-sses/ ˵sse) *von Nahrung:* consumption; *Essen:* eating,

Trinken: drinking; *Vergnügen*: enjoyment, pleasure; *Hoch2*: treat; **~mittel** *n* semi-luxury.

Geo|graphie [geogra'fi:] *f* (-/no pl) geography; **~logie** [-lo'gi:] *f* geology; **~metrie** [-me'tri:] *f* geometry.

Gepäck [gə'pɛk] *n* (-[e]s/ no pl) luggage, *Am.* baggage; **~annahme** *f* luggage (registration) office *od.* counter; **~aufbewahrung** [-'ʔaufbəva:- ruŋ] *f* left-luggage office *od.* counter, *Am.* checkroom; **~ausgabe** *f* luggage office *od.* counter; **~kontrolle** *f* luggage inspection, *Am.* baggage check; **~netz** *n* luggagerack, *Am.* baggage rack; **~schein** *m* luggage receipt (slip, ticket), *Am.* baggage check; **~schließfach** [-ʃli:sfax] *n* (-[e]s/ **¨er**) luggage locker; **~stück** *n* piece of luggage; **~träger** *m* porter; *Fahrrad*: carrier; **~wagen** *m* luggage-van, *Am.* baggage car.

gepflegt [gə'pfle:kt] *adj* neat; *Garten*: well-kept.

Ge|plapper [gə'plapər] *n* (-s/no pl) babble, chatter (-ing); **~plauder** [-'plaudər] *n* (-s/no pl) chat(ting), small talk; **~polter** [-'pɔltər] *n* (-s/no pl) rumble.

gerade [gə'ra:də] *adj* straight (*a. fig.*); *Zahl etc.*:

even; *direkt*: direct; *Haltung*: upright, erect; *adv* straight; just; **~ dabei sein, et. zu tun** be just doing s.th.; **~ an dem Tage** on that very day; **2** *f* (-/-n) straight line; **~aus** [gəra:də'ʔaus] *adv* straight on *od.* ahead; **~heraus** [-he'raus] *adv* frankly; **~(n)wegs** [-(n)ve:ks] *adv* straight, directly; **~zu** *adv* almost, really.

Gerät [gə'rɛ:t] *n* (-[e]s/ -e) tool, implement, utensil; *Radio*: set; *Apparat*: apparatus.

geraten [gə'ra:tən] *v/i* (*irr*) come, fall, get; (**gut**) **~** turn out well.

Geratewohl [gəra:tə- vo:l] *n*: **aufs ~** at random.

geräumig [gə'rɔymɪç] *adj* spacious.

Geräusch [gə'rɔyʃ] *n* (-[e]s/-e) noise; **2los** *adj* noiseless; **2voll** *adj* noisy.

gerben ['gɛrbən] *v/t* tan.

gerecht [gə'rɛçt] *adj* just; *rechtschaffen*: righteous; **2igkeit** *f* justice; righteousness.

Gerede [gə're:də] *n* (-s/no pl) talk; gossip; *Gerücht*: rumo(u)r.

gereizt [gə'raɪtst] *adj* irritable; *Haut etc.*: irritated.

Gericht [gə'rɪçt] *n* (-[e]s/ -e) *Küche*: dish, course; *jur. s.* **Gerichtshof**; **2lich** *adj* legal.

Gerichts|barkeit [gə- 'rɪçtsba:rkaɪt] *f* (-/no pl)

jurisdiction; **~hof** m lawcourt, court of justice; **~saal** m court-room; **~verhandlung** f trial; **~vollzieher** [-fɔltsiːər] m (-s/-) bailiff.

gering [gəˈrɪŋ] adj little, small; s. **geringfügig**; **~er** adj inferior, less, minor; **~fügig** [-fyːgɪç] adj insignificant, trifling, slight; **~schätzig** [-ʃetsɪç] adj contemptuous; **2schätzung** f contempt; **~st** adj least.

gerinnen [gəˈrɪnən] v/i (irr) clot; Milch: curdle; Blut: coagulate, congeal.

Gerippe [gəˈrɪpə] n (-s/-) skeleton.

gern(e) [gɛrn, ˈgɛrnə] adv willingly, gladly; **~ haben** od. **mögen** be fond of, like.

Geröll [gəˈrœl] n (-/-e) scree.

Gerste [ˈgɛrstə] f (-/-n) barley; **~nkorn** n med. sty(e).

Geruch [gəˈrʊx] m (-[e]s/ ve) smell, odo(u)r; angenehmer: scent; **2los** adj odo(u)rless; scentless.

Gerücht [gəˈrʏçt] n (-[e]s/-e) rumo(u)r.

geruhsam [gəˈruːzaːm] adj peaceful, quiet.

Gerümpel [gəˈrʏmpəl] n (-s/no pl) lumber, junk.

Gerundium [gəˈrʊndiʊm] n (-s/-dien) gr. gerund.

Gerüst [gəˈrʏst] n (-[e]s/ -e) scaffold(ing).

gesamt [gəˈzamt] adj whole, entire, total, all; **2ausgabe** f complete edition; **2betrag** m sum total; **2schule** f comprehensive school.

Gesandte [gəˈzantə] m (-n/-n) envoy; **~schaft** f legation.

Gesang [gəˈzaŋ] m (-[e]s/ ve) singing; Lied: song.

Gesäß [gəˈzɛːs] n (-es/ -e) seat, buttocks pl.

Geschäft [gəˈʃɛft] n (-[e]s/-e) business; Laden: shop, Am. store; **2ig** adj busy, active; **2lich** adj business ...; adv on business.

Geschäfts|... business ...; **~führer** m manager; **~mann** m businessman; **~partner** m (business) partner; **~räume** [-rɔymə] pl business premises pl; **~reise** f business trip; **~schluß** m closing-time; nach **~schluß** a. after business hours; **~zeit** f office od. business hours pl.

geschehen [gəˈʃeːən] v/i (irr) happen, occur, take place; **2** n (-s/-) events pl.

gescheit [gəˈʃait] adj clever, intelligent, bright.

Geschenk [gəˈʃɛŋk] n (-[e]s/-e) present, gift; **~packung** f gift-box.

Geschicht|**e** [gəˈʃɪçtə] f (-/-n) story; tale; Wissenschaft: history; **2lich** adj historical.

Geschick [gəˈʃɪk] *n* (-[e]s/-e) fate, destiny; skill; ~**lichkeit** *f* skill; **2t** *adj* skil(l)ful.

Geschirr [gəˈʃɪr] *n* (-[e]s/-e) dishes *pl*; *Porzellan*: china; *Steingut*: earthenware, crockery; *Pferde*: harness.

Geschlecht [gəˈʃlɛçt] *n* (-[e]s/-er) sex; kind, species; *Familie*: family; *gr.* gender; **2lich** *adj* sexual.

Geschlechts|krankheit *f* venereal disease; ~**teile** *pl* genitals *pl*; ~**verkehr** *m* sexual intercourse.

geschliffen [gəˈʃlɪfən] *adj* cut; *fig.* polished.

Geschmack [gəˈʃmak] *m* (-[e]s/ᵕe) taste (*a. fig.*); *Aroma*: flavo(u)r; **2los** *adj* tasteless; *pred fig.* in bad taste; **2voll** *adj* tasteful; *pred fig.* in good taste.

geschmeidig [gəˈʃmaɪdɪç] *adj* supple, lithe.

Geschnatter [gəˈʃnatər] *n* (-s/*no pl*) cackle, cackling.

Geschöpf [gəˈʃœpf] *n* (-[e]s/-e) creature.

Geschoß [gəˈʃɔs] *n* (-sses/-sse) projectile, missile; *Stockwerk*: stor(e)y, floor.

Geschrei [gəˈʃraɪ] *n* (-[e]s/*no pl*) cries *pl*; shouting; *fig.* noise, fuss.

Geschütz [gəˈʃʏts] *n* (-es/-e) gun, cannon.

Geschwader [gəˈʃvaːdər] *n* (-s/-) *mil.*: *mar.* squadron; *aer.* group, *Am.* wing.

Geschwätz [gəˈʃvɛts] *n* (-es/*no pl*) idle talk; *Klatsch*: gossip; **2ig** *adj* talkative.

geschweige [gəˈʃvaɪgə] *cj*: ~ **(denn)** let alone.

geschwind [gəˈʃvɪnt] *adj* fast, quick, swift.

Geschwindigkeit [gəˈʃvɪndɪçkaɪt] *f* (-/-en) quickness; *Tempo*: speed; ~**sbeschränkung** *f* speed limit; ~**süberschreitung** [-ˈʔyːbərʃraɪtuŋ] *f* (-/-en) speeding.

Geschwister [gəˈʃvɪstər] *pl* brother(s *pl*) and sister(s *pl*).

Geschworene [gəˈʃvoːrənə] *m*, *f* (-n/-n) juror; **die** ~**n** *pl* the jury *sg*.

Geschwulst [gəˈʃvʊlst] *f* (-/ᵕe) swelling; tumo(u)r.

Geschwür [gəˈʃvyːr] *n* (-[e]s/-e) abscess, ulcer.

Geselle [gəˈzɛlə] *m* (-n/-n) journeyman; **2en** *v/refl*: **sich zu j-m** ~ join s.o.; **2ig** *adj* social, sociable.

Gesellschaft [gəˈzɛlʃaft] *f* (-/-en) society; company (*a. econ.*); party; **j-m** ~ **leisten** keep s.o. company; ~**er(in** *f*) *m econ.* partner; **2lich** *adj* social.

Gesellschafts|reise [gəˈzɛlʃaftsraɪzə] *f* (-/-n) conducted tour, package tour; ~**spiel** n party od. round game.

Gesetz [gə'zɛts] n (-es/ -e) law; ~**buch** n (-[e]s/ ...bücher) statute-book; ~**entwurf** m bill; ~**geber** [-ge:bər] m (-s/-) legislator; ~**gebung** [-tsy:ŋ] (-/-en) legislation; 2**lich** adj lawful, legal; 2**lich geschützt** patent, registered.

gesetzt [gə'zɛtst] adj ernst: sedate; ~ **den Fall** ... supposing ...

gesetzwidrig [gə'zɛts-vi:drɪç] adj unlawful, illegal.

Gesicht [gə'zɪçt] n (-[e]s/ -er) face; Miene: countenance.

Gesichts|ausdruck m expression, countenance; ~**farbe** f complexion; ~**punkt** m point of view; ~**züge** [-tsy:gə] pl features pl, lineaments pl.

Gesindel [gə'zɪndəl] n (-s/no pl) rabble, mob.

Gesinnung [gə'zɪnʊŋ] f (-/-en) mind; sentiment(s pl).

gespannt [gə'ʃpant] adj tense (a. fig.); Seil: tight, taut; fig. intent, eager; Aufmerksamkeit: close; Verhältnis: strained.

Gespenst [gə'ʃpɛnst] n (-[e]s/-er) ghost; 2**isch** ghostly.

Gespräch [gə'ʃprɛːç] n (-[e]s/-e) talk, conversation; teleph. call; 2**ig** adj talkative.

Gestalt [gə'ʃtalt] f (-/-en) form, shape; Körperbau: figure; 2**en** v/t form, shape (a. fig.); arrange, organize.

geständig [gə'ʃtɛndɪç] adj: ~ **sein** confess; 2**nis** n (-ses/-se) confession.

Gestank [gə'ʃtaŋk] m (-[e]s/no pl) stench.

gestatten [gə'ʃtatən] v/t allow, permit; ~ **Sie!** allow me!, excuse me!

gestehen [gə'ʃte:ən] v/t (irr) confess.

Gestein [gə'ʃtaɪn] n (-[e]s/-e) rock, stone; ~**stell** [-'ʃtɛl] n (-[e]s/-e) stand, rack, shelf; Rahmen: frame.

gestern ['gɛstərn] adv yesterday; ~**rig** [-trɪç] adj of yesterday, yesterday's.

Gestrüpp [gə'ʃtrʏp] n (-[e]s/-e) brush(wood), undergrowth.

Gestüt [gə'ʃty:t] n (-[e]s/ -e) stud (farm).

Gesuch [gə'zu:x] n (-[e]s/ -e) application; Bittschrift: petition.

gesund [gə'zʊnt] adj sound; healthy; ~ **werden** get well; ~**er Menschenverstand** common sense.

Gesundheit [gə'zʊnthaɪt] f (-/no pl) health.

Gesundheits|amt [gə-'zʊnthaɪts?amt] n (-[e]s/ ...ämter) public health department; 2**schädlich** [-'ʃɛːt-lɪç] adj unhealthy, unwholesome; ~**zustand** m state of health.

Getränk [gə'trɛŋk] *n* (-[e]s/-e) drink, beverage.

Getreide [gə'traidə] *n* (-s/-) corn, grain.

Getriebe [gə'tri:bə] *n* (-s/-) *mot.* gear; **automatisches** ~ automatic transmission; **~schaden** *m* gear defect.

Ge|tue [gə'tu:ə] *n* (-s/*no pl*) fuss; **~tümmel** [-'tyməl] *n* turmoil.

getupft [gə'tupft] *adj* dotted, spotted.

Gewächs [gə'vɛks] *n* (-es/-e) growth (*a. med.*); *Pflanze:* plant; **~haus** *n* greenhouse, hothouse.

ge|wachsen [gə'vaksən] *adj:* **j-m ~ sein** be a match for s.o.; **e-r Sache ~ sein** be equal to s.th.; **~wagt** [-'va:kt] *adj* risky; bold.

Gewähr [gə'vɛːr] *f* (-/no pl) guarantee, security; **2en** *v/t* grant, allow; **2leisten** *v/t* guarantee.

Gewahrsam [gə'va:rza:m] *m* (-s/*no pl*) custody, safe-keeping.

Gewalt [gə'valt] *f* (-/-en) power; authority; *Zwang:* force; violence; **mit ~** by force; **2ig** *adj* powerful, mighty; **2sam** *adj* violent; *adv a.* forcibly; **2sam öffnen** force open, open by force; **2tätig** *adj* violent.

Gewand [gə'vant] *n*

(-[e]s/ˇer) garment; *wallendes:* robe; *bsd. eccl.* vestment.

gewandt [gə'vant] *adj* agile, nimble; clever.

Gewässer [gə'vɛsər] *n* (-s/-) water(s *pl*).

Gewebe [gə've:bə] *n* (-s/-) fabric; *feines:* tissue (*a. anat.*, *fig.*); *Webart:* texture.

Gewehr [gə've:r] *n* (-[e]s/-e) gun; rifle.

Geweih [gə'vai] *n* (-[e]s/-e) horns *pl*, antlers *pl*.

Gewerb|e [gə'verbə] *n* (-s/-) trade, business; **2lich** ['-verpliç] *adj* commercial, industrial; **2smäßig** *adj* professional.

Gewerkschaft [gə'werkʃaft] *f* (-/-en) trade(s) union, *Am.* labor union; **~ler** [-lər] *m* (-s/-) trade-unionist; **2lich** *adj* trade-union.

Gewicht [gə'viçt] *n* (-[e]s/-e) weight; *fig.* importance; **2heben** [-he:bən] *n* (-s/*no pl*) weightlifting; **2ig** *adj* weighty.

gewillt [gə'vilt] *adj* willing.

Ge|wimmel [gə'viməl] *n* (-s/*no pl*) throng; **~winde** ['-vində] *n* (-s/-) *tech.* thread.

Gewinn [gə'vin] *m* (-[e]s/-e) gain; *econ.* gains *pl*, profit; *Lotterie:* prize; *Spiel2:* winnings *pl*; **2bringend** *adj* profita-

ble; **2en** [gə'vɪnən] v/t (irr)
win; fig. gain; **~er** m
winner.

gewiß [gə'vɪs] adj certain;
~! certainly!, Am. sure!

Gewissen [gə'vɪsən] n
(-s/-) conscience; **2haft**
adj conscientious; **2los** adj
unscrupulous; **~sbisse**
[-bɪsə] pl remorse sg.

Gewißheit [gə'vɪshaɪt] f
(-/no pl) certainty.

Gewitter [gə'vɪtər] n (-s/
-) (thunder-)storm; **2n** v/i:
es gewittert there is a
thunderstorm.

gewöhnen [gə'vø:nən] v/t
accustom (**an** to); **sich ~**
an get used to.

Gewohnheit [gə'vo:n-
haɪt] f (-/-en) habit.

gewöhnlich [gə'vø:nlɪç]
adj ordinary, usual; unfein:
common, vulgar.

gewohnt [gə'vo:nt] adj
customary, habitual.

Gewölbe [gə'vœlbə] n
(-s/-) vault.

gewunden [gə'vʊndən]
adj winding.

Gewürz [gə'vʏrts] n (-es/
-e) spice; **~gurke** f pickled gherkin.

Gezeiten [gə'tsaɪtən] pl
tide(s pl).

geziert [gə'tsi:rt] adj affected.

Gezwitscher [gə'tsvɪt-
ʃər] n (-s/no pl) chirping,
twittering.

gezwungen [gə'tsvʊŋən]
adj forced, constrained.

Gicht [gɪçt] f (-/no pl) gout.

Giebel ['gi:bəl] m (-s/-)
gable.

Gier [gi:r] f (-/no pl) greed;
2ig adj greedy.

gießen ['gi:sən] v/t (irr)
pour; tech. cast, found;
Blumen: water; v/i: **es ~t** it
is pouring (with rain);
2erei [-ə'raɪ] f (-/-en)
foundry; **2kanne** f water-
ing-can.

Gift [gɪft] n (-[e]s/-e)
poison; Schlangen**2**: venom
(a. fig.); **2ig** adj poisonous; venomous (a. fig.);
~pilz m poisonous mushroom, toadstool;
~schlange f venomous
snake; **~zahn** m poison-
fang.

Gipfel ['gɪpfəl] m (-s/-)
summit, top; Spitze: peak;
~konferenz f summit
meeting.

Gips [gɪps] m (-es/-e)
plaster (of Paris); **~ab-**
druck m, **~verband** m
med. plaster cast.

Giraffe [gi'rafə] f (-/-n)
giraffe.

Girlande [gɪr'landə] f (-/
-n) garland.

Girokonto ['ʒi:rokɔnto]
n (-s/-ten) current account.

Gischt [gɪʃt] m (-es/-e), f
(-/-en) spray; spindrift.

Gitarre [gi'tarə] f (-/-n)
guitar.

Gitter ['gɪtər] n (-s/-)
lattice; Fenster: grating.

Glanz [glants] m (-es/no
pl) brightness; lustre, Am.
-er; fig. splendo(u)r.

Glas [gla:s] n (-es/ᵛer) glass.

Gläser ['glɛ:zər] pl s. **Brille**; 2n adj vitreous; glassy.

glasieren [gla'zi:rən] v/t glaze; *Kuchen:* ice, frost.

glasig ['gla:zɪç] adj glassy.

Glasscheibe ['gla:sʃaɪbə] f (-/-n) pane of glass.

glatt [glat] adj smooth (a. fig.); *glitschig:* slippery.

Glätte ['glɛtə] f (-/no pl) smoothness (a. fig.); slipperiness.

Glatteis ['glat'ʔaɪs] n glazed frost, Am. glaze.

glätten ['glɛtən] v/t smooth.

glattrasiert ['glatrazi:rt] adj clean-shaven.

Glatze ['glatsə] f (-/-n) bald head.

Glaube ['glaubə] m (-ns/ no pl) faith, belief (**an** in); 2n ['glaubən] v/t believe; *meinen:* think, suppose, Am. a. guess; ~nsbe**kenntnis** [-bəkɛntnɪs] n (-ses/-se) creed.

glaubhaft ['glaubhaft] adj plausible.

Gläubiger ['glɔybɪgər] m (-s/-) creditor.

glaubwürdig ['glaupvyrdɪç] adj credible.

gleich [glaɪç] adj equal; same; *eben:* even; level; **zur ~en Zeit** at the same time; adv alike, equally; *so~:* immediately, directly, at once; ~ **groß** the same height; ~ **gegenüber** just opposite; **es ist ~ acht** (Uhr) it is close on od. nearly eight (o'clock); ~**altrig** [-altrɪç] adj (of) the same age; ~**berechtigt** adj having equal rights; ~**bleibend** adj constant, steady; ~**en** ['glaɪçən] v/i (irr) equal; *ähneln:* resemble; ~**falls** adv also, likewise; 2ge**wicht** n balance (a. fig.); ~**gültig** adj indifferent (**gegen** to); **es ist mir ~gültig** I don't care; 2**gültigkeit** f indifference; ~**lautend** adj identical; ~**mäßig** adj regular; *Verteilung etc.:* equal; ~**namig** [-na:mɪç] adj of the same name; 2**strom** m direct current; 2**ung** f math. equation; ~**wertig** [-ve:rtɪç] adj of the same value, of equal value; ~**zeitig** [-tsaɪtɪç] adj simultaneous.

Gleis [glaɪs] n (-es/-e) rails pl, line(s pl), track(s pl).

gleiten ['glaɪtən] v/i (irr) glide, slide; 2**flug** m glide.

Gletscher ['glɛtʃər] m (-s/-) glacier; ~**spalte** f crevasse.

Glied [gli:t] n (-[e]s/-er) anat. limb; *Kette:* link (a. fig.); 2**ern** ['gli:dərn] v/t arrange; divide; ~**maßen** [-ma:sən] pl limbs pl, extremities pl.

glimmen ['glɪmən] v/i (a. irr) smo(u)lder.

glimpflich ['glɪmpflɪç] *adv:* ~ **davonkommen** get off lightly.

glitschig ['glɪtʃɪç] *adj* slippery.

glitzern ['glɪtsərn] *v/i* glittern, glisten.

Globus ['glo:bus] *m* (-ses/Globen) globe.

Glocke ['glɔkə] *f* (-/-n) bell.

Glocken|spiel ['glɔkən-ʃpi:l] *n* (-[e]s/-e) carillon, chime(s *pl*); ~**turm** *m* belfry, bell tower.

glotzen ['glɔtsən] *v/i* colloq. stare.

Glück [glyk] *n* (-[e]s/no *pl*) fortune; good luck; happiness; **auf gut** ~ on the off chance; ~ **haben** be lucky; **viel** ~! good luck!; **zum** ~ fortunately.

Glucke ['glukə] *f* (-/-n) sitting hen.

glücken ['glykən] *v/i* s. gelingen.

gluckern ['glukərn] *v/i* gurgle.

glücklich ['glyklɪç] *adj* fortunate; happy; ~**er-weise** [-'vaɪzə] *adv* fortunately.

glucksen ['gluksən] *v/i* gurgle.

Glück|sspiel ['glyks-ʃpi:l] *n* (-[e]s/-e) game of chance; **2strahlend** [-ʃtra:lənt] *adj* radiant(ly happy); ~**wunsch** *m* congratulation(s *pl*); good wishes *pl*; **herzlichen** ~**wunsch zum Ge-**

burtstag! many happy returns (of the day!)

Glüh|birne ['gly:bɪrnə] *f* (-/-n) bulb; **2en** ['gly:ən] *v/i* glow; **2end** *adj* glowing; *Eisen:* red-hot; *Kohle:* live; *fig.* ardent; **2(end)-heiß** *adj* burning hot; ~**lampe** *f* bulb; ~**wein** *m* mulled wine *od.* claret; ~**würmchen** [-vʏrmçən] *n* (-s/-) glow-worm.

Glut [glu:t] *f* (-/-en) heat; glow (*a. fig.*); embers *pl*; *fig.* ardo(u)r.

Gnade ['gna:də] *f* (-/-n) grace; favo(u)r; mercy; ~**ngesuch** *n* petition for mercy.

gnädig ['gnɛ:dɪç] *adj* gracious; merciful; *Anrede:* ~**e Frau** Madam.

Gold [gɔlt] *n* (-[e]s/no *pl*) gold (*a. attr*); ~**barren** *m* gold bar *od.* ingot; **2en** *adj* gold; *fig.* golden; **2ig** *adj* sweet, lovely, *Am. a. fig.* cute; ~**schmied** *m* goldsmith; ~**währung** *f* gold standard.

Golf[1] [gɔlf] *m* (-[e]s/-e) *geogr.* gulf.

Golf[2] *n* (-s/no *pl*) golf; ~**platz** *m* golf-course, (golf-links *f*); ~**schlä-ger** *m* (golf-)club; ~**spiel** *n* golf; ~**spieler** *m* golfer.

Gondel ['gɔndəl] *f* (-/-n) gondola; car.

gönnen ['gœnən] *v/t:* **j-m et.** ~ allow s.o. s.th.; *neidlos:* not to (be)grudge s.o. s.th.; ~**rhaft** ['gœnərhaft] *adj* patronizing.

Gorilla [go'rɪla] *m* (-s/-s) gorilla.

Gosse ['gɔsə] *f* (-/-n) gutter (*a. fig.*).

Gott [gɔt] *m* (-es/⸚er) God; **~heit:** god, deity; **~ sei Dank!** thank God!; **um ~es willen!** for God's sake!

Gottes|dienst ['gɔtəs-di:nst] *m* (-es/-e) (divine) service; **~lästerung** [-lɛstəruŋ] *f* (-/-en) blasphemy.

Gottheit ['gɔthaɪt] *f* (-/-en) deity, divinity.

Göttlin ['gœtɪn] *f* (-/-nen) goddess; **2lich** *adj* divine.

Götze ['gœtsə] *m* (-n/-n) idol.

Gouvern|ante [guvɛr-'nantə] *f* (-/-n) governess; **~eur** [-'nø:r] *m* (-s/-e) governor.

Grab [gra:p] *n* (-[e]s/⸚er) grave; tomb.

Graben ['gra:bən] *m* (-s/⸚) ditch; *mil.* trench; 2 *v/t, v/i* (*irr*) dig; *Tier:* burrow.

Grab|gewölbe ['gra:p-gəvœlbə] *n* (-s/-) vault, tomb; **~inschrift** *f* epitaph; **~mal** *n* (-[e]s/⸚er) monument; tomb, sepulchre, *Am.* -er; **~stein** *n* tombstone; gravestone.

Grad [gra:t] *m* (-[e]s/-e) degree; *mil. etc.:* grade, rank; **15 ~ Kälte** *or* **minus** 15 degrees below zero; **~einteilung** ['-ʔaɪntaɪ-luŋ] *f* graduation.

Graf [gra:f] *m* (-en/-en) count; *in England:* earl.

Gräfin ['grɛ:fɪn] *f* (-/-nen) countess.

Grafschaft ['gra:fʃaft] *f* (-/-en) county.

Gram [gra:m] *m* (-[e]s/*no pl*) grief, sorrow.

Gramm [gram] *n* (-s/-e) gram(me).

Grammati|k [gra'matɪk] *f* (-/-en) grammar; **2sch** [gra'matɪʃ] *adj* grammatical.

Granate [gra'na:tə] *f* (-/-n) *mil.* shell; *Gewehr2, Hand2:* grenade.

Granit [gra'ni:t] *m* (-s/-e) granite.

graphisch ['gra:fɪʃ] *adj* graphic.

Gras [gra:s] *n* (-es/⸚er) grass; **2en** *v/i* graze.

gräßlich ['grɛslɪç] *adj* hideous, atrocious.

Grat [gra:t] *m* (-[e]s/-e) ridge, edge.

Gräte ['grɛ:tə] *f* (-/-n) (fish)bone.

Gratifikation [gratifika-'tɪo:n] *f* (-/-en) gratuity, bonus.

gratis ['gra:tɪs] *adj* gratis, free of charge.

gratulieren [gratu'li:rən] *v/i* congratulate; **j-m zum Geburtstag ~** wish s.o. many happy returns (of the day).

grau [grau] *adj* grey, *bsd. Am.* gray.

grauen ['grauən] *v/i:* **mir graut vor** I shudder at, I

Graupen

dread; **2** *n* (-s/*no pl*) horror; **~haft** *adj* horrible.

Graupe|n ['graʊpən] *pl* pot-barley; **~ln** ['graʊpəln] *pl* soft hail *sg.*

grausam ['graʊzaːm] *adj* cruel; **2keit** *f* cruelty.

grause|n ['graʊzən] *s.* **grauen; ~ig** *adj* s. **gräßlich**.

graziös [gra'tsjøːs] *adj* graceful.

greifen ['graɪfən] *v/t* (*irr*) seize, grasp, catch hold of; **um sich ~** spread.

Greis [graɪs] *m* (-es/-e) old man; **~in** ['graɪzɪn] *f* (-/-nen) old woman.

grell [grɛl] *adj* Licht: glaring; *Farbe, Muster*: loud.

Grenze ['grɛntsə] *f* (-/-n) boundary; *Staats2*: frontier, border; **2n** ['grɛntsən] *v/i*: **~ an** border on; *fig. a.* verge on; **2nlos** *adj* boundless.

Grenzübergang ['grɛntsʔyːbərgaŋ] *m* (-[e]s/⸚e) frontier *od.* border crossing(-point).

Griech|e ['griːçə] *m* (-n/-n) Greek; **2isch** *adj* Greek; *arch.* Grecian.

griesgrämig ['griːsgrɛːmɪç] *adj* morose, sullen.

Grieß [griːs] *m* (-es/-e) semolina.

Griff [grɪf] *m* (-[e]s/-e) grip, grasp; *Tür, Messer etc.*: handle; *Schwert*: hilt.

Grille ['grɪlə] *f* (-/-n) cricket; *fig.* whim.

Grimasse [gri'masə] *f* (-/-n) grimace; **~n schneiden** pull faces.

grimmig ['grɪmɪç] *adj* grim; fierce.

grinsen ['grɪnzən] *v/i*: **~ (über)** grin (at); *höhnisch*: sneer (at); **2** *n* (-s/*no pl*) grin; sneer.

Grippe ['grɪpə] *f* (-/-n) influenza, *colloq.* flu.

grob [groːp] *adj* coarse (*a. fig.*); rough; rude.

grölen ['grøːlən] *v/i colloq.* bawl.

Groll [grɔl] *m* (-[e]s/*no pl*) grudge, ill will; **2en** ['grɔlən] *v/i*: **j-m ~** bear s.o. a grudge *od.* ill will.

Groschen ['grɔʃən] *m* (-s/-) penny.

groß [groːs] *adj* large; *dick, weit, erwachsen*: big; *hochgewachsen*: tall; *fig.* great, grand; *Hitze*: intense; *Kälte*: severe; *Verlust*: heavy; **im ~en (und) ganzen** on the whole; **~er Buchstabe** capital (letter); **~artig** [-'ʔaːrtɪç] *adj* great, grand; **2aufnahme** *f Film*: close-up.

Größe ['grøːsə] *f* (-/-n) size; *Körper2*: height; *bsd. math.* quantity; *Bedeutung*: greatness; *Person*: celebrity; *thea.* star.

Großeltern ['groːsʔɛltərn] *pl* grandparents *pl*; **~handel** *m* wholesale trade; **~händler** *m* wholesale dealer, wholesaler; **2jährig** *adj* of age;

2**jährig werden** come of age; ~**jährigkeit** f majority; ~**macht** f great power; ~**mutter** f grandmother; 2**spurig** [-ʃpu:rɪç] adj arrogant; ~**stadt** f large town od. city; 2**städtisch** adj of od. in a large town od. city.

Groß|vater ['gro:sfa:tər] m (-s/⁺) grandfather; ~**wild** n (-[e]s/no pl) big game; 2**ziehen** v/t (irr/ Kind: bring up; Kind, Tier: rear, raise; 2**zügig** [-'tsy:gɪç] adj liberal, generous.

grotesk [gro'tɛsk] adj grotesque.

Grotte ['grɔtə] f (-/-n) grotto.

Grübchen ['gry:pçən] n (-s/-) dimple.

Grube ['gru:bə] f (-/-n) pit; Bergbau: a. mine.

grübeln ['gry:bəln] v/i brood (**über** over, on).

Gruft [gruft] f (-/⁺e) tomb, vault.

grün [gry:n] adj green; 2**anlage** f (public) park(s pl).

Grund [grunt] m (-[e]s/⁺e) ground; Gewässer: bottom (a. fig.); Beweg2: motive; reason (gen, **für** of, for); ~**ausbildung** f basic training; ~**bedingung** f basic od. fundamental condition; ~**begriffe** pl rudiments pl; ~**besitz** m (landed) property; ~**besitzer** m landowner.

gründe|n ['gryndən] v/t found, establish; 2**r** m founder.

Grund|fläche ['gruntflɛçə] f (-/-n) math. base; Zimmer etc.: area; ~**gebühr** f basic fee; teleph. rental; ~**gedanke** m basic od. fundamental idea; ~**lage** f foundation; 2**legend** ['-le:gənt] adj fundamental, basic.

gründlich ['gryntlɪç] adj thorough; Kenntnisse: profound.

grund|los ['gruntlo:s] adj fig. unfounded; 2**mauer** f foundation.

Gründonnerstag [gry:n'dɔnərsta:k] m Maundy Thursday.

Grund|regel ['gruntre:gəl] f (-/-n) fundamental rule; ~**riß** m groundplan; ~**satz** m principle; 2**sätzlich** ['-sɛtslɪç] adj on principle; ~**schule** f primary school; ~**stein** m foundation-stone; ~**stück** n plot of land) (building) site; premises pl; ~**stücksmakler** m estate agent, Am. realtor.

Gründung ['gryndʊŋ] f (-/-en) foundation, establishment.

grundverschieden ['gruntfɛr'ʃi:dən] adj entirely different.

grunzen ['gruntsən] v/i grunt.

Grupp|e ['grupə] f (-/-n) group; 2**ieren** [-'pi:rən] v/t group; **sich** 2**ieren**

grus(e)lig

(form a) group; form groups; **~ierung** [-'piːruŋ] f (/-en) grouping; group.

grus(e)lig ['gruːz(ə)liç] adj creepy, weird.

Gruß [gruːs] m (-es/ᵛe) greeting; *bsd. mil.*, *mar.* salute.

Grüße ['gryːsə] pl regards pl; respects pl, compliments pl; **2n** [grysən] v/t, v/i greet; *bsd. mil.* salute; **2n Sie ihn von mir** remember me to him.

Grütze ['grytsə] f (-/-n) grits pl, groats pl.

gucken ['gukən] v/i look; peep, peer.

Gulasch ['guːlaʃ] n (-(e)s/no pl) goulash.

gültig ['gyltiç] adj valid; legal; *Münze:* current; *Fahrkarte:* valid; **2keit** f validity; currency.

Gummi ['gumi] n, m (-s/-s) gum; ~ *m Radier2:* (India-)rubber; **~band** n (-[e]s/ᵛer) elastic (band); **2eren** [-'miːrən] v/t gum; **~knüppel** m truncheon, *Am.* club; **~sohle** f rubber sole; **~stiefel** pl wellingtons pl, *Am.* rubbers pl.

günstig ['gynstiç] adj favo(u)rable; **im ~sten Fall** at best.

Gurgel ['gurgəl] f (/-n) throat; **2n** v/i gargle; gurgle.

Gurke ['gurkə] f (/-n) cucumber; *Gewürz2:* gherkin.

Gurt [gurt] m (-[e]s/-e) girdle, belt; *Trage2:* strap.

Gürtel ['gyrtəl] m (-s/-) belt, girdle.

Guß [gus] m (-sses/ᵛsse) *tech.* founding; casting; *Regen:* downpour, shower; **2eisern** ['-aɪzərn] adj cast-iron.

gut [guːt] adj good; **~es Wetter** fine weather; **~ werden** get well; *fig.* turn out well; **ganz ~** not bad; **schon ~!** I never mind!, all right!; adv well; **~ aussehen** be good-looking.

Gut [guːt] n (-[e]s/ᵛer) possession, property; *Land2:* estate.

Gut|achten ['guːt?axtən] n (-s/-) (expert) opinion; **~achter** m (-s/-) expert; **2artig** ['-aːrtiç] adj good-natured; *med.* benign.

Gute ['guːtə] n (-n/no pl): **~s tun** do good; **alles ~!** all the best!

Güte ['gyːtə] f (-/no pl) goodness, kindness; *econ.* quality; **in ~** amicably; **meine ~!** good gracious!

Güter ['gyːtər] pl goods pl; **~bahnhof** m goods station, *Am.* freight depot *od.* yard; **~wagen** m (goods) waggon, *Am.* freight car; **~zug** m goods train (*Am.* freight) train.

gut|gelaunt ['guːtgəlaunt] adj good-humo(u)red; **2haben** ['-haːbən] n (-s/-) credit (balance); **~heißen** v/t (irr) approve (of); **~herzig**

['hɛrtsɪç] adj kind(-heart-ed).

Gutsbesitzer ['gu:tsbə-zɪtsər] m (-s/-) owner of an estate.

Gutschein ['gu:tʃaɪn] m (-[e]s/-e) credit note; coupon, *Beleg*: voucher.

Guts|haus ['gu:tshaʊs] n (-es/er) farm-house; ~hof m estate, farm.

gutwillig ['gu:tvɪlɪç] adj willing.

Gymnasi|ast [gymna-'zɪast] m (-en/-en) appr. grammar-school boy; ~um [-'na:zɪʊm] n (-s/-sien) appr. grammar-school.

Gymnastik [gym'nastɪk] f (-/no pl) gymnastics pl; 2sch adj gymnastic.

Gynäkologe [gynɛko-'lo:gə] m (-n/-n) gyn(a)ecologist.

H

Haar [ha:r] n (-[e]s/-e) hair; ~e pl hair sg; **sich die ~e schneiden lassen** have one's hair cut; ~bürste f hairbrush; ~festiger ['-fɛstɪgər] m (-s/-) setting-lotion; 2ig ['ha:rɪç] adj hairy; in Zssgn: ...haired; ~klemme f hair grip, Am. bobby pin; ~nadel f hairpin; ~nadelkurve f hairpin bend; ~schnitt m haircut; ~spray n hair spray od. lacquer; ~wäsche f shampoo; ~waschmittel ['-vaʃmɪtəl] n (-s/-) shampoo; ~wasser n hair-lotion.

Habe ['ha:bə] f (-/no pl) property; belongings pl.

haben ['ha:bən] v/t (irr) have.

habgierig ['ha:pgi:rɪç] adj avaricious.

Habicht ['ha:bɪçt] m (-[e]s/-e) (gos)hawk.

Hackle ['hakə] f (-/-n)

hoe; *Ferse*: heel; 2en ['ha-kən] v/t hack; *Fleisch*: mince; *Holz*: chop; ~fleisch n mince(d meat).

Hafen ['ha:fən] m (-s/er) harbo(u)r, port; ~arbeiter m docker, longshoreman; ~stadt f (sea)port.

Hafer ['ha:fər] m (-s/no pl) oats pl; ~brei m (oatmeal) porridge; ~flocken pl rolled oats pl, rolled oats pl; ~schleim m gruel.

Haft [haft] f (-/no pl) *Gewahrsam*: custody; *Gefängnis*: imprisonment, confinement; 2bar adj responsible, jur. liable; 2en ['haftən] v/i stick, adhere (an to); 2en für answer for, be liable for.

Häftling ['hɛftlɪŋ] m (-s/-e) prisoner.

Haftpflichtversicherung ['haftpflɪçtfɛrzi:çə-rʊŋ] f (-/-en) third-party insurance; ~ung ['haftʊŋ] f jur. liability.

Hagel ['ha:gǝl] m ~s/no pl) hail; fig. a. volley; ~**korn** n hailstone; 2n ['ha:gǝln] v/i hail; ~**schauer** m (brief) hailstorm. [gaunt.)

hager ['ha:gǝr] adj lean,)

Hahn [ha:n] m (-[e]s/-e orn., tech. cock; Haus2: rooster; Wasser2: tap, Am. a. faucet.

Hai(fisch) ['hai(fɪʃ)] m (-[e]s/-e) shark.

häkeln ['hɛ:kǝln] v/t, v/i crochet.

Haken ['ha:kǝn] m (-s/-) hook; Kleider2: a. peg; fig. snag, catch.

halb [halp] adj half; e-e ~e Stunde half an hour; ein ~es Jahr six months pl; um ~ vier at half past three; 2finale n sp. semifinal; ~**gar** [-'ga:r] adj underdone, rare; ~**ieren** [-'bi:rǝn] v/t halve; 2**insel** f peninsula; 2**kreis** m semicircle; 2**kugel** f hemisphere; 2**laut** adj low, subdued; adv in an undertone; 2**mond** m half-moon, crescent; 2**pension** f (-/no pl) dinner, bed and breakfast; 2**schuh** m shoe; 2**tagsarbeit** [-ta:ks?arbaɪt] f part-time job od. employment; ~**wüchsig** [-vyksɪç] adj adolescent; ~**zeit** f sp. half(-time).

Hälfte ['hɛlftǝ] f (-/-n) half. [-) halter.)

Halfter ['halftǝr] m, n (-s/)

Halle ['halǝ] f (-/-n) hall; Hotel: lobby, lounge.

hallen ['halǝn] v/i resound, ring.

Hallenbad ['halǝnba:t] n (-[e]s/¨er) indoor swimming-pool.

hallo [ha'lo:, 'halo] int. hallo!

Halm [halm] m (-[e]s/-e) blade; Getreide: stem, stalk; Stroh: straw.

Hals [hals] m (-es/¨e) neck; Kehle: throat; ~ über **Kopf** head over heels; ~**band** n necklace; Tier: collar; ~**entzündung** f sore throat; ~**kette** f necklace; ~**schlagader** [-la:k?a:dǝr] f (-/-n) carotid; ~**schmerzen** pl: ~ haben have a sore throat; 2**starrig** [-ʃtarɪç] adj stubborn, obstinate; ~**tuch** n neckerchief; Schal: scarf.

Halt [halt] m (-[e]s/-e) hold; Stütze: support; 2**bar** adj durable, lasting.

halten ['haltǝn] v/t (irr) hold; keep; Rede: make, deliver; ~ **für** take for; **viel** od. **wenig** ~ **von** think highly od. little of; **sich** ~ last; v/i stop.

Halter ['haltǝr] m (-s/-) keeper, owner; für Geräte etc.: holder.

Halte|stelle ['haltǝʃtelǝ] f (-/-n) stop; ~**verbot** n no stopping; **eingeschränktes** ~**verbot** n no waiting.

haltmachen v/i stop.

Haltung ['haltʊŋ] f deportment, carriage; fig. attitude (**gegenüber** towards).

Hammel ['haməl] m (-s/-, ") wether; **~fleisch** n mutton.

Hammer ['hamər] m (-s/ ") hammer; **~werfen** n (-s/no pl) hammer throw.

hämmern ['hɛmərn] v/i, v/t hammer.

Hampelmann ['hampəl-man] m (-[e]s/"er) jumping jack.

Hamster ['hamstər] m (-s/-) hamster.

Hand [hant] f (-/"e) hand; **j-m die ~ geben** od. **schütteln** shake hands with s.o.; **~arbeit** f manual labo(u)r od. work; needlework; **~ball** m handball; **~brause** f handshower; **~bremse** f handbrake.

Händedruck ['hɛndə-drʊk] m (-[e]s/"e) handshake.

Handel ['handəl] m (-s/no pl) commerce; *Geschäfts-verkehr:* trade; traffic; *ab-geschlossener:* bargain; **2n** ['handəln] v/i act; *feilschen:* bargain (**um** for); **2n mit** deal od. trade in; **2n von** deal with, be about.

Handels|beziehungen ['handəlsbətsi:ʊŋən] pl trade relations pl; **~ge-sellschaft** f (trading) company; **~schule** f com-

mercial school, business college od. school.

Hand|feger ['hantfe:gər] m (-s/-) hand-brush; **~fläche** f palm; **2gear-beitet** [-gəˀarbaɪtət] adj hand-made; **~gelenk** n wrist; **~gemenge** [-gə-mɛŋə] n (-s/-) scuffle; **~gepäck** n hand-lug-gage; **2haben** [-ha:bən] v/t handle, manage; **~kof-fer** m suit-case.

Händler ['hɛndlər] m (-s/-) dealer.

handlich ['hantlɪç] adj handy.

Handlung ['handlʊŋ] f (-/-en) act(ion); deed; thea. action, plot; econ. shop, Am. store; **~sweise** [-varzə] f (-/-n) conduct.

Hand|schellen ['hantʃɛ-lən] pl handcuffs pl; **~schrift** f hand-writing; manuscript; **2schriftlich** handwritten; **~schuh** m glove; **~tasche** f handbag, Am. purse; **~tuch** n towel; **2voll** f (-/-) handful; **~werk** n (handi)craft; **~werker** [-vɛrkər] m workman; **~werkzeug** [-vɛrkstsɔyk] n (-[e]s/no pl) tools pl. [hemp.\]

Hanf [hanf] m (-[e]s/no pl)

Hang [haŋ] m (-[e]s/"e) slope, incline; fig. inclination, tendency.

Hänge|brücke ['hɛŋə-brykə] f (-/-n) suspension bridge; **~matte** f hammock.

hängen ['hɛŋən] v/i (irr),
v/t hang (**an** on, on);
an j-m ~ be attached od.
devoted to s.o.; ~**bleiben**
v/i (irr) get caught (**an** on,
in).

Happen ['hapən] m (-s/-)
morsel, bite; snack.

Harfe ['harfə] f (-/-n)
harp.

harmlos ['harmlo:s] adj
harmless, inoffensive.

Harmonie [harmo'ni:] f
(-/-n) harmony; ~**ren**
[-'ni:rən] v/i harmonize;
2**sch** [-'mo:nɪʃ] adj har-
monious.

Harn [harn] m (-[e]s/-e)
urine; ~**blase** f (urinary)
bladder.

Harpune [har'pu:nə] f (-/
-n) harpoon.

hart [hart] adj hard; fig. a.
harsh; severe.

Härte ['hɛrtə] f (-/-n)
hardness; fig. Unbill: a.
hardship; Strenge: sever-
ity.

Hartgeld ['hartgɛlt] n
(-[e]s/no pl) coin(s pl);
2**näckig** [-nɛkɪç] adj obstinate, stubborn.

Harz [ha:rts] n (-es/-e)
resin.

Hase ['ha:zə] m (-n/-n)
hare.

Haselnuß ['ha:zəlnʊs] f
(-/-sse) hazelnut.

Hasenscharte ['ha:zən-
ʃartə] f (-/-n) harelip.

Haß [has] m (-sses/no pl)
hatred.

hassen ['hasən] v/t hate.

häßlich ['hɛslɪç] adj ugly;
fig. a. nasty.

hastig ['hastɪç] adj hasty,
hurried.

Haube ['haubə] f (-/-n)
bonnet; cap, hood; mot.
bonnet, Am. hood.

Hauch [haux] m (-[e]s/no
pl) breath; fig. touch; 2**en**
['hauxən] v/i breathe.

Haue ['hauə] f (-/no pl) colloq. hiding, spanking; 2**n**
['hauən] v/t (a. irr) hew;
chop; verhauen: beat.

Haufen ['haufən] m (-s/-)
heap, pile; fig. colloq.
crowd.

häufen ['hɔyfən] v/t heap,
pile (up), accumulate;
sich ~ pile up, accumulate; fig. increase; ~**ig** adj
frequent.

Haupt [haupt] n (-es/ᵘer)
head; fig. a. leader;
~**bahnhof** m main od.
central station; ~**darstel-
ler(in** f) ['-dar[tɛlər(ɪn)] m
lead(ing man od. lady);
~**eingang** m main en-
trance; ~**fach** n main subject, Am. major; ~**film** m
feature (film); ~**gewinn**
m first prize.

Häuptling ['hɔyptlɪŋ] m
(-s/-e) chief(tain).

Haupt|mann ['haupt-
man] m (-[e]s/-leute)
captain; ~**merkmal**
[-mɛrkma:l] n (-[e]s/-e)
characteristic feature;
~**quartier** n headquarters
pl; ~**rolle** f lead(ing part);
~**sache** f main thing;

⌐sächlich *adj* main; **⌐satz** *m gr.* main clause; **⌐stadt** *f* capital; **⌐straße** *f* high street, *Am.* main street; *Hauptverkehrsstraße*: main road *od.* street; **⌐verkehrszeit** [-ferkeːrstsaɪt] *f* (-/-en) rush *od.* peak hours *pl.*

Haus [haʊs] *n* (-es/⌐er) house; home; **nach** ⌐e home; **zu** ⌐e at home; **⌐angestellte** *m, f* (-n/-n) domestic (servant); **⌐apotheke** *f* medicine-chest, medicine-cabinet; **⌐arbeit** *f* house-work; **⌐arzt** *m* family doctor; **⌐aufgaben** *pl* homework *sg*; **⌐besitzer** *m* house owner, landlord; **⌐bewohner** *m* occupant of a house; **⌐flur** *m* s.

Flur; ⌐frau *f* housewife; **⌐halt** *m* (-[e]s/-e) household; **⌐hälterin** [-hɛltərɪn] *f* (-/-nen) housekeeper; **⌐herr** *m* head of a family; *Besitzer*: landlord;

Hausierer [haʊˈziːrər] *m* (-s/-) hawker, pedlar.

häuslich [ˈhɔʏslɪç] *adj* domestic.

Haus|meister [ˈhaʊsmaɪstər] *m* (-s/-) caretaker, janitor; **⌐ordnung** *f* rules *pl* of the house; **⌐schlüssel** *m* latchkey, front-door key; **⌐schuh** *m* slipper; **⌐tier** *n* domestic animal; **⌐tür** *f* front door; **⌐wirt** *m* landlord; **⌐wirtin** *f* landlady.

Haut [haʊt] *f* (-/⌐e) skin; *Tier*⌐: hide; **⌐ausschlag** *m* rash; **⌐farbe** *f* colo(u)r of the skin; **⌐schere** *f* (**e-e** a pair of) cuticle scissors *pl*.

Hebamme [ˈheːpʔamə] *f* (-/-n) midwife.

Hebebühne [ˈheːbəbyːnə] *f* (-/-n) lifting platform.

Hebel [ˈheːbəl] *m* (-s/-) lever.

heben [ˈheːbən] *v/t* (*irr*) lift, raise; heave; **sich** ⌐ rise, go up.

hebräisch [heˈbrɛːɪʃ] *adj* Hebrew.

Hecht [hɛçt] *m* (-[e]s/-e) pike.

Heck [hɛk] *n* (-[e]s/-e, -s) *mar.* stern; *aer.* tail; *mot.* rear. [hedge.]

Hecke [ˈhɛkə] *f* (-/-n))

Heer [heːr] *n* (-[e]s/-e) army; *fig. a.* host.

Hefe [ˈheːfə] *f* (-/-n) yeast.

Heft [hɛft] *n* (-[e]s/-e) exercise book; *Zeitschrift*: issue, number.

heften [ˈhɛftən] *v/t* fasten, fix (**an** to); *Saum*: baste.

heftig [ˈhɛftɪç] *adj* violent, fierce; passionate; *Regen etc.*: heavy; *Schmerzen*: severe.

Heft|klammer [ˈhɛftklamər] *f* (-/-n) staple; **⌐pflaster** *n* adhesive *od.* sticking plaster; **⌐zwecke** *f s.* **Reißzwecke**.

hegen [ˈheːɡən] *v/t* foster, have, entertain.

Heide

Heide[1] ['haɪdə] m (-n/-n) heathen.

Heide[2] f (-/-n) heath; **~kraut** n (-[e]s/no pl) heather, heath.

Heidelbeere ['haɪdəlbeːrə] f (-/-n) bilberry, blueberry.

heidnisch ['haɪdnɪʃ] adj heathen(ish).

heikel ['haɪkəl] adj Person: particular; Problem etc.: delicate, awkward.

heil [haɪl] adj safe, unhurt; whole.

Heiland ['haɪlant] m (-[e]s/no pl) Savio(u)r, Redeemer.

Heil|anstalt ['haɪl?anʃtalt] f (-/-en) sanatorium, Am. a. sanitarium; **2bar** adj curable; **2en** ['haɪlən] v/t cure; v/i heal (up).

heilig ['haɪlɪç] adj holy; Gott geweiht: sacred (a. fig.); **Heiliger Abend** = **2abend** m Christmas Eve; **2e** ['haɪlɪgə] m, f (-n/-n) saint.

Heilmittel ['haɪlmɪtəl] n (-s/-) remedy; medicine.

heim [haɪm] adv home; **2** n (-[e]s/-e) home; **2arbeit** f outwork.

Heimat ['haɪmaːt] f (-/no pl), **~land** n mother country; native land; **2los** adj homeless; **~ort** m home town od. village.

Heim|fahrt ['haɪmfaːrt] f journey home, homeward journey; **2isch** adj home, local, domestic, bot., zo.

etc.: native; **sich 2isch fühlen** feel at home; **2kehren** v/i, **2kommen** v/i (irr) return home; **2lich** adj secret; **~reise** f s. **Heimfahrt**; **2tückisch** adj malicious; treacherous; **2wärts** [-verts] adv homeward(s); **~weg** m way home; **~weh** n (-s/no pl): **~ haben** be homesick.

Heirat ['haɪraːt] f (-/-en) marriage; **2en** v/i marry; get married; **~santrag** [-?antraːk] m offer od. proposal of marriage.

heiser ['haɪzər] adj hoarse, husky.

heiß [haɪs] adj hot; **mir ist ~** I am hot od. feel hot.

heißen ['haɪsən] v/i (irr) be called; bedeuten: mean; **wie ~ Sie?** what is your name?; **willkommen ~** v/t welcome.

heiter ['haɪtər] adj Wetter: bright; Himmel: a. clear; Person: cheerful, gay.

heiz|en ['haɪtsən] v/t Zimmer etc.: heat; Ofen: fire; **2er** m fireman; **2körper** m radiator; **2material** n fuel; **2öl** n fuel oil; **2ung** f heating.

Held [hɛlt] m (-en/-en) hero.

helfen ['hɛlfən] v/i (irr) help, assist, aid; **~ gegen** be good for.

Helfer ['hɛlfər] m (-s/-) helper, assistant, **~shelfer** ['-hɛlfər] m accomplice.

hell [hɛl] adj Klang, Stimme: clear; Licht: bright; Haare: light, fair; Farben: light; Bier: pale; 2seher(in f) ['-ze:ər(ın)] m clair-voyant.

Helm [hɛlm] m (-[e]s/-e) helmet.

Hemd [hɛmt] n (-[e]s/-en) shirt.

hemmen ['hɛmən] v/t Bewegung etc.: check, stop; behindern: hamper; 2ung f stoppage, check; psych. inhibition; ~ungslos adj uncontrolled, unrestrained.

Hengst [hɛŋst] m (-es/-e) stallion.

Henkel ['hɛŋkəl] m (-s/-) handle, ear.

Henker ['hɛŋkər] m (-s/-) executioner.

Henne ['hɛnə] f (-/-n) hen.

her [he:r] adv here; ago; **von ... ~** from.

herab [he'rap] adv down; **~lassen** v/t let down, lower; **~lassend** adj condescending; **~setzen** v/t reduce; **~steigen** v/i (irr) climb down, descend.

heran [he'ran] adv close, near; **~kommen** v/i (irr) come ad. draw near; ap-proach (a. fig.); **~wachsen** v/i (irr) grow (up) (zu into).

herauf [he'rauf] adv up (here); upstairs; **~ziehen** v/t (irr) pull up.

heraus [he'raus] adv out

(here); **zum Fenster ~** out of the window; **~bekommen** v/t (irr) get out; Geld: get back; fig. find out; **~bringen** v/t (irr) bring od. get out; fig. = **~finden** v/t (irr) find out, discover; **~fordern** v/t challenge; **~geben** v/t (irr) give back, restore; Zeitung etc.: edit; Buch: publish; Vorschriften: issue; Geld: give change (auf j-n); 2geber m editor; publisher; **~kommen** v/i (irr) come out; be published; **~ragen** v/i project, jut out; **~stellen** v/t put out; sich **~stellen** als turn out od. prove to be; **~strecken** v/t put out; **~treten** v/i (irr) come od. step out; Augen: protrude; **~ziehen** v/t (irr) pull out; Zahn: a. extract.

herb [hɛrp] adj Geschmack: tart; Wein: dry; Gesichtszüge: austere.

herbeieilen [hɛr'baı²aı-lən] v/i come hurrying; **~holen** v/t fetch.

Herberge ['hɛrbɛrgə] f (-/-n) shelter, lodging; inn.

Herbst [hɛrpst] m (-es/-e) autumn, Am. a. fall.

Herd [he:rt] m (-[e]s/-e) stove.

Herde ['he:rdə] f (-/-n) herd; Schaf2, Gänse2 etc.: flock.

herein [he'raın] adv in (here); **~!** come in!; **~fallen** v/i fig. be taken

taken in; **~legen** v/t fig. take in.

Her|fahrt ['he:rfa:rt] f (-/no pl) journey here; **2fallen** v/i (irr): ~ **über** attack; **~gang** m (-[e]s/no pl) course of events; **2geben** v/t (irr) give up; return.

Hering ['he:rɪŋ] m (-s/-e) herring.

her|kommen ['he:rkɔmən] v/i (irr) come here; **2kunft** [-kʊnft] f (-/no pl) origin; Person: a. birth.

Heroin [hero'i:n] n (-s/no pl) heroin.

Herr [her] m (-n/-en) lord, master; gentleman; eccl. the Lord; **~ Maier** Mr Maier; **mein ~** Sir; **m-e ~en** gentlemen.

Herren|friseur ['herən-frizø:r] m (-s/-e) men's hairdresser, barber; **~haus** n manor house; **~schneider** m men's tailor; **~toilette** f (gentle)men's toilet.

herrichten ['he:rrɪçtən] v/t arrange; prepare.

Herrin ['herɪn] f (-/-nen) mistress; lady.

herrisch ['herɪʃ] adj imperious.

herrlich ['herlɪç] adj glorious, splendid.

Herrschaft ['herʃaft] f (-/no pl) rule, dominion; Macht: control; (pl -en) von Dienstboten: master and mistress.

herrscheln ['herʃən] v/i

rule; Monarch: reign; fig. be, prevail; **2r m** ruler; sovereign, monarch.

her|rühren ['he:rry:rən] v/i, **~stammen** [-ʃtamən] v/i: **~ von** come from; **~stellen** v/t make, manufacture, produce; **2stellung** f manufacture, production.

herüber [he'ry:bər] adv over (here), across.

herum [he'rʊm] adv (a)round; about; **~führen** v/t show (a)round; **~lungern** [-lʊŋərn] v/i loaf about, hang about; **~reichen** v/t pass od. hand round.

herunter [he'rʊntər] adv down (here); downstairs; **von oben ~** down from above; **~kommen** v/i (irr) come down(stairs); fig. come down in the world; deteriorate.

hervor [her'fo:r] adv out, forth; **~bringen** v/t (irr) bring out, produce (a. fig.); Früchte: yield; Wort: utter; **~gehen** v/i (irr) be clear od. apparent (aus from); **~heben** v/t (irr) fig. stress, emphasize; **~holen** v/t produce; **~ragen** [-ra:gən] v/i project; **~ragend** [-ra:gənt] adj fig. outstanding; **~rufen** v/t (irr) fig. arouse, evoke; **~stechend** [-ʃtɛçənt] adj fig. striking.

Herz [herts] n (-ens/-en) anat. heart (a. fig.); Karten: heart(s pl); **~anfall** m heart attack; **~enslust** [-lʊst] f: **nach ~** to one's heart's content; **~fehler** m cardiac defect; **~haft** adj hearty; **₂ig** adj lovely, Am. a. cute; **~infarkt** [-ʔɪnfarkt] m (-[e]s/-e) cardiac infarction; **₂krank** adj having heart trouble; **₂lich** adj cordial, hearty; **₂los** adj heartless.

Herzog ['hɛrtso:k] m (-[e]s/ᵉe) duke; **~in** f (-/ -nen) duchess; **~tum** [-tu:m] n (-[e]s/ᵉer) duchy.

Herz|schlag ['hɛrtsʃla:k] m (-[e]s/ᵉe) heartbeat; *Herzversagen:* heart failure; **~verpflanzung** f heart transplant.

Hetze ['hɛtsə] f (-/no pl) hurry, rush; **₂n** v/i, v/t hurry, rush; v/i agitate.

Heu [hɔy] n (-s/no pl) hay.

Heuch|elei [hɔyçə'laɪ] f (/-en) hypocrisy; **₂eln** ['hɔyçəln] v/t, v/i feign; **~ler** m hypocrite.

heulen ['hɔylən] v/i howl; cry.

Heu|schnupfen ['hɔyʃnʊpfən] m (-s) hayfever; **~schrecke** [-ʃrɛkə] f (/ -n) grasshopper, locust.

heut|e ['hɔytə] adv today; **~e abend** this evening, tonight; **~e früh**, **~e morgen** this morning, **~e in acht Tagen**, **~e in e-r Woche** today od. this day week; **~e vor acht Tagen**, **~e vor e-r**

Woche a week ago today; **~ig** ['hɔytɪç] adj this day's, today's; *gegenwärtig:* present; **~zutage** ['-tsu:ta:gə] adv nowadays, these days.

Hexe ['hɛksə] f (-/-n) witch; **~nschuß** [-ʃʊs] m (-sses) lumbago.

Hieb [hi:p] m (-[e]s/-e) blow; **~e** pl hiding sg, thrashing sg.

hier [hi:r] adv here; **~ entlang!** this way!

hier|auf ['hi:'raʊf] adv on it od. this; after this od. that; then; **~aus** ['hi:-'raʊs] adv from it od. this; **~bei** ['hi:r'baɪ] adv here, in this case; **~durch** ['hi:r-'dʊrç] adv through this, hereby; **~für** ['hi:r'fy:r] adv for it od. this; **~her** ['hi:r'he:r] adv here, hither; **bis ~her** as far as here; **~in** ['hi:'rɪn] adv in this; **~mit** ['hi:r'mɪt] adv with it od. this, herewith; **~nach** ['hi:r'na:x] adv after it od. this; *dementsprechend:* according to this; **~über** ['hi:r'y:bər] adv over it od. this; over here; *Thema:* about it od. this; **~von** ['hi:r'fɔn] adv of od. from it od. this.

Hilfe ['hɪlfə] f (-/-n) help; *Beistand:* aid, assistance; relief (**für** to); **Erste ~** first aid; **~ruf** m shout (call, cry) for help.

hilflos ['hɪlflo:s] adj helpless.

Hilfs|arbeiter ['hɪlfsʔar-

baitar] m (-s/-) unskilled
worker od. labo(u)rer;
2**bedürftig** adj needy;
2**bereit** adj helpful, ready
to help; ~**mittel** n aid;
tech. device.

Himbeere ['hɪmbeːrə] f
(-/-n) raspberry.

Himmel ['hɪməl] m (-s/-) *of*
sky; eccl., fig. heaven;
2**blau** adj sky-blue;
~**fahrt** eccl. ascension (of
Christ); Ascension-day;
~**richtung** f direction.

himmlisch ['hɪmlɪʃ] adj
heavenly.

hin [hɪn] adv: ~ **und her** to
and fro, Am. back and
forth; ~ **und wieder** now
and again od. then; ~ **und**
zurück there and back.

hinab [hɪ'nap] adv down;
~**steigen** v/i, v/t (irr)
climb down; descend.

hinauf [hɪ'nauf] adv up
(there); upstairs; ~**gehen**
v/i, v/t (irr) go up(stairs);
Preise, Löhne etc.: go up,
rise; ~**steigen** v/i, v/t (irr)
climb up; ascend.

hinaus [hɪ'naus] adv out;
~**begleiten** v/t show out;
~**gehen** v/i (irr) go od.
walk out; ~**schieben** v/t
(irr) fig. put off; postpone;
~**werfen** v/t (irr) throw
out; j-n: turn od. throw
out; ~**zögern** v/t put off.

Hin|blick ['hɪnblɪk] m: im
~ **auf** in view of, with regard to; 2**bringen** v/t (irr)
take there.

hindern ['hɪndərn] v/t hin-

der; ~ **an** prevent from
ger; 2**is** [-nɪs] n (-ses/-se)
sp. etc.: obstacle.

hindurch [hɪn'durç] adv
through; zeitlich: all
through, throughout.

hinein [hɪ'naɪn] adv in(to);
~**gehen** v/i (irr) go in;
~**gehen** in go into; hold.

hinfahr|en ['hɪnfaːrən] v/t
(irr) drive od. take
there; et.: take there; v/i go
there; drive there; 2**t** f (-/
no pl) journey od. way
there.

hin|fallen ['hɪnfalən] v/i
(irr) fall (down); 2**flug** m
outward flight; 2**führen**
v/t lead od. take there;
2**gabe** f (-/no pl) devo-
tion; ~**geben** v/t (irr):
sich ~ give o.s. to; widmen: devote o.s. to; ~**ge-**
hen v/i (irr): ~ **(zu)** go
(to); Pfad etc.: lead (to);
~**halten** v/t (irr) hold out;
j-n: put s.o. off.

hinken ['hɪŋkən] v/i limp.

hin|legen ['hɪnleːgən] v/t
lay od. put down; **sich**
~**legen** lie down; ~**neh-**
men v/t (irr) ertragen: put
up with; 2**reise** f journey
there, outward journey;
~**richten** v/t execute;
~**setzen** v/t set od. put
down; **sich** ~**setzen** sit
down; ~**sichtlich** [-zɪçt-
lɪç] prp (gen) with regard to;
~**stellen** v/t place; abstellen: put down.

hinten ['hɪntən] adv behind; at the back; am Ende:

in the rear.

hinter ['hɪntər] *prp* (*dat*, *acc*) behind; **2bein** *n* hind leg; **2bliebene** ['bli:bə-nə] *pl* the bereaved *pl*; *Angehörige:* surviving dependants *pl*; **~einander** [-ʔaɪ-'nandər] *adv* one after the other; **~gehen** [-'ge:ən] *v/t* (*irr*) deceive; **2grund** ['-grʊnt] *m* background; **2halt** *m* (-[e]s/-e) ambush; **~her** [-'he:r] *adv zeitlich:* afterwards; **2kopf** *m* back of the head; **~lassen** ['-lasən] *v/t* (*irr*) leave (behind); **~legen** ['-le:gən] *v/t* deposit; **2n** ['hɪntərn] *m* (-s/-) *colloq.* behind, bottom; **2rad** *n* rear wheel; **2treppe** *f* backstairs *pl*; **2tür** *f* back door.

hinüber [hɪ'ny:bər] *adv* over (there); *quer:* across.

Hin- und Rückfahrkarte *f* return ticket.

hinunter [hɪ'nʊntər] *adv* down (there); **~schlucken** *v/t* swallow.

Hinweg ['hɪnve:k] *m* (-[e]s) way there *od.* out.

hinweg [hɪn'vɛk] *adv* away, off; **~kommen** *v/i* (*irr*): **~** **über** get over; **~setzen** *v/refl:* **sich ~** **über** ignore.

Hin|weis ['hɪnvaɪs] *m* (-es/-e) hint; *Anhaltspunkt:* indication; **2weisen** *v/t* (*irr*): j-n **~** **auf** draw *od.* call s.o.'s attention to; *v/i:* **~** **auf**

point at *od.* to; **2werfen** *v/t* (*irr*) throw down; **2ziehen** *v/refl:* **sich ~** stretch (**bis zu** to); *zeitlich:* drag on.

hinzu [hɪn'tsu:] *adv* in addition; **~fügen** *v/t* add; **~kommen** *v/i* (*irr*) be added; **~ziehen** *v/t* (*irr*) *Arzt:* call in.

Hippie ['hɪpi] *m* (-s/-s) hippie, hippy.

Hirn [hɪrn] *n* (-[e]s/-e) brain(*s pl fig.*).

Hirsch [hɪrʃ] *m* (-[e]s/-e) stag, hart; *Gattung:* deer; **~kuh** *f* hind.

Hirt [hɪrt] *m* (-en/-en) herdsman; *Schaf2,* *fig.:* shepherd.

hissen ['hɪsən] *v/t* hoist.

historisch [hɪs'to:rɪʃ] *adj* historic(al).

Hitze ['hɪtsə] *f* (-/no pl) heat; **~welle** *f* heat wave, hot spell.

hitzig ['hɪtsɪç] *adj Person:* hot-tempered, hot-headed; *Debatte:* heated; **2kopf** *m* hot-head; **2schlag** *m* heat-stroke.

Hobel ['ho:bəl] *m* (-s/-) *tech.* plane; **2n** *v/t, v/i* plane.

hoch [ho:x] *adj* high; *Turm, Baum:* tall; *Strafe:* heavy, severe; *Alter:* great, old; **~** *adv* high up; **2** *n* (-s/-s) high-pressure area, anticyclone.

Hoch|achtung ['ho:xʔax-tʊŋ] *f* (-/no pl) high esteem *od.* respect; **2achtungs-**

höchst

voll adj respectful; adv Brief: yours faithfully od. sincerely, bsd. Am. yours truly; **~betrieb** m intense activity, rush; **~druck** m high pressure; **~druckgebiet** n s. Hoch; **~ebene** [-ᵊe:bənə] f plateau, tableland; **~form** f (-/ no pl): **in ~** in top form; **~gebirge** n high mountains pl; **~haus** n multistor(e)y building; skyscraper; **~konjunktur** f boom; **~mut** [-mu:t] m (-[e]s/no pl) arrogance; **2mütig** [-my:tıç] adj arrogant, haughty; **~ofen** m blastfurnace; **~saison** f peak season, height of the season; **~schule** f university; academy; **~sommer** m midsummer; **~spannung** f high tension od. voltage; **~sprung** m high jump.

höchst [hø:çst] adj highest; äußerst: extreme; adv highly, most, extremely.

Hochstapler ['ho:xʃta:plər] m (-s/-) impostor.

höchstens ['hø:çstəns] adv at (the) most, at best; **2form** f (-/no pl) top form; **2geschwindigkeit** f maximum speed; mot. speed limit; **2leistung** f sp. record (performance); Maschine: maximum output.

Hoch|verrat ['ho:xferra:t] m (-[e]s/no pl) high treason; **~wasser** n flood;

2wertig [-ve:rtıç] adj high-grade.

Hochzeit ['hoxtsait] f (-/-en) wedding; Trauung: a. marriage; **~geschenk** n wedding present; **~sreise** f honeymoon.

hocke|n ['hokən] v/i squat; m/r (-s/-) stool.

Höcker ['hœkər] m (-s/-) Kamel: hump; Buckel: hump, hunch.

Hoden ['ho:dən] pl testicles pl.

Hof [ho:f] m (-[e]s/ꝶe) court(yard); farm; Fürsten2: court; ast. halo.

hoffen ['hofən] v/t, v/i hope (**auf** for); **~tlich** adv I hope, let's hope.

Hoffnung ['hofnuŋ] f (-/-en) hope; **2slos** [-lo:s] adj hopeless.

höflich ['hø:flıç] adj polite, civil, courteous; **2keit** f courtesy.

Höhe ['hø:ə] f (-/-n) height; aer., ast., geogr. altitude; An2: hill; Rechnung: amount; Summe: size; Strafe: severity; mus. pitch; **in die ~** up(wards).

Hoheitsgebiet ['ho:haitsgəbi:t] n (-[e]s/-e) (sovereign) territory.

Höhen|kurort ['hø:ənku:rᵊort] m high-altitude health resort; **~lage** f altitude; **~luft** f mountain air; **~zug** m mountain range.

Höhepunkt ['hø:əpuŋkt] m (-[e]s/-e) fig. climax.

hohl [ho:l] adj hollow.

Höhle ['hø:lə] *f* (-/-n) cave, cavern; *Tier2*: den, lair.

Hohl|maß ['ho:lma:s] *n* (-es/-e) measure of capacity; **~raum** *m* hollow, cavity.

Hohn [ho:n] *m* (-[e]s/*no pl*) scorn; *Spott*: derision.

höhnen ['hø:nən] *v/i* sneer, jeer (**über** at); **~isch** *adj* scornful; *spottend*: sneering, derisive.

holen ['ho:lən] *v/t* fetch; go for; *besorgen*: get; **~ lassen** send for; **sich e-e Krankheit ~** catch a disease.

Holländer ['hɔlɛndər] *m* (-s/-) Dutchman; **2isch** *adj* Dutch.

Hölle ['hœlə] *f* (-/*rare* -n) hell.

holperig ['hɔlpərɪç] *adj* bumpy, rough, uneven; **~n** ['hɔlpərn] *v/i* jolt, bump.

Holunder [ho'lʊndər] *m* (-s/-) elder.

Holz [hɔlts] *n* (-es/*ver* wood; *Nutz2*: timber, *bsd. Am.* lumber.

hölzern ['hœltsərn] *adj* wooden.

Holz|fäller ['hɔltsfɛlər] *m* (-s/-) woodcutter, *Am. a.* lumberjack; **2ig** *adj* woody; **~kohle** *f* charcoal; **~schnitt** *m* woodcut; **~schuh** *m* clog; **~wolle** *f* wood-wool, *Am.* excelsior.

Honig ['ho:nɪç] *m* (-s/-e) honey.

Honorar [hono'ra:r] *n* (-s/-e) fee.

Hopfen ['hɔpfən] *m* (-s/*no pl*) hop.

hopsen ['hɔpsən] *v/i* hop, jump.

Hör|apparat ['hø:r?apa-'ra:t] *m* (-[e]s/-e) hearing aid; **2bar** *adj* audible.

horchen ['hɔrçən] *v/i* listen; eavesdrop.

Horde ['hɔrdə] *f* (-/-n) gang.

hören ['hø:rən] *v/t* hear; *Radio*: listen (in) to; *Vorlesung*: attend; *erfahren*: hear, learn; *v/i* hear (**von** from); *zuhören*: listen; **~n auf** listen to; **schwer ~n** be hard of hearing; **2r** *m* hearer; *Rundfunk*: listener(-in); *univ.* student; *teleph.* receiver.

Horizont [hori'tsɔnt] *m* (-[e]s/-e) horizon, skyline; **2al** [-'ta:l] *adj* horizontal.)

Horn [hɔrn] *n* (-[e]s/*ver*) horn.

Hörnchen ['hœrnçən] *n* (-s/-) croissant.

Hornhaut ['hɔrnhaut] *f* horny skin; *anat. Auge*: cornea.

Hornisse [hɔr'nɪsə] *f* (-/-n) hornet.

Horoskop [horo'sko:p] *n* (-s/-e) horoscope.

Hör|saal ['hø:rza:l] *m* (-[e]s/-*säle*) lecture-room (-hall, -theat're, *Am. -er*); **~spiel** *n* radio play; **~weite** *f*: **in ~** within earshot.

Hose

Hose ['ho:zə] f (-/-n) (e-e a pair of) trousers pl od. Am. pants pl.

Hosen|anzug ['ho:zən-ʔantsu:k] m (-[e]s/ᵘe) trouser od. pant suit; **~schlitz** m fly; **~tasche** f trouser-pocket; **~träger** pl (ein Paar a pair of) braces pl od. Am. suspenders pl.

Hospital [hɔspi'ta:l] n (-s/-e, ᵘer) hospital.

Hostess [hɔs'tɛs] f (-/-en) hostess.

Hostie ['hɔstiə] f (-/-n) eccl. the Host.

Hotel [ho'tɛl] n (-s/-s) hotel; **~führer** m hotel guide; **~halle** f hall, lobby, foyer; **~pension** f private hotel.

Hubraum ['hu:praum] m (-[e]s/ᵘe) cubic capacity.

hübsch [hypʃ] adj pretty, nice; Männer: good-looking, handsome.

Hubschrauber ['hu:pʃraubər] m (-s/-) helicopter.

Huf [hu:f] m (-[e]s/-e) hoof; **~eisen** n horseshoe.

Hüft|e ['hyftə] f (-/-n) hip; **~gelenk** n hip-joint; **~gürtel** m girdle.

Hügel ['hy:gəl] m (-s/-) hill; **2ig** adj hilly.

Huhn [hu:n] n (-[e]s/ᵘer) fowl, hen; junges: chicken.

Hühnchen ['hy:nçən] n (-s/-) chicken.

Hühner|auge ['hy:nər-ʔaugə] n (-s/-n) med. corn;

~stall m hen-house, hen-coop.

Hülle ['hylə] f (-/-n) cover (-ing), wrapper; Buch: jacket; Schirm: sheath; **2n** ['hylən] v/t wrap, cover.

Hülse ['hylzə] f (-/-n) Schote: pod; Getreide: husk; Geschoß: case; **~nfrüchte** pl pulse sg.

human [hu'ma:n] adj humane.

Hummel ['huməl] f (-/-n) bumble-bee.

Hummer ['humər] m (-s/-) lobster.

Humor [hu'mo:r] m (-s/no pl) humo(u)r; **~ist** [-mo-'rɪst] m (-en/-en) humorist; **2istisch** adj humorous.

humpeln ['humpəln] v/i limp.

Hund [hunt] m (-[e]s/-e) dog.

Hunde|hütte ['hundəhytə] f (-/-n) dog-kennel; **~kuchen** m dog-biscuit; **~leine** f lead, leash.

hundert ['hundərt] adj hundred; **2jahrfeier** f (-/-n) centenary, Am. a. centennial; **~ste** adj hundredth.

Hündin ['hyndɪn] f (-/-nen) bitch.

Hundstage ['huntsta:gə] pl dog-days pl.

Hüne ['hy:nə] m (-n/-n) giant.

Hunger ['huŋər] m (-s/no pl) hunger; **~ bekommen** get hungry; **~ ha-**

ben be *od.* feel hungry; **2n** ['hunərn] *v/i* go hungry; **~snot** *f* famine.

hungrig ['hungriç] *adj* hungry.

Hupe ['hu:pə] *f (-/-n) mot.* horn; **2n** *v/i* hoot.

hüpfen ['hypfən] *v/i* hop, skip.

Hürde ['hyrdə] *f (-/-n)* hurdle.

Hure ['hu:rə] *f (-/-n)* whore, prostitute.

huschen ['huʃən] *v/i* slip, dart; *kleines Tier:* scurry, scamper.

hüsteln ['hy:stəln] *v/i* cough slightly.

husten ['hu:stən] *v/i* cough; **2** *m (-s/-)* cough.

Hut [hu:t] *m (-[e]s/*²*e)* hat.

hüten ['hy:tən] *v/t* guard, protect; *Schafe etc.:* tend; **sich ~ vor** beware of.

Hütte ['hytə] *f (-/-n)* hut; cabin; *tech.* smelting works *sg.*

Hydrant [hy'drant] *m (-en/-en)* hydrant.

hydraulisch [hy'draʊlɪʃ] *adj* hydraulic.

Hygiene [hy'gie:nə] *f (-/no pl)* hygiene; **2isch** *adj* hygienic.

Hymne ['hymnə] *f (-/-n)* hymn.

Hypnose [hyp'no:zə] *f (-/-n)* hypnosis; **2tisieren** [-noti'zi:rən] *v/t* hypnotize.

Hypothek [hypo'te:k] *f (-/-en)* mortgage.

Hypothese [hypo'te:zə] *f (-/-n)* hypothesis.

Hysterie [hyste'ri:] *f (-/no pl)* hysteria; **2sch** [-'te:rɪʃ] *adj* hysterical.

I

ich [ɪç] *pers pron* I.

Ideal [ide'a:l] *n (-s/-e)* ideal; **2** *adj* ideal.

Idee [i'de:] *f (-/-n)* idea, notion.

identifi|zieren [identifi-'tsi:rən] *v/t* identify; **~sch** [i'dentɪʃ] *adj* identical; **2tät** [-ti'tɛ:t] *f (-/no pl)* identity.

Ideologie [ideolo'gi:] *f (-/-n)* ideology.

Idiot [i'dio:t] *m (-en/-en)* idiot; **2isch** *adj* idiotic.

Idol [i'do:l] *n (-s/-e)* idol.

Igel ['i:gəl] *m (-s/-)* hedgehog.

ignorieren [ɪgno'ri:rən] *v/t* ignore.

ihm [i:m] *pers pron* (to) him; (to) it.

ihn [i:n] *pers pron* him; it.

ihnen ['i:nən] *pers pron pl* (to) them; **2** *sg, pl* (to) you.

ihr [i:r] *pers pron* you; (to) her; *poss pron* her; *pl* their; **2** *sg, pl* your.

illegal ['ɪlega:l] *adj* illegal.

Illustrierte [ɪlus'tri:rtə] *f (-n/-n)* (illustrated) magazine.

Imbiß ['ɪmbɪs] *m (-sses/*

Imker

-sse) snack; ~**stube** f snack-bar.

Imker ['ɪmkər] m (-s/-) bee-keeper.

immer ['ɪmər] adv always; ~ **mehr** more and more; ~ **noch** still; ~ **wieder** again and again; **für** ~ for ever, for good; ~**zu** ['-'tsuː] adv all the time.

Immobilien [ɪmo'biːliən] pl immovables pl, real estate sg; ~**makler** m estate agent, Am. realtor.

immun [ɪ'muːn] adj immune.

Imperativ ['ɪmperatiːf] m (-s/-e) gr. imperative (mood).

Imperfekt ['ɪmperfɛkt] n (-s/-e) gr. imperfect (tense).

Imperialismus [ɪmperia-'lɪsmʊs] m (-/no pl) imperialism.

impf|en ['ɪmpfən] v/t inoculate; bsd. gegen Pocken: vaccinate; 2**schein** m certificate of vaccination of. inoculation; 2**stoff** m serum; vaccine; 2**ung** f inoculation; vaccination.

imponieren [ɪmpo'niː-rən] v/i: **j-m** ~ impress s.o.

Import [ɪm'pɔrt] m (-[e]s/-e) import(ation); 2**ieren** [-'tiːrən] v/t import.

imprägnieren [ɪmprɛ-'gniːrən] v/t waterproof.

impulsiv [ɪmpʊl'ziːf] adj impulsive.

imstande [ɪm'ʃtandə] adj: ~ **sein** be able.

in [ɪn] prp (dat, acc) räumlich: wohin?: in, at; innerhalb: within; wohin? into, in; ~ **der Schule** at school; ~ **die Schule** to school; zeitlich: in, at, during; within.

inbegriffen ['ɪnbəgrɪfən] included, inclusive (of).

indem [ɪn'deːm] cj whilst, while; Mittel: by ger.

Inder ['ɪndər] m (-s/-) Indian.

Indianer [ɪn'diːanər] m (-s/-) (Red) Indian.

Indikativ ['ɪndikatiːf] m (-s/-e) gr. indicative (mood).

indirekt [ɪndirɛkt] adj indirect.

indisch ['ɪndɪʃ] adj Indian.

individu|ell [ɪndivi'dʊɛl] adj individual; 2**um** [-'viː-duʊm] n (-s/-duen) individual.

Indizien [ɪn'diːtsiən] pl, ~**beweis** m circumstantial evidence.

Industri|alisierung [ɪn-dʊstriali'ziːrʊŋ] f (-/no pl) industrialization; ~**e** [ɪn-dʊs'triː] f (-/-n) industry; attr industrial.

ineinander [ɪn'ʔaɪ'nan-dər] adv into one another.

Infektion [ɪnfɛk'tsioːn] f (-/-en) infection; ~**s-krankheit** f infectious disease.

Infinitiv ['ɪnfinitiːf] m (-s/-e) gr. infinitive (mood).

infizieren [ɪnfi'tsiːrən] v/t

infect.

Inflation [ɪnfla'tsɪoːn] f (-/
-en) inflation.

infolge [ɪn'fɔlgə] prp (gen)
owing od. due to; **~des-
sen** [-'desən] cj conse-
quently.

Information [ɪnfɔrma-
'tsɪoːn] f (-/-en) information; **2ieren** [-'miːrən] v/t
inform.

Ingenieur [ɪnʒe'nɪøːr] m
(-s/-e) engineer.

Ingwer ['ɪŋvər] m (-s/no
pl) ginger.

Inhaber ['ɪnhaːbər] m (-s/
-) owner, proprietor; Wohnung: occupant; Laden:
keeper; Paß, Amt etc.:
holder.

Inhalt ['ɪnhalt] m (-[e]s/
-e) contents pl; **~sver-
zeichnis** n list (Buch:
table) of contents.

Initiative [initsɪa'tiːvə] f
(-/-n) initiative; **die ~ ergreifen** take the initiative.

Injektion [ɪnjɛk'tsɪoːn] f
(-/-en) injection.

inklusive [ɪnklu'ziːvə] prp
(gen) inclusive of; adv inclusive.

Inland ['ɪnlant] n (-[e]s/no
pl) home (country);
Landesinnere: inland.

inländisch ['ɪnlɛndɪʃ] adj
inland, home, domestic.

Inlett ['ɪnlɛt] n (-[e]s/-e)
Bett: tick.

inmitten [ɪn'mɪtən] prp
(gen) in the midst of.

innen ['ɪnən] adv inside,

within; **nach ~** inwards.

Innen|minister ['ɪnənmɪnɪstər] m (-s/-) Minister of
the Interior, Brit. Home
Secretary, Am. Secretary
of the Interior; **~politik** f
domestic policy; **~seite** f
inner side, inside; **~stadt**
f city (centre, Am. -er).

inner ['ɪnər] adj interior;
inner; med., pol. internal;
2e n (-r[e]n/no pl) interi-
or; **~halb** ['ɪnərhalp] prp
(gen) within; **~lich** adj inward; bsd. med. internal.

innig ['ɪnɪç] adj intimate,
close.

inoffiziell [ɪn²ɔfi'tsɪɛl]
adj unofficial.

Insasse ['ɪnzasə] m (-n/
-n) inmate; Fahrgast:
occupant, passenger.

Inschrift ['ɪnʃrɪft] f (-/
-en) inscription.

Insekt [ɪn'zɛkt] n (-[e]s/
-en) insect.

Insel ['ɪnzəl] f (-/-n) island.

Inserat [ɪnzə'raːt] n
(-[e]s/-e) advertisement,
colloq. ad; **2ieren** [-'riː-
rən] v/t, v/i advertise.

insgesamt [ɪnsgə'zamt]
adv altogether.

insofern ['ɪnzoːfɛrn] cj: ~
als in so far as.

Inspektion [ɪnspɛk-
'tsɪoːn] f (-/-en) inspection.

Installateur [ɪnstala-
'tøːr] m (-s/-e) plumber;
fitter; **2ieren** [-'liːrən] v/t
instal(l).

instand [ɪn'ʃtant] adv: ~ **halten** keep in good order; *tech.* maintain; ~ **setzen** repair.

Instinkt [ɪn'stɪŋkt] m (-[e]s/-e) instinct.

Institut [ɪnsti'tuːt] n (-[e]s/-e) institute.

Instruktion [ɪnstrʊk'tsioːn] f (-/-en) instruction.

Instrument [ɪnstru'mɛnt] n (-[e]s/-e) instrument.

Inszenierung [ɪnstse'niːrʊŋ] f (-/-en) *thea.* staging, production.

Intellektuelle [ɪntelek'tüɛlə] m, f (-n/-n) intellectual, highbrow.

intelligen|t [ɪnteli'gɛnt] adj intelligent; 2z [-'gɛnts] f (-/rare -en) intelligence.

Intendant [ɪnten'dant] m (-en/-en) director.

intensiv [ɪnten'ziːf] adj intensive, intense.

interess|ant [ɪntəre'sant] adj interesting; 2e [-'resə] n (-s/-n) interest (an, für in); 2ent [-'rɛsənt] m (-en/-en) interested person *od.* party; *econ.* prospective buyer; **~ieren** [-'siːrən] v/t interest (für in); **sich ~ieren für** be interested in.

Internat [ɪntər'naːt] n (-[e]s/-e) boarding-school.

international [ɪntərnatsio'naːl] adj international.

inter|pretieren [ɪntərpre'tiːrən] v/t interpret; 2**punktion** [ɪntərpʊŋk'tsioːn] f (-/-en) punctuation; 2**view** ['ɪntərvjuː] n (-s/-s) interview.

intim [ɪn'tiːm] adj intimate.

intolerant ['ɪntolerant] adj intolerant.

intransitiv ['ɪntranzitiːf] adj *gr.* intransitive.

Invalide [ɪnva'liːdə] m (-n/-n) invalid.

Invasion [ɪnva'zioːn] f (-/-en) invasion.

invest|ieren [ɪnvɛs'tiːrən] v/t invest; 2**ition** [-ti'tsioːn] f (-/-en) investment.

inwie|fern [ɪnvi'fɛrn] adv, cj in what way *od.* respect; **~weit** [-'vait] adv, cj how far, to what extent.

inzwischen [ɪn'tsvɪʃən] adv in the meantime, meanwhile.

irdisch ['ɪrdɪʃ] adj earthly; worldly; *sterblich:* mortal.

Ire ['iːrə] m (-n/-n) Irishman; **die ~n** pl the Irish pl.

irgend ['ɪrgənt] adv in Zssg: some...; any...; ~**ein(e)** indef pron some (-one); any(one); **~einer** indef pron s. ~ **jemand;** ~ **etwas** something; anything; ~ **jemand** someone; anyone; **~wann** adv some time (or other); **~wie** adv somehow; anyhow; **~wo** adv somewhere; anywhere.

irisch ['iːrɪʃ] adj Irish.

Iron|ie [iro'niː] f (-/-n) irony; **2isch** [i'roːnɪʃ] adj ironic(al).

irre ['ɪrə] adj confused; mad, insane; 2 m, f (-n/-n) lunatic; mental patient; ~**führen** v/t fig. mislead; ~**n** ['ɪrən] v/i err; räumlich: wander; **sich ~n** v/refl be mistaken (**in** j-m: in, et.: about); be wrong.

irritieren [ɪri'tiːrən] v/t irritate; confuse.

Irrsinn ['ɪrzɪn] m (-[e]s/no pl) insanity, madness; **2ig** adj insane, mad.

Irr|tum ['ɪrtuːm] m (-s/ ⁓er) error, mistake; **im**

---

ja [jaː] yes; **wenn ~** if so.

Jacht [jaxt] f (-/-en) yacht.

Jacke ['jakə] f (-/-n)

Jackett [ʒa'kɛt] n (-s/-s, -e) jacket.

Jagd [jaːkt] f (-/-en) hunt (-ing); chase; Verfolgung: chase; s. **Jagdrevier;** ~**aufseher** m gamekeeper, Am. game warden; ~**hund** m hound; ~**revier** n hunting-ground, shoot; ~**schein** m shooting licen‹ce, Am. -se.

jagen ['jaːgən] v/t, v/i hunt; rasen: rush, dash; verfolgen: chase.

Jäger ['jɛːgər] m (-s/-) hunter.

Jaguar ['jaːgŭaːr] m (-s/ -e) jaguar.

---

jäh [jɛː] adj precipitous, steep; plötzlich: sudden, abrupt.

Jahr [jaːr] n (-[e]s/-e) year; **seit ~en** for years; **mit 18 ~en, im Alter von 18 ~en** at (the age of) eighteen; **2elang** adv for years; adj: **2elange Erfahrung** (many) years of experience.

Jahres|bericht ['jaːrəsbərɪçt] m (-[e]s/-e) annual report; ~**tag** m anniversary; ~**zahl** f date, year; ~**zeit** f season, time of the year.

Jahr|gang ['jaːrgaŋ] m (-[e]s/⁓e) age-group; Wein: vintage; 2**hundert** [-'hundərt] n (-s/-e) century.

...jährig [-'jɛ:rɪç] *in Zssgn:* ...-year-old, of ... (years).

jährlich ['jɛ:rlɪç] *adj* annual, yearly; *adv* every year.

Jahr|markt ['ja:rmarkt] *m* (-[e]s/=e) fair; **~zehnt** [-'tse:nt] *n* (-[e]s/-e) decade.

jähzornig ['jɛ:tsɔrnɪç] *adj* hot-tempered.

Jalousie [ʒalu'zi:] *f* (-/-n) (Venetian) blind, *Am. a.* window shade.

Jammer ['jamər] *m* (-s/*no pl*): **es ist ein ~** it is a pity.

jämmerlich ['jɛmərlɪç] *adj* miserable, wretched; *adv* piteously.

jammern ['jamərn] *v/i* lament (**um** for, over); moan; *greinen:* whine.

Januar ['janua:r] *m* (-s/*no pl*) January.

Japan|er [ja'pa:nər] *m* (-s/-) Japanese; **die ~er** *pl* the Japanese *pl;* **Qisch** *adj* Japanese.

jäten ['jɛ:tən] *v/t* weed.

Jauche ['jauxə] *f* (-/-n) liquid manure.

jawohl [ja'vo:l] *adv* yes; certainly.

je [je:] *adv, cj* ever; at any time; **~ zwei** two each; **sie bekamen ~ zwei Äpfel** they received two apples each; **~ nachdem** it depends; **~ Pfund** a pound; **~ mehr, desto besser** the more the better; **~ länger, ~ lieber** the longer the better.

jed|er ['je:dər], **~e** [-ə], **~es** [-əs] *indef pron* every; **~er beliebige:** any; **~er einzelne:** each; **von zweien:** either; **~en zweiten Tag** every other day; **~enfalls** *adv* at all events, in any case; **~ermann** *indef pron* everyone, everybody; **~erzeit** ['je:dər'tsaɪt] *adv* at any time; **~esmal** [-'ma:l] *adv* each *od.* every time.

jedoch [je'dɔx] *cj* however, yet.

jemals ['je:ma:ls] *adv* ever; at any time.

jemand ['je:mant] *indef pron* someone, somebody; *fragend:* somebody; *verneint:* anyone, anybody.

jen|er ['je:nər], **~e** [-ə], **~es** [-əs] *dem pron* that (one); **~e** *pl* those *pl.*

jenseits ['je:nzaɪts, 'jɛn-] *prp* (*gen*) on the other side of; beyond, across; *adv:* **~ von** beyond.

jetzt [jɛtst] *adv* now, at present; **bis ~** until now, so far; **erst ~** only now; **von ~ an** from now on.

jeweils ['je:vaɪls] *adv* at a time.

Jockei ['dʒɔke] *m* (-s/-s) jockey.

Jod [jo:t] *n* (-[e]s/*no pl*) iodine.

Joghurt ['jo:gʊrt] *m, n* (-[s]/-[s]) yog(hur)t.

Johannisbeere [jo'hanɪsbe:rə] *f* (-/-n) currant.

Journalist [ʒʊrna'lɪst] *m*

(-en/-en) journalist.

jubeln ['ju:bəln] *v/i* rejoice, exult.

Jubiläum [jubi'lɛ:um] *n* (-s/-läen) anniversary.

jucken ['jokən] *v/i* itch; 2**reiz** *m* itch.

Jude ['ju:də] *m* (-n/-n) Jew.

jüdisch ['jy:dɪʃ] *adj* Jewish.

Jugend ['ju:gənt] *f* (-/no *pl*) youth; young people *pl*; ~**amt** *n* youth welfare department; ~**fürsorge** *f* youth welfare; ~**heim** *n* youth centre; *Am.* -er; ~**herberge** *f* youth hostel; ~**kriminalität** [-krimi'nali:tɛ:t] *f* (-/no *pl*) juvenile delinquency; 2**lich** *adj* youthful, young; ~**liche** *m, f* (-n/-n) youth, teenager, adolescent.

Jugoslaw|e [jugo'sla:və] *m* (-n/-n) Yugoslav; 2**isch** *adj* Yugoslav.

Juli ['ju:li] *m* (-[s]/no *pl*) July.

jung [joŋ] *adj* young.

Junge[1] ['joŋə] *m* (-n/-n) boy, youngster, lad; *Karten:* knave, jack.

Junge[2] *n* (-n/-n) *Hund:* puppy; *Katze:* kitten; *Fuchs, Bär etc.:* cub.

jungenhaft ['joŋənhaft] *adj* boyish.

jünger ['jyŋər] *adj* younger, junior; 2 *m* (-s/-) disciple.

Jung|fer ['joŋfər] *f* (-/-n): **alte** ~ old maid, spinster; ~**frau** *f* virgin; young **geselle** *m* bachelor; ~**gesellin** *f* (-/-nen) bachelor girl.

Jüngling ['jyŋlɪŋ] *m* (-s/-e) youth, young man.

jüngst [jyŋst] *adj* youngest; *Zeit:* (most) recent, latest; **das** 2**e Gericht, der** 2**e Tag** the Last Judg(e)ment, the Day of Judg(e)ment; *adv* recently, lately.

Juni ['ju:ni] *m* (-[s]/no *pl*) June.

junior ['ju:niɔr] *adj* junior.

Jurist [ju'rɪst] *m* (-en/-en) lawyer, jurist; law-student.

Jury [ʒy'ri:, 'ʒy:ri] *f* (-/-s) jury.

Justiz [jos'ti:ts] *f* (-/no *pl*) (administration of) justice; ~**minister** *m* Minister of Justice; *Brit.* Lord Chancellor, *Am.* Attorney General; ~**ministerium** *n* Ministry of Justice; *Am.* Department of Justice.

Juwel|en [juve:lən] *pl* jewel(le)ry; ~**ier** [-ve'li:r] *m* (-s/-e) jewel(l)er.

Jux [joks] *m* (-es/-e) *colloq.* joke.

K

Kabel ['ka:bəl] *n* (-s/-) cable.

Kabeljau ['ka:bəljau] *m* (-s/-e, -s) cod(fish).

Kabine

Kabine [ka'bi:nə] *f* (-/-n) cabin; *Friseur etc.*: cubicle; *Seilbahn*: car; *Fahrstuhl*: cage.

Kabinett [kabi'nɛt] *n* (-s/-e) *pol.* cabinet, government.

Kabriolett [kabrio'lɛt] *n* (-s/-s) cabriolet, convertible.

Kachel ['kaxəl] *f* (-/-n) tile.

Kadaver [ka'da:vər] *m* (-s/-) carcass.

Käfer ['kɛ:fər] *m* (-s/-) beetle.

Kaffee ['kafe] *m* (-s/-s) coffee; **~satz** *m* (-es/no *pl*) coffee-grounds *pl*.

Käfig ['kɛ:fɪç] *m* (-s/-e) cage.

kahl [ka:l] *adj Mensch*: bald; bare, naked.

Kahn [ka:n] *m* (-[e]s/-e) boat; *Last2*: barge.

Kai [kaı] *m* (-s/-e, -s) quay, wharf.

Kaiser ['kaızər] *m* (-s/-) emperor.

Kajüte [ka'jy:tə] *f* (-/-n) *mar.* cabin.

Kakao [ka'ka:o] *m* (-s/-s) cocoa; *bot.* cacao.

Kakt|ee [kak'te:(ə)] *f* (-/ -n), **~us** ['kaktus] *m* (-/ -teen) cactus.

Kalb [kalp] *n* (-[e]s/-er) calf; *Fleisch* *n* veal; **~sbraten** *m* roast veal.

Kalender [ka'lɛndər] *m* (-s/-) calendar.

Kalk [kalk] *m* (-[e]s/-e) lime.

Kalorie [kalo'ri:] *f* (-/-n) calorie.

kalt [kalt] *adj* cold; *mir ist* ~ I am cold; **~blütig** ['-bly:tɪç] *adj* cold-blooded.

Kälte ['kɛltə] *f* (-/no *pl*) cold(ness); *s.* **Grad**; **~welle** *f* cold spell *od.* wave.

Kamel [ka'me:l] *n* (-s/-e) camel.

Kamera ['kamera] *f* (-/-s) camera.

Kamerad [kamə'ra:t] *m* (-en/-en) comrade, companion, *colloq.* pal; **~schaft** *f* comradeship.

Kamille [ka'mɪlə] *f* (-/-n) camomile.

Kamin [ka'mi:n] *m* (-s/-e) chimney; fireplace; **~sims** [-zɪms] *m, n* (-es/-e) mantelpiece.

Kamm [kam] *m* (-[e]s/-e) comb; *Hahn*: comb, crest; *Welle*: crest; *Gebirge*: ridge.

kämmen ['kɛmən] *v/t* comb.

Kammer ['kamər] *f* (-/-n) (small) room; **~musik** *f* chamber music.

Kampagne [kam'panjə] *f* (-/-n) campaign.

Kampf [kampf] *m* (-[e]s/ **-e**) combat, fight (*a. fig.*); struggle (*a. fig.*).

kämpfen ['kɛmpfən] *v/i* fight, struggle; **2r** *m* fighter.

Kampfrichter ['kampf- rıçtər] *m* (-s/-) *sp.* judge.

Kanal [ka'na:l] *m* (-s/⁀e)
künstlicher: canal; *natür-
licher:* channel (*a. tech.,
fig.*); *Abzug:* sewer, drain;
~isation [-naliza'tsjo:n] *f*
(-/-en) *Flüsse:* canaliza-
tion; *Städte etc.:* sewerage;
2isieren [-'zi:rən] *v/t*
canalize; sewer.

Kanarienvogel [ka'na:-
riənfo:gəl] *m* (-s/⁀) ca-
nary(-bird).

Kandid|at [kandi'da:t] *m*
(-en/-en) candidate;
2ieren [-'di:rən] *v/i* be a
candidate.

kandiert [kan'di:rt] *adj*
candied, crystallized.

Känguruh ['kɛŋguru] *m*
(-s/-s) kangaroo.

Kaninchen [ka'ni:nçən] *n*
(-s/-) rabbit.

Kanister [ka'nistər] *m* (-s/
-) can.

Kanne ['kanə] *f* (-/-n)
Kaffee2, Tee2: pot; *Milch2
etc.:* can.

Kanon ['ka:nɔn] *m* (-s/-s)
mus. round, catch.

Kanone [ka'no:nə] *f* (-/-n)
cannon, gun.

Kante ['kantə] *f* (-/-n)
edge.

Kantine [kan'ti:nə] *f* (-/
-n) canteen.

Kanu ['ka:nu] *n* (-s/-s)
canoe.

Kanzel ['kantsəl] *f* (-/-n)
eccl. pulpit; *aer.* cockpit.

Kanzler ['kantslər] *m* (-s/
-) chancellor.

Kap [kap] *n* (-s/-s) cape,
headland.

Kapazität [kapatsi'tɛ:t] *f*
(-/-en) capacity; *fig.* authority.

Kapelle [ka'pɛlə] *f* (-/-n)
eccl. chapel; *mus.* band.

Kapital [kapi'ta:l] *n* (-s/
-e, -ien) capital; **~an-
lage** *f* investment; **~is-
mus** [-ta'lısmʊs] *m* (-/no
pl) capitalism; **~ist** [-ta-
'lıst] *m* (-en/-en) capital-
ist; **~verbrechen**
['-ta:l-] *n* capital crime.

Kapitän [kapi'tɛ:n] *m* (-s/
-e) captain.

Kapitel [ka'pıtəl] *n* (-s/-)
chapter.

kapitulieren [kapitu'li:-
rən] *v/i* surrender.

Kaplan [ka'pla:n] *m* (-s/
⁀e) chaplain.

Kappe ['kapə] *f* (-/-n) cap.

Kapsel ['kapsəl] *f* (-/-n)
capsule; case.

kaputt [ka'pʊt] *adj colloq.*
broken; *Lift etc.:* out of
order; *erschöpft:* tired od.
fagged (out); **~gehen** *v/i*
(*irr*) *colloq.* break;
~machen *v/t colloq.*
break; ruin.

Kapuze [ka'pu:tsə] *f* (-/
-n) hood; *eccl.* cowl.

Karaffe [ka'rafə] *f* (-/-n)
carafe; *Wein, Likör:* de-
canter.

Karawane [kara'va:nə] *f*
(-/-n) caravan.

Kardinal [kardi'na:l] *m*
(-s/⁀e) cardinal; **~zahl** *f*
cardinal number.

Karfreitag [ka:r'fraita:k]
m (-[e]s/-e) Good Friday.

kariert [ka'ri:rt] *adj* check(ed), chequered, *Am.* checkered.

Karies ['ka:rĭɛs] *f* (*-/no pl*) caries.

Karikatur [karika'tu:r] *f* (*-/-en*) caricature, cartoon.

Karneval ['karnəval] *m* (*-s/-e, -s*) carnival.

Karo ['ka:ro] *n* (*-s/-s*) square, check; *Karten:* diamond(s *pl*).

Karosserie [karɔsə'ri:] *f* (*-/-n*) *mot.* body.

Karotte [ka'rɔtə] *f* (*-/-n*) carrot.

Karpfen ['karpfən] *m* (*-s/-*) carp.

Karre ['karə] *f* (*-/-n*), **~n** *m* (*-s/-*) cart.

Karriere [ka'rĭɛ:rə] *f* (*-/-n*) career.

Karte ['kartə] *f* (*-/-n*) card.

Kartei [kar'taɪ] *f* (*-/-en*) card-index; file; **~karte** *f* index-card, filing-card.

Kartoffel [kar'tɔfəl] *f* (*-/-n*) potato; **~brei** *m* mashed potatoes *pl.*

Karton [kar'tō:, -'to:n] *m* (*-s/-s*) *Pappe:* cardboard, pasteboard; *Schachtel:* cardboard box, carton.

Karussell [karu'sɛl] *n* (*-s/-s, -e*) roundabout, merry-go-round, *Am. a.* car(r)ousel.

Karwoche ['ka:rvɔxə] *f* (*-/no pl*) Holy *od.* Passion Week.

Käse ['kɛ:zə] *m* (*-s/-*) cheese.

Kaserne [ka'zɛrnə] *f* (*-/-n*) barracks *sg.*

Kasperle ['kaspərlə] *n*, *m* (*-s/-*) Punch; **~theater** *n* Punch and Judy show.

Kasse ['kasə] *f* (*-/-n*) cash-box; *Laden2:* cash register, till; *Bank:* cash-desk, pay-desk; *thea. etc.:* box-office.

Kassen|arzt ['kasən-?artst] *m* (*-es/ᵛe*) appr. panel doctor; **~patient** *m* appr. panel patient; **~zettel** *m* sales slip (*Am.* check).

Kassette [ka'sɛtə] *f* (*-/-n*) *phot., tech.* cassette; *Geld2:* box; *Schmuck2:* case; **~nfilm** *m* cartridge film.

kassieren [ka'si:rən] *v/t, v/i* take (the money); *Beitrag:* collect; **2r(in** *f*) *m* (*-s/-* [*-nen*]) cashier; *Bank:* a. teller; collector.

Kastanie [kas'ta:nĭə] *f* (*-/-n*) chestnut.

Kästchen ['kɛstçən] *n* (*-s/-*) small box *od.* case; casket.

Kasten ['kastən] *m* (*-s/ᵘ*) box; case.

Kasus ['ka:zʊs] *m* (*-/-*) *gr.* case.

Katalog [kata'lo:k] *m* (*-[e]s/-e*) catalog(ue).

Katarrh [ka'ta(:)r] *m* (*-s/-e*) cold, catarrh.

Katastrophe [kata'stro:fə] *f* (*-/-n*) disaster.

Kategorie [katego'ri:] *f* (*-/-n*) category.

Kater ['ka:tər] *m* (*-s/-*) male cat, tomcat; *colloq.* s.

Katzenjammer.

Kathedrale [kate'dra:lə] f (-/-n) cathedral.

Katholik [kato'li:k] m (-en/-en) Catholic; **2sch** [-'to:lɪʃ] adj Catholic.

Katze ['katsə] f (-/-n) cat; **~njammer** [-jamər] m (-s/no pl) colloq. hangover.

kauen ['kauən] v/t chew.

kauern ['kauərn] v/i crouch, squat.

Kauf [kauf] m (-[e]s/-e) purchase; **günstiger ~** bargain; **2en** ['kaufən] v/t, v/i buy; **2er** m (-s/-) buyer; customer.

Käufer ['kɔyfər] m (-s/-) buyer; customer.

Kaufhaus ['kaufhaus] n (-es/-er) department store.

käuflich ['kɔyflɪç] adj fig. venal.

Kaufmann ['kaufman] m (-[e]s/-leute) businessman; merchant; shopkeeper, B. grocer, Am. a. storekeeper.

Kaugummi ['kaugumi] m, n (-s/-[s]) chewing-gum.

kaum [kaum] adv, cj hardly, scarcely.

Kaution [kau'tsɪo:n] f (-/-en) security; jur. bail.

Kaviar ['ka:vɪar] m (-s/-e) caviar(e).

keck [kɛk] adj bold; saucy, cheeky.

Kegel ['ke:gəl] m (-s/-) Spiel: skittle, pin; math., tech. cone; **~bahn** f skittle (Am. bowling) alley; **2förmig** [-fœrmɪç] adj con-

ic(al), cone-shaped; **2n** ['ke:gəln] v/i play (at) skittles od. ninepins, Am. bowl.

Kehle ['ke:lə] f (-/-n) throat; **~kopf** m larynx.

Kehr|e ['ke:rə] f (-/-n) (sharp) bend od. turn; **2en** ['ke:rən] v/t, v/i sweep, brush; **~icht** m, n (-s/no pl) sweepings pl. (sold.).

keifen ['kaifən] v/i nag, scold.

Keil [kail] m (-[e]s/-e) wedge; **~er** m (-s/-) wild boar.

Keim [kaim] m (-[e]s/-e) germ; **2en** ['kaimən] v/i Samen: germinate; sprießen: sprout; **2frei** adj sterilized, sterile.

kein [kain] indef pron: **~(e)** no; **~e(r, -s)** none; no one, nobody; **~er von beiden** neither (of the two); **~er von uns** none of us; **~esfalls** [-fals], **~eswegs** [-ve:ks] adv not at all; **~mal** [-ma:l] adv not once.

Keks [ke:ks] m, n (-[es]/-[e]) biscuit, Am. cooky; ungesüßt: cracker.

Kelch [kɛlç] m (-[e]s/-e) cup; bot. calyx.

Kelle ['kɛlə] f (-/-n) Suppen2: ladle; Maurer2: trowel.

Keller ['kɛlər] m (-s/-) cellar; **~geschoß** n basement.

Kellner ['kɛlnər] m (-s/-) waiter; **~in** f (-/-nen) waitress.

kennlen ['kɛnən] v/t (irr) know, be acquainted with; **~enlernen** [-lɛrnən] v/t get od. come to know; j-n: meet s.o.; **2er m** (-s/-) expert; Kunst2, Wein2: connoisseur; **2tnis f** (-/-se) knowledge; **2zeichen n** mark, sign; mot. registration (number), Am. license number; **~zeichnen** v/t mark; fig. characterize.

kentern ['kɛntərn] v/i capsize.

Keramik [ke'raːmɪk] f (-/ -en) ceramics sg.

Kerbe ['kɛrbə] f (-/-n) notch.

Kerl [kɛrl] m (-[e]s/-e) colloq. chap, fellow, Am. guy.

Kern [kɛrn] m (-[e]s/-e) Nuß: kernel; Kirsche etc.: stone, Am. pit; Orange, Apfel etc.: pip; Erd2: core; phys. nucleus; fig. core, heart; **Kern...** s.a. **Atom...;** **~energie** f nuclear energy; **2gesund** adj thoroughly healthy; **~gehäuse n** core; **~spaltung** [-ʃpaltuŋ] f (-/-en) nuclear fission.

Kerze ['kɛrtsə] f (-/-n) candle.

Kessel ['kɛsəl] m (-s/-) kettle; boiler.

Kette ['kɛtə] f (-/-n) chain; Berg2: a. range; Hals2: necklace.

Kettenlraucher m chainsmoker; **~reaktion** f chain reaction.

keuchlen ['kɔyçən] v/i pant, gasp; **2husten m** (w)hooping cough.

Keule ['kɔylə] f (-/-n) club; Fleisch: leg.

kichern ['kɪçərn] v/i giggle, titter.

Kiefer¹ ['kiːfər] m (-s/-) jaw(-bone).

Kiefer² f (-/-n) bot. pine.

Kiel [kiːl] m (-[e]s/-e) mar. keel.

Kieme ['kiːmə] f (-/-n) zo. gill.

Kies [kiːs] m (-es/-e) gravel; **~el** ['kiːzəl] m (-s/ -) pebble.

Kilo ['kiːlo] n (-s/-[s]), **~gramm** [kilo'gram] n (-s/-e, -) kilogram(me); **~meter** [-'meːtər] m kilomet|re, Am. -er; **~watt** ['vat] n kilowatt.

Kind [kɪnt] n (-[e]s/-er) child; Klein2: baby.

Kinderlarzt ['kɪndər-ʔartst] m (-es/ˀe) p(a)ediatrician; **~bett n** Gitter2: cot, Am. crib; **~garten m** kindergarten, day nursery; **~lähmung** [-lɛːmuŋ] f polio(myelitis); **2los** adj childless; **~mädchen n** nurse; **~wagen m** perambulator, colloq. pram, Am. baby carriage; **~zimmer n** nursery.

Kindlheit ['kɪnthaɪt] f (-/ no pl) childhood; **2isch** adj childish; **2lich** adj childlike.

Kinn [kɪn] n (-[e]s/-e)

chin.

Kino ['ki:no] *n* (-s/-s) cinema, *colloq.* the pictures *pl*, *Am.* motion-picture theater, *colloq.* the movies *pl*.

Kippe ['kɪpə] *f* (-/-n) *colloq.* stub, *Am. a.* butt; **2n** ['kɪpən] *v/i, v/t* tip (over); tilt.

Kirche ['kɪrçə] *f* (-/-n) church.

Kirchen|gemeinde *f* parish; **~schiff** *n* nave; **~stuhl** *m* pew.

Kirch|gänger ['kɪrç-gɛŋər] *m* (-s/-) churchgoer; **2lich** *adj* church; **~turm** *m* steeple, *ohne Spitze:* church-tower.

Kirsche ['kɪrʃə] *f* (-/-n) cherry.

Kissen ['kɪsən] *n* (-s/-) cushion; *Kopf2:* pillow.

Kiste ['kɪstə] *f* (-/-n) box, chest; *Latten2:* crate.

Kitsch [kɪtʃ] *m* (-es/*no pl*) (sentimental) rubbish, trash.

Kitt [kɪt] *m* (-[e]s/-e) cement; *Glaser2:* putty.

Kittel ['kɪtəl] *m* (-s/-) smock, overall; *Arzt2:* (white) coat.

kitten ['kɪtən] *v/t* cement; putty.

kitzel|n ['kɪtsəln] *v/t* tickle; **~(e)lig** *adj* ticklish (*a. fig.*).

klaffen ['klafən] gape, yawn.

kläffen ['klɛfən] *v/i* yap, yelp.

Klage ['kla:gə] *f* (-/-n)

---

complaint; *Weh2:* lament; *jur.* action, suit; **2n** ['kla:-gən] *v/i* complain; *jur.* take legal action.

Kläger ['klɛ:gər] *m* (-s/-) *jur.* plaintiff.

kläglich ['klɛ:klɪç] *adj* pitiful, piteous; miserable.

klamm [klam] *adj Hände etc.:* numb.

Klamm *f* (-/-en) ravine, gorge.

Klammer ['klamər] *f* (-/-n) clamp, cramp; *Büro2:* (paper-)clip; *Wäsche2:* (clothes-)peg; *typ.* bracket, *runde: a.* parenthesis; **2n** ['klamərn] *v/refl:* **sich ~ an** cling to (*a. fig.*).

Klang [klaŋ] *m* (-[e]s/⁻e) sound; ringing.

Klappe ['klapə] *f* (-/-n) flap; **2n** ['klapən] *v/t:* **nach oben ~** tip up; **nach unten ~** lower, put down; *v/i* click, bang; *colloq.* come off well.

Klapper ['klapər] *f* (-/-n) rattle; **2n** ['klapərn] *v/i* clatter, rattle (**mit et.** s.th.); **~schlange** *f* rattlesnake.

Klapp|messer ['klapme-sər] *n* (-s/-) clasp-knife, jack-knife; **~sitz** *m* tip-up seat; **~stuhl** *m* folding chair. [slap.]

Klaps [klaps] *m* (-es/-e)

klar [kla:r] *adj* clear; bright; plain; *offenkundig:* evident.

klären ['klɛ:rən] *v/t* clarify; *fig.* clear up.

Klasse

Klasse ['klasə] f (-/-n) class; Schul2: class, form, Am. a. grade; **~nzimmer** n classroom, schoolroom.

klassisch ['klasɪʃ] adj classic(al).

Klatsch [klatʃ] m (-es/no pl) fig. colloq. gossip; **2en** ['klatʃən] v/t: **Beifall ~** applaud (**j-m** s.o.); v/i splash; applaud, clap; colloq. gossip.

Klaue ['klauə] f (-/-n) claw; fig. clutch.

Klavier [kla'vi:r] n (-s/-e) piano.

kleb|en ['kle:bən] v/t glue, paste; stick; v/i stick, adhere (**an** to); **~end** adj adhesive; **~rig** adj sticky; **2stoff** m adhesive.

Klee [kle:] m (-s/no pl) clover, trefoil.

Kleid [klaɪt] n (-[e]s/-er) dress, frock; gown; **2en** ['klaɪdən] v/t: **j-n ~** suit od. become s.o.; **sich ~** dress (o.s.).

Kleider ['klaɪdər] pl clothes pl; **~bügel** m coathanger; **~bürste** f clothes-brush; **~haken** m clothes-peg; **~schrank** m wardrobe.

Kleidung ['klaɪduŋ] f (-/no pl) clothes pl.

klein [klaɪn] adj little (nur attr); small; **2bildkamera** f miniature camera; **2bus** m minibus; **2geld** n (-[e]s/no pl) (small) change; **2igkeit** ['klaɪnɪçkaɪt] f (-/-en) trifle;

2kind n infant, baby; **~laut** adj subdued; **~lich** adj narrow-minded; geizig: mean; **2stadt** f small od. country town; **~städtisch** adj small-town, provincial; **2wagen** m small car, minicar.

Klemme ['klemə] f (-/-n) tech. clamp; Haar: (hair) grip, Am. bobby pin; **in der ~ sitzen** colloq. be in a jam; **2n** ['klemən] v/t od. v/i stick; **sich die Finger ~** v/t pinch od. nip one's fingers.

Klempner ['klempnər] m (-s/-) plumber.

Klette ['klɛtə] f (-/-n) bot. bur(r).

klettern ['klɛtərn] v/i climb.

Klient [kli'ɛnt] m (-en/-en) client.

Klima ['kli:ma] n (-s/-s, -te) climate; **~anlage** f: **mit ~** air-conditioned.

klimpern ['klɪmpərn] v/i jingle; mus. strum.

Klinge ['klɪŋə] f (-/-n) blade.

Klingel ['klɪŋəl] f (-/-n) bell; **~knopf** m bell-push; **2n** ['klɪŋəln] v/i ring (the bell).

klingen ['klɪŋən] v/i (irr) sound; ring.

Klinik ['kli:nɪk] f (-/-en) hospital, clinic.

Klinke ['klɪŋkə] f (-/-n) (door)handle.

Klippe ['klɪpə] f (-/-n) cliff, crag.

klirren ['klɪrən] *v/i Kette:* clank, jangle; *Schlüssel:* jingle; *Gläser, Münzen:* clink, chink.

klobig ['klo:bɪç] *adj* clumsy.

klopfen ['klɔpfən] *v/i, v/t* beat; knock; *auf die Schulter:* tap; *es klopft* there's a knock at the door.

Klops [klɔps] *m* (-es/-e) meatball.

Klosett [klo'zɛt] *n* (-s/-s, -e) lavatory, (water-)closet, W.C., toilet; **~papier** *n* toilet-paper.

Kloß [klo:s] *m* (-es/ᵕe) dumpling; *fig.* lump.

Kloster ['klo:stər] *n* (-s/ᵕ) cloister; *Mönchs2:* monastery; *Nonnen2:* convent, nunnery.

Klotz [klɔts] *m* (-es/ᵕe) block, log.

Klub [klʊp] *m* (-s/-s) club.

Kluft [klʊft] *f* (-/ᵕe) cleft; chasm (*a. fig.*).

klug [klu:k] *adj* clever; intelligent.

Klumpen ['klʊmpən] *m* (-s/-) lump; *Erd2 etc.:* clod.

knabbern ['knabərn] *v/i* nibble, gnaw.

Knabe ['kna:bə] *m* (-n/-n) boy, lad.

knacken ['knakən] *v/t, v/i* crack.

Knall [knal] *m* (-[e]s/-e) crack; bang; *Waffe:* report; **2en** ['knalən] *v/i* crack; bang; *Korken:* pop.

knapp [knap] *adj* tight;

spärlich: scanty; *Stil:* concise; *Vorsprung, Sieg:* narrow; *Zeit:* short; **~ werden** run short.

knarren ['knarən] *v/i* creak.

knattern ['knatərn] *v/i* rattle, roar.

Knäuel ['knɔyəl] *m, n* (-s/ -) ball.

Knauf [knauf] *m* (-[e]s/ᵕe) knob.

Knebel ['kne:bəl] *m* (-s/-) gag; **2n** *v/t* gag.

kneifen ['knaifən] *v/t* (*irr*) pinch; **2zange** *f* (-e-e) a pair of) pincers *pl.*

Kneipe ['knaipə] *f* (-/-) *colloq.* pub, local.

kneten ['kne:tən] *v/t* knead.

Knick [knɪk] *m* (-[e]s/-e) fold, crease; *Kurve:* bend; **2en** *v/t* fold, crease; bend; *brechen:* break.

Knicks [knɪks] *m* (-es/-e) curts(e)y; **e-n ~ machen = 2en** ['knɪksən] *v/i* (drop a) curts(e)y (**vor** to).

Knie [kni:] *n* (-s/-) knee; **2n** ['kni:ən] *v/i* kneel; **~scheibe** *f* knee-cap; **~strumpf** *m* knee-length sock.

Kniff [knɪf] *m* (-[e]s/-e) crease, fold; *fig.* trick, knack.

knipsen ['knɪpsən] *v/t, v/i* *colloq.* clip, punch; *phot.* take a snapshot (of).

Knirps [knɪrps] *m* (-es/-e) little chap.

knirschen ['knɪrʃən] *v/i*

crunch; **mit den Zähnen** ~ grind one's teeth.

knistern ['knɪstərn] *v/i* crackle; *Seide etc.*: rustle.

knittern ['knɪtərn] *v/t, v/i* crease, wrinkle.

Knoblauch ['kno:plaux] *m* (-[e]s/*no pl*) garlic.

Knöchel ['knœçəl] *m* (-s/-) *Fuß*: ankle; *Finger*: knuckle.

Knoch|en ['knɔxən] *m* (-s/-) bone; **~enbruch** *m* fracture; **2ig** ['knɔxɪç] *adj* bony.

Knödel ['knø:dəl] *m* (-s/-) dumpling.

Knolle ['knɔlə] *f* (-/-n) tuber; *Zwiebel*: bulb.

Knopf [knɔpf] *m* (-[e]s/*ϋe*) button.

knöpfen ['knœpfən] *v/t* button.

Knopfloch ['knɔpflɔx] *n* (-[e]s/*ϋer*) buttonhole.

Knorpel ['knɔrpəl] *m* (-s/-) cartilage, gristle.

Knospe ['knɔspə] *f* (-/-n) bud; **2n** ['knɔspən] *v/i* bud.

Knoten ['kno:tən] *m* (-s/-) knot; **2** *v/t* knot; **~punkt** *m* rail. junction.

knüpfen ['knʏpfən] *v/t* tie, knot; *Bedingungen*: attach (**an** to).

Knüppel ['knʏpəl] *m* (-s/-) cudgel.

knurren ['knʊrən] *v/i* growl; snarl; *Magen*: rumble.

knusprig ['knʊsprɪç] *adj* crisp, crunchy.

Koch [kɔx] *m* (-[e]s/*ϋe*) cook; **~buch** *n* cookery-book, *Am.* cook-book; **2en** ['kɔxən] *v/t Wasser, Eier, Fisch*: boil; *Fleisch, Gemüse*: cook, boil; *Kaffee, Tee etc.*: make; *v/i Wasser etc.*: boil; *Tätigkeit*: cook, do the cooking; **~er** *m* cooker.

Köchin ['kœçɪn] *f* (-/-nen) (female) cook.

Koch|nische ['kɔxni:ʃə] *f* (-/-n) kitchenette; **~topf** *m* pot, saucepan.

Köder ['kø:dər] *m* (-s/-) bait; **2n** ['kø:dərn] *v/t* bait.

Koffer ['kɔfər] *m* (-s/-) (suit)case; trunk; **~radio** *n* portable radio; **~raum** *m mot.* boot, *Am.* trunk.

Kognak ['kɔnjak] *m* (-s/-s) French brandy, cognac.

Kohl [ko:l] *m* (-[e]s/-e) cabbage.

Kohle ['ko:lə] *f* (-/-n) coal; *electr.* carbon; **~säure** *f* carbonic acid; **~nstoff** *m* carbon; **~papier** *n* carbon-paper.

Koje ['ko:jə] *f* (-/-n) berth, bunk.

Kokosnuß ['ko:kɔsnʊs] *f* (-/*ϋsse*) coconut.

Koks [ko:ks] *m* (-es/-e) coke.

Kolben ['kɔlbən] *m* (-s/-) *Gewehr*: butt; *tech.* piston.

Kolik ['ko:lɪk] *f* (-/-en) colic.

Kolleg|e [kɔ'le:gə] *m* (-n

-n), **~in** *f* (-/-nen) colleague. [colony.]

Kolonie [kolo'ni:] *f* (-/-n)◊

Kolonne [ko'lɔnə] *f* (-/-n) *mil.* column; *Wagen2:* convoy.

Kombi|nation [kɔmbina'tsĭo:n] *f* (-/-en) combination; *Fußball etc.:* move; **~wagen** ['kɔmbi-] *m* estate car, *Am.* station wagon.

Komfort [kɔm'fo:r] *m* (-s/ *no pl*) comfort; **2abel** [-fɔr'ta:bəl] *adj* comfortable.

Komi|k ['ko:mɪk] *f* (-/*no pl*) humo(u)r, fun; **~ker** *m* (-s/-) comedian; **2sch** *adj* comic(al), funny; *fig.* odd.

Komitee [komi'te:] *n* (-s/ -s) committee.

Komma ['kɔma] *n* (-s/-s, -ta) comma; **sechs ~ vier** six point four.

Kommando [kɔ'mando] *n* (-s/-s) *mil.* command; *Befehl(e):* a. order(s *pl*); *Abteilung:* detachment.

kommen ['kɔmən] *v/i* (*irr*) come; *an~:* arrive; **~ lassen** *j-n:* send for; *et.:* order; **~ auf** remember; **um et. ~** lose s.th.

Komment|ar [kɔmen'ta:r] *m* (-s/-e) commentary, comment; **2ieren** [-'ti:rən] *v/t* comment on.

Kommiss|ar [kɔmɪ'sa:r] *m* (-s/-e) *Polizei:* superintendent; **~ion** [-mɪˈsĭo:n] *f* (-/-en) commission; *Ausschuß:* a. committee.

Kommode [kɔ'mo:də] *f* (-/-n) chest of drawers, *Am.* bureau.

Kommunis|mus [kɔmu'nɪsmʊs] *m* (-/*no pl*) communism; **~t** [-'nɪst] *m* (-en/-en) communist; **2tisch** *adj* communist.

Komödi|ant [komø'dĭant] *m* (-en/-en) comedian; **~ie** [ko'mø:dĭə] *f* (-/-n) comedy.

Kompanie [kɔmpa'ni:] *f* (-/-n) *mil.* company.

Komparativ ['kɔmparati:f] *m* (-s/-e) *gr.* comparative (degree).

Kompaß ['kɔmpas] *m* (-sses/-sse) compass.

komplett [kɔm'plɛt] *adj* complete.

Komplex [kɔm'plɛks] *m* (-es/-e) complex; *Gebäude:* block.

Komplikation [kɔmplika'tsĭo:n] *f* (-/-en) complication.

Kompliment [kɔmpli'mɛnt] *n* (-[e]s/-e) compliment.

Komplize [kɔm'pli:tsə] *m* (-n/-n) accomplice.

kompli|zieren [kɔmpli'tsi:rən] *v/t* complicate; **~t** *adj* complicated; *Problem etc.:* complex.

kompo|nieren [kɔmpo'ni:rən] *v/t* compose; **2nist** [-'nɪst] *m* (-en/-en) composer; **2sition** [-zɪ'tsĭo:n] *f* (-/-en) composition.

Kompott [kɔm'pɔt] *n* (-[e]s/-e) stewed fruit.

Kompromiß

Kompromiß [kɔmpro-'mɪs] *m* (-sses/-sse) compromise.

kondens|ieren [kɔndɛn-'ziːrən] *v/t* condense; **≈milch** *f* evaporated milk.

Kondition [kɔndi'tsĭoːn] *f* (-/-en) *sp.* condition.

Konditional [kɔnditsĭo-'naːl] *m* (-s/-e) *gr.* conditional (mood).

Konditor|ei [kɔndito'raɪ] *f* (-/-en) confectionery, café; **~waren** *pl* confectionery *sg.*

Konfekt [kɔn'fɛkt] *n* (-[e]s/-e) sweets *pl*, *Am.* candy; chocolates *pl.*

Konfektion [kɔnfɛk-'tsĭoːn] *f* (-/no *pl*) ready-made clothes *pl.*

Konferenz [kɔnfe'rɛnts] *f* (-/-en) conference.

Konfession [kɔnfɛ'sĭoːn] *f* (-/-en) denomination.

Konfirmation [kɔnfɪrma-'tsĭoːn] *f* (-/-en) confirmation.

Konfitüre [kɔnfi'tyːrə] *f* (-/-n) preserves *pl*, (whole-fruit) jam.

Konflikt [kɔn'flɪkt] *m* (-[e]s/-e) conflict.

konfrontieren [kɔnfrɔn-'tiːrən] *v/t* confront.

konfus [kɔn'fuːs] *adj* confused.

Kongreß [kɔn'grɛs] *m* (-sses/-sse) congress.

König ['køːnɪç] *m* (-[e]s/-e) king; **~in** *f* (-/-nen) queen; **≈lich** *adj* royal; **~reich** *n* (-[e]s/-e) kingdom.

Konjugation [kɔnjuga-'tsĭoːn] *f* (-/-en) *gr.* conjugation; **≈ieren** [-ju'giːrən] *v/t gr.* conjugate.

Konjunktion [kɔnjuŋk-'tsĭoːn] *f* (-/-en) *gr.* conjunction; **~iv** ['kɔnjuŋk-tiːf] *m* (-s/-e) *gr.* subjunctive *od.* conjunctive (mood); **~ur** [-'tuːr] *f* (-/-en) economic *od.* business situation.

Konkurr|ent [kɔnku'rɛnt] *m* (-en/-en) competitor, rival; **~enz** [-'rɛnts] *f* (-/no *pl*) competition (*a. sp.*); competitor(s *pl*), rival(s *pl*); **≈enzfähig** [-fɛːɪç] *adj* able to compete; *Preise:* competitive; **≈ieren** [-'riː-rən] *v/i* compete.

Konkurs [kɔn'kurs] *m* (-es/-e) bankruptcy.

können ['kœnən] *v/aux*, *v/t*, *v/i* (*irr*) know; be allowed *od.* permitted to; ~ **Sie Deutsch?** do you speak German? **ich kann** I can, I am able to; **es kann sein** it may be.

konsequen|t [kɔnze-'kvɛnt] *adj* consistent; **≈z** [-'kvɛnts] *f* (-/-en) consistency; *Folge:* consequence.

konservativ [kɔnzerva-'tiːf] *adj* conservative.

Konserven [kɔn'zɛrvən] *pl* tinned (*Am.* canned) food *sg*; **~büchse** *f*, **~dose** *f* tin, *Am.* can.

konservieren [kɔnzer-'viːrən] *v/t* preserve.

Konsonant [kɔnzo'nant]
m (-en/-en) consonant.

konstruieren [kɔnstru-
'i:rən] *v/t gr.* construe;
tech.: construct; *entwerfen*:
design; **2ktion** [-struk-
'tsjo:n] *f* (-/-en) *tech.*: construction; design.

Konsul ['kɔnzul] *m* (-s/-n)
consul; **~at** [-zu'la:t] *n*
(-[e]s/-e) consulate.

Konsum [kɔn'zu:m] *m* (-s/
no pl) consumption; [kɔn-
zu:m] *m* (-s/-s) *Laden:* co-
operative, *colloq.* co-op;
~ent [-zu'mɛnt] *m* (-en/
-en) consumer; **~güter**
[kɔn'zu:m-] *pl* consum-
er('s) goods *pl.*

Kontakt [kɔn'takt] *m*
(-[e]s/-e) contact; **~ aufnehmen** get in touch.

Kontinent ['kɔntinɛnt] *m*
(-[e]s/-e) continent.

Konto ['kɔnto] *n* (-s/**Kon-
ten**) account.

Kontrast [kɔn'trast] *m*
(-[e]s/-e) contrast.

Kontrolle [kɔn'trɔlə] *f* (-/
-n) control; *Aufsicht:*
supervision; *Prüfung:*
check; **~eur** [-trɔ'lø:r] *m*
(-s/-e) inspector; *rail.*
conductor; **2ieren** [-'li:-
rən] *v/t* control; supervise;
check.

Konversation [kɔnvɛrza-
'tsjo:n] *f* (-/-en) conversation.

konzentrieren [kɔntsɛn-
'tri:rən] *v/t* (**sich**) concentrate.

Konzert [kɔn'tsɛrt] *n*
(-[e]s/-e) concert; *Musik-
stück:* concerto; **~saal** *m*
concert-hall.

Konzession [kɔntsɛ-
'sjo:n] *f* (-/-en) concession; licen[c]e, *Am.* -se.

Kopf [kɔpf] *m* (-es/ⁿe)
head; *fig.* brains *pl;* **~be-
deckung** ['-bədɛkuŋ] *f*
headgear; **~ende** [-'ʔɛn-
də] *n* (-s/-n) head, top;
~hörer *m* headphone;
~kissen *n* pillow; **~nik-
ken** *n* (-s/*no pl*) nod; **~sa-
lat** *m* lettuce; **~schmer-
zen** *pl* headache *sg;*
~sprung *m* header;
~tuch *n* head-scarf;
2über [-'ʔy:bər] *adv* head
first; **~weh** *n* headache.

Kopie [ko'pi:] *f* (-/-n)
copy, duplicate; **2ren**
[-'pi:rən] *v/t* copy.

Kopilot ['ko:pilo:t] *m*
(-en/-en) *aer.* co-pilot;
mot. co-driver.

Koralle [ko'ralə] *f* (-/-n)
coral.

Korb [kɔrp] *m* (-[e]s/ⁿe)
basket; **~möbel** *pl* wicker
furniture *sg.*

Korken ['kɔrkən] *m* (-s/-)
cork; **~zieher** ['-tsi:ər] *m*
corkscrew.

Korn [kɔrn] *n* (-[e]s/*rare*
-e) grain, corn; (*pl* ⁿer)
Samen: seed.

körnig ['kœrnɪç] *adj* gran-
ular; *in Zssgn:* ...-grained.

Körper ['kœrpər] *m* (-s/-)
body; **~bau** *m* (-[e]s/*no
pl*) physique; **2behin-
dert** [-bəhɪndərt] *adj*

(physically) disabled, handicapped; **2lich** adj bodily, physical; **~pflege** f hygiene.

korrekt [kɔ'rɛkt] adj correct; **2ur** f [-rɛk'tuːr] f (-/-en) correction.

Korrespond|ent [kɔrɛspɔn'dɛnt] m (-en/-en) correspondent; **2ieren** [-'diːrən] v/i correspond.

korrigieren [kɔri'giːrən] v/t correct.

Korsett [kɔr'zɛt] n (-[e]s/-s) corset.

Kosename ['koːzənaːmə] m (-ns/-n) pet name.

Kosmetik [kɔs'meːtɪk] f (-/no pl) beauty culture; **~erin** f (-/-nen) beautician, cosmetician; **~salon** [-zalɔ̃:] m (-s/-s) beauty parlo(u)r.

Kost [kɔst] f (-/no pl) food, fare; *Beköstigung:* board; **2bar** adj costly, expensive; *fig.* valuable, precious.

kosten[1] ['kɔstən] v/t, v/i taste, try, sample.

kosten[2] v/t cost; *Zeit:* take; **2** pl cost(s pl); *Ausgaben:* expenses pl; **~los** adj free (of charge).

köstlich ['kœstlɪç] adj delicious.

Kost|probe ['kɔstproːbə] f (-/-n) sample; **2spielig** [-'ʃpiːlɪç] adj expensive.

Kostüm [kɔs'tyːm] n (-s/-e) costume; suit.

Kot [koːt] m (-[e]s/no pl) excrement.

Kotelett [kɔt'lɛt] n (-[e]s/-s) chop.

Kotflügel ['koːtflyːgəl] m (-s/-) mudguard, *Am.* a. fender.

Krabbe ['krabə] f (-/-n) crab; shrimp.

krabbeln ['krabəln] v/i crawl.

Krach [krax] m (-[e]s/-e) crash; *Lärm:* noise; *Streit:* quarrel, *colloq.* row; **2en** ['kraxən] v/i crash.

krächzen ['krɛçtsən] v/i, v/t croak.

Kraft [kraft] f (-/¨e) strength; *Natur*2: force; *electr., tech.* power; *Tat*2: energy; **in ~ treten** come into operation od. force; **~brühe** f beef tea; **~fahrer** m driver, motorist; **~fahrzeug** n motor vehicle.

kräftig ['krɛftɪç] adj strong (a. fig.); powerful; *Essen:* substantial.

kraft|los ['kraftloːs] adj feeble, weak; **2stoff** m fuel; petrol, *Am.* gas(oline); **2wagen** m motor vehicle; **2werk** n power-station.

Kragen ['kraːgən] m (-s/-) collar.

Krähe ['krɛːə] f (-/-n) crow; **2n** ['krɛːən] v/i crow.

Kralle ['kralə] f (-/-n) claw; *Raubvogel:* talon.

Krampf [krampf] m (-[e]s/¨e) cramp; *stärker:* spasm, convulsion; **~ader**

['-ʔaːdər] f (-/-n) varicose
vein; 2̲haft adj convul-
sive; fig. forced.
Kran [kraːn] m (-[e]s/ᵘe)
crane.
krank [kraŋk] adj ill, bsd.
Am. 2̲sick; 2̲ werden fall
ill; 2e m, f (-n/-n) sick
person, patient.
kränken ['krɛŋkən] v/t offend, hurt.
Kranken|bett ['kraŋkən-
bɛt] n (-[e]s/-en) sickbed;
~haus n hospital; ~kas-
se f health insurance
scheme; ~pfleger [-pfleː-
gər] m (-s/-) male nurse;
~schwester f nurse;
~versicherung f health
od. sickness insurance;
~wagen m ambulance;
~zimmer n sick-room.
krank|haft ['kraŋkhaft]
adj morbid; 2̲heit f ill-
ness, sickness; bestimmte:
disease.
kränklich ['krɛŋklɪç] adj
sickly, ailing.
Kranz [krants] m (-es/ᵘe)
wreath; garland.
kratzen ['kratsən] v/t, v/i:
(sich) ~ scratch (o.s.).
kraulen ['kraulən] v/t
scratch (gently); v/i sp.
crawl.
kraus [kraus] adj curly,
crisp.
Kraut [kraut] n (-[e]s/ᵘer)
herb; Kohl: cabbage.
Krawall [kra'val] m (-s/
-e) riot.
Krawatte [kra'vatə] f (-/
-n) (neck)tie.

Krebs [kreːps] m (-es/-e)
zo. crayfish; med. cancer.
Kredit [kre'diːt] m (-[e]s/
-e) credit.
Kreide ['kraɪdə] f (-/-n)
chalk.
Kreis [kraɪs] m (-es/-e)
circle (a. fig.); district;
~bahn f orbit.
kreischen ['kraɪʃən] v/i
screech, scream.
Kreisel ['kraɪzəl] m (-s/-)
(whipping-)top.
kreis|en ['kraɪzən] v/i
(move in a) circle, revolve,
rotate; aer., Vogel: circle;
Blut: circulate; ~förmig
['kraɪsfœrmɪç] adj circular;
2lauf m circulation;
2laufstörung f circula-
tory disturbance; ~rund
[-rʊnt] adj circular; 2ver-
kehr m roundabout
traffic.
Krem [kreːm] f (-/-s)
cream.
Krempe ['krɛmpə] f (-/-n)
brim.
Kreuz [krɔʏts] n (-es/-e)
cross; crucifix; anat. small
of the back; Karten: club(s
pl); 2 adv: ~und quer in
all directions.
kreuz|en ['krɔʏtsən] v/t
cross; sich ~en cross, intersect; 2fahrt f cruise;
~igen [-tsɪgən] v/t cruci-
fy; 2otter ['-ʔɔtər] f (-/
-n) common viper; adder;
2schmerzen pl backache
sg; 2ung f cross-roads sg;
bot., zo. cross(breed);
2verhör n: ins ~ neh-

men cross-examine; 2**worträtsel** n crossword (puzzle).

kriech|en ['kri:çən] v/i (irr) creep, crawl; 2**spur** f mot. creeper lane.

Krieg [kri:k] m (-[e]s/-e) war.

kriegen ['kri:gən] v/t colloq.: get; fangen: catch.

Kriegs|beschädigte ['kri:ksbəʃɛ:dɪçtə] m (-n/ -n) disabled veteran; ~**gefangene** m (-n/-n) prisoner of war; ~**gefangenschaft** f captivity; ~**verbrechen** n war crime.

Kriminal|beamte [krimi'na:lbə²amtə] m (-n/-n) criminal investigator, plain-clothes man; ~**film** m crime film, thriller; ~**polizei** f criminal investigation department; ~**roman** m detective story, crime novel.

kriminell [krimi'nɛl] adj criminal; 2**e** m, f (-n/-n) criminal.

Krippe ['krɪpə] f. (-/-n) crib, manger; Kinderhort: crèche.

Krise ['kri:zə] f (-/-n) crisis.

Kriti|k [kri'ti:k] f (-/-en) criticism; thea. etc.: review; ~**ker** ['kri:tikər] m (-s/-) critic; 2**sch** adj critical; 2**sieren** [-'zi:rən] v/t criticize.

kritzeln ['krɪtsəln] v/i, v/t scrawl, scribble.

Krokodil [kroko'di:l] n (-s/-e) crocodile.

Krone ['kro:nə] f (-/-e) crown; Adels2: coronet.

krönen ['krø:nən] v/t crown.

Kronleuchter ['kro:nlɔʏçtər] m (-s/-) chandelier.

Krönung ['krø:nʊŋ] f (-/ -en) coronation.

Kropf [krɔpf] m (-[e]s/=e) goitre; Am. -er.

Kröte ['krø:tə] f (-/-n) toad.

Krücke ['krʏkə] f (-/-n) crutch.

Krug [kru:k] m (-[e]s/=e) jug, pitcher; mug.

Krume ['kru:mə] f (-/-n) crumb.

Krümel ['kry:məl] m (-s/-) small crumb.

krumm [krʊm] adj crooked; bent.

krümm|en ['krʏmən] v/t bend; Finger, Arm: crook; 2**ung** f bend; curve; Fluß, Weg: turn, wind; Erde, anat.: curvature.

Krüppel ['krʏpəl] m (-s/-) cripple.

Kruste ['krʊstə] f (-/-n) crust.

Kruzifix [krutsi'fɪks] n (-es/-e) crucifix.

Kubikmeter [ku'bi:kme:tər] m, n (-s/-) cubic metre, Am. -er.

Küche ['kʏçə] f (-/-n) kitchen; cuisine.

Kuchen ['ku:xən] m (-s/-) cake.

Küchen|herd ['kyçən-he:rt] *m* (-[e]s/-e) (kitchen) range, stove; **~schrank** *m* dresser.

Kuckuck ['kʊkʊk] *m* (-s/-e) cuckoo.

Kufe ['ku:fə] *f* (-/-n) aer. skid; *Schlitten etc.*: runner.

Kugel ['ku:gəl] *f* (-/-n) ball; *Gewehr etc.*: bullet; *math., geogr.* sphere; *sp.* shot; **2förmig** [-fœrmiç] *adj* spherical; **~gelenk** *n* tech., anat. ball-and-socket joint; **~lager** *n* ball-bearing(s *pl*); **~schreiber** *m* ball(-point) pen; **~stoßen** *n* (-s/*no pl*) sp. shot-put.

Kuh [ku:] *f* (-/⁓e) cow.

kühl [ky:l] *adj* cool; chilly; **~en** ['ky:lən] *v/t* cool; chill; **2er** *m mot.* radiator; **2schrank** *m* refrigerator, *colloq.* fridge.

kühn [ky:n] *adj* bold, daring.

Kuhstall ['ku:ʃtal] *m* (-[e]s/⁓e) cow-house.

Küken ['ky:kən] *n* (-s/-) chick(en).

kultivieren [kʊlti'vi:rən] *v/t* cultivate.

Kultur [kʊl'tu:r] *f* (-/-en) agr. cultivation; culture, civilization; **2ell** [-tu'rel] *adj* cultural; **~film** [kʊl-'tu:r-] *m* documentary film.

Kümmel ['kyməl] *m* (-s/-) caraway.

Kummer ['kʊmər] *m* (-s/*no pl*) grief, sorrow; *Verdruß*: trouble.

kümmer|lich ['kymərliç] *adj* miserable, wretched; **~n** ['kymərn] *v/t* bother, worry; **sich ~n** *um v/refl* look after, take care of; *see* (to it).

Kunde ['kʊndə] *m* (-n/-n) customer, client; **~ndienst** *m* service.

Kundgebung ['kʊntge:-bʊŋ] *f* (-/-en) pol. rally.

kündig|en ['kyndigən] *v/t* cancel; *Vertrag*: denounce; *v/i:* j-m **~en** give s.o. notice; **2ung** *f* notice.

Kund|in ['kʊndɪn] *f* (-/-nen) customer, client; **~schaft** *f* customers *pl*, clients *pl*.

Kunst [kʊnst] *f* (-/⁓e) art; *Fertigkeit*: skill; **~aus-stellung** *f* art exhibition; **~dünger** *m* fertilizer; **~händler** *m* art dealer; **~leder** *n* imitation leather.

Künstler ['kynstlər] *m* (-s/-), **~in** *f* (-/-nen) artist; *mus., thea.* a. performer; **2isch** *adj* artistic.

künstlich ['kynstliç] *adj* artificial; false (a. *Zähne etc.*); synthetic.

Kunst|seide ['kʊnstzaɪdə] *f* (-/-n) rayon, artificial silk; **~stoff** *m* synthetic material, plastic; **~stück** *n* feat; trick; **2voll** *adj* artistic, elaborate; **~werk** *n* work of art.

Kupfer ['kʊpfər] *n* (-s/-) copper; **~stich** *m* copperplate (engraving).

Kuppe

Kuppe ['kʊpə] f (-/-n) rounded hilltop; *Nagel etc.*: head.

Kuppel ['kʊpəl] f (-/-n) dome, cupola.

kuppel|n ['kʊpəln] v/t, v/i couple; *mot.* declutch; ℒ**lung** f *tech.* coupling; *mot.* clutch; ℒ**lungspedal** [-peda:l] n (-s/-e) clutch pedal.

Kur [ku:r] f (-/-en) cure.

Kurbel ['kʊrbəl] f (-/-n) crank.

Kürbis ['kʏrbɪs] m (-ses/-se) pumpkin.

Kur|gast ['ku:rgast] m (-[e]s/ᵛe) visitor; ℒ**ieren** [ku'ri:rən] v/t cure; ~**ort** ['ku:rʔɔrt] m health resort, spa; ~**park** m park, gardens *pl.*

Kurs [kʊrs] m (-es/-e) course (a. fig.); *Börse:* price; *Wechsel|s:* rate of exchange; *Lehrgang:* course; class; *pol.* policy, line; ~**buch** n railway (*Am.* railroad) guide.

kursieren [kʊr'zi:rən] v/i circulate.

Kurswagen ['kʊrsva:gən] m (-s/-) through carriage.

Kurtaxe ['ku:rtaksə] f visitor's tax.

Kurve ['kʊrvə] f (-/-n) curve; bend.

kurz [kʊrts] adj short; *zeitlich:* brief; ~**e Hose** shorts *pl.*; **sich ~ fassen** be brief od. concise; **vor ~em** a short time ago.

kürzen ['kʏrtsən] v/t shorten (**um** by); *Buch etc.:* abridge; *Ausgaben:* cut, reduce.

Kurz|film ['kʊrtsfɪlm] m (-s/-e) short film; ℒ**fristig** ['-frɪstɪç] adj *Kredit:* short-term; *Absage:* at short notice; ~**geschichte** f short story; ~**nachrichten** *pl* news summary *sg.*

kürzlich ['kʏrtslɪç] adv recently.

Kurz|parkzone ['kʊrtsparktso:nə] f (-/-n) limited parking zone; ~**schluß** m short circuit; ~**schrift** f shorthand; ℒ**sichtig** ['-zɪçtɪç] adj short-sighted, near-sighted; ~**waren** f haberdashery *sg*, *Am. a.* notions *pl*; ~**welle** f short wave.

Kusine [ku'zi:nə] f (-/-n) cousin.

Kuß [kʊs] m (-sses/ᵛsse) kiss.

küssen ['kʏsən] v/t kiss.

Küste ['kʏstə] f (-/-n) shore, coast.

Küster ['kʏstər] m (-s/-) verger, sexton.

Kutsche ['kʊtʃə] f (-/-n) carriage, coach; ~**r** m coachman.

Kutte ['kʊtə] f (-/-n) cowl.

Kutter ['kʊtər] m (-s/-) cutter.

Kuvert [ku've:r] n (-s/-s, -e) envelope.

L

Labor [la'bo:r] *n* (-s/-s, -e) laboratory; ~**ant** [-bo'rant] *m* (-en/-en), ~**antin** *f* (-/-nen) laboratory assistant; ~**atorium** [-ra-'to:rĭʊm] *n* (-s/-rien) laboratory.

Lache [laxə] *f* (-/-n) pool, puddle.

lächeln ['lɛçəln] *v/i* smile; 2 *n* (-s/*no pl*) smile.

lachen [laxən] *v/i* laugh; 2 *n* (-s/*no pl*) laugh(ter).

lächerlich ['lɛçərlɪç] *adj* ridiculous.

Lachs [laks] *m* (-es/-e) salmon.

Lack [lak] *m* (-[e]s/-e) varnish; 2**ieren** [-'ki:rən] *v/t* varnish; ~**leder** ['le:dər] *n* patent leather.

laden ['la:dən] *v/t* (*irr*) load; *electr.* charge.

Laden *m* (-s/⁓) shop, *Am.* store; *Fenster*: shutter; ~**dieb** *m* shop-lifter; ~**kasse** *f* till; ~**schluß** *m* closing time; ~**tisch** *m* counter.

Ladung ['la:dʊŋ] *f* (-/-en) load, freight; *mar.* cargo; *electr.* charge.

Lage ['la:gə] *f* (-/-n) situation (*a. fig.*); position (*a. fig.*); **in der ~ sein zu** be able to.

Lager ['la:gər] *n* (-s/-) couch, bed; *Vorrat*: store, stock; *mil. etc.*: camp, encampment; *s.* **Lager-**

haus; **auf ~** on hand, in stock; ~**feuer** *n* campfire; ~**haus** *n* warehouse, store-house; 2**n** ['la:gərn] *v/i mil.* (en)camp; *econ.* be stored; *v/t econ.* store, warehouse; ~**raum** *m* store-room; ~**ung** *f* storage.

Lagune [la'gu:nə] *f* (-/-n) lagoon.

lahm [la:m] *adj* lame; ~**en** ['la:mən] *v/i* be lame (**auf** in).

lähm|en ['lɛ:mən] *v/t* paraly|se, *Am.* -ze; 2**ung** *f* paralysis.

Laib [laɪp] *m* (-[e]s/-e) loaf.

Laie ['laɪə] *m* (-n/-n) layman; amateur.

Laken ['la:kən] *n* (-s/-) sheet.

lallen ['lalən] *v/i*, *v/t* babble.

Lamm [lam] *n* (-[e]s/⁓er) lamb.

Lampe ['lampə] *f* (-/-n) lamp; ~**nschirm** *m* lampshade.

Land [lant] *n* (-es/⁓er) *Fest*2: land; country; **an ~ gehen** go ashore; **auf dem ~(e)** in the country; ~**ebahn** *f* *aer.* runway; 2**einwärts** [-'?aɪnverts] *adv* upcountry, inland; 2**en** ['landən] *v/i* land.

Länder|kampf ['lɛndərkampf] m (-[e]s/-e), ~spiel n international match.

Landes|grenze ['landəsgrentsə] f (-/-n) national border, frontier; **~innere** [-'?ɪnərə] n (-n/no pl) interior, upcountry; **~regierung** f (Deutschland: Land) government.

Land|karte f ['lantkartə] f (-/-n) map; **~kreis** m rural district.

ländlich ['lɛntlɪç] rural, rustic.

Land|schaft ['lantʃaft] f (-/-en) countryside; bsd. paint. landscape; **~smann** m (-[e]s/-leute) (fellow) countryman, compatriot; **~straße** f highway, road; **~streicher** m [-ʃtrɑɪçər] m (-s/-) vagabond, tramp; **~tag** m Landtag, Land parliament.

Landung ['landʊŋ] f (-/-en) landing; **~ssteg** [-sʃteːk] m (-[e]s/-e) gangway.

Land|weg m ['lantveːk] m (-[e]s/no pl): **auf dem ~**(e) by land; **~wirt** m farmer; **~wirtschaft** f agriculture, farming; 2**wirtschaftlich** adj agricultural.

lang [laŋ] adj long; Person: tall.

Länge ['lɛŋə] f (-/-n) length; tallness; geogr. longitude.

langen ['laŋən] v/i colloq.: be enough; **~ nach** reach for.

Langeweile ['laŋəvaɪlə] f (-/no pl) boredom.

lang|fristig ['laŋfrɪstɪç] adj long-term; **~jährig** adj: **~e Erfahrung** many years of experience.

länglich ['lɛŋlɪç] adj longish, oblong.

längs [lɛŋs] prp (gen) along(side).

langsam ['laŋzaːm] adj slow; 2**schläfer** [-'ʃleːfər] m (-s/-) late riser; 2**spielplatte** f long-play record.

längst [lɛŋst] adv long ago od. since.

Langstreckenlauf ['laŋʃtrɛkənlaʊf] m (-[e]s/-e) long-distance run od. race.

langweilen ['laŋvaɪlən] v/t bore; **sich ~** an v/i refl be bored; **~ig** adj boring, dull; **~ige Person** bore.

Lang|welle ['laŋvɛlə] f (-/-n) long wave; **~wierig** [-viːrɪç] adj protracted, lengthy.

Lappen ['lapən] m (-s/-) rag; Staub2: duster; Wisch2 etc.: cloth; anat., bot. lobe.

Lärche ['lɛrçə] f (-/-n) larch.

Lärm [lɛrm] m (-[e]s/no pl) noise; 2**en** ['lɛrmən] v/i make a noise; 2**end** adj noisy.

Larve ['larfə] f (-/-n) mask; zo. larva.

Lasche ['laʃə] f (-/-n) tongue.

leben

lassen ['lasən] *v/aux, v/t, v/i (irr)* let*≈:* leave; allow, permit, let; *veran≈:* make; **laß das!** don't!; **drucken ≈** have printed.

lässig ['lɛsɪç] *adj* easy; careless.

Last [last] *f (-/-en)* load; burden; *Gewicht:* weight; **≈auto** *n s.* **Last(kraft)wagen**; 2en ['lastən] *v/t* ≈ **auf** weigh *od.* press on.

Laster ['lastər] *n (-s/-)* vice.

lästern ['lɛstərn] *v/i:* ≈ **über** speak ill of.

lästig ['lɛstɪç] *adj* troublesome; annoying.

Last|kahn ['lastka:n] *m (-[e]s/⁀e)* barge; ≈ **(kraft)wagen** *m* lorry, *Am.* truck.

Latein [la'taɪn] *n (-s/no pl)* Latin; 2**isch** *adj* Latin.

Laterne [la'tɛrnə] *f (-/-n)* lantern; street-lamp; ≈**pfahl** *m* lamp-post.

Latte ['latə] *f (-/-n)* lath; *Zaun:* pale.

Lätzchen ['lɛtsçən] *n (-s/-)* bib, feeder.

Laub [laʊp] *n (-[e]s/no pl)* foliage, leaves *pl;* ≈**baum** *m* deciduous tree.

Laube ['laʊbə] *f (-/-n)* arbo(u)r, bower.

Lauch [laʊx] *m (-[e]s/-e)* leek.

lauern ['laʊərn] *v/i* lurk, watch.

Lauf [laʊf] *m (-[e]s/⁀e)* *Gewehr:* barrel; *Fluß:* course (*a. fig.*); run; *sp. a.*

heat; ≈**bahn** *f* career; 2**en** ['laʊfən] *v/i (irr)* run; *gehen:* walk; 2**enlassen** *v/t (irr):* **j-n** ≈ let s.o. go.

Läufer ['lɔyfər] *m (-s/-)* runner (*a. Teppich*); *Fußball:* half-back.

Laufmasche ['laʊfmaʃə] *f (-/-n)* ladder, *Am. a.* run.

Lauge ['laʊgə] *f (-/-n)* lye.

Laune ['laʊnə] *f (-/-n)* humo(u)r, mood, temper; whim; 2**enhaft**, 2**isch** *adj* moody.

Laus [laʊs] *f (-/⁀e)* louse.

lauschen ['laʊʃən] *v/i* listen (*dat* to); *heimlich:* eavesdrop.

laut [laʊt] *adj* loud; noisy; *adv* aloud, loud(ly); *prp* according to; 2 *m (-[e]s/-e)* sound; ≈**en** ['laʊtən] *v/i Text:* run.

läuten ['lɔytən] *v/i, v/t* ring; **es läutet** the bell is ringing.

laut|los ['laʊtlo:s] *adj* noiseless, soundless; *Stille:* hushed; 2**schrift** *f* phonetic transcription; 2**sprecher** *m* loud-speaker; 2**stärke** *f* volume.

lauwarm ['laʊvarm] *adj* tepid, lukewarm.

Lava ['la:va] *f (-/Laven)* lava.

Lavendel [la'vɛndəl] *m (-s/-)* lavender.

Lawine [la'vi:nə] *f (-/-n)* avalanche.

leben ['le:bən] *v/i* live; alive; **leb wohl!** goodbye!, farewell!; **von et.** ≈

live on s.th.; ⌀ *n* (-s/-) life;
stir, bustle; **am** ⌀ alive;
am ⌀ **bleiben** survive;
ums ⌀ **kommen** lose
one's life; **~dig** [le'bɛndiç]
adj fig. lively.

Lebens|alter ['le:bəns-
ʔaltər] *n* (-s/-) age; **~be-
dingungen** *pl* living conditions *pl*; **~gefahr** *f* danger to life; **~gefahr!** danger!; ⌀**gefährlich** *adj*
dangerous (to life); **~hal-
tungskosten** [-haltuŋs-
kɔstən] *pl* cost *sg* of living;
⌀**länglich** *adj* for life;
~lauf *m* personal record,
curriculum vitae; ⌀**lustig**
adj gay, merry; **~mittel** *pl*
food *sg*, groceries *pl*;
~mittelgeschäft *n* grocer's (shop), grocery;
~standard [-ʃtandart] *m*
(-s/-s) standard of living;
~unterhalt *m*: **s-n** ⌀
verdienen earn one's living; ⌀**versicherung** *f*
life assurance, *Am.* life insurance; ⌀**wichtig** *adj* vital, essential; **~zeichen** *n*
sign of life.

Leber ['le:bər] *f* (-/-n) liver; **~tran** [-tra:n] *m*
(-[e]s/-e) cod-liver oil.

Lebewesen ['le:bəve-
zən] *n* (-s/-) living being
od. creature.

Lebewohl [le:bə'vo:l] *n*
(-s/-e, -s) farewell.

leb|haft ['le:phaft] *adj*
lively; vivid; *Interesse*:
keen; **~los** *adj* lifeless.

leck [lɛk] *adj* leaky; **~ sein**

leak.

lecken ['lɛkən] *v/t, v/i* lick;
v/i leak.

lecker ['lɛkər] *adj* dainty,
delicious; ⌀**bissen** *m* (-s/
-) dainty, delicacy.

Leder ['le:dər] *n* (-s/-)
leather.

ledig ['le:diç] *adj* single,
unmarried; *Kind:* illegitimate.

leer [le:r] *adj* empty; vacant; *Seite etc.*: blank; ⌀**e** *f*
(-/no *pl*) emptiness; **~en**
['le:rən] *v/t* empty; clear
out; empty; ⌀**lauf** *m*
neutral gear.

legal [le'ga:l] *adj* legal,
lawful.

legen ['le:gən] *v/t* lay;
place, put; *v/refl:* **sich** ~
Wind etc.: abate, calm
down; *v/i, v/t Henne:* lay.

Legende [le'gɛndə] *f* (-/
-n) legend.

Lehm [le:m] *m* (-[e]s/-e)
loam.

Lehn|e ['le:nə] *f* (-/-n)
Arm⌀: arm; *Rücken*⌀:
back; ⌀**en** ['le:nən] *v/i, v/t*
lean, rest (**an, gegen**
against); (**sich**) **~** lean
against; **~sessel** *m*,
~stuhl *m* armchair, easy
chair.

Lehrbuch ['le:rbu:x] *n*
(-[e]s/⁀er) textbook.

Lehre ['le:rə] *f* (-/-n) doctrine; science; *Warnung:*
lesson; apprenticeship; **in
der** ~ **sein** bei be ap-
prenticed to; ⌀**n** ['le:rən]
v/t, v/i teach, instruct.

Lehrer ['le:rər] m (-s/-) teacher, instructor; **~in** f (-/-nen) teacher.

Lehr|fach ['le:rfax] n (-[e]s/ⁿer) subject; **~herr** m master, sl. boss; **~ling** [-lɪŋ] m (-s/-e) apprentice.

Leib [laɪp] m (-[e]s/-er) body; Bauch: belly, anat. abdomen; Mutter2: womb; **~chen** ['laɪpçən] n (-s/-) bodice; **~esübungen** ['laɪbəsˀy:bʊŋən] pl physical exercise sg; **~gericht** n favo(u)rite dish; **~schmerzen** pl s. Bauchschmerzen; **~wache** f, **~wächter** m bodyguard.

Leiche ['laɪçə] f (-/-n) (dead) body, corpse; **~nschauhaus** [-ʃaʊhaʊs] n (-es/ⁿer) morgue.

leicht [laɪçt] adj light (a. fig.); einfach: easy; **~athlet** m athlete; **2athletik** ['-ˀatle:tɪk] f (-/no pl) athletics pl, Am. track and field events pl; **~gläubig** [-glɔʏbɪç] adj credulous; **2igkeit** f lightness; fig. a. ease; **2sinn** m (-[e]s/no pl) carelessness; **~sinnig** adj careless.

leid [laɪt] adj: es tut mir **~** I am sorry; er tut mir **~** I am sorry for him; 2 n (-[e]s/no pl) grief, sorrow; **~en** ['laɪdən] v/i (irr) suffer (an from); v/t: (nicht) **~en können** (dis)like; 2en n (-s/-) suffering; med. complaint; **~end** adj ailing.

Leidenschaft ['laɪdən-

schaft] f (-/-en) passion; **2lich** adj passionate.

leider ['laɪdər] adv unfortunately; **2tragende** m, f (-n/-n) mourner.

Leih|bücherei ['laɪbyːçəraɪ] f (-/-en) lending-library, circulating library; **2en** ['laɪən] v/t (irr) lend; (sich) **2en** borrow; **~haus** n pawnshop; **~wagen** m hire(d) car.

Leim [laɪm] m (-[e]s/-e) glue; **2en** ['laɪmən] v/t glue.

Leine ['laɪnə] f (-/-n) line; Hunde2: leash, lead.

leinen ['laɪnən] adj (of) linen; 2 n (-s/-) linen; **2schuh** m canvas shoe.

Leinwand ['laɪnvant] f (-/ⁿe) paint. canvas; Kino: screen.

leise ['laɪzə] adj low, soft; **~r stellen** turn down.

Leiste ['laɪstə] f (-/-n) ledge; anat. groin.

leisten ['laɪstən] v/t do; Dienst, Hilfe: render; **ich kann mir das ~** I can afford it; **Widerstand ~** offer resistance.

Leistung ['laɪstʊŋ] f (-/-en) performance; achievement; output; Arbeits2: output; Versicherung: benefit.

Leit|artikel ['laɪtˀartiːkəl] m (-s/-) leading article, leader, editorial; **2en** ['laɪtən] v/t lead, guide; conduct (a. phys., mus.); run, manage.

Leiter¹ ['laɪtər] *m* (-s/-) conductor; manager.

Leiter² *f* (-/-n) ladder.

Leitung ['laɪtʊŋ] *f* (-/-en) *Stromkreis:* circuit; *teleph.* line; *Rohr*₂: pipe; *Führen:* guidance; *fig.* management, administration, direction; **~srohr** *n* conduit, pipe; **~swasser** *n* tap water.

Lektion [lɛk'tsio:n] *f* (-/-en) lesson; **~üre** [-'ty:rə] *f* (-/-n) reading; books *pl.*

Lende ['lɛndə] *f* (-/-n) loin(s *pl*).

lenken ['lɛŋkən] *v/t* direct; *mar.* steer; *Fahrzeug:* a. drive; **2rad** *n* steering-wheel; **2stange** *f* handle-bar; **2ung** *f* steering-gear.

Leopard [leo'part] *m* (-en/-en) leopard.

Lerche ['lɛrçə] *f* (-/-n) lark.

lernen ['lɛrnən] *v/t* learn.

Lese|buch ['le:zəbu:x] *n* (-[e]s/ᵘer) reader; **~lampe** *f* reading-lamp; **2n** ['le:zən] *v/t* (*irr* lesen) read; *agr.* gather; **~r(in** *f*) *m* reader; **2rlich** [-'zərlɪç] *adj* legible; **~zeichen** *n* book-mark.

letzt [letst] *adj* last; final.

leuchten ['lɔɪçtən] *v/i* shine; *schimmern:* gleam; *luminous:* **2er** *m* (-s/-) candlestick; *s.* Kron-leuchter; **2reklame** *f* neon sign; **2turm** *m* light-house; **2ziffer** *f* luminous figure.

leugnen ['lɔɪgnən] *v/t* deny.

Leute ['lɔɪtə] *pl* people *pl*; *einzelne:* persons *pl.*

Lexikon ['lɛksikɔn] *n* (-s/ -ka) dictionary; encyclop(a)edia.

Libelle [li'bɛlə] *f* (-/-n) dragon-fly.

liberal [libe'ra:l] *adj* liberal.

Licht [lɪçt] *n* (-[e]s/-er) light; ~ **machen** switch on the light(s); **~bild** *n* photo(graph); **2empfindlich** [-'?empfɪntlɪç] *adj* sensitive to light; *phot.* sensitive.

lichten ['lɪçtən] *v/t Wald:* clear; **den Anker** ~ weigh anchor; *v/refl:* **sich** ~ thin.

Licht|hupe ['lɪçthu:pə] *f* (-/-n) headlight flash(er); **~maschine** *f* dynamo; **~reklame** *f* neon sign; **~schalter** *m* (light) switch; **~strahl** *m* ray *od.* beam of light.

Lichtung ['lɪçtʊŋ] *f* (-/ -en) clearing.

Lid [li:t] *n* (-[e]s/-er) (eye)lid.

lieb [li:p] *adj* dear (*a.* Anrede); *nett:* nice, kind; *Kind:* good.

Liebe ['li:bə] *f* (-/no *pl*) love; **2n** ['li:bən] *v/t* love.

liebenswürdig ['li:bənsvyrdiç] *adj* kind.

lieber ['li:bər] *adv* rather, sooner; ~ **haben** prefer, like better.

Liebes|brief ['li:bəsbri:f] *m* (-[e]s/-e) love-letter; **~paar** *n* lovers *pl.*

liebevoll ['li:bəfɔl] *adj* loving, affectionate.

Lieb|haber ['li:pha:bər] *m* (-s/-) lover (*a.* fig.); **2kosen** ['ko:zən] *v/t* caress; **2lich** *adj* lovely, charming; **~ling** *m* (-s/-e) darling; favo(u)rite; *Kind, Tier:* pet; *Anrede:* darling; **2los** *adj* unkind; careless; **~ste** *m, f* (-n/-n) darling; sweetheart.

Lied [li:t] *n* (-[e]s/-er) song.

liederlich ['li:dərlıç] *adj* slovenly.

Liefer|ant [li:fə'rant] *m* (-en/-en) supplier, purveyor; **~auto** *n* s. **Lieferwagen; 2bar** ['li:fərba:r] *adj* available; **2n** ['li:fərn] *v/t* deliver; supply; **~ung** *f* delivery; supply; *Ware:* consignment; **~wagen** *m* delivery van.

Liege ['li:gə] *f* (-/-n) couch; *Garten2:* deckchair.

liegen ['li:gən] *v/i* (*irr*) lie; *Haus etc.:* be (situated); **~nach** face; **es liegt an ihm** it is up to him; **~bleiben** *v/i* (*irr*) stay in bed; *Arbeit etc.:* stand over; **~lassen** *v/t* (*irr*) leave (behind).

Liege|stuhl ['li:gəʃtu:l] *m* (-[e]s/⁀e) deck chair; **~wagen** *m* couchette coach.

Lift [lıft] *m* (-[e]s/-e, -s) lift, *Am.* elevator.

Liga ['li:ga] *f* (-/-Ligen) league.

Likör [li'kø:r] *m* (-s/-e) liqueur, cordial.

lila ['li:la] *adj* lilac.

Lilie ['li:lɪə] *f* (-/-n) lily.

Limonade [limo'na:də] *f* (-/-n) orangeade; lemonade.

Limousine [limu'zi:nə] *f* (-/-n) saloon car, sedan.

Linde ['lındə] *f* (-/-n) lime(-tree), linden.

lindern ['lındərn] *v/t* alleviate, soothe; *Not:* relieve.

Lineal [line'a:l] *n* (-s/-e) ruler.

Linie ['li:nɪə] *f* (-/-n) line; *Bus etc.:* number.

link [lıŋk] *adj* left; **2e** *f* (-n/-n) left; **~isch** *adj* awkward, clumsy.

links [lıŋks] *adv* (on *od.* to the) left; **nach ~** to the left; **2händer** ['-hendər] *m* (-s/-) left-hander.

Linse ['lınzə] *f* (-/-n) *bot.* lentil; *opt.* lens.

Lippe ['lıpə] *f* (-/-n) lip; **~nstift** *m* lipstick.

lispeln ['lıspəln] *v/i, v/t* lisp.

List [lıst] *f* (-/-en) ruse, trick.

Liste ['lıstə] *f* (-/-n) list; roll.

listig ['lıstıç] *adj* cunning, crafty.

Liter ['li:tər] *m, n* (-s/-) lit|re, *Am.* -er.

litera|risch [lıte'ra:rıʃ]

Lizenz

adj literary; 2**tur** [-ra'tu:r] *f* (*-/-en*) literature.

Lizenz [li'tsɛnts] *f* (*-/-en*) licen|ce, *Am.* -se.

Lob [lo:p] *n* (*-[e]s/no pl.*) praise; 2**en** ['lo:bən] *v/t* praise; 2**enswert** *adj* praiseworthy.

Loch [lɔx] *n* (*-[e]s/⸚er*) hole; 2**en** ['lɔxən] *v/t* perforate, pierce; *Karten:* punch; ⁓**er** *m* punch, perforator; ⁓**karte** *f* punch(ed) card.

Locke ['lɔkə] *f* (*-/-n*) curl, ringlet.

locken ['lɔkən] *v/t* decoy (*a. fig.*); *fig.* allure, entice.

Lockenwickler [-vɪklər] *m* (*-s/-*) curler.

locker ['lɔkər] *adj* loose; slack; ⁓**n** ['lɔkərn] *v/t* loosen (*a. sich*), slacken; relax.

lockig ['lɔkɪç] *adj* curly.

Löffel ['lœfəl] *m* (*-s/-*) spoon.

Loge ['lo:ʒə] *f* (*-/-n*) *thea.* box.

Loggia ['lɔdʒa] *f* (*-/ -gien*) loggia.

logisch ['lo:ɡɪʃ] *adj* logical.

Lohn [lo:n] *m* (*-[e]s/⸚e*) wages *pl.*; *fig.* reward; ⁓**empfänger** *m* wageearner; 2**en** ['lo:nən] *v/t*, *v/refl.*: **sich** ⁓ pay; *fig.* **(sich)** ⁓ *chem.* dissolve; sich ⁓ loosen.

⁓**end** *adj* profitable; *fig.* rewarding; ⁓**erhöhung** *f* rise (in wages), *Am.* raise;

⁓**steuer** *f* wage(s) tax;

⁓**stopp** *m* (*-s/-s*) wage-freeze.

lokal [lo'ka:l] *adj* local; 2 *n* (*-[e]s/-e*) restaurant; public house, *Am.* saloon.

Lokomotiv|e [lokomo'ti:-və] *f* (*-/-n*) (railway) engine; ⁓**führer** *m* enginedriver, *Am.* engineer.

Lorbeer [lɔrbe:r] *m* (*-s/ -en*) laurel, bay.

Los [lo:s] *n* (*-es/-e*) lot; lottery ticket; *fig.* fate, destiny, lot.

los *adj* loose, free; **was ist** ⁓? what is the matter?; ⁓**sein** be rid of; ⁓**!** go (on, ahead)!; ⁓**binden** *v/t* (*irr*) untie.

Lösch|blatt ['lœʃblat] *n* (*-[e]s/⸚er*) blotting-paper; 2**en** ['lœʃən] *v/t* extinguish, put out; wipe off; *Tonband:* erase; *Feuer, Durst:* quench; *mar.* unload.

lose ['lo:zə] *adj* loose.

Lösegeld ['lø:zəɡɛlt] *n* (*-[e]s/-er*) ransom.

losen ['lo:zən] *v/i* cast *od.* draw lots (**um** *for*).

lösen ['lø:zən] *v/t* loosen, untie; *Karte:* buy; *fig.* solve; *Verlobung:* break off; *Vertrag:* annul, cancel; **(sich)** ⁓ *chem.* dissolve; sich ⁓ loosen.

los|fahren ['lo:sfa:rən] *v/i* (*irr*) depart, drive off; ⁓**gehen** *v/i* (*irr*) go *od.* be off; ⁓**lassen** *v/t* (*irr*) let go.

löslich ['lø:slɪç] *adj* soluble.

los||lösen ['lo:slø:zən] *v/t* detach; **~machen** *v/t* unfasten, loosen; **~reißen** *v/t* (*irr*) tear off; **sich ~reißen** *fig.* tear o.s. away.

Lösung ['lø:zʊŋ] *f* (-/-en) solution (*a. fig.*).

loswerden ['lo:sve:rdən] *v/t* (*irr*) get rid of.

Lot [lo:t] *n* (-[e]s/-e) plumb(-line), plummet.

löten ['lø:tən] *v/t* solder.

Lotse ['lo:tsə] *m* (-n/-n) *mar.* pilot.

Lotterie [lɔtə'ri:] *f* (-/-n) lottery.

Lotto ['lɔto] *n* (-s/-s) numbers pool, lotto.

Löwe ['lø:və] *m* (-n/-n) lion; **~in** *f* (-/-nen) lioness.

loyal [löa'ja:l] *adj* loyal.

Luchs [lʊks] *m* (-es/-e) lynx.

Lücke ['lykə] *f* (-/-n) gap; **2nhaft** *adj* incomplete; **2nlos** *adj* complete.

Luft [lʊft] *f* (-/⁻e) air; **frische ~ schöpfen** take the air; **in die ~ sprengen** *v/t* blow up; **~angriff** *m* air raid; **~blase** *f* air bubble; **~brücke** *f* air-lift; **2dicht** *adj* airtight; **~druck** *m* atmospheric *od.* air pressure.

lüften ['lyftən] *v/t* air; *Hut:* raise.

Luft||fahrt ['lʊftfa:rt] *f* (-/*no pl*) aviation, aeronautics *sg*; **~kissen** *n* air cushion; **2krank** *adj* airsick; **~kurort** [-'ʔɔrt] *m* climatic

health resort; **2leer** *adj:* **~er Raum** vacuum; **~linie** *f* bee-line, *Am. a.* air line; **~loch** *n* air pocket; **~matratze** *f* airbed; **~post** *f* air mail; **~pumpe** *f* bicycle pump; **~röhre** *f* windpipe; **~stützpunkt** *m* air base.

Lüftung ['lyftʊŋ] *f* (-/-en) ventilation.

Luft||veränderung [-fer-'ʔendərʊŋ] *f* change of air; **~verkehr** *m* air traffic; **~verkehrsgesellschaft** [-gəzɛlʃaft] *f* airway, airline; **~waffe** *f* air force; **~weg** *m:* **auf dem ~** by air; **~zug** *m* (-[e]s/*no pl*) draught, *Am.* draft.

Lüge ['ly:gə] *f* (-/-n) lie, falsehood; **2n** ['ly:gən] *v/i* (*irr*) lie; **~ner(in** *f*) *m* liar.

Luke ['lu:kə] *f* (-/-n) hatch.

Lump [lʊmp] *m* (-en/-en) cad, rogue.

Lumpen ['lʊmpən] *m* (-s/-) rag.

Lunge ['lʊŋə] *f* (-/-n) lungs *pl*; **~nentzündung** [-'ʔɛnttsʏndʊŋ] *f* pneumonia; **~nflügel** *m* lung.

Lupe ['lu:pə] *f* (-/-n) magnifying glass.

Lust [lʊst] *f* (-/⁻e) pleasure, delight; lust; **~ haben zu** feel like ger.

lüstern ['lʏstərn] *adj* lewd.

lustig ['lʊstiç] *adj* merry, gay; *belustigend:* amusing, funny; **sich ~ig machen**

über make fun of; **≈spiel** n comedy.
lutschen ['lutʃən] v/i, v/t suck.
luxuriös [luksu'riø:s] adj luxurious.
Luxus ['luksus] m (-/no pl)

luxury; **~artikel** m luxury; **~hotel** n luxury hotel.
Lymphdrüse ['lʏmfdry:zə] f (-/-n) lymph gland.
Lyrik ['ly:rɪk] f (-/no pl) (lyric) poetry.

M

machen ['maxən] make; do; *herstellen:* make, produce, manufacture; *Prüfung:* sit for; *Rechnung:* come *od.* amount to; **wieviel macht das?** how much is it?; **das macht nichts!** never mind!, that's (quite) all right!; **da(gegen) kann man nichts machen** it cannot be helped; **ich mache mir nichts daraus** I don't care about it; **sich et. ~ lassen** have s.th. made; **na, mach schon!** *colloq.* hurry up!
Macht [maxt] f (-/⸚e) power (a. *Staat*), *stärker:* might; authority.
mächtig ['mɛçtɪç] adj powerful (a. *fig.*); mighty; *riesig:* huge.
machtlos ['maxtlo:s] adj powerless.
Mädchen ['mɛːtçən] n (-s/-) girl; maid (servant); **~name** m girl's name; **~ Frau:** maiden name.
Madle ['ma:də] f (-/-n) maggot, mite; **≈ig** ['ma:dɪç] adj maggoty, full of mites.

Magazin [maga'tsi:n] n (-s/-e) magazine.
Magen ['ma:gən] m (-s/⸚, -) stomach; **~beschwerden** pl stomach trouble *sg;* **~bitter** m (-s/-) bitters pl; **~geschwür** n gastric ulcer; **~schmerzen** pl stomachache *sg.*
mager ['ma:gər] adj meagire, *Am.* -er (a. *fig.*); *Mensch, Tier, Fleisch:* lean; **≈milch** f skim (med) milk.
magnetisch [ma'gne:tɪʃ] adj magnetic.
mähen ['mɛːən] v/t cut, mow, reap.
Mahl [ma:l] n (-[e]s/-e) meal.
mahlen ['ma:lən] grind, mill.
Mahlzeit ['ma:ltsaɪt] f (-/-en) meal.
Mähne ['mɛːnə] f (-/-n) mane.
mahnen ['ma:nən] v/t remind, admonish.
Mai [maɪ] m (-[e]s, -/no pl) May; **~baum** m maypole; **~glöckchen** ['-glœkçən] n (-s/-) lily of the valley; **~käfer** m cockchafer.
Mais [maɪs] m (-es/no pl)

maize, Indian corn, *Am.* corn.

Majestät [majes'tɛːt] *f (/-en)* majesty.

Major [ma'joːr] *m (-s/-e)* major.

makellos ['maːkəlloːs] *adj* immaculate.

Makler [maːklər] *m (-s/-)* broker.

Mal [maːl] *n (-[e]s/-e)* mark, sign; time; **zum ersten ~** for the first time.

mal *adv* times; multiplied by.

male|n ['maːlən] *v/i, v/t* paint; **2r(in** *f) m* painter; **2rei** [-lə'raɪ] *f (/-no pl)* painting.

Malz [malts] *n (-es/no pl)* malt.

Mama ['mama] *f (/-s)* mam(m)a, mammy, ma.

man [man] *indef pron* one, you; we; they, people.

manch [manç], **~er** [-ər], **~e** [-ə], **~es** [-əs] *indef pron* many a; **~e** *pl* some, several; **~mal** [-maːl] *adv* sometimes, at times.

Mandant [man'dant] *m (-en/-en)* client.

Mandarine [manda'riːnə] *f (/-n)* tangerine.

Mandel ['mandəl] *f (/-n)* bot. almond; *anat.* tonsil; **~entzündung** *f* tonsillitis.

Manege [ma'neːʒə] *f (/-n)* (circus-)ring.

Mangel ['maŋəl] *m (-s/ᵛ)* want, lack, deficiency; *Knappheit:* shortage;

Fehler: defect; **2haft** *adj* defective; unsatisfactory; **~ware** *f:* **~ sein** be scarce.

Manieren [ma'niːrən] *pl* manners *pl.*

Mann [man] *m (-[e]s/ᵛer)* man; *Ehe2:* husband.

Männ|chen ['mɛnçən] *n (-s/-)* zo. male; orn. cock; **2lich** *adj* male; gr. masculine.

Mannschaft *f (/-en)* crew; sp. team.

Manöver [ma'nøːvər] *n (-s/-)* manoeuvre, *Am.* maneuver.

Mansarde [man'zardə] *f (/-n)* attic, garret.

Manschette [man'ʃɛtə] *f (/-n)* cuff; **~nknopf** *m* cuff-link.

Mantel ['mantəl] *m (-s/ᵛ)* (over)coat.

Manuskript [manu'skript] *n (-[e]s/-e)* manuscript.

Mappe ['mapə] *f (/-n)* portfolio, briefcase; *Aktendeckel:* folder.

Märchen ['mɛːrçən] *n (-s/-)* fairy-tale.

Marder ['mardər] *m (-s/-)* marten.

Margarine [marga'riːnə] *f (/-no pl)* margarine, *colloq.* marge.

Marinade [mari'naːdə] *f (/-n)* marinade.

Marine [ma'riːnə] *f (/-no pl)* marine; *Kriegs2:* navy.

Marionette [marĭo'nɛtə] *f (/-n)* puppet.

Mark¹ [mark] f (-/-) *Geld*: mark.

Mark² n (-[e]s/*no pl*) *anat.* marrow; *bot.* pith.

Marke ['markə] f (-/-n) *Brief*2 *etc.*: stamp; *Fabrikat*: brand.

markieren [mar'ki:rən] v/t mark.

Markise [mar'ki:zə] f (-/-n) awning.

Markt [markt] m (-[e]s/ᵘe) market.

Marmelade [marmə'la:də] f (-/-n) jam; *Orangen*2: marmalade.

Marmor ['marmɔr] m (-s/-e) marble.

Marsch [marʃ] m (-[e]s/ᵘe) march (a. *mus.*); 2**ieren** [-'ʃi:rən] v/i march.

Märtyrer ['mɛrtyrər] m (-s/-) martyr.

März [mɛrts] m (-es/*no pl*) March.

Marzipan [martsi'pa:n] n (-s/-e) marzipan, marchpane.

Masche ['maʃə] f (-/-n) mesh; *Strick*2: stitch; ∼**draht** m wire netting.

Maschine [ma'ʃi:nə] f (-/-n) machine; *Motor*: engine; *aer.* plane; 2**ll** [-ʃi-'nɛl] *adj* mechanical.

Maschinen|gewehr n machine-gun; ∼**schaden** m engine trouble.

Masern ['ma:zərn] pl measles pl.

Mask|e ['maskə] f (-/-n) mask; ∼**enball** m fancy-dress *od.* masked ball; 2**ieren** [-'ki:rən] v/t: **sich** ∼ put on a mask.

Maß¹ [ma:s] n (-es/-e) measure; *Verhältnis*: proportion; *Mäßigung*: moderation; ∼**e** pl measurements pl.

Maß² f (-/-) *Bier*: appr. quart.

Massaker [ma'sa:kər] n (-s/-) massacre.

Maßanzug ['ma:sʔantsu:k] m (-[e]s/ᵘe) tailor-made suit.

Masse ['masə] f (-/-n) mass; *Haupt*2: bulk; *Substanz*: substance; *Volk*: crowd; **e-e** ∼ a lot of.

massieren [ma'si:rən] v/t massage, knead.

massig ['masiç] *adj* massy, bulky.

mäßig ['mɛ:siç] *adj* moderate; *Ergebnis etc.*: poor.

massiv [ma'si:f] *adj* massive, solid; 2 n (-s/-e) massif.

maß|los ['ma:slo:s] *adj* immoderate; 2**nahme** [-na:mə] f (-/-n) measure, step; 2**stab** m measure, rule(r); *Karte*: scale; *fig.* standard; ∼**voll** *adj* moderate.

Mast [mast] m (-[e]s/-en, -e) mast.

mästen ['mɛstən] v/t fatten, feed; *Geflügel*: stuff, cram.

Material [mate'ria:l] n (-s/-ien) material.

Mathematik [matema-

'ti:k] f (-/no pl) mathematics sg, pl; ~er [-'ma:tikər] m (-s/-) mathematician.

Matinee [mati'ne:] f (-/-n) morning performance.

Matratze [ma'tratsə] f (-/-n) mattress.

Matrose [ma'tro:zə] m (-n/-n) sailor, seaman.

Matsch [matʃ] m (-[e]s/no pl) mud, slush.

matt [mat] adj schwach: faint, feeble; trübe: dim(t); Auge, Licht: dim; Schach: (check)mate.

Matte ['matə] f (-/-n) mat.

Mattscheibe ['mat'ʃaibə] f (-/-n) screen.

Mauer ['mauər] f (-/-n) wall.

Maul [maul] n (-[e]s/-er) mouth; ~esel m hinny; ~korb m muzzle; ~tier n mule; ~wurf m mole.

Maurer ['maurər] m (-s/-) bricklayer, mason.

Maus [maus] f (-/-ue) mouse.

Maximum ['maksimʊm] n (-s/-xima) maximum.

Mechanik [me'ça:nik] f (-/-en) mechanics mst sg; ~ker m mechanic; 2sch adj mechanical; ~smus [-ça'nısmʊs] m (-/-smen) mechanism.

meckern ['mɛkərn] v/i bleat; fig. colloq. grumble.

Medaille [me'daljə] f (-/-n) medal; ~on [-dal-'jő:] n (-s/-s) locket.

Medikament [medika-'mɛnt] n (-[e]s/-e) medicine.

Medizin [medi'tsi:n] f (-/-en) medicine; 2isch adj medical; heilkräftig: medicinal; Seife etc.: medicated.

Meer [me:r] n (-[e]s/-e) sea, ocean; ~enge ['-?eŋə] f (-/-n) strait(s pl); ~esspiegel m sea level; ~rettich m horseradish; ~schweinchen n guinea-pig.

Mehl [me:l] n (-[e]s/-e) flour.

mehr [me:r] adv more; ich habe nichts ~ I have nothing left; ~deutig ['-dɔʏtiç] adj ambiguous; ~ere ['me:rərə] indef pron several, some; ~fach adj repeated; 2heit f majority; ~malig adj repeated; ~mals adv several times, repeatedly; 2wertsteuer f value-added tax; 2zahl f majority; gr. plural.

meiden ['maidən] v/t (irr) avoid.

Meile ['mailə] f (-/-n) mile.

mein [main] poss pron my.

Meineid ['main?ait] m (-[e]s/-e) perjury.

meinen ['mainən] v/t think, believe; Am. a. reckon, guess; äußern: say; sagen wollen: mean.

meinetwegen ['mainət-'ve:gən] adv for my sake; int. I don't mind od. care!

Meinung ['mainʊŋ] f (-/-en) opinion; meiner ~

nach in my opinion; **j-m (gehörig) die ~ sagen** give s.o. a piece of one's mind; **~sverschiedenheit** f difference of opinion; disagreement.

Meise ['maɪzə] f (-/-n) titmouse.

Meißel ['maɪsəl] m (-s/-) chisel.

meist [maɪst] adj most; **am ~en** most (of all); **~ens** adv mostly.

Meister ['maɪstər] m (-s/-) master; sp. champion; **~schaft** f sp. championship; **~werk** n masterpiece.

melancholisch [melaŋ-'koːlɪʃ] adj melancholy.

meld|en ['mɛldən] v/t announce; inform; amtlich: notify; report; **sich ~en** report (bei to); Schule: put up one's hand; answer the telephone; sp. enter; 2**ung** f (-/-en) announcement; report; Behörde: registration; sp. entry.

melken ['mɛlkən] v/t (irr) milk.

Melodie [melo'diː] f (-/-n) melody, tune, air.

Melone [me'loːnə] f (-/-n) melon.

Menge ['mɛŋə] f (-/-n) quantity; amount; Menschen2: crowd; **e-e ~** plenty of, lots of.

Mensch [mɛnʃ] m (-en/-en) human being; man; einzelner: person, individual; **die ~en** pl people pl,

mankind sg; **kein ~** nobody.

Menschen|affe ['mɛn-ʃən²afə] m (-n/-n) ape; **~kenntnis** f (-/no pl) knowledge of human nature; **~leben** n human life; 2**leer** adj deserted; **~menge** f crowd; **~rechte** pl human rights pl; 2**scheu** adj shy.

Menschheit ['mɛnʃhaɪt] f (-/no pl) mankind.

menschlich ['mɛnʃlɪç] adj human; fig. humane; 2**keit** f humanity.

Menstruation [mɛn-strua'tsjoːn] f (-/-en) menstruation.

Menü [me'nyː] n (-s/-s) menu, set lunch od. dinner.

merk|en ['mɛrkən] v/t notice, perceive; **sich et. ~en** remember s.th.; 2**mal** n (-[e]s/-e) characteristic, feature; **~würdig** adj strange, odd.

Meß|band ['mɛsbant] n (-[e]s/-ver) tape-measure; 2**bar** adj measurable.

Messe ['mɛsə] f (-/-n) fair; eccl. mass; **~gelände** n fairground.

messen ['mɛsən] v/t (irr) measure.

Messer ['mɛsər] n (-s/-) knife.

Messing ['mɛsɪŋ] n (-s/no pl) brass.

Metall [me'tal] n (-s/-e) metal; **~waren** pl hardware sg.

Meter ['me:tər] *m*, *n* me-t|re, *Am.* -er.

Methode [me'to:də] *f* (-/-n) method; technique.

Metzger ['metsgər] *m* (-s/-), ~ei [-'raɪ] *f* (-/-en) s. Fleischer(ei).

Meuterei [mɔʏtə'raɪ] *f* (-/-en) mutiny.

mich [mɪç] *pers pron* me; ~ (selbst) myself.

Mieder ['mi:dər] *n* (-s/-) bodice; *Korsett:* corset; ~waren *pl* foundation garments *pl.*

Miene ['mi:nə] *f* (-/-n) countenance, air.

Miet|e ['mi:tə] *f* (-/-n) rent; *für bewegliche Sachen:* hire; 2en *v/t* rent; *Wagen, Boot:* hire; ~er *m* (-s/-) tenant; *einzelner Zimmer:* lodger; 2frei *adj* rent-free; ~shaus *n* block of flats, *Am.* apartment house; ~vertrag *m* lease; ~wagen *m* hire(d) car; ~wohnung *f* flat, *Am.* apartment.

Mikro|phon [mikro'fo:n] *n* (-s/-e) microphone, *colloq.* mike; ~skop ['sko:p] *n* (-s/-e) microscope.

Milch [mɪlç] *f* (-/no pl) milk; *Fisch2:* milt, soft roe; ~glas *n* frosted glass; 2ig *adj* milky; ~kaffee *m* white coffee; ~kännchen *n* (milk-)jug; ~reis *m* rice pudding; ~zahn *m* milk-tooth.

mild [mɪlt] *adj* mild; soft, gentle; ~ern ['dərn] *v/t*

soften; *Schmerz:* soothe, alleviate.

Milieu [mi'ljø:] *n* (-s/-s) environment.

Militär [mili'tɛ:r] *n* (-s/no pl) military, army.

Milliarde [mɪ'ljardə] *f* (-/-n) billion; *früher Brit.* milliard; ~meter ['me:-tər] *m*, *n* millimetl|re, *Am.* -er; ~on [-'ljo:n] *f* (-/-en) million; ~onär [-ljo'nɛ:r] *m* (-s/-e) millionaire.

Milz [mɪlts] *f* (-/-en) spleen.

minder ['mɪndər] *adj* less; 2heit *f* minority; ~jährig *adj* under age.

minderwertig ['mɪndər-ve:rtɪç] *adj* inferior; 2keitskomplex *m* inferiority complex.

mindest ['mɪndəst] *adj* least; *geringst:* slightest; *kleinst:* minimum; ~ens *adv* at least.

Mine ['mi:nə] *f* (-/-n) mine; *Bleistift:* lead; *Ersatz2:* refill.

Mineral [mine'ra:l] *n* (-s/-e, -ien) mineral; ~öl *n* mineral oil, petroleum; ~wasser *n* mineral water.

Minirock ['minirɔk] *m* (-[e]s/ᵁe) miniskirt.

Minister [mi'nɪstər] *m* (-s/-) minister, *Brit. a.* secretary (of state), *Am.* secretary; ~ium [mɪnɪs'te:rjʊm] *n* (-s/-rien) ministry, *Brit. a.* office, *Am.* department.

minus ['mi:nʊs] *adv*, *prp* minus, less; *s.* **Grad**.

Minute [miˈnuːtə] f (-/-n) minute.

mir [miːr] pers pron (to) me.

mischen [ˈmɪʃən] v/t mix, mingle; blend; shuffle; **2ling** [-lɪŋ] m (-s/-e) half-breed; **2ung** f mixture.

mißachten [mɪsˈʔaxtən] v/t disregard, ignore; **2bildung** [ˈmɪs-] f deformity; **2billigen** [ˈmɪs-bɪlɪgən] v/t disapprove (of); **2brauch** [ˈmɪs-] m abuse; *falsche Anwendung:* misuse; **2erfolg** m failure; **2geschick** n bad luck, misfortune; *Panne etc.:* mishap; **2handlung** [-ˈhandluŋ] f ill-treatment.

Mission [mɪˈsjoːn] f (-/-en) mission; **~ar** [-sjoˈnaːr] m (-s/-e) missionary.

Mißkredit [ˈmɪskrediːt] m (-[e]s/-e): **in ~ bringen** bring discredit upon; **2lingen** [-ˈlɪŋən] v/i (irr) fail; **2mutig** [ˈmɪsmuːtɪç] adj ill-humo(u)red; discontented; **~stand** m nuisance, grievance; **2trauen** [-ˈtrauən] v/i distrust; **2trauisch** [ˈmɪs-] adj distrustful, suspicious; **~verständnis** n misunderstanding; **2verstehen** v/t (irr) misunderstand; *Absichten etc.:* mistake.

Mist [mɪst] m (-[e]s/no pl) dung, manure; *fig. colloq.* rubbish.

Mistel [ˈmɪstəl] f (-/-n) mistletoe.

Misthaufen [ˈmɪsthaufən] m (-s/-) dunghill.

mit [mɪt] prp (dat) with; **2arbeit** f co(-)operation; **2arbeiter** m colleague; **~bringen** v/t (irr) bring (with one); **2bürger** m fellow-citizen; **~einander** [-ʔaiˈnandər] adv with each other; together; **2esser** [ˈ-ʔɛsər] m (-s/no pl) med. blackhead; **~fahren** v/i (irr): **mit j-m** go with s.o.; **j-n ~ lassen** give s.o. a lift; **~fühlend** [ˈ-fyːlənt] adj sympathetic; **~geben** v/t (irr) give s.o. s.th. (to take along); **2gefühl** n sympathy; **~gehen** v/i (irr): **mit j-m ~** go with s.o.

Mitglied [ˈmɪtgliːt] n (-[e]s/-er) member; **~schaft** f membership.

Mitinhaber [ˈmɪtʔɪnhabər] m (-s/-) partner; **2kommen** v/i (irr) come along.

Mitleid [ˈmɪtlaɪt] n (-[e]s/no pl) compassion, pity; sympathy; **2ig** adj compassionate.

mitmachen [ˈmɪtmaxən] v/t take part in; *erleben:* go through; v/i: **~machen bei** join in; **2mensch** m fellow creature; **~nehmen** v/t (irr) take along (with one); *fig.* exhaust; **j-n (im Auto) ~nehmen** give s.o. a lift; **2reisende** m, f fellow-travel(l)er; **2schüler(in** f) m schoolfellow, schoolmate; ~**spielen** v/i join in the game; sp. be on the team; thea. be on the stage.

Mittag ['mɪtaːk] m (-s/-e) midday, noon; **heute** 2 at noon today; **zu ~ essen** lunch, dine; ~**essen** n lunch(eon); Hauptmahlzeit: dinner; 2s adv at noon.

Mittags|pause f lunch hour; ~**tisch** m dinner-table; ~**zeit** f noon.

Mitte ['mɪtə] f (-/-n) middle; centre; Am. -er.

mitteil|en ['mɪttaɪlən] v/t communicate; **j-m et. ~en** inform s.o. of s.th.; 2**ung** f communication; information.

Mittel ['mɪtəl] n (-s/-) means sg, way; Heil2: remedy (**gegen** for); Durchschnitt: average; ~ pl means pl, money sg; ~**alter** ['-ʔaltər] n (-s/no pl) Middle Ages pl; 2**alterlich** adj medi(a)eval; ~**finger** m middle finger; 2**groß** adj of medium height; medium-sized; 2**los** adj destitute; 2**mäßig** adj mediocre; ~**punkt** m centre, Am. -er; ~**stürmer** m sp. centre (Am. -er) forward.

mitten ['mɪtən] adv: ~ **in (auf, unter)** in the middle of.

Mitternacht ['mɪtərnaxt] f (-/no pl) midnight.

mittler ['mɪtlər] adj mid-

dle; average.

Mittwoch ['mɪtvɔx] m (-[e]s/-e) Wednesday.

Mitwisser ['mɪtvɪsər] m (-s/-) confidant; jur. accessory.

mixen ['mɪksən] v/t mix.

Möbel ['møːbəl] pl furniture sg; ~**stück** n piece of furniture; ~**wagen** m furniture (Am. moving) van.

möblieren [mø'bliːrən] v/t furnish.

Mode ['moːdə] f (-/-n) fashion, vogue; ~**artikel** pl fancy goods pl.

Modell [mo'del] n (-s/-e) model; Muster: pattern.

Mode(n)schau ['moːdə(n)ʃaʊ] f (-/-en) fashion parade od. show.

mod(e)rig [mo:d(ə)rɪç] adj musty, mo(u)ldy.

modern [mo'dern] adj modern; fashionable; ~**isieren** [-derni'ziːrən] v/t modernize.

Mode|salon ['moːdəza'lõː] m (-s/-s) fashion house; ~**schmuck** m (-[e]s/no pl) costume jewel(le)ry.

modisch ['moːdɪʃ] adj fashionable.

mogeln ['moːgəln] v/i colloq. cheat.

mögen ['møːgən] v/aux, v/t, v/i (irr) wollen: want (to); gern ~: like, be fond of; nicht ~: dislike; ich möchte wissen I should like to know; ich möchte lieber I would rather.

möglich 188

möglich ['mø:klɪç] *adj* possible; **so bald wie ~, ~st bald** *adv* as soon as possible; **2keit** *f* possibility.

Mohammedaner [moha'me:da:nər] *m* (-s/-) Muslim, Moslem.

Mohn [mo:n] *m* (-[e]s/*no pl*) poppy.

Möhre ['mø:rə] *f* (-/-n) carrot.

Mohrrübe ['mo:rry:bə] *f* (-/-n) carrot.

Mokka ['mɔka] *m* (-s/-s) mocha.

Mole ['mo:lə] *f* (-/-n) mole, jetty.

Molkerei [mɔlkə'raɪ] *f* (-/-en) dairy.

Moll [mɔl] *n* minor (key).

mollig ['mɔlɪç] *adj colloq.*: snug, cosy; *dicklich*: plump.

Moment [mo'mɛnt] *m* (-[e]s/-e) moment, instant.

Monarchie [monar'çi:] *f* (-/-n) monarchy.

Monat [mo:nat] *m* (-[e]s/-e) month; **2lich** *adj* monthly.

Mönch [mœnç] *m* (-[e]s/-e) monk; *Bettel2:* friar.

Mond [mo:nt] *m* (-[e]s/-e) moon; **~fähre** *f* lunar module; **~finsternis** *f* lunar eclipse; **~schein** *m* moonlight.

Monolog [mono'lo:k] *m* (-[e]s/-e) monolog(ue), soliloquy; **2ton** [-'to:n] *adj* monotonous.

Montag ['mo:nta:k] *m* (-[e]s/-e) Monday.

Mont|age [mɔn'ta:ʒə] *f* (-/-n) mounting, fitting; *Zusammenbau:* assemblage; **~eur** [-'tø:r] *m* (-s/-e) fitter; **2ieren** [-'ti:-rən] *v/t* mount, fit; assemble.

Moor [mo:r] *n* (-[e]s/-e) bog, swamp; **2ig** boggy, marshy.

Moos [mo:s] *n* (-es/-e) moss.

Moped ['mo:pɛt] *n* (-s/-s) moped.

Moral [mo'ra:l] *f* (-/*no pl*) morals (*pl.*); *Lehre:* moral; *mil. etc.:* morale.

Morast [mo'rast] *m* (-[e]s/-e) mud; **2ig** *adj* muddy.

Mord [mɔrt] *m* (-[e]s/-e) murder (**an** of).

Mörder ['mœrdər] *m* (-s/-) murderer.

Morgen ['mɔrgən] *m* (-s/-) morning; **am ~** *s.* **morgens; guten ~!** good morning!; **2** *adv* tomorrow; **2 früh** tomorrow morning; **~dämmerung** *f* dawn, daybreak; **~rock** *m* dressing-gown; **2s** *adv* in the morning.

morgig ['mɔrgɪç] *adj* tomorrow's.

Morphium ['mɔrfɪʊm] *n* (-s/*no pl*) morphia, morphine.

morsch [mɔrʃ] *adj* rotten, decayed.

Mörtel ['mœrtəl] *m* (-s/-) mortar, cement.

Mosaik [moza'i:k] n (-s/ -en, -e) mosaic.

Moschee [mɔ'ʃe:] f (-/-n) mosque.

Moskito [mɔs'ki:to] m (-s/ -s) mosquito.

Moslem ['mɔslem] m (-s/ -s) Muslim, Moslem.

Most [mɔst] m (-[e]s/-e) must, grape-juice; *Apfel*₂ cider.

Mostrich ['mɔstrɪç] m (-[e]s/no pl) mustard.

Motiv [mo'ti:f] n (-s/-e) motive, reason; *paint.*, *mus.* motif.

Motor ['mo:tɔr] m (-s/-en), [mo'to:r] (-s/-en) motor, engine; **~boot** n motor-boat; **~haube** f mot. bonnet, Am. hood; **~rad** n motor-cycle; **~radfahrer** m motor-cyclist; **~roller** m (motor-)scooter; **~schaden** m engine trouble.

Motte ['mɔtə] f (-/-n) moth.

Möwe ['mø:və] f (-/-n) gull.

Mücke ['mykə] f (-/-n) gnat, midge.

müde ['my:də] adj tired, weary.

muffig ['mufɪç] adj musty.

Mühe ['my:ə] f (-/-n) trouble, pains pl; **j-m ~ machen** give s.o. trouble; **sich ~ geben** take pains; 2los adj effortless, easy; 2voll adj hard, laborious.

Mühle ['my:lə] f (-/-n) mill.

mühsam ['my:za:m] adj laborious.

Mulde ['muldə] f (-/-n) depression, hollow.

Mull [mul] m (-[e]s/-e) gauze, mull.

Müll [myl] m (-[e]s/no pl) dust, refuse, rubbish, Am. garbage; **~abfuhr** f (-/ no pl) refuse (Am. garbage) disposal od. collection; **~eimer** m dustbin, Am. garbage od. ash can.

Müller ['mylər] m (-s/-) miller.

Mülltonne ['myltɔnə] f s. Mülleimer.

multiplizieren [multipli-'tsi:rən] v/t multiply (**mit** by).

Mund [munt] m (-[e]s/ ver) mouth; **~art** ['-'?a:rt] f (-/-en) dialect.

münden ['myndən] v/i: ~ in Fluß: flow into; Straße: lead into.

mündig ['myndɪç] adj: ~ (werden) come) of age.

mündlich ['myntlɪç] adj oral, verbal; adv orally, by word of mouth.

Mundstück n mouthpiece; Zigarette: tip.

Mündung ['myndʊŋ] f (-/ -en) mouth, ins Meer: estuary; Feuerwaffe: muzzle.

Mundwasser ['muntva-sər] n (-s/ver) mouthwash.

Munition [muni'tsio:n] f (-/no pl) ammunition.

munter ['muntər] adj wach: awake; lebhaft, fröhlich: lively, merry.

Münz|e ['myntsə] f (-/-n) coin; *Hartgeld:* (small) change; *Gedenkmünze:* medal; **~fernsprecher** [-fernʃpreçər] m coin-box od. public telephone; **~wechsler** [-vekslər] m (-s/-) change giver.

mürbe ['myrbə] adj tender; *Gebäck:* crisp, short.

murmel|n ['murməln] v/i, v/t mumble, murmur; **2tier** n marmot.

murren ['murən] v/i grumble.

mürrisch ['myrɪʃ] adj surly, sullen.

Mus [mu:s] n (-es/-e) pap; stewed fruit.

Muschel ['muʃəl] f (-/-n) mussel; *Schale:* shell; *teleph.* earpiece.

Museum [mu'ze:um] n (-s/-seen) museum.

Musik [mu'zi:k] f (-/no pl) music; **2alisch** [-zi'ka:lɪʃ] adj musical; **~automat** m juke-box; **~er** ['mu:zikər] m (-s/-) musician; **~instrument** n musical instrument; **~kapelle** f band.

Muskat [mus'ka:t] m (-[e]s/-e), **~nuß** f nutmeg.

Muskel ['muskəl] m (-s/-n) muscle; **~kater** [-ka:tər] m (-s/no pl) colloq.: **~ haben** be muscle-

bound; **~zerrung** f pulled muscle.

Muskul|atur [muskula'tu:r] f (-/-en) muscles pl; **2ös** [-ku'lø:s] adj muscular.

Muße ['mu:sə] f (-/no pl) leisure; spare time.

müssen ['mysən] v/aux (irr): **ich muß ...** I must ..., I have to ...

Muster ['mustər] n (-s/-) model; design, pattern; *Probestück:* specimen, sample; *fig.* model, example; **2n** ['mustərn] v/t pattern; *prüfen:* examine.

Mut [mu:t] m (-[e]s/no pl) courage; **2ig** adj courageous; **2maßlich** adj supposed.

Mutter ['mutər] f (-/¨) mother; (-/-n) *Schraube:* nut; **~leib** m womb.

mütterlich ['mytərlɪç] adj motherly, maternal.

mutter|los ['mutərlo:s] adj motherless; **2mal** [-ma:l] n (-[e]s/-e) birthmark, mole; **2sprache** f mother tongue.

mutwillig ['mu:tvilɪç] adj wanton, mischievous.

Mütze ['mytsə] f (-/-n) cap.

mysteriös [myste'riø:s] adj mysterious.

Mythologie [mytolo'gi:] f (-/-n) mythology.

N

Nabe ['na:bə] f (-/-n) hub.
Nabel ['na:bəl] m (-s/-)
navel.

nach [na:x] prp (dat) after;
to(wards), for; Reihen-
folge: after; Zeit: after,
past; according to; adv after; ~ und ~ little by little,
gradually.

nachahmen ['na:xʔa-
mən] v/t imitate, copy; fälschen: counterfeit.

Nachbar ['naxba:r] m
(-n, -s/-n), **~in** f (-/
-nen) neighbo(u)r; **~**-
schaft f neighbo(u)r-
hood, vicinity.

nachdem [na:x'de:m] cj
after, when; **je ~** depend-
ing on.

nach|denken ['na:xdeŋ-
kən] v/i (irr) think (**über**
over, about); **~denklich**
adj pensive; **2druck** m (no
pl) fig. stress, emphasis;
~drücklich ['-drykliç]
adv: **~ betonen** empha-
size; **~eifern** ['-ʔaifərn]
v/i emulate.

nacheinander [na:xʔai-
'nandər] adv one after the
other.

nacherzähl|en ['na:xʔɛr-
tsɛ:lən] v/t retell; **2lung** f
story retold.

Nachfolger ['na:xfɔlgər]
m (-s/-) successor.

nachforsch|en ['na:xfɔr-
ʃən] v/i investigate; **2ung**
f investigation.

Nachfrage ['na:xfra:gə] f
(-/-n) inquiry; econ. de-
mand; **2n** v/i inquire.

nach|fühlen ['na:xfy:lən]
v/t: **es j-m ~** feel od. sympathize with s.o.; **~füllen**
v/t refill; **~geben** v/i (irr)
give way; fig. give in, yield;
2gebühr f surcharge;
~gehen v/i (irr) follow;
Uhr: be slow; **~giebig**
[-gi:biç] adj fig. compliant;
~haltig adj lasting.

nachher [na:x'he:r, 'na:x-
he:r] adv afterwards.

Nachhilfeunterricht
['na:xhilfə-] m private
lesson(s pl), coaching.

nachholen ['na:xho:lən]
v/t make up for.

Nachkomme ['na:xkɔ-
mə] m (-n/-n) descendant;
~n pl bsd. jur. issue sg; **2n**
v/i (irr) follow.

Nachkriegs... ['na:x-
kri:ks-] post-war ...

Nachlaß ['na:xlas] m
(-sses/ᵁe) econ. reduc-
tion, discount; jur. assets
pl, estate.

nach|lassen ['na:xlasən]
v/i (irr) Wind, Schmerz etc.:
abate; Interesse, Kräfte:
flag; **~lässig** adj careless,
negligent; **~laufen** v/i
(irr) run after; **~lesen** v/t
(irr) look up; **~lösen** v/i,
v/t take a supplementary
ticket; **~machen** v/t s.
nachahmen.

Nachmittag ['naːxmɪ-taːk] m (-[e]s/-e) afternoon; **am ~ =** 2s adv in the afternoon.

Nachnahme ['naːxnaː-mə] f (-/-n) cash on delivery; **~name** m surname, last name; **~porto** n surcharge; 2**prüfen** v/t verify; check; **~rechnen** v/t check.

Nachricht ['naːxrɪçt] f (-/-en) news sg; Botschaft: message; Bericht: report.

Nachruf ['naːxruːf] m (-[e]s/-e) obituary (notice).

nach|sagen ['naːxzaːgən] v/t repeat; 2**saison** [-zɛzõː] f dead od. off season; **~schicken** v/t s. nachsenden; 2**schlagen** v/t (irr) look up; 2**schlüssel** m skeleton key; 2**schub** [-ʃuːp] m (-[e]s/no pl) supplies pl; **~sehen** v/i (irr) look after; **~sehen ob** (go and) see whether; v/t examine, inspect; check; look up; **~senden** v/t (irr) send on, forward (dat to); **~sichtig** [-zɪçtɪç] adj indulgent, forbearing; 2**silbe** f gr. suffix; 2**sitzen** v/i (irr): **~ müssen** be kept in; 2**speise** f dessert.

nächst [nɛːçst] adj next; Entfernung, Beziehung: nearest.

nachstellen ['naːxʃtɛlən] v/t Uhr: put back; tech. readjust.

Nächstenliebe ['nɛːç-stənliːbə] f (-/no pl) charity.

Nacht [naxt] f (-/⸚e) night; **in der ~** s. nachts; **gute ~!** good night!; 2**dienst** m night duty.

Nachteil ['naːxtaɪl] m (-s/-e) disadvantage; 2**ig** adj disadvantageous.

Nacht|hemd ['naxthɛmt] n (-[e]s/-en) nightdress, nightgown; Männer2: nightshirt.

Nachtigall ['naxtɪgal] f (-/-en) nightingale.

Nachtisch ['naːxtɪʃ] m (-[e]s/-e) sweet, dessert.

Nacht|lokal ['naxtlokaːl] n (-s/-e) nightclub; **~portier** m night-porter.

nachträglich ['naːxtrɛːk-lɪç] adj, adv later.

nachts [naxts] adv at od. by night; 2**schicht** f night-shift; 2**tisch** m bedside table; 2**wächter** m (night-)watchman.

nach|wachsen ['naːx-vaksən] v/i (irr) grow again; 2**weis** [-vaɪs] m (-es/-e) proof; 2**weisen** v/t (irr) prove; 2**welt** f posterity; 2**wirkung** f after-effect; 2**wort** n epilog(ue); **~zählen** v/t count over (again); check; 2**zahlung** f additional payment.

Nacken ['nakən] m (-s/-) nape (of the neck), neck.

nackt [nakt] adj naked, nude, bare.

Nadel ['naːdəl] f (-/-n)

needle; Steck2, Haar2 etc.: pin; **~baum** m conifer(ous tree).

Nagel ['na:gəl] m (-s/¨) nail; Beschlag: stud; **~lack** m nail varnish; **~lackentferner** ['-ʔɛntfɛrnər] m (-s/-) nail-varnish remover; **~schere** f (e-e a pair of) nail scissors pl.

nage|n ['na:gən] v/i, v/t gnaw; **~n an** gnaw at; Knochen: pick; 2tier n rodent.

nah(e) [na:, 'na:ə] adj, adv near, close (**bei** to).

Nähe ['nɛ:ə] f (-/no pl) nearness; vicinity; **in der ~** close by od. to.

nähen ['nɛ:ən] v/t, v/i sew, stitch.

näher ['nɛ:ər] adj, adv nearer, closer; Weg: shorter; **~n** ['nɛ:ərn] v/refl: **sich ~** approach.

Näh|garn ['nɛ:garn] n (-[e]s/-e) cotton; **~maschine** f sewing-machine; **~nadel** f needle.

nahr|haft ['na:rhaft] adj nutritious, nourishing; **2ung** f (-/no pl) food, nourishment; **2ungsmittel** pl food sg, victuals pl.

Naht [na:t] f (-/¨e) seam; med. suture.

Nähzeug ['nɛ:tsɔyg] n sewing-kit.

naiv [na'i:f] adj naïve, naive, simple.

Name ['na:mə] m (-ns/

~n) name; **~enstag** m name-day; 2entlich adv by name; especially.

nämlich ['nɛ:mlɪç] adv that is (to say).

Napf [napf] m (-[e]s/¨e) bowl, basin.

Narbe ['narbə] f (-/-n) scar.

Narko|se [nar'ko:zə] f (-/-n) narcosis; **~tikum** [-'ko:tikum] n (-s/-ka) narcotic.

Narr [nar] m (-en/-en) fool; jester.

Närr|in ['nɛrɪn] f (-/-nen) fool(ish woman); 2isch adj foolish, silly.

Narzisse [nar'tsɪsə] f (-/-n) narcissus; **gelbe ~** daffodil.

nasal [na'za:l] adj nasal.

naschen ['naʃən] v/i: **gern ~** have a sweet tooth.

Nase ['na:zə] f (-/-n) nose.

Nasen|bluten ['na:zənblu:tən] n (-s/no pl) nosebleed; **~loch** n nostril; **~spitze** f tip of the nose.

Nashorn ['na:shɔrn] n (-s/¨er) rhinoceros.

naß [nas] adj wet.

Nässe ['nɛsə] f (-/no pl) wet(ness).

naßkalt ['naskalt] adj damp and cold, raw.

Nation [na'tsĭo:n] f (-/-en) nation.

national [natsĭo'na:l] adj national; **2hymne** f national anthem; 2**ität** [-nali'tɛ:t] f (-/-en) nationality; 2**itäts(kenn)zei-**

chen n mot. nationality plate; ♀**mannschaft** f national team.

Natter ['natər] f (-/-n) adder, viper.

Natur [na'tu:r] f (-/-en) nature; ~**forscher** m naturalist; ~**gesetz** n law of nature, natural law; ♀**getreu** [-gətɔy] adj true to nature; lifelike; ~**kunde** [-kundə] f (-/no pl) biology.

natürlich [na'ty:rlɪç] adj natural; unaffected; adv naturally; of course.

Naturschutzgebiet [na'tu:rʃutsgəbi:t] n (-[e]s/-e), ~**schutzpark** m national park, wildlife (p)reserve; ~**wissenschaft** f (natural) science; ~**wissenschaftler** m (natural) scientist.

Nebel ['ne:bəl] m (-s/-) mist; stärker: fog.

neben ['ne:bən] prp (dat, acc) beside; compared with; ~**an** [-'ʔan] adv next door; ♀**ausgang** m sideexit; ~**bei** [-'bai] adv by the way; besides; ♀**beruf** m, ♀**beschäftigung** f sideline; ~**einander** [-ʔai'nandər] adv side by side; ♀**eingang** m sideentrance; ♀**fach** n subsidiary subject; Am. minor (subject); ♀**fluß** m tributary; ♀**gebäude** n adjoining building; Anbau: annex(e); ♀**kosten** pl extra charges pl, extras pl;

♀**produkt** n by-product; ~**sächlich** [-zɛçlɪç] adj unimportant; ♀**satz** m gr. subordinate clause; ♀**straße** f by-road, sideroad; ♀**tisch** m next table; ♀**wirkung** f side-effect; ♀**zimmer** n adjoining room.

neblig ['ne:blɪç] adj foggy; misty.

Necessaire [nesɛ'sɛ:r] n (-s/-s) travel kit.

necken ['nɛkən] v/t tease, banter.

Neffe ['nɛfə] m (-n/-n) nephew.

negativ [nega'ti:f] adj negative.

Neger ['ne:gər] m (-s/-) Negro; ~**in** f (-/-nen) Negress.

nehmen ['ne:mən] v/t (irr) take.

Neid [nait] m (-[e]s/no pl) envy; ♀**isch** adj envious.

neigen ['naigən] v/t (sich) ~ bend, incline; v/i: ~ **zu** be inclined to; ♀**ung** f inclination (a. fig.), slope.

nein [nain] adv no.

Nelke ['nɛlkə] f (-/-n) carnation; Gewürze: clove.

nennen ['nɛnən] v/t (irr) name, call; mention; **sich** ... ~ be called ...; ~**swert** adj worth mentioning.

Neon ['ne:ɔn] n (-s/no pl) neon.

Nerv [nɛrf] m (-s/-en) nerve; **j-m auf die ~en**

fallen *od.* **gehen** get on s.o.'s nerves.

Nerven|arzt ['nɛrfən-ʔartst] *m* (-es/ᵂe) neurologist; **~heilanstalt** *f*, **~klinik** *f* mental hospital; **~system** *n* nervous system; **~zusammenbruch** *m* nervous breakdown.

nervlös [nɛr'vøːs] *adj* nervous; 2**osität** [-vozi'tɛːt] *f* (-/no *pl*) nervousness.

Nerz [nɛrts] *m* (-es/-e) mink.

Nessel ['nɛsəl] *f* (-/-n) nettle.

Nest [nɛst] *n* (-[e]s/-er) nest.

nett [nɛt] *adj* nice; pretty; kind.

netto ['nɛto] *adv econ.* net.

Netz [nɛts] *n* (-es/-e) net; *fig.* network; **~anschluß** *m* mains supply; **~haut** *f* retina; **~karte** *f* area season ticket.

neu [nɔy] *adj* new; *kürzlich:* recent; *modern;* **~este Nachrichten** latest news; **von ~em** anew, afresh; **was gibt es 2es?** what is the news?; *Am.* what is new?; **~artig** ['-ʔaːrtɪç] *adj* novel; 2**bau** *m* new building; **~geboren** *adj* new-born; **~gier**(-**de**) ['-giːr(də)] *f* (-/no *pl*) curiosity; **~gierig** *adj* curious; 2**heit** *f* novelty; 2**igkeit** (-e-e-a piece of) news *sg;* 2**jahr** *n* New Year('s Day); **~lich** *adv*

the other day, recently; 2**mond** *m* new moon.

neun [nɔyn] *adj* nine; **~te** *adj* ninth; 2**tel** ['nɔyntəl] *n* (-s/-) ninth part; **~tens** *adv* ninthly; **~zehn**(**te**) *adj* nineteen(th); **~zig** ['-tsɪç] *adj* ninety; **~zigste** ['-tsɪçstə] *adj* ninetieth.

neutral [nɔy'traːl] *adj* neutral; 2**alität** [-trali-'tɛːt] *f* (-/no *pl*) neutrality; 2**um** [nɔy'troːm] *n* (-s/ -tra) *gr.* neuter.

Neuzeit ['nɔytsaɪt] *f* (-/no *pl*) modern times *pl*.

nicht [nɪçt] *adv* not; **~ mehr** no more, no longer.

Nichte ['nɪçtə] *f* (-/-n) niece.

Nichtraucher ['nɪçtraux-ər] *m* (-s/-) nonsmoker.

nichts [nɪçts] *indef pron* nothing.

Nichtschwimmer *m* (-s/ -) non-swimmer.

nicken ['nɪkən] *v/i* nod.

nie [niː] *adv* never.

nieder ['niːdər] *adj* low; *fig.* inferior; *adv* down; **~geschlagen** *adj* dejected, downcast; 2**kunft** [-kʊnft] *f* (-/ᵂe) confinement; 2**lage** *f* defeat; **~lassen** *v/refl* (*irr*): **sich ~** sit down; *Vogel:* alight; settle; 2**lassung** *f* settlement; *Zweiggeschäft:* branch, agency; **~legen** *v/t* lay *od.* put down; *Amt:* resign; **sich ~legen** lie down, go to bed; 2**schläge** [-ʃlɛːgə] *pl* me-

niedlich

teor. precipitation *sg;* rain *sg;* **~schlagen** *v/t (irr)* knock down, floor; *Augen:* cast down; *Aufstand:* put down; **2ung** *f* lowlands *pl.*

niedlich ['ni:tlɪç] *adj* sweet, nice, pretty.

niedrig ['ni:drɪç] *adj* low (*a. fig.*).

niemals ['ni:ma:ls] *adv* never, at no time.

niemand ['ni:mant] *indef pron* nobody, no one; **2sland** *n* -[e]s/*no pl* no-man's-land.

Niere ['ni:rə] *f* (-/-n) kidney.

nieseln ['ni:zəln] *v/i:* es **~t** it is drizzling; **2regen** *m* drizzle.

niesen ['ni:zən] *v/i* sneeze.

nippen ['nɪpən] *v/i* sip (**an** at).

nirgends ['nɪrgənts] *adv* nowhere.

Nische ['ni:ʃə] *f* (-/-n) niche, recess.

nisten ['nɪstən] *v/i* nest.

Niveau [ni'vo:] *n* (-s/-s) level; *fig. a.* standard.

noch [nɔx] *adv* still; *v/a:* **~ ein** another, one more; **~ einmal** once more *od.* again; **~ etwas?** anything else?; **~ immer** still; **~ nicht** not yet; **~ nie** never before; **~mals** ['nɔxma:ls] *adv* once more *od.* again.

Nominativ ['no:minati:f] *m* (-s/-e) *gr.* nominative (case).

nominieren [nomi'ni:rən] *v/t* nominate.

Nonne ['nɔnə] *f* (-/-n) nun.

Nonstopflug [nɔn'stɔp-flu:k] *m* (-[e]s/*ue) nonstop flight.

Nord (*m*) [nɔrt, 'nɔr-dən] north.

nördlich ['nœrtlɪç] *adj* northern, northerly.

Nord|ost(en *m*) [nɔrt-'?ɔst(ən)] northeast; **~pol** ['nɔrtpo:l] *m* -s/*no pl* North Pole; **~see** *f* North Sea; **~west(en** *m*) northwest.

nörgeln ['nœrgəln] *v/i* nag.

Norm [nɔrm] *f* (-/-en) standard; *Regel:* rule; **2al** [-'ma:l] *adj* normal; *gewohnt:* regular; *Maß, Gewicht, Zeit:* standard.

Not [no:t] *f* (-/*ue) need, distress; want; trouble; *Elend:* misery.

Notar [no'ta:r] *m* (-s/-e) *mst* notary public.

Not|ausgang ['no:t?aus-gaŋ] *m* (-[e]s/*ue) emergency exit; **~behelf** [-bəhɛlf] *m* (-[e]s/-e) makeshift; **~bremse** *f* emergency brake; *rail.* communication cord; **~durft** [-dʊrft] *f* (-/*no pl*) *s-e* **~ verrichten** relieve o.s.; **2dürftig** *adj* scanty, poor; temporary.

Note ['no:tə] *f* (-/-n) note; *Zensur:* mark.

Not|fall ['no:tfal] *m* (-[e]s/*ue) emergency; **2falls** *adv* if necessary.

oben

notieren [no'ti:rən] *v/t* make a note of, note down. **nötig** ['nø:tɪç] *adj* necessary; **~ haben** need. **Notiz** [no'ti:ts] *f* (-/-en) notice; *Vermerk:* note; **~buch** *n* notebook. **not|landen** [no:tlandən] *v/i* make an emergency landing; **~landung** *f* emergency landing; **~lei-dend** *adj* needy, distressed; **~ruf** *m* teleph. emergency call; **~rutsche** *f* aer. emergency chute; **~signal** *n* emergency *od.* distress signal; **~wehr** [-ve:r] *f* (-/no pl) self-defen|ce, *Am.* -se; **~wendig** [-vendɪç] *adj* necessary; **~zucht** *f* (-/no pl) rape. **Novelle** [no'vɛlə] *f* (-/-n) novelette. **November** [no'vɛmbər] *m* (-s/no pl) November. **Nu** [nu:] *m*: **im ~** in no time. **nüchtern** ['nʏçtərn] *adj* sober; *sachlich:* matter-of-fact. **Nudel** ['nu:dəl] *f* (-/-n) noodle. **null** [nʊl] *adj* zero; **zwei zu ~** two-nil; **2** *f* (-/-en)

zero, nought, cipher; *teleph.* O [əu], zero; **2punkt** *m* zero. **numerieren** [nume'ri:-rən] *v/t* number. **Nummer** ['numər] *f* (-/-n) number; *Zeitung etc.:* a. copy; *Größe:* size; **~-schild** *n* mot. number plate. **nun** [nu:n] *adv* now, at present; **~?** well? **nur** [nu:r] *adv* only; but; *bloß:* merely; **~ noch** only. **Nuß** [nus] *f* (-/-sse) nut; **~kern** *m* kernel; **~knacker** *m* nutcracker. **Nüstern** ['nʏstərn] *pl* nostrils *pl.* **Nutzen** ['nʊtsən] *m* (-s/no pl) use; *Gewinn:* profit, gain; *Vorteil:* advantage; **2** *v/i, v/t s.* **nützen.** **nütz|en** ['nʏtsən] *v/i* be of use; **es ~t nichts zu** it is no use *ger; v/t* make use of; *Gelegenheit:* seize; **~lich** *adj* useful; advantageous. **nutzlos** ['nʊtslo:s] *adj* useless. **Nylon** ['naɪlɔn] *n* (-s/no pl) nylon.

O

o [o:] *int.* oh!, ah! **Oase** [o'a:zə] *f* (-/-n) oasis. **ob** [ɔp] *cj* whether, if. **Obdach** ['ɔpdax] *n* (-[e]s/no pl) shelter, lodging;

2los *adj* homeless. **oben** ['o:bən] *adv* above; up; at the top; upstairs; **von ~** from above; **~an** [-'?an] *adv* at the top; **~auf** [-'?auf] *adv* on the top; on

the surface; **~erwähnt,
~genannt** adj above-mentioned.

ober ['o:bər] adj upper, higher.

Ober ['o:bər] m (-s/-) (head) waiter.

Ober|arm ['o:bərʔarm] m (-[e]s/-e) upper arm; **~arzt** m senior physician; **~befehlshaber** [-bəfe:lsha:bər] m commander-in-chief; **~fläche** f surface; **~flächlich** adj superficial; **2halb** [-halp] prp (gen) above; **~hemd** n shirt; **~kellner** m head waiter; **~kiefer** m upper jaw; **~körper** m upper part of the body; **~lippe** f upper lip; **~schenkel** m thigh; **~schule** f secondary school, Am. appr. (senior) high school.

oberst ['o:bərst] adj uppermost, top(most); highest; **2** m (-en, -s/-en, -e) colonel.

obgleich [ɔp'glaɪç] cj (al)though.

Obhut ['ɔphu:t] f (-/no pl) care, custody.

Objekt [ɔp'jɛkt] n (-[e]s/-e) object (a. gr.).

objektiv [ɔpjɛk'ti:f] adj objective; **2** n (-s/-e) phot. lens.

Obst [o:pst] n (-[e]s/no pl) fruit; **~garten** m orchard; **~händler** m fruiterer.

obszön [ɔps'tsø:n] adj obscene, filthy.

obwohl [ɔp'vo:l] cj (al-)

though.

Ochse ['ɔksə] m (-n/-n) ox; **~nfleisch** n beef.

öd(e) [ø:t, 'ø:də] adj deserted, desolate.

oder ['o:dər] cj or.

Ofen ['o:fən] m (-s/-ü) stove; Back2.: oven; **~rohr** n stove-pipe.

offen ['ɔfən] adj open (a. fig.); Stelle: vacant; fig. frank, outspoken; **~bar** adj obvious; **~lassen** v/t (irr) leave open; **~sichtlich** adj evident, obvious.

offensiv [ɔfɛn'zi:f] adj offensive.

offenstehen ['ɔfənʃte:ən] v/i (irr) stand open.

öffentlich ['œfəntliç] adj public; **~er Dienst** civil service; **2** adv publicly, in public; **2keit** f publicity; the public.

offiziell [ɔfi'tsjɛl] adj official.

Offizier [ɔfi'tsi:r] m (-s/-e) officer.

öffn|en ['œfnən] v/t: (sich) **~** open; **2er** m opener; **2ung** f opening.

oft [ɔft] adv often, frequently.

öfter ['œftər] adv (more) often.

oh [o:] int. o(h)!

ohne ['o:nə] prp (acc) without; **~hin** [-'hin] adv anyhow, anyway.

Ohn|macht ['o:nmaxt] f (-/-en) med. unconsciousness; **in ~macht fallen** faint; **2mächtig** adj powerless; *med.* unconscious; **2mächtig werden** faint.

Ohr [o:r] *n* (-[e]s/-en) ear.

Öhr [ø:r] *n* (-[e]s/-e) *Nadel:* eye.

Ohren|arzt ['o:rən?artst] *m* (-[e]s/¨e) ear specialist; **2betäubend** *adj* deafening; **~schmerzen** *pl* earache *sg.*

Ohr|feige ['o:rfaigə] *f* (-/-n) box on the ear(s); **~läppchen** [-lɛpçən] *n* (-s/-) lobe of the ear; **~ring** *m* ear-ring.

Oktober [ɔk'to:bər] *m* (-s/no *pl*) October.

Öl [ø:l] *n* (-[e]s/-e) oil; **2en** *v/t* oil; *tech. a.* lubricate; **~gemälde** *n* oil-painting; **~heizung** *f* oil-heating; **2ig** *adj* oily.

Olive [o'li:və] *f* (-/-n) olive.

olympisch [o'lʏmpiʃ] *adj* Olympic; **2e Spiele** *pl* Olympic Games *pl.*

Omelett [ɔm(ə)'lɛt] *n* (-[e]s/-e, -s) omelet(te).

Omnibus ['ɔmnibus] *m* (-ses/-se) *s.* **Autobus.**

Onkel ['ɔŋkəl] *m* (-s/-) uncle.

Oper ['o:pər] *f* (-/-n) opera; opera-house.

Operation [opera'tsio:n] *f* (-/-en) operation.

Operette [ope'rɛtə] *f* (-/-n) operetta.

operieren [ope'ri:rən] *v/t:* **j-n ~** operate (up)on

s.o.; **sich ~ lassen** undergo an operation.

Opernglas ['o:pərngla:s] *n* (-es/¨er) opera-glasses *pl.*

Opfer ['ɔpfər] *n* (-s/-) sacrifice; victim; **2n** ['ɔpfərn] *v/t* sacrifice.

Opposition [opozi-'tsio:n] *f* (-/-en) opposition.

Optiker ['ɔptikər] *m* (-s/-) optician.

Optimist [opti'mist] *m* (-en/-en) optimist; **2isch** *adj* optimistic.

Orange [o'rã:ʒə] *f* (-/-n) orange; **~ade** [-'ʒa:də] *f* (-/-n) orangeade; **~nmarmelade** *f* marmalade.

Orchester [ɔr'kɛstər] *n* (-s/-) orchestra.

Orchidee [ɔrçi'de:ə] *f* (-/-n) orchid.

Orden ['ɔrdən] *m* (-s/-) order (*a. eccl.*); medal, decoration.

ordentlich ['ɔrdəntlıç] *adj* tidy; *richtig:* proper; *tüchtig:* good, sound.

ordinär [ɔrdi'nɛ:r] *adj* common, vulgar.

ordn|en ['ɔrdnən] *v/t* put in order; arrange; **2er** *m* file; **2ung** *f* order; class; **in 2ung bringen** put in order; **2ungszahl** *f* ordinal number.

Organ [ɔr'ga:n] *n* (-s/-e) organ.

Organisation [ɔrganiza-'tsio:n] *f* (-/-en) organization.

organisch [ɔr'ga:nıʃ] *adj* organic.

organisieren [ɔrgani'zi:rən] *v/t* organize.

Organismus [ɔrga'nısmus] *m* (-/-men) organism; *biol. a.* system.

Orgel ['ɔrgəl] *f* (-/-n) *mus.* organ.

orientalisch [ɔriɛn'ta:lıʃ] *adj* oriental.

orientier|en [ɔriɛn'ti:rən] *v/t/refl:* **sich ~** orientate o.s.; **2ung** *f* orientation; **die 2ung verlieren** lose one's bearings.

Origin|al [ɔrigi'na:l] *n* (-s/-e) original; **2al** *adj* original; **2ell** [-'nɛl] *adj* original; *kunstvoll:* ingenious.

Orkan [ɔr'ka:n] *m* (-[e]s/-e) hurricane.

Ort [ɔrt] *m* (-[e]s/-e) place; village.

Orthopäde [ɔrto'pɛ:də] *m* (-n/-n) orthop(a)edist.

örtlich ['œrtlıç] *adj* local.

Ortschaft ['ɔrtʃaft] *f* (-/-en) place, village.

Orts|gespräch ['ɔrtsgəʃprɛ:ç] *n* (-[e]s/-e) *teleph.* local call; **~kenntnis** *f* knowledge of a place; **2kundig** [-kundıç] *adj* familiar with the locality; **~zeit** *f* local time.

Öse ['ø:zə] *f* (-/-n) *tech.* eye; *Schuh:* eyelet.

Ost(en *m*) [ɔst, 'ɔstən] east.

Oster|ei ['o:stər'?aı] *n* (-[e]s/-er) Easter egg; **~hase** *m* Easter bunny *od.* rabbit; **~n** ['o:stərn] *n* (-/-) Easter.

Österreich|er ['ø:stəraıçər] *m* (-s/-) Austrian; **2isch** *adj* Austrian.

östlich ['œstlıç] *adj* eastern, easterly; *adv:* **~ von** east of.

Otter[1] ['ɔtər] *m* (-s/-) otter.

Otter[2] *f* (-/-n) adder, viper.

Ouvertüre [uver'ty:rə] *f* (-/-n) overture.

oval [o'va:l] *adj* oval.

Ox|id [ɔ'ksi:t] *n* (-[e]s/-e) oxide; **2ydieren** [ɔksy-di:rən] *v/t, v/i* oxidize.

Ozean ['o:tsea:n] *m* (-s/-e) ocean.

P

Paar [pa:r] *n* (-[e]s/-e) pair; *Ehe2 etc.:* couple; **2** *indef pron:* **ein ~** a few, some; **2er** ['pa:rər] *m:* **(sich) ~** mate; **2weise** ['-vaızə] *adv* in pairs.

Pacht [paxt] *f* (-/-en) lease; **2en** ['paxtən] *v/t* (take on) lease, rent.

Pächter ['pɛçtər] *m* (-s/-), **~in** *f* lessee, leaseholder, tenant.

Päckchen ['pɛkçən] *n* (-s/-) small parcel, *Am. a.* package; **ein ~ Zigaretten** a pack(et) of cigarettes.

pack|en ['pakən] *v/t* pack (up); *derb fassen*: grip, grasp, clutch; **2boot** *n* brown paper; **2ung** *f* pack(age), packet; *med.*: pack; *Breipackung*: poultice; *e-e* **2ung Zigaretten** *s.* **Päckchen.**

pädagogisch [pɛda'goːgɪʃ] *adj* pedagogic(al).

Paddel ['padəl] *n* (-s/-) paddle; **2boot** *n* canoe; **2n** ['padəln] *v/i* paddle, canoe.

Paket [pa'keːt] *n* (-[e]s/ -e) parcel, package.

Palast [pa'last] *m* (-[e]s/ ⁻e) palace.

Palme ['palmə] *f* (-/-n) palm(-tree); **~sonntag** *m* Palm Sunday.

panieren [pa'niːrən] *v/t* bread, crumb.

Panik ['paːnɪk] *f* (-/-en) panic.

Panne ['panə] *f* (-/-n) breakdown, *mot. a.* engine trouble; *Reifen2*: puncture; *fig.*: mishap; **~ndienst** *m mot.* breakdown service.

Panorama [pano'raːma] *n* (-s/-men) panorama.

Panther ['pantər] *m* (-s/-) panther.

Pantoffel [pan'tɔfəl] *m* (-s/-n, -) slipper.

Panzer ['pantsər] *m* (-s/-) armo(u)r; *mil.* tank; *zo.* shell; **~schrank** *m* safe.

Papa [pa'paː, 'papa] *m* (-s/-s) papa, *colloq.* dad(dy).

Papagei [papa'gaɪ] *m* (-s, -en/-en) parrot.

Papier [pa'piːr] *n* (-s/-e) paper; **~e** *pl* papers *pl*, documents *pl*; *Ausweis*: papers *pl*, identity card *sg*; **~geld** *n* paper-money; banknotes *pl*, *Am.* bills *pl*; **~korb** *m* wastepaper basket; **~waren** *pl* stationery *sg*.

Pappe ['papə] *f* (-/-n) pasteboard, cardboard.

Pappel ['papəl] *f* (-/-n) poplar.

Papp|karton [-'kartɔː] *m* (-s/-s), **~schachtel** *f* cardboard box, carton.

Paprika ['paprika] *m* (-s/ -[s]) paprika; **~schoten** *pl* peppers *pl*.

Papst [paːpst] *m* (-es/⁻e) pope.

Parade [pa'raːdə] *f* (-/-n) parade.

Paradies [para'diːs] *n* (-es/-e) paradise.

Paragraph [para'graːf] *m* (-en/-en) *jur.* article, section; *print.* paragraph.

parallel [para'leːl] *adj* parallel.

Parfüm [par'fyːm] *n* (-s/ -e, -s) perfume, scent.

Park [park] *m* (-s/-s) park; **2en** ['parkən] *v/t, v/i* park; **2en verboten!** no parking!

Parkett [par'kɛt] *n* (-[e]s/ -e) parquet; *thea.* stalls *pl*, *Am.* orchestra.

Park|gebühr ['parkgə-byːr] *f* (-/-en) parking fee;

~haus n parking garage; **~lücke** f parking space; **~platz** m car park, parking lot; **~uhr** f parking meter; **~verbot(s-schild)** n no parking (sign).

Parlament [parla'mɛnt] n (-[e]s/-e) parliament.

Parodie [paro'di:] f (-/-n) parody.

Partei [par'taɪ] f (-/-en) party; **≈isch** ['-taɪʃ] adj partial; **≈los** adj independent.

Parterre [par'tɛr(ə)] n (-s/-s) s. **Erdgeschoß.**

Partie [par'ti:] f (-/-n) Spiel: game; mus. part.

Partisan [parti'za:n] m (-s, -en/-en) partisan, gue(r)rilla.

Partizip [parti'tsi:p] n (-s/-ien) gr. participle.

Partner ['partnər] m (-s/-), **~in** f partner; **~schaft** f partnership.

Parzelle [par'tsɛlə] f (-/-n) plot, lot.

Paß [pas] m (-sses/ᵛsse) pass (a. Fußball etc.); Reise≈: passport.

Passage [pa'sa:ʒə] f (-/-n) passage.

Passagier [pasa'ʒi:r] m (-s/-e) passenger.

Passant [pa'sant] m (-en/-en), **~in** f passerby.

Paßbild ['pasbɪlt] n (-[e]s/-er) passport photo (-graph).

passen ['pasən] v/i fit; zusagen: suit (j-m s.o.), be

convenient; **~ zu** go with, match; **~d** adj fit, suitable; convenient.

passier|bar [pa'si:rba:r] adj passable; **~en** ['-si:rən] v/i happen; v/t pass; **≈schein** m pass, permit.

passiv ['pasi:f, pa:'si:f] adj passive; **≈** n (-s/-e) gr. passive (voice).

Paste ['pastə] f (-/-n) paste.

Pastete [pas'te:tə] f (-/-n) pie.

pasteurisieren [pastøri-'zi:rən] v/t pasteurize.

Pate ['pa:tə] m (-n/-n) godfather; godchild; f (-/-n) godmother; **~nkind** n godchild.

Patent [pa'tɛnt] n (-[e]s/-e) patent.

Patient [pa'tsi̯ɛnt] m (-en/-en), **~in** f patient.

Patin ['pa:tɪn] f (-/-nen) godmother.

Patriot [patri'o:t] m (-en/-en) patriot.

Patrone [pa'tro:nə] f (-/-n) cartridge.

Patsche ['patʃə] f (-/-n) fig. colloq.: **in der ~ sitzen** be in a scrape.

patzig ['patsɪç] adj rude, saucy.

Pauke ['paʊkə] f (-/-n) kettle-drum.

Pauschal|e [paʊ'ʃa:lə] f (-/-n) lump sum; **~reise** f package(d) tour; **~summe** f lump sum.

Pause ['paʊzə] f (-/-n) break, interval, intermission; *kurze:* pause; *thea.* interval, *Am.* intermission; *Schul2:* break, *Am. a.* recess; 2**nlos** *adj* uninterrupted, incessant.

Pavian ['pa:vĭa:n] *m* (-s/ -e) baboon.

Pavillon ['pavɪljõ] *m* (-s/ -s) pavilion.

Pech [pɛç] *n* (-s/-e) pitch; *(no pl) fig. colloq.* bad luck; **~vogel** *m colloq.* unlucky fellow.

Pedal [pe'da:l] *n* (-s/-e) pedal.

pedantisch [pe'dantʃ] *adj* pedantic.

peinlich ['paɪnlɪç] *adj* embarrassing; *gewissenhaft:* particular.

Peitsche ['paɪtʃə] *f* (-/-n) whip.

Pelle ['pɛlə] *f* (-/-n) skin, peel; **~kartoffeln** *pl* potatoes *pl* (boiled) in their jackets.

Pelz [pɛlts] *m* (-es/-e) fur; *Kleidung:* mst furs *pl*; **~mantel** *m* fur coat; **~mütze** *f* fur cap; **~stiefel** *pl* fur-lined boots *pl*.

pendeln ['pɛndəln] *v/i* rail. commute.

Pension [pã'zĭo:n, pen-'zĭo:n] *f* (-/-en) (old-age) pension; boarding-house; **~at** [-'na:t] *n* (-[e]s/-e) boarding-school; 2**ieren** [-'ni:rən] *v/t* pension (off); **sich** 2**ieren lassen** retire; **~sgast** *m* boarder.

perfekt [pɛr'fɛkt] *adj* per-

fect; 2 ['pɛrfɛkt] *n* (-[e]s/ -e) *gr.* perfect (tense).

Pergament [pɛrga'mɛnt] *n* (-[e]s/-e) parchment.

Periode [pe'rĭo:də] *f* (-/ -n) period (*a. med.*).

Perle ['pɛrlə] *f* (-/-n) pearl; *Glas2:* bead; 2**n** ['pɛrlən] *v/i* sparkle.

Perlmutt ['pɛrlmʊt] *n* (-s/ *no pl*), **~er** *f* (-/*no pl*) mother-of-pearl.

Person [pɛr'zo:n] *f* (-/-en) person; **für zwei ~en** for two.

Personal [pɛrzo'na:l] *n* (-s/*no pl*) staff, personnel; **~abteilung** *f* personnel department; **~ausweis** *m* identity card; **~chef** *m* personnel officer or dept. manager; **~ien** [-'na:lĭən] *pl* particulars *pl*, personal data *pl*; **~pronomen** *n gr.* personal pronoun.

Personen|wagen *m* (motor-)car; **~zug** *m* passenger train.

persönlich [pɛr'zø:nlɪç] *adj* personal; *Brief:* private; 2**keit** *f* personality.

Perücke [pe'rykə] *f* (-/-n) wig.

Pest [pɛst] *f* (-/no pl) plague.

Petersilie [petər'zi:lĭə] *f* (-/-n) parsley.

Petroleum [pe'tro:leʊm] *n* (-s/*no pl*) petroleum; *Lampen2:* paraffin (oil), kerosene.

Pfad [pfa:t] *m* (-[e]s/-e) path; **~finder** [-findər] *m*

Pfahl

Boy Scout; **~finderin** f Girl Guide (*Am.* Scout).

Pfahl [pfaːl] m (-[e]s/¬e) stake, post, pile.

Pfand [pfant] n (-[e]s/¬er) pledge; *Flaschen2*: deposit.

pfänden ['pfɛndən] v/t distrain upon.

Pfann|e ['pfanə] f (-/-n) pan; **~kuchen** m pancake.

Pfarr|er ['pfarər] m (-s/-) priest; clergyman, pastor; vicar; *Dissenterkirche*: minister; **~gemeinde** f parish; **~haus** n parsonage; rectory, vicarage.

Pfau [pfau] m (-[e]s, -en/-en) peacock.

Pfeffer ['pfɛfər] m (-s/-) pepper; **~kuchen** m gingerbread; **~minze** f peppermint; 2n ['pfɛfərn] v/t pepper; **~streuer** m pepper-castor.

Pfeife ['pfaifə] f (-/-n) whistle; *Orgel etc.*: pipe; (tobacco) pipe; 2n ['pfaifən] v/i (*irr*) whistle; *Wind, Radio*: howl.

Pfeil [pfail] m (-[e]s/-e) arrow.

Pfeiler ['pfailər] m (-s/-) pillar.

Pfennig ['pfɛniç] m (-[e]s/-e) pfennig; *fig.* penny.

Pferd [pfeːrt] n (-[e]s/-e) horse; **zu ~(e)** on horseback.

Pferde|rennen n (-s/-) horse-race; **~stall** m stable; **~stärke** f (-/-n) horsepower.

Pfiff [pfif] m (-[e]s/-e) whistle.

Pfifferling ['pfifərliŋ] m (-s/-e) chanterelle.

pfiffig ['pfifiç] adj clever, artful.

Pfingst|en ['pfiŋstən] n (-/-) Whitsun(tide); **~montag** m Whit Monday; **~sonntag** m Whit Sunday.

Pfirsich ['pfirziç] m (-s/-e) peach.

Pflanze ['pflantsə] f (-/-n) plant; 2n ['pflantsən] v/t plant.

Pflaster ['pflastər] n (-s/-) plaster; *Straße*: pavement; 2n ['pflastərn] v/t pave; **~stein** m paving-stone; *Kopfstein*: cobble(-stone).

Pflaume ['pflaumə] f (-/-n) plum; *Back2*: prune.

Pflege ['pfleːgə] f (-/-n) care; *med.* nursing; *fig.* cultivation; **~eltern** pl foster-parents pl; **~heim** n nursing home; **~kind** n foster-child; 2leicht adj wash-and-wear; 2n ['pfleːgən] v/t nurse; *fig.* cultivate; **sie pflegte zu sagen** she used to say; **~r** m (-s/-) male nurse; **~rin** f nurse.

Pflicht [pfliçt] f (-/-en) duty; **~fach** n compulsory subject.

Pflock [pflɔk] m (-[e]s/¬e) peg.

pflücken ['pflykən] v/t pick, gather, pluck.

Pflug [pfluːk] m (-[e]s/¬e)

plough, *Am.* plow.

pflügen ['pfly:gən] *v/t, v/i*
plough, *Am.* plow.

Pforte ['pfɔrtə] *f* (-/-n)
gate, door.

Pförtner ['pfœrtnər] *m* (-s/
-) gate-keeper; door-
keeper, porter.

Pfosten ['pfɔstən] *m* (-s/-)
post.

Pfote ['pfo:tə] *f*(-/-n) paw.

Pfropfen ['pfrɔpfən] *m*
(-s/-) stopper; plug; *med.*
clot (of blood).

pfui [pfʊi] *int.* ugh!, for
shame!

Pfund [pfʊnt] *n* (-[e]s/-e,
-) pound.

pfuschen ['pfʊʃən] *v/i colloq.* bungle, botch.

Pfütze ['pfʏtsə] *f* (-/-n)
puddle, pool.

Phantasie [fanta'zi:] *f* (-/
-n) imagination, fancy;
2**ieren** [-'zi:rən] *v/i med.*
be delirious, rave; 2**tisch**
[-'tastıʃ] *adj* fantastic.

Phase ['fa:zə] *f* (-/-n)
phase, stage.

Philologe [filo'lo:gə] *m*
(-n/-n), ~**in** [filo'lo:gın] *f*
(-/-nen)
philologist.

Philosoph [filo'zo:f] *m*
(-en/-en) philosopher; ~**ie**
[-zo'fi:] *f* (-/-n)
philosophy.

phlegmatisch [fle'gma:-
tıʃ] *adj* phlegmatic.

phonetisch [fo'ne:tıʃ] *adj*
phonetic.

Phosphor ['fɔsfɔr] *m* (-s/
no pl) phosphorus.

Photo... *s.* **Foto...**

Photokopie *s.* **Fotokopie.**

Physik [fy'zi:k] *f* (-/*no pl*)
physics *sg;* 2**alisch** [-zi-
'ka:lıʃ] *adj* physical; ~**er**
['fy:zikər] *m* (-s/-) physicist.

physisch ['fy:zıʃ] *adj*
physical.

Pianist [pia'nıst] *m* (-en/
-en) pianist; ~**o** ['pia:no]
n (-s/-s) piano.

Pickel ['pıkəl] *m* (-s/-)
med. pimple; 2**(e)lig** *adj*
pimpled, pimply.

picken ['pıkən] *v/t, v/i*
pick, peck.

Picknick ['pıknık] *n* (-s
-e) picnic.

Pik [pi:k] *n* (-s/-s) spade(s
pl).

pikant [pi'kant] *adj* spicy,
piquant.

Pilger ['pılgər] *m* (-s/-) pilgrim.

Pille ['pılə] *f* (-/-n) pill.

Pilot [pi'lo:t] *m* (-en/-en)
pilot.

Pilz [pılts] *m* (-es/-e)
fungus; mushroom.

Pinguin ['pıngui:n] *m* (-s/
-e) penguin.

Pinsel ['pınzəl] *m* (-s/-)
brush.

Pinzette [pın'tsetə] *f* (-/
-n) (-e-a pair of) tweezers
pl.

Pionier [pio'ni:r] *m* (-s/-e)
pioneer; *mil.* engineer.

Piste ['pıstə] *f* (-/-n)
course; *aer.* runway.

Pistole [pıs'to:lə] *f* (-/-n)
pistol, *Am. a.* gun.

placieren [pla'tsi:rən] *v/t*
place; **sich** ~ *sp.* be placed.

Plage ['pla:gə] *f* (-/-n)
trouble, nuisance; **2n** *v/t*
trouble, bother; **sich 2n**
toil, drudge.

Plakat [pla'ka:t] *n* (-[e]s/
-e) poster, placard, bill.

Plakette [pla'kɛtə] *f* (-/-n)
plaque.

Plan [pla:n] *m* (-[e]s/ʔe)
plan; *Absicht:* a. design, intention.

Plane ['pla:nə] *f* (-/-n)
awning.

planen ['pla:nən] *v/t* plan.

Planet [pla'ne:t] *m* (-en/
-en) planet.

Planke ['plaŋkə] *f* (-/-n)
plank, board.

planlos ['pla:nlo:s] *adj*
aimless; *adv* at random;
~mäßig *adj* systematic;
adv as planned.

planschen ['planʃən] *v/i*
splash, paddle.

Plantage [plan'ta:ʒə] *f* (-/
-n) plantation.

plappern ['plapərn] *v/i
colloq.* prattle.

plärren ['plɛrən] *v/i colloq.*: blubber; *schreien:*
bawl.

Plastik[1] ['plastik] *f* (-/-en)
sculpture.

Plastik[2] *n* (-s/*no pl*) plastic; **2sch** *adj* plastic.

plätschern ['plɛtʃərn] *v/i*
splash; *Wasser:* ripple,
murmur.

platt [plat] *adj* flat, level,
even; *colloq.* flabbergasted.

Platte ['platə] *f* (-/-n)

plate; dish; *Stein:* flag;
Metall, Stein, Holz: slab;
Tisch: top; *Schall2:* disc,
record; **kalte** ~ cold meat.

plätten ['plɛtən] *v/t* iron.

Platten|spieler *m* record-
player; **~teller** *m* turn-
table.

Plattform ['platform] *f* (-/
-en) platform.

Platz [plats] *m* (-es/ʔe)
place; spot; *Raum:* room,
space; *Lage, Bau2:* site;
Sitz: seat; square; *runder:*
circus; **ist hier noch** ~?
is this seat taken?; **den
dritten** ~ **belegen** *sp.*
come in third; **~an-
weiserin** [-'ʔanvaizərin] *f*
(-/-nen) usherette.

Plätzchen ['plɛtsçən] *n*
(-s/-) biscuit, *Am.* cookie.

platzen ['platsən] *v/i*
burst (*a.* fig.), split;
2karte *f* ticket for a reserved seat; **2regen** *m*
downpour.

Plauder|ei [plaudə'rai] *f*
(-/-en) chat, talk; *oberflächliche:* small talk; **2n**
['plaudərn] *v/i* (have a)
chat.

pleite ['plaitə] *adj colloq.*
broke.

Plisseerock [pli'se:rɔk] *m*
(-[e]s/ʔe) pleated skirt.

Plombe ['plɔmbə] *f* (-/-n)
(lead) seal; *Zahn:* stopping,
filling; **2ieren** [-'bi:rən]
v/t seal; stop, fill.

plötzlich ['plœtsliç] *adj*
sudden.

plump [plump] *adj*

clumsy.

plündern ['plʏndərn] v/t
plunder, loot.

Plural ['plu:ra:l] m (-s/-e)
gr. plural.

plus [plus] adv plus.

Plusquamperfekt
['pluskvampεrfεkt] n (-s/
-e) gr. pluperfect (tense).

Pöbel ['pø:bəl] m (-s/no pl)
mob, rabble.

pochen ['pɔxən] v/i
knock, rap; Herz: throb,
thump.

Pocken ['pɔkən] pl small-
pox sg; **~schutzimp-
fung** f vaccination.

Podium ['po:dĭum] n (-s/
-dien) podium, platform.

Poesie [poe'zi:] f (-/-n)
poetry.

Pokal [po'ka:l] m (-s/-e
sp. cup; **~endspiel**
[-'ʔεnt∫pi:l] n cup-final;
~spiel n cup-tie.

pökeln ['pø:kəln] v/t corn,
salt.

Pol [po:l] m (-s/-e) pole;
2ar [po'la:r] adj polar.

Pole ['po:lə] m (-n/-n)
Pole.

Police [po'li:sə] f (-/-n)
policy.

polieren [po'li:rən] v/t
polish.

Politesse [poli'tεsə] f (-/
-n) mot. appr. traffic
warden.

Politik [poli'ti:k] f (-/rare
-en) policy; Staat: politics
sg, pl; **~ker** [-'li:tikər] m
(-s/-) politician; führender:
statesman; 2sch adj politi-

cal.

Politur [poli'tu:r] f (-/-en)
polish.

Polizei [poli'tsai] f (-/rare
-en) police pl; **~beamte**
m (-n/-n) police-officer;
~revier n police-station;
~streife f police patrol;
~stunde f closing time.

Polizist [poli'tsist] m (-en/
-en) policeman, sl. bobby,
cop; **~in** f (-/-nen) police-
woman.

polnisch ['pɔlnɪʃ] adj Polish.

Polster ['pɔlstər] n (-s/-)
pad; cushion; **~möbel** pl
upholstered furniture sg;
2n v/t upholster, stuff;
wattieren: pad, wad;
~sessel m easy chair.

poltern ['pɔltərn] v/i rumble.

Pommes frites [pɔm-
'frit(s)] pl chips pl, Am.
French fried potatoes pl.

Pony ['pɔni] n (-s/-s) pony;
m (-s/-s) fringe.

populär [popu'lɛ:r] adj
popular.

Porle ['po:rə] f (-/-n) pore;
2ös [po'rø:s] adj porous;
permeable.

Porree ['pɔre] m (-s/-s)
leek.

Portemonnaie [pɔrtmɔ-
'ne:] n (-s/-s) purse.

Portier [pɔr'tĭe:] m (-s/-s)
porter.

Portion [pɔr'tsĭo:n] f (-/
-en) portion, share; bei
Tisch: helping, serving;
zwei **~en ... ...** for two.

Porto

Porto ['pɔrto] n (-s/-s, -ti) postage; **2frei** adj postfree.

Porträt [pɔr'trɛː(t)] n (-s/-s, -e) portrait.

Portugies|e [pɔrtu'giːzə] m (-n/-n) Portuguese; **2isch** adj Portuguese.

Porzellan [pɔrtsɛ'laːn] n (-s/-e) china.

Posaune [po'zaunə] f (-/-n) trombone.

Position [pozi'tsjoːn] f (-/-en) position.

positiv ['poːzitiːf] adj positive.

possessiv ['pɔsɛsiːf] adj gr. possessive.

Post [pɔst] f (-/no pl) post, Am.: mail; mail, letters pl; = **~amt** n post office; **~anweisung** f postal order; **~beamte** m post office official; **~bote** m postman, Am. mailman.

Posten ['pɔstən] m (-s/-s) post, place; Anstellung: job; mil. sentry, sentinel.

Post|fach n post office box; **~karte** f postcard, Am. a. postal card; **~kutsche** f stage-coach; **2lagernd** ['-laːgərnt] adj poste restante, Am. a. general delivery; **~scheck** m postal cheque (Am. check); **~schließfach** n post office box; **~sparbuch** n post office savings-book; **~stempel** m postmark; **2wendend** ['-vɛndənt] adv by return of post;

~wertzeichen ['-veːrttsaiçən] n stamp.

Pracht [praxt] f (-/no pl) splendo(u)r.

prächtig ['prɛçtiç] adj splendid.

Prädikat [prɛdi'kaːt] n (-[e]s/-e) gr. predicate.

prahlen ['praːlən] v/i brag, boast.

praktisch ['praktiʃ] adj practical; useful, handy; **~er Arzt** general practitioner.

Praline [pra'liːnə] f (-/-n) chocolate.

prall [pral] adj tight; drall: plump; Sonne: blazing.

Prämie ['prɛːmjə] f (-/-n) premium; bonus.

präparieren [prɛpa'riːrən] v/t prepare.

Präposition [prɛpozi'tsjoːn] f (-/-en) gr. preposition.

Präsens ['prɛːzɛns] n (-/no pl) gr. present (tense).

Präsident [prɛzi'dɛnt] m (-en/-en) president; Vorsitzender: a. chairman.

prasseln ['prasəln] v/i Feuer: crackle; Regen etc.: patter.

Präteritum [prɛ'teːritum] n (-s/no pl) gr. preterit(e) (tense).

Praxis ['praksis] f (-/-xen) practice.

predig|en ['preːdigən] v/i, v/t preach; **2er** m preacher; **2t** ['-diçt] f (-/-en) sermon.

Preis [prais] m (-es/-e)

price; cost; *Auszeichnung*: award; prize; **~aus-schreiben** *n* (-s/-) competition.

Preiselbeere ['praizəl-beːrə] *f* (-/-n) cranberry.

Preis|erhöhung *f* rise *od.* increase in price(s); **2gekrönt** ['-gəkrøːnt] *adj* prize; **~nachlaß** *m* discount; **~stopp** *m* price-freeze; **2wert** *adj*: **~ sein** be a bargain.

Prellung ['prɛlʊŋ] *f* (-/-en) contusion, bruise.

Premiere [prə'mi̯ɛːrə] *f* (-/-n) première, first night.

Press|e ['prɛsə] *f* (-/-n) press; *Saft* 2: squeezer; *Zeitungen*: the press; **2en** *v/t* press; squeeze.

prickeln ['prɪkəln] *v/i* prickle, tingle.

Priester ['priːstər] *m* (-s/-) priest.

prima ['priːma] *adj colloq.* fine.

primitiv [primi'tiːf] *adj* primitive, crude.

Prinz [prɪnts] *m* (-en/-en) prince; **~essin** ['-tsɛsɪn] *f* (-/-nen) princess.

Prinzip [prɪn'tsiːp] *n* (-s/-ien) principle.

Prise ['priːzə] *f* (-/-n): **e-e ~** a pinch of.

Pritsche ['prɪtʃə] *f* (-/-n) plank bed.

privat [pri'vaːt] *adj* private; **2adresse** *f* home address; **2klinik** *f* private hospital, nursing home; **2schule** *f* private school.

Privileg [privi'leːk] *n* (-[e]s/-ien) privilege.

pro [proː] *prp* per; **~ Jahr** per annum; **~ Person** each; **~ Stück** a piece.

Probe ['proːbə] *f* (-/-n) trial, test; *Waren*: sample, specimen; *thea.* rehearsal; **~exemplar** *n* specimen copy; **~fahrt** *f* test drive; **~flug** *m* test flight; **2n** ['proːbən] *v/t, v/i thea.* rehearse.

probieren [pro'biːrən] *v/t* try, test; *Speisen*: taste.

Problem [pro'bleːm] *n* (-s/-e) problem.

Produ|kt [pro'dʊkt] *n* (-[e]s/-e) product; *agr. a.* produce; **~ktion** [-dʊk-'tsi̯oːn] *f* production; *Menge*: output; **2ktiv** [-'tiːf] *adj* productive; **2zieren** [-'tsiːrən] *v/t* produce.

Professor [pro'fɛsɔr] *m* (-s/-en) professor; **~i** ['proːfiː] *m* (-s/-s) *sp.* (-fessional).

Profil [pro'fiːl] *n* (-s/-e) profile; *Reifen*: tread.

profitieren [profi'tiːrən] *v/i, v/t* profit (**von** by).

Programm [pro'gram] *n* (-s/-e) program(me).

Projekt [pro'jɛkt] *n* (-[e]s/-e) project; **~ion** [-jɛk-'tsi̯oːn] *f* projection; **~ionsapparat** *m*, **~or** [-'jɛktɔr] *m* projector.

Prolog [pro'loːk] *m* (-[e]s/-e) prolog(ue).

Promille [pro'mɪlə] *n* (-[s]/-) per thousand; *colloq.* pro mille content.

prominent [promi'nɛnt] *adj* prominent.

Pronomen [pro'no:mən] *n* (-s/-) *gr.* pronoun.

Propeller [pro'pɛlər] *m* (-s/-) *aer.* (air)screw, propeller.

prophezeien [profe'tsaɪən] *v/t* prophesy, predict.

Prosa ['pro:za] *f* (-/no *pl*) prose.

Prospekt [pro'spɛkt] *m* (-[e]s/-e) prospectus, leaflet, brochure.

prost [pro:st] *int.* cheers!

Prostituierte [prostitu-'i:rtə] *f* (-n/-n) prostitute.

Protest [pro'tɛst] *m* (-[e]s/-e) protest; ~ant [-tɛs-'tant] *m* (-en/-en) Protestant; 2antisch *adj* Protestant; 2ieren [-tɛs'ti:rən] *v/i* protest.

Prothese [pro'te:zə] *f* (-/-n) artificial limb; *Zahn*2: denture.

Protokoll [proto'kɔl] *n* (-s/-e) record; *Versammlungs*2: minutes *pl*.

protzig ['prɔtsɪç] *adj* showy.

Proviant [pro'vĭant] *m* (-s/no *pl*) provisions *pl*.

Provinz [pro'vɪnts] *f* (-/-en) province.

Provision [provi'zĭo:n] *f* (-/-en) commission; 2orisch [-'zo:rɪʃ] *adj* provisional.

provozieren [provo'tsi:rən] *v/t* provoke.

Prozent [pro'tsɛnt] *n* (-[e]s/-e) per cent; ~satz

m percentage.

Prozeß [pro'tsɛs] *m* (-sses/-sse) process; *jur.* lawsuit, action.

Prozession [protse'sĭo:n] *f* (-/-en) procession.

prüde ['pry:də] *adj* prudish.

prüfen ['pry:fən] *v/t Schüler etc.*: examine; try, test; *kontrollieren*: check; ~end *adj Blick*: searching; 2er *m* examiner; 2ung *f* examination, *colloq.* exam; test.

Prügel ['pry:gəl] *m* (-s/-) cudgel, club; ~ *pl colloq.* beating *sg*, thrashing *sg*; 2n *v/t* beat, thrash; **sich** 2n (have a) fight.

pst [pst] *int.* hush!

Psychiater [psyçi'a:tər] *m* (-s/-) psychiatrist; 2sch ['psy:çɪʃ] *adj* psychic(al).

Psychologe [psyço'lo:gə] *m* (-n/-n) psychologist; ~ie [-lo'gi:] *f* (-/no *pl*) psychology; 2isch [-'lo:gɪʃ] *adj* psychological.

Publikum ['pu:blikum] *n* (-s/no *pl*) the public; *Zuhörer*: audience; *Zuschauer*: spectators *pl*, crowd; *Leser*: readers *pl*.

Pudding ['pudɪŋ] *m* (-s/-e, -s) pudding.

Pudel ['pu:dəl] *m* (-s/-) poodle.

Puder ['pu:dər] *m* (-s/-) powder; ~dose *f* compact; 2n ['pu:dərn] *v/t* powder; **sich** 2n powder o.s.; ~quaste *f* powderpuff; ~zucker *m* powdered sugar.

Pullover [pʊˈloːvər] *m* (-s/-) pullover, sweater.

Puls [pʊls] *m* (-es/-e) pulse; **~ader** [-'ʔaːdər] *f* artery; **~schlag** *m* beat, pulsation.

Pult [pʊlt] *n* (-[e]s/-e) desk.

Pulver ['pʊlfər] *n* (-s/-) powder.

Pumpe ['pʊmpə] *f* (-/-n) pump; **2n** ['pʊmpən] *v/t* pump.

Punkt [pʊŋkt] *m* (-[e]s/-e) point (*a. fig.*); *Tüpfelchen*: dot; *print.*, *ling.* full stop, period; *Stelle*: spot, place; **~ zehn Uhr** 10 (o'clock) sharp.

pünktlich ['pʊŋktlɪç] *adj* punctual.

Punsch [pʊnʃ] *m* (-[e]s/-e) punch.

Pupille [puˈpɪlə] *f* pupil.

Puppe ['pʊpə] *f* (-/-n) doll; *zo.* chrysalis, pupa.

pur [puːr] *adj* pure; *Getränk*: neat.

Püree [pyˈreː] *n* (-s/-s) purée, mash.

purpur|n ['pʊrpʊrn], **~rot** *adj* purple.

Purzelbaum ['pʊrtsəlbaʊm] *m* (-[e]s/ᵛe) somersault; **2n** ['pʊrtsəln] *v/i* tumble.

Pustel ['pʊstəl] *f* (-/-n) pustule, pimple.

pusten ['puːstən] *v/i* puff, pant; *blasen*: blow.

Pute ['puːtə] *f* (-/-n) turkey(-hen); **~r** *m* turkey (-cock).

putz|en ['pʊtsən] *v/t* clean, cleanse; wipe; *Schuhe*: polish, *Am.* shine; **sich die Nase ~en** blow *od.* wipe one's nose; **sich die Zähne ~en** brush one's teeth; **2frau** *f* charwoman.

Pyjama [pyˈdʒaːma] *m* (-s/ -s) pyjamas *pl*, *Am. a.* pajamas *pl*.

Pyramide [pyraˈmiːdə] *f* (-/-n) pyramid.

Q

Quacksalber ['kvakzalbər] *m* (-s/-) quack (doctor).

Quadrat [kvaˈdraːt] *n* (-[e]s/-e) square; **2isch** *adj* square; **2meter** *n*, *m* square met|re, *Am.* -er.

quaken ['kvaːkən] *v/i* quack; *Frosch*: croak.

Qual [kvaːl] *f* (-/-en) pain, torment, agony.

quälen ['kvɛːlən] *v/t* torment (*a. fig.*); torture; *fig.* bother.

Qualifi|kation [kvalifikaˈtsi̯oːn] *f* (-/-en) qualification; **2zieren** [-ˈtsiːrən] *v/t*: (**sich**) **~** qualify.

Qualität [kvaliˈtɛːt] *f* (-/ -en) quality.

Qualle ['kvalə] *f* (-/-n) jelly-fish.

Qualm [kvalm] *m* (-[e]s/*no pl*) (dense) smoke; **2en** ['kvalmən] *v/i* smoke.

qualvoll ['kva:lfɔl] *adj* very painful; agonizing.

Quantität [kvanti'tɛ:t] *f* (-/-en) quantity.

Quarantäne [karan'tɛ:nə] *f* (-/-n) quarantine.

Quark [kvark] *m* (-s/*no pl*) curd(s *pl*).

Quartal [kvar'ta:l] *n* (-s/-e) quarter.

Quartett [kvar'tɛt] *n* (-[e]s/-e) quartet(te).

Quartier [kvar'ti:r] *n* (-s/-e) accommodation.

Quaste ['kvastə] *f* (-/-n) tassel; *Puder*2: (powder-)puff.

Quatsch [kvatʃ] *m* (-es/*no pl*) *colloq.* nonsense, *sl.* rot.

Quecksilber ['kvɛkzɪlbər] *n* (-s/*no pl*) mercury, quicksilver.

Quelle ['kvɛlə] *f* (-/-n) spring; source (*a. fig.*); *Öl*2: well; **2n** ['kvɛlən] gush, well.

quer [kve:r] *adv* crosswise; ~ **über** across; **2straße** *f* cross-road; **zweite 2straße rechts** second turning on *od.* to the right.

quetsch|en ['kvetʃən] *v/t* squeeze; *med.* contuse, bruise; **2ung** *f* contusion, bruise.

quieken ['kvi:kən] *v/i* squeak, squeal.

quietschen ['kvi:tʃən] *v/i* squeak, squeal; *Tür:* creak; *Bremsen:* screech.

quitt [kvɪt] *adj* quits, even.

Quitte ['kvɪtə] *f* (-/-n) quince.

quitt|ieren [kvɪ'ti:rən] *v/t Rechnung:* receipt; *aufgeben:* quit, abandon; **2ung** ['kvɪtʊŋ] *f* receipt.

Quote ['kvo:tə] *f* (-/-n) quota; share.

R

Rabatt [ra'bat] *m* (-[e]s/-e) discount, rebate.

Rabbiner [ra'bi:nər] *m* (-s/-) rabbi.

Rabe ['ra:bə] *m* (-n/-n) raven.

rabiat [ra'bĭa:t] *adj* violent.

Rache ['raxə] *f* (-/*no pl*) revenge, vengeance.

Rachen ['raxən] *m* (-s/-) throat.

rächen ['rɛçən] *v/t* revenge (sich o.s.).

Rad [ra:t] *n* (-[e]s/*ᵘer*) wheel; *s.* **Fahrrad**.

Radar [ra'da:r] *m, n* (-s/*no pl*) radar.

radfahr|en ['ra:tfa:rən] *v/i* (*irr fahren*) cycle, (ride a) bicycle; **2r** *m* cyclist.

radier|en [ra'di:rən] *v/t* rub out, erase; *Kunst:* etch; **2gummi** *m* (India-)rubber.

Radieschen [ra'di:sçən] *n*

(-s/-) (red) radish.

radikal [radi'ka:l] *adj* radical.

Radio ['ra:dɪo] *n* (-s/-s) radio, wireless; **im** ~ on the radio; **2aktiv** [-?ak'ti:f] *adj* radio(-)active; **~apparat** *m* radio(-set), wireless (set).

Radius ['ra:dɪʊs] *m* (-/-dien) radius.

Rad|kappe ['ra:tkapə] *f* (-/-n) hub cap; **~rennen** *n* (-s/-) cycle race; **~spur** *f* rut.

raffiniert [rafi'ni:rt] *adj* refined; *fig.* clever, cunning.

Ragout [ra'gu:] *n* (-s/-s) ragout, stew.

Rahm [ra:m] *m* (-[e]s/no *pl*) cream.

Rahmen ['ra:mən] *m* (-s/-) frame; ♀ *v/t* frame.

Rakete [ra'ke:tə] *f* (-/-n) rocket.

rammen ['ramən] *v/t* ram.

Rampe ['rampə] *f* (-/-n) ramp.

Ramsch [ramʃ] *m* (-[e]s/no *pl*) junk, trash.

Rand [rant] *m* (-[e]s/ᵛer) edge, border, margin; *bsd. Gefäß:* brim; *Gefäß, Brille:* rim; *Stadt:* outskirts *pl*; *fig.* verge, brink.

Rang [raŋ] *m* (-[e]s/ᵛe) rank (*a. mil.*); *Thea.* circle, *Am.* balcony.

rangieren [rã'ʒi:rən] *v/t rail.* shunt, switch.

Ranke ['raŋkə] *f* (-/-n) tendril; **2n** ['raŋkən]: **sich**

~ *v/refl* creep, climb.

Ranzen ['rantsən] *m* (-s/-) satchel.

ranzig ['rantsɪç] *adj* rancid, rank.

Rappe ['rapə] *m* (-n/-n) black horse.

rar [ra:r] *adj* rare, scarce.

rasch [raʃ] *adj* quick, swift; prompt.

rascheln ['raʃəln] *v/i* rustle.

rasen ['ra:zən] *v/i* rage, storm, rave; race, speed, *colloq.* scorch; **~d** *adj* raving; *Tempo:* scorching; *Schmerzen:* agonizing; *Kopfschmerzen:* splitting.

Rasen *m* (-s/-) lawn.

Raserei [ra:zə'rai] *f* (-/no *pl*) *colloq.* rage, fury; madness; *mot.* speeding.

Rasier|apparat [ra'zi:r-?aparat] *m* (-[e]s/-e) (safety) razor; **~creme** *f* shaving-cream; **2en** [ra-'zi:rən] *v/t* shave; *v/refl:* **sich 2en (lassen** get a) shave; **~klinge** *f* razor-blade; **~messer** *n* razor; **~pinsel** *m* shaving-brush; **~seife** *f* shaving-soap; **~wasser** *n* after-shave lotion.

Rasse ['rasə] *f* (-/-n) race; *zo.* breed.

rasseln ['rasəln] *v/i* rattle.

Rassen|trennung *f* racial segregation; **~unruhen** *pl* race riots *pl*.

rasserein ['rasərain] *adj s.* **reinrassig.**

Rast [rast] *f* (-/rare -en)

rest; break, pause; 2**en** ['rastən] *v/i* rest; 2**los** *adj* restless; ~**platz** *m* mot. picnic area, lay-by; ~**stät- te** *f* rest-house.

Rat|schlag *m* (-[e]s/Rat- **schläge**) advice, counsel; *Ausweg:* way out; (*pl* **Rä- te**) *Körperschaft:* council, board; *Person:* council(l)or.

Rate ['ra:tə] *f* (-/-n) instal(l)ment; **in** ~**n** by instal(l)ments.

raten ['ra:tən] *v/i, v/t* (*irr*) advise, counsel; *v/t* guess.

Ratenzahlung *f* payment by instal(l)ments.

Rat|geber ['ra:tge:bər] *m* (-s/-) adviser; ~**haus** *n* town (*Am. a.* city) hall.

Ration [ra'tsĭo:n] *f* (-/-en) ration, allowance; 2**alisieren** [-tsĭonali'zi:- rən] *v/t* rationalize; 2**ieren** [-'ni:rən] *v/t* ration.

rat|los ['ra:tlo:s] *adj* at a loss; ~**sam** [-'za:m] *adj* advisable.

Rätsel ['rɛ:tsəl] *n* (-s/-) riddle, puzzle; mystery; 2**haft** *adj* puzzling, mysterious.

Ratte ['ratə] *f* (-/-n) rat.

rattern ['ratərn] *v/i* rattle.

Raub [raup] *m* (-[e]s/*no pl*) robbery; 2**en** ['raubən] *v/t* rob.

Räuber ['rɔybər] *m* (-s/-) robber.

Raub|mord *m* murder with robbery; ~**tier** *n*

beast of prey; ~**überfall** *m* hold-up; armed robbery; ~**vogel** *m* bird of prey.

Rauch [raux] *m* (-[e]s/*no pl*) smoke; 2**en** ['rauxən] *v/i* smoke; *Rauchen ver- boten!* no smoking!; ~**er** *m*, ~**erabteil** *n* smoker.

räuchern ['rɔyçərn] *v/t* smoke, cure.

rauchig ['rauxiç] *adj* smoky.

raufen ['raufən] *v/i* fight; 2**rei** [-'rai] *f* (-/-en) fight.

rauh [rau] *adj* rough; *Klima:* inclement, raw; *Stim- me:* hoarse; 2**reif** *m* (-[e]s/ *no pl*) white frost, hoar- frost.

Raum [raum] *m* (-[e]s/~**e**) room; space; area; ~**an- zug** *m* space suit.

räumen ['rɔymən] *v/t* clear; *Gebiet:* leave; *Woh- nung:* vacate.

Raum|fahrt ['raumfa:rt] *f* (-/*no pl*) astronautics *sg, pl*; ~**flug** *m* space flight; ~**in- halt** *m* volume; ~**kapsel** *f* capsule.

räumlich ['rɔymliç] *adj* of space, spatial.

Raumschiff *n* spaceship, spacecraft.

Raupe ['raupə] *f* (-/-n) caterpillar.

Rausch [rauʃ] *m* (-[e]s/~**e**) intoxication; ~**en ha- ben** be drunk; 2**en** ['rau- ʃən] *v/i* rustle; *Wind:* roar; *Wasser:* bubble, roar; *fig.* sweep (**aus** from); ~**gift** *n* narcotic, drug, *colloq.*

dope.

räuspern ['rɔʏspərn] *v/ refl:* **sich ~** clear one's throat.

Razzia ['ratsɪa] *f* **(-/-s, -zien)** raid.

reagieren [re'a'giːrən] *v/i* react **(auf** to); *fig. a.* respond **(auf** to).

Reaktor [re'ʔaktɔr] *m* **(-s/ -en)** (nuclear) reactor.

real [re'aːl] *adj* real; **~istisch** [-a'lɪstɪʃ] *adj* realistic; **2ität** [-ali'tɛːt] *f* **(-/ -en)** reality.

Rebe ['reːbə] *f* **(-/-n)** vine.

Rebell [re'bɛl] *m* **(-en/ -en)** rebel; **2ieren** [-e'liːrən] *v/i* rebel, revolt, rise.

Rebhuhn ['reːphuːn] *n* **(-s/=er)** partridge.

Rechen ['rɛçən] *m* **(-s/-)** rake.

Rechen|aufgabe *f* sum, (arithmetical) problem; **~fehler** *m* arithmetical error, miscalculation; **~schaft** *f* **(-/no pl):** ~ **ablegen über** account for; **zur ~ ziehen** call to account.

rechn|en ['rɛçnən] *v/i* do sums, reckon; **~en auf** count *od.* rely (up)on; **2ung** *f* calculation; reckoning; *Waren:* invoice; *Gasthaus:* bill, *Am.* check.

recht [rɛçt] *adj* right; **~ haben** be right.

Recht *n* **(-[e]s/-e)** right **(auf** to); *jur.* law; *fig.* justice.

Rechte ['rɛçtə] *f* **(-n/no pl)**

right hand.

Rechteck ['rɛçt'ʔɛk] *n* **(-[e]s/-e)** rectangle; **2ig** *adj* rectangular.

recht|fertigen ['rɛçtfɛrtɪgən] *v/t* justify; **2fertigung** *f* justification; **~lich** *adj* legal; **~mäßig** *adj* legal, lawful, legitimate.

rechts [rɛçts] *adv* (on *od.* to the) right; **nach ~** to the right.

Rechtsanwalt *m* **(-[e]s/=e)** lawyer, *Am. a.* attorney; solicitor.

Rechtschreibung *f* **(-/no pl)** orthography, spelling.

rechtskräftig [-krɛftɪç] *adj* valid; *Urteil:* final.

recht|winkl|ig *adj* right-angled; **~zeitig** *adj* punctual; *adv* on time.

Reck [rɛk] *n* **(-[e]s/-e)** *sp.* horizontal bar.

recken ['rɛkən] *v/t* stretch **(sich** o.s.).

Redakt|eur [redak'tøːr] *m* **(-s/-e)** editor; **~ion** [-'tsɪoːn] *f* **(-/-en)** editorial staff, editors *pl.*

Rede ['reːdə] *f* **(-/-n)** speech; **zur ~ stellen** take to task **(wegen** for); **2n** ['reːdən] *v/i, v/t* speak; talk.

redlich ['reːtlɪç] *adj* honest; upright.

Red|ner ['reːdnər] *m* **(-s/-)** speaker; **2selig** ['-zeːlɪç] *adj* talkative.

reduzieren [redu'tsiːrən] *v/t* reduce.

Reederei

Reederei [re:də'raɪ] f (-/-en) shipping company *od.* firm.

reell [re'el] *adj* respectable, honest; *Ware:* good; *Angebot:* fair.

reflektieren [reflek'ti:rən] *v/t* reflect.

reflexiv [refle'ksi:f] *adj gr.* reflexive.

Reform [re'fɔrm] f (-/-en) reform; **2ieren** [-fɔr'mi:rən] *v/t* reform.

Regal [re'ga:l] n (-[e]s/-e) shelf.

rege ['re:gə] *adj* active, lively; busy.

Regel ['re:gəl] f (-/-n) rule; *med.* menstruation; **2mäßig** *adj* regular; **2n** ['re:gəln] *v/t* regulate; arrange; settle; **~ung** f regulation; arrangement; settlement.

regen ['re:gən] *v/t:* (sich) ~ move, stir.

Regen m (-s/-) rain; **~bogen** m rainbow; **~bogenhaut** f iris; **~mantel** m raincoat; **~schauer** m shower; **~schirm** m umbrella; **~tag** m rainy day; **~tropfen** m raindrop; **~wasser** n rainwater; **~wetter** n rainy weather; **~wurm** m earthworm; **~zeit** f rainy season.

Regie [re'ʒi:] f (-/no pl) (stage) direction.

regier|en [re'gi:rən] *v/t, v/i* reign; govern; **2ung** f government; Amtsperiode:

Am. administration; *Monarchie:* reign.

Regiment [regi'ment] n (-[e]s/-er) regiment.

Regisseur [reʒi'sø:r] m (-s/-e) (stage) director.

registrieren [regɪs'tri:rən] *v/t* register, record.

regneln ['re:gnən] *v/i* rain; **es ~t** it is raining; **~risch** *adj* rainy.

regulieren [regu'li:rən] *v/t* regulate, adjust.

regungslos ['re:guŋslo:s] *adj* motionless.

Reh [re:] n (-[e]s/-e) roe deer, roe; *weiblich:* doe; **~bock** m roebuck; **~geiß** f doe; **~kitz** [-kɪts] n (-es/-e) fawn.

Reib|e ['raɪbə] f (-/-n), **~eisen** [-'ʔaɪzən] n (-s/-) grater; **2en** ['raɪbən] *v/t* (*irr*) rub; **~ung** f friction.

reich [raɪç] *adj* rich (**an** in); wealthy.

Reich n (-[e]s/-e) empire; *Natur2:* kingdom; *poet.* realm.

reichen ['raɪçən] *v/t Speise:* serve; **j-m et.** ~ hand *od.* pass s.th. to s.o.; *v/i* reach; **genügen:** suffice; **das reicht!** that will do!

reich|haltig ['raɪçhaltɪç] *adj* rich; **~lich** *adj* ample, abundant; **~lich Zeit** plenty of time; **2tum** [-tu:m] m (-s/-er) riches *pl;* wealth; **2weite** [-vaɪtə] f (-/-en) reach; *mil.* range.

Reif [raɪf] m (-[e]s/no pl)

white frost, hoar frost.

reif *adj* ripe, mature; **~en** ['raɪfən] *v/i* ripen, mature.

Reifen *m* (**-s**/-) hoop; *Auto*2: tyre, (*Am. nur*) tire; **~druck** *m* tyre pressure; **~panne** *f* puncture, *Am. a.* flat.

Reife|prüfung *f* s. **Abitur**; **~zeugnis** *n* s. **Abschlußzeugnis**.

Reihe ['raɪə] *f* (**-**/-n) row; line; *Serie*: series; *Anzahl*: number; *thea.* row; **der ~ nach** in turn; **~nfolge** *f* order.

Reiher ['raɪər] *m* (**-s**/-) heron.

Reim [raɪm] *m* (**-[e]s**/-e) rhyme; **2en** ['raɪmən] *v/i, v/t*: (**sich**) **~** rhyme.

rein [raɪn] *adj* pure; clean; clear; **~igen** ['-ɪgən] *v/t* clean; **2igung** *f* cleaning; (*dry*) *cleaners pl*; **chemische 2igung** dry-cleaning; **~lich** *adj* clean(ly); **2(e)machefrau** ['-(ə)maxəfrau] *f* charwoman; **~rassig** ['-rasɪç] *adj* purebred, thoroughbred.

Reis [raɪs] *m* (**-es**/*no pl*) rice.

Reise ['raɪzə] *f* (**-**/-n) journey; *mar.* voyage; *Rund*2: tour; *kurze*: trip; **~andenken** *n* souvenir; **~büro** *n* travel agency or bureau; **~führer** *m* guide(-book); **~gesellschaft** *f* (tourist) party; **~leiter** *m* courier; **2n** ['raɪzən] *v/i* travel, jour-

ney; **~nde** *m, f* (**-n**/-n) passenger; tourist; *econ.* commercial travel(l)er; **~necessaire** *n* dressing-case; **~paß** *m* passport; **~scheck** *m* travel(l)er's cheque (*Am.* check); **~tasche** *f* travel(l)ing bag; **~ziel** *n* destination.

reiß|en ['raɪsən] *v/t, v/i* (*irr*) tear; **~end** *adj* rapid; **2nagel** *m* s. **Reißzwecke**; **2verschluß** *m* zip (-fastener), *besd. Am.* zipper; **2zwecke** *f* drawing-pin, *Am.* thumb-tack.

reit|en ['raɪtən] *v/i, v/t* (*irr*) ride; **2er** *m* rider; *geübter*: horseman; **2hose** *f* riding-breeches *pl*; **2pferd** *n* riding-horse; **2stiefel** *pl* riding-boots *pl*.

Reiz [raɪts] *m* (**-es**/-e) charm, attraction; *med.* irritation; **2bar** *adj* irritable; **2en** ['raɪtsən] *v/t* irritate (*a. med.*); *anziehen*: attract; *Karten*: bid; **2end** *adj* charming, *Am.* cute; lovely; **2voll** *adj* attractive.

Reklam|ation [reklama-'tsĭoːn] *f* (**-**/-en) complaint; **~e** ['-klaːmə] *f* (**-**/-n) advertising; *Anzeige*: advertisement, *colloq.* ad.

Rekord [re'kɔrt] *m* (**-[e]s**/-e) record.

Rekrut [re'kruːt] *m* (**-en**/-en) recruit.

relativ [rela'tiːf] *adj* relative; **2pronomen** *n gr.* relative pronoun.

Religi|on [reli'gĭo:n] *f* (*-/ -en*) religion; **2ös** ['-'glö:s] *adj* religious; pious.

Reling ['re:lɪŋ] *f* (*-/-s*) *mar.* rail.

Reliquie [re'li:kvĭə] *f* (*-/ -n*) (holy) relic.

Renn|bahn ['renba:n] *f* (*-/ -en*) racecourse, *Am.* race track; **2en** ['renən] *v/i* (*irr*) run, race; **~en** *n* (*-s/-*) run(ning); race; **~fahrer** *m* racing driver; racing cyclist; **~läufer** *m* ski racer; **~pferd** *n* racehorse; **~rad** *n* racing bicycle; **~sport** *m* racing; **~stall** *m* racing stable; **~wagen** *m* racing car.

renovieren [reno'vi:rən] *v/t Haus:* renovate; *Zimmer:* redecorate.

Rente ['rentə] *f* (*-/-n*) annuity; (old-age) pension.

Rentier ['renti:r, 're:n-] *n* (*-[e]s/-e*) reindeer.

Rentner ['rentnər] *m* (*-s/-*) (old-age) pensioner.

Reparatur [repara'tu:r] *f* (*-/-en*) repair; **~werkstatt** *f* repair shop; *mot. a.* garage, service station.

reparieren [repa'ri:rən] *v/t* repair.

Report|age [repɔr'ta:ʒə] *f* (*-/-n*) coverage; **~er** [-'pɔrtər] *m* (*-s/-*) reporter.

Reptil [rep'ti:l] *n* (*-s/ -ien*) reptile.

Republik [repu'bli:k] *f* (*-/ -en*) republic; **~aner** [-bli'ka:nər] *m* (*-s/-*) republican; **2anisch** *adj* republican.

Reserve [re'zervə] *f* (*-/-n*) reserve; **~rad** *n* spare wheel; **~tank** *m* reserve tank.

reservier|en [rezer'vi:rən] *v/t Platz:* keep; **~en lassen** book, reserve; **~t** *adj* reserved (*a. fig.*).

Residenz [rezi'dents] *f* (*-/ -en*) residence.

resignieren [rezi'gni:rən] *v/i* resign.

Respekt [re'spekt] *m* (*-[e]s/no pl*) respect.

Rest [rest] *m* (*-[e]s/-e*) rest, remainder; *Speise:* leftover.

Restaurant [rɛsto'rãː] *n* (*-s/-s*) restaurant.

rest|lich ['rɛstlɪç] *adj* remaining; **~los** *adv* entirely, completely.

rette|n ['retən] *v/t* save (*vor* from); deliver, rescue (*aus* from); **2r** *m* rescuer, deliverer.

Rettich ['retɪç] *m* (*-s/-e*) radish.

Rettung ['retʊŋ] *f* (*-/no pl*) rescue.

Rettungs|boot *n* lifeboat; **~gürtel** *m* lifebelt; **~mannschaft** *f* rescue party; **~ring** *m* life-buoy.

Reue ['rɔʏə] *f* (*-/no pl*) repentance, remorse.

Revier [re'vi:r] *n* (*-s/-e*) district, quarter.

Revision [revi'zĭo:n] *f* (*-/ -en*) *jur.* appeal.

Revolution [revolu-'tsĭo:n] f (/-en) revolution; **~är** [-tsĭo'nε:r] m (-s/-e) revolutionary; **2är** adj revolutionary.

Revolver [re'vɔlvər] m (-s/-) revolver, Am. colloq. a. gun.

Rezept [re'tsεpt] n (-[e]s/-e) prescription; Koch2: recipe (a. fig.).

Rezeption [retsεp'tsĭo:n] f (/-en) reception desk.

Rhabarber [ra'barbər] m (-s/no pl) rhubarb.

Rheuma ['rɔyma] n (-s/no pl), **~tismus** [-'tismʊs] m (-/-men) rheumatism.

Rhythmus ['rʏtmʊs] m (-/-men) rhythm.

richten ['rɪçtən] v/t tech. adjust; Waffe: point (**auf** at); direct (**auf, an** to); v/refl **sich ~ nach** conform to, act according to; depend on.

Richter ['rɪçtər] m (-s/-) judge.

richtig ['rɪçtɪç] adj right, correct; gehörig: proper; **~ gehen** Uhr: be right; **~stellen** v/t put od. set right.

Richtlinien ['rɪçtli:nĭən] pl directions pl.

Richtung ['rɪçtʊŋ] f (/-en) direction; **~anzeiger** ['-ʔantsaɪgər] m mot. indicator, trafficator.

riechen ['ri:çən] v/i, v/t (irr) smell (**nach** of; **an** at).

Riegel ['ri:gəl] m (-s/-) bar, bolt; Seife: bar, cake; Schokolade: bar.

Riemen ['ri:mən] m (-s/-) strap; Gürtel, tech.: belt; Ruder: oar.

Riese ['ri:zə] m (-n/-n) giant.

Riff [rɪf] n (-[e]s/-e) reef.

Rille ['rɪlə] f (/-n) groove.

Rind [rɪnt] n (-[e]s/-er) Ochse: ox; Kuh: cow; **~er** pl cattle pl.

Rinde ['rɪndə] f (/-n) bark; Käse: rind; Brot: crust.

Rind|erbraten m roast beef; **~fleisch** n beef.

Ring [rɪŋ] m (-[e]s/-e) ring.

Ringelnatter ['rɪŋəlnatər] f (/-n) ring-snake.

ring|en ['rɪŋən] v/t (irr) Hände: wring; v/i wrestle; fig. a. struggle; **nach Atem ~en** gasp (for breath); **2er** m wrestler; **2kampf** m wrestling (-match); **2richter** m referee.

Rinn|e ['rɪnə] f (/-n) groove, channel; **2en** ['rɪnən] v/i (irr) run, flow; tröpfeln: drip; **~stein** n gutter.

Rippe ['rɪpə] f (/-n) rib.

Risiko ['ri:ziko] n (-s/-s, -ken) risk.

risk|ant [rɪs'kant] adj risky; **~ieren** [-'ki:rən] v/t risk.

Riß [rɪs] m (-sses/-sse) rent, tear; Sprung: crack; Haut: chap.

Ritt [rɪt] *m* (-[e]s/-e) ride.

Ritter ['rɪtər] *m* (-s/-) knight.

Ritze ['rɪtsə] *f* (-/-n) chink; **2n** ['rɪtsən] scratch.

Rivalle [ri'va:lə] *m* (-n/-n), **~in** *f* (-/-nen) rival.

Robbe ['rɔbə] *f* (-/-n) zo. seal.

Robe ['ro:bə] *f* (-/-n) robe; gown.

Roboter ['rɔbɔtər] *m* (-s/-) robot.

robust [ro'bust] *adj* robust, sturdy.

röcheln ['rœçəln] *v/i* rattle.

Rock [rɔk] *m* (-[e]s/=e) skirt.

rodelln ['ro:dəln] *v/i* sled(ge), *Am. a.* coast; **2schlitten** *m* sled, sledge; *Am.* toboggan.

roden ['ro:dən] *v/t* clear.

Rogen ['ro:gən] *m* (-s/-) (hard) roe, spawn.

Roggen ['rɔgən] *m* (-s/-) rye.

roh [ro:] *adj* raw; rough, rude; cruel; brutal; **2kost** *f* uncooked vegetarian food.

Rohr [ro:r] *n* (-[e]s/-e) tube, pipe; *Schilf:* reed.

Röhre ['rø:rə] *f* (-/-n) tube, pipe; *Radio:* valve, *Am.* tube.

Rohstoff ['ro:ʃtɔf] *m* (-[e]s/-e) raw material.

Rolllladen ['rɔla:dən] *m* (-s/ᵘ) rolling shutter; **~bahn** *f* runway.

Rolle ['rɔlə] *f* (-/-n) roll;

tech. a. roller; *thea.* part, role; **~ Garn** reel of cotton, *Am.* spool of thread; **2n** ['rɔlən] *v/i, v/t* roll; *aer.* taxi; **~r** *m* (motor-)scooter.

Rolllfilm *m* roll film; **~kragen** *m* turtle neck; **~schuh** *m* roller-skate; **~stuhl** *m* wheelchair; **~treppe** *f* escalator.

Roman [ro'ma:n] *m* (-s/-e) novel.

romantisch [ro'mantɪʃ] *adj* romantic.

Römler ['rø:mər] *m* (-s/-) Roman; **2isch** *adj* Roman.

röntgen ['rœntgən] *v/t* X-ray; **2aufnahme** *f*, **2bild** *n* X-ray; **2strahlen** *pl* X-rays *pl.*

rosa ['ro:za] *adj* pink.

Rose ['ro:zə] *f* (-/-n) rose.

Rosenlkohl *m* Brussels sprouts *pl;* **~kranz** *m* rosary.

rosig ['ro:zɪç] *adj* rosy.

Rosine [ro'zi:nə] *f* (-/-n) raisin.

Roß [rɔs] *n* (-sses/-sse) horse.

Rost[1] [rɔst] *m* (-[e]s/*no pl*) rust.

Rost[2] *m* (-[e]s/-e) grate; *Brat2:* gridiron; grill; **~braten** *m* roast (of beef).

rosten ['rɔstən] *v/i* rust.

rösten ['rø:stən] *v/t* roast, grill; *Brot:* toast; *Kartoffeln:* fry.

rostlfrei ['rɔstfraɪ] *adj* rustless; stainless; **~ig** *adj* rusty.

rot [ro:t] *adj* red; **~ werden** blush; **~blond** *adj* sandy; **2es Kreuz** Red Cross.

röten ['rø:tən] *v/t:* (sich) ~ redden.

rotieren [ro'ti:rən] *v/i* rotate, revolve.

Rot|kohl *m* red cabbage; **~stift** *m* red pencil; **~wein** *m* red wine; clar; **~wild** *n* (-[e]s/*no pl*) red deer.

Roulade [ru'la:də] *f* (-/-n) roulade (of beef).

Rouleau [ru'lo:] *n* (-s/-s) *s.* **Rolladen:** blind, *Am.* (window) shade.

Route ['ru:tə] *f* (-/-n) route.

Routine [ru'ti:nə] *f* (-/*no pl*) routine.

Rübe ['ry:bə] *f* (-/-n) beet; **rote** ~ red beet, beetroot; **gelbe** ~ carrot.

Rubin [ru'bi:n] *m* (-s/-e) ruby.

Ruck [ruk] *m* (-[e]s/-e) jerk, jolt.

Rückblick ['rykblık] *m* (-[e]s/-e) retrospect.

rücken ['rykən] *v/t, v/i* move; shift; **näher** ~ approach.

Rücken *m* (-s/-) back; **~lehne** *f* back; **~mark** *n* spinal cord; **~schwimmen** *n* (-s/*no pl*) backstroke; **~wind** *m* following wind, tail wind; **~wirbel** *m* dorsal vertebra.

Rück|erstattung ['ryk-?ɛrʃtatʊŋ] *f* restitution,

refund; **~fahrkarte** *f* return (ticket), round-trip ticket; *Am.* round-trip ticket; **~fahrt** *f* return journey *od.* trip; **auf der ~fahrt** on the way back; **2fällig** *adj:* **~ werden** relapse; **~flug** *m* return flight; **2gängig** [-gɛŋıç] *adj:* **~ machen** cancel; **~grat** *n* (-[e]s/-e) spine, backbone; *fig.* mainstay; support; **~kehr** [-ke:r] *f* (-/*no pl*) return; **~licht** *n* taillight, rear light *od.* lamp; **~porto** *n* return postage; **~reise** *f* return journey, journey back *od.* home.

Rucksack ['rukzak] *m* (-[e]s/*ᵛe*) knapsack, rucksack.

Rück|schlag ['rykʃla:g] *m* (-[e]s/*ᵛe*) set-back; **~schritt** *m* retrogression; *pol.* reaction; **~seite** *f* back, reverse; **~sicht** *f* (-/-en) consideration; **2sichtslos** *adj* inconsiderate; *skrupellos:* ruthless; *unbekümmert:* reckless; **2sichtsvoll** *adj* considerate; **~sitz** *m* backseat; **~spiegel** *m* rear-view mirror; **~spiel** *n* return match; **~stand** *m* (-[e]s/*ᵛe*) arrears *pl;* *chem.* residue; **2ständig** *adj* old-fashioned; **~tritt** *m* resignation; **~trittbremse** *f* backpedal(l)ing brake, *Am* coaster brake; **2wärts** *adv* back, backward(s); **~wärtsgang** *m* reverse (gear); **~weg** *m* way back;

Rudel

2**wirkend** adj retrospective; ~**zahlung** f repayment; ~**zug** m retreat.

Rudel ['ruːdəl] n (-s/-) troop; Wölfe: pack; Rehe: herd.

Ruder ['ruːdər] n (-s/-) oar; mar.: rudder; helm; aer. rudder; ~**boot** n rowing boat, Am. a. rowboat; 2n ['ruːdərn] v/i, v/t row.

Ruf [ruːf] m (-[e]s/-e) call (a. fig.); cry, shout; Leumund: reputation; 2en ['ruːfən] v/i, v/t (irr) call; cry, shout; 2en **lassen** send for; ~**nummer** f telephone number.

Rüge ['ryːgə] f (-/-n) rebuke, reprimand.

Ruhe ['ruːə] f (-/no pl) rest; sleep; Stille: quiet(ness), calm; Gelassenheit: composure; **in** ~ **lassen** leave od. let alone; 2**los** adj restless; 2n ['ruːən] v/i rest; sleep; ~**pause** f pause; ~**stand** m: **im** ~ retired; ~**störung** f disturbance (of the peace); ~**tag** m rest-day.

ruhig ['ruːiç] adj quiet; calm.

Ruhm [ruːm] m (-[e]s/no pl) glory; fame.

Rühr|**ei** ['ryːrʔaiər] n scrambled eggs pl; 2**en** ['ryːrən] v/t stir, move; fig. touch, move, affect; **sich** 2**en** stir, move; 2**end** adj touching, moving; ~**ung** f (-/no pl) emotion, feeling.

Ruin [ruːiːn] m (-s/no pl)

ruin; decay; ~**e** f (-/-n) ruin(s pl); 2**ieren** [ruiˈniːrən] v/t ruin.

rülpsen ['rylpsən] v/i belch.

Rum [rʊm] m (-s/-s) rum.

Rummel ['rʊməl] m (-s/no pl) colloq. bustle; ~**platz** m amusement park.

rumpeln ['rʊmpəln] v/i colloq. rumble.

Rumpf [rʊmpf] m (-[e]s/ᵉe) anat. trunk, body; mar. hull, body; aer. fuselage, body.

rund [rʊnt] adj round; circular; adv about; ~ **um** (a panorama); 2**blick** m panorama; 2**e** ['rʊndə] f (-/-n) round; sp. lap; Boxen: round; Polizist: beat; 2**fahrt** f s. **Rundreise**; ~**flug** m sightseeing od. local flight.

Rund|**funk** m (-s/no pl) broadcast(ing); Anstalt: broadcasting company; s. **Radio**; ~**gerät** n s. **Radioapparat**; ~**hörer** m listener(-in); pl a. (radio) audience sg; ~**sender** m broadcasting od. radio station; ~**sendung** f broadcast; ~**sprecher** m broadcaster, (radio) announcer.

Rund|**gang** m (-s/no pl) tour; round; 2**herum** [-heˈrʊm] adv round about, all (a)round; 2**lich** adj roundish; plump; ~**reise** f circular tour, round trip, sightseeing trip; ~**schreiben** n circular (letter).

Runz|el ['rʊntsəl] f (-/-n)
wrinkle; 2**(e)lig** adj wrinkled; 2**eln** ['rʊntsəln] v/t:
die Stirn ~ frown.

rupfen ['rʊpfən] v/t pick;
Geflügel: pluck.

Rüsche ['ry:ʃə] f (-/-n)
ruffle, frill.

Ruß [ru:s] m (-es/no pl)
soot.

Russe ['rʊsə] m (-n/-n)
Russian.

Rüssel ['rʊsəl] m (-s/-)
Elefant: trunk; *Schwein:*
snout.

rußig ['ru:sɪç] adj sooty.

russisch ['rʊsɪʃ] adj Russian.

rüsten ['rʊstən] v/t, v/refl:
sich ~ (zu) prepare od.
get ready (for).

rüstig ['rʊstɪç] adj vigorous, strong.

Rüstung ['rʊstʊŋ] f (-/
-en) armo(u)r; *mil.* armament.

Rute ['ru:tə] f (-/-n) rod;
Gerte: switch.

Rutsch|bahn ['rʊtʃba:n] f
(-/-en), ~**e** f (-/-n) slide,
chute; 2**en** ['rʊtʃən] v/i
glide, slide; 2**ig** adj slippery.

rütteln ['rʊtəln] v/i jog,
jolt; **an der Tür ~** rattle
at the door.

S

Saal [za:l] m (-[e]s/Säle)
hall.

Saat [za:t] f (-/-en) seed
(a. fig.); *junge Pflanzen:*
growing crops pl.

Säbel ['zɛ:bəl] m (-s/-)
sab|re, *Am.* -er.

Sabotage [zabo'ta:ʒə] f
(-/-n) sabotage.

Sach|bearbeiter ['zax-
bə²arbaɪtər] m (-s/-) official in charge; 2**dienlich**
[-di:nlɪç] adj relevant; ~**e**
['zaxə] f (-/-n) thing;
affair, matter; ~**en** pl *Besitz:* things pl, belongings
pl; 2**gemäß** adj proper;
~**kenntnis** f expert
knowledge; 2**kundig** adj
expert; 2**lich** adj matter-
of-fact, businesslike; objective.

sächlich ['zɛçlɪç] adj gr.
neuter.

Sach|register ['zaxregɪs-
tər] n (-s/-) (subject) index; ~**schaden** m damage
to property.   [gentle.]

sacht [zaxt] adj soft,]

Sach|verhalt ['zaxfɛr-
halt] m (-[e]s/-e) facts pl
(of the case); ~**verstän-
dige** m, f (-n/-n) expert,
authority.

Sack [zak] m (-[e]s/⁀e)
sack, bag; ~**gasse** f blind
alley, cul-de-sac; *fig.* deadlock.

säen ['zɛ:ən] v/t sow.

Saft [zaft] m (-[e]s/⁀e)
juice; *Bäume etc.:* sap; 2**ig**
adj juicy.

Sage ['za:gə] f (-/-n)
legend, myth.

Säge

Säge ['zɛ:gə] f (-/-n) saw; **~mehl** n saw-dust.

sagen ['za:gən] v/t say; *mitteilen:* tell.

sägen ['zɛ:gən] v/t, v/i saw.

Sahne ['za:nə] f (-/no pl) cream.

Saison [zɛ'zõ:] f (-/-s) season; **~zuschlag** m seasonal surcharge.

Saite ['zaɪtə] f (-/-n) string, chord; **~ninstrument** n string(ed) instrument.

Sakko ['zako] m, n (-s/-s) (lounge) jacket.

Salat [za'la:t] m (-[e]s/-e) salad; *Kopf2:* lettuce.

Salbe ['zalbə] f (-/-n) ointment.

Salz [zalts] n (-es/-e) salt; **2en** v/t (irr) salt; **2ig** adj salt(y); **~kartoffeln** pl boiled potatoes pl; **~säure** f hydrochloric acid; **~streuer** [-ʃtrɔyər] m saltshaker; **~wasser** n salt water.

Samen ['za:mən] m (-s/-) seed; *biol.* sperm.

samm|eln ['zaməln] v/t gather; collect; **2ler** m collector; **2lung** f collection; *fig.* composure.

Samstag ['zamsta:k] m Saturday.

Samt [zamt] m (-[e]s/-e) velvet.

sämtlich ['zɛmtlɪç] indef pron all; complete.

Sanatorium [zana'to:rɪum] n (-s/-rien)

sanatorium, *Am. a.* sanitarium.

Sand [zant] m (-[e]s/-e) sand.

Sandale [zan'da:lə] f (-/-n) sandal.

Sand|bank ['zantbaŋk] f (-/~e) sandbank; **2ig** adj sandy.

sanft [zanft] adj soft; gentle, mild.

Sänger ['zɛŋər] m (-s/-), **~in** f (-/-nen) singer.

sanitär [zani'tɛ:r] adj sanitary.

Sanitäter [zani'tɛ:tər] m (-s/-) ambulance man, first-aider.

Sankt [zaŋkt] Saint, *abbr.* St.

Sard|elle [zar'dɛlə] f (-/-n) anchovy; **~ine** [zar'di:nə] f (-/-n) sardine.

Sarg [zark] m (-[e]s/~e) coffin, *Am. a.* casket.

Satellit [zate'li:t] m (-en/-en) satellite.

Satire [za'ti:rə] f (-/-n) satire.

satt [zat] adj: **sich ~ essen** eat one's fill; **ich bin ~** I have had enough; **et. ~ haben** colloq. be fed up with s.th.

Sattel ['zatəl] m (-s/~) saddle; **2n** v/t saddle.

sättigend ['zɛtɪgənt] adj substantial.

Satz [zats] m (-es/~e) *Sprung:* leap, bound; *ling.* sentence, clause; *Tennis:* set; *Boden2:* dregs pl, grounds pl; *Garnitur:* set;

~ung f statute; **~zeichen** n punctuation mark.

Sau [zau] f (-/-ᵉe, -en) sow.

sauber ['zaubɐr] adj clean; ordentlich: neat, tidy; **2keit** f (-/no pl) cleanness; tidiness; neatness; **~machen** v/t clean.

säubern ['zɔybɐrn] v/t clean(se); Zimmer: tidy, clean.

sauer ['zauɐr] adj sour; acid; Gurke: pickled; fig. colloq. peeved; **2milch** f (no pl) curdled milk; **2stoff** m (no pl) oxygen; **2teig** m leaven.

saufen ['zaufən] v/i, v/t (irr) drink; colloq. booze.

Säufer ['zɔyfɐr] m (-s/-) colloq. drunkard, boozer.

saugen ['zaugən] v/t, v/i (irr) suck.

säug|en ['zɔygən] v/t suckle, nurse; **2etier** [-tiːr] n mammal; **2ling** [-lɪŋ] m (-s/-e) baby.

Säule ['zɔylə] f (-/-n) column, pillar.

Saum [zaum] m (-[e]s/ᵉe) seam, hem; Rand: selvage, edge.

Sauna ['zauna] f (-/-s, -nen) sauna.

Säure ['zɔyrə] f (-/-n) acidity (a. Magen2); chem. acid.

sausen ['zauzən] v/i rush, dash.

Saxophon [zakso'foːn] n (-s/-e) saxophone.

Schabe ['ʃaːbə] f (-/-n) cockroach; **2n** ['ʃaːbən] v/t scrape.

schäbig ['ʃɛːbɪç] adj shabby; fig. a. mean.

Schach [ʃax] n (-s/-s) chess; **~brett** n chessboard; **~figur** f chessman; **2matt** [-'mat] adj checkmate; **~spiel** n (game of) chess.

Schacht [ʃaxt] m (-[e]s/ᵉe) shaft; Bergbau: a. pit.

Schachtel ['ʃaxtəl] f (-/-n) box.

schade ['ʃaːdə] adj: es ist ~ it is a pity; wie ~! what a pity!

Schädel ['ʃɛːdəl] m (-s/-) skull; **~bruch** m fractured skull.

schaden ['ʃaːdən] v/i injure, harm, hurt; **2** m (-s/ᵉ) damage (an to); körperlicher: injury; **2ersatz** m (-es/no pl) compensation; Geldsumme: damages pl; **2freude** f (no pl) malignant delight; **~froh** adj gloating.

schadhaft ['ʃaːthaft] adj damaged; Rohr: leaking; Zähne: decayed.

schädig|en ['ʃɛːdɪgən] v/t damage; j-n: injure; **~lich** ['ʃɛːtlɪç] adj harmful, injurious; **2linge** pl vermin pl.

Schaf [ʃaːf] n (-[e]s/-e) sheep; **~bock** m ram.

Schäfer ['ʃɛːfɐr] m (-s/-) shepherd; **~hund** m sheepdog; deutscher: Alsatian.

schaffen ['ʃafən] v/t brin

gen: carry; take; *bewälti-gen:* manage; *v/t (irr)* create.

Schaffner ['ʃafnɐ] *m* -s/-) rail. guard, *Am.* conductor; *Straßenbahn, Bus:* conductor.

Schaft [ʃaft] *m* -(e)s/ʉe) shaft; *Gewehr:* stock; *Stiefel:* leg; **~stiefel** *pl* high boots *pl.*

schal [ʃaːl] *adj* stale; *fade:* insipid.

Schal *m* -s/-s) scarf; *Woll:* comforter.

Schale [ʃaːlə] *f* -/-n) bowl, dish; *Waage:* scale; shell; *Früchte:* skin, peel; **~n** *pl* parings *pl;* *Kartoffeln:* peelings *pl.*

schälen [ʃɛːlən] *v/t* pare, peel; **sich ~** *Haut:* peel od. come off.

Schall [ʃal] *m* -(e)s/no *pl)* sound; **2dicht** *adj* soundproof; **2en** *v/i (a. irr)* sound; *klingen, dröhnen:* ring, peal; **~mauer** *f* sound barrier; **~platte** *f* record.

schalt|en [ʃaltən] *v/t* switch; *v/i* change gear; **2er** [ʃaltɐ] *m* -s/-) switch; *rail.* booking-office, ticket-office; *Post, Bank:* counter; *Auskunftsschalter:* desk; **2hebel** *m* gear lever; *tech., aer.* control lever; **2jahr** *n* leap year; **2tafel** *f* switchboard, control panel.

Scham [ʃaːm] *f* -/no *pl)* shame.

schämen [ʃɛːmən] *v/refl:* **sich ~** be *od.* feel ashamed (*gen,* **wegen** of).

Scham|gefühl *n* sense of shame; **2haft** *adj* bashful; **2los** *adj* shameless.

Schande [ʃandə] *f* -/no *pl)* shame, disgrace.

schändlich [ʃɛntlɪç] *adj* shameful, disgraceful.

Schanze [ʃantsə] *f* -/-n) ski-jump.

Schar [ʃaːr] *f* -/-en) troop, band; *Gänse etc.:* flock; **2en** *v/t, v/refl:* **sich ~ um** gather *od.* flock round.

scharf [ʃarf] *adj* sharp; pungent; *Pfeffer:* hot; *Augen, Gehör, Verstand:* sharp, keen; **~ sein auf** be keen on.

schärfen [ʃɛrfən] *v/t* sharpen.

Scharf|schütze [ʃarfʃʏtsə] *m* -n/-n) sharp-shooter; marksman; **~sinn** *m (no pl)* acumen.

Scharlach [ʃarlax] *m* -s/no *pl)* scarlet fever; **2rot** *adj* scarlet.

Scharnier [ʃarniːr] *n* -s/-e) hinge, joint.

Schärpe [ʃɛrpə] *f* -/-n) sash.

scharren [ʃarən] *v/i, v/t* scrape; *Huhn:* scratch; *Pferd:* paw.

Schatt|en [ʃatən] *m* -s/-) shadow; **~ierung** [-'tiːruŋ] *f* shade; **2ig** *adj* shady.

Schatz [ʃats] *m* -es/ʉe)

treasure; *fig.* sweetheart; darling.

schätzen [ˈʃɛtsən] *v/t* estimate, value (**auf a**); *würdigen*: appreciate; *hoch*: esteem.

Schau [ʃau] *f* (*-/-en*) show; exhibition.

Schauder [ˈʃaudər] *m* (*-s/-*) shudder, shiver.

schauen [ˈʃauən] *v/i* look (**auf a**).

Schauer [ˈʃauər] *m* (*-s/-*) *Regen etc.*: shower; *s.* **Schauder**; **2lich** *adj* dreadful, horrible.

Schaufel [ˈʃaufəl] *f* (*-/-n*) shovel; *Kehr2*: dustpan; **2n** *v/t* shovel.

Schaufenster [ˈʃaufɛnstər] *n* (*-s/-*) shop-window; *~bummel* m: ein ~ machen go window-shopping.

Schaukel [ˈʃaukəl] *f* (*-/-n*) swing; **2n** *v/i* swing; *Boot*: rock; *~pferd* n rocking-horse; *~stuhl* m rocking-chair, *Am.* rocker.

Schaum [ʃaum] *m* (*-[e]s/ve*) foam; *Bier*: froth, head; *Seife*: lather.

schäumen [ˈʃɔymən] *v/i* foam; *Seife*: lather; *Wein*: sparkle.

Schaum|gummi *m* (*-s/-[s]*) foam (rubber); **2ig** *adj* foamy, frothy; *~stoff* m expanded plastic.

Schauplatz [ˈʃauplats] *m* (*-es/ve*) scene.

Schauspiel [ˈʃauʃpiːl] *n*

(*-s/-e*) spectacle; *thea.* play; *~er* m actor; *~erin* f (*-/-nen*) actress.

Scheck [ʃɛk] *m* (*-s/-s*) cheque, *Am.* check.

Scheibe [ˈʃaibə] *f* (*-/-n*) disc, disk; *Brot etc.*: slice; *Fenster*: pane; *Schieß2*: target; *~nbremse* f disc brake; *~nwischer* [ˈ-vɪʃər] m windscreen (*Am.* windshield) wiper.

Scheide [ˈʃaidə] *f* (*-/-n*) sheath, scabbard; *anat.* vagina; **2n** [ˈʃaidən] *v/t, v/i* (*irr*) separate; **sich 2en lassen** von j—m divorce s.o.; *~ung* f (*-/-en*) divorce.

Schein [ʃain] *m* (*-[e]s/-e*) certificate; *Quittung*: receipt; *Banknote*, *Am.* a. bill; (*no pl*) light; *fig.* appearances *pl*; **2bar** [*-ba:r*] *adj* seeming, apparent; **2en** [ˈʃainən] *v/i* (*irr*) shine; *fig.* seem, appear, look; **2heilig** *adj* hypocritical; *~werfer* [ˈ-verfər] m (*-s/-*) headlight; *thea.* spotlight.

Scheiße [ˈʃaisə] *f* (*-/no pl*) *vulg.* shit.

Scheit [ʃait] *n* (*-[e]s/-e*) log.

Scheitel [ˈʃaitəl] *m* (*-s/-*) *Frisur*: parting; **2n** *v/t* part.

scheitern [ˈʃaitərn] *v/i* fail, miscarry.

Schellfisch [ˈʃɛlfɪʃ] *m* (*-[e]s/-e*) haddock.

Schelm [ʃɛlm] *m* (*-[e]s*

-e) rogue; 2**isch** adj arch, roguish, mischievous.

schelten ['ʃɛltən] v/t (irr) scold.

Schema ['ʃeːma] n (-s/-s, **Schemata**) scheme; pattern.

Schemel ['ʃeːməl] m (-s/-) stool.

Schenke ['ʃɛŋkə] f (-/-n) pub(lic house).

Schenkel ['ʃɛŋkəl] m (-s/-) Ober2: thigh; Unter2: shank.

schenken ['ʃɛŋkən] v/t give.

Scherbe ['ʃɛrbə] f (-/-n), ~n m (-s/-) (broken) piece, fragment.

Schere ['ʃeːrə] f (-/-n) (e-e a pair of) scissors pl; Krebs etc.: claw; 2n ['ʃeː-rən] v/t (irr) clip, shear; Haare: cut; Bart: shave.

Scherereien [ʃeːrə'raɪən] pl trouble sg.

Scherz [ʃɛrts] m (-es/-e) joke; 2**en** ['ʃɛrtsən] v/i joke; 2**haft** adj joking.

scheu [ʃɔy] adj shy, timid; 2 f (-/no pl) shyness; Furchtsamkeit: timidity; ~en ['ʃɔyən] v/i shy (vor at); v/t shun, avoid.

Scheuer|lappen ['ʃɔyər-lapən] m (-s/-) floor-cloth; ~**leiste** f skirting-board; 2**n** ['ʃɔyən] v/t scour, scrub; wund reiben: chafe.

Scheune ['ʃɔynə] f (-/-n) barn.

Scheusal ['ʃɔyzaːl] n (-s/-e) monster.

scheußlich ['ʃɔyslɪç] adj abominable.

Schi m etc. s. **Ski** etc.

Schicht [ʃɪçt] f (-/-en) layer (a. geol.); Arbeits2: shift; (social) class, rank; 2**en** ['ʃɪçtən] v/t pile.

schick [ʃɪk] adj chic, stylish.

schicken ['ʃɪkən] v/t send.

Schicksal ['ʃɪkzaːl] n (-s/-e) fate, destiny.

Schiebe|dach ['ʃiːbədax] n (-[e]s/ˈ/er) sliding roof; ~**fenster** n sash-window; 2**n** ['ʃiːbən] v/t (irr) push, shove; ~**tür** f sliding door.

Schiedsrichter ['ʃiːtsrɪç-tər] m (-s/-) Tennis: umpire; Fußball etc.: referee.

schief [ʃiːf] adj sloping, slanting; awry; Gesicht, Mund: wry.

Schiefer ['ʃiːfər] m (-s/-) slate; Splitter: splinter; ~**tafel** f slate.

schiefgehen v/i (irr) go wrong.

schielen ['ʃiːlən] v/i squint.

Schienbein n shin(-bone).

Schiene ['ʃiːnə] f (-/-n) rail; med. splint; 2**n** ['ʃiː-nən] v/t splint.

schießen ['ʃiːsən] v/i, v/t (irr) fire; shoot; ein Tor ~**en** score a goal; 2**erei** [-sə'raɪ] f (-/-en) shooting; 2**scheibe** f target; 2**stand** m shooting-gallery, shooting-range.

Schiff [ʃɪf] n (-[e]s/-e) ship, vessel; ~**ahrt**

['-fa:rt] f (-/-en) navigation; 2**bar** [-ba:r] adj navigable; ~**bruch** m: ~ **erleiden** be shipwrecked; 2**brüchig** adj shipwrecked.

schikanieren [ʃika'ni:rən] v/t tyrannize.

Schild [ʃɪlt] n (-[e]s/-er) sign(-board); Namens2: nameplate; Etikett: label; Mützen2: peak; ~**drüse** f thyroid gland.

schilder|n ['ʃɪldərn] v/t describe; 2**ung** f (-/-en) description.

Schildkröte f Land2: tortoise; See2: turtle.

Schilf [ʃɪlf] n (-[e]s/-e), ~**rohr** n reed.

Schimmel|el ['ʃɪməl] m (-s/-) Pferd: white horse; (no pl) Pilz: mo(u)ld; 2**eln** v/i mo(u)ld; 2**(e)lig** adj mo(u)ldy.

schimmern ['ʃɪmərn] v/i glimmer, gleam.

Schimpanse [ʃɪm'panzə] m (-n/-n) chimpanzee.

schimpf|en ['ʃɪmpfən] v/i, v/t scold; 2**wort** n swearword, abusive word.

Schindel ['ʃɪndəl] f (-/-n) shingle.

schinden ['ʃɪndən] v/t (irr) tax, sweat; **sich** ~ drudge, slave, sweat.

Schinken ['ʃɪŋkən] m (-s/-) ham.

Schirm [ʃɪrm] m (-[e]s/-e) umbrella; Lampe: shade; Mütze: peak; ~**mütze** f peaked cap.

Schlacht [ʃlaxt] f (-/-en) battle (**bei** of); 2**en** ['ʃlaxtən] v/t slaughter, butcher; ~**feld** n battlefield; ~**schiff** n battleship.

Schlacke ['ʃlakə] f (-/-n) cinder.

Schlaf [ʃla:f] m (-[e]s/no pl) sleep; ~**anzug** m (**ein** a pair of) pyjamas pl od. Am. a. pajamas pl.

Schläfe ['ʃlɛ:fə] f (-/-n) temple.

schlafen ['ʃla:fən] v/i (irr) sleep; ~ **gehen, sich** ~ **legen** go to bed.

schlaff [ʃlaf] adj slack; Muskeln: flabby; bot. limp.

schlaf|los ['ʃla:flo:s] adj sleepless; 2**losigkeit** f sleeplessness, med. insomnia; 2**mittel** n soporific.

schläfrig ['ʃlɛ:frɪç] adj sleepy, drowsy.

Schlaf|sack m sleeping bag; ~**tablette** f sleeping pill; ~**wagen** m sleeping car; ~**zimmer** n bedroom.

Schlag [ʃla:k] m (-[e]s/ :e) blow (a. fig.); flache Hand: slap; tech. stroke; electr. shock; med. apoplexy, stroke; ~**ader** ['-ʔa:dər] f artery; ~**anfall** m apoplexy, stroke; ~**baum** m barrier(s pl); 2**en** ['ʃla:gən] v/t, v/i (irr) strike, beat, hit; Faust: punch; flache Hand: slap; Bäume: fell; besiegen: beat, defeat; Uhr: strike; ~**er** m pop(ular) song; hit.

Schläger ['ʃlɛːgər] m (-s/ -) rowdy; *Kricket:* bat; *s.* **Golf-, Tennisschläger; ~ei** [-gəˈraɪ] f (-/ -en) fight.

schlagfertig ['ʃlaːkfɛr- tɪç] adj good at repartee; **2sahne** f whipped cream; **2wort** n slogan; **2zeile** f headline; **2zeug** n percussion (instruments pl).

Schlamm [ʃlam] m (-[e]s/ no pl) mud; **2ig** adj muddy.

Schlampe ['ʃlampə] f (-/ -n) slut, slattern; **2ig** adj slovenly; slipshod.

Schlange ['ʃlaŋə] f (-/-n) *zo.:* snake; serpent (a. fig.); *Menschen2:* queue, *Am. a.* line; **~ stehen** queue up, *Am. a.* line up.

schlängeln ['ʃlɛŋəln] v/ refl: **sich ~** worm one's way o.s. *Weg:* wind; *Fluß:* meander.

schlank [ʃlaŋk] adj slender, slim; **2heitskur** [-kuːr] f (-/-en): **e-e ~ machen** slim.

schlau [ʃlau] adj clever, cunning.

Schlauch [ʃlaux] m (-[e]s/ *e) tube; *Spritz2:* hose; *Auto2 etc.:* inner tube; **~boot** n rubber boat; **2los** adj tubeless.

Schlaufe ['ʃlaufə] f (-/-n) loop.

schlecht [ʃlɛçt] adj bad (a. verdorben); wicked; **mir ist ~** I feel sick; adv badly, ill.

schleichen ['ʃlaɪçən] v/i (irr) creep; *heimlich:* sneak, steal.

Schleier ['ʃlaɪər] m (-s/-) veil (a. fig.); *Dunst:* haze.

Schleife ['ʃlaɪfə] f (-/-n) loop; *Band2:* bow; *Kranz2:* streamer.

schleifen ['ʃlaɪfən] v/t drag, trail; (irr) *Messer etc.:* whet; *Steine:* cut.

Schleim [ʃlaɪm] m (-[e]s/ -e) slime; *med.* mucus, phlegm; **~haut** f anat. membrane; mucous membrane; **2ig** adj slimy (a. fig.); mucous.

schlemmen ['ʃlɛmən] v/i feast.

schlendern ['ʃlɛndərn] v/i stroll, saunter.

schlenkern ['ʃlɛŋkərn] v/i dangle, swing.

Schlepp|e ['ʃlɛpə] f (-/-n) train; **2en** v/t drag (sich o.s.); carry; *mar.* tug; **~lift** m T-bar (lift).

Schleuder ['ʃlɔydər] f (- -n) sling, catapult, *Am. a.* slingshot; *Trocken2:* spin dryer; **2n** v/t fling, hurl; *Wäsche:* spin-dry; v/i *mot.* skid.

Schleuse ['ʃlɔyzə] f (-/-n) sluice; *Kanal:* lock.

schlicht [ʃlɪçt] adj plain, simple; modest; **~en** ['ʃlɪç- tən] v/t settle.

schließ|en ['ʃliːsən] v/t (irr) shut, close; *Fabrik:* shut down; *Geschäft:* shut up; *Vertrag, Rede:* conclude; **2fach** n post office

box; *rail.* locker; ~**lich** *adv*
finally, at last; after all.

schlimm [ʃlɪm] *adj* bad;
serious; *wund:* bad, sore;
~**er** *comp* worse; **am**
~**sten** *sup* (the) worst.

Schlinge [ʃlɪŋə] *f* (-/-n)
loop; sling (*a. med.*);
zusammenziehbare: noose;
hunt. snare (*a. fig.*); ~**el** *m*
(-s/-) rascal; 2**en** [ʃlɪŋən]
v/t (*irr*) wind, twist;
~**pflanze** *f* creeper,
climber.

Schlips [ʃlɪps] *m* (-es/-e)
(neck)tie.

Schlitten [ʃlɪtən] *m* (-s/-)
sled(ge); *sp.* toboggan;
*Pferde*2: sleigh; ~**fahrt** *f*
sleigh-ride.

Schlittschuh [ʃlɪtʃuː] *m*
(-[e]s/-e) skate; ~ **laufen** skate; ~**läufer** *m*
skater.

Schlitz [ʃlɪts] *m* (-es/-e)
slit; *Einwurf*2: slot; 2**en**
[ʃlɪtsən] *v/t* slit, slash.

Schloß [ʃlɔs] *n* (-sses/
⸚**sser**) *Tür, Gewehr:* lock;
arch. castle, palace.

Schlosser [ʃlɔsər] *m* (-s/
-) locksmith.

schlottern [ʃlɔtərn] *v/i*
shake (vor with).

Schlucht [ʃluxt] *f* (-/-en)
gorge, ravine.

schluchzen [ʃluxtsən] *v/i*
sob.

Schluck [ʃluk] *m* (-[e]s/
-e, ⸚e) draught; ~**auf**
['-ʔaʊf] *m* (-s/*no pl*) hiccup,
hiccough; 2**en** *v/t, v/i*
swallow; ~**en** [ʃlukən] *m*

(-s/*no pl*) *s.* **Schluckauf.**

Schlummer [ʃlʊmər] *m*
(-s/*no pl*) slumber; 2**n**
slumber.

Schlund [ʃlʊnt] *m* (-[e]s/
⸚e) pharynx, throat.

schlüpf|en [ʃlʏpfən] *v/i*
slip, slide; 2**er** *m* knickers
pl, drawers *pl;* panties *pl,*
briefs *pl;* ~**rig** *adj* slippery.

schlurfen [ʃlʊrfən] *v/i*
shuffle.

schlürfen [ʃlʏrfən] *v/t, v/i*
sip; drink *od.* eat noisily.

Schluß [ʃlʊs] *m* (-sses/
⸚sse) close, end; *Abs2,*
~*folgerung:* conclusion.

Schlüssel [ʃlʏsəl] *m* (-s/-)
key; ~**bein** *n* collarbone;
~**bund** *m, n* bunch of
keys; ~**loch** *n* keyhole.

Schluß|folgerung [ʃlʊs-
fɔlɡəruŋ] *f* (-/-en) conclusion; ~**licht** *n s.* **Rücklicht;** ~**runde** *f sp.* final.

schmächtig [ʃmɛçtɪç] *adj*
slender, slim.

schmackhaft [ʃmakhaft]
adj palatable, savo(u)ry.

schmal [ʃmaːl] *adj* narrow; *Gestalt:* slender, slim;
Gesicht: thin; 2**spur** *f* narrow ga(u)ge.

Schmalz [ʃmalts] *n* (-es/
-e) grease; *Schweine*2:
lard.

Schmarotzer [ʃmaˈrɔt-
sər] *m* parasite.

schmatzen [ʃmatsən] *v/i*
eat noisily, smack one's
lips.

schmecken [ʃmɛkən] *v/t, v/i*

v/i taste; **~ nach** taste of; **schmeckt es?** do you like it? **das schmeckt mir** I enjoy this.

schmeichel|haft [ˈʃmaɪ-çəlhaft] *adj* flattering; **~n** *v/i* flatter (j-m s.o.).

schmeißen [ˈʃmaɪsən] *v/t* (irr) *colloq.* throw, fling, hurl; *Tür:* slam.

schmelzen [ˈʃmɛltsən] *v/i, v/t* (irr) melt; *Metall:* smelt, fuse.

Schmerbauch [ˈʃmeːr-baʊx] *m colloq.* paunch.

Schmerz [ʃmɛrts] *m* (-es/ -en), *auch* **~en** *pl* pain, *anhaltender:* ache; *fig.* grief, sorrow; **~en** *v/i, v/t* pain (*a. fig.*), hurt; ache; *fig.* grieve, afflict; **~haft** *adj* painful; **~lich** *adj* painful; **~lindernd** *adj* soothing; **~los** *adj* painless; **~stillendes Mittel** anodyne.

Schmetter|ling [ˈʃmɛtər-lɪŋ] *m* (-s/-e) butterfly; **~n** [ˈʃmɛtərn] *v/t* dash; *v/i singen:* warble.

Schmied [ʃmiːt] *m* (-[e]s/ -e) (black)smith; **~e** *f* (-/ -n) forge, smithy; **~en** [ˈʃmiːdən] *v/t* forge; *Pläne:* make, devise.

schmiegen [ˈʃmiːgən], **sich ~ an** *v/refl* nestle up to.

schmier|en [ˈʃmiːrən] *v/t* smear; *tech.* grease, oil, lubricate; *aufstreichen:* spread (**auf** on); *v/i kritzeln:* scrawl, scribble; **~ig** *adj* greasy; dirty; filthy.

Schminke [ˈʃmɪŋkə] *f* (-/ -n) make-up; **2n** *v/t* make up; **sich 2n** make (o.s.) up.

schmollen [ˈʃmɔlən] *v/i* sulk, pout.

Schmor|braten [ˈʃmoːr-braːtən] *m* pot roast; **2en** [ˈʃmoːrən] *v/t, v/i* stew (*a. fig.*).

Schmuck [ʃmʊk] *m* (-[e]s/*no pl*) ornament; decoration; *jewel(le)ry, jewels pl*; *2 adj* neat, smart.

schmücken [ˈʃmʏkən] *v/t* adorn, decorate.

schmuggeln [ˈʃmʊgəln] *v/t, v/i* smuggle.

schmunzeln [ˈʃmʊntsəln] *v/i* smile amusedly.

Schmutz [ʃmʊts] *m* (-es/ *no pl*) dirt, filth; **2en** [ˈʃmʊtsən] *v/i* soil, get dirty; **~fleck** *m* smudge, stain; *2ig* *adj* dirty, filthy.

Schnabel [ˈʃnaːbəl] *m* (-s/ **ᵛ**) bill, *gebogen:* beak.

Schnalle [ˈʃnalə] *f* (-/-n) buckle; **2n** *v/t* buckle; *festschnallen:* strap.

schnappen [ˈʃnapən] *v/i, colloq. v/t* snap, snatch; **nach Luft ~en** gasp for breath; *2schuß* *m* snapshot.

Schnaps [ʃnaps] *m* (-es/ **ᵛe**) strong liquor, *Am. a.* schnap(p)s.

schnarchen [ˈʃnarçən] *v/i* snore.

schnattern [ˈʃnatərn] *v/i* cackle.

schnauben [ˈʃnaʊbən] *v/i*

snort; v/t (sich) die Nase ~ blow one's nose.

schnaufen ['ʃnaʊfən] v/i pant, puff, blow.

Schnauze ['ʃnaʊtsə] f (-/-n) muzzle, snout; Kanne: spout.

Schnecke ['ʃnɛkə] f (-/-n) snail; Nackt2: slug.

Schnee [ʃne:] m (-s/no pl) snow; ~ballschlacht f snowball fight; 2bedeckt adj Berg: snowcapped; ~flocke f snowflake; ~gestöber ['-gəʃtø:bər] n (-s/no pl) snowflurry; ~glöckchen n (-s/-) snowdrop; ~kette f snow tyre chain; ~mann m snowman; ~pflug m snowplough, Am. snowplow; ~sturm m snowstorm, blizzard; ~wehe ['-ve:ə] f (-/-n) snowdrift; 2weiß adj snow-white.

Schneide ['ʃnaɪdə] f (-/-n) edge; 2n ['ʃnaɪdən] v/t (irr) cut; carve; ~r m (-s/-) tailor; ~rin f (-/-nen) dressmaker; ~zahn m incisor.

schneilen ['ʃnaɪən] v/i snow; es ~t it is snowing.

Schneise ['ʃnaɪzə] f (-/-n) lane.

schnell [ʃnɛl] adj quick, fast, swift; rapid; baldig: speedy; (mach) ~! be quick!, hurry up!; ~en ['ʃnɛlən] v/i jerk; 2hefter ['-hɛftər] m (-s/-) folder; 2igkeit f (-/no pl) speed;

2imbiß ['-ʔɪmbɪs] m snack(-bar); 2straße f Am. expressway; 2zug m express (train).

schnippisch ['ʃnɪpɪʃ] adj pert.

Schnitt [ʃnɪt] m (-[e]s/-e) cut; Kleid etc.: cut, make, style; fig. average; ~blumen pl cut flowers pl; ~e f (-/-n) slice; ~lauch m chives pl; ~muster n pattern; ~punkt m (point of) intersection; ~wunde f cut, gash.

Schnitzel¹ ['ʃnɪtsəl] n (-s/-) cutlet; Wiener ~ cutlet Viennese style.

Schnitzel² n, m (-s/-) colloq. scrap.

schnitzen ['ʃnɪtsən] v/t carve, cut.

Schnorchel ['ʃnɔrçəl] m (-s/-) s(ch)norkel.

schnüffeln ['ʃnʏfəln] v/i sniff, nose.

Schnuller ['ʃnʊlər] m (-s/-) dummy, comforter.

Schnulze ['ʃnʊltsə] f (-/-n) collog. tearjerker.

Schnupfen ['ʃnʊpfən] m (-s/-) cold, catarrh.

schnuppern ['ʃnʊpərn] v/i sniff.

Schnur [ʃnu:r] f (-/⁀e) string, line.

Schnur|bart ['ʃnʊrbaːrt] m (-[e]s/⁀e) m(o)ustache; 2en v/i purr.

Schnürsenkel ['ʃnyːrzɛŋkəl] m (-s/-) shoelace, shoestring.

Schock [ʃɔk] m (-[e]s/-e)

shock; **2ieren** [-'ki:rən] *v/t* shock.

Schokolade [ʃoko'la:də] *f* (-/-n) chocolate.

Scholle ['ʃɔlə] *f* (-/-n) *Erd2:* clod; *Eis2:* floe; *ichth.* plaice.

schon [ʃo:n] *adv* already; **~ lange** for a long time; **~ gut!** all right!

schön [ʃøːn] *adj* beautiful; *Mann:* handsome; *Wetter:* fair, fine.

schonen ['ʃoːnən] *v/t* spare; take care of; *Kräfte:* husband.

Schönheit ['ʃøːnhaɪt] *f* (-/-en) beauty.

Schonzeit ['ʃoːntsaɪt] *f* (-/-en) close season.

Schopf [ʃɔpf] *m* (-[e]s/ᵉe) tuft; *orn. a.* crest.

schöpfen ['ʃœpfən] *v/t* scoop, ladle; *Mut:* take; *Hoffnung:* find; **Verdacht ~en** become suspicious; **2er** *m* creator; **~erisch** *adj* creative; **2ung** *f* creation.

Schorf [ʃɔrf] *m* (-[e]s/-e) scab.

Schornstein ['ʃɔrnʃtaɪn] *m* (-[e]s/-e) chimney; *mar., rail.* funnel; **~feger** *m* chimney-sweep(er).

Schoß [ʃoːs] *m* (-es/ᵉe) lap; *Mutterleib:* womb; *Rock2:* tail.

Schote ['ʃoːtə] *f* (-/-n) *bot.* pod.

Schotte ['ʃɔtə] *m* (-n/-n) Scot, Scotchman, Scotsman; **die ~n** *pl* the Scotch

pl.

Schotter ['ʃɔtər] *m* (-s/-) crushed (road)stone.

schottisch ['ʃɔtɪʃ] *adj* Scottish, Scots, *a.* Scotch.

schräg [ʃrɛːk] *adj* slanting, sloping.

Schramme ['ʃramə] *f* (-/-n) scratch.

Schrank [ʃraŋk] *m* (-[e]s/ᵉe) cupboard; wardrobe.

Schranke ['ʃraŋkə] *f* (-/-n) barrier (*a. fig.*); rail. *a.* gate.

Schraube ['ʃraubə] *f* (-/-n) screw; *mar.* screw (-propeller); **2n** *v/t* screw.

Schrauben|mutter *f* nut; **~schlüssel** *m* spanner, wrench; **~zieher** [-tsi:ər] *m* screwdriver.

schrecklich ['ʃrɛklɪç] *adj* terrible.

Schrei [ʃraɪ] *m* (-[e]s/-e) cry; *lauter:* shout; *Angst2:* scream.

schreiben ['ʃraɪbən] *v/t* (*irr*) write; spell; **mit der Maschine ~** type(write); **2 n** (-s/-) letter.

Schreib|feder ['ʃraɪbe-dər] *f* pen; **~heft** *n* exercise-book; **~maschine** *f* typewriter; **~material** *n* *s.* **Schreibwaren**; **~papier** *n* writing-paper; **~tisch** *m* (writing-)desk; **~ung** [-buŋ] *f* spelling; **~waren** *pl* writing-materials *pl*, stationery *sg*; **~warengeschäft** *n* stationer's (shop).

schreien ['ʃraɪən] *v/i* (*irr*)

cry; *lauter*: shout; *angst-voll*: scream.

Schreiner ['ʃraɪnər] *m* ⟨-s/-⟩ *s*. Tischler.

Schrift [ʃrɪft] *f* ⟨-/-en⟩ (hand)writing; *print*. type; 2**lich** *adj* written; *adv* in writing; ~**steller** [-ʃtelər] *m* ⟨-s/-⟩ author, writer; ~**stück** *n* piece of writing, paper, document; ~**wechsel** *m* correspondence.

schrill [ʃrɪl] *adj* shrill, piercing.

Schritt [ʃrɪt] *m* ⟨-[e]s/-e⟩ step; ~ **fahren!** slow down!, dead slow!

schroff [ʃrɔf] *adj* rugged, jagged; *steil*: steep; *fig.* harsh.

Schrot [ʃro:t] *m, n* ⟨-[e]s/-e⟩ crushed grain; *Munition*: (small) shot; ~**flinte** *f* shotgun.

Schrott [ʃrɔt] *m* ⟨-[e]s/-e⟩ scrap(-iron).

schrubben ['ʃrubən] *v/t* scrub, scour.

schrumpfen ['ʃrʊmpfən] *v/i* shrink.

Schub|fach ['ʃu:pfax] *n* ⟨-[e]s/⁀er⟩ drawer; ~**karre(n** *m) f* wheelbarrow; ~**kraft** *f* thrust; ~**lade** [-la:də] *f* ⟨-/-n⟩ drawer.

schüchtern ['ʃyçtərn] *adj* shy, timid.

Schuft [ʃʊft] *m* ⟨-[e]s/-e⟩ scoundrel, rascal; 2**en** *v/i colloq.* drudge, slave.

Schuh [ʃu:] *m* ⟨-[e]s/-e⟩ shoe; ~**anzieher** ['-ʔan-

tsi:ər] *m* ⟨-s/-⟩ shoehorn; ~**bürste** *f* shoe-brush; ~**creme** *f* shoe-cream, shoe-polish; ~**spanner** *m* shoe-tree.

Schul|arbeit ['ʃu:lʔarbaɪt] *f* ⟨-/-en⟩ homework; ~**bank** *f* (school-)desk; ~**bildung** *f* education; ~**buch** *n* school-book.

Schuld [ʃʊlt] *f* ⟨-/-en⟩ *Geld2*: debt; *Vergehen*: guilt; *Fehler*: fault; **ich bin 2 it is my fault;** 2**be-wußt** *adj* guilty; 2**en** ['ʃʊldən] *v/t*: **j-m et.** ~ owe s.o. s.th.; **j-m Dank** ~ be indebted to s.o. (**für** for).

schuldig ['ʃʊldɪç] *adj* guilty; ~ **sprechen** find guilty; 2**e** *m, f* ⟨-n/-n⟩ guilty person; culprit.

schuldlos ['ʃʊltlo:s] *adj* innocent.

Schule ['ʃu:lə] *f* ⟨-/-n⟩ school; **höhere** ~ secondary school, *Am.* appr. (senior) high school; 2**n** ['ʃu:lən] *v/t* train, school.

Schüler ['ʃy:lər] *m* ⟨-s/-⟩ schoolboy, pupil; ~**in** *f* ⟨-/-nen⟩ schoolgirl, pupil.

Schul|ferien ['ʃu:lfe:riən] *pl* holidays *pl*, *Am.* vacation *sg*; ~**fernsehen** *n* educational TV; 2**frei** *adj*: **heute haben wir** ~ there's no school today; ~**freund(in** *f) m* schoolfriend, schoolfellow;

~funk m school broadcasts pl; **~mappe** f satchel; **2pflichtig** ['-pflɪçtɪç] adj of school age; **~schwänzer** m truant; **~stunde** f lesson.

Schulter ['ʃʊltər] f (-/-n) shoulder; **~blatt** n shoulder-blade.

Schulzeugnis n report.

Schund [ʃʊnt] m (-[e]s/no pl) trash, rubbish.

Schuppe ['ʃʊpə] f (-/-n) zo. scale; **~n** pl dandruff sg.

Schuppen ['ʃʊpən] m (-s/-) shed.

Schurke ['ʃʊrkə] m (-n/-n) scoundrel, villain.

Schürze ['ʃʏrtsə] f (-/-n) apron; Kinder: pinafore.

Schuß [ʃʊs] m (-sses/ ⁓sse) shot; Munition: round; kleine Portion: dash.

Schüssel ['ʃʏsəl] f (-/-n) basin; für Speisen: bowl, dish.

Schuß|waffe f firearm; **~wunde** f gunshot wound.

Schuster ['ʃuːstər] m (-s/-) shoemaker.

Schutt [ʃʊt] m (-[e]s/no pl) rubbish, refuse; Trümmer: debris; **~abladeplatz** m dump.

Schüttelfrost ['ʃʏtəl-frɔst] m (-[e]s/no pl) shivering-fit; **2n** ['ʃʏtəln] v/t shake.

schütten ['ʃʏtən] v/t pour; es schüttet v/i it is pour-ing with rain.

Schutz [ʃʊts] m (-es/no pl) protection; Zuflucht: shelter; **~blech** n mudguard, Am. fender.

schützen ['ʃʏtsən] v/t protect; shelter.

Schutz|engel ['ʃʊts-ʔeŋəl] m (-s/-) guardian angel; **~heilige** m, f (-n/-n) patron saint; **~impfung** f protective inoculation; Pocken: vaccination; **2los** adj unprotected; wehrlos: defen|celess, Am. -seless; **~umschlag** m (dust-)jacket.

schwach [ʃvax] adj weak; faint; feeble.

Schwäch|e ['ʃvɛçə] f (-/-n) weakness; **2en** v/t weaken; **2lich** adj weakly; zart: delicate, frail.

schwach|sinnig ['ʃvaxzɪnɪç] adj weak-minded, feeble-minded; **2strom** m weak current.

Schwager ['ʃvaːgər] m (-s/ᵛ) brother-in-law.

Schwägerin ['ʃvɛːgərɪn] f (-/-nen) sister-in-law.

Schwalbe ['ʃvalbə] f (-/-n) swallow.

Schwall [ʃval] m (-[e]s/-e) flood; Worte: torrent.

Schwamm [ʃvam] m (-[e]s/ᵛe) sponge.

Schwan [ʃvaːn] m (-[e]s/ᵛe) swan.

schwanger ['ʃvaŋər] adj pregnant; **2schaft** f pregnancy.

schwanken ['ʃvaŋkən] v/i

stagger, totter; *Zweige etc.*:
sway; *Preise*: fluctuate;
zögern: waver.

Schwanz [ʃvants] *m* (-es/
ॱe) tail.

schwänzen [ˈʃvɛntsən]
v/t: **die Schule** – play
truant.

Schwarm [ʃvarm] *m*
(-[e]s/ॱe) *Bienen etc.*:
swarm; *Vögel*: a. flight,
flock; *Fische*: school,
shoal; *Person*: idol, hero.

schwärmen [ˈʃvɛrmən]
v/i Bienen etc.: swarm; ~
für adore.

Schwarte [ˈʃvartə] *f* (-/
-n) rind.

schwarz [ʃvarts] *adj*
black; ~**es Brett** notice-
board, *Am.* bulletin board;
ॼ**brot** *n* brown bread;
ॼ**weißfilm** [-ˈvaisfilm] *m*
black-and-white film.

schwatzen [ˈʃvatsən] *v/i*
chat(ter).

schwätzeln [ˈʃvɛtsəln] *v/i*
chat(ter); **ॼr(in)** *f m* chatter-
box; gossip.

Schwebe|bahn [ˈʃveːbə-
baːn] *f* (-/-en) aerial railway *od.* ropeway; **ॼn**
[ˈʃveːbən] *v/i* be sus-
pended; *Vogel, aer.*: hover
(*a. fig.*); *gleiten*: glide; **in
Gefahr ॼn** be in danger.

Schwede [ˈʃveːdə] *m* (-n/
-n) Swede; **ॼisch** *adj*
Swedish.

Schwefel [ˈʃveːfəl] *m* (-s/
no pl) sulphur, *Am.* sulfur.

Schweif [ʃvaif] *m* (-[e]s/
-e) *lit.* tail.

schweig|en [ˈʃvaigən] *v/i*
(*irr*) be silent; **ॼen** (-s/*no
pl*) silence; **~end** *adj* silent; **~sam** [ˈʃvaikzaːm]
adj taciturn.

Schwein [ʃvain] *n* (-[e]s/
-e) pig, hog.

Schweine|braten *m*
roast pork; **~fleisch** *n*
pork; **~stall** *m* pigsty (*a.
fig.*).

Schweiß [ʃvais] *m* (-es/
-e) sweat, perspiration;
ॼen *v/t tech.* weld.

Schweizer [ˈʃvaitsər] *m*
(-s/-) Swiss; **ॼisch** [-tsə-
riʃ] *adj* Swiss.

schwelen [ˈʃveːlən] *v/i*
smo(u)lder.

schwelgen [ˈʃvɛlgən] *v/i*:
~ in revel in.

Schwelle [ˈʃvɛlə] *f* (-/-n)
threshold; **ॼen** [ˈʃvɛlən]
v/i (*irr*) swell; **~ung** *f* swelling.

schwenken [ˈʃvɛŋkən] *v/t*
swing; *Hut*: wave.

schwer [ʃveːr] *adj* heavy;
Wein etc.: strong;
schwierig: hard, difficult;
ernst: serious; **2 Pfund ~
sein** weigh two pounds; **~
arbeiten** work hard;
~fällig *adj* slow; *unbeholfen*: clumsy; **ॼgewicht** *n*
heavy-weight; **~hörig**
[-høːrɪç] *adj* hard of hearing; **ॼkraft** *f* gravity;
ॼkranke *m, f* (-n/-n)
seriously ill person;
ॼpunkt *m* centre (*Am.*
-er) of gravity; *fig.* emphasis.

Schwert [ʃveːrt] n (-[e]s/
-er) sword.

schwer|verdaulich
[ʃveːrfɛrdaulɪç] adj indigestible, heavy; **~ver-
ständlich** adj difficult to
understand; **~verwun-
det** adj seriously wounded; **~wiegend** [-viːgənt]
adj fig. weighty, serious.

Schwester [ʃvɛstər] f (-/
-n) sister; Kranken2:
nurse.

Schwieger|eltern [ʃviː-
gərʔɛltərn] pl parents-in-
law pl; **~mutter** f etc.
mother-in-law, etc.

schwielig [ʃviːlɪç] adj callous.

schwierig [ʃviːrɪç] adj
difficult, hard; **2keit** f difficulty, trouble.

Schwimm|bad [ʃvɪm-
baːt] n (-[e]s/-er) swimming bath, swimming
pool; **2en** [ʃvɪmən] v/i
(irr) swim; Gegensatz:
float; **~er(in** f) m swimmer; **~flosse** f flipper;
~gürtel m lifebelt;
~haut f zo. web; **~weste** f
life-jacket.

Schwindel [ʃvɪndəl] m
(-s/no pl) med. giddiness,
dizziness; colloq. swindle;
~anfall m fit of dizziness;
2n [ʃvɪndəln] v/i cheat,
swindle.

Schwindler [ʃvɪndlər] m
(-s/-) swindler; **2ig** adj
giddy, dizzy.

Schwinge [ʃvɪŋə] f (-/-n)
lit. wing; **2n** [ʃvɪŋən] v/t,

v/i (irr) swing.

Schwips [ʃvɪps] m (-es/
-e): e-n ~ haben colloq.
be tipsy.

schwitzen [ʃvɪtsən] v/i
sweat, perspire.

schwören [ʃvøːrən] v/t,
v/i (irr) swear.

schwül [ʃvyːl] adj sultry,
close.

Schwung [ʃvʊŋ] m (-[e]s/
ᵉe) swing; fig. energy,
drive; **2voll** adj full of
drive; lively.

Schwur [ʃvuːr] m (-[e]s/
ᵉe) oath; **~gericht** n (-[e]s/
ᵉe) Crown Court, Am. jury
court.

sechs [zɛks] adj six; **2eck**
[-ʔɛk] n (-s/-e) hexagon;
~eckig adj hexagonal;
~te adj sixth; **2tel** n (-s/-)
sixth (part); **~tens** adv
sixthly, in the sixth place.

sech|zehn(te) [ʒɛçtseːn
(-tə)] adj sixteen(th); **~zig**
[-tsɪç] adj sixty; **~zigste**
adj sixtieth.

See¹ [zeː] m (-s/-n) lake.

See² f (-/-n) sea, ocean; **an
der ~** at the seaside;
~bad n seaside resort;
~gang m: hoher ~
rough sea; **~hund** m zo.
seal; **2krank** adj seasick.

Seele [zeːlə] f (-/-n) soul;
2isch adj psychic(al).

See|macht [zeː maxt] f (-/
ᵉe) naval power; **~mann**
m (pl -leute) seaman,
sailor; **~meile** f nautical
mile; **~not** f (no pl) distress (at sea); **~reise** f

voyage; **~streitkräfte** pl naval forces pl.

Segel ['ze:gǝl] n (-s/-) sail; **~boot** n sail(ing-)boat; sp. yacht; **~fliegen** n (-s/no pl) gliding; **~flugzeug** n glider; **2n** ['ze:gǝln] v/i sail; sp. yacht; **~schiff** n sailing-ship, sailing-vessel; **~tuch** n canvas.

Segen ['ze:gǝn] m (-s/-) blessing (a. fig.), bsd. eccl. benediction.

Segler ['ze:glǝr] m (-s/-) yachtsman.

segnen ['ze:gnǝn] v/t bless.

sehen ['ze:ǝn] v/i (irr) see; **~ auf** look at; **~ nach** look after; v/t see; notice; watch, observe; **~swert** [-ve:rt] adj worth seeing; **2swürdigkeiten** pl sights pl.

Sehne ['ze:nǝ] f (-/-n) sinew, tendon; Bogen: string.

sehnen ['ze:nǝn] v/refl: **sich ~** long for.

Sehn|enzerrung [-tse-ruŋ] f strained tendon; **2ig** adj sinewy.

sehn|lich ['ze:nlıç] adj ardent; anxious; **2sucht** f (-/ve) longing, yearning.

sehr [ze:r] adv very; mit vb: (very) much, greatly.

seicht [zaıçt] adj shallow.

Seid|e ['zaıdǝ] f (-/-n) silk; **~enpapier** n tissue (paper); **2ig** adj silky.

Seife ['zaıfǝ] f (-/-n) soap.

Seifen|pulver n soap-

powder; **~schaum** m lather; suds pl.

seifig ['zaıfıç] adj soapy.

Seil [zaıl] n (-[e]s/-e) rope; **~bahn** f funicular (railway); cableway.

sein[1] [zaın] poss pron his; her; its.

sein[2] v/i (irr) be; bestehen: exist; **2n** (-s/no pl) being; existence.

seiner|seits ['zaınǝrzaıts] adv for his part; **~zeit** adv then; in those days.

seit [zaıt] prp (dat.), cj since; **~ drei Wochen** for three weeks; **~dem** ['de:m] adv since then; ever since; cj since.

Seite ['zaıtǝ] f (-/-n) side; Buch: page.

Seiten|straße f side-road; **~wind** m side-wind.

seit|lich ['zaıtlıç] adj lateral; **~wärts** [-vɛrts] adv sideways.

Sekretär [zekre'tɛːr] m (-s/-e), **~in** f (-/-nen) secretary.

Sekt [zɛkt] m (-[e]s/-e) champagne.

Sektor ['zɛktɔr] m (-s/-en) sector; fig. field.

Sekunde [ze'kundǝ] f (-/-n) second.

selbst [zɛlpst] pron: **ich ~** (I) myself; **von ~** Person: of one's own accord; Sache: by itself, automatically; adv even.

selbständig ['zɛlpʃtɛn-dıç] adj independent; **2keit** f independence.

Selbst|bedienung
['zɛlpstbadi:nuŋ] f self-service; **~beherrschung** f self-command, self-control; **~bestimmung** f self-determination; **2be-wußt** adj self-confident; **2gemacht** [-gəmaxt] adj home-made; **2gespräch** n soliloquy, monolog(ue); **2los** adj unselfish, disinterested; **~mord** m suicide; **2sicher** adj self-confident; **~süchtig** adj selfish; **2tätig** adj self-acting, automatic; **~unterricht** m private study; **2ver-ständlich** [-fɛrʃtɛndliç] adv of course, naturally; **~verteidigung** f self-defence, Am. -se; **~ver-trauen** n self-confidence; **~verwaltung** f self-government, autonomy.

selig ['ze:lıç] adj eccl. blessed; verstorben: late; fig. overjoyed.

Sellerie ['zɛləri] m (-s/-[s]) celery.

selten ['zɛltən] adj rare, scarce; adv rarely, seldom.

seltsam ['zɛltza:m] adj strange, odd.

Semester [ze'mɛstər] n (-s/-) term.

Semikolon [zemi'ko:lɔn] n (-s/-s) semicolon.

Seminar [zemi'na:r] n (-s/-e) univ. seminar; Priester: seminary.

Semmel ['zɛməl] f (-/-n) roll.

Senat [ze'na:t] m (-[e]s/-e) senate.

send|en ['zɛndən] v/t (irr) send, forward; Funk etc.: transmit; Rundfunk: broadcast; Fernsehen: a. telecast; **2er** m (-s/-) transmitter; broadcasting station; **2ung** f (-/-en) econ. consignment, shipment; broadcast; telecast.

Senf [zɛnf] m (-[e]s/-e) mustard.

sengen ['zɛŋən] v/t singe; **~d** adj parching.

Senk|e ['zɛŋkə] f (-/-n) depression, hollow; **2en** ['zɛŋkən] v/t lower; Kopf: bow; v/refl: **sich ~** sink; Decke etc.: sag; **2recht** [-rɛçt] adj vertical, perpendicular.

Sensation [zɛnza'tsĭo:n] f (-/-en) sensation.

Sense ['zɛnzə] f (-/-n) scythe.

sensibel [zɛn'zi:bəl] adj sensitive.

sentimental [zɛntimen'ta:l] adj sentimental.

September [zɛp'tɛmbər] m (-[s]/no pl) September.

Serie [ze:rĭə] f (-/-n) series; Satz: set.

Serpentine [zɛrpən'ti:nə] f (-/-n) serpentine.

Serum ['ze:rum] n (-s/Se-ren) serum.

Service¹ [zɛr'vi:s] n (-[s]/-) service, set.

Service² ['zœrvıs] m, n (-/ rare -s) service, set.

servieren [zɛr'vi:rən] v/t serve.

Silber

Serviette [zɛr'vjetə] f (-/-n) (table-)napkin.

Sessel ['zɛsəl] m (-s/-) armchair, easy chair; **~lift** m chair-lift.

setzen ['zɛtsən] v/t set, place, put; *pflanzen*: plant; v/refl: **sich** ~ sit down, take a seat; *Vögel*: perch; *Bodensatz etc.*: settle; v/i: ~ **auf** *Rennpferd*: back.

Seuche ['zɔʏçə] f (-/-n) epidemic (disease).

seufzen ['zɔʏftsən] v/i sigh; **2r** m sigh.

sexuell [zɛ'ksŭɛl] adj sexual.

sich [zɪç] pron oneself; sg himself, herself, itself; pl themselves; sg yourself, pl yourselves; *einander*: each other, one another.

Sichel ['zɪçəl] f (-/-n) sickle.

sicher ['zɪçər] adj safe, secure (**vor** from); *gewiß*: certain, sure; **2heit** f safety; security; certainty.

Sicherheits|gurt ['zɪçər-haɪtsgʊrt] m seat-belt; **~nadel** f safety-pin; **~schloß** n safety-lock.

sicher|n ['zɪçərn] v/t secure; guarantee; **~stellen** v/t safeguard; **2ung** f (-/-en) safeguard; *tech.* safety device; *electr.* fuse.

Sicht [zɪçt] f (-/no pl) visibility; *Auss.*: view; **in** ~ **kommen** come into view, come in sight; **2bar** [-ba:r] adj visible; **2lich** adv visibly; **~vermerk**

[-fɛrmɛrk] m (-[e]s/-e) visa, visé; **~weite** [-vaɪtə] f (-/-n) visibility.

sickern ['zɪkərn] v/i trickle, ooze, seep.

sie [zi:] pers pron she; pl they; **2** pers pron sg pl you.

Sieb [zi:p] n (-[e]s/-e) sieve; *Sand*! : riddle.

sieben[1] ['zi:bən] v/t sieve, sift; *Sand etc.*: riddle.

sieben[2] adj seven.

siebte ['zi:ptə] adj seventh; **2l** n (-s/-) seventh (part); **~ns** adv seventhly, in the seventh place.

sieb|zehn(te) ['zi:ptse:n (-tə)] adj seventeen(th); **~zig** [-tsɪç] adj seventy; **~zigste** adj seventieth.

siedeln ['zi:dəln] v/i settle.

sieden ['zi:dən] v/t, v/i (a. irr) boil; **2punkt** m boiling-point.

Siedl|er ['zi:dlər] m (-s/-) settler; **~lung** f settlement; *Stadtrand*: housing estate.

Sieg [zi:k] m (-[e]s/-e) victory; *sp. a.* win.

Siegel ['zi:gəl] n (-s/-) seal; *privat*: signet.

sieg|en ['zi:gən] v/i be victorious; *sp.* win; **2er** m (-s/-) conqueror; *sp.* winner.

Signal [zɪ'gna:l] n (-s/-e) signal; **2isieren** [-nali'zi:-rən] v/t signal.

Silbe ['zɪlbə] f (-/-n) syllable.

Silber ['zɪlbər] n (-s/no pl) silver; **2n** adj (of) silver.

Silhouette [zi'lŭɛtə] f (-/-n) silhouette; _Stadt:_ skyline.

Silvester [zil'vɛstər] n (-s/-) New Year's Eve.

Sinfonie [zɪnfo'niː] f (-/-n) symphony.

singen ['zɪŋən] v/i, v/t (irr) sing.

Singular ['zɪŋɡulaːr] m (-s/-e) gr. singular.

Singvogel ['zɪŋfoːɡəl] m (-s/⁓) songbird, songster.

sinken ['zɪŋkən] v/i (irr) sink; _Preise:_ go down.

Sinn [zɪn] m (-[e]s/-e) sense; _Verstand:_ mind; _Bedeutung:_ sense, meaning.

Sinnesänderung ['zɪnəs²ɛndəruŋ] f change of mind; **⁓organ** n sense-organ.

sinnlich ['zɪnlɪç] adj sensual; **⁓los** [-loːs] adj senseless; futile, useless.

Sippe ['zɪpə] f (-/-n) _Stamm:_ tribe; (blood-)relations pl; family.

Sirup ['ziːrup] m (-s/-e) syrup, _Am._ sirup.

Sitte ['zɪtə] f (-/-n) custom, habit; **⁓n** pl morals pl.

sittlich ['zɪtlɪç] adj moral.

Situation [zituaˈtsi̯oːn] f (-/-en) situation.

Sitz [zɪts] m (-es/-e) seat; **⁓en** ['zɪtsən] v/i (irr) sit, be seated; _passen:_ fit; **⁓en bleiben** remain seated; **⁓platz** m seat; **⁓ung** f (-/-en) meeting, conference.

Skala ['skaːla] f (-/-len, -s) scale; _Radio:_ dial.

Skandal [skanˈdaːl] m (-s/-e) scandal.

Skelett [skeˈlɛt] n (-[e]s/-e) skeleton.

skeptisch ['skɛptɪʃ] adj sceptical, _Am._ skeptical.

Ski [ʃiː] m (-s/-er, rare ⁓) ski; **⁓ laufen** od. **fahren** ski; **⁓fahrer** m, **⁓läufer** m skier; **⁓lift** m ski-lift; **⁓springen** n (-s/-) ski-jumping.

Skizze ['skɪtsə] f (-/-n) sketch; **⁓ieren** [-ˈtsiːrən] v/t sketch, outline.

Sklave ['sklaːvə, 'sklaː-] m (-n/-n) slave.

Skrupel ['skruːpəl] m (-s/-) scruple; **⁓los** [-loːs] adj unscrupulous.

Skulptur [skʊlpˈtuːr] f (-/-en) sculpture.

Slalom ['slaːlɔm] m (-s/-s) slalom.

Smaragd [smaˈrakt] m (-[e]s/-e) emerald.

Smoking ['smoːkɪŋ] m (-s/-s) dinner-jacket, _Am. a._ tux(edo).

so [zoː] adv so, thus; like this od. that; _vergleichend:_ as; **⁓ ein** such a; **⁓bald** [zoˈbalt] cj: **⁓ als** (_wie_ od. **als**) as soon as.

Socke ['zɔkə] f (-/-n) sock; **⁓l** ['zɔkəl] m (-s/-) pedestal; **⁓nhalter** m suspender, _Am._ garter.

Soda ['zoːda] n (-s/-s), **⁓wasser** n soda-water.

Sodbrennen ['zoːt-] n (-s/no pl) heartburn.

soeben [zoˈʔeːbən] adv

just (now).

Sofa ['zo:fa] n (-s/-s) sofa.

sofort [zo'fɔrt] adv at once; immediately.

Sog [zo:k] m (-[e]s/-e) suction; aer. wake; mar. undertow.

sogar [zo'ga:r] adv even.

sogenannt ['zo:gənant] adj so-called.

Sohle ['zo:lə] f (-/-n) sole; Tal: bottom.

Sohn [zo:n] m (-[e]s/ue) son.

solange [zo'laŋə] cj as long as.

solch [zɔlç] pron, adj such.

Sold [zɔlt] m (-[e]s/-e) pay.

Soldat [zɔl'da:t] m (-en/ -en) soldier.

Söldner ['zœldnər] m (-s/ -) mercenary.

solid(e) [zo'li:t, -'li:də] adj solid; fig. a. sound.

Solist [zo'lɪst] m (-en/ -en), ~in f (-/-nen) soloist.

Soll [zɔl] n (-[s]/-[s]) debit; Produktions2: target.

sollen ['zɔlən] v/aux (irr): **ich sollte** I should, I ought to; **er soll** he shall; he is said to.

Sommer ['zɔmər] m (-s/-) summer; 2lich adj summer(y); ~schlußverkauf m (-[e]s/ue) summer sale(s pl); ~sprossen [-ʃprɔsən] f/pl freckles pl; ~(s)zeit f summertime.

Sonde ['zɔndə] f (-/-n) sonde, probe (a. med.).

Sonder|angebot ['zɔn- dər⁹aŋgəbo:t] n (-[e]s/-e) special offer; ~ausgabe f special (edition); 2bar adj strange, odd; ~fahrt f special; ~ling [-lɪŋ] m (-s/-e) crank, odd person; 2n ['zɔndərn] cj but; ~zug m special (train).

Sonnabend ['zɔn⁹a:bənt] m (-s/-e) Saturday.

Sonne ['zɔnə] f (-/-n) sun; 2n v/refl: **sich** ~ sun o.s., bask in the sun.

Sonnen|aufgang ['zɔ- nən⁹aufgaŋ] m (-s/ue) sunrise; ~bad n sun-bath; ~brand m sunburn; ~brille f (e-e a pair of) sunglasses pl; ~finsternis f solar eclipse; ~licht n sunlight; ~öl n suntan lotion; ~schein m sunshine; ~schirm m sunshade; ~stich m sunstroke; ~strahl m sunbeam; ~uhr f sundial; ~untergang m sunset.

sonnig ['zɔnɪç] adj sunny.

Sonntag ['zɔnta:k] m (-s/ -e) Sunday.

sonst [zɔnst] adv otherwise; mit pron else; **wer ~?** who else? **wie** ~ as usual; ~ **nichts** nothing else.

Sorge ['zɔrgə] f (-/-n) care; sorrow; uneasiness, anxiety; **sich** ~n **machen um** be anxious od. worried about; **mach dir keine ~n** don't worry.

sorgen ['zɔrgən] v/i: ~ **für** care for, provide for;

sorgfältig

dafür ~, daß see (to it) that; *v/refl:* **sich ~ um** worry about.

sorgfältig ['zɔrkfɛltɪç] *adj* careful; **~los** [-lo:s] *adj* carefree; careless.

Sortie ['zɔrtə] *f* (-/-n) sort, kind, species; **2ieren** [-'ti:rən] *v/t* (as)sort; arrange; **~iment** [-ti-'mɛnt] *n* (-[e]s/-e) assortment.

Soße ['zo:sə] *f* (-/-n) sauce; *Braten2:* gravy.

Souvenir [zuvə'ni:r] *n* (-s/-s) souvenir.

Souveränität [zuvərɛni-'tɛːt] *f* (-/no *pl*) sovereignty.

soviel [zo'fi:l] *adv* so much, as much; **~weit** [-'vaɪt] *cj* as far as; **~wieso** [zovi'zo:] *adv* in any case, anyway.

sowjetisch [zɔ'vjɛtɪʃ] *adj* Soviet.

sowohl [zo'vo:l] *cj* ~ ... **als (auch)** both ... and, ... as well as ...

sozial [zo'tsĭa:l] *adj* social; **~demokratisch** *adj* Social Democratic; **2ist** [-tsĭa'lɪst] *m* (-en/-en) socialist; **~istisch** *adj* socialist.

Soziussitz ['zo:tsĭus-] *m* pillion (seat).

sozusagen ['zo:tsu'za:-gən] *adv* so to speak.

Spalt [ʃpalt] *m* (-[e]s/-e) crack, crevice; **~e** *f* (-/-n) *s.* **Spalt**; *print.* column; **2en** *v/t* (*a.* irr): **(sich) ~** split.

Span [ʃpa:n] *m* (-[e]s/ᵘe) chip, shaving.

Spange ['ʃpaŋə] *f* (-/-n) clasp; (hair-)slide; *Armreif:* bangle.

Spanier ['ʃpa:nĭər] *m* (-s/-) Spaniard; **2sch** [-nɪʃ] *adj* Spanish.

Spann [ʃpan] *m* (-[e]s/ᵘe) instep; **~e** *f* (-/-n) span; *econ.* margin; **2en** ['ʃpanən] *v/t* stretch; tighten; *v/i* be (too) tight; **2end** *adj* exciting, thrilling; **~ung** *f* tension (*a.* fig.); *electr.* voltage; *tech.* strain, stress; **~weite** [-vaɪtə] *f* (-/-n) spread.

Sparbuch ['ʃpa:rbu:x] *n* (-[e]s/ᵘer) savings-bank book; **2en** ['ʃpa:rən] *v/t*, *v/i* save; economize; **~er** *m* (-s/-) saver.

Spargel ['ʃpargəl] *m* (-s/-) asparagus.

Sparkasse ['ʃpa:rkasə] *f* (-/-n) savings-bank; **~konto** *n* savings account.

spärlich ['ʃpɛ:rlɪç] *adj* scanty.

sparsam ['ʃpa:rza:m] *adj* economical.

Spaß [ʃpa:s] *m* (-es/ᵘe) fun; jest, joke; **2en** ['ʃpa:sən] *v/i* joke, make fun; **~vogel** *m* wag.

spät [ʃpɛ:t] *adj* late; **zu ~** (too) late; **wie ~ ist es?** what time is it?

Spaten ['ʃpa:tən] *m* (-s/-) spade.

spätestens ['ʃpɛːtəstəns] *adv* at the latest.

Spatz [ʃpats] *m* (-en, -es/-en) sparrow.

spazieren [ʃpaˈtsiːrən] *v/i* walk, stroll; **~fahren** *v/i* (*irr*) go for a drive; *v/t* take for a drive; *Baby*: take out for a walk; **~gehen** *v/i* (*irr*) go for a walk.

Spazier|**fahrt** *f* drive, ride; **~gang** *m* walk, stroll; **e-n ~gang machen** go for a walk; **~gänger** [-gɛŋər] *m* (-s/-) walker.

Specht [ʃpɛçt] *m* (-[e]s/-e) woodpecker.

Speck [ʃpɛk] *m* (-[e]s/-e) bacon.

Spediteur [ʃpediˈtøːr] *m* (-s/-e) forwarding agent; *Möbel*: (furniture) remover.

Speer [ʃpeːr] *m* (-[e]s/-e) spear; *sp.* javelin.

Speiche ['ʃpaɪçə] *f* (-/-n) spoke.

Speichel ['ʃpaɪçəl] *m* (-s/ *no pl*) spit(tle), saliva.

Speicher ['ʃpaɪçər] *m* (-s/-) garret, attic.

speien ['ʃpaɪən] *v/i, v/t* (*irr*) spit; vomit, be sick.

Speise ['ʃpaɪzə] *f* (-/-n) food, nourishment; *Gericht*: dish; **~eis** *n* ice-cream; **~kammer** *f* larder, pantry; **~karte** *f* bill of fare, menu; **2n** ['ʃpaɪzən] *v/i* e. essen; *v/t* feed; **~röhre** *f* gullet; **~saal** *m* dining-room; **~wagen** *m* dining-car; diner; **~zimmer** *n* dining-room.

spekulieren [ʃpekuˈliːrən] *v/i* speculate.

Spende ['ʃpɛndə] *f* (-/-n) gift; contribution; **2n** *v/t* give; donate.

Sperling ['ʃpɛrlɪŋ] *m* (-s/-e) sparrow.

Sperr|**e** ['ʃpɛrə] *f* (-/-n) barrier; barrier, *Am.* gate; *sp.* suspension; **2en** ['ʃpɛrən] *v/t* close; *Licht etc.*: cut od. shut off; *Scheck*: stop; *sp.* suspend; **~holz** *n* plywood; **2ig** *adj* bulky; **~stunde** *f* closing time.

Spesen ['ʃpeːzən] *pl* expenses *pl.*

speziali|**sieren** [ʃpetsiaˈliːzirən] *v/refl*: **sich ~** specialize (**auf** *in*); **2st** [-ˈlɪst] *m* (-en/-en) specialist; **2tät** [-liˈtɛːt] *f* (-/-en) special(i)ty.

speziell [ʃpeˈtsiɛl] *adj* special, particular.

Spiegel ['ʃpiːɡəl] *m* (-s/-) mirror, looking-glass; **~bild** *n* reflection; **~ei** ['-ʔaɪ] *n* (-s/-er) fried egg; **2n** *v/i* shine; *v/t* reflect; *v/refl* **sich 2n** be reflected. **Spieg(e)lung** ['ʃpiːɡ(ə)luŋ] *f* (-/-en) reflection.

Spiel [ʃpiːl] *n* (-[e]s/-e) play; *sp.* game; *Wettkampf*: match; **auf dem ~ stehen** be at stake; **aufs ~ setzen** jeopardize; **~automat** *m* slot-machine; **~bank** *f* casino; **2en**

Spieß

['ʃpiːslən] v/i, v/t play; gamble; 2**end** adv fig. easily; ~**er** n player; gambler; ~**feld** n (playing-)field; ~**film** m feature film od. picture; ~**gefährte** m playfellow, playmate; ~**karte** f playing-card; ~**marke** f counter, chip; ~**plan** m program(me); ~**platz** m playground; ~**regel** f rule (of the game); ~**sachen** pl toys pl; ~**verderber** m (-s/-) spoil-sport; 2**waren** pl toys pl; ~**zeug** n toy(s pl).

Spieß [ʃpiːs] m (-es/-e) spear; pike; fig. colloq.: ~**er** [-ər] m (-s/-) cobweb.

Spinat [ʃpiˈnaːt] m (-[e]s/-e) spinach.

Spind [ʃpɪnt] m, n (-[e]s/-e) cupboard; locker.

Spinn|e ['ʃpɪnə] f (-/-n) spider; 2**en** ['ʃpɪnən] v/t, v/i (irr) spin; fig. colloq. be crazy, sl. be nuts; ~**webe** [-veːbə] f (-/-n) cobweb.

Spion [ʃpiˈoːn] m (-s/-e) spy; ~**age** [ʃpioˈnaːʒə] f (-/no pl) espionage.

Spirale [ʃpiˈraːlə] f (-/-n) spiral.

Spirituosen [ʃpiriˈtuoːzən] pl spirits pl.

spitz [ʃpɪts] adj pointed; sharp; Winkel: acute; 2**e** ['ʃpɪtsə] f (-/-n) point; Nase, Finger: tip; Turm: spire; Berg etc.: top, peak; Gewebe: lace; fig.: head; top; ~**en** v/t point, sharpen; ~**findig** [-fɪndɪç] adj subtle; 2**name** m nick-name.

Splitter ['ʃplɪtər] m (-s/-) splinter, shiver; 2**n** v/i splinter, shiver.

Sporn [ʃpɔrn] m (-[e]s/Sporen) spur.

Sport [ʃpɔrt] m (-[e]s/no pl) sport(s pl); fig. hobby; ~ **treiben** go in for sports; ~**kleidung** f sportswear; ~**lehrer** m games-master; ~**ler** [-lər] m (-s/-) sportsman; ~**lerin** f sportswoman; 2**lich** adj sporting; Figur: athletic; ~**nachrichten** pl sports news pl; ~**platz** m sports field; stadium; ~**tauchen** n (-s/) skin-diving; ~**verein** m sports-club; ~**wagen** m sports-car; folding pram, Am. stroller.

Spott [ʃpɔt] m (-[e]s/no pl) mockery; derision; scorn; 2**billig** adj colloq. dirt-cheap; 2**en** ['ʃpɔtən] v/i: ~ **über** mock od. sneer at.

spöttisch ['ʃpœtɪʃ] adj mocking, sneering; ironical.

Sprach|e ['ʃpraːxə] f (-/-n) Fähigkeit: speech; language; ~**führer** m phrase-book; ~**kenntnisse** pl knowledge sg of foreign languages; 2**los** adj speechless.

Spray [ʃpreː, spreː] m, n (-s/-s) spray; Gerät: atomizer.

sprech|en ['ʃprɛçən] v/i, v/t (irr) speak; talk; 2**er** m speaker; Ansager: an-

nouncer;   *Wortführer:*
spokesman; **2stunde** *f*
consulting-hours *pl*, surgery hours *pl*; **2stunden-**
hilfe *f* (*-/-n*) receptionist;
2zimmer *n* consulting-
room, surgery.

spreizen [ˈʃpraɪtsən] *v/t*
spread (out).

sprengen [ˈʃprɛŋən] *v/t*
sprinkle, water; blow up;
burst open; **2stoff** *m* explosive; **2ung** *f* blowing-
up; explosion.

sprenkeln [ˈʃprɛŋkəln] *v/t*
speckle, spot.

Sprichwort [ˈʃprɪçvɔrt] *n*
(*-[e]s/ᵘer*) proverb.

sprießen [ˈʃpriːsən] *v/i*
(*irr*) sprout.

Spring|brunnen [ˈʃprɪŋ-
brunən] *m* (*-s/-*) fountain;
2en [ˈʃprɪŋən] *v/i* (*irr*)
jump, leap; *Ball:* bounce;
Schwimmen: dive; burst,
crack, break.

Spritze [ˈʃprɪtsə] *f* (*-/-n*)
syringe; *Injektion:* injection; **2n** *v/t*, *v/i* sprinkle,
water; splash; *med.* inject;
2n aus spurt from; **~r** *m*
(*-s/-*) splash.

spröde [ˈʃprøːdə] *adj*
brittle; *fig.* coy.

Sproß [ʃprɔs] *m* (*-sses/*
-sse) shoot, sprout.

Sprosse [ˈʃprɔsə] *f* (*-/-n*)
rung, step.

Sprößling [ˈʃprœslɪŋ] *m*
(*-s/-e*) offspring.

Sprotte [ˈʃprɔtə] *f* (*-/-n*)
sprat.

Spruch [ʃprʊx] *m* (*-[e]s/*

ᵘe) saying.

Sprudel [ˈʃpruːdəl] *m* (*-s/*
-) mineral water; **2n** *v/i*
bubble; effervesce.

sprühlen [ˈʃpryːən] *v/t*
spray, sprinkle; *v/i Funken:* fly; **es ~t** it is drizzling; **2regen** *m* drizzle.

Sprung [ʃprʊŋ] *m* (*-[e]s/*
ᵘe) jump, leap, bound;
Schwimmen: dive; *Riß:*
crack; **~brett** *n* spring-
board; **~schanze** *f* ski-
jump.

Spucke [ˈʃpʊkə] *f* (*-/no pl*)
colloq. spit(tle); **2n** *v/i* spit.

Spule [ˈʃpuːlə] *f* (*-/-n*)
spool, reel; *electr.* coil.

spülen [ˈʃpyːlən] *v/t*
rinse; wash (up); *v/i* flush
the lavatory; **2mittel** *n* detergent.

Spur [ʃpuːr] *f* (*-/-en*) trace
(*a. fig.*); *mehrere:* track;
Wagen: rut; *fig.* sign.

spüren [ˈʃpyːrən] *v/t* feel;
sense.

Staat [ʃtaːt] *m* (*-[e]s/-en*)
state; government.

Staats|angehörige
[ˈʃtaːtsˀangəhøːrɪgə] *m*, *f*
(*-n/-n*) national, citizen,
bsd. Brit. subject; **~ange-**
hörigkeit *f* nationality,
citizenship; **~anwalt** *m*
public prosecutor, *Am.*
prosecuting attorney,
~bürger *m* citizen;
~dienst *m* (*no pl*) civil service; **~mann** *m* statesman;
~oberhaupt *n* (*-[e]s/ᵘer*) head
of (the) state.

Stab [ʃtaːp] *m* (-[e]s/ᵘe) staff (*a. fig.*); Metall, Holz: bar; pole.

stabil [ʃtaˈbiːl] *adj* stable.

Stachel [ʃtaxəl] *m* (-s/-n) prickle; Biene: sting; ~**beere** *f* gooseberry; ~**draht** *m* barbed wire.

stach(e)lig [ʃtax(ə)lɪç] *adj* prickly, thorny.

Stadion [ʃtaːdiɔn] *n* (-s/ -dien) stadium; ~**um** [-diʊm] *n* (-s/-dien) stage, phase.

Stadt [ʃtat] *f* (-/ᵘe) town; city.

Städter [ʃteːtər] *m* (-s/-) townsman; ~ *pl* townspeople *pl*.

Stadt|gebiet [ʃtatɡəbiːt] *n* (-[e]s/-e) urban area; ~**gespräch** *n* teleph. local call.

städtisch [ʃteːtɪʃ] *adj* municipal.

Stadt|mitte *f* town *od*. city centre; Am. -er; ~**plan** *m* town plan, map of the town; ~**rand** *m* outskirts *pl*; ~**rat** *m* town council; Person: town council(l)or; ~**rundfahrt** *f* sightseeing tour; ~**teil** *m*, ~**viertel** *n* quarter.

Staffelei [ʃtafəˈlaɪ] *f* (-/ -en) easel; ~**lauf** *m* [ʃtafəllauf] *m* relay race.

Stahl [ʃtaːl] *m* (-[e]s/ᵘe) steel.

Stall [ʃtal] *m* (-[e]s/ᵘe) stable.

Stamm [ʃtam] *m* (-[e]s/ ᵘe) stem; Baum: trunk;

Volks2: race; Eingeborenen2: tribe; ~**baum** *m* family tree, pedigree (*a. zo.*); **2eln** [ʃtaməln] *v/i* stammer; **2en** [ʃtamən] *v/i*: ~**aus** come from; zeitlich: date from; ~**gast** *m* regular customer *od*. guest, colloq. regular.

stämmig [ʃtemɪç] *adj* stocky, squat.

Stammkunde [ʃtamkundə] *m* (-n/-n) regular customer.

stampfen [ʃtampfən] *v/t* mash; *v/i* stamp; Pferd: paw.

Stand [ʃtant] *m* (-[e]s/no *pl*) stand; position; Höhe: level; Wettkampf: score; (*pl* ᵘe) Verkaufs2: stall; ~**bild** *n* statue.

Ständer [ʃtendər] *m* (-s/ -) stand, rack.

Standes|amt [ʃtandəs-ʔamt] *n* (-[e]s/ᵘer) registry office; **2amtlich** *adj*: ~**e Trauung** civil marriage.

stand|haft [ʃtanthaft] *adj* firm; ~**halten** *v/i* (*irr*) resist.

ständig [ʃtendɪç] *adj* permanent; constant.

Stand|licht [ʃtantlɪçt] *n* parking light(s *pl*); ~**ort** *m* position; ~**punkt** *m* point of view.

Stange [ʃtaŋə] *f* (-/-e) pole; Metall: rod, bar; Fahne: staff.

Stanniol [ʃtanˈiɔl] *n* (-s/ -e) tin foil.

stanzen ['ʃtantsən] *v/t* punch, stamp.

Stapel ['ʃta:pəl] *m* (-s/-) pile, stack; 2*n v/t* pile (up), stack.

stapfen ['ʃtapfən] *v/i* plod.

Star [ʃta:r] *m* (-[e]s/-e) *orn.* starling; *med.* cataract; (*pl* -s) *thea. etc.*: star.

stark [ʃtark] *adj* strong; *dick*: stout; **~e Erkältung** bad cold; **~er Raucher** heavy smoker.

Stärke ['ʃtɛrkə] *f* (-/-n) strength; *chem.* starch; 2**n** ['ʃtɛrkən] *v/t* strengthen (*a. fig.*); *Wäsche*: starch; *v/refl*: **sich** 2**n** take some refreshment(s).

Starkstrom ['ʃtark-ʃtro:m] *m* heavy current.

starr [ʃtar] *adj* rigid (*a. fig.*); stiff; *Blick*: fixed; **~en** ['ʃtarən] *v/i* stare (**auf** at); **~köpfig** ['-kœp-fiç] *adj* obstinate; 2**krampf** *m* tetanus.

Start [ʃtart] *m* (-[e]s/-e) start (*a. fig.*); *aer.* take-off; *Rakete*: lift-off; **~bahn** *f* runway; **~bereit** *adj* ready to start; *aer.* ready for take-off; 2**en** ['ʃtartən] *v/i* start; *aer.* take off; *Rakete*: lift off; *v/t* start; *Rakete*: launch.

Station [ʃta'tsĭo:n] *f* (-/-en) station; *Kranken*2: ward.

Statistik [ʃta'tɪstɪk] *f* (-/-en) statistics *pl.*

Stativ [ʃta'ti:f] *n* (-s/-e) tripod.

statt [ʃtat] *prp* (*gen*) instead of; **~ dessen** instead; *cj* **~ zu** instead of *ger.*

Stätte ['ʃtɛtə] *f* (-/-n) place, spot.

stattfinden ['ʃtatfɪndən] *v/i* (*irr*) take place.

stattlich ['ʃtatlɪç] *adj* stately, impressive; *Summe*: considerable.

Statue ['ʃta:tŭə] *f* (-/-n) statue.

Statut [ʃta'tu:t] *n* (-[e]s/-en) statute.

Staub [ʃtaup] *m* (-[e]s/*no pl*) dust.

Staubecken ['ʃtaubɛkən] *n* (-s/-) reservoir.

staub|**en** ['ʃtaubən] *v/i* make dust; **~ig** *adj* dusty; 2**sauger** ['ʃtaupzaugər] *m* (-s/-) vacuum cleaner; 2**tuch** *n* duster.

Stau|**damm** *m* dam; 2**en** ['ʃtauən] *v/t* dam (up); **sich** 2**en** *v/refl* accumulate; gather; *Fahrzeuge*: become jammed.

staunen ['ʃtaunən] *v/i* be astonished (**über** at).

Staupe ['ʃtaupə] *f* (-/-n) distemper.

Stausee ['ʃtauze:] *m* (-s/-n) reservoir.

stechen ['ʃtɛçən] *v/t*, *v/i* (*irr*) prick; *Insekten*: sting; *Floh, Mücke*: bite; *Sonne*: burn; **~d** *adj Blick*: piercing; *Schmerz*: stabbing.

Steckdose ['ʃtɛkdo:zə] *f* (-/-n) (wall) socket.

stecken ['ʃtɛkən] *v/t* stick,

put; *v/i sich befinden*: be;
stick, be stuck; 2 *m* (-s/-)
stick; **~bleiben** *v/i* (*irr*)
get stuck; **~lassen** *v/t* (*irr*)
leave; 2**pferd** *n* hobby-
horse; *fig.* hobby.

Steckler ['ʃtɛkar] *m* (-s/-)
plug; **~nadel** *f* pin.

Steg [ʃteːk] *m* (-[e]s/-e)
footbridge.

stehen ['ʃteːən] *v/i* stand;
sich befinden: be;
geschrieben ~: be written;
kleiden: suit, become; **wie
steht's mit ...?** what
about ...?; **~bleiben** remain standing; **~bleiben**
v/i (*irr*) leave standing;
~lassen *v/t* (*irr*) leave *s.o.*
standing; *Essen*: leave untouched.

Stehlampe ['ʃteːlampə] *f*
(-/-n) floor-lamp.

stehlen ['ʃteːlən] *v/t* (*irr*)
steal.

Stehplatz *m* standing-
room.

steif [ʃtaɪf] *adj* stiff (*a.
fig.*); numb (**vor Kälte**
with cold).

Steig|bügel ['ʃtaɪkbyː-
gəl] *m* (-s/-) stirrup; 2**en**
['ʃtaɪgən] *v/i* (*irr*) rise; increase; *Nebel*: ascend;
2**ern** [-gərn] *v/t* raise; increase; heighten; **~ung** *f*
rise; gradient, *Am.* grade.

steil [ʃtaɪl] *adj* steep.

Stein [ʃtaɪn] *m* (-[e]s/-e)
stone; **~bruch** *m* quarry;
~gut [-guːt] *n* (-[e]s/-e)
crockery, earthenware;
2**ig** *adj* stony; **~pilz** *m bot.*
yellow boletus; **~schlag**

m falling rocks *pl.*

Stelle ['ʃtɛlə] *f* (-/-n)
place; *Fleck*: spot; *Punkt*:
point; *Behörde*: authority;
Buch: passage; *Arbeit*: *colloq.* job; **freie ~** vacancy;
ich an deiner ~ if I were
you.

stellen ['ʃtɛlən] *v/t* put,
place; set (*a. Uhr, fig.*); *Bedingungen*: make; *Frage*:
ask, put.

Stellung ['ʃtɛlʊŋ] *f* (-/
-en) position, posture; *Beruf*: position; *Rang*: position, rank; **~nahme**
[-naːmə] *f* (-/-n) opinion,
comment; 2**slos** *adj* un-
employed.

Stellvertreter ['ʃtɛlfɛr-
treːtər] *m* (-s/-) substitute;
deputy.

stemmen ['ʃtɛmən] *v/t Gewicht*: lift; **sich ~ gegen**
press against; *fig.* resist *od.*
oppose *s.th.*

Stempel ['ʃtɛmpəl] *m* (-s/
-) stamp; *bot.* pistil; 2**n** *v/t*
stamp.

Stengel ['ʃtɛŋəl] *m* (-s/-)
stalk, stem.

Steno ['ʃteːno] *f* (-/no *pl.*)
colloq., **~graphie** [ʃteno-
graˈfiː] *f* (-/-n) shorthand;
2**graphieren** [-graˈfiː-
rən] *v/t, v/i* write (in) shorthand; **~typistin** [-tyˈpis-
tɪn] *f* (-/-nen) shorthand-
typist.

Steppdecke ['ʃtɛpdɛkə] *f*
(-/-n) quilt.

sterb|en ['ʃtɛrbən] *v/i* (*irr*)
die (**an** of); **~lich** ['ʃtɛrp-

liç] *adj* mortal.

steril [ʃteˈriːl] *adj* sterile.

Stern [ʃtɛrn] *m* (-[e]s/-e) star (*a. fig.*); **~enbanner** *n* Star-Spangled Banner, Stars and Stripes *pl*; **~schnuppe** [-ʃnʊpə] *f* (-/ -n) shooting star; **~warte** [-vartə] *f* (-/-n) observatory.

stetig [ʃteːtiç] *adj* constant; steady; **~s** *adv* always.

Steuer¹ [ʃtɔʏər] *n* (-s/-) *mar.* helm, rudder; *mot.* (steering-)wheel.

Steuer² *f* (-/-n) tax; duty.

Steuer|beamte [ʃtɔʏər-ˀamtə] *m* (-n/-n) revenue officer; **~bord** *n* starboard; **~erklärung** *f* taxreturn; **2frei** *adj* tax-free; *Waren:* duty-free; **~knüppel** *n aer.* control lever od. stick; **~mann** *m mar.* helmsman; *Boot:* coxswain; **2n** [ʃtɔʏərn] *v/t* steer, navigate; *mot.* drive; *fig.* direct, control; **~rad** *n* steering-wheel; **~ruder** *n* helm; rudder; **~ung** *f* (-/no *pl*) steering; **~zahler** *m* taxpayer.

Stich [ʃtiç] *m* (-[e]s/-e) prick; *Insekten:* sting, bite; *Messer:* stab; *Nähen:* stitch; *Karten:* trick; *Kupfer:* engraving; **im ~ lassen** desert, forsake; **2haltig** [-haltiç] *adj:* **~ sein** hold water; **~probe** *f* random test *od.* sample; **~tag** *m* fixed day; **~wort**

n (*pl* ~er) headword; (*pl* -e) note; *thea.* cue.

stick|en [ʃtɪkən] *v/t, v/i* embroider; **~ig** *adj* stuffy, close; **~stoff** *m* nitrogen.

Stiefel [ʃtiːfəl] *m* (-s/-) boot.

Stief|mutter [ʃtiːfmʊtər] *f etc.* stepmother, *etc.*; **~mütterchen** [ˈʃtiːfmʏtər-çən] *n* (-s/-) pansy.

Stiel [ʃtiːl] *m* (-[e]s/-e) handle; *Axt:* haft; *Besen:* stick; *bot.* stalk.

Stier [ʃtiːr] *m* (-[e]s/-e) bull; **~kampf** *m* bullfight.

Stift [ʃtɪft] *m* (-[e]s/-e) pin; peg; pencil; **2en** *v/t* endow; give, donate.

Stil [ʃtiːl] *m* (-[e]s/-e) style.

still [ʃtɪl] *adj* still, quiet, silent; **~!** silence! **2e** *f* (-/ no *pl*) stillness, quiet(ness); silence; **~egen** [ˈʃtɪlˌleːgən] *v/t Fabrik etc.:* shut down; *Verkehr:* stop; **~en** [ˈʃtɪlən] *v/t Schmerz:* soothe; *Hunger, Neugier:* appease; *Durst:* quench; *Blutung:* sta(u)nch; *Säugling:* nurse; **~halten** *v/i (irr)* keep still; **~schweigend** *adj fig.* tacit; **2stand** *m* (-[e]s/no *pl*) standstill, stop.

Stimm|band [ʃtɪmbant] *n* (-[e]s/~er) vocal c(h)ord; **2berechtigt** *adj* entitled to vote; **~e** [ˈʃtɪmə] *f* (-/-n) voice; *Wähler:* vote; **2en** *v/t* tune; *v/i* be true *od.* right; *Summe:* be correct; **2en für** vote for;

~recht n (-[e]s/no pl) right to vote; **~ung** f mood, humo(u)r; **~zettel** m ballot, voting-paper.

stinken ['ſtiŋkən] v/i (irr) stink (**nach** of).

Stipendium [ſti'pɛn-dɪʊm] n (-s/-dien) scholarship.

Stirn [ſtɪrn] f (-/-en) forehead, brow; fig. cheek; **~runzeln** n (-s) frown.

stöbern ['ſtøːbərn] v/i colloq. rummage (about).

stochern ['ſtɔxərn] v/i poke; pick.

Stock [ſtɔk] m (-[e]s/ᵉe) stick; Rohr2: cane; Takt2: baton; Bienen2: beehive; **~werk**: stor(e)y, floor; **erster ~** first (Am. second) floor.

stocken ['ſtɔkən] v/i stop; Milch etc.: curdle (a. fig.); Stimme: falter; Verkehr: be blocked; **2werk** n (-[e]s/-e) stor(e)y, floor.

Stoff [ſtɔf] m (-[e]s/-e) substance; material, fabric, textile; Material, Zeug: material, stuff; cloth.

stöhnen ['ſtøːnən] v/i groan, moan.

stolpern ['ſtɔlpərn] v/i stumble, trip.

stolz [ſtɔlts] adj proud, haughty; **2** m (-es/no pl) pride.

stopfen ['ſtɔpfən] v/t stuff; Pfeife: fill; Geflügel: cram, stuff; Strümpfe: darn; v/i med. constipate, be constipating; **2garn** n

darning-cotton; **2nadel** f darning-needle.

Stoppel ['ſtɔpəl] f (-/-n) stubble.

stopp|en ['ſtɔpən] v/i, v/t stop; Zeit: time, clock; **2uhr** f stop-watch.

Stöpsel ['ſtœpsəl] m (-s/-) stopper, plug.

Storch [ſtɔrç] m (-[e]s/ᵉe) stork.

stören ['ſtøːrən] v/i be intruding; v/t disturb; belästigen: trouble.

störrisch ['ſtœrɪſ] adj stubborn.

Störung ['ſtøːruŋ] f (-/-en) disturbance; trouble (a. tech.); breakdown.

Stoß [ſtoːs] m (-es/ᵉe) push, shove; Schlag: blow, knock; Schwimm2: stroke; Erschütterung: shock; Wagen: jolt; Haufen: pile, heap; **~dämpfer** m shock-absorber; **2en** ['ſtoːsən] v/t (irr) push, shove; knock; strike; v/i (v/refl: **sich**) **2en** an strike od. knock against; **2en** an adjoin, border on; **2en auf** come across; Widerstand: meet with; **~stange** f bumper; **~verkehr** m rush-hour traffic.

stottern ['ſtɔtərn] v/i stammer; Motor: sputter.

Strafanstalt ['ſtraːfʔan-ſtalt] f (-/-en) prison; **2bar** [-baːr] adj punishable, criminal; **~e** f (-/-en) punishment; jur., sp., fig.

penalty; *jur.* sentence; **2en**
['ʃtra:fən] *v/t* punish.

straff [ʃtraf] *adj* tight; *fig.*
strict.

Strafraum ['ʃtra:fraum] *m*
(-[e]s/̃e) *sp.* penalty area.

Strahl [ʃtra:l] *m* (-[e]s/
-en) ray (*a. fig.*); *Licht: a.*
beam; *Blitz:* flash; *Wasser
etc.:* jet; **2en** ['ʃtra:lən] *v/i*
radiate; *fig.* beam;
~ung *f* radiation, rays *pl.*

Strähne ['ʃtrɛ:nə] *f* (-/-n)
Haar: lock, strand.

stramm [ʃtram] *adj* tight;
fig. strict.

strampeln ['ʃtrampəln]
v/i kick.

Strand [ʃtrant] *m* (-[e]s/
̃e) beach; **am ~** on the
beach; **2en** ['ʃtrandən]
v/i strand; **~kleidung** *f*
beachwear; **~korb** *m*
beach-basket, beach-chair;
~promenade, *Am.* boardwalk.

Strang [ʃtraŋ] *m* (-[e]s/
̃e) cord (*a. anat.*); rope.

Strapaze [ʃtra'pa:tsə] *f*
(-/-n) exertion, fatigue;
2ierfähig [ʃtrapa'tsi:r-
fɛ:ɪç] *adj* durable, for hard
wear.

Straße ['ʃtra:sə] *f* (-/-n)
road, highway; street;
Meerenge: strait(s *pl*); **auf
der ~** in the street;

Straßenarbeiten *pl*
road works *pl.*; **~bahn** *f*
tram(-car), *Am.* streetcar;
~beleuchtung *f* street
lighting; **~cafe** *f* pavement (*Am.* sidewalk) café;
~karte *f* road map;

~kreuzung *f* cross-roads
sg; **~schild** *n* street *od.*
road sign; **~wacht** [-vaxt]
f (-/no pl) road maintenance squad.

sträuben ['ʃtrɔybən] *v/t
Federn:* ruffle up; **sich ~** *v/
refl Haare:* stand on end;
sich ~ gegen struggle
od. kick against.

Strauch [ʃtraux] *m* (-[e]s/
̃er) shrub, bush.

straucheln ['ʃtrauxəln]
v/i s. stolpern.

Strauß [ʃtraus] *m* (-es/-e)
orn. ostrich; (*pl* ̃e) *Blumen:* bunch, bouquet.

streben ['ʃtre:bən] *v/i:* **~
nach** strive for.

Strecke ['ʃtrɛkə] *f* (-/-n)
stretch; route; distance;
rail. etc.: line; **2n** ['ʃtrɛ-
kən] *v/t* stretch; extend;
verdünnen: dilute; **sich 2n**
v/refl stretch (o.s.).

Streich [ʃtraɪç] *m* (-[e]s/
-e) trick, prank; **2eln** ['ʃtraɪ-
çən] *v/t* (*irr streichen*)
stroke, caress; **2en** ['ʃtraɪ-
çən] *v/t (irr)* rub; paint; *s.
aus-, bestreichen;* *v/i*
mit der Hand über et.
2en pass one's hand over
s.th.; **~holz** *n* match;
~orchester *n* string band
od. orchestra.

Streife ['ʃtraɪfə] *f* (-/-n)
patrol(man); **2n** ['ʃtraɪfən]
v/t berühren: brush; *Thema:*
touch (up)on; *v/i* roam; **~n**
m (-s/-) stripe, *unregel-
mäßiger:* streak; *Land etc.:*
strip; **~nwagen** *m* police
od. patrol car.

Streik

Streik [ʃtraɪk] *m* (-[e]s/-s)
strike, *Am. a.* walkout;
2en *v/i* strike, *Am. a.* walk
out.

Streit [ʃtraɪt] *m* (-[e]s/-e)
quarrel; dispute; conflict;
2en [ʃtraɪtən] *v/i* (*irr*):
(**sich**) ~ quarrel; **~kräfte**
pl (armed) forces *pl*.

streng [ʃtrɛŋ] severe, stern
(*a. Blick etc.*); strict.

streuen [ʃtrɔʏən] *v/t*
strew, scatter.

Strich [ʃtrɪç] *m* (-[e]s/-e)
stroke; *Linie*: line.

Strick [ʃtrɪk] *m* (-[e]s/-e)
cord; rope; **2en** [ʃtrɪkən]
v/t, v/i knit; **~jacke** *f* cardigan; **~nadel** *f* knitting-needle; **~waren** *pl* knitwear *sg*; **~zeug** *n* knitting.

Striemen [ʃtriːmən] *m*
(-s/-) weal, wale.

Stroh [ʃtroː] *n* (-[e]s/*no pl*)
straw; *Dach*: thatch;
~halm *m* straw.

Strom [ʃtroːm] *m* (-[e]s/
ᵘe) stream (*a. fig.*), (large)
river; *electr.* current.

strömen [ʃtrøːmən] *v/i*
stream; flow, run; *Regen,
Menschenmenge*: pour.

Strom|kreis [ʃtroːm-
kraɪs] *m* (-es/-e) circuit;
~schnelle [-ʃnɛlə] *f* (-/
-n) rapid.

Strömung [ʃtrøːmʊŋ] *f*
(-/-en) current.

Strophe [ʃtroːfə] *f* (-/-n)
verse.

Strudel [ʃtruːdəl] *m* (-s/-)
swirl, whirlpool.

Struktur [ʃtrʊkˈtuːr] *f* (-/

-en) structure.

Strumpf [ʃtrʊmpf] *m*
(-[e]s/**ᵘe**) stocking; **~halter** *m* suspender, *Am.* garter; **~haltergürtel** *m*
girdle; **~hose** *f* tights *pl*.

struppig [ʃtrʊpɪç] *adj*
shaggy.

Stube [ʃtuːbə] *f* (-/-n)
room; **~nmädchen** *n*
chambermaid.

Stück [ʃtʏk] *n* (-[e]s/-e)
piece (*a. mus.*); fragment;
Vieh: head; *Zucker*: lump;
thea. play.

Student [ʃtuˈdɛnt] *m* (-en/
-en), **~in** *f* (-/-nen) student, undergraduate.

Studie [ʃtuːdiə] *f* (-/-n)
study; **2ieren** [ʃtuˈdiːrən]
v/t, v/i study, read; **~ium**
[ʃtuːdiʊm] *n* (-s/-dien)
study, *allgemeiner*: studies
pl.

Stufe [ʃtuːfə] *f* (-/-n) step;
Grad: degree; *Entwicklung*: stage; **2nweise**
[-vaɪzə] *adv* gradual.

Stuhl [ʃtuːl] *m* (-[e]s/**ᵘe**)
chair; seat; **~bein** *n* leg of
a chair; **~gang** *m med.*
stool, movement; **~lehne**
f back of a chair.

stumm [ʃtʊm] *adj* dumb,
mute.

Stummel [ʃtʊməl] *m* (-s/
-) stump; *Zigarette etc.*:
stub, butt.

Stummfilm [ʃtʊmfɪlm] *m*
(-s/-e) silent film.

stümperhaft [ʃtʏmpər-
haft] *adj* bungling, clumsy.

stumpf [ʃtʊmpf] *adj* blunt;

Sinne: dull; apathetic; 2 *m* (-[e]s/~e) stump, stub; **~sinnig** ['-zɪnɪç] *adj* stupid, dull.

Stunde ['ʃtʊndə] *f* (-/-n) hour; *Unterrichts2:* lesson, *Am.:* period.

Stunden|kilometer *m* kilometre (*Am.* -er) per hour; **2lang** *adv* for hours (and hours); **2nach:** after hours of waiting; **~lohn** *m* wages *pl* per hour; **~plan** *m* timetable, *Am.* schedule; **2weise** [-vaɪzə] *adv* by the hour.

stündlich ['ʃtʏntlɪç] *adj, adv* hourly.

Sturm ['ʃtʊrm] *m* (-[e]s/~e) storm.

stürm|en ['ʃtʏrmən] *v/t* storm; *v/i Wind:* rage; rush; *Am.* sp. forward; **~isch** *adj* stormy.

Sturz [ʃtʊrts] *m* (-es/~e) fall; *Regierung etc.:* overthrow; *Preis2:* slump.

stürzen ['ʃtʏrtsən] *v/i* fall; eilen: rush; *v/t Regierung:* overthrow.

Sturzhelm ['ʃtʊrtshelm] *m* (-[e]s/-e) crash-helmet.

Stute ['ʃtuːtə] *f* (-/-n) mare.

Stütze ['ʃtʏtsə] *f* (-/-n) support.

stutzen ['ʃtʊtsən] *v/t Haare:* crop; *Bart:* trim; *Flügel, Hecke:* clip; *Baum:* lop; *v/i* start (**bei** at).

stützen ['ʃtʏtsən] *v/t* support (*a. fig.*); **sich ~ auf**

lean on.

stutzig ['ʃtʊtsɪç] *adj:* ~ **machen** make suspicious.

Stützpunkt *m mil.* base.

Subjekt [zʊp'jekt] *n* (-[e]s/-e) *gr.* subject; **2iv** [zʊbjek'tiːf] *adj* subjective.

Substantiv ['zʊpstantiːf] *n* (-s/-e) *gr.* noun, substantive.

Substanz [zʊp'stants] *f* (-/-en) substance.

subtrahieren [zʊptra'hiːrən] *v/t* subtract.

Suche ['zuːxə] *f* (-/no *pl*) search (**nach** for); **auf der ~ nach** in search of; **2n** ['zuːxən] *v/t Rat etc.:* seek; *a. v/i* **~ nach** search for, look for.

Sucht [zʊxt] *f* (-/~e) mania; addiction.

süchtig ['zʏçtɪç] *adj:* ~ **sein** be addicted (**nach** to *drugs, etc.*); **2e** [-gə] *m, f* (-n/-n) addict.

Süd(en *m*) [zyːt, 'zyːdən] south; **~früchte** *pl* citrus and other tropical fruits *pl*; **2lich** *adj* south(ern), southerly; **~ost(en** *m*) [zyːt'ʔɔst(ən)] southeast; **~pol** *m* South Pole; **~west(en** *m*) [-'vɛst(ən)] southwest.

Sühne ['zyːnə] *f* (-/-n) atonement.

Sülze ['zʏltsə] *f* (-/-n) brawn, jellied meat.

Summe ['zʊmə] *f* (-/-n) sum (*a. fig.*), (sum) total; *Betrag:* amount.

summen ['zumən] *v/i* buzz, hum.

Sumpf [zumpf] *m* (-[e]s/ ⁃e) swamp, bog, marsh; **2ig** *adj* swampy, boggy, marshy.

Sünde ['zʏndə] *f* (-/-n) sin; **⁃nbock** *m colloq.* scape-goat; **⁃r** *m* sinner.

Super|(benzin) ['zu:-pər-] *n* super; **⁃lativ** ['zu:-perlati:f] *m* (-s/-e) *gr.* superlative (degree); **⁃markt** *m* supermarket.

Suppe ['zupə] *f* (-/-n) soup; **⁃nschüssel** *f* tureen; **⁃nteller** *m* soup-plate.

süß [zy:s] *adj* sweet (*a. fig.*); **⁃en** *v/t* sweeten; **2igkeiten** *pl* sweets *pl*; **2speise** *f* sweet; **2was-ser** *n* fresh water.

Symbol [zʏm'bo:l] *n* (-s/

-e) symbol; **2isch** *adj* symbolic(al).

symmetrisch [zʏ'me:trɪʃ] *adj* symmetric(al).

sympathisch [zʏm'pa:tɪʃ] *adj* lik(e)able; **er ist mir ⁃** I like him.

Symphonie [zʏmfo'ni:] *f* (-/-n) symphony.

Symptom [zʏmp'to:m] *n* (-s/-e) symptom.

Synagoge [zyna'go:gə] *f* (-/-n) synagogue.

synchronisieren [zʏn-kroni'zi:rən] *v/t* synchronize; *Tonfilm:* a. dub.

synthetisch [zʏn'te:tɪʃ] *adj* synthetic.

System [zʏs'te:m] *n* (-s/ -e) system; **2atisch** [-te-'ma:tɪʃ] *adj* systematic(al); methodical.

Szene ['stse:nə] *f* (-/-n) scene.

T

Tabak ['ta:bak, ta'bak] *m* (-s/-e) tobacco.

Tabelle [ta'belə] *f* (-/-n) table.

Tablett [ta'blet] *n* (-[e]s/ -s, -e) tray; **⁃e** [-'bletə] *f* (-/-n) tablet.

Tachometer [taxo'me:-tər] *m, n* (-s/-) speedo-meter.

Tadel ['ta:dəl] *m* (-s/-) re-proof, rebuke; **2los** *adj* faultless; excellent; **2n** *v/t* reprove, rebuke.

Tafel ['ta:fəl] *f* (-/-n) slab; *Gedenk2:* plaque, tablet;

Schiefer2: slate; *Schul2:* blackboard; *Anschlag2:* notice board, *Am.* bulletin board; *Schokolade:* bar; dinner-table; **⁃geschirr** *n* dinner-service, dinner-set.

Täfelung ['te:fəlʊŋ] *f* (-/ -en) wainscot, panel(l)ing.

Tag [ta:k] *m* (-[e]s/-e) day; **am** *od.* **bei ⁃e** by day; **guten ⁃!** how do you do?; good morning!; good afternoon!

Tage|buch ['ta:gəbu:x] *n*

(-[e]s/ver) diary; **2lang** *adv* for days; **2n** ['ta:gən] *v/i* hold a meeting.

Tages|anbruch ['ta:gəs-?anbrux] *m* (-[e]s/no *pl*): **bei** ~ at daybreak *od.* dawn; ~**ausflug** *m* day excursion *od.* trip; ~**kurs** *m* current rate; ~**licht** *n* daylight.

täglich ['tɛ:klɪç] *adj, adv* daily.

tagsüber ['ta:ks?y:bər] *adv* during the day.

Tagung ['ta:guŋ] *f* (-/-en) meeting.

Taille ['taljə] *f* (-/-n) waist.

Takt [takt] *m* (-[e]s/-e) *mus.* time, measure; *mot.* stroke; (*no pl*) *fig.* tact; ~**ik** ['taktɪk] *f* (-/-en) tactics *sg, pl*; **2los** [-lo:s] *adj* tactless; ~**stock** *m* baton; **2voll** *adj* tactful.

Tal [ta:l] *n* (-[e]s/ver) valley.

Talent [ta'lɛnt] *n* (-[e]s/-e) talent, gift.

Talg [talk] *m* (-[e]s/-e) suet; *ausgelassener:* tallow.

Talisman ['ta:lɪsman] *m* (-s/-e) talisman, charm.

Tang [taŋ] *m* (-[e]s/-e) seaweed.

Tank [taŋk] *m* (-[e]s/-s) tank; **2en** ['taŋkən] *v/i* fill up; *v/t* fill up with; ~**er** *m* tanker; ~**stelle** *f* petrol station, *Am.* gas *od.* filling station; ~**wart** [-vart] *m* (-[e]s/-e) pump attendant.

Tanne ['tanə] *f* (-/-n) fir (-tree); ~**nzapfen** *m* fir-cone.

Tante ['tantə] *f* (-/-n) aunt.

Tanz [tants] *m* (-es/-e) dance; **2en** ['tantsən] *v/i, v/t* dance.

Tänzer ['tɛntsər] *m* (-s/-), ~**in** *f* (-/-nen) dancer; partner.

Tapete [ta'pe:tə] *f* (-/-n) wallpaper.

tapezieren [tape'tsi:rən] *v/t* paper, decorate.

tapfer ['tapfər] *adj* brave, courageous.

Tarif [ta'ri:f] *m* (-s/-e) tariff.

tarn|en ['tarnən] *v/t* camouflage; *bsd. fig.* disguise; **2ung** *f* camouflage.

Tasche ['taʃə] *f* (-/-n) bag, pocket.

Taschen|buch *n* pocketbook; ~**dieb** *m* pickpocket; ~**geld** *n* pocket money; ~**lampe** *f* (pocket) torch, flashlight; ~**messer** *n* pocket knife; ~**tuch** *n* (pocket-)handkerchief; ~**uhr** *f* pocket-watch.

Tasse ['tasə] *f* (-/-n) cup.

Taste ['tastə] *f* (-/-n) *Klavier etc.*: key; **2n** *v/i* grope (**nach** *for*, *after*); **sich 2n** *v/refl* feel *od.* grope one's way.

Tat [ta:t] *f* (-/-en) action, act, deed; *Straf2:* offen|ce, *Am.*, ~*se*; crime; **2enlos** ['ta:tənlo:s] *adj* inactive.

Täter ['tɛ:tər] *m* (-s/-) perpetrator.

tätig ['tɛːtɪç] *adj* active; busy; **2keit** *f* activity; occupation, job.

tatkräftig ['taːtkrɛftɪç] *adj* active; **2ort** ['-ʔɔrt] *m* (-[e]s/-e) scene of a *od.* the crime.

Tätowierung [tɛtoˈviːruŋ] *f* (-/-en) tattoo.

Tatsache ['taːtzaxə] *f* (-/-n) fact; **2sächlich** ['-zɛçlɪç] *adj* actual, real.

tätscheln ['tɛtʃəln] *v/t* pet, pat.

Tatze ['tatsə] *f* (-/-n) paw.

Tau[1] [tau] *n* (-[e]s/no *pl*) rope, cable.

Tau[2] *m* (-[e]s/no *pl*) dew.

taub [taup] *adj* deaf; *Finger:* numb.

Taube ['taubə] *f* (-/-n) pigeon.

taubstumm ['taupʃtum] *adj* deaf and dumb; **2e** *m, f* (-n/-n) deaf mute.

tauch|en ['tauxən] *v/t* dip; *v/i* dive; *U-Boot:* submerge; **2er** *m* diver; **2sieder** ['tauxziːdər] *m* immersion heater; **2sport** *m* skin diving.

tauen ['tauən] *v/i, v/t* melt; **es taut** it is thawing; dew is falling.

Tauf|e ['taufə] *f* (-/-n) baptism, christening; **2en** *v/t* baptize; christen; **~pate** *m* godfather; **~patin** *f* godmother.

taug|en ['taugən] *v/i* be good (**zu** for); (**zu**) **nichts ~en** be good for nothing; **~lich** *adj* good, fit, useful.

taumeln ['tauməln] *v/i* reel, stagger.

Tausch [tauʃ] *m* (-[e]s/-e) exchange; barter; **2en** ['tauʃən] *v/t* exchange, trade, barter; *v/i* exchange.

täuschen ['tɔyʃən] *v/t* deceive; **sich ~en** be mistaken; **~end** *adj* striking; **2ung** *f* deception.

tausend ['tauzənt] *adj* thousand; **~ste** *adj* thousandth.

Tauwetter ['tauvɛtər] *n* (-s/no *pl*) thaw.

Taxe ['taksə] *f* (-/-n) *Gebühr:* fee; s. **Taxi**.

Taxi ['taksi] *n* (-s/-s) taxi (-cab); cab; **~fahrer** *m* taxi-driver, cab-driver; **~stand** *m* cabstand, taxi rank.

Technik ['tɛçnɪk] *f* (-/no *pl*) technology, engineering; (*pl* -en) *Fertigkeit:* skill, workmanship; *Verfahren:* technique; **~er** *m* technician.

technisch ['tɛçnɪʃ] *adj* technical; **~e Hochschule** college of technology.

Tee [teː] *m* (-s/-s) tea; **~gebäck** *n* tea-cakes *pl.*

Teer [teːr] *m* (-[e]s/-e) tar; **2en** *v/t* tar.

Teesieb ['teːziːp] *n* (-[e]s/-e) tea-strainer.

Teich [taɪç] *m* (-[e]s/-e) pond, pool.

Teig [taɪk] *m* (-[e]s/-e) dough, paste; **~waren** *pl* pasta *sg.*

Teil [taɪl] *m, n* (-[e]s/-e)
part; *Anz:* portion, share;
zum ~ partly, in part;
2bar *adj* divisible;
~chen *n* (-s/-) particle;
2en ['taɪlən] *v/t* divide;
fig. share; **2haben** *v/i*
(*irr*) participate, (have) a
share (**an in**); *op.*
~haber *m* partner;
~nahme [-na:-
mə] *f* (-/no pl) participa-
tion; sympathy; **2nahms-
los** *adj* indifferent; apathetic; **2nehmen** *v/i* (*irr*):
~ an take part in, participate in; **~nehmer** *m* par-
ticipant; *teleph.* subscrib-
er; **2s** *adv* partly; *Anz.*
division; **2weise** *adv*
partly, in part.

Teint [tɛ̃] *m* (-s/-s) complexion.

Telefon [tele'fo:n] *n* (-s/
-e) telephone, *colloq.*
phone; **~buch** *n* telephone
directory; **~gespräch** *n*
(tele)phone call; **2ieren**
[-fo'ni:rən] *v/i* (tele)phone;
2isch [-'fo:nɪʃ] *adj, adv*
over the *od.* by (tele)phone;
~istin [-fo'nɪstɪn] *f* (-/
-nen) (telephone) operat-
or; **~zelle** [-'fo:n-] *f* telephone kiosk, call-box, *Am.*
telephone booth; **~zen-
trale** [-'fo:n-] *f* (telephone) exchange.

telegrafieren [telegra-
'fi:rən] *v/t, v/i* wire;
Übersee: cable; **~isch**
[-'gra:fɪʃ] *adv, adj* by telegram *od.* wire; by cable.

Telegramm [tele'gram] *n*

(-s/-e) telegram, wire;
Übersee: cable(gram).

Teller ['tɛlər] *m* (-s/-)
plate.

Tempel ['tɛmpəl] *m* (-s/-)
temple.

Temperament [tempera-
'mɛnt] *n* (-[e]s/-e) tem-
per(ament); **2voll** *adj*
spirited.

Temperatur [tempera-
'tu:r] *f* (-/-en) temperature; **j-s ~ messen** take
s.o.'s temperature.

Tempo ['tɛmpo] *n* (-s/-s,
-pi) time; *Gangart:* pace;
Geschwindigkeit: speed.

Tendenz [tɛn'dɛnts] *f* (-/
-en) tendency, trend.

Tennis ['tɛnɪs] *n* (-/no pl)
tennis; **~platz** *m* tennis
court; **~schläger** *m* (tennis)racket.   [carpet.]

Teppich ['tɛpɪç] *m* (-s/-e)

Termin [tɛr'mi:n] *m* (-s/
-e) appointed time *od.* day;
jur., econ. date.

Terrasse [tɛ'rasə] *f* (-/-n)
terrace.

Territorium [tɛri'to:rɪʊm]
n (-s/-rien) territory.

Terror ['tɛrɔr] *m* (-s/no pl)
terror; **2isieren** [-ri'zi:-
rən] *v/t* terrorize.

Testament [tɛsta'mɛnt]
n (-[e]s/-e) (last) will; *eccl.*
Testament.

testen ['tɛstən] *v/t* test.

Tetanus ['te:tanus] *m* (-/no
pl) tetanus.

teuer ['tɔʏər] *adj* dear (*a.
fig.*), expensive; **wie ~ ist
es?** how much is it?

Teufel ['tɔyfəl] *m* (-s/-) devil.

Text [tɛkst] *m* (-[e]s/-e) text; *Lied:* words *pl*; *Oper:* book, libretto.

Textilien [tɛks'ti:liən] *pl* textiles *pl*.

Theater [te'a:tər] *n* (-s/-) theatre, *Am.* -er; **~be-sucher** *m* playgoer; **~kasse** *f* box-office; **~stück** *n* play.

Theke ['te:kə] *f* (-/-n) bar, counter.

Thema ['te:ma] *n* (-s/-men) theme, subject; *Gesprächs2:* topic.

Theologie [teolo'gi:] *f* (-/-n) theology.

theoretisch [teo're:tiʃ] *adj* theoretic(al); **2ie** [-'ri:] *f* (-/-n) theory.

Therapie [tera'pi:] *f* (-/-n) therapy.

Thermometer [termo-'me:tər] *n* (-s/-) thermometer.

Thermosflasche ['termɔs-] *f* thermos (flask).

Thrombose [trɔm'bo:zə] *f* (-/-n) thrombosis.

Thron [tro:n] *m* (-[e]s/-e) throne.

Thunfisch ['tu:nfiʃ] *m* (-[e]s/-e) tunny, tuna.

ticken ['tikən] *v/i* tick.

tief [ti:f] *adj* deep (*a.* fig.); *Seufzer, Schlaf etc.:* profound; *niedrig:* low; 2 *n* (-s/-e) *meteor.* depression; **2druckgebiet** *n* low-pressure area; **2e** *f* (-/-n) depth (*a.* fig.); **~gekühlt**

adj deep-frozen; **2kühl-fach** *n* freezing compartment; **2kühltruhe** *f* freezer.

Tier [ti:r] *n* (-[e]s/-e) animal; beast; **~arzt** *m* veterinary (surgeon), *colloq.* vet, *Am. a.* veterinarian; **~garten** *m* zoological gardens *pl*, zoo; **2isch** *adj* animal; **~kreis** *m ast.* zodiac; **~park** *m s.* Tiergarten.

Tiger ['ti:gər] *m* (-s/-) tiger; **~in** *f* (-/-nen) tigress.

tilgen ['tilgən] *v/t* wipe out; *Schuld:* pay off.

Tinte ['tintə] *f* (-/-n) ink; **~nfisch** *m* cuttlefish.

Tip [tip] *m* (-s/-s) hint, tip.

tippen ['tipən] *v/i, v/t colloq.* type; *v/i:* ~ **an** tip; ~ **auf** tap on.

Tisch [tiʃ] *m* (-[e]s/-e) table; **bei** ~ at table; **nach** ~ after dinner; **~decke** *f* table-cloth; **~ler** *m* joiner; *Möbel:* cabinet-maker; **~tennis** *n* table tennis; **~tuch** *n* tablecloth; **~zeit** *f* dinnertime; lunch-hour.

Titel ['ti:təl] *m* (-s/-) title; **~bild** *n* cover (picture); **~blatt** *n* title-page.

Toast [to:st] *m* (-[e]s/-e, -s) toast (*a. Trinkspruch*).

toben ['to:bən] *v/i* rage, storm; *Kinder:* romp; **~süchtig** ['to:p-] *adj* raving mad.

Tochter ['tɔxtər] *f* (-/-n) daughter.

Tod [to:t] m (-[e]s/*rare* -e) death.

Todes|anzeige ['to:dəs-ʔantsaɪgə] f (-/-n) obituary (notice); **~opfer** n death, casualty; **~strafe** f capital punishment, death penalty.

tödlich ['tø:tlɪç] adj deadly; fatal.

todmüde ['to:t'my:də] adj dead tired.

Toilette [töa'lɛtə] f (-/-n) toilet; lavatory; **~nartikel** pl toilet articles pl; **~npapier** n toilet paper.

tolerant [tole'rant] adj tolerant.

toll [tɔl] adj mad, crazy; **~en** ['tɔlən] v/i romp; **2wut** f (-/no pl) rabies.

tolpatschig ['tɔlpatʃɪç] adj colloq. awkward, clumsy.

Tomate [to'ma:tə] f (-/-n) tomato.

Ton¹ [to:n] m (-[e]s/-e) clay.

Ton² m (-[e]s/ˇe) sound; mus. tone, einzelner: note; Betonung: accent, stress; **~abnehmer** m (-s/-) Plattenspieler: pick-up; **2angebend** adj leading; **~art** f mus. key; **~band** n tape; **~bandgerät** n tape recorder.

tönen ['tø:nən] v/i sound, ring; v/t tint (a. Haar), tone.

Ton|fall ['to:nfal] m (-[e]s/no pl) intonation, accent; **~film** m sound

film.

Tonne ['tɔnə] f (-/-n) tun; barrel; Regen2: butt; Gewicht, mar. ton.

Topf [tɔpf] m (-[e]s/ˇe) pot.

Tor [to:r] n (-[e]s/-e) gate; Fußball etc.: goal; Skisport: gate. [peat.]

Torf [tɔrf] m (-[e]s/no pl)]

töricht ['tø:rɪçt] adj foolish, silly.

torkeln ['tɔrkəln] v/i reel, stagger.

Tor|latte ['to:rlatə] f (-/-n) crossbar; **~lauf** m Skisport: slalom; goal-line; **~pfosten** m gatepost; sp. goal-post; **~schütze** [-ʃytsə] m (-n/-n) sp. scorer.

Torte ['tɔrtə] f (-/-n) fancy cake, layer-cake.

Torwart ['to:rvart] m (-[e]s/-e) goalkeeper.

tosen ['to:zən] v/i roar.

tot [to:t] adj dead (a. fig.); **~er Punkt** fig. deadlock.

total [to'ta:l] adj total, complete.

Tote ['to:tə] m, f (-n/-n) dead man od. woman; (dead) body, corpse; **die ~n** pl the dead pl.

töten ['tø:tən] v/t kill; murder.

Totenschein m death certificate.

Toto ['to:to] n, m (-s/-s) football pools pl.

Totschlag m manslaughter, homicide; **2en** v/t (irr) kill.

toupieren [tu'pi:rən] v/t backcomb.

Tour [tu:r] f (-/-en) tour (durch of).

Tourist [tu'rıst] m (-en/-en) tourist; **~enklasse** f tourist class; **~in** f (-/-nen) tourist.

Tournee f [tur'ne:] f (-/-s, -n) tour.

traben ['tra:bən] v/i trot.

Tracht [traxt] f (-/-en) costume; uniform.

trächtig ['trɛçtıç] adj with young, pregnant.

Tradition [tradi'tsïo:n] f (-/-en) tradition.

Trag|bahre ['tra:kba:rə] f (-/-n) stretcher; **2bar** adj portable; Kleidung: wearable; fig. bearable.

träge ['trɛːgə] adj lazy, indolent.

tragen ['tra:gən] v/t (irr) carry; Kleidung: wear; stützen: support; Früchte: bear (a. fig.).

Träger ['trɛːgər] m (-s/-) carrier; Gepäck: porter; (shoulder-)strap; tech. support, girder.

Tragfläche ['tra:kflɛçə] f (-/-n) aer. wing.

trag|isch ['tra:gıʃ] adj tragic; **2ödie** [tra'gøːdïə] f (-/-n) tragedy.

Trainer ['trɛːnər] m (-s/-) trainer; coach; **~ing** f (-s/-e) training; **~ingsanzug** m track suit.

Traktor ['traktor] m (-s/-en) tractor.

trampeln ['trampəln] v/i trample, stamp.

Träne ['trɛːnə] f (-/-n) tear; **2n** v/i Augen: water.

tränken ['trɛŋkən] v/t water; et.: soak.

Transfusion [transfu'zïo:n] f (-/-en) transfusion.

Transistor [tran'zıstor] m (-s/-en) transistor.

transitiv ['tranzïti:f] adj gr. transitive.

Trans|port [trans'port] m (-[e]s/-e) transport(ation), conveyance, carriage; **2ieren** [-por'ti:rən] v/t transport, convey, carry.

Traube ['traubə] f (-/-n) bunch of grapes; Beere: grape; **~nsaft** f/m grape-juice; **~nzucker** m grape-sugar, glucose, dextrose.

trauen ['trauən] v/t marry; v/i trust (j-m s.o.); **sich ...** v/refl dare.

Trauer ['trauər] f (-/no pl) sorrow; mourning; **~feier** f obsequies pl; **~kleidung** f mourning; **2n** v/i mourn (um for); **~spiel** n tragedy.

Traum [traum] m (-[e]s/ ⸚e) dream.

träumen ['trɔymən] v/i, v/t dream.

traurig ['trauriç] adj sad.

Trau|ring ['traurıŋ] m (-[e]s/-e) wedding-ring; **~schein** m marriage certificate od. lines pl; **~ung** f marriage, wedding; **~zeuge** m witness to a marriage.

treff|en ['trefən] *v/t* (*irr*) hit, strike; *begegnen:* meet; *Vorkehrungen:* take; **nicht ~en** miss; **e-e Entscheidung ~en** come to a decision; **2en** *n* (*-s/-*) meeting; **2punkt** *m* meeting-place.

treib|en ['traɪbən] *v/t* (*irr*) drive; drift; *Knospen:* put forth; *fig.* impel; *v/i* drive; drift; *im Wasser:* float; *bot.* shoot; **2haus** ['traɪp-] *n* hothouse; **2riemen** ['traɪp-] *m* driving-belt; **2stoff** ['traɪp-] *m s.* **Kraftstoff.**

trenn|en ['trɛnən] *v/t* separate; *abtrennen:* sever; *teleph.* cut off, disconnect; **sich ~en** *v/refl* separate, part; **2ung** *f* separation; disconnection; **2wand** *f* partition.

Treppe ['trɛpə] *f* (*-/-n*) staircase, (*e-e* a flight of) stairs *pl.*

Treppen|absatz *m* landing; **~geländer** *n* banisters *pl;* **~haus** *n* staircase; **~stufe** *f* stair, step.

Tresor [tre'zoːr] *m* (*-s/-e*) safe; strong room.

treten ['treːtən] *v/i* (*irr*) tread, step (**auf** on); *v/t* kick.

treu [trɔy] *adj* faithful; loyal; **2e** (*-/no pl*) faithfulness; loyalty; **~los** [-loːs] *adj* faithless; disloyal.

Tribüne [tri'byːnə] *f* (*-/-n*) platform; *sp.* grandstand.

Trichter ['trɪçtər] *m* (*-s/-*)

funnel; crater.

Trick [trɪk] *m* (*-s/-s*) trick.

Trieb [triːp] *m* (*-[e]s/-e*) *bot.* sprout, (new) shoot; *Natur2:* instinct; (sexual) urge; **~kraft** *f* motive power; *fig.* driving force; **~wagen** *m* railcar.

Trikot [tri'koː] *n* (*-s/-s*) tights *pl; sp.* shirt.

trink|bar ['trɪŋkbaːr] *adj* drinkable; **2becher** *m* drinking-cup; **~en** ['trɪŋkən] *v/t* (*irr*) drink; **~en auf** *v/i* drink (to), toast; **2er** *m* drinker; **2geld** *n* tip; **2spruch** *m* toast; **2wasser** *n* drinking-water.

trippeln ['trɪpəln] *v/i* trip.

Tritt [trɪt] *m* (*-[e]s/-e*) tread, step; *Fuß2:* kick; **~brett** *n* running-board.

Triumph [tri'omf] *m* (*-[e]s/-e*) triumph; **2ieren** [-um'fiːrən] *v/i* triumph.

trocken ['trɔkən] *adj* dry (*a.* Wein); *Boden:* arid; **2haube** *f* (hair-)dryer; **2heit** *f* dryness; aridity; **~legen** *v/t* drain; *Baby:* change (the napkins *od.* Am. diapers *od.*); **2obst** *n* dried fruit.

trocknen ['trɔknən] *v/i,* *v/t* dry.

Troddel ['trɔdəl] *f* (*-/-n*) tassel.

trödeln ['trøːdəln] *v/i* col-*loq.* dawdle.

Trog [troːk] *m* (*-[e]s/ᵘe*) trough.

Trommel

Trommel ['trɔməl] f (-/-n)
drum; *tech. a.* cylinder;
~fell n *anat.* eardrum; **2n**
v/i, v/t drum.

Trompete [trɔm'pe:tə] f
(-/-n) trumpet.

tropfen ['trɔpfən] v/i
drop, drip; **2** m (-s/-)
drop.

tropisch ['tro:pɪʃ] adj
tropical.

Trost [tro:st] m (-es/no pl)
comfort, consolation.

trösten ['trø:stən] v/t con-
sole, comfort.

trostlos ['tro:stlo:s] adj
disconsolate; *Gegend etc.:*
desolate; *fig.* wretched.

Trottel ['trɔtəl] m (-s/-)
colloq. idiot.

trotten ['trɔtən] v/i *colloq.*
trot, bustle.

trotz [trɔts] prp (gen, dat) in
spite of, despite; **2** m (-es/
no pl) defiance; **~dem**
['-de:m] adv nevertheless;
~ig adj defiant; sulky.

trüb(e) ['try:p, 'try:bə] adj
muddy; *Licht, Augen:* dim;
Farbe, Wetter: dull.

Trubel ['tru:bəl] m (-s/no
pl) bustle.

trübsinnig ['try:pzinɪç]
adj gloomy.

trügerisch ['try:gərɪʃ] adj
treacherous.

Truhe ['tru:ə] f (-/-n)
chest.

Trümmer ['trymər] pl ru-
ins pl; *Schutt:* debris sg;
Unfall: wreckage sg.

Trumpf [trumpf] m (-[e]s/
~e) *Karten:* trump (card).

Trunkenheit ['truŋkən-
hait] f (-/no pl) drunken-
ness, intoxication; **~ am
Steuer** drunken driving.

Trupp [trup] m (-s/-s)
troop, gang; **~e** f (-/-n)
troop; *thea.* company.

Truthahn ['tru:tha:n] m
(-[e]s/**~e**) turkey(-cock).

Tschechoslowake [tʃɛ-
çoslo'va:kə] m (-n/-n)
Czechoslovak; **2isch** adj
Czechoslovak.

Tuberkulose [tubɛrku-
'lo:zə] f (-/-n) tuber-
culosis.

Tuch [tu:x] n (-[e]s/**~er**)
cloth; *s.* **Hals-, Kopf-,
Staubtuch.**

tüchtig ['tyçtiç] adj clever,
good; *fähig:* efficient; capable.

tückisch ['tykɪʃ] adj
treacherous; malicious,
spiteful.

Tugend ['tu:gənt] f (-/
-en) virtue.

Tulpe ['tulpə] f (-/-n)
tulip.

Tumor ['tu:mɔr] m (-s/
-en) tumo(u)r.

Tümpel ['tympəl] m (-s/-)
pool.

Tumult [tu'mult] m (-[e]s/
-e) tumult, uproar.

tun [tu:n] v/t (irr) do; make;
wohin ~: put; v/i: **zu ~ haben** be busy; **er tut so,
als ob er** he pretends to.

Tunke ['tuŋkə] f (-/-n)
sauce; **2n** v/t dip, steep.

Tunnel ['tunəl] m (-s/-)
tunnel.

tupfen ['tʊpfən] *v/t* dab; spot, dot; 2 *m* (-s/-) dot, spot.

Tür [ty:r] *f* (-/-en) door.

Turbine [tʊr'bi:nə] *f* (-/-n) turbine.

Türk|e ['tʏrkə] *m* (-n/-n) Turk; 2**isch** *adj* Turkish.

Türklinke ['tʏrklɪŋkə] *f* (-/-n) doorhandle.

Turm [tʊrm] *m* (-[e]s/ᵉe) tower; *Kirch*2: *a.* steeple; ~**spitze** *f* spire; ~**springen** *n* (-s/*no pl*) *sp.* high-diving.

Turn|anzug ['tʊrnʔan-tsu:k] *m* (-[e]s/ᵉe) gym-dress; 2**en** ['tʊrnən] *v/i* do gymnastics; ~**er** *m* gymnast; ~**halle** *f* gym(na-sium).

Turnier [tʊr'ni:r] *n* (-s/-e) tournament.

Turn|schuh ['tʊrnʃu:] *m* gym-shoe; ~**verein** *m* gymnastic *od.* athletic club.

Tür|rahmen ['ty:rra:mən] *m* door-case, door-frame; ~**schild** *n* door-plate.

Tusche ['tʊʃə] *f* (-/-n) India(n) ink; 2**ln** ['tʊʃəln] *v/i* whisper.

Tüte ['ty:tə] *f* (-/-n) (paper-)bag.

Typ [ty:p] *m* (-s/-en) type; *tech. a.* model.

Typhus ['ty:fʊs] *m* (-/*no pl*) typhoid (fever).

typisch ['ty:pɪʃ] *adj* typical (**für** of).

Tyrann [ty'ran] *m* (-en/-en) tyrant; 2**isieren** [-rani'zi:rən] *v/t* tyrannize (over), bully.

U

U-Bahn ['u:ba:n] *f s.* **Untergrundbahn**.

übel ['y:bəl] *adj* evil, bad; **mir ist** ~ I am evil *od.* feel sick; *adv* ill, badly; 2 *n* (-s/-) evil; 2**keit** *f* sickness, nausea; ~**nehmen** *v/t* (*irr*) take *s.th.* ill *od.* amiss.

üben ['y:bən] exercise; (*ein*)~: practi|se, *Am.* -ce.

über ['y:bər] *prp* (*dat, acc*) over, above; *in Fluß etc.*: across; *reisen* ~: via, by way of; more than; *sprechen* ~ talk about *od.* of; **nach-denken** ~ think about; ~**all** ['y:bər'ʔal] *adv*

everywhere.

über|anstrengen [y:-bər'ʔanʃtrɛŋən] *v/t* over-strain (**sich** o.s.); ~**bieten** [-'bi:tən] *v/t* (*irr*) *fig.* beat, surpass.

Überblick ['y:bərblɪk] *m* (-[e]s/-e) survey (**über** of); 2**en** [-'blɪkən] *v/t* overlook, survey.

über|bringen [y:bər-'brɪŋən] *v/t* (*irr*) deliver; ~**dauern** [-'dauərn] *v/t* outlast, outlive; ~**drüssig** ['y:bərdrʏsɪç] *adj* weary *od.* sick (*gen* of); ~**eilt** [-'ʔailt] *adj* precipitate, rash.

übereinander [y:bər'ʔaɪ-
'nandər] *adv* one upon the
other; **~schlagen** *v/t*
(*irr*): **die Beine ~** cross
one's legs.

übereinkommen [y:-
bər'ʔaɪn-] *v/i* (*irr*) agree;
~stimmen *v/i*: **~ (mit)**
Person: agree (with); *Sache*: correspond (with, to);
2stimmung *f* agreement;
correspondence.

überfahren [y:bər'fa:-
rən] *v/t* (*irr*) run over; *Signal*: go through; **2t** ['y:-
bərfa:rt] *f* (-/-en) *passage*;
Fluß: crossing.

Überfall ['y:bərfal] *m*
(-[e]s/ⁿe) hold-up;
assault; **2en** [-'falən] *v/t*
(*irr*) hold up; assault.

überfällig ['y:bərfɛlɪç]
adj overdue.

Überfallkommando
['y:bərfal-] *n* (-s/-s) flying
(*Am*. riot) squad.

überfliegen [y:bər'fli:-
gən] *v/t* (*irr*) fly over *od*.
across; *fig.* glance over;
~fließen ['y:bər-] *v/i* (*irr*)
overflow; **~fluß** *m* (-sses/
no pl) abundance, superflu-
ity; **~flüssig** *adj* superflu-
ous; **~fluten** [-'flu:tən] *v/t*
overflow, flood.

überführen [y:bər'fy:-
rən] *v/t* transport, convey;
Verbrecher: convict (*gen*
of); **2ung** *f* transport(a-
tion); *Brücke*: overpass.

überfüllt [y:bər'fylt] *adj*
crammed; *mit Menschen*:
overcrowded.

Übergang ['y:bərgaŋ] *m*
(-[e]s/ⁿe) crossing; *fig.*
transition; **~szeit** *f* period
of transition.

übergeben [y:bər'ge:-
bən] *v/t* (*irr*) deliver, hand
over; *mil.* surrender; **sich
~geben** *v/refl* vomit, be
sick; **~gehen in** ['y:bər-
ge:ən] *v/i* (*irr*) pass into;
2gewicht *n* overweight;
~greifen *v/i* (*irr*): **~ auf**
spread to; **~hand-
nehmen** [-'hantne:mən]
v/i (*irr*) increase, be ram-
pant; **~hängen** ['y:bər-]
v/i (*irr*) overhang; *v/t s.*
umhängen; **~haupt**
['-haupt] *adv*: **wenn ~** if at
all; **~ nicht** not at all; **~
kein** no ... whatever;
~heblich ['-he:plɪç] *adj*
presumptuous, arrogant.

überholen [y:bər'ho:lən]
v/t overtake, pass; *ausbessern*: overhaul; **~t** *adj*
outmoded, out of date;
2verbot *n* no overtaking
(sign).

überkleben [y:bər'kle:-
bən] *v/t* paste over;
~kochen ['y:bər-] *v/i* boil
over; **~lassen** [-'lasən] *v/t*
(*irr*): **j-m et. ~** let s.o.
have s.th.; *fig.* leave s.th.
to s.o.; **~lasten** [-'lastən]
v/t overload; *fig.* overbur-
den; **~laufen** ['y:bər-] *v/i*
(*irr*) run over, *Kochendes*:
boil over; *mil.* desert (*to*
to); [-'laufən] *adj* overcrowded.

überleben [y:bər'le:bən]

v/i, *v/t* survive; **2de** *m*, *f* (**-n/-n**) survivor.

überleglen [y:bər'le:gən] *v/t*: (**sich**) ~ consider, think about; **es sich anders** ~ change one's mind; **~en** *adj* superior (*dat* to; **an** in); **2ung** *f* consideration, reflection.

Überlieferung [y:bər-'li:fəruŋ] *f* (**-/-en**) tradition; **2listen** ['-'lıstən] *v/t* outwit; **2mäßig** ['y:bər-mɛ:sıç] *adj* immoderate; **2morgen** ['y:bər-] *adv* the day after tomorrow; **2müdet** [-'my:dət] *adj* overtired; **~mütig** ['y:bərmy:tıç] *adj* wanton, frolicsome; **2nächst** ['y:bər-] *adj* the next but one; **2nächste Woche** the week after next.

übernachtlen [y:bər-'naxtən] *v/i* stay overnight; **2ung** *f* night's lodging; **2ung und Frühstück** bed and breakfast.

übernatürlich [y:bərnaty:rlıç] *adj* supernatural; **~nehmen** [-'ne:mən] *v/t* (*irr*) take over; *Verantwortung*: assume; *Führung*: take; **~prüfen** [-'pry:fən] *v/t* check; *j-n*: screen; **~queren** [-'kve:rən] *v/t* cross; **~ragen** [-'ra:gən] *v/t* tower over; *fig.* tower above.

überraschlen [y:bər'raʃən] *v/t* surprise; *ertappen*: catch (**bei** at, in); **~end** *adj* surprising, unex-

pected; **2ung** *f* surprise.

überlreden [y:bər're:dən] *v/t* persuade; **~reichen** [-'raıçən] *v/t* present; **2reste** [y:bər'rɛstə] *pl* remains *pl*; **~rumpeln** [-'rumpəln] *v/t* surprise.

Überschallgeschwindigkeit [y:bər∫al-] *f* supersonic speed.

überlschätzen [y:bər-'∫ɛtsən] *v/t* overrate; **~schlagen** [-'∫la:gən] *v/t* (*irr*) *Seiten*: skip; *Kosten*: make a rough estimate of; **sich ~schlagen** tumble over; *Wagen*: turn over; *Stimme*: become high-pitched; **~schlagen** *adj* lukewarm, tepid; **~schneiden** [-'∫naıdən] *v/refl* (*irr*): **sich** ~ overlap (*a.* *fig.*); **~schreiten** [-'∫raıtən] *v/t* (*irr*) cross; *fig.* transgress; *Geschwindigkeit*, *Anweisungen*: exceed; **2schrift** ['y:bər-] *f* heading, title, headline; **2schuß** ['y:bər-] *m* (**-sses/¤sse**) surplus; **2schwemmung** ['∫ve-muŋ] *f* (**-/-en**) flood(ing).

Übersee... ['y:bərze:-] oversea(s).

übersehen [y:bər'ze:ən] *v/t* (*irr*) overlook (*a.* *fig.*).

übersetzlen [y:bər'zɛtsən] *v/t* translate (**in** into); **2er** *m* translator; **2ung** *f* translation.

Übersicht ['y:bərzıçt] *f* (**-/-en**) survey (**über** of); summary; **2lich** *adj* clear.

über|siedeln [y:bər'zi:-dəln] v/i remove (**nach** to); **~springen** [-'ʃprɪŋən] v/t (irr) jump, clear; Seite etc.: skip; **~stehen** ['y:bər-] v/i (irr) jut out, project; [-'ʃte:ən] v/t Unglück: survive; Krankheit: get over; **~steigen** [-'ʃtaɪgən] v/t (irr) climb over; fig. exceed; **~stimmen** [-'ʃtɪmən] v/t outvote.

Überstunden ['y:bər-ʃtʊndən] pl overtime sg; ~ **machen** work overtime.

überstürz|en [y:bər'ʃtʏrtsən] v/t rush, hurry; **~t** adj precipitate, rash.

übertrag|bar [y:bər'tra:kba:r] adj transferable; econ. negotiable; med. communicable; **~en** [-'tra:gən] v/t (irr) Blut: transfuse; tech., med., Rundfunk: transmit; Rundfunk: broadcast; **im Fernsehen ~en** televise; **~en** adj figurative.

übertreffen [y:bər'trefən] v/t (irr) j-n, et.: surpass, exceed.

übertreib|en [y:bər'traɪbən] v/t (irr) exaggerate; **2ung** f exaggeration.

über|treten [y:bər'tre:tən] v/t transgress, violate; **~trieben** [-'tri:bən] adj exaggerated; **2tritt** ['y:bərtrɪt] m (-[e]s/-e) going over (**zu** to); eccl. conversion; **~völkert** [-'fœlkərt] adj overpopu-

lated; **~vorteilen** [-'fɔr-taɪlən] v/t overreach, do; **~wachen** [-'vaxən] v/t supervise, superintend, control; polizeilich: shadow.

überwältigen [y:bər'vɛl-tɪgən] v/t overcome, overwhelm; **~d** adj overwhelming.

überweis|en [y:bər'vaɪ-zən] v/t (irr) Geld: remit (**an** to); **2ung** f remittance.

über|winden [y:bər'vɪn-dən] v/t (irr) overcome; **sich ~winden zu** bring o.s. to; **2zahl** ['y:bər-] f (-/no pl): **in der ~** superior in numbers.

überzeug|en [y:bər'tsɔy-gən] v/t convince (**von** of); **2ung** f conviction.

überziehen ['y:bərtsi:ən] v/t (irr) put s.th. on; [y:bər'tsi:ən] v/t (irr) cover; Bett: put clean sheets on; Konto: overdraw.

üblich ['y:plɪç] adj usual, customary.

U-Boot ['u:-] n (-[e]s/-e) submarine, Deutschland: a. U-boat.

übrig ['y:brɪç] adj left, remaining; **die ~en** pl the others pl, the rest; **~bleiben** be left, remain; **~ens** ['y:brɪgəns] adv by the way; **~lassen** v/t (irr) leave.

Übung ['y:bʊŋ] f (-/-en) exercise, practice; **~s-hang** [-haŋ] m sp. nurse-

ry slope.

Ufer ['u:fər] *n* (-s/-) shore; *Fluß*: bank; **am** *od.* **ans ~** ashore.

Uhr [u:r] *f* (-/-en) clock; *Armband2* watch; **um vier ~** at four o'clock; **~arm-band** *n* watch-strap; **~macher** ['-maxər] *m* (-s/ -) watch-maker; **~zeiger** *m* hand.

Uhu ['u:hu] *m* (-s/-s) eagle-owl.

ulkig ['ʊlkɪç] *adj* funny.

Ulme ['ʊlmə] *f* (-/-n) elm.

um [ʊm] *prp* (*acc*) round, about; **~ seinetwillen** for his sake; **~ zu** (in order) to; *s.* **besser.**

umändern ['ʊm?ɛndərn] *v/t* change, alter; **~armen** ['-?armən] *v/t*: (**sich**) **~** embrace; **~bauen** ['ʊm-] *v/t* rebuild, reconstruct; **~blättern** ['ʊm-] *v/t* turn over; **~bringen** ['ʊm-] *v/t* (*irr*) kill (**sich** o.s.); **~buchen** ['ʊmbu:xən] *v/t* rebook (**auf den ...** for the ...).

umdrehen ['ʊmdre:ən] *v/t* turn over; **sich ~en** turn round; **2ung** ['-dre:-ʊŋ] *f* (-/-en) *tech.* revolution.

umfallen ['ʊmfalən] *v/i* (*irr*) fall down.

Umfang ['ʊmfaŋ] *m* (-[e]s/*no pl*) circumference; *Leib, Stamm*: girth, *fig.* extent; **2reich** *adj* extensive.

umformen ['ʊmfɔrmən]

v/t remodel, transform (*a. electr.*); **2frage** ['ʊm-] *f* (-/-n) inquiry; poll.

Umgang ['ʊmgaŋ] *m* (-s/ *no pl*) company; **~ haben mit** associate with; **~sfor-men** *pl* manners *pl*; **~ssprache** *f* colloquial speech.

umgeben [ʊm'ge:bən] *v/t* (*irr*) surround; *adj* surrounded (**von** with, by); **2ung** *f Stadt*: environs *pl*; *Milieu*: surroundings *pl*, environment.

umgehen ['ʊmge:ən] *v/i* (*irr*): **~ mit** use; *j-m*: deal with; **2ungsstraße** ['-ge:ʊŋs-] *f* bypass.

umgekehrt ['ʊmgəke:rt] *adj* reverse, inverted; *adv* vice versa; **~graben** ['ʊm-] *v/t* (*irr*) dig up; **2hang** ['ʊm-] *m* (-[e]s/ ²e) wrap, cape; **~hängen** ['ʊm-] *v/t*: **sich den Mantel ~** put one's coat round one's shoulders.

umher [ʊm'he:r] *adv* about, (a)round; **~blik-ken** *v/i* look about (one).

umkehren ['ʊmke:rən] *v/i* return, turn back; **~kippen** ['ʊm-] *v/t* upset, tilt (*v/i a.* over); **~klam-mern** ['-klamərn] *v/t* clasp; *Boxen*: clinch; **~klappen** ['ʊm-] *v/t* turn down, fold (back).

Umkleidekabine ['ʊm-klaidə-] *f* dressing-cubicle; **2n** ['ʊm-] *v/refl*: **sich ~** change.

umkommen ['ʊmkɔmən]
v/i (*irr*) be killed (**bei** an);

Umkreis ['ʊmkraɪs] *m*: **im**
~ von within a radius of.

Umlauf ['ʊmlaʊf] *m*
(-[e]s/≈e) circulation;
~bahn *f* orbit.

um|leiten ['ʊmlaɪtən] *v/t*
divert; **2ung** *f* diversion,
detour.

um|liegend ['ʊmliːgənt]
adj surrounding; **~pflü-
gen** ['ʊm-] plough, *Am.*
plow.

um|rechn|en ['ʊmrɛçnən]
v/t convert; **2nungskurs**
m rate of exchange.

um|ringen [ʊm'rɪŋən] *v/t*
surround; **2riß** ['ʊm-] *m*
(-sses/-sse) outline;
~rühren ['ʊm-] *v/t* stir;
2satz *m* econ.: turnover;
Absatz: sales *pl*; *Einnah-
me(n)*: return(s *pl*);
~schalten ['ʊm-] *v/t*
switch (over); **~schauen**
['ʊm-] *v/refl*: **sich ~ s.
umsehen.**

Umschlag ['ʊmʃlaːk] *m*
(-[e]s/≈e) *Brief*: envelope;
cover, wrapper; *Buch*:
jacket; *Hose*: turn-up, *Am.
a.* cuff; *med. feuchter ~*:
compress; *Breiß.*: poultice;
2en ['ʊmʃlaːgən] *v/t Ärmel*: turn up; *Kragen*: turn
down; *v/i* turn over, upset;
Boot: capsize; *Wet-
ter, fig.*: change.

um|schnallen ['ʊmʃna-
lən] *v/t* buckle on;
2schrift ['ʊm-] *f Phone-
tik*: transcription;

~schütten ['ʊm-] *v/t* pour
into another vessel, decant;
verschütten: spill;
2schwung ['ʊm-] *m* (-s/
≈e) *Gesinnung*: revulsion;
Wetter etc.: change; **~se-
hen** ['ʊm-] *v/refl*: **sich ~**
look back; look round;
look about (**nach** for);
~sein ['ʊm-] *v/i* (*irr*) col-
loq. Zeit: be up; *Ferien etc.*:
be over.

umsonst [ʊm'zɔnst] *adv*
gratis, free of charge; *adv
vergebens*: in vain.

Umstand ['ʊmʃtant] *m*
(-[e]s/≈e) circumstance;
**unter diesen Umstän-
den** under the circum-
stances; **in anderen
Umständen sein** be ex-
pecting.

umständlich ['ʊmʃtɛnd-
lɪç] *adj* long-winded, tedious; *Methode etc.*: roundabout; *Person*: fussy.

um|steigen ['ʊmʃtaɪgən]
v/i (*irr*) change; **~stellen**
['ʊm-] *v/t* shift about *od.*
round; *Währung, Produk-
tion*: convert; **sich ~stel-
len** adapt *od.* accommo-
date o.s. (**auf** to); [-'ʃtɛ-
lən] *v/t umzingeln*: surround; **~stimmen** ['ʊm-]
v/t: **j-n ~** change s.o.'s
mind; **~stoßen** ['ʊm-] *v/t*
(*irr*) knock over; upset (*a.
Plan*); **2sturz** ['ʊm-] *m*
(-es/≈e) subversion, overthrow; **~stürzen** ['ʊm-]
v/t upset, overturn.

Umtausch ['ʊmtaʊʃ] *m*

(-es/no pl) exchange; in andere Währung: conversion; ~en v/t exchange; convert.

um|wandeln ['umvandəln] v/t transform, change; ~wechseln ['um-] v/t change; 2weg ['um-] m detour.

Umwelt ['umvɛlt] f (-/no pl) environment; ~verschmutzung f environmental pollution.

um|werfen ['umvɛrfən] v/t (irr) upset, overturn; ~wickeln [-'vɪkəln] v/t wind round; ~ziehen ['um-] v/i (irr) (re)move (nach to); sich ~ziehen v/refl change; ~zingeln [-'tsɪŋəln] v/t surround; 2zug ['um-] m procession; removal, move.

unabhängig ['un?aphɛnɪç] adj independent; 2keit f independence.

un|absichtlich ['un?apzɪçtlɪç] adj unintentional; ~achtsam ['un?axtza:m] adj careless.

unan|gebracht ['un?angəbraxt] adj inappropriate; pred a. out of place; ~genehm [-gəne:m] adj unpleasant; peinlich: awkward; ~nehmlichkeiten pl trouble sg, inconvenience sg; ~sehnlich [-ze:nlɪç] adj unsightly; unschönbar: plain; ~ständig adj indecent, stärker: obscene.

un|appetitlich ['un?apeti:tlɪç] adj unappetizing; distasteful; ~artig adj

naughty.

unauf|fällig ['un?auffɛl-lɪç] adj inconspicuous; ~hörlich ['hø:rlɪç] adj incessant, continuous; ~merksam [-mɛrkza:m] adj inattentive.

unausstehlich ['un?aus-'ʃte:lɪç] adj unbearable, insufferable.

unbarmherzig ['un-barmhɛrtsɪç] adj merciless, unmerciful.

unbe|absichtigt ['unbə-?apzɪçtɪçt] adj unintentional; ~achtet adj unnoticed; ~baut adj agr. untilled; Gelände: undeveloped; ~deutend [-bə-dɔytənt] adj insignificant; ~dingt [-'bədɪŋt] adv by all means; ~fahrbar adj impracticable, impassable; ~friedigend adj unsatisfactory; ~friedigt adj dissatisfied; disappointed; ~fugt [-'bəfu:kt] adj unauthorized; incompetent; ~greiflich [-bə'graɪflɪç] adj incomprehensible; ~grenzt ['un-] adj unlimited, boundless; ~gründet adj unfounded; ~haglich ['-bəha:klɪç] adj uneasy, uncomfortable; ~herrscht adj unrestrained, lacking in self-control; ~holfen ['-bəholfən] adj clumsy, awkward; ~kannt adj unknown; ~kümmert ['-bəkymərt] adj unconcerned; ~liebt adj unpopular; ~merkt

adj unnoticed; **~quem**
['-bøkveːm] *adj* uncomfortable; *lästig:* inconvenient;
~rührt *adj* untouched;
~schränkt *adj* unrestricted; absolute; **~schreiblich** *adj* indescribable;
~ständig ['-bəʃtɛndɪç]
adj unsettled; **~stechlich**
adj incorruptible;
~stimmt *adj* indeterminate, indefinite; *unsicher:*
uncertain; *Gefühl:* vague;
~teilig ['-bətaɪlɪç] *adj*
unconcerned, indifferent;
not involved; **~wacht**
adj unguarded; **~waffnet**
adj unarmed; **~weglich**
['-bøveːklɪç] *adj* motionless; *unbewohnt* *adj* uninhabited; *Gebäude:* unoccupied, vacant; **~zahlbar** [-bəˈtsaːlbaːr] *adj*
priceless, invaluable;
~zahlt *adj* unpaid.
unbrauchbar ['unbrauxbaːr] *adj* useless.
und [unt] *cj* and; **na ~?** so
what?
un|dankbar ['undaŋkbaːr] *adj* ungrateful; *Aufgabe:* thankless; **~deutlich** *adj* indistinct;
~dicht *adj* leaky.
undurch|dringlich [undurçˈdrɪŋlɪç] *adj* impenetrable; *Gesicht:* impassive;
~lässig ['undurçlɛsɪç] *adj*
impervious, impermeable;
~sichtig ['-durçzɪçtɪç] *adj*
opaque; *fig:* mysterious.
un|leben ['unˀeːbən] *adj*

uneven; *Weg:* bumpy;
~echt *adj* false; *Schmuck:*
imitation, counterfeit; *Bild
etc.:* fake; **~ehelich**
['-eːəlɪç] *adj* illegitimate;
~empfindlich *adj* insensitive (**gegen** to); **~endlich** [-ˀɛntlɪç] *adj* endless,
infinite.
unent|behrlich [unˀɛntˈbeːrlɪç] *adj* indispensable;
~geltlich [-ˈgɛltlɪç] *adj*
gratuitous, gratis; free (of
charge); **~schieden** ['unˀɛnt[iːdən] *adj* undecided;
~schieden enden *sp.*
end in a draw *od.* tie;
~schlossen [-ˈʃlɔsən] *adj*
irresolute.
uner|bittlich [unˀɛrˈbɪtlɪç] *adj* inexorable; **~fahren** ['un-] *adj* inexperienced; **~freulich** ['un-]
adj unpleasant; **~hört**
['unˀɛrˈhøːrt] *adj* unheard-of, outrageous; **~kannt**
['un-] *adj* unrecognized;
~klärlich ['unˀɛrˈklɛːrlɪç] *adj* inexplicable;
~laubt ['un-] *adj* unauthorized; *verboten:* illegal;
~meßlich [-ˀɛrˈmɛslɪç]
adj immense; **~müdlich**
[-ˀɛrˈmyːtlɪç] *adj* indefatigable; *Anstrengungen:* untiring; **~reicht** ['unˀɛrˈraɪçt]
adj unrival(l)ed, unequal(l)ed; **~schöpflich**
[-ˈʃœpflɪç] *adj* inexhaustible; **~schrocken** ['un-]
adj intrepid, fearless;
~setzlich [-ˈzɛtslɪç] *adj*
irreplaceable; **~träglich**

[-'trɛːklɪç] *adj* intolerable; **~wartet** ['ʊn-] *adj* unexpected; **~wünscht** ['ʊn-] *adj* unwanted.

unfähig ['ʊnfɛːɪç] *adj* incapable (**zu** of *ger*); unable; inefficient.

Unfall ['ʊnfal] *m* (-[e]s/ᵉe) accident.

un|faßbar [ʊn'fasbaːr] *adj* inconceivable; **~förmig** ['ʊnfœrmɪç] *adj* shapeless; misshapen; **~frankiert** ['ʊn-] *adj* unstamped; **~freiwillig** ['ʊn-] *adj* involuntary; *Humor:* unconscious; **~freundlich** ['ʊn-] *adj* unfriendly, unkind; *Klima, Wetter:* disagreeable; *Zimmer, Tag:* cheerless; **~fruchtbar** ['ʊn-] *adj* unfruitful, sterile; **₂fug** ['ʊnfuːk] *m* (-[e]s/*no pl*) mischief.

Ungar ['ʊŋgar] *m* (-n/-n) Hungarian; **₂isch** *adj* Hungarian.

un|gebildet ['ʊngəbɪldət] *adj* uneducated; **~bräuchlich** ['ʊngəbrɔʏçlɪç] *adj* unusual; **~bührlich** ['ʊn-] *adj* improper; **~bunden** ['ʊn-] *adj fig.* free.

Ungeduld ['ʊngədʊlt] *f* (-/*no pl*) impatience; **₂ig** *adj* impatient.

unge|eignet ['ʊngəˀaɪgnət] *adj* unfit; *Person:* a. unqualified; *Augenblick:* inopportune; **~fähr** ['ʊngəfɛːr] *adj* approximate, rough; *adv* approximately,

roughly, about; **~fähr-lich** ['ʊn-] *adj* harmless; **~fällig** ['ʊn-] *adj* disobliging; **~heizt** ['ʊn-] *adj* cold.

ungeheuer ['ʊngəhɔʏər] *adj* vast, huge, enormous; **2** *n* (-s/-) monster.

unge|hindert ['ʊngəhɪndərt] *adj* unhindered, free; **~hörig** ['ʊn-] *adj* improper; **~horsam** ['ʊn-] *adj* disobedient; **~kürzt** ['ʊn-gəkʏrtst] *adj* unabridged; **~legen** ['-gəleːgən] *adj* inconvenient; **~lenk** ['-gəlɛŋk] *adj* awkward, clumsy; **~lernt** ['ʊn-] *adj* unskilled; **~mütlich** ['ʊn-] *adj* uncomfortable; **~nau** ['ʊn-] *adj* inaccurate, inexact; **~nießbar** ['ʊn-] *adj* uneatable; undrinkable; *colloq. Person:* unbearable; **~nügend** ['ʊn-] *adj* insufficient; **~pflegt** ['-gəpfleːkt] *adj* unkempt; **~rade** ['ʊn-] *adj* odd.

ungerecht ['ʊngərɛçt] *adj* unjust (**gegen** to); **₂ig-keit** *f* injustice.

ungern ['ʊngɛrn] *adv* unwillingly, grudgingly.

unge|schickt ['ʊngəʃɪkt] *adj* awkward, clumsy; **~schützt** ['ʊn-] *adj* unprotected; **~setzlich** ['ʊn-] *adj* illegal, unlawful; **~stört** ['ʊn-] *adj* undisturbed, uninterrupted; **~sund** ['ʊn-] *adj* unhealthy, unwholesome.

ungewiß ['ʊngəvɪs] *adj*
uncertain; **j-n im unge-**
wissen lassen keep s.o.
in suspense; **♀heit** *f* uncer-
tainty; *Spannung:* sus-
pense.

unge|wöhnlich ['ʊngə-
vø:nlɪç] *adj* unusual, un-
common; **♀ziefer** ['ʊngə-
tsi:fər] *n* (-s/*no pl*) vermin;
~zogen [-gɔtso:gən] *adj*
rude, uncivil; *Kind:*
naughty; **~zwungen**
['ʊn-] free (and easy).

ungläubig ['ʊnglɔybɪç]
adj incredulous.

unglaub|lich [ʊn'glaup-
lɪç] *adj* incredible; **~wür-**
dig ['ʊnglaupvʏrdɪç] *adj*
untrustworthy; incredible.

ungleich ['ʊnglaɪç] *adj*
unequal, different; **~mä-**
ßig *adj* uneven; irregular.

Unglück ['ʊnglʏk] *n*
(-[e]s/-e) misfortune;
schweres: calamity, disaster; bad od. ill luck; **♀lich**
adj unfortunate, unlucky;
unhappy; **♀licherweise**
[-'vaɪzə] *adv* unfortunately; **~sfall** *m* (-[e]s/*~e)
misadventure; accident.

un|gültig ['ʊngʏltɪç] *adj*
invalid; *Geld:* not current;
~günstig ['ʊn-] *adj* unfa-
vo(u)rable; disadvanta-
geous; **~handlich** *adj* un-
wieldy, bulky; **♀lich**
adj incurable; **~heimlich**
adj uncanny; *fig.* tremendous; **~höflich** *adj* impo-
lite, uncivil; **~hörbar** *adj*
inaudible; **~hygienisch**

adj insanitary.

Uniform [uni'fɔrm] *f* (-/
-en) uniform.

uninteressant ['ʊnɪntə-
resant] *adj* uninteresting,
boring.

Union [u'nio:n] *f* (-/-en)
union.

Universität [univerzi-
'tɛ:t] *f* (-/-en) university.

Universum [uni'verzʊm]
n (-s/*no pl*) universe.

unkenntlich ['ʊnkɛntlɪç]
adj unrecognizable; **♀nis** *f*
(-/*no pl*) ignorance.

un|klar ['ʊnkla:r] *adj* not
clear; obscure; *Antwort:*
vague; **♀kosten** *pl* costs
pl, expenses *pl*; **♀kraut** *n*
weed; **~leserlich** ['ʊnle-
zərlɪç] *adj* illegible;
~logisch *adj* illogical;
~lösbar ['-lø:sba:r] *adj*
insoluble; **~manierlich**
['-mani:rlɪç] *adj* unman-
nerly; **~mäßig** *adj* immoderate; *Trinken:* in-
temperate; **♀menge** *f*
enormous *od.* vast quan-
tity.

Unmensch ['ʊnmɛnʃ] *m*
(-en/-en) monster, brute;
♀lich *adj* inhuman, brutal.

un|mißverständlich
['ʊnmɪsferʃtɛntlɪç] *adj* un-
mistakable; **~mittelbar**
['ʊn-] *adj* immediate, direct; **~möbliert** ['ʊn-] *adj*
unfurnished; **~modern**
adj unfashionable;
~möglich ['ʊn-] *adj* im-
possible; **~moralisch**
['-mora:lɪʃ] *adj* immoral;

~**mündig** ['ʊn-] *adj* under age; ~**natürlich** ['ʊn] *adj* unnatural; *geziert:* affected; ~**nötig** ['ʊn-] *adj* unnecessary.

unord|entlich ['ʊnʔɔr-dəntlɪç] *adj* untidy; ♀**nung** *f* disorder, mess.

un|parteiisch ['ʊnpartaɪʃ] *adj* impartial, unbias(s)ed; ~**passend** *adj* unsuitable; improper; *un-angebracht:* inappropriate; ~**passierbar** adj impassable; ~**päßlich** ['-pɛslɪç] *adj* indisposed, unwell; ~**persönlich** *adj* impersonal; ~**praktisch** *adj* unpractical; ~**pünktlich** unpunctual; ~**rasiert** *adj* unshaved, unshaven.

unrecht ['ʊnrɛçt] *adj* wrong, (*fig.*) → **haben** be wrong; ♀ **n** (*-s/no pl*) wrong, injustice; **zu** ♀ wrongly; **j-m ein** ♀ **(an-)tun** wrong s.o.; ~**mäßig** *adj* unlawful.

un|regelmäßig ['ʊnrə:gəlmɛsɪç] *adj* irregular; ~**reif** *adj* unripe; *fig.* immature.

Unruh|e ['ʊnru:ə] *f* (*-/-n*) restlessness; *pol.* unrest; *fig.:* uneasiness; alarm; ~**en** *pl* disturbances *pl*, riots *pl*; ♀**ig** *adj* restless; *Meer:* rough; *fig.* uneasy.

uns [ʊns] *poss pron* (to) us; ~ **(selbst)** ourselves.

un|sachlich ['ʊnzaxlɪç] *adj* not objective; irrelevant; ~**sauber** *adj* dirty;

fig. a. unfair; ~**schädlich** *adj* harmless; ~**scharf** *adj* blurred; ~**schätzbar** [-ʃɛtsba:r] *adj* invaluable; ~**scheinbar** ['ʊn-] *adj* plain; ~**schicklich** *adj* improper, indecent; ~**schlüssig** ['-ʃlʏsɪç] *adj* irresolute.

Unschuld ['ʊnʃʊlt] *f* (*-/no pl*) innocence; ♀**ig** *adj* innocent.

unselbständig ['ʊnzɛlp-ʃtɛndɪç] *adj* dependent (on others).

unser ['ʊnzər] *poss pron* our; ours.

un|sicher ['ʊnzɪçər] *adj* unsteady; *gefährlich:* insecure; uncertain; ~**sichtbar** *adj* invisible; ♀**sinn** *m* (*-[e]s/no pl*) nonsense; ~**sittlich** *adj* indecent; ~**sozial** *adj* unsocial; ~**sterblich** *adj* immortal; ♀**stimmigkeit** ['-ʃtɪmɪç-kaɪt] *f* (*-/-en*) discrepancy; *Meinungsverschiedenheit:* dissension; ~**sympa-thisch** *adj* disagreeable; **er ist mir** ~**sympa-thisch** I don't like him; ~**tätig** *adj* inactive; idle.

unten ['ʊntən] *adv* below; downstairs; **von oben bis** ~ from top to bottom.

unter ['ʊntər] *prp* below, under; *zwischen:* among; *weniger als:* less than; *adj* lower.

Unter|arm ['ʊntərʔarm] *m* (*-[e]s/-e*) forearm; ~**bewußtsein** *n* (*-s/no* *pl*): **im ~** subconsciously; **♀bieten** [-'biːtən] *v/t* (*irr*) **Rekord:** lower, beat; **♀ung** *f* interruption; **♀binden** [-'bɪndən] *v/t* (*irr*) stop.

unterbrech|en ['untər-'brɛçən] *v/t* (*irr*) interrupt; *Reise:* break, *Am. a.* stop over; **♀ung** *f* interruption; break, *Am. a.* stopover.

unter|bringen ['untər-brɪŋən] *v/t* (*irr*) place; accommodate, lodge; **~dessen** [-'dɛsən] *adv* (in the) meantime, meanwhile; **~drücken** [-'drʏkən] *v/t* suppress; *unterjochen:* oppress; **~einander** [-?aɪ'nandər] *adv* one beneath the other; among one another; **~entwickelt** ['untər-] *adj* underdeveloped.

unterernähr|t ['untər?ɛr-neːrt] *adj* underfed, undernourished; **♀ung** *f* malnutrition.

Unter|führung [untər-'fyːruŋ] *f* (*-/-en*) subway, *Am.* underpass; **~gang** ['untər-] *m* (*-[e]s*) *ast.* setting; *Schiff:* sinking; *fig.* ruin; **~gebene** [-'geːbənə] *m, f* (*-n/-n*) inferior, subordinate; **♀gehen** ['untər-] *v/i* (*irr*) *ast.* set; sink.

Untergrund ['untər-grunt] *m* (*-[e]s/no pl*) subsoil; *pol.* underground; **~bahn** *f* underground (railway), *London:* tube, *Am.* subway.

unterhalb ['untərhalp] *prp* (*gen*) below, underneath.

Unterhalt ['untərhalt] *m* (*-[e]s/no pl*) maintenance; *Lebens♀:* subsistence, livelihood; **♀en** [-'haltən] *v/t* (*irr*) maintain; support; *zerstreuen etc.*: entertain, amuse; **sich ♀en** converse, talk; **sich ♀ut** enjoy o.s.; **~ung** *f* conversation, talk; entertainment.

Unter|hemd ['untərhɛmt] *n* (*-[e]s/-en*) vest, undershirt; **~holz** *n* (*-es/no pl*) undergrowth; **~hose** *f* (**e-e** a pair of) drawers *pl* *od.* pants *pl*; **♀irdisch** ['untər?ɪrdɪʃ] *adj* underground; **~kiefer** *m* lower jaw; **~kunft** [-kunft] *f* (*-/-ve*) accommodation, lodging; **~lage** *f* base; *Schreibunterlage:* pad; **~lagen** *pl* documents *pl*; **♀lassen** [-'lasən] *v/t* (*irr*) omit, neglect; **~leib** [-'untər-] *m* abdomen, belly; **♀liegen** [-'liːgən] *v/i* (*irr*) (*dat*) be defeated (by), *sp. a.* lose (to); *fig.* be subject (to); **~lippe** ['untər-] *f* lower lip; **~mieter** *m* lodger.

unternehm|en [untər-'neːmən] *v/t* (*irr*) undertake; **♀en** *n* (*-s/-*) enterprise; *econ.* business; **♀er** *m* entrepreneur; *Werkvertrag:* contractor; *Arbeitgeber:* employer; *indus-*

trialist; ~**ungslustig** adj enterprising.

Unter|offizier ['ʊntər-ʔofitsiːr] m non-commissioned officer; ~**redung** [-'reːdʊŋ] f conversation; interview.

Unterricht ['ʊntərrɪçt] m (-[e]s/no pl) instruction, lessons pl; **2en** [-'rɪçtən] v/t, v/i instruct, teach; **2en von** inform s.o. of; ~**sstunde** f lesson, bes. Am. period.

Unter|rock ['ʊntərrɔk] m (-[e]s/⁻e) slip; **2schätzen** [-'ʃɛtsən] v/t underestimate; **2scheiden** [-'ʃaɪdən] v/t (irr) distinguish; **sich 2scheiden** differ; ~**schenkel** ['ʊntər-] m shank.

Unterschied ['ʊntərʃiːt] m (-[e]s/-e) difference; **2lich** adj different; varying.

unterschlag|en [ʊntər-'ʃlaːgən] v/t (irr) embezzle; **2ung** f embezzlement.

unter|schreiben [ʊntər-'ʃraɪbən] v/t (irr) sign; **2schrift** ['ʊntər-] f signature; **2seeboot** ['ʊntər-] n s. **U-Boot;** ~**setzt** [-'zɛtst] adj squat, stocky; ~**st** ['ʊntərst] adj lowest, undermost; ~**stehen** [-'ʃteːən] v/refl (irr): **sich ~ dare;** ~**stellen** ['ʊntər-] v/t Auto: garage, park; **sich ~stellen** take shelter (**vor** from); ~**stellen** [-'ʃtɛlən] v/t assume, sug-

gest; **j-m et. ~** impute s.th. to s.o.; **j-m ..., daß ...** insinuate that s.o. ...; ~**streichen** [-'ʃtraɪçən] v/t (irr) underline; fig. emphasize.

unterstütz|en [ʊntər-'ʃtʏtsən] v/t support; **2zung** f support; assistance, aid; Beihilfe: relief.

untersuch|en [ʊntər'zuː-xən] v/t inquire into, investigate (a. jur.); prüfen: examine (a. med.); explore; **2ung** f inquiry (into), investigation (a. jur.); examination (a. med.); exploration; **2ungshaft** [-haft] f detention (on remand).

Unter|tasse ['ʊntərtasə] f (-/-n) saucer; **2tauchen** v/i dive; duck (a. v/t); fig. disappear; ~**teil** m, n lower part; ~**titel** m subtitle; Film: a. caption; ~**wäsche** f underclothes pl, underclothing, underwear; **2wegs** [-'veːks] adv on the od. one's way; **2werfen** [-'vɛrfən] v/t (irr) subject (**dat** to); **sich 2werfen** submit (**dat** to); **2würfig** [-'vʏrfɪç] adj subservient; **2zeichnen** [-'tsaɪçnən] v/t sign; **2ziehen** [-'tsiːən] v/t (irr) put on underneath; [-'tsiː-ən] v/refl sich e-r Operation **2ziehen** undergo an operation.

un|tragbar ['ʊntraːkbaːr] adj unbearable; ~**trennbar** adj inseparable;

~**treu** ['ʊn-] *adj* unfaithful; ~**tröstlich** ['-ˈtrøːstlɪç] *adj* inconsolable; 2**tugend** ['ʊn-] *f* (-/-**en**) vice.

unüber|legt ['ʊnʔyːbər-ˈleːkt] *adj* inconsiderate, thoughtless; ~**sichtlich** *adj* unclear, obscure; *Kurve:* blind; ~**windlich** ['-ˈvɪntlɪç] *adj* insurmountable.

ununterbrochen ['ʊn-ʔʊntərbrɔxən] *adj* uninterrupted; *unaufhörlich:* incessant.

unver|ändert ['ʊnfɛrʔɛn-dərt] *adj* unchanged; ~**antwortlich** *adj* irresponsible; ~**besserlich** [-fɛrˈbɛsərlɪç] *adj* incorrigible; ~**bindlich** ['ʊn-] *adj* not binding; *Frage:* non-committal; ~**daulich** *adj* indigestible; ~**dient** *adj* undeserved; ~**einbar** [-fɛrʔaɪnbaːr] *adj* incompatible; ~**geßlich** [-fɛrˈgɛslɪç] *adj* unforgettable; ~**gleichlich** [-fɛrˈglaɪçlɪç] *adj* incomparable; ~**heiratet** ['ʊnfɛrhaɪraː-tət] *adj* unmarried, single; ~**käuflich** ['ʊn-] *adj* not for sale; ~**letzt** *adj* uninjured, unhurt; ~**meidlich** [-fɛrˈmaɪtlɪç] *adj* inevitable; ~**mutet** ['ʊnfɛrmuː-tət] *adj* unexpected; ~**nünftig** ['ʊn-] *adj* unreasonable.

unverschämt ['ʊnfɛr-ˈʃɛːmt] *adj* impudent;

2**heit** *f* impudence, cheek.

unver|ständlich ['ʊnfɛr-ˈʃtɛntlɪç] *adj* unintelligible; *unbegreiflich:* incomprehensible; ~**zeihlich** [-fɛr-ˈtsaɪlɪç] *adj* unpardonable; ~**züglich** [-fɛrtsyːklɪç] *adj* immediate, instant.

unvoll|endet ['ʊnfɔlʔɛn-dət] *adj* unfinished; ~**kommen** ['ʊn-] *adj* imperfect; ~**ständig** ['ʊn-] *adj* incomplete.

unvor|bereitet ['ʊnfoːr-bəraɪtət] *adj* unprepared; ~**eingenommen** ['ʊn-foːr-] *adj* unprejudiced; ~**hergesehen** *adj* unforeseen; ~**sichtig** *adj* incautious; *unklug:* imprudent; ~**stellbar** [-ˈʃtɛlbaːr] *adj* unimaginable; ~**teilhaft** ['ʊnfɔrtaɪlhaft] *adj* unprofitable; unbecoming.

unwahr ['ʊnvaːr] *adj* untrue; 2**heit** *f* untruth; ~**scheinlich** *adj* improbable, unlikely.

un|weit ['ʊnvaɪt] *prp* (*gen od.* **von**) not far from; ~**wesentlich** ['ʊn-] *adj* immaterial (**für** to); 2**wetter** ['ʊn-] *n* (-**s**/-) tempest; violent thunderstorm; ~**wichtig** ['ʊn-] *adj* unimportant.

unwider|ruflich [ʊnviː-dərˈruːflɪç] *adj* irrevocable; ~**stehlich** [-ˈʃteːlɪç] *adj* irresistible.

unwiederbringlich [ʊnviː-dərˈbrɪŋlɪç] *adj* irretrievable.

Unwill|e ['ʊnvilə] m (-ns/ no pl), **~n** [-n] m (-s/no pl) indignation; **2ig** adj indignant; unwilling; **2kürlich** [-'kyːrliç] adj involuntary.

un|wirksam ['ʊnvirk- zaːm] adj ineffective; **~wirtlich** adj inhospitable; **~wissend** adj ignorant; unwise; **~wohl** adj unwell, indisposed; **~würdig** adj unworthy (gen of); **~zählig** [-'tsɛːliç] adj innumerable.

unzer|brechlich [ʊntsɛr- 'brɛçliç] adj unbreakable; **~trennlich** [-'trɛnliç] adj inseparable.

Un|zucht ['ʊntsuxt] f (-/no pl) sexual offen|ce, Am. -se; **2züchtig** ['-tsyçtiç] adj obscene.

unzufrieden ['ʊntsufriː- dən] adj discontented, dissatisfied; **2heit** f discontent, dissatisfaction.

unzu|gänglich ['ʊntsu- gɛŋliç] adj inaccessible; **~länglich** ['-lɛŋliç] adj insufficient; **~rech- nungsfähig** ['ʊn-] adj irresponsible; **~sammen- hängend** ['ʊn-] adj incoherent; **~verlässig** adj unreliable.

üppig ['ʏpiç] adj bot. luxuriant, exuberant; Essen: sumptuous; Figur: volup tuous.

ur|alt ['uːrʔalt] adj very old; **2aufführung** f première.

Uran [u'raːn] n (-s/no pl) uranium.

Urenkel ['uːrʔɛŋkəl] m (-s/-) etc. great-grandson, etc.

Urheber ['uːrheːbər] m (-s/-) author.

Urin [u'riːn] m (-s/-e) urine.

Urkunde ['uːrkundə] f (-/-n) document, deed; certificate.

Urlaub ['uːrlaup] m (-[e]s/-e) leave (of absence) (a. mil.); Ferien: holiday(s pl), bsd. Am. vacation; **~er** m holidaymaker, Am. vacationist.

Urne ['ʊrnə] f (-/-n) urn.

Ur|sache ['uːrzaxə] f (-/ -n) cause; Grund: reason; **keine ~sache!** don't mention it, you are welcome; **~sprung** m origin, source; **2sprünglich** [-ʃprʏŋliç] adj original.

Urteil ['ʊrtail] n (-s/-e) judg(e)ment; Strafmaß: sentence; **2en** ['ʊrtailən] v/i judge (**über j-n** s.o.); **~sspruch** m verdict.

Urwald ['uːrvalt] m (-[e]s/-er) prim(a)eval od. virgin forest.

V

Vakuum ['va:kuʊm] n (-s/
-kua) vacuum.

Vanille [va'nɪl(j)ə] f (-/no
pl) vanilla.

Varieté [varie'te:] n (-s/
-s) variety theatre, music-
hall, Am. vaudeville theater.

Vase ['va:zə] f (-/-n) vase.

Vater ['fa:tər] m (-s/ˆ)
father; ~land n mother
country.

väterlich ['fɛ:tərlɪç] adj
fatherly, paternal.

Vaterunser [fa:tər'ʔun-
zər] n (-s/-) the Lord's
Prayer.

Vegeta|rier [vege'ta:riər]
m (-s/-) vegetarian; 2~
risch [-rɪʃ] adj vegetarian;
~tion [-ta'tsĭo:n] f (-/
-en) vegetation.

Veilchen ['faɪlçən] n (-s/-)
violet.

Vene ['ve:nə] f (-/-n) vein.

Ventil [vɛn'ti:l] n (-s/-e)
valve; fig. vent, outlet;
~ation [-a'tsĭo:n] f (-/
-en) ventilation; ~ator
[-'la:tɔr] m (-s/-en) ventilator, fan.

verabred|en [fɛr'ʔapre:-
dən] v/t agree upon,
arrange; Ort, Zeit: appoint,
fix; sich ~en v/refl make
an appointment; 2ung f
appointment, colloq. date.

verab|scheuen [fɛr'ʔap-
ʃɔyən] v/t abhor, detest;
~schieden [-ʃi:dən] v/

refl: sich ~ (von) take
leave (of), say good-bye
(to).

ver|achten [fɛr'ʔaxtən]
v/t despise; ~ächtlich
[-'ʔɛçtlɪç] adj contempti-
ble; 2achtung f (-/no pl)
contempt; ~allgemei-
nern [-algə'maɪnərn] v/t
generalize; ~altet [-'ʔal-
tət] adj out of date.

veränder|lich [fɛr'ʔɛn-
dərlɪç] adj changeable, var-
iable; ~n [-'ʔɛndərn] v/t:
(sich) ~ alter, change;
2ung f change, alteration.

veranlassen [fɛr'ʔanla-
sən] v/t cause.

veranstalt|en [fɛr'ʔan-
ʃtaltən] v/t organize;
2ung f event; sp. event,
meeting, Am. meet.

verantwort|en [fɛr'ʔant-
vɔrtən] v/t take the responsibility for; sich ~en für
answer for; ~lich re-
sponsible; j-n ~lich ma-
chen für hold s.o. re-
sponsible for; 2ung f (-/no
pl) responsibility; ~ungs-
los [-lo:s] adj irrespon-
sible.

verarbeiten [fɛr'ʔarbaɪ-
tən] v/t make (zu into);
process; fig. digest;
~ärgern [-'ʔɛrgərn] v/t
vex, annoy.

Verb [vɛrp] n (-s/-en) gr.
verb.

Verband [fɛr'bant] m

(-[e]s/~e) *med.* dressing, bandage; association, union; **~(s)kasten** *m* first-aid box; **~(s)zeug** *n* dressing (material); first-aid kit.

ver|bannen [fɛr'banən] *v/t* banish (*a. fig.*), exile; **~bergen** [-'bɛrgən] *v/t* (*irr*) conceal, hide (**sich** o.s.).

verbesser|n [fɛr'bɛsərn] *v/t* improve; *berichtigen:* correct; **2ung** *f* improvement; correction.

verbeugen [fɛr'bɔygən] *v/refl:* **sich ~** bow (**vor** to); **2ung** *f* bow.

ver|biegen [fɛr'bi:gən] *v/t* (*irr*) twist; **~bieten** *v/t* (*irr*) forbid, prohibit; **~billigen** *v/t* reduce in price, cheapen.

verbind|en [fɛr'bɪndən] *v/t* (*irr*) *med.* dress, bind up; link (**mit** to), join; connect (*a. teleph.*); *teleph.* put *s.o.* through (**mit** to); **2ung** *f* union; combination; connection; *a.* connexion (*a. teleph., rail., tech.*); *Verkehrsweg:* communication; *chem.* compound; **sich in 2ung setzen mit** get in touch with, contact.

ver|blassen [fɛr'blasən] *v/i* fade; **~blüffen** [-'blʏfən] *v/t* amaze, perplex; **~blühen** *v/i* fade, wither; **~bluten** *v/i* bleed to death; **~borgen** [-'bɔrgən] *adj* hidden.

Verbot [fɛr'bo:t] *n* (-[e]s/-e) prohibition; **~sschild** *n* prohibition sign.

Verbrauch [fɛr'braux] *m* (-[e]s/*no pl*) consumption (**an** of); **2en** *v/t* consume, use up; **~er** *m* consumer; **2t** *adj Luft:* stale.

Verbrechen [fɛr'brɛçən] *n* (-s/-) crime, offen|ce, *Am.* -se; **~er** *m* criminal; **2risch** *adj* criminal.

verbreite|n [fɛr'braɪtən] *v/t:* **sich ~** spread; **~rn** [-'braɪtərn] *v/t:* (**sich**) widen, broaden.

ver|brennen [fɛr'brɛnən] *v/t, v/i (irr)* burn; *Leiche:* cremate; **2ung** *f* burning; cremation; *med.* burn.

ver|bringen [fɛr'brɪŋən] *v/t (irr)* spend, pass; **~brühen** [-'bry:ən] *v/t* scald (**sich** o.s.).

Verbund [fɛr'bunt] *m* (-[e]s/~e) *econ.* compound, combine.

verbünde|n [fɛr'bʏndən] *v/refl:* **sich ~** ally o.s. (**mit** to, with); **2te** *m, f* (-n/-n) ally, confederate.

ver|bürgen [fɛr'bʏrgən] *v/refl:* **sich ~ für** vouch for; **~büßen** *v/t:* **e-e Strafe ~** serve a sentence.

Verdacht [fɛr'daxt] *m* (-[e]s/*no pl*) suspicion.

verdächtig [fɛr'dɛçtɪç] *adj* suspicious; **~en** [-tɪgən] *v/t* suspect (**j-n** s.o., *gen* of); **2ung** *f* suspicion.

verdammen [fɛr'damən] *v/t* condemn; **~t** *adj, adv*

verdampfen

damned; *int. colloq.* damn (it)!; **~t kalt** beastly cold.

ver|dampfen [fɛr'dampfən] *v/i* evaporate; **~danken** [-'daŋkən] *v/t*: **j-m et. ~** owe s.th. to s.o.

verdau|en [fɛr'dauən] *v/t* digest; **~lich** *adj*: **leicht ~** easy to digest, light; **2ung** *f* (~/no *pl*) digestion; **2ungsstörung** *f* indigestion.

Verdeck [fɛr'dɛk] *n* (-[e]s/-e) *mot.* hood, top; **2en** *v/t* cover; hide.

ver|derben [fɛr'dɛrbən] *v/t* (*irr*) spoil; *v/i* Fleisch *etc.*: go bad; **sich den Magen ~derben** upset one's stomach; **~deutlichen** *v/t* make plain *od.* clear; **~dienen** *v/t* earn; *fig.* merit, deserve.

Verdienst[1] [fɛr'di:nst] *m* (-[e]s/-e) earnings *pl*; *Gewinn*: gain, profit.

Verdienst[2] *n* (-[e]s/-e) merit.

ver|doppeln [fɛr'dɔpəln] *v/t*: (**sich**) **~** double; **~dorben** [-'dɔrbən] *adj* Fleisch: tainted; *Magen*: upset; *fig.* corrupt; **~drängen** *v/t* displace; *psych.* repress; **~drehen** *v/t* distort, twist (*a.* fig.); Augen: roll; **~dreifachen** [-'draifaxən] *v/t*: (**sich**) **~** triple; **~dunkeln** *v/t* darken (*a.* sich); **~dünnen** [-'dʏnən] *v/t* dilute; **~dunsten** *v/i* evaporate; **~dursten** *v/i* die of thirst.

verehr|en [fɛr'ʔe:rən] *v/t* adore; revere; *eccl.* worship; **2er** *m* (-s/-) admirer; worship; **2ung** *f* (-/no *pl*) adoration; reverence; worship.

vereidigen [fɛr'ʔaidigən] *v/t* swear in.

Verein [fɛr'ʔain] *m* (-[e]s/-e) society, association; club.

vereinbar|en [fɛr'ʔainba:rən] *v/t* agree upon, arrange; **2ung** *f* agreement, arrangement.

vereinfachen [fɛr'ʔainfaxən] *v/t* simplify.

vereinig|en [fɛr'ʔainigən] *v/t*: (**sich**) **~** unite; **2ung** *f* union; society, association.

ver|engen [fɛr'ʔɛŋən] *v/t*: (**sich**) **~** narrow; **~erben** [-'ʔɛrbən] *v/t* leave; *biol.* transmit.

ver|fahren [fɛr'fa:rən] *v/i* (*irr*) proceed; **sich ~** *v/refl* lose one's way; **2 n** (-s/-) procedure; *jur.* proceedings *pl*; *tech.* process.

Verfall [fɛr'fal] *m* (-[e]s/ no *pl*) decay (*a.* fig.); **2en** *v/i* (*irr*) decay (*a.* fig.); Haus *etc.*: *a.* dilapidate; *ablaufen*: expire.

ver|färben [fɛr'fɛrbən] *v/refl*: **sich ~** change colo(u)r.

ver|fass|en [fɛr'fasən] *v/t* write; **2er** *m* author; **2ung** *f* condition; *pol.* constitution.

verfaulen [fɛrˈfaulən] v/i
rot, decay.

verfilm|en [fɛrˈfɪlmən] v/t
film; **2ung** f film od.
screen adaptation.

verfluch|en [fɛrˈfluːxən]
v/t curse; **∼t** adj damned;
int. colloq. damn (it)!

verfolge|n [fɛrˈfɔlgən] v/t
pursue (a. fig.); bsd. pol.
persecute; **Spuren:** follow;
2r m pursuer.

verfrüht [fɛrˈfryːt] adj premature.

verfüg|bar [fɛrˈfyːkbaːr]
adj available; **∼en** [-ˈfyː-
gən] v/t decree, order; v/i:
∼en über have at one's
disposal; **2ung** f decree,
order; disposal; **j-m zur
2ung stehen** od. **stel-
len** be od. place at s.o.'s
disposal.

verführe|n [fɛrˈfyːrən] v/t
seduce; **∼risch** [-ˈrɔrɪʃ] adj
seductive; tempting.

vergangen [fɛrˈɡaŋən]
adj gone, past; **2heit** f (-/
no pl) past; gr. past (tense).

Vergaser [fɛrˈɡaːzər] m
(-s/-) carburet(t)or.

vergeben [fɛrˈɡeːbən] v/t
(irr) Preis: award; Auftrag:
place; forgive; **∼lich** adj
vain; adv in vain.

vergehen [fɛrˈɡeːən] v/i
(irr) pass (away); **2** n (-s/-)
offen/ce, Am. -se.

ver|gessen [fɛrˈɡesən] v/t
(irr) forget; leave; **∼geß-
lich** adj forgetful;
∼geuden [-ˈɡɔydən] v/t
dissipate, squander.

vergewalti|gen [fɛrɡə-
ˈvaltɪɡən] v/t rape; **2gung**
f rape.

ver|gewissern v/refl:
sich ∼ make sure (gen of);
∼gießen v/t (irr) shed;
verschütten: spill.

vergift|en v/t poison (a.
fig.); **2ung** f poisoning.

Vergleich [fɛrˈɡlaɪç] m
(-[e]s/-e) comparison;
jur. compromise; **2bar**
[-baːr] adj comparable;
2en [-ˈɡlaɪçən] v/t (irr)
compare.

vergnüg|en [fɛrˈɡnyːgən]
v/t amuse; **sich ∼en** v/refl
amuse; enjoy o.s.; **2en**
n (-s/-) pleasure, enjoy-
ment; **∼t** adj merry, gay.

ver|golden [fɛrˈɡɔldən]
v/t gild; **∼graben** [-ˈɡraː-
bən] v/t (irr) bury;
∼griffen [-ˈɡrɪfən] adj
Ware: sold out; Buch: out
of print.

vergrößer|n [fɛrˈɡrøːsər-
sərn] v/t enlarge (a. phot.);
opt. magnify; **sich ∼n** v/
refl increase; **2ung** f phot.
enlargement; **2ungsglas**
n magnifying glass.

verhaft|en [fɛrˈhaftən] v/t
arrest; **2ung** f arrest.

verhalten [fɛrˈhaltən] v/
refl: **sich ∼** Sachlage: be;
Person: behave; **2** n (-s/no
pl) behavio(u)r, conduct.

Verhältnis [fɛrˈhɛltnɪs] n
(-ses/-se) proportion,
rate, relation; colloq. love-
affair; **∼se** pl conditions
pl, circumstances pl;

verhandeln

2mäßig adv comparatively, relatively; proportionally.

verhandeln [fer'handəln] v/i negotiate; **2lung** f negotiation; jur. trial.

ver|hängnisvoll [fer'hɛŋnisfɔl] adj fatal, disastrous; **~härmt** [-'hɛrmt] adj careworn; **~haßt** [-'hast] adj hated; Sache: hateful, odious; **~hauen** v/t (irr) thrash; **~heerend** [-'he:rənt] adj disastrous; **~heilen** v/i heal (up); **~heimlichen** v/t hide, conceal; **~heiraten** v/refl: sich ~ marry; **~hindern** v/t prevent; **~höhnen** v/t ridicule, mock.

Verhör [fer'hø:r] n (-[e]s/-e) interrogation, examination; **2en** v/t examine, interrogate; **sich 2en** v/refl hear wrong.

ver|hungern [fer'huŋərn] v/i starve; **~hüten** [-'hy:tən] v/t prevent; **~irren** v/refl: sich ~ lose one's way; **~jagen** v/t drive away.

Verkauf [fer'kauf] m (-[e]s/⁔e) sale; **2en** v/t sell; **zu 2en** for sale.

Verkäuf|er [fer'kɔyfər] m (-s/-) shop-assistant, Am. (sales)clerk, salesman; **~erin** f (-/-nen) shop-assistant, Am. (sales)clerk, saleswoman; **2lich** adj for sale.

Verkehr [fer'ke:r] m (-[e]s/no pl) traffic; Um-gang, Geschlechts2: intercourse; **2en** v/i Bus etc.: run; **2en in** frequent; **2en mit** associate od. mix with.

Verkehrs|ader [fer'ke:rs?a:dər] f (-/-n) arterial road; **~ampel** f (-/-n) traffic light(s pl); **~büro** n tourist office; **~hindernis** n obstruction; **~insel** f traffic island; **~minister** m Minister of Transport; **~mittel** n (means pl of) conveyance od. transport, Am. transportation; **~polizist** m traffic policeman od. constable, Am. a. traffic cop; **~schild** n traffic od. road sign; **~stauung** f, **~stockung** f [-ʃtauuŋ] f traffic block (congestion, jam); **~teilnehmer** m road user; **~unfall** m road accident; **~verein** m tourist office; **~vorschrift** f traffic regulation; **~zeichen** n traffic od. road sign.

ver|kehrt [fer'ke:rt] adj inverted, upside down; fig. wrong; **~kennen** v/t (irr) mistake, misjudge; **~klagen** v/t sue (auf, wegen for); **~kleiden** v/t disguise (sich o.s.); tech. face; **~kommen** adj decayed; sittlich: depraved, corrupt; **~krachen** colloq.: sich ~ fall out with; **~krüppelt** adj crippled; **~künden** ['kyndən] v/t announce; Urteil: pronounce; **~kür-**

zen *v/t* shorten.

Verlag [fɛr'laːk] *m* (-[e]s/ -e) publishing house, *the* publishers *pl.*

verlangen [fɛr'laŋən] *v/t* demand, require; *v/i* ~ **nach** ask for; 2 *n* (-s/-) desire.

verlängern [fɛr'lɛŋərn] *v/t* lengthen; extend.

Verlängerung *f* lengthening; extension; **~s-schnur** *f* extension cord.

ver|langsamen [fɛr'laŋza:mən] *v/t* slacken, slow down; **~lassen** *v/t* (*irr*) leave; forsake, abandon; **sich ~lassen auf** *v/refl* rely on; **~läßlich** [-'lɛslɪç] *adj* reliable.

Verlauf [fɛr'lauf] *m* (-[e]s/ ~e) course; 2**en** *v/i* (*irr*) *Vorgang:* go; *Straße etc.:* run; **sich** 2**en** *v/refl* lose one's way; *Menge:* disperse.

ver|legen [fɛr'le:gən] *v/t* mislay; transfer, remove; *Kabel etc.:* lay; *Termin:* put off, postpone; *Buch:* publish; *adj* embarrassed; **at a loss (um** for); 2**nheit** *f* embarrassment; *Klemme:* difficulty; 2**r** *m* publisher.

ver|leihen [fɛr'laɪən] *v/t* (*irr*) lend, *Am. a.* loan; *gegen Miete:* hire *od.* let out; *Preis:* award; **~lernen** *v/t* unlearn, forget; **~lesen** *v/t* (*irr*) read out; *Namen:* call over; **sich ~lesen** *v/refl* read wrong.

verletzen [fɛr'lɛtsən] *v/t*

hurt (**sich** o.s.), injure; *fig. a.* offend; 2**te** *m*, *f* (-n/ -n) injured person; **die** 2**ten** *pl* the injured *pl;* 2**ung** *f* injury.

verleugnen [fɛr'lɔygnən] *v/t* deny, disown.

verleumd|en [fɛr'lɔymdən] *v/t* slander; 2**ung** *f* slander, defamation, *jur. a.* libel.

verlieb|en [fɛr'li:bən] *v/ refl* fall in love (**in** with); **~t** *adj* in love (**in** with); *Blick:* amorous.

verlieren [fɛr'li:rən] *v/t* (*irr*) lose; *Blätter etc.:* shed.

verlob|en [fɛr'lo:bən] *v/ refl:* **sich ~** become engaged (**mit** to); 2**te** *m* (-n/ -n) fiancé; *f* (-n/-n) fiancée; **die** 2**ten** *pl* the engaged couple *sg;* 2**ung** *f* engagement.

ver|lockend [fɛr'lɔkənt] *adj* tempting; **~loren** [-'lo:rən] *adj* lost; *fig.* forlorn; **~lorengehen** *v/i* (*irr*) be lost; **~losen** *v/t* raffle; 2**lust** [-'lʊst] *m* (-[e]s/-e) loss; **~machen** *v/t* bequeath, leave; 2**mählung** [-'mɛ:lʊŋ] *f* (-/-en) wedding, marriage; **~mehren** [-'me:-rən] *v/t* increase; **sich ~mehren** increase; *zo.* multiply; **~meiden** *v/t* (*irr*) avoid; 2**merk** *m* (-[e]s/-e) note, entry; **~messen** *v/t* (*irr*) measure; *Land:* survey; *adj* presumptuous; **~mieten**

vermitteln

286

v/t let, rent; *jur.* lease; *Boote etc.*: hire (out); **zu ~mieten** *on od.* for hire; *Haus*: to (be) let; **~mischen** [-'mɪʃən] *v/t* mix, mingle, blend; **~missen** [-'mɪsən] *v/t* miss; **~mißt** *adj* missing.

vermittel|n [fer'mɪtəln] *v/t* procure; *Eindruck etc.*: give; *v/i* mediate (**zwischen** between); intercede (**bei** with; **für** for); **2ler** *m* mediator, go-between; **2lung** *f* mediation; intercession; *teleph.* (telephone) exchange.

Vermögen [fer'mø:gən] *n* (-s/-) ability, power; *Besitz*: property; *Geld*: fortune.

vermut|en [fer'mu:tən] *v/t* suppose, *Am. a.* guess; **~lich** *adj* presumable; **2ung** *f* supposition.

ver|nachlässigen [fer-'na:xlɛsɪgən] *v/t* neglect; **~nehmen** *v/t* (*irr*) hear, learn; *jur.* examine, interrogate; **~neigen** *v/refl*: **sich ~** bow (**vor** to); **~neinen** [-'naɪnən] *v/t* deny; *v/i* answer in the negative.

vernicht|en [fer'nɪçtən] *v/t* destroy; **2ung** *f* (-/no *pl*) destruction.

Ver|nunft [fer'nunft] *f* (-/ no *pl*) reason; **2nünftig** [-'nʏnftɪç] *adj* sensible, reasonable (*a. Preis*).

veröffentlich|en [fer-'ʔœfəntlɪçən] *v/t* publish;

2ung *f* publication.

ver|ordnen [fer'ʔɔrdnən] *v/t med.* order, prescribe; **~pachten** *v/t* rent, *jur.* lease.

verpack|en [fer'pakən] *v/t* pack (up); wrap (up); **2ung** *f* packing; *Material*: *a.* wrapping.

ver|passen [fer'pasən] *v/t* miss; **~pfänden** *v/t* pawn, pledge; **~pflanzen** *v/t* transplant (*a. med.*).

verpfleg|en [fer'pfle:gən] *v/t* board; feed; **2ung** *f* food; board.

ver|pflichten [fer'pflɪçtən] *v/t* oblige; engage; **sich ~pflichten** *v/refl* bind o.s.; **~pfuschen** *v/t colloq.* bungle, botch; **~prügeln** *v/t colloq.* thrash; **2putz** [-'pʊts] *m* (-es/-e) plaster.

Ver|rat [fer'ra:t] *m* (-[e]s/ no *pl*) betrayal; *pol.* treason; **2raten** *v/t* (*irr*): (**sich**) **~** betray (o.s.), give (o.s.) away; **~räter** [-'rɛ:-tər] *m* (-s/-) traitor.

ver|rechnen [fer'rɛçnən] *v/t*: **sich ~** miscalculate; *fig.* make a mistake; **~regnet** [-'re:gnət] *adj* rainy, wet.

verreis|en [fer'raɪzən] *v/i* go on a journey; **~t** *adj* away, out of town.

verrenk|en [fer'rɛŋkən] *v/t* dislocate (**sich et. s.th.**), luxate; **sich den Hals ~en** *fig.* crane one's neck, rubberneck; **2ung** *f* dislocation, luxation.

ver|riegeln [fɛrˈriːɡəln]
v/t bolt, bar; **~ringern**
[-ˈrɪŋərn] *v/t* diminish,
lessen (*a.* **sich**); *Geschwindigkeit:* slow up *od.* down;
~rosten *v/i* rust.

verrück|en [fɛrˈrykən] *v/t*
move, shift; **~t** *adj* mad,
crazy (*a. fig.:* **nach**
about); **2te** *m* (**-n/-n**)
lunatic, madman; *f* (**-n/-n**)
lunatic, madwoman.

verrutschen [fɛrˈrʊtʃən]
v/i slip.

Vers [fɛrs] *m* (**-es/-e**)
verse.

versag|en [fɛrˈzaːɡən] *v/t*
deny (**j-m et.** s.o. s.th.);
v/i fail; break down; **2en** *n*
(**-s/no pl**) **2r** *m* failure.

versalzen [fɛrˈzaltsən] *v/t*
oversalt.

versamm|eln [fɛrˈzaməln] *v/t* assemble; **sich
~eln** assemble, meet;
2lung *f* assembly,
meeting.

Versand [fɛrˈzant] *m*
(**-[e]s/no pl**) dispatch, *Am.
a.* shipment; *Post:* posting;
~geschäft *n*, **~haus** *n*
mail-order business *od.*
house.

ver|säumen [fɛrˈzɔymən]
v/t Pflicht: neglect; *verpassen:* miss; *Zeit:* lose;
~schaffen *v/t* procure,
get; **sich ~schaffen** obtain, get; *Geld:* raise;
~schärfen *v/refl:* **sich ~**
get worse; **~schenken** *v/t*
give away; **~schicken** *v/t*

send (away), dispatch, forward; **~schieben** *v/t* (*irr*)
zeitlich: put off, postpone.

verschieden [fɛrˈʃiːdən]
adj different; **~artig** *adj*
various.

ver|schiffen [fɛrˈʃɪfən] *v/t*
ship; **~schimmeln** *v/i* get
mo(u)ldy, *Am. a.* mo(u)ld;
~schlafen *v/i* oversleep
(o.s.); *adj* sleepy, drowsy;
2schlag *m* (**-[e]s/ᵕe**)
shed; **~schlagen** *adj*
cunning; **~schlechtern**
v/t deteriorate, make
worse; **sich ~schlechtern** *v/refl* deteriorate, get
worse; **~schließen** *v/t* (*irr*) lock; *Haus:* lock up;
~schlimmern *v/t* make
worse; **sich ~schlimmern** *v/refl* get worse;
~schlingen *v/t* (*irr*) devour (*a. fig.*); **~schlossen** [-ˈʃlɔsən] *adj* closed,
shut; *fig.* reserved;
~schlucken *v/t* swallow;
sich ~schlucken *v/refl*
choke; **2schluß** *m*
(**-sses/ᵕsse**) fastener;
Pfropfen: plug; *Stöpsel:*
stopper; *phot.* shutter;
~schmelzen *v/i* (*irr*)
melt, blend; *v/t tech.* fuse
(*a. fig.*); *fig.* merge (**mit**
in); **~schmerzen** *v/t* get
over (the loss of);
~schmieren *v/t* smear,
blur; **~schmutzen** *v/t*
soil, dirty; *Luft, Wasser:*
pollute; **~schneit**
[-ˈʃnaɪt] *adj* snow-covered;
Berggipfel: *a.* snow-

capped; **~schnüren**
[-'ʃnyːrən] v/t tie up;
~schollen [-'ʃɔlən] adj
missing; **~schonen** v/t
spare; **~schreiben** v/t
(irr) med. prescribe (**ge-gen** for); **sich ~schrei-ben** v/refl make a slip of
the pen; **~schrotten** v/t
scrap; **~schuldet** ['ʃʊl-dət] adj indebted, in debt;
~schütten v/t spill; j-n:
bury alive; **~schweigen**
v/t (irr) conceal;
~schwenden [-'ʃvɛn-dən] v/t waste, squander;
~schwiegen [-'ʃviːgən]
adj discreet; **~schwim-men** v/i (irr) become blurr-ed; **~schwinden**
[-'ʃvɪndən] v/i (irr) dis-appear, vanish;
~schwommen [-'ʃvɔ-mən] adj vague (a. fig.);
phot. blurred.
Verschwör|er [fɛr'ʃvøː-rər] m (-s/-) conspirator;
~ung f conspiracy, plot.
versehen [fɛr'zeːən] v/t
(irr) Haushalt: look after;
mit et. ~ provide with;
sich ~ v/refl make a mis-take; 2 n (-s/-) oversight,
mistake, slip; **aus** 2 =
~tlich adv by mistake.
Versehrte [fɛr'zeːrtə] m, f
(-n/-n) disabled person.
ver|senden [fɛr'zɛndən]
v/t (irr) send, dispatch, for-ward; **~sengen** v/t singe,
scorch; Beamte: transfer;
Schule: move up, Am. pro-

mote; verpfänden: pawn;
antworten: reply; **~setzen
in Lage** etc.: put od. place
into; **~seuchen** [-'zɔy-çən] v/t contaminate.
versicher|n [fɛr'zɪçərn]
v/t assure (a. Leben); be-teuern: protest; Leben,
Eigentum: insure; **sich** ~
insure od. assure o.s.; 2te
m, f (-n/-n) the insured;
2ung f assurance; insur-ance (company).
Versicherungs|gesell-schaft f insurance compa-ny; **~police** f insurance
policy.
ver|sickern [fɛr'zɪkərn]
v/i trickle away; **~sinken**
v/i (irr) sink.
Version [vɛr'zioːn] f (-/
-en) version.
versöhn|en [fɛr'zøːnən]
v/t reconcile; **sich** (**wie-der**) **~en** v/refl become
reconciled; 2ung f recon-ciliation.
ver|sorgen [fɛr'zɔrgən]
v/t provide, supply; 2ung
f (-/no pl) supply.
verspät|en [fɛr'ʃpɛːtən]
v/refl: **sich** ~ be late; et.
adj belated; 2ung f: ~ **ha-ben** be late.
ver|speisen [fɛr'ʃpaɪzən]
v/t eat (up); **~sperren** v/t
lock (up); bar, block (up),
obstruct (a. Sicht);
~spotten v/t scoff at, ri-dicule; **~sprechen** v/t (irr)
promise; **sich ~spre-chen** v/refl make a slip of
the tongue; 2sprechen n

(-s/-) promise; **~staat-lichen** [-'ʃta:tlıçən] v/t nationalize.

Verstand [fer'ʃtant] m (-[e]s/no pl) understanding; intelligence, intellect; Geist: mind, wits pl; Vernunft: reason.

verständligen [fer'ʃtendıgən] v/t inform, notify; **sich ~igen** v/refl fig. come to an understanding, **2igung** f understanding, agreement; teleph. communication; **~lich** adj intelligible; understandable; **2nis** n (-ses/no pl) comprehension, understanding.

verstärklen [fer'ʃterkən] v/t reinforce; strengthen; Ton: amplify; steigern: intensify; **2er** m amplifier; **2ung** f reinforcement.

verstaublen [fer'ʃtaubən] v/i get dusty; **~t** adj dusty.

verstauchlen [fer'ʃtauxən] v/t: **sich den Fuß ~** sprain one's foot; **2ung** f sprain.

verstauen [fer'ʃtauən] v/t stow away.

Versteck [fer'ʃtek] n (-[e]s/-e) hiding-place; **2en** v/t hide (a. **sich**), conceal.

verstehen [fer'ʃte:ən] v/t (irr) understand, colloq. get; einsehen: see; begreifen: comprehend; Sprache: know; **ich verstehe!** I see!; **sich mit j-m gut ~**

get on well with s.o.

Versteigerung [fer'ʃtaı-gəruŋ] f (-/-en) auction (sale).

verstelllbar [fer'ʃtelba:r] adj adjustable; **~en** v/t adjust; versperren: bar, block (up), obstruct.

ver|steuern [fer'ʃtɔyərn] v/t pay duty od. tax on; **~stimmt** [-'ʃtımt] adj out of tune; colloq. cross; **~stohlen** [-'ʃto:lən] adj furtive.

verstopflen [fer'ʃtɔpfən] v/t plug (up); **~t** adj Straße: blocked, congested; med. constipated; **2ung** f med. constipation.

verstorben [fer'ʃtɔrbən] adj late, deceased; **2e** m, f (-n/-n) the deceased.

Verstoß [fer'ʃto:s] m (-es/ve) offen/ce, Am. -se; **2en** v/i (irr) offend.

verstreichen [fer'ʃtraı-çən] v/i (irr) Zeit: pass, elapse; Frist: expire; **~streuen** v/t scatter; **~stümmeln** [-'ʃtyməln] v/t mutilate; **~stummen** v/i grow silent od. dumb.

Versuch [fer'zu:x] m (-[e]s/-e) attempt; trial; experiment; **2en** v/t try, attempt; kosten: taste; **~ung** f temptation.

ver|tagen [fer'ta:gən] v/t: (**sich**) ~ adjourn; **~tauschen** v/t exchange.

verteidiglen [fer'taıdı-gən] v/t defend (**sich** o.s.); **2er** m defender; jur. counsel for the defen|ce, *Am.* -se; *Fußball:* full-back; **2ung** *f* defen|ce, *Am.* -se; **2ungsminister** *m* Minister of Defence, *Am.* Secretary of Defense.

verteilen [fɛr'taɪlən] *v/t* distribute.

vertief|en [fɛr'tiːfən] *v/t:* **(sich)** ~ deepen; *v/refl* **sich ~ in** *fig.* become absorbed in; **2ung** *f* hollow.

vertikal [vɛrti'kaːl] *adj* vertical.

Vertrag [fɛr'traːk] *m* (-[e]s/⁻e) contract; *pol.* treaty; **2en** *v/t* (*irr*) endure, bear, stand; **diese Speise 2e ich nicht** this food does not agree with me; *v/refl:* **sich gut 2en** get on well.

vertrau|en [fɛr'traʊən] *v/i* trust (*j-m* s.o.); **2en** *n* (-*s*/ *no pl*) confidence, trust; **~lich** *adj* confidential; **~t** *adj* intimate, familiar.

vertreiben [fɛr'traɪbən] *v/t* (*irr*) drive away; expel **(aus** from); **sich die Zeit ~** pass one's time.

vertret|en [fɛr'treːtən] *v/t* (*irr*) represent; substitute for; *Ansicht:* hold; **2er** *m* representative; *econ.* commercial travel|(l)er, *bsd. Am.* travel(l)ing salesman.

ver|trocknen [fɛr'trɔknən] *v/i* dry up; **~trösten** *v/t* put off.

verunglück|en [fɛr'ʔʊnglʏkən] *v/i* have an accident; **tödlich ~en** be

killed in an accident; **2te** *m, f* (-*n*/-*n*) casualty.

ver|unreinigen [fɛr'ʔʊnraɪnɪɡən] *v/t* s. **verschmutzen**; **~untreuen** [-'ʔʊntrɔʏən] *v/t* embezzle; **~ursachen** [-'ʔuːrzaxən] *v/t* cause.

verurteil|en [fɛr'ʔʊrtaɪlən] *v/t* condemn (*a. fig.*); sentence; **2ung** *f* jur. conviction.

ver|vielfältigen [fɛr'fiːlfɛltɪɡən] *v/t* duplicate; **~vollkommnen** [-'fɔlkɔmnən] *v/t* perfect; **~vollständigen** *v/t* complete.

verwahr|lost [fɛr'vaːrloːst] *adj* neglected; **2ung** [-'vaːrʊŋ] *f* charge, custody.

verwalt|en [fɛr'valtən] *v/t* administer, manage; **2er** *m* administrator; manager; *Gutsverwalter:* steward; **2ung** *f* administration, management.

verwand|eln [fɛr'vandəln] *v/t* change (*a. sich*), turn, transform; **2lung** *f* change, transformation.

verwandt [fɛr'vant] *adj* related **(mit** to); **2e** *m, f* (-*n*/-*n*) relative, relation; **2schaft** *f* relationship; *Verwandte:* relations *pl*.

verwarnen [fɛr'varnən] *v/t* caution.

verwechs|eln [fɛr'vɛksəln] *v/t* mistake **(mit** for); confound, mix up (*with*); confuse; **2(e)lung** [-s(ə)lʊŋ] *f*

(-/-en) mistake.

ver|wegen [fɛr'veːgən] *adj* bold; **~weigern** *v/t* deny, refuse.

Verweis [fɛr'vaɪs] *m* (-es/-e) reprimand; rebuke, reproof; reference (**auf** to); **2en** *v/t* (irr): **j-n ~ auf** *et. od. an* j-n refer s.o. to.

ver|welken [fɛr'vɛlkən] *v/i* fade, wither. **~wendlen** [fɛr'vɛndən] *v/t* (*a. irr*) use, employ; *Zeit etc.*: spend (**auf** on); **2ung** *f* use, employment.

ver|werfen [fɛr'vɛrfən] *v/t* (irr) reject; **~werten** ['vɛːrtən] *v/t* turn to account, utilize; **~wirklichen** *v/t* realize.

ver|wirren [fɛr'vɪrən] *v/t* confuse; **2ung** *f* confusion.

ver|wischen ['fɛrvɪʃən] *v/t* blur; *Spuren*: cover up; **~witwet** ['vɪtvət] *adj* widowed; **~wöhnen** ['vøːnən] *v/t* spoil; **~worren** ['vɔrən] *adj* confused.

verwundlbar [fɛr'vʊntbaːr] *adj* vulnerable (*a. fig.*); **~en** [-'vʊndən] *v/t* wound.

Verwundlete *m* (-n/-n) wounded (soldier), casualty; **~ung** *f* wound, injury.

ver|wünschen [fɛr'vynʃən] *v/t* curse; **~wüsten** ['vyːstən] *v/t* devastate; **~zählen** *v/refl*: **sich ~** miscount; **~zaubern** *v/t* bewitch, enchant; **~zeh-**

~ren [-'tseːrən] *v/t* consume.

Verzeichnis [fɛr'tsaɪçnɪs] *n* (-ses/-se) list, catalog(ue); register.

verzeihlen [fɛr'tsaɪən] *v/t* (irr) pardon, forgive; **~en Sie!** excuse me!; **2ung** *f*: **~!** I beg your pardon!, sorry!

ver|zerren [fɛr'tsɛrən] *v/t* distort; **sich ~** *v/refl* become distorted.

Verzicht [fɛr'tsɪçt] *m* (-[e]s/-e) renunciation (**auf** of); **2en** [-'tsɪçtən] *v/i* renounce (**auf** *et.* s.th.); do without.

Verzierung [fɛr'tsiːruŋ] *f* (-/-en) decoration, ornament.

ver|zinsen [fɛr'tsɪnzən] *v/t* pay interest on. **~zögerln** [fɛr'tsøːgərn] *v/t* delay; **sich ~n** *v/refl* be delayed; **2ung** *f* delay.

ver|zollen [fɛr'tsɔlən] *v/t* pay duty on; **haben Sie et. zu ~?** have you anything to declare?

ver|zweiflleln [fɛr'tsvaɪfəln] *v/i* despair; **~elt** *adj* hopeless; *aussichtslos*: desperate; **2lung** *f* despair.

ver|zweigen [fɛr'tsvaɪgən] *v/refl*: **sich ~** ramify; *Straße*: branch.

Veto ['veːto] *n* (-s/-s) veto.

Vetter ['fɛtər] *m* (-s/-n) cousin.

Vieh [fiː] *n* (-[e]s/*no pl*) livestock; cattle; **~zucht** *f* (-/*no pl*) cattle-breeding.

viel [fi:l] *indef pron* much; **~e** *pl* many.

viel|beschäftigt ['fi:lbəʃɛftɪçt] *adj* very busy; **~fach** *adj* multiple; **~leicht** [fi'laɪçt] *adv* perhaps, maybe; **~mehr** ['fi:lme:r] *adv* rather; **~sagend** ['-za:gənt] *adj* significant; **~seitig** *adj* many-sided, versatile; **~versprechend** *adj* promising.

vier [fi:r] *adj* four; **2eck** ['-ʔɛk] *n* (-[e]s/-e) square, quadrangle; **~eckig** *adj* square; **2linge** ['-lɪŋə] *pl* quadruplets *pl*; **2taktmotor** *m* four-stroke engine; **~te** *adj* fourth.

Viertel ['fɪrtəl] *n* (-s/-) fourth (part); quarter; ~ **fünf**, (ein) ~ **nach vier** a quarter past four; **drei** ~ **vier** a quarter to (*Am.* a. of) four; **~finale** *n sp.* quarter-finals *pl*; **~jahr** *n* three months *pl*, quarter (of a year); **2jährlich** *adj* quarterly; *adv* every three months, quarterly; **~pfund** *n* quarter of a pound; **~stunde** *f* quarter of an hour.

viertens ['fɪrtəns] *adv* fourthly.

vierzehn ['fɪrtse:n] *adj* fourteen; ~ **Tage** *pl* a fortnight *sg*, two weeks *pl*; **~te** *adj* fourteenth.

vierzig ['fɪrtsɪç] *adj* forty; **~ste** *adj* fortieth.

Villa ['vɪla] *f* (-/**Villen**) villa.

violett [vio'lɛt] *adj* violet.

Violine [vio'li:nə] *f* (-/-e) violin.

Visum ['vi:zʊm] *n* (-s/**Visa**) visa.

Vitamin [vita'mi:n] *n* (-s/-e) vitamin.

Vizepräsident ['fi:tsə-, 'vi:tsə-] *m* (-en/-en) vice-president.

Vogel ['fo:gəl] *m* (-s/ᵘ) bird; **~perspektive** ['-pɛrspɛkti:və] *f* (-/no *pl*) bird's-eye view; **~scheuche** ['-ʃɔʏçə] *f* (-/-n) scarecrow.

Vokab|el [vo'ka:bəl] *f* (-/-n) word; **~ular** [-kabu'la:r] *n* (-s/-e) vocabulary.

Vokal [vo'ka:l] *m* (-s/-e) vowel.

Volk [fɔlk] *n* (-[e]s/ᵘer) people; nation.

Volks|hochschule ['fɔlksho:xʃu:lə] *f* (-/-n) adult evening classes *pl*; **~lied** *n* folk song; **~musik** *f* folk music; **~republik** *f* people's republic; **~schule** *f appr.* elementary *od.* primary school; **~stamm** *m* tribe; **~tanz** *m* folk dance; **~wirtschaft** *f* economics *sg*; political economy.

voll [fɔl] *adj* full; **gefüllt**: filled; *ganz*: whole, complete, entire; *Gesicht*: full, round; *adv* fully; in full.

voll|automatisch ['fɔl-ʔaʊtoma:tɪʃ] *adj* fully automatic; **2bad** *n* bath; **2bart** *m* full beard; **2beschäftigung** *f* (*-/no pl*) full employment; **~enden** ['-'?ɛndən] *v/t* finish, complete; **~endet** ['?ɛn-dət] *adj* perfect; **~füllen** ['fɔl-] *v/t* fill (up); **~ge-pfropft** ['-gəpfrɔpft] *adj* crammed, packed; **~gie-ßen** *v/t* (*irr*) fill (up).

völlig ['fœlɪç] *adj* entire, complete.

volljährig ['fɔljɛːrɪç] *adj* of age; **2jährigkeit** *f* (*-/no pl*) majority; **~klimatisiert** ['-klimatiziːrt] *adj* (fully) air-conditioned; **~kommen** ['-kɔmən] *adj* perfect; **2macht** ['fɔl-] *f* (*-/-en*): **~ haben** be authorized; **2milch** *f* whole milk; **2mond** *m* full moon; **2pension** *f* full board; **~schlank** *adj* plump, stout; **~ständig** *adj* complete; **~stopfen** *v/t* stuff, cram; **~tanken** *v/t mot.* fill up; **~zählig** ['-tsɛːlɪç] *adj* complete.

Volt [vɔlt] *n* (*-, -[e]s/-*) volt.

Volumen [voˈluːmən] *n* (*-s/-, -lumina* [-ˈmina]) volume.

von [fɔn] *prp* (*dat*) *räumlich, zeitlich:* from; *gen:* of; *pass:* by.

vor [foːr] *prp* (*dat, acc*) *räumlich:* in front of, before; *zeitlich:* before; **~ acht Tagen** a week ago; **5 Minuten ~ 12** five

minutes to (*Am. a.* of) twelve.

Vorlabend ['foːr?aːbənt] *m* eve; **~ahnung** *f* presentiment, foreboding.

voran [foˈran] *adv* at the head (*dat* of), in front (*dat* of), before (*dat*); **Kopf ~** head first; **~gehen** *v/i* (*irr*) lead the way, precede.

Voranmeldung ['foːr-?anmɛlduŋ] *f* advance reservation.

Vorarbeiter ['foːr?arbaɪtər] *m* (*-s/-*) foreman.

voraus [foˈraus] *adv* in front (*dat* of), ahead (*dat* of); **im ~** [foˈraus] in advance, beforehand; **~gehen** [foˈraus-] *v/i* (*irr*) s. **vorangehen**; **~gesetzt** *cj:* **~, daß** provided that; **~sagen** *v/t* foretell, predict; forecast; **~schikken** *v/t* send on in advance; **~sehen** *v/t* (*irr*) foresee; **2setzung** *f* presupposition; **~sichtlich** *adj* presumable, probable; **2zahlung** *f* advance payment.

Vorbehalt ['foːrbəhalt] *m* (*-[e]s/-e*) reservation, reserve.

vorbei [fɔrˈbaɪ] *adv räumlich:* by, past (an *s.o., s.th.*); *zeitlich:* over, past, gone; **~fahren** *v/i* (*irr*) drive past; **~gehen** *v/i* (*irr*) pass, go by; **~an** pass; **~lassen** *v/t* (*irr*) let pass.

vorbereitlen ['foːrbərai-

tən] v/t prepare; **2ung** f
preparation.
vorbestellen ['fo:rbəʃtɛl-
lən] v/t order in advance;
Zimmer etc.: book.
vorbeugen ['fo:rbɔygən]
v/i prevent; (**-e-r Sache**
s.th.); v/refl: **sich ~** bend
forward; **~d** adj preven-
tive.
Vorbild ['fo:rbɪlt] n
(-[e]s/-er) model; *fig. a.*
pattern; **2lich** adj exemplary.
vorbringen ['fo:rbrɪŋən]
v/t (irr) bring forward;
Meinung etc.: advance;
äußern: say.
vorder ['fordər] adj front,
fore; **2achse** f front axle;
2bein n foreleg; **2grund**
m foreground; **2rad** n
front wheel; **2seite** f
front; *Münze*: obverse;
2sitz m front seat; **~st** adj
foremost; **2teil** n, m front.
vordringen ['fo:rdrɪŋən]
v/i (irr) advance; **2druck**
m form, *Am. a.* blank;
~ehelich ['-ɛːəlɪç] adj
premarital; **~eilig** hasty,
rash, precipitate; **~ein-**
genommen adj preju-
diced; **~enthalten** v/t
(irr) keep back, withhold
(**j-m et.** s.th. from s.o.);
~erst ['-ʔeːrst] adv for the
time being; **2fahr** ['-faːr]
m (-en/-en) ancestor.
vorfahren ['fo:rfaːrən]
v/i (irr) drive up; **2t**
['-faːrt] f (-/no pl) right of
way; **2t(s)straße** f major

road.
Vorfall ['fo:rfal] m (-[e]s/
ᵛe) incident, event.
vorfinden ['fo:rfɪndən] v/t
(irr) find.
vorführen ['fo:rfyːrən]
v/t jur. bring (*dat* before);
demonstrate; show, pre-
sent; **2ung** f demonstration; presentation, show-
ing; *Aufführung*: performance.
Vorgang ['fo:rgaŋ] m
(-[e]s/**ᵛe**) incident, event;
process; **~gänger**
['-gɛŋər] m (-s/-) pre-
decessor; **~garten** m
front garden; **2geben** v/t
(irr) pretend; **~gebirge** n
foothills pl; **2gehen** v/i
(irr) lead the way; *Uhr*: be
fast, gain; *verfahren*: proceed; *sich ereignen*: go on,
happen; **~gesetzte** ['-gə-
zɛtstə] m, f (-n/-n)
superior; **2gestern** adv
the day before yesterday.
vorhaben ['fo:rhaːbən]
v/t intend, be going to
do s.th.; **2** n (-s/-) intention; plan; project.
vorhanden [fo:rˈhandən]
adj available; **~ sein** exist;
2sein n (-s/no pl) existence.
Vorhang ['fo:rhaŋ] m
(-[e]s/**ᵛe**) curtain; **~hän-**
geschloß n padlock.
vorher [fo:rˈheːr, 'fo:r-
heːr] adv before, previously; in advance; **~gehend**
adj preceding.
vorherrschend ['fo:rher-

ʃənt] *adj* predominant.

vor|hin [foːrˈhɪn, ˈ--]
adv a short while ago; **~ig**
[ˈfoːrɪç] *adj* last; **~jährig**
adj of last year, last year's;
2kenntnisse *pl*: **mit
guten ~n** in well-ground-
ed in.

vorkommen [ˈfoːrkɔmən]
v/i (*irr*) be found; *passieren*:
occur, happen; **2** *n* (-s/-)
Bergbau etc.: deposit(s *pl*);
(*no pl*) occurrence.

Vorkriegs... [ˈfoːrˈkriːks-]
pre-war ...

vorlad|en [ˈfoːrlaːdən] *v/t*
(*irr*) summon; **2ung** *f*
summons.

Vor|lage [ˈfoːrlaːgə] *f* (-/
-n) copy; *Muster*: pattern;
parl. bill; *Unterbreitung*:
presentation; *Fußball*:
pass; **2lassen** *v/t* (*irr*) let
pass; *empfangen*: let
pass; **2läufig** [-ˈlɔyfɪç] *adj* provisional, temporary; *adv*
for the time being; **2laut**
adj forward, pert; **~leben**
n past (life).

vorleg|en [ˈfoːrleːgən] *v/t*
produce; present; **j-m et.
~n** lay (place, put) s.th. before s.o.; **2r** *m* rug.

vorles|en [ˈfoːrleːzən] *v/t*
(*irr*): **j-m et. ~** read s.th.
(out) to s.o.; **2ung** *f* lecture (**über** on).

vorletzt [ˈfoːrletst] *adj* last
but one; **~e Nacht** the
night before last.

Vor|liebe [ˈfoːrliːbə] *f* (-/
-n) preference; **~marsch**
m mil. advance; **2merken**

---

v/t make a note of; reserve.

Vormittag [ˈfoːrmɪtaːk] *m*
(-[e]s/-e) morning; **am ~**
= **2s** *adv* in the morning.

Vormund [ˈfoːrmʊnt] *m*
(-[e]s/-e) guardian.

vorn [fɔrn] *adv* in front;
nach ~ forward; **von ~**
from the front; from the
beginning.

Vorname [ˈfoːrnaːmə] *m*
(-ns/-n) Christian name,
first name, *Am. a.* given
name.

vornehm [ˈfoːrneːm] *adj*
distinguished; *edel*: noble;
elegant; **~ tun** only *v.o.*
airs; **~en** *v/t* (*irr*): **sich et.
~** resolve to do s.th.

vornherein [ˈfɔrnhɛraɪn]
adv: **von ~** from the first
od. start.

Vorort [ˈfoːrˌʔɔrt] *m* (-[e]s
-e) suburb; **~(s)zug** *m*
suburban train.

Vor|rang [ˈfoːrraŋ] *m*
(-[e]s/*no pl*): **~ haben
vor** take precedence over,
have priority over; **~rat**
[ˈ-raːt] *m* (-[e]s/*¨-e*) store,
stock (an of); *pl a.* provisions *pl*, supplies *pl*; **2rä-
tig** [ˈ-rɛːtɪç] *adj econ.* on
hand, in stock; **~recht** *n*
privilege; **~richtung** *f* device; **~rücken** *v/t* move
forward; *v/i* advance;
~runde *f sp.* preliminary
round; **~saison** *f* dead od.
off season; **~satz** *m* intention; **2sätzlich** *adj* intentional, deliberate; *bsd. jur.*
wil(l)ful; **~schein** *m* (-s/

no pl): **zum ~ kommen** appear, turn up.

Vorschlag ['fo:rʃlaːk] *m* (-[e]s/ᵛe) proposal, suggestion; **2en** *v/t* (*irr*) propose, suggest.

Vor|schlußrunde *f sp.* semi-final; **~schrift** *f* regulation(s *pl*); **2schriftsmäßig** *adj* correct, proper; **~schule** *f* preschool; **~schuß** *m* advance; **2sehen** *v/t* (*irr*) design; plan; **sich 2sehen** *v/refl* take care, be careful; (be on one's) guard (**vor** against).

Vorsicht ['fo:rzɪçt] *f* (-/*no pl*): *Behutsamkeit:* care; **~!** look out!, be careful!; **~, Stufe!** mind the step!; **2ig** *adj* cautious; careful; **~smaßnahme** *f* (-/-n): **~n treffen** take precautions.

Vorsilbe ['fo:rzɪlbə] *f* (-/-n) *gr.* prefix.

Vorsitz ['fo:rzɪts] *m* (-es/ *no pl*) chair, presidency; **~ende** *m* (-n/-n) chairman, president.

vorsorgen ['fo:rzɔrgən] *v/i* make provisions; take precautions *od.* care.

Vorspeise ['fo:rʃpaɪzə] *f* (-/-n) hors d'œuvre.

Vorspiel ['fo:rʃpiːl] *n* (-[e]s/-e) prelude (*a. fig.*); **2en** *v/i* play; *v/t* play; **j-m et. ~** play s.th. to s.o.

Vor|sprung ['fo:rʃprʊŋ] *m* (-[e]s/ᵛe) *arch.* projection; *sp.* lead; *fig.* start, advantage; **~stadt** *f* suburb;

~stand *m* managing committee *od.* board; **2stehen** *v/i* (*irr*) project, protrude.

vorstell|en ['fo:rʃtɛlən] *v/t* put on; introduce (**j-n j-m** s.o. to s.o.); **sich ~en bei** have an interview with; **sich et. ~en** imagine s.th.; **2ung** *f* introduction, presentation; *thea.* performance; *fig.* idea.

Vor|strafe ['fo:rʃtraːfə] *f* (-/-n) previous conviction; **2täuschen** *v/t* feign, pretend.

Vorteil ['fɔrtaɪl] *m* (-s/-e) advantage; **2haft** *adj* advantageous (**für** to).

Vortrag ['fo:rtraːk] *m* (-[e]s/ᵛe) lecture; **e-n ~ halten** (give a) lecture; **2en** *v/t* (*irr*) recite; *Meinung:* express.

vorüber [fo:r'yːbər] *adv räumlich:* by, past; *zeitlich:* over; **~gehen** *v/i* (*irr*) pass, go by; **~gehend** *adj* passing; *zeitweilig:* temporary; **2gehende** *m* (-n/ -n) passer-by.

Vor|urteil ['fo:rʔʊrtaɪl] *n* (-s/-e) prejudice; **~verkauf** *m thea.* advance booking; **~wand** *m* (-[e]s/ᵛe) pretext, preten|ce, *Am.* -se.

vorwärts ['fɔrvɛrts] *adv* forward, onward; **~!**

let's go; **~kommen** *v/i*
(*irr*) (make) progress.
vor|weisen ['fo:rvaɪzən]
v/t (*irr*) *s.* **vorzeigen**;
~werfen *v/t* (*irr*): **j-m et.**
~ reproach s.o. with s.th.;
~wiegend ['-vi:gənt]
adv chiefly, mainly,
mostly.
Vorwort ['fo:rvɔrt] *n*
(-[e]s/-e) foreword; *des*
Autors: preface.
Vorwurf ['fo:rvʊrf] *m*
(-[e]s/ⁱe) reproach; **j-m**
e-n ~ od. Vorwürfe
machen reproach s.o.
(**wegen** with); **²svoll**

adj reproachful.
Vor|zeichen ['fo:rtsaɪ-
çən] *n* (-s/-) omen;
²zeigen *v/t* produce,
show; **²zeitig** *adj* premature; **²ziehen** *v/t* (*irr*)
Vorhänge: draw; *fig.* prefer; **~zug** *m* (-[e]s/ⁱe)
preference; *Vorteil*: advantage; *Wert*: merit; **²züg-**
lich *adj* excellent, exquisite.
vulgär [vʊlˈgɛ:r] *adj*
vulgar.
Vulkan [vʊlˈka:n] *m* (-s/
-e) volcano.

W

Waag|e ['va:gə] *f* (-/-n)
balance, (**e-e** a pair of)
scales *pl*; **²e(h)recht** *adj*
horizontal, level.
Wabe ['va:bə] *f* (-/-n)
honeycomb.
wach [vax] *adj* awake; **~**
werden wake up; **²e** *f* (-/
-n) watch, guard (*a. Per-*
son); *Polizeiwache*: police-
station; **~en** ['vaxən] *v/i*
(keep) watch; sit up (**bei**
with).
Wacholder [va'xɔldər] *m*
(-s/-) juniper; **~brannt-**
wein [-brantvaɪn] *m* gin.
Wachs [vaks] *n* (-es/-e)
wax.
wachsam ['vaxza:m] *adj*
watchful.
wachsen¹ ['vaksən] *v/t*
wax.
wachsen² *v/i* (*irr*) grow;

fig. increase.
Wächter ['vɛçtər] *m* (-s/-)
guard; *bsd. Nacht*²:
watchman.
Wacht|posten ['vaxt-] *m*
sentry; **~turm** *m* watch-
tower.
wack(e)lig ['vak(ə)lɪç]
adj shaky; *Möbel*: rickety;
~eln ['vakəln] *v/i* shake;
Tisch etc.: wobble; *Zahn*:
be loose.
Wade ['va:də] *f* (-/-n)
anat. calf.
Waffe ['vafə] *f* (-/-n)
weapon (*a. fig.*); *pl* a. arms
pl.
Waffel ['vafəl] *f* (-/-n) *bsd.*
*Eis*²: wafer.
Waffenstillstand ['va-
fənʃtɪlʃtant] *m* (-[e]s/ⁱe)
armistice, truce.
wagen ['va:gən] *v/t* ven-

ture (a. **sich**); risk; *sich getrauen*: dare.

Wagen m (-s/-) carriage; *Kraft2*: car; *rail. s.* **Waggon**; **~heber** ['he:bər] m jack; **~papiere** pl car documents pl; **~spur** f rut.

Waggon [va'gō:] m (-s/ -s) (railway) carriage, *Am.* (railroad) car.

Wahl [va:l] f (-/-en) choice; alternative; *Auslese*: selection; *pol.* election.

wählen ['vɛ:lən] v/t choose; *pol.* elect (*v/i* vote); *teleph.* dial; **2r** m voter; **2risch** adj particular.

Wahl|fach f optional subject, *Am.* elective; **~kampf** m election campaign; **~kreis** m constituency; **2los** adj indiscriminate; **~recht** n franchise; **~urne** ['-?ʊrnə] f ballotbox.

Wahnsinn ['va:nzɪn] m (-[e]s/*no pl*) insanity, madness (a. *fig.*); **2ig** adj insane, mad.

wahr [va:r] adj true; *wirklich*: real.

während ['vɛ:rənt] prp (*gen*) during; *cj* while; *Gegensatz*: whereas.

Wahr|heit [va:rhaɪt] f (-/ -en) truth; **2nehmbar** adj perceptible; **2nehmen** v/t (*irr*) perceive, notice; *Gelegenheit*: avail o.s. of; *Interessen*: look after; **~sagerin** ['-za:gərɪn] f (-/-nen) fortune-teller; **2scheinlich** [-'ʃaɪnlɪç]

adv probably, most *od.* very likely; **~scheinlichkeit** f probability, likelihood.

Währung ['vɛ:rʊŋ] f (-/ -en) currency.

Wahrzeichen ['va:rtsaɪçən] n (-s/-) landmark.

Waise ['vaɪzə] f (-/-n) orphan; **~nhaus** n orphanage.

Wal [va:l] m (-[e]s/-e) whale.

Wald [valt] m (-[e]s/ᵛer) wood, forest; **2ig** adj wooded, woody.

Wall [val] m (-[e]s/ᵛe) *mil.* rampart; *Erd2*: mound.

Wallach ['valax] m (-[e]s/ -e) gelding.

Wallfahrt ['valfa:rt] f (-/ -en) pilgrimage.

Walnuß ['va(:)lnʊs] f (-/ ᵛsse) walnut.

Walze ['valtsə] f (-/-n) roller; cylinder.

wälzen ['vɛltsən] v/t: (**sich**) ~ roll.

Walzer ['valtsər] m (-s/-) waltz.

Wand [vant] f (-/ᵛe) wall.

Wandel ['vandəl] m (-s/ *no pl*) change; **2n** *v/refl* **sich ~** change.

Wander|er ['vandərər] m (-s/-) wanderer; hiker; **2n** ['vandərn] *v/i* wander; hike; **~ung** f walking-tour, hike; **~weg** m footpath.

Wand|gemälde ['vant-] n mural (painting); **~lung** ['vandlʊŋ] f change;

~schrank m wall-cupboard; **~tafel** f blackboard.

Wange ['vaŋə] f (-/-n) cheek.

wankel|mütig ['vaŋkəlmy:tıç] adj fickle, inconstant; **~n** ['vaŋkən] v/i totter, stagger.

wann [van] interr adv when; s. **dann**; **seit ~?** how long?, since when?

Wanne ['vanə] f (-/-n) tub; bath(tub), colloq. tub.

Wanze ['vantsə] f (-/-n) bug, Am. a. bed-bug.

Wappen ['vapən] n (-s/-) coat of arms, arms pl.

Ware ['va:rə] f (-/-n) commodity; pl a. goods pl, merchandise sg, wares pl.

Waren|haus n department store; **~lager** n in stock; Raum: warehouse; **~probe** f sample; **~zeichen** n trademark.

warm [varm] adj warm; Essen: hot.

Wärm|e ['vɛrmə] f (-/no pl) warmth; phys. heat; **2en** v/t warm; **~flasche** f hot-water bottle.

Warn|dreieck ['varndraı'ɛk] n (-[e]s/-e) mot. warning triangle; **2en** ['varnən] v/t: **~ (vor)** warn (of, against), caution (against); **~signal** n danger signal; **~ung** f warning, caution.

warten ['vartən] v/i wait (auf for).

Wärter ['vɛrtər] m (-s/-)

attendant; Wächter: guard; Tier2: keeper; Pfleger: (male) nurse.

Warte|saal ['vartəza:l] m, **~zimmer** n waiting-room.

Wartung ['vartuŋ] f (-/no pl) maintenance.

warum [va'rum] interr adv why.

Warze ['vartsə] f (-/-n) wart; Brust2: nipple.

was [vas] interr pron what; **~ kostet das?** how much is this?

waschbar ['vaʃba:r] adj washable; **2becken** n wash-basin, Am. washbowl.

Wäsche ['vɛʃə] f (-/no pl) wash(ing); the laundry; Tisch2, Bett2: linen; Unter2: underwear; **~klammer** f clothes-peg, clothes-pin; **~leine** f clothes-line.

waschen ['vaʃən] v/t (irr) wash; **sich ~** (have a) wash; (sich) die Haare **~** wash od. shampoo one's hair; **~ und legen** a shampoo and set.

Wäscherei [vɛʃə'raı] f (-/-en) laundry.

Wasch|lappen m facecloth, Am. washcloth; **~maschine** f washing-machine, washer; **~pulver** n washing powder; **~raum** m wash-room.

Wasser ['vasər] n (-s/-) water; **~ballspiel** n water-polo; **~dampf** m steam; ⟨2⟩**dicht** adj waterproof; bsd. mar. watertight; **~fall** m waterfall; **~flugzeug** n seaplane; **~graben** m ditch; **~hahn** m tap, Am. a. faucet.

wässerig ['vɛsəriç] adj watery.

Wasser|kraftwerk n hydroelectric power station od. plant; **~leitung** f water-pipe(s pl).

wässern ['vɛsərn] v/t Heringe etc.: soak.

Wasser|pflanze f aquatic plant; **~rohr** n waterpipe; ⟨2⟩**scheu** adj afraid of water; **~ski** m: **~ fahren** water-ski; **~sport** m aquatic sports pl; **~stiefel** pl waders pl; **~stoff** m (no pl) hydrogen; **~stoffbombe** f hydrogen bomb, H-bomb; **~weg** m waterway; **auf dem ~weg** by water; **~welle** f waterwave; **~werk** n waterworks sg, pl.

wäßrig ['vɛsriç] watery.

waten ['va:tən] v/i wade.

watscheln ['va(:)tʃəln] v/i waddle.

Watt [vat] n (-[e]s/-) electr. watt.

Watte ['vatə] f (-/-n) cotton-wool; surgical cotton.

web|en ['ve:bən] v/t weave; **2stuhl** m loom.

Wechsel ['vɛksəl] m (-s/-) change; Geldzuwendung: allowance; econ. bill (of ex-

change); **~geld** n change; **~kurs** m rate of exchange; ⟨2⟩**n** ['vɛksəln] v/t change; variieren: vary; Worte: exchange; **~strom** m alternating current; **~stube** f exchange office.

weck|en ['vɛkən] v/t wake (up), rouse (a. fig.); **2r** m alarm-clock.

wedeln ['ve:dəln] v/i Skisport: wedel; **~ mit** wag.

weder ['ve:dər] cj: **~ ... noch** neither ... nor.

Weg [ve:k] m (-[e]s/-e) way (a. fig.); Straße: road; Pfad: path; Spazier⟨2⟩: walk.

weg [vɛk] adv away, off; **~gegangen, ~verloren:** gone; **ich muß ~** colloq. I must be off; **~bleiben** v/i (irr) stay away, drop off; **~bringen** v/t (irr) take away; Sachen: a. remove.

wegen ['ve:gən] prp (gen) because of, owing to.

weg|fahren ['vɛkfa:rən] v/t cart away; v/i leave; im Wagen: drive away; **~fallen** v/i (irr) be omitted; **~gehen** v/i (irr) go away; Ware: sell; **~jagen** v/t drive away; **~lassen** v/t (irr) let s.o. go; Sache: leave out, omit; **~laufen** v/i (irr) run away; **~nehmen** v/t (irr) take s.th. away; Zeit, Raum: take up; **~räumen** v/t clear away; **~schaffen** v/t remove.

Wegweiser ['ve:kvaɪzər]

m (**-s/-**) signpost; *fig.* guide.

weg|werfen ['vɛkvɛrfən] *v/t* (*irr*) throw away; **~wi- schen** *v/t* wipe off.

weh [ve:] *adj* sore; *adv*: ~ **tun** ache; hurt (**sich** o.s.); **j-m** ~ **tun** hurt s.o.

Wehen ['ve:ən] *pl* uterine contraction, labo(u)r *sg.*

wehen *v/i* blow.

wehmütig ['ve:my:tiç] *adj* wistful.

Wehr [ve:r] *n* (**-[e]s/-e**) weir.

Wehrdienst ['ve:rdi:nst] *m* military service; **~ver- weigerer** [-fɛrvaɪgərər] *m* (**-s/-**) conscientious objector.

wehr|en ['ve:rən] *v/refl*: **sich** ~ defend o.s.; **2los** ['-lo:s] *adj* defenceless, *Am.* defenseless.

Weib [vaɪp] *n* (**-[e]s/-er**) woman; **Ehefrau**: wife; **~chen** ['-çən] *n* (**-s/-**) *zo.* female; **2lich** *adj* female; *gr.*, *Wesensart*: feminine.

weich [vaɪç] *adj* soft (*a. fig.*); *Fleisch*: tender; *Ei*: soft-boiled.

Weiche ['vaɪçə] *f* (**-/-n**) *rail.*: switch; **~n** *pl a.* points *pl.*

weichen[1] ['vaɪçən] *v/i* (*irr*) give way, yield (*dat* to).

weichen[2] *v/t*, *v/i* soak.

Weide ['vaɪdə] *f* (**-/-n**) *bot.* willow; *agr.* pasture; **~land** *n* pasture; **2n** ['vaɪ- dən] *v/t*, *v/i* pasture, graze.

weiger|n ['vaɪgərn] *v/refl*:

---

sich ~ refuse; **2ung** *f* refusal.

weihen ['vaɪən] *v/t* *eccl.* consecrate.

Weiher ['vaɪər] *m* (**-s/-**) pond.

Weihnachten ['vaɪnaxtən] *n* (**-/-**) Christmas.

Weihnachts|abend ['vaɪnaxts-] *m* Christmas Eve; **~baum** *m* Christmas-tree; **~geschenk** *n* Christmas present; **~lied** *n* (Christmas) carol; **~mann** *m* Father Christmas, Santa Claus.

Weih|rauch ['vaɪraux] *m* (**-[e]s/no** *pl*) incense; **~wasser** *n* holy water.

weil [vaɪl] *cj* because; since, as.

Weile ['vaɪlə] *f* (**-/no** *pl*): **e-e** ~ a while.

Wein [vaɪn] *m* (**-[e]s/-e**) wine; **~stock**: vine; **~beere** *f* grape; **~berg** *m* vineyard; **~brand** *m* brandy.

weinen ['vaɪnən] *v/i* weep (**um**, **vor** for), cry (**vor** *Freude*: with, *Schmerz*: with).

Weinfaß *n* butt, wine-cask; **~karte** *f* wine-list; **~lese** ['-le:zə] *f* (**-/-n**) vintage; **~rebe** *f* vine; **~stock** *m* vine; **~traube** *f s.* Traube.

weise ['vaɪzə] *adj* wise.

Weise ['vaɪzə] *f* (**-/-n**) *mus.* melody, tune; *fig.* manner, way.

weisen ['vaɪzən] *v/i* (*irr*): ~ **auf** point at *od.* to; *v/t* (*irr*):

von sich ~ reject; *Beschuldigung*: deny.

Weis|heit ['vaɪshaɪt] *f* (-/-en) wisdom; ~**heitszahn** *m* wisdom-tooth.

weiß [vaɪs] *adj* white; 2**brot** *n* white bread; 2**e** *m* (-n/-n) white (man); 2**wein** *m* white wine.

Weisung ['vaɪzʊŋ] *f* (-/-en) direction, directive.

weit [vaɪt] *adj* wide; vast; *Reise, Weg*: long; wide(ly); ~ **entfernt** far away; **bei** ~**em** adv by far; **von** ~**em** adv from a distance; ~**ab** [-'ʔap] adv far away.

weiter ['vaɪtər] adj further; *Kosten etc.*: additional, extra; ~**e fünf Wochen** another five weeks; adv furthermore, moreover; ~**!** go on!; **nichts** ~ nothing more; **und so** ~ and so on; ~**fahren** v/i (*irr*) drive on; go on; ~**geben** v/t (*irr*) pass (**an** to); ~**gehen** v/i (*irr*) go on (a. *fig.*); move on; ~**kommen** v/i (*irr*) get on; ~**können** v/i (*irr*) be able to go on; ~**machen** v/i carry on.

weit|sichtig ['vaɪtzɪçtɪç] adj far-sighted; 2**sprung** *m* long (*Am.* broad) jump; ~**verbreitet** adj widespread.

Weizen ['vaɪtsən] *m* (-s/-) wheat; ~**mehl** *n* wheaten flour.

welch [vɛlç] *interr pron*

what, which; ~**er?** which one?; *rel pron* who, which, that.

Wellblech ['vɛlblɛç] *n* (-[e]s/*no pl*) corrugated iron.

Welle ['vɛlə] *f* (-/-n) wave; *tech.* shaft.

wellen ['vɛlən] v/t: (**sich**) ~ wave; 2**länge** *f* wave length; 2**linie** *f* wavy line; 2**reiten** *n* (-s/*no pl*) surf-riding, surfing.

wellig ['vɛlɪç] adj wavy.

Welt [vɛlt] *f* (-/-en) world; ~**all** ['-'ʔal] *n* (-s/*no pl*) universe; ~**berühmt** adj world-famous; ~**krieg** *m* world war; 2**lich** adj worldly; *diesseitig*: secular, temporal; ~**meister** *m* world champion; ~**raum** *m* space; ~**reise** *f* journey round the world; ~**rekord** *m* world record; ~**stadt** *f* metropolis; 2**weit** adj world-wide.

wem [ve:m] *interr pron* to whom, whom (*colloq.* who) ... to; **von** ~ who from, from whom.

wen [ve:n] *interr pron* whom, *colloq.* who.

Wende ['vɛndə] *f* (-/-n) turn; 2**n** ['vɛndən] v/t (a. *irr*) turn (about, round); **bitte** 2**n!** please turn over!; v/refl: **sich** 2**n** an turn to; *Auskunft etc.*: apply to (**wegen** for); v/i *mot.* turn; ~**punkt** *m* turn-ing-point.

wenig ['ve:nɪç] *indef pron*

little; ~e [-gə] *pl* few *pl*; ~er less; *pl* fewer; *math.* minus; **am** ~**sten** least (of all); 2**stens** ['-stəns] *adv* at least.

wenn [vɛn] *cj* when; *bedingend:* if.

wer [ve:r] *interr pron* who; *auswählend:* which; ~ **von euch?** which of you?; ~ **auch immer** who(so)ever.

Werbe|fernsehen ['vɛrbəfɛrnze:ən] *n* (-s/no *pl*) commercial television; ~**funk** *m* commercial broadcasting; 2n ['vɛrbən] *v/i (irr)* ~ **für** advertise; ~ **um** court; ~**sendung** *f* commercial.

Werbung ['vɛrbuŋ] *f* (-/-en) publicity, advertising.

werden ['ve:rdən] *v/i (irr)* become, get; *allmählich:* grow; *plötzlich:* blaß ~ etc. turn; **was will er (einmal)** ~? what is he going to be?; *v/aux:* **ich werde fahren** I shall drive; *s.* **gesund** *od.* **krank** ~.

werfen ['vɛrfən] *v/t, v/i (irr)* throw (**mit** ~ *s.th.*; **nach** at; *zo. Junge:* throw; *Schatten, Blick:* cast.

Werft [vɛrft] *f* (-/-en) dockyard, shipyard.

Werk [vɛrk] *n* (-[e]s/-e) work; *tech.* works *pl*; *Fabrik:* works *sg, pl*, factory; ~**meister** *m* foreman; ~**statt** ['-ʃtat] *f* (-/≈en)

workshop; ~**tag** *m* workday; 2**tags** *adv* on weekdays; ~**zeug** *n* (-[e]s/-e) tool, implement; *feines:* instrument.

wert [ve:rt] *adj* worth; *würdig:* worthy (*gen* of); **nichts** ~ worthless; 2 *m* (-[e]s/-e) value, worth; 2**gegenstand** *m* article of value; ~**los** *adj* worthless, valueless; 2**papiere** *pl* securities *pl*; 2**sachen** *pl* valuables *pl*; 2**voll** *adj* valuable, precious.

Wesen ['ve:zən] *n* (-s/-) *Lebe2:* being, creature; *Natur:* nature, character; 2**tlich** *adj* essential.

weshalb [vɛs'halp] *adv* why.

Wespe ['vɛspə] *f* (-/-n) wasp.

wessen ['vɛsən] *interr pron* whose; what ... of.

Weste ['vɛstə] *f* (-/-n) waistcoat; *econ. u. Am.* vest.

West|en *m)* ['vɛstən] west; 2**lich** *adj* west(erly); *Einfluß etc.:* western.

Wettlbewerb ['vɛtbəvɛrp] *m* (-[e]s/-e) competition; ~**e** ['vɛtə] *f* (-/-n) bet; 2n *v/i, v/t* bet; **mit j-m um et.** 2**en** bet s.o. s.th.

Wetter ['vɛtər] *n* (-s/-) weather; ~**bericht** *m* weather forecast; ~**lage** *f* weather conditions *pl*; ~**leuchten** *n* (-s/no *pl*) sheet-lightning; ~**vor-**

Wettkampf

hersage [-foːrˈheːrzaː-gə] f (-/-n) weather forecast.

Wettkampf [ˈvɛtkampf] m contest, competition; ⟂**kämpfer** m contestant; ⟂**lauf** m, ⟂**rennen** n (-s/-) race; ⟂**rüsten** n (-s/no pl) armament race; ⟂**streit** m contest.

wichtig [ˈvɪçtɪç] adj important; ⟂**keit** f importance.

wickeln [ˈvɪkəln] v/t wind; Baby: change.

Widder [ˈvɪdər] m (-s/-) ram.

wider [ˈviːdər] prp (acc) against, contrary to; ⟂**haken** m barb; ⟂**legen** [-ˈleːgən] v/t refute, disprove; ⟂**lich** adj repugnant, repulsive; ekelhaft: disgusting; ⟂**setzen** [-ˈzɛtsən] v/refl: **sich** ~ oppose; ⟂**spenstig** [-ˈʃpɛnstɪç] adj refractory; ⟂**sprechen** [-ˈʃprɛçən] v/i (irr) contradict; ⟂**spruch** m contradiction; opposition; ⟂**stand** m resistance (a. electr.); opposition; ⟂**standsfähig** [-fɛːɪç] adj resistant; ⟂**strebend** [-ˈʃtreːbənt] adj reluctant; ⟂**wärtig** [ˈviːdərvɛrtɪç] adj disgusting; ⟂**wille** m (-ns/no pl) aversion, dislike; Ekel: disgust; ⟂**willig** [-vɪlɪç] adj reluctant.

widmen [ˈvɪtmən] v/t dedicate; devote (**sich** o.s.).

wie [viː] interr adv how; Vergleich: as; like.

wieder [ˈviːdər] adv again; **immer** ~ again and again; s. **hin**; ⟂**aufbau** [-ˈʔaufbau] m (-[e]s/no pl) reconstruction, rebuilding; ⟂**aufnehmen** [-ˈʔaufneː-mən] v/t resume; ⟂**bekommen** [ˈviːdər-] v/t (irr) get back; ⟂**bringen** v/t (irr) bring back; give back; ⟂**erkennen** v/t (irr) recognize (**an** by); ⟂**finden** v/t (irr) find again; recover; ⟂**geben** v/t (irr) give back, return; darbieten etc.: render; ⟂**gutmachen** [ˈguːtma-xən] v/t make up for; ⟂**herstellen** [-ˈheːrʃtɛ-lən] v/t restore; ⟂**holen** [-ˈhoːlən] v/t repeat; ⟂**holung** f repetition; ⟂**kommen** [ˈviːdər-] v/i (irr) come back; return; ⟂**sehen** [ˈviːdər-] v/t (irr) (**sich**) ~ see od. meet again; ⟂**sehen** n (-s) reunion; **auf** ⟂**sehen**! goodbye!

Wiege [ˈviːgə] f (-/-n) cradle.

wiegen¹ [ˈviːgən] v/t, v/i (irr) weigh.

wiegen² v/t rock; ⟂**lied** n lullaby.

wiehern [ˈviːərn] v/i neigh, whinny.

Wiese [ˈviːzə] f (-/-n) meadow.

wieso [viˈzoː] interr adv why.

wieviel [viˈfiːl, ˈviːfiːl] interr adv how much; **vor** pl how many.

wild [vɪlt] *adj* wild; savage; 2 *n* (-[e]s/*no pl*) game; 2**dieb** *m* poacher; 2**hüter** [-hy:tər] *m* (-s/-) game-keeper; 2**leder** *n* suede; 2**nis** *f* (-/-se) wilderness, wild; 2**schwein** *n* wild boar.

Wille ['vɪlə] *m* (-ns/*rare* -n) will; **s-n ~n durchsetzen** have one's way; **~nskraft** *f* (-/*no pl*) will-power.

willkommen [vɪl'kɔmən] *adj* welcome.

wimmeln ['vɪməln] *v/i* swarm (**von** with).

wimmern ['vɪmərn] *v/i* whimper, whine.

Wimpel ['vɪmpəl] *m* (-s/-) pennant, pennon.

Wimper ['vɪmpər] *f* (-/-n) (eye)lash.

Wind [vɪnt] *m* (-[e]s/-e) wind.

Windel ['vɪndəl] *f* (-/-n) napkin, *Am.* diaper.

winden ['vɪndən] *v/t* (*irr*) wind, twist; **sich ~ vor** *v/refl* writhe with.

windig ['vɪndɪç] *adj* windy; 2**mühle** ['vɪnt-] *f* windmill; 2**pocken** *pl* chicken-pox *sg*; 2**schutzscheibe** *f* windscreen, *Am.* windshield; 2**stille** *f* calm; 2**stoß** *m* blast of wind, gust.

Windung ['vɪndʊŋ] *f* (-/-en) winding, turn; *Weg:* bend.

Wink [vɪŋk] *m* (-[e]s/-e)

sign; *fig.* hint.

Winkel ['vɪŋkəl] *m* (-s/-) *math.* angle; *Ecke:* corner, nook.

winken ['vɪŋkən] *v/i* wave (one's hand), signal (*dat* to); *v/t her~:* beckon.

winseln ['vɪnzəln] *v/i* whimper, whine.

Winter ['vɪntər] *m* (-s/-) winter; **im ~** in winter; 2**lich** *adj* wintry; **~schlußverkauf** *m* winter sale(s *pl*); **~sport** *m* winter sports *pl*.

winzig ['vɪntsɪç] *adj* tiny, diminutive.

Wipfel ['vɪpfəl] *m* (-s/-) (tree-)top.

wir [vi:r] *pers pron* we.

Wirbel ['vɪrbəl] *m* (-s/-) whirl, swirl; *Luft, Wasser:* eddy; *anat.* vertebra; 2**n** ['vɪrbəln] *v/i, v/t* whirl; **~säule** *f* spinal column; **~sturm** *m* cyclone, tornado.

wirk|en ['vɪrkən] *v/i* have an effect, operate; **beruhigend ~en** have a soothing effect; **~lich** *adj* real; 2**lichkeit** *f* reality; **~sam** [-za:m] *adj* effective; 2**ung** *f* effect; **~ungsvoll** *adj* effective.

wirr [vɪr] *adj* confused; *Rede:* incoherent; *Haare:* dishevel(l)ed.

Wirt [vɪrt] *m* (-[e]s/-e) host; landlord; landlady; **~in** *f* (-/-nen) hostess, landlady.

Wirtschaft ['vɪrtʃaft] *f* (-/

no pl) housekeeping; *Gemeinwesen:* economy; *(pl -en) s.* **Wirtshaus;** **~erin** ['vɪrts-nen) housekeeper; **2lich** *adj* economic; *haushälterisch:* economical; **~sminister** *m* Minister for Economic Affairs.

Wirtshaus ['vɪrts-] *n (-es/¨er)* pub(lic house), inn.

wischlen ['vɪʃən] *v/t, v/i* wipe; *Staub* **~en** dust; **2lappen** *m* dishcloth; floorcloth.

wissen ['vɪsən] *v/t (irr)* know; **2** *n (-s/no pl)* knowledge.

Wissenschaft ['vɪsən-ʃaft] *f (-/-en)* science; **~ler** *m (-s/-)* scientist; **2lich** *adj* scientific.

wissen|**swert** ['vɪsəns-ve:rt] *adj* worth knowing; **~tlich** *adv* knowingly.

witter|**n** ['vɪtərn] *v/t* scent, smell; **2ung** *f* weather; *hunt.* scent.

Witwe ['vɪtvə] *f (-/-n)* widow; **~r** *m* widower.

Witz [vɪts] *m (-es/-e)* wit; *Spaß:* joke; **2ig** *adj* witty, funny.

wo [vo:] *interr adv* where.

Woche ['vɔxə] *f (-/-n)* week.

Wochen|**ende** ['vɔxən-ʔɛndə] *n (-s/-n)* weekend; **2lang** *adv* for weeks; **~lohn** *m* weekly pay *od.* wages *pl;* **~markt** *m* weekly market; **~schau** *f* newsreel; **~tag** *m* weekday.

wöchentlich ['vœçəntlɪç]

adj, adv weekly; **einmal ~** once a week.

wo|**durch** [vo'dʊrç] *adv* by what?; how?; by what, whereby; **~für** [-'fy:r] *adv* for what?, what ... for ?; (in return) for which.

Woge [vo:gə] *f (-/-n)* wave *(a. fig.).*

wogegen [vo'ge:gən] *adv* against what?; against which.

wo|**her** [vo'he:r] *adv* from where?, where ... from?; **~hin** [vo'hɪn] *adv* where (... to?)

wohl [vo:l] *adv* well; *vermutend:* I suppose; **leben Sie ~!** farewell!; **2** *n (-[e]s/no pl):* **auf Ihr ~!** your health!; **zum ~!** *colloq.* cheers!; **2befinden** *n (-s/no pl)* well-being, (good) health; **2fahrt** *f (-/no pl)* welfare; **~habend** *adj* well-to-do; **~schmeckend** *adj* tasty; **2stand** *m (-[e]s/no pl)* prosperity; **2tätigkeit** *f* charity; **~tuend** *adj* pleasant; **~verdient** *adj* well-deserved; **2wollen** *n (-s/no pl)* goodwill, benevolence; *Gunst:* favo(u)r.

Wohn|**block** ['vo:nblɔk] *m (-[e]s/-s, ¨e)* block of flats, *Am.* apartment house; **2en** ['vo:nən] *v/i* live (**in** in, at; **bei j-m** with s.o.); **~haus** *n* residential building; **2haft** *adj* resident, living; **~ort** *m* domicile; **~sitz** *m* residence; **~ung** f flat, *Am.* apartment; **~wagen** m caravan, *Am.* trailer; **~zimmer** n sitting-room, living-room.

wölben ['vœlbən] v/t: **(sich)** ~ arch.

Wolf [vɔlf] m (-[e]s/⸚e) wolf.

Wolke ['vɔlkə] f (-/-n) cloud.

Wolken|bruch m cloudburst; **~kratzer** m skyscraper; **2los** [-lo:s] adj cloudless.

wolkig ['vɔlkiç] adj cloudy, clouded.

Woll|decke ['vɔldɛkə] f (-/-n) blanket; **~e** ['vɔlə] f (-/-n) wool.

wollen ['vɔlən] v/aux, v/t, v/i (irr) wish, desire; want; be willing; intend (to); be going to; *im Begriff sein:* be about to; *lieber* ~ prefer.

Wollstoff ['vɔlʃtɔf] m (-[e]s/-e) wool(l)en fabric; **~e** pl wool(l)ens pl.

wo|mit [vo'mɪt] adv with what?, what ... with?; with od. by which; **~nach** [-'na:x] adv what ... for?; **~ran** [-'ran] adv by what?, by which?; **~ran denkst du?** what are you thinking of?; **~rauf** [-'rauf] adv on what?, what ... on?; *danach:* whereupon, after which; **~rauf wartest du?** what are you waiting for?; **~raus** [-'raus] adv what ... from?; from which; **~rin** [-'rɪn] adv in

what?; in which, wherein.

Wort [vɔrt] n (-[e]s/⸚er, -e) word; *Ausdruck:* expression.

Wörterbuch ['vœrtər-bu:x] n (-[e]s/⸚er) dictionary.

wörtlich ['vœrtlɪç] adj literal.

wort|los ['vɔrtlo:s] adj without a word; **2schatz** m vocabulary; **2stellung** f gr. word order; **2wechsel** m dispute.

wo|rüber [vo'ry:bər] adv what ... about?; **~rum** [-'rum] adv about what?, what ... about?; about od. for which; **~rum handelt es sich?** what is it about?; **~von** [-'fɔn] adv what ... from od. of?; what ... about?; of od. from which; **~vor** [-'fo:r] adv what ... of?; of which; **~zu** [-'tsu:] adv what ... for?

Wrack [vrak] n (-[e]s/-s, -e) wreck.

wringen ['vrɪŋən] v/t (irr) wring.

Wucher ['vu:xər] m (-s/no pl) usury; **2n** v/i grow exuberantly; **~ung** f med. growth.

Wuchs [vu:ks] m (-es/no pl) growth; figure.

Wucht [vuxt] f (-/no pl) force; **2ig** adj heavy.

wühlen ['vy:lən] v/i dig; *Schwein:* root; ~ **in** rummage (about) in.

wulstig ['vʊlstiç] adj thick.

wund [vunt] adj sore; **~e**

Stelle sore; 2e *f* (-/-n) wound.

Wunder ['vʊndər] *n* (-s/-) miracle; *fig. a.* wonder, marvel; 2**bar** *adj* wonderful, marvel(l)ous; 2**n** ['vʊndərn] *v/t* surprise, astonish; *v/refl:* **sich** 2**n** be surprised (**über** at); astonished (**über** at); 2**schön** *adj* very beautiful; 2**voll** *adj* wonderful.

Wundstarrkrampf ['vʊntʃtarkrampf] *m* (-[e]s/*no pl*) tetanus.

Wunsch [vʊnʃ] *m* (-[e]s/ *ᵘe*) wish, desire; *Bitte:* request.

wünschen ['vʏnʃən] *v/t* wish, desire; **~swert** [-ve:rt] *adj* desirable.

Würde ['vʏrdə] *f* (-/-n) dignity.

würdig ['vʏrdiç] *adj* worthy (*gen* of); **~en** [-gən] *v/t* appreciate.

Wurf [vʊrf] *m* (-[e]s/*ᵘe*) throw, cast; *zo.* litter.

Würfel ['vʏrfəl] *m* (-s/-) cube; *Spiel2:* die (*pl* dice); 2**n** *v/i* (play) dice; **~zuk-ker** *m* lump sugar.

Wurfgeschoß ['vʊrfgə-ʃos] *n* (-sses/-sse) missile.

würgen ['vʏrgən] *v/t* choke, strangle; *v/i* choke; *Erbrechen:* retch.

Wurm [vʊrm] *m* (-[e]s/ *ᵘer*) worm; 2**stichig** [-ʃtıçıç] *adj* worm-eaten, wormy.

Wurst [vʊrst] *f* (-/*ᵘe*) sausage.

Würstchen ['vʏrstçən] *n* (-s/-) (small) sausage.

Würze ['vʏrtsə] *f* (-/-n) *Gewürz:* spice; *Aroma:* seasoning, flavo(u)r.

Wurzel ['vʊrtsəl] *f* (-/-n) root.

würz|en ['vʏrtsən] *v/t* spice, season, flavo(u)r; **~ig** *adj* spicy, well-seasoned.

wüst [vy:st] *adj* desert, waste; *wirr:* confused; *roh:* rude; 2e ['vy:stə] *f* (-/-n) desert, wilderness.

Wut [vu:t] *f* (-/*no pl*) rage, fury.

wüten ['vy:tən] *v/i* rage; **~d** *adj* furious, *bsd. Am. a.* mad.

X, Y

x-beliebig ['ıksbə'li:-bıç] *adj:* **jede(r, -s) ~e ...** any ...

x-mal ['ıksma:l] *adv* many times, *sl.* umpteen times.

x-te ['ıkstə] *adj:* **zum ~n**

Male for the umpteenth time.

Yacht [jaxt] *f* (-/-en) yacht.

Z

Zack|e ['tsakə] f (-/-n); ~**en** m (-s/-) (sharp) point; **Zinke**: prong; **Fels**: jag; **2ig** adj jagged.

zaghaft ['tsa:khaft] adj timid.

zäh [tsɛ:] adj tough; = ~**flüssig** viscid, viscous, sticky.

Zahl [tsa:l] f (-/-en) number; **Ziffer**: figure; cipher; **2bar** ['-ba:r] adj payable.

zahlbar ['tsɛ:lba:r] adj countable.

zahlen ['tsa:lən] v/t, v/i pay; **Restaurant**: ~ (, bitte)! the bill (Am. the check), please!

zähle|n ['tsɛ:lən] v/t, v/i count; ~**n zu** count among; **2r** m tech. meter.

Zahl|karte ['tsa:lkartə] f (-/-n) appr. money-order form; **2los** [-lo:s] adj innumerable, countless; **2reich** adj numerous; adv in great number; ~**tag** m pay-day; ~**ung** f payment; ~**ungsbedingungen** pl terms pl of payment; ~**ungsmittel** n currency.

zahm [tsa:m] adj tame, domesticated.

zähmen ['tsɛ:mən] v/t tame, domesticate.

Zahn [tsa:n] m (-[e]s/ue) tooth; **tech.** tooth, cog; **e-n ~ bekommen** cut a tooth; ~**arzt** m dentist;

~**bürste** f toothbrush; ~**creme** f toothpaste; ~**fleisch** n gums pl; **2los** [-lo:s] adj toothless; ~**lücke** f gap between the teeth; ~**pasta** [-pasta] f (-/-sten) toothpaste; ~**rad** n cogwheel; ~**radbahn** f rack-railway; ~**schmerzen** pl toothache sg; ~**stocher** [-ʃtɔxər] m (-s/-) toothpick.

Zange ['tsaŋə] f (-/-n) (e-e a pair of) tongs pl; **med.**, zo. forceps sg, pl.

zanken ['tsaŋkən] v/i scold (**mit j-m** s.o.); v/refl: **sich** ~ quarrel.

zänkisch ['tsɛŋkiʃ] adj bickering, nagging.

Zäpfchen ['tsɛpfçən] n (-s/-) anat. uvula; med. suppository.

Zapf|en ['tsapfən] m (-s/-) plug; **Pflock**: peg, pin; **Spund**: bung; **Drehzapfen**: pivot; **bot.** cone; **2en** v/t tap; ~**hahn** m tap, Am. faucet; ~**säule** f petrol pump.

zappeln ['tsapəln] v/i struggle; **vor Unruhe**: fidget.

zart [tsa:rt] adj tender, soft, delicate; **sanft**: gentle.

zärtlich ['tsɛ:rtlɪç] adj tender, loving; **2keit** f tenderness; **Liebkosung**: caress.

Zauber ['tsaubər] m (-s/-)

spell, charm, magic (*alle a. fig.*); *fig.* enchantment; **~er** [-bərər] *m* sorcerer, magician; **2haft** *adj* fig. enchanting; **~künstler** *m* magician, conjurer; **2n** *v/t, v/i* conjure.

Zaum [tsaυm] *m* (-[e]s/⸚e) bridle.

zäumen ['tsɔymən] *v/t* bridle.

Zaumzeug *n* bridle.

Zaun [tsaυn] *m* (-[e]s/⸚e) fence; **~pfahl** *m* pale.

Zebrastreifen ['tse:bra-ʃtraɪfən] *m* (-s/-) zebra crossing.

Zeche ['tsεçə] *f* (-/-n) score, bill; *Bergbau:* mine; coal-mine, (coal) pit, colliery.

Zeh [tse:] *m* (-s/-en), **~e** *f* (-/-n) toe; **~enspitze** *f*: **auf ~n** on tiptoe.

zehn [tse:n] *adj* ten; **2kampf** *m* decathlon; **~te** *adj* tenth; **2tel** *n* (-s/-) tenth (part); **~tens** *adv* tenthly.

Zeichen ['tsaɪçən] *n* (-s/-) sign, token; *Merk2:* mark; *Signal:* signal; **~block** *m* drawing-block; **~papier** *n* drawing-paper; **~stift** *m* pencil, crayon; **~trickfilm** *m* (animated) cartoon.

zeichn|en ['tsaɪçnən] *v/t, v/i* draw; **2er** *m* draftsman, draughtsman; designer; **2ung** *f* drawing; design; *zo.* marking.

Zeige|finger ['tsaɪgə-fiŋər] *m* (-s/-) forefinger,

index (finger); **2n** ['tsaɪ-gən] *v/t* show, point out; demonstrate; *v/i* point (**auf** *at*; **nach** to); **~r** *m* *Uhr:* hand.

Zeile ['tsaɪlə] *f* (-/-n) line.

Zeit [tsaɪt] *f* (-/-en) time; *s.*
Zeitraum; freie ~ spare time; **laß dir ~!** take your time; **~abschnitt** *m* period; **~alter** *n* age; **2gemäß** *adj* modern, up-to-date; **~genosse** *m* contemporary; **2genössisch** ['-gənœsɪʃ] *adj* contemporary; **2ig** *adj* early; *adv* on time; **~karte** *f* season-ticket, *Am.* commutation ticket; **2lich** *adj* time ...; *adv:* **et. 2lich abstimmen** time s.th.; **2lich zusammenfallen** coincide; **~lupenaufnahme** ['-lu:pən-ʔaʊfna:mə] *f* Film: slow-motion picture; **~punkt** *m* moment; **~raum** *m* period, space (of time); **~schrift** *f* journal, periodical, magazine; **~ung** *f* (news)paper, journal.

Zeitungs|kiosk ['tsaɪ-tυŋskiɔsk] *m* (-[e]s/-e) newsstand; **~papier** *f* press item; **~verkäufer** *m* newsvendor.

Zeit|verlust ['tsaɪtfɛrlυst] *m* loss of time; **~verschwendung** *f* waste of time; **~vertreib** ['-fɛr-traɪp] *m* (-[e]s/-e) pastime; **2weise** *adv* at times; **~zeichen** *n* time signal.

Zelle [ˈtsɛlə] f (-/-n) cell; **~stoff** m, **~ulose** [tseluˈloːzə] f (-/no pl) cellulose.

Zelt [tsɛlt] n (-[e]s/-e) tent; **2en** v/i camp; go camping; **~lager** n camp; **~platz** m camping-ground.

Zement [tseˈment] m (-[e]s/-e) cement.

Zensur [tsɛnˈzuːr] f (-/-en) censorship; Schule: mark, Am. a. grade.

Zentimeter [tsɛntiˈmeːtər] m u. n (-s/-) centimetre, Am. -er.

Zentner [ˈtsɛntnər] m (-s/-) centner, metric hundredweight (50 kilograms).

zentral [tsɛnˈtraːl] adj central; **2e** [-ˈtraːlə] f (-/-n) central office; teleph. (telephone) exchange; **2heizung** f central heating.

Zentrum [ˈtsɛntrum] n (-s/-tren) centre, Am. -er.

zerbrechen [tsɛrˈbrɛçən] v/i, v/t (irr) break (into pieces); **sich den Kopf ~en** rack one's brains; **~lich** adj breakable, fragile.

zerbröckeln [tsɛrˈbrœkəln] v/i, v/t crumble; **~drücken** v/t crush; Kleid: crease.

Zeremonie [tseremoˈniː] f (-/-n) ceremony.

Zerfall [tsɛrˈfal] m (-[e]s/ no pl) decay; **2en** [-ˈfalən] v/i (irr) fall into pieces, decay (a. fig.).

zerfetzen [tsɛrˈfɛtsən] v/t tear to pieces; **~fließen** v/i (irr) melt; chem. dissolve; **~fressen** v/t (irr) eat; chem. corrode; **~gehen** v/i (irr) melt; **~kauen** v/t chew; **~kleinern** v/t cut up; mince; **~knirscht** [-ˈknirʃt] adj contrite; **~knittern** v/t (c)rumple, wrinkle, crease; **~knüllen** [-ˈknylən] v/t crumple up; **~kratzen** v/t scratch; **~legen** v/t take apart od. to pieces; Fleisch: carve; **~lumpt** [-ˈlumpt] adj ragged; **~mahlen** v/t (irr) grind; **~platzen** v/i burst; explode; **~quetschen** v/t crush, squash; bsd. Kartoffeln: mash; **~reiben** v/t (irr) grind, pulverize; **~reißen** v/t (irr) tear, rip up; v/i tear; Seil etc.: break.

zerren [ˈtsɛrən] v/t drag; tug; med. strain; v/i: **~en an** pull od. tug at; **2ung** f med. strain.

zersägen [tsɛrˈzɛːgən] v/t saw up; **~schellen** [-ˈʃɛlən] v/i be smashed; Schiff: be wrecked; **~schlagen** v/t (irr) break od. smash (to pieces); **~schmettern** [-ˈʃmɛtərn] v/t smash; **~schneiden** v/t (irr) cut in two; cut up; **~setzen** v/t: (sich) ~ decompose; **~splittern** v/t, v/i split, splinter; v/i burst; Glas: crack.

zerstäubeln [tsɛr'ʃtɔy-bən] v/t spray; **2r** m sprayer, atomizer.

zerstör|en [tsɛr'ʃtø:rən] v/t destroy; **2er** m destroyer (a. mar.); **2ung** f destruction.

zerstreu|en [tsɛr'ʃtrɔyən] v/t disperse, scatter (a. **sich**); Zweifel etc.: dissipate; **sich** ~en v/refl fig. amuse o.s.; **~t** adj fig. absent(-minded); **2ung** f diversion, amusement.

zer|stückeln [tsɛr'ʃty-kəln] v/t cut up; **~teilen** v/t divide; **~treten** v/t (irr) walk all over; crush; **~trümmern** ['-trymərn] v/t smash; **~zaust** ['-tsaust] adj tousled.

Zettel ['tsɛtəl] m (-s/-) slip (of paper); Preis2 etc.: ticket; Klebe2: label.

Zeug [tsɔyk] n (-[e]s/no pl) stuff (a. fig. contp.), material; things pl; **dummes ~!** nonsense! rubbish!

Zeug|e ['tsɔygə] m (-n/-n) witness; **2en** ['tsɔygən] v/t biol. become the father of; **~en von** show s.th.; **~enaussage** f testimony, evidence; **~in** f (-/-nen) (female) witness; **~nis** n (-ses/-se) jur. testimony, evidence; Bescheinigung: certificate; (school) report, Am. report card.

Zickzack ['tsɪktsak] m (-[e]s/-e) zigzag; **im ~ fahren** etc. zigzag.

Ziege ['tsi:gə] f (-/-n)

(she-)goat, nanny goat.

Ziegel ['tsi:gəl] m (-s/-) brick; Dach2: tile; **~stein** m brick.

Ziegen|bock ['tsi:gən-bɔk] m (-[e]s/-e) he-goat; **~leder** n kid; **~peter** ['-pe:tər] m (-s/-) med. mumps.

ziehen ['tsi:ən] v/t (irr) pull; draw (a. Strich); Hut: take off; Graben: dig; Zahn: draw, extract; **Aufmerksamkeit auf sich ~** attract attention; **sich ~** extend, stretch; **sich in die Länge ~** drag on; v/i pull (an at); draw (an Zigarre etc.: at); umziehen: (re)move (nach to); Vögel: migrate; Tee: infuse, draw; **es zieht** there is a draught (Am. draft).

Ziehharmonika ['tsi:-harmo:nika] f (-/-s) accordion.

Ziel [tsi:l] n (-[e]s/-e) aim (a. fig.); **~scheibe**: mark, target (a. fig.); sp. winning-post; mil. objective; Reise2: destination; fig. end, purpose; **~band** n (-[e]s/-er) sp. (finishing) tape; **2bewußt** adj purposeful; **2en** ['tsi:lən] v/i (take) aim (auf at); **2los** [-lo:s] adj aimless; **~scheibe** f target.

ziemlich ['tsi:mlɪç] adj considerable; adv pretty, fairly, rather.

Zier [tsi:r] f (-/no pl), **~de** ['tsi:rdə] f (-/-n) ornament; *fig. a.* credit (**für** to); **2en** ['tsi:rən] *v/refl:* **sich** ~ make a fuss; **2lich** *adj* dainty.

Ziffer ['tsɪfər] *f* (-/-n) figure, digit; ~**blatt** *n* dial, face.

Zigarette [tsiga'rɛtə] *f* (-/-n) cigaret(te).

Zigarre [tsi'garə] *f* (-/-n) cigar.

Zigeuner [tsi'gɔynər] *m* (-s/-), ~**in** *f* (-/-nen) gipsy.

Zimmer ['tsɪmər] *n* (-s/-) room; apartment; ~**mäd-chen** *n* chambermaid; ~**mann** *m* (-[e]s/-leute) carpenter; ~**vermieterin** *f* (-/-nen) landlady.

zimperlich ['tsɪmpərlɪç] *adj* prudish; squeamish.

Zimt [tsɪmt] *m* (-[e]s/-e) cinnamon.

Zink [tsɪŋk] *n* (-[e]s/*no pl*) zinc.

Zinke ['tsɪŋkə] *f* (-/-n) *Kamm:* tooth; *Gabel:* prong.

Zinn [tsɪn] *n* (-[e]s/*no pl*) tin.

Zins|en ['tsɪnzən] *pl* interest *sg;* ~**fuß** ['tsɪnsfu:s] *m* (-es/-e) rate of interest.

Zipfel ['tsɪpfəl] *m* (-s/-) corner; end, point.

Zirkel ['tsɪrkəl] *m* (-s/-) circle (*a. fig.*); *math.* (**ein** pair of) compasses *pl.*

zirkulieren [tsɪrku'li:rən] *v/i* circulate.

Zirkus ['tsɪrkus] *m* (-/-se) circus.

zischen ['tsɪʃən] *v/i* hiss; *schwirren:* whiz(z).

Zitlat [tsi'ta:t] *n* (-[e]s/-e) quotation; **2ieren** [-'ti:-rən] *v/t* quote.

Zitrone [tsi'tro:nə] *f* (-/-n) lemon; ~**nlimonade** *f* lemonade.

zittern ['tsɪtərn] *v/i* tremble, shake (**vor** with).

zivil [tsi'vi:l] *adj* civil(ian); *Preis:* reasonable; **2** *n* (-s/ *no pl*) *s.* **Zivilkleidung**; **2bevölkerung** *f* civilians *pl;* **2isation** *f* (-/-en) civilization; **2ist** [-vi'lɪst] *m* (-en/-en) civilian; **2kleidung** [-'vi:l-] *f* civilian *od.* plain clothes *pl;* **2personen** *pl* civilians *pl.*

zögern ['tsø:gərn] *v/i* hesitate.   (inch.)

Zoll [tsɔl] *m* (-[e]s/-) *s.*)

Zoll² *m* (-[e]s/**²e**) (customs) duty; *Behörde:* the Customs *pl;* ~**abferti-gung** *f* customs clearance; ~**amt** *n* customhouse; ~**beamte** *m* customs officer; ~**erklärung** *f* customs declaration; **2frei** *adj* duty-free; ~**kontrol-le** *f* customs examination; **2pflichtig** [-pflɪçtɪç] *adj* liable to duty, dutiable.

Zone ['tso:nə] *f* (-/-n) zone.

Zoo [tso:] *m* (-s/-s) zoo.

Zoologie [tsoolo'gi:] *f* (-/ *no pl*) zoology.

Zopf [tsɔpf] *m* (-[e]s/**²e**) plait, pigtail, braid.

Zorn [tsɔrn] m (-[e]s/no pl) anger; **2ig** adj angry.

zottig ['tsɔtɪç] adj shaggy.

zu [tsu:] prp (dat) Richtung: to, toward(s), up to; Ort: at, in; Zweck: for; ~ **Weihnachten** at Christmas; adv too; colloq.: closed, shut; **Tür** ~! close od. shut the door!; mit inf: **ich habe ~ arbeiten** I have to work.

Zubehör ['tsu:bəhø:r] n (-[e]s/-e) fittings pl; tech. accessories pl.

zubereiten ['tsu:bəraɪtən] v/t prepare; **2tung** f preparation.

zu|binden ['tsu:bɪndən] v/t (irr) tie up; **~blinzeln** v/i wink at.

Zucht [tsuxt] f (-/no pl) discipline; bot. growing; zo. (pl -en): breeding; breed.

züchten ['tsyçtən] v/t breed; bot. grow; **2r** m breeder; grower.

Zuchthaus ['tsuxthaus] n jur. hist. prison, Am. penitentiary; **~strafe** f jur. hist. imprisonment, confinement.

zucken ['tsukən] v/i jerk; twitch (**mit et.** s.th.); vor Schmerz: wince; Blitz: flash; s. **Achsel.**

Zucker ['tsukər] m (-s/no pl) sugar; **~dose** f sugar-basin, Am. sugar bowl; **2krank** adj diabetic; **~rohr** n (-[e]s/no pl) sugar-cane; **~rübe** f sugar-beet.

Zuckungen ['tsukuŋən] pl convulsions pl.

zudecken ['tsu:dɛkən] v/t cover (**sich** o.s.).

zudem [tsu'de:m] adv besides, moreover.

zu|drehen ['tsu:dre:ən] v/t turn off; **~dringlich** ['-drɪŋlɪç] adj colloq.: ~ **werden** get fresh with s.o.

zuerst [tsu'?e:rst] adv (at) first.

Zufahrt ['tsu:fa:rt] f (-/ -en) approach; **~sstraße** f approach (road).

Zufall ['tsu:fal] m (-[e]s/ ~e) chance; **2fällig** adj accidental; attr a. chance; adv by accident, by chance; **~flucht** f (-/no pl) refuge, shelter.

zufrieden [tsu'fri:dən] adj content(ed), satisfied; **2heit** f (-/no pl) contentment, satisfaction; **~stellen** v/t satisfy.

zufrieren ['tsu:fri:rən] v/i (irr) freeze up od. over; **~fügen** v/t add; inflict (j-m [up]on s.o.); **2fuhr** ['-fu:r] f (-/no pl) supply.

Zug [tsu:k] m (-[e]s/~e) draw, pull; procession; orn. migration; rail. train; Gesichts2: feature; Charakter2: trait; Luft2, Trinken: draught, Am. draft; Schach: move; Rauchen: puff.

Zugabe ['tsu:ga:bə] f (-/ -n) extra; thea. encore; **~gang** m entrance; access (a. fig.); **2gänglich**

[-gɛŋlɪç] *adj* accessible (**für** to) (*a. fig.*); **2geben** *v/t* (*irr*) add; admit; **2gehen** *v/i* (*irr*) walk up to, advance to; add up; *etc.*: close, shut; *geschehen*: happen; **2gehen auf** walk up to.

Zügel ['tsy:gəl] *m* (-s/-) rein (*a. fig.*); **2los** [-lo:s] *adj fig.* unbridled; **2n** ['tsy:gəln] *v/t* rein; *fig.* bridle, check.

Zulgeständnis ['tsu:gəʃtɛntnɪs] *n* (-ses/-se) concession; **2getan** [-gə-ta:n] *adj* attached (*dat* to).

zuglig ['tsu:gɪç] *adj* draughty; **2kraft** *f* traction; *fig.* draw, appeal. **zugleich** [tsu'glaɪç] *adv* at the same time.

Zugluft ['tsu:kluft] *f* (-/no *pl*) draught, *Am.* draft.

zugreifen ['tsu:graɪfən] *v/i* (*irr*) help o.s.

zugrunde [tsu'grʊndə] *adv*: **~ gehen** perish; **~ richten** ruin.

Zugschaffner *m* **s.
Schaffner.**

zugunsten [tsu'gʊnstən] *prp* (*gen*) in favo(u)r of.

Zug|verbindung *f* train connection; **~vogel** *m* bird of passage.

Zuhause [tsu'haʊzə] *n* (-/no *pl*) home.

zuheilen ['tsu:haɪlən] *v/i* heal up.

zuhören ['tsu:hø:rən] *v/i* listen (*dat* to); **2r** *m* hearer, listener; *pl* audience *sg*.

zuljubeln ['tsu:ju:bəln]

v/i cheer; **~kleben** *v/t* paste up; **~knallen** *v/t* *Tür*: bang shut, slam (to); *v/t* slam (to); **~knöpfen** *v/t* button (up); **~kommen** *v/i* (*irr*): **~ auf** come up to.

Zulkunft ['tsu:kʊnft] *f* (-/no *pl*) future; **~künftig** ['-kʏnftɪç] *adj* future; *adv* in future.

zullächeln ['tsu:lɛçəln] *v/i* smile (*dat* at); **2lage** *f* extra pay; *Gehalt*: rise, *Am.* raise; **2lassen** *v/t* (*irr*) admit (*a. fig.*); **2lassung** *f* admission; licen|ce, *Am.* -se; **~letzt** [tsu'lɛtst] *adv* finally; last; **~liebe** [tsu'li:bə] *adv*: **j-m ~** for s.o.'s sake; **~machen** ['-] *v/t colloq.*: close, shut; button (up).

zumindest [tsu'mɪndəst] *adv* at least.

zumuten ['tsu:mu:tən] *v/t*: **j-m et. ~** expect sth. of s.o.; **2ung** *f* unreasonable demand; impertinence.

zunächst [tsu'nɛ:çst] *adv* first of all; *vorerst*: for the present.

Zulnahme ['tsu:na:mə] *f* (-/-n) increase; **~name** *m* (-ns/-n) surname.

zünden ['tsʏndən] *v/i, v/t* kindle; *bsd. mot.* ignite; **2holz** *n* match; **2kerze** *f* spark(ing) plug; **2schlüssel** *m* ignition key; **2ung** *f* ignition.

zunehmen

zunehmen ['tsu:ne:mən] *v/i* (*irr*) increase (**an** in); *Person:* put on weight.

Zuneigung ['tsu:naigʊŋ] *f* (*-/no pl*) affection.

Zunge ['tsʊŋə] *f* (*-/-n*) tongue.

zunichte [tsu'nıçtə] *adv:* ~ **machen** destroy.

zu|nicken ['tsu:nıkən] *v/i* nod (*dat* to); ~**packen** *v/i* grip, clutch.

zupfen ['tsʊpfən] *v/t, v/i* pluck (an a.).

zurechnungsfähig ['tsu:reçnʊŋsfe:ıç] *adj jur.* responsible.

zurecht|finden [tsu'reçtfındən] *v/refl* (*irr*): **sich** ~ find one's way; ~**kommen** *v/i* (*irr*): ~ **mit** *et.*: manage; ~**machen** *v/t colloq.* get ready, prepare; (**sich**) ~**machen** make up.

zureden ['tsu:re:dən] *v/i:* **j-m** ~ coax s.o.; encourage s.o.

zurück [tsu'ryk] *adv* back; *rückwärts:* backward(s); *hinten:* behind; ~**bekommen** *v/t* (*irr*) get back; ~**bleiben** *v/i* (*irr*) remain *od.* stay behind; fall *od.* lag behind; ~**blicken** *v/i* look back; ~**bringen** *v/t* (*irr*) bring back; ~**drängen** *v/t* push back; *fig.* repress; ~**erstatten** *v/t Auslagen:* refund; ~**fahren** *v/i, v/t* (*irr*) drive back; *fig.* start back; ~**fliegen** *v/i, v/t* (*irr*) fly back; ~**führen** *v/t, v/i* lead back; ~**führen auf** attribute to; ~**geben** *v/t* (*irr*) give back, return, restore; ~**gehen** *v/i* (*irr*) go back, return; *fig.* diminish, decrease; ~**gezogen** *adj* retired; ~**halten** *v/t* (*irr*) hold back; ~**haltend** *adj* reserved; ~**holen** *v/t* fetch back; ~**kommen** *v/i* (*irr*) come back, return; ~**lassen** *v/t* (*irr*) leave (behind); ~**legen** *v/t* put back; lay aside; *Entfernung:* cover; ~**nehmen** *v/t* (*irr*) take back; *Worte etc.:* withdraw, retract; ~**prallen** *v/i* rebound; ~**schicken** *v/t* send back; ~**schlagen** *v/t* (*irr*) repel; *Bettdecke:* turn down; *v/i* hit back; ~**schrecken** *v/i* shrink (back) (**vor** from); ~**setzen** *v/t* put back; *fig.* slight, neglect; ~**stellen** *v/t* put back (a. *Uhr*); *fig.* defer, postpone; ~**stoßen** *v/t* (*irr*) push back; *fig.* repel, repulse; ~**treten** *v/i* (*irr*) step *od.* stand back; resign (**von** *Amt:* from); recede (**von** *Vertrag:* from); ~**weisen** *v/t* (*irr*) decline, reject; ~**werfen** *v/t* (*irr*) throw back; *fig.* set back; ~**zahlen** *v/t* pay back (a. *fig.*); ~**ziehen** *v/t* (*irr*) draw back; *fig.* withdraw; **sich** ~**ziehen** retire, withdraw; *mil.* retreat.

Zuruf ['tsu:ru:f] *m* (*-[e]s/*

-e) shout; **2en** v/t (irr) shout (**j-m et.** s.th. at s.o.).

Zusage ['tsu:za:gǝ] f (-/ -n) promise; *Einwilligung:* assent; **2n** v/t promise; v/i accept an invitation; **j-m 2n** suit s.o.

zusammen [tsu'zamǝn] adv together; at the same time; **2arbeit** f co-operation; *Gemeinschaft:* teamwork; **~arbeiten** v/i work together; cooperate; **~binden** v/t (irr) bind together; **~brechen** v/i (irr) break down; *völlig:* collapse; **2bruch** m breakdown; collapse; **~drük-ken** v/t compress, press together; **~fallen** v/i (irr) fall in, collapse; *zeitlich:* coincide; **~fassen** v/t summarize, sum up; **2fassung** f summary; **~gehören** v/i belong together; *Sachen:* form a nation, a. connexion; **2hang** m connection; *textlich:* context; **~hängen** v/i (irr) be connected; v/t hang together; **~klappen** v/t fold up; **~kommen** v/i (irr) meet; **2kunft** f (-/⁓e) meeting; **~legen** v/t fold up; *Geld:* club together, pool; **~nehmen** v/t (irr): **sich ~** pull o.s. together; **~packen** v/t pack up; **~passen** v/i match, harmonize; **~prall** [-pral] m -[e]s/-e) collision; **~prallen** v/i collide; **~rechnen** v/t add up;

~rücken v/t move together; v/i close up; **~schlagen** v/t (irr) *Hände:* clap; beat s.o. up; **~setzen** v/t put together; *tech.* assemble; v/refl: **sich ~setzen aus** consist of; **~stellen** v/t put together; *Liste etc.:* compile; **2stoß** m collision; *fig. a.* clash; **~stoßen** v/i (irr) collide; *fig. a.* clash; **~treffen** v/i meet; *zeitlich:* coincide; **~zählen** v/t add od. count up; **~ziehen** v/t (irr) pull od. draw together; contract (a. **sich**).

Zu|satz ['tsu:zats] m (-es/ ⁓e) addition; *Beimischung:* admixture; *Ergänzung:* supplement; **2sätzlich** ['-zetslıç] adj additional.

zuschau|en ['tsu:ʃaʊǝn] v/i look on, watch; **2er** m spectator, looker-on, onlooker; **2erraum** m thea. auditorium.

zuschicken ['tsu:ʃıkǝn] v/t send (dat to).

Zuschlag ['tsu:ʃla:k] m (-[e]s/⁓e) extra charge; surcharge (a. Post); rail. excess fare; **2en** v/i (irr) hit, strike; **s. zu-knallen.**

zu|schließen ['tsu:ʃli:-sǝn] v/t (irr) lock (up); **~schnappen** v/i *Hund:* snap; *Tür:* snap to; **~schneiden** v/t (irr) cut out; cut (to size); **~schrauben** v/t screw on; **2schrift** f letter;

zusichern

2schuß *m* allowance; staatlich: subsidy; ~sehen *v/i* (irr) s. zuschauen; ~sehends [-ze:ǝnts] *adv* visibly; ~senden *v/t* (irr) s. zuschicken; ~setzen *v/t*: j-m et. ~ press s.o. (hard).

zusichern ['tsu:ziçǝrn] *v/t*: j-m et. ~ assure s.o. of s.th.; 2ung *f* assurance.

zulspitzen ['tsu:ʃpitsǝn] *v/refl*: sich ~ *fig.* come to a head; 2stand *m* (-[e]s/ *ve*) condition, state.

zustande [zu'ʃtandǝ] *adv*: ~ bringen achieve; ~ kommen come off.

zuständig ['tsu:ʃtɛndiç] *adj* competent.

zustehen ['tsu:ʃte:ǝn] *v/i* (irr) be due (*dat* to).

zustellen ['tsu:ʃtɛlǝn] *v/t* deliver; 2ung *f* delivery.

zustimmen ['tsu:ʃtimǝn] *v/i* (*dat*) agree (to *s.th.*; with *s.o.*); consent (to *s.th.*); 2ung *f* consent.

zultragen ['tsu:tra:gǝn] *v/refl* (irr): sich ~ happen; ~trauen *v/t*: j-m et. ~ credit s.o. with s.th.; ~traulich ['-traoliç] *adj*

confiding, trustful, trusting; *Tier*: friendly, tame.

zutreffen ['tsu:trɛfǝn] *v/i* (irr) be true; ~ auf be true of; ~d *adj* right, correct.

zutrinken ['tsu:triŋkǝn] *v/i* (irr): j-m ~ raise one's glass to s.o., drink (to) s.o.'s health.

Zutritt ['tsu:trit] *m* (-[e]s/ *no pl*) access; *Einlaß*: admission; ~ verboten! no admittance!, no entry!

zuverlässig ['tsu:fɛrlɛsiç] *adj* reliable; 2keit *f* reliability.

Zuversicht ['tsu:fɛrziçt] *f* (-/*no pl*) confidence; 2lich *adj* confident.

zuviel [tsu'fi:l] *indef pron* too much.

zuvor [tsu'fo:r] *adv* before, previously; ~kommen *v/i* (irr): j-m *od.* e-r Sache ~ anticipate s.o. *od.* s.th.; ~kommend *adj* obliging.

Zuwachs ['tsu:vaks] *m* (-es/*no pl*) increase.

zuweilen [tsu'vailǝn] *adv* sometimes.

zulweisen ['tsu:vaizǝn] *v/t* assign; ~wenden *v/t* (*a.* irr): (sich) ~ turn (*dat.* to[wards]).

zuwenig [tsu've:niç] *indef pron* too little.

zulwerfen ['tsu:vɛrfǝn] *v/t* (irr) *Tür*: slam (to); j-m et.~werfen throw to s.o.; *Blick*: cast at s.o.; ~winken *v/i* wave to; beckon to; ~ziehen *v/t* (irr) draw together; *Vorhänge*: draw;

Arzt etc.: consult; **sich ~ziehen** incur; *med.* catch; *v/i* move in; **~züglich** ['-tsy:klɪç] *prp (gen)* plus.

Zwang [tsvaŋ] *m* -[e]s/ ᵛe) compulsion; *Gewalt:* force; **2los** [-lo:s] *adj* informal.

zwanzig ['tsvantsɪç] *adj* twenty; **~ste** *adj* twentieth.

zwar [tsva:r] *adv* indeed, it is true; **und ~** that is.

Zweck [tsvɛk] *m* -[e]s/ -e) aim, end, purpose; **keinen ~ haben** be of no use.

Zwecke ['tsvɛkə] *f* (-/-n) tack; *Reiß:* drawing-pin, *Am.* thumbtack.

zweck|los ['tsvɛklo:s] *adj* useless; **~mäßig** *adj* expedient, suitable.

zwei [tsvaɪ] *adj* two; **2bettzimmer** *n* double room; **~deutig** [-dɔytɪç] *adj* ambiguous; **~erlei** ['tsvaɪər'laɪ] *adj* of two kinds, two kinds of; **~fach** *adj, adv* double, twofold.

Zweifel ['tsvaɪfəl] *m* (-s/-) doubt; **2haft** *adj* doubtful, dubious; **2los** *adj* doubtless; **2n** ['tsvaɪfəln] *v/i* doubt (**an e-r Sache** s.th.; **an j-m** s.o.).

Zweig [tsvaɪk] *m* (-[e]s/ -e) branch (*a. fig.*); **kleiner ~** twig; **~geschäft** *n*, **~niederlassung** *f*, **~stelle** *f* branch.

Zwei|kampf ['tsvaɪkampf] *m* duel, single combat; **2mal** [-ma:l] *adv* twice; **2motorig** ['-mo:to:rɪç] *adj* twin-engined; **2seitig** *adj* two-sided; *Vertrag etc.*: bilateral; **~sitzer** ['-zɪtsər] *m* (-s/-) two-seater; **2sprachig** ['-ʃpra:xɪç] *adj* bilingual; **2stöckig** [-ʃtœkɪç] *adj* two-stor[e]yed, -ied.

zweit [tsvaɪt] *adj* second; **aus ~er Hand** second-hand; **wir sind zu ~** there are two of us.

zwei|teilig ['tsvaɪtaɪlɪç] *adj* *Anzug:* two-piece; **~tens** ['-təns] *adv* secondly.

Zwerchfell ['tsvɛrçfɛl] *n* (-[e]s/-e) diaphragm.

Zwerg [tsvɛrk] *m* (-[e]s/ -e) dwarf.

Zwetsch(g)e ['tsvɛtʃ(g)ə] *f* (-/-n) plum.

zwicken ['tsvɪkən] *v/t, v/i* pinch, nip.

Zwieback ['tsvi:bak] *m* (-[e]s/ᵛe, -e) rusk, zwieback.

Zwiebel ['tsvi:bəl] *f* (-/-n) onion; *Blumen:* bulb.

Zwie|licht ['tsvi:lɪçt] *n* (-[e]s/*no pl*) twilight; **~spalt** *m* (-[e]s/*rare* -e, ᵛe) conflict; **~tracht** *f* (-/ *no pl*) discord.

Zwilling|e ['tsvɪlɪŋə] *pl* twins *pl*; **~s...** twin ...

zwingen ['tsvɪŋən] *v/t (irr)* force; compel.

Zwinger ['tsvɪŋər] *m* (-s/

zwinkern

320

-) kennel; **Zucht:** kennel(s pl).

zwinkern ['tsvɪŋkərn] v/i wink, blink.

Zwirn [tsvɪrn] m (-[e]s/-e) thread, cotton; **~sfaden** m thread.

zwischen ['tsvɪʃən] prp (dat) **zweien:** between; **mehreren:** among; **~durch** ['-durç] adv colloq. in between; for a change; **2ergebnis** ['-ʔɛrgeːpnis] n intermediate result; **2fall** m incident; **2lan-dung** f aer. intermediate landing, stop, Am. a. stop-over; **(Flug) ohne 2lan-dung** non-stop (flight); **2raum** m space, interval;

2stecker m adapter; **2stück** n intermediate piece; adapter; **2wand** f partition; **2zeit** f interval; **in der 2zeit** meantime.

zwitschern ['tsvɪtʃərn] v/i twitter, chirp.

zwölf [tsvœlf] adj twelve; **um ~ (Uhr)** at twelve (o'clock); **(um) ~ Uhr mittags** (at) noon; **(um) ~ Uhr nachts** (at) midnight; **~te** adj twelfth.

Zylind|er [tsiˈlɪndər] m (-s/-) top hat; math., tech. cylinder.

zynisch ['tsyːnɪʃ] adj cynical.

Zypresse [tsyˈprɛsə] f (-/ -n) cypress.

A

a [ei, ə] ein(e); **not ~(n)** kein(e).

aback [ə'bæk] zurück; **taken ~** überrascht, bestürzt.

abandon [ə'bændən] auf-, preisgeben; verlassen; überlassen; **~ment** Auf-, Preisgabe f.

abashed [ə'bæʃt] verlegen.

abate [ə'beit] verringern; abnehmen, nachlassen; *Mißstand* abstellen.

abbess ['æbis] Äbtissin f; **~ey** ['~i] Abtei f; **~ot** ['~ət] Abt m.

abbreviat|e [ə'bri:vieit] (ab)kürzen; **~ion** Abkürzung f.

ABC ['eibi:'si:] Abc n.

abdicate ['æbdikeit] aufgeben; abdanken.

abdomen ['æbdəmen] Unterleib m.

abduct [æb'dʌkt] entführen.

abhor [əb'hɔ:] verabscheuen; **~rence** [~rəns] Abscheu m; **~rent** verhaßt, zuwider; abstoßend.

abide [ə'baid] (*irr*) bleiben; warten auf; (v)ertragen.

ability [ə'biliti] Fähigkeit f.

abject ['æbdʒekt] niedrig, gemein; *fig.* äußerst.

abjure [əb'dʒuə] abschwören; entsagen.

able ['eibl] fähig; geschickt; **be ~ to** imstande sein zu, können.

abnormal [æb'nɔ:məl] abnorm.

aboard [ə'bɔ:d] an Bord.

abode [ə'bəud] *pret u. pp von* abide; Aufenthalt *m*; Wohnung f.

aboli|sh [ə'bɔliʃ] abschaffen; **~tion** [æbəu'liʃən] Abschaffung f.

A-bomb ['eibɔm] Atombombe f.

abominable [ə'bɔminəbl] abscheulich.

abortion [ə'bɔ:ʃən] Fehlgeburt f; Abtreibung f.

abound [ə'baund]: **~ in, ~ with** voll sein von, wimmeln von.

about [ə'baut] *prp räumlich:* um, um ... herum; in ... umher; *herumlich:* um, um ... herum; in ... umher; *zeitlich, größen-, mengenmäßig:* ungefähr, etwa, gegen (**~ this time, ~ my height**) *fig.* über, um, wegen; bei (**I haven't any money ~ me**) im Begriff, dabei; *adv* umher, herum; in der Nähe, da; ungefähr, etwa.

above [ə'bʌv] *prp* über, oberhalb; *fig.* erhaben über; **~ all** vor allem; *adv* oben; darüber; *adj* obig, obenerwähnt.

abreast [ə'brest] nebeneinander. [kürzen.]

abridge [ə'bridʒ] (ver-)

abroad [ə'brɔːd] im od. ins Ausland; überall(hin).

abrupt [ə'brʌpt] jäh; zs.-hanglos; schroff.

abscess ['æbsis] Geschwür *n*.

absence ['æbsəns] Abwesenheit *f*; Mangel *m*; *~ of mind* Zerstreutheit *f*.

absent ['æbsənt] abwesend; *be ~* fehlen; *~-minded* zerstreut, geistesabwesend.

absolute ['æbsəluːt] absolut; unumschränkt.

absolve [əb'zɔlv] frei-, lossprechen.

absorb [əb'sɔːb] aufsaugen; *fig.* ganz in Anspruch nehmen.

abst|ain [əb'stein] sich enthalten; *~ention* [əb-'stenʃən] Enthaltung *f*.

abstinen|ce ['æbstinəns] Enthaltsamkeit *f*; *~t* enthaltsam.

abstract ['æbstrækt] abstrakt; Auszug *m*; [əb-'strækt] abziehen, trennen; *~ed* zerstreut.

absurd [əb'səːd] absurd; lächerlich.

abundan|ce [ə'bʌndəns] Überfluß *m*; Fülle *f*; *~t* reichlich.

abuse [ə'bjuːs] Mißbrauch *m*; Beschimpfung *f*; [ə'bjuːz] mißbrauchen; beschimpfen; *~ive* ausfallend; Schimpf...

abyss [ə'bis] Abgrund *m*.

academ|ic(al) [ækə'demik(əl)] akademisch; *~y* [ə'kædəmi] Akademie *f*.

accelerat|e [æk'seləreit] beschleunigen; *mot.* Gas geben; *~or* Gaspedal *n*.

accent ['æksənt] Akzent *m*.

accept [ək'sept] annehmen; (freundlich) aufnehmen; hinnehmen; *~able* annehmbar; *~ance* Annahme *f*; (freundliche) Aufnahme *f*.

access ['ækses] Zugang *m*; *~ary* [ək'sesəri] Mitwisser(in), Mitschuldige *m*, *f*; *~ible* [ək'sesəbl] zugänglich; *~ion* [æk'seʃən] Zuwachs *m*; Zunahme *f*; Antritt *m*; *~ion to the throne* Thronbesteigung *f*.

accessory [ək'sesəri] Zubehör(teil) *n*; *s.* **accessary**.

access road Zufahrtsstraße *f*; Autobahneinfahrt *f*.

accident ['æksidənt] Zufall *m*; Un(glücks)fall *m*; *by ~* zufällig; *~al* [ˌ'dentl] zufällig; nebensächlich.

acclimatize [ə'klaimətaiz] (sich) akklimatisieren od. eingewöhnen.

accommodat|e [ə'kɔmədeit] anpassen; unterbringen; versorgen; *j–m* aushelfen; *~ion* Anpassung *f*; Versorgung *f*; (*Am. pl.*:) Unterkunft *f*; Unterbringung *f*.

accompan|iment [ə'kʌmpənimənt] Begleitung *f*; **~y** begleiten.

accomplice [ə'komplis] Komplice *m*.

accomplish [ə'komplij] vollenden; ausführen; **~ed** vollendet, perfekt; **~ment** Vollendung *f*; Ausführung *f*; Leistung *f*; Fähigkeit *f*.

accord [ə'ko:d] übereinstimmen; gewähren; Übereinstimmung *f*; **with one~** einstimmig; **~ing: ~ to** gemäß, nach; **~ingly** (dem)entsprechend.

account [ə'kaunt] Rechnung *f*; Berechnung *f*; Konto *n*; Bericht *m*; Rechenschaft *f*; **on no ~** auf keinen Fall; **on ~ of** wegen; **take into ~** berücksichtigen; **call to ~** zur Rechenschaft ziehen; **~ for** Buchhalter *m*; **~ing** Buchführung *f*.

accumulate [ə'kju:mjuleit] (sich) (an)häufen *od.* ansammeln.

accura|cy ['ækjurəsi] Genauigkeit *f*; **~te** ['~it] genau; richtig.

accus|ation [ækju:'zeiʃən] Anklage *f*, Beschuldigung *f*; **~ative (case)** [ə'kju:zətiv] *gr.* Akkusativ *m*, 4. Fall; **~e** [ə'kju:z] anklagen, beschuldigen; **~ed: the ~** der *od.* die Angeklagte; **~er** Kläger(-in).

accustom [ə'kʌstəm] gewöhnen; **~ed** gewohnt, üblich; gewöhnt.

ace [eis] As *n* (*a. fig.*).

ache [eik] schmerzen; *an*haltender Schmerz.

achieve [ə'tʃi:v] ausführen; erreichen; **~ment** Ausführung *f*; Leistung *f*.

acid ['æsid] sauer; Säure *f*.

acknowledg|e [ək'nolidʒ] anerkennen; zugeben; *Empfang* bestätigen; **~(e)ment** Anerkennung *f*; Bestätigung *f*; Eingeständnis *n*.

acoustics [ə'ku:stiks] *pl* Akustik *f*.

acquaint [ə'kweint] bekannt machen; **~ s.o. with s.th.** j-m et. mitteilen; **be ~ed with** kennen; **~ance** Bekanntschaft *f*; Bekannte *m*, *f*.

acquire [ə'kwaiə] erwerben.

acquisition [ækwi'ziʃən] Erwerbung *f*; Errungenschaft *f*.

acquit [ə'kwit] freisprechen; **~tal** Freispruch *m*.

acre ['eikə] Morgen *m* (*4047 qm*).

acrid ['ækrid] scharf.

acrobat ['ækrəbæt] Akrobat *m*.

across [ə'krɔs] *prp* (quer) durch *od.* über; jenseits, über, auf der anderen Seite von; **come ~, run ~** stoßen auf; *adv* (quer) hin-*od.* herüber; quer durch; drüben; über Kreuz.

act [ækt] handeln; wirken; funktionieren; *thea.*: spielen; aufführen; Tat *f*; *thea.* Akt *m*; **~ion** Handlung *f* (*a. thea.*); Tätigkeit *f*; Tat *f*; Wirkung *f*; Klage *f*, Prozeß *m*; Gefecht *n*; Mechanismus *m*.

activ|e ['æktiv] aktiv; tätig; wirksam; **~e (voice)** *gr.* Aktiv *n*, Tätigkeitsform *f*; **~ity** Tätigkeit *f*; Betriebsamkeit *f*.

act|or ['æktə] Schauspieler *m*; **~ress** Schauspielerin *f*.

actual ['æktjuəl] wirklich. **acute** [ə'kju:t] spitz; scharf (-sinnig); brennend (*Frage*); *med.* akut.

adapt [ə'dæpt] anpassen; bearbeiten.

add [æd] hinzufügen; addieren; hinzukommen.

addict ['ædikt] Süchtige *m*, *f*; **~ed** [ə'diktid]: **~ to** dem *Rauschgift etc.* verfallen, ...süchtig.

addition [ə'diʃən] Hinzufügen *n*; Zusatz *m*; Addition *f*; **in ~** außerdem; **in ~ to** außer; **~al** zusätzlich.

address [ə'dres] *Worte etc.* richten (**to** an), das Wort richten an, *j-n* ansprechen; adressieren; Adresse *f*, Anschrift *f*; Ansprache *f*; **~ee** [ædre-'si:] Empfänger *m*.

adequate ['ædikwit] angemessen.

adhe|re [əd'hiə] haften

(**to** an); **~sive** [~'hi:siv] Klebstoff *m*; **~sive tape** *od.* **plaster** Heftpflaster *n*.

adjacent [ə'dʒeisənt] benachbart.

adjective ['ædʒiktiv] *gr.* Adjektiv *n*, Eigenschaftswort *n*.

adjoin [ə'dʒɔin] angrenzen an.

adjourn [ə'dʒə:n] (sich) vertagen.

adjust [ə'dʒʌst] in Ordnung bringen; anpassen; *tech.* einstellen.

administ|er [əd'ministə] verwalten, führen; spenden; *Arznei* (ein)geben; *Recht* sprechen; **~ration** Verwaltung *f*; Regierung *f*; *bsd. Am.* Amtsperiode *f*; **~rative** [~trativ] Verwaltungs...; **~rator** [~treitə] (Vermögens)Verwalter *m*.

admirable ['ædmərəbl] bewundernswert, großartig.

admiral ['ædmərəl] Admiral *m*.

admir|ation [ædmə-'reiʃən] Bewunderung *f*; **~e** [əd'maiə] bewundern; verehren; **~er** Verehrer *m*.

admiss|ible [əd'misəbl] zulässig; **~ion** Zulassung *f*; Eintritt(sgeld *n*) *m*; Eingeständnis *n*; **~ion fee** Eintrittsgeld *n*.

admit [əd'mit] (her)einlassen; zulassen; zugeben; **~tance** Zutritt *m*.

admonish [əd'mɔniʃ] ermahnen; warnen.

ado [ə'du:] Getue n.

adolescent [ædəu'lesnt] Jugendliche m, f.

adopt [ə'dɔpt] adoptieren; sich aneignen; **~ion** Adoption f.

ador|able [ə'dɔ:rəbl] liebenswert; entzückend; **~ation** [ædɔ:'reiʃən] Anbetung f; **~e** [ə'dɔ:] anbeten.

adorn [ə'dɔ:n] schmücken.

adult [ə'dʌlt] erwachsen; Erwachsene m, f.

adulter|ate [ə'dʌltəreit] (ver)fälschen; **~y** Ehebruch m.

advance [əd'va:ns] vorrücken; Fortschritte machen; vorbringen; Geld leihen; Preis erhöhen; Vorrücken n; Fortschritt m; Vorschuß m; Erhöhung f; **in ~** im voraus; **~d** Brit. Voranmeldung f; **~d** vorgerückt, fortgeschritten; **~ payment** Vorauszahlung f; **~ reservation** bsd. Am. Voranmeldung f.

advantage [əd'va:ntidʒ] Vorteil m; Gewinn m; **take ~ of** ausnutzen; **~ous** [ædvən'teidʒəs] vorteilhaft.

adventur|e [əd'ventʃə] Abenteuer n; **~er** Abenteurer m; **~ous** abenteuerlich.

adverb [ædvə:b] gr. Adverb n, Umstandswort n.

advers|ary [ædvəsəri] Gegner m; **~e** [ˈ~ə:s] ungünstig.

advertis|e [ædvətaiz] inserieren; Reklame machen (für), werben (für); **~ement** [əd'və:tismənt] (Zeitungs)Anzeige f, Inserat n; Reklame f; **~ing** Reklame f, Werbung f.

advice [əd'vais] Rat (-schlag) m; **take ~** e-m Rat folgen.

advis|able [əd'vaizəbl] ratsam; **~e** beraten; j-m raten; **~er** Ratgeber(in).

advocate [ædvəkeit] befürworten; (Antenne f.)

aerial [ˈɛəriəl] Luft-.

aero|nautics [ɛərəʊ'nɔ:-tiks] sg Luftfahrt f; **~plane** Flugzeug n.

aesthetic(al) [i:s'θetik (-əl)] ästhetisch.

affair [ə'fɛə] Angelegenheit f, Sache f; Geschäft f; (Liebes)Verhältnis n.

affect [ə'fekt] sich auswirken auf; (be)rühren; med. angreifen, befallen; vortäuschen; affektiert; **~ion** Liebe f, (Zu)Neigung f; **~ionate** [ˈ~ʃnit] liebevoll.

affinity [ə'finiti] chem. Affinität f; (geistige) Verwandtschaft.

affirm [ə'fə:m] bejahen, bestätigen; **~ation** [æfə:-'meiʃən] Bestätigung f; **~ative** [ə'fə:mətiv] bejahend; sub: **answer in the ~ative** bejahen.

afflict [ə'flikt] betrüben, plagen; **~ion** Elend n; Leiden n.

affluen|ce ['æfluəns] Überfluß *m*; Wohlstand *m*; **~t** reich(lich).

afford [ə'fɔːd] liefern; bieten; **I can ~** it ich kann es mir leisten. |gung *f.*|

affront [ə'frʌnt] Beleidi-

afraid [ə'freid]: **be ~ (of)** sich fürchten *od.* Angst haben (vor).

African ['æfrikən] afrikanisch; Afrikaner(in).

after ['ɑːftə] *prp* räumlich: hinter (... her), nach; *zeitlich, fig.*: nach; **~ all** schließlich; doch; **~ that** danach; *adv* nachher, hinterher, danach, später; *adj* später, künftig; *cj* nachdem; **~noon** Nachmittag *m*:**good ~** guten Tag (*nachmittags*); **in the ~** nachmittags; **this ~** heute nachmittag; **~ward(s)** ['~wəd(z)] nachher; später.

again [ə'gen] wieder (-um); **~ and ~, time and ~** immer wieder.

against [ə'genst] gegen, an, vor.

age [eidʒ] alt werden *od.* machen; Alter *n*; Zeit(alter *n*) *f*; **old ~** Greisenalter *n*; **of ~** mündig; **~ years of ~** ... Jahre alt; **at the ~ of** im Alter von ... Jahren; **for ~s** *colloq.* e-e Ewigkeit, ewig; **~d** ['eidʒid] alt, bejahrt; [eidʒd]: **~ twenty** 20 Jahre alt.

agen|cy ['eidʒənsi] Tätigkeit *f*; Vermittlung *f*;

Vertretung *f*, Agentur *f*; Büro *n*; **~t** Agent *m*, Vertreter *m*; wirkende Kraft.

aggress|ion [ə'greʃən] Angriff *m*; **~ive** aggressiv; **~or** Angreifer *m*.

agile ['ædʒail] flink, behend.

agitat|e ['ædʒiteit] agitieren; bewegen; *fig.* erregen; aufregen; **~ion** Agitation *f*; Erregung *f*; **~or** Agitator *m*.

ago [ə'gəu] vor (*zeitlich*): **long ~** vor langer Zeit; **a year ~** vor e-m Jahr.

agon|izing ['æɡənaiziŋ] qualvoll; **~y** Qual *f.*

agree [ə'griː] zustimmen, einwilligen; sich einigen; übereinkommen; übereinstimmen; bekommen (*Essen*); **~able** [~ə-] angenehm; **~ment** [~iː-] Abkommen *n*, Vereinbarung *f*; Verständigung *f*; Übereinstimmung *f.*

agricultur|al [ægri'kʌltʃərəl] landwirtschaftlich; **~e** ['~tʃə] Landwirtschaft *f*; **~ist** Landwirt *m*.

ague ['eigjuː] Wechselfieber *n*; Schüttelfrost *m*.

ahead [ə'hed] vorwärts; vor, voraus; vorn; **straight ~** geradeaus.

aid [eid] helfen; Hilfe *f.*

ailing ['eiliŋ] leidend.

aim [eim] Ziel *n*; Absicht *f*; zielen; *fig.* beabsichtigen; **~ at** Waffe richten auf; **~less** ziellos.

air[1] [ɛə] Luft *f*; Luftzug *m*; **by ~** auf dem Luftwege; **in the open ~** im Freien; **on the ~** im Rundfunk.

air¹ Miene f; Aussehen n; **give o.s. ~s** vornehm tun.

air² Weise f, Melodie f.

air| base Luftstützpunkt m; **~bed** Luftmatratze f; **~brake** Druckluftbremse f; **~conditioned** mit Klimaanlage; **~craft** Flugzeug(e pl) n; **~craft carrier** Flugzeugträger m; **~crew** Flugzeugbesatzung f; **~cushion** Luftkissen n; **~ force** Luftwaffe f; **~ hostess** Stewardeß f; **~ letter** Luftpostbrief m; **~lift** Luftbrücke f; **~line** Fluggesellschaft f, Luftverkehrsgesellschaft f; **~liner** Verkehrsflugzeug n; **~ mail** Luftpost f; **~plane** Am. Flugzeug n; **~pocket** Luftloch n; **~port** Flughafen m; **~raid** Luftangriff m; **~route** Flugstrecke f; **~show** Luftfahrtschau f; **~sick** luftkrank; **~taxi** Lufttaxi n; **~ terminal** Fluggastabfertigungsgebäude n (in der Innenstadt); **~tight** luftdicht; **~traffic** Flugverkehr m; **~ traffic control** Flugsicherung f; **~ traffic controller** Fluglotse m; **~way** s. airline; **~y** luftig.

aisle [ail] Seitenschiff n; Gang m.

ajar [ə'dʒa:] halb offen, angelehnt.

akin [ə'kin] verwandt (**to** mit).

alacrity [ə'lækriti] Bereitwilligkeit f, Eifer m.

alarm [ə'lɑ:m] alarmieren; beunruhigen; Alarm(zeichen n) m; Angst f; **give the ~** Alarm schlagen; **~clock** Wecker m.

alcohol [ˈælkəhɔl] Alkohol m; **~ic** alkoholisch.

ale [eil] Ale n, helles *englisches* Bier.

alert [ə'lə:t] wachsam; sub: **on the ~** auf der Hut.

alibi [ˈælibai] Alibi n.

alien [ˈeiljən] fremd; Ausländer(in).

alight [ə'lait] ab-, aussteigen; sich niederlassen (*Vogel*); aer. landen.

alike [ə'laik] gleich, ähnlich; gleich, ebenso.

alimony [ˈælimɔni] Unterhalt m.

alive [ə'laiv] am Leben, lebend; lebendig, belebt; **be still ~** noch leben.

all [ɔ:l] all; ganz; jede(r, -s); alles; alle pl; ganz, völlig; **~ of us** wir alle; **two ~** sp. 2:2; **at ~** überhaupt; **not at ~** überhaupt nicht; keine Ursache!; nichts zu danken!; **for ~ I care** meinetwegen; **for ~ I know** soviel ich weiß; **~ at once** auf einmal; **~ the better** desto besser; **~ but** fast.

alleged [ə'ledʒd] angeblich.

alleviate [ə'li:vieit] lindern.

alley ['æli] Gäßchen *n*; Allee *f*; (Durch)Gang *m*.

alliance [ə'laiəns] Bündnis *n*.

allot [ə'lɔt] zuteilen; **~ment** Zuteilung *f*; Parzelle *f*; Schrebergarten *m*.

allow [ə'lau] erlauben; bewilligen, zugeben; **~ for** berücksichtigen; **be ~ed** dürfen; **~ance** Erlaubnis *f*; Bewilligung *f*; Taschengeld *n*, Zuschuß *m*.

alloy ['ælɔi] Legierung *f*.

all-round vielseitig.

allu|de [ə'lu:d]: **~ to** anspielen auf; **~re** [ə'ljuə] (an-, ver)locken; **~sion** [ə'lu:ʒən] Anspielung *f*.

ally [ə'lai] (sich) vereinigen; sich verbünden; ['ælai] Verbündete *m, f*; **the Allies** *pl* die Alliierten *pl*.

almighty [ɔːl'maiti] allmächtig. **[del** *f.*]

almond ['ɑːmənd] Man-]

almost ['ɔːlmoust] fast, beinahe.

alms [ɑːmz], *pl* **~** Almosen *f*.

aloft [ə'lɔft] (hoch) oben.

alone [ə'loun] allein; **let** *od.* **leave ~** in Ruhe od. bleiben lassen; **let ~** geschweige denn.

along [ə'lɔŋ] *prp* entlang, längs; *adv* weiter, vorwärts; **all ~** die ganze Zeit; **~ with** zs. mit;

come ~ mitkommen; **~side** Seite an Seite, neben.

aloud [ə'laud] laut.

alphabet ['ælfəbit] Alphabet *n*, Abc *n*; **~ical** [~'betikəl] alphabetisch.

already [ɔːl'redi] bereits, schon.

also ['ɔːlsou] auch, ebenfalls.

altar ['ɔːltə] Altar *m*.

alter ['ɔːltə] (sich) verändern; ab-, umändern; **~ation** Änderung *f*.

alternat|e ['ɔːltəneit] abwechseln (lassen); [~'tə:nit] abwechselnd; **~ing current** Wechselstrom *m*; **~ive** [ɔːl'tə:nətiv] Alternative *f*, Wahl *f*.

although [ɔːl'ðou] obgleich, obwohl.

altitude ['æltitju:d] Höhe *f*.

altogether [ɔːltə'geðə] völlig; alles in allem.

alumin|ium [ælju'minjəm], *Am.* **~um** [ə'lu:minəm] Aluminium *n*.

always ['ɔːlweiz] immer.

am [æm, əm] *1. sg pres von* **be**.

amateur ['æmətə(:)] Amateur *m*; (Kunst- *etc.*)Liebhaber *m*.

amaze [ə'meiz] erstaunen, verblüffen; **~ment** Erstaunen *n*, Verblüffung *f*; **~ing** erstaunlich, verblüffend.

ambassador [æm'bæsədə] Botschafter *m*. **[m.]**

amber ['æmbə] Bernstein]

ambiguous [æmˈbigjuəs] zwei-, vieldeutig; unklar.

ambiti|on [æmˈbiʃən]Ehrgeiz *m*; ~ous ehrgeizig.

ambulance [ˈæmbjuləns] Krankenwagen *m*.

ambush [ˈæmbuʃ] Hinterhalt *m*; auflauern.

amen [ˈɑːmen] Amen *n*.

amend [əˈmend] (ver-)bessern; *Gesetz* (ab)ändern; sich bessern; ~ment (Ver)Besserung *f*; Änderung(santrag *m*) *f*; ~s *sg* (Schaden)Ersatz *m*; **make** ~s Schadenersatz leisten.

American [əˈmerikən] amerikanisch; Amerikaner (-in); Amerikanisch *n*.

amiable [ˈeimjəbl] liebenswürdig.

amicable [ˈæmikəbl] gütlich.

amid(st) [əˈmid(st)] (mitten) in *od.* unter.

amiss [əˈmis] verkehrt; falsch; **take** ~ übelnehmen.

ammunition [æmjuˈniʃən] Munition *f*.

amnesty [ˈæmnisti] Amnestie *f*.

among(st) [əˈmʌŋ(st)] (mitten) unter, zwischen.

amount [əˈmaunt] Betrag *m*; Menge *f*; Bedeutung *f*; **to** sich belaufen auf; hinauslaufen auf, bedeuten.

ample [ˈæmpl] weit, groß; reichlich.

amplif|ier [ˈæmplifaiə]

electr. Verstärker *m*; ~y [ˈ~ai] verstärken.

amputate [ˈæmpjuteit] amputieren.

amulet [ˈæmjulit] Amulett *n*.

amus|e [əˈmjuːz] amüsieren, unterhalten; ~ement Unterhaltung *f*, Zeitvertreib *m*; ~ing lustig, amüsant.

an [æn, ən] ein(e).

an(a)emia [əˈniːmjə] Blutarmut *f*.

an(a)esthetic [ænisˈθetik] Betäubungsmittel *n*.

analog|ous [əˈnæləgəs] analog, ähnlich; ~y [~dʒi] Analogie *f*.

analy|se, *Am. a.* ~ze [ˈænəlaiz] analysieren, zerlegen; ~sis [əˈnæləsis] Analyse *f*.

anatom|ize [əˈnætəmaiz] zergliedern; ~y Anatomie *f*.

ancest|or [ˈænsistə] Vorfahr *m*, Ahn *m*; ~ry Abstammung *f*; Ahnen *pl*.

anchor [ˈæŋkə] Anker *m*.

anchovy [ˈæntʃəvi] Sardelle *f*.

ancient [ˈeinʃənt] (ur)alt, antik; *sub*: **the** ~s die Alten (*Griechen u. Römer*).

and [ænd, ənd] und; ~ **so** und so weiter.

anecdote [ˈænikdəut] Anekdote *f*.

anew [əˈnjuː] von neuem.

angel [ˈeindʒəl] Engel *m*.

anger [ˈæŋgə] Zorn *m*, Ärger *m*. [gina *f*.]

angina [ænˈdʒainə] An-

angle ['æŋgl] Winkel *m*; *fig.* Standpunkt *m*; angeln.

Anglican ['æŋglikən] anglikanisch.

Anglo-Saxon ['æŋgləu-'sæksən] angelsächsisch; Angelsachse *m*.

angry ['æŋgri] zornig, böse, ärgerlich (**with** *s.o.*, **at** *s.th.* über).

anguish ['æŋgwiʃ] (Seelen)Qual *f*.

angular ['æŋgjulə] winkelig; eckig.

animal ['æniməl] Tier *n*; tierisch.

animat|e ['ænimeit] beleben; anregen, aufmuntern; ~**ed cartoon** Zeichentrickfilm *m*; ~**ion** Lebhaftigkeit *f*; Zeichentrickfilm *m*.

animosity [æni'mɔsiti] Feindseligkeit *f*.

ankle ['æŋkl] (Fuß)Knöchel *m*.

annex(e) ['æneks] Anhang *m*; Anbau *m*, Nebengebäude *n*.

annihilate [ə'naiəleit] vernichten.

anniversary [æni'və:səri] Jahrestag *m*.

annotation [ænəu'teiʃən] Anmerkung *f*.

announce [ə'nauns] ankündigen; ansagen; ~**ment** Ankündigung *f*; Durchsage *f*; Anzeige *f*; ~**r** Ansager(in).

annoy [ə'nɔi]: **be** ~**ed** sich ärgern; ~**ance** Ärger (-nis *n*) *m*.

annual ['ænjuəl] jährlich; Jahrbuch *n*.

annuity [ə'nju(:)iti] Jahresrente *f*.

annul [ə'nʌl] annullieren.

anodyne ['ænəudain] schmerzstillend(es Mittel).

anomalous [ə'nɔmələs] anomal.

anonymous [ə'nɔniməs] anonym.

another [ə'nʌðə] ein anderer; ein zweiter; noch ein; **with one** ~ miteinander; **for** ~ **day** noch e-n Tag.

answer ['ɑːnsə] Antwort *f*; beantworten; antworten (auf *od.* **to** auf); *Zweck* erfüllen; ~ **for** einstehen für; ~ **to** entsprechen.

ant [ænt] Ameise *f*.

antagonist [æn'tægənist] Gegner(in).

antelope ['æntiləup] Antilope *f*.

anthem ['ænθəm] Hymne *f*.

anti... ['ænti] Gegen..., gegen...; ~**aircraft** Fliegerabwehr...; ~**biotic** ['--bai'ɔtik] Antibiotikum *n*.

anticipat|e [æn'tisipeit] vorwegnehmen; zuvorkommen; voraussehen, ahnen; erwarten; ~**ion** Vorwegnahme *f*; Erwartung *f*; **in** ~**ion** im voraus.

anti|cyclone ['ænti'saikləun] Hoch(druckgebiet) *n*; ~**dote** ['--dəut] Gegengift *n*; ~**freeze** *mot.* Frostschutzmittel *n*.

antipathy [æn'tipəθi] Abneigung f.

antiquated ['æntikweitid] veraltet.

antique|[ən'ti:k] antik, alt; **~ity** [~ikwiti] Altertum n.

antiseptic [ænti'septik] antiseptisch(es Mittel).

antlers ['æntləz] pl Geweih n.

anvil ['ænvil] Amboß m.

anxiety [æŋ'zaiəti] Angst f; Sorge f.

anxious ['æŋkʃəs] ängstlich, besorgt (**about** um, wegen); gespannt (**for** auf); bestrebt (**to** zu).

any ['eni] (irgend)ein(e), (irgend)welche pl; jede(r, -s) (beliebige); irgend (-wie), etwas; **not** ~ kein; **not** ~ **longer** nicht länger, nicht mehr; **not** ~ **more** nicht(s) mehr; **~body** jeder; jemand; **~how** irgendwie; trotzdem, jedenfalls; **~one** s. **~body; ~thing** (irgend) etwas; alles; **~thing but** alles andere als; **~thing else?** (sonst) noch (irgend) etwas?; **not** ~**thing** nichts; **~way** ohnehin; s. **~how; ~where** irgendwo(hin); überall; **not** ~**where** nirgends.

apart [ə'pɑ:t] auseinander, getrennt; für sich; beiseite; ~ **from** abgesehen von.

apartment [ə'pɑ:tmənt] Zimmer n; Am. a. Wohnung f; pl Brit. möblierte (Miet)Wohnung, Apart-

ment n; ~ **house** Am. Mietshaus n.

apathetic [æpə'θetik] apathisch, gleichgültig.

ape [eip] (Menschen-) Affe m.

apiece [ə'pi:s] (für) das Stück, je.

apolog|ize [ə'polədʒaiz] sich entschuldigen; **~y** Entschuldigung f.

apoplexy ['æpəupleksi] Schlag(anfall) m.

apostle [ə'posl] Apostel m.

apostrophe [ə'postrəfi] Apostroph m.

appal(l) [ə'po:l] entsetzen.

apparatus [æpə'reitəs] Apparat m.

apparent [ə'pærənt] anscheinend, scheinbar; klar.

appeal [ə'pi:l] jur. Berufung einlegen; ~ **to** appellieren an, sich wenden an; wirken auf, zusagen; jur. Revision f; Berufung f; Aufruf m, dringende Bitte; Reiz m.

appear [ə'piə] erscheinen; sich zeigen; öffentlich auftreten; scheinen, aussehen; **~ance** Erscheinen n, Auftreten n; Aussehen n, Äußere n; Anschein m.

appease [ə'pi:z] beschwichtigen; stillen.

appendi|citis [əpendi'saitis] Blinddarmentzündung f; **~x** [ə'pendiks] Anhang m; (**vermiform**) **~x** Blinddarm m.

appeti|te['æpitait]: ~ (**for**) Appetit m (auf); fig. Verlangen n (nach); **~zing** appetitanregend.

applaud [ə'plɔːd] applaudieren; loben; **~se** [**~**z] Applaus m, Beifall m.

apple ['æpl] Apfel m; **~pie** gedeckter Apfelkuchen; **~ sauce** Apfelmus n.

appliance [ə'plaiəns] Vorrichtung f, Gerät n.

applica|nt ['æplikənt] Bewerber(in); **~tion** Auf-, Anlegen n; Anwendung f; Gesuch n; Bewerbung f.

apply [ə'plai] auf-, anlegen; anwenden; verwenden; zutreffen, gelten; sich wenden (**to** an); **~ o.s.** to sich widmen; **~ for** sich bewerben um; beantragen.

appoint [ə'point] festsetzen; ernennen; **~ment** Verabredung f, Termin m; Ernennung f; Stellung f, Stelle f.

apportion [ə'pɔːʃən] ver-, zuteilen.

appreciat|e [ə'priːʃieit] schätzen, würdigen, zu schätzen wissen; **~ion** Würdigung f; Verständnis n; Anerkennung f.

apprehen|d [æpri'hend] festnehmen; begreifen, verstehen; befürchten; **~sion** Festnahme f; Verstand m; Besorgnis f; **~sive** ängstlich, besorgt.

apprentice [ə'prentis] Lehrling m; vb: **be ~d to** in die Lehre sein bei; **~ship** [**~**ʃip] Lehre f.

approach [ə'prəutʃ] sich nähern; herantreten an; (Heran)Nahen n; Annäherung f; Zugang m, Zu-, Auffahrt f; **~ road** Zufahrtsstraße f.

appropriate [ə'prəupriit] angemessen; passend.

approv|al [ə'pruːvəl] Billigung f; **~e** billigen.

approximate [ə'prɔksimit] annähernd.

apricot ['eiprikɔt] Aprikose f.

April ['eiprəl] April m.

apron ['eiprən] Schürze f.

apt [æpt] passend; begabt; **~ to** neigend zu.

aquarium [ə'kwɛəriəm] Aquarium n.

aquatic [ə'kwætik] Wasser...; **~ sports** pl Wassersport m.

aqueduct ['ækwidʌkt] Aquädukt m.

aquiline ['ækwilain] Adler...

Arab ['ærəb] Araber(in); **~ic** arabisch; Arabisch n.

arbitrary ['ɑːbitrəri] willkürlich; eigenmächtig.

arbo(u)r ['ɑːbə] Laube f.

arc [ɑːk] Bogen m; **~ade** [ɑː'keid] Arkade f.

arch¹ [ɑːtʃ] Bogen m; Gewölbe n; (sich) wölben.

arch² Haupt...; Erz...

arch³ schelmisch.

arch(a)eolog|ist [ɑːki'ɔlədʒist] Archäologe m; **~y** Archäologie f.

archaic [ɑː'keiik] veraltet.

arch|angel ['ɑːk-] Erzengel m; **∼bishop** ['ɑːtʃ'-] Erzbischof m.

archer ['ɑːtʃə] Bogenschütze m; **∼y** Bogenschießen n.

architect ['ɑːkitekt] Architekt m; **∼ure** Architektur f.

archives ['ɑːkaivz] pl Archiv n.

archway (Tor)Bogen m.

arctic ['ɑːktik] arktisch.

ard|ent ['ɑːdənt] begeistert; glühend, feurig; **∼o(u)r** fig.: Eifer m; Glut f.

are [ɑː] pres pl u. 2. sg von **be**.

area ['ɛəriə] Fläche f; Gebiet n.

Argentine ['ɑːdʒəntain] argentinisch; Argentinier (-in).

argu|e ['ɑːgjuː] erörtern; beweisen; behaupten; streiten; Einwände machen; **∼ment** Argument n, (Beweis)Grund m; Erörterung f; **∼mentation** Beweisführung f.

arise [əˈraiz] (irr **rise**) entstehen, sich ergeben; sich erheben.

arithmetic [əˈriθmətik] Rechnen n.

ark [ɑːk] Arche f.

arm¹ [ɑːm] Arm m; Armlehne f; Ärmel m.

arm² (sich) bewaffnen; **∼ament** ['ɑːməmənt] Aufrüstung f; **∼ament race** Wettrüsten n.

armchair Sessel m.

armistice [ˈɑːmistis] Waffenstillstand m (a. fig.).

armo(u)r ['ɑːmə] Rüstung f; Panzer m (a. zo.); panzern; **∼ed car** Panzerwagen m.

armpit Achselhöhle f.

arms [ɑːmz] pl Waffen pl.

army ['ɑːmi] Heer n, Armee f.

around [əˈraund] prp um, um ... her(um), rund um; Am. colloq. etwa; adv (rund)herum; überall.

arouse [əˈrauz] aufwecken; fig. aufrütteln; erregen.

arrange [əˈreindʒ] (an-)ordnen; vereinbaren, abmachen; festsetzen; **∼ment** Anordnung f; Vereinbarung f; Übereinkommen n; Vorkehrung f.

arrears [əˈriəz] pl Rückstand m; Schulden pl.

arrest [əˈrest] Verhaftung f; verhaften; hemmen; fig. fesseln.

arriv|al [əˈraival] Ankunft f; Ankömmling m; **∼e at** (an)kommen (in), eintreffen (in); **∼e at** fig. kommen zu, erreichen.

arrogan|ce ['ærəugəns] Anmaßung f; **∼t** anmaßend.

arrow ['ærəu] Pfeil m.

arsenic ['ɑːsnik] Arsen(ik) n; [ɑːˈsenik] Arsen-.

arson ['ɑːsn] jur. Brandstiftung f.

art [ɑːt] Kunst(erziehung) f; fig. List f; pl Geisteswissenschaften pl.

arter|ial [ɑːˈtiəriəl] Arterien...; **∼ial road** Ausfallstraße f; **~y** ['ɑːtəri] Arterie f, Pulsader f; fig. (Haupt)Verkehrsader f.

artful schlau, verschlagen.

article ['ɑːtikl] Artikel m (a. Zeitung), Gegenstand m, Ware f; gr. Artikel m, Geschlechtswort n.

articulate [ɑː'tikjuleit] deutlich (aus)sprechen; [~it] deutlich; gegliedert.

artificial [ɑːti'fiʃəl] künstlich, Kunst...

artillery [ɑː'tiləri] Artillerie f.

artisan [ɑːti'zæn] Handwerker m.

artist ['ɑːtist] Künstler(-in) f; Artist(in); **~ic** [ɑː'tistik] künstlerisch, Kunst...

artless ungekünstelt; arglos.

as [æz, əz] so, (ebenso) wie; als; als; während; da, weil; (so) wie; ~ ... ~ (eben)so ... wie; **~ many ~** nicht weniger als; **~ well** auch; **~ well ... ~** sowohl ... als auch; **~ for** was ... (an)betrifft.

ascen|d [ə'send] (auf-, herauf-, hinauf)steigen; be-, ersteigen; **~sion** Aufsteigen n; ♀sion (Day) Himmelfahrt(stag m) f; **~t** Aufstieg m, Besteigung f; Steigung f.

ascertain [æsə'tein] feststellen.

ascetic [ə'setik] asketisch.

ascribe [əs'kraib] zuschreiben.

aseptic [æ'septik] aseptisch(es Mittel).

ash[1] [æʃ] Esche f.

ash[2], **~es** pl [æʃiz] Asche f.

ashamed [ə'ʃeimd] beschämt; be od. feel ~ of sich e-r S. od. j-s schämen.

ash can Am. Mülleimer m.

ashore [ə'ʃɔː]: go ~ an Land gehen.

ash|-tray Asch(en)becher m; ♀ **Wednesday** Aschermittwoch m.

Asiatic [eiʃi'ætik] asiatisch; Asiat(in).

aside [ə'said] beiseite; **~ from** Am. abgesehen von.

ask [ɑːsk] fragen; verlangen; bitten; ~ **a** question e-e Frage stellen; ~ **s.o. to dinner** j-n zum Essen einladen; ~ **for** bitten um, fragen nach.

askew [əs'kjuː] schief.

asleep [ə'sliːp] schlafend; **be (fast)** ~ (fest) schlafen; **fall** ~ einschlafen.

asparagus [əs'pærəgəs] Spargel m.

aspect ['æspekt] Aussehen n; Lage f; Aspekt m.

aspire [əs'paiə]: ~ **(after, to)** streben (nach).

ass [æs] Esel m.

assail [ə'seil] angreifen, überfallen; befallen (Zweifel); **~ant** Angreifer(in).

assassin [ə'sæsin] Attentäter(in); **~ate** [~eit] ermorden; **~ation** politischer Mord, Attentat n.

atlas

assault [ə'sɔ:lt] Angriff m; angreifen.

assembl|age [ə'semblɪdʒ] tech. Montage f; **~e** [~blɪ] (sich) versammeln; tech. montieren; **~y** Versammlung f; tech. Montage f; **~y line** Fließband n.

assent [ə'sent] Zustimmung f; **~ to** zustimmen, billigen.

assert [ə'sə:t] behaupten; geltend machen.

assess [ə'ses] Kosten etc. festsetzen; besteuern.

assets ['æsets] pl Vermögen n; econ. Aktiva pl.

assign [ə'saɪn] an-, zuweisen; bestimmen; **~ment** Anweisung f.

assimilate [ə'sɪmɪleɪt] (sich) angleichen; (sich) assimilieren.

assist [ə'sɪst] beistehen, helfen; unterstützen; **~ance** Hilfe f; **~ant** Assistent(in); Verkäufer(in).

assizes [ə'saɪzɪz] pl Brit. periodisches Schwurgericht (bis 1971).

associat|e [ə'səʊʃɪeɪt] vereinigen; verbinden; assoziieren; verkehren; [~ɪt] Teilhaber m; Gefährte m; **~ion** Vereinigung f; Verbindung f; Verein m; (Handels)Gesellschaft f; Genossenschaft f; **~ion football** (Verbands)Fußball m.

assort|ed [ə'sɔ:tɪd] gemischt; **~ment** Auswahl f; Mischung f.

assume [ə'sju:m] annehmen.

assur|ance [ə'ʃʊərəns] Versicherung f; Zusicherung f; Zuversicht f, Gewißheit f; Selbstsicherheit f; **~e** [~ʊə] (ver)sichern; **~ed** Versicherte m, f.

asthma ['æsmə] Asthma n.

astir [ə'stə:] auf (den Beinen); in Aufregung.

astonish [ə'stɒnɪʃ] überraschen; be **~ed** erstaunt sein (at über); **~ing** erstaunlich; **~ment** (Er-) Staunen n, Verwunderung f.

astray [ə'streɪ]: lead **~** irreführen, verleiten.

astride [ə'straɪd] rittlings.

astringent [ə'strɪndʒənt] zs.-ziehend(es Mittel).

astronaut ['æstrənɔ:t] Astronaut m, Raumfahrer m.

asunder [ə'sʌndə] auseinander; entzwei.

asylum [ə'saɪləm] Asyl n.

at [æt, ət] räumlich: an, auf, bei, in, zu; zeitlich: an, auf, bei, in, zu; im Alter von, auf, mit, um, zu; Richtung, Ziel: auf, gegen, nach; fig. auf, bei, für, in, nach, über, um, zu.

ate [et] pret von **eat**.

athlet|e ['æθli:t] (Leicht-) Athlet m; **~ic** ['letɪk] athletisch; **~ics** sg Leichtathletik f.

Atlantic [ət'læntɪk] atlantisch; **~ (Ocean)** Atlantik m, Atlantischer Ozean m.

atlas ['ætləs] Atlas m.

atmosphere ['ætməsfiə] Atmosphäre *f*.

atom ['ætəm] Atom *n*; ~ **bomb** Atombombe *f*.

atomic [ə'tɒmik] atomar, Atom...; ~ **age** Atomzeitalter *n*; ~ **bomb** Atombombe *f*; ~ **pile** Kernreaktor *m*; ~**powered** durch Atomkraft betrieben, Atom...

atomize ['ætəmaiz] atomisieren; ~**r** Zerstäuber *m*.

atone [ə'təun]: ~ **for** wiedergutmachen.

atroci|ous [ə'trəuʃəs] scheußlich; grausam; ~**ty** [~ɒsiti] Greueltat *f*.

attach [ə'tætʃ] anheften, befestigen; *Wert* beimessen; **be ~ed to** hängen an; ~ **o.s.** to sich anschließen an; ~**ment** Anhänglichkeit *f*.

attack [ə'tæk] angreifen; Angriff *m*; med. Anfall *m*.

attempt [ə'tempt] versuchen; Versuch *m*.

attend [ə'tend] bedienen; pflegen; *med.* behandeln; teilnehmen an; *Vorlesung etc.* besuchen; anwesend sein; *fig.* begleiten; ~**ance** Begleitung *f*, Gefolge *n*; Bedienung *f*; *med.* Behandlung *f*; Besuch *m* (*e-r Schule etc.*); ~**ant** Begleiter(in); Wärter(in); *tech.* Wart *m*; *pl* Gefolge *n*.

atten|tion [ə'tenʃən] Aufmerksamkeit *f*; ~**ive** aufmerksam.

attest [ə'test] bescheinigen.

attic ['ætik] Mansarde *f*.

attitude ['ætitju:d] (Ein-)Stellung *f*; Haltung *f*.

attorney [ə'tə:ni] Bevollmächtigte *m*; *Am.* (Rechts-)Anwalt *m*.

attract [ə'trækt] anziehen; *Aufmerksamkeit* erregen, auf sich lenken; ~**ion** Anziehung(skraft) *f*; *fig.* Reiz *m*; ~**ive** reizvoll.

attribute [ə'tribju(:)t] beimessen; zurückführen (**to** auf); ['ætribju:t] Attribut *n*, Merkmal *n*; *gr.* Attribut *n*, Beifügung *f*.

auburn ['ɔ:bən] kastanienbraun.

auction ['ɔ:kʃən] Auktion *f*; *mst* ~ **off** versteigern.

audaci|ous [ɔ:'deiʃəs] kühn; unverschämt; ~**ty** [ɔ:'dæsiti] Unverschämtheit *f*.

audible ['ɔ:dəbl] hörbar.

audience ['ɔ:djəns] Publikum *n*, Zuhörer *pl*, Zuschauer *pl*; Leser(kreis *m*) *pl*; Audienz *f*.

aught [ɔ:t]: **for ~ I care** meinetwegen.

August ['ɔ:gəst] August *m*.

august [ɔ:'gʌst] erhaben.

aunt [ɑ:nt] Tante *f*.

au pair girl [əu 'pɛə] Au-pair-Mädchen *f*.

auster|e [ɔs'tiə] streng; einfach; ~**ity** [~'teriti] Strenge *f*; Einfachheit *f*.

Australian [ɔs'treiljən] australisch; Australier(in).

Austrian ['ɔstriən] österreichisch; Österreicher(in).

axis

authentic [ɔː'θentik] authentisch, zuverlässig, echt.

author ['ɔːθə] Urheber(-in); Autor(in), Schriftsteller(in), Verfasser(in); **~itative** [ɔː'θɔritativ] maßgebend; gebieterisch; zuverlässig; **~ity** Autorität f; Vollmacht f; Fachmann m; mst pl Behörde f; **~ize** ['ɔːəraiz] bevollmächtigen; **~ship** Urheberschaft f.

auto|graph ['ɔːtəgrɑːf] Autogramm n; **~mat** ['ɔːmæt] Automatenrestaurant n; **~matic** [ˌˈmætik] automatisch; **~mation** Automation f.

autumn ['ɔːtəm] Herbst m.

auxiliary [ɔːg'ziljəri] Hilfs...; **~ (verb)** gr. Hilfsverb n.

avail [ə'veil] nützen, helfen; **~ o.s. of** sich **~r S.** bedienen; Nutzen m; **of no ~** nutzlos; **~able** verfügbar, vorhanden, benutzbar; gültig.

avalanche ['ævəlɑːnʃ] Lawine f.

avaric|e ['ævəris] Geiz m; Habsucht f; **~ious** [ˌˈriʃəs] geizig; habgierig.

avenge [ə'vendʒ] rächen.

avenue ['ævinjuː] Allee f; bsd. Am. Prachtstraße f.

average ['ævəridʒ] Durchschnitt m; durchschnittlich, Durchschnitts...

averse [ə'vəːs] abgeneigt **(to, from** dat**); ~ion** Widerwille m.

avert [ə'vəːt] abwenden; vermeiden.

aviat|ion [eivi'eiʃən] Fliegen n; Luftfahrt f; **~or** ['ˌtə] Flieger m.

avoid [ə'vɔid] (ver)meiden.

avow [ə'vau] bekennen, (ein)gestehen; **~al** Bekenntnis n, (Ein)Geständnis n.

await [ə'weit] erwarten.

awake¹ [ə'weik] wach, munter.

awake² (irr) (auf)wecken; auf-, erwachen; **~ to s.th.** sich **~r S.** bewußt werden; **~n** fig. erwecken.

award [ə'wɔːd] Urteil n; Preis m; zusprechen; verleihen.

aware [ə'wɛə]: **be ~ of** wissen von, sich **~r S.** bewußt sein.

away [ə'wei] weg, fort; immerzu, darauflos.

awe [ɔː] (Ehr)Furcht f, Scheu f; (Ehr)Furcht einflößen; einschüchtern.

awful [ɔː'ful] furchtbar, schrecklich.

awhile [ə'wail] **~e** Weile.

awkward ['ɔːkwəd] ungeschickt, linkisch; unangenehm; unpraktisch.

awning ['ɔːniŋ] Plane f, Markise f.

awoke [ə'wəuk] pret u. pp von **awake¹.**

awry [ə'rai] schief; **go ~** schiefgehen.

ax(e) [æks] Axt f, Beil n.

axis ['æksis], pl **axes** ['ˌiːz] Achse f.

axle(-tree) ['æksl(-)](Rad-) Achse f.

azure ['æʒə] azur-, himmelblau.

B

babble ['bæbl] stammeln, plappern; Geplapper n.

babe [beib] Baby n, kleines Kind.

baboon [bə'bu:n] Pavian m.

baby ['beibi] Säugling m, kleines Kind, Baby n; Baby..., Kinder...; klein; ~ carriage Am. Kinderwagen m; ~hood erste Kindheit.

bachelor ['bætʃələ] Junggeselle m.

back [bæk] Rücken m; Rückseite f; Rücklehne f; Rücksitz m; Fußball: Verteidiger m; Hinter..., Rück...; rückwärtig; rückständig; zurück; hinten grenzen an; rückwärts fahren; unterstützen; sich rückwärts bewegen, zurückgehen, -fahren; ~bone Rückgrat n; ~door Hintertür f; ~fire Fehlzündung f; ~ground Hintergrund m; ~ number alte Nummer (e-r Zeitung); ~ seat Rücksitz m; ~stairs Hintertreppe f; ~stroke Rückenschwimmen n; ~ tyre Hinterreifen m; ~ward ['-wəd] Rück(wärts)...; zurückgeblieben, rückständig; zurückhaltend; ~ward(s) rückwärts, zurück; ~ wheel Hinterrad n.

bacon ['beikən] Speck m; ~ and eggs Spiegeleier mit Speck.

bacteri|um [bæk'tiəriəm], pl ~a [-iə] Bakterie f.

bad [bæd] schlecht, böse, schlimm; not (too) ~ nicht schlecht!; that's too ~ ach wie dumm!, so ein Pech!; he is ~ly off es geht ihm schlecht (finanziell); ~ly wounded schwerverwundet; want ~ly dringend brauchen.

bade [bæd] pret von bid.

badge [bædʒ] Abzeichen n.

badger ['bædʒə] Dachs m.

badminton ['bædmintən] Federballspiel n.

baffle ['bæfl] verwirren, vereiteln.

bag [bæg] Beutel m, Sack m; Tüte f; Tasche f.

baggage ['bægidʒ] Am. (Reise)Gepäck n; ~ check Am. Gepäckschein m.

bag|gy ['bægi] bauschig; ausgebeult; ~pipes pl Dudelsack m.

bail [beil] Kaution f; ~ out gegen Kaution freibekommen.

bailiff ['beilif] Gerichtsvollzieher m, -diener m; (Guts)Verwalter m.

bait [beit] Köder m (a. fig.).

bak|e [beik] (über)backen;
braten; *Ziegel* brennen;
~er Bäcker *m*; **at the
~er's beim Bäcker**; **~ery**
Bäckerei *f*; **~ing-powder**
Backpulver *n*.

balance [ˈbæləns] Waage
f; Gleichgewicht *n* (*a. fig.*);
Unruh(e) *f* (*Uhr*); ab-,
erwägen; (aus)balancieren;
econ. ~; **~ wheel** Unruh(e) *f* (*Uhr*).

balcony [ˈbælkəni] Balkon
m.

bald [bɔːld] kahl.

bale [beil] *econ.* Ballen *m*.

balk [bɔːk] Balken *m*;
Hindernis *n*; verhindern,
-eiteln; scheuen (*bsd.
Pferd*).

ball [bɔːl] Ball *m*; Kugel *f*;
(Hand-, Fuß)Ballen *m*;
Knäuel *m*; Kloß *m*; Ball
m, Tanzveranstaltung *f*.

ballad [ˈbæləd] Ballade *f*.

ballast [ˈbæləst] Ballast *m*.

ball-bearings *pl tech.*
Kugellager *n*.

ballet [ˈbælei] Ballett *n*.

ballistic [bəˈlistik] balli-
stisch.

balloon [bəˈluːn] Ballon *m*.

ballot [ˈbælət] Wahlzettel
m; (geheime) Wahl; **~-box**
Wahlurne *f*.

ball(-point)-pen Kugel-
schreiber *m*.

balm [bɑːm] Balsam *m*;
fig. Trost *m*.

balmy [ˈbɑːmi] mild; hei-
lend.

balustrade [bæləsˈtreid]
Geländer *n*.

bamboo [bæmˈbuː] Bam-
bus *m*.

ban [bæn] (amtliches) Verbot; Bann *m*, Acht *f*; verbieten.

banana [bəˈnɑːnə] Ba-
nane *f*.

band [bænd] Band *n*; Streifen *m*; Schar *f*; Bande *f*;
(Musik)Kapelle *f*.

bandage [ˈbændidʒ] Binde *f*; Verband *m*; ban-
dagieren, verbinden.

band|master Kapellmei-
ster *m*; **~stand** Musik-
pavillon *m*.

bang [bæŋ] Knall *m*;
heftiger Schlag; Pony *m*
(*Frisur*); *Tür* zuschlagen.

banish [ˈbæniʃ] verbannen;
~ment Verbannung *f*.

banisters [ˈbænistəz] *pl*
Treppengeländer *n*.

banjo [ˈbændʒou] Banjo *n*.

bank [bæŋk] Böschung *f*;
Ufer *n*; (Sand-, Wolken-)
Bank *f*; *econ.* Bank(haus *n*)
f; *Geld* auf die Bank
legen; **~-bill** Bankwechsel
m; *Am.* Banknote *f*; **~er**
Bankier *m*; **~ing** Bank...;
~note Banknote *f*; *pl*
Papiergeld *n*; **~-rate** Dis-
kontsatz *m*; **~rupt** [ˈ~rʌpt]
bankrott.

banner [ˈbænə] Banner *n*,
Fahne *f*; Transparent *n*.

banns [bænz] *pl* Aufgebot
n.

banquet [ˈbæŋkwit] Fest-
essen *n*.

bapti|sm [ˈbæptizm] Tau-
fe *f*; **~ze** [ˌ~ˈtaiz] taufen.

bar [ba:] Stange *f*, (Gitter)Stab *m*; Riegel *m*; Tafel *f* (Schokolade); Schranke *f*; Schanktisch *m*; Bar *f* (Hotel); verriegeln, -sperren; ausschließen, -verbieten.

barb [ba:b] Widerhaken *m*.

barbar|ian [ba:'bɛəriən] Barbar(in); **~ous** ['~bərəs] barbarisch.

barbed wire Stacheldraht *m*.

barber ['ba:bə] (Herren-)Friseur *m*; **at** *od.* **to the ~'s** beim *od.* zum Friseur.

bare [bɛə] nackt, bloß; kahl; leer; entblößen; **~foot(ed)** barfuß; **~headed** barhäuptig; **~ly** kaum, gerade (noch), bloß.

bargain ['ba:gin] Geschäft *n*, Handel *m*, (vorteilhafter) Kauf; (ver)handeln, übereinkommen.

barge [ba:dʒ] Lastkahn *m*.

bark[1] [ba:k] Borke *f*, Rinde *f*.

bark[2] bellen; Bellen *n*.

barley ['ba:li] Gerste *f*.

barn [ba:n] Scheune *f*; *Am.* Stall *m*.

barometer [bə'rɔmitə] Barometer *n*.

barracks ['bærəks] *sg, pl* Kaserne *f*.

barrel ['bærəl] Faß *n*; (Gewehr)Lauf *m*; Walze *f*; **~organ** Drehorgel *f*.

barren ['bærən] unfruchtbar; öde.

barricade [bæri'keid]

Barrikade *f*; verbarrikadieren, sperren.

barrier ['bæriə] Schranke *f* (*a. fig.*), Sperre *f*; *fig.* Hindernis *n*.

barrister['bæristə] Rechtsanwalt *m*, Barrister *m*.

barrow ['bærəu] Karre(n *m*) *f*.

barter ['ba:tə] Tausch *m*; tauschen.

base[1] [beis] gemein; minderwertig.

base[2] Basis *f*; Fundament *n*; Stützpunkt *m*; *fig.* stützen; **~ball** Baseball (-spiel *n*) *m*; **~less** grundlos; **~ment** Fundament *n*; Keller(geschoß *n*) *m*.

bashful ['bæʃful] schüchtern.

basic ['beisik] grundlegend, Grund...

basin ['beisn] Becken *n*; Schüssel *f*.

bask [ba:sk] sich sonnen.

basket ['ba:skit] Korb *m*; **~ball** Korbball(spiel *n*) *m*.

bass [beis] Baß *m*.

bastard ['bæstəd] unehelich; unecht; Bastard *m*.

baste[1] [beist] Braten begießen.

baste[2] (an)heften.

bat[1] [bæt] Fledermaus *f*.

bat[2] Schlagholz *n*, Schläger *m*.

bath [ba:θ] *j–n* baden; Bad *n*; take *od.* have a ~ ein Bad nehmen, baden.

bathe [beið] baden (*a. im Freien*).

become

bathing ['beiðiŋ] Baden n; Bade...; **~cap** Badekappe f, **-mütze** f; **~costume**, **~suit** Badeanzug m; **~trunks** pl Badehose f.

bath|robe Bademantel m; **~room** Badezimmer n; **~towel** Badetuch n; **~tub** Badewanne f.

baton ['bætən] Stab m; Taktstock m.

battalion [bə'tæljən] Bataillon n.

batter ['bætə] Rührteig m; heftig schlagen; **~ed** verbeult; **~y** Batterie f.

battle [bætl] Schlacht f; **~ship** Schlachtschiff n.

baulk [bɔːk] s. balk.

Bavarian [bə'veəriən] bay(e)risch; Bayer(in).

bawl [bɔːl] brüllen; johlen, grölen.

bay¹ [bei] rotbraun.

bay² Bai f, Bucht f; Erker m; **~ window** Erkerfenster n.

baza(r) [bə'zɑː] Basar m.

be [biː, bi] (irr) sein; there is, there are es gibt; he wants to ~ ... er möchte ... werden; ~ reading gerade lesen; I am to ich soll od. muß; zur Bildung des Passivs: werden.

beach [biːtʃ] Strand m; on the ~ am Strand; **~ hotel** Strandhotel n; **~wear** Strandkleidung f.

beacon ['biːkən] Blinklicht n, Leuchtfeuer n.

bead [biːd] Perle f; Tropfen m.

beak [biːk] Schnabel m.

beam [biːm] Balken m; Strahl m; Leitstrahl m; strahlender Blick; (aus-)strahlen.

bean [biːn] Bohne f.

bear¹ [beə] Bär m.

bear² (irr) tragen; gebären; ertragen; ~ out bestätigen.

beard [biəd] Bart m; bot. Granne f.

bear|er ['beərə] Überbringer(in); **~ings** pl Richtung f.

beast [biːst] Vieh n; Tier n; fig. Bestie f; **~ly** viehisch; scheußlich; ~ of prey Raubtier n.

beat [biːt] (irr) schlagen; verprügeln; besiegen; übertreffen; ~ it! sl. hau ab!; Schlag m; Pulsschlag m; mus.: Takt m; Beat m; Runde f (e-s Polizisten); **~en** pp von beat.

beauti|ful ['bjuːtəful] schön; **~fy** ['bjuːtifai] verschönern.

beauty ['bjuːti] Schönheit f; **~ parlo(u)r** Schönheitssalon m.

beaver ['biːvə] Biber m; Biberpelz m.

because [bi'kɔz] weil; ~ of wegen.

beckon ['bekən] (zu)winken.

becom|e [bi'kʌm] (irr come) werden (of aus); sich schicken für; kleiden

(Hut etc.); **~ing** schicklich; kleidsam.

bed [bed] Bett n; Lager (-statt f) n; Unterlage f; agr. Beet n; **~clothes** pl Bettzeug n; **~ding** Bettzeug f; Streu f; **~linen** Bettwäsche f; **~ridden** bettlägerig; **~room** Schlafzimmer n; **~side**: at the **~** am (Kranken)Bett; **~side table** Nachttisch m; **~spread** Bett-, Tagesdecke f; **~stead** Bettgestell n; **~time** Schlafenszeit f.

bee [bi:] Biene f.

beech [bi:tʃ] Buche f.

beef [bi:f] Rindfleisch n; **~steak** Beefsteak n; **~ tea** (klare) Fleischbrühe f.

bee|hive Bienenkorb m, **~stock** m, **~keeper** Imker m; **~line** kürzester Weg.

been [bi:n, bin] pp von **be**.

beer [biə] Bier n.

beet [bi:t] Runkelrübe f, Bete f.

beetle [bi:tl] Käfer m.

beetroot rote Rübe.

befall [bi'fɔ:l] (irr fall) zustoßen.

before [bi'fɔ:] adv voran; vorher; (schon) früher; prp vor; cj bevor, ehe; **~hand** vorher; (im) voraus.

befriend [bi'frend] sich j-s annehmen.

beg [beg] bitten; **~ (for)** betteln od. bitten um.

began [bi'gæn] pret von **begin**.

beget [bi'get] (irr) (er-)zeugen.

beggar ['begə] Bettler (-in); colloq. Kerl m.

begin [bi'gin] (irr) beginnen, anfangen; **to ~ with** um es vorwegzusagen, erstens; **~ner** Anfänger(in); **~ning** Anfang m.

begot [bi'gɔt] pret, **~ten** pp von **beget**.

begun [bi'gʌn] pp von **begin**.

behalf [bi'hɑ:f]: **on** od. **in ~ of** im Namen von; **on s.o.'s ~** um j-s willen.

behave [bi'heiv] sich benehmen; **~io(u)r** [~jə] Benehmen n.

behind [bi'haind] prp hinter; adv hinten, dahinter; zurück.

being ['bi:iŋ] (Da)Sein n; Wesen n.

belated [bi'leitid] verspätet.

belch [beltʃ] rülpsen; Feuer, Rauch ausspeien.

belfry ['belfri] Glockenturm m; Glockenstube f.

Belgian ['beldʒən] belgisch; Belgier(in).

belief [bi'li:f] Glaube m (in an); **~ve** [~v] glauben (in an); trauen; **make ~ve** vorgeben; **~ver** Gläubige m, f.

bell [bel] Glocke f; Klingel f.

belligerent [bi'lidʒərənt] kriegführend; fig. streitlustig.

bellow ['beləu] brüllen; ~s ['⁔z] pl Blasebalg m.

belly ['beli] Bauch m.

belong [bi'lɒŋ] gehören; ~ to (an)gehören, gehören zu; ~ings pl Habseligkeiten pl.

beloved [bi'lʌvd] geliebt.

below [bi'ləu] adv unten; prp unter(halb).

belt [belt] Gürtel m, Gurt m; tech. Treibriemen m; Gebiet n, Zone f.

bench [bentʃ] Bank f.

bend [bend] Biegung f, Kurve f; (irr) (sich) biegen; (sich) beugen.

beneath [bi'ni:θ] s. below.

bene|diction [beni-'dikʃən] Segen m; ~factor ['⁔fæktə] Wohltäter m; ~ficent [bi'nefisənt] wohltätig; ~ficial ['⁔'fiʃəl] wohltuend; nützlich; ~fit ['⁔fit] Wohltat f; Nutzen m, Vorteil m; Unterstützung f; nützen; Vorteil haben; ~volent [bi-'nevələnt] mildtätig, gütig; wohlwollend.

bent [bent] Hang m, Neigung f; pret u. pp von **bend**; ~ on entschlossen zu.

benzene ['benzi:n] Benzol n.

benzine ['benzi:n] Benzin n.

bequeath [bi'kwi:ð] vermachen; ~est [⁔'kwest] Vermächtnis n.

ber|eave [bi'ri:v] (irr) berauben; ~eft [⁔'reft] pret u. pp von **bereave**.

beret ['berei] Baskenmütze f.

berry ['beri] Beere f.

berth [bə:θ] Koje f; Bett n (Zug).

beside [bi'said] neben; ~ o.s. außer sich (with vor); ~s adv außerdem; prp außer, neben.

besiege [bi'si:dʒ] belagern.

best [best] adj best; größt; ~ wishes beste Wünsche; herzliche Glückwünsche; adv am besten, am meisten; ~ of all am allermeisten; der, die, das Beste; die Besten pl; all the ~ alles Gute; do one's ~ sein möglichstes tun; at ~ höchstens, bestenfalls.

bestow [bi'stəu] geben, spenden, schenken, verleihen.

bet [bet] Wette f; (irr) wetten.

betray [bi'trei] verraten; ~al Verrat m; ~er Verräter(in).

better ['betə] besser; he is ~ es geht ihm besser; so much the ~ desto besser; das Bessere; get the ~ of die Oberhand gewinnen über; überbieten; vb: ~ (o.s. sich) verbessern.

between [bi'twi:n] adv dazwischen; prp zwischen; unter.

beverage ['bevəridʒ] Getränk n.

beware [bi'wɛə] sich in acht nehmen; ~ of the

dog! Vorsicht, bissiger Hund!

bewilder [bi'wildə] verwirren; **~ment** Verwirrung f, Bestürzung f.

bewitch [bi'witʃ] bezaubern; verzaubern.

beyond [bi'jɔnd] adv darüber hinaus; prp jenseits; über (...hinaus); mehr als; außer.

bias ['baiəs] beeinflussen; **~(s)ed** befangen.

bib [bib] Lätzchen n.

Bible ['baibl] Bibel f.

bicycle ['baisikl] Fahrrad n; radfahren.

bid [bid] Gebot n, Angebot n; (irr) befehlen; *Karten:* reizen; **~ farewell** Lebewohl sagen; **~den** pp von bid.

bier [biə] (Toten)Bahre f.

big [big] groß, dick, stark; **talk** ~ prahlen; **~ business** Großunternehmertum n; **~wig** colloq. hohes Tier (*Person*).

bike [baik] colloq. (Fahr-) Rad n.

bilateral [bai'lætərəl]

bil|e [bail] Galle f (a. fig.); **~ious** ['biljəs] Gallen...

bill[1] [bil] Schnabel m.

bill[2] [bil] Gesetzentwurf m; Rechnung f; Plakat n; Am. Banknote f; econ. Wechsel m; **~board** Am. Anschlagbrett n; Reklamefläche f; **~fold** Am. Brieftasche f.

billiards ['biljədz] sg Billard(spiel) n.

billion ['biljən] Milliarde f; *früher Brit.* Billion f.

bill| of exchange Wechsel m; **~ of fare** Speisekarte f.

billow ['biləu] Woge f; wogen.

bin [bin] Behälter m, Kasten m.

bind [baind] (irr) (an-, ein-, um-, auf-, fest-, ver)binden; verpflichten; **~ing** bindend; Binden n; Einband m; Einfassung f; (Ski)Bindung f.

binoculars [bi'nɔkjuləz] pl Feldstecher m, Fern-, Opernglas n.

biography [bai'ɔgrəfi] Biographie f.

biology [bai'ɔlədʒi] Biologie f, Naturkunde f.

birch [bəːtʃ] Birke f.

bird [bəːd] Vogel m; **~ of passage** Zugvogel m; **~ of prey** Raubvogel m; **~'s-eye view** Vogelperspektive f; allgemeiner Überblick.

birth [bəːθ] Geburt f; Herkunft f; **give ~ to** gebären, zur Welt bringen; **date of ~** Geburtsdatum n; **~control** Geburtenregelung f; **~day** Geburtstag m; **happy ~day to you** ich gratuliere dir recht herzlich zum Geburtstag; **~day party** Geburtstagsgesellschaft f, -feier f; **~place** Geburtsort m.

biscuit ['biskit] Keks n, m.

bishop ['biʃəp] Bischof m.

bison ['baisn] Wisent m; Bison m.

bit [bit] Gebiß n (am Zaum); Bißchen n, Stückchen n; kleine Münze; pret von **bite**.

bitch [bitʃ] Hündin f.

bite [bait] Biß m; Bissen m; (irr) (an)beißen; fig. beißen, schneiden.

bitten ['bitn] pp von **bite**.

bitter ['bitə] bitter; fig. verbittert; **~s** pl Magenbitter m.

black [blæk] schwarz; dunkel; finster; schwärzen; Schuhe wichsen; Schwarz n; Schwärze f; Schwarze m, f (Neger); **~berry** Brombeere f; **~bird** Amsel f; **~board** (Wand)Tafel f; **~en** schwärzen; schwarz werden; **~ eye** blaues Auge; **~head** Mitesser m; **~mail** Erpressung f; erpressen; **~ market** schwarzer Markt; **~ pudding** Blutwurst f; **~smith** Schmied m. [Blase f.]

bladder ['blædə] anat.

blade [bleid] bot. Blatt n (a. Säge, Schulter etc.); Halm m; Flügel m (Propeller); Klinge f.

blame [bleim] Schuld f; Tadel m; tadeln, die Schuld geben; **to be ~ for** schuld sein an; **~less** tadellos.

blank [blæŋk] leer (a. fig.); nicht ausgefüllt, unbeschrieben; fig. verdutzt; leerer Raum, Lücke f; Niete f; fig. Leere f.

blanket ['blæŋkit] Wolldecke f.

blasphemy ['blæsfimi] Gotteslästerung f.

blast [blɑːst] Windstoß m; Luftdruck m (Explosion); Ton m (Blasinstrument); (in die Luft) sprengen; zerstören (a. fig.); ~ (it)! verdammt!; **~-furnace** Hochofen m.

blaze [bleiz] flammen, lodern; leuchten; Flamme(n pl) f; Feuer n; **~r** Blazer m, Klub-, Sportjacke f.

bleach [bliːtʃ] bleichen.

bleak [bliːk] öde, kahl; rauh; fig. freudlos, finster, trüb(e).

blear [bliə] trüb(e); trüben.

bleat [bliːt] Blöken f; blöken.

bled [bled] pret u. pp von **bleed**.

bleed [bliːd] (irr) bluten (a.fig.); fig. schröpfen.

blemish ['blemiʃ] Fehler m; Makel m; verunstalten.

blend [blend] (irr) (sich) (ver)mischen; Mischung f; Verschnitt m.

blent [blent] pret u. pp von **blend**.

bless [bles] segnen; preisen; **~ my soul!** colloq. du meine Güte!; **~ed** ['~id] gesegnet; selig; **~ing** Segen m.

blew [bluː] pret von **blow¹**.

blight [blait] Mehltau m.

blind [blaind] blind (*fig.* **to** gegenüber); Jalousie *f*, Rouleau *n*; ~ **alley** Sackgasse *f*; ~**fold** *j-m* die Augen verbinden; *fig.* blindlings.

blink [bliŋk] blinzeln, zwinkern; blinken; schimmern.

bliss [blis] Seligkeit *f*.

blister ['blistə] Blase *f*.

blithe [blaið] *mst poet.* lustig, fröhlich, munter.

blizzard ['blizəd] Schneesturm *m*.

bloate|d ['bləutid] aufgedunsen; *fig.* aufgeblasen; ~**r** Bückling *m*.

block [blɔk] (*Stein-, Häuser- etc.*)Block *m*; Klotz *m*; Verstopfung *f*, (*Verkehrs*)Stockung *f*; blockieren; ~ (**up**) (ab-, ver-) sperren.

blockade [blɔ'keid] Blockade *f*; blockieren.

block|letters *pl* Druck-, Blockschrift *f*; ~ **of flats** *Brit.* Mietshaus *n*.

blond(e) [blɔnd] blond; Blondine *f*.

blood [blʌd] Blut *n*; **in cold** ~ kaltblütig; ~**shed** Blutvergießen *n*; ~**shot** blutunterlaufen; ~**vessel** Blutgefäß *n*; ~**y** blutig.

bloom [blu:m] Blüte *f*; blühen.

blossom ['blɔsəm] Blüte *f*; blühen.

blot [blɔt] Klecks *m*, Fleck *m*; *fig.* Makel *m*; beklecksen, beflecken; (ab-) löschen; ~ **out** ausstreichen; ~**ter** Löscher *m*; ~

ting-paperLöschpapier *n*.

blouse [blauz] Bluse *f*.

blow[1] [bləu] Schlag *m*, Stoß *m*.

blow[2] (*irr*) blasen; wehen; schnaufen; durchbrennen (*Sicherung*); ~ **out** ausblasen; ~ **up** in die Luft fliegen; (in die Luft) sprengen; *phot.* vergrößern; ~ **one's nose** sich die Nase putzen; ~**n** *pp* von **blow**[1].

blue [blu:] blau; *colloq.* traurig, schwermütig; Blau *n*; *f* Glockenblume *f*; ~**s** *pl mus.* Blues *m*; *colloq.* Trübsinn *m*.

bluff [blʌf] Irreführung *f*; bluffen.

bluish ['blu(:)iʃ] bläulich.

blunder ['blʌndə] Fehler *m*, Schnitzer *m*; stolpern; (ver)pfuschen.

blunt [blʌnt] stumpf; plump, grob.

blur [blə:] Fleck(en) *m*; *fig.* undeutlicher Eindruck; verschmieren; verschwommen machen *od.* werden; trüben.

blush [blʌʃ] Erröten *n*; Schamröte *f*; erröten, rot werden. [*m.*\

boar [bɔ:] Eber *m*, Keiler *f*

board [bɔ:d] Brett *n*; (Wand)Tafel *f*; Pappe *f*; Ausschuß *m*; Amt *n*, Behörde *f*; Verpflegung *f*; **full** ~ Vollpension *f*; **on** ~ an Bord; dielen; verschalen; beköstigen; an Bord gehen, einsteigen in.

in Kost sein; **~er** Kostgänger(in); Internatsschüler(in); Pensionsgast *m*; **~ing-house** (Fremden)Pension *f*, Fremdenheim *n*; **~ing-school** Internat *n* Am. Strandpromenade *f*.

boast [bəust] Prahlerei *f*; Stolz *m*; sich rühmen, prahlen.

boat [bəut] Boot *n*; Schiff *n*; Schiffsfahrt *f*; **~-race** Ruderregatta *f*, Bootsrennen *n*.

bob [bɔb], *pl* **~** *sl.*, *alte Währung*: Schilling *m*; sich auf und ab bewegen; **~(bed hair)** Bubikopf *m*.

bobby ['bɔbi] *Brit. colloq.* Polizist *m*.

bob-sleigh ['bɔb-] Bob (-sleigh) *m*.

bodice ['bɔdis] Mieder *n*.

bodily ['bɔdili] körperlich.

body ['bɔdi] Körper *m*, Leib *m*; Leichnam *m*; *mot.* Karosserie *f*; Gruppe *f*; Körperschaft *f*; **~guard** Leibwache *f*. [Moor *n*.]

bog [bɔg] Sumpf *m*,

boil [bɔil] Furunkel *m*; kochen, sieden; **~ over** überkochen; **~ed eggs** *pl* gekochte Eier *pl*; **~er** (Dampf)Kessel *m*; Boiler *m*.

boisterous ['bɔistərəs] rauh; lärmend, laut.

bold [bəuld] kühn; keck, dreist.

bolster ['bəulstə] Keilkissen *n*; Polster *n*,

bolt [bəult] Bolzen *m*; Riegel *m*; Blitz(strahl) *m*; verriegeln; durchgehen (*Pferd*); davonlaufen; **~ upright** kerzengerade.

bomb [bɔm] Bombe *f*; mit Bomben belegen; bombardieren.

bombard [bɔm'bɑːd] bombardieren.

bond [bɔnd] Bündnis *n*; *econ.* Obligation *f*; *pl* Fesseln *pl*.

bone [bəun] Knochen *m*; Gräte *f*.

bonfire ['bɔnfaiə] (Freuden)Feuer *n*.

bonnet ['bɔnit] Haube *f*; Mütze *f*, Kappe *f*; (Motor)Haube *f*.

bonn|ie, ~y ['bɔni] hübsch, schön; gesund, rosig.

bonus ['bəunəs] *econ.* Prämie *f*; Gratifikation *f*; Zulage *f*.

bony ['bəuni] knöchern, knochig.

book [buk] Buch *n*; Heft *n*; Block *m*; (Namens-) Liste *f*; buchen, *Platz etc.* (vor)bestellen, reservieren lassen; eintragen; *Fahrkarte etc.* lösen, kaufen; *Gepäck* aufgeben; **~ed up** ausgebucht, -verkauft; voll besetzt (*Hotel*); **~case** Bücherschrank *m*, **~-regal** *n*; **~ing-clerk** Schalterbeamt|e *m*, -in *f*; **~ing-office** Fahrkartenausgabe *f*, -schalter *m*; **~-keeper** Buchhalter *m*; **~-keeping** Buchführung *f*; **~let** ['~lit] Broschüre *f*; **~shop** Buchhandlung *f*.

boom [buːm] Aufschwung *m*, Hochkonjunktur *f*, Hausse *f*.

boomerang ['buːməræŋ] *m* Bumerang *m*.

boor [buə] Lümmel *m*.

boost [buːst] *tech.* Schub *m*; hochschieben; *fig.* fördern.

boot [buːt] Stiefel *m*; *mot.* Kofferraum *m*; **~ee** ['~tiː] (Damen)Halbstiefel *m*.

booth [buːð] (Markt- *etc.*) Bude *f*; Wahlzelle *f*; *Am.*: Telephonzelle *f*.

booty ['buːti] Beute *f*.

border ['bɔːdə] Rand *m*; Einfassung *f*; Grenze *f*; einfassen; begrenzen; grenzen (**upon** an).

bore¹ [bɔː] bohren; langweilen; langweiliger *od.* lästiger Mensch; langweilige *od.* lästige Sache.

bore² *pret von* **bear**¹.

born [bɔːn] *pp von* **bear**²: gebären; **she was ~ on** ... sie wurde am ... geboren; **~e** *pp von* **bear**²: tragen.

borough ['bʌrə] *Brit.*: Stadtgemeinde *f*; Stadt *f* mit eigener Vertretung im Parlament.

borrow ['bɔrəu] (aus)borgen, (ent)leihen.

bosom ['buzəm] Busen *m*.

boss [bɔs] *colloq.* Boß *m*, Chef *m*.

botany ['bɔtəni] Botanik *f*, Pflanzenkunde *f*.

botch [bɔtʃ] Flickwerk *n*; verpfuschen.

both [bəuθ] beide(s); **~ ... and** sowohl ... als (auch).

bother ['bɔðə] Plage *f*, Mühe *f*; belästigen, plagen; **~ about** sich Gedanken machen wegen, sich sorgen um.

bottle ['bɔtl] in Flaschen abfüllen; Flasche *f*; **a ~ of** e-e Flasche ...

bottom ['bɔtəm] Boden *m*, Grund *m*; Fuß *m* (*Berg*); (unteres) Ende; *colloq.* Hintern *m*.

bough [bau] Ast *m*.

bought [bɔːt] *pret u. pp von* buy. |block *m.*|

boulder ['bəuldə] Geröll-*f*

bounce [bauns] Sprung *m*; Aufprallen *n*; (hoch)springen.

bound¹ [baund] *pret u. pp von* bind; unterwegs (**for** nach); Sprung *m*; Grenze *f*; (an-, auf-, ab)prallen; begrenzen; **~ary** Grenze *f*; **~less** grenzenlos.

bouquet [buˈkei] (Blumen)Strauß *m*; Blume *f* (*Wein*).

bout [baut] *med.* Anfall *m*; (Wett)Kampf *m*.

bow¹ [bau] *mar.* Bug *m*; Verbeugung *f*; sich (ver)beugen (**to** vor); biegen; beugen, neigen.

bow² [bəu] Bogen *m*; Schleife *f*.

bowels ['bauəlz] *pl* Eingeweide *pl*.

bower ['bauə] Laube f.
bowl[1] [bəul] Schüssel f; Schale f; Humpen m; (Pfeifen)Kopf m.
bowl[2] Kugel f; Ball, Kugel rollen, werfen.
box [bɔks] Büchse f, Schachtel f, Kasten m; *thea.* Loge f; Box f (*für Pferde etc.*); boxen; **~ s.o.'s ear(s)** j-n ohrfeigen; **~er** Boxer m; **~ing** Boxen n; **2ing Day** zweiter Weihnachtsfeiertag; **~ing-match** Boxkampf m; **~-office** Theaterkasse f.
boy [bɔi] Junge m, Bursche m.
boycott ['bɔikət] boykottieren.
boy|-friend Freund m; **~hood** Knabenalter m; **~ish** knabenhaft; kindisch; **2 Scout** Pfadfinder m.
bra [brɑː] *colloq.* Büstenhalter m.
brace [breis] Strebe f; pl Hosenträger m; verstreben; (**o.s. [up]**) sich zs.-nehmen.
bracelet ['breislit] Armband n.
bracket ['brækit] *tech.* Winkelstütze f; *print.* Klammer f; einklammern.
brag [bræg] prahlen, **~gart** ['~ət] Prahler m.
braid [breid] (Haar)Flechte f; Borte f; Tresse f; flechten; mit Borte besetzen.
brain [brein] Gehirn n;

fig. Verstand m; **~ wave** *colloq.* Geistesblitz m.
brake [breik] Bremse f; bremsen.
bramble ['bræmbl] Brombeerstrauch m.
branch [brɑːntʃ] Zweig m (*a. fig.*), Ast m; Gebiet n; Fach n; Zweigstelle f, Filiale f; sich verzweigen; abzweigen.
brand [brænd] (Feuer-)Brand m; Brandmal n; *econ.*: Handelsmarke f, Sorte f; einbrennen; *fig.* brandmarken.
bran(d)-new nagelneu.
brass [brɑːs] Messing n; **~ band** Blaskapelle f.
brassière ['bræsiə] Büstenhalter m.
brave [breiv] tapfer, mutig; trotzen; **~ry** Tapferkeit f.
Brazilian [brə'ziljən] brasilianisch; Brasilianer(in).
breach [briːtʃ] Bruch m; *fig.* Bruch m, Verletzung f; durchbrechen.
bread [bred] Brot n; **~ and-butter letter** Dankbrief m.
breadth [bredθ] Breite f, Weite f.
break [breik] Bruch(stelle f) m; Öffnung f, Lücke f; Pause f; (*Tages*)Anbruch m; (*irr*) (zer)brechen; (zer)reißen (*Seil*); ruinieren; *Pferd* zureiten; *Bank* sprengen; *Reise etc.* unterbrechen; *Nachricht* schonend mitteilen; los-, an-, aufbre-

chen; umschlagen (*Wetter*); ~ **away** sich losreißen; ~ **down** niederreißen; zs.-brechen (*a. fig.*), einstürzen; *mot.* Panne haben; ~ **in** Pferd zureiten; einbrechen; ~ **off** abbrechen; ~ **out** ausbrechen; ~ **up** aufbrechen, -stören; schließen, in die Ferien gehen; *fig.*: (sich) auflösen; verfallen; **~able** zerbrechlich; **~down** Zs.-bruch *m*; Maschinenschaden *m*; *mot.* Panne *f*; **~down service** Abschlepp-, Pannendienst *m*.

breakfast ['brekfəst] Frühstück *n*; **~ bed and ~** Zimmer mit Frühstück; **at** *od.* **for ~** beim *od.* zum Frühstück; **(have) ~** frühstücken.

breast [brest] Brust *f*; **~stroke** Brustschwimmen *n*.

breath [breθ] Atem(zug) *m*; Hauch *m*; **hold one's ~** den Atem anhalten; **~e** [bri:ð] (ein- u. aus-)atmen; wehen; hauchen; flüstern; **~ing** ['ˈbri:ðiŋ] Atmen *n*, Atmung *f*; **~less** ['breθlis] atemlos.

bred [bred] *pret* u. *pp von* **breed**.

breeches ['britʃiz] *pl* Knie-, Reithosen *pl*.

breed [bri:d] Zucht *f*, Rasse *f*; Herkunft *f*; (*irr*) züchten; auf-, erziehen; brüten; sich fortpflanzen; **~er** Züchter(in); **~ing** (Tier)Zucht *f*; Erziehung *f*.

breeze [bri:z] Brise *f*.

brew [bru:] brauen; sich zs.-brauen; **~ery** Brauerei *f*.

bribe [braib] Bestechung(s-geld *n*, -geschenk *n*) *f*; bestechen; **~ry** Bestechung *f*.

brick [brik] Ziegel(stein) *m*; **~layer** Maurer *m*; **~work** Mauerwerk *n*; **~works** *sg* Ziegelei *f*.

bridal ['braidl] Braut...

bride [braid] Braut *f*, Neuvermählte *f*; **~groom** Bräutigam *m*, Neuvermählte *r*; **~smaid** Brautjungfer *f*.

bridge [bridʒ] Brücke *f*; e-e Brücke schlagen über; ~ **over** *fig.* überbrücken.

bridle ['braidl] Zaum *m*; Zügel *m*; (auf)zäumen; zügeln (*a. fig.*); **~path**, **~road** Reitweg *m*.

brief [bri:f] kurz, bündig; **~case** Aktenmappe *f*.

brigade [bri'geid] Brigade *f*.

bright [brait] hell, glänzend; strahlend; *fig.* gescheit; **~en** (sich) aufhellen; erhellen; aufheitern; **~ness** Helligkeit *f*; Glanz *m*; Aufgewecktheit *f*.

brillian|ce, **~cy** ['briljəns, ˈsi] Glanz *m*; **~t** glänzend; *fig.* ausgezeichnet; geistreich; Brillant *m*.

brim [brim] Rand *m*; Krempe *f*; **~ful(l)** ganz voll.

bring [briŋ] (*irr*) (mit-her)bringen; *j-n* veranlassen, dazu bringen; ~ **an**

buffet

action against s.o. j-n verklagen; **~ about** zustande bringen; **~ forth** hervorbringen; **~ in** (her-)einbringen; **~ up** auf-, erziehen.

brink [briŋk] Rand m.

brisk [brisk] lebhaft, flink.

bristle ['brisl] Borste f; sich sträuben.

Brit|**ish** ['britiʃ] britisch, selten: englisch; sub: **the ~ish** pl die Briten pl; **~on** ['~tn] Brit|e m, -in f.

brittle ['britl] spröde.

broach [brəutʃ] Thema anschneiden.

broad [brɔːd] breit; weit; hell (Tag); deutlich (Wink); allgemein; liberal; **~cast** (irr cast) Radio: senden; Rundfunksendung f; **~minded** großzügig.

brochure ['brəuʃjuə] Broschüre f; Prospekt m.

broke [brəuk] pret von **break**; sl. pleite, ohne e-n Pfennig; **~n** pp von **break**; zerbrochen, kaputt; zerrüttet; **~r** Makler m.

bronze [brɔnz] Bronze f; bronzen, Bronze...

brooch [brəutʃ] Brosche f.

brood [bruːd] Brut f; Zucht f; brüten (a. fig.).

brook [bruk] Bach m.

broom [brum] Besen m.

broth [brɔθ] (Fleisch-)Brühe f.

brothel ['brɔθl] Bordell n.

brother ['brʌðə] Bruder m; **~(s) and sister(s)** Geschwister pl; **~-in-law** Schwager m; **~ly** brüderlich.

brought [brɔːt] pret u. pp von **bring**.

brow [brau] (Augen)Braue f; Stirn f.

brown [braun] braun; Braun n; **~ paper** Packpapier n.

bruise [bruːz] med. Quetschung f; blauer Fleck; (zer)quetschen.

brush [brʌʃ] Bürste f; Pinsel m; (Fuchs)Rute f; Unterholz n; (ab-, aus-)bürsten; putzen; fegen; streifen; **~ up** fig. auffrischen.

Brussels sprouts ['brʌsl'sprauts] pl Rosenkohl m.

brut|**al** ['bruːtl] brutal, roh; **~ality** [~'tæliti] Brutalität f; **~e** [bruːt] Vieh n; fig. Scheusal n.

bubble ['bʌbl] Blase f; sprudeln.

buck [bʌk] Bock m; Am. sl. Dollar m; bocken.

bucket ['bʌkit] Eimer m.

buckle ['bʌkl] Schnalle f; (um-, zu)schnallen; **~ on** anschnallen.

buckskin Wildleder n.

bud [bʌd] Knospe f, Auge n; fig. Keim m; knospen.

buddy ['bʌdi] Am. colloq. Kamerad m.

budget ['bʌdʒit] Haushaltsplan m, Etat m.

buffalo ['bʌfələu] Büffel m.

buffer ['bʌfə] tech. Puffer m.

buffet ['bʌfit] Büfett n,

Anrichte *f*; ['bufei] Büfett *n*; Theke *f*.

bug [bʌg] Wanze *f*; *Am.* Insekt *n*, Käfer *m*.

bugle ['bjuːgl] Wald-, Signalhorn *n*.

build [bild] (*irr*) (er-)bauen, errichten; **⁓er** Baumeister *m*; Bauunternehmer *m*; **⁓ing** Bau *m*, Gebäude *n*; Bau...

built [bilt] *pret u. pp von* **build**.

bulb [bʌlb] Zwiebel *f*, Knolle *f*; (Glüh)Birne *f*.

bulge [bʌldʒ] (Aus)Bauchung *f*, Beule *f*, Buckel *m*; sich (aus)bauchen; hervorquellen.

bulk [bʌlk] Umfang *m*, Masse *f*; **the ⁓** der Hauptteil; **⁓y** umfangreich; sperrig.

bull [bul] Bulle *m*, Stier *m*.

bullet ['bulit] Kugel *f*, Geschoß *n*.

bulletin ['bulitin] Tagesbericht *m*; **⁓ board** *Am.* Schwarzes Brett.

bullion ['buljən] (Gold-*etc.*)Barren *m*.

bully ['buli] tyrannisieren.

bum [bʌm] *sl.*Vagabund *m*.

bumble-bee ['bʌmbl-] Hummel *f*.

bump [bʌmp] Schlag *m*; Beule *f*; holperige Stelle; (zs.-)stoßen; holpern; **⁓er** *mot.* Stoßstange *f*; volles Glas (*Wein*).

bun|bʌn] Rosinenbrötchen *n*; (Haar)Knoten *m*.

bunch [bʌntʃ] Bund *n*;

Bündel *n*; Strauß *m*; Büschel *n*; *colloq.* Haufen *m*; **⁓ of grapes** Weintraube *f*.

bundle ['bʌndl] Bündel *n*; *vb*: **⁓ up** (zs.-)bündeln, zs.-binden.

bungalow ['bʌŋgələu] Bungalow *m*.

bungle ['bʌŋgl] Pfuscherei *f*; (ver)pfuschen.

bunion ['bʌnjən] entzündeter Fußballen.

bunk [bʌŋk] (Schlaf)Koje *f*; **⁓ bed** Etagenbett *n*.

bunny ['bʌni] Kaninchen *n*, Häschen *n*.

buoy [bɔi] Boje *f*.

burden ['bəːdn] Last *f*; Bürde *f*; *mus.* Kehrreim *m*, Refrain *m*; belasten.

bureau ['bjuərəu] Büro *n*; Geschäftsstelle *f*; Schreibtisch *m*; *Am.* (Spiegel-)Kommode *f*.

burglar ['bəːglə] Einbrecher *m*; **⁓y** Einbruch(sdiebstahl) *m*.

burial ['beriəl] Begräbnis *n*.

burly ['bəːli] stämmig, kräftig.

burn [bəːn] Brandwunde *f*; (*irr*) (ver-, an)brennen; **⁓er** Brenner *m*; **⁓ing** brennend (*a. fig.*); **⁓t** *pret u. pp von* **burn**.

burst [bəːst] Bersten *n*; Bruch *m*; Ausbruch *m*; **⁓ of laughter** Lachsalve *f*; (irr) sprengen; bersten, platzen; zerspringen, explodieren; **⁓ into flames** in Flammen aufgehen;

~ into tears in Tränen ausbrechen;

bury ['beri] begraben, beerdigen; vergraben; verbergen. [Bus m.]

bus [bʌs] (Omni-, Auto-)

bush [buʃ] Busch m, Strauch m; Gebüsch n; Busch m, Urwald m; **~el** ['~ʃl] Scheffel m (36,37l); **~y** buschig.

business ['biznis] Geschäft n; Handel m; Angelegenheit f; Aufgabe f; Recht n; **on ~** geschäftlich; **mind one's own ~** sich um s-e eigenen Angelegenheiten kümmern; **talk ~** über geschäftliche Dinge reden; **~ hours** pl Geschäftszeit f; **~ letter** Geschäftsbrief m; **~-like** geschäftsmäßig, sachlich; **~man** Geschäftsmann m; **~ tour**, **~ trip** Geschäftsreise f.

bus stop Bushaltestelle f.

bust [bʌst] Büste f.

bustle ['bʌsl] geschäftiges Treiben; hetzen; hasten; sich beeilen.

busy ['bizi] beschäftigt; geschäftig, fleißig; Am. teleph. besetzt; **be ~ doing s.th.** mit et. beschäftigt sein; **~ o.s.** sich beschäftigen.

but [bʌt, bət] cj aber, jedoch; sondern; außer; ohne daß; adv nur, bloß; prp außer; **I cannot ~** ich muß; **all ~** fast; **the last one** der vorletzte; **the next one** der über-

nächste; **~ for** wenn nicht ... gewesen wäre; ohne; **~ that** wenn nicht; **~ then** andererseits.

butcher ['butʃə] Schlächter m, Fleischer m, Metzger m.

butt [bʌt] (Gewehr)Kolben m; Stummel m, Kippe f; Zielscheibe f (a. fig.); **~ in** colloq. sich einmischen.

butter ['bʌtə] Butter f; mit Butter bestreichen; **~cup** Butterblume f; **~fly** Schmetterling m.

buttocks ['bʌtəks] pl Gesäß n.

button ['bʌtn] Knopf m; (a. **~ up** zu)knöpfen; **~hole** Knopfloch n.

buttress ['bʌtris] Strebepfeiler m.

buxom ['bʌksəm] drall.

buy [bai] (irr) kaufen, einkaufen; **~er** Käufer(in).

buzz [bʌz] Summen n; Stimmengewirr n; summen, surren. [m.]

buzzard ['bʌzəd]Bussard f

by [bai] prp bei; an; neben; durch; über; an ... entlang od. vorbei; bis (zu); von; mit; um; nach; **~ o.s.** allein; **~ twos** zu zweien; **~ the dozen** dutzendweise; **~ the end** gegen Ende; **~ land** zu Lande; **go ~ bus (rail, train)** mit dem Bus (Zug, der Bahn) fahren; **day—day** Tag für Tag; adv nahe, dabei; vorbei, -über; beiseite; **~ and** bald;

nach und nach, allmählich.

by- [bai] Neben..., Seiten...
bye-bye ['bai'bai] *s.* good-bye (*int.*).
by|election Nachwahl *f*; **~gone** vergangen; **~name** Beiname *m*; Spitz-

name *m*; **~pass** Umgehungsstraße *f*; **~product** Nebenprodukt *n*; **~road** Seitenstraße *f*; **~stander** Zuschauer(in); **~street** Neben-, Seitenstraße *f*; **~word** Inbegriff *m*; Gespött *m*.

C

cab [kæb] Taxi *n*, Droschke *f*. [(-kopf) *m*.]
cabbage ['kæbidʒ] Kohl}
cabin ['kæbin] Hütte *f*; *mar.* Kabine *f* (*a. aer.*), Kajüte *f*; **three-berth ~** Dreibettkabine *f*.
cabinet ['kæbinit] Kabinett *n*; Schrank *m*; Vitrine *f*; **~maker** (Kunst-) Tischler *m*, Schreiner *m*.
cable ['keibl] Kabel *n*; Ankerkette *f*; *tel.* kabeln; **~car** Drahtseilbahn *f*.
cab|man Taxifahrer *m*; **~stand** Taxistand *m*.
cackle ['kækl] gackern, schnattern.
cact|us ['kæktəs], *pl* **~uses** ['~siz], **~i** ['~tai] Kaktus *m*.
café ['kæfei] Café *n*; Restaurant *n*.
cafeteria [kæfi'tiəriə] Selbstbedienungsrestaurant *n*.
cage [keidʒ] Käfig *m*; Förderkorb *m*.
cake [keik] Kuchen *m*; Riegel *m*, Stück *n*; **a ~ of soap** ein Stück Seife; zs.-backen; **~tin** Kuchenform *f*.

calamity [kə'læmiti] Unglück *n*, Katastrophe *f*.
calculat|e ['kælkjuleit] (be-, aus-, er)rechnen; **~ion** Kalkulation *f*, Berechnung *f*; Überlegung *f*.
calendar ['kælində] Kalender *m*.
calf [kɑːf], *pl* **calves** [~vz] Kalb *n*; Wade *f*.
calib|re, *Am.* **~er** ['kælibə] Kaliber *n*.
call [kɔːl] Ruf *m*; *teleph.* Anruf *m*, Gespräch *n*; Besuch *m*; Aufforderung *f*; Forderung *f*; **~ for help** Hilferuf *m*; (herbei)rufen; (ein)berufen; *teleph.* anrufen; nennen; **be ~ed** heißen; ~ **s.o. names** j-n beschimpfen, beleidigen; ~ **back** *teleph.* wieder anrufen; ~ **at** besuchen, gehen zu; *rail.* halten in; *Hafen* anlaufen; ~ **for** rufen nach, rufen um (*Hilfe*); *et.* (an)fordern; abholen; ~ **on s.o.** j-n besuchen; ~ **up** *teleph.* anrufen; *mil.* einberufen; **~box** Telephonzelle *f*; **~er** Anrufer(in); Besu-

cap

cher(in); **~ing** Beruf m.
callous ['kæləs] schwielig; fig. gefühllos, gleichgültig.
calm [ka:m] still, ruhig; (Wind)Stille f; Ruhe f; besänftigen; beruhigen; **~down** sich beruhigen.
calorie ['kæləri] Kalorie f.
calves [ka:vz] pl von calf.
cambric ['keimbrik] Batist m.
came [keim] pret von come.
camel ['kæməl] Kamel n.
camera ['kæmərə] Kamera f, Photoapparat m.
camomile ['kæməumail] Kamille f.
camouflage ['kæmuflu:ʒ] Tarnung f; tarnen.
camp [kæmp] (Zelt)Lager n; mil. Feldlager n; lagern; **~ (out)** zelten; **~aign** [~'pein] Feldzug m; **~ bed** Feldbett n; **~er** Zelt-, Lagerbewohner m; **~ground** Am. für **~ing-ground**; **~ing** Camping n, Zelten n; **go ~ing** zelten (gehen); **~ing-ground** Camping-, Zeltplatz m.
campus ['kæmpəs] Am. Universitäts-, Schulgelände n.
can¹ [kæn] v/aux ich, du etc.: kann(st) etc., darf(st) etc.
can² Kanne f; Am. (Konserven)Dose f; (-)Büchse f; eindosen.
Canadian [kə'neidjən] kanadisch; Kanadier(in).
canal [kə'næl] Kanal m.

canary [kə'nɛəri] Kanarienvogel m.
cancel ['kænsəl] (durch-)streichen; entwerten; absagen; rückgängig machen; **be ~(l)ed** ausfallen; **~ out** sich aufheben.
cancer ['kænsə] Krebs m.
candid ['kændid] aufrichtig, offen.
candidate ['kændidit] Kandidat m. [diert.]
candied ['kændid] kan-]
candle ['kændl] Kerze f; **~stick** Kerzenleuchter m.
candy ['kændi] Am. Süßigkeiten pl.
cane [kein] bot. Rohr n; (Rohr)Stock m.
cann|ed [kænd] Am. Büchsen...; **~ery** Am. Konservenfabrik f.
cannibal ['kænibəl] Kannibale m.
cannon ['kænən] Kanone f.
cannot ['kænɔt] nicht können od. dürfen.
canoe [kə'nu:] Kanu n; Paddelboot n.
canopy ['kænəpi] Baldachin m.
cant [kænt] Jargon m; Heuchelei f.
can't [ka:nt] s. cannot.
canteen [kæn'ti:n] Kantine f; Am. Feldflasche f; Kochgeschirr n.
canvas ['kænvəs] Segeltuch n; Zeltleinwand f; paint. Leinwand f.
canvass ['kænvəs] Stimmen, Abonnenten werben.
cap [kæp] Kappe f, Mütze

f; Haube *f*; Verschluß (-kappe *f*) *m*.

capab|ility [keipə'biliti] Fähigkeit *f*; **~le fähig (of** zu).

capacity [kə'pæsiti] (Raum)Inhalt *m*; Fassungsvermögen *n*; Kapazität *f*; Aufnahme-, (Leistungs)Fähigkeit *f*.

cape[1] [keip] Kap *n*, Vorgebirge *n*.

cape[2] Cape *n*, Umhang *m*.

caper ['keipə] (**cut a**) *od.* **cut ~s** Luftsprünge *od.* Kapriolen machen.

capital ['kæpitl] Hauptstadt *f*; Kapital *n*; Kapital...; Haupt...; *colloq.* vortrefflich; **~ crime** Kapitalverbrechen *n*; **~ism** Kapitalismus *m*; **~ (letter)** großer Buchstabe; **~ punishment** Todesstrafe *f*.

capricious [kə'priʃəs] launenhaft.

capsize [kæp'saiz] kentern; zum Kentern bringen.

capsule ['kæpsju:l] Kapsel *f*.

captain ['kæptin] Führer *m*; Kapitän *m*; *mil.* Hauptmann *m*.

caption ['kæpʃən] Überschrift *f*, Titel *m*; Bildunterschrift *f*; Film: Untertitel *m*.

captiv|ate ['kæptiveit] *fig.* fesseln; **~e** Gefangene *m*, *f*; **~ity** ['tiviti] Gefangenschaft *f*.

capture ['kæptʃə] Gefangennahme *f*; fangen, ge-

fangennehmen; erbeuten; *mar.* kapern; erlangen, gewinnen; *fig.* fesseln.

car [ku:] Auto *n*; (*bsd. Am.* Eisenbahn-, Straßenbahn-) Wagen *m*; Gondel *f*, Kabine *f*.

caravan ['kærəvæn] Karawane *f*; Wohnwagen *m*.

carbohydrate ['ka:bou-'haidreit] Kohlehydrat *n*.

carbon ['ka:bən] *chem.* Kohlenstoff *m*; **~ dioxide** ['~dai'ɔksaid] Kohlendioxyd *n*; **~ paper** Kohlepapier *n*.

carbure|tter, ~t(t)or['ka:-bjuretə] *mot.* Vergaser *m*.

car-carrier Autoreisezug *m*.

carca|se, ~ss ['ka:kəs] Kadaver *m*.

card [ka:d] (Post-, Geschäfts-, Visiten-, Spiel-) Karte *f*; **~board** Pappe *f*; **~board box** (Papp)Karton *m*.

cardigan ['ka:digən] Wolljacke *f*.

cardinal ['ka:dinl] Kardinal *m*; Haupt...; **~ number** Grundzahl *f*.

card index Kartei *f*.

car documents *pl* Wagenpapiere *pl*.

care [kɛə] Sorge *f*; Sorgfalt *f*; Fürsorge *f*, Obhut *f*, Pflege *f*, Aufsicht *f*; sich et. aus *e-r* S. machen; Lust haben; **~ of** (*abbr.* *c/o*) bei ...; **take ~ of** acht(geb)en auf, sich kümmern um, sorgen für; **with**

_! Vorsicht!; _vb_: **_** for sorgen für, sich kümmern um; sich etwas machen aus; **I don't _!** meinetwegen!

career [kə'riə] Karriere _f_; Laufbahn _f_; rasen.

care|free sorgenfrei; **_ful** vorsichtig; umsichtig; sorgfältig; **_less** sorglos; nachlässig, unachtsam; leichtsinnig.

caress [kə'res] Liebkosung _f_; liebkosen.

care|taker (Haus)Verwalter(in); **_worn** abgehärmt, verhärmt.

car ferry Autofähre _f_.

cargo ['ka:gəu] Ladung _f_.

caricature [kærikə'tjuə] Karikatur _f_.

car-mechanic Automechaniker _m_.

carnation [ka:'neiʃən] Nelke _f_.   [neval _m_.]

carnival ['ka:nivəl] Karneval _m_;

carol ['kærəl] (Weihnachts)Lied _n_.

carp [ka:p] Karpfen _m_.

car-park Parkplatz _m_.

carpenter ['ka:pintə] Zimmermann _m_, Tischler _m_.

carpet ['ka:pit] Teppich _m_.

carriage ['kæridʒ] (Eisenbahn- _etc_.) Wagen _m_; Transport _m_; Fracht(geld _n_) _f_; (Körper)Haltung _f_; **_-way** frachtfrei; **_-way** Fahrbahn _f_.

carrier ['kæriə] Träger _m_, Bote _m_; Fuhrunternehmer _m_; (Krankheits)Überträger _m_; Gepäckträger _m_

(_Fahrrad_); **_bag** Einkaufstüte _f_, Tragbeutel _m_.

carrion ['kæriən] Aas _n_; Aas...

carrot ['kærət] Karotte _f_, Mohrrübe _f_, Möhre _f_.

carry ['kæri] tragen, bringen, befördern; (bei sich) haben; **_ on** fortsetzen, weiterführen; _Geschäft etc._ betreiben; **_ out** aus-, durchführen.

cart [ka:t] Fuhrwerk _n_; Karren _m_, Wagen _m_; karren, fahren; **_er** Fuhrmann _m_; **_-horse** Zugpferd _n_.

carton ['ka:tən] Karton _m_, (Papp)Schachtel _f_.

cartoon [ka:'tu:n] Karikatur _f_; (**animated**) **_** Zeichentrickfilm _m_; **_ist** Karikaturist _m_

cartridge ['ka:tridʒ] Patrone _f_.

cart-wheel Wagenrad _n_; **turn _s** radschlagen.

carv|e [ka:v] _Fleisch_ zerlegen, tranchieren; schnitzen; meißeln; **_er** Schnitzer _m_; **_ing** Schnitzerei _f_.

cascade [kæs'keid] Wasserfall _m_.

case¹ [keis] Behälter _m_; Kiste _f_; Etui _n_; Schachtel _f_; kleiner Koffer; Tasche _f_.

case² Fall _m_ (_a. med., jur._); _gr._ Kasus _m_, Fall _m_; Sache _f_, Angelegenheit _f_; **in any _** auf jeden Fall.

casement ['keismənt] Fensterflügel _m_.

cash [kæʃ] einlösen; Bar-

geld *n*; Geld *n*, Kasse *f*;
~ **down** gegen bar; ~ **on delivery** per Nachnahme, zahlbar bei Lieferung; ~ **desk** Kasse *f* (*Bank etc.*); **.ier** [kæ'ʃiə] Kassierer (-in); ~ **register** (Registrier)Kasse *f*.

casing [keisiŋ] Umhüllung *f*; Verkleidung *f*.

cask [kɑ:sk] Faß *n*; **.et** ['.it] Kästchen *n*; *Am.* Sarg *m*.

cassock ['kæsək] Soutane *f*.

cast [kɑ:st] Wurf *m*; *tech.* Guß(form *f*) *m*; Abguß *m*, Abdruck *m*; *thea.* (Rollen-)Besetzung *f*; (*irr*) (ab-, aus)werfen; *tech.* gießen; *thea.* Stück besetzen; *Rollen* verteilen; **be ~ down** niedergeschlagen sein.

caste [kɑ:st] Kaste *f*.

cast| **iron** Gußeisen *n*; **~-iron** gußeisern.

castle [kɑ:sl] Burg *f*, Schloß *n*.

castor [kɑ:stə] (Salz- *etc.*) Streuer *m*.

castor oil Rizinusöl *n*.

cast| **steel** Gußstahl *m*; **~-steel** aus Gußstahl.

casual ['kæʒjuəl] zufällig; gelegentlich; zwanglos; flüchtig; **.ty** Unfall *m*; Verunglückte *m,f*; *pl* Opfer *pl*, *mil.* Verluste *pl*.

cat [kæt] Katze *f*.

catalog(ue) ['kætəlɔg] Katalog *m*.

cataract ['kætərækt] Wasserfall *m*.

catarrh [kə'tɑ:] Katarrh *m*; Schnupfen *m*.

catastrophe [kə'tæstrəfi] Katastrophe *f*.

catch [kætʃ] Fang(en *n*) *m*; Beute *f*; *tech.* Haken *m* (*a. fig.*), Klinke *f*; (*irr*) fangen; fassen; ertappen; *Zug etc.* erreichen, bekommen; sich *Krankheit* zuziehen, holen; *fig.* erfassen; einschnappen (*Schloß*); sich verfangen, hängenbleiben; ~ **(a) cold** sich erkälten; ~ **up (with)** einholen, überholen; **.er** Fänger *m*; **.ing** packend; *med.* ansteckend; **.word** Schlagwort *n*; Stichwort *n*.

category ['kætigəri] Kategorie *f*.

cater [keitə]: ~ **for** Lebensmittel liefern für; sorgen für.

caterpillar ['kætəpilə] *zo.* Raupe *f*.

cathedral [kə'θi:drəl] Dom *m*, Kathedrale *f*.

Catholic ['kæθəlik] katholisch; Katholik(in).

cattle [kætl] (Rind)Vieh *n*, Rinder *pl*.

caught [kɔ:t] *pret u. pp von* catch.

ca(u)ldron ['kɔ:ldrən] Kessel *m*.

cauliflower ['kɔliflauə] Blumenkohl *m*.

cause [kɔ:z] Ursache *f*, Grund *m*; Sache *f*; verursachen, -anlassen; bereiten; **.less** grundlos.

caution ['kɔ:ʃən] Vorsicht f; (Ver)Warnung f; (ver)warnen; **~ous** behutsam, vorsichtig.

cav|e [keiv], **~ern** ['kævən] Höhle f; **~ity** ['kæviti] Höhle f; Loch n.

cease [si:s] aufhören; **~less** unaufhörlich.

ceiling ['si:liŋ] (Zimmer-) Decke f; Preise: Höchstgrenze f.

celebrat|e ['selibreit] feiern; **~ed** berühmt; **~ion** Feier f.

celebrity [si'lebriti] Berühmtheit f.

celery ['seləri] Sellerie m.

celibacy ['selibəsi] Zölibat n.

cell [sel] Zelle f; electr. a. Element n.

cellar ['selə] Keller m.

Celt [kelt] Kelte m, -in f; **~ic** keltisch; das Keltische.

cement [si'ment] Zement m; Kitt m; zementieren; kitten.

cemetery ['semitri] Friedhof m.

censor ['sensə] zensieren; **~ship** Zensur f.

censure ['senʃə] Tadel m; tadeln.

cent [sent] Am. Cent m; per **~** Prozent n; **~enary** [~'ti:nəri], **~ennial** [~'tenjəl] hundertjährig; Hundertjahrfeier f.

centi|grade ['sentigreid]: **10 degrees ~** 10 Grad Celsius; **~metre,** Am. **~meter** Zentimeter n, m.

central ['sentrəl] zentral;

Mittel...; **2 Europe** Mitteleuropa n; **~ heating** Zentralheizung f; **~ize** zentralisieren.

cent|re, Am. **~er** ['sentə] Zentrum n, Mittelpunkt m; (sich) konzentrieren; zentrieren; **~re-forward** Mittelstürmer m; **~re-half** Mittelläufer m.

century ['sentʃuri] Jahrhundert n.

cereals ['siəriəlz] pl Frühstückskost f (aus Getreide).

cerebral ['seribrəl] Gehirn...

ceremon|ial [seri'mounjəl] Zeremoniell n; **~ial,** **~ious** zeremoniell; förmlich; **~y** ['~məni] Zeremonie f, Feierlichkeit f; Förmlichkeit(en pl) f.

certain ['sə:tn] sicher, gewiß, bestimmt; gewisse(r, -s); **~ly** sicher(lich), bestimmt, gewiß; **~ty** Gewißheit f.

certi|ficate [sə'tifikit] Bescheinigung f, Attest n, Schein f, Urkunde f, Zeugnis n; **~fy** ['sə:tifai] bescheinigen; **~tude** ['~tju:d] Gewißheit f.

chafe [tʃeif] reiben; (sich) wund reiben; toben.

chaff [tʃɑ:f] Spreu f; Häcksel n.

chaffinch ['tʃæfintʃ] Buchfink m.

chagrin ['ʃægrin] Ärger m.

chain [tʃein] Kette f; (an-) ketten.

chair [tʃɛə] Stuhl m, Sessel

m; Lehrstuhl m; Vorsitz m;
~-lift Sessellift m; **~man**
Vorsitzende m.

chalk [tʃɔːk] Kreide f.

challenge ['tʃælindʒ] Herausforderung f; mil. Anruf m; herausfordern; anrufen; anzweifeln.

chamber ['tʃeimbə] Kammer f; **~maid** Zimmermädchen n.

chamois ['ʃæmwaː] Gemse f; **~-leather** ['ʃæmi-] Sämischleder n.

champagne [ʃæm'pein] Champagner m.

champion ['tʃæmpjən] Vorkämpfer m, Verfechter m; sp. Meister(in); **~ship** Meisterschaft f.

chance [tʃɑːns] zufällig; Zufall m; Glück n; Chance f; (günstige) Gelegenheit; **by ~** zufällig, durch Zufall; **give s.o. a ~** j-m eine Chance geben; **take one's ~** es darauf ankommen lassen.

chancellor ['tʃɑːnsələ] Kanzler m.

chandelier [ʃændi'liə] Kronleuchter m.

change [tʃeindʒ] Veränderung f, Wechsel m; Abwechs(e)lung f; Wechselgeld n; Kleingeld n; **for a ~** zur Abwechslung; (sich) (ver)ändern; (aus-) wechseln, (um)tauschen; (sich) (ver)wandeln; sich umziehen; **~ one's mind** sich anders entschließen; **~ (trains)** umsteigen;

~able veränderlich.

channel ['tʃænl] Kanal m (a. fig.); Rinne f; aer. Flugsteig m; **the (English)** ♀ der (Ärmel)Kanal.

chaos ['keiɔs] Chaos n.

chap [tʃæp] colloq. Bursche m, Kerl m.

chapel ['tʃæpl] Kapelle f.

chaplain ['tʃæplin] Kaplan m.

chapter ['tʃæptə] Kapitel n.

character ['kæriktə] Charakter m; Schrift(zeichen n) f; thea., Roman: Person f; Ruf m; Zeugnis n; **~istic** charakteristisch; Kennzeichen n, f; **~ize** charakterisieren.

charge [tʃɑːdʒ] laden; Batterie (auf)laden; beauftragen; befehlen; ermahnen; beschuldigen, anklagen; fordern, verlangen, berechnen; electr. Ladung f; (Spreng)Ladung f; Obhut f; Schützling m; Anklage f; Preis m; pl Kosten pl; **be in ~ of** verantwortlich sein für, versorgen, betreuen; **free of ~** kostenlos.

chariot ['tʃæriət] zweirädriger (Streit-, Triumph-) Wagen.

charit|able ['tʃæritəbl] wohltätig; **~y** Nächstenliebe f; Wohltätigkeit f.

charm [tʃɑːm] Zauber m; Talisman m; fig. a. Reiz m; bezaubern, entzücken; **~ing** bezaubernd, reizend.

chart [tʃɑːt] Seekarte *f*; Tabelle *f*.

charter ['tʃɑːtə] Urkunde *f*; chartern, mieten; **~ plane** Chartermaschine *f*.

charwoman ['tʃɑːwumən] Putzfrau *f*.

chase [tʃeis] Jagd *f*; Verfolgung *f*; jagen; verfolgen; *colloq.* eilen.

chasm ['kæzəm] Kluft *f* (*a. fig.*).

chaste [tʃeist] rein, keusch; **~ity** ['tʃæstiti] Keuschheit *f*.

chat [tʃæt] Geplauder *n*; plaudern, **~ter** plappern, schwatzen, schwätzen, klappern; Geplapper *n*; **~terbox** Plappermaul *n*.

chauffeur ['ʃoufə] Chauffeur *m*.

cheap [tʃiːp] billig (*a. fig.*); **~en** (sich) verbilligen; *fig.* herabsetzen.

cheat [tʃiːt] Betrug *m*; Betrüger(in); betrügen.

check [tʃek] Hemmnis *n*, Einhalt *m*; Kontrolle *f*; Kontroll-, Garderobenmarke *f*; (Gepäck)Schein *m*; *Am.* Rechnung *f* (*Restaurant*); *Am.* Scheck *m*; karierter Stoff; hemmen, hindern, aufhalten; kontrollieren, (nach)prüfen; *Am.* Mantel in der Garderobe abgeben; *Am.* Gepäck aufgeben; **~ in** *Am.* in e-m Hotel absteigen; *out Am.* abreisen (*Hotel*). **~ed** kariert; **~room** *Am.*: Gar-

derobe *f*; Gepäckaufbewahrung *f*.

cheek [tʃiːk] Backe *f*, Wange *f*; Unverschämtheit *f*; **~y** frech.

cheer [tʃiə] gute Laune; Hoch(ruf *m*) *m*; Beifall (*-sruf*) *m*; (zu)jubeln; **~ (on)** anfeuern; **~ (up)** ermuntern, aufheitern; **~ up** Mut fassen; **~ful** heiter; **~io** [ˌtʃiəri'ou] *colloq.* mach's gut!, tschüs!; **~less** freudlos, trüb; **~y** heiter.

cheese [tʃiːz] Käse *m*.

chef [ʃef] Küchenchef *m*.

chemical ['kemikəl] chemisch; **~s** *pl* Chemikalien *pl.*

chemise [ʃə'miːz] (Frauen)Hemd *n*.

chemist ['kemist] Chemiker *m*; Apotheker *m*; Drogist *m*; **~ry** Chemie *f*; **~'s shop** Drogerie *f*; Apotheke *f*.

cheque [tʃek] Scheck *m*.

chequered ['tʃekəd] kariert; *fig.* bunt.

cherish ['tʃeriʃ] hegen.

cherry ['tʃeri] Kirsche *f*.

chess [tʃes] Schach(spiel) *n*; **~board** Schachbrett *n*; **~man** Schachfigur *f*.

chest [tʃest] Kiste *f*, Truhe *f*, Kasten *m*; *anat.* Brustkorb *m*.

chestnut ['tʃesnʌt] Kastanie *f*; kastanienbraun.

chest of drawers Kommode *f*.

chew [tʃuː] kauen; **~ing-gum** Kaugummi *m*.

chicken ['tʃikin] Huhn n; Hühnchen n; Hähnchen n; Küken n; ~pox ['~pɔks] Windpocken pl.

chief [tʃiːf] oberst; Ober..., Haupt...; hauptsächlich; Chef m; Anführer m; Häuptling m; ...-in-Ober...

chilblain ['tʃilblein] Frostbeule f.

child [tʃaild] pl ~ren Kind n; ~hood Kindheit f; ~ish kindlich; kindisch; ~less kinderlos; ~like kindlich; ~ren ['tʃildrən] pl von child.

chill [tʃil] Frost m, Kälte (-gefühl n) f; Erkältung f; (ab)kühlen; be ~ed durch(ge)froren sein; ~y kalt; fig. frostig.

chime [tʃaim] mst pl Glockenspiel n; Geläut n; läuten.

chimney ['tʃimni] Schornstein m; ~sweep(er) Schornsteinfeger m.

chin [tʃin] Kinn n.

china ['tʃainə] Porzellan n.

Chinese [tʃai'niːz] chinesisch; Chinese (n pl) m, Chinesin f; Chinesisch n.

chink [tʃiŋk] Ritz m, Spalt m.

chip [tʃip] Splitter m, Span m, Schnitzel n m; dünne Scheibe; Spielmarke f; pl Pommes frites pl; schnitzeln; an-, abschlagen.

chirp [tʃəːp] zirpen, zwitschern.

chisel ['tʃizl] Meißel m; meißeln.

chivalr|ous ['ʃivəlrəs] ritterlich; ~y Rittertum n; Ritterlichkeit f.

chive [tʃaiv] Schnittlauch m.

chlor|ine ['klɔːriːn] Chlor n; ~oform ['klɔrəfɔːm] Chloroform n; chloroformieren.

chocolate ['tʃɔkəlit] Schokolade f (a. Getränk); Praline f; pl Pralinen pl, Konfekt n; box of ~s Schachtel f Pralinen.

choice [tʃɔis] (Aus)Wahl f; auserlesen, vorzüglich.

choir ['kwaiə] Chor m.

choke [tʃəuk] (er)würgen; drosseln; ersticken; ~down hinunterwürgen; ~up verstopfen; sub: mot. Starterklappe f.

choose [tʃuːz] (irr) (aus)wählen; vorziehen.

chop [tʃɔp] Hieb m; Kotelett n; hauen, (zer)hacken; ~down niederhauen; Baum fällen.

chord [kɔːd] Saite f; mus. Akkord m; anat. Band n, Strang m.

chorus ['kɔːrəs] Chor m; Kehrreim m.

chose [tʃəuz] pret, ~n pp von choose.

Christ [kraist] Christus m.

christen ['krisn] taufen; ~ing Taufe f.

Christian ['kristjən] Christ (-in); christlich; ~ity [~i'æniti] Christentum n; ~ name Vorname m.

Christmas ['krisməs] Weihnachten n; Weihnachts...; **Father ~** Weihnachtsmann m; **Merry ~** Fröhliche Weihnachten!; **~ Day** erster Weihnachtsfeiertag; **~ Eve** Heiliger Abend. [Chrom n.]

chromium ['krəumjəm]

chronic ['krɔnik] chronisch; **~le** Chronik f.

chronological [krɔnə'lɔdʒikəl] chronologisch.

chubby ['tʃʌbi] pausbäckig.

chuck [tʃʌk] colloq. schmeißen.

chuckle ['tʃʌkl] in sich hineinlachen.

chum [tʃʌm] (Stuben-) Kamerad m; guter Freund.

church [tʃə:tʃ] Kirche f; Gottesdienst m; Kirch-(en)...; **~warden** Kirchenvorsteher m; **~yard** Kirch-, Friedhof m.

churn [tʃə:n] Butterfaß n; Brit. Milchkanne f; buttern; aufwühlen.

chute [ʃu:t] Stromschnelle f; Rutschbahn f, Rutsche f; colloq. Fallschirm m.

cider ['saidə] Apfelwein m.

cigar [si'gɑ:] Zigarre f.

cigaret(te) [sigə'ret] Zigarette f.

cinder ['sində] Schlacke f; pl Asche f; **2ella** [~'relə] Aschenbrödel n; **~track** sp. Aschenbahn f.

cine-camera ['sini-] Filmkamera f; **~ma** ['~əmə] Kino n; (Film)kunst f;

go to the ~ma ins Kino gehen; **~-projector** Filmprojektor m.

cipher ['saifə] Ziffer f; Null f (a. fig.); Chiffre f; chiffrieren.

circle ['sə:kl] Kreis(lauf) m; thea. Rang m; (um-) kreisen.

circuit ['sə:kit] Rundflug m, -gang m, -reise f; Stromkreis m; **short ~** Kurzschluß m.

circular ['sə:kjulə] kreisförmig; Kreis...; **~ (letter)** Rundschreiben n.

circulat|e ['sə:kjuleit] umlaufen, zirkulieren, kreisen; verbreiten; **~ing library** Leihbücherei f; **~ion** Kreislauf m; econ. Umlauf m; Verbreitung f; Auflage f (Zeitung).

circum|ference [sə'kʌmfərəns] (Kreis)Umfang m; **~navigate** [sə:kəm'-] umsegeln; **~scribe** ['~skraib] umschreiben; fig. begrenzen; **~stance** Umstand m; pl (a. finanzielle) Verhältnisse pl.

circus ['sə:kəs] Zirkus m; (runder) Platz.

cistern ['sistən] Wasserbehälter m.

cite [sait] zitieren; jur. vorladen.

citizen ['sitizn] (Staats-) Bürger(in); Städter(in); **~ship** Staatsangehörigkeit f.

city ['siti] (Groß)Stadt f; **the 2** London: die City,

das Geschäftsviertel; ~ **centre** Innenstadt f, Stadtmitte f; ~ **guide** Stadtplan m; ~ **hall** bsd. Am. Rathaus n.

civics ['siviks] sg Staatsbürgerkunde f.

civil ['sivl] bürgerlich, Bürger...; zivil; höflich; ~**ian** [si'viljən] Zivilist m; ~**ity** Höflichkeit f; ~**ization** Zivilisation f, Kultur f; ~**ize** zivilisieren; ~ **marriage** standesamtliche Trauung; ~ **rights** pl Bürgerrechte pl; ℞ **Service** Staatsdienst m; ~ **war** Bürgerkrieg m.

clad [klæd] pret u. pp von **clothe**; gekleidet.

claim [kleim] Anspruch m; Anrecht n; beanspruchen, fordern; ~**ant** Anwärter m.

clammy ['klæmi] feuchtkalt, klamm.

clamo|(u)r ['klæmə] Geschrei n; schreien; ~**rous** lärmend, schreiend.

clamp [klæmp] Klammer f.

clan [klæn] Clan m, Sippe f.

clandestine [klæn'destin] heimlich.

clank [klæŋk] Gerassel n, Geklirr n; rasseln od. klirren (mit).

clap [klæp] Klatschen n; Knall m; schlagen od. klatschen (mit).

claret ['klærət] Rotwein m.

clari|fy ['klærifai] (sich) klären; ~**ty** Klarheit f.

clash [klæʃ] Geklirr n;

Zs.-stoß m; Widerstreit m; klirren; zs.-stoßen.

clasp [klɑːsp] Haken m; Spange f; Umklammerung f; Umarmung f; einhaken, schließen; umklammern, umfassen; ~**knife** Klapp-, Taschenmesser n.

class [klɑːs] Klasse f; Stand m, Schicht f; Unterricht m, Stunde f; Kurs(us) m; Am. univ. Jahrgang m; (in Klassen) einteilen, einordnen; ~**mate** Klassenkamerad(in) f); ~**room** Klassen-, Schulzimmer n.

classic ['klæsik] Klassiker m; erstklassig; klassisch; ~**al** klassisch.

classi|fication [klæsifi-'keiʃən] Klassifizierung f, Einteilung f; ~**fy** [~.fai] klassifizieren; ~einstufen.

clatter ['klætə] Geklapper n, Poltern n, Getrappel n; klappern.

clause [klɔːz] Klausel f; gr. Satz(teil) m.

claw [klɔː] Klaue f, Kralle f.

clay [klei] Ton m.

clean [kliːn] rein, sauber; völlig; reinigen, saubermachen, putzen; ~ **out** reinigen, säubern; ~ **up** aufräumen; ~**er** Reiniger m; (**dry**) ~**ers** pl (chemische) Reinigung f; ~**ing** Reinigung f, Putzen n; ~**liness** ['klenlinis] Reinlichkeit f; ~**ly** ['klenli] reinlich; ~**ness** ['kliːnnis]

Sauberkeit *f;* **~se** [klenz] reinigen, säubern; **~ shaven** glattrasiert.

clear [kliə] klar; hell; rein; frei; ganz, voll; rein, netto; reinigen; roden; *Tisch* abräumen; räumen, leeren; freisprechen; **~ away** wegräumen; **~ up** auf-, abräumen; (sich) aufklären; **~ing** Lichtung *f,* Rodung *f.*

cleave [kli:v] festhalten (**to** an); (*irr*) (sich) spalten. [sel *m.*]

clef [klef] (Noten)Schlüssel *m.*

cleft [kleft] Spalte *f; pret u. pp von* **cleave**.

clemency ['klemənsi] Milde *f.*

clench [klentʃ] *Lippen* zs.-pressen; *Zähne* zs.-beißen; *Faust* ballen.

clergy ['klə:dʒi] Geistlichkeit *f;* **~man** Geistliche *m.* [lich.]

clerical ['klerikəl] geist-]

clerk [klɑ:k] Schreiber (-in); Büroangestellte *m,f;* (Bank-, Post- *etc.*)Beamt|e *m,* -in *f; Am.* Verkäufer(in).

clever ['klevə] gescheit, klug, gewandt, geschickt.

click [klik] Klicken *n,* Knacken *n;* klicken, knacken; (zu-, ein)schnappen.

client ['klaiənt] Klient (-in); Kund|e *m,* -in *f.*

cliff [klif] Klippe *f.*

climate ['klaimit] Klima *n.*

climax ['klaimæks] Höhepunkt *m.*

climb [klaim] klettern *od.* steigen auf; **~ up** hinaufsteigen, -klettern; **~er** Kletterer *m; bot.* Kletterpflanze *f.*

clinch [klintʃ] Umklammerung *f.*

cling [kliŋ] (*irr*) sich (an-) klammern (**to** an).

clinic ['klinik] Klinik *f.*

clink [kliŋk] klingen (lassen).

clip[1] [klip] (Büro)Klammer *f;* Spange *f.*

clip[2] [klip] Schur *f;* ab-, beschneiden; *Schafe etc.* scheren; **~pings** *pl* (Zeitungs- *etc.*) Ausschnitte *pl.*

cloak [kləuk] Mantel *m,* Umhang *m;* **~room** Garderobe *f;* Gepäckaufbewahrung *f;* Toilette *f.*

clock [klɔk] (Wand- *etc.*) Uhr *f;* **~wise** im Uhrzeigersinn. [*m.*]

clod [klɔd] (Erd)Klumpen]

clog [klɔg] Klotz *m;* Holzschuh *m;* verstopfen; belasten.

cloister ['klɔistə] Kreuzgang *m;* Kloster *n.*

close [kləus] geschlossen; nah; eng; dicht; knapp; streng; genau, sorgfältig; schwül, dumpf; geizig; verschwiegen; **~ to** *od.* **by** dicht *od.* nahe bei, an; Einfriedung *f,* Hof *m;* [~z] (Ab)Schluß *m,* Ende *n;* [~z] (ab-, ein-, ver-, zu)schließen; beenden; sich schließen; **~ down** *Fabrik etc.* schließen; **in**

hereinbrechen (*Nacht*).

closet ['klɔzit] kleines Zimmer; (Wand)Schrank *m*; *s.* **water-closet.**

close-up ['kləusʌp] Großaufnahme *f*.

closing-time ['kləuziŋ-] Geschäftsschluß *m*.

clot [klɔt] Klumpen *m*, Klümpchen *n*; gerinnen (lassen), Klumpen bilden.

cloth [klɔθ] Stoff *m*, Tuch *n*; **lay the ~** den Tisch decken; **~bound** in Leinen (gebunden).

clothe [kləuð] (*irr*) (an-, be-, ein)kleiden.

clothes [kləuðz] *pl* Kleider *pl*, Kleidung *f*; Wäsche *f*; **~brush** Kleiderbürste *f*; **~hanger** Kleiderbügel *m*; **~line** Wäscheleine *f*; **~peg**, **~pin** Wäscheklammer *f*. (dung *f*.)

clothing ['kləuðiŋ] Kleiı

cloud [klaud] Wolke *f*; (sich) bewölken, *fig.* (sich) trüben; **~y** wolkig; Wolken...; trübe.

clove¹ [kləuv] Gewürznelke *f*. [**cleave.**

clove² *pret*, **~n** *pp von*

clover ['kləuvə] Klee *m*.

clown [klaun] Clown *m*, Hanswurst *m*.

club [klʌb] Keule *f*, Knüppel *m*; Klub *m*, Verein *m*; **~s** (*pl*) *Karten:* Kreuz *n*.

clue [kluː] Anhaltspunkt *m*.

clumsy ['klʌmzi] unbeholfen, ungeschickt; plump..

clung [klʌŋ] *pret u. pp von* **cling.**

cluster ['klʌstə] Traube *f*; Büschel *n*; Haufen *m*; sich zs.-drängen; ranken.

clutch [klʌtʃ] Griff *m*; Kupplung *f*; packen, (er-)greifen; **~ pedal** Kupplungspedal *n*.

coach [kəutʃ] Kutsche *f*, Karosse *f*; (Eisenbahn-) Wagen *m*; Überland-, Reisebus *m*; Nachhilfelehrer *m*, Einpauker *m*; Trainer *m*; Nachhilfeunterricht geben, einpauken; trainieren.

coagulate [kəu'ægjuleit] gerinnen (lassen).

coal [kəul] Kohle *f*; **~field** Kohlenrevier *n*.

coalition [kəuə'liʃən] Koalition *f*.

coal|-mine Kohlengrube *f*; **~mining** Kohlenbergbau *m*; **~pit** Kohlengrube *f*.

coarse [kɔːs] grob; ungeschliffen.

coast [kəust] Küste *f*; die Küste entlangfahren; im Freilauf fahren; **~guard** Küsten(zoll)wache *f*.

coat [kəut] überziehen, anstreichen; umkleiden; Jackett *n*, Jacke *f*, Rock *m*; Mantel *m*; Fell *n*, Pelz *m*; (*Farb- etc.*)Überzug *m*, Anstrich *m*; **~hanger** Kleiderbügel *m*; **~ing** Überzug *m*, Anstrich *m*; Mantelstoff *m*; **~ of arms** Wappen(schild) *n*.

coax [kəuks] beschwatzen.

cob [kɔb] Maiskolben *m*.

collect

cobra ['kəubrə] Brillen-
schlange f, Kobra f.

cobweb ['kɔbweb] Spinn-
(en)gewebe n.

cock [kɔk] Hahn m; Ge-
wehrhahn spannen; ~ **(up)**
aufrichten; **~atoo** [~ə'tu:]
Kakadu m; **~chafer** Mai-
käfer m; **~le** Herzmuschel
f; **~ney** ['~ni] Cockney m,
(echter) Londoner f; **~pit**
(Flugzeug)Kanzel f;
roach ['~rəutʃ](Küchen-
Schabe f; **~sure** tod-
sicher; überheblich; **~tail**
Cocktail m. [palme f.]

coco ['kəukəu] Kokos-]

cocoa ['kəukəu] Kakao m.

coconut ['kəukənʌt] Kokosnuß f.

cocoon [kə'ku:n] Kokon m.

cod [kɔd] Kabeljau m,
Dorsch m.

coddle['kɔdl] verhätscheln.

code [kəud] Gesetzbuch n;
Kodex m; Code m, Schlüs-
sel m; chiffrieren.

cod-liver oil Lebertran m.

coexist [kəuig'zist] gleichzeitig bestehen; **~ence**
Koexistenz f.

coffee ['kɔfi] Kaffee m;
~bean Kaffeebohne f;
~mill Kaffeemühle f;
~pot Kaffeekanne f;
~stall Kaffeestand m,
Imbißstube f; **~wagen** m

coffin ['kɔfin] Sarg m.

cog-wheel ['kɔg-] Zahn-
rad n.

coheren|ce [kəu'hiərəns],
~cy Zs.-hang m; † zs.-
hängend.

cohesive [kəu'hi:siv] zs.-
hängend. [sur f.]

coiffure [kwɑ:'fjuə] Fri-]

coil [kɔil] Rolle f, Spirale f; electr. Spule f;
Windung f; ~ **(up)** aufrollen, (-)wickeln; ~ **o.s.**
up sich zs.-rollen.

coin [kɔin] Münze f,
Geldstück n; prägen (a.
fig.); münzen; **~age** Prä-
gung f.

coincide [kəuin'said] zs.-
treffen; übereinstimmen;
~nce [kəu'insidəns] Zs.-
treffen n; Übereinstim-
mung f.

coke [kəuk] Koks m; sl.
Koks m (Kokain).

cold [kəuld] kalt; Kälte f;
Erkältung f; bad ~ eine
Erkältung f; **~ness** Kälte
f; **~storage room** Kühlraum m.

colic ['kɔlik] Kolik f.

collaborat|e [kə'læbəreit]
zs.-arbeiten; **~ion** Zs.-ar-
beit f; **in** ~ in gemeinsam.

collapse [kə'læps] zs.-,
einfallen; zs.-brechen; Zs.-
bruch m; Falt.., **~ible** zs.-klapp-
bar, Falt.., Klapp..

collar ['kɔlə] Kragen m;
Halsband n; Kummet n;
beim Kragen packen; **~bone** Schlüsselbein n.

colleague['kɔli:g]Kolleg|e
m, -in f.

collect [kə'lekt] (ein-)
sammeln; Gedanken etc.
sammeln; einkassieren;
abholen; sich an- od.

versammeln; ~ed *fig.* gefaßt; ~ion (An)Sammlung *f*; *econ.* Einziehung *f*; Leerung *f* (*Briefkasten*); ~ive kollektiv, gesamt; ~or Sammler *m*; Einnehmer *m*; Einsammler *m*.

college ['kɔlidʒ] College *n*; Hochschule *f*; höhere Lehranstalt.

collide [kə'laid] zs.-stoßen.

colliery ['kɔljəri] (Kohlen-) Zeche *f*.

collision [kə'liʒən] Zs.-stoß *m*.

colloquial [kə'ləukwiəl] umgangssprachlich.

colon ['kəulən] Doppelpunkt *m*.

colonel ['kəːnl] Oberst *m*.

colonial [kə'bunjəl] Kolonial...; ~ism Kolonialismus *m*.

colon|ist ['kɔlənist] Siedler(in); ~ize kolonisieren; besiedeln; ~y Kolonie *f*; Ansiedlung *f*.

colo(u)r ['kʌlə] Farbe *f*; *fig.* Anschein *m*; *pl* Fahne *f*, Flagge *f*; Farbe *f*; (an-)streichen; *fig.* beschönigen, entstellen; sich (ver-)färben; erröten; ~bar Rassenschranke *f*; ~ed gefärbt; farbig, bunt; farbig, Neger...; ~ed man Farbige *m*; ~ed people Farbige *pl*; ~ful farbenreich, -freudig, bunt; ~ing Färbung *f*; Farbton *m*; ~less farblos; ~line *Am.* Rassenschranke *f*; ~print Farbabzug *m*.

colt [kəult] (Hengst)Füllen *n*.

column ['kɔləm] Säule *f*; *print.* Spalte *f*; *mil.* Kolonne *f*.

comb [kəum] Kamm *m*; [kämmen.]

combat ['kɔmbæt] Kampf *m*; ~e)kämpfen; ~ant Kämpfer *m*.

combin|ation [kɔmbi'neiʃən] Verbindung *f*; ~e [kəm'bain] (sich) verbinden; ~e-harvester Mähdrescher *m*.

combust|ible [kəm'bʌstəbl] brennbar; ~ion [~stʃən] Verbrennung *f*.

come [kʌm] (*irr*) kommen; ~ about sich zutragen, zustande kommen; ~ across *auf j-n od. et.* stoßen, *j-m od. et.* begegnen; ~ along mitkommen; ~ at erreichen; ~ by vorbeikommen; zu *et.* kommen; ~ for abholen kommen; ~ loose sich ablösen, abgehen; ~ off ab-, losgehen; abfinden; stattfinden; ~ on! los!, vorwärts!, komm!; ~ round vorbeikommen; wieder zu sich kommen; ~ to see besuchen; ~ up to entsprechen; ~back Comeback *n*.

comed|ian [kə'miːdjən] Komiker(in); ~y ['kɔmidi] Lustspiel *n*.

comet ['kɔmit] Komet *m*.

comfort ['kʌmfət] Bequemlichkeit *f*, Behaglichkeit *f*; Trost *m*; trö-

369 **communion**

sten; **~able** behaglich, bequem, komfortabel; **~er** Wollschal *f*; Schnuller *m*.

comic|(al) ['kɔmik(əl)] komisch; **~ strips** *pl* (lustige) Bildergeschichte(n *pl*).

comma ['kɔmə] Komma *n*.

command [kə'maːnd] Herrschaft *f*, Beherrschung *f* (*a. fig.*); Befehl *m*, Aufforderung *f*; *mil.* Kommando *n*, (Ober-)Befehl *m*; befehl(ig)en; verfügen über; beherrschen; **~er** Kommandeur *m*, Befehlshaber *m*; **~in-chief** Oberbefehlshaber *m*; **~ment** Gebot *n*.

commemorat|e [kə'meməreit] gedenken, feiern.

commence [kə'mens] anfangen, beginnen; **~ment** Anfang *m*.

commend [kə'mend] empfehlen; loben; anvertrauen.

comment ['kɔment] Kommentar *m*, An-, Bemerkung *f*; **~** (up)on kommentieren; **~ary** ['~əntəri] Kommentar *m*; **~ator** ['~enteitə] Kommentator *m*; Rundfunkreporter *m*.

commerc|e ['kɔmə(ː)s] Handel *m*; **~ial** [kə'məːʃəl] *Rundfunk etc.*: Reklame-, Werbesendung *f*; kaufmännisch; Handels...; **~ial travel(l)er** Handlungsreisende *m*.

commiseration [kəmizə'reiʃən] Mitleid *n*.

commission [kə'miʃən] Auftrag *m*; Vollmacht *f*;

Provision *f*; Kommission *f*; beauftragen; bevollmächtigen; **~er** [~ʃnə] Bevollmächtigte *m*, *f*; Kommissar *m*.

commit [kə'mit] anvertrauen, übergeben; *Tat* begehen, verüben; verpflichten, festlegen; **~ment** Verpflichtung *f*; **~tee** [~ti] Ausschuß *m*, Komitee *n*.

commodity [kə'mɔditi] Ware *f*, Gebrauchsartikel *m*.

common ['kɔmən] gemeinsam; allgemein; gewöhnlich (*a. fig.*); Gemeindeland *n*; **in ~** gemeinsam; **~er** Bürger *m*; **~ law** Gewohnheitsrecht *n*; **~ market** Gemeinsamer Markt; **~place** gemeinplatz *m*; alltäglich; **~s** *pl*: **House of 2s** *Brit. parl.* Unterhaus *n*; **~ sense** gesunder Menschenverstand; **~wealth** Staat (-enbund) *m*; Republik *f*; **the (British) 2wealth** das Commonwealth.

commotion [kə'məuʃən] Aufruhr *m*; Aufregung *f*.

commune ['kɔmjuːn] Gemeinde *f*; Kommune *f*.

communicat|e [kə'mjuːnikeit] mitteilen; in Verbindung stehen; **~ion** Mitteilung *f*; Verständigung *f*; Verbindung *f*; **~ive** [~ətiv] gesprächig.

communion [kə'mjuːnjen] Gemeinschaft *f*; 2 Abendmahl *n*.

communi|sm ['kɔmju-nizəm] Kommunismus m; **~t** Kommunist(in); kommunistisch.

community [kə'mju:niti] Gemeinschaft f; Gemeinde f.

commute [kə'mju:t] aus-, ein-, umtauschen; *Strafe* umwandeln; *rail. etc.* pendeln.

compact ['kɔmpækt] (Kompakt)Puderdose f; [kəm'pækt] dicht, fest; knapp, bündig.

companion [kəm'pænjən] Gefährte m, -in f, Begleiter(in); **~ship** Gesellschaft f.

company ['kʌmpəni] Gesellschaft f; Handelsgesellschaft f; *thea.* Truppe f.

compar|able ['kɔmpərəbl] vergleichbar; **~ative** [kəm'pærətiv] verhältnismäßig; **~ative (degree)** gr. Komparativ m, 1. Steigerungsstufe f; **~e** [~'pɛə] vergleichen; sich vergleichen (lassen); *sub:* **beyond (without, past) ~e** unvergleichlich; **~ison** [~'pærisn] Vergleich m; gr. Steigerung f.

compartment [kəm'pɑ:tmənt] Abteilung f; Fach n; *rail.* Abteil n.

compass ['kʌmpəs] Kompaß m; Bereich m; **(pair of) ~es** pl Zirkel m.

compassion [kəm'pæʃən] Mitleid n; **~ate** [~it] mitleidig.

compatible [kəm'pætəbl] vereinbar.

compatriot [kəm'pætriət] Landsmann m.

compel [kəm'pel] (er-) zwingen.

compensat|e ['kɔmpenseit] entschädigen; **~ion** Ausgleich m; Entschädigung f, (Schaden)Ersatz m.

compère ['kɔmpɛə] Conférencier m.

compete [kəm'pi:t] sich mitbewerben **(for** um); konkurrieren.

competen|ce ['kɔmpitəns], **~cy** Befähigung f; Zuständigkeit f; **~t** (leistungs)fähig; ausreichend; zuständig.

competit|ion [kɔmpi-'tiʃən] Wettbewerb m, -kampf m; *econ.* Konkurrenz f; Preisausschreiben n; **~or** [kəm'petitə] Konkurrent(in); *sp.* Teilnehmer(in).

compile [kəm'pail] zs.-stellen.

complacent [kəm'pleisnt] selbstzufrieden, -gefällig.

complain [kəm'plein] (sich be)klagen; **~t** Klage f, Beschwerde f; *med.* Leiden n.

complet|e [kəm'pli:t] vollständig, ganz; vollzählig; vervollständigen, ergänzen; beenden; **~ion** Vervollständigung f; Abschluß m.

complexion [kəm'plek-ʃən] Aussehen n; Gesichtsfarbe f, Teint m.

complicate ['kɔmplikeit]
komplizieren, erschweren.

compliment ['kɔmpli-
mənt] Kompliment *n*; *pl*
Grüße *pl*; ['⁓ment] be-
glückwünschen.

comply [kəm'plai]: ⁓
(with) sich fügen (*dat.*)

component [kəm'pəu-
nənt] Bestandteil *m*.

compos|e [kəm'pəuz] zs.-
setzen; komponieren, ver-
fassen; ⁓ **o.s.** sich beruhigen *od.* fassen; **be**
⁓**ed of** bestehen aus; ⁓**ed**
ruhig, gesetzt; ⁓**er** Kompo-
nist(in); ⁓**ition** [kɔm-
pə'ziʃən] Zs.-setzung *f*;
Abfassung *f*; Komposition
f; Aufsatz *m*; ⁓**ure** [kəm-
'pəuʒə] Fassung *f*.

compote ['kɔmpɔt] Kompott *n*.

compound ['kɔmpaund]
zs.-gesetzt; Zs.-setzung *f*;
[kəm'paund] zs.-setzen.

comprehen|d [kɔmpri-
'hend] begreifen; ⁓**sible**
verständlich; ⁓**sion** Verständnis *n*; Fassungskraft
f; ⁓**sive** umfassend; ⁓**sive**
school Gesamtschule *f*.

compress [kəm'pres] zs.-
drücken.

comprise [kəm'praiz] bestehen aus.

compromise ['kɔmprə-
maiz] Kompromiß *m*;
bloßstellen; einen Kom-
promiß schließen.

compuls|ion [kəm'pʌl-
ʃən] Zwang *m*; ⁓**ory** obli-
gatorisch; Pflicht...

compunction [kəm'pʌŋk-
ʃən] Gewissensbisse *pl*;
Reue *f*.

computer [kəm'pju:tə]
Computer *m*.

comrade ['kɔmrid] Ka-
merad *m*, Genosse *m*;
⁓**ship** Kameradschaft *f*.

conceal [kən'si:l] verbergen; verschweigen.

conceit [kən'si:t] Einbil-
dung *f*; ⁓**ed** eingebildet.

conceiv|able [kən'si:vəbl]
denkbar; ⁓**e** *Kind* empfangen; sich denken; pla-
nen.

concentrate ['kɔnsən-
treit] (sich) konzentrieren.

conception [kən'sepʃən]
Begreifen *n*; Vorstellung
f; *biol.* Empfängnis *f*.

concern [kən'sɔ:n] Angelegenheit *f*; *econ.* Ange-
schäft *n*; Interesse *n*;
Sorge *f*; betreffen, an-
gehen; beteiligen; beun-
ruhigen; ⁓**ed** besorgt.

concert ['kɔnsət] Konzert *n*.

concession [kən'seʃən]
Zugeständnis *n*; Konzes-
sion *f*.

conciliat|e [kən'silieit]
aus-, versöhnen; ⁓**ory**
[⁓ətəri] versöhnlich.

concise [kən'sais] kurz,
knapp.

conclu|de [kən'klu:d] (ab-,
be)schließen; folgern;
⁓**sion** [⁓ʒən] Schluß *m*,
Ende *n*; Abschluß *m*; Folgerung *f*; ⁓**sive** [⁓siv]
endgültig.

concord ['kɔŋkɔ:d] Eintracht _f_; Übereinstimmung _f_; Harmonie _f_.

concrete [ˈkɔnkriːt] Beton _m_.

concur [kənˈkəː] zs.-treffen, zs.-wirken; übereinstimmen.

concussion (of the brain) [kənˈkʌʃən] Gehirnerschütterung _f_.

condemn [kənˈdem] verurteilen; verdammen; verwerfen; **~ation** [kɔndemˈneiʃən] Verurteilung _f_; Verdammung _f_.

condense [kənˈdens] (sich) verdichten, kondensieren; _fig._ kürzen, zs.-drängen; **~r** Kondensator _m_.

condescend [kɔndiˈsend] sich herablassen, geruhen.

condition [kənˈdiʃən] Zustand _m_; Bedingung _f_; _pl_ Verhältnisse _pl_; bedingen; **~al** bedingt; **~al clause** _gr._ Bedingungssatz _m_; **~al (mood)** _gr._ Konditional _m_, Bedingungsform _f_.

condole [kənˈdəul] kondolieren; **~nce** Beileid _n_.

conduct [ˈkɔndʌkt] Führung _f_; Verhalten _n_, Betragen _n_; [kənˈdʌkt] führen; leiten; _mus._ dirigieren; **~ o.s.** sich benehmen; **~ed tour** Gesellschaftsreise _f_; **~ion** [kənˈdʌkʃən] Leitung _f_; **~or** [kənˈdʌktə] Führer _m_; Leiter _m_; Schaffner _m_; Dirigent _m_.

cone [kəun] Kegel _m_; _bot._ Zapfen _m_.

confection [kənˈfekʃən] Konfekt _n_; **~er** [~ʃnə] Konditor _m_; **~ery** Konditorwaren _pl_; Konditorei _f_.

confedera|cy [kənˈfedərəsi] Staatenbund _m_; **~te** [~it] verbündet; Bundesgenosse _m_; [~eit] (sich) verbünden; **~tion** Bund _m_, Bündnis _n_; Staatenbund _m_.

confer [kənˈfəː] verleihen; sich beraten; **~ence** [ˈkɔnfərəns] Konferenz _f_.

confess [kənˈfes] gestehen, bekennen; beichten; **~ion** [kənˈfeʃən] Geständnis _n_; Beichte _f_; **~or** Beichtvater _m_.

confide [kənˈfaid] anvertrauen; vertrauen; **~nce** [ˈkɔnfidəns] Vertrauen _n_; Zuversicht _f_; **~nt** zuversichtlich; **~ntial** [~ˈdenʃəl] vertraulich.

confine [kənˈfain] beschränken; einsperren; **be ~d** niederkommen; **~ment** Haft _f_; Niederkunft _f_.

confirm [kənˈfəːm] bestätigen; konfirmieren; firmen; **~ation** [kɔnfəˈmeiʃən] Bestätigung _f_; Konfirmation _f_; Firmung _f_.

confiscate [ˈkɔnfiskeit] beschlagnahmen.

conflagration [kɔnfləˈgreiʃən] Großbrand _m_.

conflict [ˈkɔnflikt] Konflikt _m_; [kənˈflikt] im Konflikt stehen.

conform [kənˈfɔːm] (sich) anpassen; **~ity** Übereinstimmung _f_.

confound [kən'faund] verwechseln; *j–n* verwirren; *it! colloq.* verdammt!

confront [kən'frʌnt] gegenüberstellen; konfrontieren.

confus|e [kən'fju:z] verwechseln; verwirren; ~ion [~ʒən] Verwirrung *f;* Durcheinander *n;* Verwechs(e)lung *f.*

congeal [kən'dʒi:l] erstarren *od.* gerinnen (lassen).

congestion [kən'dʒestʃən] (Blut)Andrang *m;* ~ **of traffic** Verkehrsstockung *f.*

congratulat|e [kən'grætjuleit] beglückwünschen; *j–m* gratulieren; ~**ion** Glückwunsch *m.*

congregat|e [ˈkɔŋgrigeit] (sich) (ver)sammeln; ~**ion** Versammlung *f; eccl.* Gemeinde *f.*

congress [ˈkɔŋgres] (*Am. parl.* 2) Kongreß *m.*

conjecture [kən'dʒektʃə] Vermutung *f;* vermuten.

conjugal [ˈkɔndʒugəl] ehelich.

conjugat|e [ˈkɔndʒugeit] *gr.* verbinden, beugen; ~**ion** *gr.* Konjugation *f,* Beugung *f.*

conjunction [kən'dʒʌŋkʃən] Verbindung *f;* Zs.-treffen *n; gr.* Konjunktion *f,* Bindewort *n.*

conjunctive (mood) [kən'dʒʌŋktiv] *gr.* Konjunktiv *m,* Möglichkeitsform *f.*

conjure¹ [kən'dʒuə] beschwören.

conjure² [ˈkʌndʒə] zaubern; ~**er** Zauberer *m;* ~**ing trick** Zauberkunststück *n;* ~**or** *s.* **conjurer.**

connect [kə'nekt] verbinden; *electr.* anschließen; *rail.* Anschluß haben (**with** an); ~**ed** ~s.-hängend; ~**ion** Verbindung *f;* Anschluß *m;* Zs.-hang *m.*

connexion [kə'nekʃən] *s.* **connection.**

conquer [ˈkɔŋkə] erobern; (be)siegen; ~**or** Eroberer *m;* Sieger *m.*

conquest [ˈkɔŋkwest] Eroberung *f.*

conscien|ce [ˈkɔnʃəns] Gewissen *n;* ~**tious** [~i'enʃəs] gewissenhaft; ~**tious objector** Kriegsdienstverweigerer *m.*

conscious [ˈkɔnʃəs] bewußt; **be** ~ **of** sich bewußt sein; ~**ness** Bewußtsein *n.*

consecrate [ˈkɔnsikreit] weihen.

consecutive [kən'sekjutiv] auf-ea.-folgend.

consent [kən'sent] Einwilligung *f,* Zustimmung *f;* einwilligen, zustimmen.

consequen|ce [ˈkɔnsikwəns] Folge *f,* Konsequenz *f;* Bedeutung *f;* ~**tly** folglich, daher.

conserv|ative [kən'sə:vətiv] konservativ; Konservative *m, f;* ~**e** erhalten, bewahren; *mst* ~**es** *pl* Eingemachte *n,* Marmelade *f.*

consider [kən'sidə] betrachten; erwägen, sich

überlegen;berücksichtigen; denken, meinen; **~able** beträchtlich; **~ably** bedeutend; (sehr) viel; **~ate** [~rit] rücksichtsvoll; **~ation** Überlegung *f*; Rücksicht *f*.

consign [kən'sain] liefern; anvertrauen; **~ment** Versand *m*; Sendung *f*.

consist [kən'sist] bestehen (**of** aus);**~ency** Festigkeit *f*; Übereinstimmung *f*; Konsequenz *f*; **~ent** übereinstimmend; konsequent.

consol|ation [kɔnsə'lei-ʃən] Trost *m*; **~e** [kən-'soul] trösten.

consolidate [kən'sɔlideit] (sich) festigen; vereinigen.

consonant ['kɔnsənənt] *ling.* Konsonant *m*, Mitlaut *m*.

conspicuous [kən'spik-juəs] deutlich sichtbar; auffallend; hervorragend.

conspir|acy [kən'spirəsi] Verschwörung *f*; **~ator** Verschwörer *m*; **~e** [~'spaiə] sich verschwören; planen.

constable ['kʌnstəbl] Polizist *m*.

constant ['kɔnstənt] (be-)ständig; treu.

consternation [kɔnstə(:)-'neiʃən] Bestürzung *f*.

constipation [kɔnsti'pei-ʃən] *med.* Verstopfung *f*.

constituen|cy [kən'stitju-ənsi] Wählerschaft *f*;Wahlkreis *m*, **-bezirk** *m*; **~t** Bestandteil *m*; Wähler(in).

constitut|e ['kɔnstitjuːt] ernennen, einsetzen; bevollmächtigen; einrichten; ausmachen; **~ion** Zs.-setzung *f*; körperliche Verfassung, Konstitution *f*; *pol.* Verfassung *f*, Grundgesetz *n*; **~ional** verfassungsmäßig, konstitutionell.

constrain [kən'strein] (er-)zwingen; **~t** Zwang *m*.

construct [kən'strʌkt] bauen; **~ion** Bau(en *n*) *m*, Konstruktion *f*; **~ive** aufbauend, konstruktiv; **~or** Erbauer*m*,Konstrukteur*m*.

consul ['kɔnsəl] Konsul *m*; **~ar** ['~julə] Konsulats..., Konsular...; **~ate** ['~julit] Konsulat *n*; **~general** Generalkonsul *m*.

consult [kən'sʌlt] konsultieren, um Rat fragen; in *e-m Buch* nachschlagen; sich beraten; **~ation** [kɔn-sʌl'teiʃən] Konsultation *f*; Beratung *f*; Rücksprache *f*; **~ing hours** *pl* Sprechstunde *f*.

consume [kən'sjuːm] verzehren; verbrauchen; **~r** Verbraucher *m*.

consummate [kən'sʌmit] vollendet; ['kɔnsəmeit] vollenden, -ziehen.

consumption [kən'sʌmp-ʃən] Verbrauch *m*; *med.* Schwindsucht *f*.

contact ['kɔntækt] Berührung *f*; Kontakt *m*; Verbindung *f*; [kən'tækt] sich in Verbindung setzen mit; ~ lenses pl Haft-, Kontaktschalen pl.

contagious [kən'teidʒəs] ansteckend.

contain [kən'tein] enthalten; ~er Behälter m; Großbehälter m, Container m.

contaminat|e [kən'tæmineit] verunreinigen; verseuchen; ~ion Verunreinigung f; Verseuchung f.

contemplat|e ['kontempleit] betrachten; beabsichtigen; ~ion Betrachtung f; Nachdenken n; ~ive nachdenklich; beschaulich.

contemporary [kən'tempərəri] zeitgenössisch; Zeitgenosse m, -in f.

contempt [kən'tempt]Verachtung f; ~ible verachtenswert; ~uous [~juəs] geringschätzig, verächtlich.

contend [kən'tend] kämpfen.

content [kən'tent] zufrieden; befriedigen; ~ o.s. sich begnügen; Zufriedenheit f; **to one's heart's ~** nach Herzenslust; ~s ['kontents] pl Inhalt(sverzeichnis n) m.

contest ['kontest] Wettkampf m, -bewerb m; [kən'test] bestreiten, anfechten.

context ['kontekst] Zusammenhang m.

continent ['kontinənt] Kontinent m, Erdteil m; Festland n; ~al [~'nentl] kontinental; Kontinental...

continu|al [kən'tinjuəl] fortwährend, unaufhörlich; ~ance (Fort)Dauer f; ~ation Fortsetzung f; Fortdauer f; ~e [~u(:)] (sich) fortsetzen; (fort)dauern; fortfahren; **to be ~ed** Fortsetzung folgt; ~ous ununterbrochen.

contort [kən'tɔ:t] verzerren; verdrehen.

contour ['kontuə]Umriß m.

contraceptive [kontrə'septiv] empfängnisverhütend(es Mittel).

contract [kən'trækt] (sich) zs.-ziehen; e-n Vertrag schließen, sich vertraglich verpflichten; ['kontrækt] Vertrag m; ~or[kən'træktə] Unternehmer m.

contradict [kontrə'dikt] widersprechen; ~ion Widerspruch m; ~ory (sich) widersprechend.

contrary ['kontrəri] entgegengesetzt; ungünstig; ~ to zuwider; gegen; sub: Gegenteil n; **on the ~** im Gegenteil.

contrast ['kontra:st] Gegensatz m; [kən'tru:st] gegenüberstellen, vergleichen; sich unterscheiden.

contribut|e [kən'tribju(:)t] beitragen, -steuern; ~ion [kontri'bju:ʃən] Beitrag m; ~or [kən'tribjutə] Mitarbeiter(in) (an e-r Zeitung).

contrite ['kontrait] zerknirscht.

contriv|ance [kən'traivəns] Vorrichtung f; Erfindung(sgabe) f; Plan m; ~e erfinden; planen; es fertigbringen.

control [kən'trəul] Kontrolle f; Aufsicht f; Herrschaft f, Beherrschung f; Kontrollvorrichtung f; kontrollieren; (nach)prüfen; beherrschen; econ. lenken; ~ler Kontrolleur m, Prüfer m, Aufseher m.

controvers|ial [kɔntrə'və:ʃəl] umstritten; ~y ['ˌ ˌvə:si] Streit(frage f) m.

contuse [kən'tju:z] quetschen.

convalesce [kɔnvə'les] genesen; ~nce Genesung f; ~nt Genesende m, f.

convenien|ce [kən'vi:njəns] Bequemlichkeit f; at your earliest ~ce sobald wie möglich; public ~ce öffentliche Bedürfnisanstalt; ~t bequem; passend; brauchbar.

convent ['kɔnvənt] (Nonnen)Kloster n; ~ion [kən'venʃən] Versammlung f; Abkommen n; ~ional konventionell.

convers|ation [kɔnvə'seiʃən] Gespräch n, Unterhaltung f; ~e [ˌ ˌ'və:s] sich unterhalten.

conver|sion [kən'və:ʃən] Um-, Verwandlung f; eccl. Bekehrung f; ~t um-, verwandeln; eccl. bekehren; ~tible umwandelbar; mot. Kabrio(lett) n.

convey [kən'vei] befördern; übermitteln; mitteilen; Sinn ausdrücken; ~ance Beförderung f, Transport m; Übermittlung f; Verkehrsmittel n; ~er od. ~or belt Förderband n.

convict ['kɔnvikt] Sträfling m, Zuchthäusler m; [kən'vikt] überführen (of gen); ~ion Überzeugung f; jur.: Überführung f; Verurteilung f.

convince [kən'vins] überzeugen.

convoy ['kɔnvɔi] Geleit n; Geleitzug m; geleiten.

convuls|ion [kən'vʌlʃən] Krampf m; ~ive krampfhaft, -artig.

cook [kuk] Koch m, Köchin f; kochen; ~ing Kochen n; Küche f (Kochweise).

cool [ku:l] kühl; fig. gelassen; (sich) abkühlen; ~er Kühler m; Kühlraum m; ~ness Kühle f (a. fig.).

co-op ['kəuɔp] colloq. s. **co-operative (society, store).**

co(-)operat|e [kəu'ɔpəreit] zs.-arbeiten; beitragen; ~ion Zs.-arbeit f, Mitwirkung f; ~ive [ˌ ˌətiv] zs.-arbeitend; genossenschaftlich; ~ive society Konsum(genossenschaft f) m; ~ive store Konsum(laden) m; ~or Mitarbeiter (-in).

co(-)ordinate [kəu'ɔ:dineit] koordinieren; auf-ei. abstimmen.

cop [kɔp] *sl.* Polyp *m*, Bulle *m* (Polizist).

co-partner ['kou'pɑ:tnə] Teilhaber *m*.

cope [koup]: ~ **with** fertigwerden mit.

co-pilot ['kou'pailət] Kopilot *m*. |(-lich).

copious ['koupjəs] reich∫

copper ['kɔpə] Kupfer *n*; Kupfermünze *f*; kupfern, Kupfer...

copy ['kɔpi] kopieren; abschreiben; nachbilden, -ahmen; Kopie *f*; Abschrift *f*; Durchschlag *m*; Muster *n*; (Buch)Exemplar *n*; (Zeitungs)Nummer *f*, Ausgabe *f*; druckfertiges Manuskript; fair ~ Reinschrift *f*; rough ~ erster Entwurf; ~book Schreibheft *n*; ~right Verlagsrecht *n*, Copyright *n*.

coral ['kɔrəl] Koralle *f*.

cord [kɔ:d] Schnur *f*, Strick *m*; *anat.* Band *n*, Strang *m*; (zu)schnüren, binden.

cordial ['kɔ:djəl] herzlich; (herz)stärkend; Likör *m*; ~ity [~i'æliti] Herzlichkeit *f*.

corduroys ['kɔ:dərɔiz] *pl.* Kordhose *f*.

core [kɔ:] Kerngehäuse *n*; *fig.* Herz *n*, Kern *n*.

cork [kɔ:k] Kork *m*; zukorken; ~screw Korkenzieher *m*.

corn [kɔ:n] Korn *n*; Getreide *n*; *Am.* Mais *m*; *med.* Hühnerauge *n*; (ein)pökeln.

corner ['kɔ:nə] Ecke *f*, Winkel *m*; *fig.* Enge *f*; Eck...; *fig.* in die Enge treiben; ~ed *in Zssgn*: ...eckig.

cornet ['kɔ:nit] Eistüte *f*.

corn flakes *pl* geröstete Maisflocken *pl*.

coronation [kɔrə'neiʃən] Krönung *f*.

coroner ['kɔrənə] *jur.* Untersuchungsrichter *m*, ~'s **inquest** Gerichtsverhandlung *f* (zur Feststellung der Todesursache in Fällen gewaltsamen od. plötzlichen Todes).

corpora|**l** ['kɔ:pərəl] körperlich; Unteroffizier *m*; ~**tion** Körperschaft *f*; Stadtbehörde *f*; *Am.* Aktiengesellschaft *f*.

corpse [kɔ:ps] Leiche *f*.

corpulent ['kɔ:pjulənt] beleibt.

corral [kɔ'rɑ:l, *Am.* kə'ræl] Korral *m*, Hürde *f*.

correct [kə'rekt] korrekt, richtig; korrigieren; bestrafen; ~**ion** Verbesserung *f*; Korrektur *f*; Strafe *f*.

correspond [kɔris'pɔnd] entsprechen (with, to dat); korrespondieren; ~**ence** Übereinstimmung *f*; Briefwechsel *m*; ~**ent** Korrespondent(in).

corridor ['kɔridɔ:] Korridor *m*, Flur *m*, Gang *m*.

corrigible ['kɔridʒəbl] zu verbessern(d).

corroborate [kə'rɔbəreit] bestätigen.

corro|de [kə'rəud] zerfressen; wegätzen; **~sion** [~ʒən] Korrosion f.

corrugate ['kɔrugeit] runzeln; wellen; **~d iron** Wellblech n.

corrupt [kə'rʌpt] verdorben; bestechlich; verderben; bestechen; **~ion** f; Verderben n; Verdorbenheit f; Korruption f; Bestechung f.

corset ['kɔ:sit] Korsett n.

cosmetic [kɔz'metik] kosmetisch; Kosmetik(artikel m) f; **~ian** [~ə'tiʃən] Kosmetiker(in).

cosmonaut ['kɔzmənɔ:t] Kosmonaut m, Raumfahrer m.

cost [kɔst] Preis m; Kosten pl; Schaden m; (irr) kosten; **~ly** kostbar; kostspielig.

costume ['kɔstju:m] Kostüm n; Tracht f.

cosy ['kəuzi] gemütlich.

cot [kɔt] Feldbett n; Kinderbett n.

cottage ['kɔtidʒ] Hütte f; kleines Wohnhaus; kleines Landhaus; Sommerhaus n.

cotton ['kɔtn] Baumwolle f; (Näh- etc.)Garn n; Baumwoll...; **~ wool** Watte f.

couch [kautʃ] Lager n; Couch f, Sofa n; in Worte fassen; (sich) kauern.

cough [kɔf] Husten m; husten.

could [kud] pret u. cond]

council ['kaunsl] Rat(sversammlung f) m; **~(l)or**

['~silə] Ratsmitglied n, Stadtrat m.

counsel ['kaunsəl] j-m od. zu et. raten; Beratung f; Rat(schlag) m; Anwalt m; **~ for the defence** Verteidiger m; **~ for the prosecution** Anklagevertreter m; **~(l)or** ['~slə] Ratgeber m; Am. u. Irland Anwalt m.

count[1] [kaunt] zählen; (End)Zahl f; jur. Anklagepunkt m; zählen, rechnen; **~ up** zs.-zählen.

count[2] nichtbritischer Graf.

count-down ['kauntdaun] Countdown m, n.

countenance ['kauntinəns] Gesichtsausdruck m; Fassung f.

counter[1] ['kauntə] Zähler m; Spielmarke f; Ladentisch m; Theke f; Schalter m.

counter[2] entgegen, zuwider (to dat); **~act** [~'rækt] entgegenwirken, bekämpfen; **~balance** ['~bæləns] Gegengewicht n; [~'bæləns] aufwiegen, ausgleichen; **~espionage** Spionageabwehr f; **~feit** ['~fit] nachgemacht, gefälscht; Fälschung f; nachmachen, fälschen; **~foil** ['~fɔil] Kontrollabschnitt m; **~intelligence** ['~rintelidʒəns] Spionageabwehr (-dienst m) m; **~pane** ['~pein] Tagesdecke f; **~part** Gegenstück n.

countess ['kauntis] Gräfin f.

count|ing-house Kontor n, Büro n; ~**less** zahllos.

country ['kʌntri] Land n; Gegend f; Heimatland n; Land...; **in the** ~ auf dem Land; ~**house** Landsitz m; ~**man** Landmann m (Bauer); Landsmann m; ~**seat** Landsitz m; ~**side** Gegend f; Landschaft f; ~**town** Kleinstadt f.

county ['kaunti] Grafschaft f, Kreis m.

coupl|e ['kʌpl] (zs.-, ver-)koppeln; kuppeln; verbinden; (sich) paaren; (Ehe)Paar n; Koppel f (Jagdhunde); **a** ~**e of** zwei, colloq. ein paar; ~**ing** Kupplung f; Radio, electr.: Kopplung f.

coupon ['ku:pɔn] Abschnitt m; Bon m; (Gut-)Schein m.

courage ['kʌrid3] Mut m; ~**ous** [kə'reid3əs] mutig.

courier ['kuriə] Kurier m; Reiseleiter(in).

course [kɔ:s] Lauf m; Weg m, Route f; mar., f ig.: Kurs m; Rennbahn f; Gang m (Speisen); Kursus m; **of** ~ selbstverständlich, natürlich; **matter of** ~ Selbstverständlichkeit f.

court [kɔ:t] Hof m (a. e-s Fürsten); Gericht(shof m) n; **j-m den Hof machen**; werben um; ~**eous** ['kə:tjəs] höflich; ~**esy** ['kə:tisi] Höflichkeit f; Gefälligkeit f; ~**ier** ['kɔ:tjə] Höf-

ling m; ~**martial** Militärgericht n; ~ **of justice** Gericht(shof m) n; ~**room** Gerichtssaal m; ~**ship** Werbung f; ~**yard** Hof m.

cousin ['kʌzn] Vetter m, Cousin m; Base f, Cousine f.

cover ['kʌvə] Decke f; Hülle f; Deckel m; Umschlag m; (Buch)Einband m; Mantel m (Bereifung); Gedeck n; Deckung f; Schutz m; Vorwand m; (be-, zu)decken; beziehen, verbergen, verdecken; schützen; Weg zurücklegen; Gebiet bereisen, versorgen; econ. decken; umfassen; f ig. erfassen; Zeitung: berichten über; ~**age** Berichterstattung f; ~**ing** Decke f; Be-, Überzug m; Dach n.

covet ['kʌvit] begehren; ~**ous** begehrlich.

cow [kau] Kuh f.

coward ['kauəd] Feigling m; ~**ice** ['~is] Feigheit f; ~**ly** feig(e).

cowboy Cowboy m, Rinderhirt m.

cower ['kauə] kauern; sich ducken.

cow|herd Kuhhirt m; ~**hide** Rind(s)leder n; ~**house** Kuhstall m; ~ **shed** Kuhstall m; ~**slip** Schlüsselblume f; Am. Sumpfdotterblume f.

coxcomb ['kɔkskəum] Geck m.

coxswain ['kɔkswein,

mar. 'kɔksn] Bootsführer *m*; Steuermann *m*.

coy [kɔi] schüchtern; spröde.

crab [kræb] Krabbe *f*.

crack [kræk] Krach *m*, Knall *m*; Riß *m*, Sprung *m*; derber Schlag; (zer-)sprengen; knacken *od.* krachen (lassen); (auf)knacken; platzen, (zer)springen; brechen (*a.* Stimme); **~ a joke** e-n Witz reißen; **~er** Knallbonbon *m*, *n*, Schwärmer *m*; Keks *m* (*ungesüßt*); **~le** knattern, knistern.

cradle ['kreidl] Wiege *f*; wiegen; betten.

craft [krɑːft] Handwerk *n*; *mar.* Schiff(e *pl*) *n*, Fahrzeug(e *pl*) *n*; List *f*; **~sman** (Kunst)Handwerker *m*; **~y** gerissen, schlau.

crag [kræg] Klippe *f*, spitzer Fels.

cram [kræm] (voll)stopfen.

cramp [kræmp] Krampf *m*; *tech.* Krampe *f*; (ver-)krampfen; einengen, hemmen.

cranberry ['krænbəri] Preiselbeere *f*.

crane [krein] *orn.* Kranich *m*; Kran *m*; (den Hals) recken.

crank [kræŋk] Kurbel *f*; komischer Kauz; **~ up** *Motor* anwerfen.

crape [kreip] Krepp *m*; Trauerflor *m*.

crash [kræʃ] Krach(en *n*) *m*; Zs.-stoß *m*; *aer.* Absturz *m*; krachen(d fallen *od.* einstürzen); *aer.* abstürzen; **~-helmet** Sturzhelm *m*; **~-landing** Bruchlandung *f*.

crate [kreit] Lattenkiste *f*.

crater ['kreitə] Krater *m*; (Bomben)Trichter *m*.

crave [kreiv] dringend bitten *od.* flehen um; sich sehnen (**for** nach).

crawfish ['krɔːfiʃ] Flußkrebs *m*.

crawl [krɔːl] kriechen; schleichen; wimmeln; *Schwimmen:* kraulen.

crayfish ['kreifiʃ] Flußkrebs *m*.

crayon ['kreiən] Zeichenstift *m*.

crazy ['kreizi] verrückt (**about** nach).

creak [kriːk] knarren, quietschen.

cream [kriːm] Rahm *m*, Sahne *f*; Creme *f*; Auslese *f*, *das* Beste; den Rahm abschöpfen von; sahnig rühren; **~ cheese** Weich-, Schmelzkäse *m*; **~y** sahnig.

crease [kriːs] (Bügel-)Falte *f*; falten; (zer-)knittern.

create [kriː(ː)'eit] (er-)schaffen; verursachen; **~ion** Schöpfung *f*; **~ive** schöpferisch; **~or** Schöpfer *m*; **~ure** ['kriːtʃə] Geschöpf *n*; Kreatur *f*.

credentials [kri'denʃəlz]

pl Beglaubigungsschreiben
n; Zeugnisse *pl.*
credible ['kredəbl] glaubwürdig; glaubhaft.
credit ['kredit] Glaube(n)
m; Ruf m, Ansehen n;
Ehre f; Guthaben n;
Kredit m; j-m glauben;
j-m (zu)trauen; *Betrag* gut-
schreiben; **~able** ehrenvoll (**to** für); **~ card**
Scheckkarte f; **~or** Gläubiger m.
credulous ['kredjuləs]
leichtgläubig.
creed [kri:d] Glaubens-
bekenntnis n.
creek [kri:k] Bucht f; *Am.*
kleiner Fluß.
creep [kri:p] (*irr*) kriechen; schleichen; **it made
my flesh ~** ich bekam e-e
Gänsehaut; **~er** Kletterpflanze f.
cremate [kri'meit] ein-
äschern.
crept [krept] *pret u. pp
von* **creep**.
crescent ['kresnt] Halb-
mond m.
cress [kres] Kresse f.
crest [krest] (Hahnen-,
Berg)Kamm m; (*Wellen-*)
Kamm m; Federbusch m;
Wappenfigur f; **~family
~** Familienwappen
n; **~fallen** niederge-
schlagen.
crevasse [kri'væs] (Gletscher)Spalte f.
crevice ['krevis] Riß m,
Spalte f.
crew[1] [kru:] Schar f;

mar., aer. Besatzung f,
Mannschaft f.
crew[2] *pret von* **crow.**
crib [krib] Raufe f; *bsd.
Am.* Kinderbett n;
Schule: Klatsche f; ab-
schreiben.
cricket ['krikit] *zo.*
Grille f; *sp.* Kricket n.
crime [kraim] Verbre-
chen n.
criminal ['kriminl] ver-
brecherisch; Straf...; Ver-
brecher(in).
crimson ['krimzn] karme-
sin-, feuerrot. [ken.]
cringe [krindʒ] sich duk-
cripple ['kripl] Krüppel m;
verkrüppeln; *fig.* lähmen.
crisis ['kraisis], *pl* **~es**
['~i:z] Krise f; Wende-,
Höhepunkt m.
crisp [krisp] knusp(e)rig;
kraus; forsch; *Luft:*
scharf, frisch; **(potato)
~s** pl Kartoffelchips pl.
critic ['kritik] Kritiker
(-in); **~al** kritisch; bedenklich; **~ism** ['~sizəm]
Kritik f; **~ize** ['~saiz]
kritisieren; tadeln.
croak [krəuk] krächzen;
quaken.
crochet ['krəuʃei] häkeln.
crockery ['krɔkəri] Steingut n.
crocodile ['krɔkədail]
Krokodil n.
crofter ['krɔftə] Klein-
bauer m.
crook [kruk] Krüm-
mung f; *sl.* Gauner m;
(*pret, pp* [krukt]) sich

krümmen; ~ed ['~id]
krumm, schief; unehrlich.

crop [krɔp] Kropf *m*;
Ernte *f*; kurzer Haar-
schnitt; *Haar* kurz schneiden; *Acker* bebauen; ~ **up**
auftauchen.

cross [krɔs] Kreuz *n*;
biol. Kreuzung *f*; ärgerlich, böse; (sich) kreuzen
(*a. biol.*); durch-, überqueren; *fig.* durchkreu-
zen; ~ **off** *od.* **out** ausstreichen; ~ **o.s.** sich be-
kreuzigen; **keep one's
fingers** ~**ed** den Daumen halten; ~**Channel
boat** Kanalfähre *f*; ~
examination Kreuz-
verhör *n*; ~**ing** Überfahrt
f; (*Bahn-, Fußgänger-*)
Übergang *m*; Kreuzung *f*;
~**road** Querstraße *f*; ~
roads *sg* (Straßen)Kreu-
zung *f*; ~**word (puzzle)**
Kreuzworträtsel *n*. (ken.)

crouch [krautʃ] sich duk-

crow [krəu] Krähe *f*;
Krähen *n*; (*irr*) krähen;
triumphieren; ~**bar**
Brecheisen *n*.

crowd [kraud] Ansamm-
lung *f*, Haufen *m*; (Menschen)Menge *f*; ~**s** *pl* **of
people** Menschenmas-
sen *pl*; sich drängen;
(über)füllen, vollstopfen;
~**ed** überfüllt, verstopft,
voll.

crown [kraun] Krone *f*;
Kranz *m*; krönen.

crucial ['kru:ʃəl] ent-
scheidend, kritisch.

cruci|fixion [kru:si'fikʃən]
Kreuzigung *f*; ~**fy** ['~fai]
kreuzigen.

crude [kru:d] roh; un-
fertig; grob; Roh...

cruel [kruəl] grausam;
hart; ~**ty** Grausamkeit *f*,
~**ty to animals** Tier-
quälerei *f*.

cruet ['kru(:)it] Essig-,
Ölfläschchen *n*.

cruise [kru:z] Kreuzfahrt
f; kreuzen; ~**r** Kreuzer *m*;
Jacht *f*.

crumb [krʌm] Krume *f*;
~**le** ['~l] zerkrümeln,
-bröckeln; zerfallen.

crumple ['krʌmpl] zerknittern; ~ **up** zerknül-
len.

crunch [krʌntʃ] (zer)kauen;
zermalmen; knirschen.

crusade [kru:'seid] Kreuz-
zug *m*; ~**r** Kreuzfahrer *m*.

crush [krʌʃ] Gedränge *n*;
(Frucht)Saft *m*; sich
drängen; (zer-, aus)quet-
schen; zermalmen; zer-
knittern; *fig.* vernichten;
~ **barrier** Absperrgitter *n*.

crust [krʌst] Kruste *f*,
Rinde *f*; verkrusten; ~
(over) (sich) überkru-
sten; verharschen.

crutch [krʌtʃ] Krücke *f*.

cry [krai] schreien, (aus-)
rufen; weinen; Schrei *m*,
Ruf *m*; Geschrei *n*; Weinen *n*; ~ **of rage** Wut-
geschrei *n*.

crypt [kript] Gruft *f*.

crystal ['kristl] Kristall
m, *n*; *Am.* Uhrglas *n*.

~line ['~əlain] kristallen; **~lize** kristallisieren.

cub [kʌb] (*Raubtier*)Junge *n*.

cube [kjuːb] Würfel *m*; Kubikzahl *f*; **~ root** Kubikwurzel *f*.

cubicle ['kjuːbikl] kleiner abgeteilter (Schlaf-)Raum; Kabine *f*. [*m*.]

cuckoo ['kuku:] Kuckuck]

cucumber ['kjuːkʌmbə] Gurke *f*.

cuddle ['kʌdl] hätscheln.

cudgel ['kʌdʒəl] Knüppel *m*; prügeln. [(Wink *m*.)]

cue [kjuː] Stichwort *n*;]

cuff [kʌf] Manschette *f*; (Ärmel-, *Am. a.* Hosen-)Aufschlag *m*; Schlag *m*; **~links** *pl* Manschettenknöpfe *pl*.

culminate ['kʌlmineit] gipfeln; **~ion** *fig.* Höhepunkt *m*.

culprit ['kʌlprit] Schuldige *m*, *f*.

cultivate ['kʌltiveit] kultivieren; an~, bebauen; pflegen; **~ion** Bestellung *f*; Anbau *m*; Pflege *f*; **~or** Landwirt *m*; Kultivator *m* (*Gerät*).

cultural ['kʌltʃərəl] kulturell; **Kultur...** *f*; **['~tʃə] Kultur** *f*; Pflege *f*; Zucht *f*; **~ed** kultiviert.

cumulative ['kjuːmjulətiv] sich (an)häufend.

cunning ['kʌniŋ] schlau, listig; *Am.* reizend; List *f*, Schlauheit *f*.

cup [kʌp] Becher *m*; Tasse *f*; Kelch *m*; *sp.* Pokal *m*;

a **~ of tea** e-e Tasse Tee; **~board** ['kʌbəd] Schrank *m*.

cupola ['kjuːpələ] Kuppel *f*.

cur [kəː] Köter *m*.

curable ['kjuərəbl] heilbar.

curate ['kjuərit] Hilfsgeistliche *m*.

curb [kəːb] *s.* **kerb(stone)**.

curd [kəːd] *oft pl* Quark *m*; **~le** gerinnen (lassen).

cure [kjuə] Heilung *f*; Kur *f*; Heilmittel *n*; heilen; pökeln; räuchern.

curfew ['kəːfjuː] Ausgangssperre *f*.

curio ['kjuəriəu] Rarität *f*; **~sity** [~'ɔsiti] Neugier *f*; Rarität *f*; **~us** ['~əs] neugierig; merkwürdig.

curl [kəːl] Locke *f*; (sich) kräuseln *od.* locken *od.* ringeln; **~ up** sich hochringeln (*Rauch*); sich zs.-rollen; **~y** lockig.

currant ['kʌrənt] Johannisbeere *f*; Korinthe *f*.

currency ['kʌrənsi] Umlauf *m*; Kurs *m*, Währung *f*; **~t** laufend, gegenwärtig, aktuell; geläufig, allgemein bekannt; gültig (*Geld*); Strom *m* (*a. electr.*); Strömung *f*.

curriculum [kə'rikjuləm], *pl* **~a** [~ə] Lehr-, Studienplan *m*; **~um vitae** [~'vaiti:] Lebenslauf *m*.

curse [kəːs] Fluch *m*; (ver)fluchen; **~d** ['~id] verflucht.

curt [kə:t] kurz; barsch.

curtail [kə:'teil] (ab-, ver)kürzen.

curtain ['kə:tn] Vorhang m; Gardine f.

curts(e)y ['kə:tsi] Knicks m; knicksen (**to** vor).

curve [kə:v] Kurve f, Krümmung f, Biegung f; (sich) krümmen od. biegen.

cushion ['kuʃən] Kissen n; Polster n; polstern.

custody ['kʌstədi] Haft f; Obhut f.

custom ['kʌstəm] Gewohnheit f, Brauch m, Sitte f; Kundschaft f; **~ary** üblich; **~er** Kund|e m, -in f; **~-house** Zollamt n; **~-made** Zw. maßgearbeitet.

customs ['kʌstəmz] pl Zoll (-abfertigung f) m; **~ clearance** Zollabfertigung f; **~ declaration** Zollerklärung f; **~ examination** Zollkontrolle f.

cut [kʌt] Schnitt m; Hieb m; Stich m; Schnittwunde f; Schnitte f, Scheibe f; Holzschnitt m; Schliff m; Kürzung f; **cold ~s** pl Aufschnitt m; **power ~** Stromsperre f; **short ~** Abkürzung(sweg m) f; (irr) (ab-, an-, be-, durch-, zer)schneiden; schnitzen; Edelstein schleifen; Karten abheben; Betrag etc. kürzen; j-n beim Begegnen schneiden; Zahn bekommen; **~ down** fällen;

mähen; kürzen; Preis herabsetzen; **~ in** unterbrechen; **~ mot.** einschneiden; **~ off** abschneiden; -schlagen, -hauen; unterbrechen, trennen; Strom sperren; **~ out** ausschneiden; zuschneiden; **be ~ out** for das Zeug zu et. haben.

cute [kju:t] schlau; Am. colloq. a. reizend.

cuticle ['kju:tikl] Oberhaut f; Nagelhaut f; **~ scissors** pl Hautschere f.

cutlery ['kʌtləri] (Tisch-, Eß)Besteck n.

cutlet ['kʌtlit] Kotelett n.

cut|off Am. Abkürzung(sweg m) f; **~purse** Taschendieb(in); **~ter** Zuschneider(in); Schneidewerkzeug n, -maschine f; Kutter m; **~ting** schneidend, scharf; Schneiden n; Film: Schnitt m; (Zeitungs)Ausschnitt m.

cycl|e ['saikl] Zyklus m; Kreis m; Fahrrad n; radfahren, radeln; **~ist** Radfahrer(in).

cyclone ['saikləun] Wirbelsturm m.

cylinder ['silində] Zylinder m, Walze f; tech. Trommel f.

cynic ['sinik] Zyniker m; **~al** zynisch.

cypress ['saipris] Zypresse f.

cyst [sist] Zyste f.

Czech [tʃek] Tschech|e m, -in f; tschechisch.

dash

Czechoslovak ['tʃekəu-'sləuvæk] Tschechoslowakisch.

D

dab [dæb] betupfen.

dachshund ['dækshund] Dackel m.

dad [dæd], ~dy ['~i] Papa m, Vati m; ~dy-longlegs Schnake f; Am. Weberknecht m.

daffodil ['dæfədil] Gelbe Narzisse f.

daft [dɑːft] colloq. doof.

dagger ['dægə] Dolch m.

daily ['deili] täglich; Tageszeitung f.

dainty ['deinti] lecker; zart, fein; wählerisch.

dairy ['dɛəri] Molkerei f; Milchgeschäft n; ~man Milchmann m.

daisy ['deizi] Gänseblümchen n.

dale [deil] Tal m.

dally ['dæli] herumtrödeln; schäkern; spielen.

dam [dæm] (Stau)Damm m, Deich m; (ab-, ein)dämmen.

damage ['dæmidʒ] Schaden m; pl jur. Schadenersatz m; (be)schädigen; schaden.

dame [deim] Dame f (alte Form).

damn [dæm] verdammen; ~ation [~'neiʃən]Verdammung f; Verdammnis f.

damp [dæmp] feucht; Feuchtigkeit f; an-, befeuchten; ~(en) dämp-

fen, niederdrücken.

danc|e [dɑːns] Tanz m; Ball m; tanzen; ~er Tänzer(in); ~ing Tanzen n; Tanz...

dandelion ['dændilaiən] Löwenzahn m.

dandruff ['dændrʌf] (Kopf)Schuppen pl.

Dane [dein] Däne m, -in f.

danger ['deindʒə] Gefahr f; ~ous ['~dʒrəs] gefährlich.

dangle ['dæŋgl] baumeln (lassen), hin- und herschlenkern.

Danish ['deiniʃ] dänisch.

dar|e [dɛə] es od. et. wagen; ~ing verwegen.

dark [dɑːk] dunkel; finster; Dunkel(heit f) n; ~ brown dunkelbraun; ~en (sich) verdunkeln; ~ness Dunkelheit f, Finsternis f.

darling ['dɑːliŋ] Liebling m.

darn [dɑːn] stopfen.

dart [dɑːt] Satz m; Wurfpfeil m; pl Pfeilwerfen n; schleudern; schießen; stürzen.

dash [dæʃ] Schlag m; (An)Sturm m; Klatschen n (Wellen); Prise f (Salz etc.); Schuß m (Rum etc.); Federstrich m; Gedankenstrich m; schleudern; (be)spritzen; *Hoffnung* vernichten; stürzen, stürmen, jagen, rasen; ~board Armaturenbrett n; ~ing schneidig.

data ['deitə] pl Tatsachen pl; Daten pl, Angaben pl, Informationen pl; Meßwerte pl; ~ processing Datenverarbeitung f.

date [deit] datieren; ~ from (her)stammen aus od. von; *bot.* Dattel f; Datum n; Termin m; Zeit f; *colloq.* Verabredung f; **out of** ~ veraltet, unmodern; **up to** ~ zeitgemäß, modern; auf dem laufenden.

dative (case) ['deitiv] *gr.* Dativ m, 3. Fall.

daub [dɔːb] (be)schmieren.

daughter ['dɔːtə] Tochter f; ~-in-law Schwiegertochter f.

dawdle ['dɔːdl] ~ (away) (ver)trödeln.

dawn [dɔːn] Dämmerung f; dämmern, tagen.

day [dei] Tag m; *oft pl* (Lebens)Zeit f; ~ off (dienst)freier Tag; **by** ~ am Tage; **all** ~ **long** den ganzen Tag (lang, über); **to this** ~ bis heute; **the other** ~ neulich; **this week** heute in einer Woche; **in the old** ~**s** in alten Zeiten, früher; ~break Tagesanbruch m; ~ **excursion** Tagesausflug m; ~-labo(u)rer Tagelöhner m; ~light

Tageslicht n; ~-school Tagesschule f.

daze [deiz] betäuben.

dazzle ['dæzl] blenden.

dead [ded] *tot*; unempfindlich (**to** für); völlig; plötzlich; *sub*: **the** ~ *pl* die Toten pl; **in the** ~ **of winter** im tiefsten Winter; ~**en** abstumpfen; dämpfen, (ab)schwächen; ~ **end** Sackgasse f (a. *fig.*); ~**line** letzter Termin; Stichtag m; ~**lock** *fig.* toter Punkt; ~ **loss** Totalverlust m; ~**ly** tödlich; Tod...; ~ **tired** todmüde.

deaf [def] taub; ~**en** taub machen; ~**ening** ohrenbetäubend.

deal [diːl] Menge f, Teil m; Abmachung f; *colloq.* Handel m; **a good** ~, **a great** ~ sehr od. ziemlich viel; (*irr*) (aus-, ver-, zu)teilen; handeln (**in** mit e-r Ware); ~ **with** behandeln, sich befassen mit; ~**er** Händler m; ~**ing** Geschäftsverkehr m; *oft* Umgang m; ~**t** [delt] *pret u. pp von* **deal**.

dean [diːn] Dekan m.

dear [diə] teuer; lieb; Teure m, f, Liebling m; **Sir** Sehr geehrter Herr (*in Briefen*); ~ **me!** du liebe Zeit!, ach herrje! ~**ly** sehr; innig.

death [deθ] Tod(esfall) m; ~**ly** tödlich; ~**bed**.

debar [di'bɑː] ausschließen.

debase [di'beis] verderben; verschlechtern;

debate [di'beit] Debatte *f*; debattieren.

debauchery [di'bɔ:tʃəri] Ausschweifung *f*.

debit ['debit] *econ.* Debet *n*, Schuld *f*; belasten.

debris ['deibri:] Trümmer *pl.*

debt [det] Schuld *f*; **⁓or** Schuldner(in).

decade ['dekeid] Jahrzehnt *n*.

decadence ['dekədəns] Verfall *m*.

decapitate [di'kæpiteit] enthaupten.

decay [di'kei] Verfall *m*; Fäulnis *f*; verfallen; (ver)faulen.

decease [di'si:s] *bsd. jur.* Ableben *n*; sterben.

deceit [di'si:t] Täuschung *f*, Betrug *m*; **⁓ful** (be-) trügerisch; falsch.

deceive [di'si:v] betrügen, täuschen; **⁓r** Betrüger(in).

decelerate [di:'seləreit] s-e Geschwindigkeit verringern, langsamer fahren, *mot. a.* Gas wegnehmen.

December [di'sembə] Dezember *m*.

decen|cy ['di:snsi] Anstand *m*; **⁓t** anständig.

deception [di'sepʃən] Täuschung *f*.

decide [di'said] (sich) entscheiden; sich entschließen; beschließen; **⁓d** entschieden.

decimal ['desiml] Dezimal...; ziffern.

decipher [di'saifə] ent-

decisi|on [di'siʒən] Entscheidung *f*; Entschluß *m*; **⁓ve** [di'saisiv] entscheidend; entscheidungs-.

deck [dek] (Ver)Deck *n*; **⁓ chair** Liegestuhl *m*.

declar|ation [deklə'reiʃən] Erklärung *f*; **⁓ation of Independence** Unabhängigkeitserklärung *f*; **⁓e** [di'klɛə] erklären; behaupten; deklarieren; verzollen.

declension [di'klenʃən] *gr.* Deklination *f*, Beugung *f*.

decline [di'klain] Abnahme *f*; Verfall *m*; *gr.* deklinieren; beugen; ablehnen; sich neigen; ablehnen; verfallen.

declivity [di'kliviti] (Ab-) Hang *m*.

decode ['di:'kəud] entschlüsseln.

decorat|e ['dekəreit] (ver)zieren, schmücken; tapezieren, anstreichen; dekorieren; **⁓ion** Verzierung *f*; Schmuck *m*, Dekoration *f*; Orden *m*; **⁓ive** ['‿rətiv] verzierend, Zier...; **⁓or** Dekorateur *m*; Maler *m*.

decoy ['di:kɔi] Lockvogel *m* (*a. fig.*); Köder *m*; [di'kɔi] ködern, locken.

decrease ['di:kri:s] Abnahme *f*; [di:'kri:s] (sich) vermindern, abnehmen.

decree [di'kri:] Dekret *n*, Erlaß *m*; beschließen.

decrepit [di'krepit] altersschwach.

dedicat|e ['dedikeit] widmen; **~ion** Widmung f.

deduce [di'dju:s] ableiten; folgern.

deduct [di'dʌkt] abziehen; **~ion** Abzug m; (Schluß-) Folgerung f.

deed [di:d] Tat f; Heldentat f; Urkunde f.

deep [di:p] tief; verschlagen, schlau; Tiefe f; **~en** (sich) vertiefen; (sich) verstärken; **~-freeze** tiefkühlen; Gefrierfach n; Gefrier-, Tiefkühltruhe f; **~ness** Tiefe f.

deer [diə] Hirsch m; Reh n; Rotwild n.

deface [di'feis] entstellen.

defame [di'feim] verleumden.

defeat [di'fi:t] Niederlage f; besiegen; vereiteln.

defect [di'fekt] Defekt m, Fehler m; Mangel m; **~ive** mangelhaft; fehlerhaft.

defen|ce, Am. **~se** [di'fens] Verteidigung f; Schutz m; **~celess**, Am. **~seless** schutzlos, wehrlos.

defen|d [di'fend] verteidigen; schützen; **~dant** Angeklagte m, f; Beklagte m, f; **~der** Verteidiger(in); **~sive** Defensive f; Verteidigungs...

defer [di'fə:] auf-, verschieben.

defiant [di'faiənt] herausfordernd, trotzig.

deficien|cy [di'fiʃnsi] Unzulänglichkeit f; Man-

gel m; Fehlbetrag m; **~t** mangelhaft, unzureichend.

deficit ['defisit] Fehlbetrag m.

defile [di'fail] Engpaß m.

defin|e [di'fain] definieren, erklären; **~ite** ['definit] bestimmt, klar; **~ition** (Begriffs)Bestimmung f; Erklärung f; **~itive** [di'finitiv] endgültig.

deflate [di'fleit] Luft od. Gas ablassen aus.

deflect [di'flekt] ablenken.

deform [di'fɔ:m] entstellen, verunstalten; **~ed** mißgestaltet.

defrost [di'frɔst] entfrosten, -eisen, abtauen.

defy [di'fai] trotzen; standhalten; herausfordern.

degenerate [di'dʒenərit] entartet, verderbt.

degrade [di'greid] degradieren; erniedrigen.

degree [di'gri:] Grad m; Rang m; fig. Stufe f; **five ~s centigrade** 5 Grad Celsius (abbr. 5°C); **by ~s** allmählich.

dejected [di'dʒektid] niedergeschlagen.

delay [di'lei] Aufschub m, Verzögerung f; aufschieben, verzögern; aufhalten; sich verspäten.

delegat|e ['deligeit] abordnen; übertragen; ['~it] Abgeordnete m, f; **~ion** [~'geiʃən] Abordnung f.

deliberate [di'libərit] überlegen; sich beraten; [~it] vorsätzlich.

delica|cy ['delikəsi] Leckerbissen *m*; Zartheit *f*; Feinheit *f*; **~te** ['~it] schmackhaft; zart; fein; empfindlich; **~tessen** [,~'tesn] Feinkost(geschäft *n*) *f*.

delicious [di'liʃəs] köstlich.

delight [di'lait] Freude *f*; entzücken, erfreuen; **~ful** wunderbar.

delinquen|cy [di'liŋkwənsi] Vergehen *n*; Kriminalität *f*; **~t** Verbrecher(in).

deliver [di'livə] befreien; aus-, abliefern, aushändigen; *Briefe* zustellen; *Botschaft* ausrichten; *Rede* halten; *med.* entbinden; **~ance** Befreiung *f*; **~er** Befreier(in); **~y** *med.* Entbindung *f*; (Ab)Lieferung *f*; *Post:* Zustellung *f*; Vortrag *m*.

deluge ['delju:dʒ] Überschwemmung *f*; **the** *~* 2 die Sintflut.

delus|ion [di'lu:ʒən] Täuschung *f*; Wahn(vorstellung *f*) *m*; **~ive** [~siv] trügerisch.

demand [di'mɑ:nd] Forderung *f*; Nachfrage *f*, Bedarf *m*; verlangen, fordern; fragen nach.

demeano(u)r [di'mi:nə] Benehmen *n*.

demented [di'mentid] wahnsinnig.

demi- ['demi-] Halb...)

demilitarized ['di:'militəraizd] entmilitarisiert.

demise [di'maiz] *jur.* Ableben *n*.

demobilize [di:'məubilaiz] demobilisieren.

democra|cy [di'mɔkrəsi] Demokratie *f*; **~t** ['deməkræt] Demokrat(in); **~tic** [,~'krætik] demokratisch.

demolish [di'mɔliʃ] niederreißen, abreißen.

demon ['di:mən] Dämon *m*.

demonstra|te ['demənstreit] demonstrieren; darlegen, zeigen; vorführen; **~ion** Demonstration *f*; Darlegung *f*, -stellung *f*; Vorführung *f*; **~ive** [di'mɔnstrətiv] demonstrativ.

den [den] Höhle *f*; Hütte *f*, Loch *n*; *colloq.* Bude *f*.

denial [di'naiəl] Leugnen *n*; Ablehnung *f*, Verweigerung *f*, abschlägige Antwort.

denomination [dinɔmi'neiʃən] Konfession *f*.

denounce [di'nauns] anzeigen; *Vertrag* kündigen.

dens|e [dens] dicht, dick (*Nebel*); **~ity** Dichte *f*.

dent [dent] Beule *f*; ver-, einbeulen.

dent|al ['dentl] Zahn...; **~al surgeon**, **~ist** Zahnarzt *m*; **~ure** (künstliches) Gebiß.

deny [di'nai] (ver)leugnen; verweigern, abschlagen.

depart [di'pɑ:t] abreisen, abfahren; **~ment** Abteilung *f*; *Am.* Ministerium *n*; **~ment store** Warenhaus *n*; **~ure** Abreise *f*, Abfahrt *f*; *aer.* Abflug *m*.

depend [di'pend]: **~ (up)-on** abhängen von; angewiesen sein auf; **that ~s, it all ~s** *colloq.* es kommt (ganz) darauf an; **~ence** Abhängigkeit *f*; Vertrauen *n*; **~ent**: **~ (up)on** abhängig von; angewiesen auf.

deplor|able [di'plɔːrəbl] beklagenswert; **~e** bedauern.

depopulate [diː'pɔpjuleit] entvölkern.

deport [di'pɔːt] ausweisen; **~ o.s.** sich benehmen.

depose [di'pəuz] *j-n* absetzen; (unter Eid) aussagen.

deposit [di'pɔzit] *geol.* Ablagerung *f*; (Erz)Lager *n*; Einzahlung *f*; (nieder-, ab-, hin)legen; *Geld* einzahlen; *Geld* anzahlen; (sich) ablagern; **~or** Kontoinhaber(in).

depot ['depəu] Depot *n*; Lager(haus) *n*.

depraved [di'preivd] verdorben, -kommen.

depress [di'pres] herunterdrücken; bedrücken; **~ed** niedergeschlagen; **~ion** Vertiefung *f*; Flaute *f*, Wirtschaftskrise *f*; *meteor.* Tief (-druckgebiet) *n*; Niedergeschlagenheit *f*.

deprive [di'praiv] berauben; entziehen.

depth [depθ] Tiefe *f*.

deputy ['depjuti] (Stell-) Vertreter(in); Abgeordnete *m, f*.

derail [di'reil]: **be ~ed** [entgleisen.]

derange [di'reindʒ] durchea.-bringen.

deri|de [di'raid] verspotten; **~sion** [~'iʒən] Spott *m*; **~sive** [~'aisiv] spöttisch.

derive [di'raiv]: **~ (from)** herleiten (von); *Nutzen etc.* ziehen (aus).

derogatory [di'rɔgətəri] 'nachteilig (**to** für); abfällig; herabsetzend.

descend [di'send] her-, hinuntersteigen, **-kommen**; *aer.* niedergehen; **be ~ed** abstammen; **~ant** Nachkomme *m*.

descent [di'sent] Hinuntersteigen *n*, Abstieg *m*; Gefälle *n*; *aer.* Niedergehen *n*; Abstammung *f*.

descri|be [di'skraib] beschreiben; **~ption** [~'kripʃən] Beschreibung *f*.

desegregate [diː'segrigeit] *Am.* die Rassentrennung aufheben in.

desert[1] ['dezət] Wüste *f*; öde; Wüsten...

desert[2] [di'zəːt] verlassen; im Stich lassen; desertieren; **~ed** verlassen; einsam; **~er** Deserteur *m*; **~ion** Verlassen *n*; Fahnenflucht *f*.

deserve [di'zəːv] verdienen.

design [di'zain] Plan *m*; Entwurf *m*; Zeichnung *f*;

devastate

Muster *n*; Ausführung *f*; Absicht *f*; entwerfen; planen.

designate ['dezigneit] bezeichnen; bestimmen.

designer [di'zainə] (Muster)Zeichner(in); Konstrukteur *m*.

desirable [di'zaiərəbl] wünschenswert; angenehm; **~it** [~it] öde; **~e** [~ə] verlangen *n*; verlangen; **~ousbegierig.**

desk [desk] Pult *n*; Schulbank *f*; Schalter *m*; Schreibtisch *m*; **~ set** Schreibtischgarnitur *f*.

desolate ['desəleit] verwüsten; ['~it] öde; verwüstet; verlassen, einsam; **~ion** Verwüstung *f*; Verlassenheit *f*.

despair [dis'pεə] Verzweiflung *f*; verzweifeln (**of** an); **~ing** verzweifelt.

desperate ['despərit] verzweifelt; hoffnungslos; **~ion** Verzweiflung *f*.

despise [dis'paiz] verachten. [**of** trotz.]

despite [dis'pait] (**in**) *~*]

despond [dis'pɔnd] verzagen; **~ent** verzagt.

dessert [di'zə:t] Nachtisch *m*, Dessert *n*.

destination [desti'neiʃən] Bestimmung(sort *m*) *f*; Reiseziel *n*; **~e** ['~in] bestimmen; **~y** Schicksal *n*.

destitute ['destitju:t] mittellos.

destroy [dis'trɔi] zerstören, vernichten; **~er** Zerstörer *m*.

destruction [dis'trʌkʃən] Zerstörung *f*; Zerstörend, vernichtend.

detach [di'tætʃ] losmachen, (ab)lösen; **~ed** einzeln (stehend); unbeeinflußt.

detail ['di:teil] Einzelheit *f*.

detain [di'tein] zurück-, auf-, abhalten.

detect [di'tekt] entdecken; **~ion** Entdeckung *f*; **~ive** Detektiv *m*, Kriminalbeamte *m*; **~ive story** Kriminalroman *m*.

detention [di'tenʃən] Haft *f*; Arrest *m*.

deter [di'tə:] abschrecken.

detergent [di'tə:dʒənt] Reinigungsmittel *n*.

deteriorate [di'tiəriəreit] (sich) verschlechtern.

determination [ditə:mi'neiʃən] Entscheidung *f*; Bestimmung *f*; Entschlossenheit *f*; **~e** [di'tə:min] bestimmen; (sich) entscheiden; sich entschließen.

deterrent [di'terənt] Abschreckungsmittel *n*.

detest [di'test] verabscheuen; **~able** abscheulich.

detonate ['detəuneit] explodieren (lassen).

detour ['di:tuə] Umleitung *f*.

devaluation [di:vælju'eiʃən] Abwertung *f*; **~e** ['~vælju:] abwerten.

devastate ['devəsteit] verwüsten.

develop [di'veləp] (sich) entwickeln; erschließen; ~ment Entwicklung f; phot. Entwickeln n; Erschließung f.

deviate ['di:vieit] abweichen.

device [di'vais] Plan m; Erfindung f; Trick m; Vor-, Einrichtung f; Gerät n.

devil ['devl] Teufel m; ~ish teuflisch.

devise [di'vaiz] ausdenken.

devoid [di'void]: ~ of ohne.

devot|e [di'vəut] widmen; ~ed ergeben; zärtlich; ~ion Ergebenheit f; Hingabe f; Liebe f; pl Andacht f.

devour [di'vauə] verschlingen.

devout [di'vaut] fromm; innig. [betaut.]

dew [dju:] Tau m; ~y]

dext|erity [deks'teriti] Gewandtheit f; ~(e)rous ['~(ə)rəs] gewandt.

dial ['daiəl] Zifferblatt n; teleph. Wählscheibe f; Skala f; teleph. wählen.

dialect ['daiəlekt] Mundart f.

dialog(ue) ['daiələg] Dialog m, Gespräch n.

diameter [dai'æmitə] Durchmesser m.

diamond ['daiəmənd] Diamant m; ~(s pl) Karten: Karo n.

diaper ['daiəpə] Am. Windel f.

diaphragm ['daiəfræm] Zwerchfell n; opt. Blende f; teleph. Membran(e) f.

diarrh(o)ea [daiə'riə] med. Durchfall m.

diary ['daiəri] Tagebuch n.

dice [dais] pl von die²; würfeln.

dictat|e [dik'teit] diktieren; fig. vorschreiben; ~ion Diktat n; Vorschrift f; ~or Diktator m; ~orship Diktatur f.

dictionary ['dikʃənri] Wörterbuch n.

did [did] pret von do.

die¹ [dai] sterben, umkommen; absterben; ~ of cold erfrieren. [fel m.]

die² [dai] pl dice [dais] Würf-]

diet ['daiət] Landtag m; Diät f; Nahrung f, Kost f; auf Diät setzen; diät leben.

differ ['difə] sich unterscheiden; auseinandergehen (Meinungen); ~ence ['difrəns] Unterschied m; Differenz f; Meinungsverschiedenheit f; ~ent verschieden.

difficult ['difikəlt] schwierig, schwer; ~y Schwierigkeit f.

diffident ['difidənt] schüchtern.

diffuse [di'fju:z] verbreiten.

dig [dig] (irr) (um)graben.

digest [di'dʒest] verdauen; verdaut werden; ['daidʒest] Überblick m; Auswahl f; ~ible [di'dʒestəbl] verdaulich; ~ion [di'dʒestʃən] Verdauung f.

diggings ['digiŋz] *pl colloq.* Bude *f*, Zimmer *n*.

digni|fied ['dignifaid] würdevoll; **~ty** Würde *f*.

digress [dai'gres] abschweifen.

digs [digz] *pl colloq.* Bude *f*, Zimmer *n*.

dike [daik] Deich *m*, Damm *m*; Graben *m*.

dilapidated [di'læpideitid] verfallen, baufällig.

dilate [dai'leit] (sich) ausdehnen *od.* (aus)weiten.

diligen|ce ['dilidʒəns] Fleiß *m*; **~t** fleißig.

dilute [dai'lju:t] verdünnen, (trüben.)

dim [dim] trüb(e); (sich))

dime [daim] *Am.* Zehncentstück *n*.

dimension [di'menʃən] Dimension *f*, Abmessung *f*; *pl a.* Ausmaß *n*.

dimin|ish [di'miniʃ] (sich) verringern; **~utive** [~jutiv] winzig.

dimple ['dimpl] Grübchen *n*.

dine [dain] speisen; **~r** Gast *m*; *rail.* Speisewagen *m*.

dining-**car** ['dainiŋ-] Speisewagen *m*; **~-room** Speise-, Eßzimmer *n*; **~-table** Eßtisch *m*.

dinner ['dinə] Hauptmahlzeit *f*, (Mittag-, Abend-) Essen *n*; **for ~** zum Essen; **have ~** zu Mittag *od.* Abend essen; **~, bed and breakfast** Halbpension *f*; **~-jacket** Smo-

kingjacke *f*; **~-party** Tischgesellschaft *f*.

dip [dip] (ein-, unter-) tauchen; schöpfen; *mot.* abblenden; sich senken; Eintauchen *n*; *colloq.* kurzes Bad; Senkung *f*, Neigung *f*. [Diphtherie *f*.)

diphtheria [dif'θiəriə])

diploma [di'pləumə] Diplom *n*, Abgangszeugnis *n*; **~cy** Diplomatie *f*; **~t** ['~mæt] Diplomat *m*; **~tic** [~ə'mætik] diplomatisch; **~tist** [di'pləumətist] Diplomat *m*.

direct [di'rekt] direkt; gerade; unmittelbar; offen, deutlich; *adv s.* **directly**; *Weg* zeigen; lenken, leiten; adressieren; anordnen; richten; **~ current** Gleichstrom *m*; **~ion** Richtung *f*; Leitung *f*; Direktion *f*; **~ions** *pl* Adresse *f*; Anweisung(en *pl*) *f*; **~ions** *pl* **(for use)** Gebrauchsanweisung *f*; **~ly** gerade; sofort, gleich.

director [di'rektə] *Film*: Regisseur *m*; *thea.* Intendant *m*; Direktor *m*, Leiter *m*; **board of ~s** Direktion *f*, Aufsichtsrat *m*; **~y** Adreßbuch *n*.

dirigible ['diridʒəbl] lenkbar.

dirt [də:t] Schmutz *m*; **~-cheap** spottbillig; **~y** schmutzig; (be)schmutzen.

disabled [dis'eibld] dienstunfähig; körperbehindert; kriegsbeschädigt.

disadvantage [disəd-
'va:ntidʒ] Nachteil *m*;
~ous [disædva:n'teidʒəs]
nachteilig.

disagree [disə'gri:] nicht
übereinstimmen; anderer
Meinung sein (**with** als);
nicht bekommen (**with**
s.o. j-m); **~able** [~iəbl]
unangenehm; **~ment** Un-
stimmigkeit *f*; Meinungsverschiedenheit *f*.

disappear [disə'piə] verschwinden; **~ance** Ver-
schwinden *n*.

disappoint [disə'pɔint]
enttäuschen; **~ment** Ent-
täuschung *f*.

disapprov|al [disə'pru:-
vəl] Mißbilligung *f*; **~e**
mißbilligen (**of** s.th. et.).

disarm [dis'ɑ:m] entwaff-
nen; abrüsten; **~ament**
Abrüstung *f*.

disarrange ['disə'reindʒ]
in Unordnung bringen.

disast|er [di'zu:stə] Un-
glück *n*, Katastrophe *f*;
~rous katastrophal.

disbelie|f ['disbi'li:f] Un-
glaube *m*, Zweifel *m*; **~ve**
['~'li:v] nicht glauben.

disc [disk] Scheibe *f*;
(Schall)Platte *f*.

discern [di'sə:n] unterscheiden; erkennen.

discharge [dis'tʃɑ:dʒ]ent-,
ab-, ausladen; abson-
dern; ausströmen; ab-
feuern; *Pflicht* erfüllen;
Schuld bezahlen; entlassen; freisprechen; (sich)
entladen; abfließen; Aus-

laden *n*; Entladung *f*; Ausströmen *n*, Abfluß *m*; Ab-
sonderung *f* (*Eiter*); Aus-
fluß *m*; Abfeuern *n*; Entlassung *f*; Bezahlung *f*.

disciple [di'saipl] Schüler
m; Jünger *m*; **~ine** ['disi-
plin'] Disziplin *f*.

disc jockey Ansager *m*
(*e-r Schallplattensendung*).

dis|claim [dis'kleim] (ab-)
leugnen; enthüllen; **~close** aufdek-
ken; enthüllen; **~colo(u)r**
(sich) verfärben; **~com-
fort** Unbehagen *n*; **~com-
pose** beunruhigen; aus der
Fassung bringen; *Pläne*
zunichte machen.

disconnect ['diskə'nekt]
trennen; *electr. a.* abschal-
ten; **~ed** zs.-hanglos.

disconsolate [dis'kɔn-
səlit] untröstlich.

discontent ['diskən'tent]
Unzufriedenheit *f*; **~ed** unzufrieden.

discontinue ['diskən-
'tinju(:)] aufhören.

discord [disko:d], **~ance**
['~kɔ:dəns] Mißklang *m*.

discotheque ['diskəutek]
Diskothek *f*.

discount ['diskaunt] Diskont *m*; Rabatt *m*.

discourage [dis'kʌridʒ]
entmutigen; abschrecken.

discover [dis'kʌvə] entdecken; **~er** Entdecker
(-in); **~y** Entdeckung *f*.

dis|credit [dis'kredit]
schlechter Ruf; Schande
f; Zweifel *m*; anzweifeln;

disobey

in Mißkredit bringen; **~creet** [,'kri:t] diskret, verschwiegen; **~crepancy** [,'krepənsi] Widerspruch m; **~cretion** [,'krefən] Verschwiegenheit f; Vorsicht f; Ermessen n; **~criminate** [,'krimineit] unterscheiden; **~criminate against** benachteiligen.

discuss [dis'kʌs] diskutieren, besprechen; **~ion** Diskussion f, Besprechung f.

disdain [dis'dein] Verachtung f; verachten.

disease [di'zi:z] Krankheit f; **~d** krank.

disembark ['disim'bɑːk] ausschiffen; an Land gehen.

disengage ['disin'geidʒ] los-, freimachen; **~d** frei.

dis|entangle ['disin'tæŋgl] entwirren; **~favo(u)r** Mißfallen n; Ungnade f; **~figure** entstellen.

disgrace [dis'greis] Ungnade f; Schande f; entehren; **~ful** schändlich.

disguise [dis'gaiz] verkleiden; Stimme verstellen; verbergen; Verkleidung f; Maske f; Verstellung f.

disgust [dis'gʌst] Ekel m, Abscheu m; anekeln; empören; **~ing** ekelhaft.

dish [diʃ] Schüssel f, Platte f, Schale f; Gericht n, Speise f; *the* **~es** *pl* Geschirr n; **~cloth** Spüllappen m.

dishevel(l)ed [di'ʃevəld] zerzaust, wirr.

dishonest [dis'ɔnist] unehrlich; **~y** Unehrlichkeit f.

dishono(u)r [dis'ɔnə] Schande f; entehren; *Wechsel* nicht honorieren; **~able** schändlich; ehrlos.

dish|-washer Geschirrspülmaschine f; **~-water** Spülwasser n.

dis|illusion [disi'luːʒən] Ernüchterung f, Enttäuschung f; ernüchtern; **~inclined** abgeneigt.

disinfect [disin'fekt] desinfizieren; **~ant** Desinfektionsmittel n.

dis|inherit ['disin'herit] enterben; **~integrate** (sich) auflösen; **~interested** uneigennützig.

disk [disk] s. **disc**.

dis|like [dis'laik] Abneigung f; nicht mögen; **~locate** *med.* verrenken; **~loyal** treulos.

dismal ['dizməl] düster, trüb(e), trostlos.

dis|mantle [dis'mæntl] demontieren; **~may** [,'mei] Schrecken m, Bestürzung f; **~member** zerstückeln.

dismiss [dis'mis] entlassen; wegschicken; aufgeben; **~al** Entlassung f.

dismount ['dis'maunt] demontieren; absteigen.

disobedien|ce [disə'biːdjəns] Ungehorsam m; **~t** ungehorsam.

dis|obey ['disə'bei] nicht

gehorchen; nicht befolgen; **~oblige** ungefällig sein gegen.

disorder [dis'ɔ:də] Unordnung f; Unruhe f; *med.* Störung f; **~ly** unordentlich; gesetzwidrig; aufrührerisch.

dis|own [dis'əun] nicht anerkennen; verleugnen; **~parage** [~'pærid3] herabsetzen; **~passionate** leidenschaftslos.

dispatch [dis'pætʃ] Erledigung f; Absendung f; Eile f; (amtlicher) Bericht; (ab)senden; (schnell) erledigen; töten.

dispens|able [dis'pensəbl] entbehrlich; **~e** austeilen; **~e with** auskommen ohne.

dis|perse [dis'pə:s] (sich) zerstreuen; **~place** verrücken, -schieben; absetzen; ersetzen.

display [dis'plei] Entfaltung f; Zurschaustellung n; (*Schaufenster*)Auslage f; Ausstellung f; zeigen; ausstellen; entfalten.

displease [dis'pli:z] mißfallen; **~ed** ungehalten; **~ure** [~eʒə] Mißfallen n.

dispos|al [dis'pəuzəl] Anordnung f; Verfügung(srecht n) f; Beseitigung f; Veräußerung f; **~e** (an-) ordnen; veranlassen; **~e of** verfügen über; veräußern; beseitigen; erledigen; **~ed** geneigt; **~ition** [~ə'ziʃən] Anordnung f; *freie* Verfügung; Neigung f; Wesen n, Gemütsart f.

disproportionate [disprə'pɔ:ʃnit] unverhältnismäßig.

dispute [dis'pju:t] Debatte f; Streit m; (sich) streiten; anzweifeln.

dis|qualify [dis'kwɔlifai] ausschließen; **~regard** nicht beachten; **~reputable** verrufen; schändlich; **~respectful** respektlos; unhöflich; **~rupt** [~'rʌpt] spalten.

dissatisf|action [dissætis'fækʃən] Unzufriedenheit f; **~ied** unzufrieden.

dissen|sion [di'senʃən] Zwietracht f; **~t** anderer Meinung sein (**from** als).

dis|similar ['di'similə] verschieden (**to** von); **~sipate** ['~sipeit] (sich) zerstreuen; verschwenden; **~sociate** [~'səuʃieit] trennen; **~sociate o.s.** sich distanzieren.

dissol|ute ['disəlu:t] ausschweifend, liederlich; **~ution** Auflösung f; **~ve** [di'zɔlv] (sich) auflösen.

dissuade [di'sweid] j-m abraten.

distan|ce ['distəns] Abstand m, Entfernung f; Ferne f; Strecke f; *fig.* Distanz f; **in the ~ce** in der Ferne; **~t** entfernt; zurückhaltend; Fern...

distaste ['dis'teist] Wider...

wille *m*; Abneigung *f*; **⹁ful** [⹁'teistful] unangenehm.

distend [dis'tend] (sich) ausdehnen; aufblähen.

distinct [dis'tiŋkt] verschieden; getrennt; deutlich, klar; **⹁ion** Unterscheidung *f*; Unterschied *m*; Auszeichnung *f*; Rang *m*; **⹁ive** besonder.

distinguish [dis'tiŋgwiʃ] unterscheiden; auszeichnen; **⹁ed** berühmt; ausgezeichnet; vornehm.

distort [dis'to:t] verzerren; verdrehen.

distract [dis'trækt] ablenken, zerstreuen; **⹁ed** verwirrt; von Sinnen; **⹁ion** Ablenkung *f*; Wahnsinn *m*.

distress [dis'tres] Schmerz *m*; Elend *n*; Not *f*; beunruhigen; **⹁ed** besorgt, bekümmert; notleidend.

distribut|e [dis'tribju(:)t] aus-, verteilen; verbreiten; **⹁ion** [⹁'bju:ʃən] Verteilung *f*; Verbreitung *f*.

district [distrikt] Bezirk *m*; Gegend *f*, Gebiet *n*.

distrust [dis'trast] Mißtrauen *n*; mißtrauen; **⹁ful** mißtrauisch.

disturb [dis'tə:b] stören; beunruhigen; **⹁ance** Störung *f*; Unruhe *f*.

disused [dis'ju:zd] außer Gebrauch, ausgedient.

ditch [ditʃ] Graben *m*.

dive [daiv] (unter)tauchen; e-n Kopfsprung (*aer.* Sturzflug) machen; (hastig)hineingreifen; (Kopf-)

Sprung *m*; *aer.* Sturzflug *m*; **⹁r** Taucher *m*.

diverge [dai'və:dʒ] auseinander-laufen; abweichen.

divers|e [dai'və:s] verschieden; **⹁ion** Ablenkung *f*; Umleitung *f*; Zeitvertreib *m*; **⹁ity** Verschiedenheit *f*; Mannigfaltigkeit *f*.

divert [dai'və:t] ablenken; *j-n* zerstreuen; umleiten.

divide [di'vaid] (sich) teilen; (sich) trennen; einteilen; dividieren (**by** durch); Wasserscheide *f*.

divine [di'vain] ahnen; Geistliche *m*; göttlich.

diving ['daiviŋ] Tauchen *n*; Kunstspringen *n*; Taucher...

divinity [di'viniti] Gottheit *f*; Göttlichkeit *f*; Theologie *f*.

divis|ible [di'vizəbl] teilbar; **⹁ion** [⹁'ʒən] (Ein-)Teilung *f*; Trennung *f*; *mil., math.* Division *f*.

divorce [di'vo:s] (Ehe-)Scheidung *f*; *j-n* scheiden; sich scheiden lassen von.

dizzy ['dizi] schwind(e)lig.

do [du:] (*irr*) tun; *Speisen* zubereiten; *Zimmer* (sauber)machen; handeln; sich benehmen; genügen; **⹁ you know him ? — No, I don't** kennst du ihn? — Nein; **⹁ not (don't)** nicht; **⹁ be quick!** beeile dich doch!; **what can I ⹁ for you?** was kann ich für Sie tun?;

~ London *colloq.* London besichtigen; **have one's hair done** sich die Haare machen *od.* frisieren lassen; **have done reading** fertig sein mit Lesen; **that will ~** das genügt; **~ away with** abschaffen, beseitigen; **~ well** s-e Sache gut machen; **~ up** instand setzen; zurechtmachen; einpacken; **I could ~ with** ... ich könnte ... gebrauchen *od.* vertragen; **~ without** auskommen ohne. [fügsam.]

docile ['dəusail] gelehrig;)

dock [dɔk] Dock *n*; *pl* Hafenanlagen *pl*; **~yard** Werft *f*.

doctor ['dɔktə] Doktor *m*; Arzt *m*; **~'s help** Arzthelferin *f*.

doctrine ['dɔktrin] Doktrin *f*; Lehre *f*.

document ['dɔkjumənt] Urkunde *f*; **~ary** (film) Dokumentar-, Kulturfilm *m*.

dodge [dɔdʒ] rasches Ausweichen; Schlich *m*, Kniff *m*; ausweichen; sich drücken (vor).

doe [dəu] Hirschkuh *f*; (Reh)Geiß *f*; Häsin *f*.

dog [dɔg] Hund *m*; **~eared** mit Eselsohren (*Buch*); **~gie, ~gy** Hündchen *n*; **~gie, ~gy** Hündchen *n*.

dogma ['dɔgmə] Dogma *n*, Glaubenssatz *m*.

dog tired hundemüde.

doings ['du(:)iŋz] *pl colloq.*

Ereignisse *pl*; Treiben *n*.

dole [dəul] Spende *f*; *colloq.* Arbeitslosenunterstützung *f*.

doll [dɔl] Puppe *f*.

dollar ['dɔlə] Dollar *m*.

doll's| house Puppenhaus *n*; **~ pram** Puppenwagen *m*.

dolorous ['dɔlərəs] schmerzlich, traurig.

dolphin ['dɔlfin] Delphin *m*.

dome [dəum] Kuppel *f*.

domestic [dəu'mestik] häuslich; Inlands...; einheimisch; Innen...; **~ animal** Haustier *n*; **~ate** [~eit] zähmen; **~ servant** Hausangestellte *m*, *f*.

domicile ['dɔmisail] Wohnsitz *m*.

domin|ate ['dɔmineit] beherrschen, herrschen über; **~ation** (Vor)Herrschaft *f*; **~eer** [~'niə] (despotisch) herrschen; **~eering** herrisch; tyrannisch.

donat|e [dəu'neit] spenden; **~ion** Spende *f*.

done [dʌn] *pp von* **do**; getan; erledigt; fertig; gar.

donkey ['dɔŋki] Esel *m*.

donor ['dəunə] Spender (-in) (*a. med.*).

doom [du:m] Verhängnis *n*; verurteilen; **~sday** der Jüngste Tag.

door [dɔ:] Tür *f*; **~handle** Türgriff *m*, -klinke *f*; **~keeper, ~man**, *Am. a.* **~man** Pförtner *m*; Portier *m*; **~mat** Fußmatte *f*; **~way** Türöffnung *f*.

drank

dope [dəup] *colloq.* Rauschgift *n*; Rauschgift geben; betäuben; dopen.

dormer(-window) ['dɔ:mə('-)] Dachfenster *n*.

dormitory ['dɔ:mitri] Schlafsaal *m*; *bsd.* Am. Studenten(wohn)heim *m*.

dose [dəus] Dosis *f*.

dot [dɔt] Punkt *m*; punktieren, tüpfeln; verstreuen.

dote [dəut]: ~ (up)on vernarrt sein in.

double ['dʌbl] doppelt, Doppel..., zweifach; Doppelte *n*; Doppelgänger(in); ~(s *pl*) *Tennis*: Doppel *n*; (sich) verdoppeln; ~ up zs.-legen, zs.-rollen; sich krümmen; ~ bed Doppelbett *n*; ~ französisches Bett; ~ breasted zweireihig (*Jackett*); ~decker *colloq.* Doppeldecker *m*; ~park in zweiter Reihe parken; ~ room Doppel-, Zweibettzimmer *n*.

doubt [daut] zweifeln (an); bezweifeln; Zweifel *m*; no ~ ohne Zweifel; ~ful zweifelhaft; ~less ohne Zweifel.

douche [du:ʃ] *med.*: Spülung *f*; (aus)spülen.

dough [dəu] Teig *m*; ~nut *e-e* Art Schmalzgebackenes.

dove [dʌv] Taube *f*.

down¹ [daun] Daune *f*; Flaum *m*; Düne *f*; *pl* Hügelland *n*.

down² nieder; her-, hinunter; *aer.* abschießen; ~cast niedergeschlagen; ~fall *fig.* Sturz *m*; ~hill bergab; ~pour Regenguß *m*; ~right glatt (*Lüge etc.*); *adj.* hinunter; unten; ~town *bsd.* Am. Geschäftsviertel *n*; ~ train Zug *m* von London; ~ward(s) ['~wəd(z)] abwärts, nach unten.

downy ['dauni] flaumig.

dowry ['dauəri] Mitgift *f*.

doze [dəuz] dösen; Schlummer *m*.

dozen ['dʌzn] Dutzend *n*.

drab [dræb] eintönig.

draft [drɑ:ft] Entwurf *m*; *econ.* Tratte *f*; *Am. mil.*Einberufung *f*; *s.* **draught**; entwerfen; aufsetzen; *Am. mil.* einziehen; ~sman (technischer) Zeichner.

drag [dræg] schleppen, ziehen, zerren; ~fly Libelle *f*.

dragon ['drægən] Drache *m*; ~fly Libelle *f*.

drain [drein] Abfluß(rohr *n*, -kanal) *m*; Entwässerungsgraben *m*; entwässern; ~ away, ~ off abfließen; ~age Abfluß *m*; Entwässerung *f*; Kanalisation *f*.

drake [dreik] Enterich *m*, Erpel *m*.

drama ['drɑ:mə] Drama *n*; ~tic [drə'mætik] dramatisch; ~tist ['dræmətist] Dramatiker *m*. [**drink**.]

drank [dræŋk] *pret* von

drape [dreip] drapieren; in Falten legen.

drastic ['dræstik] drastisch.

draught, *Am.* **draft** [dru:ft] Ziehen *n*, Zug *m*; Fischzug *m*; Luftzug *m*, Zugluft *f*; Schluck *m*; **~ beer** Bier *n*; **~sman** *s.* draftsman; **~y** zugig.

draw [drɔ:] *Lotterie:* Ziehung *f*; *unentschiedenes Spiel;* Attraktion *f*; Zugnummer *f*; *(irr)* (heraus-, zu)ziehen; herausholen; *Geld* abheben; anziehen; zeichnen; *unentschieden* spielen; *Luft* schöpfen; **~ near** sich nähern, heranrücken; **~ out** in die Länge ziehen; **~ up** Schriftstück aufsetzen; halten; vorfahren; **~back** Nachteil *m*; Hindernis *n*; **~er** Zeichner *m*; Aussteller *m* (*e-s Wechsels*); [drɔ:] Schublade *f*; **(a pair of) ~ers** [drɔ:z] *pl* (e-e) Unterhose *f*; (ein) Schlüpfer.

drawing ['drɔ:iŋ] Ziehen *n*; Zeichnen *n*; Zeichnung *f*; **~-pin** Reißzwecke *f*; **~room** Salon *m*.

drawn [drɔ:n] *pp von* **draw;** *unentschieden;* verzerrt.

dread [dred] Furcht *f*, Schrecken *m*; fürchten, sich fürchten vor; **~ful** schrecklich, furchtbar.

dream [dri:m] Traum *m*;

(irr) träumen; **~t** [dremt] *pret u. pp von* **dream**; **~y** verträumt.

dreary ['driəri] trostlos.

dregs [dregz] *pl* Bodensatz *m*. [nässen.]

drench [drentʃ] durch-

dress [dres] Anzug *m*; Kleid(ung *f*) *n*; zurechtmachen; (sich) ankleiden *od.* anziehen; schmücken; *med.* verbinden; frisieren; **~ circle** *thea.* erster Rang; **~ designer** Modezeichner(in), -schöpfer(in).

dressing ['dresiŋ] An-, Zurichten *n*; Ankleiden *n*; Verband *m*; (*Salat*)Soße *f*; Füllung *f*; **~-case** Reisenecessaire *f*; **~cubicle** Umkleidekabine *f*; **~-gown** Morgenrock *m*; **~-table** Frisierkommode *f*.

dressmaker Schneiderin *f*.

drew [dru:] *pret von* **draw.**

drift [drift] (Dahin-) Treiben *n*; (*Schnee*)Verwehung *f*; Tendenz *f*; (dahin)treiben; wehen.

drill [dril] (*Acker*)Furche *f*; Bohrer *m*; Sämaschine *f*; Drill *m*; Exerzieren *n*; bohren; drillen; (ein)exerzieren.

drink [driŋk] (*irr*) trinken; (geistiges) Getränk *n*; **have a ~.** et. trinken.

drip [drip] tropfen *od.* tröpfeln (lassen); **~-dry** bügelfrei; **~ping** Bratenfett *n*.

drive [draiv] (Spazier-

Fahrt *f*; Auffahrt *f*; *tech.* Antrieb *m*; Tatkraft *f*, Schwung *m*; (*irr*) (an-)treiben; fahren; ~ **away** vertreiben, -jagen; ~ **out** vertreiben; **what is he driving at?** worauf will er hinaus?

drive-in *Am.* Autokino *n*, Autorestaurant *n*; Auto...; ~ **cinema** Autokino *n*.

drive|n ['drivn] *pp von* **drive**; ~**r** ['draivə] Fahrer *m*.

driving **lesson** ['draiviŋ] Fahrstunde *f*; ~ **licence** Führerschein *m*; ~ **school** Fahrschule *f*.

drizzle ['drizl] Sprühregen *m*; sprühen, nieseln.

drone [drəun] Drohne *f*.

droop [dru:p] sinken lassen; (schlaff) herabhängen (lassen).

drop [drɔp] Tropfen *m*; (Frucht)Bonbon *m*, *n*; *econ.* Sinken *n*; tropfen (lassen); fallen lassen; *Brief* einwerfen; *Fahrgast* absetzen; senken; (herab-)fallen; sich legen (*Wind*); ~ **s.o. a few lines** j-m ein paar Zeilen schreiben; ~ **in** unerwartet kommen, vorbeikommen.

drove [drəuv] *pret von* **drive**.

drown [draun] ertrinken; ertränken; *fig.* übertönen; **be** ~**ed** ertrinken.

drowsy ['drauzi] schläfrig; einschläfernd.

drudge [drʌdʒ] sich (ab-)plagen.

drug [drʌg] Droge *f*; Rauschgift *n*; Drogen beimischen; (mit Drogen) betäuben; Drogen *od.* Rauschgift geben *od.* nehmen; ~ **addict** Rauschgiftsüchtige *m*, *f*; ~**gist** ['~gist] Drogist *m*; Apotheker *m* *Am.*; ~**store** *Am.* Drugstore *m*.

drum [drʌm] Trommel *f*; trommeln; ~**mer** Trommler *m*.

drunk [drʌŋk] *pp von* **drink**; betrunken; ~**ard** ['~əd] Trinker *m*, Säufer *m*; ~**en** betrunken; ~**en-driving** Trunkenheit *f* am Steuer.

dry [drai] trocken; herb (*Wein*); (ab)trocknen; dörren; ~ **up** austrocknen; ~**clean** chemisch reinigen; ~ **goods** *pl* *Am.* Textilien *pl*.

dual ['dju(:)əl] doppelt.

duchess ['dʌtʃis] Herzogin *f*.

duck [dʌk] Ente *f*; *colloq.* Liebling *m*; (unter-)tauchen; (sich) ducken.

dude [dju:d] *Am.* Geck *m*; ~ **ranch** *Am.* Ferienranch *f*.

due [dju:] Zustehende *n*, Anspruch *m*; *pl* Gebühren *pl*; fällig; zustehend; gebührend; angemessen, sorgfältig; erwartet; ~ **to** zuzuschreiben, verursacht durch; **be** ~ **to** sollen, müssen; **in ~ time** rechtzeitig.

duel ['dju(:)əl] Duell *n*, Zweikampf *m*. [**dig.**]

dug [dʌg] *pret u. pp von*|

duke [dju:k] Herzog *m*.

dull [dʌl] stumpf; dumpf; trüb(e); schwach (*Gehör*); langweilig; träg(e); dumm; *econ.* flau.

duly ['dju:li] ordnungsgemäß; rechtzeitig.

dumb [dʌm] stumm; sprachlos; *Am. colloq.* blöd(e); **~founded** sprachlos.

dummy ['dʌmi] Attrappe *f*; nachgemacht; Schein *m*.

dump [dʌmp] auskippen; *Schutt etc.* abladen; Schutthaufen *m*; Schuttabladeplatz *m*.

dun [dʌn] *Schuldner* mahnen, drängen.

dune [dju:n] Düne *f*.

dung [dʌŋ] Dung *m*; düngen.

dungeon ['dʌndʒən] Kerker *m*.

dupe [dju:p] anführen, täuschen.

duplicate ['dju:plikit] genau gleich; doppelt; Duplikat *n*; ['~eit] kopieren; verdoppeln.

dura|ble ['djuərəbl] dauerhaft; **~tion** Dauer *f*.

duress(e) [dju'res] Zwang *m*.

during ['djuəriŋ] während.

dusk [dʌsk] Dämmerung *f*.

dust [dʌst] Staub *m*; abstauben; Staub wischen; (be)streuen; **~bin** Mülleimer *m*; **~cart** Müllwagen *m*; **~er** Staublappen *m*; **~jacket** Schutzumschlag *m*; **~man** Müllabfuhrmann *m*; **~pan** Kehrschaufel *f*; **~y** staubig.

Dutch [dʌtʃ] holländisch; Holländisch *n*; **the ~ pl** die Holländer *pl*; **~man** Holländer *m*; **~woman** Holländerin *f*.

duty ['dju:ti] Pflicht *f*, Aufgabe *f*; Zoll *m*; **be off ~** dienstfrei haben; **be on ~** Dienst haben, im Dienst sein; **~free** zollfrei.

dwarf [dwɔ:f] Zwerg *m*.

dwell [dwel] (*irr*) wohnen; verweilen ([**up-**] **on** bei); **~ing** Wohnung *f*.

dwelt [dwelt] *pret u. pp von* **dwell.**

dwindle ['dwindl] schwinden.

dye [dai] Farbe *f*; färben.

dying ['daiiŋ] *pres p von* **die[1]**.

dyke [daik] *s.* **dike.**

dynam|ic [dai'næmik] dynamisch; **~ics** *sg* Dynamik *f*; **~ite** ['~əmait] Dynamit *n*; **~o** ['~əmou] Dynamo(maschine *f*) *m*, Lichtmaschine *f*.

dysentery ['disntri] *med.* Ruhr *f*.

E

each [i:tʃ] jede(r, -s); ~ **other** einander.

eager ['i:gə] begierig; eifrig; **~ness** Begierde *f*; Eifer *m*.

eagle ['i:gl] Adler *m*.

ear [iə] Ohr *n*; Gehör *n*; Ähre *f*; Henkel *m*; **~drum** Trommelfell *n*.

earl [ə:l] *britischer* Graf.

early ['ə:li] früh; Früh...; erst; bald.　[bringen.]

earn [ə:n] verdienen; ein-]

earnest ['ə:nist] ernst (-haft); **in** ~ ernsthaft.

earnings ['ə:niŋz] *pl* Verdienst *m*, Einkommen *n*.

ear|-phone Kopfhörer *m*; **~shot** Hörweite *f*.

earth [ə:θ] Erde *f*; Land *n*; *electr.* erden; **~en** irden; **~enware** Steingut *n*; irden; **~ly** irdisch; **~quake** Erdbeben *n*; **~worm** Regenwurm *m*.

ease [i:z] erleichtern; lindern; beruhigen; sich entspannen (*Lage*); Bequemlichkeit *f*; Entspannung *f*; Ungezwungenheit *f*; Leichtigkeit *f*; **at** ~ bequem, behaglich.

easel ['i:zl] Staffelei *f*.

east [i:st] Ost(en *m*); östlich, nach Osten, Ost...

Easter ['i:stə] Ostern *n*; Oster...; **Sly** östlich, nach Osten, Ost...; **Sn** östlich.

eastward(s) ['i:stwəd(z)] ostwärts.

easy ['i:zi] leicht, einfach; bequem; ruhig; ungezwungen; **take it** ~! immer mit der Ruhe!; ~ **chair** Lehnstuhl *m*, Sessel *m*.

eat [i:t] (*irr*) essen; (*zer-*) fressen; ~ **up** aufessen; **~en** *pp von* eat.

eaves [i:vz] *pl* überhängende Dachkante; **~drop** lauschen, horchen.

ebb(-tide) ['eb('-)] Ebbe *f*.

ebony ['ebəni] Ebenholz *n*.

eccentric [ik'sentrik] exzentrisch; *fig. a.* überspannt; Sonderling *m*.

ecclesiastical [ikli:zi'æstikəl] kirchlich, geistlich.

echo ['ekəu] Echo *n*, Widerhall *m*; widerhallen; *fig.* echoen, nachsprechen.

eclipse [i'klips] (*Sonnen-, Mond*)Finsternis *f*.

economic [i:kə'nɔmik] (volks)wirtschaftlich, Wirtschafts...; **~al** wirtschaftlich, sparsam; **~s** *sg* Volkswirtschaft(slehre) *f*.

econom|ist [i(:)'kɔnəmist] Volkswirt *m*; **~ize** sparen; **~y** Wirtschaft *f*; Sparsamkeit *f*; *pl* Einsparung *f*; **~y class** *aer.* Economy-Klasse *f*, Touristenklasse *f*.

ecstasy ['ekstəsi] Ekstase *f*.　[wirbeln.]

eddy ['edi] Wirbel *m*;]

edge [edʒ] schärfen; (um)säumen; Schneide *f*; Rand *m*; Kante *f*; **be on ~e** gereizt *od.* nervös sein; **~ing** Rand *m*; Einfassung *f*; **~y** gereizt, nervös.

edible ['edibl] eßbar.

edifice ['edifis] Gebäude *n*.

edifying ['edifaiiŋ] erbaulich.

edit ['edit] *Buch, Zeitung* herausgeben; **~ion** [i'diʃən] Ausgabe *f*; Auflage *f*; **~or** ['editə] Herausgeber *m*; Redakteur *m*; **~orial** [edi'tɔːriəl] Leitartikel *m*; Redaktions...

educat|e ['edju(ː)keit] erziehen, unterrichten, ausbilden; **~ion** Erziehung *f*; (Aus)Bildung *f*; Schulwesen *n*; **~ional** erzieherisch, Erziehungs...; **~or** Erzieher(in).

eel [iːl] Aal *m*.

effect [i'fekt] bewirken; ausführen; Wirkung *f*; Eindruck *m*, Effekt *m*; *pl* Habe *f*; **in ~** tatsächlich; *jur.* in Kraft; **take ~ in** Kraft treten; **~ive** wirksam; eindrucksvoll; tatsächlich.

effeminate [i'feminit] verweichlicht; weibisch.

effervescent [efə'vesnt] sprudelnd, schäumend.

efficien|cy [i'fiʃənsi] Leistungsfähigkeit *f*; **~t** tüchtig, (leistungs)fähig.

effort ['efət] Anstrengung *f*, Bemühung *f*.

effusive [i'fjuːsiv] überschwenglich.

egg [eg] Ei *n*; **~cup** Eierbecher *m*; **~head** *Am. sl.* Intellektuelle *m*.

egoism ['egəuizm] Egoismus *m*, Selbstsucht *f*.

egress ['iːgres] Ausgang *m*; *fig.* Ausweg *m*.

Egyptian [i'dʒipʃən] ägyptisch; Ägypter(in).

eider-down ['aidə-] Eiderdaunen *f/pl*, Daunendecke *f*.

eight [eit] acht; Acht *f*; **~een(th)** ['ei'tiːn(θ)] achtzehn(te); **~fold** achtfach; **~h** [eitθ] achte; Achtel *n*; **~hly** achtens; **~ieth** ['eitiiθ] achtzigste; **~y** achtzig; Achtzig *f*.

either ['aiðə, *Am.* 'iːðə] jede(r, -s) (von zweien), beide; irgendeine(r, -s) (von zweien); .. oder; entweder ... oder; **not ... ~** auch nicht.

ejaculate [i'dʒækjuleit] *Worte etc.* ausstoßen.

eject [i(ː)'dʒekt] ausstoßen; vertreiben; ausweisen.

elaborate [i'læbərit] sorgfältig ausgearbeitet; [~eit] sorgfältig ausarbeiten.

elapse [i'læps] vergehen, -streichen (*Zeit*).

elastic [i'læstik] elastisch, dehnbar; Gummiband *n*.

elated [i'leitid] freudig erregt.

elbow ['elbəu] Ell(en)-bogen *m*; Biegung *f*; *tech.* Knie *n*; *mit dem Ellbogen* stoßen, drängen.

elder¹ ['eldə] Holunder *m*.

elde|r² älter; *der, die* Ältere; **~rly** ältlich; **~st** |'~ist| älteste.

elect |i'lekt| designieren; wählen; **~ion** Wahl *f;* **~or** Wähler *m; Am.* Wahlmann *m.*

electric |i'lektrik| elektrisch; **~al engineer** Elektroingenieur *m,* -techniker *m;* **~ chair** elektrischer Stuhl; **~ian** |~-'triʃən| Elektriker *m;* **~ity** |'~trisiti| Elektrizität *f.*

electrify |i'lektrifai| elektrisieren; elektrifizieren.

electrocute |i'lektrəkju:t| durch elektrischen Strom töten. | tron *n.*|

electron |i'lektrɔn| Elektron *m.*

elegan|ce |'eligəns| Eleganz *f;* Anmut *f;* **~t** elegant, geschmackvoll.

element |'elimənt| Element *n; pl* Anfangsgründe *pl;* **~al** |~'mentl| elementar; **~ary** |~'mentəri| elementar; Anfangs...; **~ary school** Volks-, Grundschule *f.* | *m.*|

elephant |'elifənt| Elefant *f.*

elevat|e |'eliveit| (hoch-, er)heben; **~ion** Erhebung *f;* Erhöhung *f;* Höhe *f;* Erhabenheit *f;* **~or** *Am.* Fahrstuhl *m; aer.* Höhenruder *n.*

eleven |i'levn| elf; Elf *f;* **~th** |~θ| elfte. | eignet.|

eligible |'elidʒəbl| ge-|

eliminat|e |i'limineit| entfernen, ausmerzen; ausscheiden; **~ion** Entfernung *f,* Ausmerzung *f;* Ausscheidung *f.*

elk |elk| Elch *m; Am.* Elk *m,* Wapiti *m.*

ellipse |i'lips| Ellipse *f.*

elm |elm| Ulme *f.*

elongate |'i:lɔŋgeit| (sich) verlängern.

elope |i'ləup| davonlaufen, durchbrennen (*Frau*).

eloquen|ce |'eləkwəns| Beredsamkeit *f;* **~t** beredt.

else |els| sonst; weiter; andere; **what ~?** was sonst noch?; **~where** anderswo(hin).

elu|de |i'lu:d| ausweichen, sich entziehen; **~sive** ausweichend; schwer faßbar.

emaciated |i'meiʃieitid| abgemagert, abgezehrt.

emancipate |i'mænsipeit| emanzipieren, befreien.

embalm |im'bu:m| einbalsamieren.

embankment |im'bæŋkmənt| Damm *m;* Bahndamm *m;* befestigte Uferstraße.

embargo |em'bu:gəu| (Hafen-, Handels)Sperre *f.*

embark |im'bu:k| (sich) einschiffen (**for** nach); verladen (**for** nach); **~(up)on** *et.* anfangen.

embarrass |im'bærəs| behindern; verwirren, in Verlegenheit bringen; **~ing** unangenehm, peinlich; **~ment** (Geld)Verlegenheit *f.*

embassy |'embəsi| Botschaft *f;* Gesandtschaft *f.*

embedded [im'bedid] (ein)gebettet, eingeschlossen.

embellish [im'beliʃ] verschönern; (aus)schmücken.

embers ['embəz] *pl* glühende Asche, Glut *f*.

embezzle [im'bezl] *Geld* unterschlagen.

embitter [im'bitə] verbittern.

emblem ['embləm] Sinnbild *n*, Symbol *n*.

embody [im'bɔdi] verkörpern.

embolism ['embəlizəm] Embolie *f*.

embrace [im'breis] (sich) umarmen; Umarmung *f*.

embroider [im'brɔidə] sticken; *fig.* ausschmücken; **~y** Stickerei *f*.

emerald ['emərəld] Smaragd(grün *n*) *m*.

emerge [i'məːdʒ] auftauchen; *fig.* hervorgehen.

emergency [i'məːdʒənsi] Not(lage) *f*, -fall *m*; Not...; **~ brake** Notbremse *f*; **~ call** Notruf *m*; **~ chute** *aer.* Notrutsche *f*; **~ exit** Notausgang *m*; **~ landing** *aer.* Notlandung *f*; **make an ~ landing** *aer.* notlanden.

emigra|nt ['emigrənt] Auswanderer *m*; **~te** ['~eit] auswandern; **~tion** Auswanderung *f*.

eminent ['eminənt] berühmt; außergewöhnlich; **~ly** (ganz) besonders.

emit [i'mit] aussenden, -strömen, -stoßen.

emotion [i'məuʃən] (Gemüts)Bewegung *f*, Gefühl *n*, Rührung *f*; **~al** gefühlsmäßig; gefühlvoll; gefühlsbetont.

emperor ['empərə] Kaiser *m*.

empha|sis ['emfəsis] Nachdruck *m*; **~size** (nachdrücklich) betonen; **~tic** [im'fætik] nachdrücklich, betont.

empire ['empaiə](Kaiser-)Reich *n*.

employ [im'plɔi] beschäftigen, anstellen; an-, verwenden; *sub*: **in the ~ of** angestellt bei; **~ee** [emplɔi'iː] Angestellte *m*, *f*, Arbeitnehmer(in); **~er** Arbeitgeber(in); **~ment** Beschäftigung *f*, Arbeit *f*; **~ment agency** Stellenvermittlungsbüro *n*; **~ment exchange** Arbeitsamt *n* [*rin f*.]

empress ['empris] Kaise-

empt|iness ['emptinis] Leere *f*; **~y** leer; (aus-, ent)leeren; sich leeren.

emulate ['emjuleit] wetteifern mit, nacheifern.

enable [i'neibl] es *j-m* ermöglichen; ermächtigen.

enact [i'nækt] erlassen; verfügen; *thea.* spielen.

enamel [i'næməl] Email (-le *f*) *n*; Glasur *f*; Lack *m*; Zahnschmelz *m*.

encase [in'keis] umhüllen; verschalen.

enchant [in'tʃuːnt] be-, verzaubern.

encircle [in'səːkl] umgeben; einkreisen.

enclos|e [in'kləuz] einzäunen; einschließen; beifügen; **~ure** [~ʒə] Einzäunung *f*; Anlage *f* (*Brief*).

encounter [in'kauntə] Begegnung *f*; begegnen; auf *Schwierigkeiten etc.* stoßen.

encourage [in'kʌridʒ] ermutigen; unterstützen; **~ment** Ermutigung *f*; Unterstützung *f*.

encumber [in'kʌmbə] belasten; behindern.

end [end] enden; beend(ig)en; Ende *n*; Ziel *n*, Zweck *m*; **no ~ of** sehr viel(e); **in the ~** schließlich; **stand on ~** zu Berge stehen (*Haare*).

endanger [in'deindʒə] gefährden.

endear [in'diə] lieb *od.* teuer machen (**to s.o.** j-m.).

endeavo(u)r [in'devə] Bemühung *f*; sich bemühen.

end|ing ['endiŋ] Ende *n*, Schluß *m*; *gr.* Endung *f*; **~less** endlos, unendlich.

endorse [in'dɔːs] *Dokument* auf der Rückseite beschreiben; *et.* vermerken; billigen, unterstützen.

endow [in'dau] ausstatten; stiften.

endur|ance [in'djuərəns] Ausdauer *f*; Ertragen *n*; **~e** (aus-, fort)dauern; durchhalten; ertragen.

enemy ['enimi] Feind *m*; feindlich.

energ|etic [enə'dʒetik] energisch; **~y** Energie *f*.

enervate ['enəːveit] entnerven, -kräften.

enfold [in'fəuld] umfassen.

enforce [in'fɔːs] er-, aufzwingen; durchführen.

enfranchise [in'fræntʃaiz] das Wahlrecht verleihen.

engage [in'geidʒ] anstellen; *mil.* angreifen; sich verpflichten; sich versprechen, garantieren; sich beschäftigen (**in** mit); **be ~d** verlobt sein (**to** mit); beschäftigt sein (**in** mit); besetzt sein; **~ment** Verpflichtung *f*; Verlobung *f*; Verabredung *f*.

engine ['endʒin] Maschine *f*; Motor *m*; Lokomotive *f*; **~-driver** Lokomotivführer *m*.

engineer [endʒi'niə] Ingenieur *m*, Techniker *m*; Maschinist *m*; *Am.* Lokomotivführer *m*; *mil.* Pionier *m*; **~ing** Maschinenbau *m*; Ingenieurwesen *n*; technisch.

engine trouble Motorschaden *m*.

English ['iŋgliʃ] englisch; Englisch *n*; **the ~** *pl* die Engländer *pl*; **~man** Engländer *m*; **~woman** Engländerin *f*.

engrav|e [in'greiv] gravieren, eingraben; *fig.* einprägen; **~ing** (Kupfer-,

Stahl)Stich m; Holzschnitt
m.

engross [in'grəus] ganz in
Anspruch nehmen.

enigma [in'nigmə] Rätsel n.

enjoin [in'dʒɔin] vorschreiben, befehlen.

enjoy [in'dʒɔi] sich erfreuen an; genießen; **did
you ~ it?** hat es Ihnen
gefallen?; **~ o.s.** sich
amüsieren od. gut unterhalten; **~ment** Genuß m,
Freude f.

enlarge [in'lɑːdʒ] (sich)
vergrößern; **~ment** Vergrößerung f.

enlighten [in'laitn] fig.
aufklären, belehren.

enlist [in'list] gewinnen
(zur Mitarbeit); mil. anwerben; sich (freiwillig)
melden.

enliven [in'laivn] beleben.

enmity ['enmiti] Feindschaft f.

enormous [i'nɔːməs] ungeheuer.

enough [i'nʌf] genug.

enquire [in'kwaiə], **~y** s.
inquire, inquiry.

enrage [in'reidʒ] wütend
machen; **~d** wütend.

enrapture [in'ræptʃə] entzücken.

enrich [in'ritʃ] be-, an-
reichern.

enrol(l) [in'rəul] j-s Namen eintragen; aufnehmen.

ensue [in'sjuː] folgen, sich
ergeben.

ensure [in'ʃuə] sichern.

entangle [in'tæŋgl] verwickeln, -wirren.

enter ['entə] (ein)treten

in; betreten; einfahren in;
eindringen in; eintragen;
anmelden; sich einschreiben; **~ (up)on** Amt etc.
antreten.

enterprise ['entəpraiz]
Unternehmen n; Unternehmungslust f; **~ing** unternehmungslustig.

entertain [entə'tein] un-
terhalten; bewirten; Zweifel etc. hegen; **~er** Unterhaltungskünstler m;
~ment Bewirtung f; Veranstaltung f; Unterhaltung f.

enthusiasm [in'θjuːziæzm] Begeisterung f;
~t [~st] Enthusiast(in),
Schwärmer(in); **~tic**
[~stik] begeistert.

entice [in'tais] (ver)locken;
verleiten.

entire [in'taiə] ganz; vollständig; **~ly** völlig.

entitle [in'taitl] betiteln;
berechtigen.

entrails ['entreilz] pl Eingeweide pl.

entrance ['entrəns] Ein-,
Zutritt m; Eingang m; Eingang m; Einlaß m; **~ fee**
Eintrittsgeld n.

entreat [in'triːt] (et. er-)
bitten; **~y** dringende Bitte.

entrust [in'trʌst] anvertrauen; betrauen.

entry ['entri] Eintritt m;
Einreise f; Eintragung f;
sp. Meldung f); **~ permit**
Einreisegenehmigung f.

enumerate [i'njuːməreit]
aufzählen.

envelop [in'veləp] einhüllen; einwickeln; ~e ['envələup] Briefumschlag m.

envi|able ['enviəbl] beneidenswert; ~ous neidisch.

environ|ment [in'vaiərənment] Umgebung f; ~mental pollution Umweltverschmutzung f; ~s ['envirənz] pl Umgebung f (e-r Stadt).

envoy ['envɔi] Gesandte m.

envy ['envi] Neid m; beneiden.

epidemic (disease) [epi'demik] Seuche f.

epidermis [epi'də:mis] Oberhaut f. [lepsie f.]

epilepsy ['epilepsi] Epi-]

epilog(ue) ['epilɔg] Epilog m, Nachwort n.

episode ['episəud] Episode f.

epitaph ['epitɑ:f] Grabschrift f.

epoch ['i:pɔk] Epoche f.

equal ['i:kwəl] Gleichgestellte m, f; gleichen; gleich; **be** ~ **to** e-r S. gewachsen sein; ~ity [i(:)-'kwɔliti] Gleichheit f, -berechtigung f; ~ize ['i:kwəlaiz] gleichmachen, -stellen; ausgleichen.

equanimity [ekwə'nimiti] Gleichmut m.

equation [i'kweiʒən] Ausgleich m; math. Gleichung f; ~or Äquator m.

equilibrium [i:kwi'libriəm] Gleichgewicht n.

equip [i'kwip] ausrüsten;

~ment Ausrüstung f; Einrichtung f, Anlage f.

equivalent [i'kwivələnt] gleichwertig; entsprechend (**to** dat); Äquivalent n, Gegenwert m.

era ['iərə] Ära f, Zeitrechnung f, -alter n.

erase [i'reiz] ausradieren, -streichen, (-)löschen.

ere [εə] ehe, bevor; vor.

erect [i'rekt] aufrecht; aufrichten, -stellen; errichten; ~ion Auf-, Errichtung f; Gebäude n.

erosion [i'rəuʒən] Zerfressen n; geol. Erosion f.

erotic [i'rɔtik] erotisch.

err [ə:] (sich) irren.

errand ['erənd] Botengang m, Auftrag m; **run** ~s Besorgungen machen.

erro|neous [i'rəunjəs] irrig, falsch; ~r ['erə] Irrtum m, Fehler m.

erupt [i'rʌpt] ausbrechen (Vulkan); ~ion Ausbruch m (e-s Vulkans; a. fig.); Hautausschlag m.

escalat|ion [eskə'leiʃən] Eskalation f; ~or ['~tə] Rolltreppe f.

escape [is'keip] entgehen, entkommen; j-m entfallen; Entkommen n, Flucht f.

escort ['eskɔ:t] Eskorte f; Begleiter(in); [is'kɔ:t] eskortieren; begleiten.

especial [is'peʃəl] besonder; ~ly besonders.

espionage [espiə'nɑ:ʒ] Spionage f.

espy [is'pai] erspähen;

essay ['esei] Aufsatz m, Essay m, n.

essen|ce ['esns] Wesen n (e-r Sache); Essenz f; ~**tial** [i'senʃəl] wesentlich.

establish [is'tæbliʃ] errichten, aufbauen, gründen; ~ **o.s.** sich niederlassen od. einrichten; ~**ment** Er-, Einrichtung f, Gründung f; pol. die etablierte Macht, die herrschende Schicht; Firma f.

estate [is'teit] (Grund-)Besitz m; ~ **agent** Immobilienhändler m; ~ **car** Kombiwagen m.

esteem [is'ti:m] Achtung f; achten, schätzen.

estimat|e ['estimeit] beurteilen; schätzen, veranschlagen; ['~it] Beurteilung f; Kostenanschlag m; ~**ion** Urteil n, Meinung f; Achtung f.

estrange [is'treindʒ] entfremden.

estuary ['estjuəri] Flußmündung f (ins Meer).

etern|al [i(:)'tɔ:nl] ewig; ~**ity** Ewigkeit f.

ether ['i:θə] Äther m.

ethics ['eθiks] sg Sittenlehre f, Ethik f; pl Moral f.

etymology [eti'mɔlədʒi] Etymologie f.

European [juərə'pi(:)ən] europäisch; Europäer(in).

evacuate [i'vækjueit] entleeren, evakuieren; räumen.

evade [i'veid] ausweichen.

evaporate [i'væpəreit] verdunsten od. verdampfen (lassen).

evasi|on [i'veiʒən] Ausweichen n; Ausflucht f; ~**ve** [~siv] ausweichend.

eve [i:v] Vorabend m, -tag m.

even ['i:vən] eben; glatt; gleichmäßig; ausgeglichen; gerade (Zahl).

even² selbst, sogar; **not** ~ nicht einmal; ~ **if, ~ though** selbst wenn.

evening ['i:vniŋ] Abend m; **this** ~ heute abend; ~ **dress** Abendanzug m; Abendkleid n; ~ **paper** Abendzeitung f.

evensong ['i:vənsɔŋ] Abendandacht f.

event [i'vent] Ereignis n; sp.: Veranstaltung f; (Programm)Nummer f; **at all** ~**s** auf alle Fälle; **in the** ~ **of** im Falle; ~**ful** ereignisreich.

eventual [i'ventʃuəl] schließlich; ~**ly** schließlich.

ever ['evə] je(mals); immer; ~ **after**, ~ **since** von der Zeit an, seitdem; **for** ~ für immer; ~**lasting** ewig; dauerhaft; ~**more** immerfort.

every ['evri] jede(r, -s); all; ~ **other day** jeden zweiten Tag; ~ **few** od. **ten minutes** alle paar od. zehn Minuten; ~**body** jeder(mann); ~**day** (all)täglich; Alltags...; ~**one** jeder(mann), alle; ~**thing** alles; ~**where** überall.

eviden|ce ['evidəns] Beweis(material n) m; Zeugenaussage f; **~ give ~** aussagen; **~t** augenscheinlich, klar.

evil ['i:vl] übel, schlecht, schlimm, böse; Übel n; *das Böse*.

evince [i'vins] zeigen.

evoke [i'vəuk] (herauf)beschwören; hervorrufen.

evolution [i:və'lu:ʃən] Entwicklung f.

evolve [i'vɔlv] (sich) entwickeln.

ewe [ju:] Mutterschaf n.

ex- [eks-] ehemalig, früher.

exact [ig'zækt] genau; *Zahlung* eintreiben; (er)fordern; **~itude** [~itju:d] s. **exactness**; **~ly** genau; **~ness** Genauigkeit f.

exaggerate [ig'zædʒəreit] übertreiben; **~ion** Übertreibung f.

exalt [ig'zɔ:lt] erhöhen; erheben; verherrlichen.

exam [ig'zæm] *colloq. abbr. für* **~ination** Examen n, Prüfung f; Untersuchung f; Vernehmung f; **~ine** [~in] untersuchen; prüfen; vernehmen, -hören.

example [ig'zɑ:mpl] Beispiel n; Vorbild n; **for ~** zum Beispiel.

exasperate [ig'zɑ:spəreit] ärgern, reizen.

excavate ['ekskəveit] ausgraben, -heben.

exceed [ik'si:d] überschreiten; übertreffen; **~ingly** außerordentlich.

excel [ik'sel] übertreffen; **~lence** ['eksələns] hervorragende Leistung; Vorzug m; **2lency** Exzellenz f; **~lent** ausgezeichnet.

except [ik'sept] ausnehmen; außer; **~** vorgesehen von; **~ion** Ausnahme f; **~ional(ly)** außergewöhnlich.

excess [ik'ses] Übermaß n; Exzeß m; **~ fare** Zuschlag m; **~ive** übermäßig, -trieben; **~ luggage** Übergewicht n (*Gepäck*); **~ postage** Nachbühr f.

exchange [iks'tʃeindʒ] (aus-, ein-, um)tauschen (**for** gegen); wechseln; (Aus-, Um)Tausch m; (Geld)Wechsel m; Börse f.

exchequer [iks'tʃekə]: **the 2** *Brit.* das Finanzministerium.

excit|able [ik'saitəbl] reizbar; **~e** erregen; aufregen; (auf)reizen; **~ed** aufgeregt; **~ement** Auf-, Erregung f; Reizung f; **~ing** erregend; aufregend; spannend.

exclaim [iks'kleim] ausrufen.

exclamation [eksklə'meiʃən] Ausruf m; **~ mark** Ausrufezeichen n.

exclu|de [iks'klu:d] ausschließen; **~sion** [~ʒən] Ausschluß m; **~sive** [~siv] ausschließlich; exklusiv.

excursion [iks'kə:ʃən] Ausflug m.

excuse [iks'kju:z] entschuldigen; ~ **me entschuldige(n Sie)!**; [~s] **Entschuldigung** f.

execut|**e** ['eksikju:t] ausführen; mus., thea. vortragen, spielen; hinrichten; ~**ion** Ausführung f; mus. Vortrag m; Hinrichtung f; [~'kju:] **vollziehend**; Exekutive f; econ. leitender Angestellter, Geschäftsführer m.

exemplary [ig'zempləri] vorbildlich; abschreckend.

exempt [ig'zempt] befreit; befreien.

exercise ['eksəsaiz] Übung (-sarbeit) f; körperliche Bewegung; Ausübung f, Gebrauch m; **take ~** sich Bewegung machen; vb: gebrauchen; (aus)üben; bewegen; sich Bewegung machen; ~**book** (Schul-, Übungs)Heft n.

exert [ig'zə:t] Einfluß etc. ausüben; ~ **o.s.** sich anstrengen od. bemühen; ~**ion** Anwendung f; Anstrengung f.

exhale [eks'heil] ausatmen, -dünsten; ausströmen.

exhaust [ig'zɔ:st] entleeren, auspumpen; erschöpfen; Abgas n; Auspuff m; ~ **fumes** pl Auspuffgase pl; ~**ion** Erschöpfung f; ~**pipe** Auspuffrohr n.

exhibit [ig'zibit] ausstellen; zeigen, aufweisen; Ausstellungsstück n; Beweisstück n; ~**ion** [eksi'biʃən] Ausstellung f; Zur-schaustellung f; Brit. Stipendium n; ~**ion grounds** pl Ausstellungsgelände n.

exile ['eksail] Exil n, Verbannung f; Verbannte m, f; verbannen.

exist [ig'zist] existieren, bestehen; leben; ~**ence** Existenz f, Bestehen n, Leben n; **in ~ence**, ~**ent** vorhanden.

exit ['eksit] Ausgang m; Ausfahrt f; thea. Abgang m; thea. (geht) ab; ~ **(road)** Autobahnausfahrt f; ~ **visa** Ausreisevisum n.

expan|**d** [iks'pænd] (sich) ausbreiten od. ausdehnen od. erweitern; ~**se** [~s] Ausdehnung f, Weite f; ~**sion** Ausbreitung f; Ausdehnung f; Erweiterung f; ~**sive** ausdehnungsfähig; ausgedehnt, weit.

expect [iks'pekt] erwarten; colloq. annehmen; ~**ation** [ekspek'teiʃən] Erwartung f.

expedi|**ent** [iks'pi:djənt] zweckmäßig; Hilfsmittel n, (Not)Behelf m; ~**tion** [~pi'diʃən] Eile f; Expedition f, Forschungsreise f.

expel [iks'pel] vertreiben, ausstoßen, -schließen.

expen|**d** [iks'pend] Geld ausgeben; verwenden; verbrauchen; ~**se** [~s] (Geld-) Ausgabe f; pl Unkosten pl, Spesen pl; **at the ~se of** auf Kosten von; ~**sive** kostspielig, teuer.

experience [iks'piəriəns]

Erfahrung f; Erlebnis n; erfahren, erleben; ~d erfahren.

experiment [iks'periment] Experiment n, Versuch m; [~ment] experimentieren.

expert ['ekspə:t] Experte m, Sachverständige m, Fachmann m; ['~, pred a. ~'pə:t] erfahren, geschickt; fachmännisch.

expir|ation [ekspaiə'reiʃən] Ausatmen n; Ablauf m; ~e [iks'paiə] ausatmen; ablaufen; verfallen.

expl|ain [iks'plein] erklären, erläutern (**to s.o.** j-m); ~anation [eksplə'neiʃən] Erklärung f.

explicit [iks'plisit] deutlich.

explode [iks'plaud] explodieren (lassen).

exploit [iks'plɔit] ausverwerten; ausbeuten.

explor|ation [eksplɔ:'reiʃən] Erforschung f; ~e [iks'plɔ:] erforschen; ~er Forscher m.

explosi|on [iks'plauʒən] Explosion f; fig. Ausbruch m; ~ve [~siv] explosiv; Sprengstoff m.

export [iks'pɔ:t] exportieren, ausführen; ['~] Export m, Ausfuhr f; ~ation Ausfuhr f; ~er Exporteur m.

expos|e [iks'pəuz] aussetzen; ausstellen; phot. belichten; aufdecken; entlarven, bloßstellen; ~ition [ekspəu'ziʃən] Ausstellung f; ~ure [iks'pəuʒə] Ausgesetztsein n; phot. Belichtung f; Enthüllung f, -larvung f; ~ure meter Belichtungsmesser m.

express [iks'pres] ausdrücklich, deutlich; Expreß..., Eil...; Eilbote m; Schnellzug m; äußern, ausdrücken; auspressen; ~ion Ausdruck m; ~ive ausdrückend (**of** acc.); ~ly ausdrücklich, eigens; ~ train Schnellzug m; ~way Am. Schnellstraße f.

expulsion [iks'pʌlʃən] Vertreibung f; Ausschluß m; Ausweisung f.

exquisite ['ekskwizit] vorzüglich, ausgezeichnet.

extant [eks'tænt] (noch) vorhanden.

exten|d [iks'tend] ausdehnen; ausstrecken; vergrößern; verlängern; sich erstrecken; ~sion Ausdehnung f; Verlängerung f; Anbau m; teleph. Nebenanschluß m; fig. Vergrößerung f, Erweiterung f; ~sive [~siv] ausgedehnt, umfassend; ~t Ausdehnung f, Weite f, Größe f, Länge f; fig. Umfang m, Grad m; **to some** ~ einigermaßen.

exterior [eks'tiəriə] äußere, Außen...; Äußere n.

exterminate [iks'tə:mineit] ausrotten, vertilgen.

external [eks'tə:nl] äußere, äußerlich; Außen...

extinct [iks'tiŋkt] erloschen; ausgestorben.

extinguish [iks'tiŋgwiʃ] (aus)löschen; vernichten.

extirpate ['eksto:peit] ausrotten; *med.* entfernen.

extra ['ekstrə] zusätzlich, Extra..., Sonder..., Neben...; *extra*, besonders; Zusätzliche *n*; *pl* Nebenkosten *pl*, Zuschlag *m*; ~ **charge** Mehrpreis *m*.

extract ['ekstrækt] Auszug *m*; [iks'trækt] (heraus)ziehen; entlocken; e-n Auszug machen; *tech.* gewinnen; ~**ion** (Heraus)Ziehen *n*; Herkunft *f*.

extradite ['ekstrədait] *Verbrecher* ausliefern.

extraordinary [iks'tro:dnri] außerordentlich; ungewöhnlich.

extravagan|ce [iks'trævigəns] Verschwendung *f*;

Überspanntheit *f*; ~**t** übertrieben; verschwenderisch.

extrem|e [iks'tri:m] äußerst, größt, höchst; Äußerste *n*, Extrem *n*; ~**ity** [~emiti] Äußerste *n*; (höchste) Not; *pl* Gliedmaßen *pl*; *mst pl* äußerste Maßnahmen *pl*.

exuberant [ig'zju:bərənt] üppig; überschwenglich.

exult [ig'zʌlt] frohlocken, jubeln.

eye [ai] Auge *n*; Öhr *n*; Öse *f*; *fig.* Blick *m*; ansehen, mustern; ~**ball** Augapfel *m*; ~**brow** Augenbraue *f*; ~**d** *in Zssgn*: ...äugig; **(a pair of)** ~**glasses** *pl* (e-e) Brille; ~**lash** (Augen)Wimper *f*; ~**lid** Augenlid *n*; ~**sight** Augen(licht *n*) *pl*, Sehkraft *f*; ~**witness** Augenzeuge *m*, -in *f*.

F

fable ['feibl] Fabel *f*.

fabric ['fæbrik] Gewebe *n*, Stoff *m*; Gebäude *n*; *fig.* Struktur *f*; ~**ate** [~eit] erfinden; fälschen.

fabulous ['fæbjuləs] sagenhaft, unglaublich.

façade [fə'sɑ:d] Fassade *f*.

face [feis] Gesicht *n*; Oberfläche *f*; Vorderseite *f*; Zifferblatt *n*; *fig.* Stirn *f*; **make of. pull a** ~ *od.* ~**s** Fratzen schneiden; *vb*: ansehen; gegenüberstehen; (hinaus)gehen

auf (*Fenster*); die Stirn bieten; einfassen; ~**cloth** Waschlappen *m*.

facil|itate [fə'siliteit] *et.* erleichtern; ~**ity** Leichtigkeit *f*; Gewandtheit *f*; *pl* Einrichtung(en *pl*) *f*, Anlage(n *pl*) *f*; Erleichterung(en *pl*) *f*.

fact [fækt] Tatsache *f*; Wirklichkeit *f*, Wahrheit *f*; **in** ~ in der Tat, tatsächlich.

factor ['fæktə] Faktor *m*, Umstand *m*; ~**y** Fabrik *f*.

faculty ['fækəlti] Fähigkeit f; Gabe f; univ. Fakultät f.

fade [feid] (ver)welken od. verblassen (lassen); schwinden.

fail [feil] fehlen; nachlassen; versagen; mißlingen, fehlschlagen; versäumen, unterlassen; Kandidat: durchfallen (lassen); im Stich lassen; **he cannot ~ to er** muß (einfach); **~ure** ['~jə] Fehlschlag m, Mißerfolg m; Ausbleiben n, Versagen n; Unterlassung f; Versager m.

faint [feint] schwach, matt; in Ohnmacht fallen.

fair¹ [fɛə] (Jahr)Markt m; Messe f, Ausstellung f.

fair² gerecht, ehrlich, anständig; fair; recht gut; reichlich; schön (Wetter); günstig (Wind); blond, hellhäutig; sauber, in Reinschrift; schön, hübsch (Frau); **play ~** ehrlich od. fair spielen; fig. ehrlich sein; **~ly** ziemlich; **~ness** Gerechtigkeit f, Fairneß f.

fairy ['fɛəri] Fee f; Elf(e f) m; **~tale** Märchen n.

faith [feiθ] Glaube m; Vertrauen n; Treue f; **~ful** treu; genau; **Yours ~fully** hochachtungsvoll; **~less** treulos.

fake [feik] Schwindel m; Fälschung f; Schwindler m; fälschen.

falcon ['fɔ:lkən] Falke m.

fall [fɔ:l] Fall(en n) m; Sturz m; Verfall m; Am. Herbst m; pl Wasserfall m; (irr) (ab-, ein-, zer-, ver-) fallen; sinken; nachlassen (Wind); **~ back on** zurückgreifen auf; **~ ill**, **~ sick** krank werden; **~ in love with** sich verlieben in; **~ out** sich entzweien; **~ short of** den Erwartungen etc. nicht entsprechen; **~en** pp von **fall**.

false [fɔ:ls] falsch; **~hood** Lüge f. [fälschen.]

falsify ['fɔ:lsifai] (ver-))

falter ['fɔ:ltə] schwanken; zaudern; straucheln; stocken (Stimme); stammeln.

fame [feim] Ruhm m, Ruf m; **~d** berühmt (**for** wegen).

familiar [fə'miljə] vertraut; gewohnt; ungezwungen; Vertraute m, f; **~ity** [~i'æriti] Vertrautheit f; pl (plumpe) Vertraulichkeit f; **~ize** vertraut machen.

family ['fæmili] Familie f; Familien...; **~ name** Familien-, Nachname m; **~ tree** Stammbaum m.

famine ['fæmin] Hungersnot f; Mangel m; **~sh** verhungern.

famous ['feiməs] berühmt.

fan¹ [fæn] Fächer m; Ventilator m.

fan² colloq. begeisterter Anhänger, Fan m.

fanatic [fə'nætik] Fanatiker(in); **~(al)** fanatisch.

fanciful ['fænsiful] phantasievoll; phantastisch.

fancy ['fænsi] Phantasie *f*; Einbildung(skraft) *f*; Idee *f*, Laune *f*; Vorliebe *f*; Phantasie...; sich vorstellen; sich einbilden; gern mögen; ~ **cake** Torte *f*; ~**dress ball** Kostümfest *n*; ~ **goods** *pl* Modeartikel *pl*; ~**work** feine Handarbeit.

fang [fæŋ] Fangzahn *m*; Giftzahn *m*.

fantastic [fæn'tæstik] phantastisch.

far [fɑː] fern, entfernt; weit; (sehr) viel; **as ~ as** bis; soweit; **by ~** bei weitem, weitaus; **~ from** weit entfernt von; ~**away** weitentfernt.

fare [fɛə] Fahrgeld *n*; Fahrgast *m*; Kost *f*; (es) gehen; ~**well** lebe(n Sie) wohl!; Abschied *m*, Lebewohl *n*.

far-fetched weithergeholt.

farm [fɑːm] Bauernhof *m*, Farm *f*, Gehöft *n*; Land bewirtschaften; ~**er** Bauer *m*, Landwirt *m*; ~**hand** Landarbeiter(in); ~**house** Bauern-, Gutshaus *n*; ~**ing** Landwirtschaft *f*; ~**worker** Landarbeiter(in).

far-sighted weitsichtig; *fig.* weitblickend.

farthe|r ['fɑːðə] *comp von* **far;** ~**st** ['~ist] *sup von* **far.**

fascinat|e ['fæsineit] bezaubern; ~**ion** Zauber *m*, Reiz *m*.

fashion ['fæʃən] Mode *f*; Art *f*, Stil *m*; herstellen, machen; ~**able** ['~nəbl] modern, modisch, elegant.

fast¹ [fɑːst] schnell; fest; treu; echt, beständig (*Farbe*); **be ~** vorgehen (*Uhr*).

fast² Fasten *n*; fasten.

fasten ['fɑːsn] befestigen, festbinden, -schnallen, anbinden; *Augen etc.* richten (**on** auf); sich schließen lassen; ~**er** Verschluß *m*.

fastidious [fəs'tidiəs] anspruchsvoll, wählerisch.

fast train Eilzug *m*.

fat [fæt] fett; dick; Fett *n*.

fat|al ['feitl] tödlich; verhängnisvoll (**to** für); ~**e** [feit] Schicksal *n*; Verhängnis *n*.

father ['fɑːðə] Vater *m*; ~**hood** Vaterschaft *f*; ~**in-law** Schwiegervater *m*; ~**less** vaterlos; ~**ly** väterlich.

fathom ['fæðəm] Klafter *m, n*; *mar.* Faden *m*; loten; *fig.* ergründen; ~**less** unergründlich.

fatigue [fə'tiːg] Ermüdung *f*; Strapaze *f*; ermüden.

fatten ['fætn] fett machen *od.* werden; mästen.

faucet ['fɔːsit] *Am. tech.* Hahn *m*.

fault [fɔːlt] Fehler *m*, Defekt *m*; Schuld *f*; **find ~ with et.** auszusetzen haben an; ~**less** fehlerfrei, tadellos; ~**y** fehler-, mangelhaft.

favo(u)r ['feivə] begünsti-

gen; Gunst(bezeigung) f;
Gefallen m; **in ~ of** zugunsten von; **do s.o. a ~**
j-m e-n Gefallen tun;
~able günstig; **~ite** ['~rit]
Günstling m; Liebling m;
sp. Favorit(in); bevorzugt,
Lieblings-.

fawn [fɔ:n] (Reh)Kitz n;
Rehbraun n.

fear [fiə] Furcht f, Angst f;
(be)fürchten; sich fürch-
ten vor; **~ful** furchtsam;
furchtbar; besorgt; **~less**
furchtlos.

feast [fi:st] Fest(tag m) m,
Feiertag m; Festmahl n,
Schmaus m; (festlich)
bewirten; schmausen;
sich weiden.

feat [fi:t] Helden-, Großtat
f; Kunststück n.

feather ['feðə] Feder f,
pl Gefieder n; mit Federn
schmücken; **~bed** (Feder-)
Unterbett n; **~ed** be-,
gefiedert; **~y** federartig.

feature ['fi:tʃə] (Ge-
sichts-, Charakter)Zug m;
(charakteristisches) Merkmal; Haupt-, Spielfilm
m; Zeitung, Rundfunk:
Feature n; pl Gesicht n.

February ['februəri]
Februar m.

fed [fed] pret u. pp von
feed.

federa∥l ['fedərəl] Bundes...; **~tion** Staatenbund
m; Verband m.　　[n.]

fee [fi:] Gebühr f; Honorar

feeble ['fi:bl] schwach.

feed [fi:d] Futter n, Nah-

rung f; Fütterung f; tech.
Zuführung f, Speisung f;
(irr) (ver)füttern; (er-)
nähren, speisen, zu essen
geben; tech. speisen, zu-
führen; weiden; **be fed
up with** sl. et. satt haben;
~er road Zubringer-
straße f; **~ing-bottle**
Saugflasche f.

feel [fi:l] (irr) (sich) fühlen;
befühlen; empfinden;
sich anfühlen; **~ for**
tasten nach; **~ well** od.
bad sich wohl od. elend
fühlen; Gefühl n; Emp-
findung f; **~er** Fühler m;
~ing mitfühlend; Gefühl n.

feet [fi:t] pl von **foot**.

fell [fel] pret von **fall**;
niederschlagen; fällen.

felloe ['felou] (Rad)Felge f.

fellow ['felou] Gefährt∥e
m, -in f, Kamerad(in);
colloq. Kerl m, Bursche m;
Gegenstück n; Mit...;
being Mitmensch m;
~citizen Mitbürger m;
~countryman Lands-
mann m; **~ship** Gemein-
schaft f; Kameradschaft f.

felon ['felən] Schwer-
verbrecher m; **~y** Kapitalverbrechen n.

felt[1] [felt] pret u. pp von
feel.

felt[2] Filz m.

female ['fi:meil] weiblich;
zo. Weibchen n.

feminine ['feminin] weiblich.

fen [fen] Fenn n, Marsch f;
Moor n.

fenc|e [fens] Zaun *m*; fechten; **~e (in)** ein-, umzäunen; **~ing** Fechten *n*.

fend [fend]: **~ for** sorgen für; **~ off** abwehren; **~er** *Am.* Kotflügel *m*.

ferment ['fə:ment] Ferment *n*; [fə(:)'ment] gären (lassen); **~ation** Gärung *f*.

fern [fə:n] Farn(kraut *n*) *m*.

ferocity [fə'rɔsiti] Grausamkeit *f*; Wildheit *f*.

ferry ['feri] Fähre *f*; übersetzen; **~boat** Fähre *f*.

fertil|e ['fə:tail] fruchtbar; **~ity** [~'tiliti] Fruchtbarkeit *f*; **~ize** ['~ilaiz] befruchten; düngen; **~izer** (Kunst)Dünger *m*.

fervent ['fə:vənt] glühend (heiß); leidenschaftlich.

fester ['festə] eitern.

festiv|al ['festəvəl] Fest, *n*, Feier *f*; Festspiele *pl*; **~e** festlich, heiter; **~ities** [~'tivitiz] *pl* Fest *n*.

fetch [fetʃ] holen; *Preis* erzielen.

fetter ['fetə] Fessel *f*.

feud [fju:d] Fehde *f*.

fever ['fi:və] Fieber *n*; **~ish** fieb(e)rig; *fig.* fieberhaft.

few [fju:] wenig; **a ~** einige, ein paar; **quite a ~** e-e ganze Menge.

fiancé [fi'ã:nsei] Verlobte *m*; **~e** [~] Verlobte *f*.

fib [fib] schwindeln.

fib|re, *Am.* **~er** ['faibə] Faser *f*; **~rous** faserig.

fickle ['fikl] wankelmütig.

fict|ion ['fikʃən] Erfindung

f; Roman(literatur *f*) *m*; **~itious** [~'tiʃəs] erfunden.

fiddle ['fidl] Fiedel *f*, Geige *f*; fiedeln; herumspielen; **~r** Fiedler *m*, Geiger *m*.

fidelity [fi'deliti] Treue *f*.

fidget ['fidʒit] (herum)zappeln; **~y** unruhig, zappelig.

field [fi:ld] Feld *n*; (Sport-) Platz *m*; Bereich *m*; **~ events** *pl sp.* Sprung- u. Wurfwettkämpfe *pl*, **~glasses** *pl* Fernglas *n*; Feldstecher *m*.

fiend [fi:nd] böser Feind, Teufel *m*; *in Zssgn colloq.* Süchtige *m*, *f*; Fanatiker (-in).

fierce [fiəs] wild; heftig.

fiery ['faiəri] glühend; *fig.* feurig, hitzig.

fife [faif] Querpfeife *f*.

fif|teen(th) ['fif'ti:n(θ)] fünfzehn(te); **~th** [fifθ] fünfte; Fünftel *n*; **~thly** fünftens; **~tieth** ['~tiiθ] fünfzigste; **~ty** fünfzig; Fünfzig *f*.

fig [fig] Feige *f*.

fight [fait] Kampf *m*; Schlägerei *f*; Kampflust *f*; (*irr*) bekämpfen; erkämpfen; kämpfen, sich schlagen; **~er** Kämpfer *m*, Streiter *m*; Jagdflugzeug *n*.

figurative ['figjurətiv] bildlich.

figure ['figə] Figur *f*; Gestalt *f*; Ziffer *f*; abbilden; mit Mustern schmücken; sich *et.* vorstellen; e-e Rolle spielen; **~ out** ausrechnen; verstehen; **~-skating** Eiskunstlauf m.

file¹ [fail] Ordner m; Akte f; Akten pl, Ablage f; Reihe f; **Briefe** etc. einordnen, abheften, -legen; hinter-ea. marschieren.

file² Feile f; feilen.

fill [fil] (sich) füllen; an-, aus-, erfüllen; **~ in** Formular ausfüllen; **~** Namen einsetzen; **~ up** an-, vollfüllen, mot. volltanken.

fillet ['filit] Filet n.

filling ['filiŋ] Füllung f; **~ station** Am. Tankstelle f.

filly ['fili] (Stuten)Füllen n.

film [film] Häutchen n; Film m; (ver)filmen.

filter ['filtə] Filter m; filtern.

filth [filθ] Schmutz m; **~y** schmutzig; fig. unflätig.

fin [fin] Flosse f.

final ['fainl] letzt; endültig; End..., Schluß...; oft pl Schlußprüfung f; oft pl sp. Finale n, Endspiel n; **~ly** endlich, schließlich.

financ|e [fai'næns] Finanzwesen n; pl Finanzen pl; finanzieren; **~ial** [~ʃəl] finanziell; **~ier** [~siə] Finanzmann m; Finanzier m.

finch [fintʃ] Fink m.

find [faind] Fund m; (irr) finden, (an)treffen, entdecken; jur. for schuldig erklären; beschaffen; **~ (out)** herausfinden; **~ings** pl Befund m; Urteil n.

fine¹ [fain] Geldstrafe f; zu e-r Geldstrafe verurteilen.

fine² schön; fein; rein; spitz, dünn; vornehm; colloq. gut, bestens; **I am ~** es geht mir gut; **~ry** Putz m, Staat m.

finger ['fiŋgə] Finger m; betasten; **~nail** Fingernagel m; **~print** Fingerabdruck m.

finish ['finiʃ] (be)enden, abschließen; vollenden; polieren, glätten; Ende f; Vollendung f, letzter Schliff; **~ing line** Ziellinie f.

Finn [fin] Finn|e m, -in f; **~ish** finnisch; Finnisch n.

fir [fə:] Tanne f.

fire ['faiə] an-, entzünden; Ziegel etc. brennen; feuern; colloq. rausschmeißen, entlassen; (ab)feuern, schießen; Feuer n; **catch ~**, **take ~** Feuer fangen; **on ~** in Brand, in Flammen; **~-alarm** Feuermelder m; **~-arm** Schußwaffe f; **~-brigade**, Am. **~ department** Feuerwehr f; **~-engine** Löschfahrzeug n; **~-escape** Feuerleiter f; Nottreppe f; **~-extinguisher** Feuerlöscher m; **~man** Feuerwehrmann m; Heizer m; **~-place** Kamin m; **~-proof** feuerfest; **~-side** Kamin m; **~-wood** Brennholz n; **~-works** pl Feuerwerk n.

firm [fə:m] fest; standhaft; Firma f; **~ness** Festigkeit f.

first [fə:st] erst; best; zuerst; erstens; **~ of all** zu allererst; der, die, das Erste; **~** at zuerst, anfangs; **~ aid** Erste Hilfe; **~-aid box** Verband(s)kasten m; **~-aid kit** Verband(s)zeug n; **~-born** erstgeboren; **~ class** erster Klasse; **~-class** erstklassig; **~ floor** erster Stock, Am. Erdgeschoß m; **~ly** erstens; **~ name** Vorname m; **~-rate** erstklassig.

firth [fə:θ] Förde f, (weite) Mündung.

fish [fiʃ], pl **~(es)** ['~iz] Fisch m; fischen, angeln; **~-bone** Gräte f.

fisher|man ['fiʃəmən] Fischer m; **~y** Fischerei f.

fishing ['fiʃiŋ] Fischen n; **~-line** Angelschnur f; **~ rod** Angelrute f; **~ tackle** Angelgerät n.

fishmonger ['fiʃmʌŋgə] Fischhändler m.

fiss|ion ['fiʃən] Spaltung f; **~ure** ['fiʃə] Spalt(e f) m, Riß m.

fist [fist] Faust f.

fit [fit] Anfall m; geeignet, passend; schicklich; tauglich; in (guter) Form, fit; passen, sitzen (Kleid); passen für od. dat; anpassen, geeignet machen; **~ (on)** anprobieren; **~ out** ausrüsten; **~ up** einrichten, ausstatten; **~ness** Gesundheit f; Fähigkeit f; Schick-

lichkeit f; **~ter** Monteur m, Installateur m; **~ting** passend; schicklich; Installation f; Anprobe f; pl Einrichtung f.

five [faiv] fünf; Fünf f.

fix [fiks] befestigen; Augen etc. richten; fesseln; bestimmen; fixieren; Am. colloq. richten; **~ (up)on** sich entschließen für; **~ up** arrangieren; j-n unterbringen; colloq. heikle Lage, Klemme f; **~ed** fest; bestimmt; starr; **~tures** pl festes Inventar.

fizz [fiz] zischen, sprudeln.

flabbergast ['flæbəga:st] colloq.: **be ~ed** platt sein.

flabby ['flæbi] schlaff.

flag [flæg] Flagge f, Fahne f; Fliese f; Schwertlilie f; beflaggen; schlaff herabhängen; fig. nachlassen; **~stone** Fliese f, Platte f.

flake [fleik] Flocke f; vb: **~ off** abblättern.

flame [fleim] Flamme f, Feuer n; flammen, lodern.

flank [flæŋk] Flanke f; flankieren.

flannel ['flænl] Flanell m; Waschlappen m; pl Flanellhose f.

flap [flæp] (Hut)Krempe f; Klappe f; Klaps m, Schlag m; schlagen; flattern.

flare [flɛə] flackern; sich bauschen; **~ up** aufflammen; fig. aufbrausen.

flash [flæʃ] Blitz m; Aufblitzen n; kurze Meldung;

aufleuchten *od.* -blitzen (lassen); rasen; *Blick* werfen; funken; **~bulb** Blitzbirne *f*; **~cube** Blitzwürfel *m*; **~light** Blinklicht *n*; *phot.* Blitzlicht *n*; Taschenlampe *f*; **~ of lightning** Blitzstrahl *m*.

flask [flɑːsk] Taschenflasche *f*; Thermosflasche *f*.

flat [flæt] flach, eben; platt; schal; *econ.* flau; klar; glatt; völlig; Fläche *f*, Ebene *f*; Flachland *n*; *mot.* Plattfuß *m*; *Brit.* (Miet)Wohnung *f*; **~** (ein)ebnen; abflachen; flach werden.

flatter ['flætə] schmeicheln; **~y** Schmeichelei *f*.

flavo(u)r ['fleivə] (Bei-)Geschmack *m*; Aroma *n*; würzen.

flaw [flɔː] Sprung *m*, Riß *m*; Fehler *m*; **~less** fehlermakellos.

flax [flæks] Flachs *m*.

flea [fliː] Floh *m*.

fled [fled] *pret u. pp von* **flee.**

fledged [fledʒd] flügge.

flee [fliː] (*irr*) fliehen.

fleece [fliːs] Vlies *n*, Schaffell *m*; *fig.* prellen.

fleet [fliːt] schnell; Flotte *f*; **2 Street** die (Londoner) Presse.

flesh [fleʃ] Fleisch *n*; **~y** fleischig; dick.

flew [fluː] *pret von* **fly².**

flexible ['fleksəbl] flexibel, biegsam; *fig.* anpassungsfähig.

flick [flik] leicht u. schnell schlagen; schnellen.

flicker ['flikə] flackern; flimmern; flattern.

flier ['flaiə] *s. flyer.*

flight [flait] Flucht *f*; Flug *m*; Schwarm *m* (*Vögel etc.*); *aer.* Flug (verbindung) *f*) *m*; **~ of stairs** Treppe *f*.

flimsy ['flimzi] dünn; *fig.* fadenscheinig.

flinch [flintʃ] zurückweichen.

fling [fliŋ] Wurf *m*; Versuch *m*; (*irr*) eilen, stürzen; werfen, schleudern; **~ open** *Tür* aufreißen.

flint [flint] Kiesel *m*; Feuerstein *m*.

flip [flip] schnipsen.

flippant ['flipənt] frech.

flipper ['flipə] (Schwimm-)Flosse *f*.

flirt [fləːt] flirten, kokettieren; **~ation** Flirt *m*.

flit [flit] flitzen, huschen; (umher)flattern.

float [fləut] Schwimmer *m*; Floß *n*; flottmachen; schwimmen *od.* treiben (lassen); schweben.

flock [flɔk] (*Schaf*)Herde *f* (*a. fig.*); Schar *f*; sich scharen; zs.-strömen.

floe [fləu] Eisscholle *f*.

flog [flɔg] peitschen; prügeln.

flood [flʌd] Flut *f*; Überschwemmung *f*; Flut *f*, Strom *m*; überfluten, -schwemmen; **~lights** *pl* Flutlicht(er) *n*; **~tide** Flut *f*.

floor [flɔ:] Fußboden m; Stock(werk n) m, Etage f; **take the ~** das Wort ergreifen; vb: e-n (Fuß-) Boden legen; zu Boden schlagen; verwirren; **~ cloth** Putzlappen m; **~ lamp** Stehlampe f; **~ show** Nachtklubvorstellung f.

flop [flɔp]: **~ down** (sich) hinplumpsen lassen.

florist ['flɔrist] Blumenhändler(in).

flounder ['flaundə] Flunder f.

flour ['flauə] (feines) Mehl.

flourish ['flʌriʃ] Schnörkel m; Schwingen f; Tusch m; blühen, gedeihen; schwingen.

flow [fləu] Fließen n; Strom m, Fluß m; fließen.

flower ['flauə] Blume f; Blüte f (a. fig.); blühen.

flown [fləun] pp von **fly²**.

fluctuate ['flʌktjueit] schwanken.

flu [flu:] colloq. abbr. von **influenza**.

fluent ['flu(:)ənt] fließend, geläufig.

fluff [flʌf] Flaum m; **~y** flaumig, flockig.

fluid ['flu(:)id] flüssig; Flüssigkeit f.

flung [flʌŋ] pret u. pp von **fling**.

flunk [flʌŋk] Am. colloq. durchfallen (lassen).

flurry ['flʌri] Bö f; Schauer m; Aufregung f, Unruhe f; nervös machen, beunruhigen.

flush [flʌʃ] Spülung f; Erröten n; Erregung f; überfluten, (aus)spülen; (er)röten.

fluster ['flʌstə] Aufregung f; nervös machen, verwirren; sich aufregen.

flute [flu:t] Flöte f.

flutter ['flʌtə] Geflatter n; Erregung f; flattern (mit).

flux [flʌks] Fließen n, Fluß m.

fly¹ [flai] Fliege f.

fly² (irr) fliegen (lassen); stürmen, stürzen; flattern, wehen; verfliegen (Zeit); Drachen steigen lassen; fliehen aus; **~ north** nach Norden fliegen; **~ (across)** überfliegen; **~ into a rage** od. **passion** in Wut geraten; **~er** Flieger m.

flying ['flaiiŋ] fliegend; Flug...; **~ machine** Flugapparat m, -zeug n; **~ squad** Überfallkommando n; **~ time** Flugzeit f.

fly-over (Straßen)Überführung f; **~weight** Boxen: Fliegengewicht n.

foal [fəul] Fohlen n.

foam [fəum] Schaum m; schäumen; **~y** schaumig.

focus ['fəukəs] Brennpunkt m; opt. scharf einstellen; fig. konzentrieren.

foe [fəu] poet. Feind m.

fog [fɔg] (dichter) Nebel; **~gy** neb(e)lig; fig. nebelhaft.

foible ['fɔibl] fig. Schwäche f.

foil¹ [fɔil] Folie f; fig. Kontrast m, Hintergrund m.

foil² vereiteln.

fold¹ [fəuld] (Schaf)Hürde f, Pferch m; eccl. Herde f; einpferchen.

fold² Falte f; falten; Arme kreuzen; **~er** Aktendeckel m, Schnellhefter m; Faltprospekt m.

folding ['fəuldiŋ] zs.-legbar, Klapp...; **~ boat** Faltboot n; **~ chair** Klappstuhl m.

foliage ['fəuliidʒ] Laub (-werk) n, Blätter n/pl.

folk [fəuk] pl Leute pl; **~lore** ['‿lɔ:] Folklore f; **~s** pl colloq. Leute pl (Angehörige); **~song** Volkslied n.

follow ['fɔləu] folgen (auf); befolgen; Beruf ausüben; **~er** Anhänger(in); **~ing** Anhängerschaft f.

folly ['fɔli] Torheit f.

fond [fɔnd] zärtlich; vernarrt; **be ~ of** gern haben, lieben; **~le** liebkosen, streicheln; **~ness** Zärtlichkeit f; Vorliebe f.

food [fu:d] Speise f, Essen n, Nahrung f; Nahrungs-, Lebensmittel n/pl; Futter n.

fool [fu:l] (herum)spielen; zum Narren halten; betrügen; verleiten; Narr m, Närrin f, Dummkopf m; Hanswurst m; **make a ~ of o.s.** sich lächerlich machen; **~hardy** tollkühn; **~ish** töricht, dumm; **~ishness** Torheit

f; **~proof** narrensicher.

foot [fut], pl **feet** [fi:t] Fuß m; Fußende n; **on ~** zu Fuß; fig. im Gange; **~ the bill** die Rechnung bezahlen; **~ball** Fußball m; **~baller** Fußballspieler m; **~board** Trittbrett n; **~ brake** Fußbremse f; **~hills** pl Vorgebirge n; **~hold** fester Stand; **~ing** Stand m, Halt m; fig.: Stellung f; Beziehung f (on pl); **~lights** pl Rampenlicht n; **~path** (Fuß-)Pfad m, Gehweg m; **~print** Fußspur f; **~step** Fußstapfe f; Schritt m.

for [fɔ:, fə] für; als; Zweck, Ziel, Richtung: zu, nach; warten, hoffen etc. auf; sich sehnen etc. nach; Grund: aus, vor, wegen; **~ three days** drei Tage lang; seit drei Tagen; **walk a mile** eine Meile (weit) gehen.

forbade [fɔ'bæd] pret von **forbid**.

forbear [fɔ:'bɛə] (irr) unterlassen, sich enthalten.

forbid [fə'bid] (irr) verbieten; **~den** pp von **forbid**; **~ding** abstoßend.

forbore [fɔ:'bɔ:] pret, **~ne** pp von **forbear**.

force [fɔ:s] Kraft f, Gewalt f; Zwang m; Nachdruck m; **armed ~s** pl Streitkräfte pl; **come od. put into ~** in Kraft treten od. setzen; vb: (er-) zwingen; **~ (open)** aufbrechen; **~d landing** Notlandung f.

forceps ['fɔ:seps], pl ~ med. Zange f.

forcible ['fɔ:səbl] gewaltsam; überzeugend.

ford [fɔ:d] Furt f; durchwaten.

fore [fɔ:] vorder, Vorder-..; **~boding** [.'bəudiŋ] Ahnung f; **~cast** Voraussage f; (irr cast) vorhersehen, voraussagen; **~fathers** pl Vorfahren pl; **~finger** Zeigefinger m; **~foot** Vorderfuß m; **~ground** Vordergrund m; **~head** ['fɔrid] Stirn f.

foreign ['fɔrin] fremd; ausländisch; ~ **currency** Devisen pl; **~er** Ausländer (-in), Fremde m, f; ~ **exchange** Devisen pl; 2 **Office** Brit. Außenministerium n; ~ **policy** Außenpolitik f; ~ **trade** Außenhandel m.

fore|leg Vorderbein n; **~man** Vorarbeiter m, Werkmeister m; jur. Sprecher m (der Geschworenen); **~most** vorderst; erst; zuerst; **~noon** Vormittag m; **~see** (irr see) vorhersehen; **~sight** Voraussicht f, Vorsorge f.

forest ['fɔrist] Wald m (a. fig.), Forst m; **~er** Förster m; **~ry** Forstwirtschaft f.

fore|taste Vorgeschmack m; **~tell** (irr tell) vorhersagen. [mer.]

forever [fə'revə] (für) im-

foreword Vorwort n.

forfeit ['fɔ:fit] einbüßen, verscherzen; Strafe f.

forge [fɔ:dʒ] Schmiede f; schmieden; fälschen; **~ry** Fälschung f.

forget [fə'get] (irr) vergessen; **~ful** vergeßlich; **~me-not** Vergißmeinnicht n.

forgiv|e [fə'giv] (irr give) vergeben, -zeihen; **~eness** Verzeihung f; **~ing** versöhnlich.

forgot [fə'gɔt] pret, **~ten** pp von forget.

fork [fɔ:k] Gabel f; sich gabeln, abzweigen.

forlorn [fə'lɔ:n] verloren, -lassen; unglücklich.

form [fɔ:m] Form f; Gestalt f; Formular n; (Schul-)Bank f (Schul-)Klasse f; Kondition f; (sich) formen od. bilden od. gestalten.

formal ['fɔ:məl] förmlich; formell; äußerlich; **~ity** [.'mæliti] Förmlichkeit f, Formalität f.

format|ion [fɔ:'meiʃən] Bildung f; **~ive** [.'mətiv] formend, gestaltend.

former ['fɔ:mə] früher, ehemalig; **the ~** der erstere; **~ly** früher.

formidable ['fɔ:midəbl] schrecklich; ungeheuer.

formulate ['fɔ:mjuleit] formulieren.

forsake [fə'seik] (irr) verlassen; aufgeben; **~saken** pp, **~sook** [fə'suk] pret von forsake.

fort [fɔ:t] Fort *n*.

forth [fɔ:θ] heraus; weiter, fort(an); **~coming** bevorstehend; **~with** sogleich. [ste.]

fortieth ['fɔ:tiiθ] vierzig-

fortify ['fɔ:tifai] befestigen; *fig.* stärken.

fortnight ['fɔ:tnait] vierzehn Tage; **today ~** heute in vierzehn Tagen.

fortress ['fɔ:tris] Festung *f*.

fortunate ['fɔ:tʃnit] glücklich; **~ly** glücklicherweise.

fortune ['fɔ:tʃən] Glück *n*; Schicksal *n*; Vermögen *n*.

forty ['fɔ:ti] vierzig; Vierzig *f*.

forward ['fɔ:wəd] *adj* vorwärts; vorder; zeitig; vorlaut; fortschrittlich; *adv* (*selten* **~s**) nach vorn, vorwärts; (her)vor; *su* Stürmer *m*; (be)fördern; (ver)senden; Brief etc. nachsenden.

foster|-child ['fɔstətʃaild] Pflegekind *n*; **~parents** *pl* Pflegeeltern *pl*.

fought [fɔ:t] *pret u. pp von* **fight**.

foul [faul] schmutzig (*a. fig.*); faul, verdorben; schlecht (*a. Wetter*); übelriechend; *sp.* unfair, regelwidrig; Foul *n*; beschmutzen.

found [faund] *pret u. pp von* **find**; gründen; stiften; *tech.* gießen; **~ation** Gründung *f*; Stiftung *f*; *oft pl* Fundament *n*; *fig.*

Grundlage *f*; **~er** Gründer(in); Stifter(in); **~ling** Findelkind *n*.

fountain ['fauntin] Springbrunnen *m*; Quelle *f* (*bsd. fig.*); **~-pen** Füllfederhalter *m*.

four [fɔ:] vier; Vier *f*; **~score** achtzig; **~stroke engine** Viertaktmotor *m*; **~teen(th)** [~'ti:n(θ)] vierzehn(te); **~th** [fɔ:θ] vierte; Viertel *n*; **~thly** viertens.

fowl [faul] Haushuhn *n*; Geflügel *n*; Vogel *m*; **~ing-piece** Vogel-, Schrotflinte *f*.

fox [fɔks] Fuchs *m*.

fract|ion ['frækʃən] Bruch (-teil) *m*; **~ure** (*bsd.* Knochen)Bruch *m*; brechen. [brechlich.]

fragile ['frædʒail] zer-]

fragment ['frægmənt] Bruchstück *n*.

fragran|ce ['freigrəns] Wohlgeruch *m*, Duft *m*; **~t** wohlriechend, duftend.

frail [freil] ge-, zerbrechlich; schwach; **~ty** *fig.* Schwäche *f*.

frame [freim] Rahmen *m*; Gerüst *n*; (Brillen)Gestell *n*; Körper(bau) *m*; **~ of mind** Gemütsverfassung *f*; bilden, formen, bauen; (ein)rahmen; **~house** Holzhaus *n*; **~work** *tech.* Gerüst *n*.

franchise ['fræntʃaiz] Wahlrecht *n*; Bürgerrecht *n*.

frank [fræŋk] offen, aufrichtig.

frankfurter ['fræŋkfətə] Frankfurter Würstchen.

frankness ['fræŋknis] Offenheit f.

frantic ['fræntik] wild, rasend; wahnsinnig.

fratern|al [frə'tɜ:nl] brüderlich; **~ity** Brüderlichkeit f; Bruderschaft f.

fraud [frɔ:d] Betrug m; Schwindel m; Schwindler m.

fray [frei] (sich) durchscheuern.

freak [fri:k] (verrückter) Einfall, Laune f; verrückter Kerl, Sonderling m.

freckle ['frekl] Sommersprosse f.

free [fri:] befreien, freilassen; frei; freigebig; **~ and easy** zwanglos; **set ~** freilassen; **~dom** Freiheit f; Offenheit f; Zwanglosigkeit f; (plumpe) Vertraulichkeit; **~mason** Freimaurer m; **~ port** Freihafen m; **~ ticket** Freikarte f; **~ time** Freizeit f; **~way** Am. Schnellstraße f; **~wheel** Freilauf m.

freeze [fri:z] (irr) (ge-)frieren, erstarren; zum Gefrieren bringen; Fleisch etc. einfrieren, tiefkühlen; **~ing point** Gefrierpunkt m.

freight [freit] Fracht(geld n, -gut n) f; Am. Güter...; beladen; **~er** Frachter m.

French [frentʃ] französisch; Französisch n; **the ~** pl die Franzosen pl; **~man** Franzose m; **~ window** Balkon-, Glastür f; **~woman** Französin f.

frequen|cy ['fri:kwənsi] Häufigkeit f; phys. Frequenz f; **~t** häufig; [fri'kwent] (oft) be- od. aufsuchen.

fresh [freʃ] frisch; neu; unerfahren; **~man** Student m im ersten Jahr; **~ness** Frische f; Neuheit f; **~water** Süßwasser...

fret [fret] (sich) ärgern.

friar ['fraiə] (Bettel)Mönch m.

friction ['frikʃən] Reibung f; fig. Spannung f.

Friday ['fraidi] Freitag m.

fridge [fridʒ] colloq. Kühlschrank m.

fried [fraid] gebraten, gebacken, Brat..., Back...

friend [frend] Freund(in); Bekannte m, f; **~s** Freundschaft schließen; **~ly** freund(schaft)lich; **~ship** Freundschaft f.

frig(e) [fridʒ] s. fridge.

fright [frait] Schreck(en) m; **~en** erschrecken; **~ened: be ~ of** colloq. sich fürchten vor; **~ful** schrecklich. [stig.]

frigid ['fridʒid] kalt, frostig.]

frill [fril] Krause f, Rüsche f.

fringe [frindʒ] Franse f; Rand m; Pony m (Frisur).

frisk [frisk] hüpfen; **~y** lebhaft, munter.

fro [frəu]: **to and ~ hin und her, auf und ab.**

frock [frɔk] Kutte f; Kleid n.

frog [frɔg] Frosch m.

frolic ['frɔlik] scherzen, spaßen; **~some** ['~səm] vergnügt, ausgelassen.

from [frɔm, frəm] von; aus, von ... aus od. her, aus ... heraus, von ... herab; aus, vor, infolge von; **~ ... to** von ... bis.

front [frʌnt] gegenüberstehen, -liegen; mit der Front nach ... zu liegen; Vorderseite f; Strandpromenade f; Vorder...; **in ~** vorn; **in ~ of** räumlich: vor; **~door** Haus-, Vordertür f; **~ garden** Vorgarten m; **~ier** ['~iə] Grenze f; Grenz...; **~ page** Titelseite f; **~ seat** Vordersitz m; **~ tyre** Vorderreifen m; **~ wheel** Vorderrad n; **~wheel drive** Vorderradantrieb m.

frost [frɔst] Frost m; Reif m; mit Reif od. Eis überziehen; mit Puderzucker bestreuen; glasieren; mattieren; **~bite** Erfrierung f; **~ed glass** Milchglas n; **~y** eisig, frostig.

froth [frɔθ] Schaum m; schäumen; **~y** schaumig.

frown [fraun] die Stirn runzeln; finster blicken.

froze [frəuz] pret, **~n** pp von **freeze**; **~n meat** Gefrierfleisch n.

frugal ['fru:gəl] sparsam, bescheiden.

fruit [fru:t] Frucht f; Früchte pl; Obst n; **~erer** Obsthändler m; **~ful** fruchtbar; **~less** unfruchtbar; fig. vergeblich.

frustrate [frʌs'treit] vereiteln; enttäuschen.

fry [frai] braten, backen; **~ing-pan** Bratpfanne f.

fuchsia ['fju:ʃə] Fuchsie f.

fuel [fjuəl] Brenn-, Treib-, Kraftstoff m.

fugitive ['fju:dʒitiv] flüchtig; Flüchtling m.

fulfil(l) [ful'fil] erfüllen; ausführen; **~ment** Erfüllung f.

full [ful] voll; vollständig; ganz; ausführlich; völlig; ganz; gerade, genau; **~ of** voller ..., voll von; erfüllt von; **~ up** voll, besetzt; **in ~** voll(ständig); **~ board** Vollpension f; **~ stop** Punkt m.

ful(l)ness ['fulnis] Fülle f.

full-time employment, ~ job Ganztagsbeschäftigung f.

fumble ['fʌmbl] umhertasten, (herum)fummeln.

fume [fju:m] Dunst m, Dampf m; rauchen, dampfen; fig. wütend sein.

fun [fʌn] Scherz m, Spaß m; **for ~** aus Spaß; **it is ~** es macht Spaß; **make ~ of** sich lustig machen über.

function ['fʌŋkʃən] Funktion f; Aufgabe f; Veranstaltung *f*; funktionieren; ~ary Funktionär *m*.

fund [fʌnd] Kapital *n*, Geldsumme *f*, Fonds *m*; *pl a.* (Geld)Mittel *pl*; *fig.* Vorrat *m*.

fundamental [fʌndə'mentl] grundlegend.

funeral ['fju:nərəl] Beerdigung *f*; Trauer..., Begräbnis...

fun fair Rummelplatz *m*.

funicular (railway) [fju(:)'nikjulə] (Draht-)Seilbahn *f*.

funnel ['fʌnl] Trichter *m*; Licht-, Luftschacht *m*; *mar.*, *rail.* Schornstein *m*.

funny ['fʌni] spaßig, komisch, lustig.

fur [fə:] Pelz *m*, Fell *n*; Belag *m* (*auf der Zunge*).

furious ['fjuəriəs] wütend; wild.

furl [fə:l] zs.-rollen; sich zs.-rollen lassen.

furnace ['fə:nis] Schmelz-, Hochofen *m*; (Heiz)Kessel *m*.

furnish ['fə:niʃ] versorgen; liefern; möblieren; ausstatten.

furniture ['fə:nitʃə] Möbel *pl*, Einrichtung *f*.

furrow ['fʌrou] Furche *f*; pflügen; furchen.

further ['fə:ðə] weiter; ferner; überdies; fördern; ~more ferner, überdies.

furtive ['fə:tiv] verstohlen.

fury ['fjuəri] Zorn *m*, Wut *f*; Furie *f*.

fuse [fju:z] (ver)schmelzen; *electr.* durchbrennen; *electr.* Sicherung *f*; Zünder *m*.

fuselage ['fju:zila:ʒ] (Flugzeug)Rumpf *m*.

fusion ['fju:ʒən] Verschmelzung *f*; Fusion *f*.

fuss [fʌs] Aufregung *f*, Getue *n*; viel Aufhebens machen; (sich) aufregen.

futile ['fju:tail] nutzlos.

future ['fju:tʃə] (zu)künftig; Zukunft *f*; ~ (**tense**) *gr.* Futur *n*, Zukunft *f*.

G

gab [gæb] *colloq.* Geschwätz *n*; **have the gift of the** ~ ein gutes Mundwerk haben.

gable ['geibl] Giebel *m*.

gad-fly ['gædflai] *zo.* Bremse *f*.

gag [gæg] Knebel *m*; Gag *m*; knebeln.

gage [geidʒ] *s.* **gauge**.

gai|ety ['geiəti] Fröhlichkeit *f*; ~ly *adv* von **gay**.

gain [gein] Gewinn *m*; Zunahme *f*; gewinnen; bekommen; zunehmen (*Gewicht*); vorgehen (*Uhr*).

gait [geit] Gang(art *f*) *m*; ~er Gamasche *f*.

gale [geil] Sturm *m*.

gall [gɔ:l] Galle *f*.

gallant ['gælənt] stattlich; tapfer; galant, höflich.

gallery ['gæləri] Galerie f; Empore f.

galley ['gæli] Galeere f; Kombüse f; ~proof (Korrektur)Fahne f.

gallon ['gælən] Gallone f (4,54 Liter, Am. 3,78 Liter).

gallop ['gæləp] Galopp m; galoppieren (lassen).

gallows ['gæləuz] sg Galgen m.

galore [gə'lɔ:] im Überfluß.

gamble ['gæmbl] spielen; ~r Spieler(in).

gambol ['gæmbəl] Luftsprung m; (herum)hüpfen.

game [geim] Spiel n (a. Wettkampf, -spiel); Wild n; ~keeper Wildhüter m.

gander ['gændə] Gänserich m.

gang [gæŋ] Gruppe f, Trupp m; Bande f; ~ up sich zs.-rotten od. zs.-tun.

gangster ['gæŋstə] Gangster m.

gangway ['gæŋwei] (Durch)Gang m; Gangway f, Laufplanke f.

gaol [dʒeil] Gefängnis n; einsperren; ~er (Gefängnis)Wärter m.

gap [gæp] Lücke f; Spalt (a. f) m; fig. Kluft f.

gape [geip] gähnen; gaffen; klaffen.

garage ['gærɑ:dʒ] Garage f; Auto-, Reparaturwerkstatt f; Auto einstellen.

garbage ['gɑ:bidʒ] Abfall m.

garden ['gɑ:dn] Garten

m; ~er Gärtner(in); ~ing Gartenarbeit f.

gargle ['gɑ:gl] Mund ausspülen; gurgeln.

garland ['gɑ:lənd] Girlande f, Kranz m. [m.]

garlic ['gɑ:lik]Knoblauch

garment ['gɑ:mənt] Kleidungsstück n, Gewand n.

garnish ['gɑ:niʃ] garnieren.

garret ['gærət] Dachstube f, Mansarde f.

garrison ['gærisn] Garnison f, Besatzung f.

garter ['gɑ:tə] Strumpfband n; Am. Sockenhalter m.

gas [gæs] Gas n; Am. mot. Benzin n; ~eous ['~əs] gasförmig; ~ fire Gasheizung f.

gash [gæʃ] klaffende Wunde.

gasket['gæskit] tech. Dichtung f.

gas-meter Gasuhr f; ~oline ['gæsəli:n] Am. mot. Benzin n.

gasp [gɑ:sp] Keuchen n; keuchen, schnaufen.

gas station Am. Tankstelle f; ~stove Gasherd m; ~works Gaswerk n.

gate [geit] Tor n; Pforte f; Schranke f, Sperre f; aer. Flugsteig m; ~way Tor(weg m) n, Einfahrt f.

gather ['gæðə] sich versammeln; sich zs.-ballen (Wolken); eitern (Abszeß); (ein-, ver)sammeln; ernten, pflücken; raffen (in

schließen (**from** aus); ~
speed schneller werden;
~ing Versammlung f.

gaudy ['gɔːdi] grell; protzig.

gauge [geidʒ] (Normal-)
Maß n; rail. Spurweite f;
Meßgerät n; eichen; (aus-)
messen.

gaunt [gɔːnt] hager; finster. [m.]

gauze [gɔːz] Gaze f; Mull

gave [geiv] pret von **give**.

gay [gei] lustig, fröhlich,
heiter; bunt, lebhaft.

gaze [geiz] (fester, starrer)
Blick; ~ **at** anstarren.

gear [giə] tech. Getriebe
n; mot. Gang m; Gerät
n; **~change** Gangschal-
tung f; **~defect** Getriebe-
schaden m; **~ing** Getriebe
n; Übersetzung f; **~lever**
Schalthebel m.

geese [giːs] pl von **goose**.

gem [dʒem] Edelstein m.

gender ['dʒendə] gr. Genus n.

general ['dʒenərəl] allgemein; Haupt...; General
m; Feldherr m; **~ize** ver-
allgemeinern; **~ly** im all-
gemeinen; gewöhnlich.

general|e ['dʒenəreit] erzeu-
gen; **~ion** Erzeugung
f; Generation f; Men-
schenalter n; **~or** Generator m; mot. Licht-
maschine f.

gener|osity [dʒenə'rɔsiti]
Großmut f; Großzügig-
keit f; **~ous** großzügig;
edel; reichlich.

genial ['dʒiːnjəl] freundlich.

genitive (case) ['dʒeni-
tiv] gr. Genitiv m, 2. Fall.

genius ['dʒiːnjəs] Genie n;
fig. Geist m.

gentle ['dʒentl] sanft, mild,
zart; vornehm; **~man**
Herr m, Gentleman m;
~manlike, **~manly** vornehm, fein, gebildet; **~
ness** Güte f, Milde f,
Sanftheit f; **~woman**
Dame f.

gentry ['dʒentri] niederer
Adel; gebildete und be-
sitzende Stände pl.

genuine ['dʒenjuin] echt.

geography [dʒi'ɔgrəfi]
Geographie f, Erdkunde f.

geolog|ist [dʒi'ɔlədʒist]
Geologe m; **~y** Geologie f.

geometry [dʒi'ɔmitri]
Geometrie f.

germ [dʒəːm] Keim m;
Bakterie f.

German ['dʒəːmən]
deutsch; Deutsche m, f;
Deutsch n.

germinate ['dʒəːmineit]
keimen.

gerund ['dʒerənd] gr. Gerundium n.

gesticulate [dʒes'tikju-
leit] gestikulieren.

gesture ['dʒestʃə] Geste f,
Gebärde f.

get [get] (irr) erhalten, bekommen, colloq. kriegen;
(sich) besorgen; holen;
bringen; erwerben; verdienen; ergreifen, fassen, fangen; veranlassen; colloq.

verstehen; gelangen, (an-)kommen, geraten; *mit adj:* werden; **~ about** herumkommen; auf den Beinen sein; sich verbreiten (*Gerücht*); **~ along** auskommen; vorwärtskommen; **~ away** loskommen; entkommen; **~ in** einsteigen; **~ off** aussteigen; **~ on** einsteigen in; **~ on with s.o.** mit j-m auskommen; **~ out** aussteigen; **~ out of** heraus- *od.* hinauskommen aus; **~ to** kommen nach; **~ together** zs.-kommen; **~ up** aufstehen; **~ by heart** auswendig lernen; **~ one's hair cut** sich die Haare schneiden lassen; **~ ready** sich fertigmachen; **~ to know** kennenlernen; **have got** haben; **have got to** müssen.

geyser ['gaizə] Geiser *m*, Geysir *m*; ['gu:tli] Boiler *m*.

ghastly ['gu:stli] gräßlich, schrecklich; (toten)bleich.

gherkin ['gə:kin] Gewürzgurke *f*.

ghost [gaust] Geist *m*, Gespenst *n*; **~ly** geisterhaft.

giant ['dʒaiənt] riesig, gigantisch, Riesen...; Riese *m*.

gibbet ['dʒibit] Galgen *m*.

gibe [dʒaib] (ver)spotten.

giblets ['dʒiblits] *pl* Gänse-, Hühnerklein *n*.

giddy ['gidi] schwind(e)lig; schwindelnd; *fig.* leichtsinnig.

gift [gift] Geschenk *n*;

Begabung *f*, Talent *n*; **~ed** begabt.

gigantic [dʒai'gæntik] riesig, gigantisch.

giggle ['gigl] kichern; Gekicher *n*.

gild [gild] (*irr*) vergolden; verschöne(r)n.

gill [gil] Kieme *f*; *bot.* Lamelle *f*.

gilt [gilt] *pret u. pp von* **gild**; Vergoldung *f*.

gin [dʒin] Gin *m*, Wacholderschnaps *m*.

ginger ['dʒindʒə] Ingwer *m*; *colloq.* Schneid *m*, Feuer *n*; rötlich-gelb; **~bread** Pfefferkuchen *m*; **~ly** sachte, behutsam; zimperlich.

gipsy ['dʒipsi] Zigeuner (-in).

giraffe [dʒi'rɑ:f] Giraffe *f*.

gird [gə:d] (*irr*) (um)gürten; umgeben.

girder ['gə:də] Träger *m*, Tragbalken *m*.

girdle ['gə:dl] Gürtel *m*; Hüfthalter *m*, -gürtel *m*.

girl [gə:l] Mädchen *n*; **♀ Guide** Pfadfinderin *f*; **~hood** Mädchenjahre *pl*; **~ish** mädchenhaft; **♀ Scout** *Am.* Pfadfinderin *f*; **~'s name** Mädchenname *m*.

girt [gə:t] *pret u. pp von* **gird**.

girth [gə:θ] (Sattel)Gurt *m*; Umfang *m*.

give [giv] (*irr*) (ab-, weiter)geben; schenken; her-, hingeben; widmen; geben, reichen; liefern; verursachen; bereiten; zugeste-

glacier

hen, erlauben; nachgeben; ~ **away** verschenken; verteilen; verraten; ~ **in** nachaufgeben; *Gesuch etc.* einreichen; ~ **up** aufgeben; *j-n* ausliefern; ~ **o.s. up** sich stellen; ~ **(up)on (to)** nachgeben, hinausgehen auf (*Fenster etc.*); ~ **way** zurückweichen, Platz machen; ~**n** *pp von* **give**; ergeben; verfallen (**to** *dat.*).

glacier ['glæsjə] Gletscher *m.*

glad [glæd] froh, erfreut; **be** ~ sich freuen; ~**ly** gern(e); ~**ness** Freude *f.*

glam|orous ['glæmərəs] bezaubernd; ~**o(u)r** Zauber *m*, Reiz *m.*

glance [glɑːns] flüchtiger Blick; Aufblitzen *n*; ~ **at** (schnell, flüchtig) blicken auf.

gland [glænd] Drüse *f.*

glare [glɛə] blendendes Licht; wilder *od.* funkelnder Blick; grell leuchten *od.* scheinen; ~ **at** (wild) anstarren.

glass [glɑːs] (Trink-, Fern-, Opern)Glas *n*; Spiegel *m*; Barometer *n*; **a** ~ **of ...** ein Glas ...; **(a pair of)** ~**es** *pl* (**e-e**) Brille; gläsern, Glas...; ~**y** gläsern; glasig.

glaze [gleiz] Glasur *f*; verglasen; glasieren; glasig werden (*Auge*); ~**ier** ['~jə] Glaser *m.*

gleam [gliːm] schwacher

Schein, Schimmer *m*; leuchten, schimmern.

glee [gliː] Fröhlichkeit *f*, Freude *f*; mehrstimmiges Lied.

glen [glen] enges Tal, Bergschlucht *f.*

glib [glib] glatt, gewandt; zungenfertig.

glide [glaid] Gleiten *n*; *aer.* Gleitflug *m*; gleiten; segeln; ~**r** Segelflugzeug *n.*

glimmer ['glimə] Schimmer *m*; schimmern.

glimpse [glimps] flüchtiger Blick; flüchtig (er-)blicken.

glint [glint] schimmern, glitzern.

glisten ['glisn] schimmern, glänzen, glitzern.

glitter ['glitə] glitzern, glänzen, funkeln.

gloat [gləut]: ~ **(up)on, ~ over** sich weiden an.

globe [gləub] (Erd)Kugel *f*; Globus *m.*

gloom [gluːm] Düsterkeit *f*, Dunkel *n*; düstere Stimmung, Schwermut *f*; ~**y** dunkel, düster; niedergeschlagen.

glor|ify ['glɔːrifai] verherrlichen; ~**ious** herrlich; ruhmvoll; ~**y** Ruhm *m*, Ehre *f*; Herrlichkeit *f.*

gloss [glɔs] Glanz *m.*

glossary ['glɔsəri] (Spezial)Wörterbuch *n.*

glossy ['glɔsi] glänzend.

glove [glʌv] Handschuh *m.*

glow [gləu] Glühen *n*;

Glut *f*; glühen; **~worm** Glühwürmchen *n*.

glue [glu:] Leim *m*; Klebstoff *m*; leimen; kleben.

glutton ['glʌtn] Vielfraß *m*; **~ous** gefräßig; **~y** Gefräßigkeit *f*.

gnarled [nɑːld] knorrig; knotig, gichtig (*Finger*).

gnash [næʃ] (Stech)Mücke *f*; **~es** knirschen mit (*Zähnen*).

gnat [næt] (Stech)Mücke *f*.

gnaw [nɔː] zernagen, nagen *a*; nagen (*at an*).

go [gəu] (*irr*) gehen, fahren; verkehren (*Fahrzeuge*); (fort)gehen, abfahren; vergehen (*Zeit*); kaputtgehen; ausgehen; ablaufen, ausfallen; lassen, arbeiten, funktionieren; reichen; passen; werden; gelten; läuten, ertönen (*Glocke*); **~ to bed** ins Bett gehen; **~ to school** zur Schule gehen; **~ to see** besuchen; **let ~** loslassen; **~ at** losgehen auf; **~ by** sich richten nach; **~ for** holen; angreifen; **~ for a walk** spazierengehen; **~ in** hineingehen, eintreten; **~ in for an examination** e-e Prüfung machen; **~ off** fortgehen; **~ on** weitergehen, -fahren; *fig.*: fortfahren (**doing** zu tun); vor sich gehen, vorgehen; **~ through** durchgehen, durchmachen; **~ up** steigen; hinaufsteigen, **-gehen**; **~ without** auskommen ohne; *sub: colloq.* Schwung *m*; **have a ~ at** es versuchen mit.

goad [gəud] anstacheln.

goal [gəul] Ziel *n*; *Fußball:* Tor *n*; **~keeper** Torwart *m*.

goat [gəut] Ziege *f*.

go-between Vermittler (-in).

goblet ['gɔblit] Kelchglas *n*.

goblin ['gɔblin] Kobold *m*.

god [gɔd] (*eccl. 2*) Gott *m*; *fig.* (Ab)Gott *m*; **~child** Patenkind *n*; **~dess** Göttin *f*; **~father** Pate *m*; **~less** gottlos; **~mother** Patin *f*.

goggles ['gɔglz] *pl* Schutzbrille *f*.

going ['gəuiŋ]: **be ~ to** im Begriff sein zu, gleich tun wollen *od.* werden.

gold [gəuld] Gold *n*; golden, Gold...; **~digger** Goldgräber *m*; **~en** golden (*a. fig.*), goldgelb; **~plated** vergoldet; **~smith** Goldschmied *m*.

golf [gɔlf] Golf(spiel) *n*; Golf spielen; **~course**, **~links** *pl* Golfplatz *m*.

gondola ['gɔndələ] Gondel *f*.

gone [gɔn] *pp* von **go**; fort, weg, *colloq.* futsch.

good [gud] gut; artig, lieb (*Kind*); gütig; **~ at** gut in, geschickt in; **make s.th. ~** et. wiedergutmachen; Gute *n*, Wohl *n*; Vorteil *m*, Nutzen *m*; *pl* Waren *pl*, Güter *pl*; **that's no ~** das nützt

nichts; **for** ~ für immer;
~by(e) [.'bai] Lebewohl n; int. ['.'bai] (auf) Wiedersehen!; **~for-
nothing** Taugenichts m;
♀ **Friday** Karfreitag m;
~natured gutmütig;
~ness Güte f; **thank
~ness!** Gott sei Dank!;
~will Wohlwollen n, guter Wille.

goose [guːs], pl **geese**
[giːs] Gans f (a. fig.).

goose|**berry** ['guzbəri]
Stachelbeere f; **~flesh**
['guːs-] fig. Gänsehaut f.

gopher ['gəufə] Taschenratte f.

gorge [gɔːdʒ] enge (Fels-)
Schlucht; Mageninhalt m;
gierig verschlingen; (sich)
vollstopfen.

gorgeous ['gɔːdʒəs]
prächtig; colloq. großartig.

gospel ['gɔspəl] Evangelium n.

gossip ['gɔsip] Klatsch m;
Geplauder n; Klatschbase f; klatschen.

got [gɔt] pret u. pp von **get**.
Gothic ['gɔθik] gotisch.

gotten ['gɔtn] Am. pp von **get**.

gourd [guəd] Kürbis m.

gout [gaut] Gicht f.

govern ['gʌvən] regieren;
(be)herrschen; verwalten, lenken, leiten; **~ess**
Erzieherin f; **~ment** Regierung f; pol. Kabinett n;
~or Gouverneur m; colloq.
Alte m (Vater, Chef).

gown [gaun] (Damen-)
Kleid n; Robe f, Talar m.

grab [græb] (hastig) (er)greifen; an sich reißen,
packen.

grace [greis] Gnade f;
Gunst f; jur., econ. Frist f;
Grazie f, Anmut f; Anstand m; Tischgebet n;
Your ~ Euer Gnaden;
~ful anmutig.

gracious ['greiʃəs] gnädig;
gütig; **good** ~ ! du meine
Güte!

grade [greid] Grad m,
Stufe f; Rang m; Qualität
f; Am. Schule: Klasse f;
Note f; einstufen; planieren; **~ crossing** Am.
schienengleicher Bahnübergang; **~ school** Am.
Grundschule f.

gradient ['greidjənt]
Steigung f, Gefälle n.

gradua|**l** ['grædʒuəl] allmählich, stufenweise;
~te ['.'djueit] ein-, (sich)
abstufen; in Grade einteilen; promovieren, e-n
akademischen Grad verleihen od. erlangen;
['.'djuət] Graduierte m,
f; Promovierte m, f; Am.
Absolvent(in); **~tion** [.'dju-
'eiʃən] Abstufung f; Gradeinteilung f; Promotion f;
Am. Abschlußfeier f.

graft [grɑːft] Pfropfreis n;
pfropfen; med. verpflanzen.

grain [grein] (Samen-)
Korn n; Getreide n; fig.
Spur f.

gram [græm] s. **gramme**.

gramma|r ['græmə] Grammatik f; **~r-school** appr. Gymnasium n; **~tical** [grə'mætikəl] grammati(kali)sch.

gramme [græm] Gramm n.

gramophone ['græmə-faun] Grammophon n, Plattenspieler m.

grand [grænd] großartig; erhaben; groß, bedeutend; Groß...; Haupt...; **~child** ['~ntʃ-] Enkel(in); **~daughter** ['~nd͡ɔ:-] Enkelin f; **~eur** ['~ndʒə] Größe f, Hoheit f; Erhabenheit f; Herrlichkeit f; **~father** ['~df-] Großvater m; **~father('s) clock** Standuhr f; **~ma** ['~nma:] colloq. Oma f; **~mother** ['~nm-] Großmutter f; **~pa** ['~npa:] colloq. Opa m; **~parents** ['~np-] pl Großeltern pl; **~son** ['~ns-] Enkel m; **~stand** Tribüne f.

granny ['græni] colloq. Oma f.

grant [gra:nt] Unterstützung f, Zuschuß m; Stipendium n; bewilligen; Bitte etc. erfüllen; zugeben; **take for ~ed** als selbstverständlich annehmen.

granulated sugar ['grænjuleitid] Kristallzucker m.

grape [greip] Weinbeere f, ~traube f; **~fruit** Grapefruit f, Pampelmuse f; **~sugar** Traubenzucker m.

graphic ['græfik] graphisch; anschaulich.

grasp [gra:sp] Griff m; fig. Verständnis n; (er)greifen, packen; fig. verstehen; greifen (at nach).

grass [gra:s] Gras n; Rasen m; Weide f; **~hopper** Heuschrecke f; **~ widow** Strohwitwe f.

grate [greit] (Feuer)Rost m; (zer)reiben; knirschen (mit).

grateful ['greitful] dankbar.

grater ['greitə] Reibeisen n.

grati|fication [grætifi-'keiʃən] Befriedigung f; Freude f; **~fy** ['~fai] befriedigen; erfreuen.

grating ['greitiŋ] rauh, unangenehm; Gitter n.

gratitude ['grætitju:d] Dankbarkeit f.

gratuit|ous [grə-'tju(:)itəs] unentgeltlich; freiwillig; **~y** Gratifikation f; Trinkgeld n.

grave [greiv] ernst; Grab n; **~digger** Totengräber m.

gravel ['grævəl] Kies m.

graveyard Friedhof m.

gravit|ation [grævi-'teiʃən] Schwerkraft f; **~y** ['~ti] Ernst m; Schwere f; Schwerkraft f.

gravy ['greivi] Bratensoße f.

gray [grei] bsd. Am. für **grey.**

graz|e [greiz] (ab)weiden; (ab)grasen; streifen,

schrammen; *Haut* ab-
schürfen; ~ing-land Wei-
deland n.

greas|e [gri:s] Fett n;
Schmiere f; [~z] (be-,
ab)schmieren; ~y ['~zi]
fettig, schmierig, ölig.

great [greit] groß;
Groß...; *colloq.* groß-
artig; ~coat Überzieher
m; ~grandchild Ur-
enkel(in); ~grand-
father Urgroßvater m;
~grandmother Ur-
großmutter f; ~ly sehr;
~ness Größe f; Bedeutung
f.

greed [gri:d] Gier f; ~y
(be)gierig; habgierig.

Greek [gri:k] griechisch;
Griechle m, -in f;
Griechisch n; it's ~ to
me das sind böhmische
Dörfer für mich.

green [gri:n] grün (*a.*
fig.); unreif; *fig.* unerfahren, neu; Grün n;
Grünfläche f; *pl* grünes
Gemüse; ~grocer Ge-
müsehändler(in); ~horn
Grünschnabel m, Neuling
m; ~house Ge-
wächshaus n; ~ish grün-
lich.

greet [gri:t] (be)grüßen;
~ing Gruß m, Begrüßung
f.

grenade [gri'neid] Hand-,
Gewehrgranate f.

grew [gru:] *pret von*
grow.

grey [grei] grau; Grau n;
~hound Windhund m.

grid [grid] Gitter n; *electr.*
Überlandleitungsnetz n;
~(iron) (Brat)Rost m.

grief [gri:f] Kummer m.

griev|ance ['gri:vəns]
Grund m zur Klage, Miß-
stand m; ~e bekümmern,
kränken; bekümmert sein;
~ous schmerzlich; schwer.

grill [gril] grillen; (Brat-)
Rost m, Grill m; gegrilltes
Fleisch; ~(-room) Grill
(-room) m.

grim [grim] grimmig.

grimace [gri'meis]
Fratze f, Grimasse f;
Grimassen schneiden.

grim|e [graim] Schmutz
m; ~y schmutzig.

grin [grin] Grinsen n;
grinsen.

grind [graind] (*irr*) zer-
reiben; (zer)mahlen;
schleifen; *Kaffeemühle*
etc. drehen; mit den
Zähnen knirschen; ~stone
Schleifstein m.

grip [grip] packen (*a. fig.*),
fassen; Griff m (*a. fig.*).

gripes [graips] *pl* Kolik f.

gristle ['grisl] Knorpel m.

grit [grit] Kies m, Sand
m; *fig.* Mut m.

groan [groun] stöhnen.

grocer ['grousə] Lebens-
mittel-, Kolonialwaren-
händler m; ~ies ['~riz] *pl*
Lebensmittel *pl*; ~y Le-
bensmittelgeschäft n.

groin [groin] *anat.* Leiste f.

groom [grum] Reit-,
Pferdeknecht m; Bräuti-
gam m; pflegen.

groove [gru:v] Rinne *f*; Rille *f*.

grope [grəup] tasten.

gross [grəus] dick, fett; grob; derb; Brutto...; Gros *n* (12 Dutzend).

ground¹ [graund] *pret u. pp von* grind.

ground² [graund] Boden *m*, Erde *f*; Gebiet *n*; (Spiel- *etc.*) Platz *m*; Meeresboden *m*; *fig.* Grund *m*; *pl* Grundstück *n*, Park *m*, Gartenanlage *f*; *pl* (Kaffee)Satz *m*; (be)gründen; *electr.* erden.

ground| control *aer.* Bodenkontrollstation *f*; ~ **crew** *aer.* Bodenpersonal *n*; ~ **floor** Erdgeschoß *n*; ~ **glass** Mattglas *n*; ~**hog** Amerikanisches Murmeltier; ~**less** grundlos; ~**nut** Erdnuß *f*; ~ **staff** *aer.* Bodenpersonal *n*.

group [gru:p] Gruppe *f*; (sich) gruppieren.

grove [grəuv] Hain *m*, Gehölz *n*.

grow [grəu] (irr) wachsen; werden; anbauen; (sich) wachsen lassen.

growl [graul] knurren, brummen; grollen (Donner).

grow|n [grəun] *pp von* grow; ~**n-up** erwachsen; Erwachsene *m*, *f*; ~**th** [~θ] Wachstum *n*; (An-)Wachsen *n*; Entwicklung *f*; Wuchs *m*; Produkt *n*, Erzeugnis *n*; *med.* Wucherung *f*.

grub [grʌb] Larve *f*, Made *f*; ~**by** schmierig.

grudge [grʌdʒ] Groll *m*; mißgönnen; ungern geben.

gruel [gruəl] Haferschleim *m*.

gruff [grʌf] grob, schroff, barsch.

grumble ['grʌmbl] murren, brummen; grollen (Donner); ~**r** Nörgler *m*.

grunt [grʌnt] grunzen.

guarant|ee [gærən'ti:] Bürgschaft *f*, Garantie *f*; Kaution *f*, Sicherheit *f*; Bürge *m*; (sich ver-)bürgen für; garantieren; ~**or** [‿'tɔ:] *jur.* Bürge *m*; ~**y** ['‿ti] Bürgschaft *f*, Garantie *f*, Kaution *f*, Sicherheit *f*.

guard [gɑ:d] bewachen, (be)schützen; ~ **against** sich hüten vor; Wache *f*; Aufseher *m*, Wächter *m*, Wärter *m*; *rail.* Schaffner *m*; Schutzvorrichtung *f*; on one's ~ auf der Hut; off one's ~ unachtsam; ~**ian** ['‿jən] *jur.* Vormund *m*; Schutz...; ~**ianship** *jur.* Vormundschaft *f*; 2s *pl in England*: Garde *f*.

guess [ges] Vermutung *f*; vermuten; (er)raten; *Am.* denken.

guest [gest] Gast *m*; ~**house** (Hotel)Pension *f*, Fremdenheim *n*; ~**room** Gäste-, Fremdenzimmer *n*.

guidance ['gaidəns] Führung *f*; (An)Leitung *f*.

guide [gaid] Führer *m*;
Fremdenführer *m*; führen;
lenken, leiten, steuern;
~book (Reise)Führer *m*.

guild [gild] Gilde *f*, Zunft
f, Innung *f*; Vereinigung
f; **2~hall** Rathaus *n* (*London*).

guileless ['gaillis] arglos.

guilt [gilt] Schuld *f*; **~less**
schuldlos; *~y* schuldig.

guinea-pig ['gini-] Meer-
schweinchen *n*.

guitar [gi'tɑ:] Gitarre *f*.

gulf [gʌlf] Meerbusen *m*,
Golf *m*; Abgrund *m*,
Kluft *f*.

gull [gʌl] Möwe *f*.

gullet ['gʌlit] Speiseröhre
f; Gurgel *f*.

gulp [gʌlp] (großer)
Schluck; **~ down** hin-
unterschlingen, -stürzen.

gum [gʌm] Gummi *n*; Klebstoff *m*; *pl* Zahnfleisch *n*;
gummieren; kleben.

gun [gʌn] Gewehr *n*,
Flinte *f*; Geschütz *n*,
Kanone *f*; *Am. colloq.*
Revolver *m*; *Am. colloq.*
~powder Schießpulver *n*.

gurgle ['gə:gl] gluckern,
gurgeln, glucksen.

gush [gʌʃ] Strom *m*, Guß
m; *fig.* Erguß *m*; sich er-
gießen, schießen.

gust [gʌst] Windstoß *m*,
Bö *f*.

guts [gʌts] *pl* Eingeweide
pl; *fig.* Schneid *m*.

gutter ['gʌtə] Dachrinne
f; Gosse *f* (*a. fig.*), Rinn-
stein *m*.

guy [gai] *Am. sl.* Kerl *m*.

gym [dʒim] *sl. abbr.* für
gymnasium, **gym-
nastics**; **~nasium** [~-
'neizjəm] Turnhalle *f*;
~nastics [~'næstiks] *pl*
Turnen *n*; Gymnastik *f*.

gyn(a)ecologist [gaini-
'kɔlədʒist] Frauenarzt *m*.

gypsy ['dʒipsi] *bsd. Am.*
für **gipsy**.

H

haberdasher ['hæbə-
dæʃə] Kurzwarenhändler
m; *Am.* Herrenausstatter
m; *~y* Kurzwaren(ge-
schäft *n*) *pl*; *Am.* Herren-
bekleidungsartikel *pl*; *Am.*
Herrenmodengeschäft *n*.

habit ['hæbit] (An)Ge-
wohnheit *f*; **~ation** Wohnen *n*; Wohnung *f*; **~ual**
[hə'bitjuəl] gewohnt, üb-
lich; gewohnheitsmäßig.

hack [hæk] (zer)hacken.

hackney-carriage ['hækni-]
(Pferde)Droschke *f*.

hack-saw ['hæk-] Me-
tallsäge *f*.

had [hæd] *pret u. pp von*
have.

haddock ['hædək] Schellfisch *m*.

h(a)emorrhage ['hemə-
ridʒ] Blutung *f*.

hag [hæg] Hexe *f*.

haggard ['hægəd] ver-
härmt.

handkerchief

hail [heıl] Hagel *m*; hageln; begrüßen; anrufen.
hair [heə] Haar *n*; **~brush** Haarbürste *f*; **~cut** Haarschnitt *m*; **~do** Frisur *f*; **~dresser** (bsd. Damen)Friseur *m*; *at the* **~dresser's** beim Friseur; **~dryer** Trockenhaube *f*; Fön *m*; **~less** kahl; **~pin** Haarnadel *f*; **~y** haarig, behaart.
half [hɑːf] halb; **~ an hour** e-e halbe Stunde; **~ a pound** ein halbes Pfund; **~ way up** auf halber Höhe; **~ past ten** halb elf (Uhr); **~,** *pl* **halves** [~vz] Hälfte *f*; **~back** *Fußball*: Läufer *m*; **~breed,** **~caste** Mischling *m*; Halbblut *n*; **~penny** ['heıpnı] halber Penny; **~time** *sp.* Halbzeit *f*; **~way** auf halbem Weg *od.* in der Mitte (liegend).
halibut ['hælıbət] Heilbutt *m*.
hall [hɔːl] Halle *f*; Saal *m*; (Haus)Flur *m*, Diele *f*.
hallo [hə'ləu] *int.* hallo!
halo ['heıləu] *ast.* Hof *m*; Heiligenschein *m*.
halt [hɔːlt] Halt(estelle *f*) *m*; Stillstand *m*; (an-)halten.
halter ['hɔːltə] Halfter *m*, *n*; Strick *m* (*zum Hängen*).
halve [hɑːv] halbieren; **~s** [~z] *pl von* **half.**
ham [hæm] Schinken *m*.
hamburger ['hæmbəːgə]

Am. deutsches Beefsteak; mit deutschem Beefsteak belegtes Brötchen.
hamlet ['hæmlıt] Weiler *m*.
hammer ['hæmə] Hammer *m*; (ein)hämmern.
hammock ['hæmək] Hängematte *f*.
hamper ['hæmpə] Geschenk-, Eßkorb *m*; (be-)hindern.
hamster ['hæmstə] Hamster *m*.
hand [hænd] Hand *f* (*a. fig.*); Handschrift *f*; (Uhr-)Zeiger *m*; Mann *m*, Arbeiter *m*; *Karten*: Blatt *n*; **at ~** nahe, bei der Hand; **at first ~** aus erster Hand; **on ~** vorrätig; **on the one ~** einerseits; **on the other ~** andererseits; **on the right ~** rechter Hand, rechts; **change ~s** den Besitzer wechseln; **lend a ~** (mit) anfassen; *vb*: ein-, aushändigen, (über-)geben, (-)reichen; **~ back** zurückgeben; **~ down** überliefern; **~ in** einhändigen, -reichen; **~ over** aushändigen, -liefern; **~bag** Handtasche *f*; **~bill** Hand-, Reklamezettel *m*; **~brake** Handbremse *f*; **~cuffs** *pl* Handschellen *pl*; **~ful** Handvoll *f*; *colloq.* Plage *f*.
handi|cap ['hændıkæp] Handikap *n*; Nachteil *m*; (be)hindern, benachteiligen; **~craft** Handwerk *f*.
handkerchief ['hæŋkə-

tʃi(ː)f] Taschentuch n;
Halstuch n.

handle ['hændl] Griff m;
Stiel m; Henkel m; (Tür-)
Klinke f; anfassen; hand-
haben; umgehen mit; be-
handeln; **~bar** Lenk-
stange f.

hand|luggage Handge-
päck n; **~made** handge-
arbeitet; **~rail** Geländer
n; **~shake** Händedruck m;
~some ['hænsəm] hübsch,
beträchtlich, ansehnlich;
~work Handarbeit f; **~-
writing** (Hand)Schrift f;
~y geschickt; handlich;
zur Hand.

hang [hæŋ] (irr) (auf-,
be-, ein)hängen; Tapete
ankleben; (pret u. pp **~ed**)
(auf-, er)hängen; **~
about** (Am. **around**) herumlungern; **~ out** (heraus)hängen; **~ up** auf-
hängen.

hangar ['hæŋə] Flugzeug-
halle f.

hang|ings ['hæŋiŋz] pl
Wandbehang m; **~man**
Henker m; **~over**
Katzenjammer m, Kater
m.

hanky ['hæŋki] colloq. Taschentuch n.

haphazard ['hæp'hæzəd]
Zufall m; at **~** aufs Geratewohl.

happen ['hæpən] sich ereignen, geschehen, vor-
kommen; he **~ed to be
at home** er war zufällig
zu Hause; **~ (up)on** zu-

fällig treffen auf od. finden;
~ing Ereignis n.

happ|ily ['hæpili] glück-
lich(erweise); **~iness**
Glück n; **~y** glücklich;
froh; erfreut; **~y-go-
lucky** unbekümmert.

harass ['hærəs] belästigen,
quälen; aufreiben.

harbo(u)r ['huːbə] Hafen
m; Zufluchtsort m; be-
herbergen; Groll hegen.

hard [huːd] hart; schwer,
schwierig; kräftig; müh-
sam; fleißig; streng, stark,
heftig; Am. stark (Spiri-
tuosen); fest; **~** by ganz
nahe; **~ up** schlecht bei
Kasse; **~ of hearing**
schwerhörig; **try ~** sich
alle Mühe geben; **work ~**
schwer od. fleißig arbei-
ten; **~en** härten; hart
machen; hart werden, er-
härten; (sich) abhärten;
fig. (sich) verhärten; **~
headed** praktisch, nüch-
tern; **~hearted** hart(her-
zig), herzlos; **~ly** kaum;
~ness Härte f; Strenge f;
~ship Härte f, Not f;
Mühsal f, Beschwerde f;
~ware Eisenwaren pl; **~y**
kühn; widerstandsfähig,
abgehärtet.

hare [hɛə] Hase m; **~bell**
Glockenblume f.

hark [huːk] horchen.

harm [huːm] Schaden m,
Unrecht n; schaden, schä-
digen, verletzen; **~ful**
schädlich; **~less** harmlos,
unschädlich.

harmon|ious [hɑːˈməʊnjəs] harmonisch; **~ize** [ˈˌɔnaiz] in Einklang bringen; harmonieren; **~y** Harmonie *f*.

harness [ˈhɑːnis] (Pferde-) Geschirr *n*; anschirren.

harp [hɑːp] Harfe *f*; Harfe spielen; **~ on** *fig*. herumreiten auf.

harpoon [hɑːˈpuːn] Harpune *f*; harpunieren.

harrow [ˈhærəʊ] Egge *f*; eggen.

harsh [hɑːʃ] rauh; hart; streng, grausam.

hart [hɑːt] Hirsch *m*.

harvest [ˈhɑːvist] Ernte (-zeit) *f*; Ertrag *m*; ernten; **~er** Mähbinder *m*.

has [hæz] *3. sg pres von* **have.**

hash [hæʃ] Haschee *n*; *Fleisch* zerschneiden, -hacken.

hast|e [heist] Eile *f*; Hast *f*; **~ make ~** (sich be)eilen; **~en** [ˈˌsn] (sich be)eilen; *j-n* antreiben; *et.* beschleunigen; **~y** (vor)eilig; hastig; hitzig.

hat [hæt] Hut *m*.

hatch [hætʃ] Luke *f*; Durchreiche *f*; Brut *f*; (Junge) ausbrüten; ausschlüpfen.

hatchet [ˈhætʃit] Beil *n*.

hat|e [heit] Haß *m*; hassen; **~eful** verhaßt; widerlich; **~red** [ˈˌrid] Haß *m*.

haught|iness [ˈhɔːtinis] Hochmut *m*, Stolz *m*; **~y** hochmütig, stolz.

haul [hɔːl] Ziehen *n*; Fischzug *m*; (Transport)Strecke *f*; ziehen, schleppen; transportieren.

haunch [hɔːntʃ] *zo.* Keule *f*.

haunt [hɔːnt] (*bsd.* Lieblings)Platz *m*; Schlupfwinkel *m*; heimsuchen; spuken in; **this place is ~ed** hier spukt es.

have [hæv, həv] (*irr*) haben; bekommen; (haben) mögen, essen, trinken, nehmen; ausführen, machen; lassen; *vor inf*: müssen; **I had my hair cut** ich ließ mir das Haar schneiden; **I had better go** es wäre besser, wenn ich ginge; **I had rather** ich möchte lieber; **~ on** anhaben, tragen; **~ come** gekommen sein; **~ got** *colloq.* haben.

haven [ˈheivn] (*mst fig.* sicherer) Hafen.

havoc [ˈhævək] Verwüstung *f*; **make ~ of, play ~ with** *od.* **among** verwüsten, übel zurichten.

hawk [hɔːk] Habicht *m*; Falke *m*.

hawthorn [ˈhɔːθɔːn] Weiß-, Rotdorn *m*.

hay [hei] Heu *n*; **~cock** Heuschober *m*, -haufen *m*; **~ fever** Heuschnupfen *m*; **~loft** Heuboden *m*; **~rick**, **~stack** Heuschober *m*.

hazard [ˈhæzəd] Zufall *m*; Gefahr *f*, Wagnis *n*, Risiko *n*; wagen; **~ous** gewagt, riskant.

haze [heɪz] Dunst *m*.

hazel ['heɪzl] Haselnuß (-strauch *m*) *f*; nußbraun; ~**nut** Haselnuß *f*.

hazy ['heɪzɪ] dunstig, diesig; *fig.* verschwommen.

H-bomb ['eɪtʃbɒm] H-Bombe *f*, Wasserstoffbombe *f*.

he [hiː] er; *in Zssgn:* männlich, ...männchen *n*.

head [hed] an der Spitze stehen von; (an)führen; Fußball: köpfen; losgehen, zusteuern (**for** auf); Kopf..., Ober...; ~ Kopf *m*, Haupt *n* (*a. fig.*); Leiter *m*, Chef *m*; Direktor *m* (*Schule*); Spitze *f*; oberes Ende; Kopfende *n* (*Bett*); Kopfseite *f* (*Münze*); Vorgebirge *n*, Kap *n*; Bug *m*; Hauptpunkt *m*, Abschnitt *m*; ~ *pl* Stück *pl* (*Vieh*); ~ **over heels** Hals über Kopf; *fig.* völlig; **at the** ~ **of** an der Spitze (*gen*); **off one's** ~ verrückt, übergeschnappt; **come to a** ~ aufbrechen (*Geschwür*); *fig.* sich zuspitzen; **I cannot make** ~ **or tail of it** ich kann daraus nicht schlau werden; ~**ache** Kopfschmerz(en *pl*) *m*, -weh *n*; ~**gear** Kopfbedeckung *f*; ~**ing** Überschrift *f*, Titel *m*; Thema *n*, Punkt *m*; ~**land** Vorgebirge *n*, Kap *n*; ~**light** Scheinwerfer *m*; ~**line** Überschrift *f*; Schlagzeile *f*; ~**long** kopfüber; ~**master** Direktor *m* (*Schule*); ~**mistress** Direktorin *f* (*Schule*); ~**phone** Kopfhörer *m*; ~**quarters** *pl* mil. Hauptquartier *n*; Hauptsitz *m*, Zentrale *f*; ~**strong** eigensinnig, halsstarrig; ~**word** Stichwort *n* (*Wörterbuch*).

heal [hiːl] heilen; ~ **up**, ~ **over** (zu)heilen.

health [helθ] Gesundheit *f*; ~ **resort** Kurort *m*; ~**y** gesund.

heap [hiːp] Haufe(n) *m*; *colloq.* Haufen *m*, Menge *f*; (an-, auf)häufen (*a.* ~ **up**); *fig.* überhäufen; ~schütten.

hear [hɪə] (*irr*) (an-, zu-, Lektion ab)hören; ~**d** [hɜːd] *pret u. pp von* **hear**; ~**er** (Zu)Hörer(in) *f*; ~**ing** Gehör *n*; Anhören *n*; Hörweite *f*; ~**say** Hörensagen *n*; Gerücht *n*.

hearse [hɜːs] Leichenwagen *m*.

heart [hɑːt] Herz *n* (*a. fig.*); Innere *n*; Kern *m*; Mut *m*; Liebling *m*; ~**s** (*pl*) *Karten:* Herz *n*; **by** ~ auswendig; ~**breaking** herzzerbrechend; ~**burn** Sodbrennen *n*; [*fig.*).

hearth [hɑːθ] Herd *m* (*a.*)

heart|less ['hɑːtlɪs] herzlos; ~ **transplant** Herzverpflanzung *f*; ~**y** herzlich; aufrichtig; gesund; herzhaft.

heat [hiːt] Hitze *f*; *fig.* Eifer *m*; *zo.* Läufigkeit *f*, Brunst *f*; *sp.*: Durchgang *m*; Lauf *m*, Einzelrennen

n; heizen; (sich) erhitzen
(a. fig.); ~er Heizgerät n;
Erhitzer m; Ofen m.

heath [hi:θ] Heide(kraut
n) f.

heathen ['hi:ðən] Heid|e
m, -in f; heidnisch.

heather ['heðə] Heide-
kraut n [; Heiz...]

heating ['hi:tiŋ] Heizung ∫

heave [hi:v] (irr) (hoch-)
heben; Anker lichten;
Seufzer ausstoßen; sich
heben und senken, wogen.

heaven ['hevn] Himmel
m; mst pl Himmel m,
Firmament n; good ~s! du
lieber Himmel!; ~ly himm-
lisch.

heaviness ['hevinis]
Schwere f (a. fig.); Druck
m.

heavy ['hevi] schwer; heftig (Regen); trüb(e) (Himmel); unwegsam (Straße);
drückend, lästig; schwer-
fällig; bedrückt, trau-
rig; Schwer...; ~ current
Starkstrom m; ~-handed
ungeschickt; ~ traffic
starker od. dichter Ver-
kehr; ~-weight Schwer-
gewicht(ler m) n.

hectic ['hektik] hektisch.

hedge [hedʒ] Hecke f; ~-
hog Igel m; Am. Stachel-
schwein n.

heed [hi:d] beachten, achten auf; Beachtung f, Aufmerksamkeit f; take ~ od.
give od. pay ~ to achten
auf, beachten; ~less: ~ of
ungeachtet.

heel [hi:l] Ferse f; Absatz
m; take to one's ~s
Reißaus nehmen.

he-goat Ziegenbock m.

heifer ['hefə] Färse f (junge
Kuh).

height [hait] Höhe f;
Höhepunkt m; ~en er-
höhen; vergrößern.

heinous ['heinəs] abscheulich. [Erbin f.]

heir [εə] Erbe m; ~ess]
held [held] pret u. pp von
hold.

helicopter ['helikɔptə]
Hubschrauber m.

hell [hel] Hölle f.

hello ['he'ləu] int. hallo!

helm [helm] Ruder n,
Steuer n.

helmet ['helmit] Helm m.

help [help] Hilfe f;
(Dienst)Mädchen n, Hilfe
f; helfen; geben, reichen
(bei Tisch); ~ o.s. to sich
bedienen mit, sich neh-
men; I can't ~ it ich
kann es nicht ändern, ich
kann nichts dafür; I can-
not ~ laughing ich muß
(einfach) lachen; ~er Hel-
fer(in); Gehilfe m, -in f;
~ful hilfreich, -sbereit;
nützlich; ~ing Portion f;
~less hilflos; ~lessness
Hilflosigkeit f

helter-skelter ['heltə-
'skeltə] holterdiepolter.

hem [hem] Saum m; säumen; sich räuspern, stok-
ken (beim Reden); ~ in
einschließen.

hemisphere ['hemisfiə]

Halbkugel f, Hemisphäre f.

hemline Saum m.

hemlock ['hemlɔk] Schierling m.

hemp [hemp] Hanf m.

hemstitch Hohlsaum m.

hen [hen] Henne f, Huhn n; (Vogel)Weibchen n.

hence [hens] von jetzt an, binnen; daher, deshalb; **~forth**, **~forward** von nun an, künftig.

hen-coop ['henku:p]Hühnerstall m; **~house** Hühnerhaus n; **~pecked** unter dem Pantoffel stehend; **~pecked husband** Pantoffelheld m.

her [hə:] sie; ihr; ihr(e); sich.

herald ['herəld] Herold m; Vorbote m, ankündigen, einführen; **~ry** Wappenkunde f, Heraldik f.

herb [hə:b] Kraut n.

herd [hə:d] Herde f (a. fig.); **~sman** Hirt m.

here [hiə] hier; hierher; **~'s to ...!** auf das Wohl von ...!; **~ you are** hier (bitte)!, da hast du es!; **~after** künftig; **~by** hierdurch.

hereditary [hi'reditəri] erblich, Erb... [von.]

here|in hierin; **~of** hier-]

heresy ['herəsi] Ketzerei f.

here|upon hierauf, darauf (-hin); **~with** hiermit.

heritage ['heritidʒ] Erbe n, Erbschaft f.

hermit ['hə:mit] Einsiedler m.

hero ['hiərəu] Held m; **~ic** [hi'rəuik] heroisch; **~ine** ['herəuin] Heldin f; **~ism** ['herəuizəm] Heldentum n, Heroismus m.

heron ['herən] Reiher m.

herring ['heriŋ] Hering m.

hers [hə:z] ihr, der, die, das ihr(ig)e.

herself [hə:'self] sich (selbst); sie od. ihr selbst; **by ~** allein.

hesitate ['heziteit] zögern, Bedenken tragen; **~ion** Zögern n, Bedenken n.

hew [hju:] (irr) hauen, hacken; **~n** pp von hew.

hey [hei] int. he!, heda!

heyday ['heidei] Höhepunkt m, Blüte f.

hi [hai] int. he!, heda! Am. hallo!

hicc|ough, **~up** ['hikʌp] Schlucken m; den Schlucken haben.

hid [hid] pret u. pp, **~den** pp von hide.

hide [haid] (Tier)Haut f; (irr) (sich) verbergen od. -stecken; **~-and-seek** Versteckspiel n.

hideous ['hidiəs] abscheulich.

hiding[1] ['haidiŋ] Tracht f Prügel.

hiding[2] Versteck n; **be in ~** sich versteckt halten; **~place** Versteck n.

hi-fi ['hai'fai] colloq. s. **high-fidelity**.

high [hai] meteor. Hoch(druckgebiet) n;

hoch; stark, heftig; schrill; teuer; äußerst; angegangen (*Fleisch*); bedeutend, Haupt..., Hoch..., Ober...; erhaben, vornehm, edel; arrogant, hochmütig; *be* ~ *sl.* angeheitert sein; im Drogenrausch sein; **in ~spirits** guter Laune, in gehobener Stimmung; ~ **time** höchste Zeit; **~brow** Intellektuelle *m*, *f*; (betont) intellektuell; ~ **diving** Turmspringen *n*; **~fidelity** mit höchster Wiedergabetreue, Hi-Fi; ~ **jump** Hochsprung *m*; **~lands** *pl* Hochland *n*; **~lights** *pl* Höhepunkt(e *pl*) *m*; **~ly** hoch, sehr; **think ~ly of** viel halten von; **~ness** *fig.*: Höhe *f*; Erhabenheit *f*; 2**ness** Hoheit *f* (*Titel*); **~-pitched** schrill (*Ton*); steil (*Dach*); **~power(ed)** Hochleistungs..., Groß...; **~pressure area** Hochdruckgebiet *n*; ~ **road** Hauptstraße *f*; ~ **school** *Am. appr.* höhere Schule (*bis Mittlere Reife*), Mittelschule *f*; ~ **street** *Brit.* Hauptstraße *f*; **~ tea** kaltes Abendessen mit Tee; **~tide** Flut *f*; **~way** Landstraße *f*; 2**way Code** Straßenverkehrsordnung *f*.

hijack ['haidʒæk] (be-)rauben; entführen.

hike [haik] *colloq.* wandern; Wanderung *f*; **~r** Wanderer *m*.

hilarious [hi'lɛəriəs] vergnügt, ausgelassen.

hill [hil] Hügel *m*, Anhöhe *f*; **~billy** ['~bili] Hinterwäldler *m*; **~side** (Ab-) Hang *m*; **~y** hügelig.

hilt [hilt] Heft *n*, Griff *m*.

him [him] ihn; ihm; den(-), dem(jenigen); sich; **~self** sich (selbst); (er, ihn, ihm) selbst; **by ~self** allein.

hind[1] [haind] Hirschkuh *f*.

hind[2] [haind] Hinter...; **~er** ['hində] (ver)hindern, abhalten; ~ **leg** Hinterbein *n*; **~rance** ['hindrəns] Hindernis *n*.

hinge [hindʒ] (Tür)Angel *f*, Scharnier *n*.

hinny ['hini] Maulesel *m*.

hint [hint] Wink *m*, Hinweis *m*, Tip *m*; Anspielung *f*; andeuten; anspielen.

hinterland ['hintəlænd] Hinterland *n*.

hip [hip] Hüfte *f*.

hippopotamus [hipə-'pɔtəməs] Fluß-, Nilpferd *n*.

hire ['haiə] mieten; *j-n* anstellen; ~ **out** vermieten; *sub*: Miete *f*; (Arbeits-) Lohn *m*; **for ~** zu vermieten; frei (*Taxi*); **on ~** zu vermieten; **~(d) car** Mietauto *n*, -wagen *m*.

his [hiz] sein(e); seine(r, -s), der, die, das sein(ig)e.

hiss [his] zischen; auszischen, -pfeifen; Zischen *n*.

histor|ian [his'tɔːriən] Historiker *m*; **~ic** [~'tɔrik]

hit

hit

hit 446

historical (berühmt *od.* bedeutsam); **~ical** historisch, geschichtlich (belegt), Geschichts...; **~y** ['~əri] Geschichte *f.*

hit [hit] Schlag *m*, Stoß *m*; Treffer *m*; *thea.*, *mus.* Schlager *m*; *fig.* schlagen, stoßen; treffen (*a. fig.*); auf *et.* stoßen; **~ (up)on** (zufällig) auf *et.* stoßen, *et.* treffen *od.* finden; **~-and-run** driving Fahrerflucht *f.*

hitch [hitʃ] Ruck *m*; *fig.* Haken *m*; ziehen; festmachen, ~haken; hängenbleiben; **~hike** per Anhalter fahren **~hiker** Anhalter *m.*

hither ['hiðə] hierher; **~to** bisher.

hive [haiv] Bienenkorb *m*, **~stock** *m*; Bienenvolk *n.*

hoard [hɔːd] Vorrat *m*, Schatz *m*; horten.

hoar-frost ['hɔː'-] (Rauh-) Reif *m.*

hoarse [hɔːs] heiser, rauh.

hoax [həuks] Schabernack *m*, Streich *m*; foppen.

hobble ['hɔbl] humpeln; e-m Pferd die Vorderbeine fesseln.

hobby ['hɔbi] Steckenpferd *n*, Hobby *n*; **~-horse** Schaukelpferd *n*; Steckenpferd *n.* (Kobold *m.*)

hobgoblin ['hɔbgɔblin] (wein.)

hobo ['həubəu] *Am.* Wanderarbeiter *m*, Landstreicher *m.*

hock¹ [hɔk] weißer Rhein-

hock² *zo.* Sprunggelenk *n.*

hockey ['hɔki] Hockey *n.*

hoe [həu] Hacke *f*; hacken.

hog [hɔg] Schwein *n.*

hoist [hɔist] (Lasten)Aufzug *m*; hochziehen; hissen.

hold [həuld] (*irr*) (ab-, an-, auf-, aus-, be)halten; besitzen; Amt innehaben; Stellung halten; fassen, enthalten; Ansicht vertreten, haben; meinen; beibehalten; halten für; *fig.* fesseln; (stand)halten; (an-, fort)dauern; **~ one's ground**, **~ one's own** sich behaupten; **~ tight** sich festhalten; **~ on** sich festhalten; aushalten, ~harren; fortdauern; *teleph.* am Apparat bleiben; **~ s.th. on** *et.* (an s-m Platz fest)halten; **~ to** festhalten an; **~ up** hochheben; halten, stützen; aufrechterhalten; aufhalten; *su:* Halt *m*; Griff *m*; Gewalt *f*,Einfluß *m*; *Lade-*, Frachtraum *m*; **~ catch** (get, lay, seize, take) **~ of** (er)fassen, ergreifen; **keep ~ of** festhalten; **~er** oft in Zssgn: Halter *m*; Pächter *m*; Inhaber(in) (*bsd. econ.*); **~ing** Pachtgut *n*; *mst pl* Besitz *m* (an Effekten *etc.*); **~up** Raubüberfall *m*; Aufhalten *n*, (Verkehrs)Stockung *f.*

hole [həul] Loch *n*; Höhle *f*, Bau *m*; durchlöchern.

holiday ['hɔlədi] Feiertag

m; freier Tag, Ferientag *m*; *mst pl* Ferien *pl*, Urlaub *m*; **on** ~ in den Ferien, auf Urlaub; **~makers** *pl* Urlauber *pl*; **~ village** Feriendorf *m*.

hollow ['hɔləu] Höhle *f*, (Aus)Höhlung *f*; Loch *n*; Mulde *f*, Tal *n*; hohl (*a. fig.*); ~ **(out)** aushöhlen.

holly ['hɔli] Stechpalme *f*.

holy ['həuli] heilig; ℚ **Thursday** Gründonnerstag *m*; ℚ **Week** Karwoche *f*.

home [həum] Heim *n*; Wohnung *f*; Heimat *f*; **at** ~ zu Hause; **make o.s. at** ~ es sich bequem machen; **take s.o.** ~ j-n nach Hause bringen; einheimisch, inländisch, Inland(s)...; nach Hause; ℚ **Counties** *pl* die Grafschaften um London; **~less** heimatlos; obdachlos; **~ly** anheimelnd, häuslich; *fig.* hausbacken; schlicht; **~made** selbstgemacht; ℚ **Office** *Brit.* Innenministerium *n*; ℚ **Secretary** *Brit.* Innenminister *m*; **~sick: be** ~ Heimweh haben; **~sickness** Heimweh *n*; **~ team** *sp.* Gastgeber *pl*; **~ trade** Binnenhandel *m*; **~ward** ['~wəd] heimwärts; Heim...; **~wards** heimwärts; **~work** Hausaufgabe(n *pl*) *f*, Schularbeiten *pl*.

homicide ['hɔmisaid] Totschlag *m*; Mord *m*.

honest ['ɔnist] ehrlich; aufrichtig; ~**y** Ehrlichkeit *f*; Aufrichtigkeit *f*.

honey ['hʌni] Honig *m*; *fig.* Liebling *m*; **~comb** (Honig)Wabe *f*; **~moon** Flitterwochen *pl*; die Flitterwochen verbringen.

honk [hɔŋk] *mot.* hupen.

honorary ['ɔnərəri] Ehren...; ehrenamtlich.

hono(u)r ['ɔnə] Ehre *f*; (Hoch)Achtung *f*; Ansehen *n*; *fig.* Zierde *f*; *pl* Auszeichnung *f*, Ehrung *f*; (be)ehren; *Scheck etc.* einlösen; **~able** ehrenwert; ehrlich; ehrenvoll.

hood [hud] Kapuze *f*; *mot.* Verdeck *n*; *Am.* (Motor-) Haube *f*; *tech.* Kappe *f*.

hoodlum ['hu:dləm] *Am. colloq.* Rowdy *m*, Strolch *m*.

hoodwink ['hudwiŋk] täuschen.

hoof [hu:f], *pl* ~**s, hooves** [~vz] Huf *m*.

hook [huk] (Angel)Haken *m*; Sichel *f*; an-, ein-, fest-, zuhaken; angeln (*a. fig.*); sich (zu)haken lassen; sich festhaken.

hoop [hu:p] (*Faß- etc.*) Reif(en) *m*.

hooping-cough ['hu:piŋ-] Keuchhusten *m*.

hoot [hu:t] heulen, johlen; *mot.* hupen; auspfeifen.

Hoover ['hu:və] (*Fabrikmarke*): Staubsauger *m*; staubsaugen.

hooves [hu:vz] *pl von* **hoof.**

hop

hop [hɔp] *bot.* Hopfen *m*; Sprung *m*; hüpfen, hopsen.

hope [houp] Hoffnung *f*; hoffen (for auf); ∼**ful** hoffnungsvoll; ∼**less** hoffnungslos, verzweifelt.

horizon [hə'raizn] Horizont *m*; ∼**tal** [hɔri'zɔntl] horizontal, waag(e)recht.

horn [hɔːn] Horn *n*; *mot.* Hupe *f*; *pl* Geweih *n*.

hornet ['hɔːnit] Hornisse *f*.

horny ['hɔːni] aus Horn; schwielig.

horr|ible ['hɔrəbl] schrecklich, entsetzlich; ∼**id** ['∼id] schrecklich; ∼**ify** ['∼ifai] entsetzen; ∼**or** Entsetzen *n*; Abscheu *m* (of vor).

horse [hɔːs] Pferd *n*; Bock *m*, Gestell *n*; ∼**back**: **on** ∼ zu Pferde; ∼**hair** Roßhaar *n*; ∼**man** Reiter *m*; ∼**power** Pferdestärke *f*; ∼**race** Pferderennen *n*; ∼**racing** Pferderennsport *m*, -rennen *n*; ∼**radish** Meerrettich *m*; ∼**shoe** Hufeisen *n*.

horticulture ['hɔːtikʌltʃə] Gartenbau *m*.

hos|e [houz] Schlauch *m*; ∼**e** *pl* Strümpfe *pl*; ∼**iery** ['∼iəri] Strumpfwaren *pl*.

hospitable ['hɔspitəbl] gast(freund)lich.

hospital ['hɔspitl] Krankenhaus *n*, Klinik *f*; ∼**ity** [∼'tæliti] Gastfreundschaft *f*.

host [houst] Gastgeber *m*; Hausherr *m*; (Gast)Wirt *m*;

fig. (Un)Menge *f*; Heer *n*; *eccl.* Hostie *f*.

hostage ['hɔstidʒ] Geisel *f*.

hostel ['hɔstl] Herberge *f*; Studenten(wohn)heim *n*.

hostess ['houstis] Gastgeberin *f*; (Gast)Wirtin *f*.

hostile ['hɔstail] feindlich; feindselig; ∼**ity** [∼'tiliti] Feindseligkeit *f*.

hot [hɔt] heiß; scharf; warm; hitzig; heftig.

hot dog colloq. heißes Würstchen *n* im Semmel.

hotel [hou'tel] Hotel *n*.

hot|head Hitzkopf *m*; ∼**house** Treibhaus *n*; ∼**water-bottle** Wärmflasche *f*.

hound [haund] Haus *m*, Jagdhund *m*; jagen, hetzen; drängen.

hour ['auə] Stunde *f*; (Tages)Zeit *f*, Uhr *f*; ∼**ly** stündlich.

house [haus] Haus *n*; the 2 *colloq.* das Parlament; [∼z] unterbringen; ∼**hold** Haushalt *m*; Haushalts...; ∼**keeper** Haushälterin *f*; ∼**keeping** Haushaltung *f*, -wirtschaft *f*; ∼**warming** Einzugsfeier *f*; ∼**wife** Hausfrau *f*; ∼**work** Hausarbeit(en *pl*) *f*, Arbeit *f* im Haushalt.

housing estate ['hauziŋ] (Wohn)Siedlung *f*.

hove [houv] *pret* u. *pp* von **heave**.

hover ['hɔvə] schweben.

how [hau] wie; ∼ **do you do?** (Begrüßungsformel bei der Vorstellung); ∼ **are**

you? – **fine, thank y**ou wie geht es Ihnen? – danke, gut!; ~ **about** ...? wie steht's mit ...?; ~ **much (many)?** wieviel(e)?; ~ **much is it?** was kostet es?; ~**ever** wie auch (immer); jedoch.

howl [haul] heulen; wehklagen; pfeifen (*Wind, Radio*); Heulen *n*, Geheul *n*; ~**er** *colloq.* grober Fehler.

hub [hʌb] (Rad)Nabe *f*.

hubbub ['hʌbʌb] Stimmengewirr *n*; Tumult *m*, Lärm *m*.

hubby ['hʌbi] *colloq.* (Ehe-) Mann *m*.

huckleberry ['hʌklberi] amerikanische Heidelbeere.

huddle ['hʌdl]: ~ **together** (sich) zs.-drängen; ~**d up** zs.-gekauert.

hue [hju:] Farbe *f*.

hug [hʌg] Umarmung *f*; umarmen.

huge [hju:dʒ] sehr groß, riesig, ungeheuer.

hull [hʌl] *bot.* Schale *f*, Hülse *f*; (Schiffs)Rumpf *m*; enthülsen, schälen.

hullabaloo [hʌləbə'lu:] Lärm *m*.

hullo ['hʌ'ləu] *int.* hallo!

hum [hʌm] summen, brummen.

human ['hju:mən] menschlich, Menschen...; ~**e** [ˌ'mein] human; ~**itarian** [ˌmæni'tɛəriən] Menschenfreund *m*;

humanität; ~**ity** [~'mæniti] Menschheit *f*; Humanität *f*.

humble ['hʌmbl] demütig, bescheiden; niedrig, gering; erniedrigen, demütigen; ~**ness** Demut *f*.

humbug ['hʌmbʌg] Schwindel *m*; Schwindler *m*; beschwindeln.

humdrum ['hʌmdrʌm] eintönig, alltäglich.

humidity [hju(:)'miditi] Feuchtigkeit *f*.

humiliat|e [hju(:)'milieit] erniedrigen, demütigen; ~**ion** Erniedrigung *f*, Demütigung *f*.

humility [hju(:)'militi] Demut *f*.

humming-bird Kolibri *m*.

humorous ['hju:mərəs] humoristisch, humorvoll, komisch.

humo(u)r ['hju:mə] Laune *f*, Stimmung *f*; Humor *m*; *j-m* s-n Willen tun *od.* lassen.

hump [hʌmp] Höcker *m*, Buckel *m*; ~**back** Bucklige *m*, *f*.

hunch [hʌntʃ], ~**back** *s.* **hump(back)**.

hundred ['hʌndrəd] hundert; Hundert *n*; ~**th** [ˌ_ʊ] hundertste; ~**weight** *appr.* Zentner *m* (50,8 *kg*).

hung [hʌŋ] *pret. u. pp von* **hang**.

Hungarian [hʌŋ'gɛəriən] ungarisch; Ungar(in); Ungarisch *n*.

hunger

hunger ['hʌŋgə] Hunger *m*; **hungern** (**for, after** nach).

hungry ['hʌŋgri] hungrig; **be ~** Hunger haben.

hunt [hʌnt] Jagd *f*; jagen; **~er** Jäger *m*; **Jagdpferd** *n*; **~ing** Jagen *n*; Jagd...; **~ing-ground** Jagdrevier *n*; **~sman** Jäger *m*.

hurdle ['hɜːdl] Hürde *f* (*a. fig.*); **~r** Hürdenläufer (-in); **~-race** Hürdenlauf *m*.

hurl [hɜːl] schleudern.

hurrah [hu'rɑː], **[**~'rei] *int.* hurra!

hurricane ['hʌrikən] Hurrikan *m*, Wirbelsturm *m*, Orkan *m*.

hurried ['hʌrid] eilig, hastig, übereilt.

hurry ['hʌri] Eile *f*, Hast *f*; **be in a ~** es eilig haben; *vb*: (an)treiben, drängen (*beide a.* **~ up**); (sich be)eilen; (sich be)eilen; **~ up!** beeile dich!

hurt [hɜːt] Verletzung *f*; Schaden *m*; (*irr*) verletzen (*a. fig.*); schmerzen, weh tun; drücken (*Schuh*); (*j-m*) schaden.

husband ['hʌzbənd] (Ehe)Mann *m*; haushalten mit; **~ry** Landwirtschaft *f*.

hush [hʌʃ] Stille *f*; still sein; zum Schweigen bringen; beruhigen; **~ s.th. up** vertuschen; [ʃ:] *int.* still!, pst!

husk [hʌsk] (trockene) Hülse, Schote *f*, Schale *f*; enthülsen, schälen; **~y**

heiser; *colloq.* robust, stämmig.

hustle ['hʌsl] stoßen, (sich) drängen; antreiben; Gedränge *n*, Hütte *f*.

hut [hʌt] Hütte *f*.

hutch [hʌtʃ] (*bsd.* Kaninchen)Stall *m*; Hütte *f*.

hybrid ['haibrid] *biol.* · Mischling *m*, Kreuzung *f*.

hydrant ['haidrənt] Hydrant *m*.

hydraulic [hai'drɔːlik] hydraulisch.

hydro- ['haidrəu-] Wasser...;

hydro|carbon Kohlenwasserstoff *m*; **~chloric acid** [~'klɔrik] Salzsäure *f*; **~gen** ['~idʒən] Wasserstoff *m*; **~gen bomb** Wasserstoffbombe *f*; **~plane** Gleitboot *n*.

hyena [hai'iːnə] Hyäne *f*.

hygiene ['haidʒiːn] Hygiene *f*.

hymn [him] Hymne *f*, Kirchenlied *n*.

hyphen ['haifən] Bindestrich *m*.

hypnotize ['hipnətaiz] hypnotisieren.

hypo|crisy [hi'pɔkrəsi] Heuchelei *f*; **~crite** ['hipəkrit] Heuchler(in); **~critical** [hipəu'kritikəl] heuchlerisch.

hypothesis [hai'pɔθisis] Hypothese *f*.

hysteri|a [his'tiəriə] Hysterie *f*; **~cal** [~'terikəl] hysterisch; **~cs** *pl* hysterischer Anfall.

I

I [ai] ich.

ice [ais] Eis *n*; gefrieren (lassen); vereisen (*a.* **~ up**); mit *od.* in Eis kühlen; überzuckern, glasieren; **~age** Eiszeit *f*; **~berg** ['~bə:g] Eisberg *m*; **~-cream** (Speise)Eis *n*.

icicle ['aisikl] Eiszapfen *m*; **~ing** Zuckerguß *m*; *tech.* Vereisung *f*; **~y** eisig (*a. fig.*); vereist.

idea [ai'diə] Idee *f*; Vorstellung *f*, Begriff *m*, Ahnung *f*; Gedanke *m*, Idee *f*, Einfall *m*; **~l** ideal; Ideal *n*.

identical [ai'dentikəl] identisch, gleich(bedeutend).

identi|fication [aidentifi-'keiʃən] Identifizierung *f*; **~fication papers** *pl* Ausweis(papiere *pl*) *m*; **~fy** ['~'dentifai] identifizieren; ausweisen.

identity [ai'dentiti] Identität *f*; **~ card** (Personal-)Ausweis *m*, Kennkarte *f*.

ideological [aidiə'lɔdʒikəl] ideologisch.

idiom ['idiəm] Idiom *n*, Mundart *f*; Redewendung *f*.

idiot ['idiət] Idiot(in), Dummkopf *m*; Schwachsinnige *m*, *f*; **~ic** [~'ɔtik] blödsinnig.

idle ['aidl] müßig, untätig; träg(e), faul; nutzlos; faulenzen; *tech.* leerlaufen;

~ away vertrödeln; **~ness** Muße *f*; Faulheit *f*.

idol ['aidl] Idol *n*, Abgott *m*; Götzenbild *n*; **~ize** ['~əulaiz] vergöttern.

idyl(l) ['idil] Idyll(e *f*) *n*.

if [if] wenn, falls; ob; Wenn *n*.

igloo ['iglu:] Iglu *m*.

ignit|e [ig'nait] an-, (sich) entzünden; **~ion** [ig'niʃən] *mot.* Zündung *f*; **~ion key** Zündschlüssel *m*.

ignoble [ig'nəubl] schändlich, gemein.

ignor|ance ['ignərəns] Unwissenheit *f*; Unkenntnis *f*; **~ant** ungebildet; nicht wissend *od.* kennend; **~e** [ig'nɔ:] ignorieren, nicht beachten.

ill [il] übel, böse; schlimm, schlecht; krank; **fall ~**, **be taken ~** krank werden; Unglück *n*; Übel *n*, Böse *n*; **~-advised** schlechtberaten, unklug; **~-bred** ungezogen, -höflich.

il|legal [i'li:gəl] illegal, ungesetzlich; **~legible** unleserlich; **~legitimate** unrechtmäßig; unehelich.

ill-humo(u)red übelgelaunt.

il|licit [i'lisit] unerlaubt; **~literate** [i'litərit] ungebildet; Analphabet(in).

ill-judged unvernünftig; **~mannered** ungehobelt, mit schlechten Um-

gangsformen; **~natured**
boshaft, bösartig; **~ness**
Krankheit f; **~tempered**
schlechtgelaunt; **~timed**
ungelegen, unpassend; **~treat** mißhandeln.

illuminate [i'lju:mineit]
be-, erleuchten; fig. erläutern; **~ion** (pl Festf)
Beleuchtung f.

illus|ion [i'lu:ʒən] Illusion f, Täuschung f; **~ive**,
~ory illusorisch, trügerisch.

illustrat|e ['iləstreit] illustrieren; erläutern; bebildern; **~ion** Erläuterung
f; Illustration f; Abbildung f; **~ive** erläuternd.

illustrious [i'lʌstriəs] berühmt.

ill will Feindschaft f.

image ['imidʒ] Bild(nis)
n; Statue f; Ebenbild n;
Vorstellung f; **~ry** Bilder
pl, Bildwerk(e pl) n; Bildersprache f.

imagin|able [i'mædʒinəbl] denkbar; **~ary** eingebildet; **~ation** Phantasie
f, Einbildung(skraft) f; **~e**
[~in] sich j-m od. et. vorstellen; sich et. einbilden.

imbecile ['imbisi:l] geistesschwach; dumm; Schwachsinnige m; Narr m.

imitat|e ['imiteit] nachahmen, imitieren; **~ion**
Nachahmung f; Nachbildung f; unecht, künstlich,
Kunst...

im|material [imə'tiəriəl] unwesentlich;

~mature unreif; **~measurable** unermeßlich.

immediate [i'mi:djət]
unmittelbar, unverzüglich,
sofort; **~ly** sofort; unmittelbar.

im|mense [i'mens] ungeheuer; **~merse** [i'mə:s]
(ein)tauchen; vertiefen.

immigra|nt ['imigrənt]
Einwanderer m, -in f; **~te**
['~eit] einwandern; **~tion**
Einwanderung f.

imminent ['iminənt] bevorstehend, drohend.

im|mobile [i'məubail] unbeweglich; **~moderate**
übermäßig, maßlos; **~modest** unbescheiden; **~moral** unmoralisch.

immortal [i'mɔ:tl] unsterblich; Unsterbliche
m, f; **~ity** ['~'tæliti] Unsterblichkeit f.

im|movable [i'mu:vəbl]
unbeweglich; unerschütterlich; **~mune** [i'mju:n]
immun.

imp [imp] Teufelchen n;
Schlingel m.

impact ['impækt] Stoß m,
Zs.-prall m; fig. (Ein-)
Wirkung f.

impair [im'pɛə] schwächen; beeinträchtigen.

impart [im'pɑ:t] geben;
mitteilen; **~ial** [~ʃəl] unparteiisch; **~iality** ['~ʃiæliti] Unparteilichkeit f.

im|passable [im'pɑ:səbl] unpassierbar; **~passive** teilnahmslos. [**~t** ungeduldig.]

impatien|ce Ungeduld f;}

impotence

impediment [im'pedimənt] Behinderung f.

im|pend [im'pend] bevorstehen, drohen; **~penetrable** [~'penitrəbl] undurchdringlich; *fig.* unzugänglich.

imperative [im'perətiv] unumgänglich, unbedingt erforderlich; befehlend, gebieterisch; **~ (mood)** *gr.* Imperativ *m*, Befehlsform *f*.

imperceptible unmerklich.

imperfect [im'pə:fikt] unvollkommen; unvollendet; **~ (tense)** *gr.* Imperfekt *n*, unvollendete Vergangenheit.

imperial [im'piəriəl] kaiserlich; großartig; **~ism** Imperialismus *m*.

im|peril [im'peril] gefährden; **~perious** [im'piəriəs] herrisch; dringend; **~permeable** undurchlässig.

imperson|al unpersönlich; **~ate** [im'pə:səneit] verkörpern; *thea.* darstellen.

impertinen|ce [im'pə:tinəns] Unverschämtheit *f*; **~t** unverschämt.

im|perturbable [im'pə:'tə:bəbl] unerschütterlich; **~pervious** [~'pə:vjəs] undurchlässig; *fig.* unzugänglich (**to** für); **~petuous** [~'petjuəs] ungestüm, heftig; **~placable** [~'plækəbl] unversöhnlich.

implement ['implimənt] Werkzeug *n*, Gerät *n*.

implicat|e ['implikeit] verwickeln; **~ion** Verwick(e)lung *f*; Folge *f*; tieferer Sinn.

im|plicit [im'plisit] (mit *od.* stillschweigend) inbegriffen; blind (*Glaube etc.*); **~plore** [~'plɔ:] *j-n* dringend bitten *od.* anflehen; **~ply** [~'plai] in sich schließen; bedeuten; andeuten; **~polite** unhöflich.

import ['impɔ:t] Einfuhr *f*, Import *m*; *pl* Einfuhrwaren *f/pl*; Bedeutung *f*; Wichtigkeit *f*; [~'pɔ:t] einführen, importieren; bedeuten; **~ance** [~'pɔ:təns] Wichtigkeit *f*, Bedeutung *f*; **~ant** wichtig, bedeutend; wichtigtuerisch; **~ation** Import *m*, Einfuhr(ware) *f*.

importune [im'pɔ:tju:n] dauernd bitten, belästigen.

impos|e [im'pəuz] auferlegen, aufbürden (**on**, **upon** *dat*); **~e upon** *j-n* täuschen; **~ing** eindrucksvoll, imponierend.

impossib|ility Unmöglichkeit *f*; **~le** unmöglich.

impostor [im'pɔstə] Hochstapler(in).

impoten|ce ['impətəns] Unvermögen *n*, Unfähigkeit *f*; Machtlosigkeit *f*; *med.* Impotenz *f*; **~t** unfähig; machtlos; schwach; *med.* impotent.

impracticable undurchführbar; unwegsam.

impregnate ['impregneit] schwängern; imprägnieren.

impress ['impres] Ab-, Eindruck *m*; [.'pres] (auf-)drücken; einprägen (**on** *dat*); j-n beeindrucken; **~ion** Eindruck *m*; Abdruck *m*; **be under the ~ion** den Eindruck haben; **~ive** eindrucksvoll.

imprint [im'print] (auf-)drücken; aufdrücken; *fig.* einprägen (**on** *dat*); ['~] Abdruck *m*.

imprison [im'prizn] einsperren; **~ment** Haft *f*; Gefängnis(strafe *f*) *n*.

im|probable unwahrscheinlich; **~proper** unpassend; falsch; unanständig.

improve [im'pruːv] verbessern; sich (ver)bessern; **~ment** (Ver)Besserung *f*; Fortschritt *m*.

improvise ['improvaiz] improvisieren; **~prudent** [.'pruːdənt] unklug, unüberlegt.

impuden|ce ['impjudəns] Unverschämtheit *f*, Frechheit *f*; **~t** unverschämt.

impulse ['impʌls] Antrieb *m*; *fig. a.* Impuls *m*, Drang *m*; **~ive** (an)treibend; *fig.* impulsiv.

im|punity [im'pjuːniti] **with ~** straflos, ungestraft;

~pure [.'pjuə] unrein (*a. fig.*); schmutzig; **~pute** [.'pjuːt] zuschreiben.

in [in] *prp* in, auf, an; **~ the street** auf der Straße; **~ 1972** im Jahre 1972; **~ English** auf englisch; **~ my opinion** meiner Meinung nach; **~ Shakespeare** bei Shakespeare; *adv* hinein; herein; (dr)innen; zu Hause; da, angekommen; modern.

in|ability Unfähigkeit *f*; **~accessible** [inæk'sesəbl] unzugänglich; **~accurate** ungenau; falsch.

inactiv|e untätig; **~ity** Untätigkeit *f*.

in|adequate unangemessen; unzulänglich; **~advertent** [inəd'vəːtənt] unachtsam; unabsichtlich; **~alterable** unveränderlich; **~animate** [.'ænimit] leblos; *fig.* unbelebt; geistlos, langweilig; **~appropriate** unangebracht; unpassend; **~apt** ungeschickt; unpassend; **~articulate** undeutlich; sprachlos.

inasmuch [inəz'mʌtʃ]: **~ as** da, weil.

in|attentive unaufmerksam; **~audible** unhörbar.

inaugura|l [i'nɔːgjurəl] Antrittsrede *f*; Antritts...; **~te** [.~eit] (feierlich) einführen; einweihen, eröffnen; einleiten, beginnen.

inborn ['in'bɔːn] angeboren.

incalculable [in'kælkjuləbl] unzählbar; unberechenbar.

incapa|ble unfähig, **~citate** [inkə'pæsiteit] arbeitsunfähig *od.* untauglich machen; **~city** Unfähigkeit *f*, Untauglichkeit *f*.

incautious unvorsichtig.

incendiary [in'sendjəri] Feuer...; Brand...; Brandstifter *m*.

incense[1] ['insens] Weihrauch *m*.

incense[2] [in'sens] erzürnen, erbosen.

incessant [in'sesnt] unaufhörlich, ständig.

incest ['insest] Blutschande *f*.

inch [intʃ] Zoll *m* (= 2,54 cm).

incident ['insidənt] Vorfall *m*, Ereignis *n*; *pol.* Zwischenfall *m*; **~al** [~'dentl] beiläufig, nebensächlich; Begleit...; Neben...; **~ally** beiläufig; zufällig.

incinerate [in'sinəreit] (zu Asche) verbrennen.

incis|e [in'saiz] einschneiden; **~ion** [~'iʒən] (Ein-)Schnitt *m*; **~ive** scharf, schneidend; **~or** Schneidezahn *m*.

incite [in'sait] anspornen, anregen; aufhetzen.

inclement [in'klemənt] rauh (*Klima*, *Wetter*).

inclin|ation [inkli'neiʃən] Neigung *f* (*a. fig.*); **~e** [in'klain] (sich) neigen;

abfallen; geneigt sein (**to** *dat*); veranlassen, bewegen; Neigung *f*, Abhang *m*.

inclos|e [in'klouz], **~ure** [~ʒə] *s.* enclose, enclosure.

inclu|de [in'klu:d] einschließen; **~sive** einschließlich (**of** *gen*); **~sive terms** *pl* Pauschalpreis *m*.

incoherent unzs.-hängend.

income ['inkʌm] Einkommen *n*; **~-tax** ['~əmtæks] Einkommensteuer *f*.

incoming ['inkʌmiŋ] hereinkommend; ankommend.

in|comparable unvergleichlich; **~compatible** unvereinbar; **~competent** unfähig; unbefugt; **~complete** unvollständig; **~comprehensible** unbegreiflich; **~conceivable** unbegreiflich; **~consequent** inkonsequent.

inconsidera|ble unbedeutend; **~te** unüberlegt; rücksichtslos.

in|consistent unvereinbar; widerspruchsvoll; **~consolable** untröstlich; **~constant** unbeständig; wankelmütig.

inconvenien|ce Unbequemlichkeit *f*; Unannehmlichkeit *f*, Ungelegenheit *f*; belästigen; **~t** unbequem; ungelegen, lästig.

incorporate [in'kɔ:pəreit] (sich) vereinigen; einver-

leiben; ~[~rit], ~d [~reitid]
(amtlich) eingetragen.
in|correct unrichtig; ~
corrigible unverbesser-
lich.
increas|e [in'kri:s] zu-
nehmen, größer werden,
(an)wachsen; vermehren,
-größern, erhöhen; ['in-
kri:s] Zunahme f, Ver-
größerung f, Erhöhung
f, Zuwachs m, Steigen n;
~ingly immer mehr.
incred|ible unglaublich;
~ulous ungläubig, skep-
tisch; [neit] belasten.
incriminate [in'krimi-
incubator [in'kjubeita]
Brutapparat m.
incur [in'kə:] sich et. zuziehen; Verpflichtung eingehen; Verlust erleiden.
in|curable unheilbar;
~debted verschuldet; fig.
zu Dank verpflichtet.
indecen|cy Unanständig-
keit f; ~t unanständig, un-
sittlich.
indecis|ion Unentschlos-
senheit f; ~ive nicht ent-
scheidend; unentschlos-
sen.
indeed [in'di:d] in der
Tat, tatsächlich, wirklich,
allerdings; int. ach wirklich!, nicht möglich!
in|defatigable [indi-
'fætigəbl] unermüdlich;
~definite unbestimmt;
unbegrenzt; ~delible
[~'delibl] unauslöschlich;
untilgbar; ~delicate un-
fein; taktlos.

indemni|fy [in'demnifai]
entschädigen; sichern;
~ty Entschädigung f;
Sicherstellung f.
indent [in'dent] (ein)ker-
ben, (aus)zacken; ['~] Kerbe f; ~ure [in'dentʃə]
Vertrag m; Lehrvertrag m.
independen|ce Unab-
hängigkeit f; Selbständig-
keit f; ~t unabhängig;
selbständig.
in|describable [indis-
'kraibəbl] unbeschreib-
lich; ~determinate [~-
di'tə:minit] unbestimmt.
index [indeks] Zeiger m;
(Inhalts-, Namen-, Sach-)
Verzeichnis n, Register n;
fig. (An)Zeichen n; ~
(finger) Zeigefinger m.
Indian [indjən] indisch;
indianisch; Inder(in);
(Red) ~ Indianer(in); ~
corn Mais m; ~ file:
in ~ im Gänsemarsch; ~
summer Altweibersom-
mer m.
India-rubber ['indjə'rʌbə]
Radiergummi m.
indicat|e [indikeit] (an-)
zeigen; hinweisen auf;
andeuten; ~ion Anzeichen
n; Andeutung f; ~ive
(mood) [in'dikativ] gr.
Indikativ m, Wirklich-
keitsform f; ~or ['~eitə]
Zeiger m; Anzeigevor-
richtung f; mot. Blinker m.
indict [in'dait] anklagen;
~ment Anklage f.
indifferen|ce Gleich-

gültigkeit f; ~t gleich-
gültig; mittelmäßig.
indigent ['indidʒənt] arm.
indigest|ible unverdau-
lich; **~ion** Verdauungs-
störung f, Magenverstim-
mung f.
indign|ant [in'dignənt]
entrüstet, empört; **~ation**
Entrüstung f, Empörung f.
indirect indirekt; nicht
direkt *od.* gerade.
indiscre|et unklug; in-
diskret; **~tion** Unüber-
legtheit f; Indiskretion f.
in|discriminate [indis-
'kriminit] wahllos; **~dis-
pensable** unentbehrlich.
indispos|ed [indis'pəuzd]
unpäßlich; abgeneigt;
~ition Unpäßlichkeit f;
Abneigung f.
in|disputable ['indis-
'pju:təbl] unbestreitbar;
unbestritten; **~distinct**
undeutlich, unklar.
individual [indi'vidjuəl]
persönlich; individuell;
einzeln; Individuum n;
~ist Individualist m.
indivisible unteilbar.
indolen|ce ['indələns]
Trägheit f; **~t** träge,
lässig.
indomitable [in'dɔmi-
təbl] unbezähmbar, un-
beugsam.
indoor ['indɔ:] im Hause;
Haus..., Zimmer..., *sp.* Hallen...; **~s** [in'dɔ:z] im *od.*
zu Hause; ins Haus.
indorse [in'dɔ:s] *s.* **endorse.**

induce [in'dju:s] veranlassen; verursachen.
induct [in'dʌkt] einführen,
-setzen.
indulge [in'dʌldʒ] nachsichtig sein gegen; *j-m*
nachgeben; frönen; **~**
in s.th. sich *et.* hingeben
od. gönnen; **~nce** Nach-
sicht f; Befriedigung f;
Schwelgen n; **~nt** nachsichtig.
industrial [in'dʌstriəl] in-
dustriell, gewerblich, Industrie..., Gewerbe...; **~**
area Industriegebiet n;
~ city Industriestadt f;
~ist Industrielle m; **~ize**
industrialisieren.
industr|ious [in'dʌstriəs]
fleißig; **~y** ['indəstri] Industrie f; Gewerbe n;
Fleiß m.
in|effective, **~efficient**
wirkungslos; unfähig;
~equality Ungleichheit f.
inert [i'nə:t] träge; **~ia**
[~'ʃiə] Trägheit f.
in|estimable [in'esti-
məbl] unschätzbar; **~**
evitable [~'evitəbl] un-
vermeidlich; **~excusable**
unverzeihlich; **~exhaust-
ible** unerschöpflich;
~expensive nicht teuer,
preiswert; **~experienced**
unerfahren; **~explicable**
[~'eksplikəbl] unerklärlich.
inexpress|ible [iniks-
'presəbl] unaussprech-
lich; **~ive** ausdruckslos.
infallible [in'fæləbl] un-
fehlbar.

infam|ous ['infəməs]
schändlich; **-y** Niedertracht f; Schande f.

infan|cy ['infənsi] frühe
Kindheit; **-t** Säugling m;
kleines Kind, Kleinkind n.

infantile ['infəntail] kindlich, Kinder...; kindisch.

infantry ['infəntri] Infanterie f.

infatuated [in'fætjueitid]:
~ with vernarrt in.

infect [in'fekt] infizieren,
anstecken (a. fig.); verseuchen; **-ion** Infektion f,
Ansteckung f; **-ious** ansteckend.

infer [in'fə:] schließen;
-ence ['infərəns] Schlußfolgerung f, (Rück)Schluß
m.

inferior [in'fiəriə] Untergebene m, f; unter; minderwertig; **~ to** niedriger od. geringer als; untergeordnet; unterlegen; **-ity**
[.'ɔriti] Unterlegenheit f;
Minderwertigkeit f.

infernal [in'fə:nl] höllisch.

infest [in'fest] heimsuchen,
plagen, verseuchen.

infidelity Unglaube m;
Untreue f.

infiltrate ['infiltreit] einsickern (in); durchsetzen;
eindringen.

infinite ['infinit] unendlich.

infinitive (mood) [in-
'finitiv] gr. Infinitiv m,
Nennform f.

infinity [in'finiti] Unendlichkeit f.

infirm [in'fə:m] schwach,
gebrechlich; **-ary** Krankenhaus n; **-ity** Gebrechlichkeit f, (Alters)Schwäche f.

inflame [in'fleim] (sich)
entzünden; fig. entflammen, erregen.

inflamma|ble [in'flæməbl] feuergefährlich; **~tion** [.ə'meiʃən] Entzündung f; **-tory** [in'flæmətəri] med. Entzündungs...;
fig. aufrührerisch, Hetz...

inflat|e [in'fleit] aufblasen,
-pumpen, -blähen; **-ion**
econ. Inflation f; fig. Aufgeblasenheit f.

inflect [in'flekt] biegen; gr.
flektieren, beugen.

inflex|ible [in'fleksəbl]
starr; fig. unbeugsam;
-ion [.kʃən] Biegung f;
gr. Flexion f, Beugung f.

inflict [in'flikt] Leid zufügen; Wunde beibringen;
Schlag versetzen; Strafe
verhängen; **-ion** Zufügung f; Plage f.

influen|ce ['influəns] Einfluß m; beeinflussen; **-tial**
[.'enʃəl] einflußreich.

influenza [influ'enzə]
Grippe f.

inform [in'fɔ:m]: **~ (of)**
benachrichtigen (von), informieren (über); j-m mitteilen; **~ against s.o.**
j-n anzeigen; **-al** zwanglos.

information [infə'meiʃən] Auskunft f; Nachricht f, Information f;

~ bureau Auskunftsbüro n; **~ desk** Informationsschalter m; **~ office** Auskunftsbüro n.

inform|ative [in'fɔ:mətiv] informatorisch; lehrreich; **~er** Denunziant m; Spitzel m.

infuriate [in'fjuərieit] wütend machen.

infuse [in'fju:z] aufgießen; fig. einflößen.

ingeni|ous [in'dʒi:njəs] geistreich, klug; erfinderisch; kunstvoll, raffiniert; **~uity** [~i'nju(:)iti] Klugheit f, Geschicklichkeit f.

ingot ['iŋgət] (Gold- etc.) Barren m.

ingrati|ate [in'greiʃieit]: **~ o.s.** sich einschmeicheln (**with** bei); **~tude** [~'grætitju:d] Undank(barkeit f) m.

ingredient [in'gri:djənt] Bestandteil m; pl Zutaten pl.

inhabit [in'hæbit] bewohnen; **~able** bewohnbar; **~ant** Bewohner(in); Einwohner(in).

inhale [in'heil] einatmen.

inherent [in'hiərənt] innewohnend, angeboren, eigen.

inherit [in'herit] erben; **~ance** Erbe n; Erbschaft f.

inhibit [in'hibit] hemmen; **~ion** Hemmung f.

in|hospitable ungastlich, unwirtlich; **~human** unmenschlich.

initia|l [i'niʃəl] anfänglich, Anfangs..., Ausgangs...;

Anfangsbuchstabe m; **~te** [~ʃieit] beginnen; einführen, -weihen; **~tion** Einleitung f; Einführung f; **~tive** [~ʃiativ] Initiative f.

inject [in'dʒekt] einspritzen; **~ion** Injektion f, Spritze f.

injudicious unklug.

injur|e ['indʒə] beschädigen; schaden; verletzen, -wunden; fig. kränken; **~ed:** the ~ pl die Verletzten pl; **~ed person** Verletzte m, f; **~ious** [in'dʒuəriəs] schädlich; **be ~ious** schaden (**to** dat); **~y** ['~əri] Verletzung f, Wunde f; Schaden m; fig. Beleidigung f.

injustice Ungerechtigkeit f, Unrecht n.

ink [iŋk] Tinte f.

inkling ['iŋkliŋ] Andeutung f; leise Ahnung.

ink-pot Tintenfaß n.

inland ['inlənd] inländisch; Binnen...; Landesinnere n; Binnenland n; ['inlænd] adv im Innern des Landes; landeinwärts.

inlay ['in'lei] (irr **lay**) einlegen.

inlet ['inlet] schmale Bucht; Einlaß m. [m, -in f.]

inmate ['inmeit] Insasse m.

inmost ['inməust] innerst, fig. a. geheimst.

inn [in] Gasthaus m, -hof m.

innate ['i'neit] angeboren.

inner ['inə] inner, Innen...; **~most** s. inmost; **~ tube** (Fahrrad- etc.) Schlauch m.

innkeeper Gastwirt(in).

innocen|ce [ˈinəsns] Unschuld f; **~t** unschuldig; Unschuldige m, f.

innovation [inəuˈveiʃən] Neuerung f.

innumerable [iˈnjuːmərəbl] unzählig, zahllos.

inoculate [iˈnɔkjuleit] (ein)impfen; **~ion** Impfung f.

inoffensive harmlos.

in-patient [ˈinpeiʃənt] Krankenhauspatient(in).

inquest [ˈinkwest] jur. gerichtliche Untersuchung.

inquir|e [inˈkwaiə] fragen od. sich erkundigen (nach); **~e into** untersuchen; **~y** Erkundigung f, Nachfrage f; Untersuchung f.

inquisitive [inˈkwizitiv] neugierig; wißbegierig.

insan|e [inˈsein] geisteskrank; **~ity** [inˈsæniti] Geisteskrankheit f.

insatia|ble [inˈseiʃəbl], **~te** [~iit] unersättlich.

inscri|be [inˈskraib] (ein-, auf)schreiben; beschriften; **~ption** [~ipʃən] Inschrift f.

insect [ˈinsekt] Insekt n.

insecure unsicher.

insensi|ble unempfindlich; bewußtlos; unmerklich; gleichgültig; **~tive** unempfindlich.

inseparable untrennbar; unzertrennlich.

insert [inˈsəːt] einsetzen, -fügen; (hin)einstecken; Münze einwerfen; **~ion**

Einsetzung f, Einfügung f; Einwurf m (Münze).

inshore [ˈinˈʃɔː] an od. nahe der Küste; Küsten...

inside [inˈsaid] Innenseite f; Innere n; **turn ~ out** umkrempeln; inner, Innen...; im Innern, drinnen; nach innen, hinein; innerhalb; **~ left** sp. Halblinke m; **~ right** sp. Halbrechte m.

insight [ˈinsait] Einblick m; Einsicht f.

in|significant unbedeutend; **~sincere** unaufrichtig; **~sinuate** [~ˈsinjueit] zu verstehen geben; andeuten; **~sipid** [~ˈsipid] geschmacklos, fad.

insist [inˈsist]: **~ (up)on** bestehen auf; dringen auf.

in|solent [ˈinsələnt] unverschämt; **~soluble** [~ˈsɔljubl] unlöslich; fig. unlösbar; **~solvent** zahlungsunfähig.

insomnia [inˈsɔmniə] Schlaflosigkeit f.

insomuch [insəuˈmʌtʃ] dermaßen, so (sehr).

inspect [inˈspekt] untersuchen, prüfen; inspizieren; **~ion** Prüfung f, Untersuchung f; Inspektion f; **~or** Inspektor m.

inspir|ation [inspəˈreiʃən] Inspiration f, Eingebung f; **~e** [inˈspaiə] erfüllen; inspirieren.

insta|l(l) [inˈstɔːl] tech. installieren; in ein Amt einsetzen; **~llation** [~əˈleiʃən] *tech.* Anlage *f*; Installation *f*; (Amts)Einsetzung *f*; **~l(l)ment** [~'stɔːlmənt] Rate *f*, Teilzahlung *f*; Fortsetzung *f* (*Roman*).

instance ['instəns] Ersuchen *n*; Beispiel *n*, Fall *m*; **for ~** zum Beispiel.

instant ['instənt] dringend; sofortig, augenblicklich; Augenblick *m*; **~a~neous** [~'teinjəs] augenblicklich; **~ly** sofort.

instead [in'sted] statt dessen; **~ of** anstatt, an Stelle von.

instep ['instep] Spann *m*.

instigat|e ['instigeit] anstiften; **~or** Anstifter *m*.

instil(l) [in'stil] einflößen.

instinct ['instiŋkt] Instinkt *m*; **~ive** [in'stiŋktiv] instinktiv.

institut|e ['institjuːt] Institut *n* (*a. Gebäude*); (gelehrte *etc.*) Gesellschaft; **~ion** Institut *n*; Institution *f*, Einrichtung *f*.

instruct [in'strʌkt] unterrichten; ausbilden; anweisen; informieren; **~ion** Unterricht *m*, Ausbildung *f*; Vorschrift(en *pl*) *f*, Anweisung (*pl*) *f*; **~ive** lehrreich; **~or** Lehrer *m*; Ausbilder *m*.

instrument ['instrumənt] Instrument *n*; Werkzeug *n*.

in|subordinate [insə-'bɔːdnit] aufsässig; **~suf~ferable** unerträglich; **~sufficient** unzulänglich, ungenügend.

insulate ['insjuleit] isolieren.

insult ['insʌlt] Beleidigung *f*; [in'sʌlt] beleidigen.

insupportable [insə'pɔː-təbl] unerträglich.

insur|ance [in'ʃuərəns] Versicherung *f*; Versicherungs...; **~ance policy** Versicherungspolice *f*, **~-schein** *m*; **~e** versichern.

insurmountable [insə(ː)-'mauntəbl] unüberwindlich.

insurrection [insə'rekʃən] Aufstand *m*.

intact [in'tækt] unberührt; unversehrt, intakt.

integrate ['intigreit] zs.-schließen, vereinigen; eingliedern; integrieren.

integrity [in'tegriti] Integrität *f*, Rechtschaffenheit *f*; Ganzheit *f*, Vollständigkeit *f*.

intellect ['intilekt] Verstand *m*; **~ual** [~'lektjuəl] intellektuell, geistig; Intellektuelle *m*, *f*.

intellig|ence [in'telidʒəns] Intelligenz *f*; Nachricht *f*; **~ent** intelligent, klug; **~ible** verständlich.

intemperate [in'tempərit] unmäßig.

intend [in'tend] beabsichtigen; bestimmen.

intens|e [in'tens] intensiv, stark, heftig; angestrengt; **~ify** [~ifai] (sich) verstärken *od.* steigern; **~ity** Intensität *f*; **~ive** intensiv.

intent [in'tent] Absicht *f*;

gespannt; ~ **(up)on** bedacht auf, beschäftigt mit; **~ion** Absicht *f*; **~ional** absichtlich.

inter [in'tɜ:] beerdigen.

inter|cede [intə(:)'si:d] vermitteln; **~cept** [~'sept] abfangen; abhören; **~cession** [~ə'seʃən] Fürsprache *f*.

interchange [intə(:)-'tʃeindʒ] austauschen; abwechseln; ['~'tʃeindʒ] Austausch *m*.

intercourse ['intə(:)kɔ:s] Umgang *m*; Verkehr *m*.

interdict [intə(:)'dikt] untersagen, verbieten.

interest ['intrist] Interesse *n*; Bedeutung *f*; *econ.* Anteil *m*, Beteiligung *f*; Zins (-en *pl*) *m*; **take an ~ in** sich interessieren für; *vb*: interessieren (**in** für); **~ed** interessiert (**in** an); **~ing** interessant.

interfere [intə'fiə] sich einmischen; eingreifen; **~ with** stören; **~nce** Einmischung *f*, Eingreifen *n*; Störung *f*.

interior [in'tiəriə] inner, Innen...; Innere *n*; **Department of the** ♀ *Am.* Innenministerium *n*; **~ decorator** Innenarchitekt *m*.

inter|jection [intə(:)'dʒekʃən] Interjektion *f*, Ausruf *m*; **~lude** ['~lu:d] Zwischenspiel *n*.

intermedia|ry [intə(:)-'mi:djəri] Zwischen...; vermittelnd; Vermittler *m*; **~te** [~jət] dazwischenliegend, Zwischen..., Mittel...; **~te landing** *aer.* Zwischenlandung *f*.

inter|mingle (sich) vermischen; **~mission** Unterbrechung *f*, Pause *f*; **~mittent fever** [intə(:)-'mitənt] Wechselfieber *n*.

intern ['intɜ:n] *Am.* Assistenzarzt *m*; **~al** [~'tɜ:nl] inner(lich).

inter|national international; **~pose** *Veto* einlegen; unterbrechen; dazwischentreten; vermitteln.

interpret [in'tɜ:prit] interpretieren, auslegen; (ver-) dolmetschen; **~ation** Interpretation *f*; Auslegung *f*; **~er** Dolmetscher(in).

interrogat|e [in'terəugeit] (be)fragen; vernehmen, -hören; **~ion** Vernehmung *f*, -hör *n*; Befragung *f*; **note (mark, point) of ~ion** Fragezeichen *n*; **~ive** [intə-'rɔgətiv] fragend; *ling.* interrogativ, Frage...

interrupt [intə'rʌpt] unterbrechen; **~ion** Unterbrechung *f*.

intersect [intə(:)'sekt] sich schneiden *od.* kreuzen; **~ion** Schnittpunkt *m*; (Straßen)Kreuzung *f*.

interval ['intəvəl] Zwischenraum *m*; Abstand *m*; Pause *f*.

interven|e [intə(:)'vi:n] dazwischenkommen; sich

einmischen; vermitteln; **~tion** [~venʃən] Eingreifen *n*, Einmischung *f*.

interview ['intəvju:] Unterredung *f*, Interview *n*; interviewen; **~er** Interviewer *m*.

intestines [in'testinz] *pl* Eingeweide *n*.

intima|cy ['intiməsi] Intimität *f*, Vertrautheit *f*; **~te** ['~eit] zu verstehen geben; ['~it] intim; vertraut; gründlich; Vertraute *m*, *f*; **~tion** Andeutung *f*.

intimidate [in'timideit] einschüchtern.

into ['intu, 'intə] in, in ... hinein.

intoler|able unerträglich; **~ant** unduldsam, intolerant.

in|toxicate [in'tɔksikeit] berauschen; **~transitive** *gr.* intransitiv; **~trepid** [~'trepid] unerschrocken, furchtlos.

intricate ['intrikit] verwickelt, kompliziert.

intrigue [in'tri:g] Intrige *f*; intrigieren; neugierig machen.

introduce [intrə'dju:s] einführen; vorstellen (**to** *dat*); **~tion** [~'dakʃən] Einführung *f*; Einleitung *f*; Vorstellung *f*; **letter of ~tion** Empfehlungsschreiben *n*; **~tory** [~'daktəri] einleitend.

intru|de [in'tru:d] (sich) aufdrängen; stören; **~der** Eindringling *m*; Stören-

fried *m*; **~sion** [~ʒən] Eindringen *n*; Zudringlichkeit *f*.

intuition [intju(:)'iʃən] Intuition *f*, Eingebung *f*.

invade [in'veid] eindringen in, einfallen in; **~r** Angreifer *m*, Eindringling *m*.

invalid[1] ['invəli:d] krank; Kranke *m*, *f*, Invalide *m*.

invalid[2] [in'vælid] (rechts-)ungültig; **~ate** [~eit] (für) ungültig erklären; entkräften.

invaluable unschätzbar.

invariab|le unveränderlich; **~ly** beständig.

invasion [in'veiʒən] *mil.*: **~(of)** Einfall *m* (in), Invasion *f* (in), Angriff *m* (auf).

invent [in'vent] erfinden; **~ion** Erfindung *f*; **~ive** erfinderisch; **~or** Erfinder(in).

invers|e ['in'və:s] umgekehrt; **~ion** Umkehrung *f*.

invert [in'və:t] umkehren, umdrehen, umstellen; **~ed commas** *pl* Anführungszeichen *pl*.

invest [in'vest] investieren, anlegen.

investigat|e [in'vestigeit] untersuchen; **~ion** Untersuchung *f*; **~or** Untersuchungsbeamte *m*.

investment [in'vestmənt] Kapitalanlage *f*.

in|vincible [in'vinsəbl] unbesiegbar; unüberwindlich; **~violable** [~'vaiə-ləbl] unverletzlich, unantastbar; **~visible** unsichtbar.

invit|ation [invi'teiʃən] Einladung *f*; Aufforderung *f*; **~e** [in'vait] einladen; auffordern.

invoice ['invɔis] *econ.* (Waren)Rechnung *f*.

in|voke [in'vəuk] anrufen; beschwören; **~voluntary** unfreiwillig; unwillkürlich; **~volve** [-'vɔlv] verwickeln; -stricken, hineinziehen; mit sich bringen; **~vulnerable** unverwundbar.

inward ['inwəd] inner (-lich); **~(s)** ['~(z)] einwärts, nach innen.

iodine ['aiəudi:n] Jod *n*.

I O U ['ai'əu'ju:] (= **I owe you**) Schuldschein *m*.

irascible [i'ræsibl] jähzornig.

iridescent [iri'desnt] schillernd.

iris ['aiəris] *anat.* Iris *f*; *bot.* Schwertlilie *f*.

Irish ['aiəriʃ] irisch; Irisch *n*; **the ~** *pl* die Iren *pl*; **~man** Ire *m*; **~woman** Irin *f*.

iron ['aiən] Eisen *n*; Bügeleisen *n*; eisern, Eisen...; bügeln, plätten.

ironic(al) [ai'rɔnik(əl)] ironisch, spöttisch.

iron|ing ['aiəniŋ] Bügeln *n*, Plätten *n*; Bügel..., Plätt...; **~ lung** *med.* eiserne Lunge; **~monger** Metallwarenhändler *m*; **~mo(u)ld** Rostfleck *m*; **~works** *sg*, *pl* Eisenhütte *f*.

irony ['aiərəni] Ironie *f*.

ir|radiate [i'reidieit] bestrahlen (*a. med.*); *Gesicht* aufheitern; *et.* erhellen; **~rational** unvernünftig; **~reconcilable** unversöhnlich; unvereinbar; **~recoverable** unersetzlich; **~redeemable** *econ.* nicht einlösbar; *fig.* unersetzlich; **~regular** unregelmäßig; ungleichmäßig; **~relevant** nicht zur Sache gehörig; **~removable** unabsetzbar; **~reparable** nicht wiedergutzumachen(d); **~replaceable** unersetzlich; **~repressible** nicht zu unterdrücken(d); unbezähmbar; **~reproachable** untadelig; **~resistible** unwiderstehlich; **~resolute** unentschlossen; **~respective**: **~ of** ohne Rücksicht auf, unabhängig von; **~responsible** unverantwortlich; verantwortungslos; **~retrievable** unwiederbringlich, unersetzlich; **~reverent** [i'revərənt] respektlos; **~revocable** [i'revəkəbl] unwiderruflich, endgültig. **[sern.]**

irrigate ['irigeit] bewässern. **[bar; Reizung f.]**

irrit|able ['iritəbl] reizbar; **~ate** ['~eit] reizen; (ver)ärgern; **~ation** Reizung *f*; Gereiztheit *f*.

is [iz] *3. sg pres von* **be**.

island ['ailənd] Insel *f*.

isle [ail] Insel *f*.

isn't ['iznt] = **is not**;
~ **it?** nicht wahr?

isolat|e ['aisəleit] isolieren; **~ed** abgeschieden; **~ion** Isolierung *f*.

issue ['iʃuː] Ausgabe *f* (*Buch etc.*); Nummer *f* (*Zeitung*); Nachkommen (-schaft *f*) *pl*; Ergebnis *n*, Ausgang *m*; (Streit)Frage *f*; **point at** ~ strittige Frage; *vb*: *Befehle* erteilen; ausgeben; *Bücher etc.* herausgeben; herausströmen, -kommen.

it [it] es; er, sie, es, ihn (*für Sachen u. Tiere*).

Italian [i'tæljən] italienisch; Italiener(in); Italienisch *n*.

itch [itʃ] Jucken *n*; jucken.

item ['aitəm] Punkt *m*, Posten *m*; Zeitungsnotiz *f*.

itinerary [ai'tinərəri] Reiseroute *f*; Reiseplan *m*, Reisebericht *m*.

its [its] *von Sachen u. Tieren*: sein(e), ihr(e); dessen, deren.

itself [it'self] sich; ~ sich selbst; selbst; **by** ~ allein; von selbst.

ivory ['aivəri] Elfenbein *n*.

ivy ['aivi] Efeu *m*.

J

jab [dʒæb] stechen, stoßen.

jack [dʒæk] Wagenheber *m*; *Karten*: Bube *m*; ~ **(up)** *Auto* aufbocken.

jackal ['dʒækɔːl] Schakal *m*.

jack|ass ['dʒækæs] Esel *m*; ['~kɑːs] *fig.* Esel *m*, Dummkopf *m*; **~daw** ['~dɔː] Dohle *f*.

jacket ['dʒækit] Jacke *f*, Jackett *n*; *tech.* Mantel *m*; Schutzumschlag *m*.

jack-in-the-box ['dʒæk-] Schachtelmännchen *n*; ~ **knife** Klappmesser *n*; **2 of all trades** Alleskönner *m*; **~pot** Haupttreffer *m*.

jag [dʒæg] Zacken *m*; **~ged** ['~gid] zackig.

jaguar ['dʒægjuə] Jaguar *m*.

jail [dʒeil], **~er** *s.* **gaol (-er)**.

jam¹ [dʒæm] Marmelade *f*.

jam² [dʒæm] quetschen, pressen; versperren; blockieren; *Radio*: stören; eingeklemmt sein, festsitzen; (sich ver)klemmen; Gedränge *n*; Stauung *f*, Stockung *f*; *tech.* Blockieren *n*; *colloq.* mißliche Lage, Klemme *f*.

janitor ['dʒænitə] Portier *m*; *Am.* Hausmeister *m*.

January ['dʒænjuəri] Januar *m*.

Japanese [dʒæpə'niːz] japanisch; Japaner(in); Japanisch *n*; **the** ~ *pl* die Japaner *pl*.

jar [dʒɑː] Krug *m*, Topf *m*, (Einmach)Glas *n*.

jaundice ['dʒɔːndis] Gelbsucht *f*.

javelin ['dʒævlin] Speer *m*.

jaw [dʒɔ:] Kinnbacken *m*, Kiefer *m*; *pl*: Rachen *m*; Maul *n*; **~bone** Kiefer (-knochen) *m*, Kinnlade *f*.

jay [dʒei] Eichelhäher *m*.

jealous ['dʒeləs] eifersüchtig; **~y** Eifersucht *f*.

jeer [dʒiə] Spott *m*, Stichelei *f*; spotten, höhnen.

jellied ['dʒelid] eingedickt (*Obst*); in Gelee.

jelly ['dʒeli] Gallert(e *f n*; Gelee *n*; gelieren; zum Gelieren bringen; **~fish** Qualle *f*.

jeopardize ['dʒepədaiz] gefährden, aufs Spiel setzen.

jerk [dʒə:k] Ruck *m*; *med.* Zuckung *f*; (plötzlich) stoßen *od.* ziehen, (sich) ruckartig bewegen; werfen, schleudern; **~y** ruckartig; holperig.

jersey ['dʒə:zi] Wollpullover *m*.

jest [dʒest] Scherz *m*; scherzen; **~er** Spaßmacher *m*; Hofnarr *m*.

jet [dʒet] (*Wasser- etc.*) Strahl *m*; Düse *f*; *s.* **~ engine**, **~ liner**, **~ plane**; hervorschießen; ausstoßen; **~ engine** Strahl-, Düsentriebwerk *n*; **~ liner**, **~ plane** Düsenflugzeug *n*; **~-propelled** mit Düsenantrieb.

jetty ['dʒeti] Mole *f*; Anlegestelle *f*.

Jew [dʒu:] Jude *m*.

jewel ['dʒu:əl] Juwel *n*, *m*; Edelstein *m*; **~(l)er** Juwe-

lier *m*; **~(le)ry** Juwelen *pl*; Schmuck *m*.

Jew|ess ['dʒu(:)is] Jüdin *f*; **~ish** jüdisch.

jiffy ['dʒifi] *colloq.* Augenblick *m*.

jiggle ['dʒigl] (leicht) rütteln *od.* schaukeln.

jingle ['dʒiŋgl] Klimpern *n*; klimpern (mit).

job [dʒɔb] *ein Stück* Arbeit *f*; *colloq.* Stellung *f*, Arbeit(splatz *m*) *f*, Beschäftigung *f*, Beruf *m*; Aufgabe *f*; Sache *f*; **by the ~** im Akkord; **out of ~** arbeitslos; **~-work** Akkordarbeit *f*.

jockey ['dʒɔki] Jockei *m*.

jocular ['dʒɔkjulə] lustig; scherzhaft.

jocund ['dʒɔkənd] lustig, fröhlich.

jog [dʒɔg] (an)stoßen, rütteln; **~ along**, **~ on** dahintrotten, -zuckeln.

join [dʒɔin] Verbindungsstelle *f*; verbinden, vereinigen, zs.-fügen (**to** mit); sich anschließen (an); eintreten in, beitreten; sich vereinigen (mit); **~ in** teilnehmen an, mitmachen bei; einstimmen in.

joiner ['dʒɔinə] Tischler *m*.

joint [dʒɔint] Verbindungsstelle *f*; Gelenk *n*; Braten *m*; *Am. sl.* Spelunke *f*; *sl.* Marihuanazigarette *f*; gemeinsam, Mit...; **~-stock company** Aktiengesellschaft *f*.

joke [dʒɔuk] scherzen; Scherz *m*, Spaß *m*; Witz

m; **practical ~** Streich *m*; **play a ~ on s.o.** j-m e-n Streich spielen; **he cannot take a ~** er versteht keinen Spaß; **~r** Spaßvogel *m*; *Karten*: Joker *m*.

jolly ['dʒɔli] lustig, fidel; *colloq.*: nett; sehr.

jolt [dʒəult] stoßen; rütteln; holpern; Ruck *m*, Stoß *m*, Rütteln *n*.

jostle ['dʒɔsl] (an)rempeln.

jot [dʒɔt]: **~ down** schnell notieren.

journal ['dʒə:nl] Tagebuch *n*; Journal *n*; Zeitung *f*; Zeitschrift *f*; **~ism** ['~əlizəm] Journalismus *m*.

journey ['dʒə:ni] reisen; Reise *f*; Fahrt *f*; **~ there** Hinfahrt *f*; **~man** Geselle *m*. \

jovial ['dʒəuvjəl] heiter, froh.

joy [dʒɔi] Freude *f*; **~ful, ~ous** freudig, erfreut; froh.

jubil|ant ['dʒu:bilənt] frohlockend; **~ee** ['~li:] (fünfzigjähriges) Jubiläum.

judg|e [dʒʌdʒ] Richter *m*; Preis-, Schiedsrichter *m*; Kenner *m*; urteilen; ein Urteil fällen über; entscheiden; beurteilen; halten für; **~(e)ment** Urteil *n*; Verständnis *n*, Einsicht *f*; Meinung *f*; göttliches (Straf)Gericht; ♀**(e)ment Day, Day of** ♀**(e)ment** Jüngstes Gericht.

judici|al [dʒu:(')diʃəl] gerichtlich, Justiz...; Gerichts...; kritisch; un-

parteiisch; **~ous** vernünftig, klug. [*f.* \

jug [dʒʌg] Krug *m*, Kanne *f*. \

juggle ['dʒʌgl] Taschenspielerei *f*; Schwindel *m*; jonglieren; verfälschen; betrügen; **~r** Jongleur *m*.

juic|e [dʒu:s] Saft *m*; **~y** saftig.

juke-box ['dʒu:k-] Musikautomat *m*.

July [dʒu(:)'lai] Juli *m*.

jumble ['dʒʌmbl] Durcheinander *n*; **~sale** Wohltätigkeitsbasar *m*.

jump [dʒʌmp] Sprung *m*; (über)springen; hüpfen; **~ at** sich stürzen auf; **~er** Springer *m*; Jongleur *m*; **~ing jack** Hampelmann *m*; **~y** nervös.

junct|ion ['dʒʌŋkʃən] Verbindung *f*; *rail.* Knotenpunkt *m*; **~ure** Verbindungsstelle *f*; (kritischer) Augenblick *od.* Zeitpunkt.

June [dʒu:n] Juni *m*.

jungle ['dʒʌŋgl] Dschungel *m*.

junior ['dʒu:njə] junior; jünger; untergeordnet; *Am.* Kinder-...; Jugend...; Jüngere *m*, *f*; Junior *m*.

juris|diction [dʒuəris'dikʃən] Rechtsprechung *f*; Gerichtsbarkeit *f*; **~prudence** ['~pru:dəns] Rechtswissenschaft *f*.

juror ['dʒuərə] Geschworene *m*, *f*.

jury ['dʒuəri] *die* Geschworenen *pl*; Jury *f*, Preisrichter *pl*.

just

468

just [dʒʌst] gerecht; berechtigt; genau, richtig; gerade, (so)eben; gerade (noch); nur; ~ *like that* einfach so; ~ *now* gerade jetzt.

justice ['dʒʌstis] Gerechtigkeit *f*; Recht *n*; Richter *m*.

justif|ication [dʒʌstifi'keiʃən] Rechtfertigung *f*; ~y ['~fai] rechtfertigen.

justly ['dʒʌstli] mit Recht.

jut [dʒʌt]: ~ *out* vorspringen, herausragen.

juvenile ['dʒu:vinail] jung, jugendlich; Jugend...; Jugendliche *m, f*.

K

kangaroo [kæŋgə'ru:] Känguruh *n*.

keel [ki:l] Kiel *m*.

keen [ki:n] scharf (*a. fig.*); begeistert, eifrig; heftig, stark, groß; ~ *on colloq.* erpicht od. versessen auf.

keep [ki:p] (Lebens)Unterhalt *m*; (*irr*) (auf-, ab-, [bei]be-, ein-, er-, fest-, unter)halten; (auf)bewahren; *Versprechen* halten; *Buch, Ware etc.* führen; *Bett* hüten; bleiben; sich halten; *colloq.* wohnen, weiter... (*Handlung beibehalten*); ~ *doing* immer wieder tun; ~ *going* weitergehen; ~ (*on*) *talking* weitersprechen; ~ *s.o. company* j-m Gesellschaft leisten; ~ *s.o. waiting* j-n warten lassen; ~ *time* richtig gehen (*Uhr*); ~ *away* (sich) fernhalten; wegbleiben; ~ *from* ab-, zurückhalten; *et.* vorenthalten; sich fernhalten von; sich enthalten; ~ *in Schüler* nachsitzen lassen;

~ *off* (sich) fernhalten; ~ *on Kleider* anbehalten, *Hut* aufbehalten; *Licht* brennen lassen; ~ *to* bleiben in; sich halten an; ~ *up* aufrechterhalten; *Mut* nicht sinken lassen; sich halten; ~ *up with* Schritt halten mit.

keep|er ['ki:pə] Wächter *m*, Aufseher *m*, Wärter *m*; ~ing Verwahrung *f*, Obhut *f*, Pflege *f*; *be in* (*out of*) ~ing *with* ... (nicht) übereinstimmen mit ...; ~sake Andenken *n* (*Geschenk*).

keg [keg] kleines Faß.

kennel ['kenl] Hundehütte *f*; Hundezwinger *m*.

kept [kept] *pret u. pp von* **keep**. [Bordstein *m*.]

kerb(stone) ['kə:b(-)]

kerchief ['kə:tʃif] (Kopf-) Tuch *n*.

kernel ['kə:nl] Kern *m*.

kettle ['ketl] Kessel *m*; ~drum (*Kessel*)Pauke *f*.

key [ki:] Schlüssel *m* (*a. fig.*); (*Klavier- etc.*)Taste *f*; (Druck)Taste *f*; *mus.*

Tonart f; fig. Ton m;
Schlüssel...; **~board** Klaviatur f; Tastatur f; **~hole**
Schlüsselloch n; **~note**
mus. Grundton m (a. fig.).

kick [kik] (Fuß)Tritt m;
Stoß m; colloq. (Nerven-)
Kitzel m; (mit dem Fuß)
stoßen od. treten; e-n
Fußtritt geben; Fußball:
schießen; ausschlagen
(Pferd); **~ off** Fußball:
anstoßen; **~ out** colloq.
hinauswerfen.

kid [kid] Zicklein n;
Ziegenleder n; sl. Kind n;
sl. foppen; **~glove** Glacéhandschuh m (a. fig.).

kidnap ['kidnæp] entführen; **~(p)er** Kindesentführer m, Kidnapper m.

kidney ['kidni] Niere f;
~ bean Weiße Bohne.

kill [kil] töten; schlachten;
vernichten; **~ time** die
Zeit totschlagen; Tötung
f; Jagdbeute f, Strecke f;
~er Mörder m.

kiln [kiln] Brenn-, Darrofen m.

kilo|gram(me) ['kiləugræm] Kilo(gramm) n;
~metre, Am. **~meter**
Kilometer m.

kilt [kilt] Kilt m, Schottenrock m.

kin [kin] Familie f; **~ pl**
(Bluts)Verwandtschaft f.

kind [kaind] gütig, freundlich, nett; Art f; Gattung
f; **what ~ of ...?** was für
ein ...?

kindergarten ['kində-

gɑ:tn] Kindergarten m.

kind-hearted gütig.

kindle ['kindl] anzünden,
(sich) entzünden; fig. entflammen.

kind|ly ['kaindli] freundlich; **~ness** Güte f, Freundlichkeit f; Gefälligkeit f.

kindred ['kindrid] verwandt; Verwandtschaft f;
Verwandte pl.

king [kiŋ] König m; **~dom**
(König)Reich n; **~-size**
überlang, -groß.

kins|man ['kinzmən] Verwandte m; **~woman** Verwandte f.

kipper ['kipə] Räucherhering m. | **küssen**.}

kiss [kis] Kuß m; (sich)

kit[1] ['kit] Kätzchen n.

kit[2] Ausrüstung f; Werkzeug n; Werkzeugtasche f.

kitchen ['kitʃin] Küche f;
~ette [~'net] Kochnische
f, Kleinküche f. | [m.]

kite [kait] (Papier)Drachen}

kitten ['kitn] Kätzchen n.

knack [næk] Kniff m,
Dreh m.

knapsack ['næpsæk] Tornister m; Rucksack m.

knave [neiv] Schurke m;
Karten: Bube m; **~ry**
['~əri] Schurkerei f.

knead [ni:d] kneten; massieren.

knee [ni:] Knie n; **~cap**
Kniescheibe f; **~-joint**
Kniegelenk m.

kneel [ni:l] (irr) knien;
(sich) hin- od. niederknien
(**to** vor).

knelt [nelt] *pret u. pp von*
kneel.
knew [nju:] *pret von* **know.**
knicker|bockers ['nikə-bokəz] *pl* Kniehosen
pl; **_s** *pl colloq. für*
knickerbockers; (Da-men)Schlüpfer *m.*
knick-knack ['niknæk]
Tand *m;* Nippsache *f.*
knife [naif], *pl* **knives**
[_vz] Messer *n;* schneiden;
erstechen.
knight [nait] Ritter *m;*
Schach: Springer *m;* zum
Ritter schlagen.
knit [nit] (*irr*) stricken;
zs.-fügen, verbinden; **_
the brows** die Stirn run-zeln; **_ting** Stricken *n;*
Strickzeug *n;* Strick...
knives [naivz] *pl von*
knife.
knob [nob] Knopf *m,*
Knauf *m, runder* Griff.
knock [nok] Schlag *m,*
Stoß *m;* Klopfen *n,* Pochen
n; **there is a _** es klopft;
vb: schlagen; stoßen; (an-)
klopfen; pochen; **_ down**
niederschlagen; überfah-ren; **_ out** *Boxen:* k.o.

schlagen; **_ over** um-werfen, umstoßen; **_er**
Türklopfer *m;* **_-out** *Bo-xen:* Knockout *m,* K.o. *m*
knoll [nəul] kleiner (Erd-)
Hügel.
knot [not] Knoten *m (a*
mar., bot.); Schleife *f;*
Gruppe *f (Menschen);* *fig*
Band *m;* Schwierigkeit *f*
(ver)knoten, -knüpfen; **_ty**
knotig; knorrig; *fig*
schwierig, verwickelt.
know [nəu] (*irr*) wissen;
(es) können *od.* verstehen;
kennen; (wieder)erken-nen, unterscheiden; **_ all
about it** genau Bescheid
wissen; **_ German**
Deutsch können; **_
one's business, _ a
thing or two, _ what's
what** sich auskennen, Er-fahrung haben; **_ing** klug;
schlau; verständnisvoll,
wissend; **_ingly** absicht-lich; **_ledge** ['nolidʒ]
Kenntnis(se *pl) f;* Wissen
n; **to my _ledge** meines
Wissens; **_n** *pp von* **know;**
bekannt.
knuckle ['nʌkl] Knöchel *m*

L

label ['leibl] Zettel *m,* Eti-kett *n,* Schildchen *n;* eti-kettieren, beschriften.
laboratory [lə'borətəri]
Labor(atorium) *n;* **_
assistant** Laborant(in).
laborious [lə'bɔːriəs]
mühsam, arbeitsam;

schwerfällig *(Stil).*
labor union ['leibə] *Am.
pol.* Gewerkschaft *f.*
labo(u)r ['leibə] (schwer)
arbeiten; sich be- *od.* ab-mühen; (schwere) Arbeit *f,*
Mühe *f;* Arbeiter(schaft *f)*
pl; med. Wehen *pl;* Ar-

beiter...; Arbeits...; **Min- istry of** 2 Arbeitsministe- rium m; **~er** (bsd. unge- lernter) Arbeiter; 2 **Ex- change** Arbeitsamt n; **Labour Party** Brit. pol. Labour Party f.

lace [leis] Spitze(n pl f); Litze f, Schnur f; Schnür- senkel m (zu)schnüren; mit Spitze etc. besetzen.

lack [læk] Fehlen n, Man- gel m; nicht haben, Man- gel haben an; **be ~ing in** fehlen od. mangeln an.

laconic [lə'kɔnik] lako- nisch.

lacquer ['lækə] Lack m; lackieren.   [m.\

lad [læd] Bursche m, Junge \

ladder ['lædə] Leiter f; Laufmasche f; **~proof** maschenfest (Strumpf).

lad|en ['leidn] beladen; **~ing** Ladung f, Fracht f.

ladle ['leidl] Schöpflöffel m, Kelle f.

lady ['leidi] Dame f; Lady f; **~ help** Hausangestellte f; **~like** damenhaft.

lag [læg]: **~ behind** zu- rückbleiben.

lager ['lɑːgə] Lagerbier n.

lagoon [lə'guːn] Lagune f.

laid [leid] pret u. pp von **lay**².

lain [lein] pp von **lie**¹.

lair [lɛə] Lager n (des Wildes).

lake [leik] See m.

lamb [læm] Lamm n.

lame [leim] lahm; lähmen.

lament [lə'ment] (Weh-) Klage f; jammern; (be-) klagen; **~able** ['læmən- təbl] beklagenswert; er- bärmlich; **~ation** [læmen- 'teiʃən] (Weh)Klage f.

lamp [læmp] Lampe f; **~post** Laternenpfahl m; **~shade** Lampenschirm m.

lance [lɑːns] Lanze f; med. aufschneiden, -ste- chen.

land [lænd] landen; Land n; Grundbesitz m, Grund m und Boden m; **by ~** auf dem Landweg; **~holder** Grundpächter m; Grundbesitzer m.

landing ['lændiŋ] mar. Anlegen n; aer. Landung f; Treppenabsatz m; **~field** aer. Landeplatz m; **~gear** aer. Fahrgestell n; **~stage** Landungssteg m, Anlegeplatz m.

land|lady ['lænleidi] Ver- mieterin f, Wirtin f; **~lord** ['læn-] Vermieter m; Wirt m; Haus-, Grund- besitzer m; **~lubber** ['lænd-] mar. Landratte f; **~mark** ['lænd-] Wahr- zeichen n; **~owner** ['lænd-] Land-, Grund- besitzer m; **~scape** ['læn- skeip] Landschaft f; **~slide** ['lænd-] Erdrutsch m (a. pol.); **~slip** ['lænd-] Erdrutsch m.

lane [lein] (Feld)Weg m; Gasse f; mot. Fahrbahn f, Spur f.

language ['læŋgwidʒ] Sprache f.

langu|id ['læŋgwid] matt;
träg(e); **~ish** ermatten;
schmachten; dahinsiechen;
~or ['læŋgə] Mattigkeit f;
Trägheit f; Stille f.

lank [læŋk] lang und dünn;
glatt (Haar); **~y** schlaksig.

lantern ['læntən] Laterne f.

lap [læp] Schoß m; (sich)
überlappen; plätschern;
(auf)lecken; schlürfen.

lapel [lə'pel] Rockauf-
schlag m, Revers m, n.

lapse [læps] Verlauf m
(der Zeit); Versehen n.

larceny ['lɑːsəni] Diebstahl m.

larch [lɑːtʃ] Lärche f.

lard [lɑːd] (Schweine-)
Schmalz n; **~er** Speise-
kammer f.

large [lɑːdʒ] groß; reichlich; weitgehend; groß-
zügig, -mütig; **at ~** auf
freiem Fuß; ausführlich;
~ly weitgehend; reichlich.

lark [lɑːk] Lerche f; fig.
Spaß m, Streich m.

larva ['lɑːvə] zo. Larve f.

larynx ['læriŋks] Kehl-
kopf m.

lascivious [lə'siviəs] lüstern; schlüpfrig.

lash [læʃ] Peitschen-
schnur f; (Peitschen)Hieb
m; Wimper f; peitschen
(mit); schlagen; (fest)bin-
den.

lass [læs] Mädchen n.

lasso [læ'suː] Lasso n, m.

last¹ [lɑːst] adj letzt;
vorig; äußerst; neuest;
~ night gestern abend;

~ but one vorletzt; adv
zuletzt; als letzte(r,-s);
(but) not least nicht
zuletzt; sub: der, die, das
Letzte; **at ~** endlich.

last² dauern; (stand)halten;
(aus)reichen; **~ing** dauerhaft.

last|ly zuletzt; **~ name**
Familien-, Nachname m.

latch [lætʃ] Klinke f;
Schnappschloß n; ein-,
zuklinken.

late [leit] spät; ehemalig;
neuest; verstorben; **be ~**
(zu) spät kommen, sich
verspäten; **at (the) ~st**
spätestens; **as ~ as** erst,
noch; **of ~** kürzlich; **~r on**
später; **~ly** kürzlich.

lath [lɑːθ] Latte f.

lathe [leið] Drehbank f.

lather ['lɑːðə] (Seifen-)
Schaum m; einseifen;
schäumen.

Latin ['lætin] lateinisch;
Latein n. [Breite f.]

latitude ['lætitjuːd] geogr.]

latter ['lætə] letzt; letzter.

lattice ['lætis] Gitter n.

laudable ['lɔːdəbl] lobenswert.

laugh [lɑːf] Lachen n,
Gelächter n; lachen; **~ at**
lachen über; j-n aus-
lachen; **make s.o. ~** j-n
zum Lachen bringen; **~ter**
Lachen n, Gelächter n.

launch [lɔːntʃ] Schiff vom
Stapel lassen; Rakete starten, abschießen; **~ing-
pad** (Raketen)Abschuß-
rampe f.

laund|erette [lɔːndəˈret] Selbstbedienungswaschsalon *m*; **~ry** [ˈ~drɪ] Wäscherei *f*; Wäsche *f*.

laurel [ˈlɔrəl] Lorbeer *m*.

lavatory [ˈlævətərɪ] Waschraum *m*; Toilette *f*.

lavender [ˈlævɪndə] Lavendel *m*.

lavish [ˈlævɪʃ] freigebig, verschwenderisch.

law [lɔː] Gesetz *n*; Recht *n*; ~wissenschaft *f*) *n*; ~ **court** Gericht(shof *m*) *n*; **~ful** gesetzlich; rechtmäßig; **~less** gesetzlos; rechtswidrig.

lawn [lɔːn] Rasen *m*.

law|suit [ˈlɔːsjuːt] Prozeß *m*; **~yer** [ˈ~jə] Jurist *m*; (Rechts)Anwalt *m*.

lax [læks] locker; schlaff; **~ative** [ˈ~ətɪv] abführend; Abführmittel *n*.

lay[1] [leɪ] *pret von* **lie**[2].

lay[2] weltlich; Laien...

lay[3] Lage *f*; (*irr*) legen (*a. fig.*); *Tisch* decken; (*Eier*) legen; ~ **out** ausbreiten; auslegen; *Geld* ausgeben; *typ.* gestalten; *Garten etc.* anlegen; ~ **up** *Vorräte* hinlegen; **be laid up** das Bett hüten müssen.

lay-by [ˈleɪbaɪ] *Brit. mot.* Parkstreifen *m*.

layer [ˈleɪə] Lage *f*, Schicht *f*.

layman [ˈleɪmən] Laie *m*.

lazy [ˈleɪzɪ] faul, träg(e).

lead[1] [liːd] Führung *f*; *thea.* Hauptrolle *f*; *electr.* Leitung *f*; (Hunde)Leine *f*; (*irr*) (an)führen; leiten; *Karte* ausspielen; vorangehen.

lead[2] [led] Blei *n*; Lot *n*; **~en** bleiern (*a. fig.*), aus Blei, Blei...

lead|er [ˈliːdə] (An)Führer(in); Leiter(in); Leitartikel *m*; **~ing** leitend, Leit...; führend; erst.

leaf [liːf], *pl* **leaves** [~vz] Blatt *n*; (Tisch)Klappe *f*, Ausziehplatte *f*; **~let** [ˈ~lit] Blättchen *n*; Flugblatt *n*; Prospekt *m*.

league [liːg] Liga *f*; Bund *m*; *mst poet.* Meile *f*.

leak [liːk] Leck *n*; leck sein; tropfen; ~ **out** *fig.* durchsickern; **~age** Leckken *n*; **~y** leck, undicht.

lean[1] [liːn] (*irr*) (sich) lehnen; (sich) neigen.

lean[2] mager; mageres Fleisch.

leant [lent] *pret u. pp von* **lean**[1].

leap [liːp] Sprung *m*; (*irr*) (über)springen; **~t** [lept] *pret u. pp von* **leap**; **~year** Schaltjahr *n*.

learn [lɜːn] (*irr*) lernen; erfahren, hören; **~ed** [ˈ~nid] gelehrt; **~er** Anfänger(in); Fahrschüler (-in); **~ing** Gelehrsamkeit *f*; **~t** [lɜːnt] *pret u. pp von* **learn**.

lease [liːs] Pacht *f*, Miete *f*; Pacht-, Mietvertrag *m*; (ver)pachten; ~mieten.

leash [liːʃ] (Hunde)Leine *f*.

least [liːst] kleinst, geringst, mindest; **at ~** mindestens, wenigstens.

leather ['leðə] Leder n; ledern; Leder...

leave [li:v] Erlaubnis f; Abschied m; Urlaub m; **take (one's) ~** sich verabschieden; (irr) (hinter-, über-, übrig-, zurück)lassen; liegenlassen, vergessen; vermachen; (fort-, weg)gehen; abreisen (von); abfahren.

leaven ['levn] Sauerteig m; Hefe f.

leaves [li:vz] pl von **leaf**; Laub n.

lecture ['lektʃə] Vortrag m; Vorlesung f; Strafpredigt f; e-n Vortrag od. Vorträge halten; e-e Vorlesung od. Vorlesungen halten; abkanzeln; **~r** Vortragende m, f; univ. Dozent(in).

led [led] pret u. pp von **lead[1]**.

ledge [ledʒ] Leiste f, Sims m; Riff n.

leech [li:tʃ] Blutegel m.

leek [li:k] Lauch m, Porree m.

leer [liə] (lüsterner od. finsterer) Seitenblick; schielen (**at** nach).

left[1] [left] pret u. pp von **leave**.

left[1] links(s); **turn ~** links abbiegen; sub: Linke f; on **the ~**, links, auf der linken Seite; **to the ~** nach links; **keep to the ~** sich links halten; mot. links fahren;

~-hand link; **on the ~ hand side** links; **~-handed** linkshändig.

left-luggage office Gepäckaufbewahrung f.

leg [leg] Bein n; Keule f; **pull s.o.'s ~** fig. j-n auf den Arm nehmen.

legacy ['legəsi] Vermächtnis n.

legal ['li:gəl] gesetzlich; gesetzmäßig; Rechts...

legation [li'geiʃən] Gesandtschaft f.

legend ['ledʒənd] Legende f, Sage f; Beschriftung f, Bildunterschrift f; **~ary** sagenhaft.

legible ['ledʒəbl] leserlich.

legion ['li:dʒən] Legion f; Unzahl f.

legislat|ion [ledʒis'leiʃən] Gesetzgebung f; **~ive** ['~lətiv] gesetzgebend; **~or** ['~leitə] Gesetzgeber m.

legitimate [li'dʒitimit] legitim, rechtmäßig.

leisure ['leʒə] Muße f; **~ly** gemächlich.

lemon ['lemən] Zitrone f; **~ade** [~'neid] Zitronenlimonade f; **~ squash** Zitronenwasser n.

lend [lend] (irr) (ver-, aus)leihen.

length [leŋθ] Länge f; (Zeit)Dauer f; **at ~** endlich; **~en** verlängern; länger werden; **~wise** ['~waiz] der Länge nach.

lenient ['li:njənt] mild(e), nachsichtig.

lens [lenz] opt. Linse f.

lie

lent [lent] *pret u. pp von* **lend**; ♀ Fastenzeit *f*.

leopard ['lepəd] Leopard *m*.

leprosy ['leprəsi] Lepra *f*.

less [les] kleiner, geringer; weniger; minus; **~en** (sich) vermindern; abnehmen; herabsetzen; **~er** kleiner, geringer.

lesson ['lesn] Lektion *f*; Aufgabe *f*; (Unterrichts-) Stunde *f*; *pl* Unterricht *m*; *fig.* Lehre *f*.

lest [lest] damit nicht, daß nicht; daß.

let [let] *(irr)* lassen; vermieten; sollen; **~ alone** in Ruhe lassen; geschweige denn; **~ down** *j-n* im Stich lassen; **~ go** loslassen; **~ s.o. know** *j-n* wissen lassen.

lethal ['li:θəl] tödlich.

letter ['letə] Buchstabe *m*; Brief *m*; *pl* Literatur *f*; **~box** Briefkasten *m*; **~ carrier** *Am.* Briefträger *m*.

lettuce ['letis] (Kopf-) Salat *m*.

leuk(a)emia [lju(:)'ki:miə] Leukämie *f*.

level ['levl] Ebene *f*, ebene Fläche; (gleiche) Höhe, Niveau *n*, Stand *m*; eben; waag(e)recht; gleich (-mäßig); ebnen; gleichmachen; zielen; **~ crossing** *Brit.* schienengleicher Bahnübergang.

lever ['li:və] Hebel *m*.

levity ['leviti] Leichtfertigkeit *f*.

levy ['levi] (Steuer)Erhebung *f*; **~** erheben.

lewd [lu:d] lüstern; unzüchtig.

liability [laiə'biliti] Verpflichtung *f*, Verbindlichkeit *f*; Haftpflicht *f*.

liable ['laiəbl] verantwortlich, haftbar; verpflichtet; **be ~ to** neigen zu; **~** *e-r Sache* ausgesetzt sein *od.* unterliegen.

liar ['laiə] Lügner(in).

libel ['laibəl] *jur.* Verleumdung *f*.

liberal ['libərəl] liberal (*a. pol.*); freigebig; reichlich.

liberat|e ['libəreit] befreien; freilassen; **~ion** Befreiung *f*; **~or** Befreier *m*.

liberty ['libəti] Freiheit *f*; **be at ~** frei sein.

librar|ian [lai'brɛəriən] Bibliothekar(in); **~y** ['~brəri] Bibliothek *f*; Bücherei *f*.

lice [lais] *pl von* **louse**.

licen|ce, *Am.* **~se** ['laisəns] Lizenz *f*, Konzession *f*; lizenzieren, berechtigen; **~see** [~'si:] Lizenzinhaber *m*.

lichen ['laikən] Flechte *f*.

lick [lik] Lecken *n*; Salzlecke *f*; (be)lecken; *colloq.* verdreschen; **~ing** *colloq.* Dresche *f*.

lid [lid] Deckel *m*; (Augen)Lid *n*.

lie¹ [lai] Lüge *f*; lügen.

lie² [lai] Lage *f*; *(irr)* liegen; **~ down** sich hin- *od.* niederlegen; ~in: have a ~ sich gründlich ausschlafen.

lieutenant [lef'tenənt, mar. le'tenənt, Am. lu:'tenənt] Leutnant m.

life [laif, pl lives [~vz] Leben n; Biographie f; for ~ auf Lebenszeit, lebenslänglich; ~ assurance Lebensversicherung f; ~belt Rettungsgürtel m; ~boat Rettungsboot n; ~guard Rettungsschwimmer m; ~ insurance Lebensversicherung f; ~jacket Schwimmweste f; ~less leblos; matt; ~like lebensecht; ~ sentence lebenslängliche Freiheitsstrafe; ~time Leben(szeit f) n.

lift [lift] Heben n; phys., aer. Auftrieb m; Fahrstuhl m, Lift m, Aufzug m; give s.o. a ~ j-n (im Auto) mitnehmen; get a ~ (im Auto) mitgenommen werden; vb: (auf-, er-, hoch)heben; sich heben; ~off aer. Start m, Abheben n.

ligature ['ligətʃuə] med.: Abbinden n; Verband m.

light¹ [lait] Licht n (a. fig.); Gesichtspunkt m, Aspekt m; can you give me a ~, please? haben Sie Feuer?; put a ~ to anzünden; adj: licht, hell; vb (irr): leuchten; ~ (up) anzünden; be-, erleuchten; ~ up aufleuchten (Augen etc.).

light² leicht; ~en leichter machen od. werden; erhellen; sich aufhellen; blitzen; ~er Feuerzeug n; mar. Leichter m; ~house Leuchtturm m; ~ing Beleuchtung f; ~minded leichtfertig; ~ness Leichtigkeit f.

lightning ['laitniŋ] Blitz m; ~conductor, ~rod Blitzableiter m.

light-weight Leichtgewicht n.

like [laik] gleich; (so) wie; ähnlich; feel ~ Lust haben zu; ~ that so; what is he ~? wie sieht er aus?; wie ist er?; der, die, das gleiche; vb: gern haben, (gern) mögen; wollen; how do you ~ it? wie gefällt es dir?; if you ~ wenn du willst.

like|lihood ['laiklihud] Wahrscheinlichkeit f; ~ly wahrscheinlich; geeignet; ~ness Ähnlichkeit f; (Ab-) Bild n; Gestalt f; ~wise ['~waiz] gleich-, ebenfalls.

liking ['laikiŋ] Zuneigung f; Gefallen n, Geschmack m.

lilac ['lailək] lila; Flieder m.

lily ['lili] Lilie f; ~ of the valley Maiglöckchen n.

limb [lim] (Körper)Glied n; Ast m; pl Gliedmaßen pl.

lime [laim] Kalk m; Limonelle f; Linde f; ~light thea. Scheinwerferlicht n.

limit ['limit] Grenze *f*; **off ~s** *Am.* Zutritt verboten; **that's the ~!** *colloq.* das ist (doch) die Höhe!; *vb:* begrenzen; beschränken **(to** auf); **~ed liability company** Gesellschaft *f* mit beschränkter Haftung.

limp [limp] hinken; schlaff; weich.

line [lain] Linie *f*; Strich *m*; Reihe *f*; (Menschen-) Schlange *f*; Falte *f*, Runzel *f*; Geschlecht *n*, Linie *f*; Zeile *f*; Vers *m*; Fach *n*, Branche *f*; (Eisenbahn- etc.)Linie *f*, Strecke *f*; (Verkehrs)Gesellschaft *f*; *teleph.* Leitung *f*; Leine *f*; (Angel)Schnur *f*; *pl* Umriß *m*; **hold the ~** *teleph.* am Apparat bleiben; **stand in ~** anstehen; *vb:* linieren; *Gesicht* zeichnen; einfassen, säumen; *Kleid* füttern; **~ up** (sich) aufstellen.

lineaments ['liniəmənts] *pl* Gesichtszüge *pl*.

linear ['liniə] geradlinig.

linen ['linin] Leinen *n*, Leinwand *f*; (*Bett- etc.*) Wäsche *f*; leinen; **~closet** Wäscheschrank *m*.

liner ['lainə] Passagierdampfer *m*; Verkehrsflugzeug *n*.

linger ['liŋgə] zögern; trödeln; verweilen.

lingerie ['lÉ›nʒəri:] Damenunterwäsche *f*.

lining ['lainiŋ] (*Kleider- etc.*)Futter *n*.

link [liŋk] (Ketten)Glied

n; *fig.* (Binde)Glied *n*; (sich) verbinden.

links [liŋks] *pl* Dünen *pl*; *sg* Golfplatz *m*.

lion ['laiən] Löwe *m*; **~ess** Löwin *f*.

lip [lip] Lippe *f*; **~stick** Lippenstift *m*.

liquid ['likwid] flüssig; Flüssigkeit *f*.

liquor ['likə] alkoholisches Getränk; Flüssigkeit *f*, Saft *m.* {kritze *f.*}

liquorice ['likəris] Lakritze *f.*

lisp [lisp] Lispeln *n*; lispeln.

list [list] Liste *f*, Verzeichnis *n*; (in e-e Liste) eintragen; verzeichnen.

listen ['lisn] hören, horchen, lauschen; **~ in,** **~ to** *Radio* hören; **~ to** zu-, anhören; hören auf; **~er** Zuhörer(in); (Rundfunk-) Hörer(in).

listless ['listlis] lustlos.

lit [lit] *pret u. pp von* **light**[1].

literal ['litərəl] wörtlich.

litera|ry ['litərəri] literarisch, Literatur...; **~ture** ['~ritʃə] Literatur *f*.

lithe [laið] geschmeidig.

lit|re, *Am.* **~er** ['li:tə] Liter *m, n*.

litter ['litə] Tragbahre *f*; Abfall *m*; *zo.* Wurf *m*; **~basket, ~bin** Abfallkorb *m*.

little ['litl] klein; wenig; **a ~ bit** etwas; **~ one** Kleine *n* (*Kind*); **a ~** ein wenig, ein bißchen, etwas; **~ by ~** nach und nach.

live¹ [liv] leben; wohnen; **~ on** leben von.

live² [laiv] lebend; lebendig; lebhaft; *Rundfunk, Fernsehen*: Direkt..., Original..., Live...

live|lihood ['laivlihud] Lebensunterhalt *m*; **~long: the ~ day** den lieben langen Tag; **~ly** lebhaft, lebendig.

liver ['livə] Leber *f*.

livery ['livəri] Livree *f*.

live|s [laivz] *pl von* **life**; **~stock** Vieh(bestand *m*) *n*.

livid ['livid] bläulich; fahl.

living ['liviŋ] lebend(ig); Leben *n*; Lebensweise *f*; Lebensunterhalt *m*; *eccl.* Pfründe *f*; **~-room** Wohnzimmer *n*.

lizard ['lizəd] Eidechse *f*.

load [ləud] Last *f*; Ladung *f*; Belastung *f*; (be-, ver-)laden; *fig.* überhäufen; **~laden**; **~ up** aufladen; **~ing** (Be)Laden *n*; Ladung *f*; Lade...

loaf¹ [ləuf], *pl* **loaves** [~vz] (Brot) Laib *m*.

loaf² [ləuf] herumlungern; **~er** Herumtreiber(in).

loam [ləum] Lehm *m*.

loan [ləun] Anleihe *f*; Darlehen *n*; (Ver)Leihen *n*; Leihgabe *f*; **on ~** leihweise; *vb:* bsd. Am. verleihen.

loath [ləuθ] abgeneigt; **~e** [ləuð] sich ekeln vor; verabscheuen; **~ing** ['~ðiŋ] Ekel *m*; Abscheu *m*;

~some ['~ðsəm] ekelhaft, -erregend.

loaves [ləuvz] *pl von* **loaf¹**.

lobby ['lɔbi] Vorhalle *f*; *parl.* Wandelgang *m*; *thea.* Foyer *n*.

lobe [ləub] *anat.* Lappen *m*; Ohrläppchen *n*. [*m.*\

lobster ['lɔbstə] Hummer\

local ['ləukəl] örtlich, lokal, Orts...; *colloq.* Wirtshaus *n* (am Ort); **~ity** [~'kæliti] Örtlichkeit *f*; Lage *f*; **~ize** lokalisieren; **~ train** Vorort(s)zug *m*.

locate [ləu'keit] unterbringen; ausfindig machen; **be ~ed** gelegen sein; **~ion** Lage *f*.

loch [lɔk] *Scot.:* See *m*; Bucht *f*.

lock [lɔk] (Tür-, Gewehretc.)Schloß *n*; Schleuse(nkammer) *f*; Locke *f*; (ab-ver-, zu)schließen, (ver-)sperren; umschließen; *tech.* sperren; sich schließen (lassen); **~ in** einschließen; **~sperren**; **~ up** ver-, wegschließen; **~er** schmaler Schrank; Schließfach *n*; **~et** ['~it] Medaillon *n*; **~smith** Schlosser *m*.

locomotive ['ləukəmʌutiv] Fortbewegungs...; Lokomotive *f*.

locust ['ləukəst] Heuschrecke *f*.

lodg|e [lɔdʒ] Häuschen *n*; Sommerhaus *n*; Pförtnerhaus *n*; Jagdhütte *f*; aufnehmen, (für die Nacht) unterbringen; (in Untermiete) wohnen; **~er** (Unter)Mieter(in); **~ing** Unterkunft f; pl möbliertes Zimmer; **night's ~ing** Nachtquartier n; Übernachtung f.

loft [lɔft] (Dach)Boden m, Heuboden m, Empore f; **~y** hoch; erhaben; **~ily** et.

log [lɔg] Klotz m, Block m; (gefällter) Baumstamm; **~book** Log-, Fahrtenbuch n; **~ cabin** Blockhaus n.

loggia [ˈlɔdʒə] Loggia f.

logic [ˈlɔdʒik] Logik f; **~al** logisch. [denstück n.]

loin [lɔin] Lende f; Len-

loiter [ˈlɔitə] schlendern, bummeln, trödeln.

loll [lɔl] (sich) rekeln.

lone|liness [ˈləunlinis] Einsamkeit f; **~ly, ~some** einsam; abgelegen.

long¹ [lɔŋ] lang(e); langfristig; **be ~** lange brauchen; **so ~!** bis dann!, auf Wiedersehen!; **no ~er, not any ~er** nicht mehr, nicht (mehr) länger; sub: Länge f; lange Zeit; **before ~** bald; **for ~** lange (Zeit); **take ~** lange brauchen od. dauern.

long² sich sehnen (**for** nach).

long-distance Fern...; Langstrecken...; **~ call** Ferngespräch n.

longing [ˈlɔŋiŋ] sehnsüchtig; Sehnsucht f, Verlangen n.

longitude [ˈlɔndʒitjuːd] geogr. Länge f.

long| jump Weitsprung m; **~shoreman** [ˈlɔːʃɔːmən] Hafenarbeiter m; **~sighted** weitsichtig; **~term** langfristig; **~winded** langatmig.

look [luk] Blick m; pl Aussehen n; **have a ~ at s.th.** sich et. ansehen; vb: sehen, blicken, schauen (**at** auf); aussehen; nachsehen; **~ after** nachblicken; aufpassen auf, sich kümmern um; **~ at** ansehen; **~ for** suchen; erwarten; **~ forward to** sich freuen auf; **~ into** untersuchen, prüfen; **~ on** zuschauen; betrachten, ansehen; **~ on (to)** liegen nach, (hinaus)gehen auf (Fenster etc.); **~ out** aufpassen, sich vorsehen; **~ over** et. durchsehen; j-n mustern; **~ round** sich umsehen (a. fig.); **~ up** et. nachschlagen.

look|er-on [ˈlukərˈɔn] Zuschauer(in); **~ing-glass** Spiegel m.

loom [luːm] Webstuhl m; undeutlich zu sehen sein.

loop [luːp] Schlinge f, Schleife f; Schlaufe f; Öse f; e-e Schleife machen; in Schleifen legen, schlingen.

loose [luːs] lose(r); locker; ungenau; liederlich; lösen; lockern; **~n** [ˈluːsn] (sich) lösen; (sich) lockern.

loot [luːt] plündern; Beute f.

lop [lɔp] schlaff herunterhängen; *Baum* beschneiden; ~ (off) abhauen.

lope [ləup]: at a ~ im Galopp, mit großen Sprüngen.

lord [lɔːd] Herr m, Gebieter m; Lord m; **House of 2s** Brit. parl. Oberhaus n; the 2 der Herr (Gott); 2 **Mayor** Brit. Oberbürgermeister m; 2's **Prayer** Vaterunser n; 2's **Supper** Abendmahl n.

lorry ['lɔri] Last(kraft)wagen m; rail. Lore f.

lose [luːz] (irr) verlieren; verpassen; nachgehen (Uhr); ~o.s. sich verirren.

loss [lɔs] Verlust m, Schaden m; at a ~ econ. mit Verlust; in Verlegenheit, außerstande.

lost [lɔst] pret u. pp von lose; verloren; fig. versunken, -tieft; ~**property office** Fundbüro n.

lot [lɔt] Los n (a. fig.); Anteil m; Parzelle f; (Waren)Posten m; colloq. Menge f; **cast ~s, draw ~s** losen; the ~ alles; a ~ of, ~s of so viel, e-e Menge; a ~ (sehr) viel.

loth [ləuθ] s. loath.

lotion ['ləuʃən] (Haar-, Haut-, Rasier- etc.)Wasser n.

lottery ['lɔtəri] Lotterie f.

lotto ['lɔtəu] Lotto n.

loud [laud] laut; fig. grell, auffallend; **~speaker** Lautsprecher m.

lounge [laundʒ] sich re-

keln od. lümmeln; Bummel m; Wohnzimmer n; Hotelhalle f.

lous|e [laus], pl **lice** [lais] Laus f; ~y ['lauzi] verlaust; colloq. miserabel.

lout [laut] Tölpel m, Lümmel m.

love [lʌv] Liebe f; Liebling m, Schatz m; sp. null; **give my ~ to her** grüße sie herzlich von mir; **send one's ~ to** j-n grüßen lassen; **~ from** herzliche Grüße von (Brief); **in ~ with** verliebt in; **fall in ~ with** sich verlieben in; vb: lieben; mögen; **~ to do** gern tun; **we ~d having you with us** wir haben uns sehr über deinen Besuch gefreut; **~ly** lieblich, wunderschön, entzückend, reizend; **~r** Liebhaber(in) (a. fig.), Geliebte m, f; pl Liebespaar n.

loving ['lʌviŋ] liebend, liebevoll.

low[1] [ləu] niedrig; tief; gering; leise (Stimme, Ton); fig. niedergeschlagen; meteor. Tief(druckgebiet) n.

low[2] brüllen, muhen (Rind).

lower ['ləuə] niedriger, tiefer; unter, Unter...; fallen, sinken; niedriger machen; senken; Preis herabsetzen; herunterlassen; fig. erniedrigen; 2 **House** Brit. parl.Unterhaus n.

low|lands pl Tiefland n; **~ly** demütig; einfach; be-

scheiden; **~necked** (tief)
ausgeschnitten (Kleid);
~pressure area Tief
(-druckgebiet) n; **~ tide**
Ebbe f. [Treue f.]
loyal ['lɔiəl] treu; **~ty**
lozenge ['lɔzindʒ] Raute
f; Pastille f.
lubber ['lʌbə] Tölpel m.
lubric|ant ['lu:brikənt]
Schmiermittel n; **~ate**
['~eit] (ab)schmieren, ölen;
~ation (Ab)Schmieren n,
Ölen n. [lich.]
lucid ['lu:sid] klar; deut-]
luck [lʌk] Glück n; Schicksal n; **bad (hard, ill)**
~ Unglück n, Pech n; **good**
~ Glück n; **~ily** glücklicherweise; **~y** glücklich;
Glücks...; **be ~y** Glück
haben; **~y fellow** Glücks-
pilz m.
ludicrous ['lu:dikrəs] lächerlich.
lug [lʌg] zerren, schleppen.
luggage ['lʌgidʒ] (Reise-)
Gepäck n; **~carrier** Gepäckträger m (Fahrrad);
~ (delivery) office Ge-
päckausgabe f; **~rack**
Gepäcknetz n; **~ (regis-
tration) office** Gepäck-
annahme f; Gepäckaus-
gabe f; **~ ticket** Gepäckschein m; **~van** Gepäckwagen m.
lukewarm ['lu:kwɔ:m] lau
(-warm); fig. lau.
lull [lʌl] einlullen; (sich)
beruhigen; sich legen;
(Ruhe)Pause f; **~aby**
['~əbai] Wiegenlied n.

lumbago [lʌm'beigəu]
Hexenschuß m.
lumber ['lʌmbə] Bau-,
Nutzholz n; Gerümpel n;
~jack, am Holzfäller
m, -arbeiter m; **~room**
Rumpelkammer f.
luminous ['lu:minəs]
leuchtend; Leucht...; klar,
einleuchtend.
lump [lʌmp] Klumpen m;
fig. Kloß m; **~ of** Stück n
(Zucker etc.); **in the ~**
in Bausch und Bogen;
~ sugar Würfelzucker m;
~ sum Pauschalsumme
f.
lunar ['lu:nə] Mond...;
~ module Mondfähre f.
lunatic ['lu:nətik] irr-,
wahnsinnig; Geisteskranke
m, f.
lunch [lʌntʃ] zu Mittag
essen; Lunch m, (leichtes)
Mittagessen; **packed ~**
Lunchpaket n; **~-hour**,
Mittagspause f.
lung [lʌŋ] Lunge(nflügel
m) f; **the ~s** pl die Lunge.
lunge [lʌndʒ] losstürzen,
-fahren (at auf).
lurch [lə:tʃ] mar. schlingern; taumeln, torkeln.
lure [ljuə] Köder m; fig.
Lockung f; ködern, (an-)
locken.
lurk [lə:k] lauern; fig. ver-
borgen liegen, schlum-
mern.
luscious ['lʌʃəs] köstlich;
üppig; wollüstig.
lust [lʌst] Begierde f;
Gier f, Sucht f.
lust|re, Am. **~er** ['lʌstə]

Glanz *m*; Kronleuchter *m*.

lusty ['lʌsti] kräftig, robust.

lute [luːt] Laute *f*.

luxate ['lʌkseit] *med.* verrenken.

luxurious [lʌg'zjuəriəs] luxuriös, üppig, Luxus...;

~y ['lʌkʃəri] Luxus *m*; Luxusartikel *m*.

lying ['laiiŋ] *pres p von* lie¹ *u.* lie²; lügnerisch.

lymph [limf] Lymphe *f*.

lynch [lintʃ] lynchen.

lynx [liŋks] Luchs *m*.

lyric ['lirik] lyrisch(es Gedicht); *pl* (Lied)Text *m*.

M

ma'am [mæm, məm] *colloq. s.* **madam**.

mac [mæk] *colloq. s.* **mackintosh**.

machine [mə'ʃiːn] Maschine *f*; **~-made** maschinell hergestellt; **~ery** Maschinen *pl*; **~ist** Maschinist *m*.

mack [mæk] *colloq., intosh* ['~intoʃ] Regenmantel *m*.

mad [mæd] wahnsinnig, verrückt, toll; *bsd. Am.* wütend; **drive s.o. ~** j-n verrückt machen; **go ~** verrückt werden.

madam ['mædəm] gnädige Frau, gnädiges Fräulein.

made [meid] *pret u. pp von* **make**.

madman Verrückte *m*; **~ness** Wahnsinn *m*.

magazine [mægə'ziːn] Magazin *n*; Munitionslager *n*; Zeitschrift *f*.

maggot ['mægət] Made *f*.

magic ['mædʒik] Zauberei *f*; *fig.* Zauber *m*; **~(al)** magisch, Zauber...; **~ian**

magistrate ['mædʒistreit] (Polizei-, Friedens-) Richter *m*.

magnanimous [mæg'næniməs] großmütig.

magnet ['mægnit] Magnet *m*; **~ic** [~'netik] magnetisch.

magnificence [mæg'nifisns] Großartigkeit *f*, Pracht *f*; **~ficent** großartig, prächtig, herrlich; **~fy** ['~fai] vergrößern.

magpie ['mægpai] Elster *f*.

maid [meid] (Dienst)Mädchen *n*, Magd *f*; Mädchen *n*; **old ~** alte Jungfer; **~en** unverheiratet; Jungfern..., Erstlings...; **~enly** mädchenhaft; **~en name** Mädchenname *m* (*e-r Frau*).

mail [meil] Post(dienst *m*) *f*; Post(sendung) *f*; *Am.* (mit der Post) schicken, aufgeben; **~bag** Postsack *m*; **~box** *Am.* Briefkasten *m*; **~man** *Am.* Briefträger *m*; **~-order business**

(firm, house) Versandgeschäft n, -haus n.

maim [meim] verstümmeln.

main [mein] Haupt..., größt, wichtigst, hauptsächlich; *mst pl* Haupt(gas-, -wasser-, -strom-) leitung f; Stromnetz n; **~land** Festland n; **~ly** hauptsächlich; **~ road** Haupt(verkehrs)straße f; **~ street** *Am.* Hauptstraße f.

maintain [mein'tein] (aufrecht)erhalten; instand halten; unterstützen; unterhalten; behaupten; verteidigen.

maintenance ['meintənəns] Instandhaltung f; *tech.* Wartung f; Unterhalt m.

maize [meiz] Mais m.

majestic [mə'dʒestik] majestätisch; **~y** ['mædʒisti] Majestät f.

major ['meidʒə] größer; wichtig; volljährig; *mus.* Dur...; der ältere; Major m; Volljährige m, f; *Am.* Hauptfach n; *mus.* Dur n; Hauptfach n; *mus.* Dur m; **~ity** [mə-'dʒɔriti] Mehrheit f; Mehrzahl f; Volljährigkeit f; **~ road** Haupt-, Vorfahrt(s)straße f.

make [meik] Ausführung f; Fabrikat n; *tech.* Typ m, Bauart f; *(irr)* machen; anfertigen, herstellen, erzeugen; verarbeiten **(into** zu); bilden; **(er)**geben; machen zu, ernennen zu; *j-n* veranlassen *od.* bringen *od.* zwingen zu; *Geld* verdienen; *colloq.* Strecke zurücklegen; *colloq. et.* erreichen *od.* schaffen; **~ for** zugehen auf; sich begeben nach; **~ out** Rechnung *etc.* ausstellen; erkennen, ausmachen; ausfindig machen, feststellen; entziffern; klug werden aus; **~ over** Eigentum *etc.* übertragen; **~ up** bilden, zs.-setzen; zs.-stellen; (sich) zurechtmachen *od.* schminken; sich ausdenken, erfinden; **~ up for** ausgleichen, aufholen; wiedergutmachen; **~ up one's mind** sich entschließen; **~ it up** sich versöhnen; **~-believe** So-tun-als-ob n; Verstellung f; **~r** Hersteller m; **2r** Schöpfer m *(Gott)*; **~shift** Notbehelf m; behelfsmäßig; **~up** Schminke f, Make-up n.

malady ['mælədi] Krankheit f.

male [meil] männlich; Mann m; *zo.* Männchen n.

malediction [mæli'dikʃən] Fluch m; **~factor** ['~fæktə] Übeltäter m; **~volent** [mə'levələnt] übelwollend.

malice ['mælis] Bosheit f, Gehässigkeit f; Groll m; **~ious** [mə'liʃəs] boshaft; böswillig.

malignant [mə'lignənt] bösartig *(a. med.)*.

malnutrition

malnutrition [ˌmælnjuː(ː)-ˈtrɪʃən] Unterernährung *f*.

malt [mɔːlt] Malz *n*.

maltreat [mælˈtriːt] mißhandeln; **~ment** [ ] *(ma f.)*

mam(m)a [məˈmɑː] Ma-

mammal [ˈmæməl] Säugetier *n*.

man [mæn, *in Zssgn*: mən], *pl* **men** [men] Mann *m*; Mensch(en *pl*) *m*; Menschheit *f*; Diener *m*; männlich; bemannen.

manage [ˈmænɪdʒ] handhaben; verwalten; leiten; fertig werden mit; *et.* fertigbringen; *Betrieb etc.* leiten *od.* führen; auskommen; *colloq.* (es) schaffen; **~able** handlich; lenksam; **~ment** Verwaltung *f*, Leitung *f*; Geschäftsleitung *f*, Direktion *f*; **~r** Verwalter *m*, Leiter *m*; Manager *m*; Geschäftsführer *m*, Direktor *m*; **~ress** [ˈ~ə˟res] Geschäftsführerin *f*.

mane [mein] Mähne *f*.

maneuver [məˈnuːvə] *Am. für* **manoeuvre**.

manger [ˈmeindʒə] Krippe *f*.

mangle [ˈmæŋgl] Wäschemangel *f*; mangeln; übel zurichten; *fig.* verstümmeln.

manhood [ˈmænhud] Mannesalter *n*; Männlichkeit *f*; die Männer *pl*.

mania [ˈmeinjə] Wahn(-sinn) *m*; Sucht *f*, Manie *f*; **~c** [ˈ~iæk] Wahnsinnige *m, f*.

manifest [ˈmænifest] offenbar; offenbaren; kundtun.

manifold [ˈmænifəuld] mannigfaltig; vervielfältigen.

manipulate [məˈnipjuleit] (geschickt) handhaben *od.* behandeln; manipulieren.

man|kind [mænˈkaind] die Menschheit *f*; [ˈ~kaind] die Männer *pl*; **~ly** männlich.

manner [ˈmænə] Art *f*, Weise *f*, Art und Weise; *pl* Benehmen *n*, Manieren *pl*, Sitten *pl*.

manoeuvre [məˈnuːvə] Manöver *n*; manövrieren.

man-of-war [ˈmænə-ˈwɔː] Kriegsschiff *n*.

manor [ˈmænə] Rittergut *n*; **lord of the ~** Gutsherr *m*; **~house** Herrenhaus *n*.

man|power [ˈmæn˟pauə] Menschenpotential *n*; Arbeitskräfte *pl*; **~servant** Diener *m*.

mansion [ˈmænʃən] (herrschaftliches) Wohnhaus.

manslaughter *jur.* Totschlag *m*, fahrlässige Tötung.

mantelpiece [ˈmæntlpiːs] Kaminsims *m*.

manual [ˈmænjuəl] Hand...; Handbuch *n*.

manufacture [ˌmænjuˈfæktʃə] Herstellung *f*; herstellen, erzeugen; **~r** Hersteller *m*, Erzeuger *m*, Fabrikant *m*.

manure [məˈnjuə] Dünger *m*, Mist *m*; düngen.

manuscript ['mænju-skript] Manuskript *n*; Handschrift *f*.

many ['meni] viel(e); manch; **a good ~, a great ~** sehr *od.* ziemlich viel(e).

map [mæp] (Land- *etc.*) Karte *f*;(Stadt- *etc.*)Plan *m.*

maple ['meipl] Ahorn *m.*

marble ['mɑːbl] Marmor *m*; Murmel *f*; marmorn.

March [mɑːtʃ] März *m.*

march [mɑːtʃ] Marsch *m*; marschieren.

mare [mɛə] Stute *f.*

margarine [mɑːdʒə-'riːn], **~e** [mɑːdʒ] *colloq.* Margarine *f.*

margin ['mɑːdʒin] Rand *m*; Grenze *f*; Spielraum *m*; (Gewinn)Spanne *f.*

marine [mə'riːn] Marine *f*; Marineinfanterist *m*; See-...; Marine...; Schiffs...; **~r** ['mærinə] Seemann *m.*

maritime ['mæritaim] See-...; Küsten...

mark [mɑːk] Markierung *f*, Bezeichnung *f*, Marke *f*; Zeichen *n* (*a. fig.*); (Körper)Mal *n*; Spur *f*; Merkmal *n*; Zensur *f*, Note *f*; Ziel *n*; markieren, kenn-, bezeichnen; benoten, zensieren; sich *et.* merken; achtgeben; **~ out** abgrenzen, bezeichnen; **~ed** deutlich; auffallend.

market ['mɑːkit] Markt *m* (*Handel*, *Absatzgebiet*); Markt(platz) *m*; *Am.* (Lebensmittel)Geschäft *n*; auf

den Markt bringen; verkaufen; einkaufen; **~-garden** Handelsgärtnerei *f*; **~ing** *econ.* Marketing *n*, Absatzpolitik *f*; **~-place** Marktplatz *m.*

marksman ['mɑːksmən] (guter) Schütze.

marmalade ['mɑːmə-leid] (*bsd.* Orangen)Marmelade *f.*

marmot ['mɑːmət] Murmeltier *m.*

marriage ['mæridʒ] Heirat *f*, Hochzeit *f*; Ehe (-stand *m*) *f*; **~able** heiratsfähig; **~ articles** *pl* Ehevertrag *m*; **~ certificate**, **~ lines** *pl* Trauschein *m*; **~ portion** Mitgift *f.*

married ['mærid] verheiratet; **~ couple** Ehepaar *n.*

marrow ['mærəu] Mark *n.*

marry ['mæri] (ver)heiraten; trauen; (sich ver)heiraten.

marsh [mɑːʃ] Sumpf *m.*

marshal ['mɑːʃəl] Marschall *m*; *Am.* Bezirkspolizeichef *m*; ordnen; aufstellen; (hinein)geleiten.

marshy ['mɑːʃi] sumpfig.

marten ['mɑːtin] Marder *m.*

martial ['mɑːʃəl] Kriegs..., Militär...

martyr ['mɑːtə] Märtyrer (-in).

marvel ['mɑːvəl] Wunder *n*; sich wundern; **~(l)ous** wunderbar; fabelhaft.

mascot ['mæskət] Maskottchen *n.*

masculine ['mæskjulin]
männlich.

mash [mæʃ] zerdrücken,
-quetschen; **~ed pota-
toes** pl Kartoffelbrei m.

mask [mɑːsk] Maske f;
maskieren.

mason ['meisn] Stein-
metz m; Maurer m; **~ry**
Mauerwerk n.

masque [mɑːsk] Masken-
spiel n.

mass [mæs] eccl. Messe f;
Masse f; Menge f; Mas-
sen...; (sich) (an)sammeln.

massacre ['mæsəkə] Blut-
bad n; niedermetzeln.

massage ['mæsɑːʒ] Massage f; massieren.

massif ['mæsiːf](Gebirgs-)
Massiv n.   [schwer.]

massive ['mæsiv] massiv;}

mast [mɑːst] Mast m.

master ['mɑːstə] Meister
m; Herr m; Gebieter m;
Lehrer m; junger Herr
(als Anrede); Rektor m
(e-s College); Meister...;
Haupt...; meistern; be-
herrschen; **~ly** meister-
haft; **♀ of Arts** Magister
m Artium; **~ of ceremo-
nies** Am. Conférencier m;
~piece Meisterstück n,
-werk n; **~ship** Meisterschaft f; Herrschaft f;
Lehramt n; **~y** Herrschaft
f; Oberhand f; Beherr-
schung f.

mat [mæt] Matte f; Unter-
setzer m; mattiert, matt.

match¹ [mætʃ] Streichholz n.

match² Partie f; (Wett-)
Spiel n, Wettkampf m;
be a ~ for j-m gewachsen sein; **find od. meet
one's ~** s-n Meister finden; vb: passen zu; zs.-
passen; **to ~** dazu passend;
~less unvergleichlich;
~maker Ehestifter(in).

mate [meit] Kamerad m;
Gehilfe m; Gattle m, -in
f; zo. Männchen n, Weib-
chen n; mar. Maat m; (sich) paaren.

material [mə'tiəriəl] ma-
teriell; körperlich; wesentlich; Material n; Stoff m.

matern|al [mə'təːnl] müt-
terlich; mütterlicherseits;
~ity Mutterschaft f; **~ity
hospital** Entbindungsan-
stalt f.

mathematic|ian [mæθi-
mə'tiʃən] Mathematiker m;
~s [~'mætiks] sg, pl Mathematik f.

maths [mæθs] colloq. abbr.
für **mathematics**.

matriculate [mə'trikju-
leit] immatrikulieren; sich
immatrikulieren (lassen).

matrimony ['mætriməni]
Ehe(stand m) f.

matron ['meitrən] ältere
(verheiratete) Frau, Ma-
trone f; Wirtschafterin f;
Oberin f.

matter ['mætə] von Be-
deutung sein; **it doesn't ~
es macht nichts (aus)**
Materie f, Material n,
Stoff m; med. Eiter m;
Sache f, Angelegenheit f;

medal

Anlaß m; a ~ of course
e-e Selbstverständlichkeit;
a ~ of fact e-e Tatsache;
for that ~ was das be-
trifft; no ~ ganz gleich;
what's the ~? was ist
los?; what's the ~ with
you? was fehlt dir?; ~-of-
fact sachlich. [tratze f.\
mattress ['mætris] Ma-
matur|e ['mə'tjuə] reif;
reiflich (erwogen); econ.
fällig; zur Reife bringen;
reifen; econ. fällig werden;
~ity Reife f; econ. Fällig-
keit f.\
Maundy Thursday
['mɔːndi] Gründonnerstag
m.
mauve [məuv] hellviolett.
maw [mɔː] (Tier)Magen m.
maxim ['mæksim] Grund-
satz m; ~um ['~əm]
Maximum n; Höchst...
May [mei] Mai m.
may [mei]v aux ich, du etc.:
kann(st) etc., mag(st) etc.,
darf(st) etc.; ~be vielleicht.
may|-beetle, ~-bug Mai-
käfer m; ♀Day der 1. Mai.
mayor [mɛə] Bürgermei-
ster m.
maypole Maibaum m.
maze [meiz] Irrgarten m,
Labyrinth n; in a ~ ver-
wirrt.
me [miː, mi] mir; mich;
colloq. ich; it's ~ ich bin's.
meadow ['medəu] Wiese f.
meag|re, Am. ~er ['miː-
gə] mager, dürr; dürftig.
meal [miːl] Mahl(zeit f) n;
Mehl n.

mean¹ [miːn] gemein; niedrig, gering; armselig;
geizig, knauserig.
mean² Mitte f; Mittel n;
pl (Geld)Mittel pl; ~s od
Mittel n; by all ~s gewiß;
auf alle Fälle; by no ~s
keineswegs; by ~s of mit-
tels, durch.
mean³ (irr) meinen; be-
absichtigen; bestimmen;
bedeuten; ~ well od. ill es
gut od. schlecht meinen;
~ing bedeutsam; Sinn m,
Bedeutung f; ~ingless
bedeutungs-, sinnlos.
meant [ment] pret u. pp
von mean³.
mean|time, ~while 'in-
zwischen; [sern pl.\
measles ['miːzlz] sg Ma-\
measure ['meʒə] Maß n
(a. fig.); mus. Takt m;
Maßnahme f; beyond ~
über alle Maßen, außer-
ordentlich; made to ~
nach Maß gemacht; vb:
(ab-, aus-, ver)messen;
Maß nehmen; ~less un-
ermeßlich; ~ment Mes-
sung f; Maß n; pl Ab-
messungen pl; ~ of capac-
ity Hohlmaß n.
meat [miːt] Fleisch n.
mechanic [mi'kænik] Me-
chaniker m; ~al mecha-
nisch; Maschinen...; ~s sg
Mechanik f.
mechan|ism ['mekəni-
zəm] Mechanismus m; ~-
ize mechanisieren.
medal ['medl] Medaille f;
Orden m.

meddle ['medl] sich ein-
mischen (**with, in** in).

mediaeval [medi'i:vəl] s.

medieval.

mediate ['mi:dieit] ver-
mitteln; **~ion** Vermittlung
f; **~or** Vermittler m.

medical ['medikəl] medi-
zinisch, ärztlich; **~ certificate** ärztliches Attest.

medicated ['medikeitid]
medizinisch.

medicinal [me'disinl]
medizinisch, Heil...; **~e**
['medsin] Medizin f; Arz-
nei f.

medieval [medi'i:vəl] mit-
telalterlich.

mediocre [mi:di'əukə]
mittelmäßig.

meditate ['mediteit]
nachdenken, grübeln; im
Sinn haben; **~ion** Nachdenken n, Meditation f;
Betrachtung f; **~ive** ['~
tətiv] nachdenklich.

Mediterranean [meditə-
'reinjən] Mittelmeer n;
Mittelmeer...

medium ['mi:djəm] Mitte
f; Mittel n; Medium n;
mittler, Mittel...

medley ['medli] Gemisch
n; mus. Potpourri n.

meek [mi:k] sanftmütig;
demütig.

meet [mi:t] (irr) treffen
(auf); stoßen auf; be-
gegnen; j-n kennenlernen;
bsd. Am. j-n vorstellen;
j-n abholen; Verpflichtun-
gen nachkommen; Wunsch
etc. befriedigen; sich tref-

fen; sich versammeln; **~
with** stoßen auf; erleiden,
erfahren; **~ing** Begegnung
f, Treffen n; Versammlung
f, Sitzung f, Tagung f.

melancholy ['melənkəli]
Schwermut f; schwermü-
tig.

mellow ['meləu] reif;
weich; fig. abgeklärt.

melodious [mi'ləudjəs]
melodisch; **~y** ['melədi]
Melodie f; Lied n.

melon ['melən] Melone f.

melt [melt] (zer)schmel-
zen; fig.: erweichen; zer-
fließen; weich werden.

member ['membə] (Mit-)
Glied n; Angehörige m, f;
~ship Mitgliedschaft f;
Mitgliederzahl f; Mit-
glieds...

membrane ['membrein]
Membran(e)f; Häutchenn.

memoir ['memwa:]
Denkschrift f; pl Me-
moiren pl; **~rable** ['~mə-
rəbl] denkwürdig; **~rial**
[mi'mɔ:riəl] Denk-, Eh-
renmal n; **~rize** ['memə-
raiz] auswendig lernen;
~ry ['~əri] Gedächtnis n,
Erinnerung f; Andenken
n; **in ~ry of** zum Andenken an.

men [men] pl von man;
Leute pl.

menace ['menəs] (be-)
drohen; Drohung f.

mend [mend] ausbessern,
flicken, reparieren; (ver-)
bessern; [(Arbeit).\
menial ['mi:njəl] niedrig

mew

mental ['mentl] geistig, Geistes...; ~ **arithmetic** Kopfrechnen *n*; ~ **home**, ~ **hospital** (Nerven)Heilanstalt *f*; ~**ity** [ˌ'tæliti] Mentalität *f*.

mention ['menʃən] Erwähnung *f*; erwähnen; **don't** ~ **it** bitte!

menu ['menju:] Menü *n*; Speisekarte *f*.

meow [mi(:)'au] miauen.

mercantile ['mə:kəntail] kaufmännisch; Handels...

mercenary ['mə:sinəri] käuflich; gewinnsüchtig; Söldner *m*.

merchan|dise ['mə:tʃəndaiz] Waren *pl*; ~**t** ['ˌənt] Kaufmann *m*; *Am. a.* Krämer *m*; Handels...

merci|ful ['mə:siful] barmherzig; ~**less** unbarmherzig.

mercury ['mə:kjuri] Quecksilber *n*.

mercy ['mə:si] Barmherzigkeit *f*, Gnade *f*.

mere [miə] bloß, rein; ~**ly** bloß, rein, nur.

merge [mə:dʒ] verschmelzen (**in** mit).

meridian [mə'ridiən] Meridian *m*.

merit ['merit] Verdienst *n*; Wert *m*; *fig.* verdienen; ~**orious** [ˌ'tɔ:riəs] verdienstvoll.   [xe *f.*]

mermaid ['mə:meid] Ni-}

merriment ['merimənt] Lustigkeit *f*, Belustigung *f*.

merry ['meri] lustig, fröhlich; **make** ~ lustig sein;

~ **andrew** ['ˌ'ændru:] Hanswurst *m*; ~**-go-round** Karussell *n*; ~**-making** Lustbarkeit *f*, Fest *n*.

mesh [meʃ] Masche *f*; *pl fig.* Netz *n*, Schlingen *pl.*

mess [mes] Unordnung *f*, *colloq.* Schweinerei *f*; Patsche *f*, Klemme *f*; **what a** ~**!** eine schöne Geschichte!; *vb*: ~ **(up)** beschmutzen; in Unordnung bringen; verpfuschen.

message ['mesidʒ] Botschaft *f*; Mitteilung *f*, Nachricht *f*; **give s.o. a** ~, **give a** ~ **to s.o.** j-m et. ausrichten *od.* bestellen.

messenger ['mesindʒə] Bote *m*.

met [met] *pret u. pp von* **meet.**

metal ['metl] Metall *n*; ~**lic** [mi'tælik] metallisch, Metall...

meteor ['mi:tjə] Meteor *m*; ~**ology** [ˌ'rɔlədʒi] Meteorologie *f*.

meter ['mi:tə] Messer *m*, Zähler *m*; *Am. für* **metre.**

method ['meθəd] Methode *f*; ~**ical** [mi'θɔdikəl] methodisch.

meticulous [mi'tikjuləs] peinlich genau.

met|re, *Am.* ~**er** ['mi:tə] Meter *m*; Versmaß *n*.

metric system ['metrik] Dezimalsystem *n*.

metropolitan [metrə'pɔlitən] hauptstädtisch.

mew [mju:] miauen.

miaow [mi(:)'au] miauen.

mice [mais] pl von mouse.

micro|phone ['maikrə-faun] Mikrophon n; ~**scope** Mikroskop n.

mid [mid] Mitte, Mittel...; **in ~ winter** mitten im Winter; ~**day** Mittag m.

middle ['midl] Mitte f; mittler, Mittel...; ~**aged** mittleren Alters; **2 Ages** pl Mittelalter n; ~ **class** (-es pl) Mittelstand m; ~ **name** zweiter Vorname; ~**sized** mittelgroß; ~**weight** Boxen: Mittelgewicht n.

middling ['midliŋ] mittelmäßig; leidlich.

midge [midʒ] Mücke f; ~**t** ['.it] Zwerg m, Knirps m.

mid|land ['midlənd] binnenländisch; **the 2lands** pl Mittelengland n; ~**night** Mitternacht f; ~**st**: **in the** ~ **of** inmitten (gen); ~**summer** Sommersonnenwende f; Hochsommer m; ~**way** auf halbem Wege; ~**wife** Hebamme f.

might [mait] pret von may; Macht f, Gewalt f; ~**y** mächtig, gewaltig, groß.

migrat|e [mai'greit] (aus-) wandern, (fort)ziehen; ~**ory** ['.ətəri] Zug..., Wander...

mild [maild] mild, sanft, leicht.

mildew ['mildju:] Mehltau m.

mildness ['maildnis] Milde f.

mile [mail] Meile f (1,609 km).

mil(e)age ['mailidʒ] zurückgelegte Meilenzahl od. Fahrtstrecke; Meilen-, Kilometergeld n.

milestone Meilenstein m.

military ['militəri] militärisch, Militär...

milk [milk] melken; Milch f; **it's no use crying over spilt ~** geschehen ist geschehen; ~**ing-machine** Melkmaschine f; ~**man** Milchmann m; ~**shake** Milchmixgetränk n; ~**sop** ['.sɔp] Weichling m; ~**y** milchig; Milch...

mill [mil] Mühle f; Fabrik f; Spinnerei f; mahlen; tech. fräsen; ~**er** Müller m.

millet ['milit] Hirse f.

milliner ['milinə] Putzmacherin f, Modistin f; **million** ['miljən] Million f; ~**aire** ['.'nɛə] Millionär m; ~**th** ['.nθ] millionste; Millionstel n.

milt [milt] ichth. Milch f.

mimic ['mimik] nachahmen, -äffen.

mince [mins] zerhacken; ~**d meat** Hackfleisch n; ~**meat** ~**e** Pastetenfüllung; ~**e pie** mit mincemeat gefüllte Pastete; ~**er,** ~**ing-machine** Fleischwolf m.

mind [maind] Sinn m; Geist m, Verstand m; Meinung f; Absicht f, Neigung f, Lust f; Gedächtnis n; **to my ~** meiner Ansicht nach; **out of one's ~** von Sinnen, verrückt; **bear** od. **keep s.th. in ~** an et. denken; **change one's ~** sich anders besinnen; **give s.o. a piece of one's ~** j-m gründlich die Meinung sagen; **have s.th. on one's ~** et. auf dem Herzen haben; vb: merken, beachten, achtgeben auf, achten auf; sich kümmern um; **I don't ~ (it)** ich habe nichts dagegen, meinetwegen; **do you ~ if I smoke?, do you ~ my smoking?** stört es Sie, wenn ich rauche?; **would you ~ opening the window?** würden Sie bitte das Fenster öffnen?; **~ the step!** Achtung Stufe!; **~ your own business!** kümmern Sie sich um Ihre Angelegenheiten!; **~!** gib acht!; **never ~!** macht nichts!; **~ed** geneigt, gewillt; in Zssgn: gesinnt; **~ful:** be **~ of** achten auf, denken an.

mine¹ [main] meine(r, -s), der, die, das mein(ig)e.

mine² Bergwerk n, Grube f; mil. Mine f; fig. Fundgrube f; **~** of Erz, Kohle abbauen, gewinnen; mil. verminen; **~r** Bergmann m.

mineral ['minərəl] Mineral n; mineralisch.

mingle ['miŋgl] (ver)mi-

schen; sich mischen od. mengen (**with** unter).

miniature ['minjət∫ə] Miniatur(gemälde n) f; Miniatur..., Klein...; **~ camera** Kleinbildkamera f.

minimum ['miniməm] Minimum n; Mindest...

mining ['mainiŋ] Bergbau m.

miniskirt ['miniskə:t] Minirock m.

minister ['ministə] Geistliche m; Minister m; Gesandte m; helfen, unterstützen.

ministry ['ministri] geistliches Amt; Ministerium n.

mink [miŋk] Nerz m.

minor ['mainə] kleiner, geringer; unbedeutend; mus. Moll n; Minderjährige m, f; Am. Nebenfach n; **~ity** [~'nɔriti] Minderjährigkeit f; Minderheit f.

minster ['minstə] Münster n.

minstrel ['minstrəl] mus. hist. Spielmann m; Sänger, der als Neger geschminkt auftritt.

mint [mint] bot. Minze f; Münze f; münzen, prägen.

minus ['mainəs] minus, weniger; colloq. ohne.

minute¹ [mai'nju:t] sehr klein, winzig; sehr genau.

minute² ['minit] Minute f; Augenblick m; pl Protokoll n; **in a ~** gleich, sofort; **just a ~** e-n Augenblick.

to the ~ auf die Minute (genau).

mirac|le ['mirəkl] Wunder n; **~ulous** [mi'rækjuləs] wunderbar; **~ulously** wie durch ein Wunder.

mirage ['mira:ʒ] Luftspiegelung f, Fata Morgana f.

mire ['maiə] Schlamm m, Sumpf m, Kot m.

mirror ['mirə] Spiegel m; (wider)spiegeln.

mirth [mə:θ] Fröhlichkeit f, Heiterkeit f.

miry ['maiəri] schlammig.

mis- [mis] miß..., falsch, schlecht.

misadventure Mißgeschick n; Unfall m.

misanthrop|e ['mizən-θrəup], **~ist** [mi'zænθrə-pist] Menschenfeind m.

mis|apply falsch anwenden; **~apprehend** mißverstehen; **~behave** sich schlecht benehmen; **~calculate** falsch berechnen; sich verrechnen.

miscarr|iage Mißlingen n; Fehlgeburt f; **~y** Mißlingen; e-e Fehlgeburt haben.

miscellaneous [misi'leinjəs] ge~, vermischt; verschiedenartig.

mischie|f ['mistʃif] Unheil n, Schaden m; Unfug m; Übermut m; **~vous** ['~vəs] schädlich; boshaft, mutwillig; schelmisch.

mis|deed Missetat f, Verbrechen n; **~demeano(u)r** jur. Vergehen n.

miser ['maizə] Geizhals m.

miser|able ['mizərəbl] elend, erbärmlich; unglücklich; **~y** Elend n, Not f.

mis|fortune Unglück(s-fall m) n; Mißgeschick n; **~giving** Befürchtung f; **~guided** fehl-, irregeleitet; **~hap** ['~hæp] Unglück n, Unfall m; **~inform** falsch unterrichten; **~lay** (irr lay) et. verlegen; **~lead** (irr lead) irreführen, täuschen; verleiten; **~manage** schlecht verwalten od. führen; **~place** et. verlegen; an e-e falsche Stelle legen od. setzen; fig. falsch anbringen; **~print** [~'print] verdrucken; ['~print] Druckfehler m; **~pronounce** falsch aussprechen; **~represent** falsch darstellen, verdrehen.

Miss [mis] mit folgendem Namen: Fräulein n.

miss [mis] Fehlschlag m, -schuß m, -stoß m, -wurf m; Versäumen n, Entrinnen n; verpassen, -säumen, -fehlen; überhören; übersehen; (ver)missen; entgehen; nicht treffen; mißlingen; ~ out auslassen.

missile ['misail] (Wurf-)Geschoß n; (ballistic) ~ Rakete f.

missing ['misiŋ] fehlend,

abwesend; vermißt; **be ~** fehlen.

mission ['miʃən] Auftrag *m*; *eccl.*, *pol.* Mission *f*; *mil.* Einsatz *m*; Berufung *f*; **~ary** ['~ʃnəri] Missionar(in).

mis-spell (*irr* spell) falsch buchstabieren *od.* schreiben.

mist [mist] (feiner) Nebel, feuchter Dunst.

mistake [mis'teik] (*irr* take) verwechseln (**for** mit); mißverstehen; sich irren (in); Mißverständnis *n*; Irrtum *m*, Versehen *n*; Fehler *m*; **by ~** aus Versehen; **~n** falsch; **be ~n** sich irren.

Mister ['mistə] *s.* **Mr.**

mistletoe ['misltəu] Mistel *f*.

mistress ['mistris] Herrin *f*; Lehrerin *f*; Geliebte *f*.

mistrust mißtrauen; Mißtrauen *n*.

misty ['misti] (leicht) neb(e)lig, dunstig; *fig.* unklar.

misunderstand (*irr* stand) mißverstehen; **~ing** Mißverständnis *n*.

misuse [mis'ju:z] mißbrauchen; mißhandeln; ['~'ju:s] Mißbrauch *m*.

mite [mait] Milbe *f*.

mitigate ['mitigeit] mildern, lindern.

mitten ['mitn] Fausthandschuh *m*, Fäustling *m*; Halbhandschuh *m* (*ohne Finger*).

mix [miks] (sich) (ver-) mischen; mixen; verkehren (**with** mit); **~ up** durch-ea.-bringen; verwechseln; **be ~ed up with** in *et.* verwickelt sein; **~ture** Mischung *f*.

moan [məun] Stöhnen *n*; stöhnen.

moat [məut] Burg-, Stadtgraben *m*.

mob [mɔb] Pöbel *m*.

mobile ['məubail] beweglich.

mock [mɔk] falsch, Schein...; (ver)spotten; trotzen; **~ery** Spott *m*, Hohn *m*.

mode [məud] (Art und) Weise *f*; Mode *f*.

model ['mɔdl] Modell *n*; Muster *n*; Mannequin *n*; *fig.* Vorbild *n*; Muster...; Modell...; modellieren; (ab)formen.

moderat|e ['mɔdərit] (mittel)mäßig; ['~eit] (sich) mäßigen; *et.* leiten; **~ion** Mäßigung *f*, Maß(halten) *n*.

modern ['mɔdən] modern, neu; **~ize** (sich) modernisieren.

modest ['mɔdist] bescheiden; **~y** Bescheidenheit *f*.

modi|fication [mɔdifi-'keiʃən] Ab-, Veränderung *f*; Einschränkung *f*; **~fy** ['~fai] (ab)ändern; mäßigen.

modul|ate ['mɔdjuleit] modulieren; **~e** ['~u:l] *Raumfahrt:* Kapsel *f*.

moist [mɔist] feucht, naß;

~en ['~sn] an-, befeuchten; **~ure** ['~stʃə] Feuchtigkeit f.

molar (tooth) ['məulə] Backenzahn m.

mole [məul] zo. Maulwurf m; Muttermal n; Mole f; Hafendamm m.

molecule ['mɔlikju:l] Molekül n.

molest [məu'lest] belästigen.

mollify ['mɔlifai] besänftigen, beruhigen.

moment ['məumənt] Augenblick m, Moment m; Bedeutung f; **~ary** augenblicklich; vorübergehend.

monarch ['mɔnək] Monarch(in); **~y** Monarchie f.

monastery ['mɔnəstəri] (Mönchs)Kloster n.

Monday ['mʌndi] Montag m.

monetary ['mʌnitəri] Währungs...; Geld...

money ['mʌni] Geld n; **~ order** Postanweisung f.

monger ['mʌŋɡə] in Zssgn: ...händler m, ...krämer m.

monk [mʌŋk] Mönch m.

monkey ['mʌŋki] Affe m; **~ business** fauler Zauber; **~wrench** verstellbarer Engländer m (Schraubenschlüssel).

mono|**logue**, Am. a. **.log** ['mɔnəlɔɡ] Monolog m.

mono|**polize**[mə'nɔpəlaiz] monopolisieren; fig. an sich reißen; **~poly** Monopol n (of auf); **~tonous** [~tnəs] monoton, eintönig; **~tony** [~tni] Monotonie f.

monst|**er** ['mɔnstə] Ungeheuer n, Monstrum n; Riesen...; Monster...; **~rous** ungeheuer(lich); gräßlich.

month [mʌnθ] Monat m; **~ly** monatlich, Monats...; Monatsschrift f.

monument ['mɔnjumənt] Monument n, Denkmal n.

moo [mu:] muhen.

mood [mu:d] Stimmung f, Laune f; **~y** launisch; übellaunig; niedergeschlagen.

moon [mu:n] Mond m; **~light** Mondlicht n, -schein m; **~lit** mondhell.

Moor [muə] Maure m, Mohr m.

moor[1] [muə] Moor n, Heideland n.

moor[2] mar. vertäuen; **~ings** pl mar.: Vertäuung f; Ankerplatz m.

moose [mu:s] Elch m.

mop [mɔp] Mop m; (Haar)Wust m; auf-, abwischen.

moral ['mɔrəl] Moral f, pl Moral f, Sitten pl; moralisch; Moral..., Sitten...; **~e** [mɔ'rɑ:l] Moral f (e-r Truppe etc.); **~ity** [mə'ræliti] Moralität f, Moral f; **~ize** ['mɔrəlaiz] moralisieren.

morass [mə'ræs] Morast m, Sumpf m; **~** (haft.).

morbid ['mɔːbid] krankhaft.

more [mɔ:] mehr; noch; no **~** nicht mehr; once **~** noch einmal; **(all) the ~** (nur) um so mehr;

much the ~ as um so mehr als.

morel [mɔ'rel] Morchel f.

moreover [mɔ:'rəuvə] außerdem, ferner.

morgue [mɔ:g] Leichenschauhaus n.

morning ['mɔ:niŋ] Morgen m; Vormittag m; **this** ~ heute morgen od. früh; **tomorrow** ~ morgenfrüh.

morose [mə'rəus] mürrisch.

morph|ia ['mɔ:fjə], **~ine** ['~fi:n] Morphium n.

morsel ['mɔ:səl] Bissen m; Stückchen n, das bißchen.

mortal ['mɔ:tl] sterblich; tödlich; **~ity** [~'tæliti] Sterblichkeit f.

mortar ['mɔ:tə] Mörser m; Mörtel m.

mortgage ['mɔ:gidʒ] Hypothek f; verpfänden.

mortician [mɔ:'tiʃən] Am. Leichenbestatter m.

morti|fication [mɔ:tifi'keiʃən] Kränkung f; **~fy** ['~fai] kränken, demütigen.

mortuary ['mɔ:tjuəri] Leichenhalle f.

mosaic [məu'zeiik] Mosaik n.

mosque [mɔsk] Moschee f.

mosquito [məs'ki:təu] Moskito m; (Stech)Mücke f.

moss [mɔs] Moos n; **~y** moosig, bemoost.

most [məust] meist; die meisten; am meisten; höchst, äußerst; *das* Äußerste; *das* meiste; **at**

(the) ~ höchstens; **~ly** hauptsächlich; meistens.

moth [mɔθ] Motte f; **~-eaten** mottenzerfressen.

mother ['mʌðə] Mutter f; **~ country** Vater-, Heimatland n; Mutterland n; **~hood** Mutterschaft f; **~-in-law** Schwiegermutter f; **~ly** mütterlich; **~-of-pearl** Perlmutter f, n; **~'s help** Hausangestellte f; **~ tongue** Muttersprache f.

motif [məu'ti:f] (Leit)Motiv n.

motion ['məuʃən] Bewegung f; Gang m (a. tech.); parl. Antrag m; (j-m zu-) winken; j-m ein Zeichen geben; **~less** bewegungslos; **~ picture** Film m.

motiv|ate ['məutiveit] motivieren, begründen; **~e** Motiv n.

motor ['məutə] Motor m; Motor...; im Auto fahren; **~-bicycle**, **~-bike** Motorrad n; **~-boat** Motorboot n; **~-bus** Autobus m; **~-car** Auto(mobil) n, (Kraft)Wagen m; **~-coach** Reisebus m; **~-cycle** Motorrad n; **~-cyclist** Motorradfahrer m; **~ing** Autofahren n; **~ist** Autofahrer(in); **~ize** motorisieren; **~-lorry** Last(kraft)wagen m; **~-scooter** Motorroller m; **~-way** Autobahn f.

motto ['mɔtəu] Motto n.

mo(u)ld [məuld] Schimmel m; (Guß)Form f; formen; gießen; **~er (away)**

mo(u)lt

zerfallen; **~y** schimm(e)lig, mod(e)rig. **[**mausern.**]**
mo(u)lt [məʊlt] (sich)
mound [maʊnd] Erdhügel m, -wall m.
mount [maʊnt] Berg m; (Reit)Pferd n; be-, ersteigen; hinaufgehen; montieren; (auf-, hinauf)steigen; aufs Pferd steigen.
mountain ['maʊntin] Berg m; **pl** Gebirge n; Berg...; Gebirgs...; **~eer** [‚‿'niə] Bergbewohner(in); Bergsteiger(in); **~ous** berg, gebirgig.
mourn [mɔːn] trauern (**for**, **over** um); betrauern, trauern um; **~er** Leidtragende m, f; **~ful** traurig; **~ing** Trauer f.
mouse [maʊs], **pl mice** [mais] Maus f.
moustache [məs'tɑːʃ] Schnurrbart m.
mouth [maʊθ], **pl ~s** [maʊðz] Mund m; Maul n; Mündung f; **~ful** Mundvoll m; **~organ** Mundharmonika f; **~piece** Mundstück n; fig. Sprachrohr n; **~wash** Mundwasser n.
move [muːv] bewegen; (weg)rücken; fig. rühren; et. beantragen; sich (fort)bewegen; sich rühren; (um)ziehen (**to** nach); **~ in** einziehen; **~ on** weitergehen; **~ out** ausziehen; Schach: Zug m; Bewegung f; fig. Schritt m; **~ment** Bewegung f.

movies ['muːviz] pl colloq. Kino n.
moving ['muːviŋ] beweglich; treibend; fig. rührend.
mow [məʊ] (irr) mähen; **~er** Mäher(in); Mähmaschine f; **~n** pp von **mow**.
Mr, Mr. ['mistə] abbr. von **Mister:** Herr m (vor Familiennamen od. Titeln).
Mrs, Mrs. ['misiz] mit folgendem Familiennamen: Frau f.
much [mʌtʃ] viel; sehr; fast; vor comp: viel; vor sup: bei weitem; **too ~** zuviel; **very ~** sehr; **I thought as ~** das dachte ich mir; **make ~ of** viel Wesens machen von.
mucus ['mjuːkəs] biol. Schleim m.
mud [mʌd] Schlamm m; Schmutz m.
muddle ['mʌdl] verwirren; **~ (up)**, **~ (together)** durcheinanderbringen; Durcheinander n.
mud|dy ['mʌdi] schlammig; trüb(e); **~guard** Kotflügel m.
muff [mʌf] Muff m.
muffle ['mʌfl] **~ (up)** einwickeln; Stimme etc. dämpfen; **~r** Halstuch n, Schal m; Am. mot. Auspufftopf m.
mug [mʌg] Krug m; Becher m.
mulberry ['mʌlbəri] Maulbeerbaum m; Maulbeere f.
mule [mjuːl] Maultier n;

mull [mʌl] Mull *m*.

mulled | claret [mʌld], **~ wine** Glühwein *m*.

mullion ['mʌliən] Fensterpfosten *m*.

multi|ple ['mʌltipl] vielfach; mehrere, viele; **~ plication** [~pli'keiʃən] Vermehrung *f*; Multiplikation *f*; **~plication table** Einmaleins *n*; **~ply** ['~plai] (sich) vermehren; multiplizieren; **~tude** [~ʧju:d] (Menschen)Menge *f*.

mumble ['mʌmbl] murmeln; mummeln (*mühsam essen*).

mummy¹ ['mʌmi] Mumie *f*.

mummy² Mami *f*, Mutti *f*.

mumps [mʌmps] *sg* Ziegenpeter *m*, Mumps *m*, *f*.

munch [mʌnʧ] mit vollen Backen kauen, mampfen.

municipal [mju(:)'nisipəl] städtisch, Gemeinde..., Stadt...; **~ity** [~'pæliti] Stadtverwaltung *f*.

mural ['mjuərəl] Mauer..., Wand...

murder ['mɜ:də] Mord *m*; (er)morden; **~er** Mörder *m*; **~ess** Mörderin *f*; **~ous** mörderisch; Mord...

murmur ['mɜ:mə] Murmeln *n*; Gemurmel *n*; Murren *n*; murmeln; murren.

musc|le ['mʌsl] Muskel *m*; **~le-bound: be ~** Muskelkater haben; **~ular** ['~kjulə] Muskel...; muskulös.

muse [mju:z] (nach)sinnen, (-)grübeln.

museum [mju(:)'ziəm] Museum *n*.

mush [mʌʃ] (*Am.* Mais-) Brei *m*.

mushroom ['mʌʃrum] Pilz *m*, *bsd.* Champignon *m*.

music ['mju:zik] Musik *f*; Noten *pl*; **~al** Musical *n*; Musik...; musikalisch; wohlklingend; **~al box** *Brit.*, **~ box** *Am.* Spieldose *f*; **~-hall** Varieté(theater) *n*; **~ian** [~'ziʃən] Musiker (-in); **~stand** Notenständer *m*; **~stool** Klavierstuhl *m*.

musk [mʌsk] Moschus *m*, Bisam *m*.

musket ['mʌskit] Muskete *f*.

musk-rat Bisamratte *f*.

Muslim ['muslim] mohammedanisch; Moslem *m*.

muslin ['mʌzlin] Musselin *m*.

musquash ['mʌskwɔʃ] Bisamratte *f*; Bisampelz *m*.

mussel ['mʌsl] (Mies-) Muschel *f*.

must¹ [mʌst] Muß *n*; *v/aux* ich, du *etc.*: muß(st) *etc.*, darf(st) *etc.*; *pret* mußte(st) *etc.*, durfte(st) *etc.*; **I ~ not** ich darf nicht.

must² Schimmel *m*, Moder *m*; Most *m*.

mustache ['mʌstæʃ] *Am.* Schnurrbart *m*.

mustard ['mʌstəd] Senf *m*.

muster ['mʌstə] versammeln; **~ (up)** aufbieten.

musty ['mʌsti] mod(e)rig, muffig. [Stumme, *m*, *f*.]

mute [mju:t] stumm;]

mutilate ['mjuːtileit] verstümmeln.

mutin|eer [mjuːti'niə] Meuterer *m*; **~ous** ['~nəs] meuternd, rebellisch; **~y** ['~ni] Meuterei *f*; meutern.

mutter ['mʌtə] Gemurmel *n*; murmeln; murren.

mutton ['mʌtn] Hammel-, Schaffleisch *n*; **~ chop** Hammelkotelett *n*.

mutual ['mjuːtʃuəl] gegen-, wechselseitig; gemeinsam.

muzzle ['mʌzl] Maul *n*, Schnauze *f*; Maulkorb *m*;

(*Gewehr*)Mündung *f*; e-n Maulkorb anlegen; *fig.* den Mund stopfen.

my [mai] mein(e).

myrrh [məː] Myrrhe *f*.

myrtle ['məːtl] Myrte *f*.

myself [mai'self] (ich) selbst; mir, mich; mir *od.* mich selbst; **by ~** allein.

myster|ious [mis'tiəriəs] geheimnisvoll; **~y** ['~təri] Geheimnis *n*; Rätsel *n*.

mystify ['mistifai] verwirren, -blüffen.

myth [miθ] Mythos *m*, Mythe *f*, Sage *f*.

N

nag [næg] nörgeln; **~ (at)** herumnörgeln an.

nail [neil] Nagel *m*; (an-, fest)nageln.

naked ['neikid] nackt; bloß; kahl.

name [neim] (be)nennen; erwähnen; ernennen; Name *m*; **what is your ~?** wie heißen Sie?; **my ~ is ...** ich heiße ...; **call s.o. ~s** j-n beschimpfen; **~less** namenlos, unbekannt; **~ly** nämlich.

nanny ['næni] Kindermädchen *n*; **~goat** Ziege *f*.

nap [næp] Schläfchen *n*; **have** *od.* **take a ~** ein Nickerchen machen.

nape (of the neck) [neip] Genick *m*, Nacken *m*.

nap|kin ['næpkin] Serviette *f*; *Brit.* Windel *f*; **~py** *Brit. colloq.* Windel *f*.

narcosis [naːˈkousis] Narkose *f*.

narcotic [naːˈkotik] Betäubungsmittel *n*; Rauschgift *n*.

narrat|e [næˈreit] erzählen; **~ion** Erzählung *f*; **~ive** ['~ətiv] Erzählung *f*; **~or** [~ˈreitə] Erzähler *m*.

narrow ['nærou] eng, schmal; beschränkt; *fig.* knapp; (sich) verengen; **~minded** engherzig, -stirnig.

nasty ['naːsti] schmutzig; widerlich; unangenehm; böse; häßlich.

nation ['neiʃən] Nation *f*, Volk *n*.

national ['næʃənl] national, National..., Landes..., Volks..., Staats...; Staatsangehörige *m, f*; **~ity** [~ˈnæliti] Nationalität *f*,

negotiate

Staatsangehörigkeit *f*; **.ity plate** *mot.* Nationalitätskennzeichen *n*; **.ize** ['-∫-nəlaiz] einbürgern; verstaatlichen.

native ['neitiv] Eingeborene *m*, *f*; angeboren; eingeboren; einheimisch; gebürtig; heimatlich, Heimat...; ~ **language** Muttersprache *f*.

nativity [nə'tiviti] Geburt *f* (*bsd. eccl.*).

natural ['nætʃrəl] natürlich; angeboren; wirklich; **.ize** einbürgern; ~ **science** Naturwissenschaft *f*.

nature ['neitʃə] Natur *f*.

naught [nɔ:t] Null *f*; **.y** frech, ungezogen, unartig.

nausea ['nɔ:sjə] Übelkeit *f*; Ekel *m*; **.ting** ['-ieitiŋ] ekelerregend.

nautical ['nɔ:tikəl] nautisch; ~ **mile** Seemeile *f*.

naval ['neivəl] See..., Marine...; ~ **base** Flottenstützpunkt *m*.

nave¹ [neiv] (Kirchen-) Schiff *n*.

nave² [neiv] (Rad)Nabe *f*.

navel ['neivəl] Nabel *m*; *fig.* Mittelpunkt *m*.

naviga|ble ['nævigəbl] schiffbar; fahrbar; lenkbar; **.te** ['-eit] (be)fahren; navigieren, steuern; **.tion** Schiffahrt *f*; Navigation *f*; **.tor** Steuermann *m*; Seefahrer *m*.

navy['neivi|Kriegsmarine *f*.

nay [nei] nein; ja sogar.

near [niə] nahe; in der Nähe (von); nahe verwandt; eng befreundet; knapp; geizig; nahe an *od.* bei; sich nähern; **.by** *bsd. Am.* in der Nähe, nahe; **.ly** nahe; fast, beinahe; annähernd; **.ness** Nähe *f*; **.sighted** kurzsichtig.

neat [ni:t] ordentlich; sauber; **.ness** Sauberkeit *f*.

necess|ary ['nesisəri] notwendig; **.itate** [ni'sesiteit] erfordern, verlangen; **.ity** [ni'sesiti] Notwendigkeit *f*; Bedürfnis *n*; Not *f*.

neck [nek] Hals *m*; Nacken *m*, Genick *n*; *sl.* (sich) (ab-) knutschen; **.erchief** ['-kətʃif] Halstuch *n*; **.lace** ['-lis] Halskette *f*; **.tie** Krawatte *f*.

née [nei] geborene.

need [ni:d] nötig haben, brauchen; müssen; Not *f*; Notwendigkeit *f*; Bedürfnis *n*; Mangel *m*; **in ~** in Not; **be** *od.* **stand in ~ of** dringend brauchen.

needle ['ni:dl] (Näh-, Strick)Nadel *f*; Zeiger *m*.

needy ['ni:di] bedürftig.

negat|e [ni'geit] verneinen; **.ion** Verneinung *f*; **.ive** ['negativ] negativ; verneinen(d); Verneinung *f*; *phot.* Negativ *n*; **answer in the .ive** verneinen.

neglect [ni'glekt] vernachlässigen.

negligent ['neglidʒənt] nachlässig.

negotiat|e [ni'gəuʃieit]

verhandeln (über); ~ion Ver-, Unterhandlung f.

Negr|ess ['ni:gris] Negerin f; ~o ['~əu], pl ~oes Neger m. [wiehern.]

neigh [nei] Wiehern n;

neighbo(u)r ['neibə] Nachbar(in); Nächste m; ~hood Nachbarschaft f; Umgebung f, Nähe f; ~ing benachbart.

neither ['naiðə, Am. 'ni:ðə] kein(er, -e, -es) (von beiden); auch nicht; ~ ... nor ... weder ... noch ...

neon ['ni:ɔn] Neon n; ~ sign Neonreklame f.

nephew ['nevju(:)] Neffe m.

nerve [nə:v] Nerv m; (Blatt)Rippe f; Mut m; get on s.o.'s ~s j-m auf die Nerven gehen.

nervous ['nə:vəs] nervös; Nerven...; ~ness Nervosität f.

nest [nest] Nest n; ~le ['nesl]: ~ (down) sich behaglich niederlassen; ~ up to sich anschmiegen an.

net¹ [net] Netz n.

net² netto; Rein...

nettle ['netl] bot. Nessel f; ärgern.

network ['netwə:k] (Straßen- etc.)Netz n; Radio: Sendernetz n, -gruppe f.

neurosis [njuə'rəusis] Neurose f.

neuter ['nju:tə] gr.: sächlich; Neutrum n.

neutral ['nju:trəl] neutral; unparteiisch; Neutrale m, f; mot. Leerlauf(stellung f)

m; ~ **gear** mot. Leerlauf (-gang) m; ~ity [~'træliti] Neutralität f; ~ize neutralisieren. [tron n.]

neutron ['nju:trɔn] Neu-

never ['nevə] nie(mals); gar nicht; ~more nie wieder; ~theless nichtsdestoweniger, dennoch.

new [nju:] neu; frisch; unerfahren; ~born neugeboren; ~comer Neuankömmling m; Neuling m.

news [nju:z] sg Neuigkeit(en pl) f, Nachricht(en pl) f; ~agent Zeitungshändler m; ~cast Radio: Nachrichtensendung f; ~paper Zeitung f; Zeitungs...; ~reel Film: Wochenschau f; ~stand Zeitungskiosk m.

new year Neujahr n, das neue Jahr; 2 **Year's Day** Neujahrstag m; 2 **Year's Eve** Silvester n.

next [nekst] adj nächst; (the) ~ **day** am nächsten Tag; ~ **door** nebenan; ~ **to** neben; ~ **but one** übernächst; adv am nächste(r, -s); das nächste Mal; prp gleich neben od. bei od. an; sub: der, die, das nächste.

nibble ['nibl]: ~ (at) nagen an, knabbern an.

nice [nais] nett; hübsch; schön; fein; angenehm; heikel; (peinlich) genau; ~ly adv gut, ausgezeichnet; ~ty [~iti] Feinheit f; Genauigkeit f.

niche [nitʃ] Nische f.

nick [nik] Kerbe f; (ein)kerben.

nickel ['nikl] min. Nickel n; Am. Nickel m (Fünfcentstück); vernickeln.

nick-nack ['niknæk] s. **knick-knack.**

nickname ['nikneim] Spitzname m; j-m den Spitznamen ... geben.

niece [ni:s] Nichte f.

niggard ['nigəd] Geizhals m.

night [nait] Nacht f; Abend m; **at** ~, **by** ~, **in the** ~ bei Nacht, nachts; ~**cap** Nachtmütze f; Schlaftrunk m; ~**club** Nachtklub m, -lokal n; ~**dress**, ~**gown** (Damen)Nachthemd n; ~**ingale** ['~iŋgeil] Nachtigall f; ~**ly** nächtlich; jede Nacht od. jeden Abend (stattfindend); ~**mare** ['~mɛə] Alptraum m; ~**school** Abendschule f; ~**shirt** (Herren)Nachthemd n; ~**y** colloq. (Damen-, Kinder)Nachthemd n.

nil [nil] bsd. sp. null.

nimble ['nimbl] flink, behend(e).

nine [nain] neun; Neun f; ~**pins** sg Kegel(spiel n) pl; ~**teen(th)** ['~'ti:n(θ)] neunzehn(te); ~**tieth** ['~tiiθ] neunzigste; ~**ty** neunzig; Neunzig f.

ninth [nainθ] neunte; Neuntel n; ~**ly** neuntens.

nip [nip] scharfer Frost;

Schlückchen n; kneifen, zwicken, klemmen; schneiden (Kälte); sl. flitzen; nippen (an).

nipple ['nipl] Brustwarze f.

nit│re, Am. ~**er** ['naitə·trədʒən] Stickstoff m.

no [nəu] nein; Nein n; kein(e); ~ **one** keiner.

nobility [nəu'biliti] Adel m.

noble ['nəubl] adlig; edel; vornehm; Adlige m, f; ~**man** Adlige m, Edelmann m.

nobody ['nəubədi] niemand, keiner.

nod [nɔd] nicken (mit); (im Sitzen) schlafen; sich neigen; Nicken n, Wink m.

noise [nɔiz] Lärm m; Geräusch n; Geschrei n; ~**less** geräuschlos.

noisy ['nɔizi] geräuschvoll; laut; lärmend.

nomin│al ['nɔminl] nominell, nur dem Namen nach; ~**ate** ['~eit] ernennen; nominieren, vorschlagen; ~**ation** Ernennung f; Nominierung f.

nominative (case) ['nɔminətiv] gr. Nominativ m, 1. Fall.

non- [nɔn-] in Zssgn: nicht..., Nicht..., un...

non│-alcoholic alkoholfrei; ~**-commissioned officer** Unteroffizier m; ~**-committal** unverbindlich; ~**conductor** electr. Nichtleiter m; ~**conformist** Dissident(in), Freikirchler

(-in); **~descript** [-diskript] schwer zu beschreiben(d); nichtssagend.

none [nʌn] kein(e, -er, -es); keineswegs.

non|**-existence** Nicht(da)sein *n*; *das* Fehlen; **~fiction** Sachbücher *pl*.

nonsense ['nɔnsəns] Unsinn *m*.

non|**-skid** rutschfest, -sicher; **~-smoker** Nichtraucher(in) *m*; *rail.* Nichtraucher(abteil *n*) *m*; **~-stop** Nonstop..., *rail.* durchgehend, *aer.* ohne Zwischenlandung; **~-union** nicht organisiert (*Arbeiter*); **~-violence** (Politik *f* der) Gewaltlosigkeit *f*.

noodle ['nu:dl] Nudel *f*.

nook [nuk] Ecke *f*, Winkel *m*.

noon [nu:n] Mittag *m*; Mittags...; **at (high) ~** um 12 Uhr mittags.

noose [nu:s] Schlinge *f*.

nor [nɔ:] noch; auch nicht.

norm [nɔ:m] Norm *f*, Regel *f*; **~al** normal; **~alize** normalisieren; normen.

Norman ['nɔ:mən] normannisch; Normann|e *m*, -in *f*.

north [nɔ:θ] Nord(en *m*); nördlich, Nord...; **~east** Nordost; **~east(ern)**nordöstlich; **~erly** ['-ð-], **~ern** ['-ð-] nördlich, Nord...; **~erner** ['-ð-] *bsd. Am.* Nordstaatler(in); **2 Pole** Nordpol *m*; **2 Sea**

Nordsee *f*; **~ward(s)**['-wəd(z)] nördlich, nordwärts; **~west** Nordwest; **~west(ern)** nordwestlich.

Norwegian [nɔ:'wi:dʒən] norwegisch; Norweger (-in); Norwegisch *n*.

nose [nəuz] Nase *f*; Spitze *f*; Schnauze *f*; riechen; schnüffeln; **~gay** ['-gei] (Blumen)Strauß *m*.

nostril ['nɔstril] Nasenloch *n*, Nüster *f*.

nosy ['nəuzi] *sl.* neugierig.

not [nɔt] nicht; **~ a** kein(e).

notable ['nəutəbl] bemerkenswert.

notary ['nəutəri], *oft* **~ public** Notar *m*.

notation [nəu'teiʃən] Bezeichnung(ssystem *n*) *f*.

notch [nɔtʃ] Kerbe *f*; *Am.* Engpaß *m*; (ein)kerben.

note [nəut] bemerken,be(ob)achten; **~ down** notieren; Zeichen *n*; Notiz *f*; Note *f* (*a. mus.*); Briefchen *n*, Zettel *m*; *print.* Anmerkung *f*; Banknote *f*; *mus.* Ton *m*; **take ~s** sich Notizen machen; notebook *n*; **~d** bekannt; **~paper** Briefpapier *n*; **~worthy** bemerkenswert.

nothing ['nʌθiŋ] nichts; **~ but** nichts als, nur; **for ~** umsonst; **good for ~** zu nichts zu gebrauchen; **say ~ of** geschweige denn; **there is ~ like** es geht nichts über.

notice ['nəutis] bemerken, be(ob)achten; Notiz

f; Nachricht *f*, Bekanntmachung *f*, Anschlag *m*; Anzeige *f*, Ankündigung *f*; Kündigung *f*; Aufmerksamkeit *f*; **at short ~** kurzfristig; **without ~** fristlos; **give ~ that** bekanntgeben; **give (a week's) ~** (acht Tage vorher) kündigen; **take ~ of** Notiz nehmen von; **~able** wahrnehmbar; beachtlich.

noti|fication [nəutifi'kei-ʃən] Anzeige *f*, Meldung *f*; Bekanntmachung *f*; **~fy** ['~fai] *et.* anzeigen, melden; benachrichtigen.

notion ['nəuʃən] Begriff *m*, Vorstellung *f*; *pl Am.* Kurzwaren *pl.*

notorious [nəu'tɔːriəs] notorisch; berüchtigt.

notwithstanding [nɔtwið'stændiŋ] ungeachtet, trotz. [*f.*]

nought [nɔːt] nichts; Null *f*

noun [naun] *gr.* Substantiv *n*, Hauptwort *n*.

nourish ['nʌriʃ] (er)nähren; *fig.* hegen; **~ing** nahrhaft; **~ment** Ernährung *f*; Nahrung(smittel *n*) *f*.

novel ['nɔvəl] neu; Roman *m*; **~ist** Romanschriftsteller(in); **~ty** Neuheit *f*.

November [nəu'vembə] November *m*.

novice ['nɔvis] Neuling *m*; *eccl.* Novize *m*.

now [nau] nun; jetzt; eben; **just ~** soeben; **~ and again, (every) ~ and then** dann u. wann.

nowadays ['nauədeiz] heutzutage. [gends.\]

nowhere ['nəuwɛə] nir-\]

noxious ['nɔkʃəs] schädlich. [Mundstück *n*.]

nozzle ['nɔzl] Düse *f*;\]

nuclear ['njuːkliə] Kern...; **~ fission** Kernspaltung *f*; **~ power plant** *od.* **station** Atomkraftwerk *n*; **~ reactor** Kernreaktor *m*.

nucleus ['njuːkliəs] Kern *m*.

nude [njuːd] nackt; *paint.* Akt *m*.

nudge [nʌdʒ] *j-n* heimlich anstoßen; Rippenstoß *m*.

nugget ['nʌgit] (*bsd.* Gold-) Klumpen *m*.

nuisance ['njuːsns] Ärgernis *n*, Unfug *m*, Plage *f*.

null [nʌl]: **~ and void** null u. nichtig, ungültig.

numb [nʌm] starr, taub.

number ['nʌmbə] Nummer *f*; (An)Zahl *f*; Heft *n*, Ausgabe *f*, Nummer *f*; (*Autobus- etc.*) Linie *f*; zählen; numerieren; **~less** zahllos; **~ plate** *mot.* Nummernschild *n*.

numer|al ['njuːmərəl] Ziffer *f*; *ling.* Numerale *n*, Zahlwort *n*; **~ous** zahlreich.

nun [nʌn] Nonne *f*; **~nery** (Nonnen)Kloster *n*.

nuptials ['nʌpʃəlz] *pl* Hochzeit *f*.

nurse [nəːs] Kindermädchen *n*, Säuglingsschwester *f*; Amme *f*; Krankenpflegerin *f*, Krankenschwester f; stillen, nähren; großziehen; pflegen.

nursery ['nə:səri] Kinderzimmer n; Baum-, Pflanzschule f; ~ **rhyme** Kinderlied n, -reim m; ~ **school** Kindergarten m; ~**school teacher** Kindergärtnerin f; ~ **slope** Ski: Idiotenhügel m.

nursing ['nə:siŋ] Stillen n; Krankenpflege f; ~ **home** Privatklinik f.

nut [nʌt] Nuß f; (Schrauben)Mutter f; **be** ~**s** sl. verrückt sein; ~**crackers** pl Nußknacker m; ~**meg** ['~meg] Muskatnuß f.

nutri|ment ['nju:trimənt] Nahrung f; ~**tion** Ernährung f; ~**tious** nahrhaft.

nut|shell Nußschale f; **in a** ~**shell** in aller Kürze; ~**ty** nußartig; sl. verrückt.

nylon ['nailən] Nylon n; pl Nylonstrümpfe m/pl.

nymph [nimf] Nymphe f.

O

o [əu] int. o(h)!, ach!; bsd. teleph. Null f.

oak(-tree) ['əuk(-)] Eiche f.

oar [ɔ:] Ruder n, Riemen m; rudern; ~**sman** Ruderer m.

oas|is [əu'eisis] pl ~**es** [~i:z] Oase f (a. fig.).

oast [əust] Darre f; ~**house** Darrhaus n.

oat [əut] mst pl Hafer m; **sow one's wild** ~**s** sich die Hörner abstoßen.

oath [əuθ], pl ~**s** [~əuðz] Eid m, Schwur m; Fluch m; **on** ~ unter Eid.

oatmeal Hafermehl n, -flocken pl.

obedien|ce [ə'bi:djəns] Gehorsam m; ~**t** gehorsam.

obey [ə'bei] gehorchen; Befehl etc. befolgen.

obituary [ə'bitjuəri] Todesanzeige f; Nachruf m.

object ['ɔbdʒikt] Gegen-

stand m; Ziel n, Zweck m, Absicht f; Objekt n; gr. Objekt n, Satzergänzung f; [əb'dʒekt]: ~ (**to**) einwenden (gegen); protestieren (gegen); et. dagegen haben; ~**ion** Einwand m, -spruch m; ~**ive** objektiv, sachlich; Ziel n; opt. Objektiv n.

obligation [ɔbli'geiʃən] Verpflichtung f; Verbindlichkeit f; econ. Schuldverschreibung f; **be under an** ~ **to** s.o. j-m (zu Dank) verpflichtet sein.

oblig|e [ə'blaidʒ] (zu Dank) verpflichten; nötigen, zwingen; **much** ~**ed** sehr verbunden, danke bestens; ~**ing** gefällig, zuvorkommend. [schräg.]

oblique [ə'bli:k] schief,

obliterate [ə'blitərit] auslöschen; ausstreichen.

oblivi|on [ə'bliviən] Vergessenheit *f;* **~ous: be ~ of** s.th. *et.* vergessen (haben).

oblong ['ɔblɔŋ] länglich; rechteckig. [ständig.]

obscene [əb'si:n] unan-

obscure [əb'skjuə] dunkel; *fig.* dunkel, unklar; unbekannt; verdunkeln.

obsequies ['ɔbsikwiz] *pl* Trauerfeierlichkeiten *pl.*

observ|ance [əb'zə:vəns] Befolgung *f,* Einhaltung *f;* Brauch *m;* **~ant** aufmerksam; **~ant of** befolgend; **~ation** Beobachtung *f;* Bemerkung *f;* Beobachtungs..., Aussichts...; **~atory** [~tri] Observatorium *n;* Stern-, Wetterwarte *f;* **~e** be(ob)achten; sehen; (ein)halten; befolgen; bemerken, (sich) äußern; **~er** Beobachter (-in).

obsess [əb'ses]: **~ed by, ~ed with** besessen von; **~ion** Besessenheit *f.*

obsolete ['ɔbsəli:t] veraltet. [dernis *n.*]

obstacle ['ɔbstəkl] Hin-

obstina|cy ['ɔbstinəsi] Eigensinn *m;* Hartnäckigkeit *f;* **~te** [~it] eigensinnig; hartnäckig.

obstruct [əb'strʌkt] versperren, -stopfen, blokkieren; behindern.

obtain [əb'tein] erlangen, erhalten, erreichen, bekommen; **~able** erhältlich.

obtrusive [əb'tru:siv] aufdringlich.

obvious ['ɔbviəs] offensichtlich, augenfällig, klar.

occasion [ə'keiʒən] veranlassen, -ursachen; Gelegenheit *f;* Grund *m,* Ursache *f;* Anlaß *m;* **on the ~ of** anläßlich; **~al** gelegentlich, Gelegenheits...

Occident ['ɔksidənt]: **the ~** Okzident *m,* Abendland *n.*

occup|ant ['ɔkjupənt] Bewohner(in; Insass|e *m,* -in *f;* **~ation** Besitznahme *f; mil.* Besatzung *f;* Beruf *m;* Beschäftigung *f;* **~y** ['~pai] einnehmen, in Besitz nehmen; bewohnen; *mil.* besetzen; besitzen; in Anspruch nehmen; beschäftigen.

occur [ə'kə:] vorkommen; sich ereignen; **it ~red to me** es fiel mir ein; **~rence** [ə'kʌrəns] Vorkommen *n;* Vorfall *m,* Ereignis *n.*

ocean ['ouʃən] Ozean *m,* Meer *n.*

o'clock [ə'klɔk]: **(at) five ~** (um) fünf Uhr.

October [ɔk'toubə] Oktober *m.*

ocul|ar ['ɔkjulə] Augen...; **~ist** Augenarzt *m.*

odd [ɔd] ungerade (*Zahl*); einzeln; etwas darüber; überzählig; gelegentlich; sonderbar; **~s** *pl* (Gewinn-) Chancen *pl;* Vorteil *m;* Unterschied *m;* **the ~s are that** es ist sehr wahrscheinlich, daß; **at ~s with** im Streit mit, un-

einig mit; **~s and ends**
Krimskrams *m*; Reste *pl.*
odo(u)r ['əudə] Geruch *m*.
of [ɔv, əv] von; *Ort:* bei;
um **(cheat** s.o. **~** s.th.);
Herkunft: von, aus; *Mate-*
rial: aus, von; von, an
(die ~); aus **(~ charity);**
vor **(afraid ~);** auf
(proud ~); über **(glad**
~); nach **(smell ~);** von,
über **(speak ~** s.th.);
an **(think ~** s.th.); **the**
city ~ London die Stadt
London; **the works ~**
Dickens D's Werke; **your**
letter ~ ... Ihr Schreiben
vom ...; **five minutes ~**
twelve *Am.* fünf Minuten
vor zwölf.

off [ɔf] *adv* fort, weg; ab,
herunter(...), los(...); entfernt; *Zeit:* bis, hin; aus(-),
ab(geschaltet) *(Licht etc.)*;
zu *(Hahn etc.)*; ab(-), los
(-gegangen) *(Knopf etc.)*;
frei *(von Arbeit)*; ganz, zu
Ende; *econ.* flau; verdorben *(Fleisch etc.)*; *fig.* aus,
vorbei; **be ~** fort od. weg
sein; **(weg)gehen;** *prp* fort
von, weg von; von (... ab,
weg, herunter; abseits
von, entfernt von; frei von
(Arbeit); *adj* (weiter) entfernt; Seiten..., Neben...;
(arbeits-, dienst)frei; *econ.*
flau, still, tot; *int.* fort,
weg!

offen|ce, *Am.* **~se** [ə'fens]
Vergehen *n*, Verstoß *m*;
Beleidigung *f*, Anstoß *m*;
Angriff *m*; **~d** beleidi-

gen, verletzen; verstoßen
(against gegen); **~der**
Übeltäter(in); Straffällige
m, *f*; **~sive** beleidigend;
anstößig; ekelhaft; An-
griffs...; Offensive *f*.

offer ['ɔfə] Angebot *n*;
Anerbieten *n*; anbieten;
(sich) bieten; darbringen;
Widerstand leisten; **~ing**
Opfer(n) *n*; Angebot *n*.

office ['ɔfis] Büro *n*; Geschäftsstelle *f*; ♀ Amt *n*;
Ministerium *n*; **~r** Beam-
t(e) *m*, -in *f*; Polizist *m*,
Polizeibeamte *m*; *mil.* Offizier *m*.

official [ə'fiʃəl] offiziell,
amtlich, Amts..., Dienst...;
Beamt|e *m*, -in *f*.

officious [ə'fiʃəs] aufdringlich.

off|-licence Schankerlaub-
nis *f* über die Straße;
~side *sp.* abseits; **~spring**
Nachkomme(nschaft *f*) *m*.

often ['ɔfn] oft, häufig.

oh [əu] *int.* oh!, ach!

oil [ɔil] Öl *n*; Erdöl *n*;
ölen, schmieren; **~cloth**
Wachstuch *n*; **~y** ölig, fettig, schmierig. [be *f.*]

ointment ['ɔintmənt] Sal-
O.K., OK, okay ['əu'kei]
colloq. richtig, gut, in Ordnung.

old [əuld] alt; **ten-year-**
zehnjährig; **~ age** (das)
Alter; **~age** Alters...;
~fashioned altmodisch;
~ town Altstadt *f*.

olive ['ɔliv] Olive *f*; Oliv-
grün *n*.

open

Olympic Games [əu'lim-pik] *pl* Olympische Spiele *pl*. [lett(e *f*) n.]
omelet(te) ['ɔmlit] Ome-
ominous ['ɔminəs] un-heilvoll.
omis|sion [ə'miʃən] Unter-lassung *f*; Auslassung *f*; **.t** unterlassen; auslassen.
omni|potent [ɔm'nipə-tənt] allmächtig; **.scient** [.siənt] allwissend.
on [ɔn] *prp* auf, an, in; **. the street** *Am*. auf der Straße; *Richtung, Ziel*: auf ... (hin), an; *fig*. auf ... (hin) (**. duty, . fire**); *Thema*: über; *Zeitpunkt*: an (**. Sunday, . the 1st of April**); bei (**. his arrival**); *adv* an(geschaltet) (*Licht etc.*), eingeschaltet, laufend, auf (*Hahn etc.*); auf(legen, -schrauben etc.); *Kleidung*: an(haben, -ziehen), auf(behalten); weiter(gehen, -sprechen etc.); **and so .** und so weiter; **. and .** immer weiter; **. to ...** auf ... (hinaus); **be .** im Gange sein, los sein; *thea*. gespielt werden; laufen (*Film*).
once [wʌns] einmal; je (-mals); einst; sobald; **. again, .** more noch einmal; **. in a while** dann u. wann; **.** (**upon a time**) **there was** es war einmal; **at .** sofort;

zugleich; **all at .** plötzlich; **for .** diesmal, ausnahms-weise.
one [wʌn] ein; einzig; man; eins; Eins *f*; **. Smith** ein gewisser Smith; **. day** eines Tages; **. of these days** demnächst; **. by .** einer nach dem andern; **. another** einander; **the little .s** die Kleinen; **.self** sich (selbst); (sich) selbst; **.-sided** einseitig; **.-way street** Ein-bahnstraße *f*.
onion ['ʌnjən] Zwiebel *f*.
onlooker ['ɔnlukə] Zu-schauer(in).
only ['əunli] einzig; nur, bloß; erst.
onto ['ɔntu, '.ə] auf.
onward ['ɔnwəd] vorwärts gerichtet; **.(s)** vorwärts, weiter.
ooze [u:z] Schlamm *m*; sik-kern; ausströmen, -schwit-zen. [durchsichtig.]
opaque [əu'peik] un-|
open ['əupən] offen, ge-öffnet, auf; frei (*Feld etc.*); öffentlich; aufgeschlossen (**to** für); freimütig; frei-gebig; **in the . air** im Freien; *vb*: (er)öffnen; sich öffnen, aufgehen; führen, gehen (*Tür*) (**on** auf; **into** nach); beginnen; **.-air** im Freien, Freilicht...; Freiluft...; **.er** (*Büchsen-etc.*)Öffner *m*; **.-handed** freigebig; **.ing** (Er)Öff-nung *f*; freie Stelle; Mög-lichkeit *f*; Eröffnungs...;

~-minded aufgeschlossen.
opera ['ɔpərə] Oper *f*;
~-glasses *pl* Opernglas *n*.
operat|e ['ɔpəreit] arbeiten, funktionieren, laufen;
med., mil. operieren; *Maschine* bedienen; bewirken;
~ion Operation *f*; **~ive** ['~ətiv] wirksam; *med.*
operativ; **~or** *tech.* Bedienungsperson *f*; Telefonist(in).

opinion [ə'pinjən] Meinung *f*; Ansicht *f*; Gutachten *n*; **in my ~** meines Erachtens.

opponent [ə'pəunənt] Gegner *m*, Gegenspieler *m*.

opportunity [ɔpə'tju:niti] (günstige) Gelegenheit *f*.

oppos|e [ə'pəuz] gegenüberstellen; entgegensetzen; sich widersetzen, bekämpfen; **be ~ed to** gegen *j-n od. et.* sein;
~ite ['ɔpəzit] gegenüberliegend; entgegengesetzt; gegenüber; Gegenteil *n*, Gegensatz *m*; **~ition** [ɔpə-'ziʃən] Widerstand *m*; Gegensatz *m*; Opposition *f*.

oppress [ə'pres] unterdrücken; bedrücken; **~ion** Unterdrückung *f*; Bedrücktheit *f*; **~ive** (be-, nieder)drückend.

optic|al ['ɔptikəl] optisch;
~ian [ɔp'tiʃən] Optiker *m*.

optimism ['ɔptimizəm] Optimismus *m*.

or [ɔ:] oder; **~ else** sonst.

oral ['ɔ:rəl] mündlich; Mund...

orange ['ɔrindʒ] Orange *f*, Apfelsine *f*; Orange *n* (*Farbe*); orange(farben) *f*;
~ade ['~'eid] Orangenlimonade *f*.

orator ['ɔrətə] Redner *m*.

orbit ['ɔ:bit] (die Erde) umkreisen; Kreis-, Umlaufbahn *f*.

orchard ['ɔ:tʃəd] Obstgarten *m*.

orchestra ['ɔ:kistrə] Orchester *n*.

ordeal [ɔ:'di:l] schwere Prüfung, Qual *f*.

order ['ɔ:də] Ordnung *f*; Anordnung *f*, Reihenfolge *f*; Klasse *f*, Rang *m*; Orden *m* (*a. eccl.*); Befehl *m*; *econ.*: Bestellung *f*; (Zahlungs)Auftrag *m*; **in ~ to** um zu; **in ~ that** damit; **out of ~** nicht in Ordnung, außer Betrieb; **~** vb: (an-, *med.* ver)ordnen; befehlen; bestellen; *j-n* schicken;
~ly ordentlich; *fig.* ruhig; *mil.* Sanitätssoldat *m*.

ordinal number ['ɔ:dinl] Ordinal-, Ordnungszahl *f*.

ordinary ['ɔ:dnri] gewöhnlich; üblich; alltäglich.

ore [ɔ:] Erz *n*.

organ ['ɔ:gən] Orgel *f*; Organ *n*; **~ic** [ɔ:'gænik] organisch.

organiz|ation [ɔ:gənai-'zeiʃən] Organisation *f*;
~e ['~aiz] organisieren;
~er Organisator(in).

Orient ['ɔ:riənt] *the ~* Orient *m*, Morgenland *n*.

orient(ate) ['ɔːrient(eit)] orientieren.

origin ['ɔridʒin] Ursprung *m*; Anfang *m*; Herkunft *f*; **~al** [ə'ridʒənl] ursprünglich; originell; Original...; Original *n*; **~ality** [ɔridʒi-'næliti] Originalität *f*; **~ate** [ə'ridʒineit] hervorbringen, schaffen; entstehen.

ornament ['ɔːnəmənt] Verzierung *f*; *fig.* Zierde *f*; ['~ment] verzieren, schmücken; **~al** schmückend; Zier...

orphan ['ɔːfən] Waise *f*; **~age** Waisenhaus *n*.

oscillate ['ɔsileit] schwingen; *fig.* schwanken.

ostrich ['ɔstritʃ] *orn.* Strauß *m.*

other ['ʌðə] ander; the ~ **day** neulich; **every ~ day** jeden zweiten Tag; **~wise** ['~waiz] anders; sonst.

ought [ɔːt] *v/aux* ich, du *etc.*: sollte(st) *etc.*; **you ~ to have done it** Sie hätten es tun sollen.

ounce [auns] Unze *f* (28,35 *g*).

our ['auə] unser; **~s** unsere(r, -s), der, die, das uns(e)re; **~selves** [~'selvz] uns (selbst); wir selbst.

oust [aust] vertreiben, entfernen, hinauswerfen.

out [aut] *adv* aus; hinaus; heraus; aus(...); außen, draußen; nicht zu Hause; *sp.* aus; aus der Mode; vorbei; erloschen; aus(gegangen), verbraucht; zu

Ende; *prp*: **~ of** aus ... (heraus); hinaus; außer (-halb; (hergestellt) aus; aus *Furcht etc.*; **be ~ of** *s.th.* et. nicht mehr haben; *int.* hinaus!, 'raus!

out|balance überwiegen, -treffen; **~bid** (*irr* bid) überbieten; **~board** Außenbord...; **~break**, **~ burst** Ausbruch *m*; **~ cast** Ausgestoßene *m*, *f*; **~come** Ergebnis *n*; **~cry** Aufschrei *m*; **~door(s)** draußen, im Freien.

outer ['autə] Außen..., äußer; **~most** äußerst.

out|fit Ausrüstung *f*, Ausstattung *f*; **~going** weg-, abgehend; **~grow** (*irr* grow) herauswachsen aus; größer werden als; **~ing** Ausflug *m*; **~last** überdauern, -leben; **~law** Geächtete *m*, *f*; **~let** Abzug *m*, Abfluß *m*; *econ.* Absatzmarkt *m*; *fig.* Ventil *n*; **~line** Umriß *m*; Entwurf *m*; Abriß *m*; umreißen, skizzieren; **~live** überleben; **~look** Ausblick *m*, -sicht *f*; Auffassung *f*; **~number** an Zahl übertreffen; **~patient** ambulanter Patient; **~put** Produktion *f*, Ertrag *m*.

outrage ['autreidʒ] Ausschreitung *f*; Gewalttat *f*; gröblich verletzen; Gewalt antun; **~ous** abscheulich; empörend.

out|right [*adj* 'autrait, *adv* ~'rait] völlig; *fig.* glatt;

~run (irr run) schneller laufen als; übertreffen; ~side Außenseite f; Äußere n; äußer, Außen...; außerhalb, draußen; her-, hinaus; ~side left sp. Linksaußen m; ~sider Außenseiter(in), -stehende m, f; ~side right sp. Rechtsaußen m; ~size Übergröße f; ~skirts pl Stadtrand m; ~spoken offen, unverblümt; ~spread ausgestreckt; aus-gebreitet; ~standing hervorragend (a. fig.); ausstehend (Schuld); ~stretched s. outspread; ~ward ['~wad] äußer (-lich); nach (dr)außen gerichtet, Aus...; ~ward(s) (nach) auswärts, nach außen; ~weigh überwiegen; ~wit überlisten.

oval ['əuvəl] oval; Oval n.

oven ['ʌvn] Backofen m.

over ['əuvə] prp über; über ... hin(weg); im (~ the radio); all ~ the town durch die ganze od. in der ganzen Stadt, überall in der Stadt; adv hinüber; darüber; her-über; drüben; über(ko-chen etc.); um(fallen, -wer-fen etc.); herum(drehen etc.); von Anfang bis Ende, durch(lesen etc.); ganz, über und über; (gründlich) über(legen etc.); nochmals, wieder; übermäßig, über...; darüber, mehr; übrig; zu Ende, vorüber, vorbei, aus;

(all) ~again nochmal, (ganz) von vorn; ~and ~ again immer wieder.

over|all ['əuvərɔːl] Gesamt...; Kittel m; pl Arbeitsanzug m; ~board über Bord; ~burden überladen, -lasten; ~cast bewölkt, bedeckt; ~charge überfordern; Betrag zuviel verlangen; überbelasten, -laden; ~coat Mantel m; ~come (irr come) über-wältigen; ~crowd überfüllen; ~do (irr do) übertreiben; zu stark kochen od. braten; ~draw (irr draw) Konto überziehen; ~due überfällig; ~estimate überschätzen, -bewerten; ~flow ['~fləu] überfluten; überlaufen, -fließen; ['~fləu] Überschwemmung f; Überschuß m; ~grown überwuchert; übergroß; ~hang (irr hang) hängen über; überhängen; ~haul überholen; ~head ['~hed] adv oben, droben; ['~hed] über Hoch..., Ober...; ~hear (irr hear) belauschen, hören; ~heat überhitzen, -heizen; ~joyed überglücklich; ~lap sich überschneiden; überlappen; ~load überladen, -lasten; ~look Fehler übersehen; überblicken; ~night Nacht...; Übernachtungs...; über Nacht; stay ~night übernachten; ~pass (Straßen)Überführung f; **~rate** überschätzen; **~rule** überstimmen; ablehnen; **~run** (irr run) überschwemmen; überlaufen; überwuchern; **~sea(s)** Übersee...; **~seas** in od. nach Übersee; **~see** (irr see) beaufsichtigen; **~seer** Aufseher m; **~shadow** überschatten; **~sight** Versehen n; **~sleep** (irr sleep) verschlafen; **~strain** überanstrengen; überholen; überholen; **be ~taken** überrascht werden von; **~throw** [~'θrəu] (irr throw) umstürzen; ['~θrəu] Sturz m; **~time** Überstunden pl; **~top** überragen.

overture ['əuvətjuə] Ouvertüre f; Vorschlag m, Antrag m, Angebot n.

over|turn umstürzen; **~weight** Übergewicht n; **~whelm** [əuvə'welm] fig. überschütten; überwälti-

gen; **~work** ['~'wə:k] Überarbeitung f; ['~'wə:k] Mehrarbeit f, Überstunden pl; ['~'wə:k] (a. irr work) sich überarbeiten.

owe [əu] schulden; verdanken.

owing ['əuiŋ]: **be ~** zu zahlen sein; **~ to** infolge, wegen.

owl [aul] Eule f.

own [əun] eigen; selbst; einzig, innig geliebt; besitzen; zugeben; anerkennen.

owner ['əunə] Eigentümer(in); **~ship** Eigentum(srecht) n.

ox [ɔks], pl **~en** ['~ən] Ochse m; Rind n.

oxid|ation [ɔksi'deiʃən] Oxydation f; **~e** ['~aid] Oxyd n; **~ize** ['~daiz] oxydieren.

oxygen ['ɔksidʒən] Sauerstoff m.

oyster ['ɔistə] Auster f.

ozone ['əuzəun] Ozon n.

P

pace [peis] Schritt m; Gang m; Tempo n; (ab-, durch)schreiten.

Pacific (Ocean) [pə'sifik] Pazifik m, Pazifischer od. Stiller Ozean.

pacify ['pæsifai] besänftigen; befrieden.

pack [pæk] Pack(en) m, Päckchen n, Paket n, Ballen m; Spiel n (Karten); Am. Packung f (Zigaret-

ten); **a ~ of lies** lauter Lügen; **~ (up)** (zs.-, verein)packen; **~age** Paket n, Pack m, Ballen m; **~er** Packer(in); **~et** ['~it] Päckchen n; Packung f (Zigaretten); **~ing** Packen n; Verpackung f; **~thread** Bindfaden m.

pact [pækt] Vertrag m.

pad [pæd] Polster n; Schreib-, Zeichenblock m;

Abschußrampe f; (aus-)polstern; **~ding** Polsterung f.

paddle ['pædl] Paddel n; paddeln; planschen.

paddock ['pædək] (Pferde)Koppel f.

padlock ['pædlɔk] Vorhängeschloß n.

pagan ['peigən] heidnisch; Heid|e m, -in f.

page [peidʒ] (Buch)Seite f; (Hotel)Page m.

pageant ['pædʒənt] historisches Festspiel; Festzug m. **[pay.]**

paid [peid] pret u. pp von|

pail [peil] Eimer m.

pain [pein] j-n schmerzen; j-m weh tun; Schmerz(en pl) m; Mühe f; **be in ~** Schmerzen haben; **take ~s** sich Mühe geben; **~ful** schmerzhaft; schmerzlich; peinlich; **~less** schmerzlos.

paint [peint] Farbe f; Schminke f; Anstrich m; (an-, be)malen; (an)streichen; (sich) schminken; **~box** Mal-, Tuschkasten m; **~brush** (Maler)Pinsel m; **~er** Maler(in); **~ing** Malen n, Malerei f; Gemälde n, Bild n.

pair [pɛə] Paar n; **a ~ of** ein Paar ..., ein(e) ...; zo. (sich) paaren.

pajamas [pə'dʒæməz] pl Am. Schlafanzug m.

pal [pæl] colloq. Kumpel m, Kamerad m, Freund m.

palace ['pælis] Palast m, Schloß n, Palais n.

palate ['pælit] Gaumen m.

pale[1] [peil] Pfahl.

pale[2] blaß, bleich, fahl; erbleichen; **~ness** Blässe f.

pallor ['pælə] Blässe f.

palm [pɑːm] Handfläche f; Palme f.

palpitation [pælpi'teiʃən] Herzklopfen n.

pamper ['pæmpə] verzärteln.

pamphlet ['pæmflit] Flugschrift f; Broschüre f.

pan [pæn] Pfanne f, Tiegel m; **~cake** Pfann-, Eierkuchen m.

pane [pein] (Fenster)Scheibe f.

panel ['pænl] (Tür)Füllung f, (Wand)Täfelung f; Gremium n; Diskussionsteilnehmer pl; täfeln.

pang [pæŋ] plötzlicher Schmerz; fig. Angst f.

panic ['pænik] panisch; Panik f.

pansy ['pænzi] Stiefmütterchen n.

pant [pænt] nach Luft schnappen, keuchen, schnaufen.

panther ['pænθə] Panther m.

panties ['pæntiz] pl colloq. (Damen)Schlüpfer m; Kinderhöschen n od. pl.

pantry ['pæntri] Speise-, Vorratskammer f.

pants [pænts] pl Hose f; Unterhose f.

pap [pæp] Brei m.

papa [pə'pɑː] Papa m.

paper ['peipə] Papier n;

Zeitung *f*; ˈPrüfungsaufgabe *f*, -arbeit *f*; *pl* (Ausweis)Papiere *pl*; tapezieren; ⁓back Taschenbuch *n*, Paperback *n*; ⁓bag Tüte *f*; ⁓hänger Tapezierer *m*; ⁓hangings *pl* Tapete *f*; ⁓money Papiergeld *n*; ⁓weight Briefbeschwerer *m*.

parable [ˈpærəbl] Gleichnis *n*.

parachut|e [ˈpærəʃuːt] Fallschirm *m*; ⁓ist Fallschirmspringer(in).

parade [pəˈreid] Parade *f*; Zurschaustellung *f*, Vorführung *f*; (Strand)Promenade *f*; antreten (lassen); vorbeimarschieren; zur Schau stellen.

paradise [ˈpærədais] Paradies *n*.

paragraph [ˈpærəgrɑːf] *print.* Absatz *m*; kurze Zeitungsnotiz.

parallel [ˈpærəlel] parallel; Parallele *f*.

paraly|se, *Am.* ⁓ze [ˈpærəlaiz] lähmen; ⁓sis [pəˈrælisis] Lähmung *f*.

paramount [ˈpærəmaunt] übergeordnet, höchst; überragend.

parasite [ˈpærəsait] Schmarotzer *m*.

parcel [ˈpɑːsl] Paket *n*, Päckchen *n*; ⁓ out auf-, austeilen.

parch [pɑːtʃ] rösten, (aus)dörren; ⁓ment Pergament *n*.

pardon [ˈpɑːdn] verzeihen; begnadigen; Verzeihung *f*; Begnadigung *f*; **I beg your** ⁓ entschuldigen Sie bitte!, Verzeihung!; wie bitte?; ⁓able verzeihlich.

pare [peə] schälen; (be)schneiden.

parent [ˈpeərənt] Elternteil *m*; Vater *m*; Mutter *f*; *pl* Eltern *pl*; ⁓al [pəˈrentl] elterlich.

parenthe|sis [pəˈrenθisis], *pl* ⁓ses [⁓siːz] (runde) Klammer.

parings [ˈpeəriŋz] *pl* Schalen *pl*; Schnipsel *pl*.

parish [ˈpæriʃ] Kirchspiel *n*, Gemeinde *f*; Pfarr..., Gemeinde...; ⁓ioner [pəˈriʃənə] Gemeindemitglied *n*.

park [pɑːk] Park *m*, Anlagen *pl*; Naturschutzgebiet *n*; parken.

parking [ˈpɑːkiŋ] Parken *n*; **no** ⁓ Parken verboten; ⁓ **garage** Parkhaus *n*; ⁓ **lot** *Am.* Parkplatz *m*; ⁓ **meter** Parkuhr *f*.

parliament [ˈpɑːləmənt] Parlament *n*; **Houses of ♀ Brit.** Parlament(sgebäude) *n*; **Member of ♀ Brit. parl.** Abgeordnete *m*, *f*; ⁓**ary** [⁓ˈmentəri] parlamentarisch, Parlaments...

parlo(u)r [ˈpɑːlə] Wohnzimmer *n*; Salon *m*; Empfangs-, Sprechzimmer *n*.

parquet [ˈpɑːkei] Parkett *n* (*Am. a. thea.*).

parrot [ˈpærət] Papagei *m*.

parsley ['pɑːsli] Petersilie f.

parson ['pɑːsn] Pfarrer m, Pastor m; **~age** Pfarrhaus n.

part [pɑːt] trennen; Haar scheiteln; sich trennen (**with** von); (An-, Bestand) Teil m; Partei f; thea., fig. Rolle f; mus. Stimme f; pl Gegend f; **take ~** in teilnehmen an; **for my ~** ich für mein(en) Teil; **on the ~ of** von seiten, seitens.

partake [pɑːˈteik] (irr take) teilnehmen, -haben.

partial ['pɑːʃəl] teilweise, Teil...; parteiisch; **~ity** [~ʃiˈæliti] Parteilichkeit f; Vorliebe f.

particip|ant [pɑːˈtisipənt] Teilnehmer(in); **~ate** [~peit] teilhaben, -nehmen; **~ation** Teilnahme f.

participle ['pɑːtisipl] gr. Partizip n, Mittelwort n.

particle ['pɑːtikl] Teilchen n.

particular [pəˈtikjulə] besonder; einzeln; genau, eigen; wählerisch; **in ~** besonders; Einzelheit f; pl Nähere n; (**personal**) **~s** pl Personalien pl; **~ity** [~ˈlæriti] Besonderheit f; Ausführlichkeit f; Eigenheit f; **~ly** besonders.

parting ['pɑːtiŋ] (Haar-) Scheitel m; Trennung f; Abschieds...

partition [pɑːˈtiʃən] Teilung f; Trennwand f; Fach n; **~ off** abteilen.

partly ['pɑːtli] zum Teil.

partner ['pɑːtnə] Partner (-in); **~ship** Teilhaber-, Partnerschaft f.

partridge ['pɑːtridʒ] Rebhuhn n.

part-time Teilzeit..., Halbtags...

party ['pɑːti] Partei f; Party f, Gesellschaft f; (Reise) Gruppe f.

pass [pɑːs] (Gebirgs) Paß m; Ausweis m, Passierschein m; Fußball: Paß m; Bestehen n (e-s Examens); et. passieren, vorbeigehen an, -fahren an, -fließen an, -kommen an, -ziehen an; überholen (a. mot.); überschreiten; durchqueren, reichen, geben; Ball abspielen; Prüfung bestehen; Prüfling durchkommen lassen; Gesetz verabschieden; Urteil fallen; fig. übersteigen; vorbeigehen, -fahren, -kommen, -ziehen (**by** an); übergehen (**to** auf; [**in**]**to** in); (den Ball) zu-, abspielen; (die Prüfung) bestehen; Karten: passen; sich zutragen, geschehen; **~ (away)** Zeit verbringen; vergehen (Zeit, Schmerz); sterben; **~ for** gelten als; **~ out** colloq. ohnmächtig werden; **~ round** herumgehen; **~ through** hindurchgehen, -fahren, -kommen; **~able** passierbar; leidlich.

passage ['pæsidʒ] Durchgang m; Durchfahrt f; Korridor m, Gang m; mus.

Passage *f;* (Text)Stelle *f;*
Reise *f,* (Über)Fahrt *f,*
Flug *m.*

passenger ['pæsindʒə]
Passagier *m,* Fahr-, Flug-
gast *m,* Reisende *m, f,*
Insasse *m;* Passagier...

passer-by ['pɑː'sɔː'bai] Pas-
sant(in).

passion ['pæʃən] Leidenschaft *f;* (Gefühls)Aus-
bruch *m;* Zorn *m;* ♀ *eccl.*
Passion *f;* ~**ate** ['~it] leidenschaftlich.

passive ['pæsiv] passiv (*a.
gr.*); teilnahmslos; un-
tätig; ~ **(voice)** *gr.* Passiv
n, Leideform *f.*

pass|port ['pɑːspɔːt] (Rei-
se)Paß *m;* ~**word** Parole *f.*

past [pɑːst] Vergangenheit *f (a. gr.);* vergangen,
vorüber; vorbei, vorüber;
nach (*zeitlich*); an ... vorbei; über ... hinaus; **half**
~ **two** halb drei; ~ **hope**
hoffnungslos.

paste [peist] Teig *m;*
Paste *f;* Kleister *m;* (be-
kleben; ~**board** Pappe *f.*

pastime ['pɑːstaim] Zeitvertreib *m.*

pastry ['peistri] (Fein-)
Gebäck *n;* Blätterteig *m.*

past tense *gr.* Vergangenheit *f.*

pasture ['pɑːstʃə] Weide
(-land *n*) *f;* weiden.

pat [pæt] Klaps *m;* tätscheln, klopfen.

patch [pætʃ] Fleck *m;*
Flicken *m;* ~ **(up)** (zs.-)
flicken;~**work**Flickwerk *n.*

patent ['peitənt, *Am.* 'pæ-
tənt] patentiert; Patent *n;*
patentieren (lassen); ~
leather Lackleder *n.*

patern|al [pə'təːnl] väter-
lich(erseits); ~**ity** Vaterschaft *f.*

path [pɑːθ], *pl* ~**s** [pɑːðz]
Pfad *m;* Weg *m.*

pathetic [pə'θetik] pathe-
tisch, rührend.

patien|ce ['peiʃəns] Ge-
duld *f;* ~**t** geduldig; Pa-
tient(in).

patriot ['peitriət] Patriot
(-in); ~**ic** [pætri'ɔtik] pa-
triotisch; ~**ism** ['pætriə-
tizəm] Patriotismus *m.*

patrol [pə'troul] Pa-
trouille *f;* (Polizei)-
Streife *f;* (ab)patrouillie-
ren; ~**man** Polizist *m* auf
Streife; Pannenhelfer *m.*

patron ['peitrən] Förderer
m; Kunde *m;* ~**age**
['pætrənidʒ] Schirmherr-
schaft *f;* Kundschaft *f;*
~**ize** ['pætrənaiz] Kunde
sein bei; fördern.

patter ['pætə] trappeln
(*Füße*); prasseln (*Regen*).

pattern ['pætən] Muster *n*
(*a. fig.*); Modell *n.*

paunch [pɔːntʃ] (Dick-)
Bauch *m.*

pause [pɔːz] Pause *f;* e-e
Pause machen.

pave [peiv] pflastern; *fig.*
Weg bahnen; ~**ment** Bürgersteig *m;* Pflaster *n;*
~**ment café** Straßencafé *n.*

paw [pɔː] Pfote *f,* Tatze *f;*
scharren; *colloq.* betasten.

pawn [pɔ:n] Pfand *n*; verpfänden; **~broker** Pfandleiher *m*; **~shop** Leihhausn.

pay [pei] (Be)Zahlung *f*; Lohn *m*; Sold *m*; (*irr*) (be)zahlen; (be)lohnen; sich lohnen (für); *Besuch* abstatten; *Aufmerksamkeit* schenken; **~ down**, **~ cash** bar bezahlen; **~ for** (für) *et*. bezahlen; **~able** zahlbar; fällig; **~-day** Zahltag *m*; **~ee** [~'i:] Zahlungsempfänger(in); **~ment** (Be-, Ein-, Aus)Zahlung *f*; Lohn *m*.

pea [pi:] Erbse *f*.

peace [pi:s] Friede(n) *m*, Ruhe *f*; **~ful** friedlich.

peach [pi:tʃ] Pfirsich *m*.

peacock ['pi:kɔk] Pfau *m*.

peak [pi:k] Spitze *f*; Gipfel *m*; Mützenschirm *m*; Spitzen...; Haupt...; Höchst...; **~ hours** *pl* Hauptverkehrs-, Stoßzeit *f*.

peal [pi:l] (Glocken)Läuten *n*; Dröhnen *n*; läuten; dröhnen, krachen.

peanut ['pi:nʌt] Erdnuß *f*.

pear [pɛə] *bot*. Birne *f*.

pearl [pə:l] Perle *f*.

peasant ['pezənt] Bauer *m*; bäuerlich, Bauern...

peat [pi:t] Torf *m*.

pebble ['pebl] Kiesel(stein) *m*.

peck [pek] Viertelscheffel *m* (9,1 *Liter*); picken, hacken (**at** nach).

peculiar [pi'kju:ljə] eigen (-tümlich); besonder; seltsam; **~ity** [~li'æriti] Eigenheit *f*, Eigentümlichkeit *f*.

pedal ['pedl] Pedal *n*; (rad)fahren.

pedestal ['pedistl] Sockelm.

pedestrian [pi'destriən] Fußgänger(in); **~ crossing** Fußgängerübergang *m*; **~ precinct**, **~ zone** Fußgängerzone *f*.

pedigree ['pedigri:] Stammbaum *m*. [*m*.\]

pedlar ['pedlə] Hausierer

peel [pi:l] Schale *f*, Rinde *f*; (sich) (ab)schälen.

peep [pi:p] neugieriger *od.* verstohlener Blick; Piepen *n*; neugierig *od.* verstohlen blicken; piepen.

peer [piə] spähen, schauen.

peevish ['pi:viʃ] gereizt.

peg [peg] Pflock *m*; Zapfen *m*; Kleiderhaken *m*; (Wäsche)Klammer *f*. [*m*.\]

pelican ['pelikən] Pelikan

pelt [pelt] bewerfen; (nieder)prasseln.

pelvis ['pelvis] *anat*. Bekken *n*.

pen [pen] (Schreib)Feder *f*; Federhalter *m*; Pferch *m*; (Schaf)Hürde *f*; **~ in**, **~ up** einpferchen.

penal ['pi:nl] Straf...; **~ servitude** Zuchthaus (-strafe *f*) *n*; **~ty** ['penlti] Strafe *f*; *sp*. Strafpunkt *m*; **~ty area** Strafraum *m*; **~ty kick** Strafstoß *m*.

penance ['penəns] Buße *f*.

pence [pens] *pl von* **penny**.

pencil ['pensl] (Blei-, Farb)Stift *m*; **~sharpener** Bleistiftspitzer *m*.

perish

pend|ant ['pendənt] (*Schmuck*)Anhänger *m*; **~ing** *jur.* schwebend; während; bis zu.

penetrat|e ['penitreit] durch-, vordringen, eindringen (in); **~ion** Durch-, Eindringen *n*;Scharfsinn *m*.

pen-friend Brieffreund(in).

penguin ['pengwin] Pinguin *m*.

penholder Federhalter *m*.

peninsula [pi'ninsjulə] Halbinsel *f*.

penitent ['penitənt] reuig; **~iary** [~'tenʃəri] Besserungsanstalt *f*; *Am.* Zuchthaus *n*.

penknife Taschenmesser *n*.

penniless ['penilis] ohne e-n Pfennig (Geld), mittellos.

penny ['peni], *pl mst* **pence** [pens]Penny *m*; **~worth**: **a ~** für e-n Penny.

pension ['penʃən] Pension *f*, Rente *f*; **~ off** pensionieren; [denklich.] **pensive** ['pensiv] nach-

penthouse ['penthaus] Wetterdach *n*; Dachwohnung *f*, Penthouse *n*.

people ['pi:pl] Volk *n*, Nation *f*; **~** *pl* Leute *pl*; Angehörige *pl*; man; bevölkern.

pepper ['pepə] Pfeffer *m*; pfeffern; **~mint** Pfefferminze *f*; Pfefferminzbonbon *m*, *n*.

per [pə:] per; pro, für.

perambulator ['præmbjuleitə] Kinderwagen *m*.

perceive [pə'si:v] (be-)

merken, wahrnehmen; erkennen.

per|cent [pə'sent] Prozent *n*; **~centage** Prozentsatz *m*; Prozente *pl*.

percept|ible [pə'septəbl] wahrnehmbar; **~ion** Wahrnehmung(svermögen *n*) *f*.

perch [pə:tʃ] *auf et.* Hohem sitzen.

percussion [pə'kʌʃən] Schlag *m*, Erschütterung *f*.

peremptory [pə'remptəri] entschieden, bestimmt.

perfect ['pə:fikt] vollkommen, vollendet, perfekt; **~ (tense)** *gr.* Perfekt *n*; [pə'fekt] vervollkommnen; **~ion** Vollendung *f*; Vollkommenheit *f*.

perforate ['pə:fəreit] durchbohren, -löchern.

perform [pə'fɔ:m] ausführen, tun; *thea.*, *mus.* aufführen, spielen, vortragen; **~ance** *thea.*, *mus.* Aufführung *f*, Vorstellung *f*, Vortrag *m*; Leistung *f*; **~er** Künstler(in).

perfume ['pə:fju:m] Duft *m*; Parfüm *n*; [pə'fju:m] parfümieren.

perhaps [pə'hæps, præps] vielleicht.

peril ['peril] Gefahr *f*; **~ous** gefährlich.

period ['piəriəd] Periode *f* (*a. med.*); Zeitraum *m*; *ling.* Punkt *m*; (Unterrichts)Stunde *f*; **~ic** [~'ɔdik] periodisch; **~ical** periodisch; Zeitschrift *f*.

perish ['periʃ]umkommen,

~able leicht verderblich.

perjury ['pə:dʒəri] Meineid m.

perm [pə:m] colloq. Dauerwelle f; ~anent (fortdauernd, ständig, dauerhaft, Dauer...; ~anent wave Dauerwelle f.

permeable ['pə:mjəbl] durchlässig.

permi|ssion [pə'miʃən] Erlaubnis f; ~t [~t] erlauben; ['~t] Erlaubnis f, Genehmigung f; Passierschein m.

perpendicular [pə:pən'dikjulə] senkrecht.

perpetual [pə'petjuəl] fortwährend, ewig.

persecut|e ['pə:sikju:t] verfolgen; ~ion Verfolgung f; ~or Verfolger m.

persevere [pə:si'viə] beharren, aushalten.

persist [pə'sist] beharren (in auf); fortdauern, anhalten; ~ence, ~ency Beharrlichkeit f; ~ent beharrlich.

person ['pə:sn] Person f; ~age (hohe) Persönlichkeit; ~al persönlich; Personen...; Personal...; ~ality [.sə'næliti] Persönlichkeit f; ~ify [.'sɔnifai] verkörpern; ~nel [.sə'nel] Personal n, Belegschaft f; ~nel manager, ~nel officer Personalchef m.

perspiration [pə:spə-'reiʃən] Schwitzen n; Schweiß m; ~e [pəs'paiə] schwitzen.

persuade [pə'sweid] überreden; überzeugen; ~sion [.ʒən] Überredung (-skunst) f; Überzeugung f; ~sive [.siv] überredend; überzeugend.

pert [pə:t] frech, vorlaut.

perus|al [pə'ru:zəl] sorgfältige Durchsicht; ~e (sorgfältig) durchlesen.

pervade [pə:'veid] durchdringen, ~ziehen.

perverse [pə'və:s] verkehrt; verdorbt; eigensinnig; pervers.

pessimism ['pesimizəm] Pessimismus m.

pest [pest] Plage f; ~er belästigen, plagen.

pet [pet] Liebling(stier n) m; Lieblings...

petal ['petl] Blütenblatt n.

petition [pi'tiʃən] Bittschrift f, Eingabe f; bitten, ersuchen; ein Gesuch einreichen.

pet name Kosename m.

petrify ['petrifai] versteinern.

petrol ['petrəl] Benzin n, Kraft-, Treibstoff m; ~ station Tankstelle f.

pet shop Zoohandlung f.

petticoat ['petikəut] Unterrock m.

petty ['peti] klein, geringfügig, unbedeutend.

pew [pju:] Kirchenbank f.

pharmacy ['fa:məsi] Apotheke f.

phase [feiz] Phase f.

pheasant ['feznt] Fasan m.

philanthropist [fi'lænθrə-

519

pike

pist] Menschenfreund(in).

philolog|ist [fi'lɔlədʒist]
Philolog|e *m*, -in *f*; **~y**
Philologie *f*.

philosoph|er [fi'lɔsəfə]
Philosoph *m*; **~ize** philosophieren; **~y** Philosophie *f*.

phone [fəun] *colloq.* für
telephone.

phonetic [fəu'netik] phonetisch, Laut...

phon(e)y ['fəuni] *sl.* falsch,
gefälscht, unecht.

photo ['fəutəu] *colloq.* für
~graph ['...təgra:f] Foto
(-grafie *f*) *n*, Bild *n*, Aufnahme *f*; fotografieren.

photograph|er [fə'tɔ-
grəfə] Fotograf(in); **~y**
Fotografie *f*.

phrase [freiz] Redewendung *f*, idiomatischer Ausdruck.

physic|al ['fizikəl] physisch, körperlich; physikalisch; **~ian** [fi'ziʃən]
Arzt *m*; **~ist** ['...sist] Physiker *m*; **~s** *sg* Physik *f*.

physique [fi'zi:k] Körper
(-bau) *m*.

piano ['pjænəu] Klavier *n*.

pick [pik] (Aus)Wahl *f*;
hacken; (auf)picken; auflesen, -nehmen; pflücken;
Knochen abnagen; bohren
in, stochern in; aussuchen;
~ out *et.* auswählen; *~* **up** aufhacken; aufheben, -lesen,
-nehmen, -picken; *colloq.*
et. aufschnappen; (*im Auto*)
mitnehmen; abholen.

picket ['pikit] Pfahl *m*;

Streikposten *m*; Streikposten stehen; Streikposten aufstellen vor.

pickle ['pikl] Lake *f*; *pl*
Eingepökelte *n*, Pickles
pl; einlegen, (-)pökeln.

pick|pocket Taschendieb
m; **~up** Tonabnehmer *m*.

picnic ['piknik] Picknick *n*.

pictorial [pik'tɔ:riəl] illustriert; Illustrierte *f*.

picture ['piktʃə] Bild *n*;
Gemälde *n*; bildschöne
Sache *od.* Person; *pl colloq.*
Kino *n*; Bilder...; darstellen; beschreiben; sich
et. vorstellen; **~ postcard**
Ansichtskarte *f*; **~sque**
[~'resk] malerisch.

pie [pai] Pastete *f*.

piece [pi:s] Stück *n*; Teil
m, n (*e-s* Services); **by
the ~** im Akkord; **a ~ of
advice** ein Rat; **a ~ of
news** e-e Neuigkeit; **in
~s** entzwei; **take to ~s**
auseinandernehmen; **~
work** Akkordarbeit *f*.

pier [piə] Pfeiler *m*; Pier *m*,
Landungsbrücke *f*.

pierce [piəs] durchbohren,
-stoßen, -stechen; durchdringen.

piety ['paiəti] Frömmigkeit *f*. [kel *n.*]

pig [pig] Schwein *n*; Fer-]

pigeon ['pidʒin] Taube *f*;
~hole (Ablage)Fach *n*.

pig|-headed dickköpfig;
~skin Schweinsleder *n*;
~sty Schweinestall *m*; **~
tail** (Haar)Zopf *m*.

pike [paik] Hecht *m*.

pile [pail] Haufen *m*; Stapel *m*, Stoß *m*; *oft* ~ **up**, ~ **on** (an-, auf)häufen, (auf)stapeln, aufschichten.

pilfer ['pilfə] stehlen.

pilgrim ['pilgrim] Pilger(in *f*) *m*; ~**age** Pilger-, Wallfahrt *f*.

pill [pil] Pille *f*, Tablette *f*.

pillar ['pilə] Pfeiler *m*, Ständer *m*; Säule *f*; ~**box** Briefkasten *m*. [*m*.]

pillion ['piljən] Soziussitz]

pillory ['piləri] Pranger *m*.

pillow ['piləu] (Kopf-) Kissen *n*; ~**case**, ~**slip** (Kissen)Bezug *m*.

pilot ['pailət] Pilot *m*; Lotse *m*; lotsen, steuern.

pimple ['pimpl] Pickel *m*.

pin [pin] (Steck)Nadel *f*; Pflock *m*; Kegel *m*; (an)heften, (an)stecken, befestigen.

pincers ['pinsəz] *pl* (*a.* **a pair of** ~) (*e-e*) (Kneif-) Zange.

pinch [pintʃ] Kneifen *n*, Prise *f* (*Salz etc.*); kneifen, zwicken; drücken; *colloq.* klauen.

pine [pain] Kiefer *f*, Föhre *f*; sich abhärmen; sich sehnen, schmachten; ~ **apple** Ananas *f*.

pinion ['pinjən] Flügelspitze *f*; Schwungfeder *f*.

pink [piŋk] Nelke *f*; Rosa *n*; rosa(farben).

pinnacle ['pinəkl] Zinne *f*; Spitzturm *m*; (Berg)Spitze *f*; *fig.* Gipfel *m*.

pint [paint] 0,57 *od.* Am. 0,47 Liter.

pioneer [paiə'niə] Pionier *m*. [dächtig.]

pious ['paiəs] fromm; an-]

pip [pip] (Obst)Kern *m*; kurzer, hoher Ton.

pipe [paip] Rohr *n*, Röhre *f*; Pfeife *f* (*a. mus.*); Flöte *f*; Luftröhre *f*; Wasser etc. leiten; pfeifen; piep(s)en; ~**line** Rohr-, Ölleitung *f*, Pipeline *f*; ~**r** Pfeifer *m*.

pirate ['paiərit] Seeräuber *m*; unerlaubt nachdrucken.

pistol ['pistl] Pistole *f*.

piston ['pistən] *tech.* Kolben *m*.

pit [pit] Grube *f*; *thea.* Parterre *n*; *Am.* (Obst)Stein *m*, Kern *m*.

pitch [pitʃ] *min.* Pech *n*; Wurf *m*; *mar.* Stampfen *n*; Neigung *f* (*e-s Daches*); *mus.* Tonhöhe *f*; Grad *m*, Stufe *f* (*a. fig.*); Zelt, Lager aufschlagen; werfen, schleudern; *mus.* stimmen; *mar.* stampfen (*Schiff*).

pitcher ['pitʃə] Krug *m*.

piteous ['pitiəs] mitleiderregend.

pitfall ['pitfɔ:l] Fallgrube *f*; *fig.* Falle *f*.

pith [piθ] Mark *n*.

pit|iable ['pitiəbl] erbärmlich; ~**iful** mitleidig; erbärmlich (*a. contp.*); ~**iless** unbarmherzig; ~**y** bemitleiden; Mitleid *n*; **it is a** ~**y** es ist schade; **what a** ~**y!** wie schade!

pivot ['pivət] *tech.*: (Dreh-) Punkt *m* (*a. fig.*); Zapfen *m*.

placard ['plækɑːd] Plakat *n*; anschlagen.

place [pleis] Platz *m*; Ort *m*; Stelle *f*; Stätte *f*; (An-)Stellung *f*; Wohnsitz *m*, Wohnung *f*; in ~ of an Stelle von *od. gen*; **out of** ~ fehl am Platz; **take** ~ stattfinden; *vb*: stellen, legen, setzen; *Auftrag* erteilen; **be** ~**d** *sp*. sich placieren. [ruhig.]

placid ['plæsid] sanft; \

plague [pleig] Pest *f*; Plage *f*; plagen, quälen.

plaice [pleis] *ichth*. Scholle *f*. [Plaid.\

plaid [plæd] *schottisches* \

plain [plein] einfach; unscheinbar; offen, ehrlich; einfarbig; klar, deutlich; *Am*. eben, flach; Ebene *f*; ~**clothes man** Polizist *m od*. Kriminalbeamte *m* in Zivil.

plaint|iff ['pleintif] Kläger (-in); ~**ive** klagend.

plait [plæt, *Am*. pleit] Flechte *f*, Zopf *m*; flechten.

plan [plæn] Plan *m*; planen.

plane [plein] flach, eben; (ein)ebnen; (ab)hobeln; Ebene *f*, (ebene) Fläche; *aer*. Tragfläche *f*; Flugzeug *n*, Maschine *f*; Hobel *m*; *fig*. Stufe *f*, Niveau *n*.

planet ['plænit] Planet *m*.

plank [plæŋk] Planke *f*, Bohle *f*, Diele *f*.

plant [plɑːnt] Pflanze *f*; (Fabrik)Anlage *f*, Fabrik *f*; (an-, ein-, be)pflanzen; an-

legen; ~**ation** [plæn-'teiʃən] Pflanzung *f*, Plantage *f*; ~**er** ['plɑːntə] Pflanzer *m*, Plantagenbesitzer *m*. [tafel *f*.\

plaque [plɑːk] Gedenk-\

plaster ['plɑːstə] *med*. Pflaster *m*; (Ver)Putz *m*; bepflastern; verputzen; ~ **cast** Gipsabdruck *m*; *med*. Gipsverband *m*; ~ **of Paris** Gips *m*.

plastic ['plæstik] plastisch; Plastik...; ~**s** *sg* Plastik *n*, Kunststoff *m*.

plate [pleit] Platte *f*; Teller *m*; (Bild)Tafel *f*; Schild *n*; plattieren; panzern.

platform ['plætfɔːm] Plattform *f*; Bahnsteig *m*; Podium *n*; *pol*. Parteiprogramm *n*. [Platin *n*.\

platinum ['plætinəm] \

platter ['plætə] (Servier-)Platte *f*.

plausible ['plɔːzəbl] glaubhaft.

play [plei] Spiel *n*; Schauspiel *n*, (Theater)Stück *n*; Spielraum *m* (*a. fig*.); spielen (gegen); ~ **off** *fig*. *j-n* ausspielen; ~**back** Playback *n*, Abspielen *n*; ~**bill** Theaterzettel *m*; ~**er** (Schau)Spieler(in); ~**fellow** Spielgefährt|e *m*, -in *f*; ~**ful** verspielt; ~**ground** Spielplatz *m*; Schulhof *m*; ~**mate** *s*. playfellow; ~**thing** Spielzeug *n*; ~**time** Freizeit *f*, Zeit *f* zum Spielen; ~**wright** ['~rait] Dramatiker *m*.

plea

plea [pli:] Vorwand *m*; Gesuch *n*; *jur.*: Verteidigung *f*; Einspruch *m*.

plead [pli:d] *e–e Sache* vertreten; plädieren; sich einsetzen; **~ guilty** sich schuldig bekennen.

pleasant ['pleznt] angenehm, erfreulich; freundlich.

pleas|e [pli:z] (*j–m*) gefallen *od.* angenehm sein; zufriedenstellen; **~e!** bitte!; **~ed** erfreut, zufrieden; **~ing** angenehm, gefällig.

pleasure ['pleʒə] Vergnügen *n*, Freude *f*.

pleat [pli:t] (Plissee)Falte *f*; plissieren.

pledge [pledʒ] Pfand *n*; Versprechen *n*; verpfänden.

plent|iful ['plentiful] reichlich; **~y** Fülle *f*, Überfluß *m*; **~y of** reichlich, e–e Menge.

pliable ['plaiəbl] biegsam; *fig.* nachgiebig.

pliers ['plaiəz] *pl* (*a. a pair of* **~**) (e–e) (Draht-, Kneif-) Zange.

plight [plait] schlechter Zustand, mißliche Lage.

plimsolls ['plimsɔlz] *pl* Turnschuhe *pl*.

plod [plɔd] sich abmühen; **~ (along, on)** sich dahinschleppen.

plot [plɔt] Stück *n* (Land); Plan *m*; Komplott *n*, Anschlag *m*; Handlung *f* (e–s *Romans, Dramas etc.*); planen.

plough, *Am.* **plow** [plau] Pflug *m*; (um)pflügen; **~ share** Pflugschar *f*.

pluck [plʌk] Ruck *m*; Mut *m*, Schneid *m*, *f*; pflücken; rupfen; (aus)reißen; **~ up courage** Mut fassen; **~y** mutig.

plug [plʌg] Pflock *m*, Dübel *m*, Stöpsel *m*, Zapfen *m*; *electr.* Stecker *m*; **~ in** *electr.* einstöpseln, -stekken; **~ up** *zu.*, verstopfen.

plum [plʌm] Pflaume *f*; Rosine *f* (*im Backwerk*).

plumage ['plu:midʒ] Gefieder *n*.

plumb [plʌm] Lot *n*, Senkblei *n*; loten; **~er** Klempner *m*, Installateur *m*. {chen *m*.

plum cake Rosinenku-

plume [plu:m] Feder (-busch *m*) *f*.

plummet ['plʌmit] Lot *n*.

plump [plʌmp] drall, mollig; (hin)plumpsen (lassen). {pudding *m*.}

plum pudding Plum-

plunder ['plʌndə] Plünderung *f*; plündern.

plunge [plʌndʒ] (ein-, unter)tauchen; (sich) stürzen.

plunk [plʌŋk] *Saite* zupfen.

pluperfect (tense) ['plu:-'pə:fikt] *gr.* Plusquamperfekt *n*, Vorvergangenheit *f*.

plural ['pluərəl] *gr.* Plural *m*, Mehrzahl *f*.

plus [plʌs] plus, und; positiv; Plus *n*.

plush [plʌʃ] Plüsch *m*.

ply [plai] (Garn)Strähne *f*; (Stoff-, Holz- *etc.*)Lage *f*; **~wood** Sperrholz *n*.

pneumatic [nju(:)'mætik] pneumatisch, (Preß)Luft...

pneumonia [nju(:)'mounjə] Lungenentzündung *f*.

poach [poutʃ] wildern; **~ed egg** verlorenes Ei; **~er** Wilddieb *m*, Wilderer *m*.

pocket ['pokit] (Hosen-*etc.*)Tasche *f*; einstecken (*a. fig.*); Taschen...; **~book** Notizbuch *n*; Brieftasche *f*; Taschenbuch *n*; **~knife** Taschenmesser *n*; **~money** Taschengeld *n*.

pod [pod] Hülse *f*, Schote *f*.

poem ['pouim] Gedicht *n*.

poet ['pouit] Dichter *m*; **~ess** Dichterin *f*; **~ic(al)** [~'etik(əl)] dichterisch; **~ry** ['~itri] Dichtkunst *f*; Dichtung *f*.

poignant ['poinənt]scharf; *fig.*: bitter; ergreifend.

point [point] Spitze *f*; Punkt *m* (*a. ling.*); *math.* (Dezimal)Punkt *m*, Komma *n*; Kompaßstrich *m*; Punkt *m*, Stelle *f*, Ort *m*; springender Punkt; Sinn *f*; Zweck *m*, Ziel *n*; *pl* rail. Weichen *pl*; **beside the ~** nicht zur Sache gehörig; **on the ~ of** *ger* im Begriff *zu inf*; **to the ~** zur Sache (gehörig), sachlich; **win on ~s** nach Punkten siegen; *vb*: (zu-)spitzen; **~ out** zeigen, hinweisen auf; **~ at** *Waffe* richten auf; zeigen auf;

~ to nach *e-r Richtung* weisen *od.* liegen; zeigen auf; hinweisen auf; **~ed** spitz; *fig.*: scharf; deutlich; **~er** Zeiger *m*; Zeigestock *m*; Vorstehhund *m*. **~ of view** Stand-, Gesichtspunkt *m*, Ansicht *f*.

poise [poiz] Gleichgewicht *n*; Haltung *f*; *Kopf etc.* halten; schweben.

poison ['poizn] Gift *n*; vergiften; *fig.* verderben; **~ous** giftig.

poke [pouk] stoßen; schüren; stecken; stoßen, stechen, stochern; **~r** Schürhaken *m*.

polar ['poulə] polar, Polar...; **~ bear** Eisbär *m*.

Pole [poul] Pol|e *m*, -in *f*.

pole [poul] Pol *m*; Stange *f*; Mast *m*; Deichsel *f*; (Sprung)Stab *m*.

police [pə'li:s] Polizei *f*; **~man** Polizist *m*; **~officer** Polizeibeamte *m*, Polizist *m*; **~station** Polizeiwache *f*, -revier *n*; **~woman** Polizistin *f*.

policy ['polisi] Politik *f*; Police *f*.

polio ['pouliou] spinale Kinderlähmung *f*.

Polish ['poulif] polnisch; Polnisch *n*.

polish ['polif] Politur *f*; Schuhcreme *f*; *fig.* Schliff *m*; polieren; *Schuhe* putzen.

polite [pə'lait] höflich; **~ness** Höflichkeit *f*.

politic|al [pə'litikəl] politisch; **~ian** [poli'tiʃən]

Politiker m; ~s ['politiks] sg, pl Politik f.

poll [pəul] Umfrage f; pol. Wahl f; go to the ~s zur Wahl(urne) gehen. [m.]

pollen ['pɔlin] Blütenstaub

pollut|e [pə'lu:t] beschmutzen, verunreinigen; ~ion Verschmutzung f.

pomp [pɔmp] Pomp m; ~ous pompös; aufgeblasen; schwülstig.

pond [pɔnd] Teich m, Weiher m.

ponder ['pɔndə] nachdenken (über); ~ous schwer (-fällig).

pony ['pəuni] Pony n.

poodle ['pu:dl] Pudel m.

pool [pu:l] Teich m; Pfütze f, Lache f; (Schwimm)Becken n; (Spiel)Einsatz m; (Fußball)Toto n.

poor [puə] arm(selig); dürftig; fig. schlecht; sub: the ~ pl die Armen pl; ~ly kränklich; arm(selig),dürftig.

pop [pɔp] knallen (lassen); Am. Mais rösten; schnell wohin tun od. stecken; ~ in vorbeikommen (Besuch); ~ out hervorschießen; sub: Knall m; colloq. Schlager m; Schlager...

pope [pəup] Papst m.

poplar ['pɔplə] Pappel f.

poppy ['pɔpi] Mohn m.

popul|ar ['pɔpjulə] Volks...; volkstümlich; populär, beliebt; ~arity [~'læriti] Popularität f;

~ate ['~eit] bevölkern; ~ation Bevölkerung f; ~ous dicht besiedelt.

porch [pɔ:tʃ] Vorhalle f, Portal n; Am. Veranda f.

porcupine ['pɔ:kjupain] Stachelschwein n.

pore [pɔ:] Pore f; ~ over et. eifrig studieren.

pork [pɔ:k] Schweinefleisch n.

porous ['pɔ:rəs] porös.

porpoise ['pɔ:pəs] Tümmler m. [brei m.]

porridge ['pɔridʒ] Hafer-]

port [pɔ:t] Hafen(stadt f) m; mar. Backbord n; Portwein m.

portable ['pɔ:təbl] transportabel; tragbar.

porter ['pɔ:tə] Pförtner m, Portier m; (Gepäck)Träger m; Porter(bier n) m.

portion ['pɔ:ʃən] (An)Teil m; Portion f (Essen); Erbteil n; ~ out austeilen.

portly ['pɔ:tli] stattlich.

portrait ['pɔ:trit] Porträt n, Bild(nis) n.

pose [pəuz] Pose f; Modell stehen; posieren.

posh [pɔʃ] colloq. schick.

position [pə'ziʃən] Position f; Lage f; (fig. Ein-) Stellung f; Stand(punkt) m.

positive ['pɔzətiv] bestimmt; sicher; phot. Positiv n.

possess [pə'zes] besitzen; beherrschen; ~ed besessen; ~ion Besitz m; ~ive gr. possessiv, besitzanzeigend; ~or Besitzer(in).

possib|ility [pɔsə'biliti] Möglichkeit f; **~le** [p'ɔsəbl] möglich; **~ly** möglich(erweise), vielleicht.

post [pəust] Pfosten m; Posten m; (An)Stellung f, Amt n; Post f; Plakat etc. anschlagen; postieren; Brief etc. einstecken, abschicken, aufgeben; **~age** Porto n; **~age stamp** Briefmarke f; **~al card** Postkarte f; **~al order** Postanweisung f; **~box** Briefkasten m; **~card** Postkarte f; **~code** Postleitzahl f.

poster ['pəustə] Plakat n.

poste restante [pəust 'restã:nt] postlagernd.

posterity [pɔs'teriti] Nachwelt f; Nachkommen pl.

post-free portofrei.

posthumous ['pɔstjuməs] post(h)um.

post|man Briefträger m, Postbote m; **~mark** Poststempel m; (ab)stempeln; **~master** Postmeister m; **~ office** Post(amt n) f; **~-office box** Postfach n; **~-paid** frankiert.

postpone [pəust'pəun] ver-, aufschieben.

postscript ['pəusskript] Postskriptum n.

posture ['pɔstʃə] (Körper-) Haltung f, Stellung f.

post-war ['pəust'wɔ:] Nachkriegs...

posy ['pəuzi] Blumenstrauß m, Sträußchen n.

pot [pɔt] Topf m; Kanne f; einmachen; eintopfen.

potato [pə'teitəu], pl **~es** Kartoffel f; **~es** pl (boiled) in their jackets Pellkartoffeln pl.

potent ['pəutənt] stark.

potion ['pəuʃən] (Arznei-, Gift-, Zauber)Trank m.

potter¹ ['pɔtə]: **~ about** herumwerkeln, -hantieren.

potter² Töpfer m; **~y** Töpferei f; Töpferware(n pl) f, Steingut n.

pouch [pautʃ] Beutel m; Tasche f.

poulterer ['pəultərə] Geflügelhändler m.

poultice ['pəultis] Breiumschlag m, -packung f.

poultry ['pəultri] Geflügel n. [zen (on auf).\

pounce [pauns] sich stür-\

pound [paund] Pfund n; **~ (sterling)** Pfund n (Sterling) (abbr. £); hämmern, trommeln; (zer-)stampfen.

pour [pɔ:] strömen, rinnen; gießen, schütten; **~ (out)** Getränk eingießen.

pout [paut] Lippen aufwerfen; fig. schmollen.

poverty ['pɔvəti] Armut f.

powder ['paudə] Pulver n; Puder m; pulverisieren; (sich) pudern; **~room** Damentoilette f.

power ['pauə] Kraft f; Macht f; Gewalt f; jur. Vollmacht f; math. Potenz f; **~ful** mächtig, stark, kräftig; wirksam; **~less** macht-, kraftlos; **~plant**, **~station** Kraftwerk n.

practi|cable ['præktikəbl]
durchführbar; begeh-, befahrbar; **~cal** praktisch;
~ce ['~tis] Praxis f; Gewohnheit f; Übung f; **~ce**
Am., **~se** ausüben, tätig
sein als; (sich) üben;
~tioner [~'tiʃnə]: **general
~** praktischer Arzt.

prairie ['prɛəri] Prärie f.

praise [preiz] Lob n; loben;
~worthy lobenswert.

pram [præm] colloq. Kinderwagen m.

prance [prɑːns] sich aufbäumen, tänzeln (Pferd).

prank [præŋk] Streich m.

prattle ['prætl] plappern.

prawn [prɔːn] Garnele f.

pray [prei] beten; bitte(n);
~er [prɛə] Gebet n; Andacht f; **~er-book** Gebetbuch n.

preach [priːtʃ] predigen;
~er Prediger(in).

precarious [pri'kɛəriəs]
unsicher, bedenklich.

precaution [pri'kɔːʃən]
Vorsicht f; **~ary** (smaß-
regel) f.

precede [pri(ː)'siːd] voraus-, vorangehen; **~nce**
Vorrang m; **~nt** ['presi-
dənt] Präzedenzfall m.

precept ['priːsept] Vorschrift f, Regel f.

precinct ['priːsiŋkt] Bezirk m; Bereich m, Grenze
f; pl Umgebung f.

precious ['preʃəs] kostbar;
edel; colloq. äußerst.

precipice ['presipis] Abgrund m.

precipit|ate [pri'sipiteit]

(hinab)stürzen; (plötzlich)
herbeiführen; [~it] überstürzt; **~ation** meteor.
Niederschlag(smenge f) m;
Hast f; **~ous** steil, jäh.

précis ['preisiː], pl **~** ['~siːz]
(kurze) Zs.-fassung.

precise [pri'sais] genau;
~ion [~'siʒən] Genauigkeit f.

precocious [pri'kəuʃəs]
frühreif, altklug.

preconceived ['priːkən-
'siːvd] vorgefaßt.

predatory ['predətəri]
räuberisch, Raub...

predecessor ['priːdisesə]
Vorgänger(in).

predetermine ['priːdi-
'təːmin] vorherbestimmen.

predicament [pri'dikə-
mənt] (mißliche) Lage.

predicate ['predikit] gr.
Prädikat n, Satzaussage f.

predict [pri'dikt] vorhersagen; **~ion** Vorhersage f.

predisposition ['priːdis-
pə'ziʃən] Neigung f, Anfälligkeit f.

predomina|nt [pri'dɔ-
minənt] vorherrschend;
~te [~eit] vorherrschen.

preface ['prefis] Vorwort n.

prefect ['priːfekt] Vertrauens-, Aufsichtsschüler m.

prefer [pri'fəː] vorziehen,
bevorzugen, lieber haben
od. tun; **~able** ['prefərəbl]:
~(to) vorzuziehen(d) (dat);
~ably vorzugsweise, lieber; **~ence** ['prefərəns]
Vorliebe f; Vorzug m;

~ment [pri'fə:mənt] Beförderung f.

prefix ['pri:fiks] *ling.* Präfix n, Vorsilbe f.

pregnan|cy ['pregnənsi] Schwangerschaft f; **~t** schwanger.

prejudice ['predʒudis] Vorurteil n; **~** mit e-m Vorurteil erfüllen; beeinträchtigen, benachteiligen; **~d** (vor)eingenommen.

preliminary [pri'liminəri] vorläufig; einleitend.

prelude ['prelju:d] Vorspiel n.

premature [premə'tjuə] vorzeitig, Früh...; vorschnell.

premeditate [pri(:)'mediteit] vorher überlegen.

premier ['premjə] Premierminister m.

premises ['premisiz] *pl* Anwesen n; Lokal n.

premium ['pri:mjəm] Prämie f (Versicherungs-)Prämie f.

preoccupied [pri(:)'ɔkjupaid] beschäftigt; vertieft.

prepar|ation [prepə'reiʃən] Vorbereitung f; Zubereitung f; **make ~ations** Vorbereitungen treffen; **~e** [pri'pɛə] (sich) vorbereiten, (zu)bereiten.

prepay ['pri:'pei] (*irr* **pay**) vorausbezahlen; frankieren.

preposition [prepə'ziʃən] *gr.* Präposition f, Verhältniswort n.

prepossess [pri:pə'zes] günstig stimmen, einneh-

men; **~ing** einnehmend, anziehend.

preposterous [pri'pɔstərəs] absurd; lächerlich.

prescri|be [pris'kraib] vorschreiben; *med.* verschreiben; **~ption** [~'kripʃən] *med.* Rezept n.

presence ['prezns] Gegenwart f; Anwesenheit f; **~ of mind** Geistesgegenwart f.

present[1] ['preznt] gegenwärtig; jetzig; anwesend, vorhanden; Gegenwart f; Geschenk n; *gr. s.* **present tense**; **at ~** jetzt.

present[2] [pri'zent] (*j-n* be)schenken; (über)reichen; (vor)zeigen; präsentieren.

presentation [prezen'teiʃən] Vorstellung f; Überreichung f; Schenkung f; Darbietung f; Vorzeigen n.

presentiment [pri'zentimənt] (*mst* böse Vor-)Ahnung.

presently ['prezntli] bald; *Am.* zur Zeit, jetzt.

present| perfect [prezn] Perfekt n, 2. Vergangenheit; **~ tense** *gr.* Präsens n, Gegenwart f.

preserv|ation [prezə(:)'veiʃən] Bewahrung f; Erhaltung f; **~e** [pri'zə:v] bewahren, behüten; erhalten, konservieren; einkochen, -machen; *pl* Eingemachte n.

preside [pri'zaid] den Vorsitz haben *od.* führen.

president ['prezidənt] Präsident(in).

press [pres] (Hände)Druck m; (Wein- etc.)Presse f; (Drucker)Presse f; Druckerei f; Druck(en n) m; fig. Druck m; **the ~** die Presse (Zeitungswesen); (aus)pressen; drücken (auf); plätten, bügeln; (be)drängen; sich drängen; **~ for** dringen auf, fordern; **~ing** dringend; **~ure** ['~ʃə] Druck m.

prestige [pres'ti:ʒ] Prestige n.

presum|able [pri'zju:məbl] vermutlich; **~e** annehmen, vermuten; sich et. herausnehmen; sich anmaßen; **~ing** anmaßend.

presumpt|ion [pri'zʌmpʃən] Vermutung f; Anmaßung f; **~uous** [~tjuəs] anmaßend.

presuppose [pri:sə'pəuz] voraussetzen.

preten|ce, Am. **~se** [pri'tens] Vorwand m; Anspruch m; **~d** vorgeben, vortäuschen, so tun als ob; Anspruch erheben (**to** auf); **~der** (Thron)Prätendent m; **~sion** Anspruch m (**to** auf); pl Ambitionen pl.

preterit(e) (tense) ['pretərit] gr. Präteritum n, 1. Vergangenheit.

pretext ['pri:tekst] Vorwand m.

pretty ['priti] hübsch, niedlich; schön; ziemlich.

prev|ail [pri'veil] (vor-)herrschen; **~alent** ['prevələnt] vorherrschend.

prevent [pri'vent] verhindern; j–n hindern; **~ion** Verhütung f; **~ive** vorbeugend.

previous ['pri:vjəs] vorhergehend, Vor...; **~ to** bevor, vor; **~ly** vorher.

pre-war ['pri:'wɔ:] Vorkriegs...

prey [prei] Raub m, Beute f; **bird of ~** Raubvogel m.

price [prais] Preis m; Waren auszeichnen; **~less** unschätzbar, unbezahlbar.

prick [prik] Stich m; (durch)stechen; **~ up one's ears** die Ohren spitzen; **~le** Stachel m, Dorn m; **~ly** stach(e)lig.

pride [praid] Stolz m, Hochmut m.

priest [pri:st] Priester m.

primar|ily ['praimərili] in erster Linie; **~y** ursprünglich; hauptsächlich; grundlegend, Grund...; **~y school** Grundschule f.

prime [praim] erst, wichtigst, Haupt...; erstklassig; fig. Blüte(zeit) f; **~ minister** Premierminister m, Ministerpräsident m; **~r** Elementarbuch n.

primitive [primitiv] erst, Ur...; primitiv.

primrose ['primrəuz] Primel f, Schlüsselblume f.

prince [prins] Fürst m; Prinz m; **~ss** [~'ses, attr

~ses] Fürstin f; Prinzessin f.

principal ['prinsəpəl] erst, hauptsächlich, Haupt...; (Schul)Direktor m, Rektor m; (Grund)Kapital n.

principality [prinsi'pæliti] Fürstentum n.

principle ['prinsəpl] Prinzip n, Grundsatz m; on ~ aus Prinzip.

print [print] (Ab)Druck m; bedruckter Kattun; Druck m, Stich m; phot. Abzug m; out of ~ vergriffen; (ab-, auf-, be)drucken; in Druckbuchstaben schreiben; ~ (off) phot. abziehen; ~ed matter Drucksache f; ~er (Buch- etc.) Drucker m; ~ing-ink Druckerschwärze f; ~ing office (Buch)Druckerei f.

prior ['praiə] früher, älter (to als); ~ to vor; ~ity [~'ɔriti] Priorität f, Vorrang m.

prison ['prizn] Gefängnis n; ~er Gefangene m, f, Häftling m; take s.o. ~er j-n gefangennehmen.

privacy ['privəsi] Zurückgezogenheit f; Privatleben n.

private ['praivit] privat, Privat...; persönlich; vertraulich; geheim; (gemeiner) Soldat; ~ hotel Hotelpension f.

privation [prai'veiʃən] Not f, Entbehrung f.

privilege ['privilidʒ] Privileg n; ~d privilegiert.

prize [praiz] (Sieges)Preis m, Prämie f; (Lotterie-) Gewinn m; preisgekrönt; Preis...; (hoch)schätzen; ~ winner Preisträger(in).

pro- [prou-] für, pro...

probab|ility [probə'biliti] Wahrscheinlichkeit f; ~le ['~əbl] wahrscheinlich.

probation [prə'beiʃən] Probe(zeit) f; jur. Bewährungsfrist f.

probe [prəub] Sonde f; sondieren; untersuchen.

problem ['prɔbləm] Problem n; math. Aufgabe f.

procedure [prə'si:dʒə] Verfahren n.

proceed [prə'si:d] fortfahren; sich begeben (to nach); ~ from ausgehen von; ~ings pl jur. Verfahren n; ~s ['prausi:dz] pl Erlös m.

process ['prauses] Fortgang m; Vorgang m; Prozeß m; Verfahren n; bearbeiten; ~ion [prə'seʃən] Prozession f.

proclaim [prə'kleim] proklamieren, ausrufen; ~mation [prɔklə'meiʃən] Proklamation f, Bekanntmachung f.

procure [prə'kjuə] beverschaffen.

prodig|ious [prə'didʒəs] ungeheuer; ~y ['prɔdidʒi] Wunder n (a. Person); mst infant ~y Wunderkind n.

produce [prə'dju:s] produzieren; erzeugen, herstellen; hervorbringen;

(vor)zeigen; *fig.* hervorrufen; ['prɔdjuːs] (Natur-)
Produkte *pl*; ~r [prɔ'djuː-
sə] Hersteller *m*; *Film*,
thea.: Produzent *m*.

product ['prɔdʌkt] Produkt *n*, Erzeugnis *n*; ~ion
[prɔ'dʌkʃən] Produktion *f*,
Erzeugung *f*, Herstellung
f; Erzeugnis *n*; Vorlegen
n; *thea.* Inszenierung *f*;
~ive [prɔ'dʌktiv] produk-
tiv, fruchtbar.

profess [prɔ'fes] (sich) bekennen (zu); erklären; ~ed
erklärt; ~ Beruf *m*; Besteuerung *f*; ~ional Berufs-
.., beruflich; Berufs-
sportler(in), -spieler(in),
Profi *m*; ~or Professor(in).

proficien|cy [prɔ'fiʃənsi]
Können *n*, Tüchtigkeit *f*;
~t tüchtig, erfahren.

profile ['prɔufail] Profil *n*.

profit ['prɔfit] Nutzen *m*,
Gewinn *m*, Profit *m*; *j—m*
nützen; ~ **by** Nutzen ziehen aus; ~able gewinn-
bringend. [gründlich.]

profound[prɔ'faund]tief;]

profusion [prɔ'fjuːʒən]
(Über)Fülle *f*, Überfluß *m*.

prognosis [prɔg'nəusis],
pl ~es [~siːz] Prognose *f*.

program(me) ['prəu-
græm] Programm *n*; *Ra-
dio*: *a.* Sendung *f*.

progress ['prəugres] Fort-
schritt(e *pl*) *m*; [~'gres]
fortschreiten; ~ive pro-
gressiv; fortschreitend;
fortschrittlich.

prohibit [prɔ'hibit] ver-

bieten; ~ion [prɔui'biʃən]
Verbot *n*; Prohibition *f*.

project ['prɔdʒekt] Projekt *n*, Vorhaben *n*; [prɔ-
'dʒekt] planen, entwer-
fen; projizieren; vorste-
hen; ~ion *arch.* Vorsprung
m; Projektion *f*; ~or Pro-
jektor *m*.

pro|logue, *Am. a.* ~log
['prəulɔg] Prolog *m*.

prolong [prɔ'lɔŋ] verlängern, (aus)dehnen.

promenade [prɔmi'nɑːd,
attr '~] (Strand)Prome-
nade *f*.

prominent ['prɔminənt]
vorstehend; prominent.

promis|e ['prɔmis] Ver-
sprechen *n*; versprechen;
~ing vielversprechend.

promontory ['prɔməntri]
Vorgebirge *n*.

promo|te [prɔ'məut] (be-)
fördern; *Am. ped.* ver-
setzen; ~ter Förderer *m*;
~tion (Be)Förderung *f*.

prompt [prɔmpt] schnell;
bereit; pünktlich; *j—n* veranlassen; *thea.* soufflieren;
~er Souffleu|r *m*, -se *f*.

prong [prɔŋ] Zinke *f*.

pronoun ['prəunaun] *gr.*
Pronomen *n*, Fürwort *n*.

pron|ounce [prɔ'nauns]
aussprechen; ~unciation
[~nʌnsi'eiʃən] Ausspra-
che *f*.

proof [pruːf] Beweis *m*;
Probe *f*; Korrekturfahne *f*;
print., *phot.* Probeabzug
m; fest, (*wasser*)dicht, (*kugel*)sicher.

prop [prɔp]: ~ **(up)** (ab-) stützen.

propaga|te ['prɔpəgeit] (sich) fortpflanzen; verbreiten; ~**tion** Fortpflanzung *f*; Verbreitung *f*.

propel [prə'pel] (an-, vorwärts)treiben; ~**ler** Propeller *m*.

proper ['prɔpə] eigen (-tümlich.); passend, richtig; anständig, korrekt; *colloq.* ordentlich, gehörig; ~**ty** Eigentum *n*, (Grund-) Besitz *m*; Eigenschaft *f*.

prophe|cy ['prɔfisi] Prophezeiung *f*; ~**sy** ['~ai] prophezeien; ~**t** Prophet *m*.

proportion [prə'pɔ:ʃən] Verhältnis *n*; *pl* (Aus-) Maße *pl*; ~**al** angemessen.

propos|al [prə'pəuzəl] Vorschlag *m*, Angebot *n*; (Heirats)Antrag *m*; ~**e** vorschlagen; e-n Heiratsantrag machen (**to** *dat*); ~**ition** [prɔpə'ziʃən] Vorschlag *m*; Behauptung *f*.

propriet|ary [prə'praiətəri] gesetzlich geschützt (*Ware*), ~**or** Eigentümer *m*.

propulsion [prə'pʌlʃən] Antrieb *m*.

prose [prəuz] Prosa *f*.

prosecut|e ['prɔsikju:t] verfolgen; ~**ion** Verfolgung *f*; ~**or** (An)Kläger *m*.

prospect ['prɔspekt] Aussicht *f* (*a. fig.*); [prə'spekt] *min.* schürfen *od.* bohren (**for** nach); ~**ive** [prə-'spektiv] (zu)künftig; ~**us**

[prə'spektəs] (Werbe)Prospekt *m*.

prosper ['prɔspə] Erfolg haben, blühen; ~**ity** [~'periti] Wohlstand *m*; ~**ous** ['~pərəs] erfolgreich; wohlhabend.

prostitute ['prɔstitju:t] Prostituierte *f*, Dirne *f*.

prostrate ['prɔstreit] hingestreckt; *fig.*: erschöpft, daniederliegend; gebrochen.

protect [prə'tekt] (be-) schützen (**from** vor); ~**ion** Schutz *m*; ~**ive** (be)schützend, Schutz...; ~**or** Beschützer *m*.

protest ['prəutest] Protest *m*; [prə'test] protestieren; beteuern; **2ant** ['prɔtistənt] protestantisch; Protestant(in) *f*; ~**ation** [prəutes'teiʃən] Beteuerung *f*.

protract [prə'trækt] in die Länge ziehen, hinziehen.

protrude [prə'tru:d] (her-) vorstehen; herausstrecken.

proud [praud] stolz (**of** auf).

prove [pru:v] be-, nachweisen; sich herausstellen *od.* erweisen (als).

proverb ['prɔvə:b] Sprichwort *n*; ~**ial** [prə'və:bjəl] sprichwörtlich.

provide [prə'vaid] versehen, -sorgen; verschaffen, besorgen; ~ **for** sorgen für; ~**d (that)** vorausgesetzt, daß.

providence ['prɔvidəns] Vorsorge *f*; Vorsehung *f*.

provinc|e ['prɔvins] Provinz *f*; *fig.* Gebiet *n*; **~ial** [prɔ'vinʃəl] Provinz...; provinziell; kleinstädtisch.

provision [prə'viʒən] Vorkehrung *f*; *jur.* Bestimmung *f*; Bedingung *f*; *pl* (Lebensmittel) Vorrat *m*, Lebensmittel *pl*, Proviant *m*; **~al** provisorisch.

provo|cation [prɔvə'keiʃən] Herausforderung *f*; **~cative** [prə'vɔkətiv] herausfordernd; **~ke** [prə'vəuk] *j-n* reizen; bewegen, herausfordern; *et.* hervorrufen.

prowl [praul] herumschleichen; durchstreifen.

proxy ['prɔksi] Stellvertreter *m*; Vollmacht *f*.

prud|e [pru:d] Prüde *f*; **~ence** Klugheit *f*; Vorsicht *f*; **~ent** klug; vorsichtig; **~ish** prüde, zimperlich.

prune [pru:n] Backpflaume *f*; *Bäume etc.* beschneiden.

psalm [sɑːm] Psalm *m*.

pseudonym ['psju:dənim] Pseudonym *n*, Deckname *m*.

psychiatr|ist [sai'kaiətrist] Psychiater *m*; **~y** Psychiatrie *f*.

psycholog|ical [saikə'lɔdʒikəl] psychologisch; **~ist** [~'kɔlədʒist] Psychologe *m*, -in *f*; **~y** [~'kɔlədʒi] Psychologie *f*.

pub [pʌb] *colloq.* Kneipe *f*.

puberty ['pju:bəti] Pubertät *f*.

public ['pʌblik] öffentlich; staatlich, Staats...; Volks...; allgemein bekannt; *das Publikum*; Öffentlichkeit *f*; **in ~** öffentlich; **~ation** Bekanntmachung *f*; Veröffentlichung *f*; **~ house** Wirtshaus *n*; **~ity** ['lisiti] Öffentlichkeit *f*; Reklame *f*, Werbung *f*; **~ school** Public School *f*.

publish ['pʌbliʃ] veröffentlichen; *Buch etc.* herausgeben, verlegen; **~er** Herausgeber *m*, Verleger *m*; **~ing house** Verlag *m*.

pudding ['pudiŋ] Pudding *m*, Süßspeise *f*.

puddle ['pʌdl] Pfütze *f*.

puff [pʌf] Zug *m* (*beim Rauchen*); (Dampf-, Rauch-) Wölkchen *f*; Puderquaste *f*; schnaufen, keuchen; (auf)blasen; pusten; paffen; **~ paste** Blätterteig *m*; **~y** kurzatmig; (an)geschwollen.

pull [pul] Zug *m*; Ruck *m*; ziehen; zerren; reißen; rudern; **~ down** ab-, niederreißen; **~ in** einfahren (*Zug*); **~ out** ausscheren (*Auto*); **~ o.s. together** sich zs.-nehmen; **~ up** *Auto* anhalten; (an)halten.

pulley ['puli] *tech.*: Rolle *f*; Flaschenzug *m*.

pullover ['puləuvə] Pullover *m*.

pulp [pʌlp] Brei *m*; Fruchtfleisch *n*.

pulpit ['pulpit] Kanzel *f*.

pulpy ['pʌlpi] breiig; fleischig.

puls|ate [pʌl'seit] pulsieren, pochen; ~e Puls m.

pulverize ['pʌlvəraiz] pulverisieren, zermahlen.

pump [pʌmp] Pumpe f; Pumps m; pumpen; j-n aushorchen; ~ **attendant** Tankwart m.

pumpkin ['pʌmpkin] Kürbis m.

pun [pʌn] Wortspiel n.

punch [pʌntʃ] (Faust-) Schlag m; Lochzange f; Locher m; Punsch m; schlagen (mit der Faust), boxen; (ein)hämmern auf; (aus)stanzen; lochen.

Punch [pʌntʃ] Kasperle m, m, Hanswurst m; ~ **and Judy show** ['dʒuːdi] Kasperletheater n.

punctual ['pʌŋktjuəl] pünktlich.

punctuat|e ['pʌŋktjueit] interpunktieren, ~ion Interpunktion f, Zeichensetzung f; ~ion **mark** Satzzeichen n.

puncture ['pʌŋktʃə] (Ein-) Stich m; Reifenpanne f.

pungent ['pʌndʒənt] scharf, stechend, beißend.

punish ['pʌniʃ] (be)strafen; ~ment Strafe f; Bestrafung f.

pupil ['pjuːpl] Pupille f; Schüler(in); Mündel m, n.

puppet ['pʌpit] Marionette f, Puppe f; ~play, ~show Puppenspiel n.

puppy ['pʌpi] Welpe m, junger Hund.

purchase ['pəːtʃəs] (An-, Ein)Kauf m; Anschaffung f; (er)kaufen; ~r Käufer(in).

pure [pjuə] rein; ~bred Am. reinrassig.

purgat|ive ['pəːgətiv] abführend; Abführmittel n; ~ory Fegefeuer n.

purge [pəːdʒ] Abführmittel n; pol. Säuberung f; mst fig. reinigen; pol. säubern; med. abführen.

puri|fy ['pjuərifai] reinigen (a. fig.); ~ty Reinheit f.

purloin [pəː'lɔin] stehlen.

purple ['pəːpl] purpurn, purpurrot; Purpur m.

purpose ['pəːpəs] beabsichtigen, vorhaben; Absicht f; Zweck m; Entschlußkraft f; **on** ~ absichtlich; **to no** ~ vergeblich; ~ful zielbewußt; ~less zwecklos; ziellos; ~ly absichtlich.

purr [pəː] schnurren (Katze); summen (Motor etc.).

purse [pəːs] Geldbeutel m; Am. Handtasche f; ~ (**up**) Lippen spitzen.

pursu|e [pə'sjuː] verfolgen (a. fig.); streben nach, fortsetzen; ~er Verfolger(in); ~it [~uːt] Verfolgung f; Streben n (**of** nach); pl Studien pl, Arbeiten pl.

purvey [pəː'vei] liefern; ~or Lieferant m.

pus [pʌs] Eiter m.

push [puʃ] (An-, Vor)Stoß
m; Anstrengung *f*; Schwung
m; Tatkraft *f*; stoßen,
schieben, drücken; drän-
gen; (an)treiben; ~ **along**,
~ **on** weitergehen, -fahren;
~ **on** weitermachen.

puss [pus] Katze *f*; Kätzchen *n*; ~**y(-cat)** Katze *f*,
Kätzchen *n*, Mieze *f*.

put [put] (*irr*) legen, setzen,
stellen, stecken, tun; bringen (*ins Bett etc.*); werfen;
Frage stellen; ausdrücken,
sagen; ~ **back** zurück-
stellen (*a. Uhr*); *fig.* aufhalten; ~ **by** Geld zurücklegen; ~ **down** hin-, niederlegen, -stellen, -setzen;
aussteigen lassen; ein-
tragen; aufschreiben; zu-
schreiben; ~ **forth** Kraft
aufbieten; *Knospen etc.*
treiben; ~ **forward** Uhr
vorstellen; *Meinung etc.*
vorbringen; ~ **in** herein-,
hineinlegen, -setzen, -stel-
len, -stecken; *Wort* einlegen; ~ **off** auf-, verschieben; vertrösten; *j-n*
abbringen; ~ **on** *Kleider*
anziehen; *Hut etc.* auf-
setzen; *Uhr* vorstellen; vortäu-

schen; ~ **on weight** zunehmen; ~ **out** hinaus-
legen, -setzen, -stellen;
herausstrecken; *Feuer,
Licht* ausmachen, (-)lö-
schen; aus der Fassung
bringen; ~ **through** *teleph.*
j-n verbinden (**to** mit); ~
together zs.-setzen; ~ **up**
hochheben, -schieben, -zie-
hen; *Haar* hochstecken;
Schirm aufspannen; auf-
stellen, errichten; *Gast*
unterbringen; *Widerstand*
leisten; *Ware* anbieten;
Preis erhöhen; ~ **up at**
absteigen *od.* einkehren
in; ~ **up with** sich abfinden mit.

putr|efy ['pju:trifai] (ver-)
faulen; ~**id** ['~id] faul,
verdorben.

putty ['pʌti] Kitt *m*; ~ **(up)**
(ver)kitten.

puzzle ['pʌzl] Rätsel *n*;
Geduld(s)spiel *n*; kniffliges
Problem; Verwirrung *f*;
verwirren; *j-m* Kopfzer-
brechen machen; sich den
Kopf zerbrechen.

pyjamas [pə'dʒɑːməz] *pl*
Schlafanzug *m*.

pyramid ['pirəmid] Pyramide *f*.

Q

quack [kwæk] quaken;
Quaken *n*; ~ **(doctor)**
Quacksalber *m*.

quadrangle ['kwɔdræŋgl]
Viereck *n*; Innenhof *m*.

quadrupl|ed ['kwɔdruped]

Vierfüßer *m*; ~**le** vierfach;
(sich) vervierfachen; ~**lets**
['~lits] *pl* Vierlinge *pl*.

quail [kweil] Wachtel *f*.

quaint [kweint] wunderlich, drollig; anheimelnd.

quake [kweik] beben, zittern; Erdbeben n.

quali|fication [kwɔlifi-'keiʃən] Qualifikation f; Befähigung f; Einschränkung f; **~fied** ['~faid] qualifiziert, befähigt; eingeschränkt, bedingt; **~fy** ['~fai] (sich) qualifizieren; befähigen; einschränken; mildern; **~ty** Qualität f; Eigenschaft f.

qualm [kwɑ:m] Übelkeit f; pl Bedenken f.

quandary ['kwɔndəri] verzwickte Lage, Verlegenheit f.

quantity ['kwɔntiti] Quantität f, Menge f.

quarantine ['kwɔrənti:n] Quarantäne f; unter Quarantäne stellen.

quarrel ['kwɔrəl] Streit m; (sich) streiten; **~some** zänkisch.

quarry ['kwɔri] Steinbruch m; (Jagd)Beute f.

quarter ['kwɔ:tə] vierteln, vierteilen; mil. einquartieren; Viertel n; Viertelpfund n; Viertelzentner m; Am. Vierteldollar m; Quartal n; (Stadt)Viertel m; Gegend f, Richtung f; pl Quartier n (a. mil.); ~ of Kreise pl; **a ~ (of an hour)** e-e Viertelstunde; **a ~ to od.** past Uhrzeit: (ein) Viertel vor od. nach; **~ly** vierteljährlich; Vierteljahresschrift f.

quartet(te) [kwɔ:'tet] mus. Quartett n.

quarto ['kwɔ:təu] Quartformat n.

quaver ['kweivə] zittern); ((Stimme).

quay [ki:] Kai m.

queen [kwi:n] Königin f; **~ bee** Bienenkönigin f.

queer [kwiə] sonderbar, seltsam; wunderlich.

quench [kwentʃ] Flammen, Durst löschen; Hoffnung zunichte machen.

querulous ['kweruləs] quengelig, verdrossen.

query ['kwiəri] Frage(zeichen n) f; (be)fragen; (be-an)zweifeln.

quest [kwest] Suche f.

question ['kwestʃən] (be)fragen; jur. vernehmen, -hören; et. bezweifeln; Frage f; Problem n; **in ~** fraglich; **that is out of the ~** das kommt nicht in Frage; **~able** fraglich; fragwürdig; **~mark** Fragezeichen n; **~naire** [.stiə-'nɛə] Fragebogen m.

queue [kju:] Schlange f, Reihe f; **~ up** anstehen, Schlange stehen, sich anstellen.

quick [kwik] schnell; rasch; flink; aufgeweckt; lebhaft; aufbrausend; scharf (Auge, Gehör); **be ~** beeil dich!; **~en** (sich) beschleunigen; anregen; **~ly** schnell; **~ness** Schnelligkeit f; (geistige) Gewandtheit; Schärfe f (Gehör etc.); Lebhaftigkeit f; **~sand** Treibsand m; **~silver** Quecksilber n;

witted schlagfertig, aufgeweckt.

quid [kwid] *sg,* *pl sl.* Pfund *n* (Sterling).

quiet ['kwaiǝt] ruhig, still; leise; Ruhe *f;* beruhigen; **~ down** sich beruhigen; **~ness, ~ude** ['~itjuːd] Ruhe *f,* Stille *f.*

quill [kwil] Federkiel *m;* Stachel *m* (*des Stachelschweins*); **~(-feather)** Schwung-, Schwanzfeder *f.*

quilt [kwilt] Steppdecke *f.*

quince [kwins] Quitte *f.*

quinine [kwi'niːn, *Am.* 'kwainain] Chinin *n.*

quintal ['kwintl] Doppelzentner *m.*

quintuple ['kwintjupl] fünffach; (sich) verfünffachen; **~ts** ['~lits] *pl* Fünflinge *pl.*

quit [kwit] frei; verlassen;

aufgeben; *Am.* aufhören mit; aufhören; ausziehen; **give notice to ~** kündigen.

quite [kwait] ganz, völlig; ziemlich; recht; wirklich; ganz; **(so)!** ganz recht.

quiver ['kwivǝ] zittern, beben; Zittern *n;* Köcher *m.*

quiz [kwiz] Prüfung *f,* Test *m;* Quiz *n;* ausfragen; *j-n* prüfen.

quota ['kwǝutǝ] Quote *f;* Kontingent *n.*

quotation [kwǝu'teiʃǝn] Zitat *n;* (Börsen-, Kurs-) Notierung *f;* **~ marks** *pl* Anführungszeichen *pl.*

quote [kwǝut] zitieren, anführen; Preis berechnen; *Börse:* notieren.

quotient ['kwǝuʃǝnt] Quotient *m.*

R

rabbi ['ræbai] Rabbi *m;* Rabbiner *m.*

rabbit ['ræbit] Kaninchen *n.* [Pöbel *m.*]

rabble ['ræbl] Mob *m,*

rabi|d (*'ræbid*) wütend; tollwütig (*Tier*); **~es** ['reibiːz] Tollwut *f.*

raccoon [rǝ'kuːn] *s.* **racoon.**

race [reis] Geschlecht *n;* Rasse *f;* Volk *n,* Nation *f;* (Wett)Rennen *n,* Lauf *m;* Renn...; *fig.* Wettlauf *m;* **the ~s** *pl* das Pferderennen; rennen, rasen; um die

Wette laufen *od.* fahren (mit); **~r** Rennpferd *n,* -boot *n,* -wagen *m.*

racial ['reiʃǝl] Rassen...

racing ['reisiŋ] (Pferde-) Rennsport *m;* Renn...

rack [ræk] Gestell *n;* (*Kleider- etc.*)Ständer *m;* (Gepäck)Netz *n;* (Futter-) Raufe *f; fig.* quälen; **~ one's brains** sich den Kopf zermartern.

racket ['rækit] (Tennis-) Schläger *m;* Lärm *m;* Trubel *m; colloq.* Schwindel *m.*

racoon [rə'ku:n] Waschbär *m*.

racy ['reisi] kraftvoll, lebendig; rassig; würzig.

radar ['reidə] Radar(gerät) *n*.

radia|nce ['reidjəns] Strahlen *n*; **~nt** strahlend; **~te** ['.eit] (aus)strahlen; **~tion** (Aus)Strahlung *f*; **~tor** Heizkörper *m*; *mot.* Kühler *m*.

radical ['rædikəl] *bot., math.* radikal; *pol.* Radikale *m*, *f*.

radio ['reidiəu] funken, senden; Funk(spruch) *m*; Radio *n*, Rundfunk *m*; Radiogerät *n* Funk...; **by ~** über Funk; **~active** radioaktiv; **~-set** Radiogerät *n*; **~-therapy** Strahlentherapie *f*.

radish ['rædiʃ] Rettich *m*; Radieschen *n*.

radius ['reidjəs] Radius *m*.

raffle ['ræfl] Tombola *f*, Verlosung *f*; verlosen.

raft [rɑ:ft] Floß *n*; **~er** (Dach)Sparren *m*.

rag [ræg] Lumpen *m*.

rage [reidʒ] toben, rasen; Wut(anfall *m*) *f*, Zorn *m*; Sucht *f* (for nach).

ragged ['rægid] zerlumpt; struppig, zottig; ausgefranst; zackig.

raid [reid] (feindlicher) Überfall; (Luft)Angriff *m*; Razzia *f*; einbrechen in, plündern; überfallen.

rail¹ [reil] schimpfen.

rail² [reil] (Quer)Stange *f*; Geländer *n*; *mar.* Reling *f*; **rail.** Schiene *f*; (Eisen-)Bahn *f*; *pl* Gleis *n*; **by ~** mit der Bahn; **~ in** *od.* **off** mit e-m Geländer umgeben *od.* abtrennen; **~ing(s** *pl*) Geländer *n*; *mar.* Reling *f*; **~road** Am., **~way** Eisenbahn *f*; **~way guide** Kursbuch *n*; **~wayman** Eisenbahner *m*.

rain [rein] Regen *m*; regnen; **~bow** Regenbogen *m*; **~coat** Regenmantel *m*; **~drop** Regentropfen *m*; **~-proof** wasserdicht; **~y** regnerisch, Regen...; **save for a ~y day** für Notzeiten vorsorgen.

raise [reiz] (*oft* **~ up** auf-, hoch)heben; erheben; aufrichten; *Kinder* aufziehen; *Familie* gründen; züchten; errichten; erhöhen; *Geld* sammeln, beschaffen.

raisin ['reizn] Rosine *f*.

rak|e [reik] Rechen *m*, Harke *f*; Wüstling *m*, Lebemann *m*; (zs.-)rechen, (-)harken; **~ish** schnittig; ausschweifend; *fig.* verwegen.

rally ['ræli] Massenversammlung *f*; *mot.* Rallye *f*; (sich) sammeln *od.* scharen; sich erholen.

ram [ræm] *zo.* Widder *m*; *tech.* Ramme *f*; (fest)rammen.

ramble ['ræmbl] Streifzug *m*; umherstreifen.

ramify ['ræmifai] (sich) verzweigen.

ramp [ræmp] Rampe *f*; ~**art** ['~ɑ:t] Wall *m*.

ran [ræn] *pret von* run.

ranch [rɑ:ntʃ, *Am.* ræntʃ] Ranch *f*; Viehfarm *f*; Farm *f*; ~**er** Rancher *m*, Viehzüchter *m*; Farmer *m*.

rancid ['rænsid] ranzig.

ranco(u)r ['ræŋkə] Groll *m*, Haß *m*.

random ['rændəm]: **at** ~ aufs Geratewohl.

rang [ræŋ] *pret von* ring.

range [reindʒ] Reihe *f*; (Berg)Kette *f*; Herd *m*; Schießstand *m*; Entfernung *f*; Reichweite *f*; Bereich *m*; *econ.* Kollektion *f*; offenes Weidegebiet; (ausgedehnte) Fläche; aufstellen; einreihen, (-)ordnen; durchstreifen; sich erstrecken, reichen; (umher)schweifen (*Blick*). ~**r** Aufseher *m* e-s Forsts *etc.*; *Am.*: Förster *m*; Angehöriger e-r berittenen Schutztruppe.

rank [ræŋk] Reihe *f*; Rang *m* (*a. mil.*), Stand *m*; *mil.* Glied *n*; (ein)ordnen, einreihen; rechnen, zählen; e-n Rang einnehmen; gehören, zählen (**among**, **with** zu); üppig; stinkend; scharf.

ransack ['rænsæk] durchwühlen, -stöbern; plündern.

ransom ['rænsəm] Lösegeld *n*; Auslösung *f*; loskaufen, auslösen.

rap [ræp] Klopfen *n*;

klopfen *od.* pochen (an, auf). [(hab)gierig.\]

rapacious [rə'peiʃəs] \]

rape [reip] Vergewaltigung *f*; vergewaltigen.

rapid ['ræpid] schnell, rasch, rapid(e); steil; ~**ity** [rə'piditi] Schnelligkeit *f*; ~**s** *pl* Stromschnelle *f*.

rapt [ræpt] versunken; entzückt; ~**ure** Entzücken *n*.

rar|e [rɛə] selten; *colloq.* ausgezeichnet; dünn (*Luft*); halbgar; ~**ity** Seltenheit *f*.

rascal ['rɑ:skəl] Schuft *m*; ~**ly** schuftig.

rash[1] [ræʃ] hastig, überstürzt; unbesonnen.

rash[2] (*Haut*)Ausschlag *m*.

rasher ['ræʃə] Speckscheibe *f*.

rasp [rɑ:sp] Raspel *f*; raspeln; krächzen.

raspberry ['rɑ:zbəri] Himbeere *f*.

rat [ræt] Ratte *f*; **smell a** ~ Lunte *od.* den Braten riechen; ~**s!** *sl.* Quatsch!

rate [reit] besteuern; (ein)schätzen; rechnen, zählen (**among** zu); gelten (**as** als); (Verhältnis)Ziffer *f*, Rate *f*; Verhältnis *n*; (Aus)Maß *n*; Preis *m*, Betrag *m*; Gebühr *f*; (Kommunal)Steuer *f*; Geschwindigkeit *f*; Klasse *f*, Rang *m*; **at any** ~ auf jeden Fall; ~ **of exchange** (Umrechnungs)Kurs *m*; ~ **of interest** Zinssatz *m*.

rather ['rɑ:ðə] eher, lieber; vielmehr, besser gesagt; ziemlich, fast.

ratify ['rætifai] bestätigen; ratifizieren.

ration ['ræʃən] Ration f, Zuteilung f; rationieren.

rational ['ræʃənl] vernünftig, rational; **~ize** ['~ʃnəlaiz] rationalisieren.

rattle ['rætl] Gerassel n; Geklapper n; Klapper f; rasseln (mit); klappern; rütteln (an); röcheln; **~ off** herunterrasseln; **~snake** Klapperschlange f.

ravage ['rævidʒ] Verwüstung f; verwüsten; plündern.

rave [reiv] rasen, toben; schwärmen (**about**, **of** von).

raven ['reivn] Rabe m.

ravenous ['rævənəs] gefräßig; heißhungrig; gierig.

ravine [rə'vi:n] Schlucht f, Klamm f, Hohlweg m.

ravings ['reiviŋz] pl irres Gerede; Delirien pl.

ravish ['ræviʃ] entzücken, hinreißen.

raw [rɔ:] roh; Roh...; wund; rauh (*Wetter*); unerfahren.

ray [rei] Strahl m (a. fig.).

rayon ['reiən] Kunstseide f.

razor ['reizə] Rasiermesser n, -apparat m; **~blade** Rasierklinge f.

re- ['ri:-] wieder, noch einmal, neu; zurück, wider.

reach [ri:tʃ] (er)reichen;

(her)langen; sich erstrecken; **~ out** reichen, ausstrecken; Reichweite f; Bereich m; Fassungskraft f; **out of ~** unerreichbar; **within easy ~** leicht zu erreichen.

react [ri(:)'ækt] reagieren; einwirken; **~ion** Reaktion f; Rückwirkung f; **~ionary** [~ʃnəri] reaktionär; Reaktionär(in); **~or** (Kern-)Reaktor m.

read [ri:d] (*irr*) lesen; deuten; (an)zeigen (*Thermometer*); lauten; **~ to s.o.** j-m vorlesen; [red] pret u. pp von **read**; **~er** (Vor)Leser(in); Lektor(in); Lesebuch n.

readi|ly ['redili] bereitwillig; **~ness** Bereitschaft f; Bereitwilligkeit f.

reading ['ri:diŋ] Lesen n; (Vor)Lesung f; Lektüre f; Lesart f; Auslegung f; Lese...

readjust ['ri:ə'dʒʌst] wieder in Ordnung bringen; wieder anpassen.

ready ['redi] bereit; fertig; im Begriff (**to do** zu tun); schnell, rasch; schlagfertig, gewandt; bar (*Geld*); **get ~** (sich) fertigmachen; **~-made** Konfektions...; **~ money** Bargeld n.

real [riəl] real, wirklich, tatsächlich; echt; **~estate** Grundbesitz m, Immobilien pl; **~ism** Realismus m; **~istic** realistisch; **~ity** [ri(:)'æliti] Realität f, Wirklichkeit f; **∼ization** Realisierung f (a. econ.); Verwirklichung f; Erkenntnis f; **∼ize** erkennen, begreifen, einsehen; realisieren (a. econ.); verwirklichen; **∼ly** wirklich, tatsächlich; **not ∼ly?** nicht möglich!

realm [relm] (König-) Reich n.

realt|or ['rialtə] Am. Grundstücksmakler m, Immobilienhändler m; **∼y** jur. Grundbesitz m.

reap [ri:p] Getreide schneiden, mähen; fig. ernten; **∼er** Schnitter(in); (Getreide)Mähmaschine f.

reappear ['ri:ə'piə] wieder erscheinen.

rear [riə] auf-, großziehen; (er)heben; sich aufbäumen; Rück-, Hinterseite f; Hintergrund m; mot. Heck n; Hinter..., Rück...; **∼guard** mil. Nachhut f; **∼-lamp**, **∼-light** mot. Rück-, Schlußlicht n.

rearm ['ri:'ɑ:m] (wieder-) aufrüsten; **∼ament** (Wieder)Aufrüstung f.

rearmost hinterst.

rear-view mirror mot. Rückspiegel m.

reason ['ri:zn] Vernunft f; Verstand m; Grund m; Ursache f; **for this ∼** aus diesem Grund; vb: logisch denken; schließen;' argumentieren; **∼ out** (logisch) durchdenken; **∼ with** gut zureden; **∼able** vernünftig; billig; angemessen.

reassure [ri:ə'ʃuə] j-n beruhigen.

rebate ['ri:beit] Rabatt m.

rebel ['rebl] Rebell m, Aufständische m; aufständisch; [ri'bel] rebellieren, sich auflehnen; **∼lion** [∼'beljən] Rebellion f; **∼lious** [∼'beljəs] aufständisch; aufsässig.

re-book ['ri:'buk] umbuchen; [rückprallen.]

rebound [ri'baund] zu-∫

rebuff [ri'bʌf] Abfuhr f.

rebuild ['ri:'bild] (irr build) wieder aufbauen.

rebuke [ri'bju:k] Tadel m; tadeln.

recall [ri'kɔ:l] abberufen; sich erinnern an; j-n erinnern (**to** an); widerrufen; Abberufung f; Widerruf m; **beyond ∼, past ∼** unwiderruflich.

recapture ['ri:'kæptʃə] wieder ergreifen; fig. wiederaufleben lassen.

recede [ri(:)'si:d] zurücktreten.

receipt [ri'si:t] Empfang m; Quittung f; pl Einnahmen pl.

receive [ri'si:v] empfangen, erhalten, bekommen; auf-, annehmen; **∼r** Empfänger m; teleph. Hörer m.

recent ['ri:snt] neu, jüngst, frisch; **∼ly** kürzlich, vor kurzem, neulich.

reception [ri'sepʃən] Empfang m (a. Funk); Annahme f; Aufnahme f; **∼ desk** Empfangsschalter *m*, Rezeption *f* (*Hotel*); **~ist** Empfangsdame *f*, **-chef** *m*; Sprechstundenhilfe *f*.

recess [ri'ses] Nische *f*; *Am.* (*Schul*)Pause *f*; **~es** *pl* *fig.* Innere *n*, **~ion** Konjunkturrückgang *m*.

recipe ['resipi] Rezept *n*.

recipient [ri'sipiənt] Empfänger(in).

reciprocal [ri'siprəkəl] wechsel-, gegenseitig.

recit|al [ri'saitl] Bericht *m*, Erzählung *f*; *mus.* (Solo)Vortrag *m*, Konzert *n*; **~e** vortragen; aufsagen; erzählen.

reckless ['reklis] unbekümmert; rücksichtslos.

reckon ['rekən] (be-, er-) rechnen; halten für; **~ up** zs.-zählen; **~ing** [**~**kniŋ] (Ab-, Be)Rechnung *f*.

reclaim [ri'kleim] zurückfordern; bekehren; urbar machen.

recline [ri'klain] (sich) (zurück)lehnen; liegen.

recogni|tion [rekəg'niʃən] Anerkennung *f*; Wiedererkennen *n*; **~ze** anerkennen; (wieder)erkennen.

recoil [ri'kɔil] zurückschrecken.

recollect [rekə'lekt] sich erinnern an; **~ion** Erinnerung *f*.

recommend [rekə'mend] empfehlen; **~ation** Empfehlung *f*.

recompense ['rekəmpens] entschädigen; ersetzen.

reconcil|e ['rekənsail] aus-, versöhnen; in Einklang bringen; **~iation** [**~**sili'eiʃən] Ver-, Aussöhnung *f*.

reconsider ['ri:kən'sidə] nochmals überlegen.

reconstruct ['ri:kən'strʌkt] wieder aufbauen; rekonstruieren; *fig.* wiederaufbauen; **~ion** Wiederaufbau *m*.

record ['rekɔ:d] Aufzeichnung *f*; Protokoll *n*; Urkunde *f*; Register *n*, Verzeichnis *n*; (schriftlicher) Bericht; Ruf *m*, Leumund *m*; *(sport pl)* Rekord *m*; (Schall)Platte *f*; *sp.* Rekord *m*; [ri'kɔ:d] auf-, verzeichnen; *auf Schallplatte etc.* aufnehmen; **~er** [**~**'k-] Aufnahmegerät *n*; **~ing** [**~**'k-] *Radio etc.* Aufzeichnung *f*, Aufnahme *f*; **~player** Plattenspieler *m*.

recourse [ri'kɔ:s]: **have ~ to s-e** Zuflucht nehmen zu.

recover [ri'kʌvə] wiedererlangen, -bekommen; bergen; wieder gesund werden; sich erholen; *fig.* sich fassen; **~y** Wiedererlangung *f*; Bergung *f*; Genesung *f*, Erholung *f*.

recreation [rekri'eiʃən] Erholung *f*.

recruit [ri'kru:t] Rekrut *m*.

rectangle ['rektæŋgl] Rechteck *n*.

rectify ['rektifai] berichtigen; *electr.* gleichrichten.

rector ['rektə] Pfarrer *m*; Rektor *m*; **~y** Pfarrhaus *n*.

recur [ri'kə:] wiederkeh-

ren; *fig.* zurückkommen
(**to** auf); **~rent** [ri'kɑrənt]
wiederkehrend.
red [red] rot; Rot *n*; **~**
breast Rotkehlchen *n*; ♀
Cross das Rote Kreuz; **~**
deer Rothirsch *m*; **~den**
(sich) röten; erröten; **~**
dish rötlich.
redeem [ri'di:m] freikau-
fen; einlösen; erlösen; ♀**er**
Erlöser *m*, Heiland *m*.
redemption [ri'dempʃən]
Einlösung *f*; Erlösung *f*.
red|-handed: **catch ~**
auf frischer Tat ertappen;
♀ **Indian** Indianer(in);
~letter day Festtag *m*;
fig. denkwürdiger Tag.
redouble [ri'dʌbl] (sich)
verdoppeln.
reduc|e [ri'dju:s] redu-
zieren; herabsetzen; ver-
ringern; ermäßigen; **~tion**
[-'dʌkʃən] Herabsetzung
f; Verringerung *f*; Er-
mäßigung *f*.
reed [ri:d] Schilfrohr *n*.
re-education [ˈriːedju(ː)-
ˈkeiʃən] Umschulung *f*.
reef [ri:f] (Felsen)Riff *n*.
reek [ri:k] stinken, (unangenehm) riechen (**of** nach).
reel [ri:l] (*Garn-*, *Film-*
etc.) Rolle *f*, (-)Spule *f*; **~**
(**up** auf)wickeln, (-)spulen;
wirbeln, schwanken, tau-
meln.
re|-elect ['ri:i'lekt] wieder-
wählen; **~enter** wieder
eintreten in (*acc.*); **~establish**
wiederherstellen.
refer [ri'fəː]: **~ (to)** verwei-

sen (auf, an); übergeben;
zurückführen (auf); sich
beziehen (auf); konsultieren.
referee [refə'riː] Schiedsrichter *m*; *Boxen:* Ring-
richter *m*.
reference ['refrəns] Re-
ferenz *f*, Zeugnis *n*; Verweis *m*; Nachschlagen *n*;
~ book Nachschlagewerk
n; **~ library** Handbiblio-
thek *f*.
refill ['riː'fil] Ersatzfüllung
f, Nachfüllpackung *f*;
['·'·'fil] auf-, nachfüllen.
refine [ri'fain] raffinieren,
veredeln; (sich) läutern;
(sich) verfeinern (*a. fig.*);
fig. bilden; **~ment** Ver-
feinerung *f*; Feinheit *f*;
Bildung *f*; **~ry** Raffinerie *f*.
reflect [ri'lekt] reflektieren, zurückwerfen, (wider-)
spiegeln; nachdenken (**on**,
upon über); **~ion** Re-
flexion *f*; Reflex *m*; Spie-
gelbild *n*; Überlegung *f*.
reflex ['riːfleks] Reflex...;
Reflex *m*.
reflexive [ri'fleksiv] *gr.* reflexiv, rückbezüglich.
reform [ri'fɔːm] Reform *f*;
reformieren, verbessern;
(sich) bessern; **~ation**
[refə'meiʃən] Besserung *f*;
♀**ation** *eccl.* Reformation
f; **~er** *eccl.* Reformator *m*;
pol. Reformer *m*.
refract [ri'frækt] *Strahlen*
brechen; **~ory** widerspen-
stig; *med.* hartnäckig.
refrain [ri'frein] unterlas-

sen (**from** *acc*); Refrain *m*.

refresh [ri'freʃ]: ~ (**o.s.**) (sich) erfrischen; auffrischen; **~ment** Erfrischung *f*.

refrigerator [ri'fridʒəreitə] Kühlschrank *m*; Kühl... [tanken.]

refuel [ri:'fjuəl] (auf-)

refuge ['refju:dʒ] Zuflucht (-stätte) *f*; **~e** [~u(:)'dʒi:] Flüchtling *m*.

refund [ri:'fʌnd] zurückzahlen.

refus|al [ri'fju:zəl] Ablehnung *f*; (Ver)Weigerung *f*; **~e** verweigern; abweisen; ablehnen; sich weigern; ['refju:s] Abfall *m*, Müll *m*.

refute [ri'fju:t] widerlegen.

regain [ri'gein] wiedergewinnen, -erlangen.

regard [ri'gɑ:d] Achtung *f*; Rücksicht *f*; **with ~ to** hinsichtlich; **kind ~s** herzliche Grüße; *vb*: ansehen; (be)achten; betreffen; **as ~** halten für; **as ~s** was ... betrifft; **~ing** hinsichtlich; **~less**: ~ **of** ohne Rücksicht auf. [(-in).]

regent ['ri:dʒənt] Regent*m*

regiment ['redʒimənt] Regiment *n*.

region ['ri:dʒən] Gegend *f*, Gebiet *n*, Bereich *m*.

regist|er ['redʒistə] Register *n* (*a. mus.*), Verzeichnis *n*; (sich) eintragen (lassen), einschreiben (lassen) (*a. Postsache*); (an-)zeigen; Gepäck aufgeben; sich (an)melden (**with** bei

der *Polizei etc.*); **~ered letter** Einschreibebrief *m*; **~ration** Eintragung *f*; Anmeldung *f*.

regret [ri'gret] Bedauern *n*; bedauern; beklagen; **~table** bedauerlich.

regular ['regjulə] regelmäßig; regulär (*a. mil.*), normal; richtig; **~ity** [~'læriti] Regelmäßigkeit *f*.

regulat|e ['regjuleit] regeln; regulieren; **~ion** Regulierung *f*; *pl* Vorschrift *f*; vorgeschrieben.

rehears|al [ri'hə:səl] Probe *f*; **~e** *thea.* proben; wiederholen.

reign [rein] Regierung *f*; Herrschaft *f* (*a. fig.*); herrschen, regieren.

rein [rein] *oft pl* Zügel *m*.

reindeer ['reindiə] *sg*, *pl* Ren(ntier) *n*.

reinforce [ri:in'fɔ:s] verstärken.

reject [ri'dʒekt] wegwerfen; ablehnen; **~ion** Ablehnung *f*.

rejoic|e [ri'dʒɔis] erfreuen; sich freuen (**at** über); **~ing** Freude *f*; *pl* (Freuden)Fest *n*.

rejoin [ri'dʒɔin] wieder zurückkehren zu; [ri-'dʒɔin] erwidern.

relapse [ri'læps] Rückfall *m*; wieder fallen (**into** in); rückfällig werden.

relate [ri'leit] erzählen; sich beziehen (**to** auf); **~d** verwandt (**to** mit).

relation [ri'leiʃən] Bericht

m, Erzählung *f*; Verhältnis *n*; Verwandte *m*, *f*; *pl* Beziehungen *pl*; **in ~ to** in bezug auf; **~ship** Beziehung *f*; Verwandtschaft *f*.

relative ['relətiv] relativ; verhältnismäßig; bezüglich; Verwandte *m*, *f*; **~ (pronoun)** *gr.* Relativpronomen *n*, bezügliches Fürwort.

relax [ri'læks] lockern; (sich) entspannen.

relay ['ri:lei] Relais *n*; *Radio*: Übertragung *f*; *Radio*: übertragen; *a* [ri:'lei] Staffellauf *m*.

release [ri'li:s] Freilassung *f*; Befreiung *f*; Freigabe *f*; *tech.*, *phot.* Auslöser *m*; freilassen; befreien; freigeben; *tech.*, *phot.* auslösen.

relent [ri'lent] sich erweichen lassen; **~less** unbarmherzig.

relevant ['relivənt] sachdienlich; zutreffend.

reliab|ility [rilaiə'biliti] Zuverlässigkeit *f*; **~le** zuverlässig.

reliance [ri'laiəns] Vertrauen *n*; Verlaß *m*.

relic ['relik] (Über)Rest *m*; Reliquie *f*.

relie|f [ri'li:f] Relief *n*; Erleichterung *f*; Abwechslung *f*; Unterstützung *f*; Hilfe *f*; Ablösung *f*; *mil.* Entsatz *m*; **~ve** [~v] erleichtern, lindern; unterstützen; ablösen; befreien; *mil.* entsetzen.

religi|on [ri'lidʒən] Religion *f*; **~ous** religiös, Religions...; gewissenhaft.

relinquish [ri'liŋkwiʃ] aufgeben; loslassen.

relish ['reliʃ] (Wohl)Geschmack *m*; *fig.* Reiz *m*; gern essen; Geschmack finden an.

reluctan|ce [ri'lʌktəns] Widerstreben *n*; **~t** widerstrebend, widerwillig.

rely [ri'lai]: **~ (up)on** sich verlassen auf.

remain [ri'mein] (übrig) bleiben; *pl:* (Über)Reste *pl*; *die* sterblichen Überreste *pl*; **~der** *m*. Rest *m*.

remand [ri'mɑ:nd] (in die Untersuchungshaft) zurückschicken; **detention on ~** Untersuchungshaft *f*.

remark [ri'mɑ:k] Bemerkung *f*; bemerken; (sich) äußern; **~able** bemerkenswert.

remedy [ri'remidi] (Heil-, *jur.* Rechts)Mittel *n*; Abhilfe *f*; heilen; abhelfen.

rememb|er [ri'membə] sich erinnern an; denken an; **~er me to** her grüße sie von mir; **~rance** Erinnerung *f*; Andenken *n*.

remind [ri'maind] erinnern (**of** an); **~er** Mahnung *f*. [(sich) erinnernd.]

reminiscent [remi'nisnt]}

remiss [ri'mis] nachlässig.

remit [ri'mit] *Schuld etc.* erlassen; überweisen; **~tance** (Geld)Überweisung *f*.

remnant['remnənt](Über-) Rest *m*.

remodel ['ri:'mɔdl] umbilden, -formen.

remonstrate ['remənstreit] protestieren; einwenden.

remorse [ri'mɔ:s] Gewissensbisse *pl*, Reue *f*; **~less** unbarmherzig.

remote [ri'məut] fern, entlegen.

remov|al [ri'mu:vəl] Entfernen *n*, Beseitigung *f*; Umzug *m*; **~al van** Möbelwagen *m*; **~e** entfernen; beseitigen; (aus-, um-, ver)ziehen; *Schule:* Versetzung *f*; **~er** (*Flecken- etc.*)Entferner *m*; (*Möbel*)Spediteur *m*.

Renaissance [rə'neisəns] die Renaissance. [reißen.\

rend [rend] (*irr*) (zer-)/

render ['rendə] *berühmt, möglich etc.* machen; wiedergeben; *Dienst etc.* leisten; *Dank* abstatten; übersetzen; *mus.* vortragen; *thea.* gestalten, interpretieren; *Rechnung* vorlegen.

renew [ri'nju:] erneuern; **~al** Erneuerung *f*.

renounce [ri'nauns] entsagen; verzichten auf; verleugnen.

renovate ['renəuveit] renovieren; erneuern.

renown [ri'naun] Ruhm *m*, Ansehen *n*; **~ed** berühmt.

rent¹ [rent] *pret u. pp von* **rend**; Riß *m*; Spalte *f*.

rent² Miete *f*; Pacht *f*;

(ver)mieten; (ver)pachten.

repair [ri'peə] reparieren, ausbessern; Reparatur *f*; **in good ~** in gutem Zustand; **~ shop** Reparaturwerkstatt *f*.

reparation [repə'reiʃən] Wiedergutmachung *f*.

repartee [repɑ:'ti:]schlagfertige Antwort.

repay [ri:'pei] (*irr* **pay**) zurückzahlen; *et.* vergelten.

repeat [ri'pi:t] (sich) wiederholen.

repel [ri'pel] *Feind etc.* zurückschlagen; *fig.:* abweisen; *j-n* abstoßen.

repent [ri'pent] bereuen; **~ance** Reue *f*; **~ant** reuig.

repetition [repi'tiʃən]Wiederholung *f*.

replace [ri'pleis] wieder hinstellen *od.* -legen; ersetzen; *j-n* ablösen; **~ment** Ersatz *m*.

replenish [ri'pleniʃ] (wieder) auffüllen, ergänzen.

reply [ri'plai]: **~ (to)** antworten (auf), erwidern (auf); Antwort *f*.

report [ri'pɔ:t] Bericht *m*; Nachricht *f*; Gerücht *n*; Knall *m*; (*Schul*)Zeugnis *n*; berichten (über); (sich) melden; anzeigen; berichten; **~er** Reporter(in), Berichterstatter(in).

repose [ri'pəuz] Ruhe *f*; (sich) ausruhen; ruhen.

represent [repri'zent] darstellen (*a. fig., thea.*); vertreten; *thea.* aufführen; **~ation** Darstellung *f* (*a.*

thea.); Vertretung *f; thea.*
Aufführung *f;* **~ative** darstellend; (stell)vertretend; repräsentativ; typisch; Vertreter(in); *Am. parl.* Abgeordnete *m; ~* **House of ~atives** *Am. parl.* Repräsentantenhaus *n.*

repress [ri'pres] unterdrücken; [Aufschub *m*.]

reprieve [ri'pri:v] Frist *f.*]

reprimand ['reprima:nd] Verweis *m; j-m* e-n Verweis erteilen.

reproach [ri'prəutʃ] Vorwurf *m;* vorwerfen (**s.o. with s.th.** j-m et.); Vorwürfe machen; **~ful** vorwurfsvoll.

reproduc|e [ri:prə'dju:s] (sich) fortpflanzen; wiedergeben, reproduzieren; **~tion** [~'dʌkʃən] Fortpflanzung *f;* Reproduktion *f.*

reproof [ri'pru:f] Vorwurf *m,* Tadel *m.*

reprove [ri'pru:v] tadeln.

reptile ['reptail] Reptil *n.*

republic [ri'pʌblik] Republik *f;* **~an** republikanisch; Republikaner(in).

repugnan|ce [ri'pʌgnəns] Widerwille *m;* **~t** widerlich.

repuls|e [ri'pʌls] Abfuhr *f,* Zurückweisung *f;* zurück-, abweisen; **~ive** abstoßend, widerwärtig.

reput|able ['repjutəbl] angesehen; anständig; **~a-tion** (guter) Ruf; **~e** [ri'pju:t] Ruf *m.*

request [ri'kwest] Gesuch

n, Bitte *f;* Nachfrage *f;* **by ~, on ~** auf Wunsch; *vb:* bitten (um); ersuchen um; **~ stop** Bedarfshaltestelle *f.*

require [ri'kwaiə] verlangen; (er)fordern; brauchen; **~d** erforderlich; **~ment** (An)Forderung *f;* Erfordernis *n; pl* Bedarf *m.*

requisite ['rekwizit] erforderlich; (Bedarfs-, Gebrauchs)Artikel *m.*

requite [ri'kwait] vergelten; belohnen.

rescue ['reskju:] Rettung *f;* Befreiung *f;* Rettungs...; retten; befreien.

research [ri'sə:tʃ] Forschung *f,* Untersuchung *f;* **~er** Forscher *m.*

resembl|ance [ri'zembləns] Ähnlichkeit *f* (**to** mit); **~e** gleichen, ähnlich sein.

resent [ri'zent] übelnehmen; **~ful** übelnehmerisch; ärgerlich; **~ment** Groll *m.*

reservation [rezə'veiʃən] Reservierung *f,* Vorbestellung *f; Am.* (Indianer-) Reservation *f;* Vorbehalt *m.*

reserve [ri'zə:v] Reserve *f;* Vorrat *m;* Ersatz *m; sp.* Ersatzmann *m;* Reservat *n;* Zurückhaltung *f;* (sich) aufsparen od. -bewahren; (sich) zurückhalten mit; reservieren (lassen), vorbestellen, vormerken; vorbehalten; **~d** *fig.* zurückhaltend, reserviert.

reservoir ['rezəvwɑ:] Staubecken *n.*

reside [ri'zaid] wohnen, ansässig sein; **~nce** ['rezidəns] Wohnsitz *m*; **~nce permit** Aufenthaltsgenehmigung *f*; **~nt** wohnhaft; Einwohner(in).

residue ['rezidju:] Rest *m*.

resign [ri'zain] zurücktreten; aufgeben; verzichten auf; *Amt* niederlegen; überlassen; **~ o.s.** to sich ergeben in, sich abfinden mit; **~ation** [rezig'neiʃən] Verzicht *m*; Rücktritt (-sgesuch *n*) *m*; Resignation *f*; **~ed** resigniert.

resin ['rezin] Harz *n*.

resist [ri'zist] widerstehen; Widerstand leisten; beständig sein gegen; **~ance** Widerstand *m*; *tech.* Festigkeit *f*, Beständigkeit *f*; **~ant** widerstehend; widerstandsfähig, beständig (**to** gegen).

resolut|e ['rezəlu:t] entschlossen; **~ion** Entschluß *m*; Entschlossenheit *f*; Resolution *f*.

resolve [ri'zɔlv] auflösen; *Zweifel* zerstreuen; beschließen; **~ (up)on** sich entschließen zu; **~d** entschlossen.

resonan|ce ['reznəns] Resonanz *f*; **~t** nach-, widerhallend.

resort [ri'zɔ:t] (Aufenthalts-, Erholungs)Ort *m*; Zuflucht *f*; **~ to** oft besuchen; seine Zuflucht nehmen zu.

resound [ri'zaund] widerhallen (lassen).

resource [ri'sɔ:s] Hilfsmittel *n*; Zuflucht *f*; Findigkeit *f*; Zeitvertreib *m*; Entspannung *f*; *pl* natürliche Reichtümer *pl*, Mittel *pl*; **~ful** findig.

respect [ris'pekt] Beziehung *f*, Hinsicht *f*; Achtung *f*, Respekt *m*; Rücksicht *f*; **one's** **~s** e Grüße *od.* Empfehlungen *pl*; achten; schätzen; respektieren; **~able** ansehnlich; ehrbar; anständig; **~ful** respektvoll, ehrerbietig; **yours ~ly** hochachtungsvoll; **~ing** hinsichtlich; **~ive** jeweilig, entsprechend; **~ively** beziehungsweise.

respiration [respə'reiʃən] Atmen *n*, Atmung *f*; Atemzug *m*.

respite ['respait] Frist *f*, Aufschub *m*; Pause *f*.

resplendent [ris'plendənt] glänzend, strahlend.

respon|d [ris'pɔnd] antworten, erwidern; **~d to** reagieren auf, empfänglich sein für; **~dent** *jur.:* Beklagte *m, f*; beklagt; **~dent to** empfänglich für; **~se** [~ns] Antwort *f*, Erwiderung *f*; *fig.* Reaktion *f*.

responsib|ility [risponsə-'biliti] Verantwortung *f*; **~le** verantwortlich; verantwortungsvoll.

rest [rest] Rest *m*; Ruhe (-pause) *f*; Rast *f*; *tech.*

Stütze f; (aus)ruhen lassen; ruhen; (sich) ausruhen, rasten; (sich) stützen *od.* lehnen; **~ (up)on** *fig.* beruhen auf.

restaurant ['rest**ɔ**r**ɔ**ŋ, '**~**r**ɔ**nt] Restaurant *n*, Gaststätte *f*.

rest|ful ruhig; erholsam; **~house** Rasthaus *n*, -stätte *f*; **~less** ruhe-, rastlos; unruhig; **~lessness** Ruhe-, Rastlosigkeit *f*; Unruhe *f*.

restor|ation [restə'rei∫ən] Wiederherstellung *f*; Wiedereinsetzung *f*; Restaurierung *f*; **~e** [ris'tɔ:] wiederherstellen; wiedereinsetzen **(to)** in); zurückerstatten, -bringen, -legen; restaurieren.

restrain [ris'trein] zurückhalten; unterdrücken; **~t** Zurückhaltung *f*; Beschränkung *f*, Zwang *m*.

restrict [ris'trikt] be-, einschränken; **~ion** Be-, Einschränkung *f*.

result [ri'zʌlt] Ergebnis *n*, Resultat *n*; Folge *f*; sich ergeben **(from** aus); **~ in** zur Folge haben.

resum|e [ri'zju:m] wiederaufnehmen; *Sitz* wieder einnehmen; **~ption** [**~**'zʌmp∫ən] Wiederaufnahme *f*.

resurrection [rezə'rek∫ən] Wiederaufleben *n*; *the* 2 *eccl. die* Auferstehung.

retail ['ri:teil] Einzelhandel *m*; Einzelhandels...; [**~**'teil] im kleinen ver-

kaufen; **~er** [**~**'t-] Einzelhändler(in).

retain [ri'tein] behalten; zurückhalten.

retaliat|e [ri'tælieit] sich rächen; **~ion** Vergeltung *f*.

retell ['ri:'tel] nacherzählen.

retention [ri'ten∫ən] Zurückhalten *n*. [ge *n*.\
retinue ['retinju:] Gefol-/
retire [ri'taiə] (sich) zurückziehen, pensionieren; sich zur Ruhe setzen; in den Ruhestand treten; **~d** pensioniert, im Ruhestand (lebend); zurückgezogen; **~ment** Ausscheiden *n*; Ruhestand *m*; Zurückgezogenheit *f*.

retort [ri'tɔ:t] erwidern.

retrace [ri'treis] zurückverfolgen; rekonstruieren

retract [ri'trækt] (sich) zurückziehen; widerrufen.

retreat [ri'tri:t] sich zurückziehen; Rückzug *m*; **beat a ~** *fig.* es aufgeben.

retribution [retri'bju:∫ən] Vergeltung *f*.

retrieve [ri'tri:v] wiederbekommen; *hunt.* apportieren.

retrospect ['retrəuspekt] Rückblick *m*; **~ive** (zu-)rückblickend; rückwirkend.

return [ri'tə:n] zurückgehen, -kehren, -kommen; erwidern; antworten; vergelten; zurückerstatten, -geben, -senden; zurückstellen, -bringen, -tun;

Rück-, Wiederkehr f;
Rückgabe f; pl Umsatz m;
Gegenleistung f; Erwiderung f; amtlicher Bericht;
Rück...; **by** ~ umgehend;
in ~ dafür; **on my** ~ bei
m-r Rückkehr; **many
happy** ~**s of the day**
herzlichen Glückwunsch
zum Geburtstag; ~ **flight**
Rückflug m; ~ **(ticket)**
Rückfahrkarte f.

reunification [ˈriːjuːnifi-
ˈkeiʃən] Wiedervereini-
gung f.

reunion [ˈriːˈjuːnjən] Wie-
dervereinigung f; Treffen n.

revaluation [riːvæljuˈei-
ʃən] econ. Aufwertung f.

reveal [riˈviːl] enthüllen,
zeigen; offenbaren.

revel [ˈrevl] feiern, ausgelassen sein; schwelgen;
zechen.

revelation [reviˈleiʃən]
Enthüllung f; Offenba-
rung f.

revenge [riˈvendʒ] Rache
f; Revanche f; rächen;
~**ful** rachsüchtig.

revenue [ˈrevinjuː] Einkommen n; pl Einkünfte
pl; ~ **office** Finanzamt n.

revere [riˈviə] (ver)ehren;
~**nce** [ˈrevərəns] Verehrung f; Ehrfurcht f; (ver-)
ehren; ~**nd** ehrwürdig;
Geistliche(r).

reverse [riˈvəːs] Gegenteil
n; Rückseite f; fig. Rückschlag m; umkehren; (um-
kehren; Meinung etc. än-
dern; Urteil aufheben; ~

gear mot. Rückwärtsgang
m; ~ **side** Rückseite f;
linke (Stoff)Seite f.

review [riˈvjuː] mil. Parade
f; Zeitschrift: Rundschau
f; Rezension f; Rückblick
m; (über-, nach)prüfen;
mil. mustern; rezensieren;
fig. zurückblicken auf; ~**er**
Rezensent(in).

revis|e [riˈvaiz] revidieren;
überarbeiten; ~**ion** [~iʒən]
Revision f; Überarbei-
tung f.

reviv|al [riˈvaivəl] Wieder-
belebung f; ~**e** wiederbe-
leben.

revoke [riˈvəuk] widerrufen; aufheben.

revolt [riˈvəult] Revolte f,
Aufstand m; revoltieren,
sich auflehnen; fig. ab-
stoßen.

revolution [revəˈluːʃən]
Umdrehung f; fig. Revo-
lution f, Umwälzung f;
~**ary** revolutionär; Revo-
lutionär(in); ~**ist** Revolu-
tionär(in); ~**ize** revolutio-
nieren.

revolv|e [riˈvɔlv] sich
drehen; ~**ing** sich dre-
hend; Dreh...

reward [riˈwɔːd] Belohnung f; belohnen.

rheumatism [ˈruːmətizəm]
Rheumatismus m.

rhubarb [ˈruːbɑːb] Rhabarber m.

rhyme [raim] Reim m;
Vers m; (sich) reimen.

rhythm [ˈriðəm] Rhythmus
m; ~**ic(al)** rhythmisch.

rib [rib] Rippe f.

ribbon ['riban] Band n.

rice [rais] Reis m.

rich [ritʃ] reich (**in** an); kostbar; fruchtbar; voll (Ton); schwer, kräftig (Speise etc.); sub: the ~ die Reichen pl; ~es ['~iz] pl Reichtum m; Reichtümer pl; ~ness Reichtum m, Fülle f.

rick [rik] (Heu)Schober m.

rickets ['rikits] sg, pl Rachitis f; ~y rachitisch; wack(e)lig, klapp(e)rig.

rid [rid] (irr) befreien (of von); **get ~ of** loswerden.

ridden ['ridn] pp von **ride**.

riddle ['ridl] Rätsel n; grobes Sieb; sieben; durchlöchern, -sieben.

ride [raid] Ritt m; Fahrt f; (irr) reiten; fahren; ~r Reiter(in f).

ridge [ridʒ] (Gebirgs-) Kamm m, Grat m; (Dach-) First m.

ridicule ['ridikju:l] Verspottung f, Spott m; verspotten; ~ous [~'dikjuləs] lächerlich.   [Reit...]

riding ['raidiŋ] Reiten n;

rifle ['raifl] Gewehr n, Büchse f.

rift [rift] Riß m, Sprung m; Spalte f.

right [rait] adj recht; recht, richtig; colloq. richtig, in Ordnung, gut!; **all ~** in Ordnung, gut!; **that's all** ~ das macht nichts!, schon gut!, bitte!; **I am perfectly all ~** mir geht es ausgezeichnet; **that's ~** richtig!, ganz recht!, stimmt!; **be ~** recht haben; **put ~, set ~** in Ordnung bringen; ganz recht!, richtig; gerade(wegs), sofort; direkt; völlig, ganz; genau; **~ ahead** geradeaus; **~ on** geradeaus; **~ away** sofort; **turn ~** (sich) nach rechts wenden, rechts abbiegen; vb (aus-, auf-) richten; j-m zu s-m Recht verhelfen; Recht n; rechte Hand, Rechte f; **on the ~** rechts; **to the ~** (nach) rechts; ~eous ['~ʃəs] rechtschaffen; gerecht(fertigt); ~ful rechtmäßig; gerecht; ~hand recht; ~handed rechtshändig; ~ of way Vorfahrt(srecht n) f.

rigid ['ridʒid] starr, steif; fig. streng.

rigorous ['rigərəs] rigoros, streng, hart; ~o(u)r Strenge f, Härte f.

rim [rim] Rand m; Felge f.

rind [raind] Rinde f, Schale f; (Speck)Schwarte f.

ring [riŋ] Ring m; Kreis m; Manege f; Arena f; Geläut(e) n; Glockenläuten n; Klang m; Klingeln n; **give s.o. a ~** j-n anrufen; (irr) läuten; klingeln; klingen; **the bell klingelt; ~ off** (den Hörer) auflegen od. einhängen; ~ **s.o. up** j-n od. bei j-m anrufen; ~**leader** Rädelsführer m; ~**master** Zirkusdirektor m.

rink [riŋk] Eisbahn f; Rollschuhbahn f.

rinse [rins]: ~ (out) (aus-, ab)spülen.

riot [raiət] Aufruhr m; Krawall m; Tumult m; randalieren, toben; schwelgen; **~ous** aufrührerisch; lärmend.

rip [rip] Riß m; auftrennen; (zer)reißen.

ripe [raip] reif; **~n** reifen (lassen); **~ness** Reife f.

ripple [ripl] kleine Welle; Kräuselung f; (sich) kräuseln; rieseln.

rise [raiz] (An-, Auf)Steigen n; Anhöhe f; (Preis-, Gehalts)Erhöhung f; Ursprung m; fig. Aufstieg m; (irr) sich erheben; aufstehen; (an-, auf)steigen; aufgehen (Sonne, Samen); entspringen (Fluß); **~n** [rizn] pp von rise; **~r**: early ~ Frühaufsteher(in).

rising [raiziŋ] ast. Aufgang m; Aufstand m.

risk [risk] riskieren, wagen; Gefahr f, Risiko n; **run the ~ of** Gefahr laufen zu; **~y** riskant, gewagt.

rite [rait] Ritus m.

rival [raivəl] Rivale m, -in f, Konkurrent(in); rivalisierend; wetteifern mit; **~ry** Rivalität f.

river [rivə] Fluß m, Strom m; **~boat** Flußdampfer m; **~side** Flußufer n.

rivet [rivit] tech. Niet m; (ver)nieten; fig. heften.

rivulet [rivjulit] Flüßchen n.

road [roud] (Auto-, Land-)Straße f, Weg m; **~ map** Straßenkarte f; **~ sign** Verkehrsschild n, -zeichen n.

roam [rəum] umherstreifen, (-)wandern; durchstreifen.

roar [rɔː] brüllen; brausen, toben; Gebrüll n; Brausen n, Toben n; **~(s pl of laughter)** schallendes Gelächter.

roast [rəust] rösten, braten, schmoren, Braten m; geröstet; gebraten, Röst..., Brat...; **~ beef** Rinderbraten m; **~ meat** Bratenm.

rob [rɔb] (be)rauben; **~ber** Räuber m; **~bery** Raub (-überfall) m.

robe [rəub] (Amts)Robe f, Talar m.

robin (redbreast) [rɔbin] Rotkehlchen n.

robot [rəubɔt] Roboter m.

robust [rəuˈbʌst] robust, kräftig.

rock [rɔk] Fels(en) m; Klippe f; Gestein n; schaukeln; wiegen.

rocker [rɔkə] Kufe f; Am. Schaukelstuhl m; Rocker m, Halbstarke m.

rocket [rɔkit] Rakete f; Raketen...; **~-powered** mit Raketenantrieb; **~ry** Raketentechnik f.

rocking-chair Schaukelstuhl m.

rocky [rɔki] felsig, Felsen...

rod [rɔd] Rute *f*; Stab *m*; Stange *f*.

rode [rəud] *pret von* ride.

rodent ['rəudənt] Nagetier *n*.

roe¹ [rəu] Reh *n*.

roe² *ichth.*: (**hard**) Rogen *m*; **soft** ~ Milch *f*.

rogue [rəug] Schurke *m*; Schelm *m*; ~ish schurkisch; schelmisch.

role, rôle [rəul] *thea.* Rolle *f* (*a. fig.*).

roll [rəul] Rolle *f*; Walze *f*; Brötchen *n*, Semmel *f*; (Namens)Liste *f*; (Donner)Rollen *n*; (Trommel)Wirbel *m*; Schlingern *n*; rollen; fahren; schlingern; (g)rollen, dröhnen; (sich) wälzen; walzen; drehen; ~ **up** zs.-, aufrollen; **~er** Rolle *f*, Walze *f*; **~er coaster** *Am.* Achterbahn *f*; **~er-skate** Rollschuh *m*; ~ **film** Rollfilm *m*; **~ing mill** Walzwerk *n*.

Roman ['rəumən] römisch; Römer(in).

roman|ce [rəu'mæns] Abenteuer-, Liebesroman *m*; Romanze *f*; Romantik *f*; **~tic** romantisch.

romp [rɔmp] Range *f*, Wildfang *m*; Tollen *n*; umhertollen; sich balgen; **~er(s** *pl*) Spielanzug *m*.

roof [ru:f] Dach *n*; ~ **over** überdachen.

rook [ruk] Saatkrähe *f*.

room [rum] Raum *m*; Zimmer *n*; Platz *m*; *pl* Wohnung *f*; *pl* Fremdenzimmer

pl; **~mate** Zimmergenoss|e *m*, -in *f*; **~y** geräumig.

roost [ru:st] Schlafplatz *m* (*von* Vögeln); Hühnerstange *f*; Hühnerstall *m*; **~er** (Haus)Hahn *m*.

root [ru:t] Wurzel *f*; (ein)wurzeln;einpflanzen;(auf)wühlen; ~ **up** ausgraben, -reißen; ~ **out** ausrotten.

rope [rəup] Tau *n*, Seil *n*, Strick *m*; Lasso *n*, *m*; festbinden; anseilen; ~ **off** (durch ein Seil) absperren.

ros|e [rəuz] Rose *f*; Brause *f* (*e-r* Gießkanne); *pret von* rise; **~y** rosig.

rot [rɔt] Fäulnis *f*; faulen lassen; (ver)faulen.

rota|ry ['rəutəri] sich drehend; Rotations...; **~te** [~'teit] (sich) drehen; rotieren (lassen); **~tion** Umdrehung *f*.

rotor ['rəutə] *aer.* Drehflügel *m*, Rotor *m*.

rotten ['rɔtn] verfault, faul; morsch; *sl.* saumäßig.

rotund [rəu'tʌnd] rundlich; voll (Stimme).

rough [rʌf] rauh; roh; grob; ungefähr; **~ness** Rauheit *f*; Roheit *f*; Grobheit *f*.

round [raund] Rund *n*, Kreis *m*; (Leiter)Sprosse *f*; Runde *f*; Rundgang *m*; Kanon *m*; *adj* rund; voll; *adv* überall; *e-e* Zeit lang *od.* hindurch; ~ (**about**) rund-, rings(her)um; *prp*

rund (um); um od. in ...
(herum); vb rund machen
od. werden; ~ off abrun-
den; ~ up zs.-treiben;~
about ausschweifig;
Karussell n; (Platz m mit)
Kreisverkehr m; ~ trip Am.
Hin- u. Rückfahrt f.

rouse [rauz] aufwachen;
wecken; ermuntern; ~o.s.
sich aufraffen.

route[ru:t] (Reise-,Fahrt-)
Route f,(-)Weg m; Strecke f.

routine [ru:ˈti:n] Routine
f; üblich; Routine...

rove [rəuv] umherstreifen.

row[rau] colloq. Krach m.

row[rau] (Häuser-, Sitz-
etc.)Reihe f; Ruderpartie
f; rudern; ~boat Ruder-
boot n; ~er Ruderer m;
~ing-boat Ruderboot n.

royal [ˈrɔiəl] königlich;
~ty Königswürde f; Mit-
glied n e-s Königshauses;
(Autoren)Tantieme f.

rub [rʌb] reiben; (ab)wi-
schen; ~ down abreiben;
~ in einreiben; ~ off ab-
reiben; ~ out ausradieren.

rubber [ˈrʌbə] Gummi n,
m; Radiergummi m; pl
Am. Gummischuhe pl;
Gummi...; ~ plant Gum-
mibaum m.

rubbish [ˈrʌbiʃ] Abfall m;
Müll m; Schund m; ~!
Unsinn!

rubble [ˈrʌbl] Schutt m.

ruby [ˈru:bi] Rubin(rot n)m.

rucksack [ˈruksæk] Rucksack m.

rudder [ˈrʌdə] mar. (Steu-

er)Ruder n; aer. Seiten-
ruder n.

ruddy [ˈrʌdi] rot(backig).

rude [ru:d] unhöflich;
heftig; grob; roh; unge-
bildet.

ruff [rʌf] Halskrause f.

ruffian [ˈrʌfjən] Rohling
m; Schurke m.

ruffle [ˈrʌfl] Krause f,
Rüsche f; kräuseln; Federn
etc. sträuben; (ver)ärgern.

rug [rʌg] (Reise-, Woll-)
Decke f; Vorleger m.

Rugby (football) [ˈrʌgbi]
Rugby n.   [eben.]

rugged [ˈrʌgid] rauh; un-]

rugger [ˈrʌgə] colloq. s.
Rugby (football).

ruin [ruin] Ruin m, Zs.-
bruch m; pl Ruine(n pl)
f, Trümmer pl; vernich-
ten; ruinieren.

rule [ru:l] Regel f; Vorschrift f; Herrschaft f;
Maßstab m; as a ~ in der
Regel;(be)herrschen;herr-
schen über; leiten; ver-
fügen; liniieren; ~ out
ausschließen; ~r Herr-
scher(in); Lineal n.

rum [rʌm] Rum m.

rumble [ˈrʌmbl] rumpeln,
grollen (Donner).

ruminant [ˈru:minənt]
Wiederkäuer m.

rummage [ˈrʌmidʒ]
Durchsuchung f; Ramsch
m; durchsuchen; (durch-)
wühlen.   [rücht m.]

rumo(u)r [ˈru:mə] Ge-]

rump [rʌmp] Steiß m,
Hinterteil n; fig. Rumpf m.

rumple ['rʌmpl] zerknittern, -knüllen; zerzausen.

run [rʌn] Lauf(en n) m; Rennen n; (Schlitten)Fahrt f; Am. Laufmasche f; Serie f; econ. Ansturm m; thea., Film: Laufzeit f; (irr) (aus-, durch-, ver-, zer-) laufen; rennen; eilen; fließen; fahren, verkehren (Bus etc.); lauten (Text); gehen (Melodie); tech. arbeiten, laufen, gehen; sp. (um die Wette) laufen (mit); laufen lassen; Geschäft betreiben, leiten; ~ **across** zufällig treffen, stoßen auf; ~ **after** hinterherlaufen; ~ **away** davonlaufen; ~ **down** ablaufen (Uhr); umrennen; überfahren; herunterwirtschaften; j-n schlecht machen; ~ **in** Auto einfahren; ~ **into** hineinlaufen in, prallen gegen; geraten in (Schulden etc.); ~ **off** weglaufen; ~ **out** zu Ende gehen, knapp werden, ausgehen; ~ **out of s.th.** j-m geht et. aus od. wird et. knapp; ~ **over** überfließen; überfliegen, durchlesen; überfahren; ~ **short (of)** s. **run out (of)**; ~ **through** durchbohren; (rasch) überfliegen; ~ **up** sich belaufen auf.

rung¹ [rʌŋ] pp von **ring**.

rung² (Leiter)Sprosse f.

runner ['rʌnə] Läufer m; (Schlitten-)Kufe f; bot. Ausläufer m; ~-**up** sp. Zweite m, f.

running Rennen n; laufend; fließend; **for two days** ~ zwei Tage hintereinander; ~-**board** Trittbrett n.

runway ['rʌnwei] aer. Start-, Lande-, Rollbahn f.

rupture ['rʌptʃə] Bruch m, Riß m (beide a. med.).

rural ['ruərəl] ländlich, Land...

rush [rʌʃ] Hetzen n, Stürmen n; Eile f; Andrang m; stürmische Nachfrage; stürzen; jagen, hetzen; stürmen; drängen; ~ **at** sich stürzen auf; ~ **hours** pl Hauptverkehrs-, Stoßzeit f.

Russian ['rʌʃən] russisch; Russe m, -in f; Russisch n.

rust [rʌst] Rost m; rosten; verrosten lassen.

rustic ['rʌstik] ländlich, Bauern..., rustikal.

rustle ['rʌsl] rascheln (mit); rauschen; Rascheln n.

rusty ['rʌsti] rostig, verrostet; fig. eingerostet.

rut [rʌt] (Wagen)Spur f; Brunst f, Brunft f.

ruthless ['ruːθlis] unbarmherzig; rücksichts-, skrupellos.

rutt|ed ['rʌtid], ~**y** ausgefahren (Weg).

rye [rai] Roggen m.

S

sable ['seibl] Zobel(pelz) *m*.

sabotage ['sæbətɑ:ʒ] Sabotage *f*; sabotieren.

sabre ['seibə] Säbel *m*.

sack [sæk] Plünderung *f*; Sack *m*; **give (get) the ~** *colloq.* entlassen (werden); *vb.*: plündern; *colloq.* entlassen, rausschmeißen.

sacrament ['sækrəmənt] Sakrament *n*.

sacred ['seikrid] heilig.

sacrifice ['sækrifais] Opfer *n*; opfern.

sad [sæd] traurig; schlimm; **~den** traurig machen *od.* werden.

saddle ['sædl] Sattel *m*; satteln.

sadness ['sædnis] Traurigkeit *f*.

safe [seif] sicher (**from** vor); unversehrt, heil; Safe *m, n*, Geldschrank *m*; **~guard** Schutz *m*; sichern, schützen.

safety ['seifti] Sicherheit *f*; Sicherheits...; **~belt** Sicherheitsgurt *m*; **~lock** Sicherheitsschloß *n*; **~pin** Sicherheitsnadel *f*; **~razor** Rasierapparat *m*.

sag [sæg] durchsacken; *tech.* durchhängen.

sagacity [sə'gæsiti] Scharfsinn *m*. [**say.**]

said [sed] *pret.* u. *pp von* [

sail [seil] Segel *n*; segeln, fahren; auslaufen (*Schiff*); **~boat** *Am.*, **~ing-boat**

Segelboot *n*; **~ing-ship,** **~ing-vessel** Segelschiff *n*; **~or** Seemann *m*, Matrose *m*.

saint [seint] Heilige *m, f*; [*vor Namen:* snt] Sankt ...

sake [seik]: **for the ~ of** um ... willen, wegen; **for my ~** meinetwegen.

salad ['sæləd] Salat *m*.

salary ['sæləri] Gehalt *n*.

sale [seil] (Aus-, Schluß-) Verkauf *m*; *econ.* Ab-, Umsatz *m*; **for ~, on ~** zum Verkauf, zu verkaufen; **~s department** Verkaufsabteilung *f*; **~sman** Verkäufer *m*; **~s manager** Verkaufsleiter *m*; **~swoman** Verkäuferin *f*.

saliva [sə'laivə] Speichel *m*.

sallow ['sæləu] gelblich.

sally ['sæli]: **~ forth, ~ out** sich aufmachen.

salmon ['sæmən] Lachs *m*, Salm *m*.

saloon [sə'lu:n] Salon *m*; *Am.* Kneipe *f*.

salt [sɔ:lt] Salz *n*; *fig.* Würze *f*; Salz...; salzig; (ein)gesalzen, Salz...; Pökel...; (ein)salzen; pökeln; **~cellar** Salzfäßchen *n*; **~y** salzig.

salut|ation [sælju(:)'teiʃən] Gruß *m*, Begrüßung *f*; **~e** [sə'lu:t] Gruß *m*; Salut *m*; grüßen; salutieren.

salvation [sæl'veiʃən] Erlösung *f*; (Seelen)Heil *n*; **2 Army** Heilsarmee *f*.

salve [sɑːv] Salbe f.

same [seim] selb, gleich; **the ~** der-, die-, dasselbe; **all the ~** trotzdem; **it is all the ~ to me** es ist mir ganz gleich.

sample ['sɑːmpl] Probe f, Muster n; probieren.

sanatorium [sænə'tɔːriəm] (Lungen)Sanatorium n.

sanct|ify ['sæŋktifai] heiligen; weihen; **~ion** Sanktion f; billigen; **~uary** ['~tjuəri] Heiligtum n; Asyl n.

sand [sænd] Sand m.

sandal ['sændl] Sandale f.

sandwich ['sænwidʒ] Sandwich n; **~man** Plakatträger m.

sandy ['sændi] sandig, Sand...; sandfarben; **~ beach** Sandstrand m.

sane [sein] geistig gesund, normal; vernünftig.

sang [sæŋ] pret von sing.

sanitarium [sæni'teəriəm] Am. für sanatorium.

sanit|ary ['sænitəri] hygienisch, Gesundheits...; **~ary napkin**, **~ary towel** Damenbinde f; **~ation** sanitäre Einrichtungen pl; **~y** gesunder Verstand.

sank [sæŋk] pret von sink.

Santa Claus [sæntə'klɔːz] Nikolaus m, Weihnachtsmann m.

sap [sæp] bot. Saft m; fig. Lebenskraft f; **~py** saftig; fig. kraftvoll.

sarcasm ['sɑːkæzəm] Sarkasmus m, beißender Spott.

sardine [sɑː'diːn] Sardine f.

sash [sæʃ] Schärpe f; **~window** Schiebefenster n.

sat [sæt] pret u. pp von sit.

Satan ['seitən] Satan m.

satchel ['sætʃəl] Schulmappe f.

satellite ['sætəlait] Satellit m.

satin ['sætin] Satin m.

satir|e ['sætaiə] Satire f; **~ize** ['~əraiz] verspotten.

satis|faction [sætis'fækʃən] Befriedigung f; Genugtuung f; Zufriedenheit f; **~factory** befriedigend, zufriedenstellend; **~fy** ['~fai] befriedigen, zufriedenstellen; überzeugen.

Saturday ['sætədi] Sonnabend m, Samstag m.

sauce [sɔːs] Soße f, Tunke f; Am. Kompott n; **~pan** Kochtopf m; **~r** Untertasse f.

saucy ['sɔːsi] frech.

saunter ['sɔːntə] schlendern, bummeln.

sausage ['sɔsidʒ] Wurst f; Würstchen n.

savage ['sævidʒ] wild; grausam; Wilde m, f.

save [seiv] retten; bewahren; erlösen; (er)sparen; außer; **~ for** bis auf; **~r** Retter(in); Sparer(in).

saving ['seiviŋ] rettend; sparsam; ...ersparend; pl Ersparnisse pl; **~s-bank** Sparkasse f.

savio(u)r ['seivjə] Retter m; 2 eccl. Heiland m, Erlöser m.

savo(u)r ['seivə] (Wohl-

Geschmack *m*; *fig.* Beigeschmack *m*; **~y** schmackhaft; pikant.

saw[1] [so:] *pret von* **see**.

saw[2] (*irr*) sägen; Säge *f*; **~dust** Sägespäne *pl*; **~mill** Sägewerk *n*; **~n** *pp von* **saw**[2].

Saxon ['sæksn] sächsisch; Sachse *m*, Sächsin *f*.

say [sei] (*irr*) auf(sagen); berichten; *Gebet* sprechen; meinen; **as if to ~** als ob er sagen wollte; **that is to ~** das heißt; **he is said to be ...** er soll ... sein; **no sooner said than done** gesagt, getan; **I ~!** sag(en Sie) mal!; ich muß schon sagen!; **~ing** Sprichwort *n*, Redensart *f*; **it goes without ~ing** es versteht sich von selbst.

scab [skæb] Schorf *m*.

scaffold ['skæfəld] (Bau-)Gerüst *n*; Schafott *n*; **~ing** (Bau)Gerüst *n*.

scald [sko:ld] verbrühen; *Milch* abkochen.

scale [skeil] Schuppe *f*; Tonleiter *f*; Skala *f*; Maßstab *m*; Waagschale *f*; **(a pair of) ~s** *pl* (e—e) Waage; (sich) abschuppen *od.* ablösen.

scalp [skælp] Kopfhaut *f*; Skalp *m*; skalpieren.

scan [skæn] absuchen, -tasten; *fig.* überfliegen.

scandal ['skændl] Skandal *m*; Klatsch *m*; **~ous** ['~dələs] skandalös, anstößig.

Scandinavian [skændi'neivjən] skandinavisch; Skandinavier(in).

scant [skænt] knapp; **~y** knapp, spärlich; dürftig.

scapegoat ['skeipgəut] Sündenbock *m*.

scar [ska:] Narbe *f*; schrammen; **~ over** vernarben.

scarce [skɛəs] knapp; selten; **~ly** kaum; **~ity** Mangel *m*, Knappheit *f* (of an).

scare [skɛə] erschrecken; **~ away** verjagen, -scheuchen; **be ~d** of Angst haben vor; **~crow** Vogelscheuche *f*.

scarf [ska:f], *pl* **~s** [~fs], **scarves** [~vz] Schal *m*, Hals-, Kopf-, Schultertuch *n*.

scarlet ['ska:lit] scharlachrot; **~ fever** Scharlach *m*.

scarred [ska:d] narbig.

scarves [ska:vz] *pl von* **scarf**.

scathing ['skeiðiŋ] *fig.* vernichtend.

scatter ['skætə] (sich) zerstreuen; aus-, verstreuen.

scavenge ['skævindʒ] *Straßen etc.* reinigen.

scene [si:n] Szene *f*; Schauplatz *m*; **~ry** Szenerie *f*.

scent [sent] (Wohl)Geruch *m*, Duft *m*; Parfüm *n*; Fährte *f*; wittern; parfümieren.

sceptic ['skeptik] Skeptiker(in); **~al** skeptisch.

schedule ['ʃedju:l, *Am.* 'skedʒu:l] festsetzen; pla-

nen; Verzeichnis *n*; *Am.* Fahr-, Flugplan *m*; **on ~** (fahr)planmäßig.
scheme [ski:m] Schema *n*; Plan *m*; planen.
scholar ['skɔlə] Gelehrte *m*; Stipendiat(in); **~ship** Stipendium *n*.
school [sku:l] *ichth.* Schwarm *m*; Schule *f* (*a. fig.*); **at ~** auf *od.* in der Schule; *vb*: schulen; **~boy** Schüler *m*; **~fellow** Mitschüler(in); **~girl** Schülerin *f*; **~ing** (Schul)Ausbildung *f*; **~master** Lehrer *m*; **~mate** Mitschüler(in); **~mistress** Lehrerin *f*; **~ of motoring** Fahrschule *f*.
schooner ['sku:nə] Schoner *m*; *Am.* Planwagen *m*.
scien|ce ['saiəns] Wissenschaft *f*; Naturwissenschaft(en *pl*) *f*; **~tific** [~'tifik] (natur)wissenschaftlich; **~tist** (Natur)Wissenschaftler(in).
scissors ['sizəz] *pl* (*a.* **a pair of ~**) (e–e) Schere.
scoff [skɔf] spotten (**at** über).
scold [skəuld] (aus)schelten, auszanken; schimpfen.
scone [skɔn] weiches Teegebäck.
scoop [sku:p] Schöpfkelle *f*; schöpfen, schaufeln.
scooter ['sku:tə] (Kinder-) Roller *m*; (Motor)Roller *m*.
scope [skəup] Bereich *m*; Spielraum *m*.
scorch [skɔ:tʃ] versengen, -brennen.
score [skɔ:] Kerbe *f*; Zeche *f*, Rechnung *f*; *sp.* Spielstand *m*, Punktzahl *f*, (Spiel)Ergebnis *n*; 20 Stück; **four ~** achtzig; (ein)kerben; *sp. Punkte* erzielen, *Tore* schießen.
scorn [skɔ:n] Verachtung *f*; Spott *m*; verachten; **~ful** verächtlich.
Scot [skɔt] Schott|e *m*, -in *f*.
Scotch [skɔtʃ] schottisch; *sub*: **the ~** die Schotten *pl*; **~man, ~woman** *s.* **Scotsman, Scotswoman.**
scot-free ['skɔt'fri:] ungestraft.
Scots [skɔts] Schottische *n*; **~man** Schotte *m*; **~woman** Schottin *f*.
scoundrel ['skaundrəl] Schurke *m*, Schuft *m*.
scour ['skauə] scheuern; reinigen.
scout [skaut] Späher *m*, Kundschafter *m*; Pannenhelfer *m* (*e–s Automobilklubs*); (aus)kundschaften; erkunden; **~master** Pfadfinderführer *m*.
scowl [skaul] finster blikken; finsterer Blick.
scramble ['skræmbl] klettern; sich balgen (**for** um); **~d eggs** *pl* Rührei *n*.
scrap [skræp] Stückchen *n*, Fetzen *m*; Abfall *m*; Schrott *m*.
scrape [skreip] Kratzen *n*, Scharren *n*; *fig.* Klemme *f*; kratzen; scharren; **~ off** abkratzen; **~ out** auskratzen.

scrap-iron Schrott *m*.

scratch [skrætʃ] Kratzer *m*, Schramme *f*; (zer)kratzen.

scrawl [skrɔ:l] Gekritzel *n*; kritzeln.

scream [skri:m] Schrei *m*; Gekreisch *n*; schreien, kreischen.

screech [skri:tʃ] *s.* **scream**.

screen [skri:n] (Schutz-) Schirm *m*; (Film)Leinwand *f*; Bildschirm *m*; (Fliegen)Gitter *n*; (ab-, be)schirmen, (be)schützen; verfilmen; *j-n* überprüfen.

screw [skru:] Schraube *f*; schrauben; **~-driver** Schraubenzieher *m*.

scribble ['skribl] Gekritzel *n*; kritzeln.

script [skript] Manuskript *n*; Drehbuch *n*; **~ure** Bibel...; **the Holy ℓures** *pl* die Bibel, die Heilige Schrift.

scroll [skroul] Schriftrolle *f*.

scrub [skrʌb] Gestrüpp *n*; schrubben, scheuern.

scrup|le ['skru:pl] Skrupel *m*, Bedenken *n*; Bedenken haben; **~ulous** ['~pjuləs] gewissenhaft.

scrutin|ize ['skru:tinaiz] (genau) prüfen; **~y** (genaue) Prüfung.

scuffle ['skʌfl] raufen.

sculpt|or ['skʌlptə] Bildhauer *m*; **~ure** Bildhauerei *f*; Skulptur *f*, Plastik *f*; (heraus)meißeln, formen.

scum [skʌm] (Ab)Schaum *m*; *fig.* Abschaum *m*.

scurf [skə:f] (Kopf)Schuppen *pl*.

scurvy ['skə:vi] Skorbut *m*.

scuttle ['skʌtl] Kohleneimer *m*.

scythe [saið] Sense *f*.

sea [si:] *die* See, *das* Meer; **at ~** auf See; **go to ~** zur See gehen; **~faring** ['~fɛəriŋ] seefahrend; **~food** Meeresfrüchte *pl*; **~gull** (See)Möwe *f*.

seal [si:l] Seehund *m*, Robbe *f*; Siegel *n*; *tech.* Dichtung *f*; (ver-, *fig.* be)siegeln; **~ up** (fest) verschließen *od.* abdichten.

sea level Meeresspiegel *m*.

seam [si:m] Saum *m*, Naht *f*.

seaman ['si:mən] Seemann *m*, Matrose *m*.

seamstress ['semstris] Näherin *f*.

sea|plane Meeresflugzeug *n*; **~port** Hafenstadt *f*; **~ power** Seemacht *f*.

search [sə:tʃ] durch-, untersuchen; erforschen; suchen, forschen (**for** nach); fahnden; Suche *f*, Forschen *n*; Durchsuchung *f*; **in ~ of** auf der Suche nach.

sea|shore Meeres-, Meeresküste *f*; **~sick** seekrank; **~side** Küste *f*; **~side resort** Seebad *n*.

season ['si:zn] Jahreszeit *f*; Saison *f*; **dead ~, off ~** Vor-, Nachsaison *f*; reifen (lassen); würzen; abhärten (**to** gegen); ablagern; **~able** rechtzeitig; **~al** Saison...; **~ing** Würze *m*, **~**

ticket rail. Zeitkarte f; thea. Abonnement n.

seat [si:t] Sitz m; Sessel m, Stuhl m, Bank f; (Sitz-)Platz m; Landsitz m; **take a ~** sich setzen; nehmen Sie Platz!; **be ~ed** sitzen; nehmen Sie Platz!; **~belt** Sicherheitsgurt m.

sea|ward(s) ['si:wəd(z)] seewärts; **~weed** (See-)Tang m; **~worthy** seetüchtig.

secession [si'seʃən] Lossagung f, Abfall m.

seclu|de [si'klu:d] abschließen, absondern; **~ded** abgelegen; **~sion** [~ʒən] Abgeschiedenheit f.

second ['sekənd] zweite; **der, die, das Zweite**; Sekunde f; **~ary** sekundär; untergeordnet; **~ary school** höhere Schule; **~ floor** Am. erster Stock; **~hand** aus zweiter Hand; gebraucht; antiquarisch; **~ly** zweitens; **~rate** zweitklassig.

secre|cy ['si:krisi] Heimlichkeit f; Verschwiegenheit f; **~t** ['~it] geheim, heimlich; Geheim...; verschwiegen; Geheimnis n.

secretary ['sekrətri] Sekretär(in); **2 of State** Brit. Minister m; Am. Außenminister m.

secret|e [si'kri:t] med. absondern; **~ion** med. Absonderung f.

section ['sekʃən] Teil m; (Ab)Schnitt m; Abteilung f; Gruppe f.

secular ['sekjulə] weltlich.

secur|e [si'kjuə] sicher; sichern; schützen; sich beschaffen; gesichert; **~ity** Sicherheit f; Kaution f; pl Wertpapiere pl.

sedan [si'dæn] Limousine f.

sedative ['sedətiv] beruhigend; Beruhigungsmittel n.

sediment ['sedimənt] (Boden)Satz m.

seduc|e [si'dju:s] verführen; **~tion** [~'dʌkʃən] Verführung f; **~tive** verführerisch.

see [si:] (irr) sehen; (sich) ansehen, besichtigen; besuchen; zu j-m gehen, j-n aufsuchen od. konsultieren; sich überlegen; **live to ~** erleben; **~ s.o. home** j-n nach Hause bringen od. begleiten; **I ~!** ich verstehe!; **~ off** Besuch fortbegleiten; **~ out** Besuch hinausbegleiten; **~ through** durchschauen; j-m über et. hinweghelfen; et. durchhalten; **~ to** sich kümmern um, dafür sorgen (,daß).

seed [si:d] Samen m; Saat (-gut n) f; fig. Keim m.

seek [si:k] (irr) suchen; trachten nach.

seem [si:m] (er)scheinen; **~ing** anscheinend; scheinbar; **~ly** schicklich.

seen [si:n] pp von **see**.

seep [si:p] (durch)sickern, tropfen.

seesaw ['si:sɔ:] Wippe *f*, Wippschaukel *f*; wippen.

segment ['segmənt] Abschnitt *m*; Segment *n*.

segregat|e ['segrigeit] absondern, trennen; **~ion** Absonderung *f*; (Rassen-) Trennung *f*.

seiz|e [si:z] (er)greifen, fassen; nehmen; *fig.* erfassen; **~ure** ['~ʒə] Ergreifung *f*; *jur.* Beschlagnahme *f*.

seldom ['seldəm] selten.

select [si'lekt] auswählen, -suchen; erlesen; **~ion** Auswahl *f*, -lese *f*.

self [self], *pl* **selves** [~vz] Selbst *n*, Ich *n*; myself, etc. ich selbst etc.; **~command** Selbstbeherrschung *f*; **~confidence** Selbstvertrauen *n*; **~conscious** befangen, gehemmt; **~control** Selbstbeherrschung *f*; **~defence** Selbstverteidigung *f*; Notwehr *f*; **~employed** selbständig (*Handwerker etc.*); **~government** Selbstverwaltung *f*, Autonomie *f*; **~interest** Eigennutz *m*; **~ish** selbstsüchtig; **~made** selbstgemacht; **~possession** Selbstbeherrschung *f*; **~reliant** selbstbewußt; **~respect** Selbstachtung *f*; **~righteous** selbstgerecht; **~service** Selbstbedienung, Selbstbedienungs...

sell [sel] (*irr*) verkaufen; gehen (*Ware*); **be sold out** ausverkauft sein; **~er** Ver-

käufer(in), Händler(in); *gut-* etc. gehende Ware.

selves [selvz] *pl von* **self**.

semblance ['sembləns] Anschein *m*; Ähnlichkeit *f*.

semi|colon ['semi'kəulən] Semikolon *n*, Strichpunkt *m*; **~final** *sp.* Halbfinale *n*.

senate ['senit] Senat *m*; **~or** ['~ətə] Senator *m*.

send [send] (*irr*) senden, schicken; **~ for** kommen lassen, holen (lassen); **~ in** einsenden, -schicken, -reichen; **~er** Absender(in).

senior ['si:njə] älter; rang-, dienstälter; Ältere *m*; Rang-, Dienstältere *m*.

sensation [sen'seiʃən] Empfindung *f*; Gefühl *n*; Sensation *f*; **~al** sensationell, Sensations...

sense [sens] Sinn *m*; Gefühl *n*; Verstand *m*; Vernunft *f*; **in a** ~ in gewissem Sinne; **in (out of) one's ~s** bei (von) Sinnen; **talk ~** vernünftig reden; *vb*: spüren, fühlen; **~less** bewußtlos; gefühllos; sinnlos.

sensib|ility [sensi'biliti] Sensibilität *f*, Empfindungsvermögen *n*; Empfindlichkeit *f*; **~le** spür-, fühlbar; vernünftig; **be ~le of** sich *e-r S.* bewußt sein.

sensitive ['sensitiv] empfindlich (**to** gegen); sensibel, feinfühlig.

sensu|al ['sensjuəl] sinnlich; **~ous** sinnlich.

sent [sent] *pret u. pp von* **send**.

sentence ['sentəns] *jur.* Urteil *n*; *gr.* Satz *m*; verurteilen.

sentiment ['sentimənt] (seelische) Empfindung, Gefühl *n*; *pl* Meinung *f*; **~al** [~'mentl] sentimental, gefühlvoll; **~ality** [~men-'tæliti] Sentimentalität *f*.

sentry ['sentri] *mil.* Posten *m*.

separa|ble ['sepərəbl] trennbar; **~te** ['~eit] (sich) trennen; absondern; ['seprit] getrennt, (ab)gesondert; **~tion** Trennung *f*.

September [sep'tembə] September *m*.

septic ['septik] septisch.

sepul|chre, *Am.* **~cher** ['sepəlkə] Grab(stätte *f*, -mal *n*) *n*.

sequel ['si:kwəl] Folge *f*; (Roman-*etc.*)Fortsetzung *f*.

sequence ['si:kwəns] (Aufeinander-, Reihen)Folge *f*.

serene [si'ri:n] heiter; klar; ruhig; gelassen.

sergeant ['sɑ:dʒənt] *mil.* Feldwebel *m*; (Polizei-) Wachtmeister *m*.

seri|al ['siəriəl] fortlaufend, serienmäßig; Serien...; Fortsetzungs...; Fortsetzungsroman *m*; Folge *f*, Serie *f*; **~es** ['~ri:z], *pl* **~** Reihe *f*, Serie *f*, Folge *f*.

serious ['siəriəs] ernst.

sermon ['sə:mən] (Straf-) Predigt *f*.

serpent ['sə:pənt] Schlange *f*.

serum ['siərəm] Serum *n*.

servant ['sə:vənt] Diener (-in); Dienstbote *m*, Dienstmädchen *n*, Hausangestellte *m*, *f*.

serve [sə:v] dienen; (*j-n*) bedienen; Speisen servieren, auftragen; *Tennis:* aufschlagen; *Zweck* erfüllen; nützen; genügen; **~ (out)** aus-, verteilen.

service ['sə:vis] Dienst (-leistung *f*) *f*; Gefälligkeit *f*; Bedienung *f*; Betrieb *m*; *tech.* Wartung *f*, Kundendienst *m*; (Zug-*etc.*)Verkehr *m*; Gottesdienst *m*; Service *n*; *Tennis:* Aufschlag *m*; Nutzen *m*; warten, pflegen; **~able** brauchbar, nützlich; **~ station** (Reparatur)Werkstatt *f*; Tankstelle *f*.

session ['seʃən] Sitzung(speriode) *f*.

set [set] Satz *m*, Garnitur *f*; Service *n*; Sammlung *f*, Reihe *f*, Serie *f*; (Radio-*etc.*)Gerät *n*; Clique *f*; *poet.* (Sonnen)Untergang *m*; fest(gelegt, -gesetzt); bereit; entschlossen; (*irr*) setzen, stellen, legen; *Wecker, Aufgabe* stellen; *Knochenbruch* einrichten; *Tisch* decken; *Haar* legen; *Edelstein* fassen; *Zeitpunkt* festsetzen; *Beispiel* geben; untergehen (*Sonne*); erstarren; **~ eyes on** erblicken; **~ free** freilassen; **~ at ease** beruhigen; **~ about doing s.th.** sich daranmachen, et. zu tun; **~ off** auf-

shallow

brechen; starten; hervor-
heben; **~ out** aufbrechen;
~ to sich daranmachen;
up aufstellen; errichten;
~back Rückschlag *m*; **~**
dinner, **~ lunch** Menü *n*,
Gedeck *n*.

settee [se'ti:] *kleines* Sofa.
setting ['setiŋ] Fassung *f*
(*e-s Edelsteins*); Hintergrund *m*, Umgebung *f*;
(*Sonnen*)Untergang *m*.
settle ['setl] Sitzbank *f*;
(sich) ansiedeln; besiedeln;
Rechnung begleichen; klären, entscheiden, regeln;
Streit beilegen; vereinbaren; vermachen (**on**
dat); beruhigen; sich (ab-)
setzen; **~ (o.s., down)** sich
niederlassen; **~ment** (An-,
Be)Siedlung *f*; Bezahlung
f; Klärung *f*; Schlichtung *f*;
Abmachung *f*; **~r** Siedler *m*.
seven ['sevn] sieben; Sieben
f; **~teen(th)** ['~'ti:n(θ)]
siebzehn(te); **~th** ['~θ]
sieb(en)te; Sieb(en)tel *n*;
~thly sieb(en)tens; **~tieth**
['~tiiθ] siebzigste; **~ty** siebzig; Siebzig *f*.
sever ['sevə] (zer)reißen;
(sich) trennen; *fig.* lösen.
several ['sevrəl] mehrere;
verschiedene; einige.
severe [si'viə] streng;
hart; scharf; rauh (*Wetter*);
heftig (*Schmerz*, *Sturm*);
schwer (*Krankheit*); **~ity**
[~eriti] Strenge *f*, Härte *f*.
sew [səu] (*irr*) nähen.
sew|age ['sju(:)idʒ] Ab-
wasser *n*; **~er** Abwasser-

kanal *m*; **~erage** Kanalisation *f*.
sew|ing ['səuiŋ] Nähen *n*;
Näherei *f*; Näh...; **~n** *pp*
von **sew**.
sex [seks] Geschlecht *n*;
(der) Sex.
sexton ['sekstən] Küster *m*
(u. Totengräber *m*).
sexual ['seksjuəl] ge-
schlechtlich, Geschlechts-
..., sexuell, Sexual...
shabby ['ʃæbi] schäbig;
gemein.
shack [ʃæk] Hütte *f*, Bude *f*.
shade [ʃeid] Schatten *m*;
(*Lampen- etc.*)Schirm *m*;
Am. Rouleau *n*; Schattierung *f*; abschirmen, schützen.
shadow ['ʃædəu] Schatten
m; beschatten.
shady ['ʃeidi] schattig; *fig.*
fragwürdig.
shaft [ʃɑːft] Schaft *m*;
Stiel *m*; Deichsel *f*;
Schacht *m*.
shaggy ['ʃægi] zottig,
struppig.
shak|e [ʃeik] Schütteln *n*;
Beben *n*; (*er*) (sch)wan-
ken; beben; zittern; schütteln, rütteln; erschüttern;
~e hands sich die Hand
geben; **~en** *pp von* **shake**;
erschüttert; **~y** wack(e)lig;
zitt(e)rig.
shall [ʃæl] *v/aux ich, du etc.*:
soll(st) *etc.*; *ich werde, wir*
werden.
shallow ['ʃæləu] seicht;
flach; *fig.* oberflächlich;
Untiefe *f*.

sham [ʃæm] vortäuschen; sich verstellen; **~ ill(ness)** sich krank stellen.

shame [ʃeim] beschämen; *j-m* Schande machen; Scham *f*; Schande *f*; **for ~!, ~ on you!** pfui!, schäme dich!; **~ful** schändlich; **~less** schamlos.

shampoo [ʃæm'puː] Haare waschen; Shampoo *n*; Haarwäsche *f*; **a ~ and set** waschen und legen.

shank [ʃæŋk] Unterschenkel *m*.

shape [ʃeip] gestalten, formen, bilden; Gestalt *f*; Form *f*; **in good ~** in guter Verfassung; **~d** geformt; **...förmig**; **~less** formlos; **~ly** wohlgeformt.

share [ʃɛə] teilen; teilhaben (in an); Pflugschar *f*; (An)Teil *m*; Aktie *f*; **go ~s** teilen; **~holder** Aktionär(in).

shark [ʃɑːk] Hai(fisch) *m*.

sharp [ʃɑːp] scharf; spitz; schneidend; stechend; schlau; pünktlich, genau; **~en** (ver)schärfen; schleifen; spitzen; **~ener** ['~pnə] (*Bleistift*)Spitzer *m*; **~ness** Schärfe *f*; **~witted** scharfsinnig.

shatter ['ʃætə] zerschmettern; zerstören, -rütten.

shave [ʃeiv] (*irr*) (sich) rasieren; haarscharf vorbeikommen an; Rasur *f*; **have (get) a ~** sich rasieren (lassen); **~n** *pp von* **shave**.

shaving ['ʃeiviŋ] Rasieren

n; Rasier...; *pl* (Hobel-) Späne *pl*.

shawl [ʃɔːl] Schal *m*, Umhängetuch *n*.

she [ʃiː] sie; *in Zssgn:* zo. ...weibchen *n*.

sheaf [ʃiːf], *pl* **sheaves** [~vz] Garbe *f*; Bündel *n*.

shear [ʃiə] (*irr*) scheren.

sheath [ʃiːθ] Scheide *f*; Futteral *n*, Hülle *f*.

sheaves [ʃiːvz] *pl von* **sheaf.**

shed [ʃed] (*irr*) Blätter etc. abwerfen; *Kleider etc.* ablegen; vergießen; verbreiten; Schuppen *m*; Stall *m*.

sheep [ʃiːp], *pl* **~** Schaf(e *pl*) *n*; **~dog** Schäferhund *m*; **~ish** einfältig.

sheer [ʃiə] rein; bloß; glatt; steil; senkrecht.

sheet [ʃiːt] Bett-, Leintuch *n*, Laken *n*; (*Glas- etc.*) Platte *f*; Blatt *n*, Bogen *m* (*Papier*); **~ iron** Eisenblech *n*; **~ lightning** Wetterleuchten *n*.

shelf [ʃelf], *pl* **shelves** [~vz] Brett *n*, Regal *n*, Fach *n*.

shell [ʃel] Schale *f*, Hülse *f*, Muschel *f*; Granate *f*; schälen; enthülsen; beschießen; **~fish** Schalentier *n*.

shelter ['ʃeltə] Schutzhütte *f*; Zufluchtsort *m*; Obdach *n*; Schutz *m*; (be)schützen.

shelves [ʃelvz] *pl von* **shelf.**

shepherd ['ʃepəd] Schäfer *m*, Hirt *m*.

shield [ʃiːld] (Schutz-)

shop

Schild *m*; (be)schützen (from vor).

shift [ʃift] (um-, aus)wechseln; verändern; (sich) verlagern *od.* -schieben; Wechsel *m*; Verschiebung *f*, -änderung *f*; (Arbeits-) Schicht *f*; Ausweg *m*, Notbehelf *m*; Kniff *m*, List *f*; **make ~** sich behelfen; **~y** unzuverlässig; verschlagen.

shilling [ˈʃiliŋ] *alte Währung:* Schilling *m*.

shin(-bone) [ˈʃin(-)] Schienbein *n*.

shine [ʃain] Schein *m*; Glanz *m*; (*irr*) scheinen, leuchten, glänzen, strahlen; *colloq.* (*pp* **~d**) polieren, putzen.

shingle [ˈʃiŋgl] Schindel *f*.

shiny [ˈʃaini] blank, glänzend, strahlend.

ship [ʃip] Schiff *n*; verschiffen; **~ment** Verschiffung *f*; Schiffsladung *f*; **~owner** Reeder *m*; **~ping** Verschiffung *f*; Versand *m*; **~ping company** Reederei *f*; **~wreck** Schiffbruch *m*; **~wrecked** schiffbrüchig; **~yard** Werft *f*.

shire [ˈʃaiə, *in Zssgn:* ...ʃiə] Grafschaft *f*. [(vor).]

shirk [ʃəːk] sich drücken]

shirt [ʃəːt] (Herren)Hemd *n*; **~sleeve** Hemdsärmel *m*.

shiver [ˈʃivə] Splitter *m*; Schauer *m*, Zittern *n*; zittern; frösteln.

shock [ʃɔk] Erschütterung *f*, Schlag *m*, Stoß *m*; (Nerven)Schock *m*; schockieren, empören; *j-n* erschüttern; **~absorber** Stoßdämpfer *m*; **~ing** schockierend, empörend, anstößig.

shoe [ʃuː] Schuh *m*; **~horn** Schuhanzieher *m*; **~lace** Schnürsenkel *m*; **~maker** Schuhmacher *m*, Schuster *m*; **~string** Schnürsenkel *m*. [**shine**.]

shone [ʃɔn] *pret u. pp von*]

shook [ʃuk] *pret von* **shake**.

shoot [ʃuːt] *bot.* Schößling *m*; (*irr*) (ab)schießen; erschießen; *Film* aufnehmen, drehen; *Knospen etc.* treiben; (dahin-, vorbei)schießen; *bot.* sprießen; filmen; **~er** Schütze *m*.

shooting [ˈʃuːtiŋ] Schießen *n*; Schießerei *f*; Jagd(-recht *n*) *f*; *Film:* Dreharbeiten *pl*; **~gallery** Schießstand *m*; **~ star** Sternschnuppe *f*.

shop [ʃɔp] Laden *m*, Geschäft *n*; Werkstatt *f*; **~ talk** fachsimpeln; *vb:* **go ~ping** einkaufen gehen; **~assistant** Verkäufer(in); **~girl** Verkäuferin *f*; **~keeper** Ladeninhaber(in); **~lifter** Ladendieb(in); **~man** Verkäufer *m*; **~ping** Einkauf *m*, Einkaufen *n*; **do one's ~ping** (s-e) Einkäufe machen; **~ping centre** Einkaufszentrum *n*; **~steward** *appr.* Betriebsrat *m*; **~walker** Aufsichtsherr *m*, -dame *f*; **~window** Schaufenster *n*.

shore

shore [ʃɔː] Küste f; Ufer n; Strand m; **on** ~ an Land.

shorn [ʃɔːn] pp von **shear.**

short [ʃɔːt] adj kurz; klein; knapp; kurz angebunden; mürbe (Gebäck); **make it** ~ sich kurz fassen; ~ **of** knapp an; adv abgesehen von; sub: **in** ~ kurz(um); **~age** Knappheit f; **~coming** Unzulänglichkeit f; ~ **cut** Abkürzung(sweg m) f; ~**en** (ab-, ver)kürzen; kürzer werden; **~hand** Kurzschrift f, Stenographie f; **~hand typist** Stenotypistin f; **~ly** kurz; bald; **~ness** Kürze f; Mangel m; **~s** pl **Shorts** pl, kurze Hose; ~ **story** Kurzgeschichte f; **~-sighted** kurzsichtig; **~-term** kurzfristig; **~-winded** kurzatmig.

shot [ʃɔt] pret u. pp von **shoot**; Schuß m; Schrot (-kugeln pl) m, n; guter etc. Schütze m; (Film-) Aufnahme f; **~gun** Schrotflinte f.

should [ʃud] pret u. cond von **shall.**

shoulder [ˈʃəuldə] Schulter f, Achsel f; schultern.

shout [ʃaut] lauter Schrei od. Ruf; Geschrei n; (laut) rufen, schreien.

shove [ʃʌv] colloq. schieben, stoßen.

shovel [ˈʃʌvl] Schaufel f; schaufeln.

show [ʃəu] (irr) (vor)zeigen; ausstellen; führen;

sich zeigen; ~ **(a)round** herumführen; ~ **off** angeben, prahlen; ~ **up** auftauchen, erscheinen; Zurschaustellung f; Vorführung f, -stellung f, Schau f; Ausstellung f; ~ **business** Unterhaltungsindustrie f, Schaugeschäft n.

shower [ˈʃauə] (Regen-etc.)Schauer m; Dusche f; fig. j-n mit et. überschütten od. -häufen; **~bath** Dusche f.

shown [ʃəun] pp von **show.**

showy [ˈʃəui] prächtig; protzig.

shrank [ʃræŋk] pret von **shrink.**

shred [ʃred] Fetzen m; (irr) zerfetzen.

shrew [ʃruː] zänkisches Weib; **~d** [~d] schlau, klug.

shriek [ʃriːk] Schrei m; Gekreisch(e) n; kreischen, schreien.

shrill [ʃril] schrill, gellend.

shrimp [ʃrimp] Garnele f.

shrine [ʃrain] Schrein m.

shrink [ʃriŋk] (irr) (ein-, zs.-)schrumpfen (lassen); einlaufen; zurückschrecken (**from** vor).

shrivel [ˈʃrivl] (ein-, zs.-) schrumpfen (lassen).

Shrove|tide [ˈʃrəuvtaid] Fastnachtszeit f; ~ **Tuesday** Fastnachtsdienstag m.

shrub [ʃrʌb] Strauch m, Busch m; **~bery** Gebüsch n.

shrug [ʃrʌg] die Achseln zucken; Achselzucken n.

shrunk [ʃrʌŋk] *pp von*
shrink; **~en** (ein)ge-
schrumpft; eingefallen.

shudder ['ʃʌdə] schau-
dern; Schauder *m*.

shuffle ['ʃʌfl] *Karten*: mischen; schlurfen.

shun [ʃʌn] (ver)meiden.

shut [ʃʌt] (*irr*) (ver)schlie-
ßen, zumachen; sich schließen; **~ down** *Betrieb*
schließen; **~ up** ein-, verschließen; einsperren; **~
up!** *colloq.* halt den Mund!
~ter Fensterladen *m*; *phot.*
Verschluß *m*.

shy [ʃai] scheu; schüchtern; **~ness** Scheu *f*;
Schüchternheit *f*.

sick [sik] krank; übel;
überdrüssig; **be ~** sich
übergeben; **be ~ of** genug
haben von; **I feel ~** mir
ist schlecht *od.* übel; **~
benefit** Krankengeld *n*;
~en erkranken, krank werden; anekeln.

sickle ['sikl] Sichel *f*.

sick|-leave Krankenurlaub
m; **~ly** kränklich; **~ness**
Krankheit *f*; Übelkeit *f*; **~
room** Krankenzimmer *n*.

side [said] Seite *f*; Seiten-
...; Neben...; **~ by ~** Seite
an Seite; **take ~s with, ~
with** Partei ergreifen für;
~board Anrichte *f*, Büfett
n, Sideboard *n*; **~car** *mot.*
Beiwagen *m*; **~d** *in Zssgn*:
...seitig; **~dish** Beilage *f*;
~road Nebenstraße *f*; **~
walk** *Am.* Bürgersteig *m*;
~walk café *Am.* Straßen-

café *n*; **~ward(s)** ['~
wəd(z)], **~ways** seitlich;
seitwärts.

siege [si:dʒ] Belagerung *f*.

sieve [siv] Sieb *n*; sieben.

sift [sift] sieben; *fig.* sichten, prüfen.   [zen.]

sigh [sai] Seufzer *m*; seuf-]

sight [sait] sichten, erblicken; Sehvermögen *n*, ~kraft
f; Anblick *m*; Sicht *f*;
pl Sehenswürdigkeiten *pl*;
catch ~ of erblicken;
know by ~ vom Sehen
kennen; **(with)in ~** in
Sicht(weite); **...ed** *in Zssgn*:
...sichtig; **~seeing** Besichtigung *f* (von Sehens-
würdigkeiten); Besichti-
gungs...; **~seeing tour**
(Stadt)Rundfahrt *f*; **~seer**
Tourist(in).

sign [sain] Zeichen *n*;
Wink *m*; Schild *n*; Zeichen
geben; unterzeichnen, un-
terschreiben.

signal ['signl] Signal *n*;
signalisieren, Zeichen geben.

signature ['signitʃə] Unter-
schrift *f*; **~ tune** *Radio*:
Kennmelodie *f*.

signboard (Firmen-, Aus-
hänge-)Schild *n*.

signet ['signit] Siegel *n*.

significa|nce [sig'nifikəns]
Bedeutung *f*; **~nt** bedeutsam; bezeichnend (**of** für);
~tion Bedeutung *f*.

signify ['signifai] andeuten; ankündigen; bedeuten.

signpost Wegweiser *m*.

silence ['sailəns] (Still-)

Schweigen *n*; Stille *f*, Ruhe *f*; ~! Ruhe!; zum Schweigen bringen; ~r Schalldämpfer *m*; *mot.* Auspufftopf *m*.

silent ['sailənt] still; schweigend; schweigsam; stumm.

silk [silk] Seide *f*; Seiden-...; ~en seiden; ~y seidig.

sill [sil] Fensterbrett *n*.

silly ['sili] dumm; albern; töricht.

silver ['silvə] Silber *n*; silbern, Silber-...; versilbern; ~y silb(e)rig.

similar ['similə] ähnlich, gleich; ~ity [.'læriti]Ähnlichkeit *f*.

simmer ['simə] leicht kochen, sieden, brodeln.

simple ['simpl] einfach; simpel; schlicht; einfältig.

simpli|city [sim'plisiti] Einfachheit *f*; Einfalt *f*; ~fication Vereinfachung *f*; ~fy ['.fai] vereinfachen.

simply ['simpli] einfach; bloß, nur.

simulate ['simjuleit] vortäuschen; simulieren.

simultaneous [siməl'teinjəs] gleichzeitig.

sin [sin] Sünde *f*; sündigen. (da ja), weil.

since [sins] seit; seit(dem);

sincer|e [sin'siə] aufrichtig; Yours ~ely Ihr ergebener; ~ity ['.'seriti] Aufrichtigkeit *f*.

sinew ['sinju:] Sehne *f*; ~y sehnig; *fig.* kräftig.

sing [siŋ] (*irr*) (be)singen.

singe [sindʒ] (ver-, an)sengen.

singer ['siŋə] Sänger(in).

single ['siŋgl] einzig; einzeln, Einzel-...; einfach; allein; ledig; *vb:* ~ **out** aussuchen, -wählen; *sub:* einfache Fahrkarte; *mst pl Tennis:* Einzel *n*; ~**handed** eigenhändig, allein; ~ **room** Einzel-, Einbettzimmer *n*; ~ **ticket** einfache Fahrkarte.

singular ['siŋgjulə] einzigartig; eigentümlich, seltsam; *gr.* Singular *m*, Einzahl *f*; ~ity [.'læriti] Einzigartigkeit *f*; Eigentümlichkeit *f*.

sinister [si'nistə] unheilvoll, böse; finster.

sink [siŋk] (*irr*) (ein-, herab-, ver)sinken; untergehen; sich senken; (ver-)senken; Ausguß *m*, Spülbecken *n*; ~ing (Ein-, Ver)Sinken *n*; Versenken *n*.

sinner ['sinə] Sünder(in).

sip [sip] Schlückchen *n*; schlürfen, nippen an *od.* von.

sir [sə:] (mein) Herr (*Anrede*); ♀ Sir (*Titel*).

sirloin ['sə:loin] Lendenstück *n*.

sister ['sistə] Schwester *f*; ~**in-law** Schwägerin *f*.

sit [sit] (*irr*) sitzen; e-e Sitzung (ab)halten, tagen; setzen; sitzen auf; ~ **down** sich (hin)setzen; ~ **up** aufrecht sitzen; sich aufrichten; aufbleiben.

site [sait] Lage *f*; Stelle *f*; Bauplatz *m*.

sitting ['sitiŋ] Sitzung *f*; **~room** Wohnzimmer *n*.

situate|d ['sitjueitid] gelegen; **be ~d** liegen; **~ion** Lage *f*; Stellung *f*; Situation *f*.

six [siks] sechs; Sechs *f*; **~pence** *alte Währung*: Sixpence *m*; **~teen(th)** ['~'ti:n(θ)] sechzehn(te); **~th** [~sθ] sechste; Sechstel *n*; **~thly** sechstens; **~tieth** ['~tiiθ] sechzigste; **~ty** sechzig; Sechzig *f*.

size [saiz] Größe *f*; Format *n*; **~d** *in Zssgn*: ...groß, von *od.* in ... Größe.

sizzle ['sizl] *colloq.* zischen, brutzeln.

skate [skeit] Schlittschuh *m*; Schlitt- *od.* Rollschuh laufen; **~r** Schlittschuh-, Rollschuhläufer(in).

skeleton ['skelitn] Skelett *n*.

skeptic ['skeptik] *bsd. Am. für* **sceptic**.

sketch [sketʃ] Skizze *f*; Entwurf *m*; skizzieren; entwerfen; **~block**, **~book** Skizzenbuch *n*.

ski [ski:], *pl* **~(s)** Schi *m*, Ski *m*; Schi *od.* Ski laufen.

skid [skid] Bremsklotz *m*; *aer.* Kufe *f*; *mot.* Rutschen *n*, Schleudern *n*; rutschen, schleudern.

ski|er ['ski:ə] Schi-, Skiläufer(in); **~ing** Schilauf, Skilauf(en *n*) *m*.

skilful ['skilful] geschickt.

skill [skil] Geschick(lich-

keit *f*) *n*, Fertigkeit *f*; **~ed** geschickt; gelernt, Fach...; **~ed worker** Facharbeiter *m*; **~ful** *Am. für* **skilful**.

skim [skim] abschöpfen, entrahmen; **~ (through)** *fig.* überfliegen; **~(med) milk** Magermilch *f*.

skin [skin] Haut *f*; Fell *n*; Schale *f*; (ent)häuten; abbalgen; schälen; **~-deep** oberflächlich; **~-diving** Sporttauchen; **~ny** mager.

skip [skip] Hüpfen *n*, Sprung *m*; hüpfen, springen.

skipper ['skipə] *mar.* Schiffer *m*, Kapitän *m*; *aer., sp.* Kapitän *m*.

skirt [skə:t] (Damen)Rock *m*; *pl* Rand *m*, Saum *m*; sich entlangziehen (an).

skittles ['skitlz] *sg* Kegeln *n*; **play (at) ~** kegeln.

skull [skʌl] (Toten)Schädel *m*.

sky [skai], *oft pl* Himmel *m*; **~jacker** ['~dʒækə] Luftpirat *m*; **~lark** Feldlerche *f*, **~light** Oberlicht *n*; Dachfenster *n*; **~line** Horizont *m*; (*Stadt- etc.*)Silhouette *f*; **~scraper** Wolkenkratzer *m*, Hochhaus *n*; **~ward(s)** ['~wəd(z)] himmelwärts.

slab [slæb] Platte *f*, Fliese *f*.

slack [slæk] schlaff; locker; (nach)lässig; *econ.* flau; **~en** nachlassen (in); (sich) lockern; (sich) verlangsamen; **~s** *pl* (lange Damen-) Hose *f*.

slain

slain [slein] *pp von* slay.

slake [sleik] *Durst, Kalk* löschen; *fig.* stillen.

slam [slæm] *Tür etc.* zuschlagen, zuknallen; *et. auf den Tisch etc.* knallen.

slander ['slɑːndə] Verleumdung *f*; verleumden.

slang [slæŋ] Slang *m*; lässige Umgangssprache.

slant [slɑːnt] schräge Fläche; Abhang *m*; sich neigen; schräg liegen *od.* legen.

slap [slæp] Klaps *m*, Schlag *m*; schlagen; **~stick comedy** *thea.* derbe Posse.

slash [slæʃ] Hieb *m*; klaffende Wunde; Schlitz *m*; (auf)schlitzen; (los)schlagen.

slate [sleit] Schiefer *m*; Schiefertafel *f*; **~-pencil** Griffel *m*.

slattern ['slætə(ː)n] Schlampe *f*.

slaughter ['slɔːtə] Schlachten *n*; Gemetzel *n*; schlachten; niedermetzeln.

slave [sleiv] Sklav|e *m*, -in *f*; schuften; **~ry** ['~əri] Sklaverei *f*.

slay [slei] (*irr*) *poet.* erschlagen, ermorden.

sled(ge) [sled(ʒ)] Schlitten *m*; Schlitten fahren.

sledge(-hammer) Schmiedehammer *m*.

sleek [sliːk] glatt, glänzend; *fig.* geschmeidig.

sleep [sliːp] (*irr*) schlafen; **~ on**, **~ over** *et.* beschlafen; Schlaf *m*; **have a** good, etc. **~** gut etc. schlafen; **go to ~** einschlafen; **~er** Schläfer(in); (Eisenbahn)Schwelle *f*; Schlafwagen(platz) *m*; **~ing-bag** Schlafsack *m*; **~ing Beauty** Dornröschen *n*; **~ing-car** Schlafwagen *m*; **~ing partner** stiller Teilhaber; **~ing-pill** Schlaftablette *f*; **~less** schlaflos; **~walker** Schlafwandler(in); **~y** schläfrig; verschlafen.

sleet [sliːt] Schneeregen *m*.

sleeve [sliːv] Ärmel *m*; Plattenhülle *f*; *tech.* Muffe *f*.

sleigh [slei] (*bsd.* Pferde-) Schlitten *m*; (im) Schlitten fahren.

slender ['slendə] schlank; schmächtig; dürftig.

slept [slept] *pret u. pp von* sleep.

slew [sluː] *pret von* slay.

slice [slais] Schnitte *f*, Scheibe *f*, Stück *n*; **a ~ of bread** e-e Scheibe Brot; in Scheiben schneiden, aufschneiden.

slick [slik] *colloq.* glatt; geschickt, raffiniert; **~er** *Am.* (langer) Regenmantel.

slid [slid] *pret u. pp von* slide.

slide [slaid] (*irr*) gleiten (lassen); rutschen; schlittern; schieben; Gleiten *n*; Rutschbahn *f*, Rutsche *f*; Erd-, Felsrutsch *m*; *tech.* Schieber *m*; *phot.* Diapositiv *n*; **~rule** Rechenschieber *m*.

slight |slait| schmächtig; schwach; gering(fügig); Geringschätzung *f*; ~ly behandeln.

slim |slim| schlank, dünn; schlank(er) werden; e-e Schlankheitskur machen.

slim|e |slaim| Schleim *m*; ~y schleimig.

sling |sliŋ| Schleuder *f*; Tragriemen *m*; (med. Arm-)Schlinge *f*; (irr) schleudern; auf-, umhängen.

slip |slip| (aus)gleiten, (aus-, ver)rutschen; (hinein-, ent)schlüpfen; gleiten lassen; **have ~ped s.o.'s memory** od. **mind** j-m entfallen sein; ~ on od. **off** Kleid etc. über- od. abstreifen; ~ **(up)** (e-n) Fehler machen; (Aus)Gleiten *n*, (~)Rutschen *n*; (Flüchtigkeits)Fehler *m*; Unterkleid *n*; (Kissen)Bezug *m*; Streifen *m*, Zettel *m*, Abschnitt *m*; ~**per** Pantoffel *m*, Hausschuh *m*; ~**pery** schlüpfrig, glatt.

slit |slit| Schlitz *m*; Spalte *f*; (irr) (auf-, zer)schlitzen; reißen.

slobber |'slɔbə| sabbern.

slogan |'slougən| Schlagwort *n*, (Werbe)Slogan *m*.

sloop |slu:p| Schaluppe *f*.

slop |slɔp| Pfütze *f*; *pl* Spül-, Schmutzwasser *n*; ~ **(over)** verschütten; überlaufen.

slop|e |sloup| (Ab)Hang *m*; Neigung *f*, Gefälle *f*; abfallen, schräg verlaufen,

sich neigen; ~**ing** schräg, abschüssig, abfallend.

sloppy |'slɔpi| naß, schmutzig; *colloq.*: schlampig; sentimental.

slot |slɔt| Schlitz *m*.

sloth |slouθ| *zo.* Faultier *n*.

slot-machine (Waren-, Spiel)Automat *m*.

slouch |slau| Sumpf(loch *n*) *m*.

sloven |'slʌvn| unordentlicher Mensch, Schlampe *f*; ~**ly** liederlich, schlampig.

slow |slou| langsam; schwerfällig; träg(e); **be ~** nachgehen (Uhr); ~ **down** verlangsamen; *et.* verzögern; langsamer werden; ~-**motion** Zeitlupe *f*; ~-**worm** Blindschleiche *f*.

sluggish |'slʌgi∫| träg(e).

sluice |slu:s| Schleuse *f*.

slums |slʌmz| *pl* Elendsviertel *n*, Slums *pl*.

slumber |'slʌmbə| *oft pl* Schlummer *m*; schlummern.

slung |slʌŋ| *pret u. pp von* **sling.**|

slush |slʌ∫| Schlamm *m*; (Schnee)Matsch *m*.

slut |slʌt| Schlampe *f*; Nutte *f*.

sly |slai| schlau, verschlagen; verschmitzt.

smack |smæk| (Bei)Geschmack *m*; Klatsch *m*, Klaps *m*; Schmatzen *m*; schmecken (**of** nach); j-m e-n Klaps geben; ~ **one's lips** schmatzen.

small |smɔ:l| klein; unbedeutend; niedrig; wenig;

bescheiden; **~ change**
Kleingeld n; *the* **~ hours**
pl die frühen Morgen-
stunden *pl*; **~ish** ziemlich
klein; **~ of the back** *anat.*
Kreuz n; **~pox** ['~pɔks]
Pocken *pl*; **~s** *pl colloq.*
Unterwäsche f; **~ talk**
oberflächliche Konversa-
tion.

smart [smɑːt] klug, gescheit; schlagfertig; gerissen; geschickt; elegant,
schick; forsch; flink; hart;
scharf.

smash [smæʃ] krachen;
zerschlagen, -trümmern;
(zer)schmettern; *fig.* vernichten; **~ing** *sl.* toll.

smattering ['smætəriŋ]
oberflächliche Kenntnis.

smear [smiə] (be)schmie-
ren; *fig.* beschmutzen;
Fleck m.

smell [smel] Geruch m;
(irr) riechen; duften.

smelt [smelt] *pret u. pp
von* **smell**.

smelt[2] *Erz* schmelzen.

smile [smail] Lächeln n;
lächeln.

smith [smiθ] Schmied m;
~y ['~ði] Schmiede f.

smitten ['smitn] betrof-
fen; *fig.* hingerissen (**with**
von).

smock [smɔk] Kittel m.

smog [smɔg] Smog m,
Dunstglocke f.

smoke [sməuk] Rauch m;
have a ~ eine rauchen
(*Zigarette etc.*); *vb:* rauchen; räuchern; **~dried**

geräuchert;**~r** Raucher(in);
rail. Raucherabteil n.

smoking ['sməukiŋ] Rauchen n; Rauch...; **~car**,
~carriage, **~compart-
ment** Raucherabteil n.

smoky ['sməuki] rauchig;
verräuchert.

smooth [smuːð] glatt; ruhig (*a. tech.*); sanft, weich;
(sich) glätten; *fig.* ebnen;
~ down glattstreichen.

smother ['smʌðə] ersticken. [schwelen.]

smo(u)lder ['sməuldə]

smudge [smʌdʒ] (be-)
schmieren; Fleck m.

smuggle ['smʌgl] schmuggeln; **~r** Schmuggler(in).

smut [smʌt] Ruß(fleck) m;
Zote(n *pl*) f; beschmutzen;
~ty schmutzig.

snack [snæk] Imbiß m; **~
bar** Imbißstube f.

snail [sneil] Schnecke f.

snake [sneik] Schlange f.

snap [snæp] schnappen
(**at** nach); knallen (mit);
zuschnappen (lassen)
(*Schloß*); (zer)brechen,
zerreißen; *phot.* knipsen;
schnappen nach; schnell
greifen nach; schnalzen
mit; Knacken n; Knall m;
(Zer)Brechen n; (Zu-)
Schnappen n; **cold ~**
Kältewelle f; **~fastener**
Druckknopf m; **~pish** bissig; schnippisch; **~shot**
Schnappschuß m.

snare [snɛə] Schlinge f;
Falle f.

snarl [snɑːl] wütend

knurren; Knurren *n*, Zäh-
nefletschen *n*.

snatch [snætʃ] schneller
Zugriff; *pl* Bruchstücke *pl*;
schnappen; an sich reißen.

sneak [sniːk] schleichen;
~ers *pl Am.* leichte (Segeltuch)Schuhe *pl*.

sneer [sniə] Hohn(lächeln
n) *m*, Spott *m*; höhnisch
grinsen; spotten (sneer *n*.).

sneeze [sniːz] niesen; Niesen *n*.

sniff [snif] schnüffeln,
schnuppern; die Nase
rümpfen.

snipe [snaip], *pl* **~(s)**
(Sumpf)Schnepfe *f*; **~r**
Scharf-, Heckenschütze *m*.

snivel ['snivl] greinen,
plärren.

snoop [snuːp] Schnüffler
(-in); **~ around** herum-
schnüffeln.

snooze [snuːz] *colloq.*: Nik-
kerchen *n*; dösen.

snore [snɔː] schnarchen;
Schnarchen *n*.

snort [snɔːt] schnauben.

snout [snaut] Schnauze *f*;
(Schweine)Rüssel *m*.

snow [snəu] Schnee *m*;
schneien; **~-capped**, **~-**
clad, **~-covered** schneebedeckt; **~-drift** Schnee-
wehe *f*; **~-drop** Schnee-
glöckchen *n*; **~y** schneeig,
Schnee...; schneebedeckt,
verschneit.

snub [snʌb] verächtlich behandeln; Abfuhr *f*; **~-**
nosed stupsnasig.

snuff [snʌf] Schnupftabak
m; schnupfen.

snug [snʌg] behaglich; **~-**
gle sich schmiegen *od.*
kuscheln.

so [səu] so; deshalb; also;
I hope ~ ich hoffe es; **~**
am I ich auch; **~ far** bisher.

soak [səuk] sickern; einweichen; durchnässen,
-tränken; **~ up** aufsaugen.

soap [səup] Seife *f*; ab-,
einseifen; **~-box** Seifen-
kiste *f*; improvisierte Red-
nerbühne.

soar [sɔː] sich erheben,
(hoch) aufsteigen.

sob [sɔb] Schluchzen *n*;
schluchzen.

sober ['səubə] nüchtern;
ernüchtern; **~ up** nüchtern
machen *od.* werden.

so-called sogenannt.

soccer ['sɔkə] *colloq.* (Ver-
bands)Fußball *m*.

sociable ['səuʃəbl] gesellig.

social ['səuʃəl] gesellig;
gesellschaftlich; sozial(i-
stisch); Sozial...; **~ in-**
surance Sozialversiche-
rung *f*; **~ism** Sozialismus
m; **~ist** Sozialist(in); **~**
ist(ic) sozialistisch; **~ize**
sozialisieren, verstaatlichen.

society [sə'saiəti] Gesellschaft *f*; Verein *m*.

sock [sɔk] Socke *f*; Ein-
legesohle *f*.

socket ['sɔkit] (Augen-,
Zahn)Höhle *f*; *electr.*: Fassung *f*; Steckdose *f*.

sod [sɔd] Grasnarbe *f*;
Rasenstück *n*.

sofa ['səufə] Sofa *n*.

soft [soft] weich; mild(e);
sanft; leise; *colloq.* einfältig; ~ **drink** *colloq.* alko-
holfreies Getränk; ~**en**
['sofn] weich werden *od.*
machen; *j-n* rühren.

soil [soil] Boden *m*, Erde *f*;
(be)schmutzen.

sojourn ['sod3ə:n] Aufenthalt *m*; sich aufhalten.

sold [sould] *pret u. pp von*
sell.

soldier ['sould3ə] Soldat *m*.

sole[1] einzig, Allein-.

sole[2] *ichth.* Seezunge *f*;
Sohle *f*; besohlen.

solemn ['soləm] feierlich;
ernst.

solicit [sə'lisit] dringend
bitten; ~**or** Anwalt *m*;
~**ous** besorgt; bestrebt,
eifrig bemüht; ~**ude** [~-
tju:d] Besorgnis *f*.

solid ['solid] fest; kompakt; stabil; massiv; *fig.*
gründlich, solid(e).

solid|**arity** [soli'dæriti]
Solidarität *f*; ~**ity** Festigkeit *f*, Solidität *f*.

soliloquy [sə'liləkwi]
Selbstgespräch *n*, Mono-
log *m*.

solit|**ary** ['solitəri] einsam;
einzeln; ~**ude** ['~tju:d]
Einsamkeit *f*.

solo ['soulou] Solo *n*; allein; ~**ist** Solist(in).

solu|**ble** ['soljubl] löslich;
(auf)lösbar; ~**tion** [sə'lu:-
ʃən] (Auf)Lösung *f*.

solve [solv] lösen; ~**nt**
(auf)lösend; zahlungsfähig;
Lösungsmittel *n*.

somb|**re**, *Am.* ~**er** ['som-
bə] düster.

some [sʌm, səm] (irgend-)
ein; etwas; *vor pl:* einige,
ein paar; manche; etwa;
~ **more** noch et.; ~**body**
['sʌmbədi] jemand; ~**day**
eines Tages; ~**how** irgendwie; ~**one** jemand.

somersault ['sʌməso:lt]
Salto *m*; Purzelbaum *m*;
turn a ~ e-n Purzelbaum
schlagen.

some|**thing** (irgend) et-
was; ~**time** irgendwann;
ehemalig; ~**times** manch-
mal; ~**what** etwas, ziemlich; ~**where** irgendwo
(-hin).

son [sʌn] Sohn *m*.

song [soŋ] Lied *n*; ~**bird**
Singvogel *m*; ~**book** Lie-
derbuch *n*; ~**ster** ['~stə]
Singvogel *m*.

sonic ['sonik] Schall-.

son-in-law Schwiegersohn
m.

sonnet ['sonit] Sonett *n*.

soon [su:n] bald; früh; as
~ **as** sobald (als, wie); ~**er**
eher, früher; lieber; **no**
~**er ... than** kaum ... als;
no ~**er said than done**
gesagt, getan.   [rußen.]

soot [sut] Ruß *m*; ver-|

soothe [su:ð] beruhigen,
besänftigen; lindern.

sooty ['suti] rußig.

sophisticated [sə'fistikei-
tid] kultiviert; intellektuell;
anspruchsvoll; blasiert.

soporific [sopə'rifik]
Schlafmittel *n*.

spare

sorcer|er ['sɔ:sərə] Zauberer *m*; **~ess** Zauberin *f*, Hexe *f*; **~y** Zauberei *f*.

sordid ['sɔ:did] schmutzig; schäbig.

sore [sɔ:] schlimm, entzündet; weh(e), wund; **~ throat** Halsweh *n*.

sorrow ['sɔrəu] Kummer *m*, Leid *n*; Reue *f*; **~ful** traurig.

sorry ['sɔri] bekümmert; traurig; **(I am) (so) ~!** es tut mir (sehr) leid!, (ich) bedaure!, Verzeihung!

sort [sɔ:t] sortieren, (ein-)ordnen; Sorte *f*, Art *f*.

sought [sɔ:t] *pret u. pp von* **seek**.

soul [səul] Seele *f*.

sound [saund] gesund; *econ.* stabil; vernünftig; gründlich; fest, tief (*Schlaf*); *mar.* loten; sondieren; (er)tönen; (er-) schallen *od.* (~)klingen (lassen); *fig.* klingen; *med.* abhorchen; (aus)sprechen; Meerenge *f*; Schall *m*, Laut *m*, Ton *m*, Klang *m*; **~less** lautlos; **~proof** schalldicht; **~wave** Schallwelle *f*.

soup [su:p] Suppe *f*.

sour [sauə] sauer; *fig.* bitter, mürrisch.

source [sɔ:s] Quelle *f*; Ursprung *m*.

south [sauθ] Süd(en *m*), südlich, Süd...; **~east** Südost; **~east(ern)** südöstlich.

souther|ly ['sʌðəli], **~n** südlich, Süd...; **~ner** *Am.* Südstaatler(in); **~nmost** südlichst.

southward(s) ['sauθwəd(z)] südwärts, nach Süden.

southwest Südwest; südwestlich; **~erly** *od.* aus Südwesten; südwestlich; **~ern** südwestlich.

souvenir ['su:vəniə] (Reise)Andenken *n*, Souvenir *n*.

sovereign ['sɔvrin] Souverän *m*, Monarch(in) *m*; **~ty** ['~rənti] Souveränität *f*.

Soviet ['sɔuviet] Sowjet *m*; sowjetisch, Sowjet...

sow¹ [sau] Sau *f*, (Mutter-)Schwein *n*.

sow² [səu] (*irr*) (aus)säen; **~n** *pp von* **sow¹**.

spa [spu:] (Heil)Bad *n*.

space [speis] (Welt)Raum *m*; Platz *m*; Zwischenraum *m*, Abstand *m*; Zeitraum *m*; **~craft**, **~ship** Raumschiff *n*; **~suit** Raumanzug *m*.

spacious ['speiʃəs] geräumig; weit, umfassend.

spade [speid] Spaten *m*; **~(s** *pl*) Karten: Pik *n*.

span [spæn] Spanne *f*; Spannweite *f*; um-, überspannen; *pret von* **spin**.

spangle ['spæŋgl] Flitter *m*; **~d** *fig.* übersät.

Spani|ard ['spænjəd] Spanier(in); **~sh** spanisch; Spanisch *n*.

spank [spæŋk] verhauen; **~ing** Tracht *f* Prügel.

spanner ['spænə] Schraubenschlüssel *m*.

spare [spɛə] (ver)schonen;

entbehren; (übrig) haben;
sparen mit; spärlich, sparsam; übrig; Ersatz...; Reserve...; **~ (part)** Ersatz-
teil n; **~ room** Gästezimmer n; **~ time** Freizeit f;
~ wheel Reserverad n.
sparing ['spεəriŋ] sparsam.
spark [spɑːk] Funke(n) m;
Funken sprühen; **~ing-
plug** Zündkerze f; **~le**
Funke(n) m; Funkeln n;
funkeln, blitzen; schäu-
men, perlen; **~plug** Zündkerze f.
sparrow ['spærəu] Sperl-
ling m, Spatz m.
sparse [spɑːs] spärlich,
dünn.
spasm ['spæzəm] Krampf
m; **~odic** [~'mɔdik]
krampfhaft, -artig.
spat [spæt] pret u. pp von
spit.
spatter ['spætə] (be)sprit-
zen.   (laichen.)
spawn [spɔːn] Laich m;∫
speak [spiːk] (irr) sprechen, reden (**to** mit, zu);
sagen; (aus)sprechen; **~
out**, **~ up** laut(er) sprechen; offen reden; **~er**
Sprecher(in), Redner(in).
spear [spiə] Speer m;
Spieß m; aufspießen.
special ['speʃəl] besonder,
speziell; Spezial...; Sonder...; Sonderausgabe f;
Sonderzug m; Am. (Ta-
ges)Spezialität f; **~ist** Spe-
zialist m; **~ity** [~ʃiæliti] Besonderheit f; Spezialität f;

~ize (sich) spezialisieren;
~ty Spezialität f.
species ['spiːʃiːz], pl **~**
Art f, Spezies f.
speci|fic [spi'sifik] spezi-
fisch; bestimmt; **~fy** ['spe-
sifai] spezifizieren, einzeln
angeben; **~men** ['spesi-
min]Exemplar n; Muster n.
spectacle ['spektəkl]
Schauspiel n; Anblick m;
(a pair of) ~s pl(e–e)Brille.
spectacular [spek'tækju-
lə]eindrucksvoll.
spectator [spek'teitə] Zuschauer m.
speculat|e ['spekjuleit]
Vermutungen anstellen;
econ. spekulieren; **~ion**
Spekulation f.
sped [sped] pret u. pp von
speed.
speech [spiːtʃ] Sprache f;
Rede f; **make a ~** e–e
Rede halten; **~day** Schule: (Jahres)Schlußfeier f;
~less sprachlos.
speed [spiːd] Geschwindigkeit f, Schnelligkeit f;
Eile f; tech. Drehzahl f;
(irr) schnell fahren, rasen,
(dahin)eilen; **~ up** (pret u.
pp **~ed**) (sich) beschleunigen;
~ limit Geschwindigkeitsbe-
schränkung f; **~ometer**
[spi'dɔmitə] Tachometer
m, n; **~y** schnell.
spell [spel] (Arbeits)Schicht
f; Zeit(abschnitt m) f,
meteor. a. Periode f. a.
Zauber(spruch) m; (irr) buchstabieren; richtig schreiben; **~bound** (wie) ge-

bannt; **~ing** Rechtschreibung f. **[spell.]**

spelt [spelt] *pret u. pp von* **spell.**

spend [spend] (*irr*) Geld etc. ausgeben; verschwenden; verbringen; verwenden.

spent [spent] *pret u. pp von* **spend.** erschöpft; verbraucht.

sperm [spə:m] Sperma *n.*

sphere [sfiə] (Erd-, Himmels)Kugel f; *fig.* Sphäre f.

spic|e [spais] Gewürz(e *pl*) *n; fig.* Würze f; würzen; **~y** würzig; *fig.* pikant.

spider ['spaidə] Spinne f.

spike [spaik] *bot.* Ähre f; Stift *m,* Spitze f, Dorn *m,* Stachel *m; pl* Spikes *pl.*

spill [spil] (*irr*) verschütten; überlaufen (lassen).

spilt [spilt] *pret u. pp von* **spill.**

spin [spin] (*irr*) spinnen; (herum)wirbeln; (sich) drehen; Drehung f. **[m.]**

spinach ['spinidʒ] Spinat *f*

spinal ['spainl] Rückgrat ...; **~ column** Wirbelsäule f; **~ cord** Rückenmark *n.*

spindle ['spindl] Spindel f.

spine [spain] *anat.* Rückgrat *n,* Wirbelsäule f; Stachel *m.*

spinning-mill Spinnerei f.

spinster ['spinstə] unverheiratete Frau; alte Jungfer.

spiny ['spaini] stach(e)lig.

spiral ['spaiərəl] Spirale f; gewunden.

spire [spaiə] (Kirch-)Turmspitze f.

spirit ['spirit] Geist *m;* Gesinnung f; Schwung *m,* Elan *m,* Mut *m; pl* Spirituosen *pl,* alkoholische Getränke *pl;* **in high** *od.* **low ~s** *pl* gehobener *od.* gedrückter Stimmung; **~ed** temperamentvoll, lebhaft; mutig; **~ual** ['~tjuəl] geistig; geistlich; *mus.* Spiritual *m* f.

spit [spit] (Brat)Spieß *m;* Speichel *m,* Spucke f; (*irr*) (aus)spucken; fauchen.

spite [spait] Bosheit f; Groll *m;* **in ~ of** trotz; **~ful** gehässig, boshaft.

spittle ['spitl] Speichel *m;* Spucke f.

splash [splæʃ] Spritzer *m;* Platschen *n;* (be)spritzen; platschen, planschen; **~down** wassern (*Raumfahrzeug*); **~down** Wasserung f.

spleen [spli:n] *anat.* Milz f; schlechte Laune, Ärger *m.*

splend|id ['splendid] glänzend, großartig, prächtig; **~o(u)r** Glanz *m,* Pracht f, Herrlichkeit f.

splint [splint] *med.* Schiene f; schienen; **~er** Splitter *m;* (zer)splittern.

split [split] Spalt *m,* Riß *m; fig.* Spaltung f; gespalten; (*irr*) (zer-, auf)spalten; (zer)teilen; sich (in *et.*) teilen; sich (auf)spalten; (zer)platzen; **~ting** heftig, rasend (*Kopfschmerz*).

splutter ['splʌtə] Worte herausprudeln, -stottern.

spoil [spɔɪl] *mst pl* (*fig.* Aus)Beute *f*; (*irr*) verderben; verwöhnen; *Kind a.* verziehen; **~sport** Spielverderber(in); **~t** *pret u.* *pp von* **spoil**.

spoke [spəʊk] Speiche *f*; (Leiter)Sprosse *f*.

spoke² *pret*, **~n** *pp von* **speak**; **~sman** Wortführer *m*.

spong|e [spʌndʒ] Schwamm *m*; (mit e-m Schwamm) (ab)wischen; *colloq.* schmarotzen; **~ecake** Biskuitkuchen *m*; **~y** schwammig; locker.

sponsor [ˈspɒnsə] Bürg|e *m*, -in *f*; Pat|e *m*, -in *f*; Förderer *m*; bürgen für.

spontaneous [spɒnˈteɪnjəs] spontan; freiwillig; Selbst...

spook [spuːk] Spuk *m*.

spool [spuːl] Spule *f*; (auf)spulen.

spoon [spuːn] Löffel *m*; **~ up**, **~ out** auslöffeln; **~ful** (*ein*) Löffel(voll) *m*.

spore [spɔː] Spore *f*.

sport [spɔːt] Vergnügen *n*; Spiel *n*; Spaß *m*; *colloq.* feiner Kerl; *pl* Sport *m*; *colloq.* protzen mit; **~sman** Sportler *m*; **~swoman** Sportlerin *f*.

spot [spɒt] Fleck(en) *m*; Tupfen *m*; Tropfen *m*; Pickel *m*; Stelle *f*; Makel *m*; **on the ~** auf der Stelle, sofort; zur Stelle; (be-) flecken; ausfindig machen, entdecken, erkennen; **~-**

~less fleckenlos; **~light** *thea.* Scheinwerfer(licht *n*) *m*.

spout [spaʊt] Tülle *f*, Schnabel *m*; (Wasser-) Strahl *m*; (heraus)spritzen.

sprain [spreɪn] Verstauchung *f*; sich *et.* verstauchen. [**sprang.**]

sprang [spræŋ] *pret von*]

sprat [spræt] Sprotte *f*.

sprawl [sprɔːl] sich rekeln, ausgestreckt daliegen.

spray [spreɪ] Gischt *m*, *f*; Spray *m*, *n*; zerstäuben; (ver)sprühen; besprühen.

spread [spred] (*irr*) (sich) aus- ed. verbreiten; (sich) ausdehnen; *Butter etc.* auf*s*.eichen; *Brot* streichen; Aus-, Verbreitung *f*; (Flügel)Spannweite *f*; (*Bett*-*etc.*)Decke *f*; (Brot)Aufstrich *m*.

sprig [sprɪɡ] kleiner Zweig.

sprightly [ˈspraɪtlɪ] lebhaft, munter.

spring [sprɪŋ] Sprung *m*, Satz *m*; (Sprung)Feder *f*; Quelle *f*; *fig.* Ursprung *m*; Frühling *m*; (*irr*) springen; **~ from** entspringen; **~board** Sprungbrett *n*; **~time** Frühling *m*.

sprinkle [ˈsprɪŋkl] (be-) streuen; (be)sprengen; **~r** Berieselungsanlage *f*; Rasensprenger *m*.

sprint [sprɪnt] sprinten; spurten; Sprint *m*; Endspurt *m*; **~er** Sprinter(in).

sprout [spraʊt] sprießen; wachsen lassen; Sproß *m*.

spruce [spru:s] schmuck, adrett; ~ **(fir)** Fichte *f*, Rottanne *f*. **{spring.}**

sprung [sprʌŋ] *pp von*

spun [spʌn] *pret u. pp von* **spin**.

spur [spə:] Sporn *m* (*a. zo.*, *bot.*); *fig.* Ansporn *m*; ~ **on** *j-n* anspornen.

sputter ['spʌtə] (hervor-)sprudeln; spritzen; zischen; stottern (*Motor*).

spy [spai] Spion(in); (er-)spähen; (aus)spionieren.

squabble ['skwɒbl] sich zanken.

squad [skwɒd] Gruppe *f*.

squall [skwɔ:l] Bö *f*.

squander ['skwɒndə] verschwenden.

square [skwɛə] quadratisch, Quadrat...; viereckig; rechtwink(e)lig; breit, stämmig (*Person*); quitt; ehrlich; Quadrat *n*; Viereck *n*; *öffentlicher* Platz; quadratisch machen; *Zahl* ins Quadrat erheben; *Schultern* straffen; in Einklang bringen *od.* stehen.

squash [skwɒʃ] Gedränge *n*; (*Zitronen-*, *Orangen-*)Saft *m*; (*zer-*, *zs.-*)quetschen, (*-*)drücken.

squat [skwɒt] untersetzt; hocken, kauern.

squeak [skwi:k] quieken; quietschen.

squeal [skwi:l] grellschreien; quieken.

squeamish ['skwi:miʃ] empfindlich; heikel; penibel.

squeeze [skwi:z] (*aus-*, *zs.-*)drücken, (*-*)pressen, (*aus*)quetschen; sich zwängen *od.* quetschen; ~**r** (*Frucht*)Presse *f*.

squid [skwid] Tintenfisch *m*. {blinzeln.}

squint [skwint] schielen;}

squire ['skwaiə] Landedelmann *m*, *a.* Großgrundbesitzer *m*. {winden.}

squirm [skwə:m] sich}

squirrel ['skwirəl, *Am.* 'skwə:rəl] Eichhörnchen *n*.

squirt [skwə:t] spritzen

stab [stæb] Stich *m*, (*Dolch*)Stoß *m*; (er)stechen.

stabili|ty [stə'biliti] Stabilität *f*; Beständigkeit *f*; ~**ze** ['steibilaiz] stabilisieren.

stable[1] ['steibl] stabil, fest.

stable[2] Stall *m*.

stack [stæk] Schober *m*; Stapel *m*; (auf)stapeln.

stadium ['steidjəm] Stadion *n*.

staff [stɑ:f] Stab *m*, Stock *m*; (*Mitarbeiter*)Stab *m*; Personal *n*; Belegschaft *f*; Lehrkörper *m*; (mit Personal) besetzen.

stag [stæg] Hirsch *m*.

stage [steidʒ] Bühne *f*; *fig.* Schauplatz *m*; (*Fahr-*)Strecke *f*; Abschnitt *m*; (*Raketen*)Stufe *f*; Stadium *n*; inszenieren; ~**coach** Postkutsche *f*; ~**manager** Inspizient *m*.

stagger ['stægə] (sch)wanken, taumeln; erschüttern.

stagnant ['stægnənt] stehend (*Wasser*); stagnierend.

stain [stein] Fleck *m*; *fig.* Makel *m*; beschmutzen, beflecken; **~ed** fleckig beflecht; bunt, bemalt (*Glas*); **~less** rostfrei; *fig.* fleckenlos.

stair [stεə] Stufe *f*; *pl* Treppe *f*; **~case**, **~way** Treppe(nhaus *n*) *f*.

stake [steik] wagen, aufs Spiel setzen; Pfahl *m*; (Spiel)Einsatz *m*; **be at ~** auf dem Spiel stehen.

stale [steil] alt; schal, abgestanden; verbraucht.

stalk [stɔ:k] Stengel *m*, Stiel *m*, Halm *m*.

stall [stɔ:l] (Pferde)Box *f*; (Verkaufs)Stand *m*; (Markt)Bude *f*; *thea.* Sperrsitz *m*; *Motor* abwürgen; aussetzen (*Motor*).

stallion ['stæljən] (Zucht-) Hengst *m*.

stalwart ['stɔ:lwət] stramm, stark; treu.

stammer ['stæmə] stottern, stammeln; Stottern *n*.

stamp [stæmp] Stempel *m*; (Brief)Marke *f*; stampfen; aufstampfen (mit); prägen, stempeln; frankieren; trampeln.

stanch [stɑ:ntʃ] *s.* **staunch**.

stand [stænd] (*irr*) stehen; stellen; aushalten, (v)ertragen; sich *et.* gefallen lassen; *Probe* bestehen; **~ (still)** stehenbleiben, still-

stehen; **~ back** zurücktreten; **~ by** dabeistehen; sich bereithalten; zu' *j*-*m* halten *od.* stehen; **~ off** zurücktreten; zu' *j*-*m* halten *od.* stehen; **~ off** zurücktreten; **~ (up)on** bestehen auf; **~ out** hervortreten; *fig.* sich abheben; **~ up** aufstehen; **~ up for** eintreten für; *sub:* Stehen*n*, Stillstand *m*; (Stand)Platz *m*; (Taxi)Stand(platz) *m*; Ständer *m*; Gestell *n*; Tribüne *f*; (Verkaufs)Stand*m*.

standard ['stændəd] Standarte *f*; Standard *m*, Norm *f*; Maßstab *m*; Niveau *n*; Normal...; **~ize** normen.

standing ['stændiŋ] stehend; (be)ständig; Stehen *n*; Stellung *f*, Rang *m*, Ruf *m*; **of long ~** alt; **~ room** Stehplatz *m*.

stand|-offish ['stænd'ɔfiʃ] reserviert, ablehnend; **~-point** Standpunkt *m*; **~still** Stillstand *m*.

stank [stæŋk] *pret von* **stink**.

star [stɑ:] Stern *m*; *thea.* Star *m*; *thea.*, Film: die Hauptrolle spielen.

starboard ['stɑ:bəd] Steuerbord *n*.

starch [stɑ:tʃ] (Wäsche-) Stärke *f*; stärken.

stare [stεə] starrer Blick; (**~ at**) anstarren.

stark [stɑ:k] völlig.

star|ling ['stɑ:liŋ] *orn.* Star *m*; **~lit** sternenklar; **~ry** Stern(en)...; strahlend; **~s and Stripes** Sternenbanner *n*; **~-spangled**

sternenbesät; **⚥-Spangled Banner** Sternenbanner n.

start [stɑːt] Start m; Anfang m; Aufbruch m, Abreise f, Abfahrt f, aer. Abflug m; fig. Auffahren n, Zs.-fahren n; anfangen (**doing** zu tun); sp. starten; mot. anspringen; aufbrechen; abfahren (Zug), auslaufen (Schiff), aer. abfliegen, starten; auffahren, zs.-fahren, zs.-zucken; stutzen; et. in Gang setzen, tech. a. anlassen; aufmachen, gründen; **e-e Reise antreten, er** sp. Starter m; Läufer(in); mot. Anlasser m.

startl|e ['stɑːtl] er-, aufschrecken; **~ing** bestürzend; überraschend.

starv|ation [stɑːˈveiʃən] (Ver)Hungern n; Hungertod m; **~e** (ver)hungern (lassen).

state [steit] Zustand m; Stand m, Lage f; (pol. ⚥) Staat m; staatlich, Staats...; darlegen; angeben; feststellen; jur. Aussagen; **2 Department** Am. Außenministerium n; **~ly** stattlich; würdevoll; **~ment** Erklärung f; Behauptung f; Aussage f; Angabe(n pl) f; Darstellung f; econ. Bericht m; **~room** mar. Einzelkabine f; **~side** Am.: amerikanisch, Heimat...; in od. nach den Staaten; **~sman** Staatsmann m.

static ['stætik] statisch.

station ['steiʃən] Platz m; Station f; Bahnhof m; mil. Stützpunkt m; Australien: Schaffarm f; fig. Rang m, Stellung f; aufstellen; stationieren; **~ary** fest (-stehend); gleichbleibend; **~er** Schreibwarenhändler m; **~ery** Schreib-, Papierwaren pl; **~master** Stationsvorsteher m; **~waggon** Kombiwagen m.

statistics [stəˈtistiks] sg, pl Statistik f.

statue ['stætʃuː] Statue f.

statute ['stætjuːt] Statut n, Satzung f; Gesetz n.

staunch [stɔːntʃ] Blut(ung) stillen; treu, zuverlässig; standhaft.

stay [stei] Strebe f, Stütze f; Aufenthalt m; pl Korsett n; bleiben (**with** bei); sich aufhalten, wohnen (**with** bei); **~ away** wegbleiben; **~ up** aufbleiben.

stead [sted]: **in his ~** an s-r Statt; **~fast** ['~fəst] fest; unverwandt.

steady ['stedi] fest; gleichmäßig, stetig, (be-) ständig; zuverlässig; ruhig, sicher; fest od. sicher machen od. werden; **~o.s.** sich stützen.

steal [stiːl] (irr) stehlen; sich stehlen, schleichen.

stealth [stelθ]: **by ~** heimlich; **~y** verstohlen.

steam [stiːm] Dampf m; Dunst m; Dampf...; dampfen; Speisen dünsten, dämpfen; **~ up** (sich) beschlagen (*Glas*); **~er**, **~ship** Dampfer *m*.

steel [sti:l] Stahl *m*; stählern; Stahl...; **~works** *sg*, *pl* Stahlwerk *n*.

steep [sti:p] steil, jäh; steiler Abhang; einweichen, -tauchen; einlegen.

steeple ['sti:pl] (spitzer) Kirchturm.

steer [stiə] steuern, lenken; **~ing-gear** Lenkung *f*; **~ing-wheel** Steuerrad *n*; *mot. a.* Lenkrad *n*.

stem [stem] (Baum-, Wort-) Stamm *m*; Stiel *m*; Stengel *m*.

stench [stentʃ] Gestank *m*.

stenographer [ste'nɔgrəfə] Stenograph(in).

step¹ [step] Schritt *m*; (Treppen)Stufe *f*; schreiten; treten, gehen.

step² *in Zssgn:* Stief...; **~father** Stiefvater *m*; **~mother** Stiefmutter *f*.

stereo [stiəriəu] Stereo *n*.

sterile ['sterail] unfruchtbar; steril; **~ize** ['~ilaiz] sterilisieren.

sterling ['stə:liŋ] Sterling *m* (*Währung*).

stern [stə:n] streng; *mar.* Heck *n*; **~ness** Strenge *f*.

stew [stju:] schmoren; Schmor-, Eintopfgericht *n*; *colloq.* Aufregung *f*.

steward [stjuəd] Verwalter *m*; Steward *m*; **~ess** Stewardeß *f*.

stick [stik] Stock *m*; (Besen- *etc.*)Stiel *m*; Stange *f*; (dünner) Zweig; (*irr*) ste-

chen mit; (an)stecken; (an)kleben; *colloq.* ertragen; hängenbleiben; steckenbleiben; **~ out** ab-, hervorstehen; heraus-st(r)ecken; **~ to** bei *j—m od. et.* bleiben; **~ing-plaster** Heftpflaster *n*; **~y** klebrig.

stiff [stif] steif, starr; mühsam; stark (*alkoholisches Getränk*); **~en** (sich) versteifen; erstarren.

stifle ['staifl] ersticken.

stile [stail] Zauntritt *m*.

still [stil] still; (immer) noch; doch; dennoch; stillen, beruhigen; **~ness** Stille *f*, Ruhe *f*.

stilt [stilt] Stelze *f*; **~ed** geschraubt (*Stil*).

stimulant ['stimjulənt] Anregungsmittel *n*; Anreiz *m*; **~ate** ['~eit] anregen; **~ating** anregend; **~ation** Anreiz *m*; *med.* Reiz(ung) *f*; **~us** ['~əs] (An)Reiz *m*.

sting [stiŋ] Stachel *m* (*e—s Insekts*); Stich *m*, Biß *m*; (*irr*) stechen; brennen; schmerzen.

stingy ['stindʒi] geizig.

stink [stiŋk] Gestank *m*; (*irr*) stinken.

stipulate ['stipjuleit] ausbedingen, vereinbaren.

stir [stə:] (sich) rühren *od.* bewegen; umrühren; *fig.* erregen; [bügel *m*.]

stirrup ['stirəp] Steig-

stitch [stitʃ] Stich *m*; Masche *f*; nähen; heften.

stock [stɔk] Griff *m*; Rohstoff *m*; (Fleisch-, Gemüse)Brühe f; Waren(lager n) pl;Vorrat m; Vieh(bestand m) n; Herkunft f; pl: Effekten pl; Aktien pl; **in (out of)** ~ (nicht) vorrätig;**take** ~ Inventur machen; vorrätig; gängig, Standard... (Größe); ausstatten, versorgen;Waren führen, vorrätig haben; ~**breeder** Viehzüchter m; ~**broker** Börsenmakler m; ~**exchange** Börse f; ~**farmer** Viehzüchter m; ~**holder** Aktionär(in).

stocking ['stɔkiŋ] Strumpf m. \
~**y** stämmig.

stock|-market Börse f; \
stole [stəul] pret, ~n pp von **steal**.

stomach ['stʌmək] Magen m; Leib m, Bauch m; fig. (v)ertragen.

stone [stəun] Stein m; (Obst)Kern m; steinern, Stein...; steinigen; entkernen; ~**ware** Steinzeug n; ~**y** steinig; fig. steinern.

stood [stud] pret u. pp von **stand**.

stool [stu:l] Schemel m, Hocker m; med. Stuhlgang m. \
~ [krumm gehen.]

stoop [stu:p]sich bücken; \
stop [stɔp] aufhören (mit); Zahlungen etc. einstellen; an-, aufhalten, stoppen; hindern; Zahnplombieren; Blut stillen; (an)halten, stehenbleiben, stoppen; aer.zwischenlanden; colloq. bleiben; ~ **over** die Fahrt

unterbrechen; ~(**up**) ver-, zustopfen; Halt m; Pause f; Aufenthalt m; Station f; Haltestelle f; tech. Anschlag m; ling. Punkt m; ~**page** tech. Hemmung f; (Zahlungs-etc.) Einstellung f; ~**per** Stöpsel m; ~**ping** med. Plombe f.

storage ['stɔ:ridʒ] Lagerung f;Lager(geld) n.

store [stɔ:] Vorrat m; Lagerhaus n; Am. Laden m, Geschäft n; pl Kauf-, Warenhaus n; versorgen; ~**up** (auf)speichern, lagern; ~**house** Lagerhaus n; ~**keeper** Am. Ladenbesitzer(in).

stor|ey ['stɔ:ri] Stock(werk n) m; ~**eyed**, ~**ied** ...stökkig.

stork [stɔ:k] Storch m.

storm [stɔ:m] Sturm m; Gewitter n; stürmen, toben; ~**y** stürmisch.

story ['stɔ:ri] Geschichte f; Erzählung f; s. **storey**.

stout [staut] kräftig; dick; starkes Porterbier.

stove [stəuv] Ofen m, Herd m; Treibhaus n.

stow [stəu] verstauen, pakken; ~**away** blinder Passagier.

straggling ['strægliŋ] verstreut (liegend); lose (Haar).

straight [streit] adj gerade; glatt (Haar); ehrlich; **put** ~ in Ordnung bringen; adv gerade(aus); direkt, geradewegs; ehrlich, anstän-

dig; ~ **away**, ~ **off** sofort;
~ **ahead**, ~ **on** geradeaus;
~**en** gerademachen, gerade werden; (gerade)rich-
ten; ~**forward** ehrlich,
einfach.

strain [strein] (an)span-
nen; verstauchen, *Muskel
etc.* zerren; überanstren-
gen; durchseihen, filtern;
sich anstrengen od. ab-
mühen; Spannung *f*; Be-
lastung *f*; *med.* Zerrung *f*;
Überanstrengung *f*, An-
spannung *f*; ~**er** Seiher *m*,
Sieb *n*.

strait [streit] (*in Eigen-
namen oft:* 2*s pl*) Meerenge
f, Straße *f*; *pl* Not(lage) *f*;
~**en:** **in** ~**ed circumstances** in beschränkten
Verhältnissen.

strand [strænd] Strand *m*;
Strang *m*; Strähne *f*; *fig.*
stranden (lassen).

strange [streindʒ] fremd;
seltsam, merkwürdig; ~**r**
Fremde *m*, *f*.

strangle ['stræŋgl] erwürgen, erdrosseln.

strap [stræp] Riemen *m*,
Gurt *m*, Band *n*; Träger *m*
(*Kleid*); fest-, umschnallen.

strateg|ic [strə'ti:dʒik]
strategisch; ~**y** ['strætidʒi]
Strategie *f*; *fig.* Taktik *f*.

straw [strɔ:] Stroh(halm
m) *n*; Stroh...; ~**berry**
Erdbeere *f*.

stray [strei] sich verirren;
verirrt; streunend; verein-
zelt.

streak [stri:k] streifen;

Strich *m*, Streifen *m*; *fig.*
Ader *f*, Spur *f*; ~ **of lightning** Blitzstrahl *m*; ~**y**
durchwachsen (*Speck*).

stream [stri:m] Strom *m*,
Fluß *m*, Bach *m*; Strömung
f; strömen; flattern.

street [stri:t] Straße *f*; ~
car *Am.* Straßenbahn *f*.

strength [streŋθ] Stärke *f*,
Kraft *f*; ~**en** (er)stärken.

strenuous ['strenjuəs] rüh-
rig; tüchtig; anstrengend.

stress [stres] Nachdruck *m*;
Betonung *f* (*a.* *ling.*); Belastung *f*, Streß *m*; betonen.

stretch [stretʃ] (sich) strek-
ken; (sich) dehnen; sich erstrecken; (an)spannen; ~
out ausstrecken; (Sich-)
Strecken *n*; (Weg)Strecke
f, Fläche *f*; Zeit(raum *m*) *f*;
~**er** (Trag)Bahre *f*.

strew [stru:] (*irr*) (be-)
streuen; ~**n** *pp von* **strew.**

stricken ['strikən] *pp von*
strike; heimgesucht; er-
griffen.

strict [strikt] streng; genau.

strid|den ['stridn] *pp von*
stride; ~**e** [straid] (*irr*)
über-, durchschreiten; aus-
schreiten; großer Schritt.

strife [straif] Streit *m*,
Kampf *m*.

strike [straik] Schlag *m*,
Stoß *m*; (Luft)Angriff *m*;
fig. Treffer *m*; *econ.* Streik
m; **be on** ~ streiken; (*irr*)
(an-, zu)schlagen; (an-,
zu)stoßen; treffen; *Streichholz, Licht* anzünden; stoßen auf; einschlagen (in)

(*Blitz etc.*); *Zelt* abbrechen; *die Stunde etc.* schlagen (*Uhr*); *j-m* einfallen *od.* in den Sinn kommen; *j-m* auffallen; streichen; **~ off, ~ out** (aus)streichen; **~r** Streikende *m, f.*

striking ['straikiŋ] Schlag...; auffallend, eindrucksvoll; verblüffend.

string [striŋ] Schnur *f*, Bindfaden *m*; Band *n*; Faden *m*; Draht *m*; Reihe *f*, Kette *f*; *bot.* Faser *f*; (Bogen)Sehne *f*; Saite *f*; *pl* Streichinstrumente *pl*; (*irr*) (be)spannen; Perlen aufreihen; **~y** ['~ji] zäh (-flüssig); sehnig.

strip [strip] entkleiden (*a. fig.*), (sich) ausziehen; abziehen, abstreifen; Streifen *m*. **~d** gestreift.

stripe [straip] Streifen *m*;

strive [straiv] (*irr*): **~ (for)** streben (nach), ringen (um); **~n** ['strivn] *pp von* **strive.**

strode [stroud] *pret von* **stride.**

stroke [strouk] streichen über; streicheln; Schlag *m*; Stoß *m*; *med.* Schlag(anfall) *m*; **~ of luck** Glücksfall *m.*

stroll [stroul] schlendern; Bummel *m*, Spaziergang *m*; **~er** Spaziergänger(in); *Am.* Faltsportwagen *m.*

strong [strɔŋ] stark; kräftig; fest; scharf (*Geschmack etc.*); **~box** Stahl-

kassette *f*; **~room** Tresor (-raum) *m*; **[strive.**

strove [strouv] *pret von*

struck [strʌk] *pret u. pp von* **strike.**

structure ['straktʃə] Bau (-werk *n*) *m*; Struktur *f.*

struggle ['stragl] sich abmühen; kämpfen, ringen; sich sträuben; Kampf *m*, Ringen *n* (*auf.*).

strum [stram] klimpern.

strung [straŋ] *pret u. pp von* **string; highly ~** (über)empfindlich, nervös.

strut [strat] stolzieren; Strebe(balken *m*) *f.*

stub [stab] (Baum)Stumpf *m*; Stummel *m.*

stubble ['stabl] Stoppel(n *pl*) *f.*

stubborn ['staban] eigensinnig; stur; hartnäckig.

stuck [stak] *pret u. pp von* **stick.**

stud [stad] Beschlagnagel *m*; Kragenknopf *m*; Gestüt *n*; besetzen, übersäen.

student ['stju:dənt] Student(in); Schüler(in).

studio ['stju:diəu] Atelier *n*; Studio *n*; Aufnahme-, Senderaum *m*; **~ couch** Bettcouch *f.*

studious ['stju:djəs] fleißig; sorgfältig, peinlich.

study ['stadi] Studium *n*; Studier-, Arbeitszimmer *n*; Studie *f*; (ein)studieren.

stuff [staf] Stoff *m*, Material *n*; Zeug *n*; (aus)stopfen; vollstopfen; **~ing** Füllung *f*; **~y** muffig; *colloq.* spießig.

stumble ['stʌmbl] stolpern, straucheln; Stolpern
n.

stump [stʌmp] Stumpf m,
Stummel m; (daher)stampf-
en.

stun [stʌn] betäuben.

stung [stʌŋ] pret u. pp von
sting.

stunk [stʌŋk] pret u. pp von
stink.

stunning ['stʌnɪŋ] colloq.
toll, hinreißend.

stup|efy ['stju:pifai] betäu-
ben; **~id** dumm; **~idity**
Dummheit f; **~or** Erstar-
rung f, Betäubung f.

sturdy ['stə:di] robust,
kräftig.

stutter ['stʌtə] stottern;
Stottern n.

sty[1] [stai] Schweinestall m.

sty[2] ., med. Gerstenkorn n.

styl|e [stail] Stil m; Mode
f; **~ish** stilvoll; elegant.

suave [swɑːv] verbindlich.

subdivision ['sʌbdiviʒən]
Unterteilung f; Unterab-
teilung f.

subdue [səb'dju:] unterwerfen; dämpfen.

subject ['sʌbdʒikt] Thema
n, Gegenstand m; (Lehr-,
Schul-, Studien)Fach n;
Untertan(in); Staatsbürger
(-in), -angehörige m, f; gr.
Subjekt n, Satzgegenstand
m; ~ to vorbehaltlich;[sʌb-
'dʒekt:] ~ to unterwerfen
od. aussetzen (dat); **~ion**
Unterwerfung f.

subjunctive (mood) [səb-
'dʒʌŋktiv] gr. Konjunktiv
m, Möglichkeitsform f.

sublime [sə'blaim] erhaben.

submachine-gun ['sʌb-
mə'ʃi:ŋgʌn] Maschinenpi-
stole f.

submarine [sʌbmə'ri:n]
Unterseeboot n, U-Boot n.

submerge [səb'mə:dʒ]
(ein-, unter)tauchen.

submiss|ion [səb'miʃən]
Unterwerfung f; **~ive** un-
terwürfig.

submit [səb'mit] ~ **to**
(sich) unterwerfen (dat);
unterbreiten (dat); sich fügen (dat, in).

subordinate [sə'bɔ:dnit]
Untergebene m, f; untergeordnet; ~ **clause** gr. Neben-
satz m.

subscribe [səb'skraib]
spenden; unterschreiben
(mit); ~ **for** Buch vorbestellen; ~ **to** Zeitung abon-
nieren; **~r** Abonnent(in);
teleph. Teilnehmer(in);
Spender(in).

subscription [səb'skrip-
ʃən] Unterzeichnung f;
Abonnement n, Subskrip-
tion f; (Mitglieds)Beitrag
m; Spende f.

subsequent ['sʌbsikwənt]
(nach)folgend, später; **~ly**
hinterher.

subsid|e [səb'said] sich
senken; (ein)sinken; sich
legen (Wind); **~iary** [~-
'sidjəri] Hilfs...; untergeordnet, Neben...; **~iary
(company)** Tochterge-
sellschaft f; **~ize** ['sʌbsi-
daiz] subventionieren; **~y**

['sʌbsidi] Subvention f.

subsist [səb'sist] leben (**on** von); **~ence** (Lebens)Unterhalt m, Existenz f.

substance ['sʌbstəns] Substanz f; das Wesentliche.

substandard [sʌb'stændəd] unter der Norm; **~film** Schmalfilm m.

substantial [səb'stænʃəl] wirklich; reichlich (Mahlzeit); namhaft (Summe); wesentlich.

substantive ['sʌbstəntiv] gr. Substantiv n, Hauptwort n.

substitut|e ['sʌbstitju:t] an die Stelle setzen od. treten (**for** von); (Stell)Vertreter (-in); Ersatz m; **~ion** Ersatz m. (titel m.)

subtitle ['sʌbtaitl] Untertitel m.

subtle ['sʌtl] fein(sinnig); subtil; scharf(sinnig).

subtract [səb'trækt] abziehen, subtrahieren.

suburb ['sʌbə:b] Vorstadt f, -ort m; **~an** [sə'bə:bən] vorstädtisch, Vorort(s)...

subway ['sʌbwei] (bsd. Fußgänger)Unterführung f; Am. Untergrundbahn f.

succeed [sək'si:d] Erfolg haben; glücken, gelingen; (nach)folgen (**to** dat).

success [sək'ses] Erfolg m; **~ful** erfolgreich; **~ion** [~n] (Nach-, Erb-, Reihen)Folge f; **~ive** aufeinanderfolgend; **~or** Nachfolger(in).

succumb [sə'kʌm] erliegen.

such [sʌtʃ] solche(r, -s); derartige; **~ a man** in sol-

cher Mann; **~ as** die, welche; wie (zum Beispiel).

suck [sʌk] saugen (an); aussaugen; lutschen (an); **~le** säugen, stillen; **~ling** Säugling m.

sudden ['sʌdn] plötzlich; **all of a ~** ganz plötzlich; **~ly** plötzlich.

suds [sʌdz] pl Seifenschaum m.

sue [sju:] klagen.

suède [sweid] Wildleder n.

suet [sjuit] Talg m.

suffer ['sʌfə] leiden (**from** an, unter); (er)leiden; büßen; dulden; **~er** Leidende m, f.

suffice [sə'fais] genügen; **~ it to say** es sei nur gesagt.

suffic|iency [sə'fiʃənsi] genügende Menge; **~t** genügend, genug, ausreichend.

suffix ['sʌfiks] ling. Suffix n, Nachsilbe f.

suffocate ['sʌfəkeit] ersticken.

sugar ['ʃugə] Zucker m; zuckern; **~cane** Zuckerrohr n.

suggest [sə'dʒest] vorschlagen, anregen; hinweisen auf; andeuten; **~ion** Vorschlag m, Anregung f; Hinweis m; Andeutung f; **~ive** anregend; andeutend (**of** acc); vielsagend; zweideutig.

suicide ['sjuisaid] Selbstmord m; Selbstmörder(in).

suit [sju:t] Anzug m; Kostüm n; Karten: Farbe f; jur. Prozeß m; passen; j-m

zusagen, bekommen; *j-n*
kleiden, *j-m* stehen, passen
zu; sich eignen für *od.* zu;
~ **yourself** tu, was dir gefällt; **~able** passend, geeignet; **~case** (Hand)Kof-
fer *m.*

suite [swiːt] Gefolge *n*;
(Zimmer)Einrichtung *f*;
Zimmerflucht *f.*

suitor [ˈsjuːtə] Freier *m*;
jur. Kläger(in).

sulfur [ˈsʌlfə] *Am.* für **sulphur.**

sulk [sʌlk] schmollen; **~y**
verdrießlich, mürrisch.

sullen [ˈsʌlən] verdrossen,
mürrisch; düster.

sulphur [ˈsʌlfə] Schwefel *m.*

sultry [ˈsʌltri] schwül; *fig.*
heftig, hitzig.

sum [sʌm] Summe *f*; Betrag *m*; Rechenaufgabe *f*;
do ~s rechnen; *vb:* **~ up**
zs.-zählen, addieren; *j-n*
abschätzen; zs.-fassen.

summar|ize [ˈsʌməraiz]
(kurz) zs.-fassen; **~y** (kurze) Inhaltsangabe, Zs.-fas-
sung *f*, Übersicht *f.*

summer [ˈsʌmə] Sommer
m; **~ resort** Sommerfri-
sche *f*; **~ school** Ferien-
kurs *m.*

summit [ˈsʌmit] Gipfel *m.*

summon [ˈsʌmən] auffor-
dern; (zu sich) bestellen;
jur. vorladen; **~ (up)** Mut
etc. zs.-nehmen; **~s** [ˈ~z],
pl **~s(es)** [ˈ~ziz] Aufforderung *f*; *jur.* Vorladung *f.*

sun [sʌn] Sonne *f*; Sonnen-
...; (sich) sonnen; **~bath**

Sonnenbad *n*; **~beam**
Sonnenstrahl *m*; **~burn**
Sonnenbrand *m*, -bräune *f.*

Sunday [ˈsʌndi] Sonntag *m.*

sundial Sonnenuhr *f.*

sundr|ies [ˈsʌndriz] *pl* Ver-
schiedenes; **~y** verschiedene.

sung [sʌŋ] *pp von* **sing.**

sun-glasses *pl* (*a.* **a pair
of ~**) (e-e) Sonnenbrille.

sunk [sʌŋk] *pp von* **sink**;
~en versunken; *fig.* eingefallen.

sun|ny [ˈsʌni] sonnig; **~
rise** Sonnenaufgang *m*; **~
set** Sonnenuntergang *m*;
~shade Sonnenschirm *m*;
~shine Sonnenschein *m*;
~stroke Sonnenstich *m.*

super| [ˈsuːpə-] übermä-
ßig, Über..., über...; übergeordnet, Ober..., ober...;
Super... [reichlich.]

superabundant über-*f*

superb [sjuˈ(ː)pəːb] herrlich; ausgezeichnet.

super|ficial [suːpəˈfiʃəl]
oberflächlich; **~fluous** [~-
ˈpəːfluəs] überflüssig; **~
highway** *Am.* Autobahn
f; **~human** übermensch-
lich; **~intend** beaufsichti-
gen, überwachen; **~in-
tendent** Leiter *m*, Direktor
m; Inspektor *m.*

superior [suˈ(ː)ˈpiəriə] höher;
vorgesetzt; besser; hervorragend; überlegen;
Vorgesetzte *m, f*; **~ity** [~-
ˈɒriti] Überlegenheit *f.*

superlative [suˈ(ː)ˈpəːlə-
tiv] höchst; überragend; **~**

(degree) gr. Superlativ m.
super|man Übermensch m; **~market** Supermarkt m; **~natural** übernatürlich; **~numerary** ['~nju:mərəri] überzählig; **~scription** Über-, Aufschrift f; **~sonic** Überschall...; **~stition** [~'stiʃən] Aberglaube m; **~stitious** abergläubisch; **~vise** ['~vaiz] beaufsichtigen, überwachen; **~visor** Aufseher m, Leiter m.

supper ['sʌpə] Abendessen n, -brot n; **the Lord's** 2 das Heilige Abendmahl.

supple ['sʌpl] geschmeidig, biegsam.

supplement ['sʌplimənt] Ergänzung f; Nachtrag f; (Zeitungs- etc.)Beilage f; ['~ment] ergänzen; **~ary** Ergänzungs..., zusätzlich, Nachtrags...

supplication [sʌpli'keiʃn] demütige Bitte, Flehen n.

suppl|ier [sə'plaiə] Lieferant(in) f; **~y** [~ai] liefern; versorgen; Lieferung f; Versorgung f; econ. Angebot n; Vorrat m.

support [sə'pɔ:t] Stütze f; tech. Träger m; Unterstützung f; (Lebens)Unterhalt m; (unter)stützen; unterhalten, sorgen für (Familie etc.).

suppos|e [sə'pəuz] annehmen, voraussetzen; vermuten; halten für; sollen; **~ed** vermeintlich; angeblich; **~edly** [~idli] vermutlich.

~ition [sʌpə'ziʃən] Voraussetzung f, Annahme f; Vermutung f.

suppress [sə'pres] unterdrücken; **~ion** f Unterdrückung f.

suppurate ['sʌpjuəreit] eitern.

suprem|acy [su'preməsi] Oberhoheit f; Vorherrschaft f; Überlegenheit f; Vorrang m; **~e** [~'pri:m] höchst, oberst, Ober...

surcharge [sə:'tʃɑ:dʒ] überlasten; Zuschlag od. Nachgebühr erheben für; ['~] Überlastung f; Zuschlag m; Nachgebühr f; Überdruck m (auf Briefmarken).

sure [ʃuə] adj: **~ (of)** sicher, gewiß, überzeugt (von); **feel ~ of** sicher od. überzeugt sein, daß; **make ~ that** sich (davon) überzeugen, daß; adv: **~! enough** tatsächlich; **~!** klar!, bestimmt!; **~ly** sicher(lich); **~ty** [~'rəti] Bürge m; Bürgschaft f, Kaution f.

surf [sə:f] Brandung f.

surface ['sə:fis] Oberfläche f; auftauchen (U-Boot).

surf-riding Wellenreiten n.

surge [sə:dʒ] Woge f, (hohe) Welle; wogen.

surg|eon [sə:dʒən] Chirurg m; **~ery** Chirurgie f; Sprechzimmer n; **~ery hours** pl Sprechstunde (n pl) f; **~ical** chirurgisch.

surly ['sə:li] mürrisch.

surmise ['sə:maiz] Vermutung f; [~'maiz] vermuten.

surmount [sə:'maunt] überwinden; **~ed by** überragt von.

surname ['sə:neim] Familien-, Nach-, Zuname m.

surpass [sə:'pɑ:s] fig. übersteigen, -treffen; **~ing** unübertrefflich.

surplus ['sə:pləs] Überschuß m, Mehr n; überschüssig, Über(schuß)...

surprise [sə'praiz] Überraschung f; überraschen; **~d** überrascht, erstaunt.

surrender [sə'rendə] Übergabe f; Kapitulation f; Aufgeben n; übergeben; aufgeben; sich ergeben (**to** dat).

surround [sə'raund] umgeben; **~ings** pl Umgebung f.

survey [sə:'vei] überblicken; begutachten; Land vermessen; ['~vei] Überblick m; (Land)Vermessung f; (Lage)Karte f. **~or** [~'v~] Land-, Feldvermesser m, (amtlicher) Inspektor.

surviv|al [sə'vaivəl] Überleben n; **~e** überleben; bestehen bleiben; **~or** Überlebende m, f.

suscept|ible [sə'septəbl] leicht zu beeindrucken; empfänglich (**to** für); empfindlich (**to** gegen).

suspect [sə'spekt] verdächtigen; vermuten; befürchten; ['sʌspekt] Verdächtige

m, f; verdächtig; **~ed** [~'pektid] vermuten.

suspend [sə'spend] (auf-) hängen; aufschieben; Zahlung einstellen; suspendieren, sperren; **~ed** hängend, Hänge...;schwebend; **~er** Strumpf-, Sockenhalter m; pl Am. Hosenträger pl.

suspens|e [sə'spens] Ungewißheit f; Spannung f; **~ion** Aufhängung f; Aufschub m; Einstellung f; Suspendierung f; sp. Sperre f; **~ion bridge** Hängebrücke f.

suspici|on [sə'spiʃən] Verdacht m; **~ous** verdächtig; mißtrauisch.

sustain [sə'stein] stützen, tragen; aushalten; erleiden; unterhalten, versorgen; stärken.

sustenance ['sʌstinəns] (Lebens)Unterhalt m; Nahrung f; Nährwert m.

swab [swɔb] Mop m; med.: Tupfer m; Abstrich m; **~ up** aufwischen.

swagger ['swægə] stolzieren; prahlen, renommieren.

swallow ['swɔlou] Schwalbe f; (hinunter-, ver-) schlucken; verschlingen.

swam [swæm] pret von **swim.**

swamp [swɔmp] Sumpf m; überschwemmen (a. fig.); **~y** sumpfig.

swan [swɔn] Schwan m.

swap [swɔp] s. **swop.**

swarm [swɔ:m] Schwarm

m; Schar *f*; schwärmen; wimmeln.

swarthy ['swɔːði] dunkel (-häutig).

swathe [sweið] (ein-, um)wickeln.

sway [swei] schwanken; (sich) wiegen; schaukeln; beeinflussen.

swear [sweə] (*irr*) (be-)schwören; fluchen; ~ s.o. in j-n vereidigen.

sweat [swet] Schweiß *m*; Schwitzen *n*; (*irr*) (aus-)schwitzen; ~er Sweater *m*, Pullover *m*; ~y verschwitzt.

Swede [swiːd] Schwed|e *m*, -in *f*; **2ish** schwedisch; Schwedisch *n*.

sweep [swiːp] (*irr*) fegen (*a. fig.*), kehren; gleiten *od.* schweifen über (*Blick*); (majestätisch) einherschreiten *od.* (dahin)rauschen; schwungvolle Bewegung; Schornsteinfeger *m*; ~er (Straßen)Kehrer *m*; Kehrmaschine *f*; **2ing** schwungvoll; umfassend; **2ings** *pl* Kehricht *m*, Müll *m*.

sweet [swiːt] süß; frisch; lieb, reizend; Bonbon *m*, *n*; süßer Nachtisch; **2en** (ver)süßen; **2heart** Schatz *m*, Liebste *m*, *f*; **2ness** Süße *f*; Sanftheit *f*; Lieblichkeit *f*; **~pea** Gartenwicke *f*.

swell [swel] (*irr*) (an-)schwellen (lassen); sich (auf)blähen; sich (auf)bauschen; anblähen; Am. pri-

ma; **2ing** Schwellung *f*, Geschwulst *f*.

swept [swept] *pret u. pp* von **sweep**.

swerve [swɜːv] (plötzlich) ab- *od.* ausbiegen.

swift [swift] schnell; eilig; flink; **2ness** Schnelligkeit *f*.

swim [swim] (*irr*) (durch)schwimmen; **my head ~s** mir ist schwind(e)lig; Schwimmen *n*; **2mer** Schwimmer(in); **2ming** Schwimmen *n*; Schwimm...; **~ming-bath** (*bsd. Hallen*)Schwimmbad *n*; **~ming-pool** Schwimmbecken *n*; Freibad *n*; **~suit** Badeanzug *m*.

swindle ['swindl] betrügen; beschwindeln; Schwindel *m*. [*n*.]

swine [swain], *pl* **~Schwein**|

swing [swiŋ] (*irr*) schwingen; schwenken; schlenkern; baumeln (lassen); schaukeln; sich drehen (*Tür*); *colloq.* baumeln, hängen; Schwingen *n*; Schwung *m*; Schaukel *f*; **~boat** Schiffsschaukel *f*; **~bridge** Drehbrücke *f*; **~door** Drehtür *f*.

swirl [swɜːl] (herum)wirbeln; Wirbel *m*, Strudel *m*.

Swiss [swis] schweizerisch, Schweizer...; Schweizer(-in); **the ~** *pl* die Schweizer *pl*.

switch [switʃ] *rail.* Weiche *f*; *electr.* Schalter *m*; *rail.* rangieren; *electr.* (um)schalten; *fig.* wechseln; ~

off ab-, ausschalten; **~ on** an-, einschalten; **~board** Schaltbrett n, -tafel f.

swollen ['swəulən] pp von swell.

swoon [swu:n] Ohnmacht f; in Ohnmacht fallen.

swoop [swu:p]: **~ down on** herabstoßen auf, sich stürzen auf.

swop [swɔp] colloq. (ein-, aus)tauschen; Tausch m.

sword [sɔ:d] Schwert n, Degen m.

swor|e [swɔ:] pret, **~n** pp von swear. [swim.\

swum [swʌm] pp von\

swung [swʌŋ] pret u. pp von swing.

syllable ['siləbl] Silbe f.

symbol ['simbəl] Symbol n, Sinnbild n; **~ic(al)** [~'bɔlik(əl)] symbolisch, sinnbildlich; **~ism** Symbolik f.

symmetr|ic(al) [si'metrik(əl)] symmetrisch, ebenmäßig; **~y** ['simitri] Sym-

metrie f; fig. a. Ebenmaß n.

sympath|etic [simpə-'θetik] mitfühlend; **~ize** sympathisieren, mitfühlen; **~y** Sympathie f; Mitgefühl n.

symphony ['simfəni] Symphonie f.

symptom ['simptəm] Symptom n.

synchronize ['siŋkrənaiz] synchronisieren.

synonym ['sinənim] Synonym n; **~ous** [si'nɔniməs] synonym, sinnverwandt.

syntax ['sintæks] ling. Syntax f, Satzbau m, -lehre f.

synthe|sis ['sinθisis], pl **~ses** [~'si:z] Synthese f; **~tic** [~'θetik] synthetisch.

syringe ['sirindʒ] Spritze f; (ein)spritzen.

syrup ['sirəp] Sirup m.

system ['sistim] System n; (Eisenbahn-, Straßen- etc.) Netz n; Organismus m, Körper m; **~atic** systematisch.

T

tab [tæb] (Mantel- etc.) Aufhänger m.

table ['teibl] Tisch m; Tafel f; Tabelle f, Verzeichnis n; **at ~** bei Tisch; **~cloth** Tischtuch n, -decke f; **~land** Plateau n, Hochebene f; **~spoon** Eßlöffel m; **~spoonful** (ein) Eßlöffel(voll) m.

tablet ['tæblit] Täfelchen n; Stück n (Seife); Tablette f.

tacit ['tæsit] stillschweigend; **~urn** ['~ə:n] schweigsam.

tack [tæk] Stift m, Zwecke f; Heftstich m; heften.

tackle ['tækl] Gerät n, Ausrüstung f; Flaschenzug m; (an)packen.

tact [tækt] Takt m, Feingefühl n; **~ful** taktvoll; **~ics** sg, pl Taktik f; **~less** taktlos.

tadpole ['tædpəul] Kaulquappe *f*.

tag [tæg] Anhänger *m*, Schildchen *n*, Etikett *n*; etikettieren, auszeichnen; anhängen (**to** an).

tail [teil] Schwanz *m*, Schweif *m*; (hinteres) Ende, Schluß *m*; Rückseite *f* (e-r Münze); **~coat** Frack *m*; **~light** Rücklicht *n*, Schlußlicht *n*.

tailor ['teilə] Schneider *m*; schneidern; **~made** Schneider..., Maß...

taint [teint] (verborgene) Anlage (*zu* e-r *Krankheit*); **~ed** *Fleisch*: verdorben.

take [teik] (*irr*) (an-, ein-, entgegen-, heraus-, hin-, mit-, weg)nehmen; ergreifen; fangen (hin-, weg-) bringen; halten (**for** für); *Speisen* zu sich nehmen; *Platz* einnehmen; *Fahrt, Spaziergang, Ferien* machen; *Zug, Bus etc.* nehmen, benutzen; *Temperatur* messen; *phot. Aufnahme* machen; *Prüfung* machen, ablegen; *Preis* gewinnen; *Gelegenheit, Maßnahmen* ergreifen; *Vorsitz etc.* übernehmen; *Eid* ablegen; *Zeit, Geduld* erfordern, brauchen; *Zeit* dauern; **along** mitnehmen; **~ from** *j-m etc.* wegnehmen; **~ in** *Gast* aufnehmen; *Zeitung* halten; *et.* kürzer od. enger machen; *fig.*: *et.* in sich aufnehmen; *Lage* überschauen; *colloq. j-n*

reinlegen; **be ~n in** reingefallen sein; **~ off** *j-n* fortbringen; *Hut etc.* abnehmen; *Kleidungsstück* ablegen, ausziehen; *e-n Tag etc.* Urlaub machen; *aer.* aufsteigen, abfliegen, starten; **~ out** heraus-, entnehmen, entfernen; *zum Essen* ausführen; **~ over** *Amt, Aufgabe etc.* übernehmen; **~ to** Gefallen finden an, sich hingezogen fühlen zu; **~ up** auf-, hochheben; aufnehmen; sich befassen mit; *Idee* aufgreifen; *Platz, Zeit etc.* in Anspruch nehmen; **~n** *pp von* **take**; besetzt; **~off** *aer.* Start *m*.

tale [teil] Erzählung *f*, Geschichte *f*; Märchen *n*.

talent ['tælənt] Talent *n*, Begabung *f*; **~ed** begabt.

talk [to:k] Gespräch *n*; Unterhaltung *f*; Unterredung *f*; Vortrag *m*; sprechen, reden; **~ to** sich unterhalten mit; **~ative** ['~ətiv] geschwätzig.

tall [to:l] groß, hochgewachsen; lang; hoch.

tallow ['tæləu] Talg *m*.

talon ['tælən] *orn.* Kralle *f*, Klaue *f*.

tame [teim] zahm; folgsam; harmlos; zähmen.

tamper ['tæmpə]: **~ with** sich (unbefugt) zu schaffen machen an.

tan [tæn] Lohfarbe *f*; (Sonnen)Bräune *f*; lohfarben,

gelbbraun; gerben; bräunen. [gente f.]

tangent ['tændʒənt|Tangerine [tændʒə'ri:n] Mandarine f.

tangle ['tæŋɡl] Gewirr n; Verwicklung f, Durcheinander n; verwirren, verwickeln.

tank [tæŋk] Tank m (a. mil.); Zisterne f, Wasserbecken n, -behälter m.

tankard ['tæŋkəd] (Bier-) Krug m.

tanner ['tænə] Gerber m.

tantalizing ['tæntəlaiziŋ] quälend, verlockend.

tantrum ['tæntrəm] Wut (-anfall m) f.

tap [tæp] leichtes Klopfen, Zapfen m; (Wasser-, Gas-, Zapf)Hahn m; pl mil. Am. Zapfenstreich m; klopfen, pochen; an-, abzapfen.

tape [teip] schmales Band, Streifen m; sp. Zielband n; (Ton)Band n; ~-measure Bandmaß n.

taper ['teipə]: ~ off spitz zulaufen.

tape| recorder Tonbandgerät n; ~ **recording** (Ton)Bandaufnahme f.

tapestry ['tæpistri] Gobelin m.

tapeworm Bandwurm m.

tar [tɑː] Teer m; teeren.

target ['tɑːɡit] (Schieß-) Scheibe f; mil. Ziel n; fig. Zielscheibe f.

tariff ['tærif] Zolltarif m; Preisliste f (im Hotel).

tarnish ['tɑːniʃ] matt od.

blind machen; anlaufen (Metall).

tart [tɑːt] sauer, herb; fig. scharf; (Obst)Torte f.

tartan ['tɑːtn] Tartan m, Schottentuch n, -muster n.

task [tɑːsk] Aufgabe f, Arbeit f; **take to ~** j-n ins Gebet nehmen **(for** wegen). [Quaste f.]

tassel ['tæsəl] Troddel f,

tast|e [teist] Geschmack m; kosten, probieren; (heraus)schmecken; fig. kennenlernen, erleben; **~eful** geschmackvoll; **~eless** geschmacklos; **~y** schmackhaft; geschmackvoll.

ta-ta ['tæ'tɑː] int. colloq. auf Wiedersehen!

tattoo [tə'tuː] mil. Zapfenstreich m; Tätowierung f; tätowieren.

taught [tɔːt] pret u. pp von teach.

taunt [tɔːnt] Spott m; verhöhnen, -spotten.

tax [tæks] Steuer f, Abgabe f; besteuern; **~ation** Besteuerung f; Steuern pl; **~ collector** Steuereinnehmer m.

taxi| (-cab) ['tæksi(-)] Taxe f, Taxi n, (Auto-) Droschke f; **~-driver** Taxifahrer m; **~ rank** Taxistand m.

tax|payer Steuerzahler m; **~return** Steuererklärung f.

tea [tiː] Tee m.

teach [tiːtʃ] (irr) lehren, unterrichten, j-m et. beibringen; **~er** Lehrer(in).

tea|cup Teetasse f; **~ket-**

tle Tee-, Wasserkessel *m*.

team [ti:m] Team *n*, (Arbeits)Gruppe *f*; Gespann *n*; *sp.* Team *n*, Mannschaft *f*; **~work** Zs.-arbeit *f*, Zs.-spiel *n*, Teamwork *n*.

teapot Teekanne *f*.

tear[1] [tɛə] *(irr)* zerren; (aus-, zer)reißen; Riß *m*.

tear[2] [tiə] Träne *f*.

tearoom Tearoom *m*, Teestube *f*.

tease [ti:z] necken, hänseln; ärgern; quälen.

tea|spoon Teelöffel *m*; **~spoonful** *(ein)* Teelöffel (-voll) *m*.

teat [ti:t] Zitze *f*.

techni|cal ['teknikəl] technisch; Fach...; **~cian** [~'niʃən] Techniker(in); **~que** [~'ni:k] Technik *f*, Verfahren *n*.

tedious ['ti:djəs] langweilig; ermüdend.

teens [ti:nz] *pl* Jugendjahre *pl (von 13–19)*.

teeny ['ti:ni] winzig.

teeth [ti:θ] *pl von* tooth; **~e** [ti:ð] zahnen.

teetotal(l)er [ti:'təutlə] Abstinenzler(in).

telegram ['teligræm] Telegramm *n*.

telegraph ['teligrɑ:f] Telegraf *m*; telegrafieren; **~ic** [~'græfik] telegrafisch; **~y** [ti'legrəfi] Telegrafie *f*.

telephone ['telifəun] Telefon *n*, Fernsprecher *m*; telefonieren; anrufen; **~ booth** Telefonzelle *f*; **~ call** Telefongespräch *n*,

Anruf *m*; **~ directory** Telefonbuch *n*; **~ exchange** Fernsprechamt *n*; **~ kiosk** ['~ ki:ɔsk] Telefonzelle *f*.

tele|printer ['teliprintə] Fernschreiber *m*; **~scope** ['~skəup] Fernrohr *n*; **~typewriter** ['~taip-]Fernschreiber *m*.

televise ['telivaiz] im Fernsehen übertragen.

television [~'teliviʒən] Fernsehen *n*; **on ~** im Fernsehen; **watch ~** fernsehen; **~ set** Fernsehapparat *m*.

tell [tel] *(irr)* sagen; erzählen; erkennen; unterscheiden; sagen, befehlen; **~er** (Bank)Kassierer *m*; **~tale** verräterisch.

temper ['tempə] mäßigen, mildern; Charakter *m*; Laune *f*; Wut *f*; **keep one's ~** sich beherrschen; **lose one's ~** in Wut geraten; **~ament** Temperament *n*; **~ance** Enthaltsamkeit *f*; **~ate** ['~rit] gemäßigt; zurückhaltend; **~ature** ['~pritʃə] Temperatur *f*; Fieber *n*.

tempest ['tempist] Sturm *m*; **~uous** [~'pestjuəs] stürmisch.

temple ['templ] Tempel *m*; *anat.* Schläfe *f*.

tempor|al ['tempərəl] zeitlich; weltlich; **~ary** vorläufig, zeitweilig, vorübergehend; Not..., Behelfs...

tempt [tempt] *j-n* versuchen; verleiten; verlocken; ~ation Versuchung f; ~ing verführerisch.

ten [ten] zehn; Zehn f.

tenacious [ti'neiʃəs] zäh, hartnäckig.

tenant ['tenənt] Pächter m; Mieter m.

tend [tend] sich bewegen (**to** nach, auf ... zu); fig. tendieren, neigen (**to** zu); pflegen; hüten; ~**ency** Tendenz f, Richtung f; Neigung f.

tender ['tendə] zart; weich; empfindlich; zärtlich; (formell) anbieten; ~**loin** Filet n; ~**ness** Zartheit f; Zärtlichkeit f.

tendon ['tendən] Sehne f.

tendril ['tendril] Ranke f.

tenement-house ['tenimənthaus] Mietshaus n.

tennis ['tenis] Tennis (-spiel) n; ~**court** Tennisplatz m.

tense [tens] gr. Tempus n, Zeitform f; (an)gespannt (a. fig.); straff; ~**ion** Spannung f.

tent [tent] Zelt n.

tentacle ['tentəkl] zo. Fangarm m.

tenth [tenθ] zehnte; Zehntel n; ~**ly** zehntens.

tepid ['tepid] lau(warm).

term [tə:m] (bestimmte) Zeit, Dauer f; Amtszeit f; Frist f; Termin m; jur. Sitzungsperiode f; Semester n, Quartal n, Trimester n; (Fach)Ausdruck m, Bezeichnung f; pl: (Ver-

trags- etc.)Bedingungen pl; Beziehungen pl; **be on good od. bad ~s with** gut od. schlecht stehen mit; (be)nennen, bezeichnen.

termina|l ['tə:minl] Endstation f; ~**te** [~eit] begrenzen; (be)enden; ~**tion** Beendigung f; Ende n.

terminus ['tə:minəs] Endstation f.

terrace ['terəs] Terrasse f; ~**d** terrassenförmig (angelegt).

terri|ble ['terəbl] schrecklich; ~**fic** [tə'rifik] schrecklich; colloq. phantastisch; ~**fy** ['terifai] erschrecken.

territor|ial [teri'tɔ:riəl] territorial; Land...; ~**y** ['~təri] Territorium n, (Hoheits-, Staats)Gebiet n.

terror ['terə] Schrecken m, Entsetzen n; Terror m; ~**ize** terrorisieren.

test [test] Probe f; Untersuchung f; Test m; (Eignungs)Prüfung f; prüfen, testen; [Testament n.]

testament ['testəmənt]]

testify ['testifai] bezeugen; (als Zeuge) aussagen.

testimon|ial [testi'məunjəl] (Führungs- etc.)Zeugnis n; ~**y** ['~məni] Zeugenaussage f.

testy ['testi] gereizt.

text [tekst] Text m; Bibelstelle f; ~**book** Lehrbuch n.

textile ['tekstail] Textil..., Gewebe...; pl Textilien pl.

texture ['tekstʃə] Gewebe n; Struktur f, Gefüge n.

than [ðæn,ðən] als.

thank [θæŋk] danken, **(no), ~ you** (nein), danke; *pl* Dank *m*; **~s** to dank; **~s!** vielen Dank!, danke!; **~ful** dankbar; **~less** undankbar; **2sgiving (Day)** *Am.* (Ernte)Dankfest *n*.

that [ðæt, ðət], *pl* **those** [ðəuz] *pron, adj*: das; jene(r,-s), der, die, das, der-, die-, dasjenige; solche(r, -s); *adv colloq.* so; *rel pron* (*pl* that): der, die, das, welche(r, -s); *conj* daß; damit; weil; da, als.

thatch [θætʃ] Dachstroh *n*; Strohdach *n*; mit Stroh decken.

thaw [θɔː] Tauwetter *n*; (auf)tauen, schmelzen.

the [vor Konsonanten ðə, vor Vokalen ði; betont ðiː] der, die, das; *pl* die, desto, um so; **~ ... ~** je ... desto.

theatr|e, *Am.* **~er** [ˈθiətə] Theater *n*; **~rical** [θiˈætrikəl] Theater-. [dir.\

thee [ðiː] *Bibel, poet.* dich; [

theft [θeft] Diebstahl *m*.

their [ðɛə] *pl* ihr(e); **~s** [~z] der, die, das ihr(ig)e.

them [ðem, ðəm] *pl* sie (*acc*); ihnen.

theme [θiːm] Thema *n*.

themselves [ðəmˈselvz] *pl* sie selbst; sich (selbst).

then [ðen] dann; damals; denn; damalig; **by ~** bis dahin, inzwischen.

theolog|ian [θiəˈləudʒiən] Theologe *m*; **~y** [θiˈɔlədʒi] Theologie *f*.

theor|etic(al) [θiəˈretik(əl)] theoretisch; **~y** [ˈ~ri] Theorie *f*; Lehre *f*. [pie *f*.\

therapy [ˈθerəpi] Thera-\

there [ðɛə] da, dort; darin; (da-, dort)hin; *int.* da!, na!; **~ is,** *pl* **~ are** es gibt, es ist, es sind; **~about(s)** da herum; so ungefähr; **~after** danach; **~by** dadurch; **~fore** darum, deshalb; **~upon** darauf(hin); **~with** damit.

thermo|meter [θəˈmɔmitə] Thermometer *n*; **~s (bottle, flask)** [ˈθɔːmɔs] Thermosflasche *f*.

these [ðiːz] *pl* von **this.**

thes|is [ˈθiːsis], *pl* **~es** [ˈ~iːz] These *f*; Dissertation *f*.

they [ðei] *pl* sie; man.

thick [θik] dick; dicht; dick(flüssig); legiert (Suppe); **~en** (sich) verdicken; legieren; (sich) verstärken; (sich) verdichten; dick(er) werden; **~et** [ˈ~it] Dickicht *n*; **~ness** Dicke *f*, Stärke *f*; Dichte *f*.

thief [θiːf], *pl* **thieves** [~vz] Dieb(in). [kel *m*.\

thigh [θai] (Ober)Schen-\

thimble [ˈθimbl] Fingerhut *m*.

thin [θin] dünn; mager; schwach; *fig.* spärlich; verdünnen; (sich) lichten; abnehmen.

thine [ðain] *Bibel, poet.* der, die, das dein(ig)e; dein.

thing [θiŋ] Ding *n*; Sache *f*; Gegenstand *m*.

think [θiŋk] (*irr*) denken (**of** an); sich vorstellen; halten für; meinen, glauben; überlegen, nachdenken (**about**, **over** über); ~ **of** sich erinnern an; sich *et.* (aus)denken; daran denken; halten von; ~ **s.th. over** sich et. überlegen.

third [θɔːd] dritte; Drittel *n*; ~**ly** drittens; ~-**party insurance** Haftpflichtversicherung *f*; ~-**rate** drittklassig.

thirst [θɔːst] Durst *m*; ~**y** durstig; **be** ~**y** Durst haben.

thirt|een(th) [ˈθɔːˈtiːn(θ)] dreizehn(te); ~**ieth** [ˈ~tiiθ] dreißigste; ~**y** dreißig; Dreißig *f*.

this [ðis], *pl* **these** [ðiːz] diese(r, -s) dies, das; der, die, das (da).

thistle [ˈθisl] Distel *f*.

thorn [θɔːn] Dorn *m*; ~**y** dornig, stach(e)lig.

thorough [ˈθʌrə] gründlich; vollkommen; ~**bred** Vollblut(pferd) *n*; Vollblut...; ~**fare** Durchfahrt *f*; Durchgangsstraße *f*.

those [ðəuz] *pl von* **that.**

thou [ðau] *Bibel*, *poet.* du.

though [ðəu] obgleich, obwohl, wenn auch; (je)doch; **as** ~ als ob.

thought [θɔːt] *pret u. pp von* **think**; Gedanke *m*; Denken *n*; Überlegung *f*; ~**ful** nachdenklich; rücksichtsvoll; ~**less** gedan-

kenlos, unüberlegt; rücksichtslos.

thousand [ˈθauzənd] tausend; Tausend *n*; ~**th** [ˈ~tθ] tausendste; Tausendstel *n*.

thrash [θræʃ] verdreschen, -prügeln; (um sich) schlagen; sich hin u. her werfen; *s.* **thresh**; ~**ing** (Tracht *f*) Prügel *pl*.

thread [θred] Faden *m* (a. *fig*.); Zwirn *m*, Garn *n*; *tech.* Gewinde *n*; einfädeln; durchziehen; sich (hindurch)schlängeln; ~**bare** fadenscheinig.

threat [θret] Drohung *f*; ~**en** (be-, an)drohen; ~**ening** drohend; bedrohlich.

three [θriː] drei; Drei *f*; ~**fold** dreifach; ~**pence** [ˈθrepəns] *alte Währung:* Dreipencestück *n*; ~**score** sechzig; ~**stage** dreistufig, Dreistufen...

thresh [θreʃ] dreschen; ~**er** Drescher *m*; Dreschmaschine *f*; ~**ing** Dreschen *n*; ~**ing-machine** Dreschmaschine *f*.

threshold [ˈθreʃhəuld] Schwelle *f*. (**throw.**)

threw [θruː] *pret von*}

thrice [θrais] dreimal.

thrifty [ˈθrifti] sparsam.

thrill [θril] erregen, packen; (er)beben, erschauern; Schauer *m*; (Nerven-)Kitzel *m*, Sensation *f*; *colloq.* Reißer *m*, Thriller *m*; ~**ing** spannend.

thrive [θraiv] (*irr*) gedei-

tie

hen; *fig.* blühen; **~n**
['θrivn] *pp von* **thrive.**
throat [θrəut] Kehle *f*,
Gurgel *f*, Schlund *m*; Hals
m.
throb [θrɔb] pochen, klopfen, hämmern (*Herz etc.*).
throne [θrəun] Thron *m*.
throng [θrɔŋ] Gedränge *n*;
(Menschen)Menge *f*; *sich*
drängen (in).
throstle ['θrɔsl] Drossel *f.*
throttle ['θrɔtl] (ab-, er-)
drosseln; **~(-valve)** *tech.*
Drosselklappe *f.*
through [θru:] durch;
durchgehend, Durchgangs-
...; **~ carriage** Kurswagen *m*; **~out** überall u. in;
durch u. durch, ganz u.
gar; **~ train** durchgehen-
der Zug. [**thrive.**\
throve [θrəuv] *pret von*\
throw [θrəu] Wurf *m*; (*irr*)
(ab)werfen; schleudern;
würfeln; **~ up** hochwerfen;
(sich) erbrechen; **~n** *pp von*
throw. [**through.**\
thru [θru:] *Am. für*\
thrum [θrʌm] klimpern
(auf).
thrush [θrʌʃ] Drossel *f.*
thrust [θrʌst] Stoß *m*;
tech.: Druck *m*; Schub *m*;
(*irr*) stoßen.
thud [θʌd] dumpf (auf-)
schlagen; dumpfer (Auf-)
Schlag.
thumb [θʌm] Daumen *m*;
Buch etc. abgreifen *od.*
durchblättern; **~ a lift** per
Anhalter fahren; **~tack**
Am. Reißzwecke *f.*

thump [θʌmp] (dumpfer)
Schlag; schlagen (häm-
mern, pochen) gegen *od.*
auf; (auf)schlagen; pochen
(*Herz*).
thunder ['θʌndə] Donner
m; donnern; **~storm** Gewitter *n*; **~struck** wie vom
Donner gerührt.
Thursday ['θə:zdi] Don-
nerstag *m.*
thus [ðʌs] so; also, somit.
thwart [θwɔ:t] durchkreu-
zen.
thy [ðai] *Bibel, poet.* dein(e).
tick [tik] *zo.* Zecke *f*; Inlett *n*; Matratzenbezug *m*;
Ticken *n*; (*Vermerk*)Häk-
chen *n*; ticken; anhaken; **~
off** abhaken.
ticket ['tikit] (Eintritts-,
Theater- *etc.*)Karte *f*;
Fahrkarte *f*, -schein *m*;
Flugkarte *f*; (Preis- *etc.*)
Schildchen *n*, Etikett *n*;
etikettieren, *Ware* aus-
zeichnen; **(automatic)
machine** Fahrkartenau-
tomat *m*; **~ office** *Am.*
Fahrkartenschalter *m.*
tickle ['tikl] kitzeln; **~ish**
kitz(e)lig (*a. fig.*).
tid|al wave ['taidl] Flut-
welle *f*; **~e** [taid] Gezeiten *pl*, Ebbe *f u.* Flut *f*;
fig. Strom *m*, Strömung *f.*
tidy ['taidi] ordentlich, sauber; **~ up** aufräumen.
tie [tai] Band *n* (*a. fig.*);
Krawatte *f*, Schlips *m*;
rail. Am. Schwelle *f*; *sp.*
Unentschieden *n*; *fig.* Fessel *f*, Last *f*; (an-, fest)bin-

den; **~ up** (an-, zs.-, zu-) binden.

tier [tiə] Reihe f, Lage f; *thea.* (Sitz)Reihe f.

tiger ['taigə] Tiger m.

tight [tait] dicht; fest; eng; knapp (sitzend); straff; *fig.* zs.-gepreßt; eng machen; (sich) straffen; fester werden; **~en (up)** (sich) zs.-ziehen; fest-, anziehen; **~rope** (Draht)Seil n (*der Artisten*); **~s** pl Trikot n, Strumpfhose f.

tigress ['taigris] Tigerin f.

tile [tail] (Dach)Ziegel m; Kachel f, Fliese f; (mit Ziegeln) decken; kacheln, fliesen. [erst (als).|

till¹ [til] bis; bis zu; **not ~.|**

till² Ladenkasse f.

till³ Boden bestellen, bebauen. [kippen.|

tilt [tilt] Plane f; (um-)

timber ['timbə] (Bau-, Nutz)Holz n; Balken m; Baumbestand m, Bäume pl.

time [taim] Zeit f; Uhrzeit f; Frist f; *mus.* Takt m; Mal n; *pl* mal, ...mal; **~ is up** die Zeit ist um *od.* abgelaufen; **for the ~ being** vorläufig; **have a good ~** sich gut unterhalten *od.* amüsieren; **what's the ~?**, **what is it?** wieviel Uhr ist es?, wie spät ist es?; **~ and again** immer wieder; **all the ~** ständig, immer; **at a ~** zugleich, zusammen; **at any ~**, **at all ~s** jederzeit; **at the**

same ~ gleichzeitig, zur selben Zeit; **in ~** rechtzeitig; **in no ~** im Nu, im Handumdrehen; **on ~** pünktlich; *vb:* messen, (ab-) stoppen; zeitlich abstimmen; den richtigen Zeitpunkt wählen *od.* bestimmen für; **~ly** rechtzeitig; **~table** Fahr-, Flugplan m; Stundenplan m.

tim|id ['timid] **~orous** ['~ərəs] furchtsam; schüchtern.

tin [tin] Zinn n; (Blech-, Konserven)Büchse f, (-) Dose f; verzinnen; (in Büchsen) einmachen, eindosen; **~foil** Aluminiumfolie f, Stanniol(papier) n.

tinge [tindʒ] Färbung f; *fig.* Anflug m, Spur f; (leicht) färben.

tingle ['tiŋgl] prickeln.

tinkle ['tiŋkl] hell (er)klingen; klirren; klingeln mit.

tin|ned Büchsen..., Dosen...; **~opener** Büchsen-, Dosenöffner m.

tint [tint] (Farb)Ton m, Schattierung f; (leicht) färben.

tiny ['taini] winzig.

tip [tip] Spitze f; Mundstück n; Trinkgeld n; Tip m, Wink m; (um)kippen; *j-m* ein Trinkgeld geben; **~ (off)** *j-m* e-n Wink geben; **~ped** mit Mundstück (*Zigarette*).

tipsy ['tipsi] *colloq.* beschwipst, angeheitert.

tiptoe ['tiptəu] auf Zehenspitzen gehen; **on ~** auf Zehenspitzen.

tire¹ ['taiə] *s*. **tyre**.

tire² ermüden; müde werden; **~d** ermüdet; erschöpft; *fig.* überdrüssig (**of** *gen*); **~some** ermüdend; lästig.

tissue ['tiʃu:] Gewebe *n*; **~-paper** Seidenpapier *n*.

tit¹ [tit] Meise *f*.

tit²: **~ for tat** wie du mir, so ich dir. [sen *m*.]

titbit ['titbit] Leckerbis-]

titillate ['titileit] kitzeln.

title ['taitl] (*Buch*)Titel *m*; (Adels-, Ehren-, Amts-*etc.*)Titel *m*; Überschrift *f*; (*Rechts*)Anspruch *m*; **~d** betitelt; ad(e)lig.

titmouse ['titmaus] Meise *f*.

to [tu:, tu, tə] *prp* zu, an, auf, für, gegen, in, mit, nach, vor, (um) zu; bis, (bis) zu, (bis) an; *zeitlich*: bis, bis zu, auf; vor; *adv* zu, geschlossen; **pull ~ Tür** zuziehen; **come ~** (wieder) zu sich kommen; **~ and fro** hin und her, auf und ab.

toad [təud] Kröte *f*.

toast [təust] Toast *m*, geröstetes Brot; Trinkspruch *m*; toasten, rösten; *fig.* trinken auf.

tobacco [tə'bækəu] Tabak *m*; **~nist** [-ʃɔnist] Tabak(waren)händler *m*.

toboggan [tə'bɔgən] Toboggan *m*; Rodelschlitten *m*; rodeln.

today [tə'dei] heute.

toddle ['tɔdl] unsicher gehen, watscheln.

toe [təu] Zehe *f*; Spitze *f*.

toffee ['tɔfi], **~y** ['tɔfi] Sahnebonbon *m*, *n*, Toffee *n*.

together [tə'geðə] zusammen; gleichzeitig; *Tage etc.* hintereinander.

toil [tɔil] Mühe *f*, Plackerei *f*; sich plagen.

toilet [tɔilit] Toilette *f*; **~-paper** Toilettenpapier *n*.

toils [tɔilz] *pl fig.* Schlingen *pl*, Netz *n*.

token ['təukən] Zeichen *n*; Andenken *n*.

told [təuld] *pret u. pp* von **tell**.

tolera|ble ['tɔlərəbl] erträglich; leidlich; **~nce** Toleranz *f*; **~nt** tolerant (**of** *gegen*); **~te** ['..eit] dulden; ertragen; **~tion** Duldung *f*.

toll¹ [təul] schlagen, läuten.

toll² Straßenbenutzungsgebühr *f*, Maut *f*; *fig.* Tribut *m*, Todesopfer *pl*; **~bar**, **~gate** Schlagbaum *m*.

tomato [tə'mɑ:təu, *Am.* tə'meitəu], *pl* **~es** Tomate *f*.

tomb [tu:m] Grab(mal) *n*; **~stone** Grabstein *m*.

tomcat ['tɔm'kæt] Kater *m*.

tomorrow [tə'mɔrəu] morgen; **the day after ~** übermorgen. [*wicht*).]

ton [tʌn] Tonne *f* (*Ge-*]

tone [təun] Ton *m*, Klang *m*, Laut *m*.

tongs [tɔŋz] *pl* **a pair of ~**(*-e*-) Zange *f*.

tongue [tʌŋ] Zunge *f*; Sprache *f*.

tonic ['tɔnik] Tonikum *n*.

tonight [tə'nait] heute abend; heute nacht.

tonnage ['tʌnidʒ] Tonnengehalt *m*.

tonsil ['tɔnsl] *anat.* Mandel *f*; **~itis** [~si'laitis] Mandelentzündung *f*.

too [tu:] zu, allzu; *nachgestellt:* auch, noch dazu; ebenfalls.

took [tuk] *pret von* **take.**

tool [tu:l] Werkzeug *n*, Gerät *n*.

tooth [tu:θ], *pl* **teeth** [ti:θ] Zahn *m*; **~ache** Zahnschmerzen *pl*; **~brush** Zahnbürste *f*; **~less** zahnlos; **~paste** Zahnpasta *f*, **~creme** *f*, **~pick** Zahnstocher *m*.

top [tɔp] Kreisel *m*; oberstes Ende; Oberteil *n*, **~site** *f*; Spitze *f* (*a. fig.*); Gipfel *m* (*a. fig.*); Wipfel *m*; Kopf(ende *n*) *m; mot.* Verdeck *n*; Stulpe *f* (*am Stiefel etc.*); **at the ~ of** oben an; **on** (**the**) **~ of** oben auf; *adj* oberst; höchst, Höchst..., Spitzen...; **~ secret** streng geheim; *vb* bedecken; überragen; an der Spitze stehen; **~ up** (auf-, nach)füllen.

topic ['tɔpik] Thema *n*.

topple ['tɔpl]: **~** (**down, over** *um*)kippen.

topsy-turvy ['tɔpsi'tə:vi] auf den Kopf (gestellt); drunter und drüber.

torch [tɔ:tʃ] Fackel *f*; Taschenlampe *f*.

tore [tɔ:] *pret von* **tear**¹.

torment ['tɔ:ment] Qual *f*; [~'ment] quälen.

torn [tɔ:n] *pp von* **tear**¹.

tornado [tɔ:'neidəu], *pl* **~es** Wirbelsturm *m*.

torrent ['tɔrənt] Sturzbach *m*; reißender Strom; *fig.* Strom, Schwall *m*.

tortoise ['tɔ:təs] (Land-) Schildkröte *f*.

torture ['tɔ:tʃə] Folter(ung) *f*; foltern.

toss [tɔs] (Hoch)Werfen *n*, Wurf *m*; Zurückwerfen *n* (*Kopf*); werfen, schleudern; **~ about** (sich) hinu. herwerfen; **~ up** hochwerfen.

total ['təutl] ganz, gesamt, Gesamt...; total; Gesamtbetrag *m*; sich belaufen auf; **~itarian** [~tæli'tɛəriən] totalitär.

totter ['tɔtə] (sch)wanken, torkeln.

touch [tʌtʃ] Berührung *f*; Verbindung *f*, Kontakt *m*; leichter Anfall; Anflug *m*; (sich) berühren; anrühren, anfassen; *fig.* rühren; **~down** *aer.* landen; **~down** *aer.* Landung *f*; **~ing** rührend; **~y** empfindlich; heikel.

tough [tʌf] zäh (*a. fig.*); grob, brutal.

tour [tuə] (Rund)Reise *f*, Tour(nee) *f*; (be)reisen.

tourist ['tuərist] Tourist (-in) Touristen..., Fremden(verkehrs)...; ~ **agency**, ~ **bureau**, ~ **office** Reisebüro n; Verkehrsverein m.

tournament ['tuənəmənt] Turnier n.

tousle ['tauzl] (zer)zausen.

tow [təu] Schleppen n; **give s.o. a** ~ j-n abschleppen; **have od. take in** ~ ins Schlepptau nehmen; vb: (ab)schleppen.

towards(s) [tə'wɔ:d(z)] gegen; auf ... zu, nach ... zu; (als Beitrag) zu.

towel ['tauəl] Handtuch n.

tower ['tauə] Turm m; (hoch)ragen, sich erheben.

town [taun] Stadt f; Stadt...; ~ **council** Stadtrat m (Versammlung); ~ **council(l)or** Stadtrat m (Person); ~ **hall** Rathaus n.

tow-rope Schlepptau n; Abschleppseil n.

toy [tɔi] Spielzeug n; pl Spielsachen pl, -waren pl; Spielzeug..., Kinder...; spielen.

trace [treis] Spur f; nachspüren; verfolgen.

track [træk] Spur f, Fährte f; rail. Gleis n; sp. (Renn-, Aschen)Bahn f; Pfad m; nachspüren, verfolgen; ~ **down**, ~ **out** aufspüren; ~**and-field events** pl Leichtathletik f; ~ **events** pl Laufdisziplinen pl.

tract|ion-engine ['træk-ʃənendʒin] Zugmaschine f; ~**or** Traktor m.

trade [treid] Handel m;

Gewerbe n, Handwerk n; Handel treiben, handeln (in mit); ~**mark** Warenzeichen n; ~**r** Händler m, Kaufmann m; ~**(s) union** Gewerkschaft f; ~**unionist** Gewerkschaftler(in).

tradition [trə'diʃən] Tradition f; ~**al** traditionell.

traffic ['træfik] Verkehr m; Handel m; handeln (in mit); ~ **island** Verkehrsinsel f; ~ **jam** Verkehrsstauung f; ~ **light(s** pl) Verkehrsampel f; ~ **regulations** pl Verkehrsvorschriften pl; ~ **sign** Verkehrszeichen n; ~ **warden** mot. appr. Politesse f.

trag|edy ['trædʒidi] Tragödie f; ~**ic(al)** tragisch.

trail [treil] Spur f; Pfad m, Weg m; fig. Streifen m; hinter sich herziehen; verfolgen; schleifen; ~**er** mot.: Anhänger m; Wohnwagen m.

train [trein] (Eisenbahn-) Zug m; Reihe f, Kette f; Schleppe f (am Kleid); schulen; abrichten; ausbilden; trainieren; ~**er** Ausbilder m; Trainer m; ~**ing** Ausbildung f; Training n. [Zug m.]

trait [treit] (Charakter-)]

traitor ['treitə] Verräter m.

tram(-car) [træm(-)] Straßenbahn(wagen m) f.

tramp [træmp] Getrampel n; Wanderung f; Landstreicher m; trampeln; (durch)wandern; ~**le** (herum-, zer)trampeln.

tranquil ['træŋkwil] ruhig; ~(l)ity Ruhe f; ~(l)ize beruhigen; ~(l)izer Beruhigungsmittel n.

transact [træn'zækt] erledigen, abwickeln; ~ion Durchführung f; Geschäft n, Transaktion f.

trans|alpine ['trænz'ælpain] transalpin(isch); ~atlantic transatlantisch.

transcend [træn'send] fig.: überschreiten, -steigen; übertreffen.

transcribe [træns'kraib] abschreiben; Kurzschrift übertragen.

transcript ['trænskript] Abschrift f; ~ion Abschrift f; Umschrift f.

transfer [træns'fə:] versetzen; verlegen; übertragen; abtreten; verlegt od. versetzt werden; umsteigen; ['~] Übertragung f; Versetzung f; Verlegung f; Umsteigefahrschein m; ~able [~'fə:rəbl] übertragbar.

transform [træns'fɔ:m] umformen, um-, verwandeln; ~ation Umformung f, Um-, Verwandlung f.

transfus|e [træns'fju:z] Blut übertragen; ~ion [~3ən] (Blut)Transfusion f.

transgress [træns'gres] überschreiten; übertreten, verletzen; ~ion Überschreitung f; Übertretung f; Vergehen n; ~or Missetäter(in).

transient ['trænziənt] ver-

gänglich, flüchtig; Am. Durchreisende m, f.

transistor [træn'sistə] Transistor m.

transit ['trænsit] Durchgang(sverkehr) m; econ. Transport m; ~ion [~'si-ʒən] Übergang m.

transitive ['trænsitiv] gr. transitiv.

translat|e[træns'leit]übersetzen; ~ion Übersetzung f; ~or Übersetzer(in).

translucent [trænz'lu:snt] lichtdurchlässig.

transmi|ssion [trænz'miʃən] Übermittlung f; Übertragung f; Radio etc.: Sendung f; ~t übermitteln; übertragen; senden; ~tter Sendegerät n; Sender m.

transparent [træns'pɛərənt] durchsichtig.

transpire [træns'paiə] schwitzen; fig. durchsickern.

transplant [træns'plɑ:nt] um-, verpflanzen; ~(ation) Verpflanzung f.

transport [træns'pɔ:t] befördern, transportieren; ['~] Beförderung f, Transport m; Beförderungsmittel n; ~ation Beförderung f, Transport m.

trap [træp] (in e-r Falle) fangen; Falle f (a. fig.); **set a ~ for** j-m e-e Falle stellen; ~door Falltür f.

trapeze [trə'pi:z] Trapez n.

trapper ['træpə] Trapper m, Fallensteller m, Pelztierjäger m.

trash [træʃ] *bsd. Am.* Abfall *m*; *fig.* Plunder *m.*

travel ['trævl] (be)reisen; *das* Reisen; *pl* Reisen *pl*; **~ agency** Reisebüro *n*; **~(l)er** Reisende *m*, *f*; **~(l)er's cheque** (*Am.* **check**) Reisescheck *m*; **~(l)ing bag** Reisetasche *f.*

traverse ['trævə(:)s] durch-, überqueren.

trawl [trɔ:l] (Grund-) Schleppnetz *n*; mit dem Schleppnetz fischen; **~er** Trawler *m* [lage *f.*\]

tray [trei] Tablett *n*; Ab-

treacherous ['tretʃərəs] verräterisch, treulos, trügerisch; **~y** Verrat *m.*

treacle ['tri:kl] Sirup *m.*

tread [tred] (*irr*) treten; schreiten; Tritt *m*, Schritt *m*; **~le** Pedal *n*; **~mill** Tretmühle *f* (*a. fig.*).

treason ['tri:zn] Verrat *m.*

treasure ['treʒə] Schatz *m* (*a. fig.*); (hoch)schätzen; **~ up** sammeln; **~r** Schatzmeister *m.*

treasury ['treʒəri] Schatzkammer *f*; Staatsschatz *m*; Staatskasse *f*; **2 Department** *Am.* Finanzministerium *n.*

treat [tri:t] behandeln; betrachten; bewirten (**to** mit); **~ s.o. to s.th.** j-m et. spendieren; **~ of** handeln von; *sub*: Vergnügen *n*, (Hoch)Genuß *m*; **~ise** ['~iz] Abhandlung *f*; **~ment** Behandlung *f*; **~y** Vertrag *m.*

treble ['trebl] dreifach; (sich) verdreifachen.

tree [tri:] Baum *m.*

trefoil ['trefɔil] Klee *m.*

trellis ['trelis] *agr.* Spalier *n*; am Spalier ziehen.

tremble ['trembl] zittern (**with** vor).

tremendous [tri'mendəs] gewaltig; enorm.

trem|or ['tremə] Zittern *n*; Beben *n*; **~ulous** ['~juləs] zitternd, bebend.

trench [trentʃ] (Schützen-) Graben *m.*

trend [trend] Richtung *f*; *fig.* Tendenz *f*, Trend *m.*

trespass ['trespəs] Übertretung *f*, Vergehen *n*; unbefugt eindringen (**on, upon** in); **~er** Unbefugte *m*, *f.*

tress [tres] Haarlocke *f*, -flechte *f.*

trestle ['tresl] Gestell *n*, Bock *m.*

trial ['traiəl] Versuch *m*, Probe *f*, Prüfung *f* (*a. fig.*); *jur.* Verhandlung *f*, Prozeß *m*; **on ~** auf Probe.

triang|le ['traiæŋgl] Dreieck *n*; **~ular** ['~æŋgjulə] dreieckig.

tribe [traib] (Volks)Stamm *m.*

tribun|al [trai'bju:nl] Gericht(shof) *n*) *m*; **~e** ['tribju:n] Tribun *m*; Tribüne *f.*

tribut|ary ['tribjutəri] Nebenfluß *m*; **~e** ['~ju:t] Tribut *m* (*a. fig.*).

trick [trik] betrügen; Kniff *m*, List *f*, Trick *m*; Kunststück n; Streich m; **play a ~ on** s.o. j-m e-n Streich spielen.

trickle ['trikl] tröpfeln; rieseln; sickern.

tricycle ['traisikl]Dreirad n.

trident ['traidənt] Dreizack m.

trifl|e ['traifl] Kleinigkeit f; spielen; spaßen; **~ing** geringfügig, unbedeutend.

trigger ['trigə] Abzug m (e-r *Feuerwaffe*).

trill [tril] Triller m; trillern.

trillion ['triljən] Trillion f; *Am.* Billion f.

trim [trim] schmuck, gepflegt; zurechtmachen; (~ **up** heraus)putzen, schmücken; *Hut etc.* besetzen; stutzen; (be)schneiden; trimmen; **~mings** pl Besatz m; Zutaten pl, Beilagen pl (e-r *Speise*).

Trinity ['triniti] *eccl.* Dreieinigkeit f.

trinket ['triŋkit] (wertlose) Schmuckstück.

trip [trip] (kurze) Reise, Fahrt f; Ausflug m, (Spritz)Tour f; Stolpern n; *fig.* Fehler m; trippeln; stolpern.

tripe [traip] Kaldaunen pl.

triple ['tripl] dreifach; **~ts** ['~its] pl Drillinge pl.

tripod ['traipɔd] Dreifuß m; *phot.* Stativ n.

triumph ['traiəmf] Triumph m; triumphieren; **~al** ['~amfəl] Triumph...; **~ant** triumphierend.

trivial ['triviəl] unbedeu-tend; trivial, alltäglich.

trod [trɔd] pret, **~den** pp von **tread**.

troll(e)y ['trɔli] Karren m; Tee-, Servierwagen m.

trombone [trɔm'boun]Posaune f.

troop [tru:p] Schar f, Haufe(n) m; pl *mil.* Truppe(n pl) f; sich scharen od. sammeln; (*herein- etc.*)strömen.

trophy ['troufi] Trophäe f.

tropic ['trɔpik] *geogr.* Wendekreis m; pl Tropen pl; **~al** tropisch.

trot [trɔt] Trott m, Trab m; traben (lassen); trotten.

trouble ['trʌbl] (sich) beunruhigen; j-m Sorgen machen; j-n bitten (**for** um); (sich) bemühen; j-m Mühe machen; plagen; Mühe f, Plage f; Störung f (a. *tech.*); Unannehmlichkeiten (pl); Schwierigkeit f; Not f, Sorge(n pl) f; Leiden n, Beschwerden pl; *pol.* Unruhe f; **ask** od. **look for ~** das Schicksal herausfordern; **take the ~** sich die Mühe machen; **what's the ~?** was ist los?; **~some** lästig.

trough [trɔf] Trog m.

trousers ['trauzəz] pl (a. **a pair of ~**) (e-e) (lange) Hose, Hosen pl.

trousseau ['tru:səu] Aussteuer f.

trout [traut], pl **~(s)** Forelle f.

truant ['tru(:)ənt] Schulschwänzer(in); **(play)**

(bsd. die Schule) schwän- zen.   [stand m.]

truce [truːs] Waffenstill-}

truck [trʌk] (offener) Gü- terwagen; Last(kraft)wa- gen m; *Am.* Gemüse m.

trudge [trʌdʒ] Last (da- hin)schleppen, stapfen.

true [truː] wahr; echt, wirklich; genau; treu; *(it is)* ~ gewiß, freilich, zwar; **come** ~ sich erfüllen.

truly ['truːli] wirklich; auf- richtig; **yours** ~ Hochach- tungsvoll *(Briefschluß).*

trump [trʌmp] Trumpf m; übertrumpfen; ~ **up** er- dichten.

trumpet ['trʌmpit] Trom- pete f; trompeten; **~er** Trompeter m.

truncheon ['trʌntʃən] (Po- lizei)Knüppel m.

trunk [trʌŋk] (Baum-) Stamm m; Rumpf m; Rüs- sel m; (Schrank)Koffer m; *Am. mot.* Kofferraum m; pl Bade-, Turnhose(n pl) f; **~call** Ferngespräch n; **~- exchange** Fernamt n; **~- line** rail. Hauptstrecke f; *teleph.* Fernleitung f.

trust [trʌst] Vertrauen n, Glaube m; *jur.* Treuhand (-vermögen n) f; *econ.* Trust m, Konzern m; ver- trauen; hoffen; (ver)trauen, sich verlassen auf; **~ee** [~- 'tiː] Sach-, Verwalter m; Treuhänder m; **~ful, ~ing** vertrauensvoll; **~worthy** vertrauenswürdig

truth [truːθ] *pl* **~s** [~ðz]

Wahrheit f; **~ful** wahr (-heitsliebend).

try [trai] versuchen, pro- bieren; *vor* Gericht stel- len; ~ **on** anprobieren; ~ **out** ausprobieren; *sub:* Versuch m; **have a** ~ e-n Versuch machen; **~ing** an- strengend.

tub [tʌb] Faß n; Zuber m, Kübel m; Badewanne f.

tube ['tjuːb] Rohr n; *(Am. bsd.* Radio)Röhre f; Tube f; (Gummi)Schlauch m; Tunnel m; *die (Londoner)* Untergrundbahn.

tuberculosis [tjuˈbəːkjuˈ- 'ləusis] Tuberkulose f.

tuck [tʌk] stecken; ~ **in**, ~ **up** (warm) zudecken, *ins Bett* packen; ~ **up** hoch- schürzen, aufkrempeln.

Tuesday ['tjuːzdi] Diens- tag m.

tuft [tʌft] Büschel n, Busch m; *(Haar)*Schopf m.

tug [tʌg] Zug m, Ruck m; *mar.* Schlepper m; ziehen, zerren; *mar.* schleppen.

tuition [tjuˈ(ː)ʃən] Unter- richt m; Schulgeld n.

tulip ['tjuːlip] Tulpe f.

tumble ['tʌmbl] fallen, stürzen, purzeln, taumeln; sich wälzen; ~ r Becher m.

tummy ['tʌmi] *colloq.:* Bäuchlein n; Magen m.

tumo(u)r ['tjuːmə] Tumor m.

tumult ['tjuːmʌlt] Tumult m; **~uous** [~'mʌltjuəs] stürmisch.

tun [tʌn] Tonne f, Faß n.

tuna ['tu:nə], *pl* ~(s) Thunfisch *m*.

tune [tju:n] Melodie *f*, Weise *f*; **out of** ~ verstimmt; *vb*: stimmen; ~ **in** (das Radio) einstellen (**to** auf); ~ **up** die Instrumente stimmen.

tunnel ['tʌnl] Tunnel *m*.

turbine ['tə:bin] Turbine *f*.

turbot ['tə:bət] Steinbutt *m*.

turbulent ['tə:bjulənt] ungestüm, stürmisch, turbulent.

turf [tə:f] Rasen *m*; Torf *m*; **the** ~ (Pferde)Rennbahn *f*; (Pferde)Rennsport *m*; **mit** Rasen bedecken.

Turk [tə:k] Türk|e *m*, *-in f*.

turkey ['tə:ki] Truthahn *m*, *-henne f*, Pute(*r m*) *f*.

Turkish ['tə:kiʃ] türkisch; Türkisch *n*.

turmoil ['tə:mɔil] Aufruhr *m*; Durcheinander *n*.

turn [tə:n] (Um)Drehung *f*; Reihe(nfolge) *f*; Biegung *f*, Kurve *f*; Wende *f*; Dienst *m*, Gefallen *m*; Zweck *m*; *colloq*. Schrecken *m*; **it is my** ~ ich bin an der Reihe; **by** ~**s** abwechselnd; **take** ~**s** sich abwechseln (**at** an, bei); *vb*: (sich)(um-,herum)drehen; wenden; zukehren, -wenden; drechseln; lenken, richten; (sich) verwandeln; (sich) verfärben (*Laub*); sich (ab-, hin-, zu-)wenden; ab-, einbiegen; e-e Biegung machen (*Straße*); grau *etc*. werden; ~

away (sich) abwenden; abweisen; ~ **back** zurückkehren; ~ **down** *Kragen* umschlagen; *Decke* zurückschlagen; *Gas* kleiner stellen; *Radio* leiser stellen; (sich) ~ **off** *Wasser*, *Gas* abdrehen; *Licht*, *Radio etc*. ausschalten, -machen; abbiegen; ~ **on** *Gas*, *Wasser etc*. aufdrehen; *Gerät* anstellen; *Licht*, *Radio* anmachen, einschalten; ~ **out** hinauswerfen; abdrehen, ausschalten, -machen; *gut etc*. ausfallen *od*. ausgehen; sich herausstellen; ~ **over** *Ware* umsetzen; (sich) umdrehen; umwerfen; übergeben (**to** *dat*); ~ **round** (sich) (herum)drehen; ~ **to** nach *rechts etc*. abbiegen; sich zuwenden; sich an *j-n* wenden; ~ **up** nach oben drehen *od*. biegen, *Kragen* hochschlagen; *Gas etc*. aufdrehen; *Radio etc*. lauter stellen; *fig*. auftauchen; ~**coat** *pol*. Überläufer(in).

turning Querstraße *f*, Abzweigung *f*; ~**point** *fig*. Wendepunkt *m*.

turnip ['tə:nip] (*bsd.* Weiße) Rübe.

turn|**out** Gesamtproduktion *f*; ~**over** *econ*. Umsatz *m*; ~**pike** *Am*. gebührenpflichtige Schnellstraße; ~**stile** Drehkreuz *n*; ~**up** *Brit*. Hosenaufschlag *m*.

turret ['tʌrit] Türmchen *n*.

turtle ['tə:tl] (See)Schildkröte f; ~dove Turteltaube f. [Hauer m.]

tusk [tʌsk] Stoßzahn m;

tutor ['tju:tə] Privat-, Hauslehrer m, Erzieher m; univ. Tutor m; ~ial [~'to:riəl] univ. Tutorenkurs m.

TV ['ti:'vi:] Fernsehen f; Fernsehapparat m.

twang [twæŋ] Schwirren n; näselnde Aussprache; Saiten zupfen, klimpern auf; schwirren; näseln.

tweet [twi:t] zwitschern.

tweezers ['twi:zəz] pl (a. a pair of ~) (e-e) Pinzette.

twelfth [twelfθ] zwölfte.

twelve [twelv] zwölf; Zwölf f.

twentieth ['twentiiθ] zwanzigste; ~y zwanzig; Zwanzig f.

twice [twais] zweimal.

twiddle ['twidl] (herum-) drehen; spielen (mit).

twig [twig] (dünner) Zweig.

twilight ['twailait] Zwielicht n; Dämmerung f.

twin [twin] Zwillings...; Doppel...; pl Zwillinge pl.

twine [twain] Schnur f; (sich) schlingen od. winden.

twin-engined zweimotorig.

twinkle ['twiŋkl] funkeln, blitzen; huschen; zwinkern; Blitzen n; (Augen-) Zwinkern n, Blinzeln n.

twirl [twɔ:l] Wirbel m; wirbeln.

twist [twist] Drehung f; Windung f; Verdrehung f;

(Gesichts)Verzerrung f; Garn n, Twist m; (sich) drehen od. winden; wikkeln; verdrehen; (sich) verzerren od. -ziehen.

twitch [twitʃ] zupfen (an); zucken (mit).

twitter ['twitə] zwitschern.

two [tu:] Zwei f; put ~ and ~ together es sich zs.-reimen; adj zwei; ... in ~ entzwei...; ~fold zweifach; ~pence ['tʌpəns] zwei Pence pl; ~piece zweiteilig; ~stroke mot. Zweitakt...; ~way adapter Doppelstecker m; ~way traffic Gegenverkehr m.

type [taip] Typ m; Vorbild n, Muster n; Art f; print. Type f, Buchstabe m; ~ (-write) [irr write]) mit der Maschine schreiben; maschineschreiben; ~writer Schreibmaschine f.

typhoid (fever) ['taifɔid] Typhus m.

typhoon [tai'fu:n] Taifun m. [ber n.]

typhus ['taifəs] Fleckfie-

typical ['tipikl] typisch.

typist ['taipist] Stenotypist (-in).

tyrannical [ti'rænikəl] tyrannisch; ~ize ['tirənaiz] tyrannisieren; ~y Tyrannei f. [(-in).]

tyrant ['taiərənt] Tyrann f

tyre ['taiə] (Rad-, Auto-) Reifen m.

Tyrolean [ti'rəuliən], ~se [tirə'li:z] Tiroler(in); Tiroler...

U

udder ['ʌdə] Euter n.

ugly ['ʌgli] häßlich; schlimm.

ulcer ['ʌlsə] Geschwür n.

ultimate ['ʌltimit] äußerst, letzt; endgültig; End...

ultimat|um [ʌltiˈmeitəm], pl a. ⁓a [⁓ə] Ultimatum n.

umbrella [ʌmˈbrelə] Regenschirm m.

umpire ['ʌmpaiə] Schiedsrichter m.

un- [ʌn-] un..., Un..., nicht..., Nicht...; ent..., auf..., los...

un|abashed unverfroren; unerschrocken; ⁓abated unvermindert; ⁓able unfähig, außerstande; ⁓acceptable unannehmbar; ⁓accountable unerklärlich, seltsam; ⁓accustomed ungewohnt; nicht gewöhnt (to an); ⁓acquainted: ⁓ with unerfahren in, nicht vertraut mit; ⁓affected ungerührt; ungekünstelt, natürlich.

unanimous [juˈnæniməs] einmütig, -stimmig.

un|approachable unnahbar; ⁓ashamed schamlos, ⁓asked ungebeten; ⁓assisted ohne Hilfe od. Unterstützung; ⁓assuming anspruchslos, bescheiden; ⁓authorized unberechtigt; unbefugt; ⁓avoidable unvermeidlich.

⁓unaware ['ʌnəˈwɛə]: be ⁓

of et. nicht bemerken; ⁓s ['⁓z] unversehens; versehentlich.

un|balanced unausgeglichen; gestört (Geist); ⁓bar aufriegeln; ⁓bearable unerträglich; ⁓becoming unkleidsam; unschicklich.

unbeliev|able unglaublich; ⁓ing ungläubig.

un|bending unbeugsam; ⁓bias(s)ed unbefangen, unparteiisch; ⁓bidden unaufgefordert; ungebeten; ⁓born (noch) ungeboren; ⁓bounded fig. grenzenlos; ⁓broken ungebrochen; unversehrt, ganz; ununterbrochen; ⁓button aufknöpfen; ⁓called-for unerwünscht; unpassend; ⁓canny [ˈ⁓kæni] unheimlich; ⁓cared-for vernachlässigt; ⁓ceasing unaufhörlich; ⁓certain unsicher, ungewiß; unzuverlässig; unbeständig; ⁓challenged unangefochten.

unchange|able unveränderlich; ⁓d unverändert.

unchecked ungehindert.

uncivil unhöflich; ⁓ized unzivilisiert.

unclaimed nicht beansprucht; unzustellbar (bsd. Brief).

uncle ['ʌŋkl] Onkel m.

un|clean unrein; ⁓comfortable** unbehaglich, ungemütlich; **~common** ungewöhnlich; **~communicative** wortkarg, verschlossen; **~complaining** ohne Murren, geduldig.

unconcern Unbekümmertheit *f*; Gleichgültigkeit *f*; **~ed** unbeteiligt; unbekümmert; gleichgültig.

un|conditional bedingungslos; **~confirmed** unbestätigt.

unconscious unbewußt; bewußtlos; **~ness** Bewußtlosigkeit *f*.

un|constitutional verfassungswidrig; **~controllable** unkontrollierbar; unbeherrscht; **~conventional** unkonventionell.

unconvinc|ed nicht überzeugt; **~ing** nicht überzeugend.

un|couth [ʌn'ku:θ] ungeschlacht; **~cover** aufdecken, freilegen; entblößen; **~cultivated**, **~cultured** unkultiviert; **~damaged** unbeschädigt, unversehrt; **~decided** unentschieden; unentschlossen; **~deniable** unleugbar.

under ['ʌndə] *prp* unter; in (*dat*); *adv* unten; darunter; unter; *adj* in Zssgn: unter, Unter...; **~bid** (*irr* bid) unterbieten; **~carriage** aer. Fahrwerk *n*; *mot.* Fahrgestell *n*; **~clothes** *pl*, **~clothing** Unterwäsche *f*; **~developed** unterentwickelt; **~done** nicht gar;

~estimate unterschätzen; **~fed** unterernährt; **~go** (*irr* go) durchmachen; sich unterziehen; **~graduate** Student(in); **~ground** unterirdisch; Untergrund...; **~**ground (-bewegung *f*) *m*; *pol.* Untergrund *m*; **~growth** Unterholz *n*; **~line** unterstreichen; **~mine** unterminieren; *fig.* untergraben; **~most** (zu)unterst; **~neath** [ˌ'ni:θ] unter (-halb); unten, darunter; **~pass** Unterführung *f*; **~privileged** benachteiligt; **~shirt** Unterhemd *n*; **~signed** Unterzeichnete *m*, *f*; **~sized** zu klein; **~staffed** unterbesetzt; **~stand** (*irr* stand) verstehen; (als sicher) annehmen; erfahren, hören; **~standable** verständlich; **~standing** verständnisvoll; Verstand *m*; Verständnis *n*; Einigung *f*; Bedingung *f*; **~statement** Understatement *n*, Untertreibung *f*; **~take** (*irr* take) unternehmen; übernehmen; **~taker** Leichenbestatter *m*, Bestattungsinstitut *n*; **~taking** Unternehmung *f*; **~value** unterschätzen; **~wear** Unterwäsche *f*; **~wood** Unterholz *n*; **~world** Unterwelt *f*.

un|deserved unverdient; **~desirable** unerwünscht; **~developed** unentwickelt; unerschlossen; **~dig-**

nified würdelos; ~diminished unvermindert; ~disciplined undiszipliniert; ~disputed unbestritten; ~disturbed ungestört; ~do (*irr* do) aufmachen; ungeschehen machen; ~ vernichten; ~dreamt-of unaged.

undress (sich) entkleiden *od.* ausziehen; ~ed unbekleidet.

un|due ungehörig; übermäßig; ~dutiful pflichtvergessen; ~easy unbehaglich; unruhig; ~educated ungebildet.

unemploy|ed arbeitslos; *the* ~ed *pl* Arbeitslose *pl*; ~ment Arbeitslosigkeit *f.*
unendurable unerträglich.
unequal ungleich; nicht gewachsen (**to** *dat*); ~(l)ed unerreicht.

un|erring unfehlbar; ~even uneben; ungleich (-mäßig); ungerade (*Zahl*); ~eventful ereignislos; ~expected unerwartet; ~failing unfehlbar; unerschöpflich; ~fair ungerecht; unfair; ~faithful un(ge)treu; treulos; ~familiar unbekannt; nicht vertraut; ~fashionable unmodern; ~favo(u)rable ungünstig; ~feeling gefühllos; ~finished unfertig; unvollendet; ~fit ungeeignet, untauglich; ~fold (sich) entfalten *od.* öffnen; enthüllen; ~foreseen unvorhergesehen; ~forget-

table unvergeßlich; ~forgiving unversöhnlich; ~forgotten unvergessen.
unfortunate unglücklich; ~ly unglücklicherweise, leider.

un|founded unbegründet; ~friendly unfreundlich; ungünstig; ~furnished unmöbliert; ~generous nicht freigebig; kleinlich; ~gentle unsanft; ~-at-able [~'get'ætəbl] unzugänglich; ~governable zügellos; wild; ~graceful ungraziös; unbeholfen; ~gracious ungnädig, unfreundlich; ~grateful undankbar; ~guarded unvorsichtig; ~happy unglücklich; ~harmed unversehrt; ~healthy ungesund; ~heard-of unerhört.

unheed|ed unbeachtet; ~ing sorglos.

un|hesitating ohne Zögern; ~hoped-for unverhofft; ~hurt unverletzt.
unicorn ['ju:nikɔ:n] Einhorn *n.*
unification [ju:nifi'keiʃən] Vereinigung *f.*
uniform ['ju:nifɔ:m] gleich; einheitlich; Uniform *f.* [einseitig.\
unilateral ['ju:ni'lætərəl]\
unimagina|ble unvorstellbar; ~tive einfallslos.
unimportant unwichtig.
uninhabit|able unbewohnbar; ~ed unbewohnt.
un|injured unbeschädigt,

unverletzt; ~intelligible unverständlich; ~intentional unabsichtlich; ~interesting uninteressant; ~interrupted ununterbrochen.

uninvit|ed un(ein)geladen; ~ing nicht od. wenig einladend.

union ['ju:njən] Vereinigung f; Verbindung f; Einigkeit f; Verband m, Verein m; pol. Union f; Gewerkschaft f; ~ist Gewerkschaftler(in); ♀ Jack Union Jack m (britische Nationalflagge).

unique [ju:'ni:k] einzigartig, einmalig. [m.]

unison ['ju:nizn] Einklang]

unit ['ju:nit] Einheit f; ~e [~'nait] (sich) vereinigen; verbinden; ~ed vereint, -einigt; ~y Einheit f; Einigkeit f.

univers|al [ju:ni'və:səl] allgemein; allumfassend, universal, Universal...; ~e ['~ə:s] Weltall n, Universum n; ~ity [~'və:siti] Universität f.

unjust ungerecht; ~kempt ['~'kempt] ungepflegt; ungekämmt; ~kind unfreundlich; lieblos; ~known unbekannt; ~lace aufschnüren; ~lawful ungesetzlich; ~learn (irr learn) verlernen.

unless [ən'les] wenn ... nicht; außer.

unlike ungleich; anders als; ~ly unwahrscheinlich.

un|limited unbegrenzt, unbeschränkt; ~load ab-, aus-, entladen.

unlock aufschließen; ~ed unverschlossen.

un|looked-for unerwartet; ~loose lösen, lockermachen; ~lucky unglücklich; be ~lucky Pech haben; ~manageable schwer zu handhaben(d); schwierig; ~manly unmännlich; ~married unverheiratet, ledig; ~mistakable unverkennbar; unmißverständlich; ~moved unbewegt, ungerührt; ~natural unnatürlich; anomal; ~necessary unnötig; ~noticed, ~observed unbemerkt; ~obtrusive unaufdringlich, bescheiden; ~occupied unbesetzt; unbewohnt; ~offending harmlos; ~official nichtamtlich, inoffiziell; ~pack auspacken; ~paid unbezahlt; ~paralleled beispiellos, ohnegleichen; ~pardonable unverzeihlich; ~perceived unbemerkt; ~perturbed ['~pə(:)'tə:bd] ruhig, gelassen; ~pleasant unangenehm, unerfreulich; ~polished unpoliert; fig. ungehobelt; ~polluted nicht verschmutzt od. verseucht.

unpopular ['ʌn'pɔpjulə] unpopular, unbeliebt; ~ity [~'læriti] Unbeliebtheit f.

unpracti|cal unpraktisch;

~sed, *Am.* ~ced ungeübt.
un|precedented beispiellos, noch nie dagewesen; ~prejudiced unbefangen, unvoreingenommen; ~premeditated unbeabsichtigt; ~prepared unvorbereitet; ~principled ohne Grundsätze, gewissenlos; ~productive unfruchtbar; unergiebig; unproduktiv; ~profitable unrentabel; nutzlos; ~provided: ~ for unversorgt, mittellos; ~qualified ungeeignet; unberechtigt; uneingeschränkt.
unquestion|able unzweifelhaft, fraglos; ~ed ungefragt; unbestritten.
unreal unwirklich; ~istic unrealistisch.
un|reasonable unvernünftig; unmäßig; ~recognizable nicht wiederzuerkennen(d); ~refined ungeläutert, Roh...; *fig.* ungebildet; ~reliable unzuverlässig; ~reserved uneingeschränkt; offen(herzig); ~resisting widerstandslos; ~rest Unruhe *f*; ~restrained ungehemmt; hemmungslos; ~restricted uneingeschränkt, unbeschränkt; ~ripe unreif; ~rival(l)ed unerreicht; ~roll ent-, aufrollen; ~ruffled glatt; *fig.* gelassen; ~ruly ungebärdig; ~safe unsicher; ~sanitary unhygienisch.
unsatisf|actory unbefrie-

digend; unzulänglich; ~ied unbefriedigt; unzufrieden.
un|savo(u)ry widerlich, -wärtig; ~screw ab-, los-, aufschrauben; ~scrupulous bedenken-, gewissen-, skrupellos; ~seen ungesehen; ~selfish selbstlos; ~settled unsicher; unbeständig; unerledigt; unbesiedelt; (geistig) gestört.
unshave|d, ~n unrasiert.
unshrink|able nicht einlaufend (*Stoff*); ~ing unverzagt.
unskil(l)ful ungeschickt; ~led ungelernt.
unsoci|able ungesellig; ~al unsozial.
unsolv|able unlösbar; ~ed ungelöst.
un|sound ungesund; nicht stichhaltig; verkehrt; ~speakable unsagbar.
unspoil|ed, ~t unverdorben; nicht verzogen (*Kind*).
unspoken un(aus)gesprochen; ~of unerwähnt.
un|stable nicht fest, unsicher; unbeständig; labil; ~steady unsicher; schwankend; unbeständig; ~stressed unbetont; ~successful erfolglos, ohne Erfolg; ~suitable unpassend; ungeeignet; ~sure unsicher; ~surpassed unübertroffen.
unsuspect|ed unverdächtig(t); unvermutet; ~ing nichts ahnend, ahnungslos.

unsuspicious nicht argwöhnisch; unverdächtig.

unthink|able undenkbar; **~ing** gedankenlos.

un|tidy unordentlich; **~tie** aufbinden; aufknoten.

until [ən'til] bis; **not ~** erst (als, wenn).

un|timely vorzeitig; ungelegen, unpassend; **~tiring** unermüdlich; **~told** unermeßlich; **~touched** unberührt; *fig.* ungerührt; **~tried** unversucht; **~troubled** ungestört; ruhig; **~true** unwahr; untreu; **~trustworthy** unzuverlässig.

unus|ed ['ʌn'juːzd] unbenutzt, ungebraucht; ['~st] nicht gewöhnt (**to** an); **~ual** ungewöhnlich; ungewohnt.

un|utterable unaussprechlich; **~varying** unveränderlich; **~voiced** *ling.* stimmlos; **~wanted** unerwünscht; **~warranted** [ˌ~'wɔrəntd] unberechtigt; ['~'wɔrəntd] unverbürgt; **~wholesome** ungesund, schädlich; **~willing** unwillig, widerwillig, abgeneigt; **~wind** (*irr* **wind**) auf-, loswickeln; (sich) abwickeln; **~wise** unklug; **~worthy** unwürdig (**of** *gen*); **~wrap** auswickeln, -packen; **~yielding** unnachgiebig.

up [ʌp] *adv* (her-, hin)auf, aufwärts, nach oben, hoch, in die Höhe, empor; oben; auf ... zu; **~ to** bis (zu);

be ~ to *et.* vorhaben; *j-s* Sache sein, abhängen von; *prp* auf ... (hinauf), hinauf, empor; oben an *od.* auf; in das Innere (*e-s Landes*); *adj* oben; hoch; gestiegen; auf(gestanden); aufgegangen (*Sonne*); abgelaufen, um (*Zeit*); **~ and about** wieder auf den Beinen; **what's ~?** *colloq.* was ist los?; **~ train** Zug *m* nach der Stadt; *sub:* **the ~s and downs** die Höhen und Tiefen (*des Lebens*).

up|bringing Erziehung *f*; **~hill** bergan, -auf; *fig.* mühsam; **~holster** [~'houlstə] *Möbel* polstern; **~holsterer** Polsterer *m*; **~holstery** Polstermaterial *n*; **~keep** Instandhaltung(skosten *pl*) *f*.

upon [ə'pɔn] *s.* **on**.

upper ['ʌpə] ober, Ober..., höher; **2 House** *Brit. parl.* Oberhaus *n*; **~most** oberst, höchst.

up|right auf-, senkrecht, gerade; **~rising** Aufstand *m*; **~roar** Aufruhr *m*; **~set** (*irr* **set**) umwerfen; *Plan etc.* durcheinanderbringen; *Magen* verderben; *j-n* aus der Fassung bringen, bestürzen; **be ~set** aufgeregt *od.* aus der Fassung *od.* durcheinander sein; **~side-down** das Oberste zuunterst; verkehrt (herum); **~stairs** die Treppe hinauf, (nach) oben; **~start** Emporkömmling *m*; **~stream** stromaufwärts; gegen den Strom; **~-to-date** modern; auf dem laufenden; **~ward(s)** ['~wəd(z)] aufwärts; nach oben.

uranium [ju'reinjəm] Uran *n*. [Stadt...]

urban ['ə:bən] städtisch,}

urchin ['ə:tʃin] Bengel *m*.

urge [ə:dʒ] drängen; **~ on** (an)treiben; Drang *m*, Trieb *m*; **~nt** dringend, dringlich, eilig.

urine ['juərin] Urin *m*, Harn *m*.

urn [ə:n] Urne *f*.

us [ʌs, əs] uns.

usage ['ju:sidʒ] (Sprach-) Gebrauch *m*; Behandlung *f*; Brauch *m*.

use [ju:s] Gebrauch *m*; Benutzung *f*, Verwendung *f*; Nutzen *m*; **(of) no ~** nutz-, zwecklos; [~z] gebrauchen, benutzen, an-, verwenden; **~ up** auf-, verbrauchen; **~d** [~zd] gebraucht; [~st] ge-

wöhnt (**to** an); gewohnt (**to** zu, *acc*); **~d to** pflegte zu; **get ~d to** sich gewöhnen an; **~ful** brauchbar, nützlich; **~less** nutz-, zwecklos, unnütz.

usher ['ʌʃə] Gerichtsdiener *m*; Platzanweiser *m*; **~ in** (hinein)führen; **~ette** [~'ret] Platzanweiserin *f*.

usual ['ju:ʒuəl] gewöhnlich, üblich; **as ~** wie gewöhnlich; **~ly** gewöhnlich, meist(ens).

usur|er ['ju:ʒərə] Wucherer *m*; **~y** ['~ʒuri] Wucher *m*.

utensil [ju(:)'tensl] Gerät *n*.

utili|ty [ju(:)'tiliti] Nützlichkeit *f*, Nutzen *m*; **~ze** (aus)nutzen, sich zunutze machen.

utmost ['ʌtməust] äußerst.

utter ['ʌtə] äußerst, völlig; äußern; *Seufzer etc.* ausstoßen; **~ance** Äußerung *f*, Ausdruck *m*; Aussprache *f*.

uvula ['ju:vjulə] *anat.* (Gaumen)Zäpfchen *n*.

V

vacan|cy ['veikənsi] Leere *f*; Lücke *f*; freie *od.* offene Stelle; **~t** leer; frei, unbesetzt (*Zimmer, Sitzplatz etc.*); frei, offen (*Stelle*).

vacat|e [və'keit, *Am.* 'vei keit] räumen; *Platz* frei machen; **~ion** (Schul- *etc.*) Ferien *f*; *bsd. Am.* Urlaub *m*.

vaccin|ate ['væksineit]

impfen; **~ation** (*bsd.* Pokken)Schutzimpfung *f*; **~e** ['~i:n] Impfstoff *m*.

vacuum ['vækjuəm] Vakuum *n*; **~ bottle** Thermosflasche *f*; **~ cleaner** Staubsauger *m*; **~ flask** Thermosflasche *f*.

vagabond ['vægəbɔnd] Landstreicher(in).

vagary ['veigəri] Laune *f*.

venal

vague [veig] vag(e), un-klar.

vain [vein] eitel; vergeblich; **in ~** vergebens, vergeblich, umsonst.

vale [veil] Tal n.

valerian [vəˈliəriən] Baldrian m. {Diener m.}

valet [ˈvælit] (Kammer-)

valiant [ˈvæljənt] tapfer.

valid [ˈvælid] (rechts)gültig; stichhaltig.

valley [ˈvæli] Tal n.

valo(u)r [ˈvælə] Tapferkeit f.

valu|able [ˈvæljuəbl] wertvoll, **~ables** pl Wertsachen pl; **~ation** Bewertung f; Schätzungswert m; **~e** [ˈvuː] Wert m; (ab)schätzen; **~eless** wertlos.

valve [vælv] Ventil n; Klappe f; (Radio)Röhre f.

van [væn] Möbelwagen m; Lieferwagen m; rail. Güter-, Gepäckwagen m.

vane [vein] Wetterfahne f; (Windmühlen-, Propeller)Flügel m.

vanilla [vəˈnilə] Vanille f.

vanish [ˈvæniʃ] verschwinden.

vanity [ˈvæniti] Eitelkeit f; **~ bag**, **~ case** Kosmetikkoffer m.

vantage [ˈvɑːntidʒ] Tennis: Vorteil m.

vap|orize [ˈveipəraiz] verdampfen, -dunsten (lassen); **~orous** dunstig; **~o(u)r** Dampf m; Dunst m.

varia|ble [ˈvɛəriəbl] veränderlich; **~nce** Uneinig-

keit f; **be at ~nce** uneinig sein; **~nt** abweichend; **Variante** f; **~tion** Schwankung f, Abweichung f; Variation f.

varicose vein [ˈværikəus] Krampfader f.

varie|d [ˈvɛərid] bunt, mannigfaltig; **~ty** [vəˈraiəti] Mannigfaltigkeit f, Vielzahl f; **~ty show** Varietévorstellung f.

various [ˈvɛəriəs] verschieden(artig); mehrere.

varnish [ˈvɑːniʃ] Firnis m; Lack m; firnissen, lackieren.

vary [ˈvɛəri] (sich) (ver-)ändern; wechseln (mit et.).

vase [vɑːz, Am. veis, veiz] Vase f.

vat [væt] Faß n, Bottich m.

vault [vɔːlt] (Keller)Gewölbe n; Gruft f; (Bank-)Tresor m; sp. Sprung m; (über)springen; **~ing-horse** Pferd n (Turngerät).

veal [viːl] Kalbfleisch n.

vegeta|ble [ˈvedʒitəbl] ein Gemüse; pl Gemüse n; **~rian** [**~ˈtɛəriən**] Vegetarier(in); vegetarisch.

vehemen|ce [ˈviːiməns] Heftigkeit f; **~t** heftig.

vehicle [ˈviːikl] Fahrzeug n.

veil [veil] Schleier m; (sich) verschleiern.

vein [vein] Ader f.

velocity [viˈlɔsiti] Geschwindigkeit f.

velvet [ˈvelvit] Samt m; Samt...; samten, aus Samt.

venal [ˈviːnl] käuflich.

vend

vend [vend] verkaufen; **~er** (Straßen)Händler *m*, Verkäufer *m*; **~ing machine** (Verkaufs)Automat *m*; **~or** *s.* **vender**, **vending machine**.

venera|ble ['venərəbl] ehrwürdig; **~te** ['~eit] verehren; **[schlechts...]**

venereal [vi'niəriəl] Geschlechts...

Venetian [vi'ni:ʃən] venetianisch; Venetianer(in); **~ blind** (Stab)Jalousie *f*.

vengeance ['vendʒəns] Rache *f*; **with a ~** *colloq.* mächtig, gehörig. [*n*.]

venison ['venzn] Wildbret [ ]

venom ['venəm] (Schlangen)Gift *n*; Gehässigkeit *f*; **~ous** giftig.

vent [vent] (Abzugs)Öffnung *f*, (Luft)Loch *n*; Schlitz *m*; **give ~ to** s-m Zorn *etc.* Luft machen.

ventilat|e ['ventileit] ventilieren, (be-, ent-, durch)lüften; **~ion** Ventilation *f*, Lüftung *f*; **~or** Ventilator *m*.

ventriloquist [ven'trilokwist] Bauchredner *m*.

venture ['ventʃə] Wagnis *n*, Risiko *n*; riskieren; (sich) wagen.

veranda(h) [və'rændə] Veranda *f*.

verb [və:b] *gr.* Verb(um) *n*, Zeitwort *n*; **~al** wörtlich; mündlich.

verdict ['və:dikt] *jur.* Urteil *n* (*a. fig.*).

verdure ['və:dʒə] Grün *n*.

verge [və:dʒ] Rand *m*,

Grenze *f*; **on the ~ of** am Rande (*gen.*); *vb*: **~ on** grenzen an.

verify ['verifai] (nach)prüfen; bestätigen.

vermicelli [və:mi'seli] Fadennudeln *pl*.

vermiform appendix ['və:mifə:m] Wurmfortsatz *m*, Blinddarm *m*.

vermin ['və:min] Ungeziefer *n*; *hunt.* Raubzeug *n*.

vernacular [və'nækjulə] Landessprache *f*.

versatile ['və:sətail] vielseitig, wendig.

vers|e [və:s] Vers(e *pl*) *m*; Strophe *f*; **~ed** bewandert; **~ion** Übersetzung *f*; Fassung *f*; Lesart *f*.

vertebra ['və:tibrə], *pl* **~e** ['~i:] *anat.* Wirbel *m*.

vertical ['və:tikəl] vertikal, senkrecht.

very ['veri] sehr; *vor sup*: aller...; genau; bloß; der, die, das gleiche; **the ~ best** das allerbeste; **the ~ thing** genau das (richtige); **the ~ thought** der bloße Gedanke.

vessel ['vesl] Gefäß *n* (*a. anat., bot.*); Schiff *n*.

vest [vest] Unterhemd *n*; *bsd. Am.* Weste *f*.

vestry ['vestri] *eccl.*: Sakristei *f*; Gemeindesaal *m*.

vet [vet] *colloq.* Tierarzt *m*.

veteran ['vetərən] alt-, ausgedient; erfahren; Veteran *m*.

veterinary (surgeon) ['vetərinəri] Tierarzt *m*.

virtual

veto ['vi:təu], *pl* **~es** Veto *n*; ablehnen.

vex [veks] ärgern; **~ation** Ärger *m*; **~atious** ärgerlich.

via ['vaiə] über, via.

vibrat|e [vai'breit] vibrieren; zittern; **~ion** Zittern *n*, Vibrieren *n*; Schwingung *f*.

vicar ['vikə] Vikar *m*, Pfarrer *m*; **~age** Pfarrhaus *n*.

vice [vais] Laster *n*; Schraubstock *m*; Vize...

vice versa ['vaisi'vɜ:sə] umgekehrt.

vicinity [vi'siniti] Nachbarschaft *f*, Nähe *f*.

vicious ['viʃəs] lasterhaft; bösartig, boshaft.

victim ['viktim] Opfer *n*.

victor ['viktə] Sieger(in); **~ian** [~'tɔ:riən] Viktorianisch; **~ious** siegreich; Sieges...; **~y** Sieg *m*.

victuals ['vitlz] *pl* Lebensmittel *pl*, Proviant *m*.

Viennese [viə'ni:z] wienerisch, Wiener...; Wiener (-in).

view [vju:] (sich) ansehen; betrachten; Sicht *f*; Aussicht *f*, (Aus)Blick *m*; Ansicht *f*, Bild *n*; Meinung *f*; **in ~ of** angesichts (*gen*); **on ~** zu besichtigen; **~er** Zuschauer(in); **~point** Gesichts-, Standpunkt *m*.

vigil ['vidʒil] Wachen *n*; Nachtwache *f*; **~ance** Wachsamkeit *f*; **~ant** wachsam.

vigo|rous ['vigərəs] kräf-

tig; energisch; **~(u)r** Kraft *f*, Vitalität *f*; Energie *f*.

vile [vail] gemein; abscheulich.

village ['vilidʒ] Dorf *n*; **~r** Dorfbewohner(in).

villain ['vilən] Schurke *m*, Schuft *m*; **~ous** schurkisch; **~y** Niederträchtigkeit *f*.

vindicat|e ['vindikeit] rechtfertigen; verteidigen; **~ion** Rechtfertigung *f*.

vindictive [vin'diktiv] rachsüchtig.

vine [vain] Wein(stock) *m*, Rebe *f*; **~gar** ['vinigə] (Wein)Essig *m*; **~yard** ['vinjəd] Weinberg *m*.

vintage ['vintidʒ] Weinlese *f*; Jahrgang *m* (*Wein*).

violat|e ['vaiəleit] verletzen; *Eid etc.* brechen; vergewaltigen; **~ion** Verletzung *f*; (*Eid- etc.*)Bruch *m*; Vergewaltigung *f*.

violen|ce ['vaiələns] Gewalt(tätigkeit) *f*; Heftigkeit *f*; **~t** heftig; gewalttätig, **~-sam.**

violet ['vaiəlit] Veilchen *n*; violett; [Geige *f*.]

violin [vaiə'lin] Violine *f*,]

viper ['vaipə] Viper *f*, Natter *f*.

virgin ['və:dʒin] Jungfrau *f*; jungfräulich; Jungfern...; **~ity** Jungfräulichkeit *f*.

viri|le ['virail] männlich; **~ity** [~'riliti] Männlichkeit *f*.

virtu|al ['və:tʃuəl] eigentlich; **~ally** praktisch; **~e**

virus 620

['ˈↄju:, 'ˌↄju:] Tugend f; Wirksamkeit f; **by** od. **in ˌe of** auf Grund (gen); **ˌous** ['ˌↄjuəs] tugendhaft.

virus ['vaiərəs] Virus n, m.

visa ['vi:zə] Visum n.

vise [vais] Am. Schraubstock m.

visib|ility [vizi'biliti] Sichtbarkeit f; meteor. Sicht (-weite) f; **ˌle** sichtbar;' fig. (er)sichtlich.

vision ['viʒən] Sehvermögen n, Sehkraft f; Vision f.

visit ['vizit] besuchen; besichtigen; e-n Besuch od. Besuche machen; Besuch m; Besichtigung f; **pay a ˌ to** j-n besuchen; **ˌor** Besucher(in), Gast m.

visual ['viʒjuəl] Seh...; Gesichts...; visuell; **ˌize** sich vorstellen.

vital ['vaitl] Lebens...; lebenswichtig; **ˌity** [ˌˈtæliti] Lebenskraft f, Vitalität f. [amin n.\

vitamin ['vitəmin] Vit-\

vivaci|ous [vi'veiʃəs] lebhaft; **ˌty** [ˌˈvæsiti] Lebhaftigkeit f. [bendig.\

vivid ['vivid] lebhaft, le-\

vixen ['viksn] Füchsin f; zänkisches Weib.

vocabulary [vəˈkæbjuləri] Wörterverzeichnis n; Wortschatz m.

vocal ['vəukəl] stimmlich, Stimm...; mus. Vokal..., Gesang(s)...; **ˌist** Sänger (-in).

vocation [vəuˈkeiʃən] (innere) Berufung; Beruf m.

vogue [vəug] Mode f; Beliebtheit f.

voice [vↄis] Stimme f; **ˌd** ling. stimmhaft.

void [vↄid] leer; jur. ungültig; **ˌ of** ohne.

volatile ['vↄlətail] chem. flüchtig. [**ˌes** Vulkan m.\

volcano [vↄlˈkeinəu], pl\

volley ['vↄli] Salve f, (Pfeil-, Stein- etc.)Hagel m; Tennis: Flugball m; fig. Schwall m.

volt [vəult] electr. Volt n; **ˌage** electr. Spannung f.

voluble ['vↄljubl] redegewandt; fließend (Rede).

volume ['vↄljum] Band m (e-s Buches); Volumen n; electr. Lautstärke f.

volunt|ary ['vↄləntəri] freiwillig; **ˌeer** [ˌˈtiə] Freiwillige m, f; sich freiwillig melden; sich freiwillig anbieten; sich e-e Bemerkung erlauben.

voluptuous [vəˈlʌptʃuəs] sinnlich; üppig.

vomit ['vↄmit] (er)brechen; (sich er)brechen.

voracious [vəˈreiʃəs] gefräßig, gierig.

vote [vəut] (Wahl)Stimme f; Abstimmung f, Wahl f; Wahlrecht n; Beschluß m; abstimmen (über); wählen; s-e Stimme abgeben; **ˌ for** stimmen für; **ˌr** Wähler(in).

voting ['vəutiŋ] Abstimmung f; Stimm(en)..., Wahl...; **ˌpaper** Stimmzettel m.

vouch [vautʃ]: ~ **for** sich verbürgen für; ~**er** Beleg *m*; Unterlage *f*; Gutschein *m*; ~**safe** [ˌˈseif] gewähren; geruhen.

vow [vau] Gelübde *n*; Schwur *m*; geloben; schwören.

vowel [ˈvauəl] *ling.* Vokal

m, Selbstlaut *m*.

voyage [ˈvɔiidʒ] *längere* (See-, Flug)Reise.

vulgar [ˈvʌlgə] gewöhnlich, vulgär.

vulnerable [ˈvʌlnərəbl] verwundbar.

vulture [ˈvʌltʃə] Geier *m*.

W

wad [wɔd] (*Watte*)Bausch *m*, Polster *n*; wattieren, auspolstern; zustopfen; ~**ding** Wattierung *f*, Polsterung *f*.

waddle [ˈwɔdl] watscheln.

wade [weid] (*durch*)waten.

wafer [ˈweifə] Waffel *f*; Oblate *f*.

waffle [ˈwɔfl] Waffel *f*.

waft [wɑːft] wehen; Hauch *m*.

wag [wæg] wackeln *od.* (wedeln (mit).)

wage|-earner [ˈweidʒəːnə] Lohnempfänger(in), ~**s** [ˌˈiz] *pl* Lohn *m*.

wager [ˈweidʒə] Wette *f*; wetten.

wag(g)on [ˈwægən] (*offener* Güter)Wagen.

wail [weil] (Weh)Klagen *n*; (weh)klagen, jammern.

wainscot [ˈweinskət] (*bsd. untere*) (Wand)Täfelung.

waist [weist] Taille *f*; ~**coat** [ˈweiskəut] Weste *f*; ~**line** Taille *f*.

wait [weit] warten (**for** auf); abwarten; warten auf; ~ **at** (*Am.* **on**) **table** bedienen; ~ (**up)on**

j-n bedienen; ~**er** Kellner *m*, Ober *m*; ~**ing** Warten *n*; **no** ~**ing** *mot.* Halteverbot *n*; ~**ing-room** Wartezimmer *n*; *rail.* Wartesaal *m*; ~**ress** Kellnerin *f*.

wake [weik] Kielwasser *n* (*a. fig.*); (*irr.*); ~ (**up**) aufwachen; (auf)wecken; ~**ful** schlaflos; ~**n** *s.* **wake** (*vb.*).

walk [wɔːk] gehen; spazierengehen; (durch)wandern; ~ **about** umhergehen, -wandern; ~ **out** *colloq.* streiken; ~ **out on** *sl. j-n* im Stich lassen; (Spazier)Gang *m*; (Spazier)Weg *m*; ~**er** Spaziergänger(in).

walkie-talkie [ˈwɔːkiˈtɔːki] *colloq.* tragbares Funksprechgerät.

walking| papers *pl colloq.* Entlassung(spapiere *pl*) *f*; ~**stick** Spazierstock *m*; ~**tour** Wanderung *f*.

walk-out *colloq.* Streik *m*.

wall [wɔːl] Wand *f*; Mauer *f*; ~ **up** zumauern.

wallet [ˈwɔlit] Brieftasche *f*.

wall|-flower fig. Mauer-
blümchen n; **~paper** Tapete f.

wall|nut ['wɔːlnʌt] Wal-
nuß(baum m) f; **~rus**
['~rəs] Walroß n.

waltz [wɔːls] Walzer m;
Walzer tanzen.

wan [wɔn] blaß, bleich,
fahl. [Stab m.]

wand [wɔnd] (Zauber-)

wander ['wɔndə] wan-
dern; fig.: abschweifen;
phantasieren; **~er** Wanderer m.

wane [wein] abnehmen
(Mond); fig. schwinden.

want [wɔnt] Mangel m (of
an); pl Bedürfnisse pl; be-
dürfen, brauchen; müs-
sen, wünschen, (haben)
wollen, mögen; ermangeln;
it **~s** s.th. es fehlt an; **~ed**
gesucht; **~ing** be- be fehlen; es fehlen lassen (in
an).

war [wɔː] Krieg m; Kriegs...

warble ['wɔːbl] trillern,
singen.

ward [wɔːd] Mündel n;
Abteilung f; (Kranken-
haus)Station f; (Stadt)Be-
zirk m; **~ off** abwehren;
~en Aufseher m; Her-
bergsvater m; **~er** (Ge-
fangenen)Wärter m.

wardrobe ['wɔːdrəub]
Garderobe f; Kleider-
schrank m.

ware [wɛə] Geschirr n; in
Zssgn: ...waren pl; pl Waren; **~house** Lager(haus)
n; Warenlager n.

warm [wɔːm] warm (a.
fig.); heiß; hitzig;
(up) (auf-, an-, er)wär-
men; sich erwärmen, warm
werden; **~th** [~θ] Wärme f.

warn [wɔːn] warnen (of,
against vor); **~ing** Warnung f; Kündigung f.

warp [wɔːp] (sich) verziehen (Holz).

warrant ['wɔrənt] et.
rechtfertigen, garantieren,
verbürgen; Vollmacht f;
Rechtfertigung f; **~ of
arrest** Haftbefehl m; **~y**
Garantie f; Berechtigung f.

warrior ['wɔriə] Krieger m.

wart [wɔːt] Warze f.

wary ['wɛəri] vorsichtig,
wachsam.

was [wɔz, wəz] 1. u. 3. sg
pret von be; pass von be.

wash [wɔʃ] (sich) waschen;
um-, überspülen; **~e-n** Teller
etc. (ab)waschen; **~away**
weg-, fortspülen; **~up**
Geschirr spülen; sub: Wa-
schen n; Wäsche f; Wasch-
...; **~ and wear** pflege-
leicht; **~basin**, Am.
~bowl Waschbecken n;
~cloth Am. Waschlappen
m; **~er** Waschmaschine f;
~ing Waschen n; Wäsche f;
Wasch...; **~ing-machine**
Waschmaschine f; **~ing
powder** Waschpulver n;
~ing-up Abwasch(en n) m;

wasp [wɔsp] Wespe f.

waste [weist] wüst, öde;
überflüssig; Abfall...; Ver-
schwendung f; Wüste f,
(Ein)Öde f; Abfall m; ver-

schwenden; verwüsten;
~away dahinsiechen, verfallen; ~paper-basket
Papierkorb m; ~pipe Abflußrohr n.

watch [wɔtʃ] (Armband-,
Taschen)Uhr f; Wache f;
keep ~ Wache halten, aufpassen; vb: (be)wachen;
beobachten; zuschauen; ~
for warten auf; ~ out colloq. aufpassen; ~dog
Wachhund m; ~ful wachsam; ~maker Uhrmacher m; ~man (Nacht-)
Wächter m.

water ['wɔ:tə] Wasser n;
pl Gewässer pl; bewässern; sprengen; (be)gießen; tränken; wässern
(Mund); tränen (Augen);
~(down) verwässern (a.
fig.); ~bottle Wasserflasche f; Feldflasche f;
~closet (Wasser)Klosett
n; ~colo(u)r Aquarell
(-malerei f) n; ~course
Wasserlauf m; ~cress
Brunnenkresse f; ~dog
Wasserratte f (Schwimmer);
~fall Wasserfall m.

watering|-can Gießkanne
f; ~place Wasserloch n,
Tränke f; Bad(eort m) n;
Seebad n.

water|-level Wasserspiegel m; ~proof wasserdicht;
Regenmantel m; ~shed
Wasserscheide f; ~side
Küste f, Fluß-, Seeufer n;
~tight wasserdicht; fig.
unangreifbar; ~way

Wasserstraße f; ~works
sg, pl Wasserwerk(e pl) n;
~y wässerig.

watt [wɔt] electr. Watt n.

wave [weiv] Welle f; Woge f; Winken n; wellen;
schwingen; schwenken;
wogen; wehen, flattern;
winken (mit); ~ to j-m
zuwinken.

waver ['weivə] (sch)wanken; flackern. [wellt.]
wavy ['weivi] wellig, ge-}
wax [wæks] Wachs n; bohnern; zunehmen (Mond).

way [wei] Weg m; Strecke
f; Richtung f; Art u.
Weise f; (Eigen)Art f;
(Aus)Weg m; Hinsicht f;
this ~ hierher, hier entlang; the other ~ round
umgekehrt; by the ~
übrigens; by ~ of durch;
on the ~, on one's ~
unterwegs; out of the ~
abgelegen; ungewöhnlich;
give ~ (zurück)weichen;
nachgeben; mot. die Vorfahrt lassen (to dat); have
one's own ~ s-n Willen
durchsetzen; lead the ~
vorangehen; ~back Rückweg m, -fahrt f; ~ in Eingang m; ~of life Lebensart f, -weise f; ~out Ausgang m; ~side Wegrand
m; (by the ~side am
Wege; ~ward ['~wəd]
eigensinnig.

we [wi:, wi] wir.

weak [wi:k] schwach; dünn
(Getränk); ~en schwächen;
schwach werden; ~ling

Schwächling *m*; ~ly schwächlich; ~-minded schwachsinnig; ~ness Schwäche *f*.

wealth [welθ] Reichtum *m*; ~y reich, wohlhabend.

wean [wi:n] entwöhnen.

weapon ['wepən] Waffe *f*.

wear [wɛə] (*irr*) am Körper tragen, anhaben, Hut etc. aufhaben; halten, haltbar sein; sich gut etc. tragen; ~ (away, down, off, out) (sich) abnutzen *od.* abtragen; ~ off sich verlieren; ~ out erschöpfen; *sub*: Tragen *n*; (Be)Kleidung *f*; Abnutzung *f*.

wear|iness ['wiərinis] Müdigkeit *f*; *fig.* Überdruß *m*; ~y müde; ermüden(d).

weasel ['wi:zl] Wiesel *n*.

weather ['weðə] Wetter *n*, Witterung *f*; ~-beaten verwittert; vom Wetter gegerbt (*Gesicht*); ~-chart Wetterkarte *f*; ~-forecast Wetterbericht *m*, -vorhersage *f*.

weave [wi:v] (*irr*) weben, flechten; ~r Weber *m*.

web [web] Gewebe *n*; Netz *n*; *zo.* Schwimmhaut *f*.

wed [wed] heiraten; ~ding Hochzeit *f*; Hochzeits...; ~ding-ring Ehe-, Trauring *m*.

wedge [wedʒ] Keil *m*; (ein)keilen, (-)zwängen.

Wednesday ['wenzdi] Mittwoch *m*.

weed [wi:d] Unkraut *n*; jäten; ~-killer Unkraut-

vertilgungsmittel *n*.

week [wi:k] Woche *f*; ~ in, ~ out Woche für Woche; this day ~ today heute in 8 Tagen; ~day Wochentag *m*; ~-end Wochenende *n*; ~ly wöchentlich.

weep [wi:p] (*irr*) weinen; tropfen; ~ing willow Trauerweide *f*.

weigh [wei] (*a.* ~ out ab-) wiegen; *fig.* ab-, erwägen; ~t Gewicht *n*; *fig.*: Last *f*; Bedeutung *f*; ~tless leicht; schwerelos; ~lifting *sp.* Gewichtheben *n*; ~ty schwer(wiegend); wichtig.

weir [wiə] Wehr *n*.

weird [wiəd] unheimlich, *colloq.* sonderbar.

welcome ['welkəm] Empfang *m*; willkommen (heißen); *fig.* begrüßen; you are ~ to ... Sie können gern ...; (you are) ~! gern geschehen!, bitte sehr! **weld** [weld] (zs.-)schweißen.

welfare ['welfɛə] Wohlfahrt *f*; ~ state Wohlfahrtsstaat *m*; ~ work Fürsorge *f*; ~ worker Fürsorger(in).

well[1] [wel] Brunnen *m*; *tech.* Quelle *f* (*a. fig.*), Bohrloch *n*.

well[2] [wel] gut; wohl; gesund; ~ off wohlhabend; I am *od.* feel ~ ich fühle mich wohl, es geht mir gut; *int.* nun!, na!, gut!, schön!;

very ~ (na) gut!; ~**being**
Wohl(ergehen) n; ~**born**
aus guter Familie; ~**bred**
wohlerzogen.

wellingtons ['welıŋtənz]
pl Schaft-, Gummistiefel pl.

well-known wohlbekannt;
~**mannered** mit guten
Manieren; ~**timed** rechtzeitig, im richtigen Augenblick; ~**to-do** wohlhabend; ~**wisher** Gönner
m, Freund m; ~**worn** abgetragen; fig. abgedroschen.

Welsh [welʃ] walisisch;
Walisisch n; **the** ~ pl die
Waliser pl; ~ **rabbit,** ~
rarebit [~ 'reəbıt] überbackene Käseschnitte.

wench [wentʃ] veraltet:
Mädchen n.

went [went] pret von **go.**

wept [wept] pret u. pp von
weep.

were [wə:, wə] pret pl u.
2. sg von **be;** pret pass
von **be;** subj pret von **be.**

west [west] West(en m);
westlich, West...; nach
Westen; ~**erly,** ~**ern** westlich; ~**ward(s)** ['~wəd(z)]
westwärts.

wet [wet] naß, feucht; ~
through durchnäßt; Nässe f; Feuchtigkeit f; (irr)
naß machen, anfeuchten;
~**nurse** Amme f.

whack [wæk] schlagen;
(knallender) Schlag.

whale [weıl] Wal m.

wharf [wɔ:f], pl a. ~**ves**
[~vz] Kai m, Anlegeplatz m.

what [wɔt] was; wie; was
für ein(e), welche(r, -s);
(das,) was; was!, wie!;
was?, wie?; ~ **about ...?**
wie steht's mit ...?; ~ **is
all this about?** worum
handelt es sich eigentlich?;
~ **for?** wofür?, wozu?; ~
next? was sonst noch?;
so ~? na, wenn schon?;
~**(so)ever** was (auch immer), alles was; was auch;
welche(r, -s) ... auch
(immer).

wheat [wi:t] Weizen m.

wheel [wi:l] Rad n; Steuer
(-rad) n; fahren, rollen,
schieben; (sich) drehen;
~**barrow** Schubkarren m;
~**chair** Rollstuhl m.

whelp [welp] Welpe m.

when [wen] wann; wenn;
wenn; als; ~**(so)ever** immer od. jedesmal wenn.

where [weə] wo; wohin;
~ ... **from?** woher?; ~
... **to?** wohin?; ~**about(s)**
wo ungefähr; Aufenthalt(s-
ort) m; ~**as** während; ~**by**
wodurch, womit; ~**fore**
weshalb; ~**in** worin; ~
(up)on worauf; ~**ver** wo
(-hin) (auch) immer.

whet [wet] wetzen, schärfen.

whether ['weðə] ob.

which [wıtʃ] welche(r, -s);
der, die, das; was; ~**(so)-
ever** welche(r, -s) ...(auch)
immer.

whiff [wıf] Hauch m; Geruch m; Zug m (beim Rauchen).

while [wail] während; Weile *f*, Zeit *f*; for a ~ e-e
Zeitlang; *vb*: ~ **away** sich
die Zeit vertreiben.

whim [wim] Schrulle *f*,
Laune *f*. [mern.]

whimper ['wimpə] wim-]

whims|ical ['wimzikəl]
launenhaft, wunderlich; ~**y**
Laune *f*, Grille *f*.

whine [wain] winseln;
wimmern; greinen, jam-
mern.

whinny ['wini] wiehern.

whip [wip] Peitsche *f*; peitschen; verprügeln; schla-
gen; ~**ped cream** Schlag-
sahne *f*; ~**ping** Prügel *pl*;
~**ping-top** Kreisel *m*.

whirl [wə:l] wirbeln, sich
drehen; Wirbel *m*; Strudel
m; ~**pool** Strudel *m*.

whir(r) [wə:] schwirren.

whisk [wisk] (Staub-, Fliegen)Wedel *m*; *Küche*:
Schneebesen *m*; schlagen;
~ **away**, ~ **off** (ab-, weg-)
wischen; *j-n* schnell weg-
bringen; ~ (**away** weg-)
huschen, (-)flitzen.

whiskers ['wiskəz] *pl* Bak-
kenbart *m*.

whisper ['wispə] flüstern;
Geflüster *n*, Flüstern *n*.

whistle ['wisl] pfeifen;
Pfeife *f*, Pfiff *m*.

white [wait] weiß; Weiß(e)
n; Weiße *m*, *f*.; ~ **coffee**
Milchkaffee *m*; ~**collar**
worker Angestellte *m*, *f*;
~ **frost** (Rauh)Reif *m*; ~
heat Weißglut *f*; ~ **lie**
fromme Lüge; ~**n** weiß

machen *od.* werden; ~**ness**
Weiße *f*; Blässe *f*; ~**wash**
Tünche *f*; weißen; *fig.*
reinwaschen.

Whit|monday ['wit'mʌn-
di] Pfingstmontag *m*; ~**sun**
['..sn] Pfingst...; ~**suntide**
Pfingsten *n*, *pl*.

whiz(z) [wiz] zischen, sausen, schwirren.

who [hu:, hu] wer?; *colloq.*
wem?, wen?; wer; welche(r, -s), den; *fig.*

whodunit [hu:'dʌnit] *sl.*
Krimi *m*.

whoever [hu(:)'evə] wer
(auch) immer; jeder, der.

whole [həul] ganz; heil,
unversehrt; Ganze *n*; (**up-**)
on the ~ im ganzen; ~
meal bread Vollkorn-
brot *n*; ~**sale dealer**,
~**saler** Großhändler *m*;
~**sale trade** Großhandel
m; ~**some** gesund.

wholly ['həuli] ganz.

whom [hu:m] *acc von* **who.**

whoop [hu:p] Schrei *m*,
Geschrei *n*; laut schreien;
~**ing cough** Keuchhusten
m.

whore [hɔ:] Hure *f*.

whose [hu:z] *gen sg u. pl
von* **who:** wessen?; dessen;
deren (*a. gen von* **which**).

why [wai] warum, weshalb;
~ **so?** wieso?; **that is** ~
deshalb; *int.* nun (gut);
aber (... doch).

wick [wik] Docht *m*.

wicked ['wikid] böse;
schlecht; schlimm; ~**ness**
Bosheit *f*, Gemeinheit *f*.

wipe

wicker| basket ['wikə]
Weidenkorb m; **~ chair**
Korbstuhl m.

wicket ['wikit] Pförtchen
n; Kricket: Dreistab m,
Tor n.

wide [waid] weit; ausgedehnt; breit; **~ awake**
hellwach; fig. aufgeweckt;
~n (sich) verbreitern; (sich)
erweitern; **~spread** weitverbreitet.

widow ['widəu] Witwe f;
~er Witwer m.

width [widθ] Breite f,
Weite f.

wife [waif], pl **wives** [~vz]
(Ehe)Frau f, Gattin f.

wig [wig] Perücke f.

wild [waild] wild; **run ~**
wild aufwachsen, verwildern; **~cat** wild (Streik);
Schwindel...; **~erness**
['wildənis] Wildnis f, Wüste f; **~fire: like ~** wie ein
Lauffeuer.

wil(l)ful ['wilful] eigensinnig; vorsätzlich.

will [wil] Wille m; Wunsch
m; Testament n; v/aux
ich, du etc.: will(st) etc.;
ich, du etc.: werde, wirst
etc.; **~ing** gewillt, willens,
bereit. [de f.]

willow ['wiləu] bot. Weidef.]

wilt [wilt] (ver)welken.

win [win] (irr) gewinnen;
erlangen; siegen; Sieg m.

wince [wins] (zs.-)zucken.

winch [wintʃ] tech. Winde f.

wind¹ [wind] Wind m;
Blähung f; wittern; **be
~ed** außer Atem sein.

wind² [waind] (irr) sich
winden od. schlängeln;
winden, wickeln; **~ up** Uhr
aufziehen; **~ing** Windung
f; sich windend; **~ing
staircase** Wendeltreppe f.

wind-instrument Blasinstrument n. [(Winde f.)]

windlass ['windləs] tech.]

windmill ['winmil] Windmühle f.

window ['windəu] Fenster
n; Schaufenster n; **~ shade**
Am. Rouleau n, Jalousie f;
~-shopping: go ~-ing
Schaufensterbummel machen; **~sill** Fensterbrett n.

wind|pipe Luftröhre f; **~screen**, Am. **~shield**
Windschutzscheibe f; **~screen wiper**, Am. **~shield wiper** Scheibenwischer m; **~y** windig.

wine [wain] Wein m.

wing [wiŋ] Flügel m;
Schwinge f; mot. Kotflügel m; aer. Tragfläche f.

wink [wiŋk] Blinzeln n,
Zwinkern n; blinzeln od.
zwinkern (mit).

winn|er ['winə] Gewinner
(-in) f; Sieger(in) f; **~ing** siegreich; fig. einnehmend;
~ing-post sp. Ziel n;
~ings pl Gewinn m.

wint|er ['wintə] Winter m;
überwintern; **~ry** ['~tri]
winterlich; fig. frostig.

wipe [waip] (ab-, auf-)
wischen; (ab)trocknen; **~off** ab-, wegwischen; tilgen; **~ out** auswischen; tilgen; (völlig) vernichten.

wire ['waiə] Draht *m*; *colloq.* Telegramm *n*; Draht...; *colloq.* telegraphieren; **~less** drahtlos, Funk...; **~less (set)** Radio(apparat *m*) *n*; **~ netting** Drahtgeflecht *n*.

wiry ['waiəri] drahtig.

wisdom ['wizdəm] Weisheit *f*; **~tooth** Weisheitszahn *m*. [erfahren.]

wise [waiz] weise, klug,] **wish** [wiʃ] Wunsch *m*; wünschen; wollen; **~ s.o. well** od. **ill** j-m Gutes od. Böses wünschen; **~ for** (sich) *et.* wünschen.

wistful ['wistful]sehnsüchtig, wehmütig.

wit [wit] Witz *m*; *sg, pl* Verstand *m*; **be at one's ~'s end** mit s-r Weisheit am Ende sein.

witch [witʃ] Hexe *f*; **~craft**, **~ery** Hexerei *f*.

with [wið] mit; bei; für; von; durch, vor.

withdraw [wið'drɔː] (*irr* **draw**) (sich) zurückziehen; *Truppen etc.* abziehen; *Geld* abheben.

wither ['wiðə] (ver)welken; verdorren lassen.

withhold [wið'həuld] (*irr* **hold**) zurückhalten; *et.* vorenthalten, **~in** [.'ðin] in(nerhalb); **~ in call** in Rufweite; **~out** [.'ðaut] ohne; **~stand** (*irr* **stand**) widerstehen.

witness ['witnis] Zeug|e *m*, -in *f*; Zeugnis *n*, Beweis *m*; (be)zeugen; Zeuge sein

von; **~box**, *Am.* **~ stand** Zeugenstand *m*, -bank *f*.

witty ['witi] witzig, geistreich.

wives [waivz] *pl von* **wife**.

wizard ['wizəd] Zauberer *m*; Genie *n*.

wobble ['wɔbl] schwanken; wackeln (mit); schlottern (*Knie*).

woe [wəu] Weh *n*, Leid *n*; **~begone** ['.bigɔn] jammervoll; **~ful** jammervoll, elend.

woke [wəuk] *pret u. pp*, **~n** *pp von* **wake**.

wolf [wulf], *pl* **wolves** [.vz] Wolf *m*; **~ (down)** (gierig) verschlingen.

woman ['wumən], *pl* **women** ['wimin] Frau *f*; weiblich; **~ doctor** Ärztin *f*; **~hood** Frauen *pl*; Weiblichkeit *f*; **~kind** Frauen *pl*; **~ly** fraulich, weiblich.

womb [wuːm] Gebärmutter *f*, Mutterleib *m*; *fig.* Schoß *m*.

women ['wimin] *pl von* **woman.** [win.] **won** [wʌn] *pret u. pp von* win]

wonder ['wʌndə] Wunder *n*; Verwunderung *f*; sich wundern; gern wissen mögen, sich fragen; **~ful** wunderbar, -voll.

won't [wəunt] *für* will not.

wont [wəunt] Gewohnheit *f*; gewohnt; **be ~ to** do zu tun pflegen; **~ed** gewohnt; üblich.

woo [wuː] werben um.

wood [wud] *oft pl* Wald *m*,

Gehölz n; Holz n; **~cut** Holzschnitt m; **~cutter** Holzfäller m; **~ed** bewaldet, waldig; *an* hölzern (*a. fig.*); Holz...; **~pecker** Specht m; **~wind** Holzblasinstrument n; **~work** Holzwerk n; Holzarbeit(en pl) f; **~y** waldig; holzig.

wool [wul] Wolle f; **~(l)en** wollen, Woll...; *pl* Wollsachen pl; **~(l)y** wollig; Woll...

word [wə:d] (in Worten) ausdrücken, formulieren; Wort n; Nachricht f; pl: (Lied)Text m; fig. Wortwechsel m; **have a ~ with** *j-m* sprechen; **~ing** Wortlaut m, Fassung f.

wore [wɔ:] *pret von* **wear.**

work [wə:k] Arbeit f; Werk n; pl (Räder-, Trieb-, Uhr)Werk n; pl *als sg konstruiert*: Werk n, Fabrik f, Betrieb m; **at ~** bei der Arbeit; **out of ~** arbeitslos; **set to ~** an die Arbeit gehen; (*a. irr*) arbeiten (**at, on** an); *tech.* funktionieren, gehen; wirken; *fig.* gelingen, klappen; ver-, bearbeiten; *Maschine etc.* bedienen; (an-, be)treiben; *fig.* bewirken; *Gefühle* abreagieren; **~ off** aufarbeiten; *Gefühle* abreagieren; **~ out** ausrechnen, *Aufgabe* lösen; *Plan* ausarbeiten; **~day** Werk-, Arbeitstag m; **~er** Arbeiter (-in); **~house** Armenhaus n; *Am.* Besserungsanstalt f, Arbeitshaus n.

working arbeitend; Arbeits...; Betriebs...; **~ class** Arbeiterklasse f; **~ day** Werk-, Arbeitstag m; **~ hours** pl Arbeitszeit f.

workman (Fach)Arbeiter m; **~ship** Kunstfertigkeit f; *gute etc.* Ausführung.

work| of art Kunstwerk n; **~s council** Betriebsrat m; **~shop** Werkstatt f.

world [wə:ld] Welt f; **~ly** weltlich; irdisch; **~ power** pol. Weltmacht f; **~ war** Weltkrieg m; **~-wide** weltweit, auf der ganzen Welt, Welt...

worm [wə:m] Wurm m; **~-eaten** wurmstichig.

worn [wɔ:n] pp von **wear**, **~-out** abgenutzt, abgetragen; verbraucht; erschöpft.

worr|ied ['wʌrid] besorgt, beunruhigt; **~y** quälen, plagen; (sich) beunruhigen; (sich) Sorgen machen; Sorge f; Ärger m.

worse [wə:s] *comp von* **bad, evil, ill.**

worship ['wə:ʃip] Anbetung f, Verehrung f; Gottesdienst m; verehren, anbeten; **~(p)er** Kirchgänger(in).

worst [wə:st] *sup von* **bad, evil, ill.**

worsted ['wustid] Kammgarn n; Woll...

worth [wə:θ] Wert m; Verdienst m; wert; **~** reading lesenswert; **~ seeing** sehenswert; **~less** wertlos;

~while der Mühe wert; **~y** ['~ði] würdig.

would [wud] pret u. cond von will; pflegte(st, -n, -t).

wound¹ [wu:nd] Wunde f, Verletzung f; verwunden, -letzen (a. fig.).

wound² [waund] pret u. pp von **wind¹**.

wove [wəuv] pret, **~n** pp von **weave**.

wrangle ['ræŋgl] (sich) streiten od. zanken; Streit m, Zank m.

wrap [ræp] wickeln, hüllen; **~ up** (ein)wickeln, (-)packen, (-)hüllen; **be ~ped up in** fig. ganz in Anspruch genommen sein von, ganz aufgehen in; Decke f; Schal m; Mantel m; **~per** Hülle f, Verpackung f; (Buch)Umschlag m; **~ping** Verpackung f.

wrath [rɔθ] Zorn m.

wreath [ri:θ], pl **~s** [~ðz] (Blumen)Gewinde n, Kranz m.

wreck [rek] Wrack n; Schiffbruch m; vernichten, zerstören; **be ~ed** Schiffbruch erleiden; **~age** Trümmer pl; Wrack(teile pl) n; **~ed** gestrandet, gescheitert; schiffbrüchig.

wrecking| company Am. Abbruchfirma f; **~ service** Am. mot. Abschleppdienst m.

wren [ren] Zaunkönig m.

wrench [rentʃ] reißen, zerren, ziehen; med. verren-

ken, -stauchen; **~ open** aufreißen; Ruck m; med. Verrenkung f, -stauchung f; Schraubenschlüssel m.

wrest [rest] reißen; **~ from** j-m entreißen od. fig. abringen; **~le** ringen (mit); **~ling** Ringkampf m, Ringen n.

wretch [retʃ] armer Kerl; Schuft m; **~ed** ['~id] elend; erbärmlich, schlecht.

wriggle [rigl] sich winden od. schlängeln; zappeln (mit).

wring [riŋ] (irr) (**~ out** aus)wringen; **Hände** ringen.

wrinkle ['riŋkl] Runzel f, Falte f; sich runzeln, runz(e)lig werden; knittern; **~ up** Stirn runzeln.

wrist [rist] Handgelenk n; **~ watch** Armbanduhr f.

writ [rit] Erlaß m; jur. Verfügung f.

write [rait] (irr) schreiben; **~ down** auf-, niederschreiben; **~ out** (ganz) ausstellen; Scheck etc. ausstellen; **~r** Schreiber(in); Verfasser(in), Autor(in), Schriftsteller(in).

writhe [raið] sich krümmen.

writing ['raitiŋ] Schreib...; Schreiben n; Schrift f; Stil m; pl literarische Werke pl; **in ~** schriftlich; **~desk** Schreibtisch m; **~paper** Schreib-, Briefpapier n.

written ['ritn] pp von

write; schriftlich.

wrong [rɔŋ] unrichtig; falsch, verkehrt; **be ~** falsch sein; nicht in Ordnung sein, nicht stimmen; falsch gehen (*Uhr*); unrecht haben; **what is ~ with you?** was ist los mit dir?; *sub*: Unrecht *n*; *vb*:

j-m Unrecht tun.

wrote [rəut] *pret von* **write.**

wrought [rɔːt] *pret u. pp von* **work;** **~-iron** schmiedeeisern, **~-up** erregt.

wrung [rʌŋ] *pret u. pp von* **wring.**

wry [rai] schief, verzerrt.

X, Y

Xmas ['krisməs] *für* **Christmas.**

X-ray ['eks'rei] Röntgenaufnahme *f*; Röntgen...; röntgen.

xylophone ['zailəfəun] Xylophon *n*.

yacht [jɔt] (Segel-, Motor-)Jacht *f*; Segelboot *n*; **~ing** Segeln *n*; Segelsport *m*.

yap [jæp] kläffen.

yard [jɑːd] Yard *n* (= 0,914 *m*); Hof *m*.

yarn [jɑːn] Garn *n*; *colloq.* Seemannsgarn *n*.

yawn [jɔːn] gähnen; Gähnen *n*.

ye¹ [jiː] *alte Form für* you.

ye² [jiː, ði:] *alte Form für* the.

yea [jei] *veraltet* ja.

yeah [jei] *sl.* ja.

year [jəː] Jahr *n*; **~ly** jährlich.

yearn [jəːn] sich sehnen.

yeast [jiːst] Hefe *f*.

yell [jel] (gellend) schreien; (gellender) Schrei.

yellow ['jeləu] gelb; Gelb *n*.

yelp [jelp] kläffen, jaulen.

yeoman ['jəumən] freier Bauer.

yes [jes] ja; doch; Ja *n*.

yesterday ['jestədi] gestern; **the day before ~** vorgestern.

yet [jet] noch; bis jetzt; schon; (je)doch, dennoch, trotzdem; **as ~** bis jetzt; **not ~** noch nicht.

yew [juː] Eibe *f*.

yield [jiːld] (ein-, hervor-)bringen; *agr.* tragen; nachgeben, weichen; Ertrag *m*; **~ing** *fig.* nachgiebig.

yoke [jəuk] Joch *n* (*a. fig.*); **~** *pl* (*Ochsen*)Gespann *n*; (an)spannen.

yolk [jəuk] (Ei)Dotter *m, n*, Eigelb *n*.

yonder ['jɔndə] *lit.* dort drüben.

you [juː, ju] du, ihr, Sie; dir, euch, Ihnen; dich, euch, Sie; man.

young [jʌŋ] jung; (Tier-)Junge *pl*; **~ster** ['~stə] Junge *m*.

your [jɔː] dein(e), euer(e), Ihr(e); **~s** [~z] deine(r, -s), euer, euere(s), Ihre(r, -s),

der, die, das dein(ig)e *od.*
eur(ig)e *od.* Ihr(ig)e; **self**,
pl **selves** (du, ihr, Sie)
selbst; dir (selbst), dich,
sich, euch, sich; **by self**
allein.

youth [ju:0], *pl* **s** [ðz]

Jugend *f*; junger Mann;
Jugend...; **ful** jung; jugendlich; **hostel** Ju-
gendherberge *f*.

Yugoslav ['ju:gəu'sla:v]
jugoslawisch; Jugoslaw|e
m, -in *f*; Jugoslawisch *n*.

Z

zeal [zi:l] Eifer *m*; **ous**
['zeləs] eifrig; eifrig bedacht (**to do** zu tun).

zebra ['zi:brə] Zebra *n*; **crossing** Fußgängerübergang *m*, Zebrastreifen *m*.

zenith ['zeni0] Zenit *m*;
fig. Höhepunkt *m*.

zero ['ziərəu] Null(punkt
m) *f*.

zest [zest] Begeisterung *f*,
Schwung *m*; Reiz *m*.

zigzag ['zigzæg] Zickzack
m.

zip| code [zip] *Am.* Post-
leitzahl *f*; **fastener**, **per**
Reißverschluß *m*.

zodiac ['zəudiæk] Tier-
kreis *m*.

zone [zəun] Zone *f*.

zoo [zu:] Zoo *m*.

zoolog|ical [zəuə'lɔdʒikəl]
zoologisch; **y** [ðlədʒi]
Zoologie *f*.

Numerals

Cardinal Numbers

0	*nought, zero, cipher* null	50	*fifty* fünfzig
1	*one* eins	60	*sixty* sechzig
2	*two* zwei	70	*seventy* siebzig
3	*three* drei	80	*eighty* achtzig
4	*four* vier	90	*ninety* neunzig
5	*five* fünf	100	*a* or *one hundred* hundert
6	*six* sechs	101	*a hundred and one* hundert(und)eins
7	*seven* sieben	200	*two hundred* zweihundert
8	*eight* acht	572	*five hundred and seventy-two* fünfhundert(und)zweiundsiebzig
9	*nine* neun		
10	*ten* zehn		
11	*eleven* elf		
12	*twelve* zwölf		
13	*thirteen* dreizehn	1000	*a* or *one thousand* tausend
14	*fourteen* vierzehn	1986	*nineteen hundred and eighty-six* neunzehnhundertsechsundachtzig
15	*fifteen* fünfzehn		
16	*sixteen* sechzehn		
17	*seventeen* siebzehn		
18	*eighteen* achtzehn		
19	*nineteen* neunzehn	500 000	*five hundred thousand* fünfhunderttausend
20	*twenty* zwanzig	1 000 000	*a* or *one million* eine Million
21	*twenty-one* einundzwanzig	2 000 000	*two million* zwei Millionen
22	*twenty-two* zweiundzwanzig	1 000 000 000	*a* or *one billion* eine Milliarde
23	*twenty-three* dreiundzwanzig		
30	*thirty* dreißig		
40	*forty* vierzig		

Ordinal Numbers

1st	*first* erste	**30th**	*thirtieth* dreißigste
2nd	*second* zweite	**40th**	*fortieth* vierzigste
3rd	*third* dritte	**50th**	*fiftieth* fünfzigste
4th	*fourth* vierte	**60th**	*sixtieth* sechzigste
5th	*fifth* fünfte	**70th**	*seventieth* siebzigste
6th	*sixth* sechste	**80th**	*eightieth* achtzigste
7th	*seventh* siebente	**90th**	*ninetieth* neunzig-
8th	*eighth* achte		ste
9th	*ninth* neunte	**100th**	*(one) hundredth*
10th	*tenth* zehnte		hundertste
11th	*eleventh* elfte	**101st**	*(one) hundred and*
12th	*twelfth* zwölfte		*first*
13th	*thirteenth*		hundert(und)erste
	dreizehnte	**200th**	*two hundredth*
14th	*fourteenth*		zweihundertste
	vierzehnte	**572nd**	*five hundred and*
15th	*fifteenth*		*seventy-second*
	fünfzehnte		fünfhundert(und)-
16th	*sixteenth*		zweiundsiebzigste
	sechzehnte	**1000th**	*(one) thousandth*
17th	*seventeenth*		tausendste
	siebzehnte	**1970th**	*nineteen hundred and*
18th	*eighteenth*		*seventieth* neun-
	achtzehnte		zehnhundert(und)-
19th	*nineteenth*		siebzigste
	neunzehnte	**500 000th**	*five hundred thou-*
20th	*twentieth*		*sandth* fünfhundert-
	zwanzigste		tausendste
21st	*twenty-first*	**1 000 000th**	*(one) millionth*
	einundzwanzigste		millionste
22nd	*twenty-second*	**2 000 000th**	*two millionth*
	zweiundzwanzigste		zweimillionste
23rd	*twenty-third*		
	dreiundzwanzigste		

Fractional Numbers and other Numerical Values

$^1/_2$ one half, a half halb
half a mile eine halbe Meile

$1^1/_2$ one and a half anderthalb or eineinhalb

$2^1/_2$ two and a half zweieinhalb

$^1/_3$ one or a third ein Drittel

$^2/_3$ two thirds zwei Drittel

$^1/_4$ one fourth, one or a quarter ein Viertel

$^3/_4$ three fourths, three quarters drei Viertel

$1^1/_4$ one hour and a quarter ein und eine viertel Stunde

$^1/_5$ one or a fifth ein Fünftel

$3^4/_5$ three and four fifths drei vier Fünftel

.4 point four null Komma vier (0,4)

2.5 two point five zwei Komma fünf (2,5)

einfach single
zweifach double, twofold
dreifach threefold, treble, triple
vierfach fourfold, quadruple

fünffach fivefold, quintuple einmal once
zweimal twice
drei-, vier-, fünfmal three or four or five times
zweimal soviel(e) twice as much or many

erstens, zweitens, drittens first(ly), secondly, thirdly; in the first or second or third place

$2 \times 3 = 6$ twice three are or make six, two multiplied by three are or make six zwei mal drei ist sechs, zwei multipliziert mit drei ist sechs

$7 + 8 = 15$ seven plus eight are fifteen sieben plus acht ist fünfzehn

$10 - 3 = 7$ ten minus three are seven zehn minus drei ist sieben

$20 : 5 = 4$ twenty divided by five make four zwanzig (dividiert) durch fünf ist vier

German Weights and Measures

I. Linear Measure

1 mm _Millimeter_ millimeter = 0.039 inch

1 cm _Zentimeter_ centimeter = 10 mm = 0.394 inch

1 m _Meter_ meter = 100 cm = 1.094 yards = 3.281 feet

1 km _Kilometer_ kilometer = 1000 m = 0.621 mile

II. Square Measure

1 mm² _Quadratmillimeter_ square millimeter = 0.002 square inch

1 cm² _Quadratzentimeter_ square centimeter = 100 mm² = 0.155 square inch

1 m² _Quadratmeter_ square meter = 10 000 cm² = 1.196 square yards = 10.764 square feet

1 a _Ar_ are = 100 m² = 119.599 square yards

1 ha _Hektar_ hectare = 100 a = 2.471 acres

III. Cubic Measure

1 cm³ _Kubikzentimeter_ cubic centimeter = 1000 mm³ = 0.061 cubic inch

1 m³ _Kubikmeter_ cubic meter = 1 000 000 cm³ = 35.315 cubic feet = 1.308 cubic yards

1 RT _Registertonne_ register ton = 2,832 m³ = 100 cubic feet

IV. Measure of Capacity

1 l _Liter_ liter = 1.760 pints = U.S. 1.057 liquid quarts _or_ 0.906 dry quart

1 hl _Hektoliter_ hectoliter = 100 l = 2.75 bushels = U.S. 26.418 gallons

V. Weight

1 g _Gramm_ gram(me) = 15.432 grains

1 Pfd. _Pfund_ pound (German) = 500 g = 1.102 pounds avdp.

1 kg _Kilogramm_ kilogram(me) = 1000 g = 2.205 pounds avdp. = 2.679 pounds troy

1 Ztr. _Zentner_ centner = 100 Pfd. = 0.984 hundredweight = 1.102 U.S. hundredweights

1 t _Tonne_ ton = 1000 kg = 0.984 long ton = U.S. 1.102 short tons

German Proper Names

Aachen ['aːxən] *n* Aachen, Aix-la-Chapelle.

Adler ['aːdlər] *Austrian psychologist.*

Adria ['aːdria] *f* Adriatic Sea.

Africa ['aːfrika] *n* Africa.

Allgäu ['algɔy] *n* Al(l)gäu *(region of Bavaria).*

Alpen ['alpən] *pl the* Alps *pl.*

Amerika [a'meːrika] *n* America.

Ärmelkanal ['ɛrməlkanaːl] *m* English Channel.

Asien ['aːziən] *n* Asia.

Atlantik [at'lantɪk] *m the* Atlantic.

Australien [aʊs'traːliən] *n* Australia.

Bach [bax] *German composer.*

Baden-Württemberg ['baːdənˈvyrtəmbɛrk] *n Land of the German Federal Republic.*

Barlach ['barlax] *German sculptor.*

Basel ['baːzəl] *n* Bâle, Basle.

Bayern ['baɪərn] *n* Bavaria *(Land of the German Federal Republic).*

Beckmann ['bɛkman] *German painter.*

Beethoven ['beːthoːfən] *German composer.*

Berlin [bɛr'liːn] *n* Berlin.

Bern [bɛrn] *n* Bern(e).

Beuys [bɔɪs] *German sculptor.*

Bloch [blɔx] *German philosopher.*

Böcklin ['bœkliːn] *German painter.*

Bodensee ['boːdənzeː] *m* Lake of Constance.

Böhm [bøːm] *Austrian conductor.*

Böhmen ['bøːmən] *n* Bohemia.

Böll [bœl] *German author.*

Bonn [bɔn] *n capital of the German Federal Republic.*

Brahms [braːms] *German composer.*

Braunschweig ['braʊnʃvaɪk] *n* Brunswick.

Brecht [brɛçt] *German dramatist.*

Bremen ['breːmən] *n Land of the German Federal Republic.*

Bruckner ['brʊknər] *Austrian composer.*

Daimler ['daɪmlər] *German inventor.*

Deutschland ['dɔytʃlant] *n* Germany.

Diesel ['diːzəl] *German inventor.*

Döblin ['døːbliːn] *German author.*

638

Dolomiten [dolo'miːtən] *pl the Dolomites pl.*

Donau ['doːnaʊ] *f Danube.*

Dortmund ['dɔrtmʊnt] *n industrial city in West Germany.*

Dresden ['dreːsdən] *n capital of Saxony.*

Dünkirchen ['dyːnkɪrçən] *n Dunkirk.*

Dürer ['dyːrər] *German painter.*

Dürrenmatt ['dyrənmat] *Swiss dramatist.*

Düsseldorf ['dysəldɔrf] *n capital of North Rhine-Westphalia.*

Egk [ɛk] *German composer.*

Eichendorff ['aɪçəndɔrf] *German poet.*

Elger ['aɪɡər] *Swiss mountain.*

Einstein ['aɪnʃtaɪn] *German physicist.*

Elbe ['ɛlbə] *f German river.*

Elsaß ['ɛlzas] *n Alsace.*

Engels ['eŋəls] *German philosopher.*

Essen ['ɛsən] *n industrial city in West Germany.*

Europa [ɔʏ'roːpa] *n Europe.*

Feldberg ['fɛltbɛrk] *German mountain.*

Fontane [fɔn'taːnə] *German author.*

Franken ['fraŋkən] *n Franconia.*

Frankfurt ['fraŋkfʊrt] *n Frankfort.*

Freud [frɔʏt] *Austrian psychologist.*

Frisch [frɪʃ] *Swiss author.*

Garmisch ['garmɪʃ] *n health resort in Bavaria.*

Genf [ɡɛnf] *n Geneva;* ~**er See** *m Lake of Geneva.*

Goethe ['ɡøːtə] *German poet.*

Grass [ɡras] *German author.*

Graubünden [ɡraʊ'byndən] *n the Grisons.*

Grillparzer ['ɡrɪlpartsər] *Austrian dramatist.*

Gropius ['ɡroːpiʊs] *German architect.*

Großglockner [ɡroːs'ɡlɔknər] *Austrian mountain.*

Grünewald ['ɡryːnəvalt] *German painter.*

Habsburg *hist.* ['haːpsbʊrk] *n Hapsburg (German dynasty).*

Hahn [haːn] *German chemist.*

Hamburg ['hambʊrk] *n Land of the German Federal Republic.*

Händel ['hɛndəl] *Handel (German composer).*

Hannover [ha'noːfər] *n Hanover (capital of Lower Saxony).*

Harz [haːrts] *m Harz Mountains pl.*

Hauptmann ['haʊptman] *German dramatist.*

Haydn ['haɪdən] *Austrian composer.*

Hegel ['heːɡəl] *German philosopher.*

Heidegger ['haɪdɛgər] *German philosopher.*

Heidelberg ['haɪdəlbɛrk] *n university town in West Germany.*

Heine ['haɪnə] *German poet.*

Heisenberg ['haɪzənbɛrk] *German physicist.*

Heißenbüttel ['haɪsənbytəl] *German poet.*

Helgoland ['hɛlgolant] *n Heligoland.*

Hesse ['hɛsə] *German poet.*

Hessen ['hɛsən] *n Hesse (Land of the German Federal Republic).*

Hindemith ['hɪndəmɪt] *German composer.*

Hohenzollern *hist.* ['hoːən-'tsɔlərn] *n German dynasty.*

Hölderlin ['hœldərliːn] *German poet.*

Inn [ɪn] *m affluent of the Danube.*

Innsbruck ['ɪnsbruk] *n capital of the Tyrol.*

Jaspers ['jaspərs] *German philosopher.*

Jung [juŋ] *Swiss psychologist.*

Jungfrau ['juŋfrau] *f Swiss mountain.*

Kafka ['kafka] *Czech poet.*

Kant [kant] *German philosopher.*

Karajan ['kaːrajan] *Austrian conductor.*

Karlsruhe ['karlsruːə] *n city in South-Western Germany.*

Kärnten ['kɛrntən] *n Carinthia.*

Kassel ['kasəl] *n Cassel.*

Kästner ['kɛstnər] *German author.*

Kiel [kiːl] *n capital of Schleswig-Holstein.*

Klee [kleː] *German painter.*

Kleist [klaɪst] *German poet.*

Koblenz ['koːblɛnts] *n Coblenz, Koblenz.*

Kokoschka [ko'kɔʃka] *Austrian painter.*

Köln [kœln] *n Cologne.*

Konstanz ['kɔnstants] *n Constance.*

Leibniz ['laɪbnɪts] *German philosopher.*

Leipzig ['laɪptsɪç] *n Leipsic.*

Lessing ['lɛsɪŋ] *German poet.*

Liebig ['liːbɪç] *German chemist.*

Liszt [lɪst] *Hungarian-German composer and pianist.*

Lothringen ['loːtrɪŋən] *n Lorraine.*

Lübeck ['lyːbɛk] *n city in West Germany.*

Luther ['lutər] *German religious reformer.*

Mahler ['maːlər] *Austrian composer.*

Main [maɪn] *m German river.*

Mainz [maɪnts] *n Mayence (capital of Rhineland-Palatinate).*

Mann [man] *name of three German authors.*

Marx [marks] *German philosopher.*

Matterhorn [ˈmatərhɔrn] *Swiss mountain.*

Meißen [ˈmaɪsən] *n* Meissen.

Meitner [ˈmaɪtnər] *Austrian female physicist.*

Menzel [ˈmɛntsəl] *German painter.*

Mies van der Rohe [ˈmiːs fan der ˈroːə] *German architect.*

Mittelmeer [ˈmɪtəlmeːr] *n* Mediterranean (Sea).

Moldau [ˈmɔldaʊ] *f Bohemian river.*

Mörike [ˈmøːrɪkə] *German poet.*

Mosel [ˈmoːzəl] *f* Moselle.

Mössbauer [ˈmœsbaʊər] *German physicist.*

Mozart [ˈmoːtsart] *Austrian composer.*

München [ˈmʏnçən] *n* Munich (*capital of Bavaria*).

Musil [ˈmuːzɪl] *Austrian author.*

Naab [naːp] *f German river.*

Nahe [ˈnaːə] *f German river.*

Niedersachsen [ˈniːdərzaksən] *n* Lower Saxony (*Land of the German Federal Republic*).

Nietzsche [ˈniːtʃə] *German philosopher.*

Nordrhein-Westfalen [ˈnɔrtraɪnvestˈfaːlən] *n* North Rhine-Westphalia (*Land of the German Federal Republic*).

Nordsee [ˈnɔrtzeː] *f* German Ocean, North Sea.

Nürnberg [ˈnʏrnbɛrk] *n* Nuremberg.

Oder [ˈoːdər] *f German river.*

Orff [ɔrf] *German composer.*

Ostende [ɔstˈɛndə] *n* Ostend.

Österreich [ˈøːstəraɪç] *n* Austria.

Ostsee [ˈɔstzeː] *f* Baltic.

Pfalz [pfalts] *f* Palatinate.

Planck [plaŋk] *German physicist.*

Porsche [ˈpɔrʃə] *German inventor.*

Prag [praːk] *n* Prague.

Preußen *hist.* [ˈprɔʏsən] *n* Prussia.

Regensburg [ˈreːgənsbʊrk] *n* Ratisbon.

Rhein [raɪn] *m* Rhine.

Rheinland-Pfalz [ˈraɪnlantˈpfalts] *n* Rhineland-Palatinate (*Land of the German Federal Republic*).

Rilke [ˈrɪlkə] *Austrian poet.*

Röntgen [ˈrœntgən] *German physicist.*

Ruhr [ruːr] *f German river;* **Ruhrgebiet** [ˈruːrgəbiːt] *n* industrial centre of West Germany.

Saale [ˈzaːlə] *f German river.*

Saar [zaːr] *f affluent of the Moselle;* **Saarbrücken** [zaːrˈbrʏkən] *n capital of the*

Saar; **Saarland** [ˈzaːrlant] *n* Saar (*Land of the German Federal Republic*).

Sachsen [ˈzaksən] *n* Saxony.

Schiller [ˈʃɪlər] *German poet.*

Schlesien [ˈʃleːziən] *n* Silesia.

Schleswig-Holstein [ˈʃleːsvɪçˈhɔlʃtaɪn] *n* Land of the German Federal Republic.

Schopenhauer [ˈʃoːpənhaʊər] *German philosopher.*

Schubert [ˈʃuːbərt] *Austrian composer.*

Schumann [ˈʃuːman] *German composer.*

Schwaben [ˈʃvaːbən] *n* Swabia.

Schwarzwald [ˈʃvartsvalt] *m* Black Forest.

Schweiz [ʃvaɪts] *f:* **die ~** Switzerland.

Siemens [ˈziːməns] *German inventor.*

Spitzweg [ˈʃpɪtsveːk] *German painter.*

Steiermark [ˈʃtaɪərmark] *f* Styria.

Stifter [ˈʃtɪftər] *Austrian author.*

Storm [ʃtɔrm] *German poet.*

Strauß [ʃtraʊs] *Austrian composers.*

Strauss [ʃtraʊs] *German composer.*

Stuttgart [ˈʃtʊtgart] *n* capital of Baden-Württemberg.

Thoma [ˈtoːma] *German author.*

Thüringen [ˈtyːrɪŋən] *n* Thuringia.

Tirol [tiˈroːl] *n* the Tyrol.

Trakl [ˈtraːkəl] *Austrian poet.*

Vierwaldstätter See [fiːrˈvaltʃtɛtərˈzeː] *m* Lake of Lucerne.

Wagner [ˈvaːgnər] *German composer.*

Wankel [ˈvaŋkəl] *German inventor.*

Weichsel [ˈvaɪksəl] *f* Vistula.

Weiß [vaɪs] *German dramatist.*

Weizsäcker [ˈvaɪtszɛkər] *German physicist and philosopher.*

Werfel [ˈverfəl] *Austrian author.*

Weser [ˈveːzər] *f* German river.

Westdeutschland *pol.* [ˈvɛstdɔʏtʃlant] *n* West Germany.

Wien [viːn] *n* Vienna.

Wiesbaden [ˈviːsbaːdən] *n* capital of Hesse.

Zeppelin [ˈtsɛpəliːn] *German inventor.*

Zuckmayer [ˈtsʊkmaɪər] *German-Swiss dramatist.*

Zweig [tsvaɪk] *Austrian author.*

Zürich [ˈtsyːrɪç] *n* Zurich.

German Abbreviations

Abb. *Abbildung* illustration.

Abf. *Abfahrt* departure, *abbr.* dep.

Abk. *Abkürzung* abbreviation.

Abt. *Abteilung* department, *abbr.* dept.

a. D. *außer Dienst* retired.

AG *Aktiengesellschaft* joint-stock company, *Am.* (stock) corporation.

allg. *allgemein* general.

a. M. *am Main* on the Main.

Ank. *Ankunft* arrival.

Art. *Artikel* article.

atü *Atmosphärenüberdruck* atmospheric excess pressure.

bes. *besonders* especially.

Betr. *Betreff, betrifft* subject, re.

Bhf. *Bahnhof* station.

BRD *Bundesrepublik Deutschland* Federal Republic of Germany.

bzw. *beziehungsweise* respectively.

C *Celsius* Celsius, *abbr.* C.

ca. *circa, ungefähr, etwa* about, approximately.

CDU *Christlich-Demokratische Union* Christian Democratic Union.

CSU *Christlich-Soziale Union* Christian Social Union.

DB *Deutsche Bundesbahn* German Federal Railway.

DDR *Deutsche Demokratische Republik* German Democratic Republic.

DGB *Deutscher Gewerkschaftsbund* Federation of German Trade Unions.

d. h. *das heißt* that is, *abbr.* i. e.

DIN, Din *Deutsche Industrie-Norm(en)* German Industrial Standards.

Dipl. *Diplom* diploma.

DM *Deutsche Mark* German Mark.

Dr. *Doktor* doctor.

DRK *Deutsches Rotes Kreuz* German Red Cross.

ev. *evangelisch* Protestant.

e. V. *eingetragener Verein* registered association, incorporated, *abbr.* inc.

E(W)G *Europäische (Wirtschafts)Gemeinschaft* European (Economic) Community, *abbr.* E(E)C.

Fa. *Firma* firm; *letter:* Messrs.

FDP *Freie Demokratische Partei* Liberal Democratic Party.

Forts. *Fortsetzung* continuation.

Frl. *Fräulein* Miss.

geb. *geboren* born; *geborene* née; *gebunden* bound.

Gebr. *Gebrüder* Brothers.

gest. *gestorben* deceased.

gez. *gezeichnet* signed, *abbr.* sgd.

GmbH *Gesellschaft mit beschränkter Haftung* limited liability company, *abbr.* Ltd., *Am.* closed corporation under German law.

Hbf. *Hauptbahnhof* central or main station.

i. A. *im Auftrage* for, by order, under instruction.

inkl. *inklusive, einschließlich* inclusive.

Ing. *Ingenieur* engineer.

Inh. *Inhaber* proprietor.

jr., jun. *junior, der Jüngere* junior, *abbr.* jr, jun.

kath. *katholisch* Catholic.

Kfm. *Kaufmann* merchant.

kfm. *kaufmännisch* commercial.

Kfz. *Kraftfahrzeug* motor-vehicle.

kW *Kilowatt* kilowatt, *abbr.* kw.

Lkw. *Lastkraftwagen* lorry, truck.

lt. *laut* according to.

MEZ *mitteleuropäische Zeit* Central European Time.

n. Chr. *nach Christus* After Christ, *abbr.* A. D.

No., Nr. *Numero, Nummer* number, *abbr.* No.

PKW, Pkw. *Personenkraftwagen* (motor-)car.

Prof. *Professor* professor.

PS *Pferdestärke(n)* horsepower, *abbr.* H.P., h.p.;

postscriptum, Nachschrift postscript, *abbr.* P.S.

Rel. *Religion* religion.

S. *Seite* page.

s. *siehe* see, *abbr.* v., vid. (= vide).

sen. *senior, der Ältere* senior.

sog. *sogenannt* so-called.

SPD *Sozialdemokratische Partei Deutschlands* Social Democratic Party of Germany.

St. *Stück* piece; *Sankt* Saint.

St(d)., Stde. *Stunde* hour, *abbr.* h.

Str. *Straße* street, *abbr.* St.

Tel. *Telefon* telephone; *Telegramm* wire, cable.

TH *Technische Hochschule* technical university *or* college.

u. *und* and.

UKW *Ultrakurzwelle* ultra-short wave, very high frequency, *abbr.* VHF.

U/min. *Umdrehungen in der Minute* revolutions per minute, *abbr.* r.p.m.

usw. *und so weiter* and so on, *abbr.* etc.

v. *von, vom* of; from; by.

V *Volt* volt; *Volumen* volume.

v. Chr. *vor Christus* Before Christ, *abbr.* B. C.

vgl. *vergleiche* confer, *abbr.* cf.

z. B. *zum Beispiel* for instance, *abbr.* e. g.

z. T. *zum Teil* partly.

zus. *zusammen* together.

List of Suffixes

normally given without phonetic transcriptions

1. Nouns

		Gender	Genitive	Plural	Example
-chen	[-çən]	n	-chens	-chen	Mädchen
-de	[-də]	f	-de	-den	Gemeinde
-e	[-ə]	m, f	-en	-en	Verwandte, Adelige
-ei	[-aɪ]	f	-ei	-eien	Traube
-er	[-ər]	m	-ers	-er	Bäckerei
-heit	[-haɪt]	f	-heit	-heiten	Fahrer
-ie	[-iː]	f	-ie	-ien [-iːən]	Einheit
-ik	[-ɪk]	f	-ik	-iken	Industrie
		f	(-ik)	(-iken)	Musik
		f	-ik	-iken	Plastik
-in	[-ɪn]	f	-in	-innen	Freundin
-ismus	[-ɪsmʊs]	m	-ismus	(-ismen)	Realismus
-ist	[-ɪst]	m	-isten	-isten	Artist
-keit	[-kaɪt]	f	-keit	-keiten	Heiterkeit
-ling	[-lɪŋ]	m	-lings	-linge	Säugling
-nis	[-nɪs]	f	-nis	-nisse	Wildnis
		n	-nisses	-nisse	Erlebnis
-or	[-ɔr]	m	-ors	-oren [-oːrən]	Doktor
-schaft	[-ʃaft]	f	-schaft	-schaften	Freundschaft

Singular		Gender	Genitive	Plural	Example
-tät	[-tɛːt]	f	-tät	-täten	Qualität
-tion	[-tsioːn]	f	-tion	-tionen	Aktion
-tiv	[-tiːf]	m, n	-tiv(e)s	-tive [-tiːvə]	Kollektiv
-tum	[-tuːm]	m, n	-tums	-tümer [-tyːmər]	Irrtum, Bistum
-ung	[-ʊŋ]	f	-ung	-ungen	Richtung

Phonetic changes in plurals:

Singular	Plural	Example
-g [-k]	-ge [-gə]	Flug – Flüge
-d [-t]	-de [-də]	Grund – Gründe
-b [-p]	-be [-bə]	Abend – Abende
	-bien [-biən]	Stab – Stäbe
-iv [-iːf]	-ive [-iːvə]	Adverb – Adverbien
		Massiv – Massive

2. Adjectives

-bar	[-baːr]	fruchtbar
-end(e)	[-ant; -əndə]	abweisend
-haft	[-haft]	ernsthaft
-ig(e)	[-ɪç; -ɪgə]	sonnig
-isch	[-ɪʃ]	wählerisch
-lich	[-lɪç]	möglich
-los(e)	[-loːs; -loːzə]	achtlos
-sam	[-zaːm]	langsam
-ste	[-stə]	erste

3. Verbs

-eln	[-əln]	lächeln
-en	[-ən]	arbeiten
-ern	[-ərn]	klettern
-ieren	[-iːrən]	servieren

German Irregular Verbs

The list of irregular verbs below contains the following forms:

> infinitive,
> 1st, 2nd, 3rd sg present,
> 1st, 3rd sg past,
> past participle.

[h] and [sein] refer to the use of *haben* and *sein* respectively to form the present perfect tense.

Forms not in general use are given in brackets.

For derivative verbs (e.g. ,,empfinden'') and compound verbs (e.g. ,,zurückgeben'') look up the basic forms (in this case ,,finden'' and ,,geben'').

Infinitive	Present (1st, 2nd, 3rd sg)	Past	Past Participle
backen	backe/backst (backst)/bäckt (backt)	backte	gebacken [h]
befehlen	befehle/befiehlst/befiehlt	befahl	befohlen [h]
beginnen	beginne/beginnst/beginnt	begann	begonnen [h]
beißen	beiße/beißt/beißt	biß	gebissen [h]
bergen	berge/birgst/birgt	barg	geborgen [h]
bersten	berste/birst/birst	barst	geborsten [sein]
betrügen	betrüge/betrügst/betrügt	betrog	betrogen [h]
bewegen	bewege/bewegst/bewegt	bewog	bewogen [h]
biegen	biege/biegst/biegt	bog	gebogen [h, v:i sein]
bieten	biete/bietest/bietet	bot	geboten [h]
binden	binde/bindest/bindet	band	gebunden [h]

Infinitive	Present (1st, 2nd, 3rd sg)	Past	Past Participle
bitten	bitte/bittest/bittet	bat	gebeten [h]
blasen	blase/bläst/bläst	blies	geblasen [h]
bleiben	bleibe/bleibst/bleibt	blieb	geblieben [sein]
braten	brate/brätst/brät	briet	gebraten [h]
brechen	breche/brichst/bricht	brach	gebrochen [h u. sein]
brennen	brenne/brennst/brennt	brannte	gebrannt [h]
bringen	bringe/bringst/bringt	brachte	gebracht [h]
denken	denke/denkst/denkt	dachte	gedacht [h]
dreschen	dresche/drischst/drischt	drosch	gedroschen [h]
dringen	dringe/dringst/dringt	drang	gedrungen [h u. sein]
dürfen	darf/darfst/darf	durfte	gedurft $(v/t$ u. v/i gedurft) [h]
empfehlen	empfehle/empfiehlst/empfiehlt	empfahl	empfohlen [h]
entsinnen	entsinne/entsinnst/entsinnt	entsann	entsonnen [h]
erschrecken	erschrecke/erschrickst/erschrickt	erschrak	erschrocken [sein]
erwägen	erwäge/erwägst/erwägt	erwog	erwogen [h]
essen	esse/ißt/ißt	aß	gegessen [h]
fahren	fahre/fährst/fährt	fuhr	gefahren [sein, v/t h]
fallen	falle/fällst/fällt	fiel	gefallen [sein]
fangen	fange/fängst/fängt	fing	gefangen [h]
fechten	fechte/fichst/ficht	focht	gefochten [h]
finden	finde/findest/findet	fand	gefunden [h]
flechten	flechte/flichst/flicht	flocht	geflochten [h]
fliegen	fliege/fliegst/fliegt	flog	geflogen [sein, v/t h]
fliehen	fliehe/fliehst/flieht	floh	geflohen [sein]

Infinitive	Present (1st, 2nd, 3rd sg)	Past	Past Participle
fließen	fließe/fließt/fließt	floß	geflossen [sein]
fressen	fresse/frißt/frißt	fraß	gefressen [h]
frieren	friere/frierst/friert	fror	gefroren [sein u. h]
gären	gäre/gärst/gärt	gor (gärte)	gegoren (gegärt) [h u. sein]
gebären	gebäre/gebärst (gebierst)/gebärt (gebiert)	gebar	geboren [h]
geben	gebe/gibst/gibt	gab	gegeben [h]
gedeihen	gedeihe/gedeihst/gedeiht	gedieh	gediehen [sein]
gehen	gehe/gehst/geht	ging	gegangen [sein]
gelingen	gelingt	gelang	gelungen [sein]
gelten	gelte/giltst/gilt	galt	gegolten [h]
genesen	genese/genest/genest	genas	genesen [sein]
genießen	genieße/genießt/genießt	genoß	genossen [h]
geraten	gerate/gerätst/gerät	geriet	geraten [sein]
geschehen	geschieht	geschah	geschehen [sein]
gewinnen	gewinne/gewinnst/gewinnt	gewann	gewonnen [h]
gießen	gieße/gießt/gießt	goß	gegossen [h]
gleichen	gleiche/gleichst/gleicht	glich	geglichen [h]
gleiten	gleite/gleitest/gleitet	glitt (gleitete)	geglitten (gegleitet) [sein]
glimmen	glimme/glimmst/glimmt	glomm (glimmte)	geglommen, geglimmt [h]
graben	grabe/gräbst/gräbt	grub	gegraben [h]
greifen	greife/greifst/greift	griff	gegriffen [h]
haben	habe/hast/hat	hatte	gehabt [h]

Infinitive	Present (1st, 2nd, 3rd sg)	Past	Past Participle
halten	halte/hältst/hält	hielt	gehalten [h]
hängen v/i	hänge/hängst/hängt	hing	gehangen (gehängt) [h (sein)]
hängen v/t	hänge/hängst/hängt	(hängte)	gehängt [h]
hauen v/t	haue/haust/haut	haute (hieb)	gehauen [h]
heben	hebe/hebst/hebt	hob	gehoben [h]
heißen	heiße/heißt/heißt	hieß	geheißen [h]
helfen	helfe/hilfst/hilft	half	geholfen [h]
kennen	kenne/kennst/kennt	kannte	gekannt [h]
klingen	klinge/klingst/klingt	klang	geklungen [h]
kneifen	kneife/kneifst/kneift	kniff	gekniffen [h]
kommen	komme/kommst/kommt	kam	gekommen [sein]
können	kann/kannst/kann	konnte	gekonnt [h], v/aux können, v/t u. v/i gekonnt [h]
kriechen	krieche/kriechst/kriecht	kroch	gekrochen [sein]
laden	lade/lädst (ladest)/lädt (ladet)	lud	geladen [h]
lassen	lasse/läßt/läßt	ließ	gelassen [h], v/aux lassen, v/t u. v/i. gelassen [h]
laufen	laufe/läufst/läuft	lief	gelaufen [sein/h]
leiden	leide/leidest/leidet	litt	gelitten [h]
leihen	leihe/leihst/leiht	lieh	geliehen [h]
lesen	lese/liest/liest	las	gelesen [h]
liegen	liege/liegst/liegt	lag	gelegen [h u. sein]
lügen	lüge/lügst/lügt	log	gelogen [h]

Infinitive	Present (1st, 2nd, 3rd sg)	Past	Past Participle
mahlen	mahle/mahlst/mahlt	mahlte	gemahlen [h]
meiden	meide/meidest/meidet	mied	gemieden [h]
melken	melke/melkst, milkst/melkt, milkt	melkte, molk	gemolken, gemelkt [h]
messen	messe/mißt/mißt	maß	gemessen [h]
mißlingen	mißlingt	mißlang	mißlungen [sein]
mögen	mag/magst/mag	mochte	v/aux mögen, v/t u. v/i gemocht [h]
müssen	muß/mußt/muß	mußte	v/aux müssen (v/i gemußt) [h]
nehmen	nehme/nimmst/nimmt	nahm	genommen [h]
nennen	nenne/nennst/nennt	nannte	genannt [h]
pfeifen	pfeife/pfeifst/pfeift	pfiff	gepfiffen [h]
quellen	quelle/quillst/quillt	quoll	gequollen [sein]
raten	rate/rätst/rät	riet	geraten [h]
reiben	reibe/reibst/reibt	rieb	gerieben [h]
reißen	reiße/reißt/reißt	riß	gerissen [h (v/i sein)]
reiten	reite/reitest/reitet	ritt	geritten [sein, v/t h]
rennen	renne/rennst/rennt	rannte	gerannt [sein]
riechen	rieche/riechst/riecht	roch	gerochen [h]
ringen	ringe/ringst/ringt	rang	gerungen [h]
rinnen	rinne/rinnst/rinnt	rann	geronnen [sein]
rufen	rufe/rufst/ruft	rief	gerufen [h]

Infinitive	Present (1st, 2nd, 3rd sg)	Past	Past Participle
salzen	salze/salzt/salzt	salzte	gesalzen (gesalzt) [h]
saufen	saufe/säufst/säuft	soff	gesoffen [h]
saugen	sauge/saugst/saugt	sog, saugte	gesogen, gesaugt [h]
schaffen	schaffe/schaffst/schafft	schuf, schaffte, (create;)	geschaffen, (create;)
		schaffte	geschafft [h]
schallen	schalle/schallst/schallt	scholl	geschallt [h]
scheiden	scheide/scheidest/scheidet	schied	geschieden [h, v/i sein]
scheinen	scheine/scheinst/scheint	schien	geschienen [h]
schelten	schelte/schiltst/schilt	schalt	gescholten [h]
scheren	schere/scherst/schert	schor (scherte)	geschoren (geschert) [h]
schieben	schiebe/schiebst/schiebt	schob	geschoben [h]
schießen	schieße/schießt/schießt	schoß	geschossen [h]
schinden	schinde/schindest/schindet	schindete	geschunden [h]
schlafen	schlafe/schläfst/schläft	schlief	geschlafen [h]
schlagen	schlage/schlägst/schlägt	schlug	geschlagen [h]
schleichen	schleiche/schleichst/schleicht	schlich	geschlichen [sein (v/refl h)]
schleifen	schleife/schleifst/schleift	schliff	geschliffen [h]
schließen	schließe/schließt/schließt	schloß	geschlossen [h]
schlingen	schlinge/schlingst/schlingt	schlang	geschlungen [h]
schmeißen	schmeiße/schmeißt/schmeißt	schmiß	geschmissen [h]

Infinitive	Present (1st, 2nd, 3rd sg)	Past	Past Participle
schmelzen	schmelze/schmilzt/schmilzt	schmolz	geschmolzen [h, v/i sein]
schneiden	schneide/schneidest/schneidet	schnitt	geschnitten [h]
schreiben	schreibe/schreibst/schreibt	schrieb	geschrieben [h]
schreien	schreie/schreist/schreit	schrie	geschrie(e)n [h]
schreiten	schreite/schreitest/schreitet	schritt	geschritten [sein]
schweigen	schweige/schweigst/schweigt	schwieg	geschwiegen [h]
schwellen	schwelle/schwillst/schwillt	schwoll	geschwollen [sein]
schwimmen	schwimme/schwimmst/schwimmt	schwamm	geschwommen [sein u. h]
schwingen	schwinge/schwingst/schwingt	schwang	geschwungen [h]
schwören	schwöre/schwörst/schwört	schwor	geschworen [h]
sehen	sehe/siehst/sieht	sah	gesehen [h]
sein	bin/bist/ist/wir sind/ihr seid/sie sind	war	gewesen [sein]
senden	sende/sendest/sendet	sandte (broadcast: sendete)	gesandt (broadcast: gesendet) [h]
sieden	siede/siedest/siedet	sott, siedete	gesotten, gesiedet [h]
singen	singe/singst/singt	sang	gesungen [h]
sinken	sinke/sinkst/sinkt	sank	gesunken [sein]
sitzen	sitze/sitzt/sitzt	saß	gesessen [h u. sein]
sollen	soll/sollst/soll	sollte	(v/i u. v/t sollen) gesollt [h]

Infinitive	Present (1st, 2nd, 3rd sg)	Past	Past Participle
spalten	spalte/spaltest/spaltet	spaltete	gespalten [h], gespalte(n)n [h]
speien	speie/speist/speit	spie	gespie(e)n [h]
spinnen	spinne/spinnst/spinnt	spann	gesponnen [h]
sprechen	spreche/sprichst/spricht	sprach	gesprochen [h]
sprießen	sprieße/sprießt/sprießt	sproß	gesprossen [sein]
springen	springe/springst/springt	sprang	gesprungen [sein]
stechen	steche/stichst/sticht	stach	gestochen [h]
stehen	stehe/stehst/steht	stand	gestanden [h u. sein]
stehlen	stehle/stiehlst/stiehlt	stahl	gestohlen [h]
steigen	steige/steigst/steigt	stieg	gestiegen [sein]
sterben	sterbe/stirbst/stirbt	starb	gestorben [sein]
stinken	stinke/stinkst/stinkt	stank	gestunken [h]
stoßen	stoße/stößt/stößt	stieß	gestoßen [h u. sein]
streichen	streiche/streichst/streicht	strich	gestrichen [h]
streiten	streite/streitest/streitet	stritt	gestritten [h]
tragen	trage/trägst/trägt	trug	getragen [h]
treffen	treffe/triffst/trifft	traf	getroffen [h]
treiben	treibe/treibst/treibt	trieb	getrieben [h u. sein]
treten	trete/trittst/tritt	trat	getreten [h u. sein]
trinken	trinke/trinkst/trinkt	trank	getrunken [h]

Infinitive	Present (1st, 2nd, 3rd sg)	Past	Past Participle
tun	tue/tust/tut	tat	getan [h] sein}
verderben	verderbe/verdirbst/verdirbt	verdarb	verdorben [h, v/i]
vergessen	vergesse/vergißt/vergißt	vergaß	vergessen [h]
verlieren	verliere/verlierst/verliert	verlor	verloren [h]
verschwinden	verschwinde/verschwindest/verschwindet	verschwand	verschwunden [sein]
verzeihen	verzeihe/verzeihst/verzeiht	verzieh	verziehen [h]
wachsen	wachse/wächst/wächst	wuchs	gewachsen [sein]
waschen	wasche/wäschst/wäscht	wusch	gewaschen [h]
weichen	weiche/weichst/weicht	wich	gewichen [sein]
weisen	weise/weist/weist	wies	gewiesen [h]
wenden	wende/wendest/wendet	wendete, wandte	gewendet [h], gewandt [h]
werben	werbe/wirbst/wirbt	warb	geworben [h]
werden	werde/wirst/wird	wurde	v/aux worden, v/i geworden [sein]
werfen	werfe/wirfst/wirft	warf	geworfen [h]
wiegen	wiege/wiegst/wiegt	wog	gewogen [h]
winden	winde/windest/windet	wand	gewunden [h]
wissen	weiß/weißt/weiß	wußte	gewußt [h]
wollen	will/willst/will	wollte	v/aux wollen, v/t u. v/i gewollt [h]
wringen	wringe/wringst/wringt	wrang	gewrungen [h]
ziehen	ziehe/ziehst/zieht	zog	gezogen [h u. sein]
zwingen	zwinge/zwingst/zwingt	zwang	gezwungen [h]